ASHER & ADAMS'
PICTORIAL ALBUM
— OF —
AMERICAN INDUSTRY

1 8 7 6

ASHER & ADAMS'
PICTORIAL ALBUM
— OF —
AMERICAN INDUSTRY

1876

with illustrations and descriptions of
mercantile and manufacturing establishments, machinery, works of art,
mechanism, trade-marks, etc., etc.

Compiled, Written, Drawn and Engraved under
the Supervision of the Publishers, by their own Corps of
Editors, Engineers and Artists.

Entered according to Act of Congress,
in the Year One Thousand Eight Hundred and Seventy-Four, by
ASHER & ADAMS,
In the Office of the Librarian of Congress, at Washington,
District of Columbia. All Rights Reserved.

New York:
ASHER & ADAMS, 59 BEEKMAN STREET,
London: George Phillip & Son, 32 Fleet St.
1876

Rutledge Books
New York
1976

Published in 1976 by Rutledge Books, 25 West 43 Street,
New York, N.Y. 10036
Copyright © 1976 by Rutledge Books, a division of Arcata
Consumer Products Corporation.
Printed in the United States of America

Library of Congress Cataloging in Publication Data
Asher and Adams.
    Asher & Adams' pictorial album of American industry,
1876.
    Reprint of selections from the 1876 ed. published by
Asher & Adams, New York, under title: Asher & Adams'
New Columbian rail road atlas and pictorial album of
American industry.
    Includes index.
    1. United States—Manufactures—Pictorial works.
2. United States—Industries—Pictorial works. I. Ti-
tle.
HD9725.5.A72   1976   338′.0973   76-9832
ISBN 0-87469-000-5

Celebration of an Era

American industry—perhaps more than other facets of our national life—has grown at a headlong pace, so much so that in its earlier days little effort was made to record its beginnings. It is only in our own time that interest in "industrial archeology" is becoming keen, as we seek to reconstruct the past.

Of particular import, then, is the discovery and reprinting here of *Asher & Adams' Pictorial Album of American Industry*. However, this volume offers not only a meticulously accurate picture of business in the days of truly free enterprise. It is also a charming and nostalgic vista on life in the United States a century ago.

Asher & Adams created their album to commemorate one hundred years of industrial growth and progress in America. On the occasion of the national Centennial, they commissioned artists to capture the look and spirit of the age in a now almost vanished art form, the copperplated steel engraving. This form permits the reproduction of illustrations in the finest and most accurate detail. Through lavish use of these illustrations—there are more than a thousand of them in this volume—the artists managed to portray the many-faceted life of the times. We see not only the factories, their intricate and powerful machines, and their products; but also farms and farm machinery; early modes of transportation—coal-burning engines with bulging smokestacks, omnibuses, carriages, wagons, sleighs; company showrooms; life in office and on the streets; mines and quarries; bird cages, tombstones, office safes, and stoves wrought with an artistry that now makes them prized as antiques. Here, too, are the first of the myriad products designed to improve life in the home—graceful or elaborate, and of remarkable inventiveness: folding beds, chairs, and tables; pianos and picture frames; ornate clocks; bronze chandeliers; bathtubs, boilers, and billiard tables.

The era of the early 1870s, celebrated by Asher & Adams in these pages, is one of the most significant in the history of American industrial growth. It was a time when the spotlight was on the individual entrepreneur, the man who started his own business and watched with pleasure and pride as it attracted customers and grew. Another decade or so later, the character and activities of the small venture capitalist would be obscured and the spotlight shifted to intricate forms of corporate organization, to trusts, combines, and monopolies.

The 1870s were also a time when American ingenuity and inventiveness were running rampant, a source of wonder, enthusiasm, and national pride, as the potential for materially improving the quality of life became evident. (Doubts, questionings, and restraints were to come only later.)

The spirit of the age could scarcely be expressed more succinctly than was done by Asher & Adams themselves in their preface, where they asserted that their album would "herald to the world, and perpetuate to futurity, the achievements which by skill, energy, enterprise, and indomitable perseverance a free and enlightened people have accomplished."

In addition to the delightful illustrations, the text in itself is rewarding, reflecting a kind of ingenuous self-belief (sometimes approaching pomposity), which is both revealing and occasionally endearing. The publishers' selection of subject matter seems to be quite haphazard, evidently made on the casual basis of whoever was willing to pay for the space. The very lack of any preordained structure, however, contributes a pleasing aura of informality. In seeming contradiction, the texts—whether they are the history of an invention, a product, or a company, or simply the description of how a piece of machinery operates—are written (and, apparently, researched) with such detailed care as to command our respect. In view of the paucity of such information available from other sources, the *Pictorial Album* takes on another value—as a unique storehouse of the odd and little-known fact.

Who were Asher & Adams? Their business lives were almost as varied as the many companies and individuals highlighted in this album. According to the records of the Mercantile Agency (a forerunner of Dun & Bradstreet, depicted here on page 41), John R. Asher and George H. Adams began in business together in Indianapolis in the late 1850s, as "Book Agents, Pills, etc." Like most businessmen of that era, they did a little of this and a little of that. They made and sold patent medicine pills (evidently composed mostly of cayenne pepper!), and later they also made and sold schoolhouse furniture. But mostly they published and sold maps and books, initially in Indiana and then in New York City. Their products included Civil War maps, atlases and gazetteers, maps and guides to New York, statistical and historical books on the United States and Canada, and so on.

In 1874 they copyrighted the first version of the present volume. It appeared in the midst of a brief national depression, when money was tight. Asher & Adams expected the book to put them back on their feet, as we can see from some interesting facts recorded by the Mercantile Agency in July, 1875: "Asher & Adams . . . are bringing out a new work, the 'Pictorial Album of American Industry.' This is a $40 book and involved a large outlay, but they have taken a great many contracts for advertising for it and they anticipate making a good deal of money by it."

How crucial this book was to their subsequent continued success is impossible to say, but Asher & Adams did prosper, until their partnership was terminated at the end of the 1870s because of Asher's failing health.

It seems likely that so expensive a book—forty dollars was an enormous sum in the 1870s—was sold to wealthy individuals and libraries; but most copies probably went to the companies and individuals described in the book itself. The lavish illustrations and comments about the firms and their products were, of course, thinly disguised advertising—a common practice in those days, before publishers were required to label such material as advertisements. In part the book was also a kind of vanity publication, in which you could pay to have yourself or your business described and praised. The advertisements were aimed more at other businessmen (or at "the trade," as the phrase went) than at final consumers, which was the case with many business publications before the development of mass consumer advertising.

We are fortunate that Asher & Adams gathered these wonderful illustrations and descriptions of American industry as it was a decade after the close of the Civil War. In these pages we see a people proclaiming their material accomplishments and the vitality of their economy, which had recently seized the position of industrial leadership in the world. Here a technically oriented society, bursting with energy, flaunts its achievements with boundless self-confidence. "In spite of all opposition," Asher & Adams asserted in their preface, "the products of the United States have advanced to the front rank in the markets of the world." In the pages of this book we can take a beautifully illustrated tour of the factories, products, and people of a very different and distant era, when business still had an individual and highly personal flavor.

GLENN PORTER
HARVARD UNIVERSITY
GRADUATE SCHOOL OF BUSINESS ADMINISTRATION

Editor's Note
The original edition of this album included an atlas and gazetteer of the United States. That section has been omitted from this reprint edition, as have a small number of pages in which subject matter is duplicated. Some of the texts have been condensed from the original in order to fit into the reprint format. However, the majority of the texts, the design of the pages, and all illustrations appear here just as they were in the original.

Preface to the 1876 edition

American Industry, its Progress

At an early period in its colonial history the manufactures of America, though small, were capable of supplying the wants of the colonists. The British manufacturers, foreseeing that the enterprising colonies would prove a dangerous rival, petitioned the British Parliament, which, in compliance, passed onerous laws burdening the commerce, and suppressing the weak and limited manufacturing interests of America; and even to the present time they have exerted a powerful influence in the endeavor to injure and supplant American industry; but in spite of all opposition the products of the United States have advanced to the front rank in the markets of the world, and her wares are now found and prized in every quarter of the globe.

In view of these facts and on the eve of the first Centennial Anniversary of American Independence, it is eminently proper that a standard work should be prepared, which will herald to the world, and perpetuate to futurity, the achievements which by skill, energy, enterprise, and indomitable perseverance, a free and enlightened people have accomplished.

The great variety of fine engravings of mercantile, manufacturing establishments, etc., diagrams and illustrations of inventions, machinery, works of art and mechanism, presents a varied attractiveness unsurpassed in any other publication; while the letter-press descriptions go behind the scenes, and give to the reader some idea of the magnitude of these interests, the immense capital employed, the many marvelous inventions, and the vast products of these industries, which minister to the necessities and refinements of life, and add wealth and prosperity to the country.

Owing to the magnitude of the work, the diversity of subjects and interests treated, the difficulty of obtaining information, most of which must be procured from interested parties, the necessity of employing many persons to collect the data and edit the articles, we may have given more prominence to some, and less to others than deserved. In order to make this work reliable on American Industry, instructions were given each editor to use great care, and much pains were taken to procure the facts from the highest and best authority, and should any misstatements or errors be found, the responsibility rests with those who furnished the information.

The standard character and intrinsic merits of the work have justly made it popular; the cordial reception and generous patronage accorded it enable us to present to our patrons a perfect epitome of American industry; and here we gladly embrace the opportunity to express our thanks for the many flattering courtesies extended to ourselves, our editors and agents.

ASHER & ADAMS.

A GRAPHIC DESCRIPTION

OF THE

Interior of Various Halls.

TOGETHER WITH

VIEWS OF THE Centennial Buildings

PUBLISHED BY ORDER OF THE

BOARD OF FINANCE.

ENGRAVINGS SUPPLIED BY THE

BOARD OF REVENUE.

PHILADELPHIA U. S. AMERICA
MAY 10TH NOVEMBER 10TH 1876.
MAIN EXHIBITION BUILDING.
1776 INTERNATIONAL EXHIBITION. 1876

The desire for information on the part of the public not only in this country, but in other parts of the world, has led to the preparation of these views, which are intended as far as possible to meet the necessities of the case. We cannot too much exaggerate the great importance of this exhibition to the future interests of the nation; it presents the first opportunity ever offered to our inventors, mechanics and manufacturers to display the great progress made in our various industries to the inspection not only of our own people, but also of the thousands from other lands who will visit Philadelphia on that occasion. There can be no question but that there will be secured in this way a largely increased demand for our own manufactures and attention will also be turned to a more close competition with our foreign rivals. To the farmer and landholder the opportunity is offered to secure both capital and labor by the proper presentation of the great resources of the various States and the advantages for investment; an impetus will also be given to the introduction of new staples, such as silk, useful fibres for paper, coffee, tea, tropical fruits, etc., etc.

The occasion is one that appeals to the national pride of every citizen, and the managers of this great enterprise feel justified in the expectation that there will not be a branch of manufacturing industry unrepresented, however simple may be its character. In all the World's Fairs of Europe Americans have carried off the majority of prizes in proportion to the articles on exhibition, and it would be a standing discredit to our people should we not meet our competitors successfully on our own ground. No better evidence of the value of a free government can be given than an exhaustive exhibit of all its resources; and the credit due to those who risked their lives and fortunes for our independence will be most justly rendered by this tribute of industry and invention. Let every manufacturer who may receive this work, use his best endeavor to give success to the International Exhibition of 1876, and thus make some return for the position he occupies as an American citizen.

THE EXHIBITION BUILDINGS.

The Main Buildings, erected by the Building Committee of the Centennial Board of Finance, for the uses of the Exhibition, are five in number, admirably located so that each is within easy distance of its neighbor, and so arranged that parties wishing to visit any one department, can by carriage or horse cars arrive directly at the gate opening into that department. This is a special advantage not heretofore available in European exhibitions. These buildings will be known as follows: I. Main Exhibition Building. II. Art Gallery. III. Machinery Hall. IV. Horticultural Building. V. Agricultural Building. In addition there will be a special edifice erected for the exhibit made by the Government of the United States, forming the sixth, and the Judges Hall, which will be the seventh of the Grand Exhibition Buildings.

I.

MAIN EXHIBITION BUILDING.

Engineer and Architect: HENRY PETTIT, JOS. M. WILSON.

This building is in the form of a parallelogram, extending east and west one thousand eight hundred and eighty feet in length, and north and south four hundred and sixty-four feet in width.

The larger portion of the structure is one story in height, and shows the main cornice upon the outside at forty-five feet above the ground, the interior height being seventy feet. At the centre of the longer sides are projections four hundred and sixteen feet in length, and in the center of the shorter sides or ends of the building are projections two hundred and sixteen feet in length. In these projections, in the center of the four sides, are located the main entrances, which are provided with arcades upon the ground floor, and central facades extending to the height of ninety feet. The East Entrance will form the principal approach from carriages, visitors being allowed to alight at the doors of the building under cover of the arcade. The South Entrance will be the principal approach for street cars, the ticket offices being located upon the line of Elm Avenue, with covered ways provided for entrance into the building itself. The Main Portal on the north side communicates directly with the Art Gallery, and the Main portal on the west side gives the main passage way to the Machinery and Agricultural Halls.

Upon the corners of the building there are four towers seventy-five feet in height, and between the towers and the central projections or entrances there is a lower roof introduced, showing a cornice at twenty-four feet above the ground.

In order to obtain a central feature for the building as a whole, the roof over the central part, for one hundred and eighty four feet square, has been raised above the surrounding portion, and four towers, forty-eight feet square, rising to one hundred and twenty feet in height, have been introduced at the corners of the elevated roof.

The areas covered are as follows:

Ground Floor, - - -	872,320	sq. ft.	20.02	acres
Upper floors in projections,	37,344	"	.85	"
" " in towers,	26,344	"	.60	"
	936.008		21 47	

A complete system of water supply with ample provision of fire cocks, etc., is provided for protection against fire and for sanitary purposes.

Offices for Foreign Commissions are placed along the sides of the building in the side aisles, in close proximity to the products exhibited; as many of the twenty-four feet spaces being partitioned off for that purpose as may be required.

Offices for the administration may be placed in the ends of the building and on the second floor.

The form of the building is such that all exhibitors will have an equally fair opportunity to exhibit their goods to advantage. There is comparatively little choice of location necessary, as the light is uniformly distributed and each of the spaces devoted to products is located upon one of the main thoroughfares.

The Departments of the Classification will be placed in parallel sections running lengthwise of the building, from east to west and will be wider or narrower in proportion to the bulk of the articles exhibited.

The countries exhibiting will be located geographically, in sections running crosswise of the building, from north to south.

This building will cost $1,600,000, and is to be completed and placed in the hands of the Centennial Commission on the first of January, 1876.

Contractor, Richard J. Dobbins, Philadelphia.

ART GALLERY.

II.

THE ART GALLERY AND MEMORIAL HALL.

Architect: H. J. SCHWARZMANN.

This structure, which is one of the affixes to the great Exhibition, is located on a line parallel with and northward of the Main Exhibition Building.

It is on the most commanding portion of the great Lansdowne Plateau and looks southward over the city.

It is elevated on a terrace six feet above the general level of the plateau—the plateau itself being an eminence one hundred and sixteen feet above the surface of the Schuylkill River.

The entire structure is in the modern Renaissance. The materials are granite, glass and iron. No wood is used in the construction, and the building is thoroughly fire-proof. The structure is three hundred and sixty five feet in length, two hundred and ten feet in width, and fifty-nine feet in height, over a spacious basement twelve feet in height, surmounted by a dome.

The main entrance opens on a hall eighty-two feet long, sixty feet wide, and fifty-three feet high, decorated in the modern Renaissance style; on the farther side of this hall, three doorways, each sixteen feet wide and twenty-five feet high, open into the centre hall; this hall is eighty-three feet square, the ceiling of the dome rising over it eighty feet in height.

From its east and west sides extend the galleries, each ninety-eight feet long eighty-eight feet wide and thirty-five feet in height. These galleries admit of temporary divisions for the more advantageous display of paintings. The centre hall and galleries form one grand hall two hundred and eighty-seven feet long and eighty five feet wide, capable of holding eight thousand persons, nearly twice the dimensions of the largest hall in the country. From the two galleries doorways open into two smaller galleries twenty-eight feet wide and eighty-nine feet long. These open north and south into private apartments which connect with the pavilion rooms, forming two side galleries two hundred and ten feet long. Along the whole length of the north side of the main galleries and central hall extends a corridor fourteen feet wide, which opens on its north line into a series of private rooms, thirteen in number, designed for studios and smaller exhibition rooms.

All the galleries and central hall are lighted from above; the pavilions and studios are lighted from the sides. The pavilions and central hall are designed especially for the exhibition of sculpture.

This building will cost $1,500,000 and is to be completed on January 1st, 1876.

Contractor: R J. Dobbins, Philadelphia.

III.

MACHINERY HALL.

Engineer and Architect: HENRY PETTIT, JOS. M. WILSON.

This structure is located west of the intersection of Belmont and Elm Avenues, at a distance of five hundred and forty-two feet from the west front of the Main Exhibition Building, and two hundred and seventy-four feet from the north side of Elm Avenue. The north front of the building will be upon the same line as that of the Main Exhibition Building, thus presenting a frontage of three thousand eight hundred and twenty-four feet from the east to the west ends of the Exhibition Buildings upon the principal avenue within the grounds.

The building consists of the Main Hall, three hundred and sixty feet wide by one thousand four hundred and two feet long, and an annex on the south side of two hundred and eight feet by two hundred and ten feet. The entire area covered by the Main Hall and annex is 558,440 square feet or 12.82 acres. Including the upper floors the building provides fourteen acres of floor space.

The annex for hydraulic machines contains a tank sixty feet by one hundred and six feet, with depth of water of ten feet. In connection with this it is expected that hydraulic machinery will be exhibited in full operation. At the south end of this tank will be a water fall, thirty-five five feet high by forty feet wide, supplied from the tank by the pumps upon exhibition.

The Machinery Hall, which is to cost $792,000, will be completed by the first of October, 1875.

Contractor: Philip Quigley, Wilmington, Del.

BUREAU OF MACHINERY.

Chief of Bureau: JOHN S. ALBERT.

No Department of the Exhibition will be as closely scanned by foreigners as this. American invention in labor saving machinery has done more in all foreign Expositions to indicate the progress of our country than all other Departments together, and a careful analysis of the awards received by our citizens exhibiting abroad will prove this fact. Under these circumstances there should be in our Machinery Hall, not only duplicates of what has been before presented, but, in addition, a specimen of every practical invention connected with machinery known in the United States. If this one Department alone is made perfect, our foreign visitors will leave with very strong impressions not only of the great natural resources of the United States, but also of the ability of our mechanics to secure the greatest results from these resources at the least expense of time and labor. It has been estimated that sixteen lines of shafting, including hangers and couplings, will be required for driving the machinery in the Machinery Hall, each line of shafting to be six hundred and fifty feet in length, and to transmit one hundred and eighty horse power, to be applied at the middle of the shaft, the bearings to be eight feet apart. There will be twelve lengths of this shafting to run at a speed of one hundred and twenty revolutions, and four lengths to run at a speed of two hundred and forty revolutions per minute; the diameter of the shafts, exclusive of "head" and "second" shafts will be three and two and one half inches respectively.

PHILADELPHIA U. S. AMERICA
MAY 10TH TO NOVEMBER 10TH 1876
INTERNATIONAL EXHIBITION.
1776 MACHINERY HALL. 1876

IV

HORTICULTURAL HALL.

Architect: H. J. SCHWARZMANN. CHARLES H. MILLER, Chief of Bureau of Horticulture.

The liberal appropriations of the City of Philadelpia have provided the Horticultural Department of the Exhibition with an extremely ornate and commodious building, which is to remain in permanence as an ornament of Fairmount Park. It is located on the Lansdowne Terrace, a short distance north of the Main Building and Art Gallery, and has a commanding view of the Schuylkill River and the northwestern portion of the city. The design is in the Mauresque style of architecture of the twelfth century, the principal materials externally being iron and glass. The length of the building is three hundred and eighty-three feet; width, one hundred and ninety-three feet, and height to the top of the lantern, seventy-two feet.

The main floor is occupied by the central conservatory, two hundred and thirty by eighty feet, and fifty-five feet high, surmounted by a lantern one hundred and seventy feet long, twenty feet wide, and fourteen feet high. Running entirely around this conservatory, at a height of twenty feet from the floor, is a gallery five feet wide. On the north and south sides of this principal room are four forcing houses for the propagation of young plants, each of them one hundred by thirty feet, covered with curved roofs of iron and glass. Dividing the two forcing houses in each of these sides is a vestibule thirty feet square. At the centre of the east and west ends are similar vestibules, on either side of which are the restaurants, reception room, offices, etc. From the vestibules ornamental stairways lead to the internal galleries of the conservatory, as well as to the four external galleries, each one hundred feet long and ten feet wide, which surmount the roofs of the forcing houses. These external galleries are connected with a grand promenade, formed by the roofs of the rooms on the ground floor, which has a superficial area of 1,800 square yards.

The east and west entrances are approached by flights of blue-marble steps from terraces eighty by twenty feet, in the center of each of which stands an open kiosque twenty feet in diameter. The angles of the main conservatory are adorned with eight ornamental fountains. The corridors which connect the conservatory with the surrounding rooms open fine vistas in every direction.

In the basement, which is of fire-proof construction, are the kitchen, store-rooms, coal-houses, ash-pits, heating arrangements, etc. Near this principal building will be a number of structures, such as Victoria Regia House, Domestic and Tropical Orchard Houses, a Grapery, and similar Horticultural buildings. The surrounding grounds will be arranged for out-door planting, and it is expected that an imposing and instructive display will be made. It is proposed to plant, among other things, representative trees of all parts of the Continent, so that side by side the visitor may see the full variety of the forest products and fruits of the country, from the firs of the extreme north, to the oranges and bananas of Florida, and the wondrous grapes and other fruits of California. In this great work it is important that the most perfect success should be achieved, so that vastness of territory, variety of product, and perfection of species, which constitute the marvel and the might of America, may be displayed in such a way as to be realized at a glance. This building is to cost $251,937.

Contractor: John Rice, Philadelphia.

AGRICULTURAL BUILDING.

Architect: James H. Windrim. Burnet Landreth, Chief of Bureau of Agriculture.

This structure will stand north of the Horticultural Building, and on the eastern side of Belmont Avenue. It will illustrate a novel combination of materials, and is capable of erection in a few months. Its materials are wood and glass. It consists of a long nave crossed by three transepts, both nave and transept being composed of Howe truss arches of a Gothic form. The nave is eight hundred and twenty-six feet in length by one hundred feet in width, each end projecting one hundred feet beyond the square of the building, with a height of seventy-five feet from the floor to the point of the arch. The central transept is of the same height, and a breath of one hundred feet; the two end transepts seventy feet high and eighty feet wide.

The four courts inclosed between the nave and transepts, and also the four spaces at the corners of the building, having the nave and end transepts for two of their sides, will be roofed and form valuable spaces for exhibits. Thus the ground plan of the building will be a parallelogram of four hundred and sixty-five by six hundred and thirty feet, covering a space of seven and one quarter acres. In its immediate vicinity will be the stock yards for the exhibition of horses, cattle, sheep, swine, poultry, etc.

Contractor: Philip Quigley.

GROUNDS OF THE INTERNAL EXHIBITION, FAIRMOUNT PARK.

H. J. Schwazmann, Chief Engineer Centennial Grounds.

The ground selected for the site of the Exhibition in Fairmount Park, containing two hundred and thirty-six acres, is west of the Schuylkill River, and north of Girard and Elm Avenues, on a plateau ninety feet above the river, heretofore known as Lansdowne. The boundaries of the exhibition are: South, Elm Avenue from Forty-first to Fifty-second Streets; west, the Park drive to George's Hill, with the concourse; north, Belmont drive from George's Hill to the foot of Belmont; and east, Lansdowne drive from Belmont to Forty-first Street. The whole of the Exhibition being enclosed, thirteen entrances have been established along the boundary drive, which might be named after the thirteen original States.

1st. The main approach for carriages and entrance at the east end of the Main Building.
2d. The central entrance between the Main Building and Machinery Hall, with the concourse for street cars and the approach from the Pennsylvania railroad depot.
3d. The entrance from George's Hill.
4th. The Belmont Avenue entrance at the intersection of the avenue with the Park Drive
5th. The Belmont entrance for visitors arriving on the Reading Railroad through Belmont Glen.
6th. An entrance in Belmont Valley for visitors arriving in steamboats.
7th. The east entrance in front of Horticultural Hall.
8th. The Lansdowne Valley entrance for visitors arriving on the Junction Railroad and by steamboats.
9th. The entrance to the Art Gallery, the only carriage entrance if desirable.

These entrances or gates will be ornamented and fitted up for the sale of tickets with self-registering turnstiles.

FAC-SIMILE of the Centennial Medal

PRICE:
Gilt, $5.00,
Bronze, $2.00,
Silver, $3.00,
Small Gilt, $1.00.

In neat case, Sent by Mail on Receipt of Price.

Address,
Centennial Bureau of Revenue,
904 WALNUT STREET,
Philadelphia, Pa.

Entered according to Act of Congress in the year 1875, by LONGACRE & CO, in the Office of the Librarian of Congress at Washington, D. C.

Birds Eye View of

CENTENNIAL GROUNDS AND BUILDINGS.

1776 AGRICULTURAL BUILDING. 1876

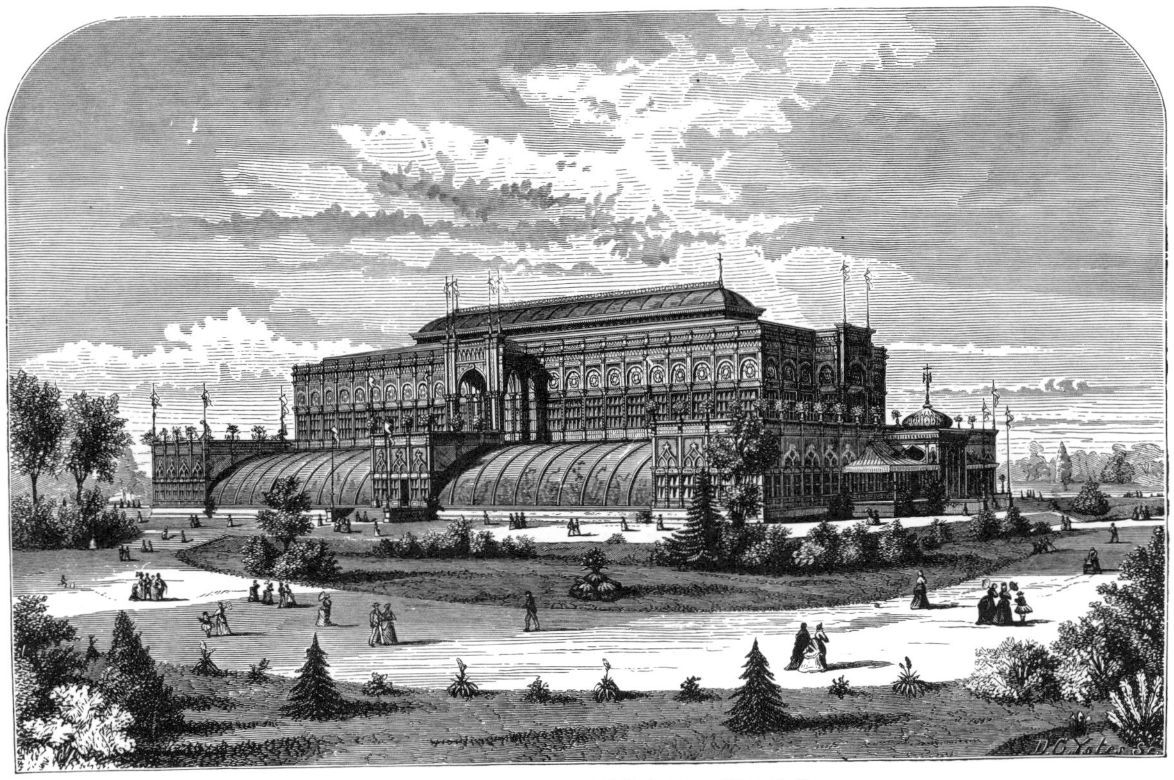

HORTICULTURAL HALL.

The proposed circuit drive necessitates changes in the present Park roads, which will be, at the same time, a long desired improvement of the present Park Drive. In the place of Belmont Avenue the boundary avenue in George's Run will be opened and a connection can be made over the inclined plane with the River Road.

The location of the buildings inside the enclosure is as follows: Main Exhibition Building occupies the most level territory with the Art Gallery north, elevated on a commanding plateau. The Machinery Hall occupies the next level portion, leaving a distance of five hundred feet between each, required for the entrance of the railroad tracks. The Horticultural Hall, most admirably situated, is in the centre of the grounds, containing sixteen acres, well sheltered and admirably adapted for horticultural purposes. Two bridges, over deep ravines, connect the Horticultural Grounds north and south with the other building. The Agricultural Grounds (thirty acres) and Building, at the north, are also well located and the ground is likewise well adapted for its purpose. The Exhibition Building of the United States Government is in the most central and prominent situation, with equal distance from all other buildings.

Economy and adaptability of the territory have been the guiding points in the selection of the various locations. The main line of connection between the buildings are straight and correct; and, for the still greater convenience of visitors, it is proposed to have cars running on the same. The meadow ground between the main avenues, reserved for private exhibition building, will be treated in regular Park style, with walks and planting, to unite the whole into a handsome picture. Lakes and fountains, fine and rare specimens of trees and shrubs, statuaries and vases, etc, etc., will be added to the ornamentation.

The entire control of the contracts for building the various edifices designed for the use of the International Exhibition, is in the hands of the

BUILDING COMMITTEE OF THE BOARD OF FINANCE:

Thomas Cochran, Chairman.
John Baird, Wm. Sellers,
Clement M. Biddle, Saml. M. Felton,
James M. Robb.

United States Centennial Commission, OFFICES, 903 WALNUT STREET.

ORGANIZATION.

President:
JOSEPH R. HAWLEY.

Vice-Presidents.
THOMAS H. COLDWELL, ORESTES CLEVELAND,
JOHN D. CREIGH, ROBERT LOWRY.
WILLIAM GURNEY, JOHN McNEIL.

Director General.
ALFRED T. GOSHORN.

Secretary:
JOHN L. CAMPBELL.

Assistant Secretaries:
DORSEY GARDNER. MYER ASCH.

Counsellor and Solicitor:
JOHN L. SHOEMAKER.

Executive Committee:

DAN'L J. MORRELL, Ch'm'n,	Pennsylvania,
ALFRED T. GOSHORN,	Ohio.
J. E. DEXTER,	Dist't of Col.
E. A. STRAW,	New Hamp.
N. M. BECKWITH,	New York.
GEORGE B. LORING,	Mass.
GEORGE H. CORLIS,	Rhode Island
JOHN G. STEVENS,	New Jersey.
ALEXANDER R. BOTELER,	West Virginia
RICHARD C. McCORMICK,	Arizona.
F. L. MATTHEWS,	Ill.
JOHN LYNCH,	Louisiana.
JAMES BIRNEY,	Michigan.
W. P. BLAKE,	Conn.
CHARLES P. KIMBALL,	Maine.
SAMUEL F. PHILLIPS,	North Carol'a
J. F. BERNARD,	Fla.

BOARD OF FINANCE.

OFFICES, 904 WALNUT ST., PHILA., PA

President.

John Welsh,	Philadelphia.

Vice-Presidents.

William Sellers,	Philadelphia.
John S. Barbour,	Virginia.

Directors.

Samuel M. Felton,	Philadelphia.
Daniel M. Fox,	Philadelphia.
Thomas Cochran,	Philadelphia.
Clement M. Biddle,	Philadelphia.
N. Parker Shortridge,	Philadelphia.
James M. Robb,	Philadelphia.
Edward T. Steel,	Philadelphia.
John Wanamaker,	Philadelphia.
John Price Wetherill,	Philadelphia.
Henry Winsor,	Philadelphia.
Henry Lewis,	Philadelphia.
Amos R. Little,	Philadelphia.
John Baird	Philadelphia.
Thos. H Dudley,	New Jersey.
A. S. Hewitt,	New York.
John Cummings,	Mass.
John Gorham,	Rhode Island
Charles W. Cooper,	Pennsylvania.
William Bigler,	Pennsylvania.
Robert M. Patton,	Alabama.
J. B. Drake,	Illinois.
George Bain,	Missouri.

Secretary and Treasurer.

Frederick Fraley,	Philadelphia.

Financial Agent. Hon. Wm. Bigler. *Auditor.* H. S. Lansing.

THE CENTENNIAL BUREAU OF REVENUE.

The above department, officially appointed by the Board of Finance, has control of the sale of stock and medals; organized July 1st, 1874, it has steadily and energetically pushed its agents throughout the various States, resulting in a success which it only needs time to complete. As the work of this Bureau, althongh national, must be continually followed up, its Directors are composed of such members of the Board of Finance as can render daily attention to its demands, as follows:

Chairman:

Clement M. Biddle,	Philadelphia.

Financial Agent:

William Bigler,	Pennsylvania.
Edmund T. Steel,	Philadelphia.
Amos R. Little,	"
John Wanamaker,	"
Daniel M. Fox,	"
James M. Robb,	"
John Baird,	"
Thos. H. Dudley,	New Jersey.
John Cummings,	Massachusetts.
William L. Strong,	New York.
George Bain,	Missouri.

Secretary:
C. B. Norton.

MAPLEWOOD MUSIC SEMINARY FOR LADIES,

East Haddam, Conn.

Maplewood Music Seminary is situated in the village of East Haddam, on the bank of the noble Connecticut River, a few rods from the Hartford and New York steamboat landing. The boats and the Valley Road, running between Hartford and Saybrook—connecting with the New York and New Haven and Air Line Roads at Middletown; with the Shore Line and Providence and New London Roads at Saybrook, and at Hartford with all points, affording daily communication with the above named cities—renders the place easy of access from all parts of the country.

The favorable locality of this institution commends itself to the public for its noted scenery, and also as a place of resort for health and pleasure seeking. The view (some eight miles in extent) is unsurpassed in beauty, and the constant passing of steamers and sailing vessels makes it very pleasant for pupils during their moments of leisure.

Early in life Professor Babcock gave evidence of marked musical ability, which, being cultivated under the best masters, was so enlarged and perfected as to place him among the first musicians of the country. As a composer, he is widely known. He is the author of many very beautiful and popular pieces, among which are: "My Home on the Mountain Side," "Thoughts of Happy Hours," "Star of Promise," "Lulu Mazurka," "La Baisir (the Kiss) Galop," "The Angel Mother," "I Never can Forget Thee," "Drifting Away," "Last Hope," (from Gottschalk's Last Hope,) "Maplewood Polka," "Romanza," "Maplewood Waltzes," "Forsaken," "Christine," and several others equally good. As a teacher Prof. Babcock has no superior, and the course of instruction given under his immediate supervision at the Maplewood Music Seminary is thorough. The staff of teachers is selected from the best talent of the country—those who are good practical musicians and have the faculty for teaching others. The number of teachers exceeds that of any other school of the kind in the United States.

PROF. D. S. BABCOCK.

This institution gives its pupils a thorough knowledge of music, also a good style of performance upon the Piano, Organ, Harp, and Guitar, as well as the proper use of the voice.

Four hours daily practice on the piano is required of pupils, and two hours each additional, on other instruments. Each pupil has a teacher with her three or four hours each day, viz: One hour in Harmony, one in Thorough Bass and Composition of Music, one in scale practice and technical studies and one in piano phrasing and voice.

For the benefit of the pupils, Prof. Babcock writes many of the exercises used in his Institution, thereby enabling him to give them such as are best adapted to their different dispositions and capacities. He deems this a great advantage, because instruction books, such as are generally used in musical institutions and seminaries, are not adopted to all minds.

From three to five operas are given by Prof. Babcock and pupils each year. The study and practice thus derived are of great advantage to the pupils. The design of the opera and oratorio practice is, to fit the pupils for singing in concert and church. A specialty is made of this part of musical education. We believe this to be the only school in the United States where pupils receive practical opera instruction.

In voice culture the Italian method (Carlo Bassini's), is used. Prof. Babcock was a pupil of his and thoroughly understands his method, and we believe it is pronounced by all well-informed teachers, the best method to form the registers of the voice.

All lessons are given as private lessons except the scales and mechanical studies which are given in class.

Prof. Babcock devotes from one to two hours every Monday evening, to lectures upon Harmony, Thorough Bass, Composition of Music, Adaptation of Language, Modulation, Transposition of Keys, and other points pertaining to music, with illustrations and exercises upon the blackboard.

The building is in two sections, three stories high, and connected by a large Opera House. The rooms throughout the institution are furnished with good beds and bedding, looking-glasses, chairs, carpets, etc.

Students take their meals with the family.

The academical year is divided into three terms of fourteen weeks each commencing the first week in September. Commencement exercises and regular Graduate Class, the third week in July. Through this vacation of five weeks, pupils from a distance may remain with the Principal's family if they desire, by paying five dollars per week for board, subject to the regulations of the school. Pupils are allowed two weeks vacation between each term. (This vacation is optional.)

The new opera house is an elegant affair, with a large and commodious stage, fitted with traps scenery, etc., suitable for the presentation of any opera. There are four stage boxes, two on each side, and the hall has a seating capacity of 1,500. The interior is tastefully frescoed in brilliant colors, and altogether East Haddam can probably boast of a finer hall than any other town of its size in the country. The Opera House is furnished with three of the finest Concert Grand Pianos, which pupils use every day for practice, and at all public rehearsals.

In combination with the Musical Institute is an Art Department, where the most complete instruction can be received in all branches.

Two evenings each week pupils are expected to practice "Parlor Gymnastics." In most schools, pupils obtain too little physical exercise, being occupied the greater part of the day with their studies; and without exercise of some kind, they become nervous and debilitated; to obviate which Prof. Babcock has introduced Calisthenics and Gymnastics. A suit adapted to their practice is required. The best material is, red Opera flannel, trimmed with white. One hour in the morning is allowed for out door exercises.

Prof. Babcock may well be proud of his Institution. If we had room to print the names of the eminent musicians who have spoken in its praise, their number would astonish our readers, while the complimentary notices of Journals, would fill a good sized volume.

Further particulars may be obtained by addressing Prof. D. S. Babcock, East Haddam, Conn.

MAPLEWOOD MUSIC SEMINARY FOR LADIES, EAST HADDAM, CONN.
(ESTABLISHED 1863.)
Prof. D. S. Babcock, Principal and Proprietor.

THE SEWING MACHINE CABINET CO.,

Cor. Washington Avenue and Pembroke Street, Bridgeport, Conn.

Branch Manufactory, Head of Malott Avenue, Indianapolis, Indiana.

This Company was organized in 1870 for the extensive manufacture of cabinets and other wood work used by sewing machine companies, the old and well known firm of S. Morris & Co. forming the nucleus. That they might keep pace with the great and rapidly increasing demand for their goods the company built extensive works for their manufacture at Indianapolis, Indiana, in the very heart of the walnut region of America, this being in addition to the immense buildings occupied by them at Bridgeport, Conn., where the general business office of the company is located.

Their factories are fitted up with the latest improved and very best wood working machinery, they having secured every appliance that can aid the mechanic in producing the finest work. Their aim has been, and is, to excel, and to reach this ultimatum they have spared neither pains nor expense. In their works at Indianapolis (a correct representation of which is given in the engraving here presented) they have erected special machinery for the production of veneers, and have gathered a corps of highly skilled workers in that branch of business.

There are few who have not both wondered at and admired the figures sometimes found in the grain of wood, but there are fewer still who know that the beauty of the figure depends largely, if not entirely, upon the skill of the man who placed the original log in the machine which cut it into veneers. Had its position been altered in the least the figure produced would have been destroyed. It is generally conceded that the section of country immediately surrounding Indianapolis, Indiana, is the richest in fine black walnut of any part of the United States, if not of the world. Taking advantage of this fact, and securing the best talent to utilize and develop the beauties hidden in the wood, this Company are now securing the very finest figures obtainable, and are producing goods of this kind second to none in this or any other country. They also have extensive mills for the manufacture of lumber, making a specialty, however, of thickness less than one inch.

Sheldon Morris, the President of the Company has been connected with its interests since the organization, and was previously, for a great number of years, a manufacturer of this special line of goods.

Visitors to the various fairs and expositions in this country, can hardly have failed to notice, in the departments occupied by the Wheeler & Wilson Manufacturing Co. and the Secor Sewing Machine Company, the elegant cabinets on exhibition, without doubt as fine as ever were constructed.

Attendants at the Vienna exposition report that there was nothing exhibited there which could compare with the beautiful specimens of skill in design and construction, which are daily produced by this company. As a direct consequence of the superiority of their goods they do an immense business, turning out about one hundred and fifty thousand pieces of cabinet furniture per year for sewing machines alone, not to mention the vast quantity of other work produced; this in addition to their very large business in the manufacture of veneers of black walnut and other fancy woods, and the sawing of lumber. A business of such proportions can only be built up by close attention. Those only are successful whose representations are always fully filled and the fact that the wares of this company are in such great demand, is of itself absolute proof of their superiority

Those desirous of entering into contracts for the manufacture of special articles made of wood, would do well to examine the ample premises and manufacturing facilities of this company, both at Bridgeport, Conn., and Indianapolis Indiana. We feel satisfied that all who do this will be convinced of their ability to turn out the best of work in the largest quantities.

They are fully prepared to contract for the manufacture of every description of fine wood work, and their great facilities for procuring the choicest of materials; their large factories, in which are every mechanical contrivance that can aid the workman, or cheapen the cost of the finished article; with their large corps of skilled mechanics, many of whom might more properly be termed artists, enable them to furnish the very best work at exceedingly low prices.

In their business relations their reputation is of the highest class. Whatever they agree to furnish the buyer will surely obtain. They make no "slop work." They slight nothing. Every article turned out from their factories is critically inspected before delivery, and if a fault in construction, or an imperfection in the material, (in short if any blemish) is found, the work is not delivered.

Their works are well worth a visit from those interested in mechanical progress. They are very hives of industry. The buzzing of saws and whirring of other machinery is full of sweet music to those who can appreciate the labor they are made to preform.

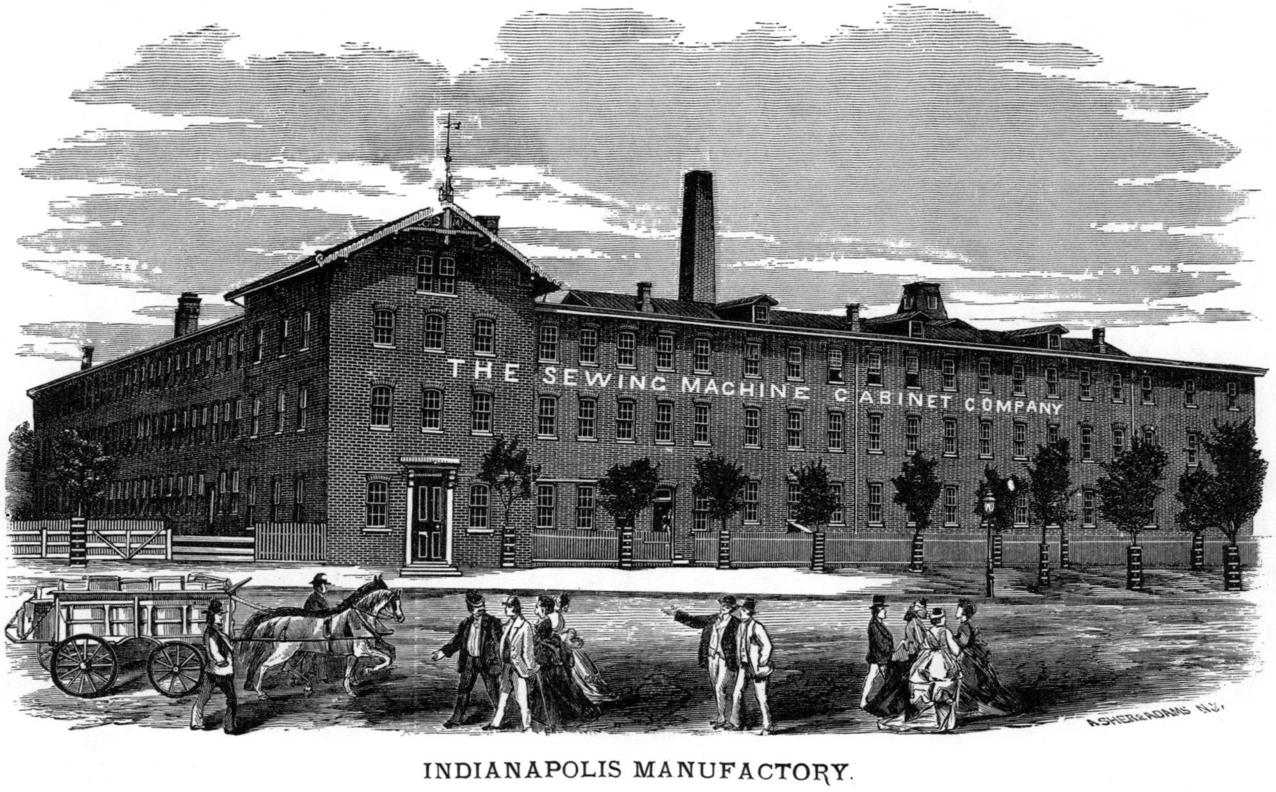

INDIANAPOLIS MANUFACTORY.
THE SEWING MACHINE CABINET COMPANY, BRIDGEPORT, CONN.

DR. ANGELL'S BATHING ESTABLISHMENT, CORNER LEXINGTON AVE. AND TWENTY-FIFTH STREET, NEW YORK CITY.

THE LEXINGTON AVENUE TURKISH AND ROMAN BATHS.

Soap has been wittily classed as the touchstone of a nation's sanitary progress, but the true scientific test of popular advancement in the art of healthful living is the people's use of the Turkish or hot air bath (which soon makes soap a needless impertinence) while the proverbial kinship between a clean skin and a clear conscience raises the question of perfect bathing to the dignity of a problem in moral science.

No one can study the history of the hot air bath among the Romans, or explore the ruins of the magnificent Thermae built by that wonderful people wherever their reign extended, without justly concluding that the use of this exquisite and effectual form of bathing was one of the grand secrets of Roman preëminence. The Turks, too, before they reached the summit of that power which threatened to devastate Christian Europe, had practised the use of the hot air bath with a devotion which has fastened the name "Turkish" upon it in modern speech, though it was in prosperous vogue nearly two thousand years before the crescent of Mahomet became a terror to the militant followers of the cross.

Nevertheless the history of hot air bathing in Europe is of little moment to the American citizen compared with the record of the efforts made to give his native land the benefits of a bath so luxuriously vitalizing as to render the fountain of youth and the elixir of life as unnecessary as they are fabulous. The first Turkish bath established in the United States was built in Brooklyn, in 1863, and since then numerous attempts have been made, with varying success, to establish the Turkish bath in the leading cities of the United States. But it was reserved for Dr. Emerson C. Angell to open, in 1867, at the corner of Lexington Avenue and Twenty-fifth Street, in New York City, a bathing establishment approaching as nearly to perfection as any of its kind on this continent or in the Old World.

Dr. Angell was born in 1822, in Rhode Island. He attended lectures at Brown University, studied medicine in Providence and New York, and received his diploma from the Bellevue Medical College in the latter city. In 1855 he established himself at San Francisco. Returning east in 1862, he became satisfied that the baths of the ancient Romans were imperatively demanded by modern American civilization, and since then he has devoted himself, to introducing and popularizing them in the home of his adoption, New York City.

In the year 1866 he bought the private residence 61 Lexington Avenue, north-east corner of Twenty-fifth Street, and with the aid of the best architects proceeded to remodel it into baths unsurpassed and perhaps unequaled, in the new world or the old, for perfection of heating and ventilation, convenience of arrangement and luxury of finish and furniture. The visitor approaching from the opposite corner sees before him a lofty and imposing structure of brick, six stories high, including the Mansard roof, which towers above the adjoining buildings, and is surmounted in turn by a sanitary chapel, in the shape of a pyramid-topped sun-bath, on which the word "Baths" appears in enormous letters of ruby glass, which gleam half way across the city when the bath is lighted at night.

The bather, after disrobing in the privacy of his dressing room, girds a sash about his loins Turkish fashion, and then ascends by easy carpeted stairs to the landing on the main floor of the building. Here, at the right, he finds the entrance to a series of three hot rooms with tiled floors, stained-glass windows, glazed partitions and graceful nymphs posing in walnut frames upon the walls. On entering he discovers none of the suffocating vapor which characterizes certain half-civilized, pseudo-baths, but finds instead a pure, dry atmosphere which he breathes with surprising facility, and, after slight experience, with a positive sense of rest and refreshment although the regulation temperatures of the three rooms are, respectively, 150°, 175° and 200°, and the thermometer sometimes marks 250° and even 300° without inconvenience to the practiced bather.

At the close of this process (which is given dry to make lean men fat, and with copious drenching to make fat men lean) the bather, having taken the plunge bath or not at his own option, is once more girded with a modest wrapper and is then conducted to the spacious and elegant cooling parlors, also on the main floor. In these unrivaled rooms the cushioned couches and chairs, velvet carpets, gilt chandeliers and cornices, lace curtains, heavy plate mirrors, illustrated newspapers, and entertaining volumes together with coffee, and choice cigars, persuade the bewildered and delighted bather that the Arabian Nights must have returned and that yonder affable host in Oriental garb must be the good Haroun al Raschid himself.

Here the Turkish bath ends and the lingering bather at last dresses slowly and betakes himself regretfully to his every day affairs. But at this establishment it has been possible since January, 1874, to take the last step, the "luxury of the Caesers," the perfumed anointing with which the Roman patricians closed their baths in the days of Augustus. In "Romaleon" the genius of Dr. Angell has secured an unguent substantially equivalent to that exhumed from the baths of Pompeii, and no one of intelligence who tries here the complete Roman bath, even as a novelty, will fail thereafter to adopt it as a luxury and a benefit, and, in short, as the only perfect bath in the world.

These baths are never closed, night or day, while upon the floor above is an entirely separate bath for ladies, equally perfect and luxurious, and kept open from 9 a. m. to 9 p. m. The bathers here include the metropolitan leaders in every department of business and of professional and mental activity, and the eulogies they have uttered or written concerning these baths would fill a volume. Three must serve as specimens. Grace Greenwood says of the Roman bath, "Do as the Romans did, whether in Rome or no." Anna E. Dickinson says, "A Turkish bath is always a taste of Paradise; at 61 Lexington Avenue, it is a full meal." And Ole Bull writes to Dr. Angell: "Allow me to congratulate you upon having succeeded in establishing the most perfect baths, to my knowledge in any land, Wishing you the success you so highly deserve for a thousand years or so, I remain, dear sir, your highly benefited and most obedient servant."

11

BENHAMS & STOUTENBOROUGH,

Manufacturers of

Stamped, Plain, Planished and Japanned

TIN WARES,

HOUSE FURNISHING GOODS, Etc.,

270 and 272 Pearl Street, N. Y.

Factory at Glen Cove, Long Island.

—:o:—

The business of the firm of Benhams & Stoutenborough was established in 1840, at 111 John Street, New York, by Andrews & Benham. Through various subsequent changes of partnership, Mr. D. Benham remained actively identified with the business, and is at the head of the present house of Benhams & Stoutenborough. Within the limited space at our disposal, it is impossible to give a history of the firm, suffice it to say, that in 1860, Mr. Stoutenborough, who entered the establishment as a boy in 1846, and risen through successive gradations,

not be marred by contact with others. The second floor is supplied with every convenience for the final packing of goods into crates, boxes, barrels, etc., preparatory to shipment to all parts of the United States, Canada, South America—in fact almost everywhere on the habitable globe. The offices are located on the first floor, the remainder of the space being used as a general salesroom. The basement is chiefly appropriated to the storage of heavy articles, Tin Plate in boxes, Coal Hods, Galvanized Well Buckets, etc., etc.

In addition to the premises above briefly described, Messrs. Benhams & Stoutenborough have extensive works at Glen Cove, Long Island, under the immediate supervision of Mr. J. C. Benham, where are made the heaviest articles of Stamped Ware, etc. The grounds are about one acre in extent; the principal factory is a large two-story structure, where "stamped" or "struck up" work is made by the use of powerful drop presses. A 30 horse engine furnishes the power for this department. Another large building is occupied for the manufacture of Coal Hods and general blacksmithing. Still another for painting the hods, and a fourth for general decoration and packing of goods preparatory to shipment. About 60 hands are employed, and the amount of goods produced seems adequate to supplying the wants of the entire civilized world.

Benhams & Stoutenborough's Manufactory, Glen Cove, Long Island.

was admitted to a partnership, that in 1869, Mr. D. Benham's brother, Mr. J. C. Benham, was taken in, and the firm name became, as at present, Benhams & Stoutenborough.

The factory and salesrooms at 270 and 272 Pearl Street, New York, is a five-story building, with basement, 40 feet in width and 100 feet long. As the upper stories are devoted to manufacturing, we commence our necessarily brief description with the fifth floor. Here some fifty mechanics are employed in the manufacture of the finer qualities of tin ware. The shop is fully equipped with all the approved mechanical appliances, and three large presses are constantly in operation, stamping out the parts; the dies for this work being worth not less than $16,000. The fourth floor is devoted to decorative work: lithographing, ornamentation by flexible blocks; crystalizing, by which the semblance of ice is given to water coolers, etc.; hand painting, Japanning, and other processes by which a degree of beauty is imparted to utensils of common use, which entitles them to rank among art productions. The third floor is devoted to the storage of fine finished goods and their preparation for market, each article being wrapped separately, that in packing they may

Many heavy contracts are assumed by this house for furnishing the Government with articles of tin and sheet iron for use in the army and navy, and for the United States hospitals; tin tubes for enclosing nitro-glycerin to be used in removing obstructions to navigation in American waters—the tubes used at Hell Gate were made here—and no house in this line has undertaken so many or such heavy contracts for furnishing the Government with articles included in its manufacture.

Of the beauty of their designs for household tinware, etc., the numerous engravings on this page bear ample testimony. In conclusion, we would simply say that Messrs. Benhams & Stoutenborough either manufacture or import every imaginable article in the way of House Furnishing Goods, in Iron, Steel, Tin, Willow, Wood, Wire; also Silver Plated and Britannia Ware; Tin Ware, plain, planished and Japanned; Lanterns, Tinners' Trimmings, Tinmen's Machines, Tools, etc., etc. In quality, their goods are certainly unsurpassed by any other manufacturers, and their long experience and great facilities give them unusual advantages which redound to the benefit of their customers.

Toilet Set.

Chafing Dish.

Toilet Set.

Nurse Lamp.

History of
TIN WARE MANUFACTURES.
Their Rise and Progress.

———

The history of no branch of industry affords a more striking example of sudden and marvelous growth than that of Tin Ware. Its development has been most extraordinary. When our country was passing through the Revolutionary struggle it is probable that no such thing as Tin Ware for house-keeping purposes was known. Afterwards as towns and cities sprang up and the wants of the people grew apace, the tin merchant could be found on the back street with his scanty stock of pots and pails, made during spare hours and rainy days in his rickety shop at the rear. His tools were few and clumsy—totally inadequate to produce anything beyond the requirements of absolute necessity. No thing was attempted that involved taste or suggested ornament; such articles were imported in rare instances from the mother country, the attention of the colonists being confined to ideas of the strictest utility.

Not until a generation ago was the project conceived of making house-furnishing Tin Wares a separate branch of manufacture. A factory or two were then built for the purpose of supplying this class of goods in larger and better style and at prices that made competition from the small dealer impossible.

The first important movements to enlarge the scope of the trade were made about twenty-five years since, and were confined at that

Their pans were sold in all parts of the country, and not a few were sent to England and South America. About the year 1865, not content with the improvements in machinery and goods already accomplished, this same house undertook to make stamped work of deeper and better shape than before. The machinery for this purpose was designed and built at their own works, and, at first, was kept secreted, so eager was the desire of others to copy it. By plans and processes entirely new and original they produced a seamless vessel varying from two to seven inches in depth, perfectly smooth, and with sides of eighty-five degrees flare, or almost straight. It was never before dreamed that cold sheet metal could be so manipulated, but such was proved to be the fact. A market was soon made for these articles and at the present time there is hardly a kitchen in the land where they are not to be found.

A little incident will serve as an illustration. Some years since, a man asked for work at the factory of E. Ketcham & Co. "Can you make a gross of six quart pieced pans in ten hours?" said Mr. Hodgetts. "Oh, no!" said our friend, "that is more than I ever heard asked of any man." "It is not more than we do here every day," was the reply. So sure was the man that such a thing was impossible, that it was agreed the matter should be tested. In the morning a gross of trimmings was placed before the man and a similar gross before Mr. Hodgetts. At five o'clock Mr. Hodgetts had finished his pans; at six, under the spur of a sharp associate, our friend had finished his. To-day, an ordinary workman, sitting at a machine can put into shape 4,500 medium sized pans, which require but a slight finishing to make them perfect goods!

Machinery is no inconsiderable item in the outfit of a large Tin Ware establishment. To compete successfully, the largest ex-

Gridiron.

Hip Bath.

Seamless Dish Pan.

Bowl and Pitcher.

Seamless Milk Pan.

Fluted Funnel.

Canister.

Seamless Milk Pail.

Cake Mold.

Cake Closet.

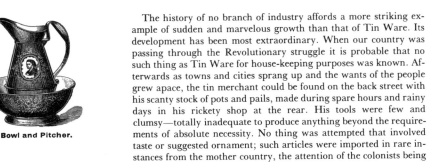

E. KETCHAM & CO'S TIN WARE MANUFACTORY, BROOKLYN.
Office & Warerooms, 100 Beekman St., & 289 Pearl St., N Y

Coffee Biggin.

Seamless Wash Bowl.

Coal Hod.

Cash Box.

Water Cooler.

time chiefly to what is called "Stamped Ware." The primeval tinsmith used to shape the covers for his vessels upon a block which had been gouged into form and the first years of an apprentice's life were usually devoted to the tedious routine of hammering. "Stamps" or "Drops" were then called into requisition, which consisted of heavy dies made to fall upon the circle or blank of tin plate with sufficient force to drive it into the shape desired. This lightened the work of the tinner by furnishing him with trimmings of a uniform size, which he simply placed in position for use. The depth of various articles so made did not exceed one inch, many being even shallower than that. It was not until about the year 1858 that anything greater was attempted. At that time the firm of E. Ketcham & Co., of New York, made experiments in stamping pans of one piece of sheet metal. Before this all the pans used by dairymen and housewives had been constructed of soldered pieces. Their first success was a pan whose sides projected at an inclination of about forty-five degrees. They were not so deep or straight as the old style; but being smooth and without seams, were eagerly sought for and formed the staple of sales for some years. Other parties soon began to make the same goods, which had the effect of driving the piece-made stock almost entirely out of the market. It was in this special branch of "Seamless Goods" that E. Ketcham & Co., achieved its greatest reputation.

penditures must be made to secure adequate facilities of production. In addition to this, one must expect to make continual outlays, as new goods are introduced or older styles superseded.

The departments in a modern Tin Ware Factory are a study by themselves. "Planishing" is a process which renders goods of heavier metal almost equal to silver. Hotel and table services of this ware are in great demand and give universal satisfaction. The "Chafing Dish" and "Coffee Urn" represented on this page are fair samples of this class of goods. The late William Taylor made this department a specialty, and ever stood at its head. "Japanning" is another branch that calls for prominent mention. Articles made of sheet metal are sometimes ornamented in the very highest style of the art. Water Coolers, Trays, Coal Vases, &c., are produced in designs that are suited for the best houses in the land.

The firm of E. Ketcham & Co., has been in existence many years, has all the facilities necessary to furnish goods of every style, and being fully alive to the growing wants of the trade, is ready to anticipate all demands. While they are manufacturers of special lines, they are also in position to make a larger assortment of Tin Wares than any other establishment. The articles exhibited on this page are but a few of the many produced in their works, their complete list covering one hundred and forty-four pages of an eight vo. book.

Seamless Kettle.

Seamless Teapot.

Well Bucket.

Polished Teapot.

Coal Vase.

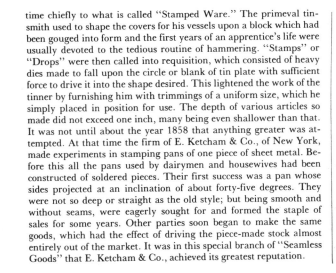

Vegetable Dish.

Crumb Tray and Brush.

Coffee Urn.

Frame of Pans.

Oyster Dish.

Plate Warmer.

THE HOWE SEWING MACHINE,

With sketch of the inventor.

This vast industry owes its existence to the original inventive genius of one man, the late Elias Howe Jr., whose first machine, an illustration of which may be seen on this page, embodied all the important features which distinguish the whole ; and which, as since improved by himself and others, is now the representative sewing machine.

As such we propose to give a brief history of its origin and present capacities, with other facts of interest to the public.

Elias Howe Jr., Inventor of the Sewing Machine, was born at Spencer, Mass., in 1819. (He died in Brooklyn, L. I., in 1867.) His father was a farmer and miller. He worked in the mill at an early age, and there received his first idea of machinery. He was subsequently employed in factories and machine shops in Lowell, Cambridge and Boston. He married at the age of 21, being then a journeyman machinist, working at $9 per week. In 1843, when extremely poor, he first conceived the idea of a machine for sewing. At first he invented a needle, pointed at both ends, with the eye in the middle, that should work up and down through the cloth, and carry the thread through at each thrust, but this did not form the common stitch. In October, 1844, he formed a rough wood and wire model, which sewed by using two threads, with the aid of a shuttle and curved needle, with the eye near the point. He had not the means to buy the raw material necessary to make a machine after his model. A friend, Mr. George Fisher, advanced the money, and he completed his first sewing machine in May, 1845. This machine sewed all the seams of two suits of woolen clothes, and the sewing outlasted the cloth

Mr. Howe's invention met with strong opposition and he was told that if this machine should prove successful it would reduce all tailors to beggary. Its practical value was also doubted. It was smiled at as an ingenious toy, although on one occasion it sewed five seams faster and better than they could be sewed by five of the swiftest sewers that could be found. However, he succeeded in obtaining a patent for it in September, 1846. Still, not a purchaser could be had, and his friend Fisher—who had advanced him about $2,000 for tools and materials, and to maintain his family while he was completing his invention—became disheartened and gave up all hopes of it.

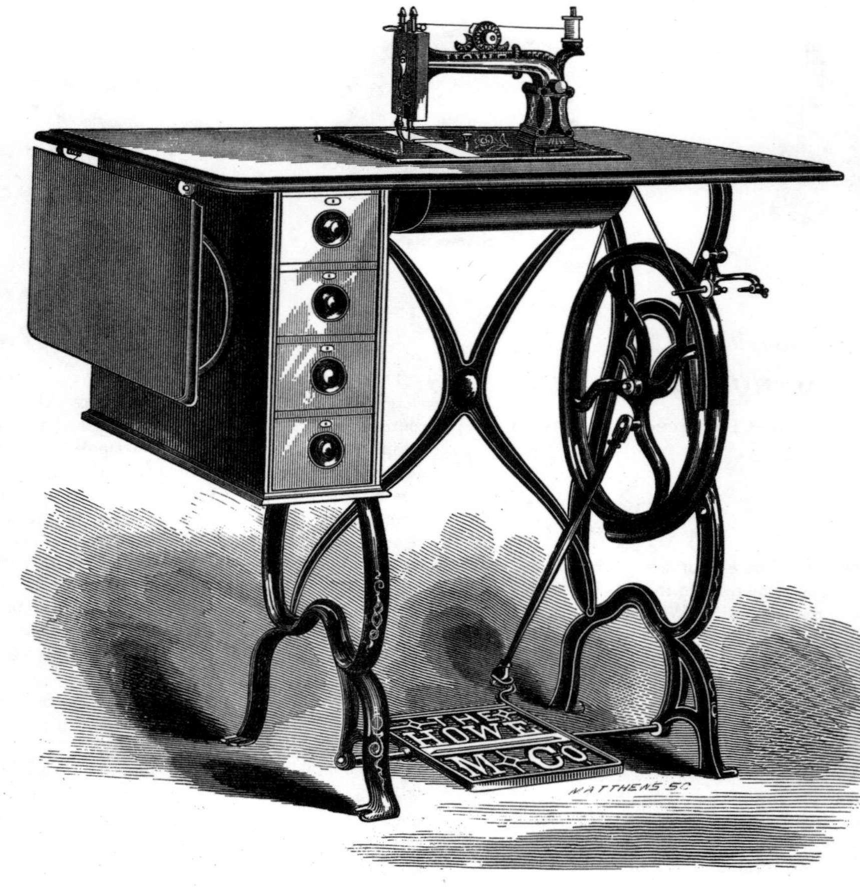

THE HOWE SEWING MACHINE.

In October, 1846, his brother, Amasa B. Howe, took the machine to England, where it was approved and purchased by William Thomas, of Cheapside, London, for 250 pounds sterling. This sum also gave Mr. Thomas the right to use as many others in his business as he desired. Mr. Thomas then had the invention patented in England ; but he broke his promise to pay Mr. Howe 3 pounds for every machine sold, and it has been estimated that Mr. Thomas has received a profit of $1,000,000 from the 250 pounds he invested in this machine.

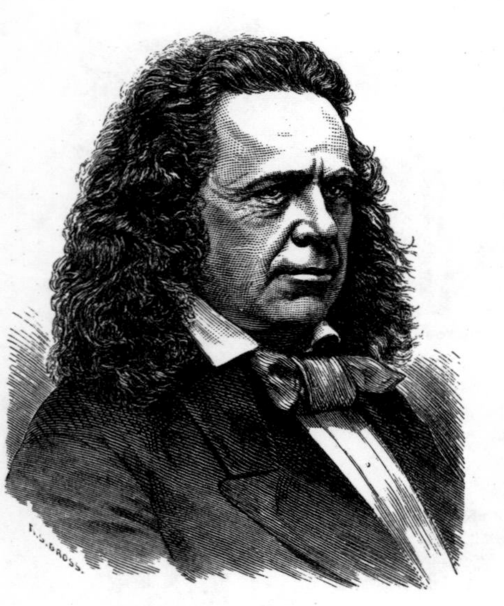

ELIAS HOWE, Jr.,

The Inventor of Sewing Machines.

Being extremely poor, with a family to support, and receiving no encouragement in this country, Elias Howe Jr., went to London with his family, in 1847, and there worked for Mr. Thomas, adapting the machine to the manufacture of corsets. But owing to dishonorable treatment, Mr. Howe separated from Thomas, although his exigencies were such that he was compelled to sell a machine for four ponnds, (though worth 50 pounds) and also to pawn his first machine and letters patent, to pay his expenses back to America. He reached New York, after two years' absence, in April, 1849, with but fifty cents in his pocket.

On his return, much to his surprise, he discovered that his machine had become famous, while he seemed forgotten, others had been infringing, and that it would require the strong hand of the law to vindicate his patent. One machine was exhibited in Western New York, as a great curiosity—"The Yankee Sewing Machine, 12½ cents a ticket." He was receiving only weekly wages as a journeyman machinist ; but he resolved to prosecute the infringers of his patent. The legal contest was long but he was finally victorious ; and thus a leading branch of our national industry became tributary to him, the founder of it. In 1850, Elias Howe Jr., produced 14 Sewing Machines, in a small shop in Gold Street, New York; and in 1851 they were all in successful operation in New York and Worcester, sewing gaiters, pantaloons, boot-legs, etc., so that he demonstrated that, besides inventing the Sewing Machine, and making the first one with his own hands, he was entitled to the credit of having brought his invention into successful use in manufacturing. In 1850 Isaac M. Singer invented three improvements; but Mr. Howe reminded him that he was infringing upon the Howe patent of 1846. In 1854, after a long trial, Judge Sprague, of Massachusetts, decided thus: "The patent of Elias Howe Jr., the plaintiff, is valid, and the defendant's machine is an infringement. There is evidence in this case that leaves no shadow of doubt that, for all the benefit conferred upon the public by the introduction of a Sewing Machine, the public are indebted to Mr. Howe."

In 1856 the principal manufacturers of Sewing Machines, were about to have their several claims tested at law; but finally, upon consultation, they came to an amicable agreement and compromise, the results of which are that every honestly made sewing machine pays the Howe Sewing Machine Company one dollar; while every sewing machine which includes any device patented by any other member of the combination, pays seven dollars to the combination. Thus the Howe Machine Company receives one of the seven dollars, and the other six go into the General Fund for defending the patents against dishonest and unlawful infringers.

Thus we see that after having devoted about 30 years to the invention and development of the Sewing Machine the persevering genius of Elias Howe Jr., was at last compensated, and this was at the rate of about $75,000 a year. But it cost him vast sums of money to defend his rights.

During the period from 1856 to the end of 1866, the number of Sewing Machines made in the United States was about 750,000. But during only the three months ending Dec. 10, 1866, the number made by licensed Companies was 52,219, or, at the rate of 200,000 a year, at an average price of $60 each. Of the three leading Companies, in 1870, the largest number was made by the Howe Machine Company, they producing in that year 75-156. The number sold by the Howe Machine Company in 1873 reached the enormous total of 153,244, in one year; and they now manufacture them at the rate of about 800 per day.

It is only upon a great scale that Sewing Machines can now be made well or profitably. About one-fifth of all made in the United States are sent to foreign countries. Some single establishments in New England employ 500 machines, and the shirt-makers in Troy, N. Y., run over 3,000 of them.

The Howe Sewing Machine now accomplishes nearly every variety of work that the needle ever did. It seams, hems, tucks, binds, stitches, quilts, gathers, fells, braids embroiders and makes button-holes. It is used in the manufacture of every garment worn by man, woman or child ; and among the singularly wide variety of articles made by its aid are sole leather trunks, men's and ladies' boots, shoes and gaiters, harness, engine hose, firemen's caps, horse collars, carriage curtains and linings, buffalo robes, horse blankets, powder flasks, whips, saddles, sails, awnings, mailbags, valises, hats, caps, corsets, pocket-books, kid gloves, suspenders, trusses, parasols, straw hats, bonnets, shirts, and even the most delicate and tasteful items of female apparel, etc., etc., from the strongest and heaviest to the finest and richest fabrics. Some of the finest stitches cannot be clearly seen without the aid of a magnifying glass.

The total value of the labor done by the sewing machine in 1863, (war time,) was $342,000,000; and an expert, under oath, testified, by careful estimate, that as far back as 1862 sewing machines had saved in labor at least $19,000-000 a year. Let us now examine and realize its relative speed:—A good hand-sewer averages 35 stitches in a minute; while the fastest machines on some kind of work, perform 3,000 stitches in the same time. To stitch a man's hat by hand takes 15 minutes; by machine only 1 minute; and one girl can sew as many boys' hats by machine as ten men can by hand in the same length of time. A first-class overcoat requires six days steady sewing, by hand, and only three days by machine. In the general work of a tailor, the machine saves a journeyman four hours in twelve.

For several years immediately previous to his death, Mr. Howe was actively engaged in increasing the facilities for manufacturing these sewing machines at Bridgeport, Conn. He succeeded in organizing a complete system, combining perfection of workmanship with the largest production, at the smallest cost. In order to obtain these results, time, labor, money, and the experience of his life as a practical mechanic were freely contributed; and, further to facilitate the manufacture and sale, the Howe Machine Company was organized, and the business is carried on in that name under the supervision of his sons-in-law, Alden B. Stockwell, President; and Levi S. Stockwell, Treasurer of the Company. The number of hands employed at Bridgeport, Conn., on machines alone, is about 1,500; at Peru, Indiana, on all the wood-work used, about 750; in Glasgow, Scotland, on machines alone, about 1,000; and in New York city, about 750; making a total of about 4,000 operatives, when all the factories are running in full, and producing, as we have said, about 800 machines per day. The number of styles is about 15, ranging from $60 to $250, according to amount of ornamentation.

All the machines are fully warranted, and in every case satisfaction is guaranteed. Each Family Machine is furnished with a hemmer, braider, quilter, gage, gage-screw, twelve assorted needles, six bobbins, needle-plate, screw-driver, oil-can, belt, two wrenches, and a book of instruction for using the machine. The trade-mark, a medallion likeness of Elias Howe Jr., is imbedded in every genuine Howe Sewing Machine. The Howe Sewing Machines are sent in annually increasing quantities, throughout every civilized country, even to Japan, and among the First Premiums awarded to them were the following: a Gold Medal at the International Exhibition of All Nations, London, 1862; a Gold Medal at the New York State Fair, 1866; a Gold Medal at the Exposition Universelle, Paris, 1867, and the Cross of the Legion of Honor, to Elias Howe Jr., as original Inventor; First Premiums at the State Fairs of Ohio, New York, Vermont, and New Hampshire, 1868; and their latest and crowning triumph was at the great Vienna Exhibition, in 1873, where they received no less than Five Testimonials for Superior Merit, viz: one for Merit, one for Progress, and three for Co-operation. Geo. W. Howe, their representative at Vienna, was decorated with the Order of Francis Joseph, and besides received a medal from the Society of Arts and Sciences of Vienna.

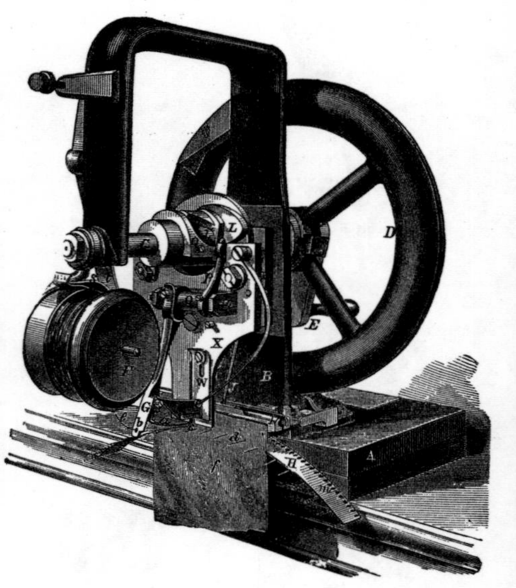

THE FIRST SEWING MACHINE

Elias Howe, Jr., Inventor, May, 1845.

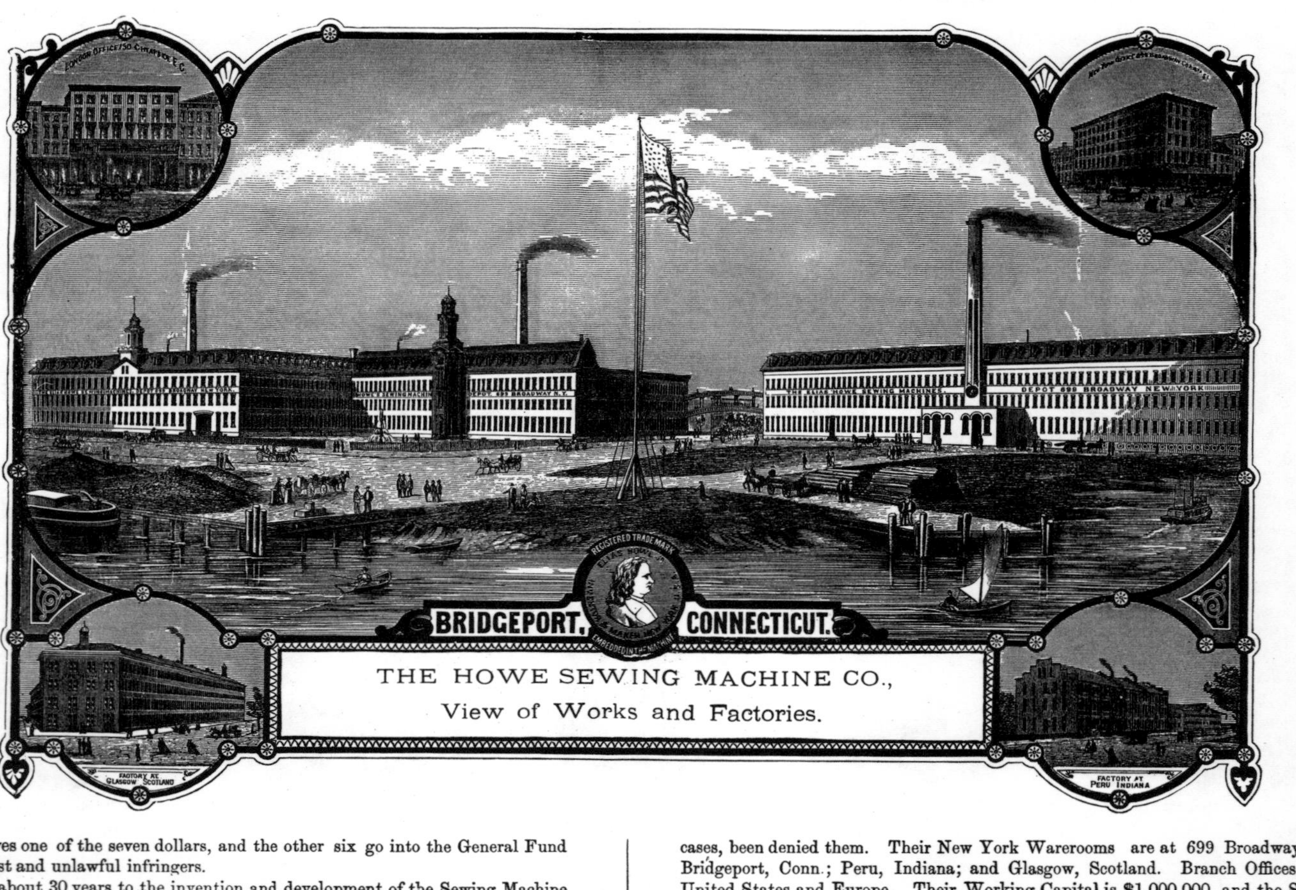

THE HOWE SEWING MACHINE CO.,

View of Works and Factories.

Such are the world's unbought tributes in honor of the Father of the Sewing Machine Industry, who fortunately, unlike the majority of great inventors and benefactors of mankind, did not go unrewarded to his grave. But far more precious than these golden testimonials is the constant homage of thanks, rendered by hundreds of thousands of faithful hearts, whose hands are strengthened and whose toil is eased in the perpetual struggle for life, for raiment, for bread and Home, which, but for this talismanic creation of Elias Howe, had in many cases, been denied them. Their New York Warerooms are at 699 Broadway, corner 4th Street. Factories at Bridgeport, Conn.; Peru, Indiana; and Glasgow, Scotland. Branch Offices in all the principal cities of the United States and Europe. Their Working Capital is $1,000,000, and the Surplus Capital, $10,000,000.

INTERIOR VIEW OF THE WILSON SEWING MACHINE ROOMS, NEW YORK.

THE WILSON SEWING MACHINE CO.

Among the industries of which America can boast of leading the world, that of the manufacture of Sewing Machines stands in the front rank, and of the numerous machines produced, the Wilson is one of the best and most popular.

The Sewing Machine is an American invention, and since the first one was produced, hundreds of thousands have been made, and at this time they are to be found in all parts of the world. At first they were constructed in Eastern cities, but gradually the march of Empire has been toward the West; and now the people of the Land of the Rising Sun look toward the Land of the Setting Sun, and see immense buildings devoted to the manufacture of sewing machines, while the warerooms of palatial magnificence lift their lofty fronts on the broad thoroughfares of the wonderful cities of the Great West. This company produce over 1600 machines per week, 266 per day or one in every three minutes; no business in the country has had a more rapid growth than that of this company, in the face of formidable competition, and it may be said to have now only just passed the point bey nd which it practically commands the market. There is not a question that to-day the Wilson Shuttle Sewing Machine is the favorite with the mass of the people and has a very strong hold upon the popular confidence. Its invariable success over all other machines at the Industrial Exhibitions in this country, and its magnificent triumph at Vienna, have established its superiority beyond all question, while the universal experience of those who have used it is a continual influence, more valuable than all else, in its behalf.

Every machine turned out by this company is warranted for a term of years, and therefore the utmost care is taken in the manufacture of them. The business policy of this company is of the most liberal character, and tens of thousands of people are daily experiencing the beneficent effects of its system of dealing with the public. Having no connection with "rings" or combinations organized to filch from the pockets of the people exorbitant profits, this company has been instrumental in saving to the people in the aggregate millions of money, which, but for its freedom of action, and its refusal to enter into combination against the public, would have gone into the coffers of the would-be exacting sewing machine companies.

The Wilson Sewing Machine Company has its headquarters at Cleveland, Ohio, where its machines are manufactured, the establishment being one of the most extensive and complete among the numerous large manufactories of that city. It has branch houses in New York, Philadelphia, Boston, Chicago, St. Louis and New Orleans—see

INTERIOR VIEW OF THE WILSON SEWING MACHINE ROOM, PHILADELPHIA.

interior views of three of their most prominent salesrooms on this page—and distributing offices in all the principal cities of the U.S. and Europe. The success which this company has achieved is but the foreshadowing of what lies beyond, the proportions of which can only be adequately apprehended by those who can estimate future growth.

The machine has been everywhere remarkably successful at all competitive exhibitions. At the Agricultural, mechanical and Horticultural Association, at Indianapolis, Indiana, in 1870, it carried off the gold medal, and at the State Agricultural Society of Michigan in the year 1871, two diplomas were awarded it. At the fairs in 1872 it carried off seven first premiums at the Northern Michigan Agricultural and Mechanical Society, and fourteen first premiums at the Ohio State Fair, for the best sewing machines and for various qualities and classes of work done on the machine, together with a silver medal and diploma at the Cincinnati Industrial Exposition for the best work done on sewing machines. A gold medal, two large silver medals, a bronze medal, and silver cup were awarded to the Wilson Machine and work done by it, over nineteen competitors, at the Louisiana State Fair, held at New Orleans in the spring of 1873; and similar honors in Missouri and other States, are among its trophies. It has been exhibited in Vienna at great expense, where Mr. Wilson received the highest medal awarded in that important department of manufacture.

Success long and continued is no accident, and to win it in this practical age of sharp competition, there must be real merit at the foundation coupled with an unusual amount of perserverance, business tact, foresight and rare executive ability.

Mr. Wilson, the inventor of the machine, the president of the company and general director of its affairs, has justly merited the success he has attained and deserves great credit from the public not only for the superior qualities of his sewing machine, but also for placing it on the market at a price far below its competitors; thereby enabling thousands to avail themselves of what is now considered a household necessity at a reasonable price.

It may be inferred that this liberal Sewing Machine Company have caught the inspiration for the character of their business from the spirit of Western industry and from the broad prairies which supply the world with cheap food, their design being to extend their business among the people by selling their productions at a price that would place them within reach of all. They have so organized their business that they can produce a shuttle sewing machine, second to none, and of the quality and reputation of which this country may justly be proud.

INTERIOR VIEW OF THE WILSON SEWING MACHINE ROOMS, CHICAGO.

No. 2 Band Saw.

Double Surfacing, Tonguing and Grooving Machine.

Combined Scroll and Band Saw.

Rip Saw Bench.

Pony Planer and Matcher.

Iron Frame Railway Cut-Off Saw.

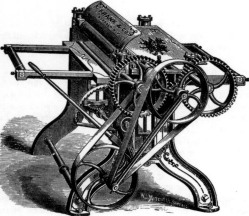

The Economist—Planer and Matcher.

Pony Planer,

FRANK & COMPANY,

Representing

WOOD WORKING MACHINERY.

Cor. Terrace and Charles Streets,
Buffalo, N. Y.

Before calling the attention of our readers particularly to the merits of the machines represented on this page, we wish to refer briefly to the extensive experience of the manufacturers, Messrs. Frank & Co., of Buffalo, N. Y., in the use and manufacture of Wood Working Machinery. After ten years practical experience in the use of this class of machinery, they commenced, and have continued to manufacture and use the same. Their experience as manufacturers covers a period of twenty years, and extends to every department of the business, from designing and making the patterns and castings, to finishing, testing, and operating the machines. Neither is their experience as manufacturers confined to the use of wood working machinery alone, but to the laborious process of working wood by hand, having devoted fourteen years to the manufacture of sash and doors in that way.

They are thus enabled to appreciate and meet the wants of those using wood-working machines, not only more promptly, but more satisfactorily than their competitors with less experience. The limits of this article forbid our making special mention of but few of the great variety of machines manufactured by these parties.

The popular idea of a planing machine, seems to have been, until a very recent date, that of a huge mass of iron, weighing from three to four tons, and equal in size to a two horse lumber wagon. In fact, those who gave the subject any consideration judged of the power, and capacity of the machine, as to the amount and quality of the work it would perform, mainly by its size and weight.

Messrs. Frank & Co., whose machines are here represented, appreciating the necessity of a lighter and cheaper machine that would do the required work successfully, and be manufactured at a price sufficiently low to be available by those whose means would not warrant the purchase of machines then in the market, resolved, some twelve years ago, upon the construction of a machine that would meet this demand. The result of their efforts in this direction, was the production of the "Pony Planer," represented on this page.

These machines vary in price from $100. to $165. and will surface from 10,000 to 18,000 feet of lumber in ten hours and do the work better than the average of large planers. More than 1000 of these planers are now in use, in almost every State in the Union, in the Canadas, Mexico, Cuba, England, Spain and Germany and notwithstanding the great depression in business the demand is still increasing.

Four-Sided Moulding Machine.

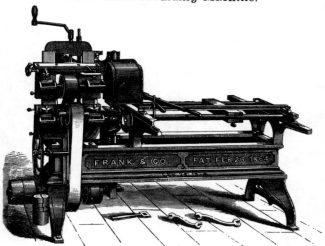

Iron Frame Tenon Machine.

Pony Planer.

This machine has a capacity for working lumber from sixteen to twenty-four inches wide and from one-eighth to six inches in thickness. Its extremely low price brings it within the reach of parties of moderate means, while it is so compact that it may be used in shops too small to admit machines of the ordinary size. Its simplicity of construction is an admirable feature, as it may be easily and successfully operated by inexperienced men.

As the Pony Planer could do only plain surfacing, but had demonstrated the fact that the power and capacity of a machine were not in proportion to its weight and price, there soon arose a demand for a cheaper and more practical machine for planing and matching material for floors and ceilings, than was then manufactured. The cost of such planers manufactured by other parties being from $500 to $3,000, they were too expensive for most parties in want of machines for this purpose. To meet the demand thus arising, Messrs. Frank & Company have perfected a machine which has proved a complete success, which they have very appropriately named The "Economist." (see cut on this page.) The object of the manufacturers was to construct a machine at the lowest price possible, to have it efficient and durable, which they have succeeded in accomplishing. This Planer and Matcher is sold at prices varying from $275 to $350, being the lowest price of any machine of equal capacity and durability in the market. It possesses sufficient strength to reduce the lumber one-half inch in thickness and one and one-half inch in width, to accomplish which it requires but four horse power. In proof of this latter statement, it may be said, it is driven with a four inch belt, and pulley ten inches in diameter, on back counter shaft, with speed of the cutter heads four, to the counter one.

Much care and judgment have been exercised in concentrating the principal part of the heft of this planer at the point, where it is most needed, rendering it sufficiently strong for all practical purposes. It will plane and match lumber as thick as two inches, or will surface that which is five and one-half inches thick.

It may be very readily changed from matching to surfacing, and vice versa. As the matcher spindles do not rise above the bed of the planer, it is not necessary to lower them after the heads are removed.

The guides are easily removed and returned to the same position as they are brought to the same line by the use of dowel pins on the guides which fit into corresponding holes in the planer frame.

The steps of the matcher spindles run in a patent self-oiling box, and the cylinder journals in C. Purdy's patent self-oiling boxes. It has a safe and reliable weighted chipper, of entirely new construction, which has a wide range of adjustment, and every part of it may be easily reached for that purpose.

Those of our readers who desire further information should address Messrs. Frank & Co., of Buffalo, New York, for their illustrated descriptive catalogue.

Patent Improved Band Saw Machines.

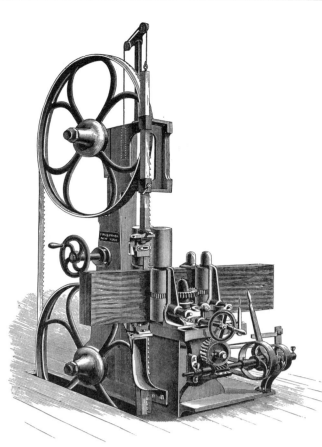

Slitting Saw.

Band Saw for Ship Builders, etc.

PATENT BAND SAW SETTING MACHINE.

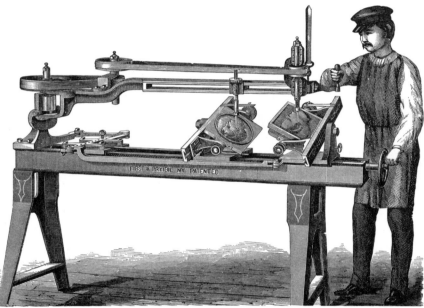

Carving Machine. To Carve Heads and other Ornaments.

BAND SAW GUIDE. Patented January 7th, 1873.

PONY PLANER.

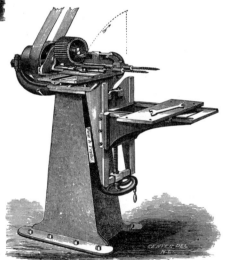

BORING MACHINE.

FIRST & PRYIBIL'S

BAND-SAW & WOOD WORKING MACHINERY,

The nearer we can approximate a proper comprehension of the extent to which the products of the American forests are being utilized, the better can we appreciate the importance of the branch of industry represented on this page. Within the memory ot the readers of this article, wood working machinery of real utility was comparatively unknown ; but a demand for an increased amount, as well as improved quality of work, created a necessity for improved facilities for securing this result. This necessity, without which development in any enterprise is very slow, has accomplished its purpose quite as satisfactorily in this as in any of the important branches of manufacture.

Among those to whom this country is most indebted for the results of their genius and enterprise in this respect is the well known firm of Messrs. First & Pryibil of New York City. A few of the great variety of wood working machines manufactured by these parties are represented on this page. The limits of this article will allow us to call special attention to but few of those here represented.

The exclusive control of most of these machines is secured to the manufacturers by Letters Patent. In addition to the machinery here represented they manufacture all kinds of general and oval Turning Lathes, Hard Wood and Waved Moulding Machines, Swing Saws, Sand Paper Rollers, &c., &c. A complete assortment of the best constructed Pulleys, Hangers and Shafting, for fitting up entire Factories, may always be found ready for immediate use at their warerooms.

Purschasers should appreciate the fact that all machinery manufactured by this house, is of the best material, carefully selected, and the work done under the personal supervision of the proprietors. The best evidence of these, as well as of all mechanical productions, is the very large number now in use.

We would also call attention to their new and most approved Carving and Saw-Setting Machinery, Circular Saw Tables, and Slitting Saws, on Bent Saw Principles, Bevel Hand Saws for Ship Builders, and other wood working machinery equal to the best which the inventive genius of the age has yet originated. Parties desiring further particulars, should apply for circulars to First & Pryibil, 461 to 467 West 40th Street, cor. 10th Avenue, New York.

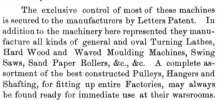

CIRCULAR SAW TABLES.

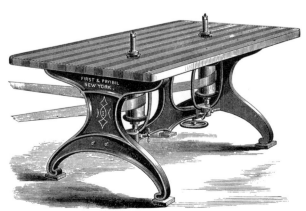

SHAPING or UPRIGHT MOULDING MACHINE.

NEW STYLE SOUNDER.

CHESTER'S PATENT DIAL TELEGRAPH.

RELAY MAGNET.

TELEGRAPHY IN THE UNITED STATES.

Charles T. Chester, Inventor and Manufacturer of Telegraph Instruments, &c.

Mr. Chester graduated from Yale College, and soon after secured the acquaintance and friendship of Professor Morse, which was retained through his life. Being much attracted by the practical science of telegraphy, then in its infancy, he devoted himself to it and soon made improvements in the construction of the various apparatus. Among other things he introduced a new and economical battery into very general use. When in 1856-7 the Australian lines were built, the English contractors sent to him for the entire equipment of the forty stations. In the same year he obtained a patent for a new signal instrument for fire alarms in cities by means of which an unskilled person could by a single pull send a perfect signal. This system of signals rapidly drove out all others and is now employed in all the principal cities in the United States and Canada.

The battery called by him "Electropoion" and of which millions have been and are used in North America and Cuba was introduced by him, and if he had obtained patents at the time of its first introduction a handsome fortune could have been realized from its sale.

In 1869-70 he constructed the New York Fire Alarm Telegraph, probably the most complete in the world. To equip this it was necessary to invent several new and complicated machines, of which two are shown on this page. The object of these several machines was to make it easy for a single man to receive from any part of Manhattan Island, instant notice of a fire and to notify any or all of 625 stations of the same. A complete description of the functions of one of these instruments engraved here would occupy a page. This system has saved millions of dollars to New York City.

Among other successful inventions and patents of Mr. Chester, the Alphabetical Telegraph has been largely used almost 500 of them are now in the hands of commercial men and municipalities. To illustrate the ease with which this system may be learned: The Mayor of St. Louis when it was proposed to introduce it as the police telegraph, opposed it on the ground of the incapacity of the police to become telegraphists. He promised to sign the contract if a man chosen by him could in 30 minutes be taught so that from a distant point he could send a message perfectly to the Mayor. The pupil was a stupid one, but the contract was signed.

Mr. Chester has lately introduced a stock quotation and private line printer, whose capacity in speed is so great that it can print 800 distinct letters in one minute. Each of these imprints requires 5 distinct actions either mechanical or electrical, that is, in other words, 4000 changes in the relation of the parts occur in one minute, and as 400 such machines are operated at once by a single controlling machine, 1,600,000 movements follow its dictation each minute.

Among other applications of electricity that have engaged his attention are the lighting of galleries, theatres and churches with the electric spark, the Electric Cautery in Surgery, the Hotel Annunciators and Telegraph Systems, Electric Lights and Submarine Blasting. He has applied to submarine torpedoes, magnetic apparatus by which they may be steered and controlled from the shore.

When Mr. Chester commenced the manufacture of Electro Telegraph Machines, but few understood the mystery, but now communication by electricity has become

BELL MAGNET.

BATTERY.

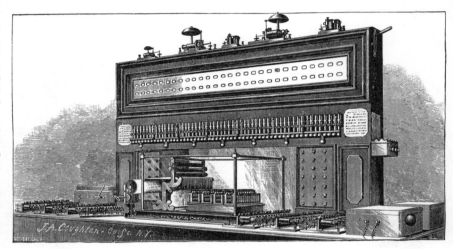

CHESTER'S FIRE ALARM REGISTER.

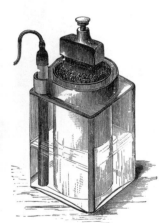

"LECLANCHÉ" BATTERY

FIG. 117.

CATON KEY.

POCKET RELAY.

BELL ALARM CONNECTION.

everywhere a necessity. Bells in hotels and houses are now rung by the subtle current. The stable boy hears the signal from the mansion, which orders him to do any one of fifty things as easily and quickly as the tongue can speak. The stock broker and merchant know through the magic tape the news of every passing moment, the fluctuations of markets at home and abroad. The manufacturer from his down town office sends his orders to the factory on the river shore, and the President of the great company calls quickly to his side any of the fifty employees whose names are designated on the little call instrument on his desk And now within a few weeks the first names of the legal profession are pledged to a scheme set on foot by Mr. Chester, by which with the courts and with one another, through all the city they can converse, arrange their cases, keep up with the progress of trials, with the registry of deeds and mortgages and all that interests and benefits the profession.

In telegraphy the machines for signalling, recording in dots and lines mechanically or chemically and printing have been infinitely numerous and ingenious, and have shown a steady progress. In the Voltaic battery not so much progress has been made. The want of the world now is a motor which shall relieve the wearied hands and feet that drive the lesser machinery of the household and the farm The time and money spent to obtain this is incredible. The electric motor would be perfect, compact, always ready to start or stop. But the one great unattained requirement is the battery. Its combinations are infinite, but none yet made is clean, cheap, or small enough for the Motor. Three types of batteries are shown, essentially different and each valuable. The Bunsen, for heavy work, as in Motors, Electric light, printers plating, surgical use, its duration four hours. The sulphate of copper gravity, for steady long continued, moderate work, its duration three months. The Leclanché, for occasional sudden brilliant work, then rest, its duration one year. The knowledge of what work each will do or will not do is now general. Though the variety of telegraph machines is so infinite, yet no one has the value of the "Morse Sounder." This conveys to the ear a new language. Inside of a thimble can a perfect talking machine be placed, and now that the appetite of wealth getters is so eager for new means of rapid conveyance of ideas, it is to be predicted that clerks in counting houses will find the language of the Morse Sounder as requisite as French or German or a rapid pen and lightning figures. Within a few months Mr. Chester has designed and published a school machine so cheap and easy to manage as to be available to all even as a plaything.

At this time Mr. Chester stands in the novel position of defender of the right to telegraph against a monopoly with forty millions capital. The Morse patent for years controlled all valuable telegraphy and gave immense wealth to the holders. Soon after its expiration these men made an attempt through a most extraordinary patent, granted by act of Congress, under gross misrepresentation to secure again privileges even more exclusive than they had enjoyed through Morse. Should this patent be sustained they alone would control almost all telegraphy. The Goliaths in legal controversy are all arranged on the side of these Philistines, and the first victim who is to be destroyed is the subject of this sketch. After his destruction free telegraphy is to end and the people of the United States are to pay tribute for another fourteen years.

We prophesy from proofs already given of the inventive genius of Charles Chester, further inventions of moment to the world's industries and civilization, which will write him down as one of the advance men of our age. His place of business is at 104 Centre street, N. Y.

IMPROVED REGISTER.

CHESTER'S FIRE ALARM TELEGRAPH.

BATTERY.

VIEW OF H. A. DELAND & COMPANY'S CHEMICAL WORKS, FAIRPORT, NEW YORK, U. S. A.

H. A. DE LAND & CO.,

Successors to

D. B. DE LAND & CO.,

Sup Carb. Soda, Saleratus, Baking Powder,

Cream of Tartar, Sal Soda, etc ,

FAIRPORT, N. Y.

—:o:—

Fairly entitled to high rank among the important industries of the United States is the manufacture of Soda in its various forms. Few chemical compounds are used in so wide a range of manufactures; few have such an extensive application in the arts; few have contributed so largely to the general diffusion of knowledge; few have as efficiently aided to scientific investigation, and fewer still enter so directly, so minutely or in so many different ways into the home life of the people. The glass that allows the sunlight to freely enter and cheer the humble home of the poorest, but for it, would be an expensive luxury that only the rich could afford. Of the same glass are formed the lenses that unfold to us a view of other worlds moving in spheres far beyond the reach of unaided human vision, or reveal the hidden beauties of Nature's most minute handiwork. To Soda we are indebted for the whiteness of the paper on which these words are printed, and only by its use are we enabled to obtain cheap paper, and consequently cheap books and journals with all their attendant blessings. Soda opens a cheap way to metallic sodium, and thus to the rare metals—aluminum and magnesium; it affords us borax for soldering and a score of other uses, and it gives us soluble glass. It cleanses and bleaches the cotton and scours the wool of which our garments are made; it cleanses the petroleum we burn, purifies our table salt, and refines our sugar. It gives us saleratus to raise our own bread, and without it, soap would become a luxury and the use of candles exclusively the privilege of the rich.

It is not our intention to give a complete history of Soda—nor could we, for its use ante–dates all recorded history, and consequently we could not possibly commence at the beginning. The plains of Egypt abound in Soda in a crude form; it has been found in Hungary, and on the plains of our own western country. These natural deposits of Soda, however, cannot be cheaply worked into a marketable commodity and are therefore not valuable at the present time. The Carbonate of Soda, (Soda-ash of Commerce) is now most cheaply produced from the chloride of sodium, (common sea salt) and the general process of manufacture is subtantially the same as that invented during the wars of the first Napoleon when French ports were blockaded by English vessels. Previously it had been largely manufactured from sea

weeds, Spain having produced the largest quantity. The blockade effectually cut off this supply, and the deprivation so seriously affected the industries of the country that the government offered a large reward to the discoverer of a successful method of converting sea salt into Soda–ash. No blockade could prevent the manufacture of salt from sea water by solar evaporation, what was needed was a process by which the salt could be converted into Carbonate of Soda. Various methods were suggested by chemists, but that of Le Blanc was the most successful, and, with some modifications and improvements it is still commonly used. The process is very simple, and, briefly stated was as follows: Equal weights of chloride of sodium and sulphuric acid were mixed together, placed in a reverbratory furnace and subjected to a high heat. The sulphuric acid expels the chlorine in the form of hydrochloric acid and takes possession of the Soda, forming a sulphate, known to commerce as salt-cake. The salt–cake is then mixed with charcoal and line-stone, and in a second furnace is reduced to ball-soda. The ball–soda is dissolved in water and crystalized if sal soda is required, or is dried and calcined into soda-ash. The incidental product mentioned, hydrochloric acid, was at first allowed to escape by the chimneys into the open air, and proved so destructive to vegetation that the soda works were driven from the mainland to the islands off the coast, but subsequently a method of catching the acid was devised, and so many uses to which it could be put were discovered, that the demand for it soon became equal to the supply.

One of the oldest, largest, and most widely and favorably known Soda Manufacturing Establishments in this country is that of H. A. De Land & Co. These works have been in the hands of the family for three generations, the house having been originally established by Mr. Justus Parce, grandfather of the junior member of the present firm. To the long incessant toil and indomitable perseverence of Mr. D. B. De Land—who became interested in the business in 1845, and senior partner of the firm of D. B. Deland & Co. in 1851,—associated with his brother, Mr. H. A. De Land, the present senior member, are due the credit of developing the business to the great magnitude which it has attained.

Mr. D. B. De Land, who died in 1872, was a man of sterling character, strictly honest in all his dealings with his fellow men, and blessed with that force and those graces of character that command respect and win lasting approbation. His untiring energy, his unyielding perseverence, his sound judgment and prompt action, tided his business bark over many petty difficulties, and though at times great obstacles loomed up, he safely guided it to success. A thorough man of business, a model citizen and a generous friend, he left behind him that best of all monuments,—a good name.

Mr. H. A. De Land is a fitting successor to his brother and under his management the business has continued to grow. An important element of

the great success of this house is found in the superiority of its productions. The first great care of the firm was to reach the highest attainable excellence, that reached, they have maintained it. In the fierce competition and the low prices at which inferior goods have been offered, prices which they must nearly or quite meet, they took no less care in the manufacture and produced no less perfect goods than during more profitable seasons. The laws of trade rendered it necessary that they should sell at low prices; but the, with them, paramount laws of honesty would not allow of any reduction of quality. The reward comes in the shape of a continuous demand for their goods, so great as to render it necessary to run their extensive works to their full capacity.

The firm have generally found it to their interest to import the crude alkali and re-work and refine it. They have many machines and processes invented by and peculiar to themselves which we cannot, for obvious reasons, here describe. The object of these new processes and machines, is, of course, to lessen the cost of production and at the same time to make more perfect goods.

The works occupy an area of ground measuring between four and five acres; the buildings are largely two and three story structures, many of them built of wood. The capacity of the works is from twenty to twenty-five tons of Soda and Saleratus per diem. The works contain nine run of stone, eleven packing and weighing machines, and many other mechanical devices used in the business. They have a box and barrel shop, also supplied with machinery, where the cases are made in which the goods are packed for shipment, and large warehouses, and storage buildings for the proper shelter of crude materials and refined manufactures. A magnificent steam engine of fifty horse power supplies the motor, and the establishment furnishes constant employment to from one hundred and twenty-five to one hundred and fifty persons.

Their specialties are Sup. Carbonate of Soda, Best Chemical Saleratus, Baking Powder, Cream of Tartar, Sal Soda and Dome Stove Polish. The work is constantly going on, there is no cessation, day or night, it still continues, and still the demand is always equal to the supply.

The shipments of the firm are principally directed to the West and Southwestern sections of the country, comparatively little going East, and as these sections require their entire production no effort need be made to secure Eastern trade.

The present firm is composed of Mr. H. A. De Land and Mr. L. J. De Land, gentlemen well known in commercial circles, and the house has long been very popular not only in this country but in Europe where they are well known as large purchasers of Alkali, while in this country they are ranked high as producers of pure articles—articles not excelled by any of like character in the world.

NELLIS'

ORIGINAL

HARPOON HORSE HAY FORK,

AND FIXTURES.

Pittsburgh, Pa.

——:o:——

The Harpoon Horse Hay Fork was originally invented by Mr. Edward L. Walker, and patented by him September 6th, 1864. The fork devised by Mr. Walker was far in advance of any that had preceded it; the principle was a good one, but the instrument itself was comparatively crude, and susceptible of great improvement. The first really valuable improvement on the original fork was made by Mr. Seymour Rogers, of Pittsburgh, Pa., and by him patented January 24th, 1865; subsequently, May 29, 1866, this patent was re-issued. Mr. Seymour Rogers being at that time a member of the firm of D. B. Rogers & Sons, of Pittsburgh, which firm, deeming the Harpoon Fork a meritorious implement, purchased the first patent from the original inventor, and, adding the improvements patented by Mr. Seymour Rogers, began their manufacture on a large scale, confident that they were perfect in every respect, and sanguine of their great success. Undoubtedly the principle of the Harpoon Fork as made by them was correct, and, when properly made, the fork was capable of doing more and better work in a given time than any other, and, indeed, the merits of other horse forks seemed to have been combined in this; but unfortunately there was a deficiency in the mechanism, and so great was the defect that nearly all the forks first put on the market were returned to have the tripping device reconstructed. This defect seriously interfered with the success of the fork, its many good points were lost sight of in the one defect, and the Harpoon Horse Hay Fork, instead of being generally recognized as an improvement entitled to a prominent place in the front rank of labor-saving agricultural implements, was consigned by its former admirers to a dark corner in the back ground, where it remained until it passed into the hands of its present owner, Mr. A. J. Nellis.

Mr. Nellis, after a long series of costly experiments, made many improvements, and the Forks manufactured by his firm have met with unqualified success. The patents of the Nellis Original Harpoon Horse Hay Fork are dated as follows: September 6, 1864; re-issued December 18, 1866; January 24, 1865; re-issued May 29, 1866; March 20, 1866; December 18, 1866; August 13, 1867; November 9, 1867; January 11, 1870; January 18, 1870; October 21, 1873; June 30, 1874; July 21, 1874. Most of these patents for improvements were issued to Mr. Nellis, and they are all owned and controlled by him; they cover every thing embraced in the single or double harpoon principle, all harpoon forks not manufactured by them, or by his license, are infringements on his patents for which makers, sellers and users are each liable. Messrs. Nellis & Co. grant no license for their manufacture.

Since the patents previously noted were issued, further and valuable improvements have been made, and it is now generally recognized as equal to any if not superior to all other Horse Forks. It is believed to be the greatest labor-saving agricultural instrument, in comparison with its cost, and is certainly the last one a farmer would think of dispensing with. It is warmly endorsed by over 100,000 farmers who use it, and after practical tests it has received seventy-six State Fair First Premiums in seventy-six months, a record of success which we think none can excel.

NELLIS' PATENT STACKER.

In addition to the Fork but a fitting connection to it for the convenience of the farmer, and worthy of special mention, is the Nellis grapple and Nellis' patent method for moving and stacking hay. The cut at the top of this page represents Nellis' patent stacker, the patent covering an improvement in pulleys and for their arrangement. The right to use this arrangement will be given to all purchasers of Nellis' Forks and Fixtures. This method of stacking requires four poles—poles A A about 35 feet in length, and poles B about 25 feet long. Now fasten these poles together at the small end by rope or chains (see G G in cut), fasten swivel pulley and two-wheeled pulley at E, first passing rope through same; raise poles B, and secure them in an upright posiiton by means of guy H and pin I, letting the poles lean a little forward (these poles B can also be used on front of barn); then tie (or fasten with floor hook) pulley at F. This done, pass your hoisting rope through the fork pulley (or small S hook pulley) then through dead eye pulley C, which is tied at G, on long poles; then tie this end of rope to neck of fork pulley and graduating cord at last named place also; now, by hitching your horse, you can raise your poles A A, and secure them by guy rope H and pin I, letting them lean slightly towards poles B. Now with graduating cord pull your fork pulley down, put horse fork in S hook pulley, attach your trip cord, and you are ready for operation.

This arrangement enables you to make your stack of any desired height or length, and renders easy the attainment of an important object when stacking, which is, to keep the centre of the stack solid, as the fork deposits its load in the centre or at any desired point of a long stack, at the disposal of a man on the stack, who, by this arrangement, is enabled to do the work of from two to three men, in from one-fourth to one-third of the time required by or in the old method of stacking; a fair trial of which must convince one of the correctness of this principle.

To load hay from stack back to wagon: Take pulley F, and fasten at bottom of either long poles. Fasten end of rope to pole at point formerly occupied by pulley F. Loosen the end of the rope from the fork and pass through pulley at bottom of long pole, and hitch now to this end. This operation will run your material successfully back to your wagon.

This stacking principle can be readily adopted inside of barn to unload into bays or mows either side of the wagon way, and the point C answering to any desired point in the roof over the mow. (See cut in centre of page). The adoption of this method enables one to convey the material to be unloaded in any direction and distance desired, and with the Nellis Grapple for putting up pulleys, the direction for running the hay can be changed with little, if any inconvenience or delay, as it can be done between forkfuls. It is deemed indispensable by all farmers who have become familiar with its convenience.

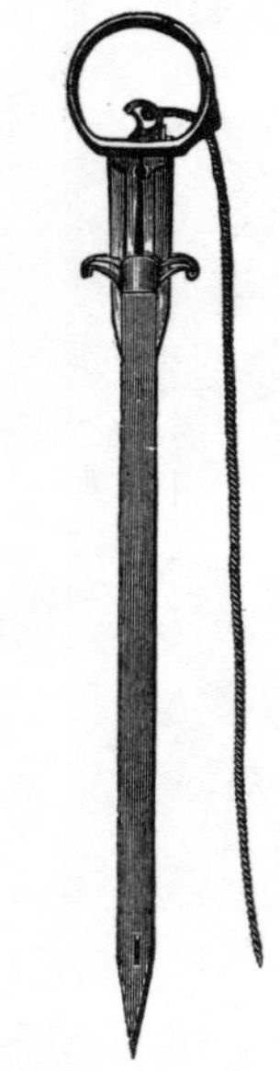

Nellis' Harpoon Fork.

Nellis' Grapple.

Trade Mark.

NELLIS' PATENT METHOD OF CONVEYING HAY, STRAW, Etc.

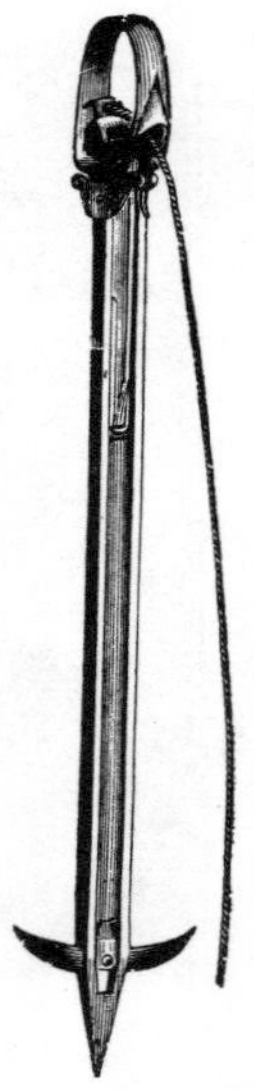

Nellis' Harpoon Fork.

Nellis' Grapple.

Trade Mark.

A. J. NELLIS & CO.,

Pittsburgh, Pa.

Manufacturers of Every Description of

AGRICULTURAL STEELS AND IRONS.

——:o:——

The facilities of the above named firm for manufacturing Agricultural Steels and Irons are not excelled, and the high quality of their productions are amply attested by the fact that even during the most depressed times their goods have always found a ready sale. This steady demand conclusively proves that their productions are not only good, but that they are cheap. Their production embraces almost everything made of steel or iron used by farmers or manfacturers of agricultural implements. One of the most valuable features ever known in the manufacture of Agricultural Steels is the Nellis' process in tempering, by his invention in heating-furnaces and chemicals, plow steels are hardened so they cannot be scratched with a file, and at the same time and by the same process, toughened so they cannot be scarcely broken with a hammer, and when it yields under the hammer it bends before breaking, and when broken you can cut glass with the same piece. This is an accomplishment never before attained, and these advantages are better appreciated than can be described by the farmer that cultivates the soil. We could if we had the room, interest the reader with notices of many other practical inventions of Mr. Nellis. One of which we can only mention, which is a cheap but very effectual Horse Power Potato Digger, the merits of which will be given on application.

Iron Fencings.

Also their Malleable and Wrought Iron Fencings, Railings, Crestings, &c., &c., the cut on this sheet showing three different designs.

We cannot describe the immense establishment operated by this firm, but can perhaps convey some idea of the magnitude of their business to the mind of the reader by giving a partial list of their specialties which embrace Steel Harrow Teeth, Iron Harrow Teeth, Nut Cultivator Teeth, Wedge Cultivator Teeth, Diam. Reversable Cultivator Teeth, Oval Reversable Cultivator Teeth, Circular Coulters, Share's Patent Harrow Teeth, Coulter Standards, Coulter Clamps, Steel Coulters, Iron Coulters, Steel Faced Coulters, Steel Mold Boards, Steel Land Sides, Cast Cast Steel Shears, Walking Cultivator Shovels, Riding Cultivator Shovels, Three River Blades, Double Shovel Blades, Single Shovel Blades, Hinged Horse Hoe Shovels, Horse Hoe Wings, Oval Reversable Points, Diamond Reversable Points, Corn Planter Runners, Grain Drill Points, Nellis' Patent Cotton Ties, Steel Bull Tongues, Dixon Cotton Sweeps, Magnolia Cotton Sweeps, Allen Cotton Sweeps, Cotton Scrapers, Cotton Scooters, Cotton Turning Shovels, Wrought Single Tree Clips, Wrought Double Tree Clips, Open Plow Links, Agricultural Malleables, Malleable Clevises, Wrought Clevises, Nellis' Original Harpoon Horse Hay Fork, Nellis' Patent Grapple, Nellis' Patent Pulley, Floor Hooks, Hart's Post Auger, Lee's Post Hole Digger, Nellis' Potato Digger, Transparent, Wrought and Malleable Iron Fences, and many other articles which we have not room to mention. Their patterns number upwards of 6,000, each for a different size or shape of article. We present cuts of a very few of their articles on this page, but for a complete catalogue, we must refer the reader to the firm themselves, who will furnish it upon application personally or by mail. Implement manufacturers and agricultural and hardware dealers should examine the goods manufactured by Messrs. A. J. Nellis & Co., compare them and their prices with others, purchase—and save a large percentage. The firm guarantee both in quality and prices.

Convinced that no manufacturer of a first-class article can compete successfully with, or can protect the consumers from those who imitate the appearance of his wares, and then foist them upon an unsuspecting public as genuine, Messrs. A. J. Nellis & Co., have designed and patented a Trade Mark, of which we present a *fac simile*, which is imprinted on all their Agricultural Steels and Irons, and such goods are warranted to be second to none offered.

The works are equipped with the latest improved furnaces and labor saving machinery, and an ample force of skilled workmen are always present. The facilities of the firm for securing the choicest stock are unsurpassed, and neither poor materials or faulty workmen find any place in their establishment. The aim of the firm ever has been and still is to furnish the best possible goods at the lowest possible prices. Much of the production of this establishment is on order from agricultural implement manufacturers, and such orders the firm are always ready to promptly fill.

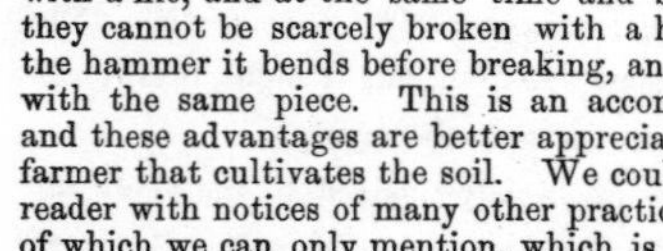

Corn Planter Runner.

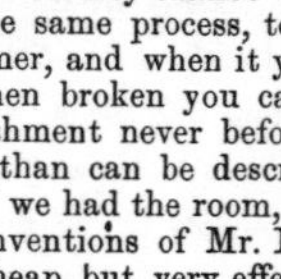

Coulter.

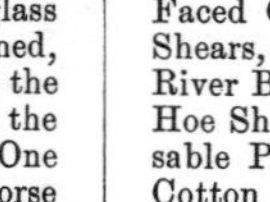

Magnolia Sweep.

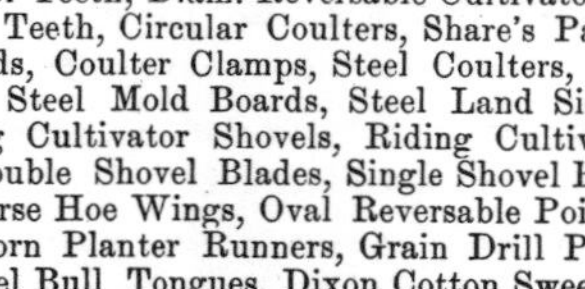

Nellis' Cotton Tie.

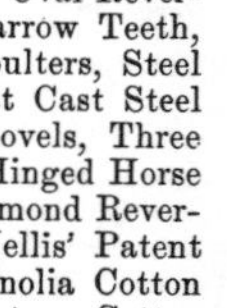

Dixon Sweep.

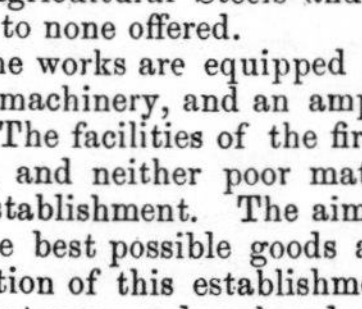

Cultivator Tooth and Shovel.

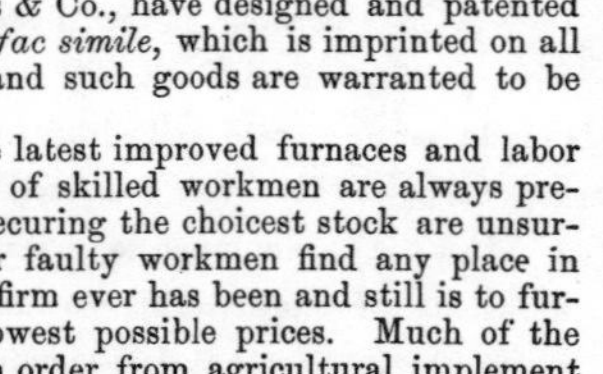

Mould Board.

H. L. EMERY & SONS,

Proprietors of the Albany Agricultural Works, Hamilton, Liberty & Union Sts., Albany, N. Y.

These extensive works were originally projected and established during the years 1847,-8 and 9, by the senior co-partner of the present firm, under the title of Horace L. Emery, since which time the firm name has been changed to Emery & Co., Emery Bros., Horace L. Emery & Son, and now is H. L. Emery & Sons. Mr. H. L. Emery has maintained an almost continuous personal supervision of the works from their inception to the present time,—and under his skillful management, they have acquired a fame which extends over all the world.

The present firm, on the first of May 1872, purchased the entire outstanding interest in property, and the business of the Albany Agricultural Works, including the large stock of Farm and Plantation Machinery and Implements then on hand, since which they have largely increased their facilities, and are now manufacturing and dealing in almost every description of machine and tool used by the husbandman.

Prominent among the many articles produced at these works and specially worthy of mention, are Horace L. Emery's Patent Endless Railway Horse-Power, with its changeable gearing for the different degrees of force and motion required for driving the various machines and processes for the plantation, farm and workshop, without changing the travel or labor of the horses; also, the Portable Lever Horse-Power, (same patent), for two to eight horses, with its double pinions and balanced gearing, without dead points of leverage, friction or wear. The Threshing Machines with Cleaners for all grains, rice, grass seeds, etc., patented by Mr. Emery, are so widely

He who by the Plow would thrive.
Himself must either hold or drive.

and favorably known, that to write a word of praise for them, would be superfluous. They are made all sizes, from two to eight horse-power.

Another very useful contrivance for the farmer or planter is Felton's Patent Portable Farm Feed Mills, suited for two horses, or for steam and water power, with a capacity per hour of from six to ten bushels with horses, and from ten to twenty-five bushels when propelled by steam or water power.

A reliable Seed Planter has for many years, been one of the greatest needs of the agriculturist, scores if not hundreds of worthless drills and broadcast seeders having been palmed off upon the farmer, but in the Seed Planter, manufactured at the Albany Agricultural Works, the highest possible degree of excellence has been obtained. The firm also manufactures a neat, light, and easy running but strong dog-power, which is in great favor among dairymen, and others who require a light motor. Clark's Patent Steam Generator, or Portable Safety Sectional Steam Boiler, manufactured by this firm, for price, efficiency, economy in rapid production of steam, and absolute safety from fire or explosion, has no superior—and is adapted for warming dwellings, workshops, hothouses, heating water, steaming and cooking food for stock, driving small steam engines, for cutting fodder, sawing wood, pumping, churning, and other uses upon the farm or plantation, and will carry with safety one hundred and fifty pounds pressure.

In addition to the articles above enumerated, they manufacture Portable Presses for hay, cotton, rags, etc., all sizes, for hand and power; also, Portable Cross-Cut, Circular and Drag Saws and Shingle Mills, Power and Hand Corn Shellers, Horse and Hand Power Corn and Seed Planters, Power and Hand Cider Mills, Dog Power Churning Machines, Plows, Harrows, Cultivators, Field Rollers, Scrapers, etc.

Such of our readers as may desire further information in relation to the various manufactures of H. L. Emery & Sons, may, by addressing them, obtain a handsomely illustrated catalogue and price list, containing carefully prepared descriptions of the leading machines which they manufacture.

We have represented on the upper portion of this page, engravings of a few of the labor saving machines manufactured at the Albany Agricultural Works, while the lower portion contains illustrations of EMERY'S UNIVERSAL

H. L. Emery & Sons Endless Railway Horse Power, Grain Thresher and Cleaner, Combined.

H. L. Emery & Sons Endless Railway, Horse Power, Grain Thresher and Cleaner on the Road.

COTTON GIN AND CONDENSER ATTACHMENT, to which we call attention.

The perfecting of these machines has for twelve to fifteen years past, received a great share of the time and efforts of the inventor, whose experience in this and other countries, and with growers, merchants and manufacturers of the staple, has thoroughly acquainted him with their customs and necessities.

It is believed that with these advantages he has succeeded in producing the most complete and desirable machinery specially adapted for the preparation of the staple for market, thereby enabling the grower and producer to effect a quicker sale, and invariably obtain the highest prices in any of the leading markets of the world.

During the years 1862, 3, and 4, these machines were placed on exhibition, by the inventor, at

H. L. Emery & Sons Endless Railway Horse Power, with Drag and Circular Cross-Cut Saw Mills.

H. L. Emery & Sons Plantation Lever Horse Power, with Cotton Gin and Condenser.

the World's Expositions in London, also at Manchester, England, where they received the most complimentary reports and honors for their merits. At a trial in Manchester, under the auspices of the Manchester Cotton Supply Association, in competition with a large number of other and most approved cotton gins then in use, these were most favorably endorsed and commended, after a trial, in which all participated.

Each gin was allotted an equal amount of several different kinds of seed cotton, from as many different quarters of the world as Egypt, Smyrna, India, China, Burmah, Venezuela, Peru, Jamaica, Honduras, and the

United States. Each competing gin was permitted to make three samples, and the competitor selected from them one sample, and these selected samples were registered and numbered by the Secretary of the Association, and afterwards forwarded to the Liverpool Cotton Exchange or Board for inspection, and report as to the quality, value, condition and other features concerning them.

When the report was received in Manchester, it appeared that those from the Universal Cotton Gin and Condenser were the only samples which were reported as entirely clean and free from foreign matter, and the staple

pronounced entirely uninjured by the process of ginning. Some of them were long and fine samples from South Carolina, Sea Island and Venezuela cotton. This was the highest and only like compliment which the Manchester Cotton Supply Association has ever given to any Saw Cotton Gin before or since.

The Manchester Cotton Supply Association was, for many years, prejudiced against the use of the Saw Cotton Gin, believing, as they did, that the defective preparation of the staple of commerce was attributable almost wholly to the action of the saws, and that it was inseparable from the very

H. L. Emery & Sons Endless Railway Horse Power, Cotton Gin and Condenser Combined, and Press.

H. L. Emery & Sons Endless Railway Horse Power, Cotton Gin and Condenser on the Road.

nature of their action and process. Their necessities, however, caused by the cotton famine, in consequence of the war then (in 1863) existing in this country, forced them to seek a supply at all hazards, even if through the hated channel—the Saw Gin, and to enable them to select from among the several kinds they consented to the trial of Saw, Roller, and other kinds of cotton gins before alluded to.

The encomiums received during the past ten years from all cotton growing countries, certifying to the merits of the Universal Cotton Gin and Condenser, would fill a large volume. We have only room to say that, like all the other machines manufactured by H. L Emery & Sons, they are perfect in their mechanism. We heartily commend them to the consideration of our cotton planters, believing them to be among the best.

With a complete stock on hand, perfectly equipped works, machinery, tools and facilities unsurpassed by any similar establishment, they are enabled to, and do offer as good terms and as low prices, considering the cost of production and the value and efficiency of their manufactures, as any other house in the same line in the country.

H. L. Emery & Sons Universal Cotton Gin and Condenser Combined.

H. L. Emery & Sons Universal Cotton Gin and Condenser Combined.

FIRE PUMP.

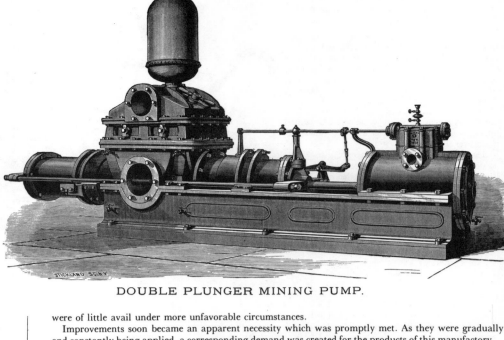

DOUBLE PLUNGER MINING PUMP.

Steam Pumps. Manufactured by the Knowles Steam Pump Works, Warehouses, 92 & 94 Liberty Street, N. Y., and 14 & 16 Federal Street, Boston, Mass. Manufactory, Warren, Mass.

The application of steam as a motive power is of uncertain origin. Hero, of Alexandria, who flourished in the third century before the Christian era, in his "Pneumatics," describes various methods of using steam for this purpose, and to him is ascribed " Eolipile," which, although a toy, possessed the properties of the steam engine. Roger Bacon, a learned Franciscan of the thirteenth century, and the first experimental natural philosopher of England, it is supposed from his writings, foresaw the application of steam power.

In 1615 Solomon de Caus, a French Protestant published a work which Arago, a modern philosopher, considers to have contained the germs of the steam engine.

The Marquis of Worcester alludes to steam power in his "Century of Inventions" in 1663. Near the close of the same century we have the account of Captain Savery's engine constructed for raising water. This machine was much used for draining mines and the water thus obtained was often used for driving other machinery. The invention for performing condensation in a separate vessel from the cylinder is ascribed to Watts in 1766, on which he took out his first patent in 1769. Thomas Payne proposed the application of steam in America in 1778; and during the same year was invented engines for producing rotary motion. Three years later Watt's Double Engine was patented.

The invention of Pumps has also been ascribed to Alexandria. Although by some ascribed to Danaus, of Lindus, in 1485, B. C.; but this invention with other hydraulic instruments, is doubtless due to Ctesibius of Alexandria, about 224, B. C.

Pumps were in general use in England early in the fifteenth century. The invention of the Air Pump is ascribed to Otto Guericke in 1654, and was improved by Boyle in 1657.

We have already sketched many of these triumphs of enterprise and on this page we

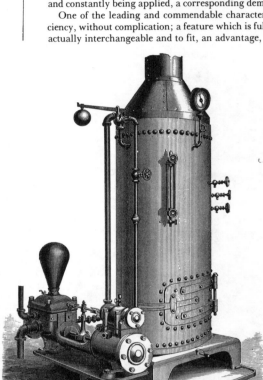

Vertical Pumps for Syrups, &c.

Small Pump and Boiler, Complete

were of little avail under more unfavorable circumstances.

Improvements soon became an apparent necessity which was promptly met. As they were gradually and constantly being applied, a corresponding demand was created for the products of this manufactory.

One of the leading and commendable characteristics of the Knowles Steam Pumps is their great efficiency, without complication; a feature which is fully appreciated by all engineers. By making all the parts actually interchangeable and to fit, an advantage, which it is claimed belongs exclusively to this pump, it tends greatly to facilitate and expedite repairs, should they become necessary.

Mr. Knowles has so far succeeded in meeting all demands for improvements, that his pumps have always stood highest in market, and consequently have secured an immense sale; not less than ten thousand of them being now in use, and the demand still increasing. He now manufactures about five hundred styles or varieties of Pumps, and his is doubtless the largest establishment of this kind in the world.

As an evidence of the high esteem in which the Knowles Pump is held, and of its real merits, not less than twenty-four first premiums have been received at the largest exhibitions held in the various parts of the United States.

Of late, special attention has been paid to the manufacture of pumps to secure protection against fire. This fire apparatus is represented in a section of a high city building, by the cut at the bottom of this page. The power is supplied from the boilers necessarily used in the building, or an independent boiler may be constructed. The pump is placed in the basement, and is so constructed as to start quickly and work up to full capacity, even when steam is at a low pressure on the boilers, as is usually the case in the night, or at other than business hours. From this pump, as will be seen, a delivery or "stand" pipe passes up through each story of the building to the roof. On each floor this pipe has one or more outlets to which hose is attached ready for instant use. Similar attachments are made on the

present our readers with another branch of industry, which is not surpassed by either in real merit and utility. Mr. L. J. Knowles the manufacturer of the Steam Pumps here represented, occupies a position far in advance of all competitors in this branch of manufactures.

His extensive manufactory is located in Warren, Mass. and his warerooms at 92 and 94 Liberty Street, N. Y. City and 14 & 16 Federal St., Boston.

Mr. Knowles commenced business in a comparatively small way more than twenty years ago. The pumps manufactured at that time were decidedly primitive in their designs and defective and inefficient in their operations.

It was found that while pumps would work successfully in pumping clear water, they

roof, thus with ordinary care and promptness in applying the remedy, an extensive conflagration among buildings supplied with this apparatus would be almost an impossibility.

The great extent to which mining is now carried on in this country, has created an extensive demand for mining pumps.

Mr. Knowles, from his long experience as manufacturer, and careful observation of what is required to meet this demand, is now able to furnish the most approved, and successful machines for these purposes, making a specialty of Pumps for deep mines and bad water, where strength is required.

Knowles' Fire Extinguishing Apparatus.

Independent Stationary Steam Fire Engine.

Mining Shaft, showing position of Vertical and Horizontal Steam Pump.

DELAMATER IRON WORKS.—View of Reynold's Hoisting Machine, Driven by the Rider Governor Cut-Off Engine.

The History of the DeLamater Iron Works is interwoven with that of the United States during the recent conflict between the North and the South. This prosperous and enterprising firm constructed the noted Iron clad gunboats "Monitor," and "Dictator," also the machinery for the Stevens Battery, all of which have a world wide reputation. Some idea of the magnitude and capacity of this establishment may be formed from the fact that they turned out a fleet of 30 Spanish Gunboats, built entirely by their works in seven months. They have constructed the large Iron Derricks for the city of New York Department of Docks of 100 Tons capacity, the engines for the Alexandria Steamship Line, City of Merida and City of Havana, for Mallory's Line City of Galveston City of Dallas and Austin.

The DeLamater Iron Works succeeded to the Phoenix Foundry established in 1825. Cornelius H. DeLamater and Peter Hogg purchased the establishment in 1842. C. H. DeLamater became its owner in 1856 and remained sole proprietor until May 1873, when George H. Robinson was admitted to a partnership with him. This establishment Employ an average of 1200 men, and are prepared to turn out work in their line with unusual despatch as they have Boiler shops, Machine shops, Smith shops, Iron and Brass Foundries, Floating Steam Derricks and ample Dock accommodations connected with the works, which are located on 55 city lots at the foot of West 13th street, New York City.

THE NEW TRIBUNE BUILDING (now in process of erection), THE LARGEST NEWSPAPER OFFICE IN THE WORLD.

The new Tribune building, an accurate illustration of which is published herewith, is now in course of erection on the old historic site of *The Tribune*, the corner of Spruce and Nassau streets, one of the most important central points in the City of New York, and the most eligible on Manhattan Island, for a great newspaper office. The new Tribune building will be the largest newspaper office in the world.

The building when complete will front 91 feet on Printing House Square, 100 feet on Spruce street, and will extend through to Frankfort street, a clear depth of 168 feet, and with a front of 29 feet on the street last named. Only a portion of the building, that fronting on Printing House Square, 91 feet, and on Spruce street, 52 feet, is now erecting, and this will be so far completed as to allow its occupation by *The Tribune* before the remaining section is begun. On Printing House Square, above huge foundations, laid in with granite bondplates and cap-stones, a majestic tower will rise nearly 260 feet. The main entrance will be in the front of this tower, which from the starting point of the foundation, 25 feet below the sidewalk level, to the top of the finial, will measure 285 feet. At the height of 150 feet a little balcony appears on the front of the tower, and from this the national flag will be displayed on suitable occasions. One hundred and sixty-seven feet from the ground will be an immense clock with four dials each 12 feet in diameter, which will be illuminated at night.

Just within the doorway will be placed a life-size statue of Mr. Greely of marble or bronze, the material for the work not having been decided.

Imposing and unrivalled as the new home for *The Tribune* will be, that newspaper is in every way worthy of it. Its facilities for the collection and transmission of intelligence from all parts of the world are unequalled. Its staff of associate editors, correspondents, and reporters contains the ablest men in the profession; and the editor has resolved to spare neither pains nor money in the effort to make *The Tribune* the very first newspaper in the world.

While *The Tribune* has retained all the excellent features that make it such a favorite in former days, it has exhibited an enterprise and acuteness in its news department which may have been the wonder of all its old friends. Remembering that the chief function of a daily journal is to give its readers the fullest, the best arranged, the most attractive, and the most readable history of the occurrences of the time, it has devoted its energies to this business, and its success has been universally recognized and applauded. It devotes especial attention to the proceedings of learned bodies, to education, to scientific discoveries and explorations, to new inventions, to agriculture, to the promotion of American industry, and to books, pictures, music, and the drama. Its financial articles have won a peculiarly high reputation. Its reports of the markets have long been distinguished for fullness and accuracy, and its quotations have been accepted as standards in the cattle, produce, and the provision trades for many years. Its reports of local affairs are acknowledged to be the most accurate, intelligent and complete; its domestic correspondence is always fresh and valuable; and abroad it is served by the ablest writers and keenest observers engaged upon any American periodical.

While it never can be neutral in politics, *The Tribune* is entirely independent of all parties. It believes that the mere organ of a clique can not be a thoroughly good newspaper, and will always defend the Republican principles which it was for over thrity years identified. But it values parties solely as means for procuring honest government on sound principles. For the partisans who insist that a journal of their faith must follow their lead, and defend their acts, it has no feeling save contempt.

VALLEY MACHINE CO.'S PUMPS,

EASTHAMPTON, MASS.

These pumps are adapted to all purposes for which pumps are used. They are of graded sizes, from the small boiler feed, which sells at ninety dollars to the large pumping engine for supplying cisterns with water or for raising the heaviest liquids in breweries, distilleries or oil works. The Valley Machine Company, Easthampton, Mass., will give full particulars to those interested.

NEW YORK SLATE ROOFING CO.

New York

Among the inventions introduced for rendering wooden and other buildings fire-proof, none is more worthy of mention than Gline's Patent Slate Roofing Paint, which article has won golden opinions from all who have used it and has slowly but steadily increased its fame until it may be found upon roofs in nearly every section, having been used either as a matter of economy or for keeping out the elements. It has the peculiar quality of causing warped shingles to become flat, of preserving the most decayed ones, making those which are otherwise worthless, durable and water-tight. The roof is a most important part of our home and often a serious annoyance as well as expense by reason of frequent leaks.

The article derives its name from the inventor, Mr. Geo. E. Glines; "Slate," from the fact that slate is one of its principal ingredients, being finely pulverized to an impalpable substance; "Roofing," because intended more particularly for roofs, although used for many other purposes; "Paint," because it is in liquid form and of proper consistency to be readily applied with a brush. The company have branch houses in five of our largest cities, and about one thousand agents for the sale of this article. Their principal offices are at 4 and 6 Cedar Street, New York, and under the personal management of Mr. Geo. E. Glines, the patentee.

The demand for the paint has increased so rapidly, that in 1873 large additions were made to the manufactory, but, these proving insufficient, in 1874 the facilities of 1873 were doubled, and the company now have such spacious warehouses, ingenious machinery and practical workmen, as to enable them to fill all orders with promptness, their weekly shipments being some two thousand barrels and upwards. Their references are many, embracing large corporations, rail road companies, public institutions, scientific men and builders, and are from all sections of this country as well as from the provinces and foreign lands. Such highly favorable results have placed this company in possession of the most desirable testimonials, and in

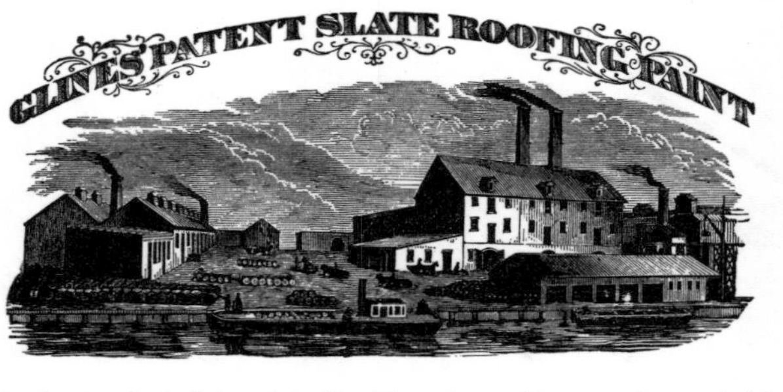

the front rank, both in point of quality and quantity, as roofing material manufacturers, their articles having taken the first premium at many of the State Fairs.

A few of the important considerations which have rendered this paint so widely known, are: it contains no tar, a most objectionable article in any form as a roof coating or paint; it is very ornamental, not only giving an old, decayed, mossy and warped shingle roof, the handsome, durable and uniform appearance of a slate roof, but also saving the expense of re-shingling, one coat being equal to a new layer of shingles. Pitch roofs frequently mar the attractiveness of buildings. and nothing helps like a slate coating to impart an elegant aspect to the whole structure, though slate itself is too heavy besides being costly. A desirable substitute, therefore is a valuable acquisition, more particularly in large towns where there are no engines and fires are spread by sparks falling on dry, decayed shingles, as readily ignited as tinder. Such roofs are prohibited in cities and also in many towns unless covered with this paint, in accordance with special acts of the Common Councils of such towns.

Nowhere else is an ounce of prevention so invaluable as when expended as a safeguard against fire. The most careful and thorough investigations, as well as extensive tests, have served to strengthen the proofs that this article will free shingles from all the defects of combustibility and leakage, admirably covering and filling up all the interstices of worn shingles, the ingredients of slate rendering the roof absolutely fireproof as well as totally impervious to water.

Last, but not least, and of no secondary importance, is its cheapness, being less in price than ordinary paint. It is sold by the gallon and not by weight, there being therefore, no necessity of adding the cheap minerals used by many paint manufacturers to produce weight, rather than quality. The genuine paint for shingles is chocolate color, all imitations containing tar and are black. This paint is largely in demand for felt and composition roofs, containing an oil which permeates the felt, causing it to become elastic pliable and durable, and is much superior to the coal tar mixture usually applied.

All house owners in cities know how often the roofer is called in to repair leaks in the tin roofs of buildings, and how considerable is the cost of such repairs. This company have added to their manufacturing business a large force of practical roofers and adopted the motto, "Leaky Roofs made water-tight or no charge." Their cement is an excellent substitute for and saves the expense of soldering. While the slate roofing paint alone, serves as the "paint" covering, which is absolutely necessary for tin or iron, (being unsurpassed for preserving metal, and preventing corrosion or decay to which such exposed surfaces are liable) it gives a glossy surface and obviates repainting every year. This paint is very elastic, will expand or contract, and never peal off, and at the same time fills up the numerous cracks and holes. No one need longer suffer the annoyance, discomfort, inconvenience and damage of a leaky roof, with an article so effectual, well tested and strongly recommended within his reach. Illustrated book circulars, with full particulars and numerous testimonials, references, etc., mailed on application to The New York Slate Roofing Co., P. O. Box 1761, or 4 and 6 Cedar Street, New York.

HOWE'S CAVE,

Schoharie County, New York.

It not unfrequently occurs that tourists make long and expensive journeys to other lands to visit places of interest, most of which have been made artificially, rather than naturally attractive. But the American seeker after what is beautiful, grand and picturesque in nature, can find within the borders of his own country, that which is excelled on no other Continent. Prominent among the wonderful natural phenomena in this country, is the celebrated Howe's Cave, in Schoharie County, New York. This Cave is situated three miles from Central Bridge or thirty-nine miles west from Albany and a few rods from the Albany and Susquehanna Railroad.

It was discovered by Lester Howe, May 22, 1842, and in extent and thrilling interest is second only to the world renowned Mammoth Cave of Kentucky. Possibly when as thoroughly explored as the latter, it may be found to have no equal among the subterranean caverns of the earth. Its arches and walls extend away for unknown miles. For want of space we are obliged to omit the mention of even the most prominent points of interest which have already been explored in this wonderful cavern. Its Halls and Castles, Mountains and Crystal Lake; its Stalagmites and Stalactites, which are among the most wonderful formations in the cave, and of special interest to the geological and scientific student, must be seen to be appreciated. It may be of interest to some to state that it contains a "Bridal Chamber" (Temperature 48 deg. Fah.) where many have been nuptially tied, including

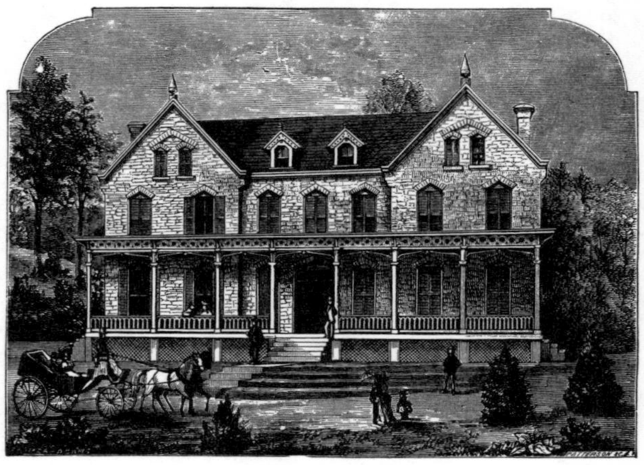

Cave House, Howe's Cave, Schoharie, Co., N. Y.

the two daughters of the discoverer. At the foot of the lake there are several gas burners, which give the visitor a beautiful view of that portion of the cave and lake, and the side grotto near by. From thence visitors proceed by boats across the lake to pursue their labyrinthian walks among these wonderful phenomena of nature.

We present the readers of this article with a view of "Cave House," an elegant hotel, recently built, near the mouth of the cave, arranged and fitted up with special reference to the convenience and comfort of the travelling public. The convenience of access, the attractive surroundings with its own unrivaled excellence have rendered the "Cave House" deservedly popular.

There is also manufactured in the vicinity of this cave, "Howe's Cave Association" Cement. This cement has become very popular, and is warranted superior to any Native Cement now in use; and by recent improvements in manufacture, it has been rendered nearly, or quite equal to the Portland and other foreign and artificial Cements. It has been used and approved by the engineers of many of our principal Railroads, including the Delaware and Hudson Canal Company's Railroads, the New York Central and Hudson River Rail Road; also by the State Engineer of New York, the engineer of the New Capitol at Albany, and many others. It is being used in the construction of many public buildings and other extensive works, in preference to any other Native Cement; including the large Anthracite Furnaces, at Albany and Crown Point, the new State capitol at Albany, and in building new locks upon the Erie and Champlain Canals; in repairs, and upon new work upon Brooklyn and Troy Gas Works; New Water Works at Albany; the masonry upon portions of the new double tracks of the New York Central Railroad, and many others. It has been practically tested by Hon. James Hall, State Geologist, and many other competent judges, and found to be first-class in all respects.

Parties wishing to learn further particulars should communicate with "Howe's Cave Association," Howe's Cave, N. Y. or J. H. Ramsay, Treasurer, 262 Broadway, Albany, N. Y.

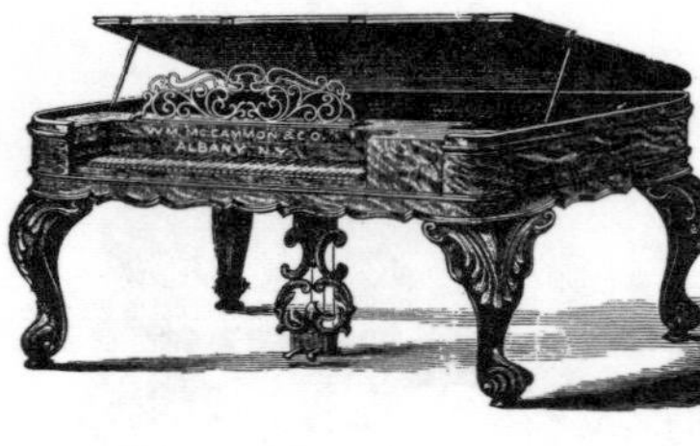

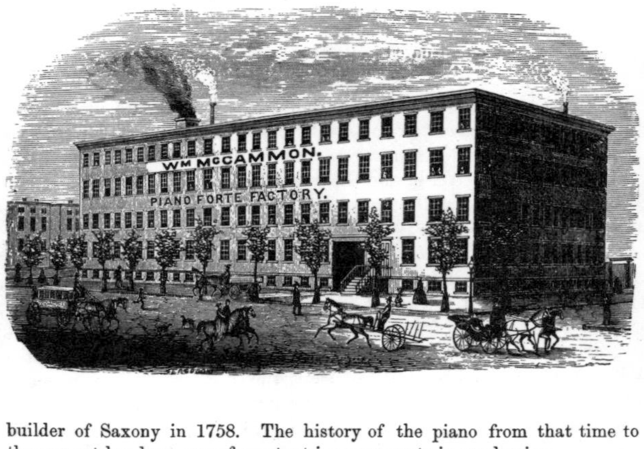

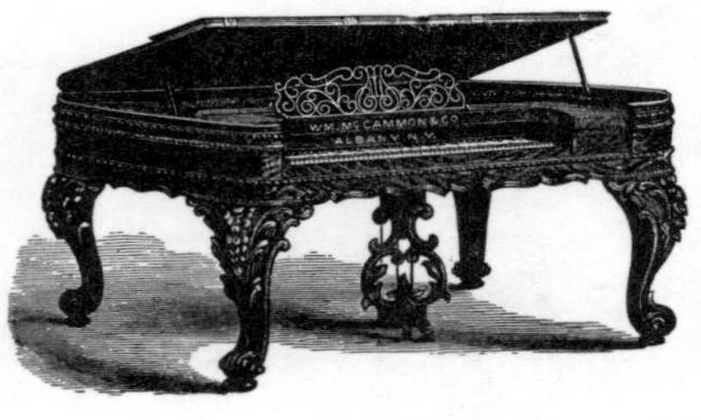

THE PIANO FORTE BUSINESS,

Represented by

WM. McCAMMON, ALBANY. N. Y.

Music is the most entirely human of the fine arts, and charms not only by its accordance with the ear, but by its power of recalling associations that are least easily recalled, and of giving depth and intensity to the most usually recurring associations. In genuine music, too, there is always something more than, and beyond the immediate expression implied, whence arises the chief part of its power.

The origin of music like that of most other arts or inventions of antiquity, is unknown. Lucretius ascribes the invention to the whistling of the winds in hollow reeds; Franckinus to the various sounds produced by the hammers of Tubal-Cain; Cameleon Pontique and others to the singing of birds, and Zarlin to the dropping of water. Pythagoras, in the middle of the sixth century, B. C., maintained that the motion of the twelve spheres must produce delightful sounds, inaudible to mortal ears, which he called "the music of the spheres."

It would be interesting to trace the gradual improvements and note the more important changes in the names and character of musical instruments, from the Harp of the Hebrews to the Grand Piano of to-day, for it is only by such comparisons that these improvements can be fully appreciated. But we can only refer to a few of those which succeeded the Harp, nearly in the order named; the Organ, the Lyre, the Psaltery, the Dulcimer and the Lute. In Queen Elizabeth's time we read of the Virginals, which somewhat resembled the Piano. These were succeeded by what was known as the Spinet; the latter, in the last century expanding into the harpsichord, the immediate predecessor of the Piano.

The original name of the Piano—"Hammer-Harpsichord"—indicates the difference between the two instruments; the Piano being a harpsichord, the strings of which are struck with hammers. It was afterward called Forte-Piano, signifying soft with power. This was finally changed to Piano-Forte, the name by which the instrument is still known.

The invention of the Piano has been ascribed to J. C. Schröter of Dresden, in 1717. Also to Bartolomeo Christofali of Florence in 1710. The Square Piano is said to have been first made by Frederica, an organ builder of Saxony in 1758. The history of the piano from that time to the present has been one of constant improvements in mechanism.

A late writer says, "the moment the idea was conceived of striking the strings with hammers, unlimited improvements were possible; and though the piano of to-day is covered all over with ingenious devices, the great essential improvements are few in number. The hammer for example may contain one hundred ingenuities, but they are all included in the device of covering the first wooden hammers with cloth; and the master thought of making the whole frame of the piano of iron, suggested the line of improvement which secures the supremacy of the piano over all other stringed instruments forever."

It is but about half a century since any practical effort was made to manufacture pianos in this country.

Among the oldest and most favorably known piano-forte manufactories in the United States is that of Mr. Wm. McCammon of Albany, N. Y. This house was founded about forty years ago by Messrs. Boardman & Gray, who were succeeded in 1862 by the present proprietor. The accumulated experience of so many years, and a successful effort to profit by every new development in the art, the pianos of this house have gradually yet constantly increased in favor and popularity until they now stand in the first rank of distinction in every respect, among those most competent to judge.

This extensive establishment is one of the largest and most complete in its appointments in the United States. It is a brick structure, five stories high, and divided into five fire-proof compartments, secured by iron doors. The building is 175 feet front, with a wing 100 feet long, the whole containing 36,750 square feet of floor. The building is on three streets, and with the lumber yard, covers a space of 26,250 square feet. The entire establishment is heated by steam, which passes through over two miles of pipe, fed by an engine of one hundred horse power. A magnificent engine of forty horse power propels an almost endless variety of new machinery, of the most approved designs.

An immense quantity of all kinds of lumber required for the construction of Piano- Fortes is constantly piled in the lumber yard, exposed to all kinds of weather, from six months to two years, after which it is put into three extensive drying rooms, which are heated by steam and capable of holding 150,000 feet of lumber, where it is kept from six months to two years longer. Contracts or lumber are made annually, with the parties who cut it, thus giving the purchasers the advantage of first prices.

The basement of the building is devoted to the manufacture of iron work. The first floor is occupied by the regulators and tuners. The packing room and machine shop are also on this floor. The second floor is devoted to the fly finishers and case makers; the third floor to finishers, carvers, sound board makers, &c.; and the upper part of the building to the varnishers, polishers and rubbers. He occupies elegant warerooms including two floors, on Broadway. No piano is allowed to leave the factory until it is thoroughly examined by the superintendent, and known to be perfect.

When we consider that the number of pieces in a piano is about 20,000 we may be able to appreciate in some measure the value of a perfect piano. Few persons we apprehend, as they look upon a piano, or listen to its enchanting music, consider the vast amount of labor, the perfection of material and the superior mechanism, requisite for the construction of such an instrument. The great number of workmen required in the construction of a piano, and the great variety of woods essential to impart the requisite properties to the different portions of the instrument, require, as may be imagined, the exercise of the greatest judgment, to secure such pieces, and so combine them, that they will produce that harmony of action and its results—sound—toward which all should tend. It is indispensable that these pieces be securely and proportionately adjusted to each other in the massing together of all the parts. The slightest vibration in any part desired to be fixed, or immobility in any part intended to vibrate, mars the effect of the most perfect performer, and often renders the player an object of deserved sympathy.

This establishment has now turned out about 11,000 pianos of superior merit as is attested by testimonials of many of the best artists; among whom are Thalberg, Gottschalk, Jenny Lind, Jules Benedict, Strakosch, and Charles Halle.

A peculiar and very important characteristic of these pianos and which is appreciated by all who use them, is their power to be kept in tune for an unusual length of time. This Mr. McCammon has introduced into his instruments, by the great care and unique manner of constructing the frames.

They are also absolute proof against climatic changes, a quality which should be considered by the purchasers. A visit to these extensive works and ware-rooms will well repay those who can appreciate what can be accomplished by well directed effort, accompanied by the highest genius, and backed by the requisite capital.

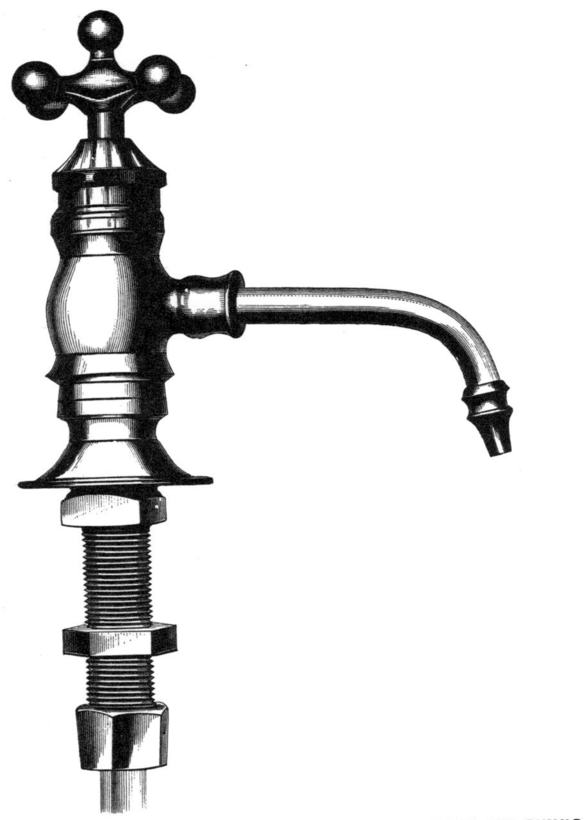

BROWNELL'S PATENT COMBINED COMPRESSION AND SWING FAUCET. Full View. Patented Nov. 16th, 1875.

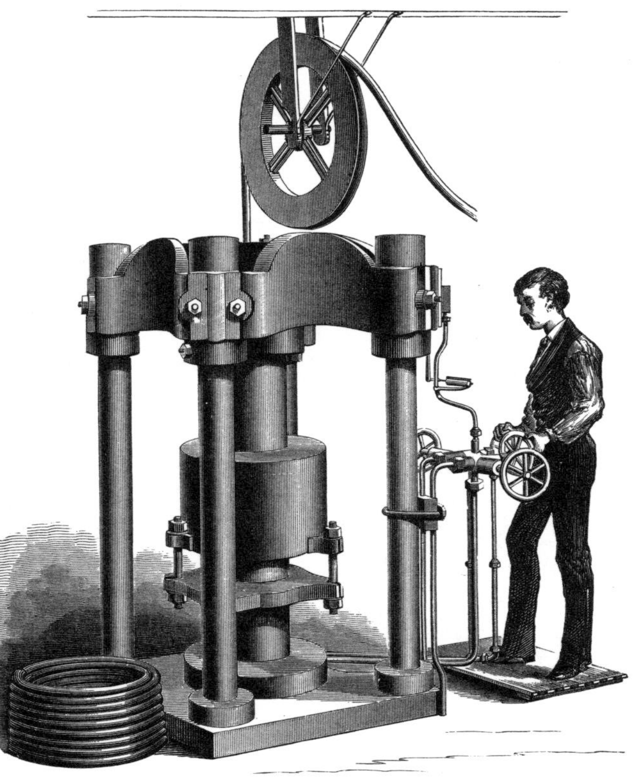

LEAD PIPE MACHINE.

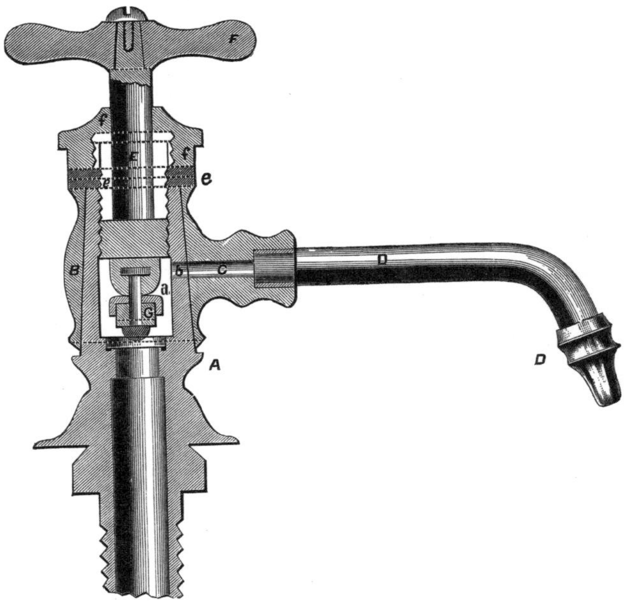

BROWNELL'S PATENT COMBINED COMPRESSION AND SWING FAUCET. Sectional View.

A.	Body of Faucet.	D.	Swinging Nozzle.
B.	Outer shell.	E.	Screw Plug.
a.	Valve chamber.	e.	Spring.
b.	Outlet in body.	F.	Handle.
C.	" " outer shell.	f.	Cap.

G. Valve swiveled to plug E.

BROWNELL MANUFACTURING CO.,

Manufacturers of

LEAD PIPE, COPPER AND BRASS GOODS,

Including

Pumps, Water Boilers, Combined Compression and Swing Faucets, and Automatic Compression Faucets. Also, Brownell's Patent Overflow Bath Tub and Plumbers' Materials Generally.

43 to 61 BOERUM PLACE, BROOKLYN, N. Y.

——:o:——

All buildings, public or private, in city or country, having any pretensions to the possession of "modern improvements" must be supplied with water, hot and cold, on every floor; with convenient bathing rooms, wash basins, sinks, etc.; consequently the manufacture of Plumbers' Materials, has become a business of great magnitude, involving the investment of an immense capital and affording employment for many thousand skilled workmen.

One of the oldest, best known and most extensive establishments in the United States for the manufacture of this class of goods is that of the Brownell Manufacturing Company, of Brooklyn, N. Y., the business having been originally established by Mr. A. C. Brownell, in the year 1854, at No. 555 Pearl Street, New York City.

Mr. Brownell was and is one of those active, persistent men with whom to will is to accomplish; he determined to manufacture goods as nearly perfect as human skill could fashion, and to merit the success which surely follows honest efforts; so successful was he, that within a few short months the demand for his goods had outgrown his facilities for production, and, in 1855, he erected, equipped and moved into a factory opposite the site of the present establishment where he remained for ten years.

In 1865, Mr. Brownell admitted his eldest son, Mr. Willis L. Brownell, into partnership, and continued the business under the firm style of A. C. Brownell & Co. At that time, the steady expansion of trade demanding ampler accommodations, the firm erected the capacious factory and warehouse now occupied by the Brownell Manufacturing Company, a rather small but very accurate engraving of which will be found at the centre of this page. The premises have a frontage on Boerum Place of 160 feet, and on Schermerhorn Street of 50 feet. The main building is a substantial brick structure, 50x100 feet in size and four stories in height, above the basement. Adjoining is the Brass Foundry 60x50 feet and two stories high. In addition to these premises, the Company have a factory on State Street for the manufacture of the wood work for their Bath Tubs, etc., (the machinery of which is driven by power conveyed from the main factory by a shaft passing under the street,) also buildings and ample grounds for the storage of the lumber and all other materials kept in stock.

The basement floor of the main building contains the powerful engine and boilers that furnish the motor to the machinery on the upper floors, and the machinery for manufacturing lead pipe; the space not thus occupied being used for crude metals and some of the coarser descriptions of manufactured goods, iron sinks, basins, etc. The coal vaults extend under the side walk, and hold from 150 to 200 tons of coal. The ground floor is occupied as offices and warerooms, in which will be found a complete stock of every description of Plumbers' Goods of the best quality. The upper floors are devoted to the manufacture of Brass and Copper Work, Water Boilers, Pumps, Common Cocks, Patent Faucets of various descriptions, and the fashioning of the metal (Tinned and Planished Sheet Copper) portions of their Patent Bath Tubs.

The Brass Foundry, in the rear of the main building, is complete in all its appointments. In a few words, the establishment is complete and has facilities for manufacturing perhaps a greater variety of plumbing materials than any other concern in this country. There are many larger producers of Lead Pipe, or Copper Goods, or Brass and Plated Goods, but this is claimed to be the only establishment in the United States that combines them all and manufactures everything belonging to the different departments.

This is a matter of great importance to the trade, as it enables them to purchase from this Company all the various goods requisite for plumbing, which otherwise could only be obtained from several dealers and manufacturers. In addition to the goods of their own manufacture, the Company keep constantly on hand and supply the trade with Iron, Enameled and Earthenware Plumbers' Miscellaneous Goods from the best makers of America and England.

The Messrs. Brownell possess a practical familiarity with the business in all its details, and have originated many valuable improvements in the manufacture of Plumbers' materials, illustrations of two of their recent and most valuable inventions being presented on this page. The reader's attention is particularly called to the following specialties:

Brownell's Patent Combination Bath Tub, of which we give at the bottom of the page a sectional and a full view, combines the conveniences of the Plunge, Sitz and Foot Bath in one tub. The space it occupies is the same as the ordinary tub, but it is set with less expense and in far less time. Each compartment is supplied with hot or cold water at pleasure by a skillful arrangement of faucets made especially for this article. The overflows and wastes are discharged into a Patent Combination Bath Plug, thus saving the expense of making joints and preventing leaking. The construction of the wood-work is novel, it being made of narrow tongued and grooved boards, and the main body of the tub placed in a frame-work, preventing the possibility of shrinkage, and thereby securing the metal lining from wrinkling or becoming loose. Heretofore there has been no convenient and economical accommodations for the Sitz and Foot Bath, but this important invention supplies the long needed apparatus which is indispensable to every household. The Sitz Bath can be used with the greatest pleasure to the bather, and is so constructed as to make it as comfortable to occupy as an easy chair. For bathing children the Combination Tub presents unequalled facilities, and this accommodation alone should recommend it to every family.

Brownell's Patent Overflow Bath Tub, with faucets and soap dish on slab, is essentially the same as the Combination Tub, except that it lacks the Sitz and Foot Bath. This Tub can be set at the minimum of cost, the plumber only having to attach pipes to the waste coupling and cocks, and it is ready for use. On the end of the tub is a slab of either Enameled Iron, Earthenware or Wood, as the purchaser may desire, and sunk in the slab is a soap dish which drains directly into the waste pipe.

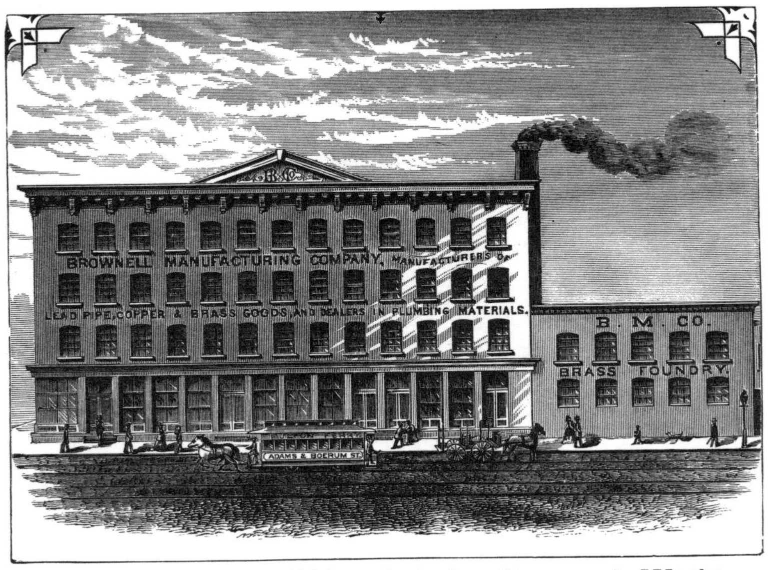

View of the Brownell Manufacturing Company's Works.

Brownell's Patent Combined Compression and Swing Faucet, Patented November 16th, 1875, (of which two illustrations are given, one a full view, the other a sectional view, accompanied with an explanation of the various parts, which will enable the reader to readily understand its operation,) has already become very popular. It completely fills a want long felt and will, without doubt, supersede at no distant day the imperfect faucets which have been in common use. For years Swing Faucets were generally used, but Compression Faucets, on account of the great durability of the valve, have of late superseded the Swing Faucets, in all first-class work. Great objection, however, is made to the stationary nozzle of the compression faucets, as being in the way and not allowing a full use of basin, and a continual annoyance in the bruising of hands and heads of persons using the basin. This objection is entirely overcome by the use of Brownell's Patent Combined Faucets, they being constructed in such a manner as to unite the advantages of the swinging nozzle and compression valve, and improve the ordinary Swing Faucets by providing them with a screw or compression valve, to permit the shutting off of the water independently of the swing faucets and prevent them from leaking. The water may be turned on and off by turning the nozzle, or by operating the screw plug, or both. When the compression valve is in its seat the water is turned off from the upper or swinging part of the faucet, so there can be no leakage.

Brownell's Patent Automatic Compression Faucets are self-closing without the use of springs. They are simple in construction and will not readily get out of order. In their use there is no concussion in the pipes owing to the peculiar construction of the valve which acts as a safety valve does to a boiler. The pressure of the water always closes the faucet, of course the heavier the pressure the tighter the faucet, but the lightest pressure, will close this faucet so effectually that it cannot leak. Other self-closing Faucets are operated by springs which soon get out of order and render the cock useless.

The Company pride themselves on the superior quality of the Lead Pipe they produce, in no branch of their diversified manufactures is more careful judgment required than in this. At the top of the page will be found a cut of the Lead Pipe Machine proper, though there are many accessories to the manufacture not here presented. To the left of the machine, for instance, is the furnace and cauldron in which the lead is melted, rising to a height considerably greater than the machine itself, that the moulton mass may readily flow into the chamber of the machine. To the right is the reel upon which the finished pipe is coiled. The machine as here represented is in operation, and has worked up about one-half of the metal with which it was originally charged. When at rest, the heavy iron cylinder, strongly bolted to a plate below, (shown between the four upright posts,) and by this means attached to the lower piston, is disengaged from the upper piston. Before the first charge, the cylinder is surrounded by a movable jacket, the space between the two being filled with charcoal fire to heat the cylinder so that the metal will not cool too soon. The core, a bar of steel of the exact size of the bore of the pipe to be made, is then placed in the cylinder, and a steel die with an interior diameter equal to the outside of the pipe is placed in the lower end of the upper piston. The moulton metal is then allowed to flow from the cauldron, through a spout to the cylinder, and to fill it. Hydraulic pressure is then applied to the bottom of the lower piston and the cylinder is forced up, until the hollow (upper) piston enters the cylinder. After waiting a moment or two, so that the lead may not be forced too suddenly, a greater pressure is applied and the cylinder being forced upward the pipe is slowly formed, the core in the cylinder of course preserving the interior bore and the die in the piston forming the outer proportion, the finished product emerging from the top of the machine and being carried over a pulley as shown, to the reeling machine, which coils it ready for market. The charge of lead which the cylinder contained being exhausted, the pressure is reversed and the cylinder lowered to its original position ready for a new supply of lead. The pumps are not shown in the engraving. The press altogether weighs about six tons.

The manufacture of lead pipe is apparently very simple, but it really requires much skill on the part of the man who operates the machine to produce a first class article. Mr. Willis L. Brownell, superintends this important branch of the Company's work, and the pipe he produces is not excelled by any made.

Owing to their long experience and perfect familiarity with the requirements of the trade, the Brownell Manufacturing Company are enabled to offer unusually advantageous terms, and buyers will find it to their interest to examine the comprehensive stock always to be found at their establishment before making purchases.

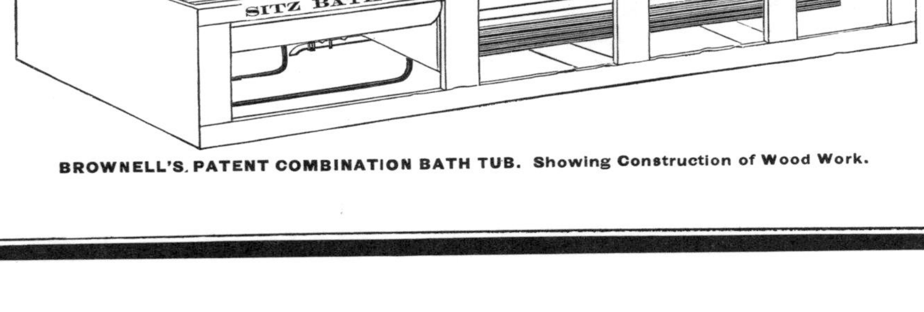

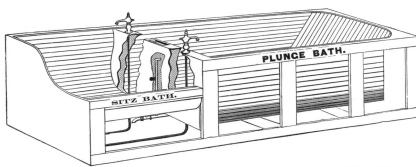

BROWNELL'S PATENT COMBINATION BATH TUB. Showing Construction of Wood Work.

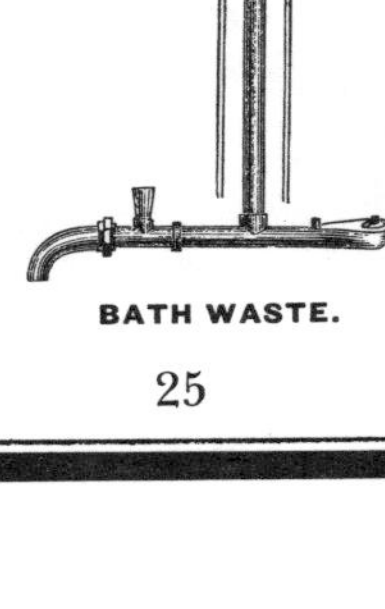

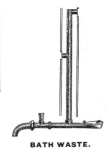

BATH WASTE.

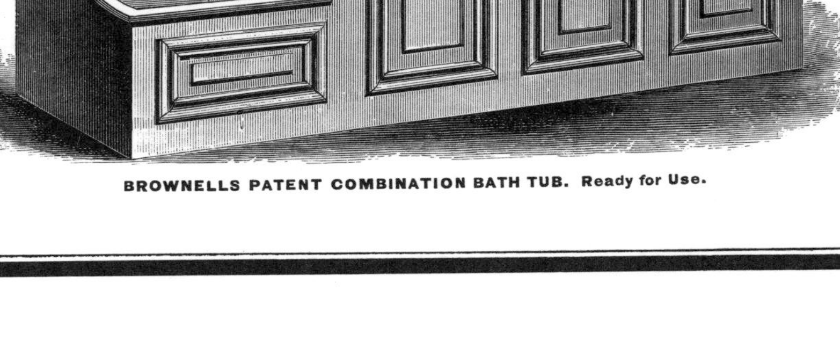

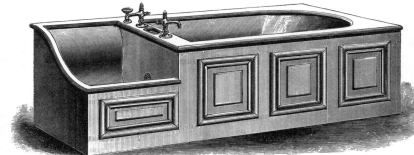

BROWNELLS PATENT COMBINATION BATH TUB. Ready for Use.

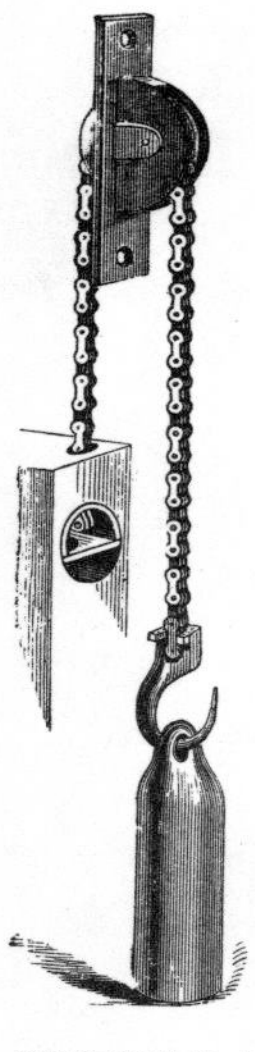

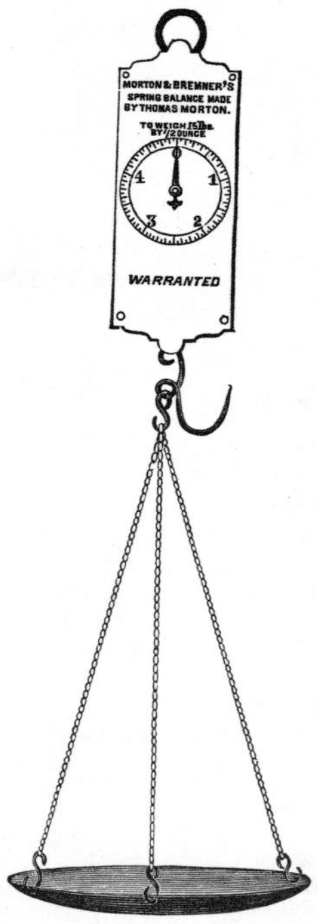

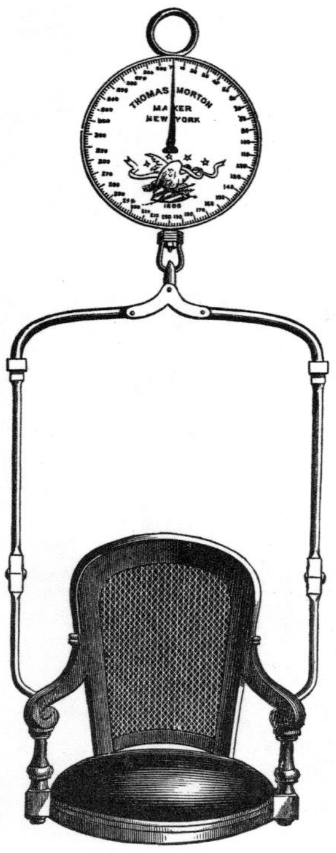

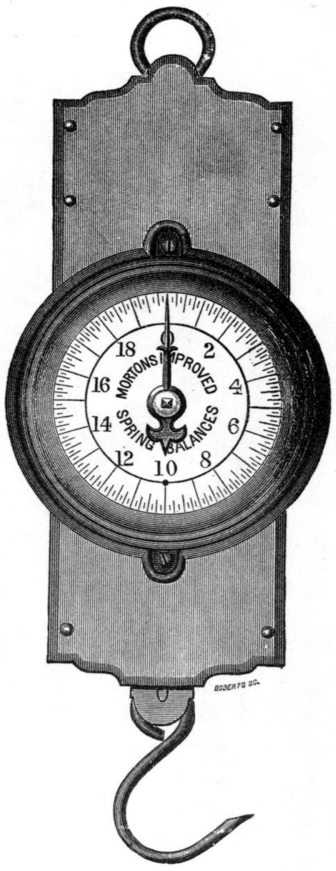

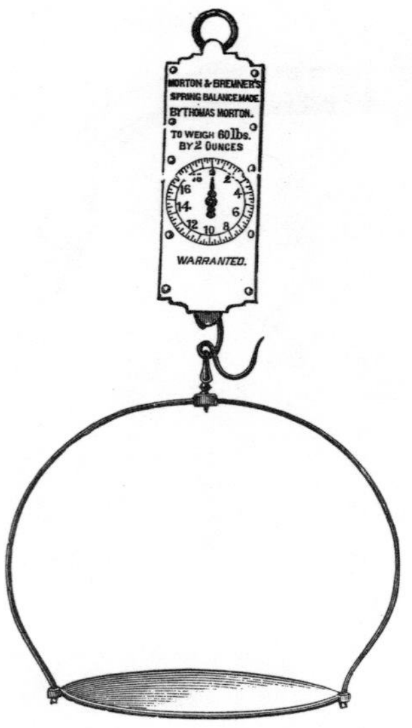

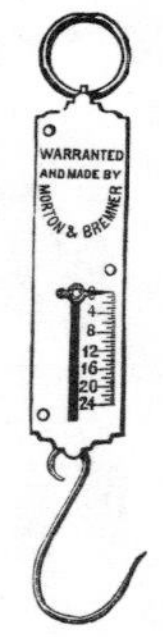

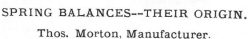

SPRING BALANCES--THEIR ORIGIN.

Thos. Morton, Manufacturer.

Since the invention, nearly half a century ago, of the spring balance by one George Salters, of West Bromwich, in England, we suppose no article of a mechanical nature in itself has obtained so universal a practical character as this. Scarcely a butcher or grocer in any country where modern customs prevail but finds its utility second only to his knife and hatchet, or his counter and scoop, and, since the development of the ice trade, its service has been almost as essential to that business as the wagon wherein the ice itself is borne, to say nothing of the hundreds of other classes of service to which it is put in preference to ordinary balance scales.

When spring balances were first introduced in America our people had but little confidence in them. The principle of springs was deemed unreliable, but they soon began to work their way forward. As soon as their real value was known, competitors in the field of their production sprang up with great rapidity, and the market was flooded with unreliable scales and balances, that in some instances begot for the principle a condemnation which has, however, been overridden and almost entirely dissipated by the scrupulous measures of one or two fair and competent makers, one of the foremost of whom in the United States is Mr. Thomas Morton, whose present establishment is at 15 Murray Street, New York.

In 1842, in conjunction with Mr. A. A. Bremner, Mr. Morton introduced to the American public the first domestic made spring balance, the construction of which was based upon Salter's method. This was a hook balance scale to weigh up to 24 lbs. From that day to this the principle upon which the action of the balances has been produced has remained intact, though the number of varieties of spring scales now made by Mr. Morton amounts to more than 150, rising from balances that will weigh a ten sent stamp—whose weight by the way is only a quarter of a dram—up to heavy instruments capable of weighing accurately 2000 lbs. at a time, all graded to suit any particular service, illustrations of a few of which grace this page. The assortment in store comprises single and double hook balances with vertical and circular indices, with circular and square pan, with single and double bow and triple chain attachments, the average stock on hand varying in value from $20,000 to $30,000.

Mr. Morton's goods rank with the best. None but the very best iron, steel and brass that can be bought are used in his manufactures, all of which are "warranted in every respect when delivered." So special and peculiar are the Morton scales that their maker can detect at sight upon opening them if they have been subjected to any abuse. Moreover, especially as regards their accuracy, Mr. Morton pits them in a published challenge against the best scales in common use, which he is willing to back with a stake of $1,000 to be given by the winner to some charitable institution.

As a striking evidence of their excellence it might be remarked that one of the Morton & Bremner spring scales has been in use in the Boston market for the last twenty years, and has never faltered or required any repairs whatever, remaining throughout as accurate as when new.

In addition to his spring balances Mr. Morton has recently introduced a new article of special service in the shape of a simple attachment for suspending chains with weights, windows, etc., moved more or less on the pulley principle. By its use the required attachment to either weight, window or what else, can be made in less than half the time required to tie the knot in the cord commonly used for the purpose of suspension, and is at the same time so secure as to be removed only by design or violence. This simple but highly serviceable invention has been patented by Mr. Morton, and has already obtained unqualified approbation wherever used. The attachments are capable of sustaining weights from 100 to 1500 lbs.

The business of the house is now principally managed by Mr. Thomas S. Morton, son of the founder. An illustrated catalogue of his wares, with prices, is worthy of attention. Address, 15 Murray Street, New York. P. O. Box, 3597.

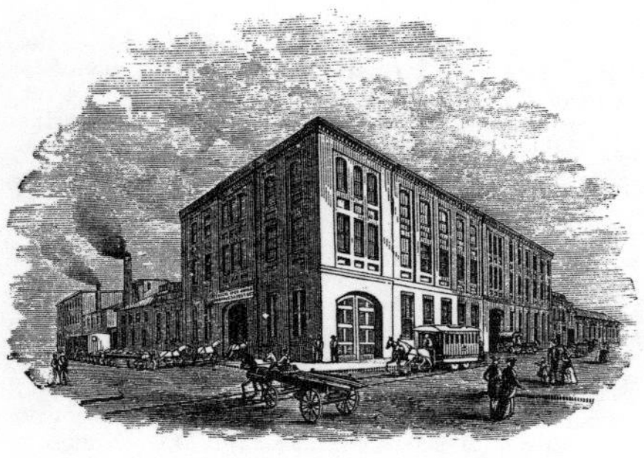

Pascal Iron Works, Philadelphia, Pa.

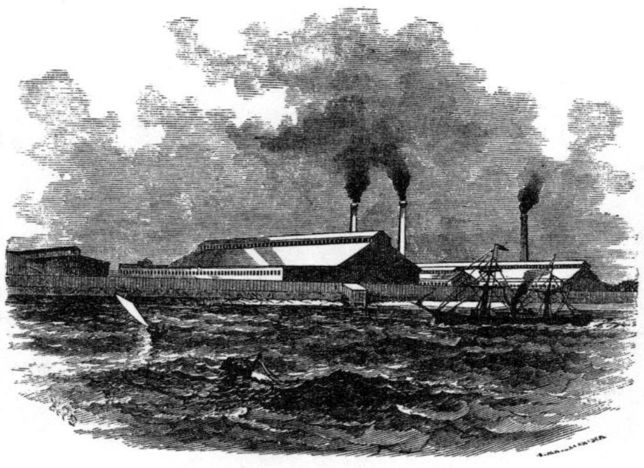

Tasker Iron Works, New Castle, Del.

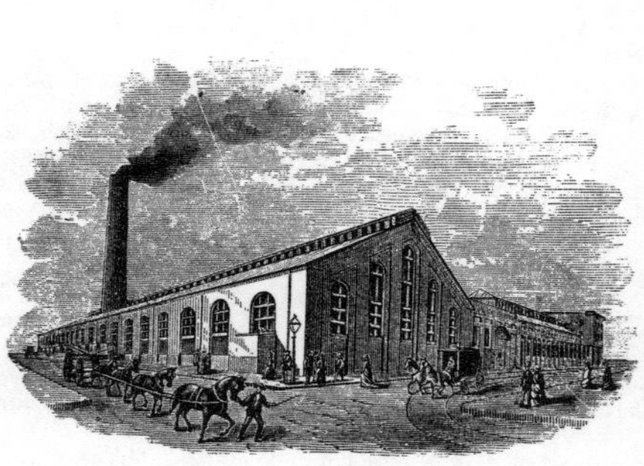

Pascal Iron Works, Philadelphia, Pa.

MORRIS, TASKER & CO.,

Proprietors of the Pascal Iron Works, Philadelphia; and Tasker Iron Works, New Castle, Delaware.

One of the marvels of our progressive age is the house of Morris, Tasker & Co., a short sketch of whose history will doubtless prove interesting to the reader. In 1821, Stephen P. Morris commenced manufacturing stoves, grates, etc., in a comparatively unpretending way, in the city of Philadelphia. By careful management and the excellence of his work, his business prospered and he became favorably known as a manufacturer of these specialities. In 1835 a partnership was formed between Stephen P. Morris, Henry Morris and Thomas T. Tasker Sr., for the manufacture of stoves, grates, etc., and their business wes conducted at the corner of Third and Walnut streets, where the central offices of the present company are now located. In the same year, gas was first introduced into Philadelphia, and a proposition was made to the firm by Wm. Griffiths, a skilled English workman, to engage in the manufacture of gas pipes, previously confined to England. Acting upon this proposition, gas pipe was added to their list of manufactures, and at that time the business which has rendered their reputation national and won for them magnificent fortunes, may be said to have commenced. Imperfections in the English process of manufacture were soon discovered and improved methods adopted. It was their determination to reach the highest excellence in this branch of manufacture. In this they were successful and their business rapidly grew to such proportions that it became necessary to build new and larger buildings. In 1836 they commenced erecting new buildings at their present location, to which they gave the name of the "Pascal Iron Works." Additional buildings were erected as the requirements of the business demanded, until now they comprise an area of twelve acres, covering two entire squares within the boundaries of Third and Fifth, and Morris and Tasker streets, in addition to the large building on the opposite side of Morris street. To the manufacture of gas pipe the firm added other articles connected with the business, such as gas fittings, gas fitters' tools, etc., and from these followed the construction of machinery for generating, washing, purifying and storing illuminating gas. Then the manufacture of pipes for other purposes, tubes for conveying water, lap-welded boiler tubes, boilers themselves, water fittings, hot water apparatus for the most varied uses, was added, together with all the tools for the erection of the same, ventilating apparatus, etc., until at present the firm manufacture every variety of apparatus necessary to heat, light, ventilate, or furnish with water, buildings of all descriptions.

The firm is now composed of the sons of Thomas T. Tasker Sr.—Messrs. Thos. T. Tasker Jr. and Stephen P. M. Tasker, who, inheriting the business capacity which distinguished their father, and being thoroughly and practically educated in all the details of the business, ably carry forward the comprehensive designs of the founders of the house, and by their broad and vigorous policy are enlarging its scope, and making it a monument of enterprise and sagacity, such as its progenitors scarcely dreamed of. Twelve boilers and seven steam engines representing one thousand horse-power, are in constant operation in the works.

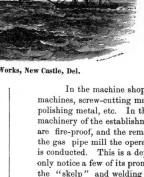

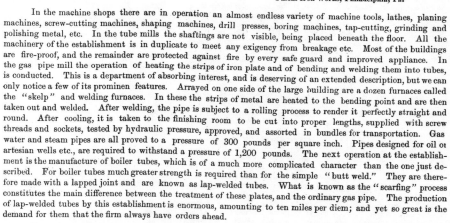

In the machine shops there are in operation an almost endless variety of machine tools, lathes, planing machines, screw-cutting machines, shaping machines, drill presses, boring machines, tap-cutting, grinding and polishing metal, etc. In the tube mills the shaftings are not visible, being placed beneath the floor. All the machinery of the establishment is in duplicate to meet any exigency from breakage etc. Most of the buildings are fire-proof, and the remainder are protected against fire by every safe guard and improved appliance. In the gas pipe mill the operation of heating the strips of iron plate and of bending and welding them into tubes, is conducted. This is a department of absorbing interest, and is deserving of an extended description, but we can only notice a few of its prominen features. Arrayed on one side of the large building are a dozen furnaces called the "skelp" and welding furnaces. In these the strips of metal are heated to the bending point and are then taken out and welded. After welding, the pipe is subject to a rolling process to render it perfectly straight and round. After cooling, it is taken to the finishing room to be cut into proper lengths, supplied with screw threads and sockets, tested by hydraulic pressure, approved, and assorted in bundles for transportation. Gas water and steam pipes are all proved to a pressure of 300 pounds per square inch. Pipes designed for oil or artesian wells etc., are required to withstand a pressure of 1,200 pounds. The next operation at the establishment is the manufacture of boiler tubes, which is of a much more complicated character than the one just described. For boiler tubes much greater strength is required than for the simple "butt weld." They are therefore made with a lapped joint and are known as lap-welded tubes. What is known as the "scarfing" process constitutes the main difference between the treatment of these plates, and the ordinary gas pipe. The production of lap-welded tubes by this establishment is enormous, amounting to ten miles per diem; and yet so great is the demand for them that the firm always have orders ahead.

From the consideration of these, the principal productions of Messrs. Morris, Tasker & Co., we would be glad to turn to describe in detail the multitude of other articles of their manufacture; but must content ourselves with a simple mention of some of them, all being closely related to the employment of gas, water, steam and air, in every form. They have the facilities for erecting gas works complete, from the retorts and buildings to the gas holder and the pipes for supplying it to the consumer, with every variety of fittings and tools for the gas fitter's trade. For their hot water and steam heating apparatus they have long been famous.

They have agencies for the distribution of goods in most of the large cities on the Atlantic and Pacific seaboards and throughout the interior.

The city authorities of Philadelphia, hesitating to accord to them such privileges as they deemed indispensable to the proper conduct of their business, Messrs. Morris, Tasker & Co., purchased a large tract of land at New Castle, Delaware, extending over a mile on the river front. They took possession in January, 1873, and on the 27th of May opened their foundry, machine, blacksmith, carpenter and pattern shops. Buildings for other branches of their work are being rapidly pushed forward with a view to their speedy occupation.

The manufactures of this firm have been so favorably known for many years that they need no commendation at our hands. Their principal offices and warehouses are located as follows: Corner of Fifth and Tasker Streets, Philadelphia; No. 15 Gold Street, New York; and No. 36 Oliver Street, Boston, Mass.

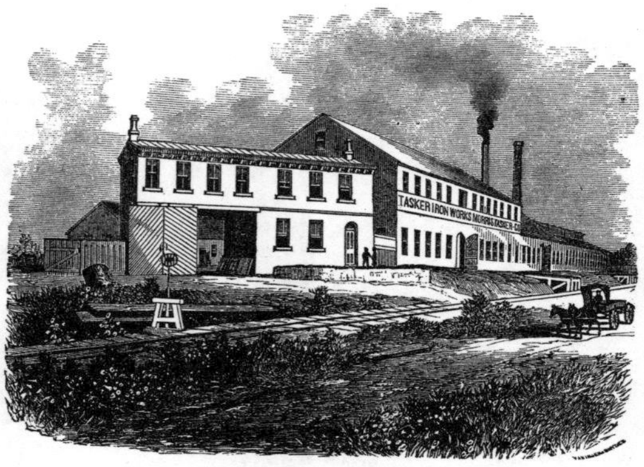

Tasker Iron Works, New Castle, Delaware.

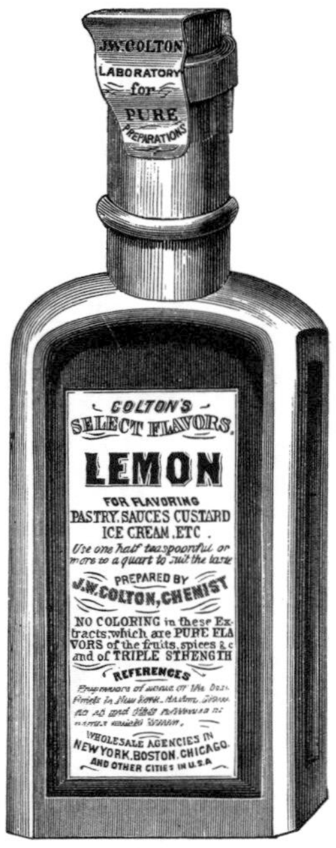

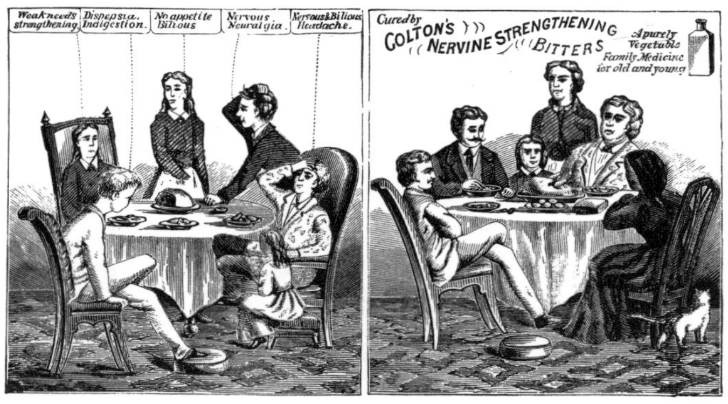

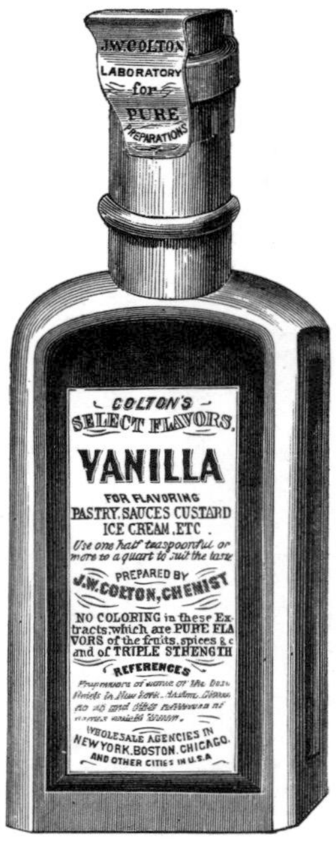

J. W. COLTON,

Manufacturer of the Celebrated Colton's Select Flavors of the Choicest Fruits and Spices, put up in sizes for family use; also, Pint and Quart Bottles for Hotels and Confectioners. Colton's Toilet Articles, Colognes and Perfumes, Nervine Strengthening Bitters and Preparations.

Laboratory and Home Depot, Westfield, Mass.

New York Agency, Bogle & Lyles, 87 and 89 Park Place

——:o:——

There are few articles of every day consumption in the preparation of which there is so great an opportunity for fraudulent adulterations as in the manufacture of Fruit Flavors. Men void of principle have gained a foothold in every calling and have foisted upon a too gullible public inferior articles of every description which they offer at a price less than the genuine can be afforded at. Some of these adulterations are comparatively harmless and the purchaser is wronged only so far as his pocket is concerned—that is, he is simply swindled out of the money he paid for the article purchased—but others are absolutely detrimental to life and health, and the purchasers of such articles are not only swindled out of the money paid, but are doubly wronged in the injury to health which too frequently follows their use.

The general public are well aware of many of the frauds constantly practised upon them. So far as we countenance such frauds by using goods which we know are not pure, we become parties to the wrong and are entitled to no redress.

In the purchase of preparations in which the introduction of foreign or impure parts is difficult of detection, too much caution cannot be used. As before stated, the manufacture of flavoring extracts furnish peculiar facilities for adulteration, while the practice is not easily discovered. We can, however, extract fruit flavors from the fruit itself, and so prepare them that without loss of strength or taste, they will last for years in any clime. To this great work the gentleman whose name heads this article has for years devoted his time and talent.

About 1860, Mr. J. W. Colton, after having given the subject of the manufacture of Fruit Extracts much careful study, and being well aware that many of the so-called Extracts of Fruits and Spices then in common use, were in no sense what they pretended to be, but vile decoctions largely composed of deleterious substances, quietly began the preparation of those Select Flavors which have since rendered his name a veritable "household word." A conscientious man, with an indomitable will and perseverence, he determined to make the best. With this aim in view he made a careful personal selection of the materials to be used and supervised the various processes through which they had to pass before the concentrated flavor of the fruits and spices assumed a useful form. From their first introduction down to the present time they have met with uninterrupted success. They have been tested in every possible manner, and have been universally recommended for their strict purity, rich flavor and unequalled strength. They are used by our first-class hotels, confectioners and families, and are sold by first-class grocers and druggists in many cities, towns and hamlets in the United States, and largely exported to foreign lands. They embrace Lemon, Vanilla, Orange, Rose, Almond, True Cinnamon, Peach, Jamaica Ginger, Nutmeg, Clove, Celery, Wintergreen, etc. It is not claimed that Colton's Flavors are sold at the lowest price per bottle; but it is claimed that one-third of the quantity is more than equal to the ordinary Flavoring Extracts and that they are true delicious flavors of the fruits, that they are strictly pure, and that it is a great saving in actual cost to use them—The Best.

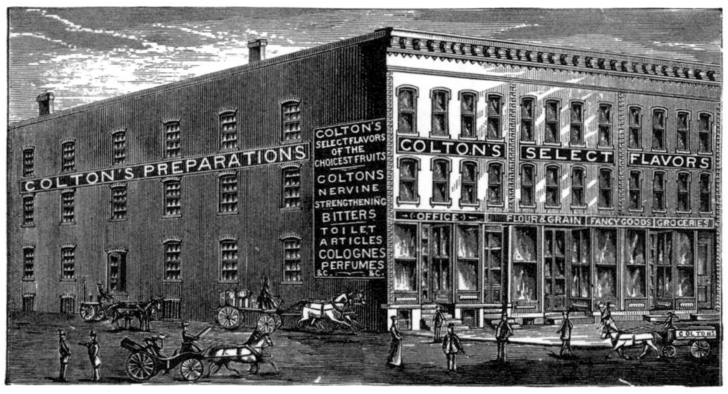

MANUFACTORY OF COLTON'S SELECT FLAVORS AND PREPARATIONS.

As a proof of the high esteem in which Mr. Colton and his preparations are held by men of world-wide fame, we annex a letter from Dr. J. G. Holland, ("Timothy Titcomb,") the Author and Poet, Springfield, Mass., (later of Scribner's Magazine:)—"To the business community: Mr. J. W. Colton I have known for many years as bearing a character for thorough integrity, a man whose position in the business world is well established; his Flavors are the standard in all this vicinity."

G. & C. Merriam, the well-known publishers of Webster's Unabridged Dictionary, writes:—"J. W. Colton is a long-time and long-tried acquaintance of ours, and his Extracts give entire satisfaction to all who use them."

We might add scores of others from men equally well-known—Hotel-keepers, Confectioners and Grocers. Families and Consumers (everywhere) would do well to know the delicious purity, great strength and economy of each and every one of Colton's Select Flavors (12 kinds.) The Extracts of Spices will be found so concentrated that for choice cookery all should try them. The Extract or Essence of Pure Jamaica Ginger is a favorite for medicine as well as for cooking.

Mr. Colton, however, does not stop in his good work for humanity here, but has prepared for the suffering ones a medical preparation of great merit. Colton's Nervine Strengthening Bitters or Tonic Elixir, which is prepared from Calisaya and Peruvian Barks, Golden Seal, Wormwood, Valerian and others of the choicest vegetable medicines. A Pure Vegetable Cordial, to strengthen or invigorate old or young, at all seasons of the year. Tonics for the stomach, a regulator for the bowels, and quieting medicines for nervous systems.

For the special use of the ladies, Colton's Toilet Article for the Compexion and Skin has no superior. Its fragrance and perfect safety for the skin of child or adult makes it almost indispensable in every family. Mr. Colton also makes a specialty of Perfumes, embracing extracts of Choice Flowers, Jockey Club, Orange Blossom, Magnolia, Rose Geranium, Musk, etc., among the finest of perfumes, and no toilet is complete without Colton's Triple and German Cologne Waters.

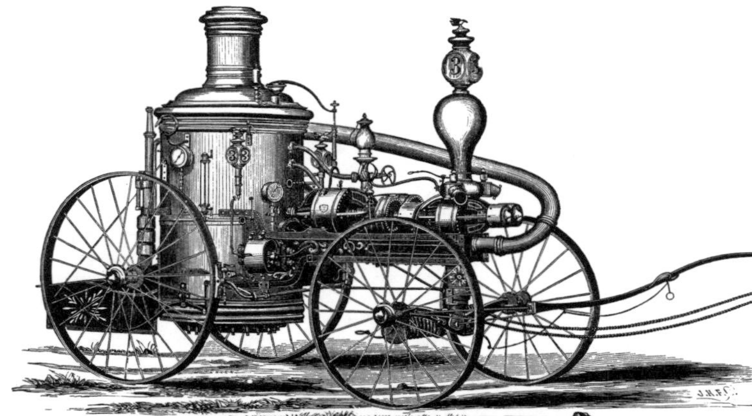

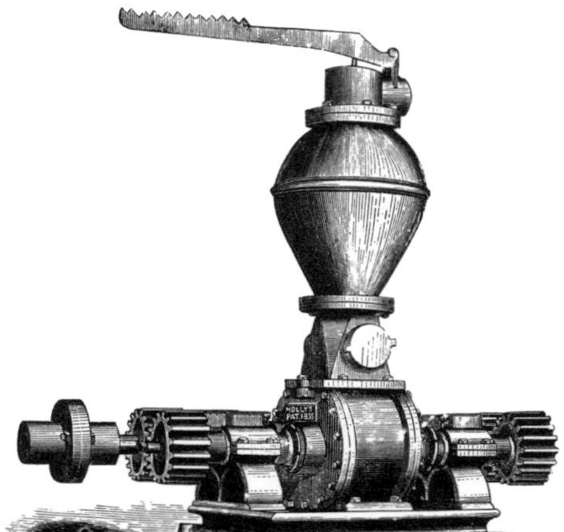

THE SILSBY MANUFACTURING CO.,

Seneca Falls, New York. Western Depot, Chicago, Ill.

Experience has proven, that when uncontrolled, fire and water are the two most powerful agencies for the destruction of life and property. Yet when properly applied, the latter becomes an efficient antidote for the former, and, paradoxical as it may appear, by recent achievements of genius and mechanism, fire is made a means for subduing itself. Prominent among the manufacturers of apparatus for extinguishing fires is the Silsby Manufacturing Company, of Seneca Falls, N. Y. These works are devoted exclusively to the manufacture of Rotary Steam Fire Engines, Rotary Pumps, Hose Carts, and Hose and Fire Department supplies.

The Rotary Steam Fire Engines manufactured by this Company are without a rival in this country. The leading feature or characteristic which has given these engines their superior efficiency and popularity is the rotary principle involved in their construction. Rotary Engines have been brought to that degree of perfection, that they have achieved a complete victory over those known as reciprocating engines. The practical difficulties growing out of contraction and expansion, packing, etc., having been entirely overcome, there is an immense gain of power as between the rotary and the reciprocating principles. In all other respects, as well as the more correct principle, these engines are constructed in the best possible manner, no effort having been spared to exhaust the resources of modern scientific engineering, to place them above all successful competition, a purpose which has been accomplished.

The space here allotted will not permit us to enter minutely into all the distinguishing features of these machines, the universal testimony of competent judges in their behalf has rendered such particulars unnecessary. The following are a few of the many advantages claimed, all of which are highly important.

They cost less to keep in repair than any other engine built; they will work more consecutive hours without stopping; they require from 50 to 75 per cent. less pressure to do the same amount of work; they will do fire duty through longer lines of leading hose, than any other machine; they will pump sandy or dirty water that would cut a piston pump all to pieces; they will throw a larger quantity of water a greater distance than any other engine; in short these machines have proved the most efficient, durable and reliable steam fire engine yet invented. More than five hundred of these machines are now in use, and wherever brought in competition with others they have been victorious.

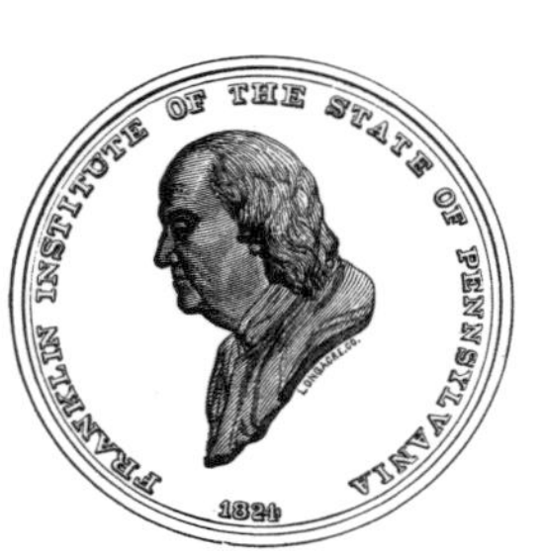

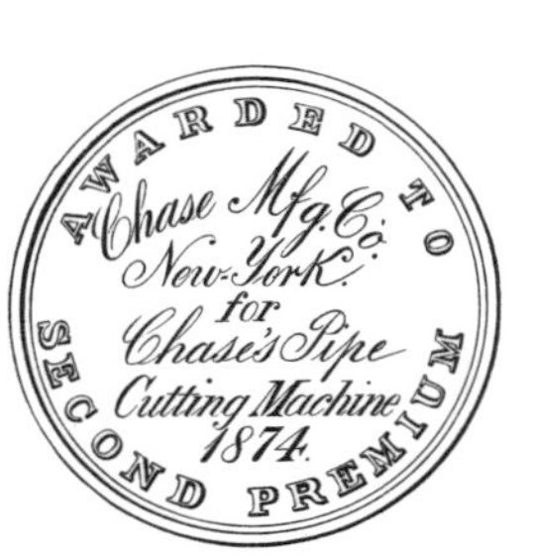

Fig. 1.

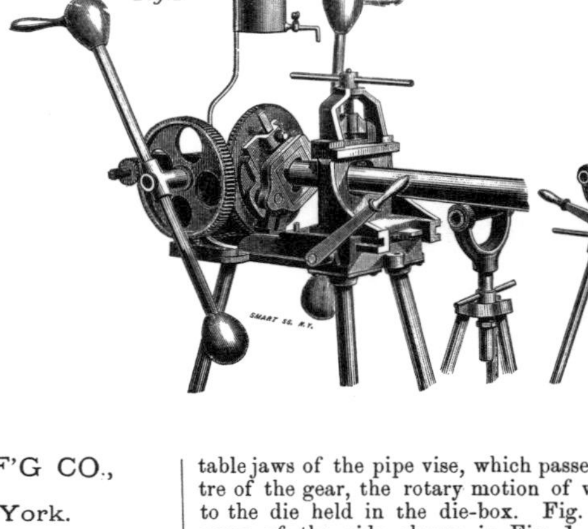

Fig. 2.

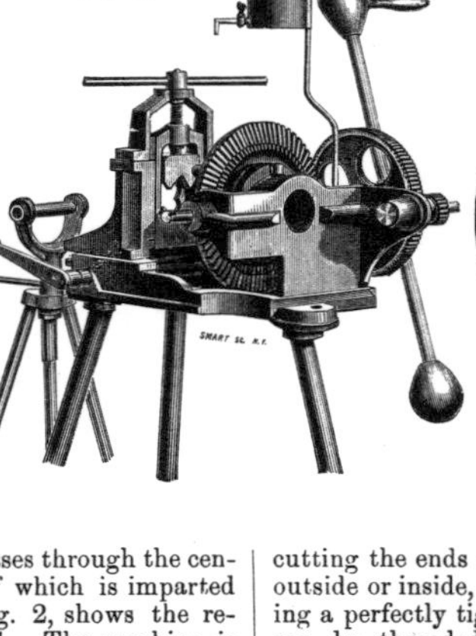

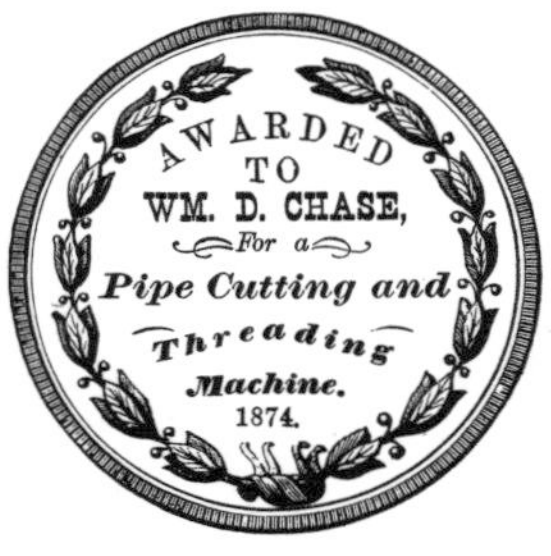

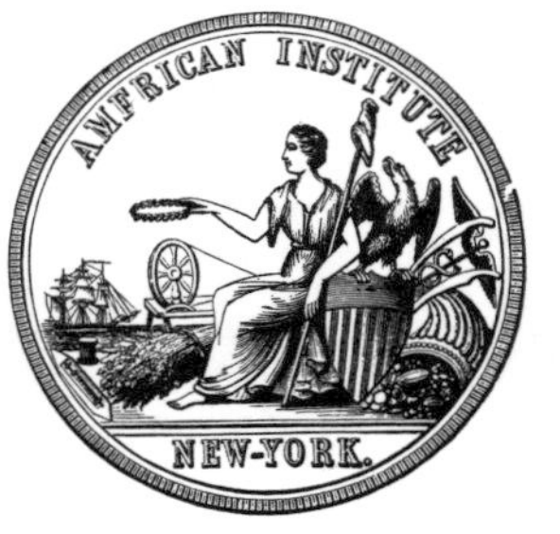

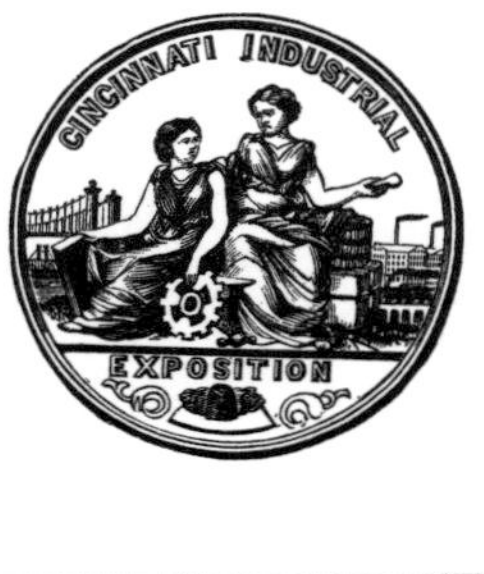

THE CHASE MANUF'G CO.,

120 Front Street, New York.

The W. D. Chase Machine for Cutting and Threading Pipes and Bolts, Tapping Nuts and Couplings and Cutting Round Bar Iron and Steel, completely fills a want long felt by gas and steam fitters and machinists. The engraving marked Fig. 1, shows the machine fitted for hand power, the motion being transmitted to the several parts by gearing as shown, while on the right is seen the pipe-rest and pipe held stationary by the adjustable jaws of the pipe vise, which passes through the centre of the gear, the rotary motion of which is imparted to the die held in the die-box. Fig. 2, shows the reverse of the side shown in Fig. 1. The machine is strongly made of cast steel, malleable iron and cast iron, the gears all being cut, with every part interchangable. It is a portable machine, one man can lift it from place to place, and as it may be worked by hand as well as power it especially recommends itself to gas and steam fitters, who by its use are enabled to cut and thread pipes and make their own nipples where the work is being done. The cutting off tool has an automatic feed cutting the ends of pipe perfectly smooth, with no bevel outside or inside, and allows the ends to fit closely, making a perfectly tight joint. Pipe as large as two inches can be threaded without splitting, with perfect ease. The thread cannot be put on otherwise than straight, and by its manner of working dies will wear much longer than as used at present, the chipping of the teeth being entirely avoided.

Our very limited space prevents us from mentioning a tithe of its advantages. It has received the several highest prizes at prominent fairs and expositions, as will be seen by a glance at this page.

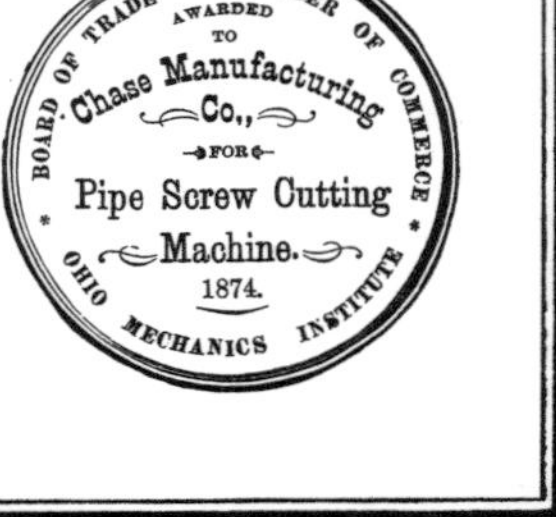

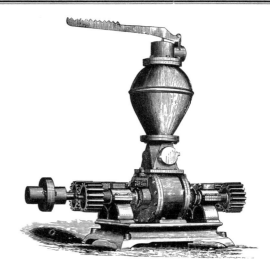

ARGAND PARLOR OVEN STOVE.

FIRE PLACE HEATER.

ARGAND PARLOR FURNACE.

PERRY & CO., STOVE WORKS,
Albany, N. Y.

The firm of John S. Perry & Co., of Albany, N. Y., are among the largest manufacturers of stoves in the world. The growth of their business is one of the many evidences of what can be accomplished by an active and well managed mercantile establishment. In 1804 the making of plows and machinery of various kinds was commenced on the site of the present offices, 115 Hudson Avenue, by Warner, Daniels & Co., and was continued till 1835; the concern having in the meantime changed owners twice. In the latter year the proprietors, W. V. Many & Co., added the manufacture of stoves and hollow-ware to the work then in hand. In 1843 the establishment was purchased by Treadwell & Perry, and the business continued by them till 1851, when they decided to confine their attention solely to the manufacture and sale of stoves. The present proprietors, John S. Perry, Nathan B. Perry and Andrew Dickey, assumed control in 1864, and by their sagacity, energy and perseverance have brought the business to its present proportions. The works cover an area of nearly five acres, and can turn out fifty thousand stoves per annum. The consumption of coal per day exceeds eight tons and the production of finished castings thirty tons. About six hundred men are employed, with a weekly pay of about $10,000.

One hundred and ninety-nine varieties of stoves and heaters are made by this firm, engravings of a few of which we here present, including eighty-three of cook stoves and heaters, sixty-six of parlor stoves, and fifty of heaters, besides an endless variety of hollow ware, registers, copper and tin work. To keep pace with the requirements of the times Messrs. Perry & Co. are constantly bringing out new patterns of all classes, some of their latest novelties being the now well-known "Argand Parlor," the "Argand Double Oven Cabinet Range," the "Model," the "Bulkley Steam Warm Air Furnace," and the "Standard Furnace." In the Bulkley Furnace, the air, instead of being brought into contact with metal at a high temperature, is heated in a very simple manner by steam, thus securing perfectly pure and healthful air of the requisite temperature at a comparatively moderate cost. The establishment gained much reputation by the manufacture of base burning stoves, which originated with them in 1853. Their fame now extends across the continent from New York to San Francisco. In every place accessible by rail or wagon their wares are to be found. Recently a dealer from Montana, while in Albany, bought one hundred cook stoves, and two hundred and fifty of Perry & Co.'s parlor stoves. Within the last two years a considerable trade has sprung up in Japan, and quite recently an order for several hundred stoves to be shipped to that market came to hand. The original location on Hudson Street, containing fifty-five thousand feet, has been utilized in every possible manner. A substantial brick building, 172 feet in length and five stories high, standing upon the street, gives room for the offices, sample rooms, &c. The sample room occupies the whole area of the second floor, and affords a fine opportunity for the display of the various stoves, ranges and furnaces made by the establishment. The offices are fitted up in excellent style, with every convenience. The shipping, financial and accountants departments are so arranged as to give every facility for the transaction of business and for communication with each other. Other buildings adjoining the main one are arranged for the accommodation of pattern makers, pattern fitters, carpenters, tin and copper-smiths, cleaners of castings and stove mounters while a large shop well lighted and ventilated is reserved for the moulders, numbering here about seventy. These extensive facilities proving insufficient for the growing business of the firm some time since they secured a larger foundry not far distant, which gave them eighty-two thousand feet of additional

ARGAND DOUBLE OVEN STOVE.

space, with floors for ninety moulders, thus enabling them to more than double their yearly productions. More room still has been found necessary, however, to meet the demands of their growing trade, and they have therefore obtained possession of a third foundry, between Broad and Grand Streets, and opposite the one last described, which will increase their ground area by 74,000 feet, and give room for sixty additional moulders, making the whole number employed of this single class of mechanics 220, or an entire force of 600 men, giving direct support to not less than 3,000 of the population of Albany. The two Grand Street foundries are connected with the offices in Hudson Avenue by telegraph, thus combining the advantages of concentration of mind with diffusion of space. It has ever been a cardinal principle with this firm to do well whatever they attempt. Their patterns and designs are all made in their own shops under their own directions, and to this department the most attention—sometimes extending to months on one special point—is uniformly given. No stove is allowed to appear until the patterns are as perfect as they can be made. When after much exhaustive experiment the patterns are completed, the next step is to make the castings. To this department, also, great attention is given. The most competent foremen and inspectors are provided, whose sole duty it is to see that not one imperfect piece goes into the finished work. In the mounting department the most complete machinery is used, and no stove is accepted until it has passed under a rigid scrutiny.

With this excellence of work it is not surprising that their stoves and other wares should have acquired great popularity, though this is also largely attributable to the new and useful inventions they have from time to time introduced. They are the owners of all the controlling patents for the "Clinkerless Grate," or "Anti-Clinker," so called, and of the devices for illuminating the base sections of stoves; patents which they do not wish to monopolize, however, but offer to other manufacturers on liberal terms, believing that they thus further the interests of the public and promote the general prosperity of the trade.

For years this firm have felt obliged to keep up a branch house in New York, as that is the most convenient shipping port in the United States, and during the season it is almost impossible to supply goods from Albany fast enough.

Their New York store, under the skillful management of Mr. C. R. Adams, is located in the St. George Building, No. 86 Beekman Street. The building is of iron, painted white, and presents a graceful and imposing front to the passer-by. Perry & Co. opened here in December, 1870, and have ever since kept up an assortment of their goods, embracing besides stoves, ranges and furnaces, a large assortment of hollow ware, both plain and enameled, registers, &c. The store is 30 x 100 feet. On the first and second floors are the offices and salesrooms, the other four floors and cellar being filled with goods, of which they carry a stock of about $75,000.

A prosperous and successful business can only be developed by enterprise, skill and honest worth. Such success as Messrs. Perry & Co. have attained is a proud monument for them. More, it is a beacon light for the young. An ever present aim of this firm has been to make only the best possible articles, to always amply fulfill every representation made as to the superior excellence of their goods. Let this same principle be carried out by all manufacturers and business men, and we would have more marked successes and fewer failures to record.

Neither pictures nor words of ours can convey to the mind of the reader the merit of the different varieties of stoves manufactured by this firm so well as does the fact of their universal use.

The great number of kinds and styles produced and kept in stock by them, will readily enable the purchaser to select something that will just suit.

One of the chief sources of prosperity in our country is found in its manufacturing industry, and a wise government will, therefore, by every means in its power, protect and foster it.

PERRY & CO., STOVE WORKS, ALBANY, NEW YORK.

BOYNTON'S "NEW CABINET" PORTABLE RANGE,
With Large Oven and Warming Closet.

"RADIANT LIGHT" SELF FEEDING PARLOR STOVE.

BOYNTON'S "1875 BALTIMORE" FIRE PLACE HEATER.

RICHARDSON, BOYNTON & CO.,

Manufacturers of

Boynton's "Improved Gas–Tight" Furnace, Boynton's "Wrought Iron" Furnace,
Boynton's "Baltimore" Fire Place Heater, Boynton's "Cabinet"
Hot Closet Range, Laundry, Heating and Cooking
Stoves, Hotel Ranges, etc., etc.

232 and 234 Water Street,
NEW YORK.

—:o:—

How to heat our dwellings, business houses, churches and other public buildings, thoroughly and economically, has been for many years the special study of some of our most noted scientists, and has called forth the best efforts of inventors. Among the many names connected with the invention and manufacture of heating apparatus, none are better, or more favorably known than that of the firm of Richardson, Boynton & Co. The older members of this firm are thoroughly practical men, each of them having learned everything pertaining to the business from the bench up, and having had several years experience in the trade before the co-partnership was entered into. The firm was organized some twenty-four years ago, and immediately assumed a prominent position in the trade, from the fact that they introduced new designs and new methods for heating, put them into successful operation, and by practical illustration demonstrated their superiority over other systems of heating. Mr. N. A. Boynton, is the inventor of the designs and personally oversees their manufacture at the foundry, while Mr. H. A. Richardson attends to the financial part of the business.

While, as will be seen from the cuts here presented, this firm manufacture stoves of various designs, their leading specialties are Furnaces and Heaters. Boynton's "Improved Gas-tight" Furnace, to be set in brick work, is completely perfect in principle and construction. Space forbids an elaborate description, but from the cut the reader will at once see that it presents an immense radiating surface, and must have great power. Boynton's Portable "Salamander" Furnace, and Boynton's Portable "Wrought Iron" Furnace, (of which last we give an illustration) are equally well known, and, for the purposes for which intended are equally as good as the first named.

All the furnaces manufactured by the firm of Richardson, Boynton & Co., possess and are noted for the following peculiarities. The castings are made without seams, and consequently no gases can escape; they are made from the best quality of iron, and are very heavy, and being without joints are more durable than others; they are remarkable for their great radiating surface, which renders them more powerful than others of the same size, enabling them to heat a greater volume of air with the same, or even a less consumption of fuel. Over 40,000 of their furnaces are in use in different parts of the country, heating many of the most prominent churches, schools and public buildings in the United States. Thousands of them have been in use for from ten to twenty years without any necessity for repairs, and every one that has been properly put in place has given satisfaction.

As an example of the estimation in which these Furnaces are held we quote from a letter dated, St. Johnsburg, Vt., December, 1875. After stating that the thermometer out of doors recorded 30 degrees below zero, while in the house it was 70 degrees above zero, the writer says: "There are many furnaces well suited for warm weather, but few that are suited to heat such arctic regions as we have here." This is a fair sample of hundreds of unsolicited letters of praise sent to the proprietors every year.

Boynton's "Baltimore" Fire Place Heaters has achieved a world-wide reputation. It is now some sixteen years since the plan was first conceived of constructing a heater which would set under the mantel, heating the room where it was located, and at the same time warming the rooms on the floors above. The first fire place heater was devised and introduced by this firm, and was, from the start a great success,

BOYNTON'S "WROUGHT IRON" FURNACES.
For Portable or Brick Set.

and were soon in such demand that other firms also deemed it advisable to manufacture fire place heaters. Some forty or fifty different styles have since then been introduced in this market, but the great majority of them have failed totally for lack of power or for some serious defect, and have been withdrawn from sale. Boynton's "Baltimore" has been and is considered by many to be the most powerful and successful heater in use. They have been greatly improved within the past three years, both in power and brilliancy.

We also present a cut of Boynton's "Cabinet," Portable Hot Closet Range. When the "Cabinet" Hot Closet Range was first presented to the trade, the trade laughed. The idea embodied in the design was ridiculed, and "Boynton's Failure" suggested as a fitting name for the new device. The "Cabinet" however proved a wonderful success, and portable ranges are succeeding the old-fashioned cook stoves about as rapidly as the latter wear out. Boynton's "Cabinet" Portable Range met with as much success as his "Baltimore" Heater, and to-day is not surpassed, for convenience and perfect working.

The "Radiant Light" Base-burning Parlor Stove and Heater is another wonderfully successful production of this firm. It is a stove of great heating capacity, and withal is economical in its consumption of fuel. Its double illumination gives it a cheerful look, and adds much to the comfortable appearance of the room.

The Franklin for burning coal carries us back in imagination to the days of our boyhood, when we sat by the hearth and watched the merry dance of the leaping flames. These Open Franklin's are powerful heaters and afford all the advantages that can be desired from an open grate fire.

Hotel Ranges is another of their specialties. They make ranges with two, three and four ovens, as required. These ranges are of great capacity, and easily managed. We cannot spare room to describe, but advise those interested to examine them.

In addition to the goods above named, Messrs. Richardson, Boynton & Co., manufacture Laundry Stoves, Cooking Stoves and Heating Stoves in great variety and are always prepared to supply the wants of customers.

The firm occupy the large four story buildings known as 232 and 234 Water Street, New York, as warehouses and salesrooms. Their trade extends over the Eastern, Middle and Western States. They keep constantly on hand a large stock comprising a complete assortment of all the goods they manufacture, and are always ready to fill orders at short notice.

The foundry is located in Brooklyn, on Van Brunt Street, one block from the Atlantic Dock Water Front. It is furnished with cupola furnaces, capable of melting twenty-four tons of metal per day. The appliances of the establishment are of the most approved kind,—complete in every respect. Every portion of the work is done on their own premises (including the drawing of designs and making the patterns) and under the immediate supervision of the firm.

The Foundry affords employment to 225 hands and is compelled to run fifty weeks per year.

Some idea of the immense business of the firm may be formed from the fact that their retail trade alone, amounts to $150,000 per year. This trade is necessarily confined to New York City, Brooklyn, and the cities and towns immediately contiguous, but it does not represent a tithe of their goods sold in these places, where there are scores of retailers who deal with them, but whose purchases are not included in the above figures. When parties purchase direct from the firm they put up the furnaces, heaters and ranges themselves, and thus practically prove the merits of their own productions.

The best furnace, heater or, even common stove, if badly put up, may not do good work, but, if properly set up, every article manufactured by Richardson, Boynton & Co., will prove itself to be all that they claim; that is, as nearly perfect in principle, in material and workmanship as human skill can make it.

LAUNDRY STOVE.

BOYNTON'S "IMPROVED GAS TIGHT" BRICK SET FURNACE.

"OUR FRANKLIN" OPEN GRATE COAL STOVE.

STOVES & RANGES,

Exhibited by

SWETT, QUIMBY & PERRY, TROY, N. Y.

Stoves, or their substitutes, are indispensable for human existence, in civilized society. Food and warmth are dependent on them, and these cannot be secured without fire, which, if uncontrolled, becomes an engine of destruction rather than a preserver of life. It is true the food upon which the thousands fed during the forty years journey from the Red Sea to the Jordan, needed no artificial preparation, and the speechless winged messengers fed the ancient prophet in his solitude; but such instances of feeding the hungry are not in profusion, and such precedents it would be dangerous to rely upon in later days. By what process the pre-historic nations prepared food we can have no knowledge.

Cooking, as an art, it is believed is peculiar to civilized society. Animals were granted to Noah as food, at the time of the Deluge, 2,348 years before the Christain Era, the eating of blood being expressly forbidden. (Gen. IX., 3, 4.) We read that a calf was cooked by Abraham, to entertain his guests, about 1900 B. C.

Previous to the invention of chimneys, chafing-dishes, or vessels for heating anything set upon them, are known to have been in use. Portable Grates, or Braziers, were also used for heating apartments. Chimneys were first introduced into these countries about the year 1,200, when they were confined to the kitchen or large hall.

Stoves are mentioned in 1,300, as having been so placed in the centre of the room that the family could sit around them, the funnel of the stove passing up through the ceiling. In the stoves of the ancients, the fire was concealed in a similar manner to the German stoves of modern times. The ancients, also, sometimes lighted a fire in a large tube in the centre of the room, the roof being open. Stoves of these primitive designs, somewhat modernized, continue in use in many houses and public establishments in England, and quite generally on the continent of Europe.

The first step in advance from the old-fashioned fire-place, still the comfort and center of attraction for the groups in many rural homes, was such modification of the fire-place, as is found in the various kinds of grates set in the fire-places, or in the "Franklin stoves," and their more recent modifications.

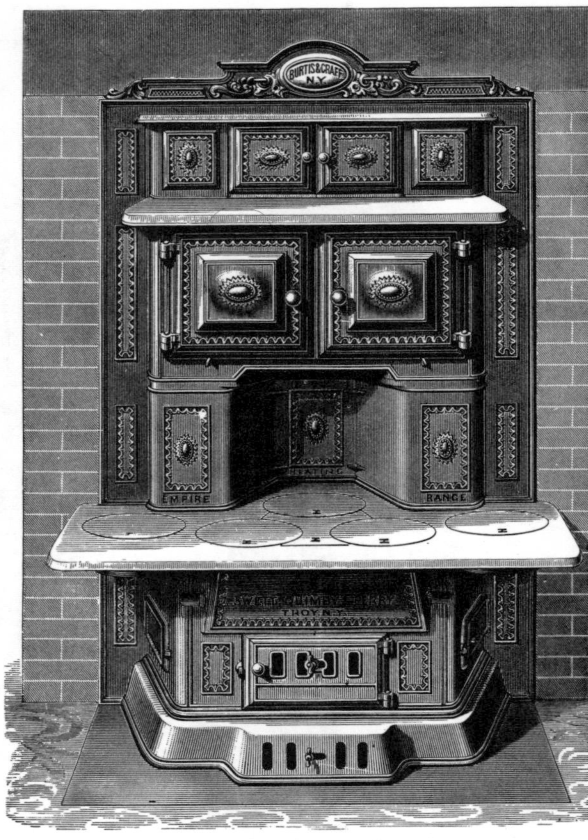

Empire Heating Range.

Of the great variety of stoves made of cast and sheet iron, and in the bewildering number and variety of patterns, the United States no doubt surpasses all other nations in the manufacture, three Americans—Dr. Franklin, Count Rumford and Dr. Eliphalet Mott, of Union College, being the acknowledged pioneers in the invention of improvements which are essential to the utility of any stove.

The principle adapting stoves for burning bituminous coal as well as wood, is said to have first been applied by Count Rumford; while Franklin designed a stove for English use, to burn bituminous coal and consume its own smoke, and which secured both warmth and ventilation. To him also belongs the credit of inventing and applying the flues and regulating valves with a register, by which the draught could be increased or checked at pleasure. The Franklin open stove which burned either wood or coal, was for a long time very popular. The decreasing supply of wood for fuel led to the invention by Dr. Mott, of an upright close stove, for the burning of anthracite coal, which had been fortunately discovered. The larger sizes of this stove were for a long time very generally used in the Northern and Eastern States for warming halls in houses, churches and public rooms. The Mott stove no doubt furnished suggestions which led to the more complete and perfect stoves of the present day.

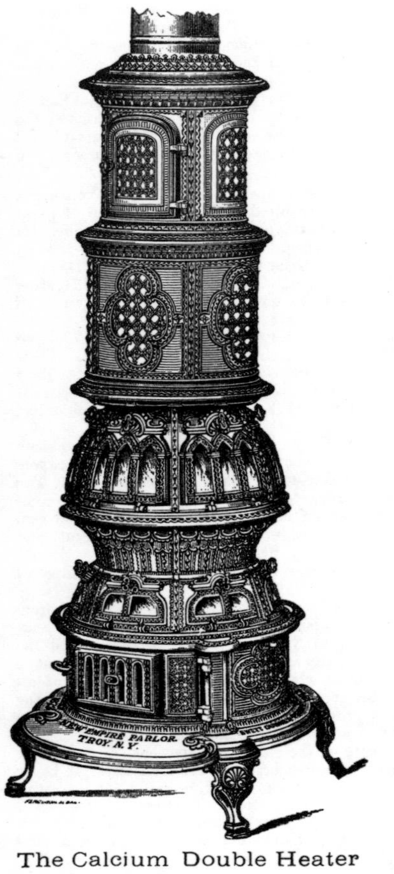

The Calcium Double Heater Base Burner.

We cannot here enumerate the successive improvements, or mention even the more popular patterns of stoves now in use; but we think it safe to say that in the variety and quality of stoves manufactured for wood or coal, America rivals all the world, and any American household that cannot be supplied with a cooking-stove—an indispensable utensil for the kitchen—which will give perfect satisfaction, can rest assured that the fault is not with the stove.

Among the most prominent and favorably known manufacturers in this branch of industry, are Messrs. Swett, Quimby & Perry, the proprietors of the Empire Stove Works, of Troy, New York.

This firm are the successors of Anson Atwood, who established business as a stove manufacturer about 1845. Their establishment includes an extensive foundry for making castings for machinery purposes, and a general assortment of Cooking and Parlor Stoves; also, a Heating Range, designed especially for heating upper rooms in connection with cooking; and a superior Hot Air Furnace for heating dwellings, churches, halls, etc.

Their new Empire Cooking Stove possesses many unique features of great merit. Among other desirable points secured in this stove, are its great economy of fuel; the ease with which a coal or wood fire may be maintained throughout the whole year without rekindling; a perfect consumption of gas and smoke, thus allowing the damper in the smoke pipe to be kept closed most of the time, and retaining the heat without the escape of gas or smoke into the room, and its perfect adaptation to all varieties of cooking. This stove has been awarded many premiums at different State and County Fairs, which, with the vast number of flattering testimonials received, and the fact that not less than forty thousand have been sold during the last six years, are sufficient proof of its superior merits.

This firm are the inventors of the celebrated Empire Heating Range, which was first placed in the market four years ago, since which time over twenty-five hundred of them have been put into use, under a guarantee that they should give entire satisfaction as to cooking perfectly, and heating the adjoining and upper rooms.

Its design is very plain and neat, the castings very smooth and proportions beautiful. Some of the principal features which combine to make it one of the best ranges in the world, are the peculiar arrangement of the fire chamber, location and arrangements of the flues, application of cold air, and its superior broiling arrangement.

This Range, unlike most elevated oven Ranges, has the cooking surface entirely outside of the chimney jambs, thus overcoming a fault of other Ranges, that they do not heat the room in which they stand sufficiently in cold weather. Yet in warm weather, by opening the direct draft damper, the heat is carried up the chimney, and not thrown into the kitchen. There is also an arrangement for throwing all the heat to one oven, so that baking can be done with a very small fire. The cooking surface or top of the Empire is larger than most elevated oven Ranges, projecting several inches from the body of the Range and forming a perfect protection to dresses, and rendering a fender unnecessary, which is always in the way and very inconvenient.

The flues of this Range are at the front, on each of the two sides—an advantage over center-flue Ranges, as the heat from the fire box is carried under each of the five boiler holes—thus rendering every hole available for cooking purposes, while in center-flue Ranges, the ovens project over the back holes, so as to render them nearly useless; consequently, only three holes are of practical use. Another advantage of side flues at front of Range, instead of back, is that the heat has not so far to pass to reach the ovens, thus making the Empire the quickest baker and most economical Range in the market.

This Range has large double ovens and capacious warming closet. The fire-box passes from front to back of Range, and is constructed with two grates—the rear grate being stationary, and a horizontal moving and dumping grate in front, so arranged that by no possibility can any dust or ashes pass into the room. The fire-chamber is divided in the middle by a very easily adjusted division-plate, in which a brick is fitted, which forms the back of summer fire-box; so that in warm weather the size of the fire may be reduced to simply sufficient for cooking purposes, making the fire-box no larger than in an ordinary cooking stove, and with this summer fire one or two fair-sized rooms may be warmed comfortably in ordinary winter weather. This peculiar construction of fire-box of the Empire Heating Range, is protected by Letters Patent, and is the great feature which has given this Range such signal success over others. The Water Back is so constructed that the stationary boiler may stand on either side of the Range, and can be arranged so as to furnish any amount of hot water that may be desired.

The manufactory of this firm is located on Second and Ida Streets, on the Poestenkill Creek, by which it is supplied with power. The buildings occupy an entire block, and over two hundred men are constantly employed by the firm.

Messrs. Swett and Quimby are both practically acquainted with the details of the manufacturing business, an almost indispensable requisite for the successful prosecution of any great manufacturing enterprise. Mr. Perry, who became a member of the firm in 1867, brought to the house very valuable business qualifications, developed by a successful business career, as an extensive railroad manager.

As an evidence of the reliability of this firm and the confidence they have secured among their patrons, we need only refer to the rapid progress which has rewarded their energy. The sales of Mr. Atwood, their "illustrious predecessor," amounted to about $10,000 per year, while the annual sales of Messrs. Swett, Quimby & Perry, amount to over half a million dollars. They have a fine salesroom at No. 277 River Street, Troy, New York.

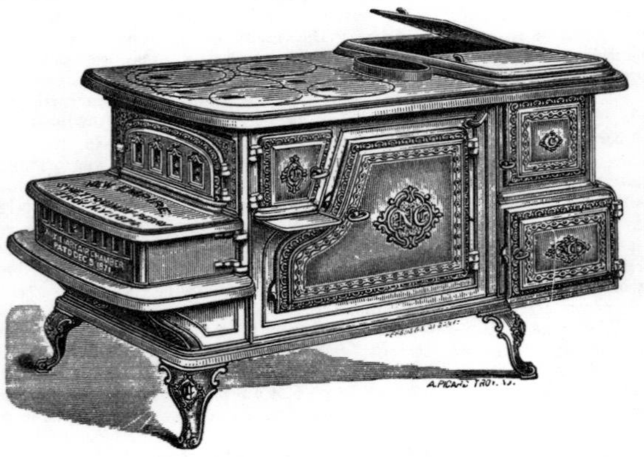

New Empire Cook Stove.

Swett, Quimby & Perry have also a half interest in the "Empire Car Wheel Works," the business of which is conducted on their premises, under the firm name of Jonas S. Hunt & Co., who do a business of about $300,000 per year. They run a Blast Furnace at South Shaftsbury, Vermont, where they manufacture a large amount of Charcoal Iron, about half of which is required for their car wheels.

The castings from this firm for stoves and other purposes, are from the best material, and are cast so exactly that duplicate parts of any particular pattern can be promptly furnished at any time.

If our space would allow, we might detail at length the improvements which have been designed and executed by the genius and enterprise of this firm, but a visit to the warerooms or manufactory will more clearly demonstrate the characteristics of the manufactures than can be done in any other way.

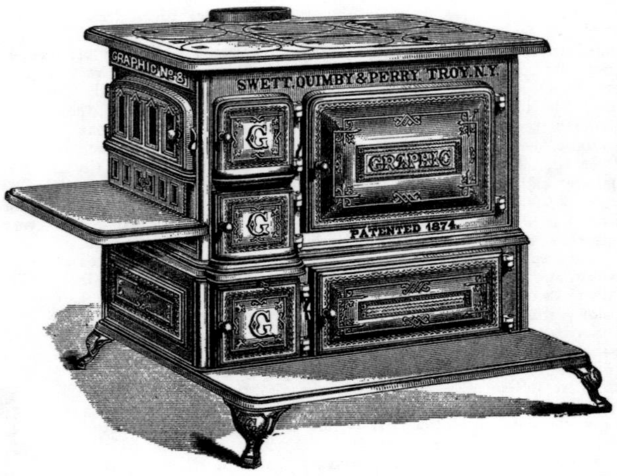

Graphic Range.

Troy has long been noted for its manufactures, and especially for thé excellence of its stoves. It is characteristic of American enterprise, that certain localities become famous, each for some special branch of industry. This concentration of enterprise, is considered advantageous to the producers, but is even more so to the consumers. Rivalry among manufacturers not only leads to a desire to excel in the quality of their products, but also in the economy of prices; and when a manufacturer in one kind of business is enabled successfully to compete with his rivals and so far sustain the reputation of his wares as to create a rapidly increasing demand for them, no further evidence is needed of their superior merits.

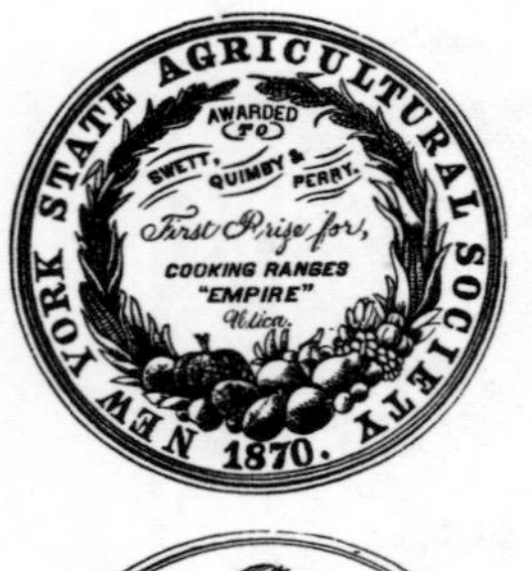

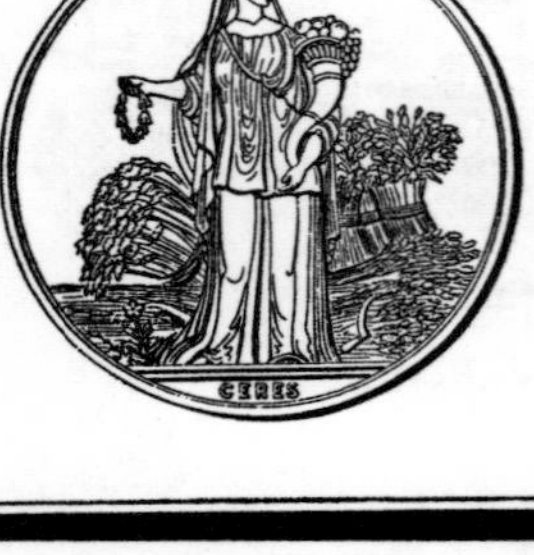

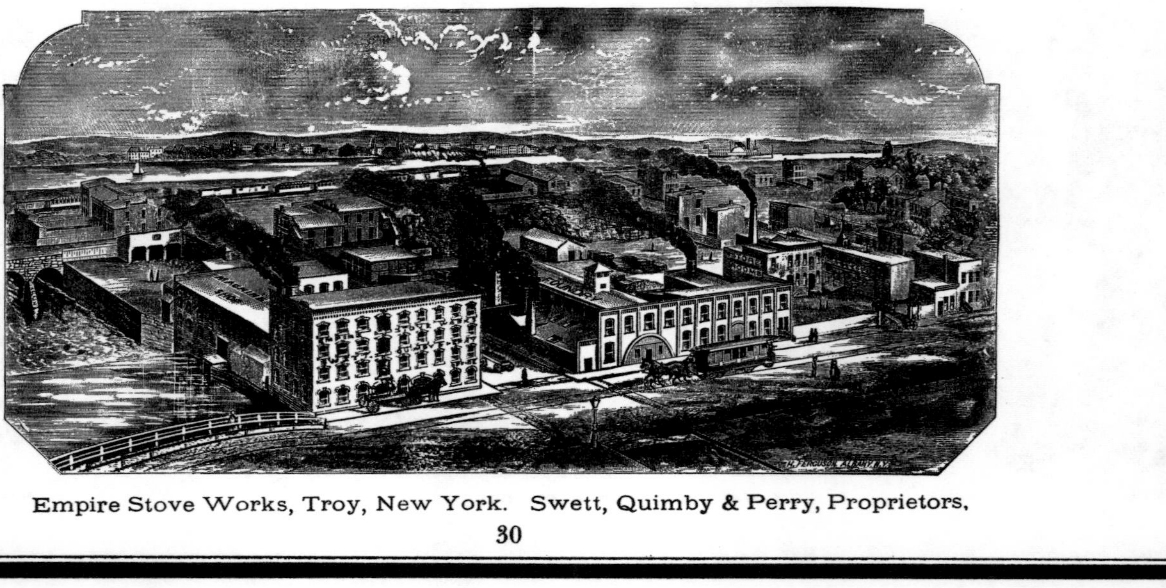

Empire Stove Works, Troy, New York. Swett, Quimby & Perry, Proprietors.

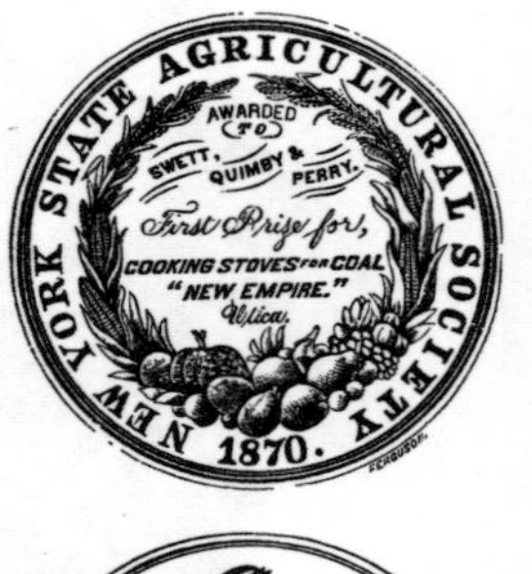

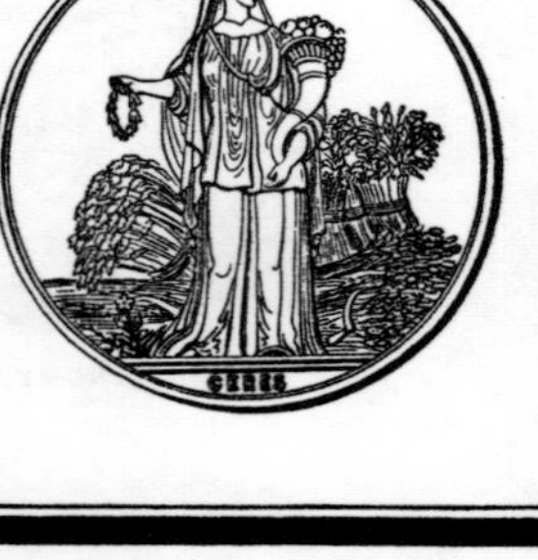

BURDON'S ENGINE.

BURDON'S PATENT.

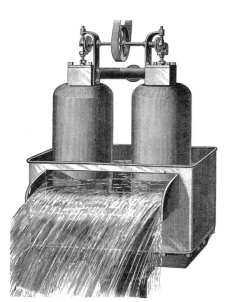

BURDON'S PATENT.

CERRICK'S PATENT TURBINE.

BURDON'S PATENT.

BURDON'S PATENT.

BUSH'S PATENT.

The New York Hydraulic & Drainage Co.,

Office 35 Wall St., N. Y. Factory, cor. Front & Pearl Sts., Brooklyn.

Wm. Burdon, Pres't. Chas V. Ware, Sec'y.

These Pumps are specially adapted for raising large quantities of water at low lifts, and therefore are peculiarly applicable to the drainage and improvement of wet lands, the drainage of city sewers, and supplying cities and towns with water; for feeding canals, overflowing rice-fields and other irrigating purposes; for Railroad stations, mines, quarries, clay pits, and for manufacturing establishments where large quantities of water are required, as ship and marine pumps, they have no superior, either for pumping out the hold in case of accident or for fire purposes. These pumps will not get out of order, as there is no machinery about them, and they can be started in a second by an ordinary laborer or common sailor. The Steam Pressure Pump is a most complete and reliable Steam Fire Engine, simply cheap and durable. The Steam Vacuum or Low Pressure Pump is of equal importance with the one above mentioned. It is not as affective as a Fire Apparatus, but will raise water much cheaper than the other Pump. It is well known that a Vacuum of fifteen pounds will raise water thirty feet high. Most low-pressure condensing engines accomplish this; but to keep up a Vacuum in the condenser an air pump must be attached to pump out the condensed water. The Vacuum Pump is a condenser without an air pump raising the water as high as the Vacuum will draw it, and then letting it fall by its own weight. This pump may be effectively used in every establishment where there is a steam boiler, very little steam—just enough to expel the air from the pump chamber is sufficient to operate it.

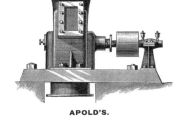

APOLD'S.

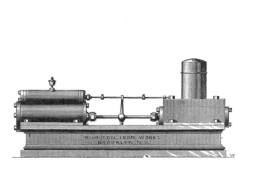

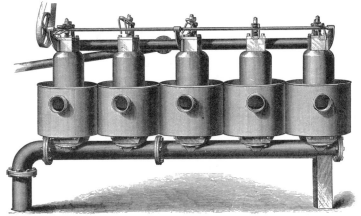

BURDON'S PATENT.

Fig. 1

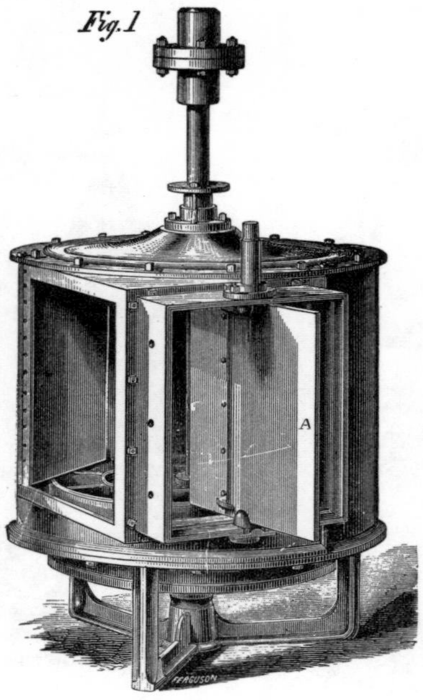

WASHINGTON M. MACHINE CO.,

Manufacturers of and Dealers in

Turbine Water Wheels, Circular Saw Mills, Saw Mill Machinery, etc.,

Leroy Mowry, Agent, Sandy Hill, Washington Co., New York.

The manufactures of the Company above named extend over so wide a range that within the limits of the space assigned to it we can but briefly mention a few of them. Among the most prominent are Portable Circular Saw Mills, for which they received the First Premium of the New York State Agricultural Society, over all competitors; Iron Gang and Mulay Mills, Patent Double Parallel Edgers, Patent Log and Timber Canting Machines, and Lath Machinery. In brief, they produce every appliance necessary for the complete equipment of Saw Mills, and deal largely in Portable and Stationary Engines, and in Paper Mill Machinery.

The Company have recently secured the right and patterns for the manufacture of Wait's Improved Turbine Water Wheels, (one of the best known and most popular wheels ever invented,) and are making a specialty of its manufacture. Having every facility for the speedy and perfect construction of these celebrated wheels they are prepared at all times to promptly execute orders for them.

The mills and other machinery manufactured by this Company have a world-wide reputation and they spare no pains to make every article they produce as perfect in material and construction as possible. They have every facility that long experience can suggest to aid them, and have such confidence in the merit of their machinery as to warrant it (if properly set up) to work to the entire satisfaction of the purchaser.

Those interested in Saw Mills or Saw Mill Machinery, or in want of a perfect Water Wheel, or a reliable Steam Engine, will do well to communicate with this Company before purchasing. Illustrated catalogues, price lists, etc., promptly furnished on application.

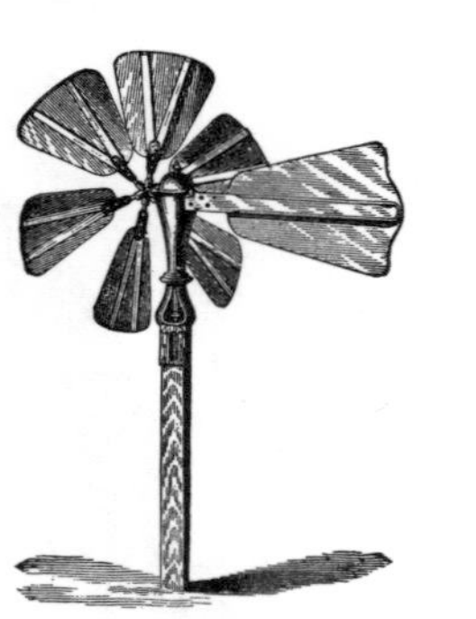

WINDMILL.

HARTFORD PUMP COMPANY,

Sigourney, cor. Cushman Street, Hartford, Conn.

Numerous applications of compressed air have already been made, many of them novel; one of the most interesting being that arrived at by the Hartford Pump Company. They employ it to force water from a distance to the place where needed and to raise it to the upper stories of buildings, making principally small machines for supplying country houses. To compress the air, a wind mill, steam, water or any other power may be used, and the source of power need not be near the spot from which the water is to be raised, as the air can be carried a quarter of a mile, or more, without difficulty.

The pumping apparatus manufactured by the Hartford Pump Company, known as the "Automatic Pump," is submerged; it has no piston or stuffing box, and is always ready to start when supplied with air. The contrivance is a very ingenious one and well worthy an examination by

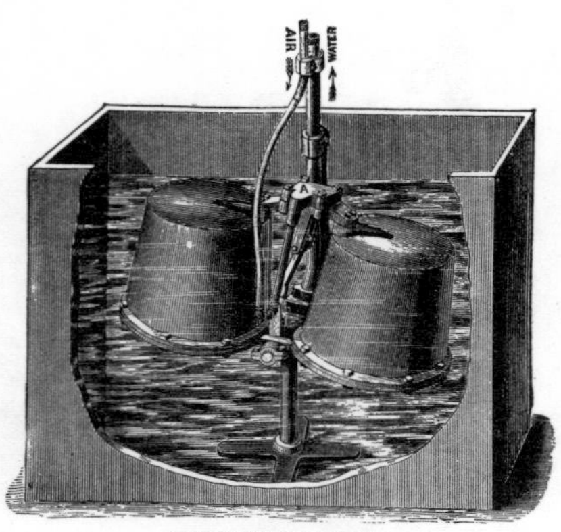

AUTOMATIC PUMP.

those who feel an interest in mechanical progress. A glance at the engravings accompanying this article will enable the reader to understand the object for which this pump was specially devised, and the manner in which its work is accomplished. By its use the convenience of running water is secured in a country house, and through the grounds adjoining, almost as perfectly as it can be obtained in the large cities. The complete machine comprises a Windmill, Air Pump, Safety Valve and Automatic Pump. They are made of various sizes and capacity; No. 2, for instance, has a six foot Windwheel, and will raise one hundred gallons of water per hour to a height of forty feet, while No. 6, with a ten foot wheel will raise two hundred gallons of water per hour to a height of eighty feet. It is difficult to give the capacity of a windmill pump with any accuracy, as its power is dependent upon the speed and prevalence of the wind, but the above amounts was obtained with a moderate breeze, the wheel making seventy revolutions per minute. It will sometimes run at twice or even three times that speed. If the air is compressed by steam or any other steady power the results do not vary.

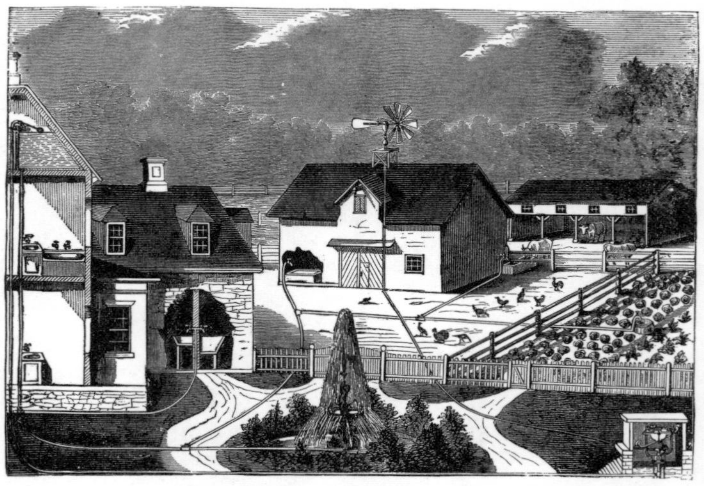

House, Barn, Cattle Sheds, etc. supplied by an 8 foot Wheel, erected on a Barn, and taking water from a distance.

Prof. Baird, U. S. Commissioner of Fish and Fisheries has used one of these Machines to supply a 5,000 gallon aquarium with salt water and in a letter to the company says:—"The apparatus works admirably, and is everything that you have claimed for it. Notwithstanding the fact that the water is constantly drawn off, we have at no time been without the full supply, using, as we do not infrequently, over 5,000 gallons per day." The high position of Prof. Baird in the scientific world, necessarily gives great weight to his opinion, and his adoption and commendation of this device is good proof of its value.

The Hartford Pump Company began the manufacture of these pumps in 1873, previous to which time a large amount of money had been spent in experiments and many devices constructed to accomplish the end in view, viz.: the construction of a simple, effective and durable contrivance to force water to considerable dstances and heights, by means of compressed air. The company is possessed of ample capital; their factory is thoroughly equipped, and they will spare no pains to produce perfect work. Their Machines will be on exhibitlon and in practical operation at the Centennial Exposition where those interested may obtain absolute proof of its value, in watching its operations.

THE ROGERS UPRIGHT PIANO CO.,

Warerooms, 608 Washington St.,

Factory, 486, 488, 490, 492, 494, 496, 498 & 500

Harrison Avenue, Boston, Mass.

——:o:——

Until the commencement of the present century but few attempts to manufacture pianos had been made in the United States, and no important improvement was made until about the year 1825, when iron frames were first introduced, the object being to give the instrument greater durability by relieving the case from the strain caused by the pull of the strings. At the time mentioned Square Pianos were most used in the United States, no other style being manufactured here to any extent, and but few imported, and consequently in Square Pianos the iron frame was first tested. From the first it was indisputable that instruments with iron frames would remain in tune longer than those without, but it was claimed that they did not possess that fullness of tone which marked the wooden frame instruments, and soon the new invention had quite as many opponents as admirers. It was not until many radical changes had been made in the construction of the wooden cases, and in iron plates or frames that the latter were generally adopted, about the year 1855.

Before any attempts were made to manufacture pianos in this country, quite a number of instruments had been imported, most of them "Uprights." For some reason imported instruments did not give satisfaction—they would not keep in tune, pins loosened, and as expressed in a letter written in 1772 to a foreign manufacturer, "ye piano gave forth jingling sounds—not full, rich music." Upright Pianos were peculiarly unfortunate, and became so unpopular that for many years none were made in this country, and not until within the past few years has there been any considerable demand for them.

From the first it has been generally conceded that the Upright Piano from its compactness of form, and its superior elegance as an article of parlor furniture, possessed great advantages over other styles. The obstacles heretofore attending the manufacture and successful introduction of this form of instrument, have been the liability to get out of order and the difficulty of keeping it in tune.

After years of patient investigation and unremitting toil, these obstacles have been triumphantly surmounted, and in the Rogers Upright Pianos we have an instrument, possessing a volume of tone not excelled by the productions of any other maker, combined with a strength and simplicity of construction, which render it entirely proof against the failings which for so long a time have made Upright Pianos unpopular.

This piano is constructed on entirely new principles, and possesses marked peculiarities which are deserving of a more detailed description than we can here give. Among the most prominent of the many new features introduced in this instrument, and peculiar to it are the following:

The iron plate is cast in one single solid piece and requires no support of timbers at its back, as do the plates in other Upright Pianos. The difficulties with other Upright Pianos, as before stated, have been their liability to get out of order and out of tune. These drawbacks were the natural results of defective construction—a lack of strength to stand the pull of the strings; the frame gave to the strain, the pitch flattened, and the full, round tone of the instrument was lost. In the Rogers Upright Piano the plate is strung, and the strings are tuned before being placed in the case. Thus the iron plate is forced to bear all the pull of the strings, and there can be no giving way of wood work, and consequently no loss in the pitch or quality of tone from the lack of strength in the case of the instrument.

The patent tuning arrangement of the Rogers Upright Pianos is well worthy of special notice. It consists of metallic levers and set screws, (all

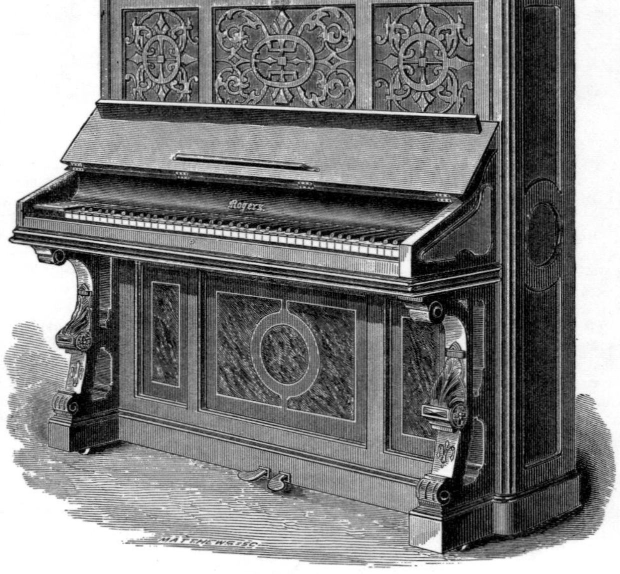

THE ROGERS UPRIGHT PIANO.

fastened to the iron frame), in place of tne wooden pin block used in all other pianos. It ensures the absolute certainty of the piano standing in tune a much longer time than by any other method and is a step in advance of the plan used by other makers. The adoption of this simple but effective method renders the Rogers Upright Pianos capable of being perfectly tuned much easier than other pianos. This arrangement is used only on these instruments.

The Action is a model of simplicity and strength combined; it is prompt and sure in its motion, and as durable as any ever made. This Patent Action is peculiar in having but one action rail, which is bolted to the iron frame, whereas in other pianos there are from four to six rails which are fastened to the wooden case, and are liable to get out of order. The Rogers Upright Piano Company have such implicit confidence in the superiority of this action that they fully warrant it never to stick or get out of order, as it is proof against atmospheric changes.

In all the points that go to make up a perfect instrument, the Rogers Upright Pianos stand in the front rank.

The singing quality of tone so desirable and so rarely found in other Pianos is richly illustrated in this instrument. The faultless purity of its higher notes cannot be excelled, while the full, round tones of its bass are wonderfully perfect. In quantity and quality of tone the Rogers Upright Pianos are all that can be desired.

The touch is delicate and well defined. The damper is controlled directly by the pedal, without levers. All the mechanism of the instrument, is extremely simple. and direct in action, there being none of the complication of parts which are found in other instruments, and there is consequently far less liability to get out of order. The durability of the Rogers Upright Piano is unquestionable.

The case is as elegant as it is original, and in beauty of design and completeness of finish it has no superior.

At the Exhibition of the Massachusetts Charitable Mechanics' Association, held in October 1874, the Highest Award was given the Rogers Upright Piano over all competitors and in view of the fact that this association is one of the most critical in the country, their endorsement is an honor of which the company may well feel proud, and which a thoughtful public will not overlook in making selections.

In presenting these Pianos, with all the vital improvements above noted, the company have the assurances of leading musicians and the press that they are supplying a want that has long been felt.

The extent of the cultivation of the fine arts is generally admitted to be a proper gauge by which to measure the civilization and education of a people. Music is properly classed as a fine art, and if the advancement of our people can be properly measured by its progress in this art we certainly have achieved a very high position. While the United States cannot claim to have produced as famous composers as some other countries, she can and does claim to have popularized music and made it an element of the home life of the masses of her people. Go where you will in this country, among the wealthy and middle classes, in the cities and villages of the older settled States or on the Western frontier and you will find Pianos in common use.

American Pianos too have received the highest commendations from Artists of all nationalities, and are generally ranked by musicians as superior to any made in other climes.

In the front rank of American Manufacturers, in their specialty of Upright Pianos, is the Rogers Upright Piano Company. Their instruments combine all the requisites of a perfect Piano and are deservedly popular at home and abroad. Every Piano leaving their warerooms is fully warranted to stand in tune and order in any climate. Parties seeking for further information in regard to these instruments upon application in person, or by letter, at the Company's Warerooms, No. 608 Washington Street, Boston, Massachusetts, will receive full particulars as to styles, prices, etc.

THE ERIE RAILWAY.

The route of the Erie Railway is peculiarly rich among American Railroads in the variety and extent of its scenery. The Valley of the Neversink, as seen from the grade east of Port Jervis, presents a picture of beauty which has no superior in the world; and the panorama of beauty in the Valley of the Delaware is continually interesting in the rapidly alternating glimpses of rivers, gaps and mountains. Passing their summit the pastoral beauties of the valleys of the Susquehanna and Chemung Rivers widen into broader and more cultivated landscapes, reaching back to the receding mountains. Ascending again to the "Summit" which divides the waters between the ocean and the great lakes and rivers, the Genesee and Alleghany rivers present new varieties of picturesque scenery, which will interest the observing business or pleasure traveler.

There is no better gauge by which to measure the immense through travel which passes over the Erie Railway, than the number of Sleeping and Drawing Room Coaches which are daily sent from the depot at Jersey City, for each of the prominent Western cities.

Here, for instance, is one in which the traveler, without alighting, may be carried to Buffalo and Niagara Falls; another which crosses the great Suspension Bridge, and goes over the Great Western Railway of Canada to Detroit; and then continues on, via the Michigan Central to Chicago; another which runs through by way of the Atlantic and Great Western Railway, to Cleveland; and another which carries its passengers by the same road and without change to Cincinnati and pauses not until it has crossed the Father of Waters and reached the City of St. Louis.

No amount of experience or habit, however much it familiarizes us with American travel, can ever seem to render commonplace to the thoughtful ob-

PALACE SLEEPING COACH.

DRAWING ROOM COACH.

server the grandeur of such a scheme as this, which daily sends out its coaches to cross half a continent. Not less worthy of admiration and remark are the interior of the coaches themselves. The upholsterer and the car builder have combined to render them moving palaces in which by day or by night the traveler may be surrounded with all the luxurious appointments of a first-class hotel. The traveler, after breakfasting in New York, may take his seat in one of the Pullman Coaches at the Erie Depot and at supper time find himself in sight of the clear waters of Lake Erie, or within hearing of the thunders of Niagara's mighty cataract; he may breakfast at Detroit, and dine at Chicago.

But more delightful than the mere achievement of such a victory over time and space are the manner and method in which it is accomplished. The train passes over the landscape, along mountain sides, through valleys, over bridges, and across broad meadow lands with the speed of a winged charger. The traveler meanwhile ensconced in his cozy drawing room or easy chair, protected from dust and cinders, looks out upon the rapidly changing landscape with undisguised delight as in a varied picture of town, city, hamlet, forest and farm land it passes before him. It is to him one continued scene of entertainment and enjoyment, and his first advice to a friend contemplating a trip eastward or westward will be, as our's is, "Don't fail to enjoy, if you can, a ride through by daylight over the Erie Railway."

There is no railway company in the world which provides better accommodations for its Patrons, or which keeps its passenger equipment in better condition than the Erie. The Drawing Room and Sleeping Coaches which are attached to express trains, both west and east, are, as shown in the illustrations given, perfect paragons of beauty and models of comfort and luxury. Indeed the entire traveling accommodations of the road are unsurpassed, and contribute in no small degree to the wonderful growth and increase of its traffic.

The broad gauge of the Erie Railway, the solidity of its road-bed, its double track of steel rails, its system of track watchers, its telegraph

NIAGARA FALLS.

lines, all aid in rendering it a peculiarly good line over which to travel. The tourist for profit as well as for pleasure will note with surprise the number and variety of trains that continually throng the track, and will, perhaps, for the first time, realize how great is the volume of traffic in daily transit, and how complete and thorough must be the organization that can handle it with promptitude and dispatch. Cars laden with live stock, coal, lumber, petroleum, ore, iron, and every conceivable form of manufacture and merchandise, pass in apparently exhaustless numbers, justifying the statement that the Erie Railway, in respect to the magnitude of its tonnage traffic, is in the front rank among the great trunk lines of the country.

But the eye will lead the mind away from the contemplation of the enormous business of the road to the scenic beauties which are ever presenting themselves. It would fill a large volume to describe them in words, or picture them in engravings, and then the words, however choice their selection, or the plates, though of the highest artistic merit, could not fully convey them to the mind.

The entire line is a panorama of loveliness. We can make but passing mention of only a very few of its many points of interest. As popular places of summer resort, might be named, Rutherfurd Park, with its splendid boating facilities on the Passaic; Clifton, overlooking the picturesque Lake Dundee; Ridgewood and Hohokus, in the historic Paramus Valley; Suffern and Ramapo, with their bracing mountain air; Cornwall and Newburgh, nestling among the Highlands of the majestic Hudson; Greenwood Lake, surrounded by mountains; Goshen, Florida and Middletown, in the heart of the famous dairy region of Orange County, a land literally flowing with milk and honey; Seven-Spring Mountain, a picturesque resort; Guymard, a charming retreat on the Shawangunk mountain side, overlooking the Neversink Valley; Port Jervis, on the Delaware, almost shut in by mountain peaks, and most romantically located; Milford, eight miles from it, famed for its scenery; Monticello and White Lake, in the centre of the finest trout and game region in the State and Lake Mohonk, a beautiful body of

WATKINS GLEN.

water, 1,200 feet above the Hudson, within a few miles easy ride of New Paltz on the Wallkill Valley branch. From this point or from Eagle's Cliff near by, may be gained a view that is surpassingly grand and impressive. It pains us to pass by many beautiful places unnoticed, but our space is so limited that we must omit a number of scenes deserving mention.

The upper waters of the Delaware abound in scenery of the wildest and most picturesque description, the river banks at many points, descending in precipitous abrupt cliffs of rock to the water's edge, rendering the original construction of the railway through this valley a work of no ordinary difficulty. At other points the river has left deposits of soil along its margin, where trees have grown, and cattle may find a pasture ground. It is one of these latter spots that the artist has chosen to portray in the accompanying beautiful engraving

One of the greatest engineering achievements on the route of the Erie Railway is the Starucca Viaduct, which spans a great valley near the village of Susquehanna, Pa., by eighteen arches of solid masonry, each of them fifty feet in width. Its total length is 1,200 feet, its height 110, and its cost was $320,000. The roadway passes directly over the viaduct. In sunshine or in storm, by night or by day, amid the snows of winter or the leafy beauties of summer, this grand work stands out boldly upon the landscape about it, a tribute to the genius and energy of man, and a source of admiration and wonder to the traveler, to whom it is plainly visible from the car windows at either end of the long curve of which the viaduct forms the centre. Many are familiar with it as the salient feature in that world-wide famed painting by Cropsey, entitled "An American Autumn."

Among the natural beauties and curiosities in the regions traversed by the Erie Railway, is the picturesque gorge, known as Watkins Glen, famous as a resort for tourists. It is reached by taking the Erie Railway to Elmira, and thence by another ride of twenty-two miles, over the Nothern Central railroad. The adjacent village of Watkins is at the head of Seneca Lake. The Glen is, in brief, a vertical split or gorge some five or six hundred feet deep, in a bluff of solid rock, through which a stream passes in successive falls and other watery antics. A ramble through Watkins Glen, even in the height of a summer noonday, is cool and delightful. Passing through a series of alcoves, stairways and bridges, each ending in some delightful surprise, with some fresh beauty beyond it, one looks up from the darkened depths of the cliff in which he stands, to see above, the little narrow strip of sky, which reminds him of the accustomed sights of the outer world.

Niagara Falls are so world famous for their majestic grandeur, that we need write no word to excite the curiosity of those who have not viewed their wondrous torrent. We think all Americans, and all foreign visitors to our land, hope to see these falls ere they lay down life's pleasures. Those who have visited them, are only waiting for an opportunity to do so again. Suffice it to say that when one has reached Niagara, via the Erie Railway, he has arrived at a fitting end to a journey through as magnificent scenery as is to be found in the whole world.

SCENE ON THE DELAWARE.

1794. [HOUSE.] 1794.

By the Preſident and Directors of the Inſurance Company of North America.

No. 19

WHEREAS John Hall of the City of Philadelphia, Physician

hath paid to the Preſident and Directors of the Inſurance Company of North America Six Dollars & Seventy five Cents for Insurance of Fifteen hundred Dollars on an unfinished Three Story Brick House & Kitchen number Thirty One, situate in Filbert Street in the City of Philadelphia

Attest Eben Hazard Secy.

from Loſs or Damage by Fire, for One Year from this Twentieth Day of January One Thousand Seven hundred & Ninety Five NOW KNOW ALL MEN BY THESE PRESENTS that in conſideration thereof the Capital Stock, Eſtate and Securities of the ſaid Corporation ſhall be ſubject to pay unto the ſaid John Hall or to his Executors, Adminiſtrators or Aſſigns any Loſs or Damage which ſhall or may happen by or by means of Fire to the ſaid House and Kitchen within the term aforeſaid, unleſs they the ſaid Preſident and Directors ſhall forthwith give Directions for putting the ſaid House and Kitchen in as good a State of Repair as it was in before it was ſo injured by Fire; or ſhall make good the ſaid Loſs or Damage by paying therefor according to the Eſtimate thereof to be made by Two disinterested persons chosen by the Parties — or provided the ſaid House and Kitchen ſhall be wholly deſtroyed by or by means of fire within the term aforeſaid then the ſaid Capital Stock, Eſtate and Securities of the Corporation ſhall be ſubject to pay to the ſaid John Hall or to his Heirs, Executors, Adminiſtrators or Aſſigns the entire ſum of Fifteen hundred Dollars and ſo ſhall continue, remain and be ſubject as aforeſaid from time to time to be computed from the Twentieth Day of January in every year for ſo long time as the ſaid John Hall ſhall well and truly pay, or cauſe to be paid the ſum of Six Dollars and Seventy five Cents to the Preſident and Directors of the ſaid Inſurance Company of North America on or before the Twentieth Day of January, which ſhall be in each ſucceeding Year, and the ſaid Corporation ſhall agree thereto by accepting the ſame, which ſaid Loſs or Damage ſhall be paid or indemnified in manner aforeſaid within thirty days after proof thereof; and if any diſpute ſhall ariſe reſpecting the ſame between the Corporation and the ASSURED, ſuch difference ſhall be ſubmitted to the judgment and determination of Arbitrators indifferently choſen, whoſe award in writing ſhall be concluſive and binding to all parties. PROVIDED always neverthelefs, and it is hereby declared to be the true intent and meaning of this Policy, that the ſaid Stock, Eſtate and Securities of the ſaid Corporation ſhall not be ſubject or liable to pay, or make good to the Aſſured, any loſs or Damage by Fire, which ſhall happen by Invaſion, Foreign Enemy, Civil Commotion, or any Military or uſurped power whatever; And provided alſo, that this Policy ſhall not take effect, or be binding to the ſaid Corporation, in caſe the ſaid Aſſured ſhall have already made, or ſhall hereafter make any other Aſſurance upon the House and Kitchen aforeſaid, unleſs the ſame ſhall be allowed of and ſpecified on the back of this Policy: Or if the House and Kitchen abovementioned ſhall, at the time when any ſuch fire ſhall happen, be in whole or in part occupied by any perſon who ſhall uſe or exerciſe therein the Trade of a Carpenter; Joiner; Cooper; Tavern-keeper, or Innholder; Stable Keeper; Bread or Biſcuit Baker; Sugar Baker; Ship Chandler; Boat Builder; Malt Drier; Brewer; Tallow Chandler; Apothecary; Chemiſt; Oil and Colourman; China, Glaſs or Earthen Ware Seller; or ſhall be made uſe of for the Storing or keeping of Hemp, Flax, Tallow, Pitch, Tar, Turpentine, Roſin, Salt Petre, Sulphur, Gun Powder Spirits of Turpentine, Shingles, Hay, Straw. Fodder of any kind, Corn unthreſhed, Oil, Wax, Diſtilled Spirits,

but that in all, or any of the ſaid caſes, this Policy, and every clauſe, article and Thing herein contained ſhall be void and of none effect; otherwiſe it ſhall remain in full force and virtue.

IN WITNESS whereof the ſaid Corporation have cauſed their Common Seal to be hereunto affixed on the Twentieth Day of January in the Year of our Lord One thouſand ſeven hundred and Ninety Five

N. B. This Policy to be of no force if aſſigned, unleſs ſuch aſſignment be allowed by an entry thereof in the Books of the Company.

1500 Fifteen hundred Dollars J. M. Nesbitt presid.

On House & Kitchen Ds. 1500.

FAC-SIMILE OF POLICY No. 19, ISSUED BY THE INSURANCE COMPANY OF NORTH AMERICA, in 1795.

The Insurance Company of North America,

Philadelphia, Pa.

The venerable and famed corporation whose name stands at the head of this article was not the earliest company formed on this continent for the purpose of insuring against loss by fire, (though it was the Pioneer Marine Company) but it was the first organized as a Stock Company, and is, consequently, the oldest Joint Stock Fire Insurance Company in the United States.

It origin was peculiar. Soon after the close of our war for independence, when the country was girding its loins for a long stride ahead in the path of material greatness, and new interests were springing into life, schemes for life insurance were numerous and popular. Among these the Tontine plan had many admirers. Several gentlemen of means in Philadelphia projected a company which they christened "The Universal Tontine," the object of which was to raise a sum upon lives, to be applied to charitable and other uses specified in the article of agreement. Many subscribers came forward, and a considerable fund was secured; but further investigation led to the abandonment of the Tontine Association. On November 3, 1792, the subscribers met at the State House, and it was determined to employ the funds subscribed in such other manner as would be most feasible and advantageous to those interested. A committee was appointed with instructions (to use the exact language of the report) to "devise, digest and report such other use or uses as they shall deem eligible and most beneficial to the subscribers for employing the funds raised for the aforesaid purpose." At a subsequent meeting, it was resolved unanimously, that the Universal Tontine Association should be changed from its original objects, and converted into a society to be called the "Insurance Company of North America." and that the capital should be fixed at $600,000.

This was the beginning of the career of the company. On the following day, December 11, the Board of Directors met, and elected John Maxwell Nesbitt, President, and Ebenezer Hazard, Secretary. A committee was appointed to prepare a petition to the legislature of Pennsylvania for an act of incorporation. A table of premiums, and rules to be observed in transacting business, were also adopted.

The charter was granted by the legislature during its session of 1794 and received the sanction of the Governor, April 14, 1794.

The officers elected at the first meeting of the Board of Directors were gentlemen of distinction in the community. The first President, John Maxwell Nesbitt, was a wealthy and respected merchant, a member of the well-known firm of Conyngham, Nesbitt & Co. The first Secretary, Mr. Hazard, came to the service of the company with a national reputation. He was born in Philadelphia in 1745, and was educated at the College of New Jersey, from which he graduated in 1762. Just before the close of the revolution he was appointed by the Continental Congress Post Master General of the United States, which position he filled until the formation of the regular government under the constitution in 1789. He was connected with the Insurance Company of North America from the birth of the institution in 1792, to 1800 when he retired.

When the Company began business it occupied a small and unpretending building on Front Street, near Walnut Street. But that humble office was the scene of heavy transactions from the outset. The times were propitious for an extensive marine business. The sails of our young merchant navy were beginning to whiten every sea, and this company, with one other started four months later in the same city, were all that were in the American market offering to underwrite marine risks. In the year 1787 upwards of $700,000 in marine premiums were received by the Insurance Company of North America. In 1798 nearly $1,500,000 were received. But notwithstanding the immense income derived from the business during these early years of the company's life, the losses kept pace, and by the close of the century had not only absorbed the entire revenue of the company, but had nearly swept away its capital. One of the results was that no dividends were paid to the stockholders for a period of nearly eight years.

On the last day of January, 1796, a change occurred in the presidency of the company. Mr. Nesbitt resigned on account of failing health, and Colonel Charles Pettit, one of the original directors, was chosen in his place. This gentleman had been a conspicuous officer in the Revolutionary war, and a statesman of commanding influence under the civil government which had followed, and at the time of his elevation to the Presidency of the Insurance Company of North America, was a leading merchant of Philadelphia.

Col. Pettit's first adminstration lasted but two years. His health was indifferent, and in January, 1798, he sent his resignation to the Directors, and that body chose another of its members, Joseph Ball, as his successor. Mr. Ball was a prominent citizen of Philadelphia and the possessor of great wealth. He occupied the Presidency of the Company but one year; Col. Pettit, in the meantime, recovering his health, so that he was enabled to resume office in July, 1798.

President Pettit, died September 4, 1806, in the 69th year of his age, subsequently, the Board of Directors met and elected John Inskeep, a former mayor of the city, President.

In 1831, John C. Smith, a prominent merchant, was chosen President. His activity and influence secured for the company a large increase on its former business and greatly promoted its success. In 1832 Mr. Stephens retired from the company, after a continuous service of thirty-two years. His successor, as Secretary, was Arthur G. Coffin, the present honored President of the company. With President Smith he carried it through the trying financial troubles of 1837-41. The company suffered so much by the shrinkage in the value of its investments that in 1842 it became necessary to obtain authority from the legislature to reduce the capital stock to the sum of $300,000, and the value of the shares to $5 each. But skilful management triumphed over all these reverses. Prosperity in the finances of the company returned, and in 1850 the Directors increased the capital to $500,000 and restored the par value of the shares to $10 each. This increase was made out of the profits of the business.

In 1835, the charter of the company had been extended by the legislature for twenty years. In 1839, it was made perpetual. President Smith died in 1845. He had been greatly esteemed, and it is said of him by a brother officer that "he discharged his duties with great intelligence, promptness, and fidelity; and the popularity and success of the institution was fully sustained during his administration."

Mr. Coffin was elected President, his commission dating from July 1, 1845. Of this gentleman, it may be said that his familiarity with the business of the company, his rare executive skill, his sterling integrity and his affable manners all contributed to fit him admirably for the management of its concerns. In 1850 there came a "great fire" to Philadelphia. It burned three hundred buildings, and inflicted a damage on the citizens of $1,500,000, which was thought to be a large loss in those days. The Insurance Company of North America was a sufferer to some extent, but its loss was a bagatelle to what it had to undergo in the great fires which visited other cities in late years.

The office of the company was removed about this time from the old building in Front Street to the present commodious quarters, No. 232 Walnut Street. On June 1, 1858, Mr. Sherrerd resigned the office of Secretary to assume the Presidency of the Insurance Company of the State of Pennsylvania, and Matthias Maris, an underwriter of experience, was appointed in his stead. Important additions to the managing force of the company have since been made. Charles Platt, one of the most accomplished gentlemen in the profession, was made Vice-President in January, 1869. He had successfully served the company for many years. In March, 1874, William S. Davis, previously President of the Bay State Insurance company of Worcester, Massachusetts, also a widely respected underwriter, was elected second Vice-President by the Board of Directors.

To return, however, to the chronological record of the company. Mr. Maris resigned the secretaryship in 1860, and was succeeded by Mr. Platt. In the following year an event happened in the history of the company of great importance to its future fortunes. It went into the agency business. The war of secession broke out and then there was a vast increase in business, particularly in the marine department. The company planted agencies throughout the Union, and everywhere it was cordially received; thanks to the grand reputation it had been building up for more than half of a century at home. In 1866, the company began to reap some of the disadvantages as it had already reaped many of the benefits of an extended agency business. It was struck by the great Portland fire to the extent of $50,000.

Chicago blazed on the 8th of October, 1871, and in its ashes the Insurance Company of North America laid away $580,000 of its hard-earned accumulations. Sister companies went down by the score before this fiery blast, but the old Philadelphia institution stood as firm as a rock. It paid every dollar of its losses, and continued its business wherever its banner had been raised as before. A year later came the Boston calamity with a still greater loss to the company. Nearly a million of dollars more of its funds were swept away. But it never flinched; again it paid the claims against it to the last dollar. Then came the reward. Its solid worth, its integrity, its good faith with its customers had been tried, as circumstances had never permitted them to be tried before, and the public came trooping to its doors to ask for its protection. Business poured in, the lost funds were rapidly restored and in 1872, affairs were so prosperous that the Company raised its capital stock to $1,000,000.

THE NEW YORK LIFE INSURANCE CO.,

Home Office, 346 and 348 Broadway, N. Y.

——:o:——

MORRIS FRANKLIN, President.
WILLIAM H. BEERS, Vice-Pres. & Actuary.
THEODORE M. BANTA, Cashier.
CORNELIUS R. BOGERT, M. D. }
GEORGE WILKES, M. D. } Med. Exam'rs.
CHARLES WRIGHT, M. D., Ass't. Med, Exam'r.
D. O'DELL, Supt. of Agencies.

——:o:——

A THIRTY YEARS RECORD.

The New York Life Insurance Company completed its thirtieth year December 31, 1874. At that time its history and condition were, in brief and in round numbers, as follows:

HISTORY.

Number of Policies Issued,	112,000.
Premium Receipts,	$57,000,000.
Death-Claims Paid,	$12,000,000.
Dividends and Return Prem's,	$17,000,000.

CONDITION.

Number of Policies in Force,	45,000.
Total Amount Insured,	$123,000,000.
Cash Assets,	$27,000,000.
Surplus, State Standard,	$4,520,400.

BUSINESS, 1874.

New Policies Issued,	7,000.
Amount Insured,	$22,000,000.
Income,	$8,000,000.
Increase in Assets,	$3,000,000.

This Company was the third Life Insurance Company organized in New York State, and its history covers not only the period in which life insurance has been prominent and popular, but it passed through the trials and discouragements of that earlier period in which the business was made prominent and popular by the fair dealing, energy and success of the few companies then in existence.

The Company has never swerved from the straight path of prudence and safety; but, while it has been conservative in its methods, it has made substantial additions to the modes by which life insurance is made to promote the greatest good of the greatest number. It originated the non-forfeiture system, since adopted by all companies, and it has so applied the Tontine principle to the distribution of surplus, that, in the judgment of experts, its "Tontine Investment Policies" offer more and greater advantages than any other form of policy now issued.

PROMINENT FEATURES OF THE COMPANY.

1. *Ample Security.* (1.) It has accumulated an immense fund which is securely invested and rapidly increasing. The interest received from this more than pays its death-losses. (2.) Its standard for estimating its liabilities is the highest in use in this country, and its reserve is thus kept over two and a half million dollars larger than is required by the legal standard of the state of New York. (3.) The large experience of its officers and managers, gained during its long and eminently successful career, guarantees the prudent management of its affairs.

2. *Pure Mutuality.* (1.) It has no capital stock to absorb the profits of policy-holders. All the earnings of funds intrusted to its keeping, after paying death losses, are returned to policy-holders in proportion to their contributions to the same. (2.) The dividends declared are available immediately, in the settlement of the second and all subsequent annual premiums.

3. *Economy.* (1.) The affairs of the Company have been so economically managed that for years the ratio of its expenses to premium receipts have been less than that of any other New York Company. In 1874 the ratio of its expenses to its income was less than half the average ratio of other companies doing business in the state. (2.) Special care is exercised in the selection of risks, and no anxiety to secure a large business ever induces it to accept any but first-class lives for insurance.

4. *Non-Forfeiture Policies.* Non-Forfeitable Policies originated with this Company, and all policies now issued by it, except Tontine Investment Policies, contain a "Non-Forfeiture" clause, providing for their surrender to the Company, for cash or a paid-up policy, in case the assured should desire, for any cause to discontinue the payment of premiums after having made three full yearly payments on a Whole Life Policy, or two full yearly payments on a Limited Payment Life Policy, or on an Endowment Policy.

5. *Liberality in the Settlement of Losses.* Experience has shown that cases arise where policies, although equitably claims, are not legally so. The records of this Company bear many acknowledgments from widows and relatives of deceased members of its liberality and fairness in the settlement of all such losses.

A NEW FORM OF LIFE INSURANCE.

The New York Life Insurance Company calls the special attention of business men to its "Tontine Investment Policy," as offering more and greater advantages to business men than any other plan of life insurance now before the public. The plan is, in brief, as follows: Those selecting this form of insurance are placed in classes, the Tontine periods of which terminate in ten, fifteen or twenty years; the election of the period to be made at the time of making the application for the Policy. The annual surplus arising in each of these classes is accumulated for the benefit of the class, but no division is made until the expiration of the selected period, and then only to such Policies as are actually in force; those terminating prior thereto receiving no dividend. To the representatives of those who die during the period, the original amount insured will be paid. Those who discontinue their Policies will receive neither Paid-up Policies nor surrender values; but profits from this source, as well as from the dividends of those who die during the period, will be placed to the credit of the class to which they belonged.

It may be urged in behalf of this form of insurance that:

1. It has received the unqualified approval of the ablest Consulting Actuaries of the United States, including Mr. Sheppard Homans, until recently the distinguished Actuary of the Mutual Life of New York, and Mr. Edwin W. Bryant.

2. It is a form of policy which effectually answers all objections offered to Life Insurance.

3. It divides the profits of insurance equitably between those who die early and those who live long.

4. It gives the assured the option at the end of his Tontine period, of withdrawing his entire Equity, *i. e.*—the accumulations upon his policy, and which it is estimated will exceed the amount of premiums paid; and, taking into account the cost of his insurance, give a handsome interest on the investment.

5. It practically offers an Endowment Policy at a Life Rate.

6. It allows, if preferred, at the end of the Tontine period, a paid up policy of nearly double the amount that can be secured in any other way, at the same expense.

7. If preferred, it places one in the annual receipt of by far the largest cash annuity, upon any given sum, that was ever paid to an annuitant.

To illustrate the practical working of policies on this plan, estimates have been prepared, based upon rates of mortality, interest, expenses and lapsing, less favorable than past experience has indicated. The age 40, at entry, at which the calculations are made, is selected as being a fair average age, but of course the results at different ages of entry, and in different classes of policies, would vary from these given. See tabular view of estimated results of a $10,000 policy on this page.

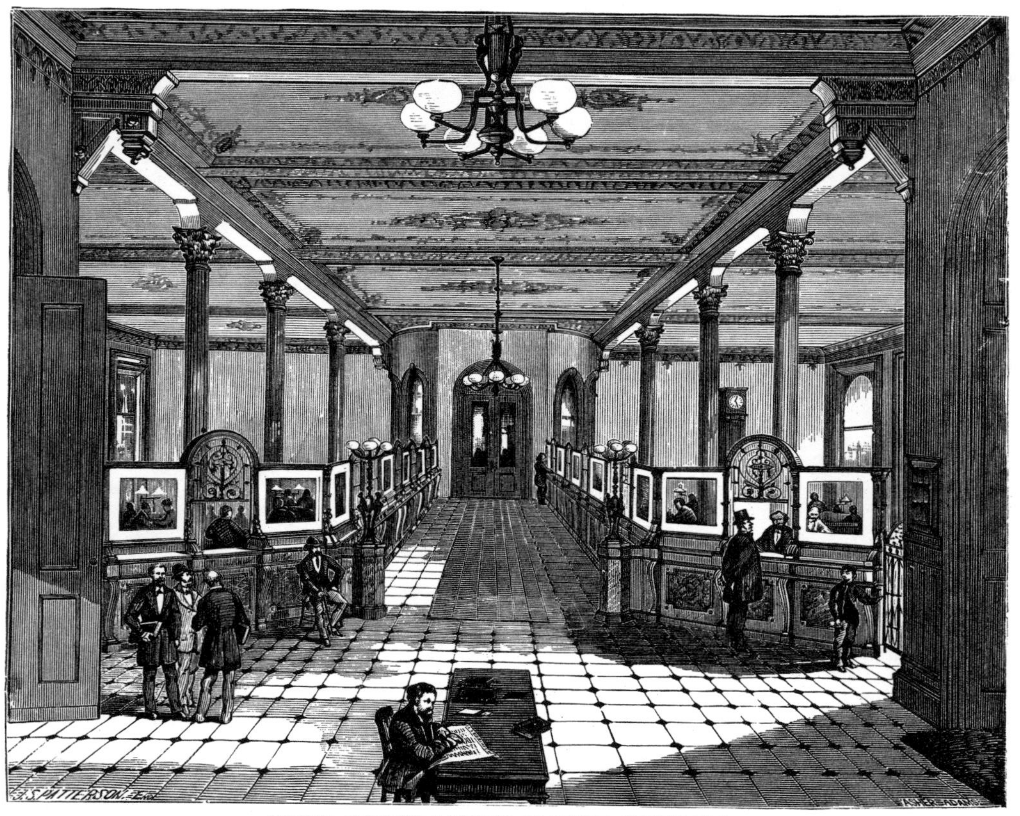

THE COMPANY'S HOME OFFICE

Estimated Results of a

TONTINE INVESTMENT POLICY OF $10,000

As issued by the NEW YORK LIFE INSURANCE CO. on the Ordinary Life Table of Rates.

Age, 40 years; Premium, **$313** Annually.

The BENEFITS PROPOSED, at the option of the Policy Owner, are:	After the completion of the TEN-YEAR Tontine Period.	After the completion of the FIFTEEN-YEAR Tontine Period.	After the completion of the TWENTY-YEAR Tontine Period.
To Withdraw the Accumulated Surplus in Cash, the Payment of Premiums being Continued by the Assured.	56 per cent. Of Premiums Paid.	101 per cent. Of Premiums Paid.	150 per cent. Of Premiums Paid.
OR, Surplus Purchases an Annuity for Life, Combined with Dividend.	$227.90 To Pay Premiums and Continue Policy.	$546.30 Will Pay Premium and leave a Surplus for Increasing Income.	$1,160 10 Will Pay Premium and leave a Surplus for Increasing Income.
OR, Sale of Policy to the Company, for Cash.	107 per ct. Cash Returns of Premiums Paid.	154 per ct. Cash Return of Premiums Paid.	207 per ct. Cash Return of Premiums Paid.
OR, Sale of Policy and Purchase, with the Proceeds, of a Yearly Income for Life.	$286.20	$699.50	$1,450.00
OR, Sale of Policy, and Purchase, with the Proceeds, of a Paid-Up Policy, without Profits.	$7.500	$15,000*	$23,500*

* Provided, that when the amount of the Paid-Up Policy exceeds the original amount of the Insurance, as a condition precedent to its issue, a satisfactory certificate of good health, from an examiner of the Company and subject to its approval, shall be furnished.

THE COMPANY'S BUILDING.

The enterprise and farsightedness with which the affairs of the New York Life Insurance Company have been conducted are well illustrated in the location and management of its Home Office. It began business in 1845, at No. 68 Wall Street. In 1851 it removed to 106 Broadway, and in 1858 it purchased the building No. 112 Broadway, which gave it excellent offices for twelve years at a merely nominal rent, and afforded a profit of $200,000, when the premises were finally sold. Its present quarters are in its commodious building, Nos. 346 and 348 Broadway, which was erected by the Company in 1868-70, and of which an illustration is given on this page. The ground dimensions are 60 feet on Broadway, 196 feet on Leonard Street, 71 feet wide in the rear and 197 feet on Catharine Lane. The site has long been a favorite one with New Yorkers, having been occupied by the "Society Library," by Appletons' book store, and by the dry goods firm of S. B. Chittenden & Co. When the old building was destroyed by fire in 1867, the refusal of the site was secured by an officer of the Company while the fire was still burning.

The building presents an imposing exterior. It is built of pure white marble, in the Ionic style, the design having been taken from the Temple of Erectheus at Athens.

The portico at the principal entrance is twenty feet in width, projects four feet from the main building, and has double columns on each side. Upon these rest a cornice, with a broken pediment, in which is set, in sculptured marble, the insignia of the Company, viz: an eagle's nest and an eagle feeding her young. The coat of arms of New York City, appropriately crowns the front of the edifice. The roof is of iron, and the building is fire-proof throughout.

The interior of the building is in keeping with its general character—simple, elegant and perfectly adapted to the purpose for which it was erected. The offices of the Company are at the end of the hall on the first floor. The main room takes in the whole width of the building, and is 110 feet long through its center. The desks of the cashier and clerks are arranged on each side behind counters of Italian marble, which are surmounted by an elaborately wrought frame work of bronze, the latter serving as a sash for immense panes of plate glass. Side rooms at the rear end serve as offices for the President and Vice-President, Medical Examiners and Directors, and as fire and burglar proof vaults for the securities and books of the Company. The walls are elegantly frescoed and the whole building is heated by steam. Agents of the Company occupy a part of the second floor, and the remainder of the building is rented for stores and offices.

The substantial character of the building, its great beauty and its perfect adaptation to the purpose for which it was constructed, combine to make it symbolical of the financial soundness and honorable dealing of the Company, and of that complete adaptability to the wants of the age which have ever characterized its systems of insurance.

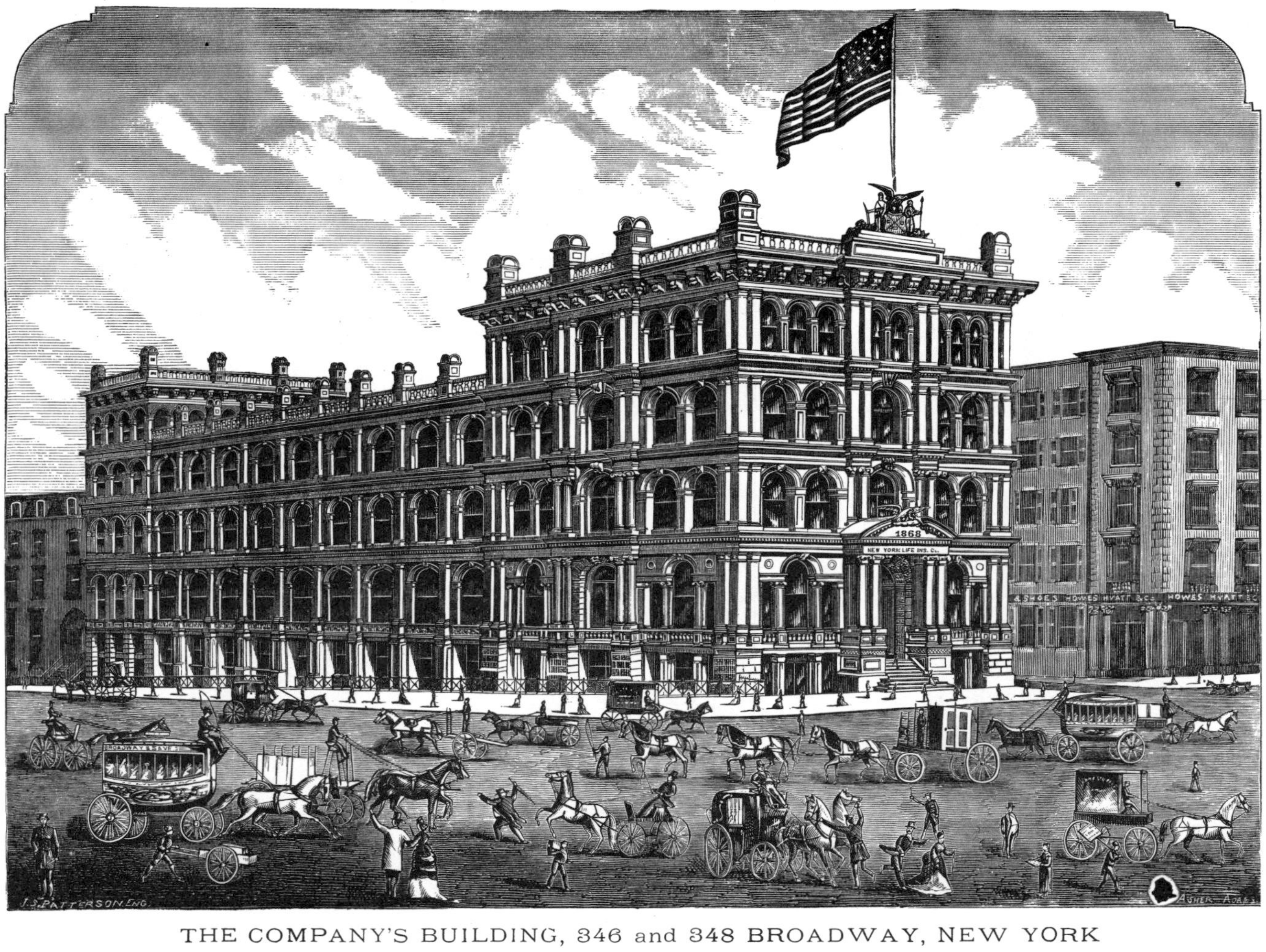

THE COMPANY'S BUILDING, 346 and 348 BROADWAY, NEW YORK

THE COMPANY'S HISTORY.

Sixty-four years have elapsed since, under the inspiration of pure experiment, and with neither precedent nor prognostic as their guide, a few Hartford men conceived the idea of crystallizing a part of their capital into organic form for the protection of their fellow-citizens against the effects of fire, and for the accumulation of such profit as they might be able to rake out of the ashes of their speculation. On the 27th of June, 1810, the Hartford Fire Ins. Co. was organized and sent forth on its somewhat daring mission, with a capital of $150,000. They have a saying among the Mississippi boatmen that "luck attends the daring sportsman," and, curiously enough, that was just the experience of the new candidate for financial martyrdom.

Whoever has the opportunity to look over the early policy registers of the Hartford, will be amazed to see the brave way in which large lines were accepted, and the rates of premiums at which its policies were sold. Of course we mean as compared with what modern underwriting dares to do. Here was a company fighting shadows in the twilight, rushing in where the insuring angels of our day would fear to tread, and risking all the cash it had in the world upon dwelling, drug store or distillery alike, writing the first at 50 cents per $100, and the last two at $1.00 or $1.25, but, nevertheless, losing not a cent of the premiums of its first two years, and expending less than $1,000 in that time! Nor was this recklessness; for, if the number of insurance companies could have been kept conveniently small, and if the public morals had not been debauched by the reward their millions of dollars paid in losses have, of late years, offered to fraud and arson, insurance to-day would be a safe and paying venture at the rates, and under the plucky practices, of sixty years ago. Those halcyon days are gone, never to return.

The first president of the company was Nathaniel Terry, and Walter Mitchell was its Secretary.

The directors of the company are among the well-known citizens and influential capitalists of Hartford, that city so rich in worldly-wise and wealthy men. It is not to be forgotten that in the keeping of these successive boards lies the guaranty of continued success; what they are and what they will do will shape the future policy of the company. Of such a board as the company now has it may well feel proud, and their names, to all who recognize them, convey a sense of fullest confidence.

Before leaving the historical branch of our subject, we will give some figures illustrative of the company's management, experience and progress, which we feel sure that many of our readers will appreciate. It is proper to repeat that so systematically has the business been conducted, from the outset, that every record, book, paper, etc., connected therewith, has been filed and preserved; and hence there can be no guesswork about statistics, no mystification about facts.

THE HARTFORD FIRE INSURANCE COMPANY'S BUILDING, Hartford, Conn.

Erected 1870.

CAPITAL

The company's capital has from time to time been increased, from the original $150,000 with which it started until the present handsome sum of $1,000,000 has been reached. These several changes have taken place in the following order:

The original capital was - - -	$ 150,000
1854, February 17, increased by - - -	150,000
	$ 300,000
1857, July 14, increased by - - -	200,000
	$ 500,000
1864, June 6, increased by - - -	500,000
Since when the capital has been as now -	$1,000,000

There is something astounding in the figures which tell us how much money the company has taken in during all these years. And yet the records vouch for a premium income of $18,288,392.59, to which must be added receipts from interest, etc., $1,419,031.11—together $19,707,423.70! Its present income is nearly $2,500,000 a year.

LOSSES PAID

Since its organization, the Hartford has paid to policy-holders for losses $16,000,000. Strictly speaking, this company has restored to the productive interests of the country more than sixteen million dollars, which otherwise had been entirely annihilated. One cannot suppress the curiosity to know how certain celebrated conflagrations affected this one company which has passed safely through them all:

New York City, Dec. 16,1835, - -	$ 64,973.55
New York City, July 19,1845, - - -	69,691.33
Nantucket, July 14, 1846, - -	54,521.63
Albany, New York, Aug. 17, 1848, -	57,673.44
St. Louis, Mo., May 18, 1849, -	58,676.85
Augusta, Me., Sept. 16, 1865, -	57,022.16
Portland, Me., July 4, 1866, -	151,288.31
Vicksburg, Miss., Dec. 24, 1866, -	55,077.55
Chicago, Oct, 8, 1871, - -	1,500,000.00
Boston, Nov. 9, 1872, - -	480,000.00
Total of losses paid at ten fires,	$2,548,924.82

What a blessed record of ruins rebuilt, capital restored, bankruptcy prevented, poverty banished and despair dispelled is fully written up in these registers, over against the policies which have been cancelled by the fires of sixty-four years.

The Hartford may justly lay claim to the distinction of being a national company. Nothing but its name and the personnel of its officers could justify any other idea; for its home office would be just as appropriately located in New York, or Chicago, or Richmond, or San Francisco, so far as the transaction of its cosmopolitan business is concerned. Its agencies are planted all over the country, in every state and territory of the United States—two only excepted, and in the Dominion of Canada as well. By the aid of 1600 agents of the various grades, all of them carefully selected as representative men in their respective localities, the company cultivates the entire insurance field. In the larger cities it ranks next only to the local companies in popularity and amount of business.

ARCHITECTURE IN THE UNITED STATES.

Until within a few years it has been "the custom of the country" to erect only the plainest structures for business purposes, consisting in most instances of a box-like building, with no visible roof, and with square openings for doors and windows, that being long deemed "good enough" for any structure designed for the purposes of trade. Some added ornamentation in details of porticos, windows, and cornices transformed the generally accepted business building into a first-class residence, and for a long time this mere addition of details—with, of course, a difference of size—was about the only architectural distinction to be made between a store and a dwelling. Within the last decade a rapid growth of good taste has been developed in architecture in all its departments, but in none to so marked a degree as in its adaptation to business structures. All of our large cities show a wonderful disparity between the "good enough" buildings of ten years ago and the more recent structures.

Chicago, before the late fire destroyed the business portion of the city, afforded, perhaps, the best illustration of the advance to which allusion has been made. Its growth since 1860 has been much more rapid than that of any other city in the country, and it therefore afforded much the best opportunity to manifest the latest "American idea" of business architecture in one of its styles. It must be confessed that the "florid style" was the favorite in that ill-fated city, but nevertheless the general effect was admirable, and the visitors to Chicago left it with the firm impression that the business part of the city was the finest in the country. But the combination of elegance and solidity which makes the perfect business structure is more largely shown in Boston than in any other American city. The near proximity of the Quincy granite quarries has aided not a little to give the appearance of solidity to the warehouses and chief business buildings of "the Hub." It cannot be denied that granite is the stone best adapted to structures devoted to purposes which call for an appearance of durability. Marble and all kinds of lime stone, with free-stone, lacking as they do the suggestion of permanence which should belong to materials entering into the construction of public and business buildings, seem better fitted for a lighter class of structures. Granite, when worked into forms of architectural beauty, is not liable to the disintegration which almost surely takes place in the marbles and free-stones used for building

CHARTER OAK LIFE INSURANCE COMPANY. Hartford Conn.

purposes in this country, and it admits of as sharp and well-defined lines as can be worked upon any other material. Its general adaptation to buildings of all kinds will doubtless lead ere long to its general adoption in preference to any other stone.

Among the most notable structures erected for business purposes in the last ten years, the imposing office building of the Charter Oak Life Insurance Company, at Hartford, Conn., has deservedly a high rank. This noble building is built of the finest granite quarried in the United States, and is a rare example of the union of beauty and strength of material. This building, so far as mere matters of *details* are concerned, might well be called a plain structure; but the architectural effect is one of wonderful grace of proportions, great harmony in all the parts, with an admirable adaptation to business purposes. It is doubtful if any business building in the country excels it in what may be called "general effect," and yet it is certain that, compared with the principal structures of like character, it is exceedingly plain. One of the most noticeable features of this building is the idea which it gives of *permanence*. Everywhere, inside and outside, this idea seems to have been worked into the entire building, and it was well that it should be so, for it is the home of an institution suggestive of permanency and stability. Indeed, its very name indicates the same idea. No better name for an institution intended to be perpetual, and whose trusts are as sacred as any business trusts can be, could be adopted, and in taking it for the Charter Oak Life Insurance Company, its originators accepted the omen of this good name as indicative of what the company must be in all its history. For the full period of twenty-one years this company has prosecuted its business in a manner which has won for it an enviable position and an honorable name. It has issued sixty-nine thousand policies, insuring in amount at least one hundred and fifty millions of dollars, and has now in force fully one-half of this number and amount. It has paid to the families of those who have held its policies the large sum of about six millions, and has returned premiums to its policyholders to the amount of six millions.

They have witnessed the growth of the business of life insurance in the United States from the feeble existence of a few companies, with aggregate assets of less than ten millions, to the present time, when nearly one hundred companies hold in possession as a sacred trust nearly or quite four hundred millions of dollars.

To such a company, the public may give their full confidence, resting assured that the permanence, ability, and integrity requisite in a Life Insurance Company will be found within.

WATERBURY CLOCK CO.,
Manufacturers of
CLOCKS AND CLOCK MATERIALS.

The Waterbury Clock Company, fine engravings of whose factories adorn this page, was incorporated in 1857. Its founders who were also pioneers in the brass and copper business of Connecticut, and more immediately identified with that branch of American industry, had been, for many years previous to the organization of this company, interested in the manufacture of clocks in other parts of the State, and were fully conversant with the business in all its details. Wisely foreseeing the growth and development of our own country, the widening area of our territory, and the rapid increase of population, they were led to anticipate a demand for American clocks greatly exceeding that of any other period of our national life, and far beyond the capacity of production of the factories at that time devoted to this class of manufactures.

American clocks were rapidly winning foreign recognition; it was apparent that the demand from abroad would soon assume proportions of considerable magnitude, and that in the near future, Connecticut, in the matter of its horological productions, would have the world for its market.

Thoroughly impressed with the soundness of these views, Messrs. Benedict, Burnham, Mitchell, Booth and other enterprising residents of Waterbury, organized this company under the general law relating to manufactures, and operations were immediately commenced in buildings adjoining those of the Benedict & Burnham Manufacturing Company, then, as now, among the foremost brass manufacturers in this country.

Having ample capital, the company obtained every known mechanical appliance that could aid them in producing perfect work, and employed skilled labor. Their first productions immediately attracted marked attention.

The year 1857 was one of disaster. The manu-

CASE FACTORY, WATERBURY CLOCK CO., WATERBURY, CONN.
ESTABLISHED, 1857.

MOVEMENT FACTORY, WATERBURY CLOCK CO., WATERBURY, CT.

facturing and mercantile interests of the country were sorely tried, but Waterbury clocks were brought to the favorable notice of the community, and from that time until the present, every succeeding year has witnessed an increasing popularity of these goods testifying alike to the quality of the article and the distinguishing taste of the buyer.

The premises originally occupied by the company were soon found insufficient to accommodate their rapidly growing business, and they erected two large and commodious factories, where with increased room, power, machinery and every necessary facility for manufacturing clocks, they are now prosecuting their work which has grown to immense proportions. The capacity of their mills is now about twenty thousand clocks per month.

They make a great variety of the cheapest and least pretentious clocks as well as those most expensive and it may be said with equal truth, that they are reliable time-keepers.

Waterbury clocks are a staple article of commerce in all the principal cities of the Union, and find a ready distribution throughout the country through the agencies of the company in New York, Chicago and San Francisco. They can be bought almost everywhere. Leading jewelers in the larger cities always have a stock on hand, while country store-keepers at cross-roads-corners generally have " a few more left."

The export trade has also kept pace with the growth of the home trade, so that in Great Britain and Ireland, on the continent of Europe, the British Dependencies and possessions, East Indies, Australia, China and Japan, they are every where known and every where appreciated as among the best results of American industry.

The magnitude of this business can scarcely be appreciated without visiting their works. Thousands of workers are constantly employed in this branch of manufacture, and millions of dollars are invested in it. The principal warerooms of the Waterbury Clock Company are at No. 4 Courtlandt Street, New York, and 160 Clark Street, Chicago. They also have an agency at San Francisco.

HARTFORD
ACCIDENT INSURANCE
COMPANY,
OF
Hartford, Conn.

The name of Hartford has become, wherever the English language is spoken, the synonym of whatever is secure, successful or lasting in the business of underwriting, its insurance companies being known throughout the commercial world, and are known only to be trusted and admired. Their agents are to be found in every city, town and hamlet of America; and the record of their prompt and bountiful benefactions is written in a multitude of homes and hearts to which the disasters of fire and death would have meant ruin irretrievable had it not been for the kindly protection of a Hartford Insurance Policy.

The aggregate capital invested in the business of insurance in the city of Hartford, on the first day of January, 1874, amounted to no less than $8,189,056; the total assets of Hartford insurance companies to $98,618,-879; while their annual income had grown to be $37,408,284 and the aggregate of all their then outstanding policies reached the enormous sum of $1,267,433,825.

Every kind of insurance policy which time has denominated safe for companies to issue, and experience has shown desirable to have, is issued at Hartford. The latest, and certainly by no means the least valuable kind of insurance offered by Hartford underwriters, is that against the pecuniary loss by disability or death, arising from any one of the numberless forms of accident to which we are exposed. In respect to this form of insurance it may be truly said, that "the best is the cheapest;" for it is certain that there is no other insurance which covers so many or so common perils, or the benefactions of which are so numerous and so welcome as Accident Insurance.

The uncertainty of life is, in itself, matter for serious reflection; but added to the many causes which may naturally bring it to a close, there is the large class of adverse influences, which we call accidents. Against organic influences, precautions may be taken; it is possible to regulate health and baffle disease, but what is to be said of the many sudden, unlooked-for,

impossible-to-be-guarded-against accidents which appear, like the phantom of Banquo, to "push us from our stools?" Against these, precaution is powerless, and fore-sight disquieteth itself in vain.

This has ever been so, and has served as the theme of the poet, and the homily of the philosopher. But in these days the tendency to accident is increased a thousand fold. Our fast lives—the habit we have acquired of rushing from place to place, of annihilating distance and defying time—is alone chargeable with the result.

Home staying folks, such as our ancestors were, if they saw little of the pleasures of life, encountered few of its dangers. We on the other hand, expose ourselves to them; seek them out, in manner of speaking, and ought not to be startled at the result. Added to this are many of the fresh conditions of life with which chemistry has surrounded us,—for though chemistry does much to lighten the burden of human affliction, it is undoubtedly pregnant with accidents. A certain increased recklessness, consequent on the utter change in our natural habits, may further be credited with a tendency in this direction, and, to sum up, taking life as a whole, there can be little question but that accident enters into it as an element of integral fact, to an extent without parallel in the experience of past ages.

In view of these considerations, it is the most natural thing in the world that insurance, ever adapting itself to the requirements of society, should have applied itself specially to the mitigation of trouble as the specific result of accidents.

The officers of the Hartford Accident Insurance Company did not enter into this business as an untried experiment. They have had the advantage of official connection for many years with the most successful companies of the country, and bring to their new duties the ripe results of years of experience. While not claiming for themselves any undue share

of the credit for the success of this branch of underwriting, they do claim that having been from the start familiar with all the methods through which that success has been secured, they are, so far as experience can make them so, entirely qualified to make this company equally a success.

Confining itself solely to an accident business, no part of the company's assets are pledged for the payment of life policies, nor for a reserve upon the same, and the energies of the direction are not divided, but will be concentrated upon making the Hartford Accident Company the leading accident insurance company of the United States.

Among the thousands of favorable notices which this company has received from the press of America, the following from the Hartford Times, where the company is best known, is worthy of reproduction.

"This new insurance Company starts under unusually favorable auspices. The Board of Directors is composed of some of our best and ablest citizens —men who have been successful in all the various business enterprises with which they have been connected, several of them being practical insurance men of large experience. We do no injustice to the many very able insurance officers in Hartford, when we say that no company in the city has started with abler or more experienced officers. It will be universally conceded that the President, the Hon. R. D. Hubbard, is one of the ablest men in New England; Vice-President Wilson, Secretary Lester, and Assistant Secretary Brainard, have all had many years experience in Accident Insurance, and are thoroughly conversant with the business in all its various departments."

The Hartford Accident Insurance Co., of Hartford, Connecticut, insures against death by Accident, and grants indemnity for loss of time by totally disabling injuries. It is the only company in the United States devoted exclusively to Accident Insurance, issuing both long and short term policies; and its managers have had an experience in the business extending over the entire history of accident insurance in the United States. Cash Capital, $200,000.

OFFICERS:

R. D. Hubbard,	- -	President.
Chas. E. Wilson,	-	Vice-President.
Geo. B. Lester,	-	Sec'y and Actuary.
Lewis H. Brainard,		Ass't Secretary.

DIRECTORS:

David Clark, Retired Merchant,	Hartford.
R. D. Hubbard, Attorney,	"
T. O. Enders, Pres't Ætna Life Ins. Co.,	"
Wm. A. Healy, Pres't National Screw Co.,	"
Chas. E. Wilson, Vice-President,	"
Sam'l L. Clemens, (Mark Twain)	"
Geo. B. Lester, Secretary and Actuary,	"
Sam'l F. Jones, Attorney,	"
T. M. Maltbie, Pres't Granby Manufacturing Co., Granby.	

OF HARTFORD, CONN.

37

CAZENOVIA SEMINARY.

Cazenovia, Madison County, New York.

Rev. W. S. SMYTH, M. A., Principal.

:o:

ORIGIN.

In the United States educational movements under Methodist auspices were, for many years, too insignificant to be of much credit to the denomination. Until near 1820 the denomination did nothing successfully for the establishment of schools; not because ministers and people did not appreciate the importance of education, but because the great work of awakening the people to a sense of religious things occupied the time of the ministers, and because the comparative poverty of the people prevented any special effort in the direction of schools.

The first Seminary that introduced the revival of education in American Methodism was established in New Market, New Hampshire, in 1817. It prospered for several years. In 1825, through financial embarrassment, it closed its halls. But in the same year Wilbraham Academy was opened, and the New Market Academy was merged in this.

The initiatory movement for the establishment of the Seminary at Cazenovia was made in 1823, by the Genesee Conference, then in session in Westmoreland, Oneida County, New York. It was determined to open the school in the old Madison County Court House with all dispatch. A local committee was appointed consisting of Charles Giles, George Gary, Elias Bowen, Solomon Root, Luther Buell, John Peck, Jacob Ten Eyck, David B. Johnson and Charles Stebbins. The committee met Aug. 14, 1823. The name of the Seminary was, "The Seminary of the Genesee Conference." Charles Giles and George Gary were appointed the first agents. The school was to be opened Dec. 1, 1824. On that day, in the basement of the old court house, with eight scholars it began its successful career.

BUILDINGS.

As before remarked, the first building was the Madison County Court House—which was built in 1810 under the superintendence of Col. John Lincklaen and Col. Eliphalet Jackson. The characteristic style of architecture belonging to the old Court House, readily distinguishes it from the other buildings, but for durability it is in no wise inferior to those which have been since added to it. It was used for recitations and chapel services, and is still used for such purposes. There were at the early organization of the Seminary no dormitories.

In 1831 the building next west of the Court House building, was erected for domitories for gentlemen, and a few years subsequently another building still further west for dormitories for ladies. In 1852 the building known as "William's Hall" was erected. This is a commodious and substantial edifice of brick, and devoted to lecture, society and reading rooms. In 1866 the building erected for dormitories for ladies was replaced by a large and beautiful building for dormitories. In 1870 this was still further enlarged by the addition of another building for the domestic department.

The group as it now (1876) stands is therefore varied in style of architecture and in material. It is picturesque and unique, and although lacking in symmetry, yet it is so historic and such an exponent of the development and growth of the Institution that its friends will regret when it shall undergo the transformation which it soon is to undergo by the construction of the imposing structure represented on this page.

This proposed building is the outgrowth of a movement by the *alumni* of the Seminary as a Semi Centennial Monument of their devotion to their *Alma Mater.* The design is to raise one hundred thousand dollars for the building, and one hundred thousand dollars toward an endowment fund. Much of this fund is already pledged. When these objects shall have been reached, no Academy in the country will be in superior condition as to its buildings and means of income.

CHARACTER OF THE SEMINARY.

1. It has ever maintained a high character for thoroughness, and no institution in the State of New York stands higher in the estimation of the Regents. The design has never been to make a college of it, although one-half of the so called colleges in the land do not equal it in the extent of its curriculum of studies, or in the facilities for academic culture. Its friends believe that there are too many colleges already, and that this Institution should be made, even still more than it is now, one in which the most thorough prepartion for our best colleges can be given, and also furnish a four years course of instruction in language, science, mathematics and literature for such young men and women as cannot complete a regular college course. This is its legitimate field of labor, and in this field the purpose of its friends is to make it second to no other institution.

2. Although, under the auspices of the Methodist Episcopal Church, the Seminary is not sectarian. From its foundation to the present time several religious denominations have been represented in its Board of Trustees, its faculty and its students. At the present time out of the 700 students, who are in attendance, not one-half are from Methodist patronage. No sectarian tenets are allowed to be taught in the Institution.

3. It is a boarding shool, and at present has facilities for boarding about one hundred and fifty students. The other students board in private families, or at their own homes in the village. The dormitories, halls, dining-room, &c., are good and well heated, ventilated and lighted.

4. It is a mixed school. The question of co-education was here successfully settled more than fifty years ago. The six thousand young women and the seven thousand young men who have been educated together here are a living commentary upon the wisdom of the system.

5. It is a religious school—not sectarian—but eminently a religious school. Thousands of every creed have been brought to Christ under the influence of the religious sentiment that has prevailed all through its history among teachers and students. The chapel services—the conference meetings—the prayer and other social meetings have been marvelous in their power of soul culture.

6. The government of the school is paternal, mild but strict. The students who attend here, and who only are invited to attend, are generally of such maturity as to be governed by appeals to their manhood and womanhood and to their sense of duty. Very few cases of expulsion have occurred during the entire history of the Seminary.

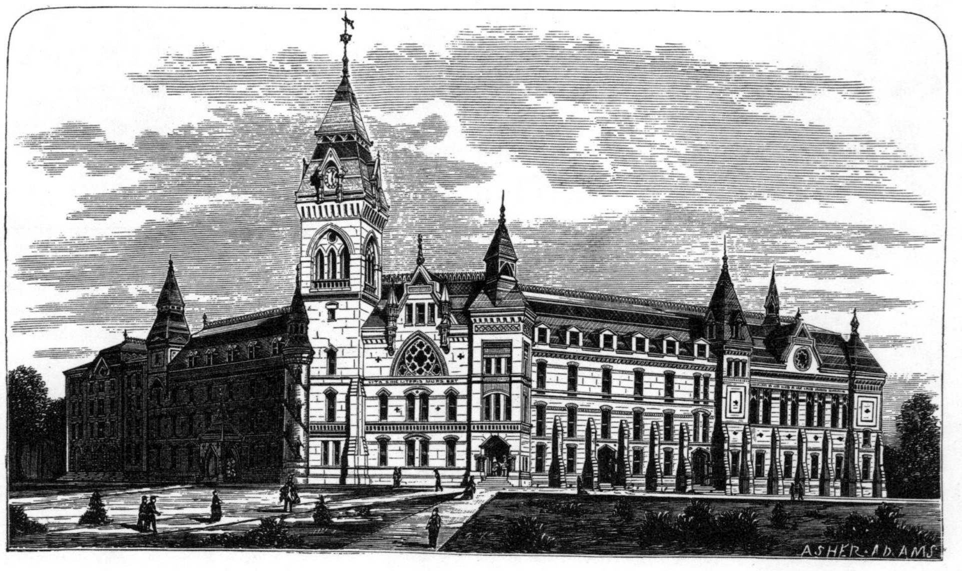

CAZENOVIA SEMINARY, CAZENOVIA, NEW YORK.

TEACHERS.

Nathaniel Porter, A. M., of Connecticut, was its first Principal. The following distinguished men have been connected with its faculties: Augustus W. Smith, L.L. D., afterwards President of the Wesleyan University at Middletown, Ct.; D. D. Whedon, D. D., LL. D., now editor of the *Methodist Quarterly Review*; Wm. C. Larabee, D. D., a distinguished educator; J. Wadsworth Tyler, A. M.; John Johnston, LL. D., the author of several text books on Physics and Chemistry, and now Emeritus Professor in Wesleyan University; Wm. H. Allen, LL. D., now President of Girard College in Philadelphia; George Peck, D. D., the editor, author and preacher; Herman M. Johnson, D. D., afterwards President of Dickinson College; Nelson Rounds, D. D., after President of Williamette University; George G. Hapgood, D. D.; Henry Bannister, D. D, Senior Professor in the Garret Biblical Institute, at Evanston, Ill.; Bostwick Hawley, D. D.; Horatio R. Clarke, D. D.; Edward Bannister, D. D., afterward of the University of California; Ami B. Hyde, D. D., now of Allegheny College; John W. Armstrong, D. D., Principal of the State Normal School, at Fredonia; Edward G. Andrews, D. D., Bishop of the M. E. Church; Edward Searing, Supt. of Public Instruction in the State of Wisconsin.

Its Principals, in order, have been as follows: Nathiel Porter, Augustus W. Smith, J. Wadsworth Tyler, Wm. C. Larabee, John Johnston, George Peck, Hanford Colburn, George G. Hapgood, Henry Bannister, Edward G. Andrews, A. S. Graves and W. S. Smyth.

STUDENTS.

During the half century of its existance there have attended the Seminary about thirteen thousand young men and women from all parts of the United States and Canada. Among them are numbered some of the most eminent men in the nation. Senators, Governors, Generals, Judges, Litterateurs, Millionaires and Bishops have received their early education within its walls. They are found in Canada, in Florida, in Mexico, on the Pacific Slope, in South America, in Europe, in Egypt, in China, in the energy and stir of the city and on the frontiers of civilization. No human arithmetic can estimate the intellectual and moral power which such an Institution wields through so large a body of alumni. From careful estimate over six hundred young men have been prepared for college here; three thousand have been converted to God; one thousand have entered the ministry; four hundred, the law; four hundred medicine; more than a thousand are successful business men; one thousand and five hundred are engaged in teaching in colleges, academies and other schools; and nearly all pursuing some honorable and useful calling.

GROWTH.

In 1824 the Seminary opened with only eight scholars. It now has a yearly attendance of over seven hundred. It then had one instructor. It now has twenty. Then it was confined to one small and inconvenient building. It now has several large and commodious buildings. Then its work was simply elementary. Now it has extensive and thorough courses of instruction. Then its income was a few hundred dollars. It has now an income of nearly forty thousand dollars. Then it annually paid its teachers about enough to keep soul and body together. Now it pays liberal salaries. Then it was poor, almost friendless, a puny child out upon the desert. Now it has hosts of friends all over the world, and a body of alumni who constitute a never failing source of support and encouragement. Though fifty years old, the institution is fresh and vigorous, and is reaching out with strong faith in the successful issue of new and largely increased enterprises.

LOCATION.

Cazenovia village is located in one of the most delightful sections of the State of New York. Elevated twelve hundred feet above the sea, its atmosphere is pure, and no place of the same population can show less sickness and mortality. The surrounding country is rolling, cut into farms under high cultivation, adorned by tasteful residences and giving evidence at once of the presence of intelligence and culture. Better roads are not to be found anywhere—smooth, broad, well shaded by maple and elm, they afford unsurpassed opportunities for riding. Near the village lies the lake—a gem of beauty—and giving excellent opportunity for boating and fishing. The number of inhabitants is about two thousand. From the incipiency of the Seminary they have been interested in its success, and have been ever ready to give it of their time and money. Cazenovia is easily accessible by Rail Roads. The Cazenovia, Canastota and De Ruyter Road connecting with the New York Central Road at Canastota, and the Syracuse and Chenango Road, running from Syracuse to Norwich, passing through the village. At the head of the lake, about four miles from the village, are located the extensive and beautiful grounds of the Cazenovia Lake Camp-meeting Association, an Association organized under the laws of the State. There are three small but handsome steamers upon the lake which give ample means of transportation between the village and grounds. On these grounds are held annually a Camp-meeting and a Sunday School Assembly, and besides they are used for summer residence by many from the cities.

SEMI CENTENNIAL JUBILEE.

In December 1874 the Seminary completed fifty years of successful work, and its friends proposed to have in, the following July, in connection with the Commencement Exercises, a Semi Centennial Celebration. The following call, signed by more than four hundred alumni, was issued: "The undersigned, former students, teachers and officers of Cazenovia Seminary, believing that the close of the fiftieth year of the noble work of this institution ought to be recognized in some way valuable to the cause of Education, respectfully invite a reunion of all students, teachers and officers of the Institution in Cazenovia on the 7th and 8th of July, 1875. We ask the resident students, faculty and officers to make all neccessary arrangement for the reunion."

When the time arrived thousands of old students and teachers from all parts of the nation and from Canada thronged to the place. No greater gathering has been seen in Central New York than was that on the 7th and 8th of July, 1875, in the village of Cazenovia. Every one was astonished to find that so eminent and large a body of men and women had been educated here. The addresses, the poems, the music, the reminiscences, the renewing of associations that had slumbered ten, twenty, thirty, forty, and, in some cases, fifty years, conspired to make it an occasion most memorable.

ALUMNI RECORD.

In commemoration of that event and of the half century's work of the institution, a book, to be called the "First Fifty Years of Cazenovia Seminary," is to be published. The book will contain a history of the Seminary, biographical sketches of the most eminent alumni and teachers, a chronological and alphabetical list of all the students who have attended here, together with such items of a personal nature as can be obtained, and a full account of the Jubilee proceedings.

While it is doubtless true that the chief interest in this book will be among the *alumni* and friends of the Seminary, still the book will have more than a mere local interest and value. For in the first place, it will enter at length into the early efforts of Methodists in this country to establish educational institutions; then, it will review the question of co-education, and from abundant facts and illustrations throw much light upon the question; moreover, it will show such relation between the work of the Institution and the development of the various interests, and remarkable growth and development of the country, as to furnish instruction and hope to all friends of Republican Government.

PROSPECTS.

An Institution with such a history and such a firm hold on the affections of the thousands of *alumni* must have a successful future. The momentum which the experience of fifty years has furnished, must give to it a steady onward movement. As population shall increase and the Alumni become more wealthy, the Seminary will not fail to be remembered in patronage by being supplied with more students and richer endowment. We cannot read the future, but Cazenovia Seminary has never been more prosperous, and has never had greater promise of perpetuity than it has now.

ROCHESTER BUSINESS UNIVERSITY,

Rochester, New York.
—:o:—

A thorough business education is an essential requisite to complete success in life.

Conceding that every man is naturally better adapted to some special pursuit than to any other, and that many failures to achieve success are attributable to errors in the selection of proper callings, our original proposition still holds good. Every profession, trade or pursuit is a business, and certain general, fundamental laws underlie them all. The very ground work of success is an intimate knowledge of, and a strict compliance with these laws; the requirements of correct general business principles and habits of thought and action. That special knowledge which enables one to discriminate between the qualities of various samples of goods of the same class, and to fix their relative values, will always aid the merchant, but it only bears that relation to success that the visible walls bear to a building whose foundation is beneath the surface ground and bedded on a rock. The walls may be of the very best materials, well put together; their exterior may present an appearance of solidity and strength, and the interior may seem beautiful; but if the foundation is not broad and strong, the very elements which, under other circumstances, would have rendered it enduring, will but destroy it—it will fall under its own weight.

Until within a comparatively few years no attempt was made to educate our young men for active business life by any regular course of instruction. The young man entered a bank, office, counting-room, warehouse or store, and "picked up" such information in relation to the special business pursued, as his duties rendered necessary. If he was quick to learn and gave evidence of being "smart" in any particular branch he was "pushed" in that direction, and eventually became, perhaps, a good office clerk or a good salesman, but outside of his special department of labor, he probably knew little or nothing of business. Or, if he had influence, or was for any cause favored, he may in time have learned all about business, as it was transacted by the special house with whom he was employed. At best he was but a specialist. He could succeed, perhaps, in the business to which he had been brought up, but was rarely qualified to engage in any other.

The youth of to-day are more favored than their fathers were. Commercial Colleges enable them to obtain a perfect theoretical and practical business education in less time than, under the old system they could have made the first real advance. The foundations of their future successful business careers are laid in the school room, and broad and sure foundations they are too. We can best make this plain by selecting a first-class commercial institute and briefly enumerating the advantages it presents.

The Rochester Business University, of Rochester, New York, was founded in the year 1863, and at once took prominent rank among the leading commercial schools of America, a rank which it still maintains. The design was and is to prepare young men for the duties of actual business life, and to fittingly do this, its curriculum embraces six regularly organized departments of study and instruction, viz:

The Department of Book-keeping;

The Department of Actual Accountantship;

The Department of Business Law;

The Department of Mercantile Mathematics;

The Department of Business Penmanship; and

The Department of Ornamental Penmanship; which last, if it does not teach an art absolutely indispensable to a thorough business education, at least affords the student an opportunity to acquire an accomplishment of great practical value.

Each of the departments is under the immediate supervision of a Professor of the highest qualifications in his specialty. In each the course of instruction is practical and so eminently thorough that the graduate is fitted to at once enter upon the business duties of life. We lack the room necessary to minutely describe the methods of teaching, but the most superficial reader must see at a glance that he who masters these studies must have obtained a very complete knowledge of the

fundamental principles of business. All that remains for him to do is to make a wise choice of profession or calling, and to as thoroughly educate himself in that special pursuit as he has been educated in the general laws and customs of trade, and if he possesses such ability as will enable him to apply his acquired knowledge to a useful purpose, success must follow.

There are still a few who distrust commercial schools and who claim that business can only be learned in business houses—by absolute contact with and personal interest in *bona-fide* business transactions. One might as well argue that a foreign language could only be learned in the country to which it is germane. The student fresh from college who carried off the highest prize is but a child in knowledge compared to the man of ripened age who has spent all the years between his college days and the present in unwearied study. The education acquired at the Rochester

HALL OF THE THEORY DEPARTMENT OF THE ROCHESTER BUSINESS UNIVERSITY.

Business University bears the same relation to the future success of its graduates in the business world, that the classical education of a college does to the future success of its graduate who enters the field of science or letters. Certainly none will argue that the youth who desires to follow a literary life, could best accomplish it by entering a publisher's office, and rising step by step. No, he must receive a liberal education, and on the good use of that rests all his hopes of success. It is the base, the foundation of his work, and to obtain it he must enter college. His school course ended, the absolute battle for success begins; then he first comes in practical contact with the busy world; but his previous study, his acquired knowledge, have prepared him for the contest. With the youth who chooses a business career the early training should be equally methodical,

and the Rochester Business University offers facilities for making it far more practical.

The student learns not only how to do business theoretically, but before he can graduate he must reduce his theory to practice, and must give tangible evidence of his perfect knowledge before he can pass examination. No matter what pursuit in life a man may follow, a thorough business education is essential to complete success. The very ground-work of the education of a lawyer, for instance, is the acquirement of a knowledge of the unwritten general laws of trade, to which should be added a comprehensive acquaintaince with the details of keeping accounts. If he is engaged in a cause growing out of a disagreement between the books of the contending principals, it must be evident to the most casual reasoner that he can present the case of his client much more clearly and forcibly if he understands how such accounts should be kept. The physician, the minister, the farmer, the mechanic, even the day laborer, should be the possessor of a practical knowledge of book-keeping. Yet, except among men who propose to follow mercantile pursuits, too little attention has heretofore been given to this important branch of education.

That the course of instruction offered at the Rochester Business University is thorough, is amply evidenced by the continued success of the institution. Notwithstanding the recent depression of business, the patronage of the University has continuously increased, and during the year 1875, dull as times were throughout the world, the number of students was larger than ever before during a similar period, and nearly fifty per cent. greater than during the preceding year.

The institution is located in one of the most beautiful, healthful and flourishing cities in the Union. It occupies one of the finest buildings, and has, perhaps, the most conveniently arranged and elegantly appointed suite of rooms on the American Continent devoted to such purposes. The reader will be enabled to form some idea of their size and general appearance from the engravings of two of the halls presented on this page. The reputation of the University is National; its graduates are everywhere, and occupy positions in all the higher walks of life. Its students are from all sections of the country, from Maine to California. It is not a cheap commercial college, but a thoroughly organized and officered institution, in which all those branches of study that every business man should be perfectly familiar with are thoroughly and practically taught by a corps of gentlemen who understand the requirements of business life, and who know how to best convey the information which they possess to young men who contemplate entering the business world.

In the selection of a school the scholar cannot be too exacting as to the qualifications of the teachers. There are many men in all the walks of life who have all the knowledge necessary for a first-class instructor, save the ability to impart the information they possess to others. To be a successful teacher a special talent is required which comparatively few men possess; therefore, the student in selecting his school, college or university should thoroughly inform himself not only as to the qualifications of the faculty and instructors, so far as their knowledge of the subject matter is concerned, but also as to their success in imparting that information to others. A really good teacher must be able to explain the same question by several different methods of reasoning, or modes of expression. The set phrases which adequately express a truth to some, will utterly fail with others of equal ability, and he only is a thoroughly good teacher who can meet the requirements of all pupils of ordinary ability. As we have previously said, the instructors of the Rochester Business University possess these qualifications.

We would gladly extend this notice, and really there is much more to be said than we have said, but our too brief space is exhausted, and for further particulars we must refer the reader to the Annual Catalogue, of the institution, which contains full statements of the rates of tuition, conditions of admission and information regarding the courses of study pursued, and the objects, rules, etc., of the University. Those may be obtained without cost by calling on or addressing, L. L. Williams, President, Rochester, New York.

HALL OF THE BUSINESS AND OFFICE DEPARTMENTS OF THE ROCHESTER BUSINESS UNIVERSITY.

L. S. LAWRENCE & CO.,
BANKERS,
Cor. Fulton and Nassau Sts., N. Y.

The firm of L. S. Lawrence & Co. was organized about the year 1856 by Luther S. Lawrence. Mr. Lawrence, for many years preceding, had been the confidential agent and correspondent in the city of New York for the banking firm of Drexel, Sather & Church, of San Francisco., California, at that time one of the most widely known and highly esteemed banking houses in that city.

Mr. Lawrence's long and practical experience, and extensive acquaintance with the business and banking firms of the country, fitted him in no ordinary degree to be the founder of a successful and honorable firm, whose record and prestige remain untarnished, and whose business ability and reputation are unquestioned.

The firm of L. S. Lawrence & Co. owned and occupied the premises No. 164 Nassau Street for nearly twenty years, where they did a large and profitable business. They disposed of this property to the New York Tribune Association, and it forms a portion of the site on which now stands the new Tribune Building, one of the most magnificent and unique structures of the age.

On the death of Mr. Luther S. Lawrence, the direct management of the firm devolved upon Mr. Charles Frazier, and under his supervision the popularity of the Banking House continues to increase.

The present location of the firm of Messrs. L. S. Lawrence & Co., corner of Nassau and Fulton Streets, is one of great prominence for the transaction of a financial and banking business. The Bennett Building being one of the most substantial and beautiful in the city, is also in a location most easily accessible for those who have business to transact either in Drafts, Notes, Bonds, Stocks, Collections, or in the sale or purchase of Foreign Coin—Gold or Silver, They buy and sell Gold, Government Securities, Stocks, and Bonds of all descriptions on most favorable terms, and on commission.

Particular attention is given to the making of collections on all parts of the United States and the Canadas, for which prompt returns are made. They also receive deposits and issue certificates bearing interest at a fixed rate, or on demand, and available in all parts of the United States. Favorable terms are made with banks, bankers, merchants, and private individuals, who open accounts with them subject to check or draft at sight. Also Drafts on England, Ireland and Scotland may be had from them at favorable rates.

Through the changes of many years, this house has established and maintained a reputation for business integrity of which any firm might well be proud—and their ability and facilities are equal to their rapidly increasing business.

Banking House of L. S. Lawrence & Co., New York.

Birmingham Iron and Steel Works.
Birmingham, Conn.

These works are the largest of their class in Connecticut, and among the largest in the United States. The capital of the Company is $200,000. Their factories cover three acres, and they constantly employ upwards of two hundred men. The power used is steam and water, the latter drawn from the Naugatuck. The company was established in 1843, and has since been in successful operation, turning out enormous quantities of work. They have an iron capacity of 6,000 tons per year, and produce yearly 300 tons of steel carriage and cart springs and 1,000 tons of axles. They make merchant iron, squares, rounds, flats, ovals, half-ovals, half-rounds, etc., of all sizes known to the trade, and of the finest quality.

In their spring and axle works is the latest and most improved machinery, and, with their greatly increased facilities, their long experience of thirty-one years—using the best brands of English and Swedish steel for springs and a very superior iron of their own manufacture for axles—and accomplished workmen of long experience, they have always given perfect satisfaction. In point of quality, finish and style, their productions cannot be excelled by any manufactory in the United States. They make springs of almost every conceivable shape and weight, and axles suitable for every kind of vehicle. Their goods are shipped to all parts of the United States, and they do a large trade in South America, the Sandwich Islands, Australia and other foreign countries. The business is principally managed by the President, Mr. Charles Atwater, and Mr. Thomas Elmes, Secretary.

The Middletown Plate Company,
Middletown, Conn.

The engraving here presented represents the latest design in Tea Sets just introduced by the Middletown Plate Company.

This company was organized in 1866, with a small capital and employing only a few workmen, but—in consequence of great energy, skill and enterprise in devising and introducing new designs, and the fine quality of their goods—has grown rapidly in popular favor. They now occupy the whole building, (of which they at first, used but a portion), have added an additional factory, and, to such large proportions has their business grown, they now require a third.

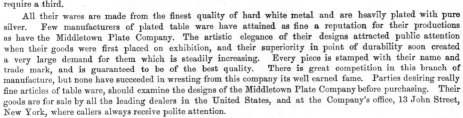

All their wares are made from the finest quality of hard white metal and are heavily plated with pure silver. Few manufacturers of plated table ware have attained as fine a reputation for their productions as have the Middletown Plate Company. The artistic elegance of their designs attracted public attention when their goods were first placed on exhibition, and their superiority in point of durability soon created a very large demand for them which is steadily increasing. Every piece is stamped with their name and trade mark, and is guaranteed to be of the best quality. There is great competition in this branch of manufacture, but none have succeeded in wresting from this company its well earned fame. Parties desiring really fine articles of table ware, should examine the designs of the Middletown Plate Company before purchasing. Their goods are for sale by all the leading dealers in the United States, and at the Company's office, 13 John Street, New York, where callers always receive polite attention.

Calcium, or Oxy-Hydrogen Lights and Light Apparatus.

The Calcium Light was introduced by Prof. Hare, M. D., of Pennsylvania. The light is produced by the combination in combustion of oxygen and hydrogen gas, the flame playing on a piece of lime. The light thus obtained is the most intense known. It is rapidly being introduced into general use, and is adapted to a great variety of purposes. In these pushing times of ours, the sun is too chary of its shine; we must work by night as well as by day, in doors and out of doors, and to accomplish this we must have a bright and reliable light. It is now not uncommon for builders to carry their work along day and night without cessation—excavations being made, and in some instances, walls carried up by night—to admit of which, no artificial light, except the calcium, is sufficiently powerful. By its aid the photographer may take negatives by night and print them too. As an illuminator for parks or pleasure grounds it has no equal, and for theatrical illusions, tableaux, stereoptican exhibitions, etc., it is indispensable.

But if the oxygen and hydrogen gases are not absolutely pure, or if they are not combined in exactly right proportions, the brilliant effect is not produced. The New York Calcium Light Company have for years made a study of the best methods of producing, retaining and utilizing oxygen and hydrogen for illuminating purposes, and their long experience has resulted in perfect success. Their improved machinery and methods of manufacture enable them to furnish gases absolutely pure, and under such perfect control that any one of ordinary intelligence can operate them. They have different pumps for the gases, and the cylinders are painted—the oxygen red, the hydrogen black, leaving no chance for a mistake. They are submitted to a hydraulic pressure of 700 pounds to the square inch before using, and the charge never exceeds 225, leaving a safety margin of 475 pounds. They are made from 12 to 60 feet capacity, and can be shipped with perfect safety. The reflectors, retorts, lenses, burners, regulators, limes, etc., are of various patterns. This company also manufacture perfectly pure oxygen gas for anaesthetic and chemical purposes. Their place of business is at 414 and 416 Bleecker Street, New York, where the inquirer can find everything in their line.

NEW YORK BUSINESS OFFICE OF THE MERCANTILE AGENCY,—DUN, BARLOW & CO.,—335 BROADWAY, NEW YORK, U. S. A.

THE MERCANTILE AGENCY,

DUN, BARLOW & CO.—R. G. DUN & CO.,
335 Broadway and 80 Wall Street, New York.

—:o:—

The system of granting commercial credits in vogue forty years ago would not at all answer at the present time. Then, if a retail dealer desired to open an account with a wholesale house, he obtained letters of introduction from other customers of the house, or from firms with whom he had previously traded, and on these and his own representations as to the amount of his capital, the extent and profitableness of his business, etc., the desired credit was granted or refused. A few of the largest houses employed traveling agents who reported as best they could the local reputation of debtors, but such sources of information were unreliable. The consequence was that those who freely granted credit were frequent losers, and that those who were too chary of favors often turned away those who would have become large and profitable customers.

All this has been changed, however, through the successful establishment of The Mercantile Agency, whose object is to supply reliable information to its subscribers as to the Capital, Capacity and Character of parties engaged in trade; and in supplying such information it not only enables the manufacturer and wholesale merchant to readily determine to whom and how far he may safely grant credit, but it at the same time affords to the purchaser equal advantages in opening to him the entire markets of the country.

Some thirty-five years ago Lewis Tappan laid the foundation of the gigantic business, which is now conducted by his legitimate and only successors, Messrs. Dun, Barlow & Co., in New York; R. G. Dun & Co., in fifty other cities in the United States. From a small beginning in 1841, The Agency has reached out its branches in every direction, over this continent, and by its many branch offices abroad afford to international commerce the same friendly assistance it has always guaranteed at home. Besides

the home office in New York City, an interior view of which is here presented, where all the lines of communication centre, more than seventy branch offices are now in successful operation in this country and in Europe, which are supported by upwards of twelve thousand yearly subscribers, comprising the leading manufacturers, merchants and bankers of each centre of trade.

Twenty thousand local correspondents are employed by The Agency, each of whom is made a subject of careful investigation before receiving the appointment. They have small, compact districts (the whole country being thus districted) over which they are expected to keep careful oversight, promptly reporting all occurrences that would be likely to affect the pecuniary interests of creditors. The Agency employ travelers of their own training, who (generally without knowing the names of local correspondents) travel the country and gather information as to traders seeking credit. Such information is compared with that furnished by the local correspondents, and if a material discrepancy exists the inquiries are pushed further until the truth is, if possible, arrived at. To compile and arrange the information thus obtained requires the services of over one thousand clerks.

In the year 1875, this Agency paid out in postage alone, over $60,000, implying a transmission of two millions of letters in the year, considerably over six thousand every day. In telegraphic service The Agency paid $25,000. These figures not only indicate the activity of The Agency, but they imply a use of its facilities by merchants and bankers to an extent hardly dreamed of years ago. Unless the information was found reliable this costly use of mail and telegraph would hardly long continue.

If these figures do not convey an idea of the scope and comprehensiveness of The Agency, it is only necessary to briefly notice the Reference Book. This work is issued in January, March, July and September of each year. It contains a complete list of all the Merchants, Bankers, Manufacturers and Traders throughout the entire United States and British Provinces, alphabetically arranged under heads of States, Territories or Provinces, which are again divided into towns, and opposite each name is an estimate of the capital of each firm, company, or individual named, and independent of this the credit is defined. Thus a man may be reported with large capital and low credit, or with small capital and high credit.

Incredible as it may seem to the uninitiated, this book is printed, bound and delivered within six weeks, the corrections are brought down to the latest possible moment prior to publication, and the information it contains is therefore much more reliable than it could possibly be without the aid of such marvelous facilities.

The private printing establishment, under the management of Mr. Wiman, one of the partners, includes twenty tons of agate type.

This type is all set in narrow columns, which if strung out in a single column would extend over a mile in length. Imagine a list of names over a mile long, set in the smallest type, each name costing five cents to print alone, and some idea will be formed of the amount of detail involved and capital required.

They issue quarterly a circular to subscribers showing, from their varied resources, the state of trade, etc., throughout the country, pointing out causes of any unhealthy symptom, and suggesting remedies. This is accompanied by financial statistics.

During its existence of thirty-four years The Mercantile Agency never approached the position which it occupies today. Its success is best shown by the esteem in which the institution is held.

PRINTING OFFICE OF THE MERCANTILE AGENCY, NEW YORK.

Moresque Cage, No. 1.

Moresque Cage, No. 2.

Moresque Cage, No. 6.

Gray Squirrel Cage.

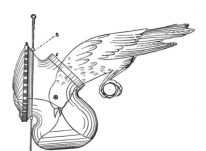

Patent Feed Cup.

Doric.

Moresque Cage, No. 7.

OSBORN MANUF'G CO.,

79 Bleecker Street, New York.

The oldest historian of whom we have any knowledge, whose records cover a period of 2553 years, closing 1451 years before the Christian Era, announces the advent of birds into the world as follows,—"And God said let the waters bring forth abundantly the moving creature that hath life and fowl that may fly above the earth in the open firmament of heaven." History furnishes no record or intimation that birds were ever held in involuntary captivity for the next sixteen and a half centuries, but were left to the free exercise of the privilege originally granted, "to fly above the earth in the open firmament of heaven." The same historian tells us that at the close of this period, a huge cage was constructed into which was gathered representatives of every species of living things, including "the fowls of the air by sevens, the male and female." This cage or ark, is represented of sufficient capacity to accommodate twenty thousand men. It is supposed to have been built of cypress, a kind of wood afterwards used extensively for the manufacture of coffins by the Athenians, and of mummy cases among the Egyptians.

From that time to the present century we have no historic evidence that any improvement in the art of manufacturing cages for the confinement of pet animals of any kind was ever attempted, on the original model of the antedeluvian architect.

To the careless observer the construction of a bird cage may seem a very simple process; but if we may judge from the results of efforts made since the recollection of many of the readers of this article we must conclude that the manufacturers were much more simple than the tasks they undertook. There are certain indispensable prerequisites for the construction of a perfect bird cage as well as in that of any tenement designed to be the abode of any species of the animal kingdom. Without the observance of such rules in construction, any place of residence becomes intolerable and fatal to its occupants.

The first to comprehend these wants and to meet them seems to have been the Osborn Manufacturing Company, of New York City. The cages manufactured at the time this Company commenced business have been aptly described by one who has given the subject much thought, as follows,—"The material was cheap and weak, the designs crude, the construction frail; the devices for feeding, connecting the different parts, suspending, etc, clumsy and insufficient. The finish was of tawdry paints made from

poisonous oxides which soon cleaved in particles from the cage, became mixed with the food, the result of course being disastrous to the bird.

The ornamentation was cheap, superfluous and profuse, which, with the methods of construction, furnished innumerable hiding and breeding places for vermin. It also made them peculiarly susceptible to the accumulation of dust and filth, and very difficult to cleanse."

It is now about ten years since this company took their "new departure" and the improvements during this decade seem almost incredible. The errors enumerated above have all been overcome, and cages are now produced which are perfectly adapted for the purposes for which they are designed, and any "bird that can sing and wont sing" in one of those antiquated cages can "be made to sing" by furnishing him with one of those marvels of beauty made by the Osborn Manufacturing Company.

As an evidence of the enterprising energy of this Company, and their determination to do more than all their competitors in this branch of industry, it appears from the records that during the last ten years they have secured letters patent on fifteen original designs or improvements, while the other manufacturers in this country have secured about half as many more. We understand also that at the time this Company first exhibited their cages at the American Institute they found many competitors, but so decidedly superior were the cages of the former, that but two efforts at competition have since been made at that Institute, both of which were entire failures. It is true of this as of all other products of merit and utility, that it finds many imitators, and it reflects great credit upon this Company that they have been able constantly to lead the van in originating new designs and improvements.

The space allotted for this article will not admit of any extended description of the many patterns of cages manufactured by the Osborn Manufacturing Company, a few of which are represented on this page, neither is it essential to do so, for in point of design, material, construction, and style of finish, the wants and comfort of the occupants, the taste of the owner, durability and economy have all been consulted and their wants fully met. Among the latest improvements we wish to call attention to the "Moresque" Cage, beautiful and unique in its design, and being supplied with the "Star Parlor Feed Cup" and the "Parlor Cage Screen" it is next to impossible for the bird to scatter any of its food or to blow by its wings any of the light husks from the seeds, upon the floor of the room. This company pay particular attention to the manufacture of Special Cages.

Special Cage.

Mocking Bird.

Screen Closed.

Screen Opened.

Parrot.

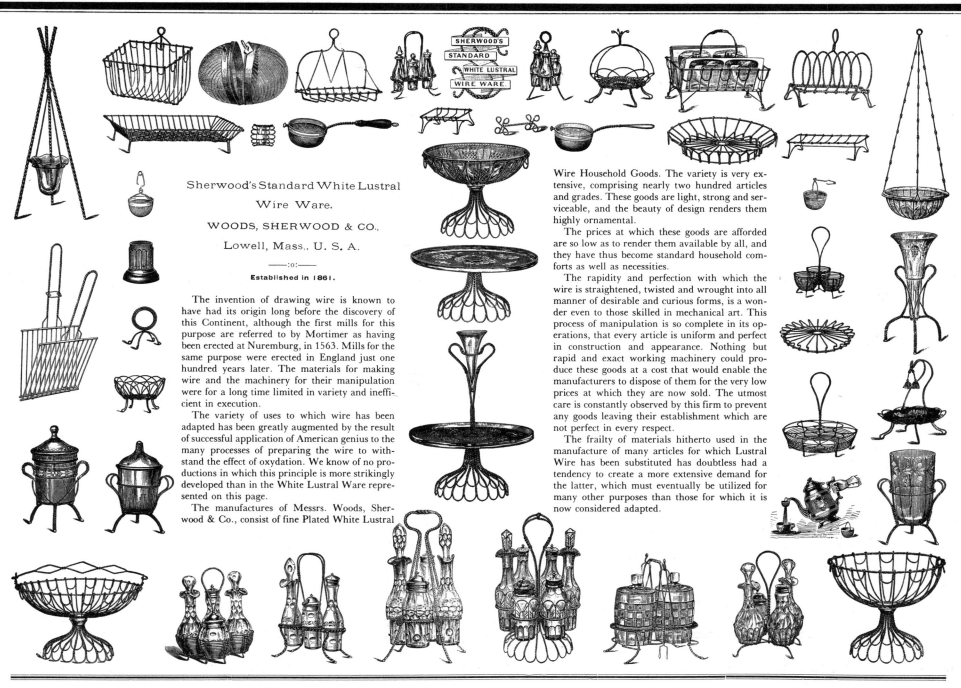

Sherwood's Standard White Lustral Wire Ware.

WOODS, SHERWOOD & CO.,
Lowell, Mass., U. S. A.
—:o:—
Established in 1861.

The invention of drawing wire is known to have had its origin long before the discovery of this Continent, although the first mills for this purpose are referred to by Mortimer as having been erected at Nuremburg, in 1563. Mills for the same purpose were erected in England just one hundred years later. The materials for making wire and the machinery for their manipulation were for a long time limited in variety and inefficient in execution.

The variety of uses to which wire has been adapted has been greatly augmented by the result of successful application of American genius to the many processes of preparing the wire to withstand the effect of oxydation. We know of no productions in which this principle is more strikingly developed than in the White Lustral Ware represented on this page.

The manufactures of Messrs. Woods, Sherwood & Co., consist of fine Plated White Lustral Wire Household Goods. The variety is very extensive, comprising nearly two hundred articles and grades. These goods are light, strong and serviceable, and the beauty of design renders them highly ornamental.

The prices at which these goods are afforded are so low as to render them available by all, and they have thus become standard household comforts as well as necessities.

The rapidity and perfection with which the wire is straightened, twisted and wrought into all manner of desirable and curious forms, is a wonder even to those skilled in mechanical art. This process of manipulation is so complete in its operations, that every article is uniform and perfect in construction and appearance. Nothing but rapid and exact working machinery could produce these goods at a cost that would enable the manufacturers to dispose of them for the very low prices at which they are now sold. The utmost care is constantly observed by this firm to prevent any goods leaving their establishment which are not perfect in every respect.

The frailty of materials hitherto used in the manufacture of many articles for which Lustral Wire has been substituted has doubtless had a tendency to create a more extensive demand for the latter, which must eventually be utilized for many other purposes than those for which it is now considered adapted.

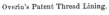

Overin's Patent Thread Lining.

American Whip Company's Manufactory, Westfield, Mass.

Coach Whip with New Haven Patent adjustable Tops.

Malacca Whip with New Haven Patent adjustable Bone Top, with wire centre.

The only durable Malacca Whip Manufactured.

AMERICAN WHIP COMPANY,
Store, No. 30 Warren Street, New York.
—:o:—

Persons who are unacquainted with the various ingenious processes by which a whip is manufactured, cannot appreciate what an interesting and important branch of our American industry the manufacture of whips has become.

The ocean, the mines, the forest and the, fields, and the animal kingdom of various climates, all bring their contributions of raw material to the making up of the finished whip; all these are subjected to the operation of the most delicate and complicated machinery, and to various other skillful processes before the work is complete. The number of patent rights, and some of them of wonderful ingenuity, involved in the machinery and other labor saving devices in the manufacture of a single whip is almost legion. A visit to a whip Factory will surprise and amply reward any one interested in ingenious mechanical contrivances.

No country in the world manufactures so many, or so elegant whips as the United States. And of all the towns or cities in this country, there is not one which equals Westfield, Massachusetts, in the amount of capital invested, in the number of operatives employed, or in the quantity or excellence of the manufactured product. Previous to 1820 it was exclusively an agricultural town, but that year was an important epoch in its history, for it marked the introduction of this new branch of industry, which has been the means of adding largely to its population, and forms a leading element of its wealth, and from that day to this the business has constantly augmented until now it is the dominant and controlling business, and the whip factory may be seen in all its important business streets. The number of separate establishments is large, probably now less than formerly, but the capital invested and the aggregate amount of production is very much greater. This is due principally to the immense amount of business done by a single prominent concern, which is properly named the American Whip Co. This great establishment is not only one of the largest whip manufactories in the world, but stands in the foremost rank in many other respects; in the amount of its capital, in the high character of the men who are at its head, and especially in the admirable and genuine quality of its manufactured products. These advantages have been secured by attracting to itself other smaller corporations and companies which from time to time have been absorbed in it, interchanging values and facilities to their mutual advantage, and thus bringing to this single corporation, not only the most skilled labor, but also giving to it the exclusive control of many valuable inventions and improvements, by which it is able to furnish its patrons a superior article, selected from the largest variety and highest style of manufactured goods and at the same time at greatly reduced cost and price.

To the long list of valuable patents upon inventions of their own, may be added the recently acquired "Overin's Patent Linen Thread Lining for Whips." Annexed is a diagram representing the complex and ingenious machinery, by which is secured a whip which has elicited the verdict of drivers, turfmen and trainers, as superior to any other whip ever made. They have also bought the Westfield Whip Co., securing thereby its "Patent Metallic Lined Whip." They have also purchased the patents and machinery of the New Haven Whip Co.

The American Whip Co. has an office and Store at No. 30 Warren Street, New York, but Westfield is now the emporium of its merchandise, as well as its place of manufacture. In the third story of their immense factory is a bazaar of every variety of manufactured articles, from the dainty and elegant riding whip for ladies use, to the cumbrous whip wielded by the cattle drivers on the plains of South America.

DELAWARE RIVER IRON SHIP BUILDING AND ENGINE WORKS, CHESTER, PA.

DELAWARE RIVER IRON SHIP BUILDING

AND ENGINE WORKS.

Chester, Penn.

JOHN ROACH, President.

—:o:—

While it is not our intention in this article to enter into a history of American Ship Building nor to discuss the relative merits of the marine of the nations of the earth, we cannot refrain from expressing the conviction that there is nothing in all our history as a nation of which we are more justly proud than our achievements upon the sea. During our colonial days we won a high reputation as naval constructors, and since we became an independent people, we have taught the world many new and valuable lessons in the art of building ships. From the close of the war of 1812 we made rapid advancement, until we became the maritime rival of Great Britain, largely excelling all other nations, and second only to her—if indeed we were second—upon the high seas. Our tonnage in foreign trade increased 60 per cent. between 1830 and 1840; it increased 75 per cent. between 1840 and 1850; it increased 60 per cent. between 1850 and 1860. In the latter decade the increase of British tonnage was but 40 per cent. In 1861 the American tonnage, in foreign trade, was 2,642,628 against 3,179,683 tons British, much of the latter being commercially antiquated and inferior to our own, and none of it equal to our renowned clipper-built ships.

At the outbreak of our civil war a great revolution was slowly taking place in the sea-going marine of the world. Sailing vessels were yielding to steamers, while among these, the paddle wheel was giving place to the screw, and wood to iron. From 1861 to 1866 all our energies were absorbed in a struggle, which for the time excluded us from all commercial enterprise or competition. During this period the navy purchased from our merchant marine 215,978 tons of our best steam tonnage, and the war department absorbed by charter and otherwise 757,611 tons more. Of the remainder, to avoid war rates of insurance or destruction by Confederate cruisers 801,311 tons sought refuge under European flags, while 104,605 tons were actually destroyed by the Alabama and other Confederate crafts. But, though from 1861 to 1866, 53 per cent of our ocean tonnage was lost, and though the premium on gold for some years greatly retarded our activity in naval construction, we are now rapidly regaining our former position among ship building nations.

Toward the close of the last decade and after the close of the war, the coasting trade of the United States began to call for iron steam propellers, and the ship building interests prepared to meet the demand. We shortly began to realize the immense resources of which we are possessed, not the least of which is an abundant supply of skilled labor, equal to any in the world for intelligence and capacity.

To describe all these departments within the limits to which these articles must be confined, is simply impossible. The capacity of the Delaware River Iron Ship Building and Engine Works is only limited by the ability of the Rolling Mills of the country to produce the necessary iron, and that is almost beyond limit.

Until recently it has been the prevailing impression that the best iron steamships can be built abroad cheaper than at home, but Mr. Roach has within the past year, in the building of vessels for the Pacific Mail Steamship Company and others, proved that they can be constructed here as rapidly and as cheaply as any where in the world. The fact that every one of the iron ships built at these Works for the foreign trade, is required by contract to be equal to the best in the world, and to receive the highest rating, "A1. for twenty years," at the English Lloyds, before the owner shall make his final payment or take the vessel off the builders' hands, is proof that they are fully equal to any made.

The French *Bureau Veritas* is the highest standard authority now in existence on iron steamship building. Taking a given thickness of iron, this authority rates American iron steamships twenty-five per cent. higher than any other steamers built of the same thickness of iron. In a communication to the Pacific Mail Company, after assigning the highest classification to the "City of Peking," and "City of Tokio," they say that they "are glad to see the United States build such magnificent vessels and sincerely hope that they [the iron steamship builders of the United States] may have every success.

The following is a list of the Iron Steamships built at the Delaware River Iron Ship Building and Engine Works, Chester, Penn., between October, 1871, and July, 1875.

STEAMER.	Tonnage.	Horse Power.
City of Peking,	5,500	4,500
City of Tokio,	5,500	4,500
City of San Francisco,	3,500	3,000
City of Washington,	3,500	3,000
City of New York,	3,500	3,000
Colima,	3,000	1,700
Colon,	3,000	1,700
G. W. Elder,	1,600	1,000
City of Guatemala,	1,600	1,000
State of Texas,	1,500	1,000
City of Waco,	1,500	1,000
City of San Antonio,	1,500	1,000
City of Chester,	1,000	750
Perkiomen	1,200	800
Albert, } U. S. War Sloops.	650	560
Alliance,	650	560
Garden City,	800	550
Erie,	800	550
Berks,	600	500
Spanish Gun Boat,	75	86
G. E. Weed——Wooden	120	100

CHESTER ROLLING MILL,

Chester, Penn.,

JOHN ROACH, President.

—:o:—

In the construction of iron ships it is of the utmost importance that the plates should be made of the best quality of iron, and that in the various manipulations through which the metal must pass before it becomes a finished plate the utmost care should be exercised, and that all should be under the immediate supervision of skilled and thoughtful men.

The easiest and perhaps the best way to describe this mill will be to follow the iron through the processes through which it passes before it assumes a finished shape. The metal reaches the mill in the shape of Pig Iron, which must be refined and reduced to Wrought Iron. The Puddling Furnace is the most common means of reducing Pig Iron to Wrought Iron and is the means here employed. This is a covered furnace like an oven, a grate being placed at one end, and a pit or trough made in the centre. The pig iron is placed in the puddling furnace and subjected to intense heat until melted, after melting it is continually stirred with a suitable hook or poker, worked by a "puddler" who has charge of the furnace. Literally, the iron is boiled and continually stirred until every particle of the puddle has been thoroughly exposed to the fire, and until the iron adheres in a spongy mass. It is then divided into balls or lumps of suitable size at the furnace, and removed to the puddle train where it passes through hugh rollers which press out the coarse cinder contained in the iron. This runs off in a melted condition leaving the bulk malleable and possessing the distinctive features of wrought iron.

The 24 inch Puddle train of the Chester Rolling Mill is operated by a Corliss Steam Engine with a 26 inch cylinder, a piston stroke of 48 inches, and a fly wheel 24 feet in diameter and weighing 50,000 pounds, in which is stored an immense amount of power, not easily calculated.

The plate after leaving the puddle train forms the foundation for a "pile" That is, on it is carefully arranged small pieces of scrap iron, the clippings from plates previously finished, etc., and, simple and easy as this seems to be to the uninitiated, it requires considerable skill to make a good "pile." There are many who have not thought that the grain of iron runs in nearly straight lines in one direction like the grain of wood, and that it is only by crossing and re-crossing the grain that the strongest possible iron can be obtained. The ability to make a "pile" is gauged by the skill of the workmen in placing the scrap in such positions as to produce the best results. The "pile" is built to a height of from twenty to twenty-four inches, according to the thickness of the plate to be rolled, and placed in the furnace where it is brought to a welding heat, preparatory to the final rolling.

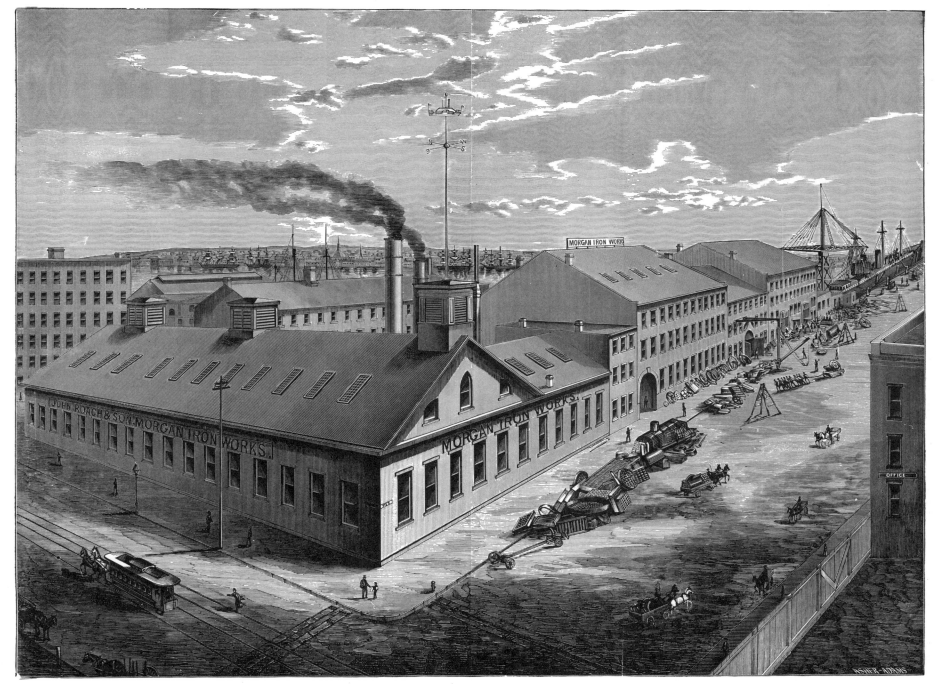

MORGAN IRON WORKS, FOOT OF EAST NINTH STREET, NEW YORK.

MORGAN IRON WORKS,

Foot of East Ninth Street, New York.

John Roach & Son, Prop's.

——:o:——

As a fuel for this heat, Gas, and Gas only is used. None will dispute that Gas is the best fuel because devoid of all deleterious matter, and that iron refined in this manner is entirely free from such impurities as other fuels sometimes leave behind them. The Gas used is manufactured on the premises, and experience has proved it to be not only the best but the cheapest fuel.

The "pile," having been brought to the proper heat, is withdrawn from the furnace and passed through the plate rollers. These rollers are driven by a Corliss Engine, having a cylinder 30 inches in diameter, and a stroke of piston of 72 inches; a fly wheel 30 feet in diameter and weighing 98,000 pounds. If a high pile is being rolled into a thin, long plate, towards the last, when the iron begins to cool, the huge fly wheel moves quite slow, sometimes sinking to twenty revolutions per minute.

There are two sizes of plate rollers in use in the mill, the largest size being 110 inches in length, and the second size 78 inches in length; both lengths being 30 inches in diameter.

The Mill itself and every appurtenance belonging to it is of the most substantial character. The trains of rollers are set up on foundations of rock built deep in the ground, as are the two large steam engines before spoken of. Among the appurtenances of the establishment are five huge shears either of which will cut through an inch plate of rolled iron, apparently with as much ease as if it was cheese. Each of these shears, indeed every piece of machinery in the Mill, is worked by a separate engine. The advantage gained by this is, that no ordinary accident can possibly stop all the work. This Mill was built and is operated for the express purpose of supplying the Delaware River Iron Ship Building and Engine Works.

The superiority in toughness and durability of American iron has long been generally conceded, even to brands with which no special care is taken in their manufacture, but the plates made at the Chester Rolling Mill are far superior to the ordinary productions of other mills.

The same may truthfully be said of all work with which the name of John Roach is connected; whether it appears as president of a corporation or as member of a private firm, his name is a stamp which attests the value of the production to which it is attached, and certainly no man has, during the past twenty years, done more to advance the industrial interests of the country.

The construction of hydraulic machinery, of stationary, locomotive and marine steam engines, the machinery used in mines, mills,

furnaces, forges and factories; in the building of roads, bridges, canals, railroads, etc., for all the purposes of the engineer and manufacturer, has become a pursuit of immense magnitude, involving the investment of many millions of capital, and affording employment to hundreds of thousands of working men. In 1870, the value of the machinery made in New York was $20,062,028, being an increase of 91 per cent over the production of 1860, and in Pennsylvania $29,258,153, an increase of 303 per cent.

The Morgan Iron Works, only a portion of which are represented in the above engraving were established about 1843, since which time they have gradually increased in dimensions and facilities, until they now extend from Eighth Street to Tenth Street, and from Avenue D to the pier line in the East River, a distance of 1112 feet, covering 130 city lots. Along the river front are three large and substantial piers, affording ample room for steamers to lay up while under repairs or receiving machinery, and allowing within their own grounds the loading of machinery for shipment, or the unloading of material to be used in the works.

There is a Foundry, Brass Foundry, Copper Shop, Boiler Shop, Blacksmith Shop, Machine Shop, and Forge Shop, the whole forming an establishment as complete as any of its kind in this country.

The Foundry contains cupola furnaces capable of melting at one heat 70 tons of iron, which can be deposited in one mould, making a single casting of that weight if required. Within this foundry and below the surface of the ground, are enormous moulding pits, the sides of which are firmly secured by plates of boiler iron riveted together. In a word, the Foundry is fitted with every convenience for the heaviest class of work.

The Boiler Shop is provided with shears to cut the iron plates into proper form, rollers to give them the required curvature, punching machines to make the holes along the edges in which the rivets are inserted, and numerous drilling and boring machines.

In the Smiths' Shop where all the wrought iron parts of the machinery are formed and fitted, there are thirty forges, with the requisite number of men to each.

The Forge is fitted with furnaces of great size, with steam hammers and all the appliances that can aid in the accomplishment of the work to be done. Shafts twenty-five inches in diameter are forged here with perfect ease.

The Machine Shop, where the cylinders, pistons, and close fitting or polished parts, whether of wrought or cast iron, are finished, is amply provided with lathes, cutting mills, and planers of vast size and strength, and is fitted with the most approved facilities for doing heavy Marine Engine Work, including a traveling crane capable of hoisting fifty tons.

At these works, in connection with the Aetna Works, formerly owned by the same proprietors, was built the machinery for the Steam Ram Dunderberg, and the United States war vessels, Onondaga, Neshaning, and many other vessels of similar size. Also the machinery for the magnificent steamers Providence, Bristol, Rhode Island, and a score or more of other equally well known boats, navigating Long Island Sound and other waters adjacent to New York.

The proprietors of the Morgan Iron Works are at all times ready to contract for anything in their line of manufacture from a first-class ocean iron steamship, fully equipped for a voyage, down to the smallest piece of machinery; and the customer may rest assured that the work will not only be well done, but that it will be finished and delivered at the time specified in contract.

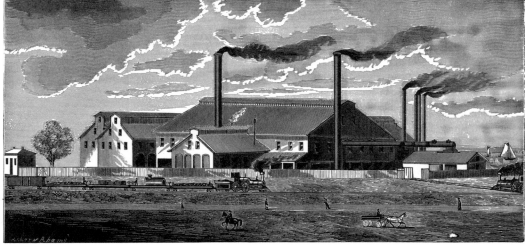

CHESTER ROLLING MILL

TETE-A-TETE TEA SET.

SOUP TOURINE.

FRUIT STANDS.

HENRY ROWLANDS,

Successor to Benjamin Marsh,

JEWELER AND SILVERSMITH,

27 North Pearl Street, cor. Maiden Lane,

Albany, New York.

In the same proportion as the world has advanced in cultivation and wealth, has the character of its adornments advanced, viewed as works of art, and also as articles of intrinsic value, because of the greater care taken in securing pure metal and the greater skill displayed in fashioning it. The United States has not fallen behind the other nations in these matters, and we have to-day several firms of world wide reputation. One of the most reliable establishments (and oldest, outside of the city,) in the state is that of Henry Rowlands of Albany. Its history dating back to 1832. For many years the business was successfully conducted on the corner of Broadway and State Street, but the steadily increasing trade demanded larger and more commodious quarters for a fitting display of their large and elegant stock of valuable goods, and for manufacturing purposes.

Among the almost endless assortment of beautiful and expensive articles, is one large case filled with fine Watches of both Foreign and American manufacture, and varying in size from the tiny little one, hardly larger than a silver dime, up to the largest sizes worn. Watches for ladies and gentlemen, with cases to suit all tastes—some with but little engraving, and others elaborately and beautifully carved; cases beautifully enameled, and studded with jewels, and others perfectly plain.

Then comes a case of precious gems—Diamonds. The must studious care has always been given to this important branch of the busi-

ness of the house, and an unusually large and fine collection of gems is now presented in single stones and matched pairs, which will repay the attention of thoughtful purchasers. As they are large and direct importers, one can always find at this establishment an extensive stock of Diamonds of the purest lustre, and at the very lowest market price.

A little farther on is another case much larger than the last, in which is displayed an elegant assortment of Sets in Pin and Ear

EPERGNE.

Rings, embracing all the latest designs from the leading foreign and American manufactories; Stone and Coral Cameoes, Amethyst and Onyx, mounted in the newest and most fashionable manner.

In the next case is displayed a large and remarkably fine selection of Lockets, Pendants and Necklaces of the most beautiful designs, either singly or in sets, as suits the purchaser; also a magnificent assortment of Band and Chain Bracelets, plain or richly chased in ornamental designs.

Above all worthy of special notice is the large and well selected stock of Sterling Silver Ware. Counters as well as side cases are filled with the latest and finest productions of the Gorham Manufacturing Company, to which new designs are added almost daily, making it certain that you will always find what you desire. If for wedding gifts, there is a large variety of the latest novelties in every conceivable shape, all of which are suitable and very appropriate; or if silver for family use, you may likewise depend upon being suited. A large assortment of Solid Silver Tea Sets is always kept on hand.

In the rear of the store, on an elevation of two feet, is a magnificent display of Clocks, of their own importation, with cases of Marble, Bronze and other fine and expensive materials, and of both modern and antique designs. In addition to the clocks there is in this part of the store, scattered over about a dozen tables, a fine collection of Birds and Animals in bronze and marble, Statuettes and Groups, Mantle Sets, Vases, etc., etc., large figures and small ones, reproductions of the finest works of French and Italian art.

Taken all in all, there is a completeness about this establishment seldom found and never surpassed. It is a pleasant place to visit. Purchasers are always sure to find in the large and varied stock something which exactly pleases them and completely fills their want. The attendants are polite and are always ready to answer questions and display goods until customers are satisfied.

NATIONAL WHIP CO.,

Jas. T. Smith & Co., Prop's,

Westfield, Mass.

——:o:——

The manufacture of whips and whip lashes has become, within a comparatively few years, a business of far greater importance than many people suppose, giving employment to thousands of hands and necessitating the investment of hundreds of thousands of dollars as a working capital.

The whip of the present day and the whip our forefathers used are very different articles. Time was, and not far distant either, when farmer, teamster and jockey all cut their whips in the woods, generally using only the "switch" or "gad" as the case might be, but for an unruly team, a lash cut from a side of sole leather, or a green hide, and fastened to a stout stock of hickory or ash, formed what they considered a "first-rate whip." In those days every man cut or made his own whip. But it soon became apparent that some men could cut straighter and better lashes than others, and those who could cut the straightest and best were frequently called on to make them for their neighbors. Then came stocks whittled with a jack knife and smoothed with glass—and braided lashes closely followed. These were soon in great request, and farmers' sons were wont to spend the long winter evenings making them. They were left at the village store for sale, but the supply soon exceeded the country demand and the storekeepers exchanged them for other goods in the city, where they found a ready sale.

Many a sturdy farmer uses these old whips yet, or at least whips of the same kind, for every day use on the farm but for driving to town, for Sundays and holidays he must now have a "store" whip. The developement of our country and its growth in wealth has fostered the finer tastes of the people, and that which was good enough for the fathers will not answer for the sons. When our people began to ride in

VIEW OF THE NATIONAL WHIP CO'S MANUFACTORY, WESTFIELD, MASS.

more stylish vehicles, they must needs have more stylish whips, and whip making became a business.

Mr. James T. Smith, the senior partner of the National Whip Company, has been engaged in the manufacture of whips and lashes for many years, and to his thorough knowledge of the business—his comprehension of the wants of the public, and his indomitable perseverance is largely attributable the success of the Company. The annexed engraving is a correct representation of their large factory. They manufacture every description of whips and lashes, whips for the cattle drivers of Texas and the herdsmen of South America, whips for stage drivers and teamsters, whips for coachmen, and for gentlemen who drive their own teams, delicate whips for ladies' use, and whips for jockeys; they confine them to no special class of whips, but take special care to manufacture the best whips of every class. Their productions are known throughout all the states and territories of the Union, they are largely sold in the British provinces, and exported to the various states of South America, and to the Sandwich Islands, and wherever known they are favorably known.

There are many whip factories in the United States, a few large ones, but the greater number small concerns, employing but few hands. Among the leading manufacturers there is a strong competition, each firm or company striving to acquire a leading reputation, but generally relying mainly upon the popularity of some special kind of whip; but the aim of the National Whip Company has always been and is to make the very best whips of every description that can be made, and, judging from the demand for their work, they have not failed in this very laudable endeavor.

Parties interested in the whip business will obtain all desired information in relation to their manufactures—descriptions of the various styles made, price lists, etc., by calling upon or addressing a letter to the National Whip Company, Westfield, Mass.

SIMPSON, HALL, MILLER & CO.,

Manufacturers of Fine Electro-Plated Wares.

Wallingford, Conn.

Sales-Rooms, 676 Broadway, New York.

This is one of the oldest and most extensive establishments of the kind in the country. Every article known to the trade or to housekeepers, made of silver and gold, is produced at their works in silver or gold plate, upon a fine white metal of great hardness and durability. The design of all their work is chaste and elegant, and the ornamentation of some of their sets is of the most elaborate description. Only those possessing natural æsthetic tastes of the highest order, cultivated by long years of practical study and experience could design and execute works of such artistic beauty. The rapid cultivation of the sense of the beautiful by the American people has caused a great demand for such articles among those who are unable to procure them in solid gold or silver, and has made their use in

SIMPSON, HALL, MILLER & CO'S. MANUFACTORY,
Wallingford. Conn.

hotels and other public places an absolute necessity. To meet this growing demand seems to have been the special object of this firm, and they are constantly producing Tea Sets, Ice Pitchers, Waiters, Epergnes, Fruit, Cake and Butter Dishes, Castors, Spoons, and every other of the endless variety of articles for table and ornamental use known in silver and gold, which are manufactured by them in such a manner as not to be distinguished from those of the more precious metals, equally as durable, as artistic in design and finish, and at a comparatively trifling cost. We present cuts of a few, selected at haphazard, from the many beautiful articles they manufacture.

The table ware manufactured by Simpson, Hall, Miller & Co., for families, hotels and steamships challenges comparison with any goods of the same kind in the world; and those wanting outfits in their line would do well to examine their stock, at their salesrooms, 676 Broadway, New York, before giving their orders; or should a personal examination be inconvenient, a communication addressed to the factory at Wallingford, Connecticut, or to their New York place of business will receive prompt and polite attention.

A HARTFORD INSTI-
TUTION.

The new State Capitol of Connecticut, a picture of which is here given, stands on College Hill, in the Western portion of the City Park, a commanding and beautiful site. It is of white marble, quarried in Connecticut, and is to be completed in 1876. Mr. James G. Batterson, designer and builder of the Worth, Gettysburg and Antie' m monuments, who also furnished the cut granite for the Connecticut Mutual building, in Hartford, the Masonic building, in New York, the Mutual Life building, in Philadelphia, and many other public and private edifices, from his extensive quarries at Westerly, R. I., is the contractor and builder of the Capitol.

One of the institutions of the beautiful city of Hartford, known as The Insurance City, is THE TRAVELERS LIFE AND ACCIDENT INSURANCE COMPANY, of which Mr. Batterson was the originator and is the President. Observing the practice of selling tickets and policies of insurance against accidents, while traveling in England, he recognized the value of the principle. Returning home, he obtained a charter from the Connecticut Legislature in June, 1863, for The Travelers Insurance Company. It was so named because the primary idea at the start, was the insurance of travelers against the accidents incident to journeying. In June of the same year, an amendment to its charter was obtained, authorizing the company to transact a general accident insurance business. In 1865, the company was authorized to grant full life insurance; and its life department was commenced in July, 1866.

STATE CAPITOL AT HARTFORD, CONN.
R. M. Upjohn, Architect, Jas. C. Batterson, Contractor and Builder.

It has also, for eight years, issued all forms of Life and Endowment policies, on the popular and satisfactory Low Rate Cash Plan, having written about twenty thousand life policies to date. The principal points of advantage claimed for this department are: 1. The most ample and unquestioned financial security; 2. a definite contract; 3. prudent and conservative management; 4. A fixed premium, never increasing, at a rate so low as to be fully equivalent to any prospective dividend of a "mutual" company; 5. a policy always worth its face, with a cash surrender value (after the third year) stated in the contract.

Its accident policies insure, not travelers merely, but men of all professions and occupations, not only against "accidents of travel," but also against general accidents of business or recreation. A policy guarantees a fixed sum, (from $1,000 to $10,000) in the event of a fatal accident, and an indemnity, (of $5 to $50 per week,) for wholly disabling injury by accident. The cost varies from $5 to $25 per year for each $1,000, according to the occupation or profession. A policy of $5,000 against death by accident, and $25 per week against wholly disabling injury, would cost $25 per year for a banker, editor, merchant, lawyer, physician, etc.; $37.50 per year for a commercial agent, insurance adjuster, machinist, book binder, printer or railroad superintendent; $50 for a carpenter, blacksmith, farmer, house painter, mason or passenger conductor. Any agent will write a policy, and no medical examination is required.

The home office of The Travelers is on Prospect Street, a few steps

In the ten years of successful business since 1864, The Travelers has written three hundred and twenty-five thousand general accident policies, and paid upwards of twenty thousand claims of its policy holders, for death or injury by accident. In this manner it has disbursed about two million dollars, a larger sum returned in direct benefits to policy holders than by any other insurance company of its age in the world. Its payments on claims have averaged seven hundred dollars a day for the past ten years. It fairly rivals the oldest and largest English companies, and stands at the head of accident insurance in America.

from the new United States Post Office; and its agencies are throughout the United States and Canadian Dominion. The officers of the company are: James G. Batterson, president; G. F. Davis, vice-president; Rodney Dennis, secretary; John E. Morris, assistant Secretary. Among its Board of Directors are Postmaster General Jewell, Senator Buckingham, Geo. M. Pullman, of palace car fame, and other gentlemen less widely known, but of acknowledged financial and business ability. The company has a high reputation throughout the country, and is an honor to the city of Hartford.

Vienna, 1873.

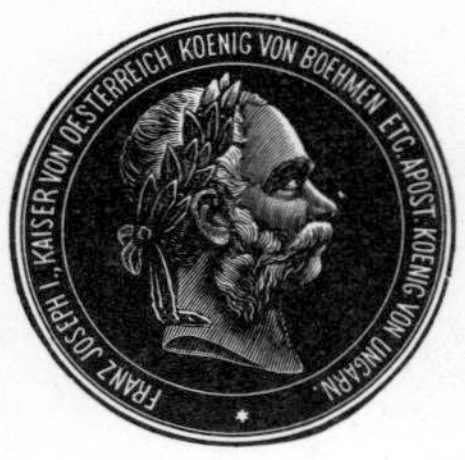

Trade Mark.

The Manufacture of Wrought Iron and Steel DROP FORGINGS.

Trade Mark.

For Progress.

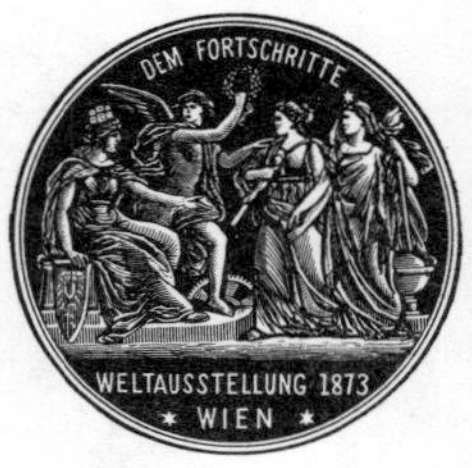

From the slow and tedious hand labor of the blacksmith and machinist, in transmuting the crude rolled or hammered metal into the forms it is designed to permanently retain, to the process and results belonging to Drop Forging by dies, is a stretch much greater than is reached by any other change in the manufacture of iron. The processes of working cast iron are essentially the same now as those employed a century ago; but in forging the improvement is wonderful. Rough dies for forming wrought iron have long been used as an attachment of the blacksmith's anvil, restricted by their crudeness, and their employment only as aids to the hand hammer; but as means for the indefinite production of pieces which are exact duplicates of each other, needing no after forging, it is but recently that they have been extensively employed, and their use has been mostly restricted to the production of the smaller parts of Fire Arms in large armories. As often the improvement in one branch of business is applicable to other branches, it was found that this way of shaping iron and steel might be applied to a great many different purposes, especially where a large number of pieces of the same form and size are required.

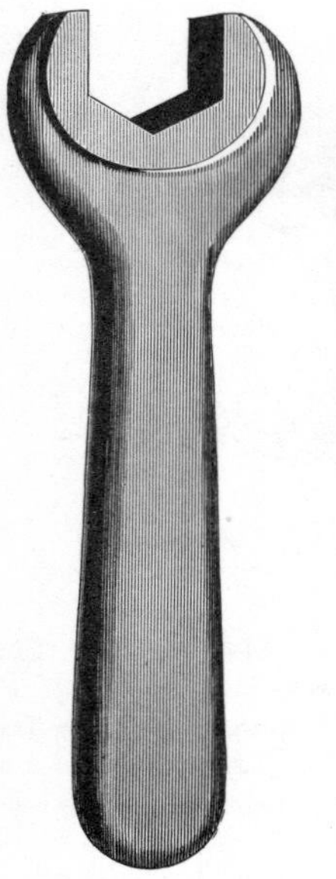

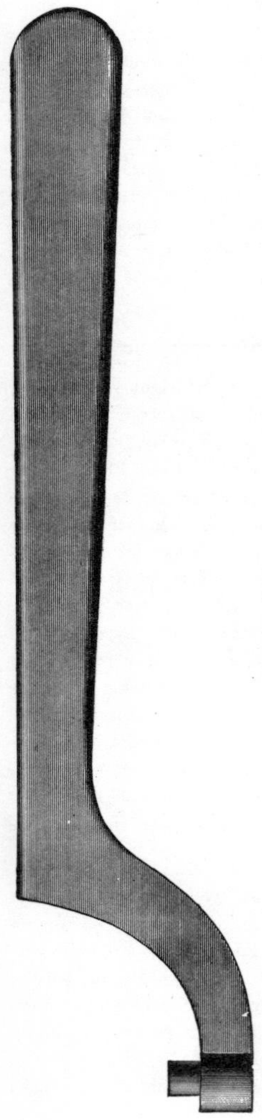

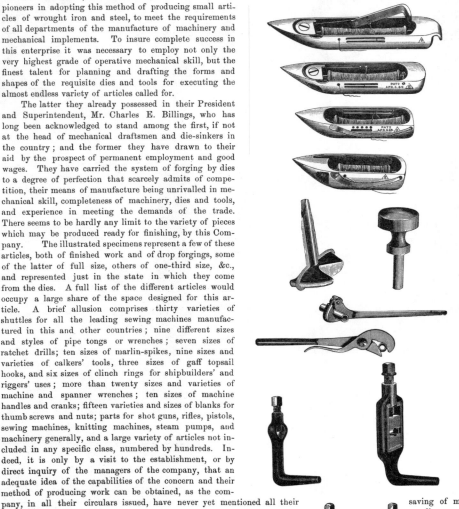

THE BILLINGS & SPENCER CO.,

Of Hartford, Connecticut, U. S. A., are the pioneers in adopting this method of producing small articles of wrought iron and steel, to meet the requirements of all departments of the manufacture of machinery and mechanical implements. To insure complete success in this enterprise it was necessary to employ not only the very highest grade of operative mechanical skill, but the finest talent for planning and drafting the forms and shapes of the requisite dies and tools for executing the almost endless variety of articles called for.

The latter they already possessed in their President and Superintendent, Mr. Charles E. Billings, who has long been acknowledged to stand among the first, if not at the head of mechanical draftsmen and die-sinkers in the country; and the former they have drawn to their aid by the prospect of permanent employment and good wages. They have carried the system of forging by dies to a degree of perfection that scarcely admits of competition, their means of manufacture being unrivalled in mechanical skill, completeness of machinery, dies and tools, and experience in meeting the demands of the trade. There seems to be hardly any limit to the variety of pieces which may be produced ready for finishing, by this Company. The illustrated specimens represent a few of these articles, both of finished work and of drop forgings, some of the latter of full size, others of one-third size, &c., and represented just in the state in which they come from the dies. A full list of the different articles would occupy a large share of the space designed for this article. A brief allusion comprises thirty varieties of shuttles for all the leading sewing machines manufactured in this and other countries; nine different sizes and styles of pipe tongs or wrenches; seven sizes of ratchet drills; ten sizes of marlin-spikes, nine sizes and varieties of calkers' tools, three sizes of gaff topsail hooks, and six sizes of clinch rings for shipbuilders' and riggers' uses; more than twenty sizes and varieties of machine and spanner wrenches; ten sizes of machine handles and cranks; fifteen varieties and sizes of blanks for thumb screws and nuts; parts for shot guns, rifles, pistols, sewing machines, knitting machines, steam pumps, and machinery generally, and a large variety of articles not included in any specific class, numbered by hundreds. Indeed, it is only by a visit to the establishment, or by direct inquiry of the managers of the company, that an adequate idea of the capabilities of the concern and their method of producing work can be obtained, as the company, in all their circulars issued, have never yet mentioned all their productions.

This company was organized in 1869, and in July, 1872, received from the Legislature of the State of Connecticut a special charter of incorporation, conferring very favorable privileges, with a capital of $150,000, and liberty to increase the same to $300,000. Its manufactory is located between Lawrence and Broad Streets, nearly in the geographical centre of the city of Hartford, a short distance from the new State House now in process of building, its real estate occupying a front of three hundred and twelve feet on Lawrence and eighty-six feet on Broad Street.

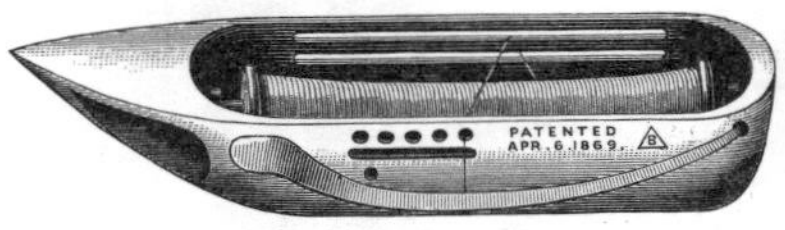

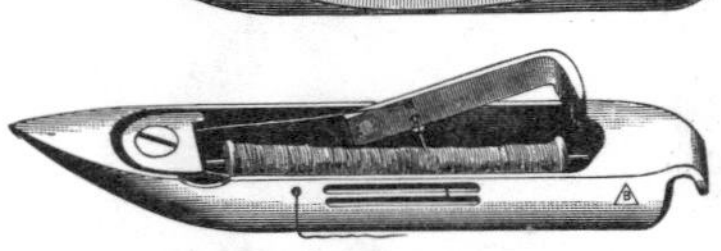

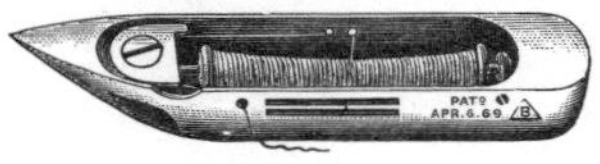

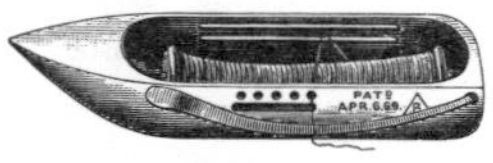

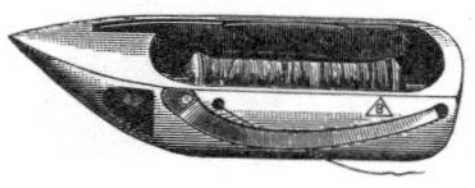

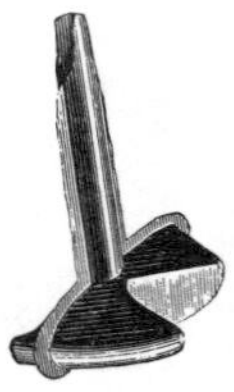

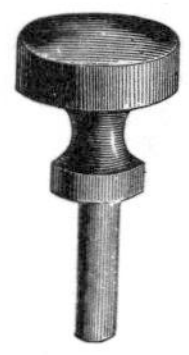

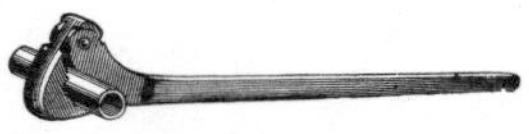

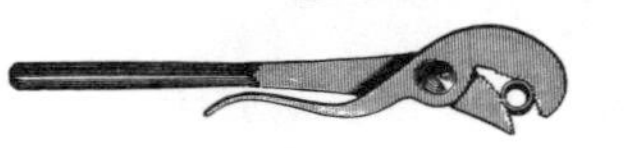

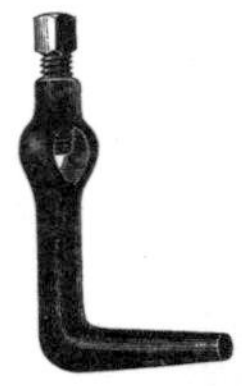

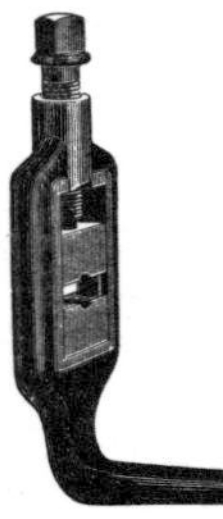

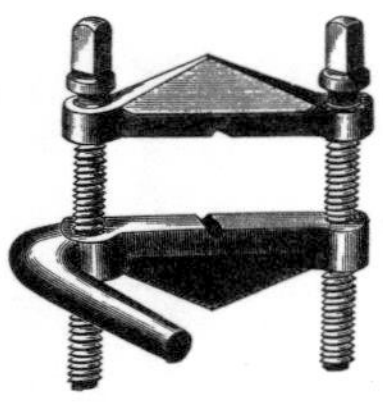

without drilling through to the outside; this is accomplished by minute gears and spindles, rotating within the cavity of the shuttle. When the diminutiveness of the shuttle itself is considered, this arrangement is worthy attention, apart from its really mechanical excellence. Mr. Billings has also contrived a very convenient Drill Press for using very small drills, which by a simple arrangement of the table on the standard, admits of a large range between the end of the spindle and the table.

Most of the forging is done by Drops, with hammers, weighing from four to six hundred pounds or more, so arranged that a blow can be struck with the whole weight of the hammer, falling four or five feet, or by a simple manipulation of the treadle the blow can be regulated so as to strike heavy or light or continuously; but there are articles that require handling under the tilt or trip hammer, and the perfection of this work is surprising, the surfaces being perfectly smooth, the forms round and straight, and lacking only polish to perfect them. Handles for Cranks, Wheels, Lathes, Carriage Work, and Machinery generally, and Marlin-Spikes, Round Thumb Screw Blanks, Pinions for Chucks, &c., &c., are among these articles.

Some of the die blanks required for drop forging are made to order of solid steel, eight inches or more square. These large sizes are forged by the steel makers in blocks to size, smaller dies are made from bars of English Steel, from three and one-half to six inches square. All of the finishing dies are made from cast steel of the finest quality; only the "breaking down," or dies for preliminary work on large articles, being of iron.

The processes of producing from the bar of steel or iron a shapely article ready for the finishing touches, are interesting in many instances; take for example a Musket or Rifle Band made from Norway Iron, which to begin with is merely a rough cut from a round bar; it undergoes six operations under the drop, and comes out apparently larger than before and wonderfully transformed. It began as a cylindrical "chunk," and comes out a symmetrical, shapley form, with all its parts and proportions suggestive of its uses. Other articles pass through as singular transmutations; notably the shells of cast steel for the caps and bodies of the Beach Drill Chuck, made for holding small drills, and used almost universally by machinists. These shells are "dropped" or formed by single blows for each grade of progress from an unsightly piece of steel, made hollow and shaped on the outer surface, ready for the finishing touches by the machinist, with a saving of more than one-half of the stock required by the old turning and boring process. In many other articles made by "drop forging" processes, there is not only a great saving of material, but a superiority of workmanship and increased excellence of stock assured by this working of the metal. The Machinists' Dogs used in turning metals are greatly cheapened and improved by the drop forging process as compared with the old style of hand forging or casting and annealing. Of these three varieties are made, the die, clamp, and common dog, and of each variety there are several sizes.

At present the Company has on hand and in process of completion, orders for goods of their manufacture, which would require more than eight months to finish, comprising a large variety of Sewing Machine Shuttles and Bobbins, Shuttle Blanks, Machinists' Tools, Pipe Tongs and Wrenches,

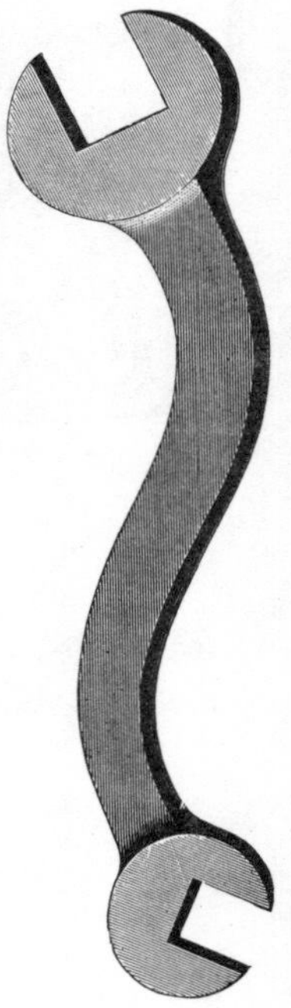

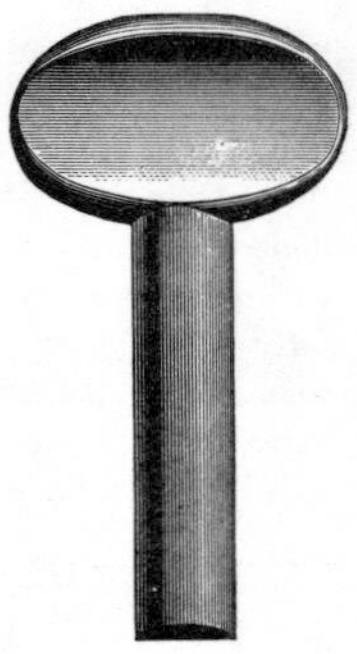

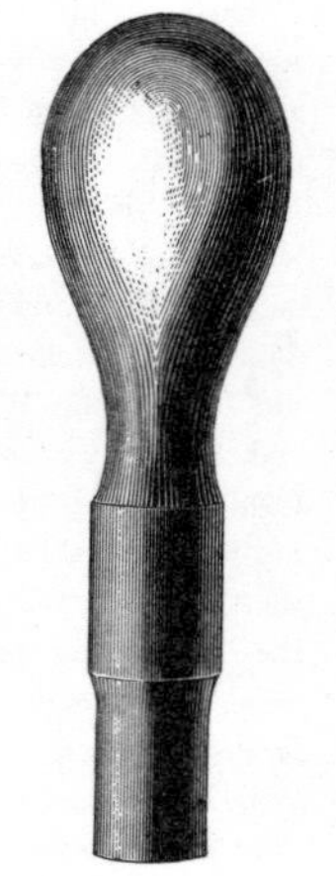

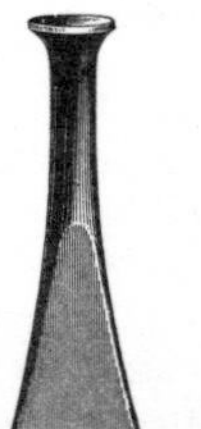

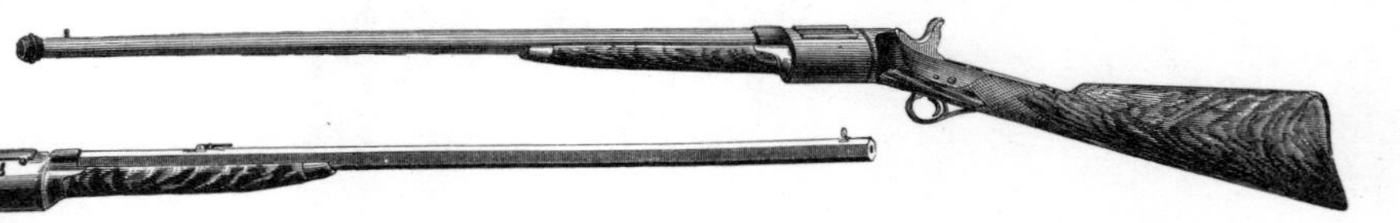

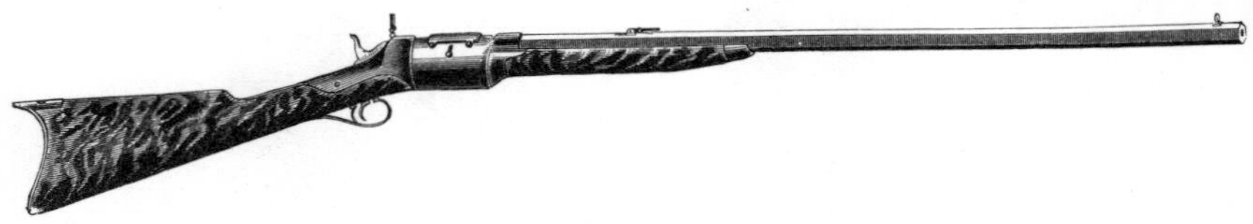

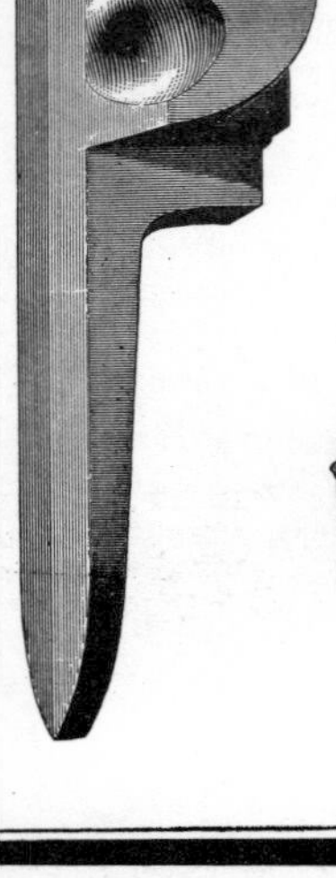

Its main factory is three stories high, with attic and basement, and covers an area of forty by one hundred and thirty feet, with engine and boiler house thirty-two by twenty-eight feet, two stories high. The forging shop is thirty by eighty-two feet and both forge shop and factory are covered throughout with corrugated iron. There are several smaller buildings connected with the works, one of which, a two-story building, thirty by twenty-two feet, is occupied for nickel plating purposes. These buildings are filled with the newest and most improved styles of machinery adapted to their special business.

A full description of the tools used would occupy too much of the space to which this notice is limited. It may not be amiss however, in this connection to notice briefly, several machines specially adapted to specific departments of their works, some of them being the result of the inventive faculty of Mr. Billings, the President of the Company, and Mr. C. M. Spencer, the inventor of the famous Spencer Rifle, from whom, jointly, the company derives its name. Of these, the Automatic Machine for making the heads of the bobbins for Sewing Machine Shuttles, is worthy of mention. From a solid rod or coil of brass, the machine straightens the rod, drills, turns, and finishes the heads, at the rate of four hundred per hour. Formerly these heads were made from sheet brass, punched, drilled, and turned, exacting several manipulations, where now one automatic machine does all the work, and insures a better product, and one tool maker is sufficient to keep in order and run several of these machines at once. Another Automatic Machine alike labor saving, is that which produces the shanks or spindles for the bobbins. These are made from English steel wire, and the machine takes the wire from a coil, on a reel, straightens it, cuts it to the proper length, points or shapes two ends at once, and delivers the spindle complete, requiring no after finishing except the hardening of the points and the attachment of the heads, which is rapidly done in a hand press. Another ingenious device, the invention of Mr. Billings, is one for drilling the holes from the inside, in the ends of Sewing Machine Shuttles,

Ratchet Drills, Saw Sets, Spinning Rings, Ship Chandlery Work, Tap Wrenches, Screw Plates, Top Blanks, Machine Handles, Wrenches and Thumb Screws, parts of Shot Guns, Rifles, Pistols, Sewing Machines, Knitting Machines and machinery generally. A large portion of the work made by the drop forging processes is finished by the company, and much of it is held in stock for sale, as finished shuttles, bobbins and shuttle blanks for all the leading sewing machines, appliances for sewing machine manufacturers, gun and pistol makers, and machinists generally.

This company also owns and manufactures the celebrated Roper Breech-Loading Repeating Sporting Arms. The styles made at present are the Twelve Gauge Four-Shooting Shot Gun, and the Six-Shot Sporting Rifle. These Guns combine all the advantages of the best Muzzle and Breech-loaders, being entirely independent of fixed ammunition, the charges being loaded in steel shells, (which will last as long as the gun,) by the sportsman himself, heavy or light, to suit his game, as in a muzzle loading gun, and with the addition of great superiority in accuracy and rapidity of execution over other sporting arms. The small parts of these guns are accurately finished to work interchangeably, so that the sportsman can at any time order parts wanted from the company, without the trouble of sending his gun for repairs.

The great perfection of this Company in the departments of Die Sinking and Forging for these purposes, is shown in the fact that they have recently completed a contract, in manufacturing from four to five hundred pairs of Steel Dies to furnish the Forging Shops of three National Armories for the Prussian Government, for the production of the far famed "Needle Gun," with the capacity for turning out the parts for nearly 1,000 guns per day. For the perfection of their finished works, and improvements and excellencies in Die Sinking and Drop Forging, they received the Medal of Progress from the Exposition at Vienna in 1873; also a Diploma the same year, from Am. Inst. of New York.

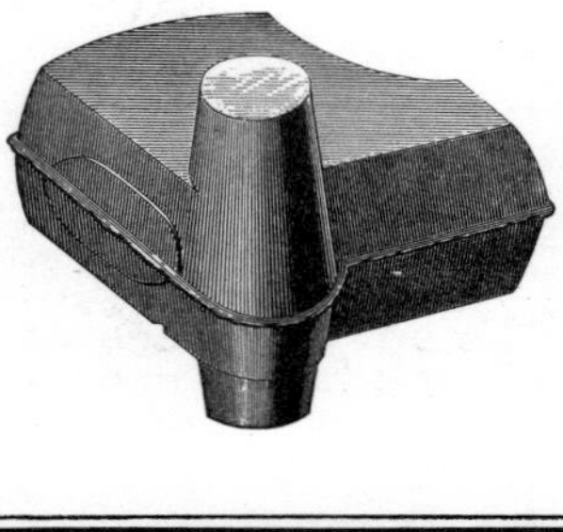

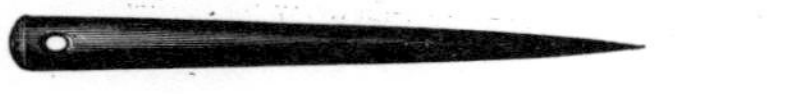

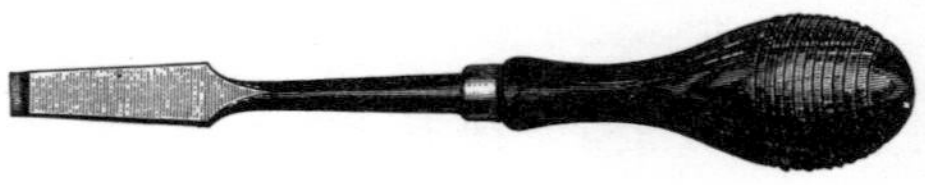

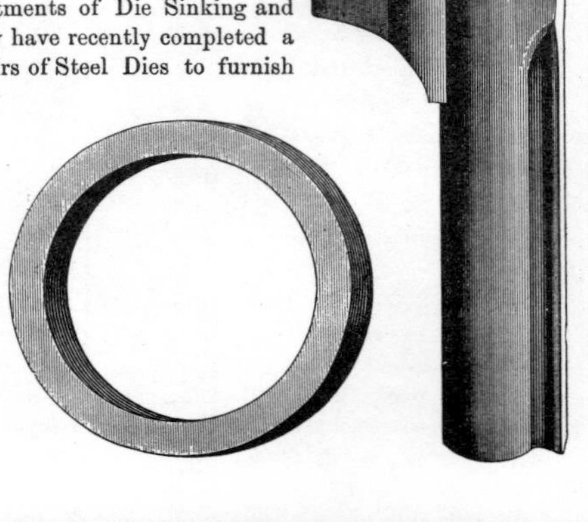

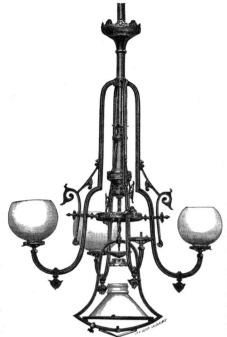

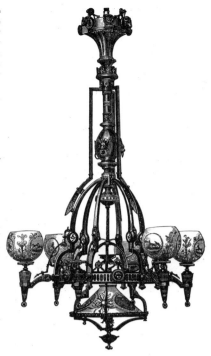

ARCHER & PANCOAST M'F'G CO.,

Designers and Manufacturers of

GASALIERS, CANDELABRA,

ARTISTIC BRONZES, Etc,

67 Greene St., and 68, 70 and 72 Wooster St.,

NEW YORK.

In all the great cities of the country, and in nearly all the villages of three thousand inhabitants or more, gas is commonly used as the illuminating agent. From this general introduction of gas has grown one of the largest and most important of our art-industries, the manufacture of bronzes. Till within a comparatively few years, nearly all the better class of gas fixtures used in this country were imported from England or France; but now the reverse is the case, and the large show rooms of the cities, rich in Gasaliers, Candelabra and artistic figures, owe their wealth of beauty to American, not to foreign manufacturers. To be sure, we import bronzes—real and imitation—but only to a very limited extent, as compared with the quantity manufactured at home. Since 1860, the bronze manufacture—the most important feature of which is the production of gas fixtures, has greatly increased in importance. The development of the zinc mines of Lehigh Valley, Pa., and the late discoveries of spelter, as zinc is called in the trade, in New Jersey, Illinois and Missouri, have made American manufacturers altogether independent of foreign mines, and they now turn out goods with

is not the difference in cost of metal which accounts for the comparative cheapness of the immitation bronze. It is the economy in the cost of labor. Real bronze can be cast only in sand moulds, hence the process is difficult and slow, a new mould being required for every piece cast; while zinc is readily cast in metal moulds which last for years. All the castings of real bronze are made on this floor, and here may be seen lying in heaps the various parts of the gas fixtures, ornaments, stop-cocks, arms and brackets—the thousand and one configurations which go to make up the finished whole. Here, also, the castings are separated, classed and prepared for the after processes, and here is the chemical room where the work is cleansed, stained, gilt, and so on, as required.

On the fifth floor the castings pass into the hands of skilled workmen, who bring them into perfect form. Gas brackets of every description are manufactured on this floor, and the workmen are supplied with every mechanical device that can aid them.

The fourth floor is devoted in part to the furnaces, where all spelter work or imitation bronze is cast into forms, this work entering largely into the manufacture of chandeliers, the brackets of which are usually made of this material. Here also is the machine shop, where all tools are made and kept in order as also the polishing room, where much of the polishing is done on emery wheels.

On the third floor the various parts are assembled, fitted together and brazed to each other, so that they form complete objects ready for the finishing touches. The gilding and varnishing is also done on this floor, and the laying on of color—where the objects are for the purpose of Mediæval

which foreign manufacturers cannot successfully compete.

The Archer & Pancoast Manufacturing Company, one of the largest and most popular manufacturers of this class of goods, originated with Mr. Archer, in 1841, in Philadelphia, and in 1859 was removed to New York, where it has grown to immense proportions. The building in which this important industry is carried on is located on Wooster Street, above Broome Street, and is sixty feet front and six stories in height, running through to Greene Street, with a frontage of twenty-five feet. The building was constructed by the company named, for the purposes of their manufacture exclusively and is remarkably adapted to its requirements. It is thoroughly ventilated and lighted in every respect, indeed, a model of fitness and cleanliness and, in its line, an exposition of the fine arts not excelled, we imagine, in this or any other country.

The visitor to the workshop who desires to follow the process of manufacture from the beginning to the end, must start at the top of the house. Here, as in some of our modern dwellings, the kitchen is nearest the roof; and in great measure for the same reason, that the disagreeable and noxious smells incidental to the business may pass away directly into the atmosphere. So, passing through the large exhibition room, around which are the offices of salesmen, bookkeepers and so forth, we enter the steam elevator and are quickly carried to the sixth story. On a portion of this floor workmen are engaged in casting real bronzes. Real bronzes are cast in sand. Immitation bronzes are cast in metal moulds. Real bronze is composed of copper and zinc, with sometimes, for special purposes, an alloy of tin. Imitation bronze has for its base pure spelter. But it

decoration—as the candelabra of churches, lecterns, etc.

A portion of the second floor is occupied as a fitting room, where the parts of the gas fixtures, chandeliers, &c., are fitted together; also by the department for fine bronzing, chiefly of church work.

The designer's department, on the second floor is in charge of a thoroughly competent artist. Here the new designs are carefully drawn by skilled artists and critically examined by the chief. When accepted the drawings are sent to the modeling room where the designs are formed in plaster and prepared as patterns for the foundry.

The first floor constitutes as fine an exposition of Chandeliers and Gas Fixtures of all kinds, Candelabra, Bronzes, &c., as can be found here or elsewhere. We cannot go into extensive particulars at this point, as it would fill a volume to do so. Suffice it to say, that every choice and desirable style of these goods are on exhibition here, including the most expensive Chandeliers, Candelabra, Bronzes and Statuettes of all kinds that are known to or wanted in the trade. Many of the gas fixtures, chandeliers and candelabra are finished in part in brilliant blue, vermillion, and salmon colors, imparting to them a cheerful and beautiful effect.

In a side room on this floor there is a display of Chandeliers, Brackets, Lecterns, Vases, Candlesticks, Crosses, &c., for churches. It is literally a scene of splendor, this Company making a specialty of this department of art.

Our attention was called to a novel and useful Gasalier, patented by this Company, so managed as to admit of the centre light being drawn down from the main body of the chandelier to any desirable distance, especially adapting it to libraries, dining rooms and offices.

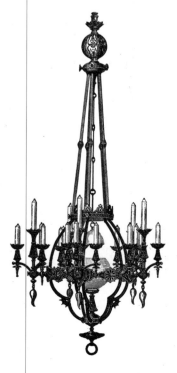

MANCHESTER LOCOMOTIVE WORKS,

Manchester, New Hampshire.

—:o:—

We believe that all thinking men will concede that no single discovery has been of as much importance to the world, as that of the expansive force or power of steam, and that no inventions have aided so much in the development of our material resources as have those connected with the restraining and utilization of that force. Electro-magnetism we class as next in importance.

If those two subtle powers were unknown, or if means by which they could be controlled and made to do our bidding had not been discovered, the world to-day would be but little better off than it was a hundred years ago. The importance of the *role* which Steam has played in the advancement of the world cannot be over-rated. It has rendered not only possible, but easy, the accomplishment of many works, which, without its aid would not have been attempted, and has made available many things, which, in its absence would have been lost. For instance, without the use of steam, or some equivalent power,—and no equivalent has as yet been discovered and controlled—it would have been an utter impossibility to develope the mineral resources of the world, as they have been developed, if from no other cause than that the mines would have flooded.

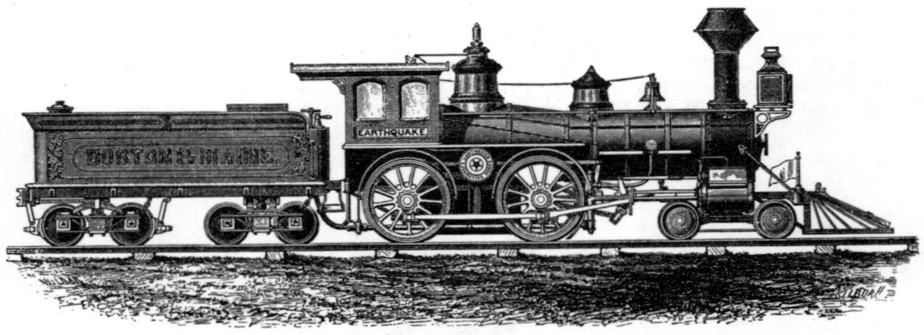

LOCOMOTIVE BUILT BY MANCHESTER LOCOMOTIVE WORKS.

Few people have ever thought of steam as a power in the body politic, or assigned it a place in the world of government; yet it is such a power and has such a place. A recent writer says: "There is an important political necessity for ease, speed, safety, cheapness, and comfort in travel, transportation, and communication of thought. It is steam and electro-magnetism that makes so large a single country as the United States possible. With no other means of inter-communication than existed at the time of the Revolution, our present existence would be mechanically out of the question. The Pacific States, for instance, would not endure the authority of a government seated at the extreme opposite verge of a continent, distant by a tenth of the earth's whole circumference, and at the end of a land journey of certainly not less than six months, or of a sea voyage of not far from the same length of time around Cape Horn. It is because we can travel between Washington and San Francisco in a few days, and can communicate between them in a few seconds, that our country still extends from ocean to ocean."

Railroads bear a like relation to the country that the arteries do to the human organization. They are the circulating system, the medium by which we distribute to the several sections the goods they need, and steam is the motive power.

There are some two thousand railroad companies in the United States, operating in the year 1871, nearly 50,000 miles of road, with a yearly extension which has run as high as 20,000 miles in a single year, (1871,) the average for many years being about 2,000 miles. It is computed that the construction and equipment of the railroads of the world has cost on an average one hundred thousand dollars per mile. Assuming these figures to be correct, and that it has not cost more than the average in this country, the capital invested in railroads in the United States is not less than five thousand millions of dollars—an amount easily written, but too vast to be clearly comprehended.

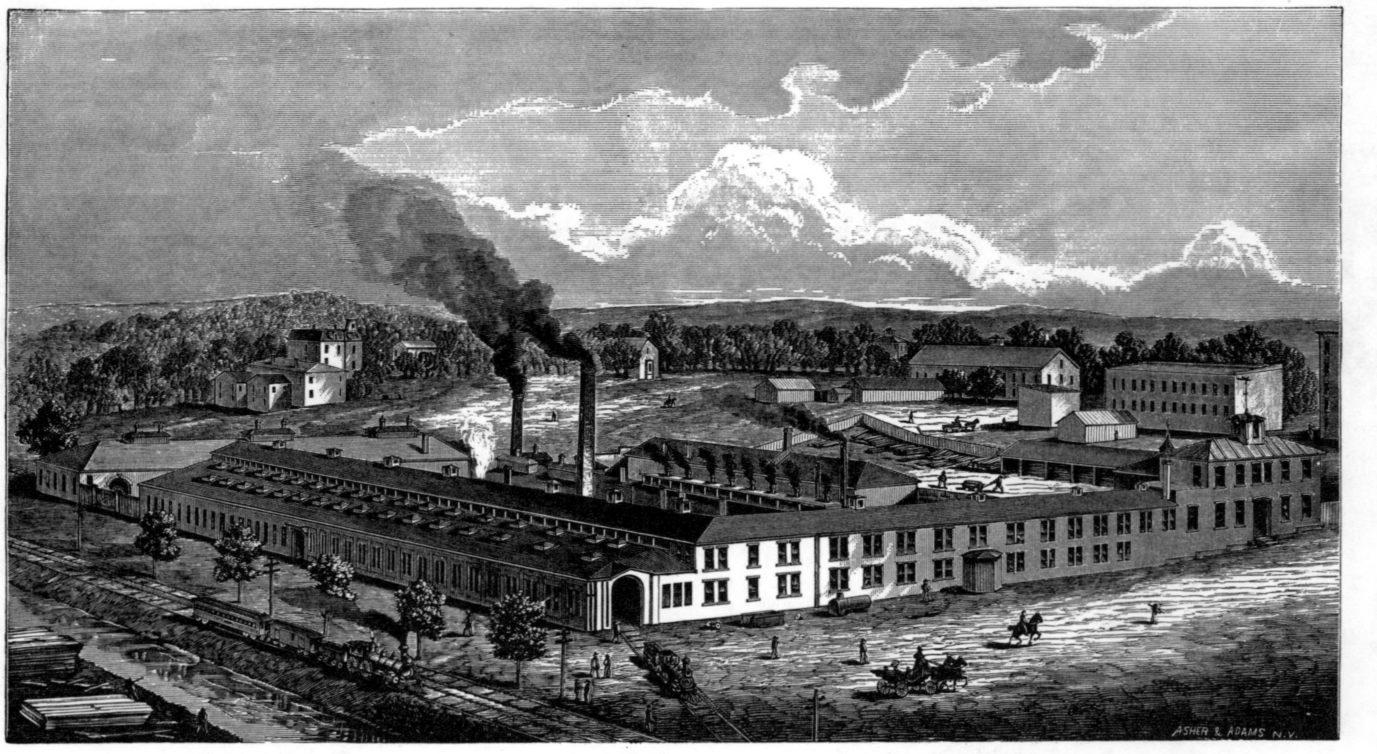

VIEW OF MANCHESTER LOCOMOTIVE WORKS, MANCHESTER, N. H.

With the successful application of steam as a motor on railroads, and their consequent popularization and rapid extension, came the necessity for the establishment of new and special branches of industry in order to furnish the railroad companies with their required outfits. Perhaps the most important of these is the manufacture of Locomotives. It involves the investment of a large capital, and the employment of the very highest grade of mechanical engineering skill—a combination of scientific knowledge and practical workmanship not easily obtained. In the construction of a locomotive, every part is important, and the utmost care is required in forming each distinct piece, be it ever so small, that forms any portion of the finished whole.

Prominent among Locomotive Builders is the Manchester Locomotive Works, Manchester, New Hampshire. The works were established in 1853 as a private enterprise, but in 1854 a charter was obtained and the Company became a corporation under the name of the Manchester Locomotive Works.

The new Company began to prepare for work, and during the spring and summer of 1854, erected shops and stocked them with the needed machinery—the capacity of the works being twenty locomotives a year. In the fall, operations were commenced in earnest, and the first born of the new company was placed upon the road to contest with the productions of older makers. Others followed as rapidly as the facilities of the works would allow, and as every new engine was a perfect success, order followed order, and the business increased with such rapidity that the Company were compelled to enlarge their shops and increase their force, until now the works have a capacity of fifteen locomotives a month—a complete engine every seventeen working hours, and, when in full operation, giving employment to seven hundred men, whose pay roll amounts to thirty thousand dollars per month.

The shops are eligibly situated on Canal Street, between Hollis and Dean Streets, and occupy five acres of land, besides the Iron Foundry and an acre of land at the lower end of Elm Street. The Machine Shop is a substantial building running parallel with Canal Street, four hundred feet in length, eighty-four feet in width and two stories in height. A stranger unused to such sights would be bewildered at entering this vast building. All the available space within its walls is filled with machinery especially constructed to meet the requirements of this establishment. There are lathes and planers, and—well if the reader desires an enumeration of the various labor saving devices there in operation, a description of the work that they perform and an explanation of how they do it—the better way will be to visit the Company's works; we haven't space to give the information here, and can only say that every appliance that can aid in the accuracy or rapidity with which the parts can be produced are gathered here, and that to the perfectness of their machinery is largely attributable the excellence of their locomotives. But the most perfect machines cannot think; they need constant and careful attention by thoughtful and skillful men, and without such care cannot produce good work. The Company have spared neither care nor expense to procure thorough workmen and only skilled men can retain a situation in these works.

The Wood Shop is also a two story building, one hundred feet long and forty feet wide. One would hardly think that the wood work connected with the manufacture of locomotives, even in so large an establishment as the Manchester Locomotive Works, would require so much room, but most of us when we question the necessity of so large a wood shop, forget that large numbers of patterns have to be made. With every variation in the size, with every alteration of style, or improvement of any part, comes a necessity for new patterns, and perhaps no branch of mechanical labor requires more skill than pattern making.

The Blacksmith Shop is three hundred and thirty feet long and fifty feet wide, and gives employment to many brawny men.

The Boiler Shop is two hundred and five feet long and fifty-two feet wide. Right merry is the music produced here, a little loud perhaps, and a continual repetition of the same strain, but pleasant music notwithstanding.

The Brass Foundry is two hundred and thirty feet in length and thirty-six feet in width.

All the Iron Castings—three million five hundred thousand pounds are required annually—are made at the Company's Foundry, at the foot of Elm Street. The Brass Castings used each year weigh two hundred thousand pounds; and two million five hundred pounds of Forgings are made each year.

One special feature of this establishment worthy of note is that the Company manufactures all the heavy forgings, frames, axles, etc., which it uses, indeed it makes in its own works every part of a locomotive. This places the supervision of the construction of their engines entirely under their own control. It renders them wholly responsible for everything they produce and entitles them to all the credit for the production of their work. Smaller establishments may purchase axles of one firm, wheels of another, boilers of a third, and so on until the business of the so called manufacturers dwindles down to merely collecting and fitting together the various parts. If the finished work of such a maker proves imperfect it takes much longer to replace the faulty part, than it would if the same error had occurred in a shop where all the parts are made.

In an establishment of this size there is a continual and very large accumulation of scrap iron, which is here utilized and remanufactured; two furnaces being constantly employed in this work.

Since the commencement of its operations the Manchester Locomotive Works have turned out a very large number of locomotives which have been distributed throughout the United States, engines of their make being in use on railroads in every part of the country, and also in the Canadas. The various States of South America are large purchasers of locomotives, and in supplying their demand the Manchester Works fully holds its own.

The Company has an ample capital, which is carefully and skillfully managed. John A. Burnham, of Boston, is President of the Company, and William G. Means, of Andover, Mass., is Treasurer. The immediate management of the immense business is under the personal superintendence of Aretas Blood, who resides in Manchester, N. H., and is the agent of the Company.

The Pattern Shop, the Foundry, the Boiler Shop, the Machine Shop, and all the various departments of the business are superintended by men of the highest skill, who are aided by accomplished foremen who personally supervise the various branches into which the labor of each department is sub-divided. Each separate piece of work is critically examined before it is accepted, and the slightest flaw in a casting, the least deviation in shape or size from the model pattern, or ever so small a lack of finish, discovered in any of the various processes through which each part must pass, at once consigns it to destruction. It must be absolutely perfect, so far as the skill of man can render it so, or it can have no place in an engine turned out of these works. It is this careful attention to the most minute details that has made the enviable reputation of the Manchester Locomotive Works, and given it so high a rank among the engine builders of the world.

Among the important industries of the United States, there is none of which our citizens have more good cause for pride, than in the manufacture of Locomotives. In this branch we claim to be far ahead of the old world. American locomotives are lighter in proportion to their drawing capacity than those of any other country. This of course is not generally conceded in European countries, but European engineers who have visited this country, and become familiar with American locomotives have almost universally acknowledged their superiority. Nowhere has the relative merits of the locomotives of different countries been so thoroughly tested as in the States of South America. These States having no manufactories within their own borders, go out into the markets of the world and select their goods. After careful tests made over the same roads, and under the same circumstances, (the trial trains closely following each other) between American and other locomotives, the palm of superiority has been accorded to the American engines. The verdict of the South American Railroad companies was rendered only after a most exhaustive trial and a careful record of the results attained by the different engines while performing absolute work. Within the past few years scarcely a locomotive has been purchased for South America from any country but the United States.

The Company are now building Engines specially designed for Lightning Express trains. Several of them are now in use on leading roads, and give perfect satisfaction, having attained the highest rate of speed. The "Earthquake" an engraving of which is presented above, is one of these fast Locomotives. This Company is always prepared to furnish Locomotives of any desired size, weight and power, from designs furnished, or to design and build locomotives for special kinds of work.

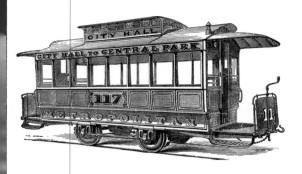

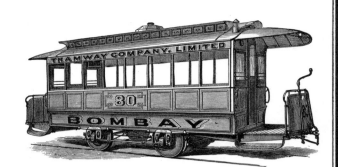

Omnibus & Street Railway Car Business,

REPRESENTED BY

John Stephenson & Co.,

New York.

The history of all modern enterprises is largely that of some single individual, who has conceived them and devoted his life to their development. The world is thus forever indebted to its heroes, for these men are as emphatically heroes, as they who die for their country upon the battle-field.

Such men are not always successful, as the world esteems success; yet, in a proper sense of the term they are, as without them civilization and development would be at a stand-still.

Who counts Fulton a blockhead to-day? and yet that was the opinion entertained of him by so-called practical men, before his little boat was launched. Who calls Professor Morse, to-day, an idle dreamer? Who believed a quarter of a century ago, that the labor of sewing by hand would soon be done away with? and yet, through the persistent trials and inventive genius of Elias Howe, such a result has been reached, to the great advantage of the human race. Instances of like character might be indefinitely multiplied. The principle announced holds, not only in regard to novelties, respecting which there has been no experience, but it is also true of any well established and important special branch of industry.

The example of these is of untold and incalculable value to the world, especially to young men embarking in commercial life, who are thereby enabled to perceive the sure path to success in business, without a laborious personal experience. The success of any enterprise soon becomes historical, and the means by which it was established, is therefore within the reach of all, and those engaging in it subsequently commence with advantages derived from the experience of their predecessors. The world is already rich in historical experience of this kind; and it is not surprising, therefore, that business of all kinds is more successfully carried on than heretofore. The philanthropists of the world—we use the term thoughtfully—are fortunately not all dead yet, they will ever flourish and increase. There is not a more useful man in the world than the successful business man who devotes his time, talent and energies to good purposes. His example in business is of great importance; and if, in addition, he is a considerate, public-spirited man, faithfully discharging all his duties to society and the world, he is justly numbered among the most valued members of the community.

In illustration of the general business principles we have set forth, it is our pleasure, to call attention to a house now of historical importance; which signally confirms all we have said. We refer to the world-renowned Omnibus and Street Car builders, Messrs. John Stephenson & Co. The firm is composed of Mr. John Stephenson, the senior member, Leander M. de Lamater, Daniel W. Pugh, and John A. Tackaberry.

Mr. Stephenson is the originator and founder of this branch of industry; and as the manufacture of omnibuses and street cars in this country is largely in his hands, to write a history of the business, would involve, of necessity, frequent reference to him

and his establishment.

Having previously served a thorough apprenticeship, Mr. Stephenson established himself in business in 1831, on Broadway, on the ground now occupied by the Grand Central Hotel; he being at the time quite a young man. New York, as a city, was but the mere promise of what it has since become. At that time there being no street railways in existence, omnibuses or stages then subserved the general purposes of locomotion and it was to the manufacture of these that Mr. Stephenson first turned his attention. He commenced operations on a moderate scale, but being well known for his thorough and painstaking attention to business, he was at once liberally patronized by stage proprietors, whose confidence and patronage he has ever held to this time. Mr. Stephenson continued at this location but a short time, the premises, with others adjoining, being burned in 1832. This misfortune led to his removal to 264 Elizabeth St. About this time the Harlem Railroad Company commenced operations, and Mr. Stephenson, constructed the first street car used by them, which is fully represented on this page. This was the commencement of a department of business which has grown into enormous proportions. The construction of these original cars, in form and otherwise, was entirely unlike anything prevailing at this day. The entrance was upon the sides, as was that of the first of the larger steam railway cars, each department affording accommodations for six or eight persons, there being three departments in each car.

The main building of the establishment is six stories in height, built of brick in the most substantial manner, and the whole includes a smith shop and iron works; wood machinery shop; wheel shop; body shop; paint shop; trimming shop and a cabinet shop; besides store rooms, which are of necessity very large.

The firm employ about 300 skilled hands in the various departments, all of whom are practical men, many of whom are artists and special experts in their business. The painting and ornamentation of omnibuses and street cars is a delicate matter, and can be performed only by skillful artists. Most of these men have been long in the employ of Mr. Stephenson, who ranks them high among his friends.

His chief trimmer has been with him forty years—during almost his entire business life—and his foremen generally have grown up in the establishment, owning and living in their own houses, and having become possessed of considerable means. Mr. Stephenson, while devoting himself assiduously to business, has ever taken a deep interest in the welfare of all engaged in his service; and has, in every possible way, labored to advance their interests.

As already stated, the business of Messrs. Stephenson & Co., is confined to the manufacture of omnibuses and street cars, therefore the vast increase in street railways which has taken place within the last few years, has taxed the establishment to its full capacity. Although the street railway system is comparatively, in its infancy, it prevails in Mexico, Cuba, South America, on the west as well as the east coast; in Europe, to some extent though not largely; in eastern Russia, Japan, the East Indies, &c. &c. Messrs. Stephenson & Co., are shipping their cars and omnibuses to all these countries, even to London.

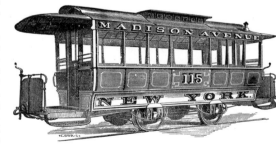

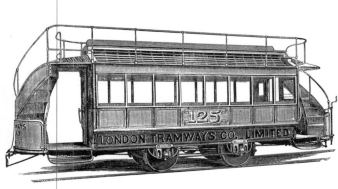

ORIGINAL STREET CAR MANUFACTURED IN 1831,
By JOHN STEPHENSON NEW YORK.

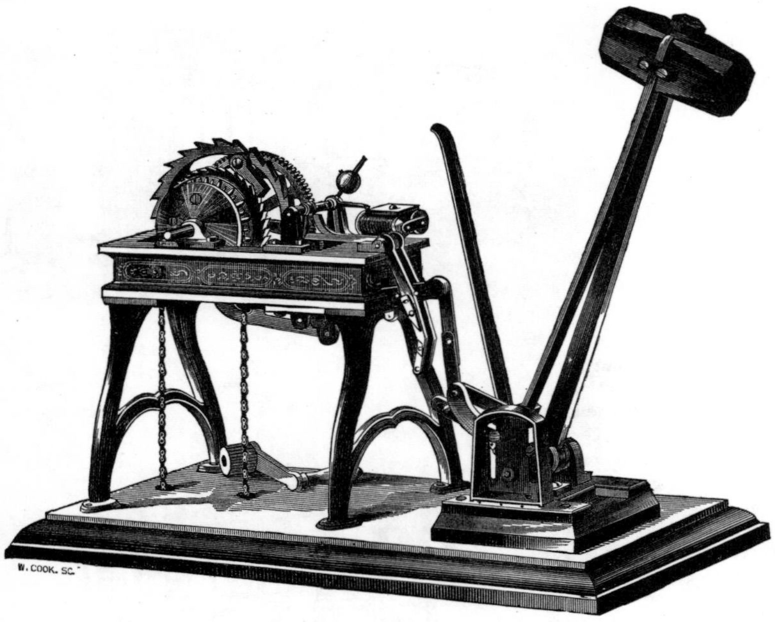

The Electro Mechanical Bell Striker.

THE AMERICAN FIRE ALARM AND POLICE TELEGRAPH.

General Office, 62 Broadway, New York.

Next to the use of the telegraph as a means for general communication between distant points, its application to the fire alarm is most important and valuable.

The Morse telegraph had scarcely been placed in successful operation, when Dr. Wm. F. Channing, of Boston, suggested its application for the giving of instantaneous, universal and definite alarms in case of fire.

In May, 1845, he published several articles calling the attention of city governments to the importance of the subject and suggesting in detail some of the necessary arrangements.

But little, however, was accomplished until six years later, (1851,) when Dr. Channing became associated with Moses G. Farmer, of Salem, Mass., an eminent electrician and a gentleman of superior inventive genius. They agreed to unite their efforts in pursuit of the object in view, and shortly after, they exhibited before the city government in Boston, a complete system of fire alarm telegraph. In June, 1861, their plan was adopted by that city and an appropriation made to test the "experiment." In the then state of electro-mechanical knowledge, progress was necessarily slow, and it was a year before the first official fire alarm was sounded by electricity. From that day to the present, this faithful agent has kept watch and ward over thousands of lives and millions of property all over the United States. The development of all great modern inventions has been the work of years, and fire alarm telegraphy is not an exception. For while Channing & Farmer are without question entitled to the same position in this wonder working art, that is accorded to Watts & Fulton, in the use of steam as a motor, yet many able minds and profound electrical research combined with inventive genius of no common order, have contributed to its recent almost perfect operations.

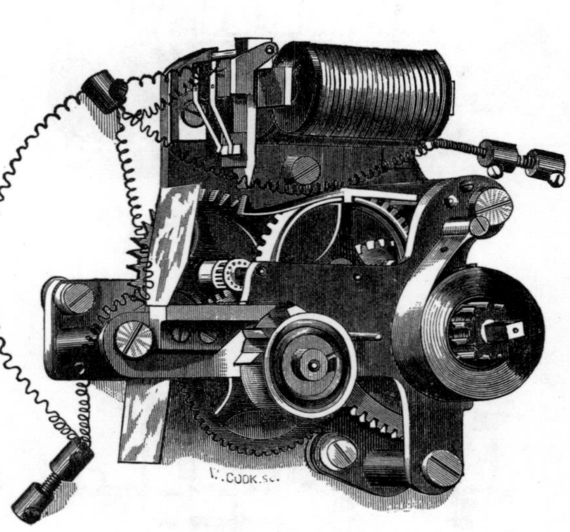

The Automatic Signal Box.

Originally the signals were made by turning a crank, which revolved the stereotyped "break wheels" in the "signal box." Of course irregular turning sometimes caused such irregularity in the signals that at times they were difficult to comprehend. Still as an evidence of the crude state of electro mechanical knowledge only twenty years ago, and of the slow and cautious progress of great improvements; it was three or four years before the mechanical or "automatic" (as it is called) signal box—plainly foreshadowed by Channing & Farmer in their patent "specifications"—was first successfully introduced in Philadelphia as the joint invention of Chas. T. Chester and Chas. Robinson, of New York. About the year 1855–6 John N. Gamewell & Co., became the sole owners of all the patents of Channing & Farmer for the South and West, and shortly afterwards for the entire country, and a little later of the Chester & Robinson, and Chester patents, thus combining all the fire telegraph patents under one control. From that time, under the energetic management of Mr. Gamewell, the art of fire alarm telegraphy made rapid progress. Not content with relying upon his own inventive talent, he counselled freely and frequently with the best experts in electrical science in this country, and spent scores of thousands of dollars, in experimenting with and securing the best fire telegraph products of the electro-mechanical genius of such well known leaders in that field, as Moses G. Farmer, Chas. T. Chester, Stephen Chester, Jos. B. Stearnes, Edwin Rogers, M. G. Crane, Jos. W. Stover, and a host of others not so generally known in fire telegraphy.

In short his rule was to incorporate in the system every feature or detail however insignificant in itself, that promised to add to the value and efficiency of a perfect whole. As the natural result, the original plan and apparatus, although the soul or moving principle of the system are, like the soul in the body, only discovered when the beautiful modern apparatus is in action. The "Automatic Repeater,"—invented by Gamewell, Rogers & Crane, and described by the jurors at the Cincinnati Exposition of 1873, who awarded the gold medal to the system, as a "splendid specimen of mechanical skill and progress in the use of electricity,"—does away with the necessity of watchmen and operators at a central station. It enables a party giving an alarm of fire to reach the fire department directly—without intermediate human agency—a great saving of expense, and of valuable time. The Automatic Signal Box as modernized and improved upon by Chester, Crane, Gamewell and Rogers, has superceded the original crank. In this box the circuit breaker is moved by clock work released by pulling a hook or lever, and the signals are transmitted with the utmost precision, an error being next to impossible.

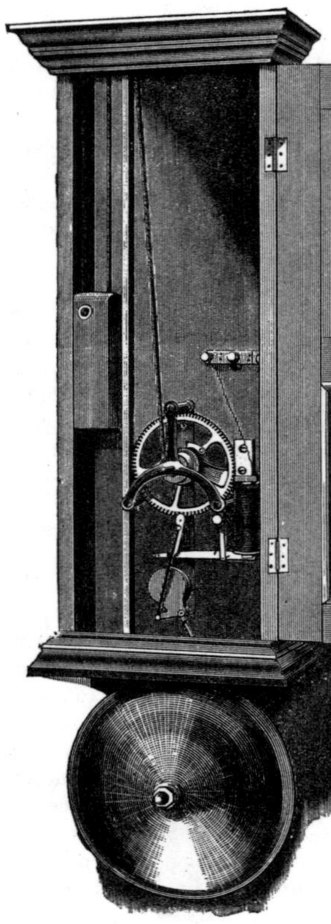

The Electro Mechanical Gong Striker.

The machinery for striking large tower bells and gongs has also been greatly improved by Messrs. Gamewell & Co., of New York, so that any amount of mechanical force can be used, giving the full tones for large bells, while the whole is held under check and control by a very small amount of battery power.

But while the Automatic system of Fire Telegraph has been regarded for some years as nearly perfect, yet further improvements have been made within a few months which add greatly to its efficiency and reliability.

The Automatic Repeater and the Signal Boxes are now constructed in a manner which almost precludes the liability of interference, and a confused alarm when two or more boxes are pulled at nearly the same time. Let one signal box have one or two seconds the start, and it secures the "right of way" and cannot be interfered with, nor can any other alarm be sounded until it has completed the work assigned it. It is confidently believed that the Automatic Non-Interfering system of Fire Alarm Telegraph as now constructed under the patents of Gamewell & Co., is as near perfection as the ingenuity of man can make it. The Central Office system of Fire Telegraph as originally introduced by Messrs. Channing & Farmer, or the Automatic system as developed by Gamewell & Co., is now in use in the following cities and towns of the United States and British Provinces.

Albany, New York.
Alleghany, Pennsylvania.
Boston Massachusetts.
Bridgeport, Connecticut.
Buffalo, New York.
Baltimore, Maryland.
Chicago, Illinois.
Cincinnati, Ohio.
Columbus, Ohio.
Cambridge, Massachusetts.
Charlestown, Massachusetts.
Chelsea, Massachusetts.
Covington, Kentucky.
Detroit, Michigan.
Dayton, Ohio.
Elizabeth, New Jersey.
Fall River, Massachusetts.
Fitchburg, Massachusetts.
Halifax, Nova Scotia.
Harrisburg, Pennsylvania.
Hartford, Connecticut,
Indianapolis, Indiana.
Jersey City, New Jersey.
Lansingburg, New York.
Louisville Kentucky.
Lowell, Massachusetts.
Lawrence, Massachusetts.
Lynn, Massachusetts.
Mobile, Alabama.
Montreal, Canada.
Milwaukee, Wisconsin.
Minneapolis, Minnesota.
Manchester, New Hampshire,
Nashville, Tennessee,
New York City.
New Orleans, Louisiana.
Newport, Kentucky.
New Bedford, Massachusetts.
New Haven, Connecticut.
Newark, New Jersey.
Newton, Massachusetts.
Omaha, Nebraska,
Pawtucket, Rhode Island.
Paterson, New Jersey.
Philadelphia, Pennsylvania.
Pittsburg, Pennsylvania.
Portland, Maine.
Peoria, Illinois.
Providence. Rhode Island.
Quebec, Lower Canada.
Rochester, New York.
Reading, Pennsylvania.
Richmond, Virginia.
St. Louis, Missouri.
St. John, New Brunswick.
Springfield, Massachusetts.
San Francisco, California.
Savannah, Georgia.
Somerville, Massachusetts.
St. Paul, Minnesota.
Syracuse, New York.
Troy, New York.
Taunton, Massachusetts.
Terre Haute, Indiana.
Toledo, Ohio.
Toronto, Canada.
Washington, D. C.
Worcester, Massachusetts.
West Roxbury, Massachusetts.

In the limited space at our command, we cannot even partially describe this "wonderful triumph of American genius" as has been aptly said of it, but shall refer only briefly to the four leading instruments used in Fire Telegraphs, and illustrated on this page.

The Automatic Signal Box.—The figure on the upper right hand corner, represents the signal mechanism, (clock work with spring or weight motors,) so arranged as to open and close an electric circuit a definite number of times at certain intervals, in such a manner as to indicate, by the number of blows upon the alarm bells—and the intervals between—the exact location, or number of the signal mechanism in action. This clock work is enclosed in a dust tight cast iron round box, which is placed in one corner of a square iron case, having a hinged door, and lock with key under the exclusive control of such city officers as may be authorized or required to give special signals. The case contains in addition to the round box a lightning arrester, also a telegraph key and call bell for engineers or police signals—thus every signal station may be used as a telegraph office for any city purposes. A small starting lever—spread into a thumb piece on the outside—passes through the door of the case and projects through a closely fitting aperture into the round box, where its end rests immediately under the detent lever of the signal mechanism. Lifting the detent lever by pressing the thumb piece of the starting lever lightly downward once, sets the signal mechanism and through it the whole system of fire telegraph in operation. The square case with contents, is enclosed in the neat little cottage shaped iron boxes seen on the corners of streets in most of our principal cities. These outside boxes are locked with combination locks, the keys of which are placed in the hands of the police and one or more responsible property holders in the immediate vicinity of each box. It will thus be seen that the mechanism is secured inside of the inner of three distinct iron boxes, and that opening the outer door reveals nothing but a square iron case with a thumb piece projecting from its door.

The Electro-Mechanical Bell Striker.—The figure in the upper left hand corner represents the apparatus for striking large bells, the size of hammer and force of blow depending entirely upon the amount of weight suspended by the chain. The weight power operating the machine is held under check by an electro-magnetic escapement controlled by a very light electric force. There is practically no limit to this power, as the apparatus gives the full tone of a ten thousand pound bell as readily as it operates upon a bell of an hundred pounds. These bell strikers are placed in church, school, or engine house towers and do not interfere with the use of a bell for its ordinary purposes.

The Electro Mechanical Gong Striker.—The central figure represents the Gong Striker placed in engine houses, factories, residences of the officers of the fire departments, police stations, or any place where a loud and certain alarm is deemed requisite; operated like the bell striker by using electricity to control mechanical power.

The Automatic Repeater.—The figure at the bottom of the page represents this wonderfully ingenious instrument, which is placed with all the batteries, galvanometers, and commutators at some central point constituting the heart of the whole system By its use the signal boxes, bell and gong strikers are distributed upon a number of wire lines or circuits—according to the size of a city—so arranged that an accidental or malicious interruption of any one will not impair the efficiency of the others. In case a battery becomes too weak to be efficient, or an interruption from any cause occurs in the "continuity" of any of the circuits, in an instant the automatic repeater gives notice by one blow upon all the alarm bells and gongs, calling attention to the imperfection; thus keeping watch, not only over the city, but actually watching itself and guaranteeing reliability every moment.

How an Alarm is Given—When a fire occurs, the person first discovering it, runs to the key holder of the nearest signal box, who either entrusts him with the key or goes himself—the outer door of the box is opened, and one simple pressure on the thumb piece, plainly in sight, instantly sounds the number of that box upon every alarm bell, gong and call bell in the system. Suppose box 23 has been touched off! the blows will be given thus: 1–1 (two blows) then a pause of four or five seconds, and then 1–1–1 (three blows) making 23; this is repeated three, four or five times as may be desired. The localities of these numbers and of all the boxes being well known by the firemen, they start at once direct to the scene of danger.

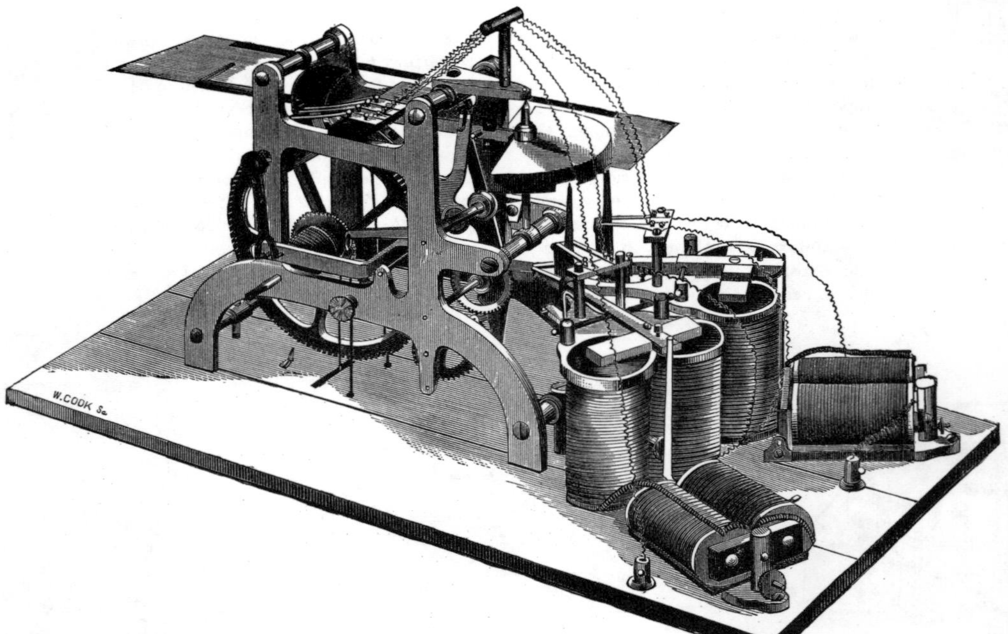

The Automatic Repeater.

The value of the Fire Alarm Telegraph as a primary agent in the suppression of fires—in the saving of lives and property—cannot be over estimated.

Most fires are discovered before they have made great progress and at a time when they might be easily subdued if the means were at hand, but left alone their progress is rapid and destructive. It is obvious then that the saving of a very few minutes, often times the saving of a minute even, is of the utmost importance and may make the difference between a trifling loss and a destructive conflagration. A city may be provided with an unlimited supply of water and a thoroughly organized and efficient fire department, but to render either available the department must first know that a fire has broken out and its exact locality.

It is indeed a great triumph of inventive genius, that electricity, the swiftest messenger known to man, has been tamed to the giving of prompt and definite alarms, in the complete and reliable manner illustrated in the working of this system of Fire Alarm Telegraph.

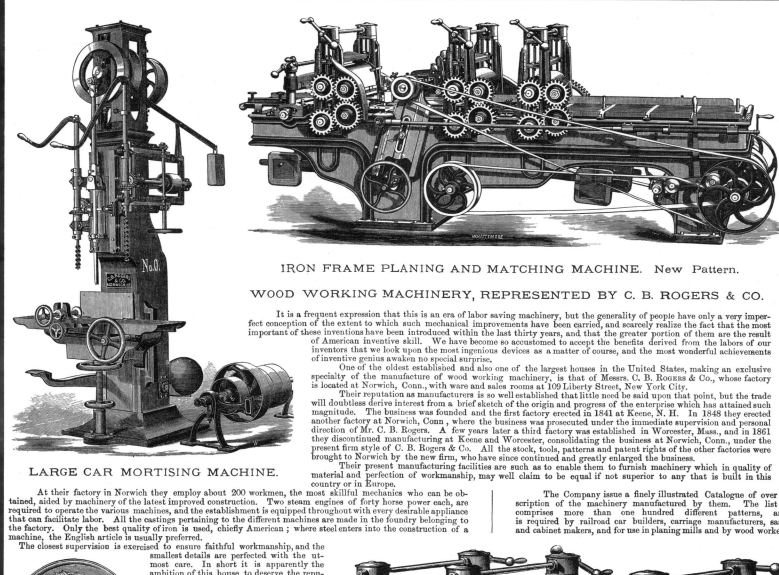

IRON FRAME PLANING AND MATCHING MACHINE. New Pattern.

LARGE CAR MORTISING MACHINE.

MEDIUM POWER MORTISING MACHINE.

With Boring Apparatus.

WOOD WORKING MACHINERY, REPRESENTED BY C. B. ROGERS & CO.

It is a frequent expression that this is an era of labor saving machinery, but the generality of people have only a very imperfect conception of the extent to which such mechanical improvements have been carried, and scarcely realize the fact that the most important of these inventions have been introduced within the last thirty years, and that the greater portion of them are the result of American inventive skill. We have become so accustomed to accept the benefits derived from the labors of our inventors that we look upon the most ingenious devices as a matter of course, and the most wonderful achievements of inventive genius awaken no special surprise.

One of the oldest established and also one of the largest houses in the United States, making an exclusive specialty of the manufacture of wood working machinery, is that of Messrs. C. B. Rogers & Co., whose factory is located at Norwich, Conn., with ware and sales rooms at 109 Liberty Street, New York City.

Their reputation as manufacturers is so well established that little need be said upon that point, but the trade will doubtless derive interest from a brief sketch of the origin and progress of the enterprise which has attained such magnitude. The business was founded and the first factory erected in 1841 at Keene, N. H. In 1848 they erected another factory at Norwich, Conn., where the business was prosecuted under the immediate supervision and personal direction of Mr. C. B. Rogers. A few years later a third factory was established in Worcester, Mass., and in 1861 they discontinued manufacturing at Keene and Worcester, consolidating the business at Norwich, Conn., under the present firm style of C. B. Rogers & Co. All the stock, tools, patterns and patent rights of the other factories were brought to Norwich by the new firm, who have since continued and greatly enlarged the business.

Their present manufacturing facilities are such as to enable them to furnish machinery which in quality of material and perfection of workmanship, may well claim to be equal if not superior to any that is built in this country or in Europe.

At their factory in Norwich they employ about 200 workmen, the most skillful mechanics who can be obtained, aided by machinery of the latest improved construction. Two steam engines of forty horse power each, are required to operate the various machines, and the establishment is equipped throughout with every desirable appliance that can facilitate labor. All the castings pertaining to the different machines are made in the foundry belonging to the factory. Only the best quality of iron is used, chiefly American ; where steel enters into the construction of a machine, the English article is usually preferred.

The closest supervision is exercised to ensure faithful workmanship, and the smallest details are perfected with the utmost care. In short it is apparently the ambition of this house to deserve the reputation of making the best possible work that can be produced, and that their enterprise has been crowned with complete success is attested by the general commendation of the mechanics and manufacturers of the country.

The Company issue a finely illustrated Catalogue of over 140 pages, giving the most complete and full description of the machinery manufactured by them. The list of machines built by Messrs. Rogers & Co., comprises more than one hundred different patterns, and embraces everything of the kind that is required by railroad car builders, carriage manufacturers, sash, door and blind makers, house builders, chair and cabinet makers, and for use in planing mills and by wood workers generally. The manufacture of machinery and

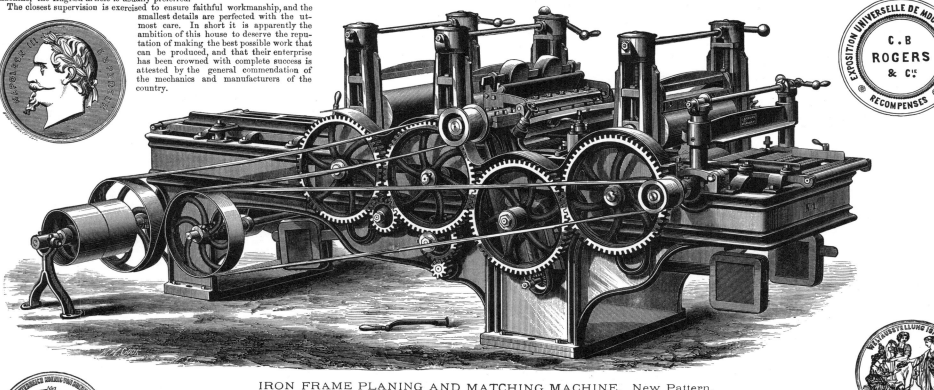

IRON FRAME PLANING AND MATCHING MACHINE. New Pattern.

tools for car builders is a leading specialty, and the firm supply many of the principal railroad car shops in the United States.

To show how universal is the high estimation in which the wood working machinery manufactured by this firm is held, we may mention that aside from large sales in nearly every State and Territory in the Union, frequent shipments are made to Mexico, Brazil, Chili, Peru, Egypt, Germany, Sweden, and even to China and Japan.

The machinery manufactured by this establishment, wherever exhibited, has invariably received the highest premiums. At the exposition in Paris, in 1867, the only gold medal bestowed for machinery of this class was awarded to Messrs. Rogers & Co. They also obtained the silver medal at the World's Fair, at London, in 1851 ; five medals, with diplomas, at the American Institute Fair of 1867 ; six silver medals, with diplomas, at the Maryland Institute Fairs of 1867 and 1868 ; also

numerous medals from the American Institute, New York ; Metropolitan Institute, Washington ; Maryland Institute, Baltimore ; Franklin Institute, Philadelphia ; Crystal Palace Exhibition, New York ; Massachusetts Charitable Association, Boston ; and many other fairs and exhibitions, including the recent Vienna Exposition, where the Medal of Merit, the highest award given for this description of machinery, was bestowed upon Rogers & Co. Space will not admit of a further description of this superior machinery, but we advise the searcher after knowledge in this direction to apply for their illustrated catalogue, which will be found very complete.

PATENT FOUR SIDE MOULDING MACHINE. Inside Heads.

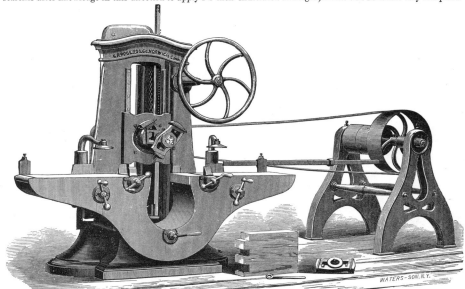

VERTICAL CAR TENONING MACHINE.

ESTABLISHED 1857.

WM. H. HASKELL & CO.,

Manufacturers of

Machine and Plow Bolts, Coach Screws,

(with Gimlet Point), Forged and Milled

Set Screws, and Top Bolts.

277 MAIN STREET, PAWTUCKET, R. I.

——:o:——

It is not many years since Machinists, Blacksmiths, Carriage and Wagon Makers, indeed all workers in metal, or metal and wood combined, made all their own Bolts, Nuts, and Screws by hand as required for use, while if a worker in wood required bolts or screws larger than the ordinary ones made for Carpenters' use, the only way to obtain them was to have them made by a machinist or blacksmith. There has always been and probably always will be a decided aversion on the part of many to the introduction of anything made by machinery, but in the matter of screws, bolts and nuts, the opposition was soon overcome, the machine-made goods not only being much cheaper, but much better than those made by hand, and now every hardware machinist, large or small, in city and country, keeps con-

View of Wm. H. Haskell & Co.'s Works, Pawtucket, R. I.

stantly on hand an assortment of Bolts, Nuts and Screws, of a variety of sizes and adapted to a large number of uses, and machinists, blacksmiths, indeed all who use bolts and screws, purchase the machine-made goods.

There are a number of establishments in the United States devoted to this branch of manufacture, prominent among which is that of Wm. H. Haskell & Co., of Pawtucket, R. I., prominent for its extent and the variety of its styles of manufacture, but more prominent for the excellent quality of its productions. The numerous cuts presented on this page will give the reader a hint as to the number of kinds of screws and bolts made,—but only a hint. They manufacture everything within the range of Machine Bolts, Plow Bolts, Coach Screws of various sizes and kinds, with Gimlet Points, Forged and Milled Set Screws and Top Bolts. Their goods are sold everywhere in the United States and Territories, and in the Canadas.

The works of this firm are models of completeness in their arrangement and equipment, being supplied with all the mechanical appliances that can lighten the labor of the workmen, or that tend to increase the excellence or the rapidity of their production. Should we attempt here to state the total number of Screws, Bolts, Nuts, etc., manufactured at this establishment in a single year, the figures, we fear, would scarcely be credited. The success of the firm has been remarkable, there has been and is a brisk competition in the business—older firms and younger ones, but none have attained a prouder position than they, and their productions have long been considered a fitting standard of excellence by which others may be judged.

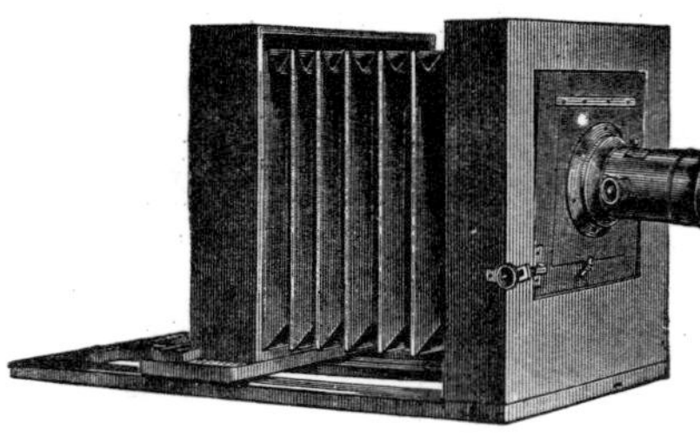

Patent Swing Front Camera.

W. KURTZ, PHOTOGRAPHS,

Twenty-Third Street, Near Broadway, N. Y.

Some inventions are happy accidents, others are developed by slow and pains-taking diligence. In reveiwing the history of great discoveries, we sometimes wonder by what brilliant chance a great idea occurred to the mind of an obscure searcher after some better way; and sometimes we see a number of persistent investigators, all fascinated with the importance of the end to be obtained, one proposing to master the difficulty in one way, the others pursuing entirely different methods, and each contributing his own good part to the final success. In the latter way has the marvelous art of photography been developed.

Almost a century ago chemists had observed that nitrate of silver is a substance curiously affected by the rays of the sun, and it had occurred to them that somehow this property might be utilized in the pictorial art; near the beginning of the present century, two of the ablest chemists of England, Joseph Wedgewood and Humphrey Davy, succeeded in producing sun pictures by smearing a piece of leather with a solution of nitrate of silver and laying over it a picture on glass. The dark lines of the glass picture protected the silvered surface, and the sunlight passing through the other unshaded parts, would fix upon the leather a copy of the picture on the glass, but with inversion of light and shade. At this point photography remained for nearly forty years, no substance or treatment having been hit upon that could dissolve the salt of silver and fix the picture.

Between 1830 and 1840 two French chemists devoted much time to the mastery of the difficulties which begirt the problem. These men were Niepce and Daguerre. Niepce discovered that by coating a metal plate with a thin film of bitumen and exposing it for several hours to the sun's rays, the actinism of the rays would act unequally on the bitumen according to the lines on the glass alone; and after removing the negative, as we now call it, he found that certain essential oils, as that of lavender, would develope the positive by rendering the thin film of bitumen insoluble.

Daguerre aimed at the same results but sought them through a medium which has since proved more effective. He prepared his plate by exposing a polished silver surface to the vapor of iodine. In this way he obtained a sensitiveness which enabled him to use the camera and to obtain results with a few seconds exposure, the picture was developed with the vapor of mercury, and fixed by the hyposulphite of soda. The plates he used were silver or copper well plated. The highly polished surface was exposed to a vapor of iodine in a dark chamber, then in a camera exposed to the rays which come from the object to be pictured. Since then the marvelous art of drawing by the chemical power of sunbeams has emerged from the dimness and shadows which had previously surrounded it, growing clearer and better defined, overcoming faults, mastering objections, throwing old methods into the background, till now it has as nearly reached absolute perfection as the advancement of chemical science and the keenness of human faculties will allow.

Now and then we may find one of those weird, shadowy pictures made in 1840 and 1841, when Daguerre's discovery was first presented to an admiring public. When held at a proper angle, and in a strong light the likeness they present is admirable, and when the materials were well handled there are as yet no traces of "decay's effacing fingers," but in clearness, force and brilliancy they are so far beneath the magnificent pictures which come from the first-class galleries of to day—notably that of Kurtz—that one can hardly believe the later picture to be the direct descendent of the earlier.

The photograph was mainly an English invention. Six months before Daguerre published his invention, Mr. Talbot, an English Chemist, in a paper laid before the Royal Society described a sensitive paper for copying drawings or paintings by direct contact. The paper was prepared by baths, first in a solution of chloride of sodium and then in a solution of nitrate of silver. Thus he obtained on paper a film of chloride of silver, and the copying was effected by placing the object, (which must be in parts transparent,) upon the sensitive paper and exposing it to the rays of the sun. In this way as early as 1840 Talbot produced a negative, that is, a picture in which the lights and shades were reversed. This inverted picture being fixed, he produced positives by placing it on another piece of sensitive paper and again subjecting it to the sun's rays. This was the beginning of photographic printing.

The next year, 1841, Talbot's constant experiments were successful in giving the art another grand advance. He prepared paper with iodide of silver, thus making it sensitive to light, fixed it in the camera, threw an image upon it with a lens, and then developed the shadow into a picture and fixed it with the chemical used by Daguerre, the hyposulphite of soda. Thus Talbot made paper negatives from which good positives could be printed; but there was an essential difficulty with them—a want of unity of structure and delicacy of lines inseparable from the use of even the best paper. It was evident that paper could be sensitized so as to receive a printed impression, and that impression be fixed so as to be imperishable,—no better material could be desired for a positive picture, but for a negative something else must be found. Scores if not hundreds of artists and chemists sought assiduously during ten years for a suitable material on which to fix the negative picture but without success, and from 1840 to 1850 most sun pictures were made, upon silver plate and very properly called Daguerreotypes.

About the year 1851 the art of making glass negatives was discovered. At first albumen was used as a film or coating on plate glass, and albumen plates are still used by some artists. Legray was the first to suggest that collodion would make a better film for photographic manipulation than albumen. Collodion is produced by dissolving gun cotton in alcohol and ether. When the solution is poured on a plate of clean glass it forms a very thin, even and transparent film, which quickly dries and can scarcely be distinguished from the glass beneath. This delicate collodion surface can be made as sensitive to light as a silver plate, an image can be thrown upon it, it may be developed by combinations of iron with sulphur and with nitrate, and it may be fixed with a combination of potash.

There are two ways of finishing this collodion shadow into a picture. It may be deepened or intensified, fixed and set against a dark back ground, when it becomes a glass positive, sometimes called a melanotype, on account of its prevailing dark or shadowy tints, but the method which is far more common, is to wash this collodion shadow into a glass negative or type from which any number of pictures may be taken by allowing the light to shine through upon properly sensitized paper.

The development and perfection of this process has given modern civilization a new and wonderful art. By it in a few seconds a portrait is thrown upon a film covering, a bit of plate glass and there fixed. After that the sitters may go their way, may travel to the ends of the earth. Time may work wondrous changes on them—the fair, smooth face may become wrinkled with age, disease or accident may scar and deform it, but the true and perfect likeness—more correct than the most gifted artist in the world could paint—remains upon the glass unchanged, and from it thousands of images on paper may be printed.

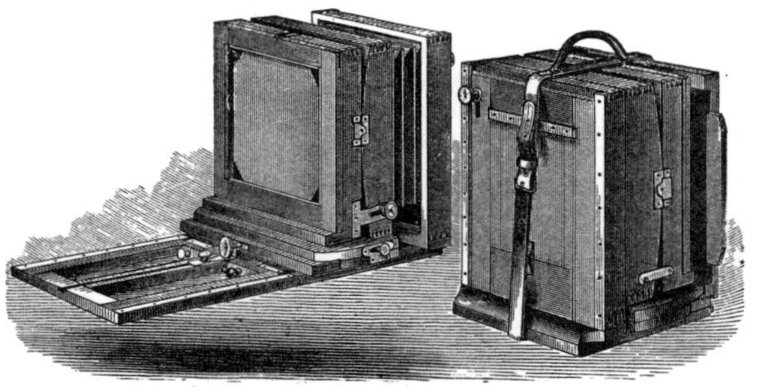

American Optical Company's View Camera Boxes.

Within twenty years since collodion came to be a promiment chemical in photography, a thousand delicate and strictly chemical improvements have been made in every step of the process. The quality of the coating material has been carefully studied, and artists have discovered just the right combinations of gun cotton, ether and alcohol to use. The best mode of making this film sensitive, the best method of developing the shadows thrown upon it, the manipulation best adapted to remove defects in the impression, the bath that will set the lines, and, as important as either of these, the most approved and skilful handling of the glass as a type to print from, the various modes of toning, softening, intensifying and fixing the pictures thrown from the glass to the paper, have been studied with enthusiasm.

The perfect photograph is the finished result of a rare combination of natural æsthetic taste, aided by careful study, chemical knowledge, and that quick, impulsive faculty of perception which enables the operator to determine with the greatest nicety the precise moment when the best effect is produced. All the various pursuits of life are to a greater or less degree divided. This is true in the mechanical, professional and art worlds. The making of a piano involves numerous departments. Before an instrument reaches the wareroom it has passed through a dozen or more sets of hands. We have lawyers among us who have attained world wide fame for their success in certain classes of causes. We have great property lawyers, great patent lawyers and great criminal lawyers; men who in the special branches of their profession are almost invincible, but who in other branches would hardly rise above mediocrity. Some painter's have achieved a fame as durable as history because they were great colorists, some as portrait painters, others for their landscapes. In many pursuits better general results can be obtained through divisions of the necessary labor into separate branches, each branch or department being presided over by those specially skillful in that particular kind of work. But to obtain an absolutely perfect result the whole must be directed and supervised by one skilled in everything pertaining to the business. The art of Photography has such a man in Mr. William Kurtz, an excellent engraving of whose new and magnificent building adorns this page.

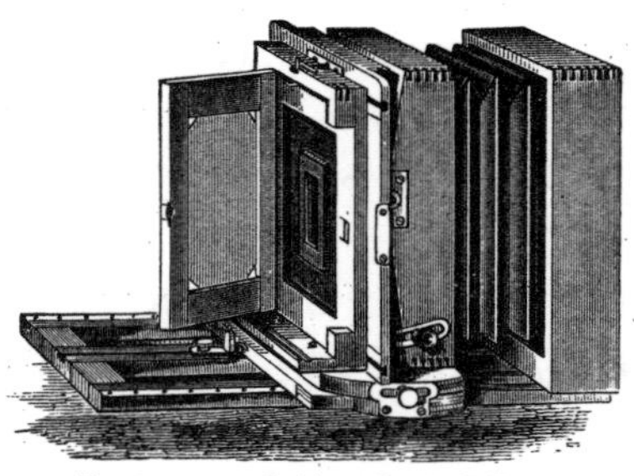

The Imperial Cabinet Portrait Box.

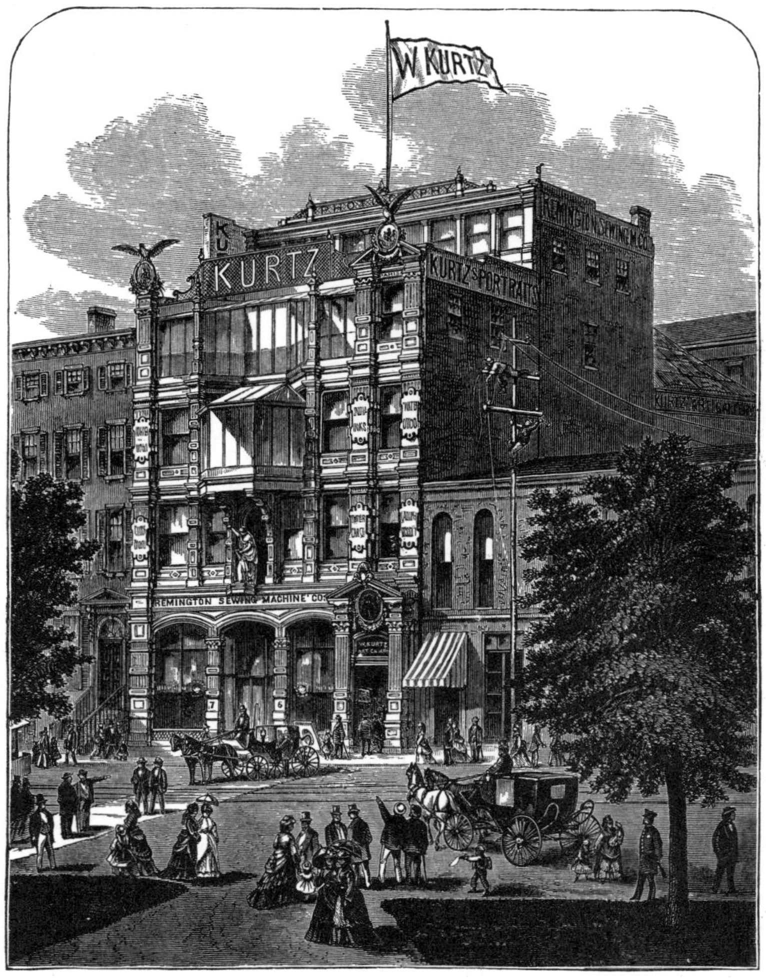

WM. KURTZ'S ART BUILDING.

Long experience having taught Mr. Kurtz that many of the failures in Photographic Ateliers are attributable to improperly arranged sky-lights (work-rooms), and to imperfect lights caused by the reflections from surrounding buildings, he determined to place his new building in a locality free from all objections, and was fortunate enough to secure the three valuable lots on the Twenty-third Street side of Madison Square, formerly known as the "Corlies Estate," where he has erected the beautiful studios which are the admiration of artists and photographers. Directly opposite the centre of a fine square, with an uninterrupted northern light, a more admirable situation for photographic and artistic purposes could not be found.

The building has its entrance on Twenty-third Street, one door east of Broadway. Above the spacious store, on the first or ground floor, is the Photographic establishment, and as fine an exhibition room for works of art as New York can boast of. The *Herald* in its notice of the Third Annual Exhibitions of "The Palette," recently held in this room, mentions: "Mr. Kurtz, whose interest in the progress of art has induced him to spare no expense in making the building worthy of its destiny, as the future art centre of the city."

On Twenty-Second street are the Club Rooms and Art School Rooms, constructed expressly to meet the requirements of the "Palette Art Association."

The building commenced in 1873 and now completed, at a cost of One Hundred and Thirty Thousand Dollars, is constructed of iron and brick, after the plans, and under the supervision of the eminent architects, Schulze & Schoen. It has all the desirable modern improvements, is heated throughout by steam (to avoid dust,) and has a system of telegraphic wires throughout, to facilitate communication between the different departments; separate stair-cases are provided for the employees, so that the principal stair-case may always be kept neat and clean and exclusively for the use of visitors.

One great trouble of Photographers, who work on thoroughfares, is the necessity, which forces them to work on the uppermost floors of high buildings, in order to obtain the light required by their process. The weary ascent of several flights of stairs is, in a great measure, obviated in the new building. The stairs have an easy rise, and the abundance of light, furnished through an extensive glass front, by the clear, wide space of Madison Square, enables Mr. Kurtz to arrange his work rooms on the lower floors, while the upper are occupied by the Studios of Artists, who can be summoned, by the electric wire, to the separate studios provided for those who desire to sit for Pictures to be finished in Oil, Pastel, Crayon, Water Colors, Porcelain Miniatures, India Ink, etc.

For the accommodation of gentlemen in business, who find it inconvenient to make an appointment for a particular day and hour, he has arranged three Operating Rooms. No appointment will be necessary, and they will be subject to no delay, as he has facilities to make one hundred and fifty negatives per day; moreover, on account of the ample light now available, a perfectly clear day is no longer required, to produce a good portrait.

The technical department is under the supervision of Mr. Elbert Anderson (who received the "Medal of Co-operation" at Vienna;) the artistic will be conducted by Mr. Kurtz, assisted by some of the best talent of the country.

For many years it was (and still is to some extent) a general impression that photography had reached a much higher degree of excellence in Europe than in America. To counteract this impression Mr. Kurtz was induced to send specimens of the work executed at his establishment to the Great International Expositions at Paris and Vienna, where they were brought into competition with the works of the most celebrated photographers of the world. At both Expositions Mr. Kurtz received the highest premiums awarded, of which he may well be proud. Not only the jury of experts but photographers generally awarded to him the highest praise for his work and skill, and the noted newspapers of the world pronounced his collection of portraits the finest specimens of the Photographic Art ever exhibited.

JOHN SOUTHER & CO.,

Exclusive Manufacturers of the

OTIS PATENT STEAM EXCAVATOR,

With

O. S. CHAPMAN'S IMPROVEMENTS,

Also, Dredges and Contractors' Machinery, etc.

Works on A Street, South Boston,

Office, No. 1 Pemberton Square, Boston, Mass.

——:o:——

Prominent among the noteworthy manufacturing establishments of the United States is that of John Souther & Co. These works were established by Lyman & Souther in 1846, who began business in a comparatively small way as Steam Engine Builders. The co-partnership did not last long, however, Mr. Souther soon bought the interest of Mr. Lyman, and extended the business by making the construction of Locomotives the leading branch. Mr. Souther had previously had much experience in the building of Locomotive Engines. In 1838, he made the models, drawings and patterns for the first locomotives built by the Hinkley Locomotive Works, then called the Hinkley & Drury Locomotive Works. During the succeeding seven years, Mr. Souther made all the working drawings and patterns of the locomotives produced by that company, and then, as previously noted, engaged in business on his own account. In 1854, a joint stock company was formed and incorporated by the State, under the name of the Globe Locomotive Works.

At the commencement of the War of the Rebellion, the Globe Locomotive Works made heavy contracts with the United States Government for marine work, such as the hulls and machinery for Monitors; the steam machinery for Frigates, Sloops of War, and Side Wheel Steamers; also the Engines for two Revenue Vessels; making marine work their principal business. In consequence of this change in the character of their business, the Company changed their title to the Globe Works, entirely dropping the word Locomotive.

At the close of the war the former name—John Souther & Co.,—was resumed. The firm now consists of John Souther, Charles H. Souther, and George A. Souther, and is largely engaged in the building of Steam Excavators and Contractors' Machinery, making this branch of business their leading specialty.

At these works have been made as great a variety of heavy steam machinery as has been produced in any establishment in this country. Machinery original with them, and so completely successful in accomplishing the purposes for which it was designed, that they have introduced it not only in all parts of our own land, but in Europe.

From the first organization of this business it has been an immense success, and one of its peculiarities has been the practice of the firm to change their appliances and adopt their tools to the class of machinery most in demand at any given time, whether it be Locomotives, Sugar Mills, Steam Excavators, or Steamships. They were largely in the Locomotive business for thirteen years, from 1847 to 1860, and made the first engines for several Eastern, Western and Southern Railroads. They furnished the first locomotive used on the Pacific coast. It was shipped to James Cunningham, San Francisco, Cal., in 1847, with a Steam Excavator, for grading, digging and filling in purposes, and when the Sacramento Valley Railroad was opened, (the first railroad built on the Pacific coast) this engine was the first used on that road and is still in use.

This firm built the engines that took the first train from the Pacific to Ogden, on the opening of the railroad across the Continent from Ocean to Ocean. These engines were originally shipped to San Francisco, there to be re-shipped to Oregon for use on the first railroad, then being built, in that State, but the Central Pacific Railroad, not being supplied with locomotives, took them to open their line with. The annual reports of many of our Eastern, Western and Southern Railroad Companies, in which are found tables showing the number of miles made by each of their locomotives during the year, record no engines doing better service or making more miles than those from these works.

At these works was built the machinery for Messrs. Munn & Co., contractors, to bore a twenty-four foot hole through the Hoosac Mountain. The machine constructed at these works is believed to have been the largest portable machine, mounted on wheels, ever built up to that time; it weighed about one hundred tons, and was driven by a one-hundred horse power steam engine. The machine had a working wheel of 23½ feet in diameter, with a rim 4½ feet on the face; from this several revolving steel cutters projected which were forced against the face of the rock. The revolutions of this huge wheel rapidly cut a groove one foot in width, and penetrating a distance of four feet at each cutting; at the same time a hole six inches in diameter was bored in the centre five feet deep; the whole machine was then backed on its own wheels, and the centre hole charged with powder and the blast made, the effect being to remove the stone clean to the groove or channel made by the cutters. This part of the work was a great success, and at the speed these cutters worked, the mountain could have been tunneled in about one-sixth of the time it took to accomplish the work with small drills. The drawback of this machine was that after blasting the centre charge the pieces were so large that they could not be moved past the machine without re-blasting. It is believed that if the boring machine had been 15 feet in diameter instead of 23½ feet, making a hole large enough for one track, and to run a locomotive through, the centre charge would have so broken up the stone that it could easily have been taken out. Unfortunately, the contractor died about the time this difficulty was developed, a smaller machine was not made, and this plan of boring the mountain was abandoned.

For twenty years the construction of Sugar Mills and Sugar Refining Machinery was a very important branch of their business. In addition to the large demand for such machinery among the planters of the Southern States, and the refiners of the North, there was an immense amount of such machinery exported to Cuba, St. Domingo, the Sandwich Islands and Mexico, and there is no sugar machinery in either of these countries that has a better reputation than that from the Globe Works. Previous to the outbreak of the Cuban Rebellion there were 2,500 estates on that island that had sugar houses fitted with steam machinery, which, in some instances, was worth two hundred thousand dollars. Mr. Souther deemed this trade of such importance that he spent two years in Cuba studying the wants of the sugar planters, and in devising the machinery best adapted to supply those wants. The advantage of thus practically acquainting himself with the needs of his patrons met its reward in the immense demand for the machinery built at his works. Cuba alone having purchased to the extent of $200,000 in a single year. These Works built and shipped the first steam sugar mill used in the Sandwich Islands; also, the first on the Island of St. Domingo. They sent the first steam engine used on the Island of Sicily used for grinding sumach.

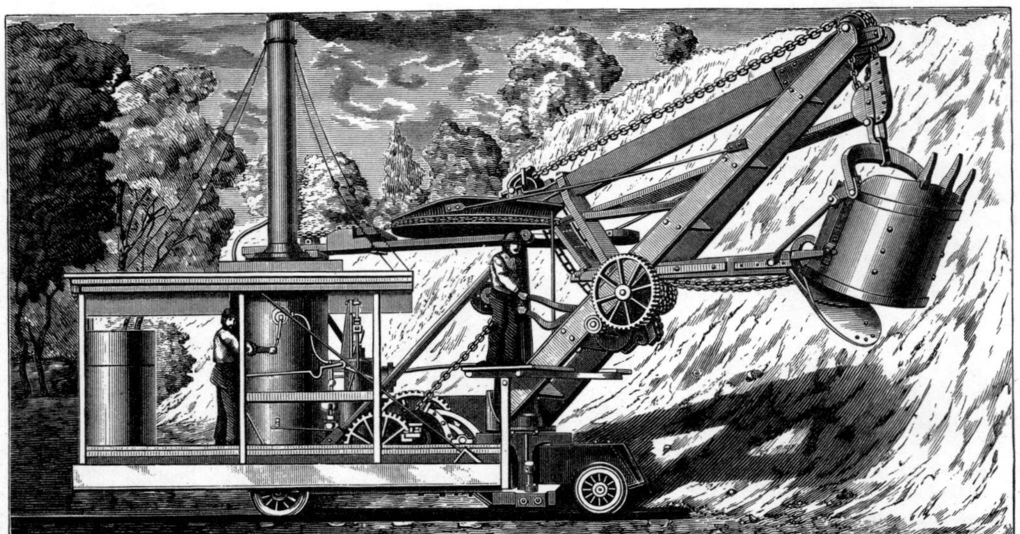

Otis Steam Excavator with Chapman's Improvements.

This Company also built the first American dredging boats and machinery for the Egyptian Government, used on the Nile at Cairo and Alexandria; also the first dredge boat and steam machinery used by the Japanese Government, and supplied the Russian Government with dredge boats and machinery for use on the Amoor River, Eastern Russia.

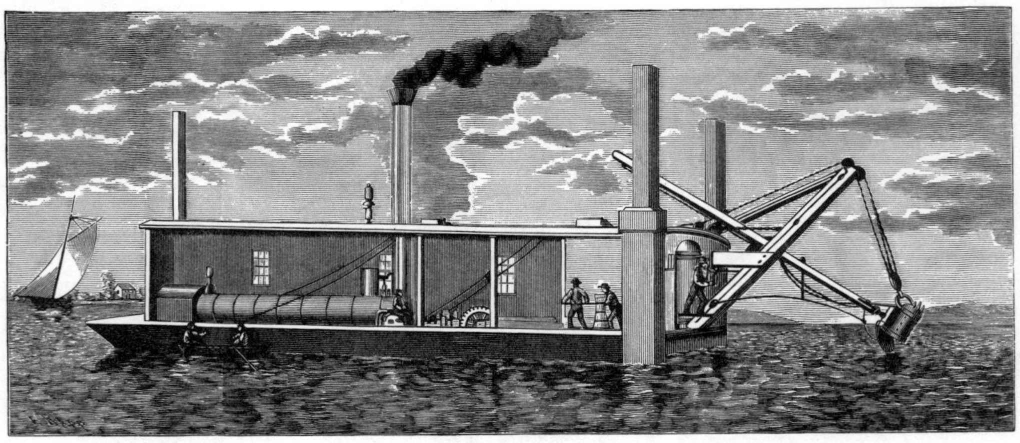

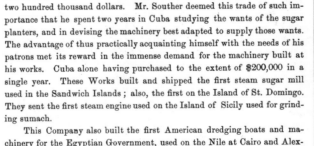

Steam Dredge Boat.

Recently they sent to England and put in successful operation the first steam excavator ever used there for excavating on dry land. The machine is working at Hull (1875), and gives complete satisfaction. They have also shipped one to the Chincha Islands, in the South Pacific Ocean, for digging guano. During eighteen years they have been the exclusive builders of the Otis Patent Steam Excavator, with O. S. Chapman's Improvements.

It is a singular fact that in this great age of invention of labor saving machinery, in carrying out so vast an enterprise as the construction of the railroads of the world, there has been no machine produced and successfully used by railroad contractors for handling earth, except the Otis Excavator with Chapman's Improvements. When we stop to consider that in the United States alone during the past forty years, there has been built over seventy thousand miles of railroad, at a cost of four thousand million dollars, and that a very large proportion of the expense of construction was paid for hand labor with pick and shovel—excavating through hills, throwing up and ballasting road beds, filling trestle work, etc.—it seems passing strange that no other inventive genius has surmounted the difficulties and produced a machine that can perform so apparently simple a labor as to dig.

The demand for digging machines has been for many years well known to engineers, mechanics and laborers, but no one seems to have cared to enter the field in competition with the single machine that has heretofore proved successful. We cannot account for this seeming lack of interest on the part of inventors, on any other ground than that they acknowledge that the Otis Excavator as completely fills the want and as nearly approaches perfection as anything they could produce.

The Excavator is a somewhat complicated machine, and cannot be otherwise, as it has five motions, where a locomotive has but one. It has distinct motions to force the shovel forward into the bank, to drive it back, to raise it up, to swing it to the right or left over the spot where it is to deposit its load, and another to drop its contents—all executed by steam power, and most of them graduating and under the control of the engineer, so that where but little power is required, none need be wasted, or when crowding the shovel through a hard-pan bank, mixed with boulders, increased power can be instantly applied. Here allow us to remark that most of the hills in this country are hard-pan mixed with stone, and that cuttings through them by hand labor is very hard and very expensive work.

The Otis Excavator was originally designed for digging in loose material. The first machines built weighed about seventeen tons, and were more nearly perfect than such complicated machinery usually is at the start. The original inventor did not live to perfect the machine and bring it into general use, but it fell into good hands. Mr. O. S. Chapman, a practical railroad contractor who has been steadily engaged in the construction of railroads from the commencement of the first road in America, believing the invention had merit in it, and appreciating the advantages to be derived from the use of such machines, set himself to work to discover and remedy its defects, and to make it the practical success he believed it capable of becoming. Only the absolute use of a machine can ever thoroughly test its value for the purpose for which invented, and Mr. Chapman, when he subjected the original machine to the crucial test of absolute labor under unfavorable circumstances, discovered and overcame the obstacles that presented themselves. He made such alterations as were necessary to adapt it to digging in hard material, and greatly strengthened all its parts, increasing its weight some ten tons. Mr. Chapman secured seven patents for his improvements.

Since the Company commenced building these machines they have completed about two hundred and fifty for use in the United States. They have been used extensively in building railroads—cutting through hills, filling trestle work and for ballasting the road beds; also for filling in low and valueless lands in and about cities. The Back Bay and South Bay of Boston were filled in by these machines, adding more than one-third to the available territory of the original city proper; and transforming that portion of the city which was worthless and a nuisance into available and valuable property; some of the finest private residences being built on this made ground.

These machines are also used in large brick yards for shoveling clay, and by coal companies to load the coal into cars and boats; and their value can scarcely be overrated for any kind of shoveling where large quantities of heavy material is to be rapidly moved. We may here mention as a proof of their capacity to do heavy work expeditiously that one machine has shoveled sixteen hundred tons of broken coal into cars in one day.

Necessarily, the Excavator is a somewhat complicated machine, yet its movements are wonderful in their harmony and it has been said to approach nearer to "a thing of life" than any other large machine ever built. It requires only two men to operate it, one engineer, and a helper to work the crane; it consumes about 800 pounds of coal in ten hours, and accomplishes as much per day as would be done by from fifty to sixty laborers. It is operated on six sections of portable track of four foot lengths, and as fast as it digs ahead the hind sections are carried forward, and the machine advanced.

The advantages over hand labor derived from the use of the Excavator are many. For instance, in cutting through hills for a railroad bed, much more rapid progress can be made; the width of the cut affords room for the employment of but few men, while the Excavator does the work more rapidly than the largest practicable force of men could.

The Excavator can be controlled and kept to work at all times, while the class of laborers who shovel on railroads are not very reliable. Generally there is much time lost by them after pay day; a strike may occur at any time and the whole work be stopped for days or even weeks; while stormy weather necessarily prevents them from working during its continuance. The Excavator never loses time after pay day; it engages in no strikes, and as the two men who operate it are under cover, and the machine not only scoops up the earth from its native bed, but deposits it just where wanted on the car, bad weather does not effect its operations.

The strongest reason in favor of the Excavator however, is the great saving in expense over hand labor. One of these machines has excavated in gravel, and loaded into cars two thousand (2,000) cubic yards in one day;—but from ten hundred to twelve hundred cubic yards would be a fair day's work with the ordinary delays in making up trains for a long haul, and from three hundred to eight hundred cubic yards when working in hard material, varying with the hardness.

THE MANUFACTURE OF CLOCKS.

A Sketch of the American Clock Company.

Some method of recording the passing hours, has been in use from time immemorial, and the history of early devices for this purpose is replete with interest, but even a brief synopsis of the development of mechanical skill in this direction, from the construction of the primitive sun dial to the manufacture of the marvelous time pieces of the present day, would furnish material for an elaborate essay, and it is too expansive a topic for the limited space we are enabled to allow to this department.

To a very limited extent clocks were manufactured in this country prior to the war of the Revolution, but the business assumed no considerable magnitude until about the year 1807, when the introduction of machinery gave a marked impulse to the manufacturing interests. At this time a few enterprising parties commenced the manufacture of clocks in large quantities, a venture which was regarded as extremely hazardous, destined to certain failure. Happily, however, these forebodings were not realized.

The pioneer in this progressive movement was the late Mr. Seth Thomas, and the company which he organized in 1813, and which still bears his name, is the oldest established corporation in this department of manufactures in the United States. Their factory at Thomaston, Conn., is now the most extensive of its kind in the country.

Five of the largest clock manufactories in Connecticut have for some years been consolidated for general business purposes under the name of the American Clock Company, which represents them as Sole Agents, with headquarters at No. 581 Broadway, New York City.

The clock manufacturing companies represented in the consolidation are: the Seth Thomas Clock Co., Thomaston, Conn.; New Haven Clock Co., New Haven, Conn.; E. N. Welch Manufacturing Co., Forrestville, Conn.; Welch, Spring & Co., Forrestville, Conn., and Seth Thomas' Sons & Co. The combined productions of these establishments are about two-thirds of all the clocks made in the United States.

The Seth Thomas Clock Co's factory is a very extensive and completely equipped establishment, giving employment to about 500 workmen in the production of a class of goods which are perhaps as widely known and highly esteemed as any made. They include ordinary one and eight day time pieces, low priced but accurate and reliable; levers, with and without striking apparatus and alarm attachment, ranging somewhat higher in price; spring and weight striking clocks, wholesaled at from $3 to $18 each; and calendars, regulators and office clocks, both spring and weight, of the most finished styles varying in price from $10 to $40.

The calendar clocks are not only reliable time keepers, but combine the advantage of a perpetual and infallible calendar, showing the day of the week, the month and the day of the month (including the 29th of February in leap year,) and require no attention other than the regular winding of the time movement. This style is also furnished to order,

with the days of the month or week in French, Spanish or German.

The New Haven Clock Co. and the E. N. Welch Manufacturing Co., employ, respectively, 350 and 300 hands in the production of various popular styles of medium and low-priced clocks, ranging from $2 to $15, for office and household use. The patterns are very numerous, and their simplicity of construction and moderate cost render them emphatically the clocks for the million. These establishments each turn out clocks at the average rate of one per minute for each working hour of the day, and the demand is such as to prevent any accumulation of stock, even at this rapid rate of production.

Messrs. Welch, Spring & Co., manufacture a variety of one and eight day spring clocks, also fine mantel and regulator calendars, office clocks, etc., all of a high grade of workmanship, both as regards the movements and style of cases.

Messrs. Seth Thomas' Sons & Co., make a specialty of the very finest description of clock movements that mechanical skill can produce, equalling in every respect the work of the most celebrated European manufacturers, though offered at considerably lower prices. Their fine mantel clocks run for eighteen days, strike the hours and half hours, and tick almost noiselessly. Some are elegantly finished with black walnut or rosewood cases, but the majority are mounted upon standards of French bronze, slate, marble or verde antique bronze, wrought into the most elaborately artistic designs and forming parlor ornaments of the richest description. These beautiful time pieces vary in price from about $18 to $135, wholesale rates. The bronze and marble bases and ornamental figures are manufactured in this city, and show conclusively that we have no need to go abroad for the finest possible work in this department of decorative art.

The domestic trade of the five establishments before named is carried on exclusively through the medium of the New York Agency, and amounts annually to not less than $1,250,000. Each Company transacts its own export business separately, the aggregate value of foreign shipments reaching the yearly total of about $1,000,000.

The American Clock Co. have branch establishments at Chicago and San Francisco, the former located at No. 172 State Street, in charge of Mr. W. F. Tompkins, the latter at No. 520 Market Street.

Both at the New York warehouse and the branch stores a complete assortment of clock materials, including all the various parts required for repairs, is constantly on hand, also watch signs and other emblematic devices for dealers in clocks, watches, jewelry and fancy goods. It is certainly a matter wherein every true citizen may take pardonable pride when he reflects that the world has been so greatly benefited by the achievements of American inventive genius and mechanical skill in this important branch of industry, a fact which the publishers of "The Pictorial Album of American Industry" are truly proud to be able to chronicle and place by the side of other American achievements worthy of mention.

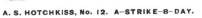

A. S. HOTCHKISS, No. 12. A-STRIKE-8-DAY.

Interior View of Rutland Marble Co's North Quarry.

Rutland Marble Co's (8 Gangs) Branch Mill, Salem, N. Y.

Interior View of Rutland Marble Co's South Quarry.

THE RUTLAND MARBLE COMPANY,

West Rutland, Vermont.

—:o:—

The Marble industry of Vermont, from small beginnings, has assumed large, and constantly increasing proportions. With the exception of some localities on the Southern extension of the Alleghany Mountain belt, Vermont contains nearly all the most valuable Marble known in this country East of the Rocky Mountains, and has within her borders, in a developed or undeveloped state, sufficient in quantity to supply the world and of a quality and variety surpassed by no other country.

Nearly all the marble quarries found in the State are located in the great valley immediately west of the Green Mountains, the deposit running northerly and southerly through the State. Experience having shown that the deposit at West Rutland is richer in extent and variety, better adapted to all the uses of marble and more accessible than any other, it is here that works on the most extensive scale have been established, and the largest amount of capital invested.

West Rutland is located in Vermont about eighty miles north of Troy, New York, twenty miles from the head of Lake Champlain, and on the Rensselaer and Saratoga Railroad, now leased and operated by the Delaware and Hudson Canal Company.

The first opening for marble was made in West Rutland in 1838. At that early date the process of quarrying was rude in the extreme, and being before the days of railroad facilities, the then slow method of transportation did not foster the business. In 1843, the late William F. Barnes, the pioneer in the marble business, commenced work upon the rich deposit that is now the property of the Rutland Marble Company. In 1850 a new impetus was given to the business by reason of the completion of railroads connecting with the quarries, and from that time to the present there has been a continued onward march of improvement and development. The introduction of machinery, and a world-wide demand for Rutland Marble, has extended and built up a business which is now one of the leading industries of the country.

The largest and most valuable part of the Marble Territory at West Rutland, is owned and worked by the Rutland Marble Company, extending northerly and southerly a distance of about 1600 feet, and embracing an upper and lower deposit of marble, with about seventy feet of lime rock between the two, (thus comprising a total length of 3,200 feet in the two deposits upon which to locate quarries, of which only one-third have been opened up,) the marble in both deposits lying in layers or strata, with a pitch or dip to the east at the surface, at an angle of about forty-five degrees.

The principal quarries worked upon the property are mainly on the lower deposit. One of these quarries having been worked to the depth of 250 feet, and at this depth is producing a fine quality of marble.

The layers in the deposits are classified as "White" and "Blue" the latter being the top and bottom strata, and the White lying in a body between the Blue in well defined layers, with natural riving beds between them, comprising an aggregate thickness in each deposit of from 50 to 70 feet.

These quarries are worked both by hand cutting and by steam channelling machines. In the former process the men stand upon the layer to be removed and by means of drills sharpened for the purpose, cut a channel of about one and one-half inches in width round a certain section of the

layer exposed, and to the depth of the layer which is afterward raised from its bed by wedges and broken or cut into square blocks of any size required (the usual size being six feet long by four feet wide) and the blocks are then taken out by means of Power Hoisting Derricks. After one layer is quarried, the same process is pursued with the next layer until all are removed.

Where quarrying is prosecuted by means of machinery such as the "Wardwell Steam Stone Channelling Machine" or the "Diamond Drill," a floor is first obtained, over which the machine traverses across all the layers cutting a channel to the required depth, producing a block from each layer in the deposit. Where the vein dips at an angle of 45 degrees, and the floors are level, as they must be for machine cutting, the blocks following the angle of dip come out in the figure or shape of a rhomb. Hand cutting where practicable possesses an advantage over machine cutting, in the production of better shaped blocks. The blocks of marble are sawed into various thicknesses depending upon the quality of marble, and the purposes to which it is to be put.

The marble of the Rutland Marble Company is very largely used for

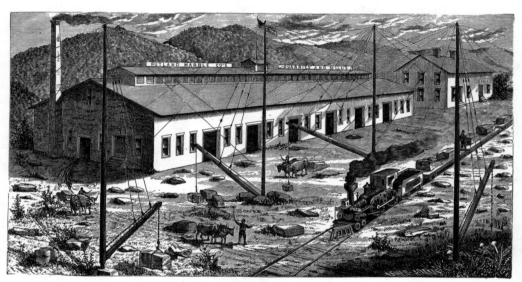

RUTLAND MARBLE CO'S MILLS, [24 Gangs] WEST RUTLAND, VT.

furniture, mantels, wainscoting, and interior decorative work, in addition to immense quantities required for cemetery uses, monumental and building purposes.

Different shades of Blue, dark, mottled, dove and common are obtained, and the White in all grades from Statuary to No. 3, with intervening shades, the value in market being regulated by the presence and degree of color.

All grades of marble produced by these quarries are used in commerce. The pure white is highly valued for Statuary and other purposes, and practically has no rival in the world. The Heroic Statue of Ethan Allen, at the Capitol of the State, Montpelier, was executed by Larkin G. Mead, from a statuary block produced from the quarries of this Company.

The annual product in gross sales of Marble taken from the West Rutland Quarries is now over $1,000,000 in value, about $500,000 of which is realized from the production of the Rutland Marble Company's quarries alone. In the sawing of the Company's product four mills are employed, with a combined capacity of sixty gangs of saws, of which the main one is a steam mill of twenty-four gangs, located at the quarries at West Rutland; one of eight gangs near Salem, New York; one of sixteen and one of twelve gangs, both located at Centre Rutland, as shown by the accompanying engravings, turning out the largest production of marble by any one company in the world.

The blocks of marble after being taken from the quarries, are placed on cars and taken to the mills, where they undergo the process of being sawed into slabs of various sizes, and thicknesses required by the trade. This process is accomplished by means of iron bands rolled from soft, tough iron three inches in width and of No. 10 wire guage in thickness, stretched within an iron or wooden frame and keyed tight into position. These frames under which the blocks are placed are called gangs, and are of different widths and lengths to accommodate blocks of all dimensions, and the iron bands, called saws, are more or less in number, depending upon the number and thickness of slabs to be obtained from the block, and are moved by power back and forth usually at the rate of 100 strokes per minute; geared, with a constant downward pressure, they penetrate the block by the use of sand and water, at the rate of one and one half to two inches per hour. So much of the product of the block as is

intended for or suitable for headstones or other purposes for which special dimensions are required, is removed from the mill to the coping or trimming shops, where by the use of proper tools for the purpose, it is broken out and trimmed to required sizes, when it is ready for shipment to dealers and manufacturers.

The annual product of the quarries of the Rutland Marble Company is about one million square feet of two inch marble (this being the standard thickness for computation,) and the shipments of block and sawed marble to and from the mills in which the Company are interested will reach 30,000 tons annually. The different quarries or openings made upon their property are five in number, and will aggregate over 1,000 feet in length, varying in depth as worked down upon the layers, from 100 to 250 feet, and the number of men employed, in the production of their marble, and fitting it for market ranges from 400 to 500.

The means and appliances at West Rutland for working the quarries, sawing the marble and general conduct of the business, consist of sixteen steam and horse power derricks, (most of them constructed to sustain and hoist blocks of from ten to fifteen tons weight); fourteen machines adapted to the cutting, splitting and raising the marble, each operated by independent steam engines of from four to ten horse power; four large power pumps for keeping water out of the quarries; two stationary engines, twenty and thirteen horse power; and large stationary engine of two hundred and fifty horse power, which operates the twenty-four gang steam mill, and other machinery, (the mill being 275 ft. long x 82 ft. wide); coal and sand house, 300 ft. long x 30 ft. wide; two coping shops, 60 x 30 feet; a covered storage and loading building 50 x 100, with switch and side tracks; a machine shop for making all repairs on the premises, a stone house and twenty-five tenement buildings constructed to accomodate one hundred and twenty-five families.

The sixteen and twelve gang mills at Centre Rutland, operated by Messrs. Clements and Ripleys, and the eight gang mill at Salem, New York, operated by the Baxter Manufacturing Company, are engaged solely in sawing the product of the Rutland Marble Company's quarries, employ a large force of men, and are fitted with the most improved appliances for the business.

In comparison with imported marbles of similar description it is the opinion of the most prominent judges that Rutland Marble equals, if not excels, them all in durability, beauty and cheapness. In the finer grades it has no competitor, but in the inferior qualities, it meets with strong competition from imported marbles, although of late years its superiority has come to be acknowledged and it is now in general use throughout the country, especially for monumental and interior ornamental work.

In the limits of so brief an article it is not possible to convey to the minds of casual readers a just conception of the magnitude of this home industry, and of its importance to the State of Vermont and the country at large. The removal of the marble from the quarries and its preparation at the mills furnishes employment to thousands of men in the aggregate, in addition, its transportation requires the use of the railroad, canal and shipping interests to a very large extent, and in its sale, diffusion and preparation for consumption, it is not beyond the truth to say that it provides occupation for tens of thousands of the active workers of the country, and for many millions of its capital.

Centre Rutland Mill, (16 Gangs,) Clement & Sons.

Centre Rutland Mill, (12 Gangs,) Ripley Sons.

of marble into suitable sizes and shapes for market. It is undoubtedly the largest mill in the world used for sawing marble. It has forty-eight gangs of saws, running day and night, with from ten to forty saws in each gang. The machinery is driven by engines of three hundred horse power. The blocks of marble are hoisted from the quarries by the same power that moves the machinery of the mill. In quarrying, sawing and shifting marble, they now employ three hundred and fifty men, besides Steam Stone Channelling Machines in their quarries. Sheldons & Slason ship to the trade, in sawed marble, about ten thousand tons annually.

An estimate of the large facilities of the firm may be formed from the fact that they have agreed to furnish the contractors, two hundred and forty thousand Soldiers' Head Stones for the National Cemeteries during the years 1875-76. This will involve an additional shipment over six thousand tons of sawed marble annually. This they can do without interfering with their regular business, which, with the Government contract, will make the production from their quarries over sixty thousand tons of blocks in the next two years and sawing and fitting the same for shipment.

The Soldiers' Headstones are finished upon the premises of Sheldons & Slason. They are lettered by the use of "Sand Blast," an invention of B. C. Tilghman of Philadelphia, Pa., but first brought into extensive practical use in connection with this work by the contractors for the government cemeteries. The stones, after being headed and polished by machinery, go into the hands of boys who set the inscription with metallic letters or type on the face with shellac. An iron shield protects the outer edges of the face of the stone, which now comes under the blast. This is simply a process by which sand is driven upon the face of the stone by steam under a high pressure, through a short gun barrel, cutting out every part not protected by the metallic letters and shield, which, being removed, leaves a raised inscription in a sunken shield or panel, of about one-eighth of an inch in depth. The process is very rapid, finishing one stone, having any number of letters, in about four minutes, thus doing the work of as many hours by hand labor. The lettering is uniform and regular, and the finished slab is exceedingly artistic and acceptable. About four hundred and fifty headstones are turned out daily at the Company's mill. In addition to the quarries of Sheldons & Slason, there are six others, supplying mills, having in the aggregate ninety six gangs of saws. Two of the mills, one with twenty-four and one with eight gangs of saws, are situated at the quarries, the balance of the ninety-six gangs are in mills at Center Rutland, Castleton, Hydeville and Fairhaven. All of the mills have railroad connection

MARBLE QUARRIES AND MILL
OF
SHELDONS & SLASON,
WEST RUTLAND, VERMONT.

The village of West Rutland, near which the largest and most valuable marble quarries in America are located, is in the West Parish of Rutland, State of Vermont, about eighty miles north of the city of Troy, New York.

At a distance of eighty rods north from the railroad depot is a range of hills rising two hundred feet above the bottom lands. On the western slope of these hills and near the base, crops out the world famous "Rutland Marble." Starting from the railroad depot and going north, a short walk places the visitor at the three large quarries of Sheldons & Slason. That the reader may at once obtain some idea of the magnitude of the business of this firm we deem it well to state just here that during the past twenty-five years, marble has been taken from a portion of these quarries to the depth of two hundred and fifty feet. The amount of labor required to excavate this immense "hole in the ground," and to prepare its product for market seems so enormous that naturally, the first enquiry of the beholder is, "How was all this stone taken out?" and then, "To what useful purpose has it been applied?"

A ramble through the works in company with one of the genial gentlemen attached to the firm, and an examination of the mechanical appliances which they have introduced will answer the first question, while a few moments time spent in recounting the many uses to which marble is adapt-

ed will answer the second. The quarries at West Rutland were first opened about the year 1845. In the beginning the business was limited and not very profitable, as, in the absence of railroads, the entire product had to be hauled by teams from the quarries to Whitehall, New York, the nearest shipping point, a distance of twenty-one miles. The completion of railroads in 1851 gave an impetus to the business and notwithstanding the strong prejudice of the American people in favor of anything foreign, the business has been steadily increasing, the demand being in excess of the capacity to supply.

In the spring of 1850, Messrs. Sheldons & Slason erected an "eight gang" mill, running nine months in the year, in day-time only, and then more nearly met the demand than they can do now with a "forty-eight gang" mill running day and night all the months of the year. This new steam mill is situated near the quarries, and is used for sawing the blocks

with the quarries. In addition to the blocks supplied to mills connected in interest with the quarries, from three to five thousand tons of blocks are sold annually and shipped to mills in various parts of the country.

The marble from the West Rutland quarries has heretofore been principally used for mantels, monuments and gravestones, but within a few years it has been quite extensively used by sculptors for statuary purposes and largely introduced in the internal ornamental work in public buildings. With other marbles, but under an assumed name, it appears prominently in the elaborate finish of the "Gold Room," at Washington, D. C., and also in the "Art Building" and the "Mutual Life" in Philadelphia. In banks and other large buildings in New York and other large cities throughout the Union, it is being used for panels, mouldings, counters, etc. The best and most expensive mantles in this country are manufactured from the statuary marble taken from these quarries. One of

the great drawbacks in the introduction of new American products, whether they be the natural productions of the country, or the result of native inventive genius, is the disposition of our people to give foreign articles the preference. In reference to marble this has notably been the case. When the American stone was first offered in competition with imported goods there were few who were willing to test its merits or even to acknowledge that it might possess any, that is, for the finer uses to which marble is put. Its purity of color could hardly be questioned, for those possessing eyes to see, upon comparing it with the choicest foreign stones, at once acknowledged that on that point there was no room for cavil. Its fineness of grain and its susceptibility of the most beautiful polish were equally apparent.

Its purity of color, its fineness and its adaptability to fine finish being conceded, the only remaining point was: Is it durable? Time and exposure to the elements must settle that point, and after a thirty years test, the Rutland Marble is immeasurably in advance of all foreign competitors. As to the durability of the Rutland, as compared with Italian marble for monumental purposes. Messrs. Strothers & Son, of Philadelphia, (one of the oldest and most eminent marble manufacturing firms in America) say:

"We have yet to see a monument or any out door work in Italian marble which has been exposed to our climate for twenty years that is not comparatively a ruin. Having been familiar with Rutland marble for monumental or other out door work, a quarter of a century and having as yet, seen no signs of its decay, we recommend Rutland marble as being in our judgment far superior to Italian where it is to be exposed to the effects of our variable climate."

Certainly no better evidence as to the merits of the Rutland marble could be given to convince those who doubt its durability, (if such there be) that they are in error, than the test of time, which has in every instance of our observation resulted in its favor. But we think the period of doubting has passed, and to-day the Rutland marbles are generally conceded to be as nearly perfect as any in the world.

These quarries are approached from Troy by the Rutland and Washington Railroad, via: Salem, N. Y., by the Troy and Boston and Western Vermont Railroads, through Bennington, Manchester and Rutland. From Troy or Schenectady, by the Delaware and Hudson Canal Co's Roads, through Saratoga Springs and Whitehall, N. Y., and by the Central Vermont Railroads from Montreal, Ogdensburgh and Burlington on the North, and from Boston through Bellows Falls on the East. A branch road runs from the depot at West Rutland to the quarries.

SCAPPLING-GROUND [SHALER & HALL'S QUARRY.]

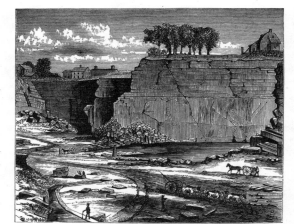

STRATA OF ROCKS IN BRAINERDS' QUARRY.

SCAPPLING-GROUND [BRAINERDS' QUARRY].

BROWN FREESTONE QUARRIES

OF THE MIDDLESEX QUARRY COMPANY, BRAINERDS & CO., and
THE SHALER & HALL QUARRY COMPANY,
PORTLAND, CONN.

——:o:——

On the banks of the Connecticut River, at Portland, Middlesex Co., Conn., are situated the celebrated Brown Freestone Quarries, from whence come the no less celebrated "brown stone fronts" which ornament with their palatial proportions and adornments, the aristocratic portions of New York City.

These quarries have been worked to a greater or less extent for more than two centuries.

They are by far the largest quarries in the world. Some idea of their magnitude may be formed from our illustrations, and from the fact that they cover an area of 175 acres. During the busy season they give employment to 1500 laborers, and 100 horses and mules; the cities of New York, Brooklyn, Boston, Washington and Philadelphia being the principal markets, though there is considerable demand for it from all parts of the Union.

VIEW OF AREA IN MIDDLESEX QUARRY.

at Windsor, Rocky Hill, Cromwell and Portland in Connecticut; but only at the latter place is the stone of perfect quality and suitable from its color and durability for building purposes. Even at Portland itself, out of the five hundred acres of deposit, only two hundred acres contain merchantable stone.

Most of the tombstones in the old grave yards at Middletown and Portland are of this material; the oldest inscription we can discover is 1689, as clear and legible as when first carved.

In these yards the marble monuments of equal antiquity have disappeared or are crumbling to pieces, while their more humble and less assuming companions of brown stone, still bid defiance to the elements. In 1836 an association of Hartford undertook to repair the monuments in the old burial ground in that city, which had been abandoned about thirty years. They re-set all the monuments, in number about five hundred. This step was taken with a view of determining the most durable stone for a monument to be erected as a memorial of the first settlers of the town of Hartford. They decided upon the Portland stone, having discovered that other stones, including marble, were very much decayed, the parts being decomposed and crumbling, whereas the tombs of Portland stone, many of them bearing inscriptions two centuries old, had not been affected by the weather.

We quote two extracts relating to the early history of these quarries:

"Sept. 4th, 1665. At a towne-meeting it was voated that whosoever shall dig or raise stones at ye rocks on the east side of the river for any without the towne, the said digger shall be none but an inhabitant of Middletown, and shall be responsible to ye towne twelve pence per tunn, for every tunn of stones that he shall digg; this money to be paid in wheat and pease."

The historical Hancock House at Boston, was built of this stone 139 years ago; the contract was made between Mr. Thomas Hancock and

Again, when the old Hancock House was taken down, after having defied the elements for over 130 years, it was found that the stone was as sound and perfect as when first used.

It is impossible to produce any stronger evidence of the durability of this stone.

The avenues and streets of New York, where this stone is most extensively used, present a striking and unique picture to one accustomed to the gray, red and yellow stones of European cities; these in hot glaring sunshine, tire the eye with their brilliant reflections; our brownstone fronts present an agreeable and soothing aspect.

VIEW OF THE BROWN FREESTONE QUARRIES ON THE CONNECTICUT RIVER, PORTLAND, CONN.

"Thomas Johnson of Middletown, in the County of Hartford and Colony of Connecticut, in New England, stone-cutter." The equivalent paid to Johnson was "the sum of Three Hundred Pounds, in goods as the said stone-cutter's work is carryed on."

Deposits of freestone occur at various localities through the valley of the Connecticut, notably at Long Meadow in Massachusetts, and

One advantage which they possess over marble or other material that glistens in sunlight is that they reveal the beautiful points of architecture at a glance.

OLD BURIAL GROUND, PORTLAND.

RIVER FRONT OF MIDDLESEX QUARRY.

EXCAVATIONS IN MIDDLESEX QUARRY, LOOKING TOWARD THE RIVER.

VIEW OF GENERAL QUARRY WORK IN BRAINERD'S QUARRY.

SOUTH-EASTERN CORNER OF SHALER & HALL'S QUARRY.

VIEW OF SHALER & HALL'S QUARRY.

CABINET CASE.
OPEN.

THE TYPE WRITER,

DENSMORE, YOST & COMPANY,

GENERAL AGENTS.

707 BROADWAY. N. Y.

——:o:——

Among the most important inventions of the present era certainly may be classed the Type-Writer. It is the culmination of successive efforts to develop an instrument to print easily and rapidly one letter or character at a time, and one after another, as in writing with the pen.

During the winter of 1866–67, Mr. C. Latham Sholes, a native of Pennsylvania, but an active, prominent citizen of Wisconsin, residing at Milwaukee, and Collector of Customs at that port, was engaged in developing a numbering and paging-machine—an instrument to print numerals following each other in any desired order, on checks, certificates, blank book pages, and the like. And during the same winter Mr. Carlos Glidden, also a citizen of Milwaukee, Wisconsin, but a native of Ohio, was engaged in developing an improved "Digger," an instrument to dig instead of plow the ground for agriculture. These gentlemen chanced to have their machines constructed at the same establishment and, became acquainted with each other's work. Mr. Glidden closely watched the progress of the paging machine and became impressed with the idea that the principle involved might be more widely employed than in the mere numbering of pages and checks. "Why not print letters and words as well as figures and numbers?" he asked. Mr. Sholes caught the idea, and the finished result is the Type-Writer. But it was not made at one happy stroke of genius: the inventors found many difficulties to overcome and it was only after years of patient experiment that the end sought for was fully attained. An instrument which would work was made in 1867; another and better, early in 1868; still another and better later that same year; and yet others and better thereafter; till, early in 1873, there had been fifty experimental machines made, each succeeding one different from and an improvement on its predecessor, and the invention was substantially completed.

In 1873, E. Remington & Sons, proprietors of the Remington Amory, Ilion, New York, undertook the manufacture of the Type-Writer, and Mr. Jefferson M. Clough, the superintendent, and Mr. William K. Jenne their chief artist took the machine as Mr. Sholes left it and dressed it in its present beautiful form.

The Type-Writer in size and appearance resembles the family sewing machine. It is graceful and ornamental, making it a beautiful piece of furniture for any office, study, or parlor.

The Type-Writer is simple in principle and construction. It is worked by means of forty-four circular keys in four rows, banked like those of an organ. Its simple mechanism consists of a series of types or type-levers pivoted on the circumference of a circle, at an angle of about forty-five degrees, the circle being fixed in a horizontal position, and the fulcra of its type-levers so adjusted that a slight depression of the outer arm or lever brings its type up to the centre of the common circle, and thus the types, when raised in succession, arrive at a common printing point. The paper, by suitable mechanism, is caused to pass over the types at this printing point, and the "writing" is effected after the manner of the familiar hand-stamp, but reversed i. e., a type is thrust up against the paper, and the ink is supplied by an intervening ribbon, previously saturated with the desired coloring matter—red, blue, mauve, or black. A system of "stringing" connects the type-levers with the keys, which are compactly arranged, each having upon its surface a plain impression of the character or figure which it represents. Any child who can read and understand the use of these characters, has only to spell out the desired word by striking the keys

BUSINESS DESK AND TYPE WRITER COMBINED.
CLOSED.

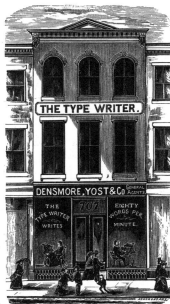

THE TYPE WRITER.

DENSMORE, YOST & Co. GENERAL AGENTS

THE TYPE WRITER WRITES 707 EIGHTY WORDS PER MINUTE.

TYPE WRITER SALESROOM, 707 BROADWAY.

with about the same force required in practising the five-finger exercise on a piano, and the "writing" is neatly and correctly done. Rapidity is acquired by good "fingering" and practice, just as it is attained on musical instruments.

The speed of rapid writers with the pen seldom reaches thirty

TYPE WRITER, SHOWING KEY BOARD.

words a minute. An expert operator on the Type-Writer will easily accomplish sixty words a minute, while some claim to be able to continuously write from ninety to one hundred words a minute. The only limit to its speed is the ability of the operator to strike the keys and the relative difference between writing with the pen and with it may be stated as the difference between making a . (dot) and forming a letter, as a single stroke prints the character. It writes on any kind or quality of paper, from the thinest, finest tissue to the thickest, coarsest wrapping, and it is adapted to sheets of any width or length—the paper may be in ordinary sheets or in a continuous roll. It "manifolds" twenty copies at once if desired, without any of the fatigue incident to the use of the stylus, while an almost infinitely better result is secured, [to merchants and bankers who send out daily statements, and to telegraph companies, news agencies, and many others this feature is of the greatest importance], and when copying ink is used from one to three copies can be taken by an ordinary copy-press.

The writing of this machine is fully as legible as print, and nearly as uniform and beautiful. There are several styles of type used; letters somewhat smaller but very similar to those forming the first and third lines of the heading to this article, being those most frequently selected by purchasers. The vexatious mistakes, annoyances, and waste of time incident to illegible pen-writing are therefore avoided.

A person of ordinary intelligence will learn the location of the key for every character in a couple of hours; this accomplished, an hours'

practice every day for a month will enable one to write faster than with the pen : and as the operator on the machine can write with any finger of either hand, and can sit in any desired position, it is manifest that the drudgery of writing with the pen, whereby a single set of muscles is used and a constrained position of the body necessitated, is overcome. Editors, copyists, and others whose time is largely occupied with writing, need have no fear of pen paralysis, loss of sight, or curvature of the spine from using the machine. It is little else than recreation to use it for any reasonable length of time.

No piece of mechanism produced within the present century has met with a more unqualified success than this. The first of the perfected machines were placed upon the market in July 1874, and on the 30th day of June 1875, 1005 had been made, sold, and shipped to the purchasers, and the sale is increasing most rapidly. It has been bought by merchants, lawyers, editors, bankers, ministers, stenographers, telegraph and railroad companies, essayists, copyists, teachers,—by all cultured classes, and all are more than satisfied with it. Mr. Anson Stager, General Superintendent of the Western Union Telegraphic Company, and President of the Western Electric Manufacturing Company, in behalf of those companies has contracted for a large number of Machines and in speaking of the merit of the invention, says : "Having used the Type-Writter two years, I express my conviction of its great value. It is a complete writing machine. Writing can be done with it easier, faster, and better than is possible with the pen." General Meigs, Quartermaster General of the United States Army, bought one to test it, and then took seven more for the use of his office, and certifies, that his clerks can write faster and better with the Machine than without. Mr. James O. Clephane, late clerk and official stenographer of the Supreme Court of the District of Columbia, has eight Machines in use in his business, and says of them, "Not only does the Type-Writer combine expedition, compactness, uniformity, neatness, and legibility, but it affords entire relief from the severe labor of the pen. I have myself worked it ten to twelve consecutive hours, with little or no fatigue, and having used it two years, I have found it two to three times the speed of the pen." Mr. E. Payson Porter, President of the National Telegraphic College, at Chicago, receives messages with it with a facility no sender can equal ; indeed, with only one hand he can receive with it so no sender can "rush" him ; and he says of it, "I unhesitatingly affirm that twice the work of the pen may be done with it, and with less fatigue." The great commercial agents, Dun, Barlow & Co., who have offices in every principal city of the country, have bought and put seventy-five machines into use in their business.

We might add scores of equally strong indorsements from well known men, but these are sufficient to prove its value. In a few words : It is to the pen what the sewing-machine is to the needle, and its use is destined to become as universal as culture and enlightenment.

Messrs. Densmore, Yost & Co., the General Agents for the Type-Writer, 707 Broadway, between Fourth Street and Washington Place, New York, or the local agents in the important cities throughout the country, will gladly exhibit and explain the operation of the machine to all who call at their warerooms, or if such a visit is not practicable, they will, in answer to inquiries through the mail, forward descriptive circulars and pamphlets which will give the reader all the further information desired in regard to this, which, if it be not the crowning achievment is at least a very meritorious production of American ingenuity, and one destined to become as popular and of as universal use in the counting room and office as the sewing machine is in the dwelling—for the simple reason that it will save as much time and labor in our business houses as the sewing machine saves in our dwellings.

CABINET CASE.
CLOSED.

BUSINESS DESK AND TYPE WRITER COMBINED.
OPEN.

Oliver's Patent Revolving Self-Setting Trap.

Heavy Window Guard.

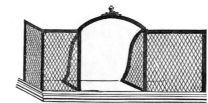

Desk, Bank and Counter Railing.

Galvanized Twist Netting.

Brass and Iron Wire Riddles.

THE AMERICAN WIRE WORKS,

Nos. 106 and 108 Beekman Street, New York

Established 1835

E. Oliver, having a life-long practical experience in manufacturing wire goods of all descriptions, of which Rat Traps have been a leading feature, has invented several improvements of ingenious construction, some of which are illustrated here.

Moulders Brass and Iron Wire Riddles, extra heavy, Heavy Crimp Wire Window Guards suitable for Asylums, Prisons, Factories &c., Brass, Copper and Iron Wire Cloth for all kinds of purposes. Flower Pot Stands, Wire Chairs and Settees for Cemeteries and Gardens, Meal and Flour Sieves. Wire Railing for Offices, Bank Counters, Cemeteries, &c., and Wire goods in general. Galvanized Twist Wire, Netting for Fencing for Sheep, Goats, Dogs, Hogs, Poultry, &c. The cheapest fence made. Garden and Lawn Fencing, &c.

The Patent Decoy Trap, is one of the most effectual Rat Catchers that was ever

Office Railing.

invented, the principle on which it is constructed being the secret of its success. Seventeen rats have been caught in one setting. Mr. Oliver has received letters from numbers of individuals who have used this trap, speaking of its success in freeing them of their troublesome neighbors, the rats. An experience of over forty years, enables him to state that the Decoy Trap is decidedly the simplest and cheapest. One person has caught from one to eight hundred Rats in this simple Decoy Trap. It catches more rats, is not liable to get out of order and gives the best proof of its superiority over other traps. From three to four thousand of these traps have been sold on their own merits, no special effort having been made to introduce it. With proper management we see no failure with this trap.

There could be much more said upon the merits of the Decoy Trap, as also upon the many other articles which Mr. Oliver manufactures, but our limited space will not permit us to mention them, but to any one desiring any thing in his line, we say "call and examine his wares."

For further information our readers are refered to the illustrated catalogue of this house, or they may call on Mr. E. Oliver at his extensive warerooms, No. 106 & 108 Beekman St. New York.

Oliver's Patent Decoy Rat Trap.

Garden Arch.

INSIDE MOULDER.

DAVIS & GLEDHILL,

Manufacturers of Wood Working Machinery,

48 De Witt St., Albany, New York.

Prominent among the manufacturers of Wood Working Machinery is the firm of Davis & Gledhill. In the limited space at our command we can mention but few of the many labor saving appliances made by them, among which are: Woodworth's Planing

DOUBLE SLAT PLANER.

WOODWORTH'S PLANING MACHINE.

Machine, which is so well and favorably known as to need no encomium from us; the Double Slat Plane, which will dress Blind Slats, Blind Stiles, Sash Muntins and Small Mouldings of any description, a machine not excelled; the Excelsior Stile Boring Machine, indispensable to Sash and Blind Makers who wish to executework with accuracy and dispatch; a Dovetail Machine, which will Dovetail Sash more rapidly than they can be tenoned and mortised, besides doing it with perfect accuracy; a machine for sand papering doors, or any other flat surfaces; Knowles Cutter Head, superior for tonguing and grooving or jointing plank or boards, combining strength and simplicity; Surface Planing Machines for surfacing plank and boards, and in fact any material from four inches down to as thin as required; The Blind Slat Sawing Machine, for sawing blind slats, cutting one and one-quarter inch stuff into three slats; a Blind Rail Boring Machine, designed for cutting the recess in the rail, or the reception of blind rod,

when the slats are closed; machines for pinning sash, and scores of other ingenious devices, which automatically perform the labor of skilled mechanics and consequently cheapen production. All the machines manufactured by this firm are made of the best material, and by practical workmen.

RITCHIE & SON, MANUFACTURERS OF PATENT PAD-LOCKS.

15 Railroad Avenue, Newark, N. J.

The Railroad Car and Switch Padlock of Ritchie & Son, has been in constant use upon nearly all the railroads in the United States, Canada and South America for the past twenty-four years, during which time many improvements have been made in its construction. A long and severe test has proved it to be a first-class and reliable padlock for railroads, stores, safes, etc. Their work shop is under the supervision of a first-class mechanic of over twenty-four years experience in this business, and affords every facility for maintaining the high standard of excellence which is accorded to their goods. Their manufactory is situated at 15 Railroad Avenue, Newark, N. J.

BROCKETT & TUTTLE, CARRIAGE MANUFACTURERS,

New Haven, Conn.

This firm, established in 1862, determined to make none but the best work. Having adhered to this resolution their business has grown with astonishing rapidity, and they stand to-day among the first carriage manufacturers in the country. They now turn out about six hundred carriages a year. A speciality with Brockett & Tuttle is their fine Light Family Phaeton, and the careful attention they bestow upon its manufacture has created for it a great demand. Their gentlemen's road wagons, too, are marked favorites. That this firm have in so short a time taken rank with acknowledged first-class makers of thrice their age, is proof of the superiority of their work.

The Celebrated Patent Agraffe Piano-Fortes.

Sohmer & Co., Manufacturers.

The wonderful increase in the manufacture of Piano Fortes in the United States, is exemplified by the fact that it has reached the rank of the Third Estate in our manufacturing industries; paying over $3,000,000 annually in wages; consuming about $3,000,000 in materials; and reaching about $9,000,000 in the annual amount of sales. The piano-forte is in reality first in importance among musical instruments, whether we consider its high place in popular esteem, its wide spread social influence, or the extent of its manufacture. The number sold for use in the United States alone, in 1870, amounted to twenty-three thousand, independent of the many additional thousands exported to European and other countries. The piano is now found even in the farm houses and dwellings of the humbler classes of artisans and laborers in our cities, as well as in the palatial residences of the wealthy.

Sohmer & Co., Piano Manufactory, Cor. of 14th St., and 3rd Ave., N. Y.

Two Doors from the Academy of Music.

Our manufacturers possess many advantages in the selection of woods, of which a considerable variety is used in the piano-forte. The perfect tone of this instrument greatly depends upon the complete seasoning of the woods, especially in the sound-board. The clearness and dryness of our climate materially contribute to the superior adaptability of American woods for the construction of a first-class piano.

Few are aware of the amount of care, patient experiment, expense and skill required to produce pianos, in their present state of perfection in all their numerous parts, so harmoniously put together, and exhibiting so much thought, that, when played upon by a master-hand, their tones seem almost those of an intelligent being.

No home can now be considered completely furnished without the presence of a good piano-forte, and it appears scarcely necessary to remark, that by proper care in selecting the best at the outset, purchasers will always find themselves in possession of a reliable, never failing source of pleasure, in the circles of domestic life.

THE LEIGHTON BRIDGE AND IRON WORKS, ROCHESTER, NEW YORK.

BRIDGE BUILDING,

Represented by

THE LEIGHTON BRIDGE & IRON WORKS,

Rochester, N. Y.

At what date in the world's progress, bridges were first constructed, history does not inform us ; neither are we informed by what method streams were originally crossed which could not be forded.

The first bridges of which we have any account were built of wood. But very ancient stone bridges of great magnitude are found in China.

Abydos, a City of Asia, directly opposite Sestos in Europe, with which, from the narrowness of the Hellespont, it seemed to those who approached it by sea, to form only one town, became famous in Classic history for the bridge of boats which Xerxes built there across the Hellespont, about 480 years before the Christian era. The insecurity of such bridges is well illustrated in the fact that when Xerxes reached the Hellespont he found the bridge of boats destroyed by the storms, and he crossed the strait in a small fishing vessel.

The emperor Trajan, also entered the enemy's country by throwing a bridge across the rapid streams of the Danube, A. D. 105, and a battle was fought in which the slaughter was so great, that in the Roman Camp, linen was wanted to dress the wounds of the soldiers. This bridge is said to have been 4,770 feet in length.

Brotherhoods for building bridges existed in South France as early as A. D. 1180. A Triangular bridge is refered to at Croyland Abbey, in a Charter dated, 943. From 1100-18, the first stone bridge was erected at Bow, near Stratford, by Queen Matilda, during the reign of Henry I., of England. A bridge is known to have existed at London as early as 978. The first iron bridge was built over the Severn at Shropshire, England,1777. Sunderland bridge was built by Wilson, 100 feet high, with a span 236 feet, in 1796.

The fine Suspension Bridge at Menai Strait was built in 1825. The celebrated Suspension Bridge two miles below Niagara Falls is one of the finest structures of the kind in the world. It is a single span of 800 feet, suspended about 250 feet above water. It is supported by more than 8,000 wires, whose estimated strength is supposed to equal a strain of 10,000 to 12,000 tons. This bridge was completed in 1855.

One of the widest bridges in the world is that across the Thames by which the London, Chatham and Dover Railway enters Victoria Station, Pimlico. This bridge was founded by Lord Harris, 1865.

The Britannia Tubular Suspension Bridge, one of the most wonderful enterprises of engineering in the world, was constructed about one mile south of the Menai Strait Suspension Bridge, already referred to.

VIEW OF RAILROAD BRIDGE OVER CONNECTICUT RIVER, SPRINGFIELD, MASS.

At the centre of the Strait is a rock called the Britannia Rock, the surface of which is about ten feet above low water level, on which is built a tower, two hundred feet above water. This tower supports two lines of tubes, strong enough for laden trains. The ends of these tubes rest on abutments on the shore and each tube is more than one fourth mile in length. The height of the tube within is thirty feet at Britannia tower and diminishing to twenty feet at either abutment. The lifting of these tubes to their places was considered the most gigantic operation of the kind, ever successfully performed. The first locomotive passed through this bridge in 1850.

One of the most stupendous tubular bridges in the world, is that over the St. Lawrence River in Canada.

The rapid increase in the extension of railroads and highways in this country especially through the more hilly or mountainous regions, where streams and mountain gorges are numerous, has tended largely to increase the demand for substantial iron bridges especially those made of wrought iron which experience has proved to be the safest and most economical.

One of the most extensive and favorably known manufacturers of Iron Bridges is Mr. Thomas Leighton, owner and manager of the celebrated Leighton Bridge and Iron Works, Rochester, New York.

Bridge making calls for a special class of engineering skill, and Americans, to-day, stand prominent among the bridge builders of the world. Iron bridges devised and erected by American skill are used in every country of the civilized world, and have universally received unqualified approbation. American bridges are noted for their strength, their graceful appearance, the rapidity with which the parts can be put together, and the great ease with which an impaired part can be replaced.

The Hudson River is crossed at Albany, N. Y., by an iron double track railroad bridge, built by the Leighton Bridge and Iron Works, of which Mr. Thos. Leighton is owner and manager. The engraving at the foot of this page affords a fine view of this magnificent structure. The cut heading this page represents the works of this company at Rochester, N. Y., and the centre picture is a view of the railroad bridge across the Connecticut River, at Springfield, Conn., also built by Thos. Leighton. The works of this company are scattered over all the land, and each separate structure is an enduring monument to their fame.

With ample capital, every aid that inventive genius can supply, and a complete corps of skilled workmen, they are always ready to undertake works of every degree of magnitude, and to promply and faithfully execute them.

VIEW OF BRIDGE OVER THE HUDSON AT ALBANY, N. Y. BUILT BY THE LEIGHTON BRIDGE AND IRON WORKS.

No. 2, Incline Power Press, with Spring Barrel Attachment.

BLISS & WILLIAMS,

Manufacturers of

PRESSES, DIES and SPECIAL MACHINERY

for Sheet Metal Workers,

167 to 173 PLYMOUTH STREET,

Cor. Jay Street,   BROOKLYN, N. Y.

:o:

A sketch of the improvements that have been made in the manufacture of tin and other sheet metal wares during the past half century would doubtless prove interesting to many of our readers, but within the brief space at our disposal, such a sketch is impossible. Suffice it to say that the first attempts to manufacture tin or similar wares from a single sheet were only made some twenty-five years ago; the apparatus used was a drop hammer, and the productions were known as "stamped" or "dropped" wares. These goods were favorably received by the public, and there was soon a demand for a wider range of goods than was first made. To meet this demand larger and better machinery must be devised; several of the leading manufacturers planned machines, and had them built at great expense, only to find that they did not fully meet their requirements.

In 1867 the firm of Mays & Bliss was

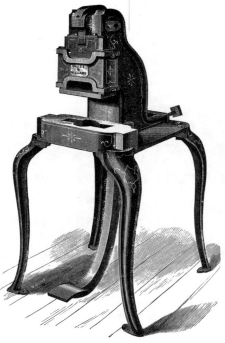

Pendulum Press, No. 3.

the same year the present firm, Bliss & Williams, was organized. The new firm were fully determined to overcome the difficulties which had beset previous inventors and manufacturers. In this they were successful, and in a short time they extended their manufactures so as to embrace the larger class of machines desired by sheet metal workers. Within the space at our disposal it is impossible to describe the machines manufactured by them. They embrace almost everything of value in the shape of power machines used by sheet metal workers. They make nearly every size and description of Power Cutting, Drawing, and Double Action, also Screw,

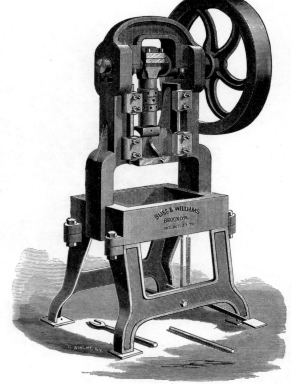

Straight Sided Power Press,

ments, spoons, forks, silver and plated ware, watches and jewelry; and in the manufacture of metallic powder kegs, powder flasks, miners' lamps, white lead and lard pail, tin cans and boxes for varnishes, oils, paints, spices, meats, fish, oysters, fruits, vegetables, condensed milk, baking and seidlitz powders, shoe blacking, etc. They also make Power Presses, with feed attachments, for cutting photographic, playing and other cards, pail ears, buttons, etc.; machines for threading small screws and for making sheet metal screws; machines for polishing and capping paint cans and crimping tops on white lead pails; slitting shears with gang cutters for paste board and sheet metals; automatic machines for forming rings and handles for cans, dripping pans, etc; lantern presses, —in fact they are prepared at all times to give estimates upon dies and special machinery upon receipt of pattern or specifications, or to devise and construct new machines for working sheet metals.

In this class of machinery the United States is far ahead of the balance of the world, and the firm of Bliss & Williams rank first among American manufacturers,

Upright Lever Press, No, 1.

No. 6, Power Drawing Press.

Bench Drop Press.

formed for the purpose of manufacturing small Presses and Dies. Their factory was originally located at No. 120 Plymouth Street, Brooklyn, but they subsequently secured the present premises, 167 to 173 Plymouth Street, corner of Jay.

The firm of Mays & Bliss was dissolved in 1870, and in December of

Lever, Pendulum, and Drop Presses; the uses to which they are applicable are very numerous, being employed by manufacturers of house-furnishing wares, sheet iron goods, gas fixtures, lanterns, lamp burners and trimmings, copper bottoms, coal hods, shovels, agricultural implements, lock work, carriage parts, curry combs, bird cages, toys, buttons, and brass orna-

both in quantity and quality of production. They have not only sent machinery to every part of the United States, including California, Oregon and Washington Territory, but they have shipped Presses and other machinery to England, Scotland, France, Switzerland, Norway, Sweden, China, Java, the West Indies, Australia and South America.

Double Action Power Blacking Box Press.

No. 6, Spinning Lathe.

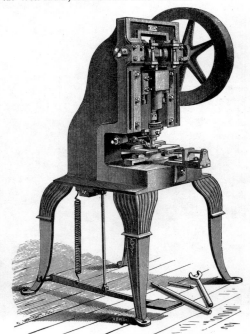

Double Action Cam Power Press.

STANDARD EIGHT WHEEL PASSENGER AND FREIGHT LOCOMOTIVE, BUILT BY THE BROOKS LOCOMOTIVE WORKS, DUNKIRK, N. Y.

BROOKS LOCOMOTIVE WORKS,

Dunkirk, N. Y.

The thriving little city of Dunkirk, Chautauqua county, New York, is located on the southern shore of Lake Erie, forty miles west of Buffalo and about sixty miles southeast of the Falls of Niagara. It is the western terminus of the Erie Railroad; the northern terminus of the Dunkirk, Allegheny Valley and Pittsburg Railroad, and a point of much importance on the line of the Lake Shore and Michigan Southern Railroad. Its harbor is one of the finest on the lake, being well protected from storms, and having a depth of water sufficient for the largest vessels that navigate our great inland seas. It is a thoroughly active, an eminently wide-awake town; its growth has not been as rapid as that of some other places "farther west," but it has been a steadier and more substantial growth, and we know of no place in the States that transacts a larger business in proportion to its population than Dunkirk. Its superior facilities for the reception of raw materials and the shipment of finished products to all parts of the country by water or rail, naturally attracted the attention of manufacturers, and in the extent of its mechanical productions Dunkirk far excels many older and larger places, and bids fair to become, at no distant date, one of the busiest hives of mechanical industry in the country.

Pre-eminent among the industrial interests of Dunkirk is the Brooks Locomotive Works. The Company was organized in 1869 by Mr. H. G.

Brooks and his associates, with Mr. Brooks—a gentleman of large general railroad experience, and possessing a thorough, practical knowledge of the general and specific details and necessities of the work—as President and Superintendent, and Mr. M. L. Hinman, who possesses qualifications which specially fit him for the double office as Secretary and Treasurer. Although the Company was organized at the comparatively recent date above noted, and in entering the field was forced to compete with many old established and favorably known manufacturers in the same line, and though closely following there came a season of general depression of all business which forced old Railroad Companies to curtail expenses, and to defer many contemplated improvements, including additions to their rolling stock until some future day and brighter time, while work on extensions of old or construction of new lines was almost entirely suspended, yet the Brooks Locomotive Works have succeeded in establishing a large and rapidly growing business and have gained an enviable reputation for the character of their work. Many older Locomotive builders within the last few years have found it necessary to close their shops for lack of work, but this Company have been kept comparatively busy even during the dullest times.

The Works are very extensive, are complete in all their appointments—as thoroughly equipped as any of their class in the world—and the system adopted in the various departments of the manufactory is most admirable. Neither effort nor expense has been spared to supply the several shops with all the latest and best machine tools and labor saving devices to aid the workmen, and the plant includes several special machines invented

and constructed for their own use and to be found in no other establishment. All the essential parts of each Locomotive built at these works are fitted to templates and permanent gauges, and consequently the corresponding details of each class of their engines are as thoroughly interchangable as are parts of a Remington Rifle, or a first-class American Watch. Corresponding with the completeness of their mechanical equipment is their ample force of workmen, a force that in point of skill is not surpassed by any establishment of like size.

When run to their full capacity the Brooks Locomotive Works are capable of producing ten Locomotives per month; they are not, of course, running to their full capacity during the present dull times, (May, 1876), nor do we know of any large establishment that is, while some are entirely closed—but they are turning out five locomotives per month, and have orders for several months in advance at the same rate of production.

From the many classes of locomotives constructed by this Company we show an engraving of their standard eight wheel Passenger and Freight Locomotive. We cannot, of course, describe it fully, nor even point out its many marked advantages over others within the little space left at our disposal (those desiring such particulars can obtain the fullest information by addressing the Company), but knowing them, as we do, we do not wonder at the marked success the builders have achieved. Excellence will always make itself felt—it will overcome all difficulties that may beset it, remove every obstacle from its path and attain the highest position. Excellence is the one great secret of the success of the Brooks Locomotive Works.

GRIFFITH & WEDGE,

MANUFACTURERS OF

Patent Vertical Portable
ENGINES AND SAW MILLS.

STATIONARY

STEAMBOAT AND PROPELLER ENGINES,

Zanesville, Ohio.

The works of the firm above named are located on Fifth Street, and consist of a large two-story office ; foundry, 60 by 120 feet ; machine and erecting shops, each 40 by 70 feet and two stories high ; boiler room, 80 by 100 feet ; blacksmith shop, 40 by 70 feet ; a large engine room, coal and coke sheds and other outhouses, storage sheds, etc. Our limited space forbids a description of any of these machines; we can only sum up the equipment of the foundry, machine and erecting shops, and all the appointments of the entire establishment in the single word, complete. The 40-horse power steam engine, which furnishes the motor for the Works, is of their own construction, and is a model of workmanship. The boiler is 24 feet long, 44 inches in diameter, and is worthy of special remark from the fact that the shell is made of four pieces of iron.

Messrs. Griffith & Wedge make all kinds of stationary engines, from 6 to 150 horse power, and also general saw and grist mill machinery, propellers for canal and river boats, and do a large business in furnishing mills complete. Their specialty, however, is in the manufacture of the patent Vertical Portable Engines, of which we give a cut and a description. Both Messrs. Griffith and Wedge commenced life at the bottom of the ladder, and have, by industry, economy and shrewd business tact, placed themselves in the front rank of the great manufacturers of the West. Mr. Griffith commenced in these works as an apprentice, and worked up through the various stations of workman, foreman, superintendent, to senior proprietor. Mr. Wedge passed through a similar course. Their business amounts now to about $400,000 per annum.

The principal feature of the Improved Portable Engine illustrated herewith is its Vertical engine, by the construction of which it is claimed that more power is gained on less fuel, that there is less friction to overcome, consequently less wear and tear on the working parts, and that greater safety is secured than with horizontal engines.

VERTICAL PORTABLE ENGINE FOR SAW MILLS, &c.

By counter or even balancing, the engine can be driven, from 275 revolutions, the regular speed for saw mills, to 400 revolutions per minute without undue strain on the boiler. Nearly three hundred of these machines, we are informed, are now in operation, to no one of which any accident has ever taken place. The cylinder of the engine is attached to one end of a base or box, in which is placed a water heater, and which supports the front end of the boiler directly under the tube sheet. The cold water becomes heated by part of the exhaust steam passing into it. The box has its open end covered by a cap, which also forms the foot of the force pump. The force pump is driven by an eccentric placed immediately over it on the main shaft. On the side of the eccentric is cast a small pulley, which belts on to a larger pulley attached to the boiler by means of a stud, and which carries a crank wrist from which power is transmitted to the pump ; the crank pin is also made square at the end, so that by the application of a crank it can be worked by hand to fill up the boiler. This pump is attached to the fire box and is placed at the top. The saddle, together with the two pillow blocks for the main shaft to run in, as well as the smoke stack base, are all cast in one piece. This saddle is bolted to the boiler over the tube sheet, and is connected to the lower box or base by means of a flat bar, which receives part of the strain between the saddle and base, and also forms the bearing for the guide yoke. The steam chest is placed in such a position on the cylinder that the valve motion is direct without the use of a rock shaft. The steam chest, piston rod, cross head, wrist and crank pin are all made of steel, which enables lightness to be combined with strength. A weight cast at the back of the crank plate counterbalances the weight of the parts described. One of the advantages claimed for this engine is the attachment of the machinery to the strongest part of the boiler, the saddle being placed immediately over the tube sheet, and the base immediately under, doing away in a great measure with strain of the machinery through the expansion and contraction caused by the varying heat of the boiler. It will be seen that, by placing the machinery below the waist of the boiler, it is not so likely to upset in transportation. The throttle is placed at the top of the steam pipe, in the steam dome, and the pipe, passing through the boiler and smoke arch, is protected from the cold atmosphere, thereby preventing condensation.

VERTICAL PORTABLE THRESHING MACHINE ENGINE.

SAW MILL AND VERTICAL PORTABLE ENGINE.

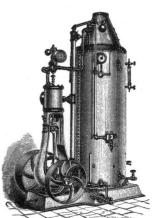

UPRIGHT STATIONARY ENGINE.

Wire Cloth, Wire Work, Fence and Railing.

The old testament gives us the earliest information we have concerning the manufacture of wire, at which remote period the metal was beaten out into thin plates which were cut into threads or wire. The Greeks and Romans had carried wire work to such perfection that Ovid speaks of an invisible net of vulcan rendered so by the fineness of the wire gauze. In the beginning of the fourteenth century we find wire workers at "Nuremburg" where Rudolph, about the middle of that century, vastly improved upon the method of his time, that of hammering out the thread, and invented the present system of drawing wire.

Wire and wire work are each so wondrously varied in their nature that the already astonishing number of their useful applications is daily increasing and promises soon to embrace a world of industries. Wire—drawn from rods one-half inch in diameter down to one-thirty thousandth part of an inch in thickness, one hundred and fifty threads of which equal a filament of common raw silk, and a grain in weight of which measures a mile in length—and wire cloth, made in meshes of four inches clear space down to that which has 22,500 holes to the square inch, naturally suit an infinite variety of purposes, from the hair spring of a watch to strands of the cables for a suspension bridge—how wide the range. Needles, pins, hooks and eyes, springs, carding machines, chains, fish hooks, telegraph lines, riddles, rope, screens, cages, traps, fences, office railing, garden ornamental work or furniture, fire and spark guards, provision and meat safes, paper makers' cloth, cloth for sugar, milk and rosin strainers, duster wires and bolting clothes, are a few of the articles made from wire. To give a full enumeration of separate articles is almost an impossibility as the firm of Howard & Morse manufacture over two thousand. A synopsis of their thirteenth catalogue, containing a price list of the most prominent articles manufactured by them, will give an idea of their vast facilities and the numerous inventions upon which they hold patents.

Howard & Morse have displayed great skill and taste in the manufacture of plain and ornamental wire work, in which branch they are unsurpassed, if equalled, by any house in the United States. They manufacture a great variety of plain and ornamental wire work for the park, pleasure ground and garden, consisting in part of galvanized summer houses, pillar, border and plain arches or arbors, tables, settees, chairs, stools, tree guards; also rose and vine trainers of every design and description. They also manufacture a general variety of wire work for plants in the winter which may be embraced under the head of "Hot House Wire Work." We consider it unnecessary to enlarge upon the importance of their nursery fenders and fire guards as a protection against the loss of life and property. They are made in a great variety of styles and patterns to suit the taste and ornament the fire place. This firm also manufacture and keep in stock a general assortment of screens for screening coal, sand, gravel, ore and grain.

The increasing demand for iron wire bolting cloth has induced this house to turn their attention more particularly to this branch of their business. The universal complaint which every manufacturer has to contend with, is its liability to rust. This they have overcome most effectually by coating the cloth with a preparation (known only to themselves) in such manner that rust cannot

WAREHOUSE, 45 FULTON STREET,
New York.

touch it. Aside from this advantage, the article made is said to be superior to any being made of a larger wire and driven up square, making it upon an average equal to ten meshes finer per square inch.

The spark wire cloth is in general use on locomotives and this house being one of the heaviest manufacturers of the article furnish it largely to the railroads.

They manufacture from either steel or iron wire, twilled and crimped cloth for both wood and coal burning engines, from the fine ten mesh to the two and a half, and are always able to furnish any size required.

They are also extensively engaged in the manufacture of the very heavy grades of screen wire cloth, which are used in screening ore and coal upon breakers and crushing machines. This grade of cloth is made of wire ranging from three-eighths to one thirty-second part of an inch in diameter, the meshes of which vary from one-sixteenth to three inches space. The firm find their customers for this article in those interested in coal and minerals.

In looking through their works we find them to be very extensive producers of the different grades and meshes of copper and brass wire cloth, which cloth is used in an infinite number of articles and ways to accomplish different results. In the manufacture of all grades of paper it has to be used, there being no substitute known. The meshes used by paper manufacturers vary according to the grade of paper made, from ten to eighty meshes each way per square inch.

In the lantern department the bivalvular lantern seems worthy of attention, as it opens at the center to allow the glass to be removed and replaced at pleasure for the purpose of cleaning. The star lantern patented by this house is manufactured without the use of solder, and being made of extra large sized wire is unusually strong and durable. The necessity for solder is obviated by the manner in which the guards are knuckled or hooked through flanges at the bottom, and at the tops turned over the round guard itself. This lantern is considered by the railroad companies as the most economical and best in use. The miners safety lamp, is manufactured in the United States solely by this house, and is the facsimile of the Davies lamp made in England and used by government order.

There are but few houses in the United States and perhaps in the world that manufacture so great a variety of wire work articles as Howard & Morse. Mr. Howard, who has charge of the factory, is one of the most thorough master mechanics in wire goods in the United States and Mr. Morse is a man of extra-ordinary business qualifications, which, combined with the facilities afforded by large buildings and expensive machinery, have enabled the National Wire and Lantern Works to build up an enviable trade. Wire has an almost infinite field of usefulness from its known qualities of elasticity and conductiveness of heat and electricity. Wire work has an amazing number of applications from its ability to separate smaller from larger bodies, solids from fluids, or to admit air and yet exclude other intruders. No other substance is as capable of receiving such variety of pleasing forms, or of uniting so much strength with light and graceful lines. We may therefore safely prognosticate a new world of uses and of beauty for wire work, already foreshadowed in the infinitely varied designs and effects produced by the garden furniture and office railing manufactured by this firm.

Howard & Morse have just effected an arrangement with Mr. Henry F. Parsons, of San Francisco, Cal., for the entire and exclusive manufacture of his patent fire proof scenery and improved machinery for working the stage.

No. 4 Mesh, No. 14 Wire.

Above we show the interior view of a Banking Room, in which the Tellers are enclosed with No. 9 and No. 14 Pattern Wire Railing. The great advantage in Tellers being thus securely enclosed from intrusion of fellow clerks, or others, is apparent. It is appreciated, and has been adopted by many of the largest Banking Institutions of the country.

Wire Fence, Guards or Railing, No. 12.

Pillar Garden Arch.
5 Feet Span, 6 Feet High, 12 Inches Deep.

No. 1.
Tree Guard.

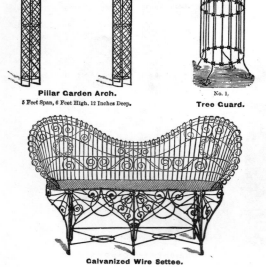

Galvanized Wire Settee.

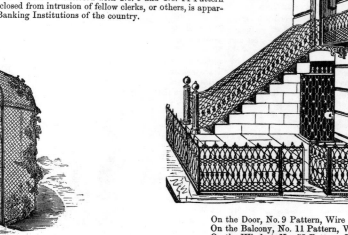

On the Door, No. 9 Pattern, Wire Guard.
On the Balcony, No. 11 Pattern, Wire Railing.
On the Window, No. 53 Pattern, Flat Iron Guard.
Balustrade from No. 12 Pattern Railing.
Fence from No. 15 Pattern Railing.

Galvanized Arbor or Summer House.
8 Feet Diameter, 12 Feet High. Made in sections, and strongly bolted together.

Wire Cloth Partly Unrolled.

Man'f'y., Nos. 9, 11, 13, 15 & 17 Chestnut St., Cor. Bushwick Ave., Brooklyn, E. D.

Star Fire Department Lantern.

MANUFACTORY OF CLARK'S **(O. N. T.)** SPOOL COTTON.

SPOOL COTTON.

ITS ORIGIN AND MANUFACTURE.

The materials and sources for the production of thread for domestic use are still limited to four—two in the animal kingdom, and two in the vegetable kingdom—silk, wool, linen and cotton. It is with the latter only, that we now have to do.

Cotton is a vegetable wool, the product of the "Gossypium," a shrub, indigenous in the tropical regions of India and America. Indian cotton cloth is mentioned by Herodotus in the fifth century, B. C. It is known to have been used in Arabia in the time of Mahomet, about A. D. 625, and was brought into Europe by his followers.

It was in use among the Chinese in the thirteenth century, and to them are we indebted for the cotton fabric, termed nankeen.

Cotton was also the material of the principal articles of clothing among the Aborigines of America when first visited by Columbus, although we are not informed as to the source whence this cloth came.

About the close of the American Revolution, the growth of cotton was commenced in the state of Georgia. In 1784, eight bales were exported, and were seized by the custom house officials on the ground that the United States could not have produced that amount.

In 1793, Eli Whitney invented the saw-gin, a machine by which cotton wool is separated from the pod, and cleaned with great ease and expedition. Before that time it required a day's work of a field hand to separate the seed from a pound of the fibre.

This machine gave an immense impetus to the growth of American cotton, and in 1795, the United States exported 5,250,000 pounds. In 1860, the year before the secession of the Southern States, 1,115,890,608 pounds were exported.

Spinning was ascribed by the ancients to Minerva, the Goddess of

Wisdom. Arcas, king of Arcadia, is said to have taught his subjects the art about 1500, B. C. The spinning-wheel was invented in Brunswick, England, about A. D., 1530. The spinning of cotton was performed by the hand spinning-wheel until about 1767.

It is said that Dr. Franklin and Dr. Priestly met one evening at the Royal Society Club in London, and during the conversation the question arose: "What was the most desirable invention that remained to be made;" upon which Dr. Franklin expressed himself thus: "A machine capable of spinning two threads at once."

Soon after this an ingenious mechanic near Blackburn, England, named Hargreaves, invented a spinning jenny with eight spindles.

The Mule, a spinning machine called also, Mule-Jenny, is said to have been invented by Sam'l. Crompton, of Bolton, Lancashire, England, in 1779; named from Crompton's residence, "Hall-in-the-wood-wheel;" "Muslin-wheel," from its giving birth to the British Muslin and Cambric manufacture; and "Mule" from its combining the advantages of Hargreaves' spinning jenny and Arkwright's adaptation. It is supposed that Crompton knew nothing of the latter invention, and did not patent his own but gave it up in 1780. It produced thread treble the fineness and very much softer than any ever before produced in England. In 1812 Parliament voted him an inadequate compensation of five thousand pounds. The self-acting mule was invented by a Mr. Roberts in 1825.

With these inventions and others the era of hand labor was abolished, and the foundation laid for that wonderful revolution and success which have since been achieved in this branch of industry.

Thread spinning has been an important branch of manufacture in the United States from an early date in our history. It was here, as in England, for many years an entirely domestic industry, and a spinning-wheel was considered a utensil as indispensable in every well furnished household as the sewing machine is at the present time.

Could the manufacturing and cotton growing interest be so combined that the machinery for carding, spinning and weaving could be propelled by the same power that moves the gin, one of the greatest

problems of political economy would be solved, for it is really at the plantation and gin house that the manufacture of cotton begins.

The cotton when received at the factory in bales, has first to be placed in a "picker," so called, to remove the seeds and foreign substances. This machine is provided with several cylinders, with iron teeth and is run at the rate of more than two thousand revolutions a minute, through which the cotton is passed.

It is claimed that the fibres of cotton in their passage through the various parts of the machinery necessary to produce a perfect six-cord cotton thread, undergo, from the time they are taken from the bale to completion, sundry operations in which they are "doubled" or inter-combined over twenty billions of times.

The process for winding the thread on spools, is so ingeniously and honestly contrived, that consumers may be assured of getting two hundred yards.

The modern application of machinery to spinning thread began in England, in 1767; but the first sewing thread ever made of cotton was produced in Pawtucket, Rhode Island, in 1784. Previous to that date flax was the material principally used for that purpose. The idea of using cotton for thread is said to have been suggested by Mrs. Samuel Slater, who, while spinning some Sea Island cotton noticed the evenness and beauty of the yarn it made. The manufacture was introduced by her husband, who is so well known as the pioneer of the cotton industry in the United States.

It is now but about ten years since six-cord cotton thread was first manufactured in this country. During this period the manufacture has increased very rapidly until the annual sales of six-cord spool cotton of two hundred yards each in the United States, exceed fourteen million dozens.

The almost incredible number of sewing machines manufactured and in use in this country has had a powerful influence to increase the demand and supply, as well as to improve the quality of the spool cotton. The number of sewing machines sold in the United States during the year 1873 was nearly 600,000.

LIME ROCK FURNACE.

BARNUM-RICHARDSON CO.,
Salisbury, Conn., P. O. Address, Lime Rock, Conn.
Manufacturers of
CHARCOAL PIG IRON from SALISBURY ORES AND CHILLED CAR WHEELS,
Also, all other descriptions of Castings for Railroad Super-
structure and Equipment   All work made from
Salisbury Iron Exclusively.

NEW FURNACE, EAST CANAAN.

erected and has continued in operation up to the present time.

About the year 1748 a forge was erected in the present village of Lakeville, (then called Furnace Village,) and in 1762, John Haseltine, Samuel Forbes and ETHAN ALLEN purchased the property and built a Blast Furnace, the first built in the State.

The forge on Mt. Riga was built about the year 1781, by Abner or Peter Woodin. Daniel Ball succeeded him and for many years, the works were known as Ball's Forge. Seth King and John Kelsey, commenced building a furnace there, about 1806, but were not able to finish it, and in 1810, it came into possession of Messrs. Holley & Coffing.

These works, and those at Lakeville, have long been abandoned, however, and the property at Mt. Riga, including the water privilege which is very valuable and one of the finest in the State, is now owned by Barnum-Richardson Co., and used by them to supply, in part, the power used in running the furnace and foundries at Lime Rock.

At East Canaan two Blast Furnaces were built for the manufacture of pig iron from Salisbury ore—one about 1840, by Samuel Forbes, the other about 1847, by John A. Beckley.

The first foundry for the remelting of pig iron was built in Lime Rock, about the year 1830, and soon after came under control of Milo Barnum the founder of the present company. Milo Barnum, was born in Dover, Dutchess County, New York, July 16, 1790. In the spring of 1820 he settled in Lime Rock and engaged in business as a merchant. Soon after coming into possession of the foundry he associated with him his son-in-law, Leonard Richardson, and a few years later his son, Wm. H. Barnum was made a partner, the firm now being Barnum, Richardson & Co. The foundry business was

The great tensile strength, about 30,000 pounds to the square inch, and natural chilling qualities of the Salisbury iron renders it specially valuable for the manufacture of cast chilled car wheels.

In 1852, Milo Barnum retired from active participation in the business and the firm name was changed to Richardson, Barnum & Co. In 1858 they obtained possession of the Beckley Furnace, and in 1862 they purchased the Forbes Furnace. They also about this time purchased the foundry at 64 South Jefferson Street, Chicago, Ills., and organized a joint stock company under the name of the Barnum

OLD HILL ORE BED.

DAVIS ORE BED.

CHATFIELD ORE BED.

The mines from which the celebrated Salisbury Iron Ores are obtained are called respectively the "Old Hill," "Davis" and "Chatfield" ore beds and are situated in the town of Salisbury, Connecticut.

The "Old Hill" ore bed is a tract of land of one hundred acres, originally granted 1731 to Daniel Bissell, of Windsor. It was soon after surveyed and located by Ezekiel Ashley and John Pell. The supply of ore from this mine has been very abundant, but latterly the cost of mining has been increased. Up to about 1840 the average yield was estimated to be about four thousand five hundred tons per annum; since then the production has gradually increased, and the present annual yield is estimated at fifteen thousand tons.

The "Davis" ore bed was originally known as "Hendrick's" ore bed, and was partly owned, before the organization of the town of Salisbury, by Thomas Lamb, one of the first settlers in the town. The ore was mined in this bed as early as 1730 or '31, and was taken by Lamb to supply his forge at Lime Rock.

The "Chatfield" ore bed was originally owned by Philip Chatfield, from whom it takes its name, and was opened about the same time as the beds above mentioned, or soon after. It has been steadily worked since first opened, showing as do the others, an increased production. Its annual yield at present is estimated to be twelve thousand tons. In addition to the mines mentioned above, this company is working mines at Amenia and Riga, both on the line of the New York and Harlem Railroad.

The pioneer forge in the vicinity of the mines first mentioned was erected in Lime Rock by Thomas Lamb as early as 1734, the ore for which was taken from the "Hendrick's" (now "Davis") ore bed. It came into possession of its present owners in 1863, and in 1864 a new Blast Furnace was

carried on in a small way in connection with the store, their production consisting chiefly of clock and sash weights, plow castings and other small work.

The business gradually increased, however, and about 1840, they began the manufacture of railroad work, chairs, frogs, heel blocks, etc., for the Boston and Albany Railroad, then being built from Springfield, Massachusetts, to Albany, New York.

& Richardson Manufacturing Co. Leonard Richardson died in January, 1864, and in the May following the Barnum-Richardson Co., a joint stock company was organized with Wm. H. Barnum as President.

The new company succeeded to all the iron interests of Richardson, Barnum & Co. and since its organization have largely increased their facilities and have, from time to time, acquired further interests in mining companies and furnace companies already in operation. They erected a second foundry at Lime Rock in 1870, and built a third furnace at East Canaan in 1872, with many improvements upon the old method of construction. A new wheel foundry was built in Chicago in 1873 by the company there.

The foundries in Chicago use the Salisbury iron and have a capacity, in the two shops of 300 wheels per day. The Company in their Lime Rock Works have a capacity of 300 wheels per day.

A test of the strength of these wheels was made before a number of prominent English Engineers and Railway Officials, in August, 1875, at the machine works of Mr. Horn, Millbank, Row, Westminster. The wheel was struck with two sledges, and it was not until the 367th blow that the iron partially gave way.

As an illustration of the rapid growth of the business of this Company, and the development of the Salisbury iron interest we offer the following. In 1840 there were in the vicinity of Lime Rock 4 Blast Furnaces, in operation, each producing 3 tons of pig iron per day, now there are eight Blast Furnaces, producing 11 tons to each furnace per day. The new furnace at East Canaan, at its last blast ran 104 consecutive weeks, making an average of 80 tons of iron per week, being the longest and best blast on record as having been made in a charcoal furnace.

FOUNDRIES AND OFFICE OF BARNUM-RICHARDSON CO., LIMEROCK, CONN., U. S. A.

Circular Top 11 x 13 In.

12 x 15 In.

Register Set in Iron Border.

Ceiling Ventilator for Churches, &c.

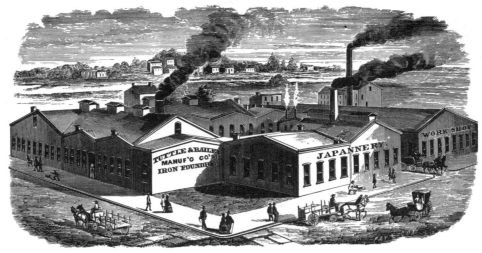

Tuttle & Bailey Manuf'g Co's. Works, 2nd, North 10th & 11th Sts., Brooklyn, N. Y.

10 In. Round.

Register or Ventilator for Shallow Flues.

14 x 18 In.

THE TUTTLE & BAILEY MANUF'G CO.,
Warm Air Registers and Ventilators.

In connection with and incident to the apparatus for the warming and ventilation of apartments, are the articles of Warm Air Registers, Ventilators, and Ornamental Screens for covering steam heating coils.

The Register for regulating the admission of the warmed air into the apartment ; the Ventilator for regulating the emission of the vitiated air from the same ; the Ornamental Screen for covering the unsightly radiator when the warming is done by steam and the radiator placed within the room.

The branch of industry here illustrated are these manufactures, which for many years were as crude in design as imperfect in mechanism, and seemingly not until their manufacture was made a specialty was there anything like artistic skill brought to bear in their construction.

For nearly thirty years Messrs. Tuttle & Bailey, or their successors, THE TUTTLE & BAILEY MANUFACTURING CO., have been engaged in the manufacture of these articles as a specialty, and as a result may justly claim to have produced an assortment which in its variety of kinds, sizes, styles of finish and beauty of designs would seem to leave no want unsupplied in this line.

Various Japans, Bronzes, Plating, whether Nickel, Copper or Silver, and the celebrated white Porcelain Enamel finish, are all brought into use.

To meet the wants of the trade promptly and to produce their wares cheaply the company have erected works adapted especially to the manufacture of these goods upon an extensive scale.

The few illustrations here presented can only convey some idea of the perfection of design attained by these manufacturers, but a visit to their warerooooms, at 83 Beekman Street, New York, will give a much better idea of the variety and beauty of finish, which cannot well be here shown, also the extent of this branch of industry.

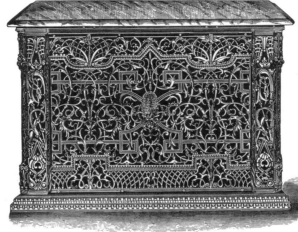

Ornamental Screen, Pattern No. 3, 36 in. high.

Circular-Top Register, 16 x 22.

3. LOUNGING POSITION.

2. EASY CHAIR.

1. PARLOR POSITION.

7. HEELS HIGHER THAN HEAD.

10. BED WITH SHOULDER REST.

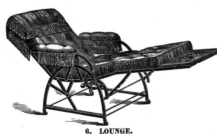

6. LOUNGE.

5. CHILD'S CRIB AND SWING.

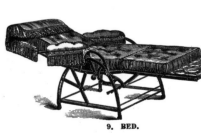

9. BED.

11. MEDICAL CHAIR.

4. INVALID POSITION.

8. READING POSITION.

12. SHIPPING.

The Wilson Adjustable Chair Mf'g Co.,
592 Broadway, New York.

A late writer in a popular scientific journal gives some very plain and convincing statements as to the causes which produce so much of the physical weakness and deformity among our youth, as well as people of mature years ; and considers it one of the strangest problems of the nineteenth century, that no parent, teacher or mechanic has given any attention to their remedy. The small of the back is the centre of voluntary motion, and is the weak or strong point of every person. Physiologists tell us that nearly three hundred muscles are directly or indirectly connected with motions of which the small of the back is the pivotal center. Hence, while the strong and the robust may fortunately live in blissful ignorance of spinal weakness or vertebral distortion, invalids are forever complaining of this part of the body.

People of sedentary habits are constantly complaining of the back. We presume there are comparatively few persons who do not know by bitter experience what this means. It is more intolerable than ague or neuralgia, or any other of the ills to which flesh is heir.

The date of the origin of household furniture is pre-historic. As long as kings have had thrones their subjects have had chairs. The remaining monuments of Egypt and Assyria give abundant representations of the conveniences of ancient households in these countries. It is known that the Egyptians had in their houses chairs and couches of the most elaborate designs, made of the best and most costly material, and finished in the most expensive style of ornamentation.

The acme in the improvement of chairs, in point of comfort, health and economy seems to have been reached in the Wilson Adjustable Chair represented on this page.

This Chair is made of the best wrought iron and rivets. The castors are made expressly for it, and very strong. Everything is arranged on strictly scientific principles. It is susceptible of Thirty Changes of Position, hence its great economy, and value in a hygienic point of view. By reference to the cuts it will be seen that the chair is pivoted to arch that forms the legs. Cut No. 3 represents the four points at which the directions are marked.

A—Braces riveted on each side of the arch, lock the chair firm to the legs; if unlocked at A, the entire chair is suspended at the pivot, and in whatever position will oscillate by the action of two springs, at option of patient, and cannot tip over.

B—At this point is a small knob on a flat bar so secured as to lock both sides of the chair on that half circle, while the back or front is retained at any angle desired by the patient. The back and front of the chair work conjointly, and very simply, the chair locking itself, and remaining as firm as if built to retain that angle.

C represents a ratchet to elevate the front part to any level; while the back may be retained at any angle.

D—Braces to adjust foot board for any position; as a lounge, the foot board locks itself.

We can allude but briefly to a few particulars in regard to the different positions of the chair as represented on this page.

The Parlor Chair.—When in this position the back may be changed to any angle. If left free at A, it forms a Rocking Chair. The Easy Chair is represented with footboard carpeted. The Reading Chair represents a position in which every part of the body is comfortable, with head and shoulders resting on the pillow. The Invalid Chair, with adjustable pillow thrown back, will admit of several other positions. No. 5 can be adjusted to any length. No. 6 is a comfortable lounge. It will swing or rest on rod across arch, but cannot tip. No. 7 unlocked at A, exhibits the entire principle of the Chair. In No. 8 the back may be lowered and front dropped to four or five changes. No. 9 represents bed with pillow, and standard dropped from the back to form support. No. 10, a bed with head reversed ; can be placed in any room with head to the north, the proper position for sound sleep. No. 11, a medical chair, endorsed by the medical fraternity as being scientifically adapted to all requirements. No. 12 is compactly folded for shipment ; frame weighs about 55 pounds ; with upholstery, but about 70 pounds. Circular with price list, &c., can be had on application.

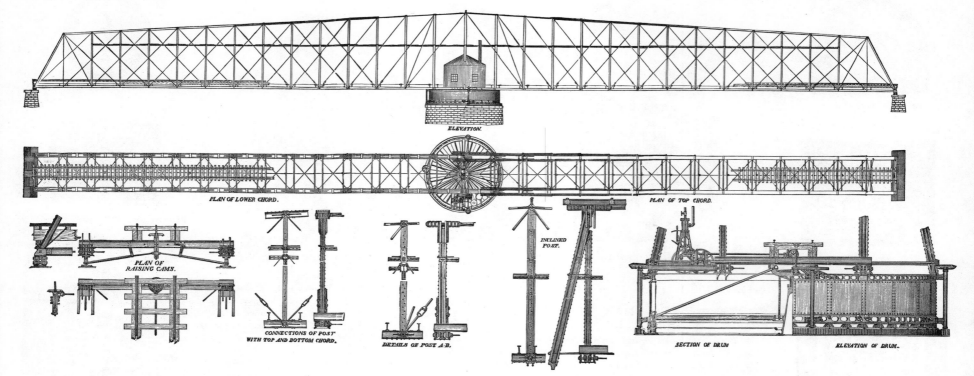

SINGLE TRACK DRAW BRIDGE, 444 FOOT SPAN. KELLOGG BRIDGE CO., BUFFALO, N. Y.

IRON BRIDGE WORKS OF NEW YORK.

Kellogg Bridge Company, Buffalo, N. Y.

CHARLES KELLOGG, Pres't.   GEORGE BEALS, Vice-Pres't.   S. D. BARLOW, Jr., Sec'y & Treas'r.

—:o:—

The art of bridge building must have been of ancient origin, and like so many other useful inventions, seems to be but the result of a necessity. To the careless observer the construction of a bridge may seem to require no unusual skill or mechanical ingenuity, and judging from many of the structures the tourist crosses, even at the present day, it is apparent that this idea was the dominant one in the minds of those who constructed them.

But bridge building is now among the most important enterprises of the day. The great uncertainty, inconvenience and peril attending travel where streams have to be forded or crossed by frail structures, constructed to meet a sudden emergency, or even by the ordinary ferry-boats in unfavorable seasons, have brought into requisition the inventive genius of many of the best architects of the present century.

Roads for ordinary travel or for steam carriage, sometimes require much engineering skill where no streams are crossed or gorges spanned. But to construct a bridge which will bear a heavy laden train safely across a broad river, or a rapid mountain stream, and withstand all the disintegrating influences to which it is exposed, is an achievement in engineering worthy the ambition of any man. Although the piers and abutments may be laid ever so strong, and defy the powers of frost and heat, of flood and ice, if the structure which spans the gorge is inefficient the unsuspected danger often proves frightfully disastrous to life and property.

To build an iron bridge hundreds of miles from the stream it was destined to span, was formerly entirely impracticable with the facilities afforded for transportation. The necessity, however, for wooden bridges, exposed to destruction, alike from fire and water, is now very limited.

As an illustration of the wonderful revolution which has been effected in bridge-building within the last few years we present our readers, at the top of this page, with a fine view of a single track draw-bridge, constructed by the Kellogg Bridge Company, of Buffalo, N. Y.; also, on the same page, a cut of the Company's works.

The Kellogg Bridge Company was organized in November, 1870. Their extensive works are located on lands fronting on Katherine Street, Buffalo, and adjoining the premises of the Union Iron Company's Works. The buildings of this establishment are built of brick, in the form of an L, containing machine, pattern and blacksmith shops.

The machine shop, a commodious building of fine appearance facing on Katherine Street, is 200 feet long, 118 feet wide, and two stories in height,

the second story being occupied by the pattern shop.

The blacksmith shop which is situated on a line with the south end of the machine shop, one end adjoining and opening into the same, is 200 feet in length, and 70 feet wide, with a foundry in process of construction, 50 x 100 feet, extending across the east end of the blacksmith shop, with hip-roof, and walls twenty-four feet high, and with the blacksmith shop forming another L.

These works are thoroughly and substantially built, and arranged in every department with special reference to convenience and adaptability to the purposes for which they were designed. They are complete in all their appointments, thoroughly furnished with such tools and machinery as are requisite for the construction of iron bridges of every descriptions, trestle work, roofs, turn-tables, etc. The buildings and surroundings are so arranged as to afford the best facilities for receiving materials, and handling and shipping the work manufactured.

We would call special attention to the Solid Die-Forged Eye Bars, for tensile members of bridges, manufactured by this Company, having no welds, and thereby avoiding the uncertainty of welds and risk of injury by upsetting. This work is performed by machinery gotten up especially for this purpose, which enables them to manufacture material of superior workmanship with great rapidity, and insures that perfect uniformity and regularity of shapes so essential to material for bridges or other similar structures.

Much of this Company's work is done with machines and tools built for special purposes, which perform their particular parts perfectly and with dispatch. Among these are machines for cutting and boring compression members as well as tensile members for bridges and other structures with a

greater degree of accuracy than can possibly be attained by any other method.

In the structures which this Company builds there is necessarily a large amount of riveting, which work, until quite recently, was done entirely by hand. They now have in operation two power riveting machines—which like many of their special machines and tools, are of their own invention and construction—and which enables them to do this kind of work more rapidly and satisfactorily than was ever before possible. They have now in process of construction, at the works of Messrs. Wm. Sellers & Co., Philadelphia, Pa., a hydraulic riveting machine, which they purpose erecting in their shops, which, together with their other machines, will give them facilities for doing this kind of work in a manner unsurpassed by any concern in the world.

The Kellogg Bridge Co's Works being situated in the immediate vicinity of the Union Iron Co's extensive Rolling Mills, enables them to procure their supplies of iron on short notice and without the delays of transportation. They have orders on hand at this time for over seven thousand tons of finished bridge material, a large portion of which is to be erected in Pennsylvania and New Jersey.

They are now preparing a new book of illustrations of their work, which will be sent by mail free, upon application. They are prepared to furnish plans and specifications for any work in their line, and are also prepared to furnish bridge or roof material to engineers and contractors on the most favorable terms.

This Company has now been organized less than five years, during which time they have erected the extensive works we have described, and constructed and erected iron bridges and trestles amounting to more than 16,000 lineal feet.

Prominent among the bridges erected are three long spans across the Mississippi River at Louisiana, Missouri, recently completed; one being a draw span of 444 feet in length, the longest draw ever built, and the others, fixed spans of 225 and 255 feet respectively. This company also furnished the iron

work for the magnificent new post office building, now nearly completed, in New York city, also, a large amount of other work for contractors, such as roofs, bridge materials, etc. They manufacture all kinds of wrought iron bridge structures, also combination bridges of wood and iron, wrought iron trestle work, viaducts, turn-tables, roofs, etc.

With their present facilities, this company can execute promptly all orders for anything in their line of manufacture, the capacity of their works being at present equal to one, 100 foot span per day. They are prepared to fill all orders for Chas. H. Kellogg's Patent Wrought Iron Columns of various sizes and sections, and can furnish these columns, fitted up for bridge posts, top chords, end braces and trestle work. They are also prepared to furnish every description of bridge material with promptness and to the satisfaction of all who favor them with their patronage.

KELLOGG BRIDGE COMPANY'S WORKS, BUFFALO, N. Y.

No. 75 CALL BELL.

REVOLVING CHIME.

TEA BELL.

OPEN TOY BELL.

'CHIME SLEIGH BELL.

ACORN RATTLE.

No. 80. CALL BELL.

GLOBE HAND BELL.

"YANKEE" ALARM DOOR BELL.

"YANKEE" GONG DOOR BELL.

"SILVER CHIME" HAND BELL.

"ABBES" GONG DOOR BELL.

GONG BELL MANUF'G CO.,

SOLE MANUFACTURERS OF

"Abbes" and the "Yankee" Patent Gong Door and

Alarm Door Bells, "Cone's" Patent Globe and Silver

Chime Hand Bells, "Cone's" Patent Acorn-

Shaped Sleigh and Toy Bells, "Bar-

ton's" Patent Revolving and Spring

Table Call Bells, Revolving Chimes,

and Chime Sleigh Bells

East Hampton, Connecticut.

——:o:——

In no State in the Union is the manufacture of the lighter articles of metal so extensively carried on as in Connecticut. Almost every village is the seat of several manufactories where skilled labor and ingenious machinery are employed in the production of small articles of utility made of metal. Nearly all of these villages, too, are distinguished for its prominence in some particular branch of manufacture. East Hampton is not an exception to this general rule: its special production being Bells—not church bells nor fire bells—but Hand Bells, Door Bells, Call Bells, Sleigh Bells, etc.

The first Sleigh Bells ever made in the United States were made in East Hampton by William Barton, who, while manufacturing andirons and other small articles of brass in the city of New York, in 1790, received some hints from a foreign mechanic in regard to the making of Sleigh Bells. Mr. Barton gave the subject much thought, devised a system of manufacture far in advance of any then in use and removed to East Hampton, where, in 1808, he commenced the manufacture of Hand and Sleigh Bells. Previous to this, all the Sleigh Bells used in this country had been imported, and as up till then they had been cast in halves and the parts afterward soldered or riveted together, the expense of manufacture had been very great and the production small, consequently Sleigh Bells were not only

very expensive but very scarce. Mr. Barton was the first man who cast Sleigh Bells whole in their present form, and he was also the first man who turned bells in a lathe.

At the outset of Mr. Barton's business the only power he had to run the lathe on which he turned and finished the bells and to work the bellows that supplied the blast necessary to smelt the metal for casting, was hand power; the water lying back in the beautiful lake had not then been utilized for running machinery. It was slow and very tiresome work, yet incomparably quicker and in every way better than the process which it superseded.

From this small beginning the business has steadily grown until it has assumed proportions far beyond the most sanguine expectations of its founder. To some extent new methods of manufacture have been adopted, and new patterns and styles of bells, almost numberless, have been designed for new uses. The single small shop has given place to a number of large factories, and at the present time there are eight firms engaged in the manufacture of Sleigh, Hand, Gong and Door Bells, Call and Toy Bells. The Gong Bell Manufacturing Company commenced business in the spring of 1866, making at first only "Abbes" Patent Gong Door, and Alarm Door Bells, but soon adding "Cone's" Patent Globe Hand Bells, and Acorn-Shaped Sleigh and Toy Bells. In 1871, "Barton's" Revolving Table Call Bells were added, and during the same year, the Silver Chime Hand Bells were first put upon the market. During the spring of 1873, a new toy called Revolving Chimes was introduced. In 1874 the "Yankee" Patent Gong Door and Alarm Bell were got out.

We present on this page cuts of several of the special production of the Gong Bell Manufacturing Company, but cannot illustrate all their manufactures. They make patterns and furnish bells of any shape or kind that parties may wish for special use. Their establishment is completely equipped with all the appliances that can aid them in the production of thoroughly good work.

ACORN SHAPED SLEIGH BELLS.

GOODSPEED & WYMAN,

MANUFACTURERS OF

TUB, PAIL AND CHAIR MACHINERY,

Woodworth Planers, Guage Lathes, Stave Saws,

Screw Machines, &c.

WINCHENDON, MASSACHUSETTS.

A little less than half a century ago, in the town of Winchendon, Massachusetts, the Cylinder Saw for sawing staves was invented, not a "circular" saw, as many suppose when they hear or see the term, but really a cylinder, on an open end of which are the teeth which, as the cylinder revolves, cuts the flat wood into curves or parts of a circle. Although the first Cylinder Saw was rude in construction, it was the dawn of a new era in the manufacture of staves

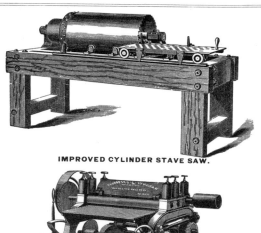

IMPROVED CYLINDER STAVE SAW.

NEW AND IMPROVED SURFACE PLANER.

for the finer kinds of cooper work, tubs, pails, etc., which are smooth both inside and out. At about the same time, and in the same town, the manufacture of Tubs, Pails and Churns by machinery was commenced on a small scale at first, but gradually increasing, until Winchendon became as famous for Tubs and Pails, as Scranton is for coal.

In the year 1850, Messrs. Goodspeed & Wyman (being convinced that the manufacture of wooden-ware, which had been so successfully carried on in their own town, was to become an important industry in other places) commenced the manufacture of Wood Working Machinery, making a specialty of such machines as were adapted to the wants of wooden ware manufacturers. They have since continuously and successfully carried on this business; a large proportion of all the Tub and Pail Machinery used in this country having been made at their works.

PAIL OR TUB LATHE.

IMPROVED GAUGE LATHE.

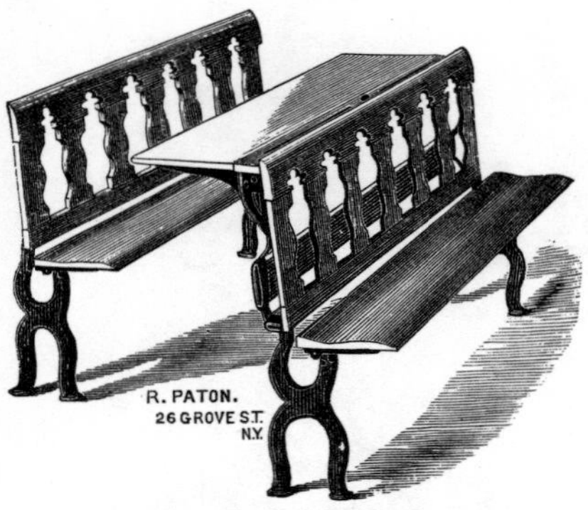

Excelsior Folding Desk.
(Ready for use)

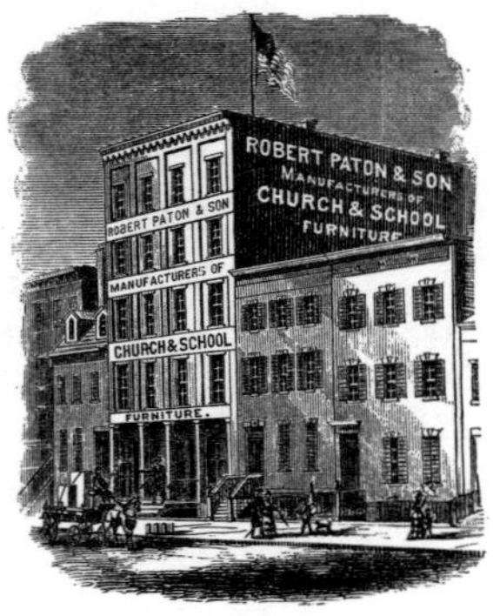

Established 1848.

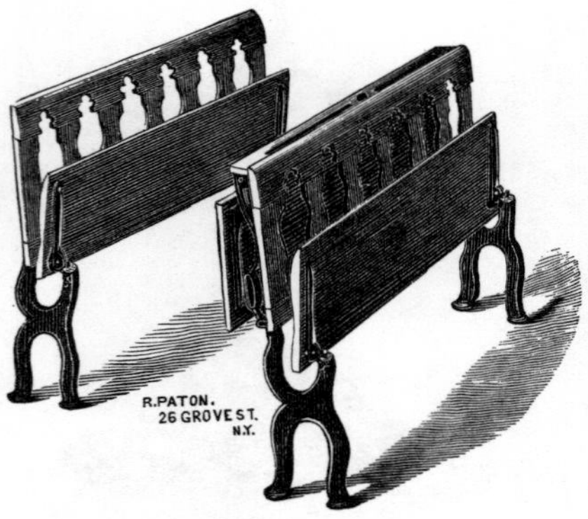

Excelsior Folding Desk.
Folded.

ROBERT PATON & SON,

Manufacturers of

SCHOOL & CHURCH FURNITURE,

Sunday School & Lecture Room Settees,

26 GROVE ST., N. Y.

——:o:——

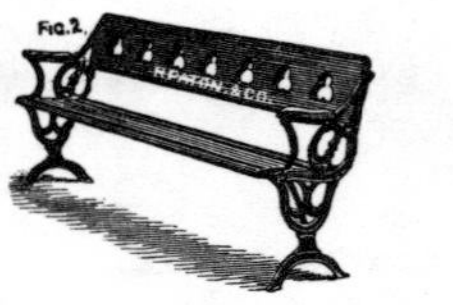

Patent Reversible Sunday School Settee.

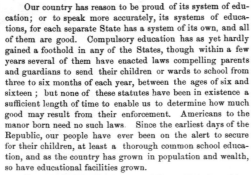

Our country has reason to be proud of its system of education; or to speak more accurately, its systems of educations, for each separate State has a system of its own, and all of them are good. Compulsory education has as yet hardly gained a foothold in any of the States, though within a few years several of them have enacted laws compelling parents and guardians to send their children or wards to school from three to six months of each year, between the ages of six and sixteen ; but none of these statutes have been in existence a sufficient length of time to enable us to determine how much good may result from their enforcement. Americans to the manor born need no such laws. Since the earliest days of the Republic, our people have ever been on the alert to secure for their children, at least a thorough common school education, and as the country has grown in population and wealth, so have educational facilities grown.

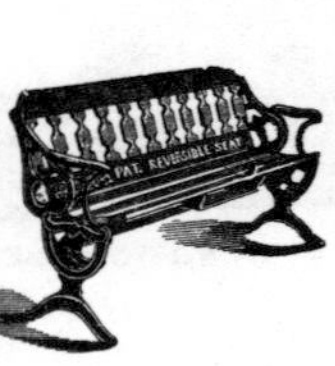

Patent Reversible Sunday School Settee.

Few persons who have not specially studied the subject have a just conception of the value, in a business point of view, of our educational machinery. Leaving for the time the intellectual and moral entirely out of the question and viewing it as a business, it ranks, in its money importance, in the same grade with the cotton business, the grain trade or the shipping interest.

At the present time there are not far from eight millions of pupils, and about one hundred and sixty thousand teachers who are continously engaged in attending public schools and other educational institutions. The books used by this grand army costs at least twenty millions of dollars; the seats, desks and other apparatus, thirty millions of dollars, together fifty millions of dollars. The investment of capital in school-houses and other buildings, in lands, college endowments, etc., amounts to hundreds of millions of dollars ; one single item, viz., fifty millions of acres of public lands, given at one time by Congress to the several States for educational purposes, at the minimum Government price $1 25, per acre, amounts to $62,500,000. But all of this land is eligibly located, and if put in market and sold at auction to-day, would bring from five to ten dollars per acre Then we must add the capital derived from bequests and legacies, the interest of which amounts to several millions of dollars per year. Another considerable item is the value of the libraries, to which we must add another large amount for reference books and professional works owned by teachers. Add all these together, and the total amount of the business investment of the United States in education becomes absolutely gigantic.

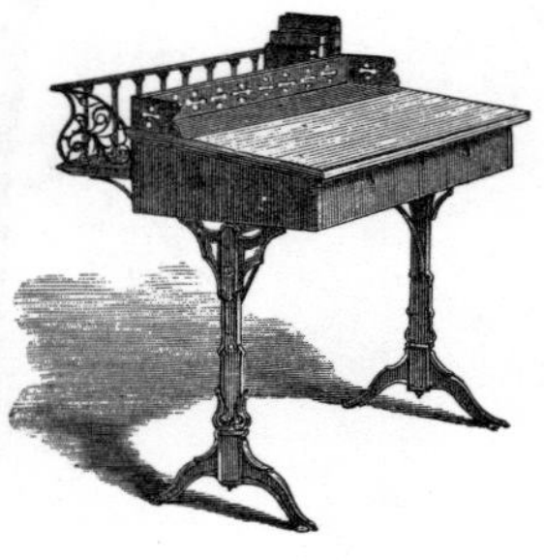

Teachers' Desk.

Since the time of the revival of classical education in Europe, just before the Protestant Reformation, one line of progress, more distinct than any other, can be clearly traced through the whole history of modern education, viz., improvement in its practical character. This practical tendency has characterized all the improved educational systems of modern times.

Passing at once to the nffairs of the present day, we find that the educational interest, so far as it is to be looked at on the business side, presents two especially striking features. First, the rapidly advancing practice of educating through the senses, and as a means of accomplishing this, the increased use of improved apparatus of all kinds, from the school house itself with its elegant furniture and fittings, its models and instruments used to clearly demonstrate facts in philosophy, astronomy and kindred studies, which the average pupil of former times could never fully understand, down to the minute details of crayons, ink stands and hat pegs; second, the extensive use of capital, machinery and inventive ability for supplying the improved instrumentalities at cheap rates.

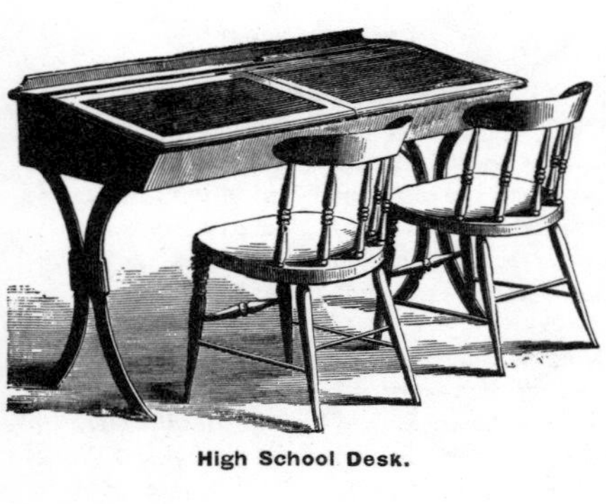

High School Desk.

The old-fashioned district school has, within the memory of many persons now living, been the prevailing type of school house and apparatus, and indeed stray specimens of it may yet be found. Not a few of our readers, we are confident will remember the old clap board shanty, or perhaps log hut, in which they conned their first lessons. There may be some pleasant memories associated with that old house, but we venture the assertion that the hard slab bench with its straddling legs is not one of them How few were the aids, we who are beginning to grow old, received in our school days, compared with the pupils of the present time. Our school house was a dismal hole at best, and the master always cross; we had no wall-maps, no globes, no apparatus of any kind, and if we learned at all, we simply learned that the books said this and that, but the truth of the assertion was not demonstrated.

Happily those days have gone by and the school-house of to-day is a very different affair. Its neat and comfortable desks and seats, abundance of text-books, well chosen library, its maps, charts, globes and scientific apparatus, form an array of contrivances for shortening, clearing, and easing the way of the scholar, and for spreading his progress on the road to knowledge.

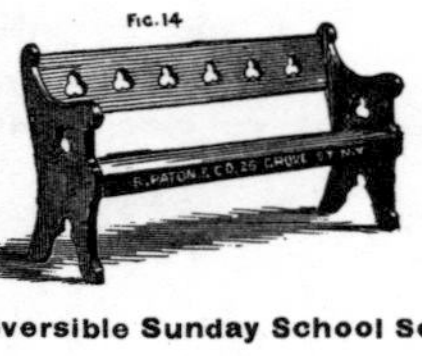

Patent Reversible Sunday School Settee.

The vast improvements in the modes of education at which we have thus briefly glanced have created a demand for school appliances of various kinds, the furnishing of which has become a business of great magnitude. For many years the manufacture of school and church furniture has held a prominent place in the great industries of the United States. Mr. Robert Paton, the senior member of the firm of Robert Paton & Son, has been extensively and exclusively engaged in this special branch of manufacture nearly thirty years, he having established the business in 1848. During that year he supplied the first of the Public School Houses in the City of New York, with what was then called "modern school furniture." Previous to that time they had been using rough, uncouth and uncomfortable seats and desks, scarcely better than those of the country schools. The improvement in the appearance of the school room, and the increased comfort of the scholars after the introduction of the new furniture, was so apparent, that Mr. Paton's furniture was at once endorsed as the best in use, and since that time, all the Public School Houses erected in the city of New York have been, to a great extent, supplied with furniture from this manufactory, until now there are in the neighborhood of one hundred of them furnished by Robert Paton & Son.

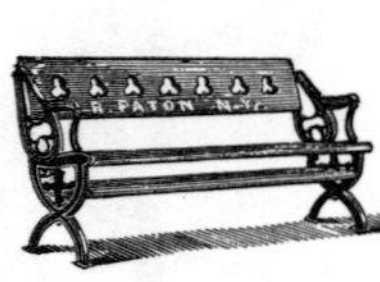

Combination Folding Settees.
For Children or Adults.

From the very start the business has continued to grow, until now it has assumed collossal proportions. The firm have constantly striven to improve their wares and have succeeded to such an eminent degree that they hold a first position in the trade. Letters Patent of the United States, No. 1,756, dated August 20, 1861, and August 30, 1864, were granted to Robert Paton, for improvement in school seat and desk. This seat was the first to be used exclusively for school furniture. The success with which it met, is seen by its general use in schools throughout the United States. This patent is controlled exclusively by Mr. Paton, and is applied to his desks as well as to his folding chairs. The great success which this invention has attained has induced some parties to appropriate it to themselves, to the manifest injury of the legal owner, and Mr. Paton, in order that he may enjoy the full and just reward of his skill, has determined to prosecute to the fullest extent of the law all who manufacture or use any article infringing on his patents.

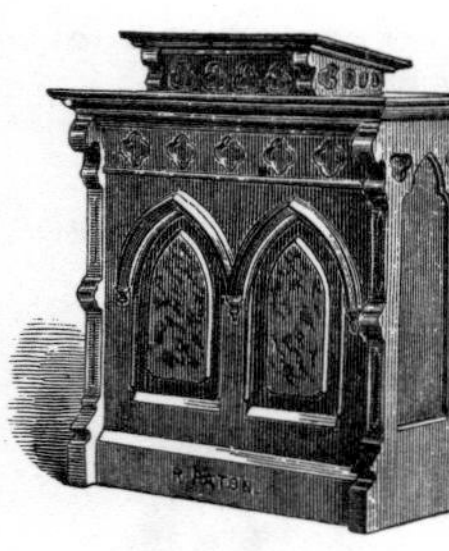

Pulpit Desk.

From the numerous engravings which surround this page the reader can gain but a faint idea of the many articles manufactured by this firm, and yet the pictures here given speak so forcibly of the beauty and utility of the articles they represent, that none who look and read can fail to acknowledge their manifest fitness for the purposes for which they are intended.

To attempt to describe all the various kinds of desks, chairs, settees, etc., manufactured by this firm, would more than fill the space we have allotted them; to even enumerate them would occupy too much room. Suffice it to say that everything necessary for the complete and comfortable furnishing of a school house, lecture room, public hall or Sunday school can be obtained at their establishment. In general terms, we may say of their school furniture, that it is made of ash or cherry and put together in the most substantial manner, mounted on cast iron stanchions. The chairs are very strong and furnish a natural support for the back. The seats are so constructed as to be readily thrown up parallel with the back of the desk, thus giving an easy mode of ingress and egress, as well as affording better accommodations for sweeping.

Particular attention is paid to the furnishing of churches with seats upholstered in sofa style. The Church Settee is beautiful to look at, convenient of access and comfortable, and is cheaper than many styles of pews. The Lecture Room Settees are strong and simple in construction, and have turn-up seats. The Sunday School Settees have either reversible backs or are made in three sections, so as to be connected into squares for classes, or used as straight seats for lecture room purposes.

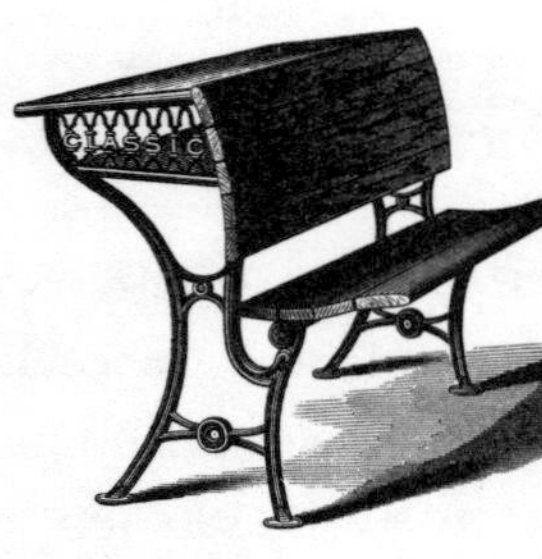

Classic Grammar School Desk.

In addition to their school furniture above spoken of, Messrs. Robert Paton & Son are always prepared to supply Blackboards, Easels and Supports, Book Cases, Slates, Silicate Slate Books, Wall Maps, Globes, Clocks, Bells, in fact anything and everything used in a School. For further information we must refer our readers to the gentlemen themselves, or if any cannot conveniently call upon them, by enclosing stamps to pre-pay the postage they can obtain an illustrated catalogue which fully describes the various articles of their manufacture.

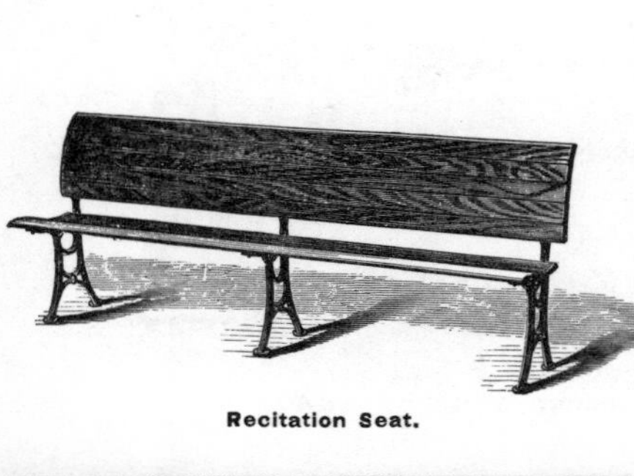

Recitation Seat.

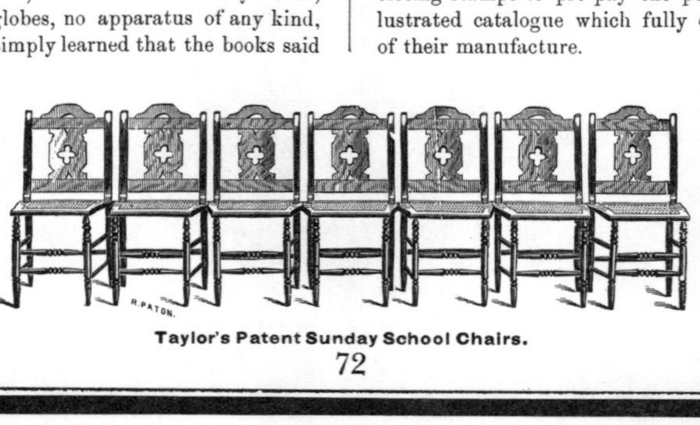

Taylor's Patent Sunday School Chairs.

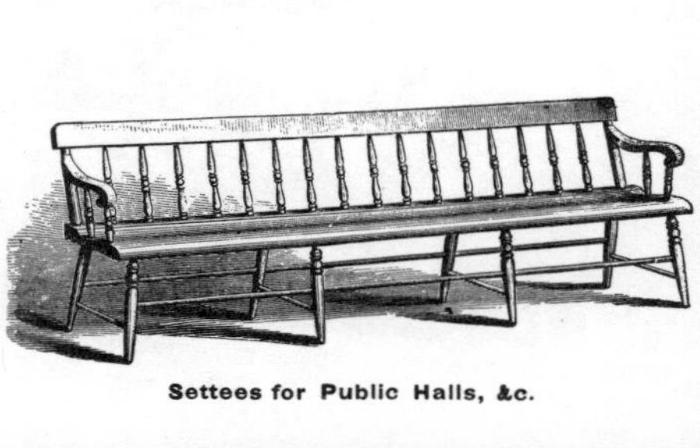

Settees for Public Halls, &c.

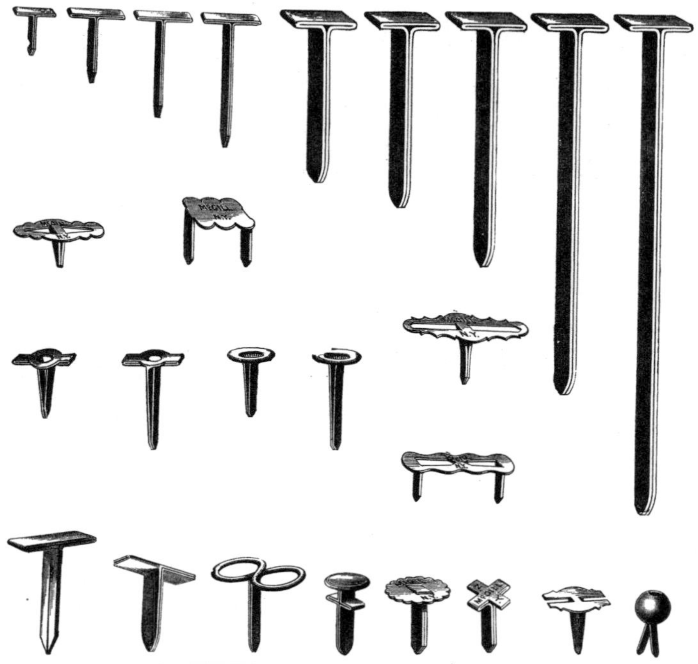

McGILL'S PAT. T FASTENERS.

GEO. W. McGILL, Patentee.

HOLMES, BOOTH & HAYDENS,

Manufacturers,

WATERBURY, CONN.

49 Chambers Street, New York.

18 Federal Street, Boston, Mass.

——:o:——

So large a portion of the space allotted for the consideration of Mr. McGill's simple and ingenious invention of, and really artistic designs for Metal Clasps and Rings is occupied by illustrations of the articles, that there is little room left for any description, nor is any description necessary, they speak for themselves. The merest glance at the cuts presented, will convince any reasoning being of their utility for and adaptability to many uses, and that for fastening and binding papers they are vastly superior to "red tape" or other materials used in by-gone days. The great variety of sizes and styles made, enables one to select the exact thing wanted, whether it be "flat head," "round head," "eyelet," or almost any imaginable style of head. They are useful for binding legal or ill-legal papers, samples of dry or fancy goods, such as woolens, cottons, linens, silks, ribbons, etc., for making paper and light wooden boxes, and for innumerable other purposes Then there are various styles of Suspendory Rings and Braces for hanging cards, calenders, and hundreds of other uses which we cannot here enumerate. Indeed, we believe that an entire page would not hold the list.

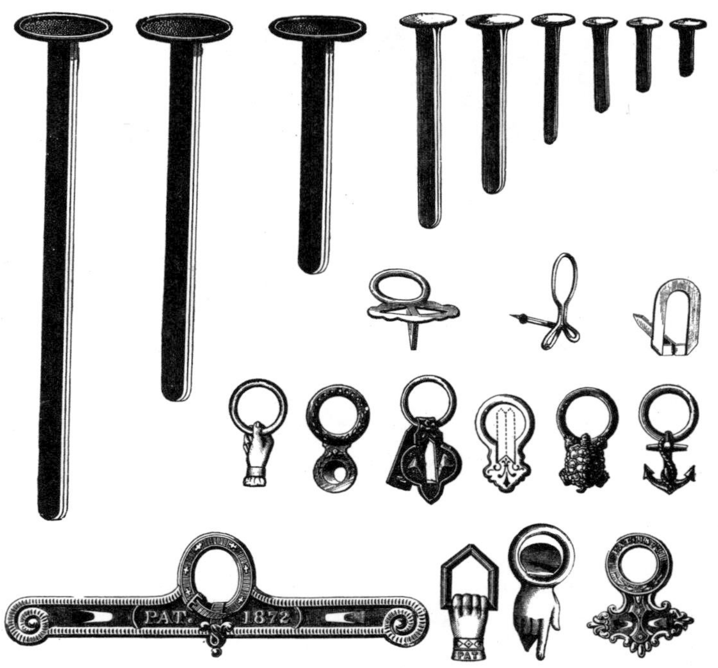

THE MERCHANTS' SHOT TOWER

Baltimore, Md.

HENRY D. HARVEY, Pres't.

——:o:——

The corner-stone of the Merchants' Shot Tower was laid by Charles Carroll, of Carrolton, (one of the signers of the Declaration of Independence,) on the 4th of July, 1828; the same day Mr. Carroll laid the corner-stone of the Baltimore and Ohio Railroad. The tower stands on a solid rock, fifteen feet below the surface, and is built of good, hard, red brick, mortar and cement; it is circular in form, two hundred and seventeen feet and eight inches high, the walls being five feet thick at the pavement, and tapering to eighteen inches at the top; the inside diameter is thirty feet and seven inches in the clear at the pavement, and seventeen feet at the roof. This tower is believed to be the finest brick and mortar structure on this continent without crack, flaw or blemish from foundation to summit. To the perfect steadiness of the tower is attributed the perfection of the shot made by this Company.

In the tower there are several floors, but only two of them are used for dropping shot: the one next to the roof, 200 feet high, from TTTT's to B shot are dropped; the other, 135 feet high, from which Nos. 1 to 13 are dropped. On each of these floors is a brick furnace, with an iron kettle large enough to hold five tons of metal; here the lead is melted and flows from the kettle through a spout into a circular dropping pan, the bottom of which is perforated, the holes being perfectly shaped, and both sides of the bottom smoothly finished. The pan is suspended over a wall or tank of water at the bottom of the tower, which both cools and preserves them from indentation. A continuous supply of metal is kept up by adding pigs of lead and pigs of temper (for without the temper the lead would not form into globes, but run through the pan in streams) until the dropping for the day is finished. As the shot falls in the well, an elevator, with shot buckets, dips it up, carrying it to a height of some sixty feet, and discharges it into a spout which leads to a large receiver, where it is drained of water. From the receiver the shot passes through another spout to a steam drying-pan on the floor below; as rapidly as it dries, it is emptied into another receiver, and from thence through another spout, and is fed into the polisher. From the polisher it is transferred to the seperating table, where all the imperfect shot are mechanically separated from the perfect ones, the imperfect being consigned to "graves," and the perfect, welcomed by another receiver, in the bottom of which are four hoppers holding thirty pounds each. The hopper being opened, the shot falls into a chest of twenty drawers, called a "sifter," which has a rocking motion from front to back, and thoroughly separates the different sizes. This being done, the shot is transferred into pipes and run into the packing room below where it is filled into bags of twenty-five pounds each, and is now ready for market. The whole operation, from placing the lead in the kettles to packing the bag can be done here in twenty-seven minutes, which is much quicker, we are told, than it can be done at any other tower in the world.

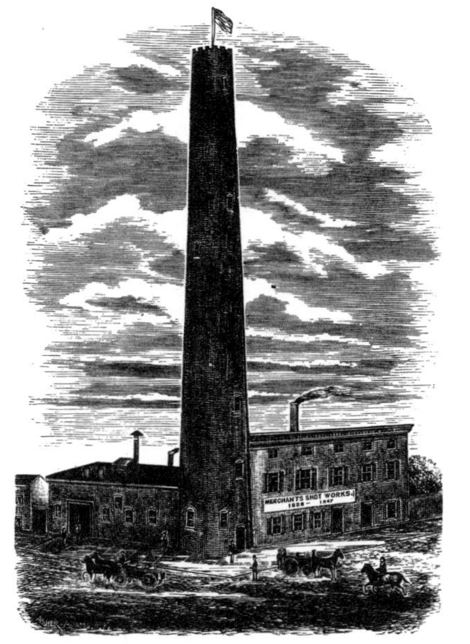

For each size of shot made a different dropping pan is used, with holes punched by machinery, each hole in a pan used for a given size of shot being exactly alike in shape and size, but all the globes that form in dropping are not of the same size. The sizes are separated by the sifter, the bottoms of the drawers are made of parchment—sheep, goat or hog skin—prepared expressly for shot manufacturers, and are punched with perfect accuracy to the standard of the Company. To briefly illustrate: In dropping for No. 6 shot there will be a few No. 5, about ninety per cent. of No. 6, and some No. 7, and so with every size dropped for. In sifting, twenty drawers are used, four for No. 4, four for No. 5, four for No. 6, four for No. 7, and four blanks. When the sifter is charged, about 120 lbs. immediately drop into the first set of drawers No. 4. When the rocking motion is applied, each size falls into its respective drawer, then the top and bottom drawers, containing the largest and smallest pellets, are set aside until those numbers are to be finished, and all the shot in the No. 5, 6, and 7 drawers are perfect.

The great improvements in machinery made by this Company in 1875, the remarkably fine results produced by their new polishing machine, and their distributor for feeding the shot at the "separating tables," devices which no other manufacturers use, and which patents have been applied for, warrant them, they believe, in claiming to make the best shot in the world. Their list of sizes runs from TTTT to No. 13, an assortment of twenty distinct sizes, and they drop two larger and two smaller sizes than any other concern. Their present rate of production is two thousand bags of finished shot per day, but should the demand necessitate it, they could produce four thousand bags per day.

Mr. Henry D. Harvey, the President of this Company, has been engaged in the manufacture of shot the past forty-nine years, and is doubtless the oldest shot maker living.

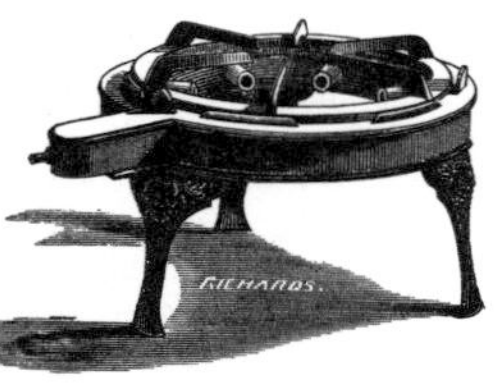

GAS COOKING WITH ECONOMY.

JOHN R. SHIRLEY,

Inventor and Manufacturer of

SHIRLEY'S NEW GAS STOVES and OVENS,

Cor. Pine and Eddy Sts., Providence, R. I.

——:o:——

In introducing to the public Shirley's New Gas Cooking Stoves and Ovens, we desire to call attention to the comfort and convenience of cooking by gas, especially during the summer months when a fire is not required for other purposes. The advantages derived by the use of gas as fuel for cooking can only be fully appreciated by those who have had experience in its extremely useful application for that purpose, but to obtain all the advantages, one must be careful to select a stove so constructed as to develop and utilize the greatest heat attainable from a given quantity of gas.

In the construction of these Stoves, great care has been taken that the gas should be so applied as to ensure perfect combustion and the smallest amount of consumption practical. That it generates and completely utilizes heat in large quantities compared with the quantity of gas consumed, is abundantly proven by the fact that it will roast a joint of meat weighing seven or eight pounds for the trifling sum of three cents.

To obtain a perfect estimate of the relative money value of Gas and Coal as calorific agents, we must take a comprehensive view of all the contingencies inseparately attached to each.

The use of coal entails first the trouble of purchase, then it must be stored away, and when it is safely in the bin, the side-walk on which it was dumped presents such an unseemly appearance that it must needs be scrubbed. Then kindlings must be purchased and stored, and as they are wanted, perhaps for use on an upper floor, both coal and wood must be carried from the cellar. When each new fire is built, the ashes from the last one must be removed from the premises, involving, no matter how careful, the scattering of some over the room, to the destruction of carpets, furniture, etc.; then comes the time lost in waiting for the fire to burn. If only a little fire is needed to boil a pint of water, substantially the same operations must be gone through with, that would be necessary to make a fire to cook a dinner. After it is built it must be watched, or it may get too hot and burn the meat, or go out and leave the water unboiled.

With gas all this is changed—it entails no journeys up and down stairs, it makes no dirt, necessitates no labor; it does not smoke, nor burn too fast or too slow; it requires no care. The gas has only to be lighted and adjusted to give the flame required, the food placed in the oven and, with very little experience, the time required for properly cooking it may be so correctly determined, that no further attention need be paid to either fire or oven until done. The gas is instantly turned off, and thereby all the waste which occurs with a coal fire is saved.

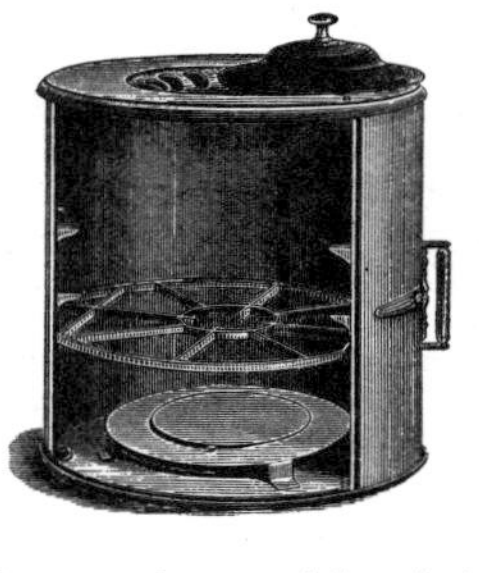

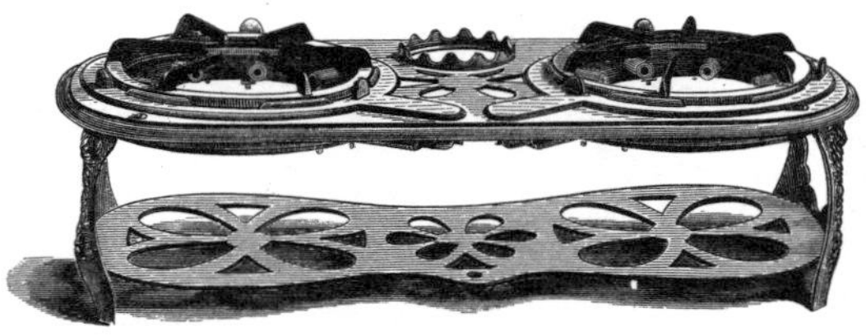

The Oven connected with these Stoves is of much larger capacity than those usually furnished with Gas Stoves, and by the peculiar arrangement of its interior, a greater amount of heat is utilized than by methods heretofore employed. These Stoves and Ovens are for sale by the inventor, John R. Shirley, at his Show Room and Manufactory, corner of Pine and Eddy Sts., Providence, R. I., where also may be seen a good assortment of Crystal, Bronze and Gilt Gas Fixtures of his own make, and at reasonable prices.

Prices of Stoves—Single Stove, $1.75; Double Stove, $4.50; Oven, can be used on either Stove, $4.50. Liberal discount to the Trade. These Stoves sent to any address, free of package, upon receipt of price.

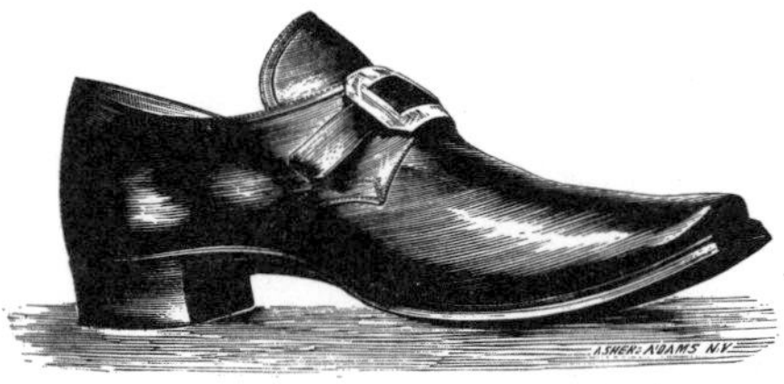

HATHAWAY & SOULE,

MANUFACTURERS OF

MEN'S BOYS' AND YOUTHS' FINE

BOOTS AND SHOES,

Cor. North Second & North Sts., New Bedford, Mass.

——:o:——

The above named firm commenced business in October, 1865, occupying a single room 14x18 feet, a rather modest beginning. Now they occupy the four story brick building, 100x32 feet, a cut of which is presented below. In 1866 their sales were $28,000; in 1875, $190,000, and thus far their sales for the current year, (1876), show a considerable gain over the same months of last year. The great increase in their business will be better appreciated from the fact that prices have decreased nearly one-third since 1866. Their factory is well lighted, well ventilated and heated by steam. Such substantial success is the best proof that can be offered of the superiority of their productions.

The manufactures of the firm consist of Men's, Boys' and Youths' Fine Boots and Shoes of all styles. Their goods are sold through New England, and in some portions of the West, directly to retail dealers. Our cuts show a few leading styles of their Shoes, but they also manufacture a full line of Boots.

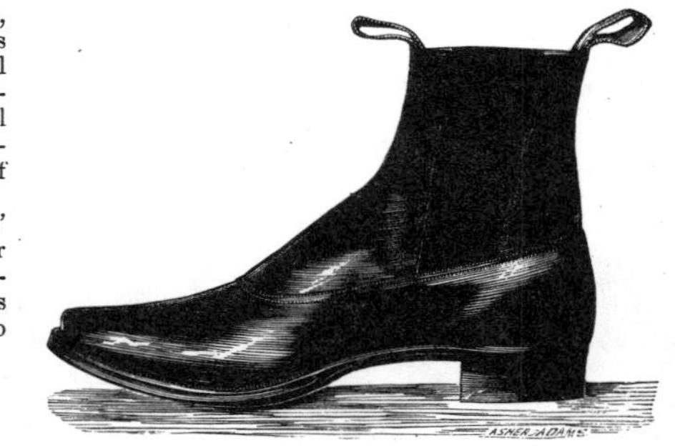

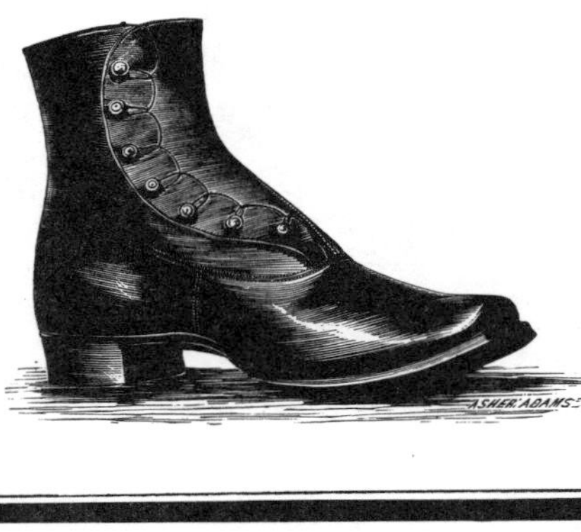

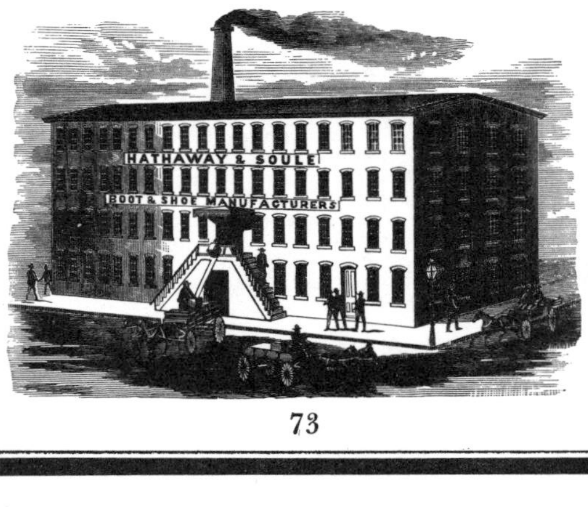

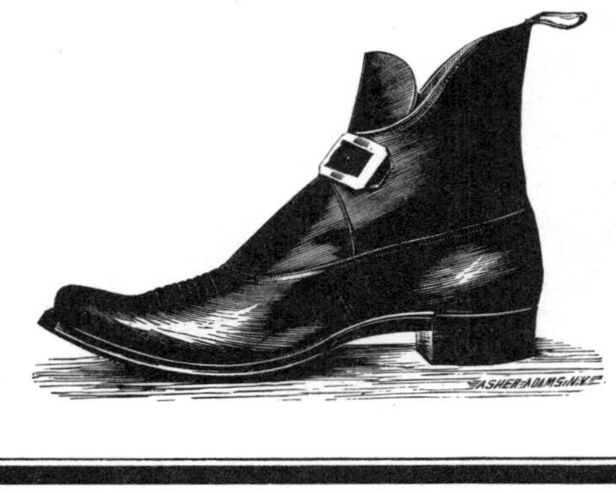

CENTRAL SHAFT.

FIG.2.   FIG.1.   FIG.3.

"POWDER KEG" BATTERY AND EXPLODERS.

WEST PORTAL.

Nitro-Glycerin and the Hoosac Tunnel.

—:o:—

GEO. M. MOWBRAY,

Manufacturer of

Mowbray's Frictional "Powder Keg" Battery.

Nitro-Glycerin, Mica Powder, Gutta Percha Works, etc.

North Adams, Mass.

—:o:—

While the British, German and French Governments have been expending millions and millions of pounds sterling on experiments with "big guns" and "defensive armour" for warlike purposes, in another direction various parties, and among them the subject of this paper, have been devoting all their energies to the application of higher explosives than gunpowder, for internal improvements.

In 1866, Thomas A. Doane, Chief Engineer of the Hoosac Tunnel, clearly foresaw that unless some higher explosive than gunpowder was applied to that work, it could not be completed within any reasonable period. He corresponded with Geo. M. Mowbray, which led the latter, in 1867, to erect nitro-glycerin works at North Adams, in the state of Massachusetts, near to the tunnel. These have been in successful operation ever since, having manufactured nearly a million pounds of nitro-glycerin.

Mr. Mowbray, during that time, has been perfecting the manufacture of this explosive with a view to rendering it non-explosive, except at the precise moment when its force is required and has been successful.

During his labors, occupying eight years, he discovered and applied various facts, opposed to the received and published views of French and German Savans, who have undoubtedly asserted erroneous conclusions.

Among the facts discovered or applied by Mr. Mowbray are the following:

1. That nitro-glycerin, in a congealed state, cannot be exploded by any ordinary means.

2. That if nitro-glycerin be mixed with one-third of nitro-benzole or nitro-toluol it cannot be exploded by percussion; but can be exploded by a heavy charge of fulminate.

3. That nitro-glycerin, by means of a fulminate, can be exploded in an open saucer. (A. Nobel, asserted that it was practically impossible to explode it, except when confined, and obtained a patent for such alleged discovery.)

4. Mowbray, subsequently, so improved the method of exploding by electricity, that it is now practicable with fuses costing only five cents each, and his new friction "powder keg" battery, so-called from its case, to explode fifty holes at one blast.

5. Finding that absorbents, such as rottenstone, sawdust and charcoal, which have been used to form the explosive compounds known as dynamite, dualin, giant powder and rend rock, when mixed with nitro-glycerin, diminished the force of the latter nearly one half, he devised and invented a compound of nitro-glycerin and mica scales, which, although absolutely safe and impossible to explode during transportation, rough handling, etc., can nevertheless be made to develope immense force, when surrounding a heavy charge of a fulminating mixture, to be exploded inside the cartridge containing this mica powder, and this compound in no way diminishes the explosive force of the nitro-glycerin it contains when so fired.

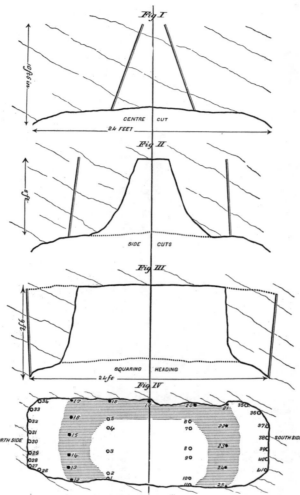

Fig I

CENTRE CUT
24 FEET

Fig II

SIDE CUTS

Fig III

SQUARING HEADING

Fig IV

NORTH SIDE   SOUTH SIDE.

SCHEME FOR DRILLING THE HEADING OF HOOSAC TUNNEL.

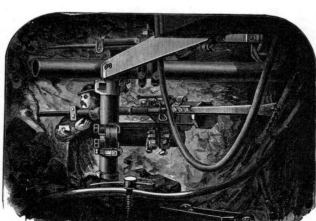

MACHINE DRILL IN TUNNEL.

During the eight years that Mr. Mowbray has devoted to the examination, improvement and development of these higher explosive forces, and while manufacturing nearly a million pounds of nitro-glycerin, no accident whatever has occurred; either in the manufacturing, teaming or transporting any of the explosives prepared by him.

Mr. Walter Shanly, the eminent engineer, and contractor for the Hoosac Tunnel, thus certifies to the new explosive, "Mica Blasting Powder."

"Hoosac Tunnel" Contract.
North Adams. Mass.
20 August, 1874.

Dear Sir:
Within the last six months we have used some 30,-000 lbs. of your "Mica Powder" and with the exception of the "Tri-Nitro-Glycerin" itself, have had no better explosive in our works here. It is light to carry. Safe (as far as that term can be applied to any explosive) to handle. "Nimble" to explode and thorough in combustion—a very essential quality in preparations of Nitro-Glycerin.
Where pure Nitro-Glycerin is not wanted we do not ask any better substitute than Mica Powder.
Yours truly,
W. SHANLY.
Geo. M. Mowbray, Esq.,
North Adams.

In a previous note the firm had stated.

To Geo. M. Mowbray:
Mr. Geo. M. Mowbray has supplied us with his Tri-Nitro-Glycerin ever since we have been engaged upon the Hoosac Tunnel, upwards of four years; during which time our consumption of the article has frequently exceeded four tons a month. We have had the greatest satisfaction in our dealings with Mr. Mowbray and have no hesitation in saying that, without the assistance of the admirable explosive he manufactures, the time within which this work will be completed would have extended over two years beyond what it will actually be when, within the next few months, the tunnel will be open to the world. (Signed,)
F. SHANLY & Co.,
Contractors,
North Adams, Mass.

July 11, 1873.

In blasting, the greater safety of firing the charges by electricity, saving twenty per cent of explosive, owing to the increased effective force of simultaneously firing each drilled hole, and the absence of smoke occasioned by the burning of the common fuse, naturally attracted many minds to this method ; among them in England, Col. Pasley, half a century ago, in removing the Royal George at Spithead, Professors Abel and Wheatstone, Col. Verdue, Siemens Brothers; in Austria, Baron Lenk, and in America, Moses Farmer, Ritchie, Smith and others, have each designed various methods or apparatus; it is only necessary to state that at the commencement of operations at the Hoosac Tunnel, when the Wheatstone apparatus was used with the Abel fuses, there was difficulty and uncertainty in firing five holes at once, whereas now with the Mowbray Frictional "Powder Keg" Battery, costing but seventy-five dollars and lasting a man's life time, one hundred of his fuses have been fired at one discharge, and fifty can as easily be fired now as five could have been fired ten years ago, and this with perfect safety to the operator.

European nations have shrunk from using nitro-glycerin, erroneously inferring that it possessed properties which do not belong to it, and using it imbued with these erroneous impressions, many fatal accidents of course resulted; hence the public mind has been wrongly impressed with an idea that this explosive cannot be handled without imminent peril to life and limb. The danger lies now in a revulsion from this extreme view, because, paraphrasing Prof. Tyndall's warning as regards Alpine climbing, and applying it to explosives:

"For rashness, ignorance and carelessness, explosives leave no margin; and to rashness, ignorance and carelessness three-fourths of the catastrophes which shock us are to be traced."

The manufacture of nearly a million pounds of these explosives, without accident, covering a term of eight years; the teaming of this quantity over the roughest roads of the United States safely to its destination, and the fact of a consumption reaching four tons a month, during five years in one work, which, to quote the language of the consulting engineer, E. S. Philbrick, Esq., before a Committee of the Massachusetts Legislature, "I think the Tunnel would not have been finished in this generation without the use of nitro-glycerin," indicate the future of nitro-glycerin; and assuredly the experience gained, the details so carefully perfected, will secure for it a market in the various public works of the United States. In order to cover his customers from litigation, Mr. Mowbray has obtained fourteen patents for his improvements in this direction. They are as follows: No. 76,499, April 7, 1868; No. 93,113, July 20, 1869; No. 94,969, September 21, 1869; No. 96,465, November 2, 1869; No. 106,606, August 23, 1870; No. 106,607, August 23, 1870 ; No. 124,397, March 5, 1872; No. 128,241, June 25, 1872; No. 139,686, June 10, 1873; No. 150,428, May 5, 1874; No. 161,430, March 30, 1875; No. 161,431, March 30, 1875; No. 161,432, March 30, 1875; No. 162,675, April 27, 1875.

NITRO-GLYCERIN CONVERTING ROOM

EAST PORTAL.

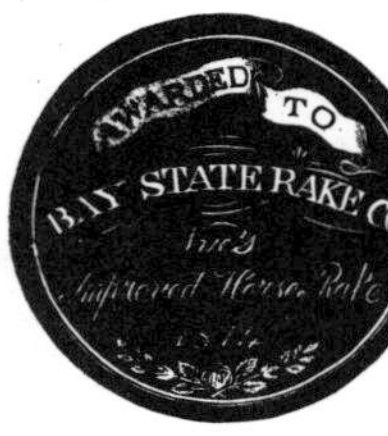

S. R. NYE BAY STATE RAKE COMPANY,

Winchendon, Mass

——:o:——

The original Bay State Rake was invented and patented by Mr. S. R. Nye, in the year 1866, and manufactured at West Fitchburg, Mass. Subsequently the inventor made a number of improvements, and, in 1871, the manufacture of the perfected machine was begun at Winchendon, Mass., by an association of gentlemen under the name of the S. R. Nye Bay State Rake Company—which was incorporated as a Joint Stock Company, under the same name, January 3d, 1874. This Company manufactures the Improved Bay State Rake, under patents granted as follows: March 13, 1866; January 12, 1869; July 19, 1870, and re-issued, October 5, 1875.

The marked advantages of this rake are found: 1st. In the peculiar shape of the Teeth, those at each end being brought forward of those in the center, which prevents the hay from scattering or roping out. This is particularly advantageous when raking on a side hill or gleaning. 2d. In the manner of holding each tooth in its proper position, laterally, by what is called the Guide, which prevents them from flopping about, as is the case with other rakes. 3d. Each tooth is independent of all the others, which with spring arrangement enables it to pass over an obstruction twenty inches high, without in the least affecting the teeth on either side of it. 4th. The Dumping Arrangement, which enables any boy or girl, who can drive a horse, to rake as well as a man, as the dumping is done entirely by the power of the

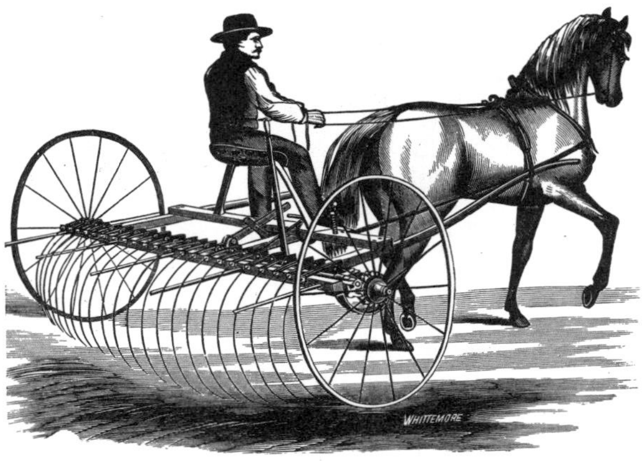

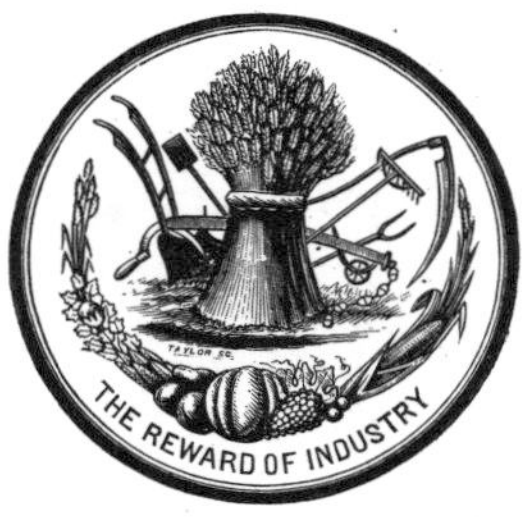

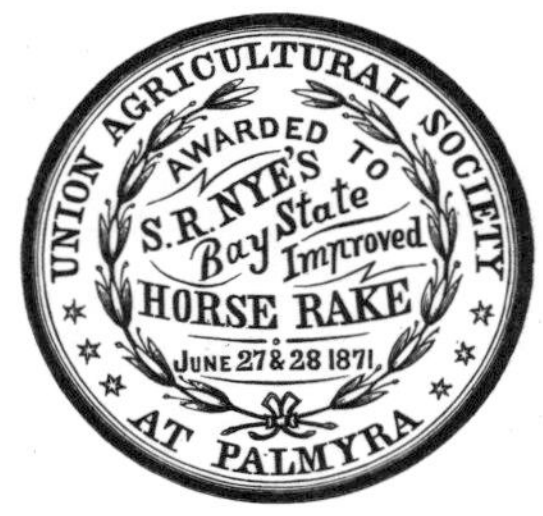

horse, and only two pounds pressure by the foot is required. 5th. The simple and effective manner of holding down the teeth in green or heavy grass.

The superiority of this Rake will readily be inferred from the fact that First Premiums were awarded to it at Fairs during the falls of 1874 and 1875, as follows:

Schenectady, N. Y.; Western N. Y., Rochester; Saratoga County, N. Y.; Bristol County, Vt.; Chittenden County, Vt.; Eastern N. Y., at Albany; Vermont State, at Rutland; Strafford County, at Dover, N. H.; Hampshire, Franklin and Hampden, at Northampton, Mass.; Connecticut Valley Fair, at Claremont, N. H.; Silver Medal at Maine State Fair; Fitchburg, Northern Worcester County; Berkshire County Fair, Silver Medal; Franklin County, at Sheldon, Vt.; Windham County, at Newfane, Vt. The Rake was shown at seventy fairs in the Fall of 1875, and First Premiums taken in all cases where Premiums were offered.

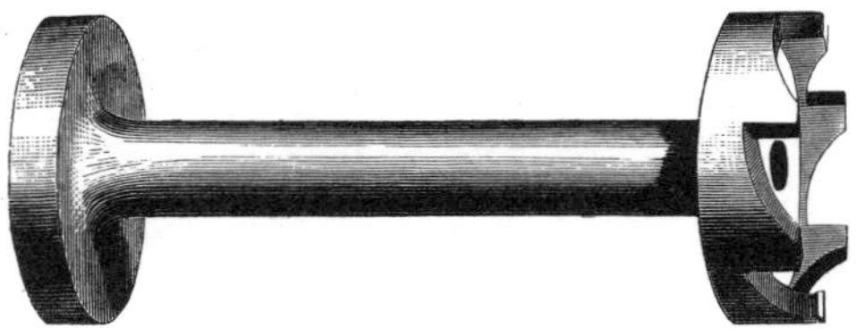

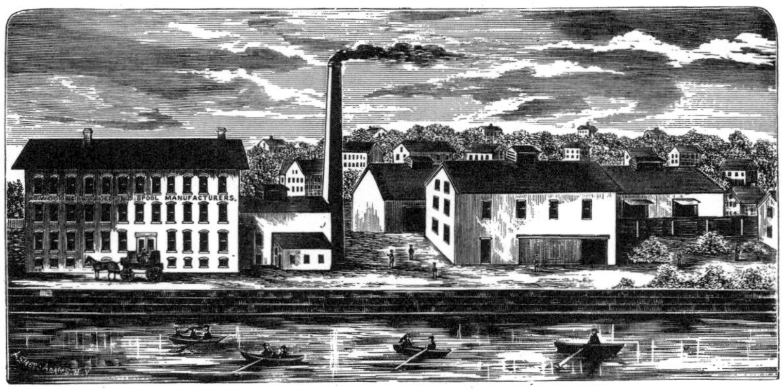

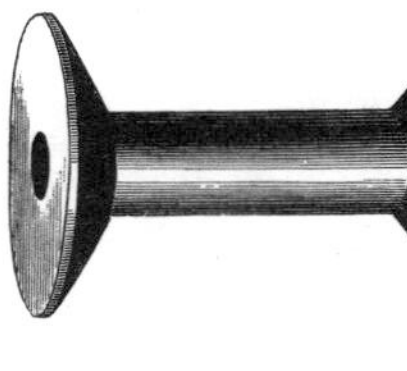

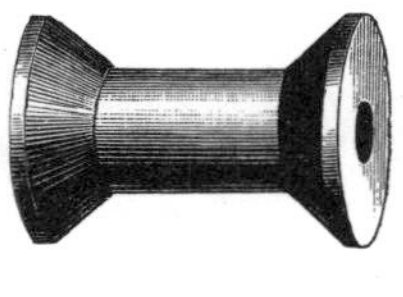

ATWOOD, CRAWFORD & CO.,

Successors to CUSHMAN, PHILLIPS & CO.,

Manufacturers of

Spools for Cotton, Linen and Silk Thread.

ALSO,

Braider Bobbins, Wooden Balls, Button Molds, &c.

PAWTUCKET, R. I.

This establishment, one of the first of its kind in the United States, so nearly perfect in this year, 1876, in its equipment for the production of spools of all kinds, is in strong contrast with its very modest beginning. The factory was started by its former proprietor (in whole or in part until last year) Robert Cushman, who in 1848 commenced operations in a power blacksmith's shop in the country. Alone, almost without means and possessed of but few tools, the prospect scarce seemed a bright one, but Mr. C. determined to merit success whether he achieved it or not, and closely applied himself to business. Perseverent effort proved the entering wedge for success, and slowly but surely he gathered capital and tools, and

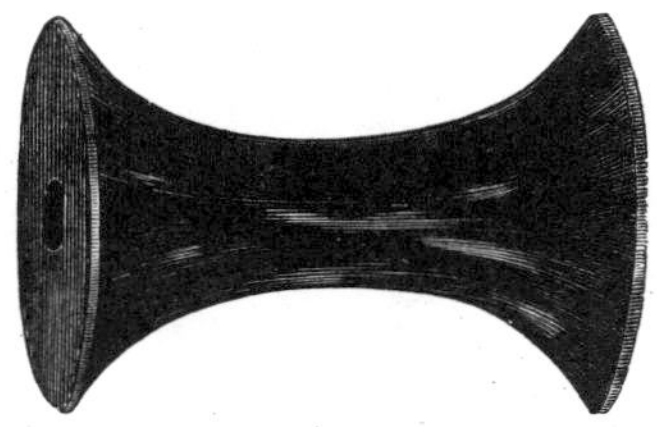

from the small beginning the business gradually grew despite many discouraging circumstances until it reached its present large proportions: consuming some years about 800,000 feet of lumber, and affording employment to some forty hands. Under its former management, the establishment gained the enviable reputation of being superior to any of its kind in the United States in the quality of its products, and it is confidently believed that its present claim to such superiority is generally acknowledged by consumers of such goods. Of the present proprietors, one was a former partner in the old firm; another was brought up in the shop and office from a boy, and the other has had many years experience in the business. None of them are new to the trade and all of them are actuated by a sincere desire not only to maintain the high reputation gained by the former proprietors, but if possible to increase and extend it.

In addition to the manufacture of silk and thread spools the firm does a great variety of Fancy Turning. Their work is sent to all parts of the United States, to the Canadas and some to foreign lands, notably Ireland, Scotland, and England, and we have no hesitancy in saying that we have the utmost confidence in their ability satisfactorily to serve those who may favor them with orders, and to suit the most particular.

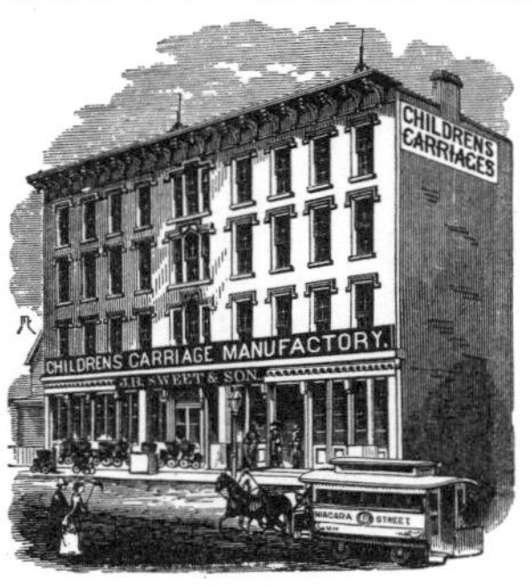

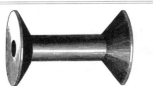

J. B. SWEET & SON,

MANUFACTURERS OF

CHILDREN'S CARRIAGES,

297, 299 and 301 Niagara St, Buffalo, N. Y.

Before us as we write is the eleventh annual catalogue of Children's Carriages, issued by the above named firm; and after a careful examination of its beautifully illustrated pages, containing descriptions of no less than forty different Carriages for Children manufactured by them, we are convinced that within the space at our disposal we cannot do the subject justice. No opportunity is afforded us to describe the delight of baby when the new equipage first arrives nor to tell of the solid comfort it afterwards finds in pleasant rides, nor can we count the advantages accruing to mamma and to nurse through its introduction.

Mr. J. B. Sweet has been engaged in the business of manufacturing Children's Carriages since the year 1866, and the present firm, J. B. Sweet & Son was formed in 1872. During this time they have introduced many new styles, and have built up a very large trade, especially through the West.

We cannot describe all their different styles, but deem it a duty to call attention to the Novelty Carriage

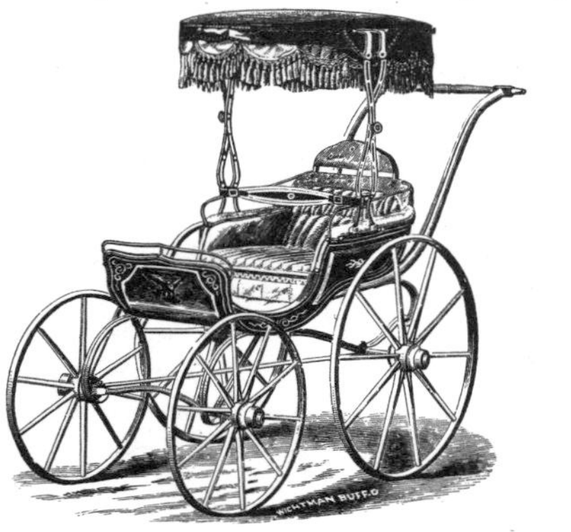

which they first introduced to the general trade less than two years ago. It is at once handsome, stylish and comfortable and its general advantages may be briefly stated as follows:

1st. It is absolutely safe—no danger of the child being thrown out. 2d. Perfect protection from the sun, and the circulation of the air equalized. 3d. The child can be placed in a reclining position. This is important, as children often go to sleep when exposed to the open air, and the old style of carriage does not admit of their being placed in a comfortable and healthy position. 4th. It can instantly be converted into a cradle by pushing

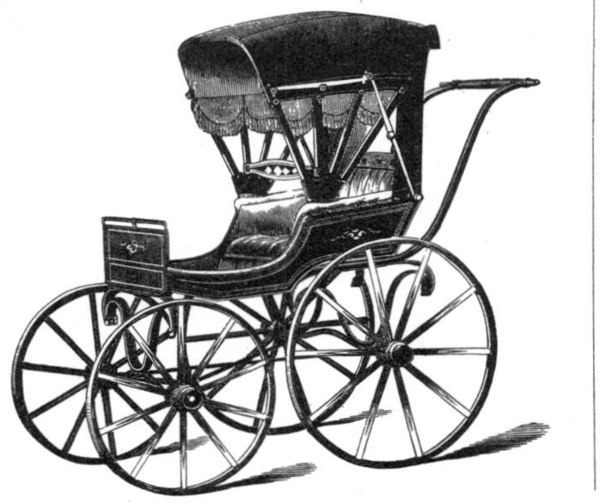

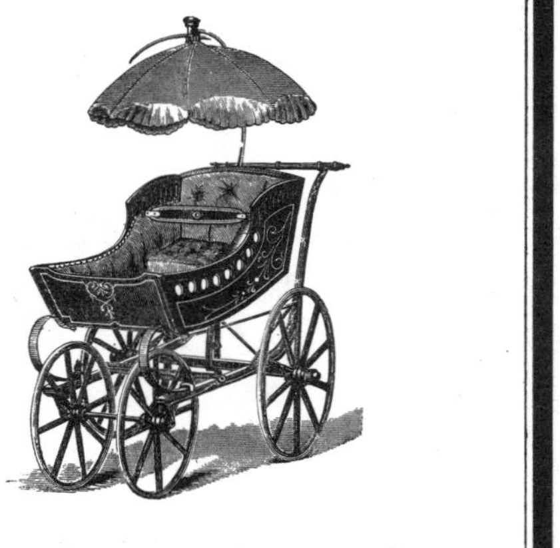

the bottom up, which fastens with a button. Does not swing, or rock from side to side, but the motion is upward and downward, the only proper way to rock a child. 5th. The springs can be adjusted to the weight of the child by pushing the clamps forward or backward. 6th. By adjusting the strap behind, little or much spring may be given to the carriage. 7th It is not complicated. As will be seen by the engraving, it is a very stylish carriage, and particular attention is called to the adjustable canopy top. It shields the child from the rays of the sun, and admits of a free circulation of the air.

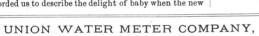

UNION WATER METER COMPANY,

Nos. 31 and 33 Hermon Street,

WORCESTER, MASS.

——:o:——

This Company was organized in November, 1868. As the name indicates, its purpose was the manufacture and introduction of Water Meters. The Meter made by this Company is the joint invention of Phinehas Ball and Benniah Fitts. Mr. Ball has been President of the Company since its formation, while Mr. Fitts has served in the capacity of Mechanical Engineer. The Treasurer has been Mr. John C. Otis.

The meter is known as the Ball & Fitts Water Meter. It is of the double reciprocating piston class, and is positive in its measurement. For the accuracy of its measurement of the quantity of water passing through under all conditions of high and low pressures and small and large streams it has attained a very high reputation, standing, in this respect, at the head of its class. Since the organization of the Company there has been made over 5,000 of these meters which are now used by over 100 different Water Companies in this country and Canada.

The need and the utility of a good reliable Water Meter is now acknowledged by the best Hydraulic Engineers and Managers of Water Works, Their usefulness is to furnish a standard by which to levy a rate based upon the actual quantity of water used, and not upon a guess of the assessor; and further, to protect the water companies from the abuse of consumers in the form of reckless and fraudulent use, and to point out waste from pipes and inferior or worn out fixtures, and bad workmanship in plumbing. The value of a Meter for these last named purposes is quite as great as for that of an equitable assessment.

This meter was the result of much study on the part of the patentees, and its manufacture was commenced not until after about two years of experimenting. During this time no less then seven different styles were made, all of the piston variety, in order to find the best form and to eliminate as far as possible all error in measurement.

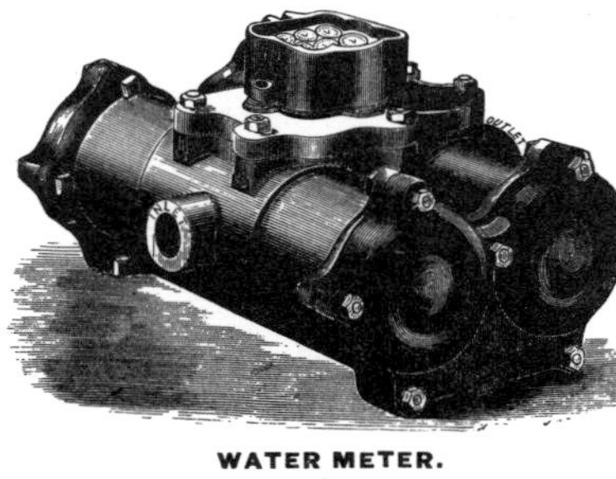

WATER METER.

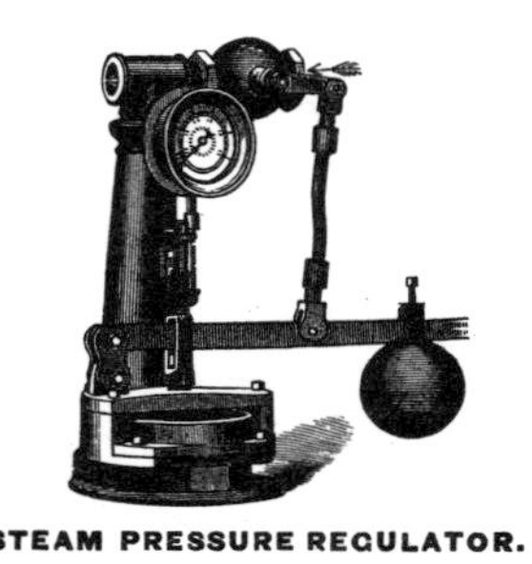

STEAM PRESSURE REGULATOR.

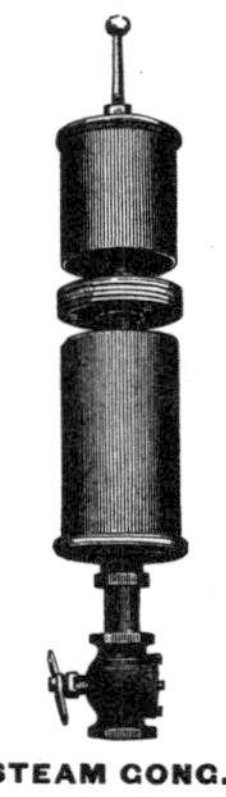

STEAM GONG.

The difficulties to be met and overcome in the making of a good, durable and reliable Meter are greater than with almost any other piece of mechanism. The Meter must run well and take care of itself. No attendant, as in the case of a steam engine, stands by to lubricate its working parts and correct minor defects in time to prolong its working life. It must care for and lubricate itself. For this reason very cheap materials and a small amount of inferior work can never produce a good Meter, however desirable a cheap Meter may be. The peculiar difficulties in this case, as in all other departments of the mechanic arts, have to be met and overcome by the use of the proper quantity of good materials, put together in a thorough and workmanlike manner.

The Piston Meter can probably never be excelled for the accurate measurement of limited quantities of water. The Rotary principle has advantages for large quantities, and when it is combined with the accurate Piston principle, a great gain in Water Meters will be achieved. Acting upon this fact the Company has been testing for about two years a device of Mr. B. Fitts that is a positive measuring Rotating Piston Meter. Thus far it promises a success.

In addition to Water Meters the Company manufacture a variety of articles, as Steam Pressure Regulators, much used in paper mills and cotton and woolen manufactories, for reducing a high pressure to a low pressure, and maintaining the low pressure uniformly. Also, Steam Gongs, much used as a fire alarm signal. These were the invention of Mr. B. Fitts. They also make a Water Pressure Regulator for reducing a high head to a low one and keeping the low head uniform. This is automatic in its operation and of great utility in many places.

In addition to these leading articles they make Fitts' Patent Stop and Chronometer Valve, a rotary valve fitted to and resting upon a conical seat, and all the fixtures for tapping cement lined wrought iron water pipes, the invention of Mr. Ball.

The Company though young in years, has won an honorable reputation for fair dealing and honest workmanship in its various specialties.

BLAKE'S PATENT STEAM PUMPS.

Made by
GEO. F. BLAKE MANUFACTURING CO.,
Sole Proprietors.
BOSTON, NEW YORK, CHICAGO.

—:o:—

New York Warerooms:

No. 86 and 88 LIBERTY ST.,

—:o:—

We are often reminded of the truth of the trite saying, "Nothing succeeds like success," and never more so than by the remarkable success of the Blake Pump, from its invention in 1862 up to the date it was placed on the market in 1864, and onward to the present time, when there are

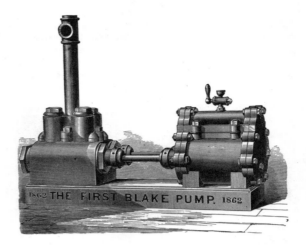

1862 THE FIRST BLAKE PUMP. 1862

The proprietors of the Blake Pump claim it is not only simple in construction and positive under pressure, but that the steam valve will work off the cold water of condensation, and that the pumps have frequently been submerged in tunnels and mines and worked themselves free. A notable instance was the flooding of the tunnel at the Buffalo Water Works, submerging six Blake Pumps to the depth of forty-five feet. Three hours from the time steam was turned on the tunnel was pumped dry.

To conclude, the success of the Blake Pump is no matter of astonishment to the initiated, for, aside from the ingenuity displayed in its construction, every step in the process of manufacture is conducted under the experienced eye of the inventor and his associates, and agents who are well known, not only as business men of integrity but also as practical engineers, are selected at the different trade centres to represent the manufacturers. Hence, with this combination of mechanical ingenuity, business tact, and practical engineering ability, it is no matter of surprise that the Blake Pump is a reminder that "Nothing succeeds like success."

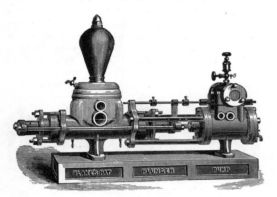

No. 2. Plunger Pump, Double Acting.

probably more Blake Pumps in actual use than those of any other manufacture.

Yet the secret of the well deserved reputation of the Blake Pump is an open one. It is, and has been, the constant aim of the inventor, Mr. Geo. F. Blake, to adapt the various pumps built by him to the peculiar work each had to perform, never sacrificing utility to embellishment.

It has always been his constant practice in bringing out his many and valuable improvements, to subject them to a series of exhaustive experiments, reaching over a period of months, and sometimes (as notably in the case of the first Blake Pump) over a period of years before placing them on the market, so that the Blake Pump, from its reliability, has to-day a reputation that is literally world-wide.

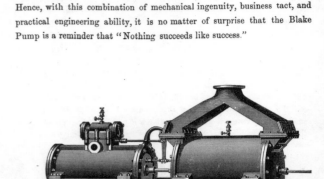

Blowing Engine.
18 inch Steam Cylinder. 30 inch Air Cylinder. 36 inch Stroke.

No. 3. Boiler Feed Pump.

Double Plunger Mining Pump.
16 inch Steam Cylinder. 7 inch Plunger. 24 inch Stroke.

No. 1. Boiler Feed Pump.

No. 8. Boiler Feed Pump.

A glance at the accompanying cuts will show the growth of the Blake Pump from '62 to '74, but of the magnitude of the business, one cannot get a conception without visiting personally the factory of the Geo. F. Blake Manufacturing Company, Friend and Causeway Streets, Boston, or their warerooms either at 86 and 88 Liberty Street, New York, or 50 and 52 South Canal Street, Chicago.

To meet the English and Colonial demand for the Blake Pump, a manufactory has recently been established in the heart of London—"within sound of Bow Bells"—while the German and Continental markets are supplied from works located in the centre of Germany.

Notwithstanding the unprecedented success that has attended the introduction and sale of the Blake Pump, the manufacturers have never lost sight of the fact that the secret of their success has been in adapting the means to the end, and being thorough in all the details of manufacture; so that the pumps being built with special tools for special work, from carefully selected material, and each pump being subjected to a severe practical test before leaving the factory, the manufacturers are enabled to guarantee each and every one, and hold themselves under obligations to return the purchase money in case a pump fails to do the work for which it is warranted.

These pumps are put to almost every conceivable use, from the pumping of alcohol to that of white-lead. They are used almost exclusively by the Navy and Merchant Marine, while, as Mine Pumps, Oil Line Pumps, Fire Pumps, Boiler Feed Pumps, &c., they lead the van.

Blake Pumps have recently been placed in the New York Post-Office, the U. S. Frigate "Tennessee" the Philadelphia and Boston Fire Tugs, and as Fire Pumps in the largest Grain Elevators in the world, at Locust Point, Baltimore. We might specify many important places where the Blake Pump has been selected, simply on its merit and for its well known reliability, but their name is legion.

As these pumps are sold not only in this country, but are exported to a large extent, it became necessary at an early date to make special tools so as to turn out parts fitted to templet and gauge, and that were interchangeable, so that, should any part become unfit for use, either from wear or accidental breakage, it could readily be duplicated.

Recognizing from the first the fact that the pump which was so constructed as to combine simplicity with durability, and was at the same time positive under any pressure, would prove a success, the inventor has used throughout, the plain flat slide valve, to control the movement of the steam piston, a feature peculiar to this alone of all positive direct-acting steam pumps.

Combined Boiler and Pump.

Mining Pump, with Removable Cylinder.
14 inch Steam Cylinder. 8 inch Water Cylinder. 12 inch Stroke.

Special Fire Pump.
14 inch Steam Cylinder. 7 inch Water Cylinder. 12 inch Stroke.

1800.

CRANE BROTHERS,

Manufacturers of

BANK LEDGER AND RECORD PAPERS,

Westfield, Mass.

——:o:——

In 1799, Zenas Crane came,—from the employ of General Burbank at Worcester, then the great paper maker of the State,—to Dalton prospecting for a location, the result of which was the issue in the *Pittsfield Sun*, in 1801, of the following advertisement:

Encourage your own Manufactories,
and they will Improve.
Ladies, save your R A G S.

A S the Subscribers have it in contemplation to erect a PAPER MILL in Dalton, the ensuing Spring; and the business being very beneficial to the community at large, they flatter themselves that they shall meet with due encouragement. And every woman who has the good of her country, and the interests of her own family at heart, will patronize them by saying her rags, and sending them to their Manufactory, or to the nearest Storekeeper, for which the subscribers will give a generous price.
HENRY WISWELL,
ZENAS CRANE,
JOHN WILLARD.

We suppose the ladies must have fulfilled their part of the contract, for the mill was immediately erected, and thus commenced the great paper manufacturing business of this beautiful village. Crane & Co., the successors of their father, who died in 1842, have seen the business grow to one of the most important manufacturing interests in the State, and divide and sub-divide itself into specialties, so that now, instead of making all sorts and kinds of paper, as did their father in the early days, they are one of three companies in the country who are making Bank and Bond Papers, running on these exclusively, manufacturing for several foreign governments the paper on which is printed their bank notes and bonds, thus getting money for their paper, and their patrons paper for their money. They also have the patronage of our own government.

The firm is composed of two brothers, J. A. & R. B. Crane, sons of J. B. Crane.

The mill in Westfield is divided into two departments, Paper and Rag. The Rag Building is 40 x 90 feet, and three stories high. The mill is situated about three quarters of a mile south-west from town.

At first the paper was made with the common river water such as most mills use, but of late years the water used in the manufacture has been brought three quarters of a mile from what is known as Wolf Pit Spring, from which circumstance their Writing Paper is all stamped "Wolf Pit Springs." The water obtained here is as clear as crystal, the spring boiling up at the rate of 100 gallons per minute from a seam in the solid rock, and its value is proven in the extraordinary snow white purity of the pulp, and by the clear, perfect quality of the paper produced, well sustaining the claim of the Brothers, that it is the finest made in the country. The capacity of the mills is two tons daily of Ledger Paper. This paper has never failed to receive the highest award when placed in competition with other papers, after a thorough test by competent judges; it therefore stands commended to the public as the best article of its kind in the world. Below, in tabular form, we give their standing prices for various sizes and weights, which, of course, is subject to alteration from time

to time, discounts, which, upon application, the firm will send to dealers or consumers.

The work of the mill is done by five rag beating engines, one sixty-six inch Fourdrinier and one ninety inch double cylinder machine. A new beating engine is soon to be added. The protection against fire is very complete, wisdom having been gained by sad experience. Numerous hydrants about the buildings are supplied by the Town Wa-

Every Sheet of Ledger Paper made by us contains the above "Water-Mark" together with the year produced.

ter Works (than which there are no better in the country).

Both male and female help is employed, about one hundred hands in all. The firm own eighty acres of land directly north of the mill property, part of which has been laid out and built up for their employés. The whole establishment is under the superintendence of Mr. F. A. Thompson, who was for many years connected with

1800.

significant of weakness. This prejudice, however, has been gradually overcome, actual trial having demonstrated their great strength, and to-day, Crane Brothers have paper belts running that were made during the year in which they were invented, and are apparently as good as when first used,—running beside leather and rubber belts, and doing the work much better, for the simple reason that they nev r stretch nor slip, while the others will stretch. Another great advantage is their perfect uniformity in thickness—being a manufactured article—which insures a perfectly straight running Belt, while other Belts are universally liable to unevenness. Soft, spongy leather, coarse and fine grain get in, even in the best appointed establishments, rendering the Belt liable to crooked and uneven places in actual use. This is more especially the case in extra wide Belts. The Paper Basket is another invention growing out of the manufacture of Paper Belting. These baskets possess many points of excellence, and are claimed by those who have used them to be superior to others, being light, strong, durable, elastic and smooth.

Paper Cans for cotton and woolen mills to take the place of tin cans, are also made under the same patent. These cans are Jappaned inside and out, and are as smooth as glass. They are elastic and will not jam as tin cans do and are consequently, more durable—they are also much lighter to handle—Paper Trunks, Guitar and Fiddle Boxes, Paper Dishes for Photographers Baths and Chemical use generally, are also made here.

Not content with transforming the shapeless rags into enduring belts to run huge machinery, into baskets, boxes, trunks and dishes, they change them also into light and graceful boats, which "skim the waters like a thing of life." The Crane Brothers have one of these paper boats at their mill. It is about fifteen feet long and three feet wide, but yet so light that a couple of men can carry it with ease. The frame of the boat is made of wood and then covered with this paper, about one-eighth to one-quarter inch thick.

This mill furnishes the entire supply for E. Waters & Sons of Troy, N. Y., two of whose boats have just won the two great races at Saratoga. The lightness and

PAPER DEPARTMENT.   CRANE BRO.'S PAPER MILLS, WESTFIELD, MASS.   **RAG DEPARTMENT.**

Crane & Co., of Dalton.

Although this firm, like their ancestors, claim to make the strongest paper in the market, they realize full well that still greater strength is needed in the heavy Record Papers now in use. They have therefore invented and are about to introduce to the public an entire new article of Ledger and Record Paper. This produces the strongest and most durable paper ever conceived of, and is a great improvement for books of Public Record, and all books of reference that have to be handled often, and through a long series of years.

Paper Belts were invented and manufactured by James B. Crane, Esq., of Dalton, Berkshire Co., Mass., (father of Crane Brothers,) and he was granted patents in 1867 and 1868. There was great prejudice against them when they were first introduced, as the very name, Paper, to persons unacquainted with the strength of paper made from material such as is used for the manufacture of Belts, was

durability of these boats will doubtless cause an extended use of them. But one of the most important of the various uses of this invention is its application in the manufacture of Buggy Boxes. In fact this paper can be applied to all the purposes of like nature as the above, where wood is now generally used and which it must largely supersede. Paper possesses great advantages over wood for many purposes for which wood alone has heretofore been employed—paper such as is made for the uses above noted has no grain, and consequently cannot check or split, it does not largely shrink or swell with every change of weather or variation of climate. It can readily be moulded into any desired shape and in times not far distant will be largely used for decorative purposes. There is scarcely a limit to its strength, and its ability to retain its texture or to withstand sudden and continuous shocks and jars is amply proven by the fact that it is largely used in the construction of car and locomotive wheels in preference to the best qualities of iron. The value of an article from which wash tubs and car wheels, articles of clothing and piano cases, belting, wagon boxes and artistic ornaments are made cannot be overrated.

1875.

Price per Ream of CRANES' Bank Ledger & Record Paper.				
Name.	Size.	Weight.	Price per Ream. P.	M.
Crown... ...	15 x 19	22	$7 00	$6 50
Demy..........	16 x 21	28	9 50	8 50
Medium...	18 x 23	36	13 00	12 00
Royal	19 x 24	44	17 00	15 00
Super Royal....	20 x 28	54	22 00	20 00
Imperial........	23 x 31	72	29 00	27 00
Demy	16 x 21	30	10 50	9 50
Double Demy.	21 x 32	60	21 00	19 00
Medium.......	18 x 23	40	15 00	14 00
Double Medium.	23 x 36	80	30 00	28 00
Double Medium.	18 x 46	80	30 00	28 00
Double Royal ..	24 x 36	88	34 00	30 00
Elephant.......	23 x 28	65	29 00	27 00
Colombier.. ...	23 x 34	80	35 00	32 00
Atlas..........	26 x 33	100	50 00	45 00
Double Elephant	27 x 40	125	60 00	55 00
Antiquarian ..	31 x 53	200	125 00	100 00

Each ream contains 480 perfect sheets, and is put up in our Trade Mark Wrapper and is Warranted.

Each ream is trimmed on a form and is perfectly square and ready for the ruling machine. This paper writes and erases perfectly.

Price per 1,000 Sheets of CRANES' Linen Lined Ledger Paper.		
Name	Price per M.	Size.
Demy... ...	30 00	16 x 21
Medium	40 00	18 x 23
Royal	44 00	19 x 24
Super Boyal	62 00	20 x 28
Elephant........	90 00	23 x 28
Imperial	82 00	23 x 31
Columbia	104 00	23 x 34
Atlas............	130 00	26 x 33
Double Elephant..	157 00	27 x 40

Put up in Reams of 500 sheets each, in our Trade Mark Wrapper. Every ream warranted.

Each ream is trimmed on a form and is perfectly square and ready for the ruling machine. This paper writes and erases perfectly.

VANDERBURGH, WELLS & CO.,

Manufacturers of and Dealers in

PRINTERS' SUPPLIES

Of Every Description,

East Corner of Fulton and Dutch Streets,

Two Blocks from Broadway, NEW YORK.

——:o:——

In the year 1827, Mr. Darius Wells, a practical printer, and but lately deceased, and a man of much mechanical skill, began the manufacture of Wood Type as a distinct business. His productions being far superior to any wood type previously made, the business was a successful one, and Darius Wells and his Printers' Warehouse were soon known all over the land. Vanderburgh, Wells & Co., as a firm only date back to 1864, but as they succeeded to the old established business of Darius Wells, they might well claim that their house was founded in 1827, and that they are the oldest manufacturers of wood type in the United States.

From the comparatively small beginning of Mr. Wells, the business has grown to large proportions, and the crude tools, patterns, and methods of manufacture then in use have been supplanted by improved devices, which enable Messrs. Vanderburgh, Wells & Co., to furnish better goods than could be made twenty years ago, and at less comparative cost. They continue the manufacture of Wood Type, Borders, Rules, etc., of various styles, and of an evenness of height and finish which is not excelled; but in addition to these they have added the manufacture of Cabinets of various styles,—the "Eagle" and "California" being favorites,—Racks, Cases of all "regular" sizes and styles and some of later design, Galleys and Galley Racks, Paper Boards, Form Racks, Standing Galleys, and Printing Office "Furniture" Generally.

They prepare Turkey Boxwood, Maple, Mahogany, Pine, etc., for Engravers' uses, and also have done the various kinds of Printers' and Engravers' jobbing, such as Plugging Engravers' Blocks, Blocking Plates on Mahogany, making special sizes of Patent Plate Blocks, and all similar work, with great care, by skilled men.

They are at all times ready to furnish all the Paraphernalia of a Printing Office; Cylinder Presses from all the celebrated makers,—Paper Presses, Screw or Hydraulic, Paper Cutters, and Printers' Machinery generally. Book, News, Poster and Job Type, Brass Rules, Dashes, Ornaments, and first-class materials of every description pertaining to the trade, at regular makers' prices.

They generally have a fair assortment of Presses, Type, Cases, Stands, Cabinets, Chases, etc., which have been used, but which they warrant to be as good as represented, and many bargains are made in the purchase of such material.

There are few first-class establishments in any branch of business but are noted for the marked superiority of some one article of production. Messrs. Vanderburgh, Wells & Co., are not exceptions to this rule. While all the articles manufactured or sold by them are universally ranked as "first-class," their Imposing Stones and Frames have become specially famous for the perfectly level and smooth finish of the stones and the great stiffness and strength of the frames.

LUTHER BROTHERS,

Manufacturers of

GILT JEWELRY.

No. 94 Orange Street, Providence, Rhode Island.

The firm of Luther Brothers—consisting of Edward A. and Wm. H. Luther—was established January 1, 1864, since which time their business has steadily increased, and has now reached such proportions as to give employment to over one hundred and fifty hands. At present they are largely engaged in the production of Prize Package Goods—that being the cheapest class of jewelry manufactured. They also produce the higher grades of goods; in fact, every description of Brass Jewelry, from the cheapest to the best. Mr. James S. Sprague, one of the most capable men in the business, is foreman of the Jewelry Department.

The specialties of the firm are Sleeve Buttons, Combination Sets, Onyx Studs, and Collar Buttons. The immense production of and demand for this class of goods may be inferred from the fact that during the year ending January 1st, 1876, Luther Brothers manufactured and sold two millions five hundred and ninety-two thousand Collar Buttons alone; we hardly dare to state the figures of other articles, but as the man who wears a collar button generally wears at the same time three studs and two sleeve buttons, the reader will at once see that the business must be of great magnitude, even if these three articles were their sole productions. An interesting department of their business is their Lapidary Work, which is under the immediate supervision of Mr. James H. Luther, who has the reputation of being one of the most skillful workmen in that line of art in this country. A large number of other skilled artificers are employed in this branch, and each one of the large number of precious stones here cut, polished and engraved, is an attest of the tasteful and intelligent care which is bestowed upon this branch of the business of the firm.

The numerous productions of Luther Brothers are well known to the trade throughout the United States and the Canadas; in South America and the Islands of the Sea; and they are always ready to exhibit samples to or supply orders from responsible dealers.

M. W. CHASE,

Manufacturer of

SCHOOL AND CHURCH FURNITURE,

212 and 214 Seventh Street, Buffalo, New York.

The manufacture of School and Church Furniture has, within a comparatively few years, assumed an important place among the special industries of the country, and prominent among the several manufacturers of this class of work is the gentleman whose name heads this article.

Mr. Chase, manufactures School Furniture of all varieties of style and finish, suited to the country district school of modest proportions and limited means, or the flourishing academy. The stock embraces appropriate Desks for teachers and scholars, Chairs, Settees, Blackboards, in fact every article of furniture needed in a school room.

There is the same completeness in the variety of Church Furniture, and a cathedral or a chapel may be furnished wholly or in part at this establishment. Mr. Chase makes a specialty of Settees, of which he manufactures twenty varieties, suitable for Churches, Sabbath Schools, Public Halls, etc., and Pews will be furnished complete, or ends seperately. Mr. Chase is prepared to give estimates for work to be delivered at any point, and guarantees perfect satisfaction to all who may favor him with their patronage.

EUGENE F. PHILLIPS,

Manufacturer of

Hoxie and Reed's Patent Flexible Gas Tight Tubing, and Reed & Phillips' Patent Insulated Telegraph Wire

Providence, Rhode Island.

This Tubing is made on a spiral spring over which there are several fibrous braids, over and between some of which are drawn, whole and intact, six animal intestines saturated with a suitable compound which preserves them in their natural and live condition and renders the Tubing absolutely Gas-Tight. It is braided on the outside, according to cost, with cotton, mohair or silk, and finished in all desirable colors and plaids, in six, eight, ten and twelve feet lengths. This Tubing is used all over the world where gas is used, and is claimed to be The Best.

Mr. Phillips also manufactures Patent Finished Office Wire, Magnet Wire, Insulated Line Wire, Patent Rubber Covered Wire, for underground and line use, Insulated Wire incased by patent process in Lead Pipe for underground or water, and Patent and other Electric Cords. The very large demand for these goods in this and other countries and almost exclusive sale in this country for some of these wires amply attest their merits, challenge competition, and invite patronage.

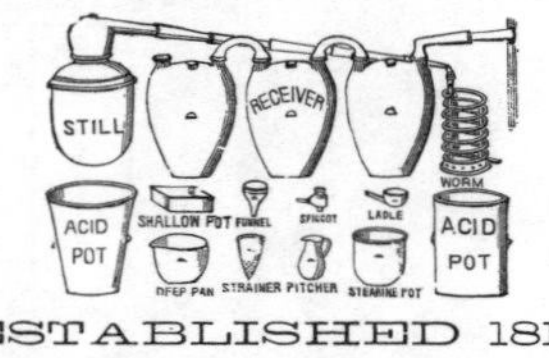

ESTABLISHED 1810.

PHILADELPHIA CHEMICAL STONEWARE MANUFACTORY,

Cor. Frankford Road and Amber St., Philadelphia, Pa.

RICHARD C. REMMEY, Prop.

The manufacture of Chemical Stoneware, for Manufacturing Chemists, Silver Platers, Photographers, Nickle Platers, Dyers, Druggists, and others requiring vessels that combine strength with lightness, and that will withstand the extremes of heat and cold without injury, and which are not affected by, and do not affect acids, is a special business of much greater importance than the casual observer would suppose. Every potter and manufacturer of stoneware could fashion vessels of the proper shape, perhaps; but there are few who have or can procure materials such as are used by those who make the manufacture of Chemical Ware a business, and still fewer, even if the proper materials were placed in their hands, who could perfectly bake or burn the ware. The business requires a special skill which but few possess.

Mr. Richard C. Remmey, proprietor of the Philadelphia Chemical Stoneware Manufactory, cor. Frankford Road and Amber Street, Philadelphia, is the only and sole manufacturer of Chemical Stoneware in America. These works have been in operation for sixty-five years, during which time their productions have not been excelled on this Continent or in England, France or Germany.

Mr. Remmey also manufactures the celebrated American Porcelain Stoneware, such as Precipitating Pots for Mints and Assayers, and Evaporating Dishes for Chemists and others. Vessels are made to hold from one gallon to one hundred gallons. Orders by mail will receive prompt attention.

The Angell Turbine Water Wheel,

Manufactured by the

ANGELL WATER WHEEL CO.,

Providence, R. I.

——:o:——

In presenting to our readers the following description of the Angell Turbine Water Wheel, we do not claim that it is the best Water Wheel in the world in every respect, nor do we pretend to assert that the art of constructing water wheels has yet reached perfection; but we do say that within the past few years there has been rapid advancement in the art, and at the present time there are a number of good water wheels in the market. The inventors of the Angell Wheel, Messrs. Otis N. Angell & Son, about fourteen years ago began to practically study water wheels, but it was not until after they had made over two hundred experiments with wheels of different constructions that they presented one to the public. Since its introduction different sizes have been tested at Holyoke, Mass., and certain improvements made, which render it a wheel suited to the wants of all manufacturers using water power.

The Angell Turbine Water Wheel, since first introduced, has given universal satisfaction; and many parties after having thoroughly tested one, have purchased two or three more for other places where new wheels were required. It has by reason of its actual merit displaced many other wheels, some of which are in the market rated as first-class, and we are satisfied that it can compete with any wheel made in economy of water at partial gate, in regularity of speed, in durability and in quality of workmanship.

The Wheel proper as shown in Fig. 1, is a cast iron irregular shaped cylinder, with a flange at the top, extending to the full diameter of the wheel, while below it is contracted in size as it approaches the bottom, thus leaving the floats larger at the bottom than at the top, thereby giving a larger space for the discharge of water. The floats which form the buckets of the wheel are made of either cast iron or bronze, and are bolted firmly to the wheel and its flanges. This enables one to replace the floats readily (which may become broken by hard substances which at times get into water-wheels, where there are poor racks,) without taking the wheel out of the flume. Where the floats, whether of steel or wrought or cast iron, are cast into the wheel, or cast on to it, no repairing can be done, and the users of them are obliged to run them as they are or purchase an entire new wheel.

Fig. 2.
Represents the Wheel proper, without the case.

Fig. 1.
Represents the Wheel as when finished.

Fig. 3.
Represents the Guides and Gates, with the cover removed and part of the Gates closed.

The Case of the wheel is of the ordinary construction, having a cover which can be removed, and the wheel taken out without disturbing the case.

Between the upper and lower parts of the case are placed a number of Stationary Guides, each fastened by two bolts, as seen in Figure 3. These guides serve the double purpose of braces to support the upper part of the case, and make it rigid and firm, but also to give the water its proper direction as it enters the wheel, and as they are stationary, the direction of the water is always the same, however small the amount used. Some wheels are constructed with movable guides, which give a different direction to the water at every stage of opening the gate, thus varying the angle at which the water strikes. It is evident that no wheel which varies the direction of the water can give the best results under all circumstances.

By a peculiar form given to the wheel, the step is relieved of nearly all the weight upon it, when the wheel is in motion, and of all the Angell Wheels now running, none have yet required a new step.

The following is the result of a test of an Angell Wheel, made at Holyoke, Mass., by Mr. James Emerson: Full gate, 85.39 per cent; 15.16 gate, 84.65 per cent; 7-8 gate, 83.32 per cent; 3-4 gate, 81.14 per cent; 5-8 gate, 72.60 per cent.

The above results at part gate were obtained by taking the fractional amount of water discharged, instead of the fractional opening of the gates of the wheel, and shows a percentage that has never been excelled by any other water wheel, at part gate, and in this point it is claimed that the Angell Wheel is in advance of all others.

When desired, the Company will build wheels with bronze floats, guides, and gates, at the extra cost of the material. They also furnish to order, heavy shafting, gearing, pulleys and regulators.

Please send for a circular. Address, Angell Water Wheel Company, Providence, R. I.

THE GATLING GUN.

The inventor of this wonderful arm is Dr. Richard J. Gatling, at the time of its invention a resident of Indianapolis, Indiana, but now of Hartford, Conn. He first conceived the idea of a machine gun in 1861, and is justly entitled to the proud distinction of being the originator of the first successful weapon of the kind ever invented. His first gun was completed in Indianapolis in the early part of 1862, and his first American patent bears date November 4, 1872. The gun was fired repeatedly during that year in Indianapolis, before thousands of persons with the most gratifying results. These guns have been adopted by the United States, England, Russia, Turkey, Egypt and most of the principal governments of the world. They have been subjected to the severest tests in the United States and abroad in competition with other arms of different descriptions and have always maintained their superiority. Their average firing capacity is about 400 shots per minute, but in some cases 600 have been fired. At Shoeburyness, England, in 1870, at a distance of 600 yards, 720 rounds were deliberately fired at a target 90 ft. x 9 ft. and 618 hits were made, and at 800 yards, firing 555 rounds at the same target, 440 hits were made. In October, 1873, at Fortress Monroe, Virginia, firing at a target 9 ft. by 40 in., distant 800 yards, 600 shots were fired in 1 minute and 26 seconds, and 534 hits were made—this with a severe wind almost at right angles to the line of fire. At a distance of 1200 yards, under similar conditions of wind, out of 600 shots fired at the same target in one minute and a half, 415 struck. At a trial of this gun at Fort Madison, Annapolis, Maryland, one hundred thousand rounds were fired consecutively, and sixty-five thousand without stopping to clean the gun. In 1873 a Board consisting of army officers representing the different branches of the service, was appointed in accordance with a special act of Congress to examine and

THE CELEBRATED GATLING GUN.

report upon the Gatling gun. The Board after protracted and severe test trials at Fortress Monroe, unanimously recommended its adoption for the service. The high character of the officers composing the Board and their close investigation and exhaustive experiments give great weight to whatever opinion they express. We quote from their report: "Among the advantages possessed by the "Gatling gun may be enumerated, the "lightness of its parts, the simplicity and "strength of its mechanism, the rapidity "and continuity of its fire without sensi- "ble recoil, its effectiveness against "troops at all ranges for which a flanking "gun is required, its general accuracy at "all ranges attainable by rifles, its com- "parative independence of the excite- "ment of battle, the interchangeableness "of its ammunition with the same calibre "of small arms, its great endurance, its "peculiar power for the defense of in- "trenched positions and villages; for "protecting roads, defiles and bridges; "for covering the embarkation or de- "barkation of troops, or the crossing of "streams; for silencing field-batteries or "batteries of position; for increasing the "infantry-fire at the critical moment of "a battle; for supporting field-batteries "and protecting them against cavalry and "infantry charges; for covering the retreat "of a repulsed column; and generally, "the accuracy, continuity, and intensity "of its fire, and its economy of men for "serving, and animals for transporting it."

The guns are generally mounted on carriages as shown in the accompanying engraving, but lighter guns are made for mounting on tripods and on the backs of horses and camels. Some are so light as to be easily carried by two men and the heaviest of them are so constructed as to be taken apart and packed on horses or mules for transportation over mountains and can easily be reassembled in a few moments. These guns are made solely by the Gatling Gun Company of Hartford, Conn., principally at Colt's Armory in that city, but also at the works of Sir William G. Armstrong & Co, newcastle-on-Tyne, England.

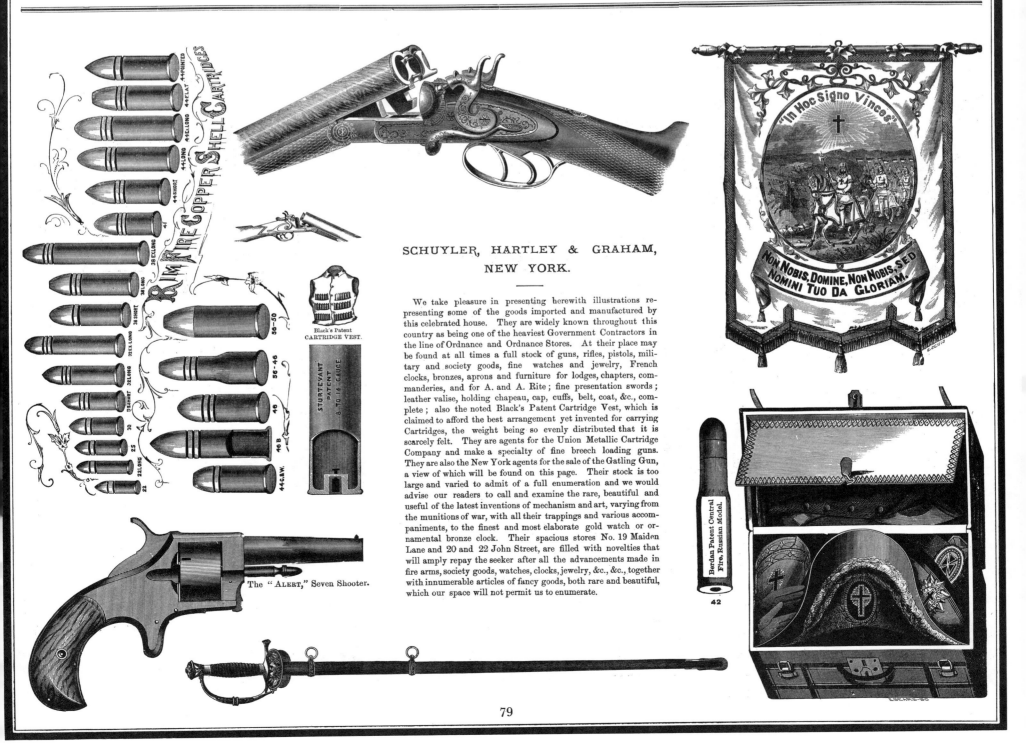

SCHUYLER, HARTLEY & GRAHAM, NEW YORK.

We take pleasure in presenting herewith illustrations representing some of the goods imported and manufactured by this celebrated house. They are widely known throughout this country as being one of the heaviest Government Contractors in the line of Ordnance and Ordnance Stores. At their place may be found at all times a full stock of guns, rifles, pistols, military and society goods, fine watches and jewelry, French clocks, bronzes, aprons and furniture for lodges, chapters, commanderies, and for A. and A. Rite; fine presentation swords; leather valise, holding chapeau, cap, cuffs, belt, coat, &c., complete; also the noted Black's Patent Cartridge Vest, which is claimed to afford the best arrangement yet invented for carrying Cartridges, the weight being so evenly distributed that it is scarcely felt. They are agents for the Union Metallic Cartridge Company and make a specialty of fine breech loading guns. They are also the New York agents for the sale of the Gatling Gun, a view of which will be found on this page. Their stock is too large and varied to admit of a full enumeration and we would advise our readers to call and examine the rare, beautiful and useful of the latest inventions of mechanism and art, varying from the munitions of war, with all their trappings and various accompaniments, to the finest and most elaborate gold watch or ornamental bronze clock. Their spacious stores No. 19 Maiden Lane and 20 and 22 John Street, are filled with novelties that will amply repay the seeker after all the advancements made in fire arms, society goods, watches, clocks, jewelry, &c., &c., together with innumerable articles of fancy goods, both rare and beautiful, which our space will not permit us to enumerate.

The "ALERT," Seven Shooter.

Black's Patent CARTRIDGE VEST.

STURTEVANT PATENT. 8 TO 16 GAUGE.

Berdan Patent Central Fire, Russian Model.

HAINES BROTHERS,

PIANO FORTE MANUFACTURERS,

Both Corners of 21st Street and Second Avenue,

NEW YORK.

—:o:—

The manufacture of pianos has become a business of far greater proportions than is generally supposed, involving the investment of over $6,000,000 as capital, and affording remunerative employment to thousands of skilled mechanics. The last United States census makes record of no less than one hundred and fifty-six establishments engaged in the business which produced 24,306 instruments valued at $8,225,204; more than one-half of the whole number of instruments (12,181), valued at $4,001,219, were made in the State of New York; New York City, of course, being the great centre of the trade. Fully one-third of the whole number of firms engaged in the manufacture of pianos in the United States are located in New York City, and considerably over one-third of all the instruments produced are made here. By far the greater number of these manufacturers are small producers, there being scarce a dozen large manufacturers in the United States.

Though it is little more than twenty-five years since the first really fine instruments were produced in this country, yet so rapid has been our improvement that in this special branch of industry America is generally confessed to lead the the world and American pianos are exported in large numbers to the musical cities of the Old World, while the demands for such instruments in the States of Central and South America is almost entirely supplied by the United States.

In no other branch of business, perhaps, is there so warm a rivalry, as between the leading piano makers of this country—mainly an honest, friendly rivalry, each earnestly striving to excel the other in producing instruments that combine the largest number of desirable qualities—but there are manufacturers whose object seems to be

to make a piano that will please the eye and ear when first seen and heard and thus meet with ready sale, without reference to its ability to withstand the effects of time and use.

Among the most widely and favorably known manufacturers of pianofortes in this country, is the firm of Haines Bros., engravings of whose large establishments, east side of Second Avenue and both corners of Twenty-first Street, are here presented. This firm has worked its way up from a small beginning to a prominent place in the front rank of leading makers by a faithful adherence to a rule early adopted by them; to make a good substantial instrument, one that will not only prove thoroughly reliable for and capable of withstanding parlor playing, but one that will bear the wear and tear incidental to school practice, for years without de-

terioration—and to sell at a fair and moderate profit to themselves. Practical mechanics, thoroughly conversant with every branch of their trade, and by long experience in the business, experts in all that pertains to it, the Haines Brothers posssess advantages not excelled by any. The extent of their business makes them large purchasers of wood and other materials, and as they buy exclusively for cash, they receive the special favor of the largest dealers in piano merchandise, and are thus enabled to secure not only the best that the market affords, but to obtain the lowest prices. Their factories are fitted with every appliance in the shape of machinery and tools that can facilitate the production of thoroughly good work, and their force of mechanics is selected from among the most skillful in the trade.

Without any noise, bustle or show, Haines Brothers, since their business was first founded—years ago—have quietly but surely advanced their trade, until it now ranks among the first of its class in the United States. Of all the pianos made in this country, few find such ready sale as theirs, and in dull times or in good times there is always a market for their productions. Their effort has always been to give satisfaction, and that they have fully accomplished this is amply testified by their constantly increasing sales. Haines Brothers believe in the superiority of their instruments and as an attest of that belief they guarantee every Piano to give satisfaction for five years, or no sale, claiming to give a better instrument for less money than any other house. At their warerooms, corner Twenty-first Street and Second Avenue, may be seen every variety of their own excellent manufactures, together with a stock of second-hand Pianos of others' make, taken in exchange for their own. These exchanges are very often made.

The Haines Brothers give constant personal superintendence to these manufactures, early and late, insuring thorough excellence, even to the most minute details. Their Pianos have established a just and world wide fame, ministering to the delight of the lovers of *la belle musique* throughout all the States and Territories of the Union; in the East Indies and in Europe, as well as in every country in our Western Hemisphere.

Manufactory and Warerooms, Twenty-first Street and Second Avenue, New York.

THE BUFFALO BISCUIT WORKS,

R. OVENS & SON,

159, 161, 163, 165 and 167 Ellicott Street,

BUFFALO, NEW YORK.

—:o:—

The baking of Ship Bread, Biscuits and Crackers of various kinds has become, in this country, a business of great importance—far greater than is generally supposed—giving constant employment to very many hands, and affording an investment for capital, amounting in buildings, machinery and stock, to millions of dollars. Impelled by the success of the old established houses, within a few years a number of small concerns have been started in various parts of the country, but they have utterly failed to wrest from the old reliable firms the prestige which years of honest effort have given them.

Among the most successful of the old established leading houses in this branch of trade is that of R. Ovens & Son, of Buffalo, New York, who operate one of the most complete bakeries in the State of New York, or, indeed, in the United States.

The business was founded by Mr. Robert Ovens, in the year 1848, and was conducted solely by him until the year 1864, when his son, Walter S. Ovens, was admitted into partnership and the firm name became R. Ovens & Son. In the beginning the business was, comparatively a small one, but the superior quality of the goods produced soon made many friends and customers for the new bakery, and the business grew continuously until, to meet the increasing demand, it became necessary to erect the large and commodious building now occupied by the firm, an exterior view of which is here given. Mr. Ovens' bakery, was, we believe, the first in this country where Aerated Bread was made, and was the first to use the now celebrated McKenzie Rotary Ovens. Aerated Bread is still an important product of the establishment—but the manufacture of Biscuits and Crackers forms the bulk of the business.

In 1871 the firm began the manufacture of the celebrated English or London Biscuit, for which purpose they imported, at great expense, a complete set of English Machinery, which in addition to their other machinery of American manufacture, enabled them to produce the highest grade of goods, in immense quantities and at the minimum of cost. They now manufacture about one hundred varieties or kinds of Biscuits and Crackers, many of which originated with and are peculiar to them, and ship their products to

all parts of the country, frequently finding it difficult, with all their facilities, to supply the demand.

But few of our readers who have not visited an establishment such as that of Messrs. R. Ovens & Son, have any idea of the processes by which delicate Biscuits and Crackers are made, nor can we describe them without the aid of many cuts of machines and explanations of their working parts. Suffice it to say, that it is largely machine work. The flour, having been passed through sieves to free it from pieces of stick or nails that may possibly have fallen in the barrel in coopering or opening it, is placed into

mixing machines, where two barrels of flour are worked at one time; all the kneading is done by machinery, the dough is rolled in sheets and cut in shapes by machinery, and baked in two of McKenzie's Reel Ovens. Two of Ruger's Cracker Machines, in addition to the English Machinery previously mentioned, and numerous other mechanical appliances are used in this establishment, and are run day and night the year round. Over fifty hands are constantly employed, but were it not for the machinery used, five times that number could not perform the work. About two hundred barrels of manufactured goods are turned out of this establishment every day, in the production of which nearly one hundred barrels of flour are consumed.

Messrs. R. Ovens & Son make no second class goods—their constant endeavor is to attain the highest possible excellence. With this end in view the utmost care is exercised in the selection of materials and only the finest qualities of flour, sugar, butter and other ingredients that enter into their manufactures are ever used in their establishment. In competition with others, Messrs. Ovens & Son have exhibited their goods at leading fairs and expositions, and wherever exhibited they have taken the first prize, but the best proof of their superiority is found in the wide spread and constantly increasing demand for them, a demand which has become so common that all first class grocers keep them in stock.

The building occupied by the firm on Ellicott Street has a frontage of 98 feet and a depth of 150 feet; it is a four story brick structure of elegant and imposing appearance, being adorned with the Mansard roof. Every department is conveniently arranged for the proper prosecution of the business. The location may be termed as central, the establishment being some two blocks from the principal thoroughfare, Main Street, and adjacent to the County Court House, within easy communication with all the leading railroads centering in the city, and convenient to the lake and canal. The private and business offices of the firm are situate on the main floor, contiguous to the wholesale and retail departments, in which full stocks of their special goods, etc., will always be found, and their quality and freshness ascertained. The mixing and storerooms for flour, etc., located on the second floor; the storeroom for Crackers and Biscuits for shipment on the third floor, and the packing room which is one of the best in the country, on the fourth floor. Access to the different stories by one of Howard's elevators. The stables are in the rear, where are usually from 10 to 13 horses, and a number of wagons, made expressly to accommodate the trade they carry on. The arrangement of the entire establishment is methodical, and it is complete in all its appointments.

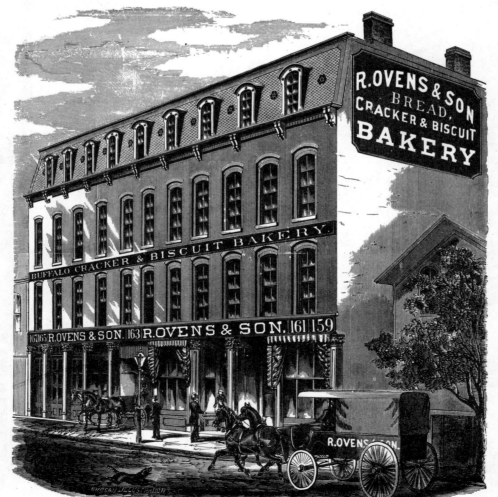

VIEW OF R. OVENS & SON'S BAKERY, BUFFALO, NEW YORK.

WIRING MACHINE.

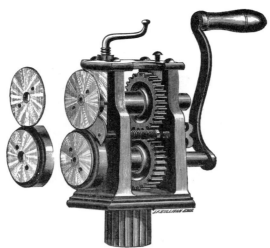

LARGE TURNING MACHINE.

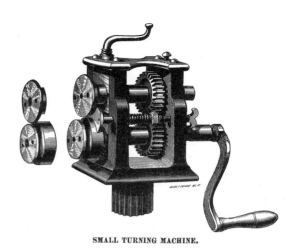

SMALL TURNING MACHINE.

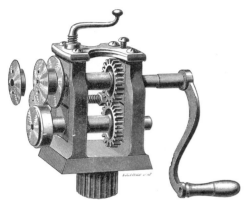

LARGE BURRING MACHINE.

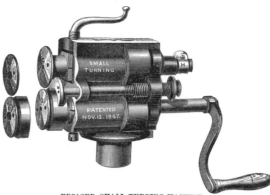

ENCASED SMALL TURNING MACHINE.

SETTING DOWN MACHINE.

TINSMITHS' TOOLS AND MACHINERY,

Represented by

THE PECK, STOW & WILCOX COMPANY,

Warerooms, 43 Chambers Street, New York,

Factories at Southington, Plantsville and East Berlin, Conn.

The various, and constantly increasing uses to which tin is applied, have called into requisition, a correspondingly increased variety of tools and machinery adapted to its proper and more expeditious manipulation. Although softer and more malleable than most metals, it does not require machinery of the same power, but its susceptibility of application to different purposes, renders the manufacture of this kind of machinery quite as important as almost any other.

Tin is not an abundant element in nature, but is one of the metals longest known to man. It is said that the Phœnicians carried on an extensive trade in tin, with Great Britain, then called Tin Islands, more than one thousand years before the Christian era, and that by this traffic, they acquired their first commercial importance. These mines were the only ones known to have been worked to any extent, prior to the thirteenth century, when tin mines were discovered in Germany. England now exports an average of 1,500 tons of unwrought tin annually, besides manufactured tin and plate to the value of about £400,000.

Tin has been discovered and mined in several places in the United States, the most productive mines being in San Diego County, California. The Vanderbilt ledge, owned by the California Company has produced specimens found to contain at least 80 per cent. of the pure metal. Although the tin mines in this country are not yet sufficiently developed to afford an intelligent estimate of their capacity, there can be no doubt that the production of tin will soon form an important branch of industry in the United States.

For the benefit of those interested in manufactures requiring the use of tinsmiths' tools and machinery, we present on this page illustrations and a brief sketch of the manufactory of The Peck, Stow & Wilcox Co., of New York.

We can in this connection mention but few of the principal articles, to the manufacture of which this Company devote special attention ; although of many others which we cannot here enumerate, they are very extensive manufacturers.

They are undoubtedly the largest manufacturers of tools and machinery for tinsmiths' use, in the world ; and in perfection of design, material and workmanship, they are unrivaled. Their machines for the manipulation of tin, such as Beading, Burring, Crimping, Seaming, Grooving, Wiring, &c., exhibit as much perfection in Mechanism and finish as a first-class watch. The several parts are made to actual gauges, and each numbered or lettered so that duplicates can always be promptly furnished ; an important advantage, peculiar to the products of this company, and one that will be appreciated by all who use this class of tools. The high character of these goods is shown in the fact that they have invariably secured the prize when offered in competition with those of other manufacturers, and have been awarded Gold and Silver Medals by the American and Maryland Institutes and many other societies.

Their variety of Tinners' and Builders' Hardware, Housefurnishing Goods, Saddlery and General Hardware, is complete. In the line of Carriage Bolts, Wrenches, Dividers, Compasses, Calipers, Steel-Traps, Steelyards, Meat-Cutters, Coffee-Mills, etc., etc., they exceed all other producers in the United States. Their trade is exclusively with the jobbers and their goods are well and favorably known in all parts of the world ; large quantities being shipped to England, France, Germany, Russia, South America, the Pacific Coast, Canada, &c.

ENCASED LARGE TURNING MACHINE.

ENCASED SMALL BURRING MACHINE.

WIRING MACHINE.

This Company has extensive factories at Southington, Plantsville and East Berlin, Connecticut. At Southington, special attention is devoted to the manufacture of Tinners' and Builders' Hardware, Carriage Bolts, and Hardware generally,—at Plantsville to Tinners' Machines, and House-Furnishing Goods, and at East Berlin, to Tinners' Tools, Compasses, Dividers, Calipers, and flat and round-nosed Plyers. The latter they control by virtue of a patent and it is said to be the best in the United States. These works include Brass Foundries, shops for making Handles and work generally. They contain five steam engines which aggregate four hundred horse power, and three water wheels by which the ponderous machinery is propelled.

The buildings are favorably located so that all freight is received into the yard directly from the Railroad and all goods shipped are packed directly into the cars. The tools and machinery used by this company are valued at not less than $200,000; from 900 to 1,000 men are employed, and a capital of $800,000.

The Peck, Stow & Wilcox Company are successors to the following firms,—The Peck Smith Manufacturing Company, the Stow Manufacturing Company, the Roys & Wilcox Company, whose various interests were consolidated under the present management in 1870.

Tinners' machines were first made in 1820 by Seth Peck, who was succeeded by S. Peck & Co., which concern after various changes merged into the Peck, Smith Manufacturing Company in 1850.

It is now half a century since Tinners' Tools were first made ; Mr. Jedediah North, whose business passed into the hands of the Roys & Wilcox Company, being the first manufacturer.

In 1847, S. Stow & Son, commenced the manufacture of Tinners' machines. Six years later this firm was succeeded by the S. Stow Manufacturing Company. These three concerns, although carrying on business separately, were the largest manufacturers of the classes of goods already alluded to, in the country ; but the proximity of their establishments, and the belief that their mutual interests would be subserved, led to a consolidation, under the direction of the most prominent men in the three firms. They also bought out other firms, and by combining such an amount of ability, experience and capital, they seem to have been placed entirely beyond competition.

During the half century which has elapsed since the commencement of this business, it has grown from a comparatively small beginning to its present gigantic dimensions, through the inventive genius, business ability, and persevering energy of the firms above mentioned. The Company have at different times secured many valuable patents, which they still control.

The officers of the Company are as follows : President, Mr. R. A. Neal, a native of Bristol, Conn.

The Vice President, Mr. O. W. Stow, is a graduate of Yale College, and has charge of everything connected with the patents owned by the company; has also invented about thirty valuable improvements, among which the Adjustable Bar Folder and Encased Machines are the best known, and are in general use throughout the country.

Mr. M. W. Beckley is Secretary and Treasurer of the Company ; Messrs. S. C. Wilcox and W. R. Walkley are the New York Managers, and Messrs. E. E. Stow and J. B. Carpenter, the General Superintendents of the several factories.

The Office and Warerooms of the Company are at 43 Chambers Street, New York, extending through to 27 Reade Street, occupying three floors, each 175 by 25 feet, where an almost endless variety of samples are always on exhibition.

Although the above engravings only represent Tinners' Machines, the company also manufacture a full line of Tools—Shears, Punches, &c. They publish a catalogue of two hundred and fifty-six pages, giving a full and complete description, and prices of goods manufactured by them which they furnish to parties desiring further information regarding their production of Machinery, free of expense.

O. W. STOW'S PATENT ADJUSTABLE BAR FOLDER.

ENCASED LARGE BURRING MACHINE.

SETTING DOWN MACHINE.

H. W. COLLENDER, BILLIARD TABLE MANUFACTURER,

Warerooms, 738 Broadway, N. Y.

No truth is more firmly established than that man cannot always labor or attend to business, but must have time for relaxation and amusement. These will ordinarily be of a nature in contrast with the daily employment, and are provided in such variety as to gratify every taste and every capacity. The love of society leads some to frequent clubs, or other places of resort; others remain at home with their families, ride, walk, attend concerts or theatres, lectures, balls or parties.

Playing at games has always been a favorite relaxation. Of these some are purely mental, some chiefly physical, while others call for the exercise of both mind and body. The game of billiards is of remote antiquity, yet it appears to have no written history. It is only within a comparatively short time, however, that the beauties and intricacies of the game have been fully developed. The billiard table of thirty years ago was a rude, roughly constructed affair, on which balls of imperfect sphericity were punched about with sticks, with a curious uncertainty as to where they would roll or where they would stop. Started by a stroke of the cue, they went as straight as their own shape and the uneven bed of the table would permit, unless they either struck the cushion or an intervening ball, or were lost in one of the wide mouthed pockets. After contact, their course was wholly erratic and beyond the reach of calculation. After pointing the cues with leather and discovering the utility of chalk, spread shots assumed a wider range and force shots became possible, but no advance in accuracy was secured, and the eccentric movements of the balls became more evident and more provoking.

Improvements have been made in the table bed by drawing a cloth tightly over the level wood, but every change of atmosphere, from moist to dry or from hot to cold, tended to produce irregularities which were fatal to accurate playing. The balls were more carefully turned, various materials were tried for cushions, and many ingenious devices were adopted to overcome the obstacles, but all with very unsatisfactory results, until Mr. Collender applied himself to the task. He has revolutionized the game of billiards by first substituting marble and then slate for table beds, by the invention of his combination cushions, and by a radical change in all the accessories of the game. A billiard table is now a work of consummate art, and all the incidentals of cues, maces, bridges, balls, cue racks and the multitude of lesser items which make up a well-furnished billiard room, are in keeping with the table.

Enter any place where Mr. Collender's tables are in use, and observe the wondrous manipulation to which the ivories are subjected. A faint touch with the cue causes a ball to roll gently to the desired contact, and it starts back from the cushion in mathematical angles and with undiminished speed. Now spinning from the well-chalked leather, in graceful curves the cue ball accomplishes the calculated carom, or rushes up to an object ball, sends it flying across the table, while the cue ball returns to seek another object. Direct caroms, cushion, force and follow shots, succeed with an accuracy limited only by the skill of the player, who in the practice of this noblest of all games, soon acquires a delicacy of nerve, an accuracy of eye and an almost instinctive appreciation of angles which make the exercise a pleasure in which the spectators fully share.

Billiards may now be classed among the exact sciences. Let us take a trip to Stamford and visit the headquarters of the magician who has wrought this wondrous change. Directly opposite the depot is a massive brick building whose foundations are sunk deep into the soil and whose solid walls inclose a space of sixty-five by eighty-five feet, and rise six stories with a mansard, which is surmounted by a clock tower whose roof is one hundred and fifty feet above the sidewalk. On entering the building we

H. W. Collender's New Design Bevel Billiard Table.

H. W. COLLENDER'S BILLIARD TABLE MANUFACTORY.

find scores of men busily at work, while the hum of machinery almost drowns our voices. On the lower floor are the machines which do the rough and dirty work, while in the yards of more than two acres surface, are the heavy lumber and the unworked material. Here are a thousand slates, cut thirty-five by sixty-eight inches and one inch thick, whose dressed faces are as plain and as smooth as a geometric ideal. To these are affixed substantial frames for protection and convenience in handling. Here, also, is a seasoning house on a new plan. It is air tight except one place for the admission of pure air, which, heated by a steam coil, passes over and around the lumber laid in racks for seasoning, and then, after licking up its charge of moisture, passes out of an exit at the bottom. Timber so seasoned loses neither its fiber nor any of its strength, and is rapidly and admirably fitted for its destined purposes.

After inspecting the huge piles of lumber, we return to the first floor of the building, see the fifty horse-power engine quietly and steadily at work, inspect the slate borers and the rough planers, visit the veneer room, where a large and varied assortment of grain and end veneers await the demand of the workmen, and go above to follow the work from one machine to another thence to the hands of the artists who give the finishing touches and proudly exhibit to us the completed table.

Here is a machine which takes in an oblong block of squared timber and cuts away on all sides at once, until, in two or three minutes, it delivers to you a completely shaped table leg. Other machines plane the sides, grade the bevels, shape the mouldings, carve the ornaments, press, punch, stamp and drive until one almost concludes that machinery does all the work. But be not too hasty. After these ingenious automatons have done, the table is still in the rough. The glue pot has yet an important function to perform, for these closely fitting pieces must be incorporated into a unit, whose crossing grains so brace and support each other that the strength of iron is made to rest in the wooden fabric. The practiced eye and skilled hand of the educated workman is still required to attend to the multitude of details which must precede and accompany the finished work. Every part must be put in place and all inaccuracies or imperfections must be corrected. Then it is again taken apart and the veneers are applied, and scoured and rubbed into smoothness and polish. The varnisher and the ornamenter next take possession, and still the work is not completed. It must again be erected and leveled, the cloth strained on, the cushions put in place and all carefully tested.

The completed table is a combination of science and art, a triumph of skill, a firm, strong, graceful and beautiful contribution to the public saloon, the quiet club or the private residence. Indeed, special tables are manufactured for this latter purpose, capable, when not opened for games, of serving as ornamental and useful pieces of furniture.

We have followed the billiard table through its course of manufacture, but have noted only a small part of the work performed in Mr. Collender's establishment. The cues and maces are rapidly and accurately turned to any desired taper by a machine especially invented for that purpose; the billiards, uniform in all respects, drop from another lathe like grain from a hopper; a curiously constructed machine handles rough pieces of ivory with almost human intelligence, and only releases them when they are turned to perfect spheres of any required size. Cue tips are cut by one machine, fastened by another and finished by a third. Cue racks are made by one set of machinery and fitted by another. In fact, throughout the whole establishment, the genius of man is embodied in machines, and these do the work more rapidly and accurately than the most rapid and accomplished workmen.

As the tables and accessories made by Mr. Collender combine every desired requisite and are far beyond any present competition, so also are his facilities for manufacturing. There is no break in the essential harmony of the whole, from the initial step to the completed work which has so uniformly been accepted as the best, and on the whole the cheapest the world has yet produced.

NEW YORK AND STATEN ISLAND FIRE BRICK AND CLAY RETORT WORKS,

B. Kreischer & Son.

This house was established in 1845 by Balthazar Kreischer and Charles Mumpeton, under the firm name of Kreischer and Mumpeton, and so continued until 1849, when, by the decease of the latter, B. Kreischer carried on the business in his own name. In 1859 his nephew becoming associated, changed the style to Kreischer & Nephew, and two years later, upon the admission of Ad. Weber, again changed to Kreischer & Co. In 1861, the partnership was dissolved, and the style B. Kreischer again adopted. The success of this house in their branch of manufacture has been marked and satisfactory. From the commencement of its career, their productions took a high rank, their fame extended rapidly and the amount of their business has constantly increased. During the first eight or nine years, Mr. Kreischer purchased the raw material as it was needed but considerable difficulties had been experienced about 1854 in procuring a reliable supply of Clay, and the proprietor feeling the necessity of having his own mines, purchased the Clay property (discovered by B. Kreischer) situated at Westfield, Richmond County, Staten Island, and there erected extensive works for the manufacture of Fire-Brick and Clay Retorts.

This purchase gave them, for a time, an ample supply of first-class material, taken from its native bed and manipulated under their own direction. The Clay here prepared was transported to the New York Works by means of a propeller built expressly for that purpose; but the business of the house increased so rapidly that in a few months large additions were made to these premises, and such was the growth and prosperity of this little village by reason of Mr. Kreischer's enterprise and success that a post-office was established in 1855, and the place named Kreischerville. In 1873 still larger additions were made to the Staten Island property making its capacity three times larger.

In 1865 very valuable clay beds at Woodbridge, New Jersey, and others at Chester, Pennsylvania, were purchased. The had become so prosperous that largely increased facilities for manufacturing became an imperative necessity to meet the constantly growing demand. The New York manufactory was rebuilt during 1865, and supplied with new and vastly improved machinery, and a new style of drying and burning was introduced. The fame of their productions had now spread over all the land, and from north and south, east and west came orders in such numbers and for such quantities as to task their ability to manufacture to its utmost extent; soon, in fact, to exceed it; but Mr. Kreischer was not to be daunted. He called to his aid Messrs. W. A. Loughridge and George Ellis, and in 1867 large and complete works were built in the city of Philadelphia, Pa., where immense quantities of Fire-Bricks, Drain-Tiles and Clay Retorts are daily turned out.

In 1872 Mr. George Kreischer was admitted a partner and the present style of B. Kreischer & Son was adopted.

For a period of more than a quarter of a century Mr. B. Kreischer has given careful study and personal supervision to this important branch of manufacture. The European systems have been carefully examined by him, and such good points as they possessed he has adopted. He has constantly striven to improve the quality of his work and the methods of producing it, his object being to produce the best article possible to be obtained, at the lowest price. Many valuable improvements have been made from time to time, the direct result of his careful study.

Such untiring energy, industry and perseverence have met with the just reward of an unqualified success. The goods of this house rank among the very best of their class, and none excel them either in quality of material, ingenious improvements, or superiority of workmanship.

The best workmen are employed and every facility which inventive genius could suggest in the way of improved machinery, has been adopted at the various manufactories of the firm.

The New York Works are located on the corner of Goerck and Delancy Streets, a reference to the engraving of them on this page, though small, will give the reader a faint idea of their size and capacity. The number of men employed in their various works located in New York City; at Kreischerville, Richmond County, Staten Island; Woodbridge, New Jersey; Philadelphia and Chester, Pennsylvania, is very large and hundreds of others are more or less directly employed in pursuits growing out of their manufactures.

In short, the house is one of the largest and oldest in the United States and widely known from one side of the continent to the other. We heartily recommend those in need of articles in their line to call upon or address B. Kreischer & Son, 58 Goerck Street, New York. Polite attention will always be shown to strangers, and every facility given for examining their extensive manufactories and ware rooms together with their productions, for which the firm is justly celebrated.

B. KREISCHER & SON'S, WORKS, New York.

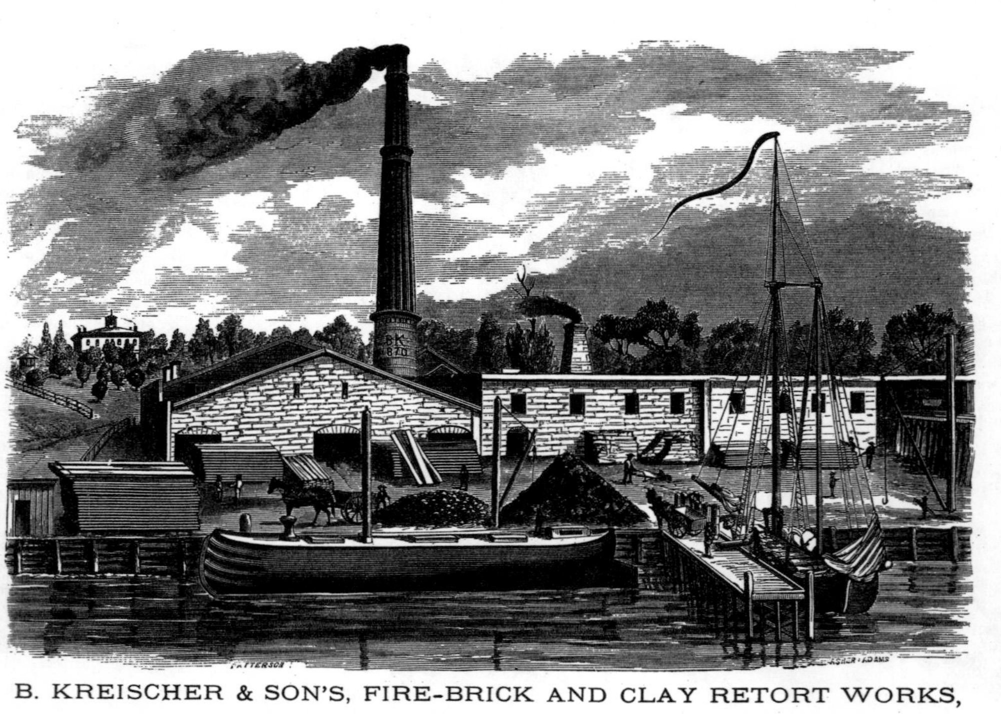

B. KREISCHER & SON'S, FIRE-BRICK AND CLAY RETORT WORKS, Kreischerville, New York.

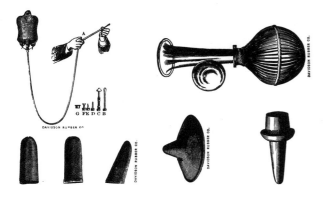

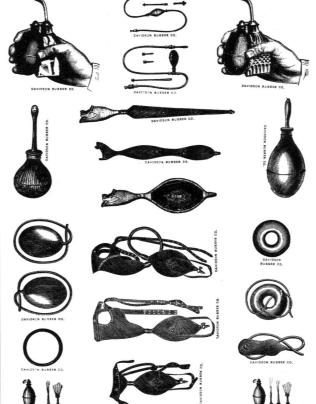

DAVIDSON RUBBER COMPANY,

Manufacturers of and Dealers in

Druggists,' Surgical and Stationers'

Rubber Goods.

265 Washington St., opp. Water, Boston, Mass.

——:o:——

Caoutchouc, as it is more generally called India Rubber, is the juice of a tree which is found in parts of Mexico, Central and South America, Africa, and in the East Indies. The process of gathering the juice is very simple. The tree is tapped in the morning, and a clay cup placed beneath each incision to receive the fluid which flows from the wound. It comes from the tree, purely colorless, like milk, but when dried in the sun the outer parts become a yellowish brown. If the drying and hardening are hastened by exposure to the heat and smoke of a fire it becomes black. To completely dry the juice in the sun requires several days, but to expedite matters, fire is generally used. It has usually been brought to this country in flat cakes, but a new method has recently been devised by which it may be shipped in air tight vessels of tin or glass, just as it comes from the tree. The natives of South America call the hardened juice *Cahuchu*, from which the word *Caoutchouc* is derived, while the term India Rubber, comes from the fact that specimens of it imported from the East Indies previous to 1770, proved to be admirably suited for rubbing out pencil marks.

Previous to 1839, rubber had been applied to but few useful purposes, but after the discovery of a successful method of vulcanization, its manufacture soon became an important item in the industries of the country. To attempt to enumerate the various uses to which rubber is now applied would be to catalogue the various utensils needed in the occupation of our daily life. It is made into Tires and Springs, Jewelry, Combs, Pails, Drinking Cups, Boats, Knife Handles, Coats, Boots, Tents, Life Preservers, Water Beds, and a patent has been taken out for making it into rails for railroads. In the beginning of the present century *Caoutchouc* was valued merely as a

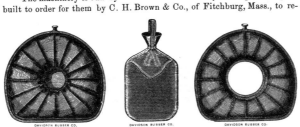

for vulcanizing the rubber, and warming the building. In the rear of the factory is their storehouse, a building 50 by 60 feet and four stories high.

The machinery is run by a one hundred and fifty horse power engine, built to order for them by C. H. Brown & Co., of Fitchburg, Mass., to re-

which the Davidson Rubber Company have bestowed upon the most minute workings of their establishment have enabled them to manufacture goods whose fine quality and durability have gained for them a prominent place in the front rank of manufacturers. One of their rules is never to sacrifice quality to cost of production but to produce as perfect and durable articles as possible, and if they find that they cannot dispose of them at a fair profit, they discontinue the manufacture of such goods, rather than reduce the quality. Through their strict adherence to this rule they have gained the confidence, not only of the trade, but of the public. The manufacture of many of the special articles now produced by this Company was commenced in response to the earnest solicitation of the trade. In many branches of the business there was formerly great difficulty in obtaining from time to time goods of uniform quality, and dealers being aware that the productions of this Company did not vary, induced them to add to their line of manufactures many articles which they originally did not intend to produce. Since the commencement their business has steadily increased, and is still increasing very rapidly.

The business of the Davidson Rubber Company, was organized in a very small way in the year 1857, by Mr. C. H. Davidson, he at that time having all his rubber and machine work done for him by outside parties. In 1860 Mr. Davidson sold the business to his nephew, Hamilton D. Lockwood, who, in 1865, on the expiration of the patent for vulcanizing soft rubber, commenced the manufacture of the crude rubber, in a small wooden factory in Malden, Mass., giving the entire process his personal supervision. In 1868, Mr. Lockwood formed a copartnership with his brother, Rhodes Lockwood, and they built and moved into the present quarters—or a part of them at least—for at various times since then they have found it necessary to enlarge, to meet the requirements of their increasing business.

On the 12th of May, 1875, Mr. H. D. Lockwood died, leaving the business in the hands of the surviving partner, Rhodes Lockwood, who by reason of his intimate knowledge of the business in all its details, derived from long experience, is fully able to carry on the manufactory and maintain the high reputation for quality which the productions of this establishment have already attained.

This Company has never attempted to force its manufactures upon the market by establishing agents in the principal cities, either in this country

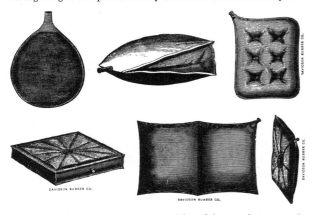

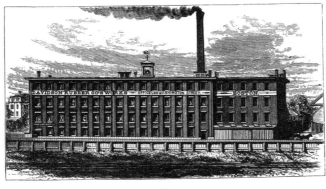

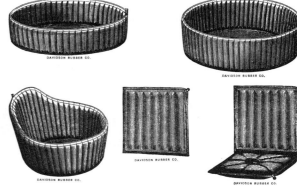

curious natural product, now it is a material used in manufactures to the amount of millions yearly.

The Davidson Rubber Company, an engraving of whose factory occupies the centre and numerous cuts of whose products are grouped in other portions of this page, are largely engaged in the manufacture of Fine Rubber Goods, which are largely sold to dealers in Druggists', Surgical, and Stationers' supplies.

Among the great variety of articles manufactured by them are included Air Work of all kinds, such as Beds, Pillows and Cushions of every description; Bath Tubs, Bed Pans and Gas Bags; Stationers' articles are represented by Elastic Bands and Rings, Erasive Rubber, etc; their line of Druggists' goods include Rubber Nipples, Tubing, Teething Rings, Ice Bags, and Cups, Breast Pumps, Finger Cots, Atomizers, etc; and in Medical goods they make Syringes of various sizes, Dilators Pessaries, Cupping Cups, Urinals, Umbilical Belts, etc. In addition to these they produce sundry other goods, such as Gloves, Dress Shields, Bulbs, Water Bags and Bottles, and an almost endless variety of other articles.

The line of their manufactures is constantly being extended to meet the demands of dealers, and they do a very large business, manufacturing special articles to order.

The popularity of the Davidson Rubber Company with dealers is accounted for in the fact that their goods are carefully and skillfully made of the finest stock, and that every effort is put forth to as nearly reach perfection as possible.

The factory of the Company is located on the line of the Eastern, and Boston and Maine Railroads, in that part of Boston formerly known as Charlestown. The establishment consists of a brick building, 170 feet long by 60 feet wide and four stories high, with two ells over 50 feet square, in which are situated the boilers which furnish steam for the engine, and heat

place a sixty horse power engine which was too small to meet their requirements. The new engine was put in place in June, 1875. The Company give steady employment to an average of one hundred and fifty hands, and consume in their manufactures about 50,000 lbs. of rubber per year.

The Company receive their supplies of rubber in the crude state, and in their own works submit it to every process through which it must pass before it reaches the pulp, in the shape of a finished article. The utmost care is exercised in the selection of the material, and every detail of its preparation is closely watched by experts who have spent many years in the business. The amount of stock worked up by this Company is very much smaller than is consumed in many other establishments where heavy goods are made, the production of this Company being generally light goods, requiring but little stock, but the finest workmanship, consequently the most skillful workmen only are employed.

To secure a uniform quality of productions a constant supervision of the manufacture in all its details must be kept up, and the careful attention

or abroad, but have preferred to sell direct to the wholesale trade, and so be in constant communication with their customers. The object of this is to enable the Company to hear at once of any defect that might be found in their goods, and to receive from first hands suggestions as to possible improvements in old or the necessity for new articles that might be needed. The Company has always been quick to act upon such information and suggestions, and their trade has rapidly increased in this and in other countries, and their goods may now be found in all the large cities over all the world, and in almost every village and hamlet throughout the United States.

In addition to the classes of goods already spoken of the Company is largely engaged in the manufacture of special articles for parties who make goods which are in part constructed of rubber, and from such parties many highly complimentary letters have been received.

The factory is fitted with every appliance that can aid the workman in the production of first-class work, and there is a system of rigid inspection of every separate article produced, which renders it almost impossible for an imperfection to escape detection. A private telegraph connects the factory with the store, in the business centre of the city, and instant communication between the two can be had at any time.

It is the intention of the proprietor, as it was of his late partner, to exhibit a full line of their goods at the Centennial Exhibition, knowing that it will afford an opportunity of placing them before a great number of people from all parts of the civilized world. They will be compared with the productions of other makers and of other countries, but he is confident that they will not suffer by the comparison.

The Davidson Rubber Company does a strictly manufacturing business, selling in full packages only, so as not to interfere with the Jobbing Trade. All orders or inquiries addressed to the Davidson Rubber Company, Boston, Massachusetts, will receive prompt attention.

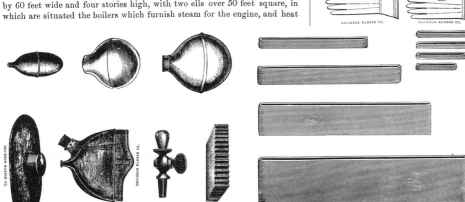

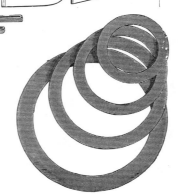

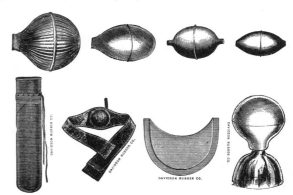

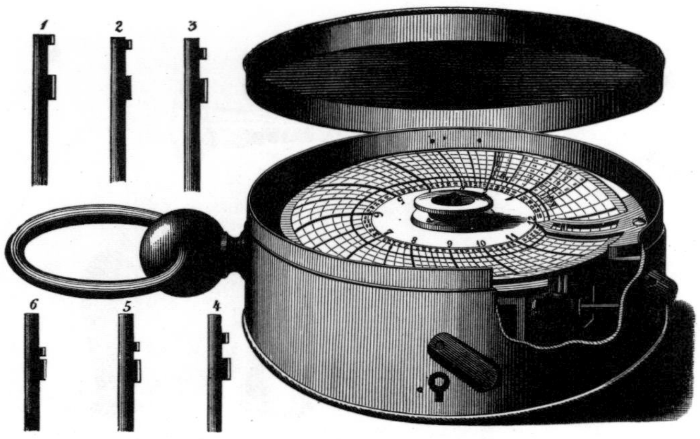

IMHAUSER & COMPANY,
WATCHMAN'S IMPROVED TIME DETECTORS,
U. S. PATENT, APRIL 22, 1873.
212 Broadway, cor. Fulton Street, N. Y.

—:o:—

In all large factories, warehouses, banks, railroad depots, machine shops, stables, etc., it is absolutely necessary that watchmen be employed to watch and guard during the night for the better protection of such buildings, and the property contained therein. With a faithful watchman the risk of loss, either by robbery or fire, is reduced to the minimum. But how to know that the watchman is faithful is the question; for a watchman who deserts his post, or "sleeps on guard," is worse than none at all. On the various stations of the watchman's beat, keys are placed and fastened within or outside the buildings, to indicate the stations by the number, up to twelve. The watchman, before entering on his duties in the evening, receives the watch, which is provided with a fresh paper dial, wound up on the arbor, in the centre of the disk, to the right, and locked. He makes his rounds and visits the different stations, according to the instructions received from his employer. In making his rounds and arriving at a station, the watchman will insert the key into the key-hole on the side of the watch opposite the ring and turn it round to the right once, and while doing this a hole will be pricked in the dial of the watch at exactly the minute the hand on the watch shows the time; in short, it tells the history of the night's doings, or the carelessness of the watchman.

In the watch represented, six different keys—Nos. 1 to 6—mark one hole in circles 1, 2, 3, 4, 5, 6, on a paper disk, which is slowly revolving; six other combination keys, Nos. 7 to 12, make a double mark, but in the same circles as before, so that the one does not interfere with the other, as seen in the cut above.

These Detectors are the latest and most complete invented, are portable and reliable time-pieces, and guaranteed in every respect as perfect. The watch can be cleaned and repaired by any watch-maker. These instruments are invaluable for all establishments that employ watchmen, as they enable them to check and control all their movements.

No person employing a night watchman will, after examining this Watchman's Time Detector, do without it for a day. No person interested in this instrument will appreciate it so fully as the watchman himself; that is, provided he means to discharge his duty in good faith, as it will clearly show to all interested that he has done so, and that, too, without any question or doubt.

The Safety Lock Attachment is a very important addition to this valuable instrument, as an effectual guard against dishonest watchmen, who, but for it, might open the watch and mark the dial without going their rounds; and as an additional guard the Time Detector is supplied with a marker, which marks the dial whenever the watch is opened.

The reliability and usefulness of these watches have been certified and confirmed by many proprietors of large establishments, who have thoroughly tested them, and whose certificates are on file at the office of Messrs. Imhauser & Co.

The Watchman's Time Detector is covered by United States Patent 138,084, dated April 22, 1873; Safety Lock Attachment patented November 30, 1875. All parties using or selling these instruments without authority from Messrs. Imhauser & Co. will be dealt with according to law; and they will protect their customers against all claims of other patentees. The instrument is supplied with pouch, box of dials, and twelve different keys, for twelve stations, complete.

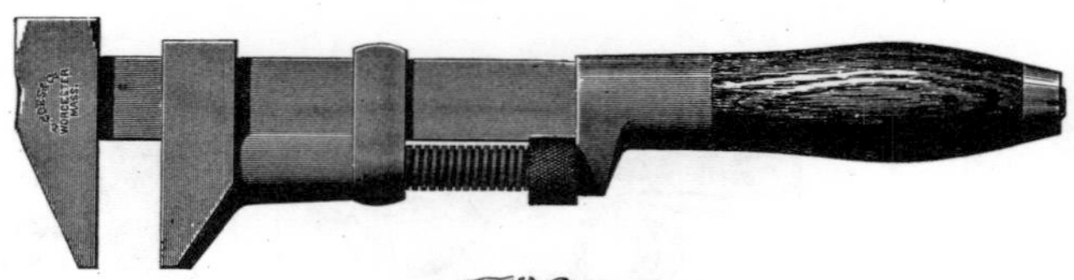

Established **in 1839.**

Registered, March 31, 1874.

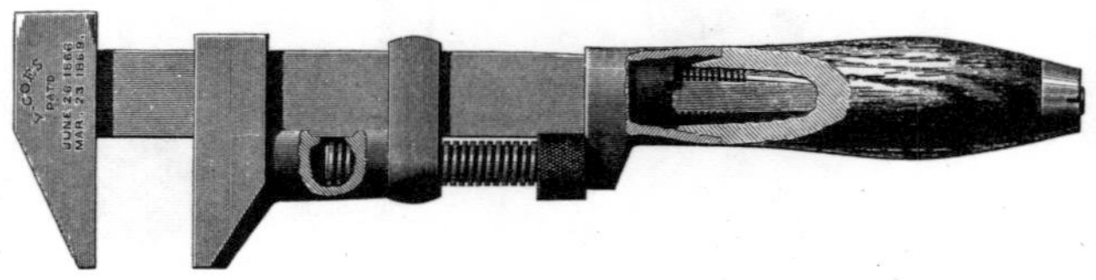

L. COES & COMPANY,
MANUFACTURERS OF SCREW WRENCHES,
Worcester, Mass.

—:o:—

There is no tool, perhaps, more generally known than the Screw Wrench; to machinists—indeed to mechanics generally it is absolutely indispensable—and there is scarcely a business of any description in which it is not frequently used. It is certainly the only effective wrench for general use ever devised, simple in its principle and mechanism. The necessity of a wrench which could be adapted to bolts, nuts, etc., of different sizes, was keenly felt many years before such a device was invented, and no really practicable adjustable wrench was known until the Screw Wrench was invented by Mr. Loring Coes, formerly senior partner of the well-known firm of L. & A. G. Coes, established in 1839—now the senior partner of the firm of L. Coes & Co.

The new wrench rapidly won its way in public favor, and was from time to time greatly improved. Upon the expiration of the original patents, several manufacturers attempted the manufacture of screw wrenches; but the name of "Coes" had become so completely identified with reliable wrenches, that other makers have had but indifferent success, and the original house and its successors have, by the superiority and continual improvement of their productions, monopolized a very large proportion of the trade. Within the past four years many important improvements have been made in the screw wrench, which have been patented. By making the Bar straight and widened to full size of the larger part of the so-called reinforced or jog bar; by enlarging the jaw, made with ribs on the inside, having a full bearing on front of the bar (see sectional view), making the jaw fully equal to any strain to which the bar may be subjected; by screwing a nut up firmly against square, solid bearings inside the ferrule, thereby effectually preventing the ferrule from being thrust back into the handle, or becoming loose, and using a larger screw than in the old wrench, a 12-inch wrench is made stronger than a 15-inch of the usual kind.

The wrenches are made of a superior quality of wrought iron, manufactured expressly for them by the Rome Merchant Iron Mill, and are sold over the whole civilized world.

The wrench factory of L. Coes & Co., situated in the outskirts of Worcester, comprises a three-story brick building, 50 by 100 feet, with a front projection 34 by 16 feet (the ground room of the projection being used for an office, and the rooms above for machinists and tools); also a forge shop, 50 feet square, both run by a 67-horse power iron-cased turbine water-wheel, in a wheel-house between the two structures.

They own three reservoirs, containing together 400 acres, all utilized so as to furnish power for machinery.

A quarter of a mile from the wrench factory, this firm also has a shop for the manufacture of machine cutters, hay cutter knives, die stock, shear blades and strips, planing machine knives, and edge tools generally. The building is 75 by 50 feet, with two stories and a basement. The power is transmitted from two turbine water-wheels. They have besides a saw-mill and a carpenter shop, both run by water power.

From 60 to 75 men are employed by the firm, and from 15,000 to 20,000 wrenches are made per month, besides a large amount of edge tools.

These works have the most beautiful natural surroundings of any in the city of Worcester, consisting of groves, gentle hills, green sward, and clear running water.

RODNEY HUNT MACHINE COMPANY,
Manufacturers of
WOOL MACHINERY,
Hunt's Double Acting Turbine Water Wheel,

—AND—

Every Branch of Mill Work,

ORANGE, MASS.

Rodney Hunt, *Pres't.* David B. Flint, *Treas.* Rufus Livermore, *Sec'y.*

—:o:—

The manufacture of Turbine Water Wheels is fairly entitled to be ranked as one of the most important industries of this country, important not only for the capital invested in the business, or the value of the wheels produced, (if we measure their value by their cost), but for that greater value which is found in their complete utilization of power. During the past fifteen years great improvement has been made in their construction and consequently in their efficiency, and Breast and Overshot Wheels are rapidly giving place to Turbines, which require much less space and afford much steadier power, with far less waste of water.

For many years the Rodney Hunt Machine Co., have given special attention to the manufacture and improvement of Water Wheels. The business was founded by Rodney Hunt, the President of the Company, in 1840. At first he gave his attention almost entirely to the manufacture of Breast Wheels, of which he probably made a larger number than any other builder in New England, but, keeping pace with the demands of the age, he gave much time to the study of Turbines, making numerous improvements—which were ultimately combined in the well and favorably known "Hunt's Double Acting Turbine Water Wheel," which was patented in June, 1869. Since that time several valuable improvements have been added to the wheel, which, also, are secured by letters patent. The manufacture of these improved wheels is a very important branch of the work carried on by the Rodney Hunt Machine Company, they having supplied many of the largest cotton and woolen mills, and other manufacturing establishments in the country with these wheels. In connection with their Machine Shop, the Company has a large and well equipped Foundry, with a full list of gear and pulley patterns and everything necessary for the execution of the heaviest mill work.

In addition to the mill work department the Company gives special attention to the manufacture of Wool Machinery for wet finishing, particularly Washers and Fulling Mills, which have been shipped to nearly every State in the Union, and to the British Provinces. Besides what they term their common Rotary Fulling Mill, a machine with which all woolen manufacturers are familiar, they make an Improved English Mill, the improvements on which are secured to them by letters patent. This Mill combines all that seems desirable in a machine of its class; it has an iron frame with wood casings; improved squeeze rollers which are remarkably durable; and all the inside surfaces are made of either wood or brass, thus protecting even the finest goods from being injured by rust.

An experience of upwards of twenty years in the manufacture of Fulling Mills enables the Company to fully meet the wants of woolen manufacturers in this branch of their business, and the high reputation which their productions have attained is a sufficient guarantee of the real merits of their mills. As only the best materials are used and none but thorough workmen employed in their establishment, purchasers may always rely on all machines manufactured by the Rodney Hunt Machine Company as being first-class in every respect—as near perfection in all their parts and in their operation, as can be attained. Circulars and descriptive catalogues will be sent on application to the Company, at their works in Orange, Mass.

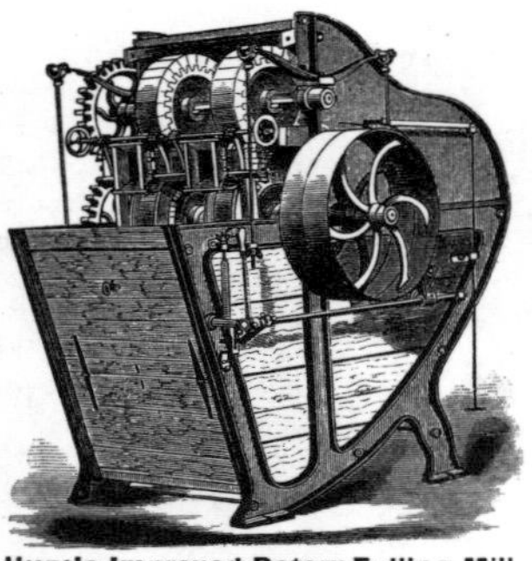

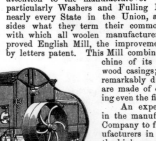

Hunt's Improved Rotary Fulling Mill.
TOP REMOVED.

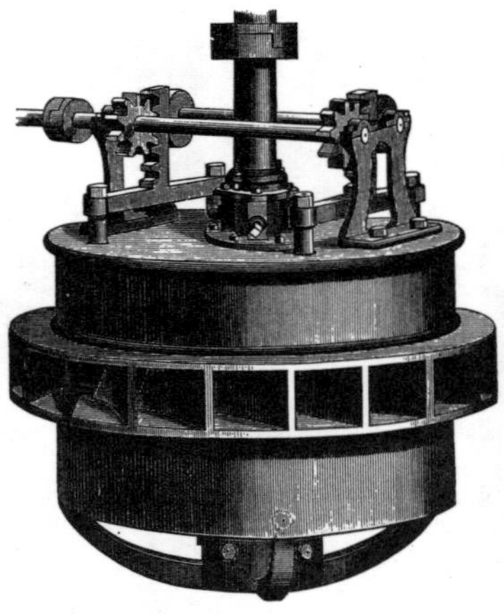

HUNT'S DOUBLE ACTING TURBINE WATER WHEEL.

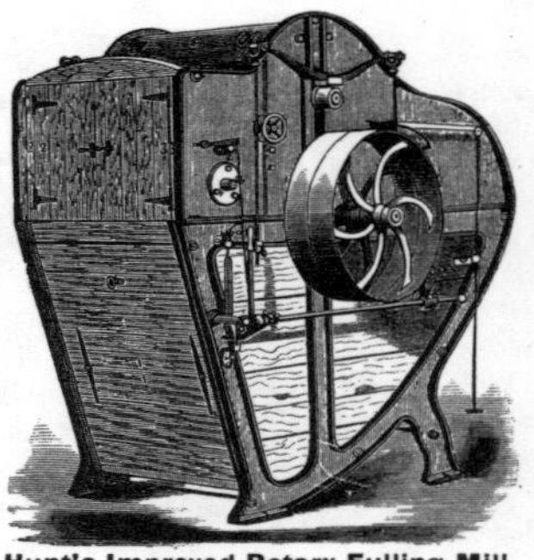

Hunt's Improved Rotary Fulling Mill.
CLOSED.

WORKS ESTABLISHED 1836.

G. WESTINGHOUSE & CO.,
Manufacturers of
THRESHING MACHINES,
Schenectady, New York

There are two styles of Grain Threshing Machines now in use, known respectively as the "Vibrator" and the "Endless Apron." The Endless Apron style of machine was the first made, the Vibrator being of more recent invention, and, as is claimed, a simpler and more perfectly operating machine than those made after the original plan.

The Westinghouse Threshing Machine to which we desire to call the reader's attention, but which we cannot describe in the limited space at our disposal, belongs to the Vibrator class, but is in many respects different from and superior to other Vibrator machines. One of the most important features of this machine is the Improved Bar Cylinder and Concaves. This cylinder is so constructed that the spikes do not work loose and are far less liable to break than in other cylinders. The Concaves are made of the same kind of bars as the cylinder, and are easily changed to any position required for the different kinds of grain.

For a long time these machines have been in advance of others in their separating capacity, and late important improvements without an increase of machinery, has added materially to this desirable qualification. For perfection in cleaning all kinds of grain they are not surpassed.

The Powers furnished with these machines possess every desirable feature for obtaining the full value of the force applied, and are durable and easily handled.

The aim of the firm has been to make the very best machine, and with this end in view, improvements such as have suggested themselves have been made from year to year, during the past twenty years. To those who are acquainted with these machines, the improvements made speak for themselves, but for the information of those who are not, it is well to say that during the entire threshing season, at least one member of the firm is in almost constant attendance upon and witnessing the operations of their machines in different sections of the country, learning the wants of every community, and the appliances and conditions necessary for most successfully handling the different varieties of grain, including Flax, Grass and Clover Seeds, and each year brings out some new feature that seems desirable.

There are machines in the market sold for a less price than the Westinghouse Threshers are sold for, but as this firm produces nothing but first-class work, they do not attempt to compete with cheaply made and inferior articles, and we believe that, as a rule, the best made and most substantial machines, although costing more at first, are by far the cheapest in the end. And we have no hesitancy in asserting that in all essential and desirable qualities requisite to first-class Threshing Machines, the Westinghouse Vibrator Thresher and Cleaner, or Separator has no superior, if an equal, in the market.

During the year 1874, the works were destroyed by fire, but new and better ones have replaced them, and the firm with perfected and increased facilities are now prepared to turn out a larger number of and better made machines than ever before.

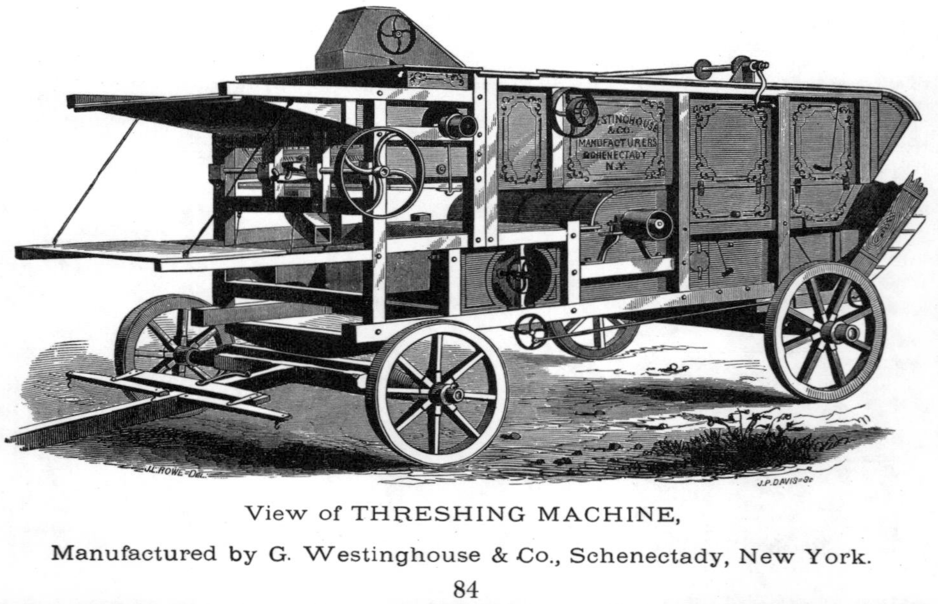

View of THRESHING MACHINE,

Manufactured by G. Westinghouse & Co., Schenectady, New York.

POWERS'
COMMERCIAL FIRE-PROOF BUILDING,
Rochester, New York.

—:o:—

Powers' Commercial Fire-Proof Building is certainly one of the finest structures on the American continent—indeed, there are but few buildings in the world, erected and occupied for business purposes, that are its equals in size, in beauty of design, in complete adaptability to the purposes for which it is intended, in strength, or in artistic finish. The block has a frontage of 176 feet on State Street, 175 feet on West Main Street, and 150 feet on Pindell Alley. The front of the centre or corner building is faced with Ohio Free- or Sandstone, elaborately carved—the blocks being alternately vermiculated and cut in panel. The great wings present uniform fronts of plate glass and cast iron, the brick which enters so largely into the construction being visible only in the tower and in the rear on the alley. The building is seven stories in height, exclusive of the basement. The Mansard Roof, twenty-five feet in height, is built wholly of iron and slate. Back of the French roof, which makes one immense hall, another story is gained, or, rather, the story is divided into two floors, and the roof is raised eight feet above the Mansard. The building is quadrangular in form, and is, we are informed, the only perfectly tubular block in the United States. It has light on all sides, with an open area in the centre for the purpose of lightning all the halls and rooms above the ground floor. The ground floor contains the Powers' Banking House, and fifteen stores, (besides two offices partly under ground), covering the entire lot, and which vary from 13 to 30 feet in width and from 50 to 150 feet in length, all being 14 feet 6 inches in height, with finely finished basements that are 11 feet 6 inches high and well lighted by knobs in the pavement. The upper stories contain 220 rooms, which are used for almost every conceivable kind of business and occupation. The halls of all the stories above the ground are circuitous, very spacious—most of them being 11 feet wide—their floors are laid with square marble tiles, with marble surbase, and each hall is lighted with eight pendants. There are three broad entrances, and one narrow one from the street to the second story—two on each street or front—the stairs of which are entirely of Italian marble. Of the three staircases leading from the second to the upper stories, two are wholly of iron, with silver bronze railings and balustrades, having a half landing or platform in the centre of each story. The grand, or principal staircase, contains fifty tons of iron, and cost $20,000. All of the floors of the entire block are built of rolled iron, with brick arches; all of the partitions throughout are of brick and the window frames and castings are made principally of iron. The building is thus rendered proof against fire, while the walls stand upon solid foundations of New Hampshire granite, literally built upon a rock, rendering it equally proof against flood or hurricane. All the stores and offices are furnished with radiators heated by steam from eleven boilers in the basement. Two of these boilers are high pressure, one of 35 horse power. A very powerful steam pump forces an abundant supply of water through pipes to the top floor, and also supplies one of the high pressure boilers during the cold weather when large quantities of steam are required to heat the immense building, the second being kept in reserve. Within the brief space to which this article must be confined we cannot describe the building as it deserves, but a few figures will perhaps, aid the reader in forming an estimate of the extent and value of the structure: The glass, best English polished plate, cost upwards of $30,000; the French roof alone cost over $70,000, and the dormer windows in it $1,000 each; $6,500 was paid for the sidewalk on which stand five elegant candelabra that cost $200 each. The building contains over one mile of marble wainscoting, in addition to the 75,000 square feet of Italian and Vermont marbles used for other purposes. Of iron there is 8,000,000 pounds, or 4,000 tons; 8,000,000 brick are in the walls, there are over 80,000 yards of plastering in the building, and 12,000 wagon loads of sand were used in making mortar. So spacious is this building, that computing the aggregate superficial feet of all the floors, the result would show standing room for 80,000 people; or, in other words, the whole population of Rochester might be comfortably assembled at one time beneath its roof. The number of tenants is about 1,600, and the variety of business here carried on makes it a miniature city in itself, in which all the ordinary wants of civilization are supplied, so that one could live in the block without being obliged to go outside of it for anything. Not only does it provide a place of occupation for so many individuals and corporations, for merchants, lawyers, painters, bankers, physicians, clergymen and others, but several departments of the National Government, the State, the County and the City have offices here.

The most conspicuous portion of the building, and the one that will be most generally visited by sight-seers, is the tower, which rises 60 feet above the roof, and is 40 feet long by 24 wide—that is on the average, like the block itself, to which it corresponds, it is an irregular quadrilateral, the northern side being narrower than the southern. Flights of iron stairs, of the same general character as the larger ones below, lead up through the first three stories, each of which contains a large room suitable for an artist's studio or any similar purpose, while the fourth floor is set apart for visitors, for whom it is a general gathering place. Doors open from all sides of this on a balcony that runs around the tower, built of iron and resting on heavy beams of the same metal, which run through from side to side, and which could not give way under a pressure of 500 tons at either end. The east and west walls of the tower run up straight from the solid rock, and the iron girders upon which the floors rest bind them so firmly that the structure will be as immovable against the stormiest visitations as against the gentlest zephyrs that play around its summit. Many callers will rest content with reaching this elevation, but the majority will mount higher and climb the spiral staircase that lands them upon the sky floor, which is paved with marble and surrounded with a coping of that stone, and finished with a substantial railing. Even above this is a square brick section, twelve feet high, (whose only purpose, however, is to serve as a bulkhead, or protection to the stairs), which is 175 feet above the sidewalk, and beside which rises a flag-staff from whose top a massive gilded eagle spreads his wings at an altitude of sixty-three feet more.

From this exalted station, 400 feet above the level of the lake; the view is peculiarly beautiful to any eye, but most attractive to those who are interested in the development of material wealth and the prosperity of an enterprising community. We cannot stop to describe the scene, but we feel it a duty to advise all visiting Rochester to make the ascent, and promise them one of the most magnificent views ever unfolded to the sight of man. While viewing the gorgeous panorama, the visitor can hardly fail to notice on the roof below an immense vane. This is one of the appurtenances of the weather office, which is located in the room just below. Again lack of space forbids description—visitors will find much of interest.

Descending from the tower to the Mansard roof we enter one of the two Otis Brothers elevators with which the building is furnished, and begin our downward journey. Stop!—we had well nigh forgotten the Art Gallery, which occupies spacious apartments on the seventh floor, and embraces over 400 oil paintings, including many very valuable originals of the old masters, copies of famous works, selected from the principal galleries of Europe, and very many meritorious original productions of American and foreign artists of the present time. Mr. Powers is a gentleman of culture, and as a connoisseur in art he has few equals; possessed of ample wealth, and earnestly desiring to aid in developing the artistic tastes of our people, he some years ago determined to gather and open to the public an Art Gallery—not a collection of cheap paintings by unknown artists in tawdry frames, but a carefully selected gallery of the finest works of art that money could buy. Mr. Powers, with this end in view, visited Europe and spent some months in the art centres of the Old World, during which time he succeeded in purchasing some of the rarest works of the old masters, at large prices, of course. The gallery is well lighted and the pictures are well hung, and the collection is really one of the most valuable in the United States. Visitors may here spend several hours, and we should like to linger with them, but must hurry on.

Entering the car of the nearest elevator, we begin the descent. This car is worthy of a special description. It is 7½ by 8 feet on the floor and 11 feet high; it is domed with cut-glass sky-lights and ventilators, is richly carpeted, is supplied with gas by a flexible tube which it carries, and is furnished with sofas on three sides and two large mirrors facing each other, in which the repeated reflection of the gas-light produces the appearance of a long train of palace cars. The sides and the dome are furnished throughout with panels, pilasters, brackets, cornices, moldings and carvings of highly polished American woods. For a description of the mechanism of these vertical railways the reader is referred to the opposite page. These elevators are absolutely safe, there is no possibility of a person in one of the cars being injured by any accident to the apparatus. The entire vertical railways in the Powers' Block, embracing car, engine and the entire mechanism cost upwards of $20,000 each, and their usefulness is shown by the fact that they carry from four to six thousand persons daily.

Rochester has good reason to be proud of her general prosperity and can point to many large establishments as monuments of her progress, but beyond a doubt, the noblest structure of all is Powers' Commercial Fire-Proof Building.

It has not been our intention, in this article, to call particular attention to any of the many kinds of business transacted in this building, but merely to briefly describe the structure itself. We are aware that we have done this very imperfectly; a full description would require a good size column, but we trust we have said enough to excite the interest of those of our readers who are interested in, or who propose to erect buildings for similar purpose. Such parties will undoubtedly find it to their interest to visit Rochester and critically examine Powers' Block before deciding upon plans or selecting materials from which to erect their own contemplated structures. The building is a perfect model of solidity and strength, artistic in its design, beautiful in its proportions, convenient in its arrangement, supplied with all the modern and most approved appliances of every description that can be of advantage to its numerous tenants, it can hardly fail to give some valuable suggestions to other builders.

A monument commemorative of the progress of Rochester, as we have previously called it, it is to a still greater extent a monument, and a fitting one, too, to the enterprise, the practical good sense and the æsthetic tastes of its public spirited owner. It is a daily and an enduring educator, and if other architects would follow Mr. Powers' example, and erect in our larger cities structures that were elegant in appearance instead of the huge piles, whose outward forms are forbidding, and whose interior present nothing that is pleasant to the eye of their care-worn occupants, we would have fewer complaints from business men. All business is, to a greater or less extent, a drudgery, but the labor is much lightened if when the weary eye is raised it meets some cheerful object which affords immediate rest. It is much more pleasant to work, no matter what the work may be, in a well lighted, neatly furnished, well ventilated apartment than in a dark and dingy one, and in offering such accommodations to so large a number of the business and professional men of Rochester Mr. Powers has done a noble work. The magnificent panoramic view from the tower, and the art gallery, form an attraction for, and are educators of the great masses of the people.

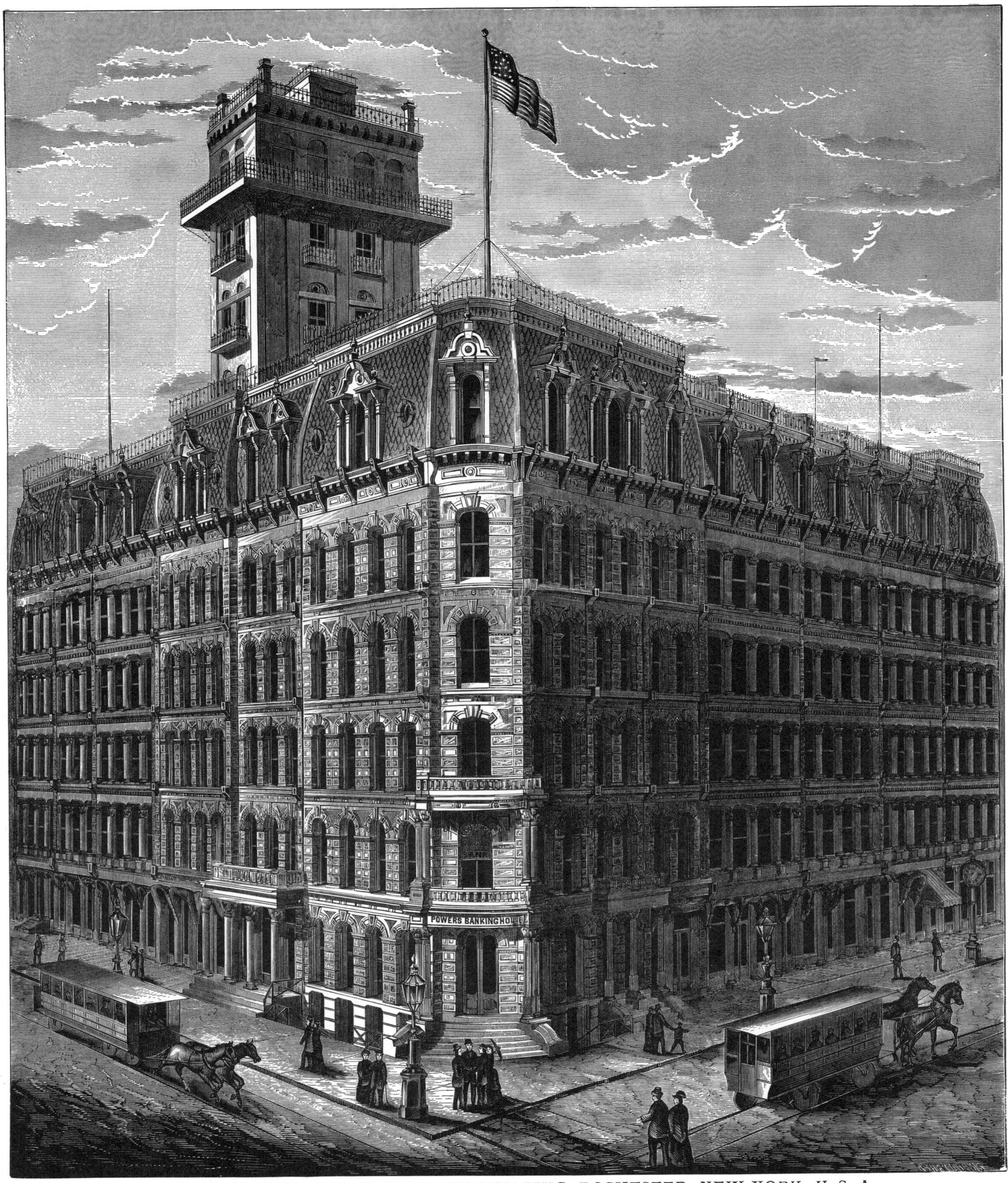

POWERS' COMMERCIAL FIRE-PROOF BUILDING, ROCHESTER, NEW YORK, U. S. A.

PATENT BUCKEYE SAFETY BIT.

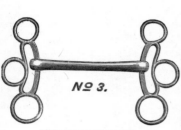

N⁰ 3.

BUCKEYE SAFETY BIT.

THE CELEBRATED P. & L. PATENT LOOP PAD HOOKS.

PATENT BOX SNAP.

BUFFALO PATENT WHIP HOLDER.
For Leather Dash.

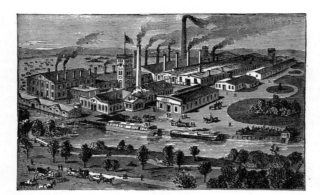

TRADE MARK.

THORNTON'S PATENT SELF ADJUSTING COLLAR BUCKLE.

BUFFALO MALLEABLE IRON WORKS,

Saddlery and Carriage Hardware Manufactory.

The above cut represents the very extensive works of Messrs. Pratt & Letchworth, at Buffalo, N. Y., probably the largest manufacturers of Malleable Iron and Saddlery Hardware in this country.

They have been established now nearly thirty years, and in their long experience have gained an enviable reputation for supplying goods of superior quality, being the makers of the well known Buffalo Hames, which are still, as for many years they have been the standard of excellence in this widely used article; many of the most valuable patents on Hame improvements are owned by this firm, and are to be found only on their Hames.

In the accompanying illustrations we show but a very few of the many valuable articles which they have introduced to the trade. The Buckeye Safety Bit, acknowledged the best in use for the management of the horse, the Buffalo Patent Whip Holder, the Patent Breast Strap Slide, Thornton's Patent Collar Buckle, Kroh's Patent Carriage Knobs, the P. & L. Patent Pad Hooks, and the Patent Box Snaps, all are too well known and appreciated to require extended notice; suffice it to say, the line of their manufactures embraces everything in the way of Saddlery Hardware, and in every variety of finish, including an extended assortment of Buckles, Rings, and Dees; Cockeyes, Harness Terrets and Hooks, Self-Adjusting Trees, and Tree Trimmings; Snaffles, Ring Bits, Mule, Port and Gig Bits in great variety, including many new and desirable styles. Patent Star Bits, Rubber Mouth Bits and Wire Bits; the celebrated Cooper's Patent Trace Carrier, Patent Halter Trimmings, Halter Squares and Bolts, Swivels, Pad Screws, Stirrups, Toggles, etc., etc.; also, an extended line of Carriage and Wagon Malleables, which are unsurpassed in strength, neatness of pattern and beauty of finish. Custom work in Malleable Iron is also made a specialty.

PETTINGILL'S PATENT BREAST STRAP SLIDE.

No. 3.   No. 1.   No. 2.   No. 4.

BUFFALO PAT. WHIP HOLDER.
For Wood Dash.

KROH'S PATENT CARRIAGE KNOBS.

Advantages of this Knee.
LIGHTER,
STRONGER,
AND
Costs no more than
Best Wood Knee.

Wrought Angle Iron Ship Knee.

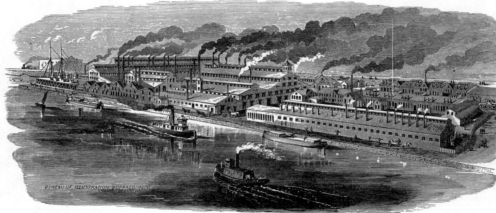

VIEW OF THE BUFFALO IRON & NAIL WORKS, BUFFALO, N. Y.

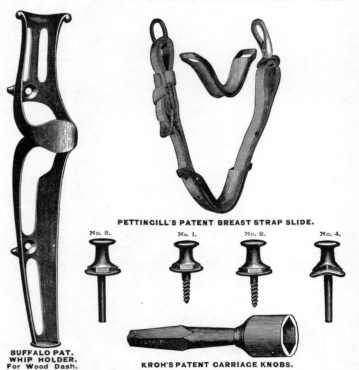

Wrought Iron Beams, Girders and Joists,
Made from Angle and Plate Iron riveted together.

Buffalo Iron and Nail Works.

PRATT & CO., Proprietors.

ADAM'S NUT LOCK:
It is simple and certain. It never gets out of place. Will hold the nut perfectly secure. A valuable invention for railroads, bridges, etc. Acts as a washer and lock for nut at the same time.

PATENTED JUNE. 15. 1869

Mine and Yard Strap Rail.
Sizes as desired.

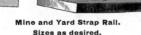

T Rail.—Weight 16 lbs. per yard, 2 in. high, 1 3-4 in. wide, base.

Street Rail. Ordinary.—Weight 47 lbs. per yard, 5 inch wide.

The manufacturing establishments of this company are owned and controlled by Messrs. Pratt & Co., of Buffalo, New York. Their Blast Furnace, called the "Fletcher" has Niagara River with deep water navigation on one side, and the Erie Canal (with private slip on the premises) on the other side and is in the 12th ward of the city. This Furnace the company run on quality, and therefore select their stocks of Ore, Coal and Lime, with reference to their own wants for consumption in their works. First class Lake Superior ores are mainly used with first quality Anthracite Coal and Coke for smelting. The furnace is a close top, 14 x 45 and makes thirty tons pig metal per day.

The Rolling Mill and Factories are situated in the 11th ward, a short distance from the Furnace and also on the river and Erie Canal, having side tracks for railway purposes on the premises, which are in connection with all the railroads leading from the city. The works are a few rods above the American shore end of the "International Bridge" across the Niagara River. These works cover altogether about fifteen acres and consist of a Rolling Mill containing twenty-two puddling and eight heating Furnaces, also eight inch, nine inch, ten inch, fifteen inch, seventeen inch and twenty inch trains. Eight Double Muck Trains, and Universal Mill with all the appliances of Squeezer Steam Shears, Ore Mill, etc., of a well appointed Rolling Mill, having a capacity of seventy tons finished iron per day.

Connected with the mill are hot and cold Nail Factories, Nut, Bolt, and Washer Factory, Forging and Blacksmith Shops, Spike Factory, Hammered Horse Nail Factory, also a Bridge Shop seven hundred feet in length, with railroad tracks for shipping, and all the necessary repair shops and appendages for the manufacture, handling and shipping of its products. These embrace all sizes and shapes of Bar Iron; flat, round and square, also, Band, Hoops, Scroll, Stake, Merchant Iron, etc.; Plate Iron, two to twenty-four wide, by one-fourth to three inch thick, by fractions of inches both in width and thickness. Angle Iron, Bridge Bolts and Plates, Nuts, Washers, Horse Nails, Bolt Blanks, Boat, Bridge and Railroad Spike, Crow-Bars, Drag Teeth, and Drift Bolts; also, Wrought Iron Work for Bridges, Roofs, Vessels, Dock and Architectural purposes.

Railroad supplies a specialty, including Switch Stands, Splice Plates, Spikes, Bolts, etc., for building or repairing; also, street railroad iron of any pattern, Mine, Strap and Small T Rail, and Patent Angle Iron Knees, for ocean, lake, river, or canal craft. Wrought Riveted Girders made up from Angles and Plates, said to be the safest beam in use.

The hardware store, warehouses and the business and private offices of Messrs. Pratt & Co., are centrally located on Terrace Square, in the city. The offices at the store, the rolling mill and the blast furnace are connected by private telegraph line giving the best facility for prompt transaction of business. This firm is of over forty years standing, and numbers among its friends and customers, dealers, manufacturers and consumers in all parts of the States and Canada.

Being, as shown above, manufacturers as well as merchants, and carrying as they do at all times a complete stock of Iron, Nails and Hardware, they are able to fill orders promptly, and compete successfully with parties in any part of the country.

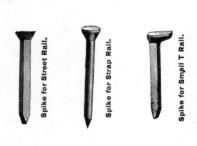

Spike for Street Rail.   Spike for Strap Rail.   Spike for Small T Rail.

Miners' Rail, Oval.—Weight 5 1-2 lbs. per yard, 1 1-4 inch wide.

Street Rail, Dental.—Weight 57 lbs. per yard, 6 3-8 inch wide.

Street Rail, [Improved.]—Weight 32 lbs. per yard, 4 3-8 in. wide.

THE AMERICAN BRIDGE COMPANY.

Chicago, Ill.

CAPITAL STOCK, (FULL PAID) $600,000.00.

Organization.

OFFICERS:

A. B. Stone, President, No. 64 Wall Street, New York.
H. A. Rust, Vice-President and Gen'l Manager, Chicago.
Edward Hemberle, Engineer, Chicago.
W. G. Coolidge, Secretary and Engineer, Chicago.
J. F. Barney, Superintendent, Chicago.

Hammers, one Hotchkiss Patent Atmospheric Hammer, one Punch, one pair of Shears, and forty Forges.

The Foundry has inside dimensions of eighty by one hundred and forty feet, and fifty by one hundred and fifteen feet, height of walls thirty feet. It contains two cupolas, with capacity for melting fifty tons of metal per day, one twenty-five ton crane, one ten ton crane and one five ton crane.

The arrangement for casting pneumatic cylinders consists in a pit, fourteen and one-half feet deep and forty-eight feet in diameter, walled up, the bottom of which is concrete, to make it water-tight. Inside of this pit there are eight others, with a spider frame placed about two and a half feet from the bottom, in which there is inserted, in the centre, a wrought iron spindle, which passes up through a cast iron sleeve of the core barrel, and centering the barrel accurately. The core barrel is made

gines and Hoisting Machinery for sinking pneumatic substructures, &c.

An abundant supply of Water is furnished by a tank of ninety-two thousand gallons capacity, filled from Lake Michigan by force pump. Pipes are laid through every building. Hydrants are located at proper points inside and outside the buildings, and supplied with hose; also fifty feet of hose, attached to pipes running through the entire shops, at intervals of one hundred feet, alternately upon each side.

Gas Works, are located in the southeast corner of the Company's property, several hundred feet from the shops, and the gas distributed throughout all the buildings, which are lighted by eight hundred burners.

The buildings are all heated by steam. The city office and the office at the works are connected by telegraph with each other and with the office of the Western Union Telegraph Company.

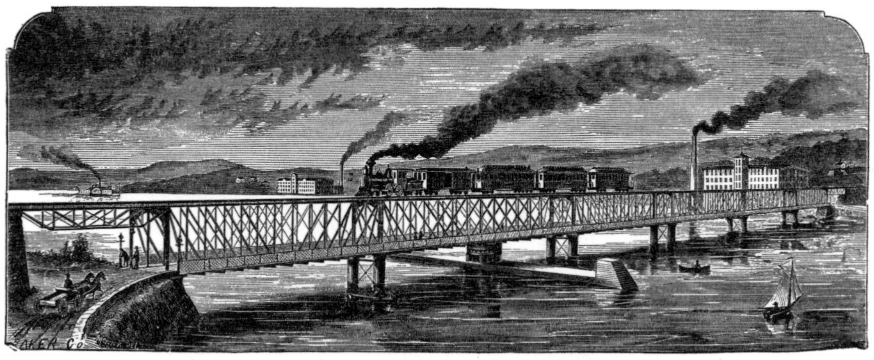

FALL RIVER BRIDGE. BUILT BY THE AMERICAN BRIDGE CO. 1875.

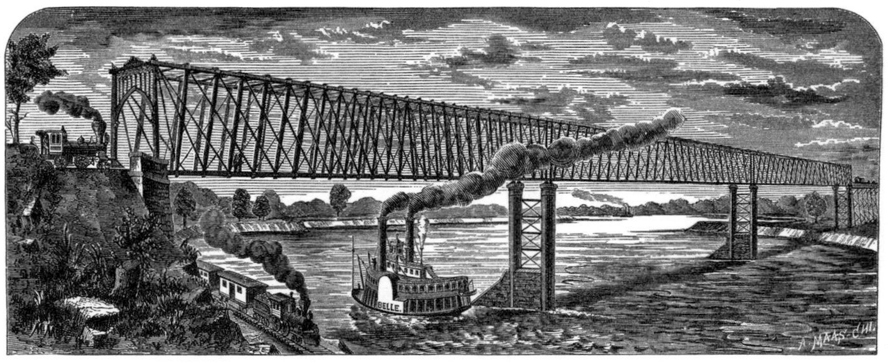

LEAVENWORTH BRIDGE. BUILT BY THE AMERICAN BRIDGE CO. 1872.

BOARD OF DIRECTORS.

A. B. Stone, New York, President Sundry Iron Companies.
W. G. Coolidge, Chicago, Ill., Secretary of Company.
L. B. Boomer, Chicago, Ill., Retired Bridge Builder.
J. Condit Smith, Buffalo, N. Y., Rail Road Builder.
H. A. Rust, Chicago, Ill., Vice-President & Gen'l Mang'r of Company.

The construction of Railroad Bridges upon an extensive scale was commenced by A. B. Stone and L. B. Boomer in the City of Chicago, in 1851, and every one who has been connected with the extension of the numerous lines of rail road which radiate from that city throughout the Northwest will remember the firm of Stone & Boomer, as the builders of nearly all the original large bridges upon those lines, especially those of the Michigan Central Railroad, the Michigan Southern Railway, the Illinois Central Railroad, and the Chicago and Rock Island Railroads, including the first bridge across the Mississippi River, at Rock Island.

The bridge building business having assumed large dimensions which were constantly increasing, necessitated the aggregation of capital, coupled with systematic and comprehensive organization; and induced Messrs. L. B. Boomer & H. A. Rust, (who has been identified with the business since 1854, either in connection with the firm of Stone & Boomer, or by himself,) and others to unite in the organization of the American Bridge Company. To this Company were transferred by the corporators the ownership of sundry patents throughout the Western States; it was also determined to introduce upon the Missouri River Pneumatic Pile Piers. This, together with the building of iron superstructures, involved the necessity of erecting extensive and costly works, which have been built by the Company in Chicago, and are described as follows:

The Real Estate, owned by the Company, and upon which the bridge works are situated, consists of thirty-two acres, lying between Thirty-ninth and Forty-third streets. The Pittsburgh, Fort Wayne and Chicago Railroad track adjoins it on the west, and the Union Stock Yard track runs directly through the premises from east to west, and affords a connection with all the railroads centering in Chicago.

This connection is made available by the many side tracks built by the Company, by which all their shops can be easily reached and heavy freight landed at the precise points where the materials are to be used.

There are about three acres under roof, and all the shops are supplied with the most approved modern machinery and fixtures.

with eight wings, which complete the circle, and braced to the cast iron sleeve, and so constructed that one or two wings can be taken out at a time after the cylinder is poured; these wings are perforated to allow the gas to escape, and made to lap each other so as to provide for the contraction and expansion of the iron. A man-hole is arranged so that a man can go into the pits, which is done immediately after the metal is poured, to relieve the keys of the core barrel. The core barrel and the inside of the pits are covered with loam, and struck up accurately before the core barrel is placed in the core oven, and the loam in the inside of the pits is baked by means of a coal fire in each pit.

These core barrels and pits are built under Cartright's Patent which the Company controls. By this system all strains upon the castings are

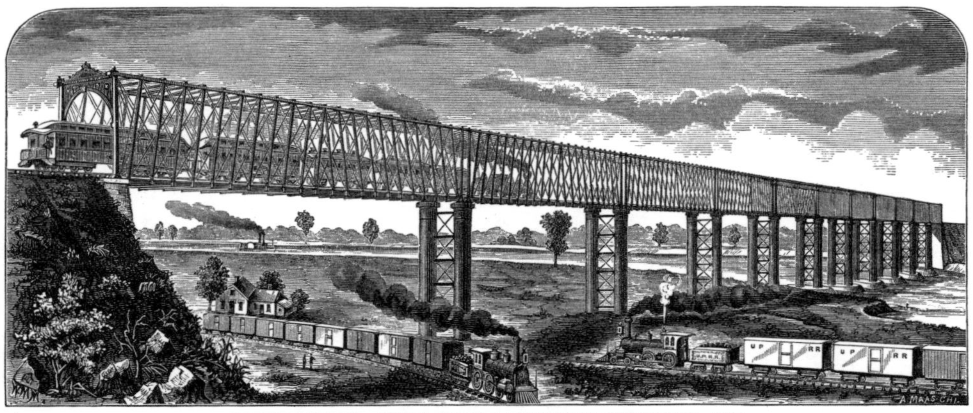

OMAHA BRIDGE. BUILT BY THE AMERICAN BRIDGE CO. 1871.

relieved, the castings are perfect, and there is no loss of cylinders in pouring, which is a decided improvement upon the ordinary method of casting them on brick cores.

The Engine and Boiler House, is fifty by fifty feet, height of walls eighteen feet, it contains one hundred and fifty horse power Engine with Force Pump, Hose and four Boilers; also three Portable Engines.

The Pattern Shop, in the second story of Machine shop, is a room eighty by eighty feet, height of walls eighteen feet, and is amply supplied with machinery for making patterns of all kinds, for Bridges, Roofs, Turntables, &c. Vast quantities of patterns are also on hand.

The Miscellaneous Buildings consist of:

Riveting Shop - - - - - - - - - -	32x104 feet.
Storehouse - - - - - - - - - - -	32x124 "
Casting Cleaning House - - - - - - -	26x70 "

New Machinery especially adapted to engineering construction is provided as fast as improvements therein are made, while the Engineering Department and Superintendent of Works have designed and the Company have themselves built many special machines.

The Company's field of operations comprises the entire Territory of the country; engineering structures being by them now in process of construction in fifteen of the States in the Union, giving employment to more than one thousand men.

Iron Bridges and Roofs upon the principal Railroads and many of the Highway Bridges of magnitude in the United States illustrate in practical form the skillful designs and thorough workmanship of the structures built at the Works of this Company.

Among the more important of said structures may be named the following, viz.:

Missouri River (R. R.) Bridge at Omaha, Neb., for Union Pacific R. R. Co. Missouri River (R. R. and Highway) Bridge at Leavenworth, Kansas, for Kansas and Missouri Bridge Co. Missouri River (R. R. and Highway) Bridge at Boonville, Mo., for Missouri, Kansas & Texas Railway Co. Red River Bridge, and all others for Missouri, Kansas & Texas Railway Co. Mississippi River (R. R.) Bridge at Hastings, Minn., for Milwaukee & St. Paul R. R. Co. Mississippi River (R. R.) Bridge at Winona, Minn., for Chicago & Northwestern Railway Co. Mississippi River (R. R. lesser channel) Bridge at Rock Island, Ill., for C. R. I. & P. R. R. Co. Mississippi River (R.R.) Bridge at Clinton, Iowa, for Chicago & Northwestern Railway Co. Two Iron Draws at South Chicago, for the Lake Shore & Michigan Southern and the Pittsburgh, Ft. Wayne and Chicago Railway Co. Brazos, Trinity & Sabine River (R. R.) Bridges for International & Great Nortwestern R. R. Co. Illinois River (R. R.) Bridge at Grand Pass, Ill., for Chicago & Alton R. R. Co. Illinois River (R. R.) Bridge at Peoria, Ill., for Indianapolis, Bloomington & Western R. R. Co. Arkansas River (R. R. and Highway) Bridge at Little Rock, Ark., for Cairo & Fulton R. R. Co. Union Passenger Depot Roof at Chicago, Ill., for L. S. & M. S. and C., R. I. & P. R. R. Co's. Railroad Shops Roofs at Chicago, Ill., for Chicago, Rock Island & Pacific R. R. Co. Railroad Shops Roofs at Elkhart, Ind., for Lake Shore & Michigan Southern R. R. Co. Railroad Shops Roofs at Chicago, Ill., for Chicago & Northwestern Railway Co. Railroad Shops Roofs at Parsons, Kansas, for Missouri, Kansas & Texas Railway Co. Union Rolling Mill Roof, at Chicago, Ill.

The Company now have in hand larger contracts than at any previous period in its history. The following list indicates the more prominent

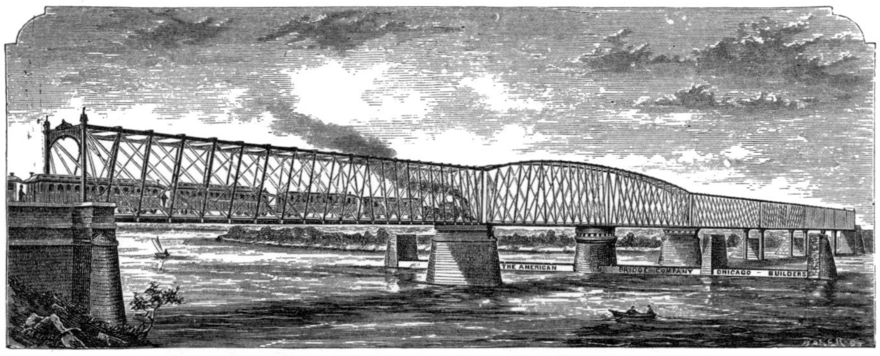

BOONVILLE BRIDGE. BUILT BY THE AMERICAN BRIDGE CO. 1873-74.

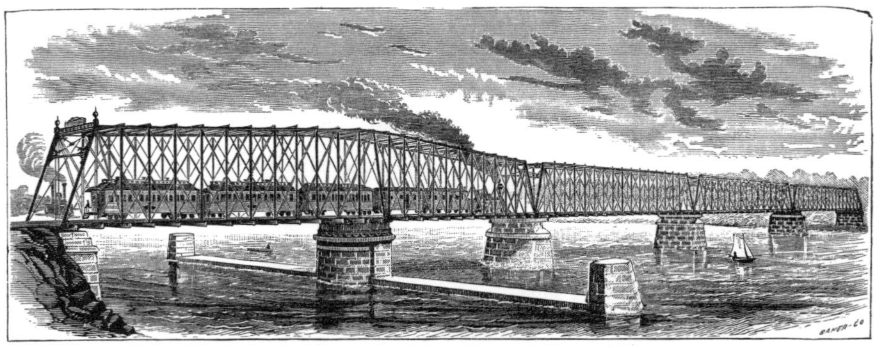

ATTCHISON BRIDGE. BUILT BY THE AMERICAN BRIDGE CO. 1875.

The Machine Shop is eighty by four hundred and twenty feet, height of walls eighteen feet, and contains a full range of various sized lathes, planers, drill-presses, horizontal and double-drills, combined punches and shears, and tappers, screw cutting and straightening machines, a hydraulic testing machine of the largest capacity, a nine foot engine lathe, for pneumatic cylinder work, and sloting machines, together with all the appurtenances.

The Hammer Shop, is sixty by one hundred and forty feet, height of walls eighteen feet, and contains two Watt Steam Hammers with vertical boilers and iron furnaces. A one thousand pound Bement Vertical Hammer, and one of the largest size Hornig's Patent Combined Punch and Shears.

The Blacksmith Shop, is eighty by one hundred and forty feet, height of walls eighteen feet, and contains two Bement Patent Vertical Steam

Forge Shop - - - - - - - - - - - -	16x30 feet.
Four Coal and Coke Houses, superficial area - - -	6,310 "
One Sand Storehouse - - - - - - - - -	30x70 "
Flak Shop - - - - - - - - - - - -	16x30 "

Office Buildings and Drafting Rooms, two stories, forty-six by thirty.

There are also Tool Shops and Barn, and a Steam Derrick for loading and unloading cars.

About ten thousand feet of railroad tracks have been laid by the Company upon its grounds, which connect with side tracks of the Pittsburgh, Fort Wayne and Chicago Railway, the Chicago, Rock Island and Pacific Railroad and the Stock Yard tracks, and the Company has six freight cars.

The Portable Machinery, consists of Six Floating Steam Pile Drivers, six sets of barges, supplied with Air Pumps, Air Locks, powerful Engines and Hoisting Machinery for sinking pneumatic substructures, &c.

works now in process of construction by this Company, viz.

LOCATION.	FOR	RIVER.	L'g'h	REMARKS.
Atchison, Kan.	Chicago & Atchison Bridge Co.	Missouri,	1150	Ap. Cost. $1,000,000.
Fall River, Mass.	Old Colony R. R. Co.	Taunton,	955	" " 300,000.
Pitsburgh, Pa.	Point Bridge Co.	Monongahela.	1245	" " 500,000.
Line	Cincinnati So. Ry. Co.	Cumberland & others.	3950	" " 250,000.
Quincy, Ill.	Western Ill. Bridge Co.	Mississippi.	2847	" " 1,000,000.
So. St. Louis, Mo.	St. Clair & Carondelet Bridge Co.	Mississippi.	3500	" " 5,000,000.
New York.	New York Elevated Ry. Co.		7100	9th ave. 36th to 61st st.
Dale Creek.	Union Pacific R. R. Co.		536	Iron Trestle.
Madison St.	City of Chicago.	Chicago.	154	Pivot Spans.
Harrison St.	City of Chicago.	Chicago.	173	Pivot Spans.
Kansas City, Mo.	Hannibal & St. Joseph R. R. Co.	Missouri.		Repairing Pivot Pier.
	Chicago & Alton R. R. Co.			TrussSpans.
Keokuk, Iowa.	Mississippi Valley & West'n Ry. Co	Des Moines.		TrussSpans.
Cleveland, Ohio.	Cleveland Rolling Mill Co.			Iron Roofs.
Stevens P't, Wis.	Wisconsin Central R. R. Co.			Machine Shop Roof.
Garrett, Ind.	Baltimore & Ohio R. R. Co.			Shop Roofs.
Hot Springs, Ark.	Hot Spring Narrow Gauge R. R. Co			3 Iron Spans.
Neosho, Mo.	Atlantic & Pacific R. R. Co.			Truss Spans.
Byron, Ills.	Chicago & Pacific R. R. Co	Rock.	800	5 Truss Spans.

"SINGLE LARGE CYLINDER PRESS"
For Job Printing.

PRINTING MACHINES,

And all articles connected with the Art of Printing,

Represented by R. HOE & CO., New York.

The histories of great firms, engaged more particularly in mechanical pursuits, though all bearing certain fixed traits of resemblance, are not invariably the same. One constant point of similarity is, that all such enterprises have commenced in a comparatively humble way, and have grown up in time to gigantic proportions, with the increased demand for the particular class of machinery produced. But there are certain rare exceptions, where the singular talent of individuals as originators of novel devices, has placed their special machines among the remarkable inventions of the world, and given untold impetus and development to their enterprise.

The difficulties in the way of constructing a printing machine adapted to the wants of the present period are very great. To the peculiar nature of the paper, its want of strength and general flimsy character, is added the necessity of impressing on it characters, exceeding in delicacy the imprint made on stronger textile fabrics. When it becomes requisite to make any thing in a continuous or constant way by machinery, when the element of rapidity of execution is a necessity, there has been heretofore a limit to the excellence of production. To turn out the greatest amount of newspapers, all perfectly printed, and to do it in the very shortest period, seemed to be a mechanical paradox. This wonderful result was first attained by the Hoe Lightning Press.

The founder of the present well-known house of R. Hoe & Co., Robert Hoe, was born in England, in 1784, and came to the United States in 1803. Early in this century, he devoted his attention to the manufacture of printing presses, so that the present firm has the advantage of over fifty years of practical experience in the business. About 1823, the original premises in Cedar Street becoming too small for the constantly increasing business, works were started in Gold Street, near Fulton, and shortly afterwards at the present location on Grand, Broome, Sheriff and Columbia Streets. At first it was a factory of modest size, but has gradually extended until it occupies to-day nearly two large blocks. It was in 1833 that, in addition to the making of printing presses, was commenced the manufacture of saws, which has been continued with success up to this time. From 1833 to 1846, Hoe Presses for newspaper, book and general printing, had become more and more in demand. For simplicity of construction, mechanical excellence, and quality of work produced, they were the earliest and best examples of American machinery.

It was in 1846, that Mr. Richard M. Hoe, son of the original founder of the firm, invented the famous Hoe Lightning Press, or Type Revolving Printing Machine. This press was the greatest mechanical advance ever made in rapid printing, and for its production the firm of R. Hoe & Co. became known all over the world. Its advantages were so manifest, its speed and perfection of work so great, that the Type Revolving Printing Machine was accepted in England and Europe generally, as indicative of that remarkable inventive genius and mechanical ability existing in the United States, which had not been recognized before.

The necessity of having power presses, capable of meeting the extra demand for newspapers, first felt in the United States, extended to England. Leading journals in England and France were quick to appreciate the vastly superior merits of the Hoe Machines. A speed of 300 impressions a minute, as an inside limit, had never been before attained. This Type Revolving Printing Machine might have seemed then, some twenty years ago, to have exhausted the inventive capabilities of the firm, and have satisfied all demands; but every perfecting of a mechanical process in this world only seems to increase our wants, and although then, as to-day, the "Lightning" Press was sufficient for the immense impressions required by almost all daily journals even of extended circulation, the growing requirements of newspapers were rapidly increasing. Announced by Hoe & Co. in 1872, as in progress, during the year, 1874, the Perfecting Web or Endless Sheet Press has been invented and completed, and is now brought before the world. The Web Press so named because a continuous roll or web of paper is used, is the last improvement in newspaper printing. In the former presses for newspapers, as in the Type Revolving Printing Machine, the paper was printed on one side only. Two presses were then necessary in order that a newspaper might be printed with celerity, one for each side; or the same machine might serve, first for one side, and with new type, print the last side. The Web Machine prints off both sides of the paper at the same time; a perfectly printed paper, at one operation, being the remarkable result. The paper fed from a roll, by a simple mechanical device, receives impressions from two stereotyped cylinders, on both sides at once. From its rapidity, some 14,000 papers, as the lowest limit of production are given off every hour. By an ingenious device, after the paper is cut in the proper lengths by the machine, a certain number of papers, six in all, are collected and these six are deposited at a time. If the Lightning Press is still admirably adapted for ordinary newspaper printing, it requires to work it, eight feeders, one foreman and two fly-boys. The Web Machine turns out the same number of papers, but they are perfect, printed on both sides at once. therefore the Web Press is twice as fast, and it can be worked by three men. The inking process, the distribution of the ink on the stereotypes, is absolutely perfect. There are many wonderful points about the Web Press, such as the facility with which every

STOP CYLINDER PRESS,
For Wood Cut Printing.

of all the tools and machinery required in printing, lithographing, stereotyping and electrotyping. Every thing appertaining to the general furniture of a printing office is manufactured by them, even to steam engines. Among these innumerable objects may be named, Proof Presses, Inking Machines, Imposing Stones, Newspaper Addressing Machines, Case-stands, Chases, Brass Rules, Dashes, Mitring Machines, Hydraulic Presses, Black-leading Machines, Bronzing Machines, Filling and Heating Tables, Stereotype Planing and Sawing Machines, Stereotype Shaving Machines, and all apparatus necessary for stereotyping or electrotyping, with the tools employed in Book-Binding, and Letter Copying Presses.

The buildings occupied for the construction of their innumerable presses, for which an endless variety of tools and machinery are necessary, are, as before stated, very extensive and in the heart of the city, covering an area of 600 feet by 300 feet. As everything is manufactured on the premises, within these buildings are foundries, forge shops, carpenter shops, and numerous work rooms where the most modern machinery is kept constantly employed in shaping the iron, steel and brass necessary for the business. The large corner building fronting on Grand Street, has lately been erected and is used for offices and warerooms where extensive stocks of completed presses, capable of performing every variety of work, are constantly kept on hand. On the upper floor of the building is a spacious drawing office, where the mechanical details of every press made are designed, and where such drawings are kept for future reference. Should any portion of a press furnished wear out, it can thus be immediately made anew, and promptly furnished. In one end of this drawing office are held the free classes of the firm; where all the apprentices of the establishment are gratuitously taught reading, writing, mathematics and mechanical drawing. At the rear of the factory are the Saw Works, where the cutting, adjusting, tempering and grinding of saws is accomplished. In saws, the firm are owners of various important patents, under which, by an ingenious adaptation of teeth, important results are gained.

In addition to their extensive factory on Grand Street, Hoe & Co., have a depot for their manufactures in Gold Street, New York, and a branch establishment in Tudor Street, Salisbury Square, London, where they manufacture for England and the Continent, their various patented machines. They also have a branch house at Chicago.

There is not, perhaps, a city, town or village in the United States where presses manufactured by this Firm are not in

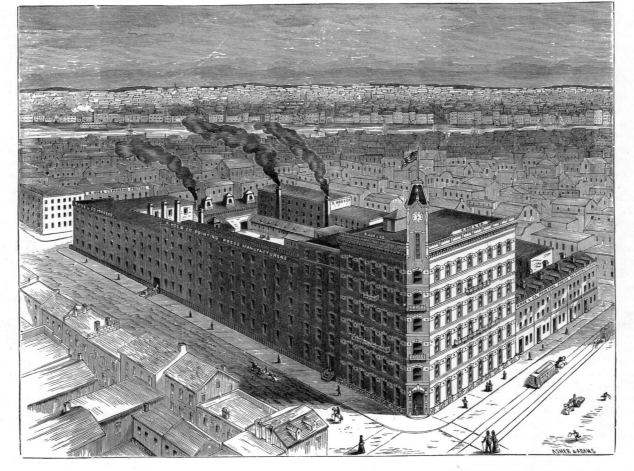

R. HOE & CO'S. WORKS, ON GRAND, SHERIFF, BROOME and COLUMBIA Sts., New York.

portion of the mechanism can be seen, and the rapidity with which all adjustments can be made, and the stereotypes put in position.

In addition to the presses manufactured by Hoe & Co. especially devoted to newspaper printing, every description of press used in book, lithographic or copper plate work, is made by them. Their catalogue embraces all varieties of presses, from the pioneer presses, the advance heralds of civilization, to the Web Press, such as Type Revolving, Book Perfecting Presses, the Flat Bed Perfecting Presses, Double and Single Cylinder Printing Machines, Single Large Hand Cylinder Printing Machines, Stop Cylinder Wood-cut Presses, Hand Stop Cylinder Printing Machines, Railway Coupon Ticket Printing and Numbering Machines, Railway Rotary Ticket Machines, the Patent Washington Printing Press, &c., &c.

The firm is perhaps the only one in the world who, in addition to manufacturing every variety of printing press, combine the production

constant use, and their printing machinery has found its way to England, France, Mexico, South America, and even Australia, China, Japan and India. It is not too much to say, that in special branches of press work the machinery invented by Hoe & Co. has completely revolutionized the art of printing.

The machinery made by this firm is remarkable for solidity and simplicity of construction. An absolute perfection of mechanical excellence is required in every article, from the Rotary and Web Perfecting Presses to the smallest circular saw. Their high standard of excellence in these particulars has never been surpassed, and is the foundation and secret of their original and continued success.

Space will not permit of our entering more fully into the details of the enormous business of this house. Suffice it to say that those interested can obtain on application to them a finely illustrated catalogue, descriptive of the various kinds of machinery made by them.

ROTARY "LIGHTNING" NEWSPAPER PRESS.   **PATENT "WEB" NEWSPAPER PERFECTING PRESS.**

MAIL COACH.

PASSENGER WAGON.

HOTEL COACH.

THE ABBOT DOWNING COMPANY,

Manufacturers of

COACHES AND WAGONS,

Concord, N. H.

——:o:——

Should we attempt to introduce this article by writing a history of wheeled vehicles we fear that we and our readers would be entirely lost in the mist that surrounds everything ancient. Antiquarians have not settled when or where wheeled vehicles were first introduced, but there is little doubt that "war chariots," with two wheels, were the first production in this line of invention, as they are mentioned in the *Book of Exodus*, are painted on ancient Egyptian tombs, and carved on the ruins of the Assyrian palaces; from which it is evident that they were in use two centuries or more before the birth of Christ.

Descending to later times, we find that it was not till about A. D. 1500 that covered carriages were introduced, and that for a long time subsequent it was considered discreditable for men to ride in them. Coaches, however, gradually crept into use despite the determined opposition they encountered, and were used at the wedding of the Emperor Leopold, about 1657. A German writer describing them, says: "In the Imperial coaches no great magnificence was to be seen. They were covered with red cloth and black nails. The panels were of glass, and on this account they were called the 'imperial glass coaches.' The imperial coaches were distinguished only by their having leather traces, but the ladies in the imperial suite were

the fame of the Concord Coach and Wagon was soon in everybody's mouth. Since then the business has increased from year to year and been handed down from generation to generation.

The Abbot Downing Company is the direct outgrowth of and the immediate successors to the originator of the Concord Coach and Wagon Manufacturing business. The present Company was formed in 1873 by the surviving partners of the old firm. The manufacture

AUSTRALIAN BUGGIE.

of Mail and Hotel Coaches, originated with the founders of this firm, and the production of the world famous Concord Coach has been exclusively confined to them. And here let us say that this establishment was the first to manufacture and introduce the Side Spring Concord Buggy so justly popular at home and abroad, and so frequently imitated (but never equaled) by other makers.

The importance of thoroughly seasoned wood for the manufacture

parts of the world where American Vehicles are in use;—when we make that assertion we take in every civilized country on the face of the globe, and some of the semi-barbarous ones—and there is no man who has traveled at all in this country but has rode in their coaches.

In the largest cities and many of the smaller towns the Hotel Coaches that convey passengers to or from the trains or boats are generally Concord Coaches. The stage lines between points which railroads have not yet connected, run Concord Coaches. In the far West, where journeys of scores and even hundreds of miles are still done by stages, Concord Coaches are used. Hundreds of mail routes are supplied by stage, and Concord Coaches are the vehicles used, and if the reader will but take notice, he will find that over all the land the Express Wagons of the larger companies, and many belonging to the smaller ones, bear the name of the Abbott Downing Company as makers.

Through agencies at Boston, New York, Chicago and San Francisco, their productions reach every part of the Union. As will be seen from the numerous cuts that are presented on this page, they make a large variety of different styles, embracing, Mail, Stage and Hotel Coaches, Buggies, and Road Wagons, Express and Tradesmen's wagons of all sizes, Trucks, light and heavy, Sprinklers—in fact every thing in the Coach and Wagon line. In looking at a vehicle of their make the eye will first take in the gracefulness of its appearance, and then be interested in the exquisite finish; a closer examination will convince him of the great strength of every part and the durability of the whole.

The reputation of this Company stands so high, and is so extended over all the land, that a Concord Wagon has become, by al-

EXPRESS BUGGIE.

SINGLE DRAY.

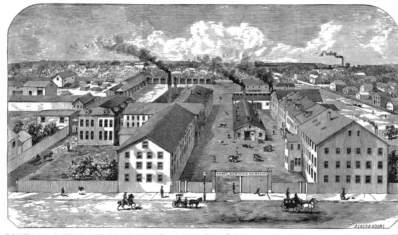

VIEW OF THE WORKS AT CONCORD, NEW HAMPSHIRE.

CONCORD BUGGIE.

SINGLE CONCORD EXPRESS.

obliged to be contented with carriages the traces of which were made of ropes." The Ambassador of Brandenburgh, at the election of the Emperor Matthias, in 1612, it is reported, had three coaches, but they are spoken of as "coarse coaches, composed of four boards put together in a clumsy manner." Judging from the drawings of these early coaches, they were not of graceful shape, and as they had no springs, and as the roads in those days were "exceedingly rough" coaching could hardly have been a very easy mode of travel.

But little improvement was made in these lumbering old machines for many years, and not until the present century were easy riding vehicles at all common. The manufacture of coaches and wagons became a business of considerable importance in America, even during colonial days, and made rapid growth after the close of the Revolution. As the older settlements became more wealthy, and as new sections of the country were opened up, the demand for more coaches and wagons, and of a better class than those imported by the earliest settlers, became imperative. The extent of our territory and the considerable distances between important points in those early days, before railroads were thought of and nearly all the travel must be done by stage or on horse back, and when goods of every description must be transported from the place of production to the consumer by teams over rough and hilly roads, made the construction of coaches and wagons, lighter, and at the same time stronger than had previously been in use, an absolute necessity.

To Concord, New Hampshire, undoubtedly belongs the credit of the first production of vehicles which in every particular satisfied the wants of the people. As early as the year 1813 the manufacture of coaches and wagons was begun in Concord. The vehicles turned out were decided improvements on those produced in other places and

of wagons or other vehicles is well known to all owners of such property, and very many know, to their great and frequent annoyance and cost, that all vehicles (especially "cheap" ones) are not made of well seasoned stuff. The shrinkage and cracking of panels, the warping and twisting of side and bottom boards, the loosening of spokes and cracking of felloes of wheels, are daily and expensive evidences of want of honest care and skill on the part of manufacturers. No

PACKAGE EXPRESS.

such defects are found in the productions of the Abbot Downing Company. They have the skill to select the very best material, and all the facilities for preparing it in the most perfect manner, and the room to store it, so that no order, no matter how large nor how quickly it must be filled, ever necessitates the use of hastily selected or improperly prepared wood.

The business of this Company embraces connections with all

most universal consent of manufacturers and purchasers, the standard of excellence by which the work of other makers is to be judged, and it is no uncommon occurrence to find in the advertisements and circulars of other manufacturers the assertion that their productions "are equal to the celebrated Concord Wagons."

The Company employ in the different departments of their works about three hundred men. Their workmen usually serve their apprenticeship with them, and then year after year continue to labor in the factory, until they acquire sufficient means to keep them the balance of their days, or old age or disease ends their labor. Consequently they have thoroughly skilled men—men who have a pride and who look upon the good name of the Company as a part of themselves.

They are a very different class of workmen from those who travel from city to city and shop to shop caring nothing for the quality of their work, so long as it brings them enough money to feed and clothe themselves. The Abbot Downing Company's mechanics are a "well-to-do" "forehanded" class of men, who have good homes and good situations of which they are proud and which they wish to retain.

Old establishments are always reliable, their age is a proof of their skill and of their honor, and it is a rule with many of our most successful business men to give the oldest establishments the preference.

Parties wishing to order goods of the Abbot Downing Company may address them at the works or at either of their agencies—Boston, Mass.; 142 Bleecker Street, New York; Ann and West Randolph Streets, Chicago, Ill.; 415 Battery Street, San Francisco, Cal.; where they can always obtain full information and descriptive price lists if desired.

DOUBLE DRAY.

MONITOR SPRINKLER.

DOUBLE CONCORD EXPRESS.

LOOKING GLASSES
and
PICTURE FRAMES,
W. J. GRAHAM,
82 Bowery, New York.
—:o:—

There are but few articles in household economy in which utility and embellishment are more happily blended, than in mirrors and pictures. The time was, not very far remote, when these, especially the latter, were regarded as ornamental rather than essential. But the prejudice probably originated in the undue extravagance to which the use of these articles was carried by those whose means would allow a full indulgence of their vanity.

Various causes have been suggested as probably leading to the discovery of mirrors manufactured from metallic substances. The reflection of bodies in a quiet silvery lake, or in any smoothly polished metal, are the same in appearance as results from the use of the modern Looking-glass, and it is probable that mirrors were made as soon as men were sufficiently skilled in the manipulation of metals and stone to be able to produce a surface sufficiently smooth to cause the necessary reflection. Looking-glasses (mirrors) are frequently mentioned in the Old Testament, scriptures clearly showing that they were in use many centuries before the Christian Era. In the Book of Job it is written, "Hast thou with him spread out the sky, which is strong, and as a *moulten looking-glass?*" Also in later days, Isaiah in enumerating the varieties and the extravagences of female dress, speaks among other things of the rings, the nose-jewels, crisping-pins and *Glasses*.

Plutarch says of Demosthenes that he had a Looking-glass (mirror) in his house before which he was accustomed to stand and declaim, and adjust all his motions. Mirrors of large size were in quite general use among the Ancients, and they were probably made of polished plates of silver, of sufficient length to reflect the whole person.

Metallic mirrors were generally used until about the thirteenth century. Those of the ancient Jewish women were made of brass. In the year 1279, Johannes Peckham, an English Fraccascian Monk, wrote a treatise on optics, in which he speaks of mirrors made of iron, steel and polished marble; also of glass mirrors, which were covered on the back with lead, and that no image was reflected when the lead was removed. This is supposed to be very soon after the invention of preparing mirrors in this way.

The improvement in the manufacture of mirrors since that time, and especially during the past century has been very great, and the improved method of producing plate glass of large size has had a tendency to reduce the price of the better quality of mirrors so to bring them into more general use.

Among the longest established and most favorably known manufacturers of Looking-glasses and Picture Frames is the house of Mr. W. J. Graham, represented on this page. He has had twenty years experience in New York, and has been five years in his present location. He makes a specialty of manufacturing Looking-glasses and Connecting Sets for parlors, as shown in the center of this page; also Picture and Portrait Frames of the most new and approved patterns, and of superior mechanism. By strict attention to business, by a careful supervision and personal attention to his manufactures, and promptness and honorable dealing, Mr. Graham has secured the patronage of the best class of our citizens. His goods adorn the walls of many of the finest residences in this vicinity. In addition to the testimony of many prominent citizens who are his patrons, he has the official award of a diploma from the American Institute, for Looking-glasses and picture frames of elegant design and workmanship. The *Independent* says: "The award was richly deserved, and the Institute did itself credit in its bestowment. Mr. Graham makes the best dressing mirror we have ever seen." The *Christian Advocate* says: "He employs none but the best experienced workmen in the various branches of his manufactory. He has had from the first a very enviable reputation for good work, fair dealing and low prices. Orders from the country are treated the same as though presented in person. Some of the most beautiful and desirable styles of picture frames we have ever seen were manufactured by Mr. Graham.

It is often a difficult matter to make appropriate selections of Mirrors and Picture Frames by persons inexperienced in house-furnishing, and in such cases it is a great satisfaction and relief to be able to secure the aid of one whose long experience and good judgment abundantly qualify him for making such selections. This opportunity is highly appreciated by Mr. Graham's patrons, especially those for whom it is difficult to be present and make selections for themselves, or who feel incompetent for the task when they are present, as all are not proficient in selecting tastefully.

D. ARTHUR BROWN & CO.,
CONCORD AXLE WORKS,
Concord, [Fisherville,] N. H.
—:o:—

The manufacture of wagon axles as a special business has been established in Concord for a number of years. Axles were manufactured as early as 1835 by a blacksmith named Warren Johnson, who is still interested in the business, being employed in the forge shops of the Concord Axle Works. From 1835 to 1859, the axle business in Fisherville passed through the hands of some seven different firms, but during all this time the business was almost entirely of a local character. The goods being made first only to meet a demand from the neighboring towns; then the hardware and iron dealers began to keep them in stock, and gradually extended the sales through the State, and into the neighboring State of Vermont.

In the year 1862, the business being in the hands of L. & A. H. Drown & Co., the amount of goods manufactured was somewhat increased, and the first shipment of Concord Axles to California was made, the goods going from Boston by sailing vessel around Cape Horn.

The business came into the hands of the present management in 1864. From this date it has shown a steady increase. So rapidly did the business increase, not only in New England and California, but in the growing West, that as early as 1866 it became necessary to establish an agency in Chicago. To supply the New England demand, in 1870, a general distributing depot was established in Boston, arrangements being made with the well known iron and metal merchants, Fuller, Dana & Fitz, of 110 North Street, to keep at their warehouse a large stock of the now famous Concord Axles, for general distribution to all parts of New England.

A little later these goods were taken up by the trade in nearly every section of the United States and Canada, so that to-day the Concord Axles are generally known throughout the entire country, and wherever known are highly esteemed.

When the business came into the hands of the present management only that style of Axles was made now known as the "Original Concord," (fig. 1) and designed for use in freight, express and business wagons—also in the smallest sizes for the medium grades of carriages. These goods have been for many years, and are now, used extensively by the makers of the celebrated Concord Coaches and Wagons, at Concord, N.H. The Original Concords are made with light Cast Iron Boxes. The arms are turned a plain smooth taper, without oil grooves, chambers or anything of that kind, nicely filled and polished, with boxes and nuts all fitted up in the very best manner. For Coaches, Freight, Express or Business Wagons in daily use, these Original Concord Axles are unexcelled. This class of goods is still the leading one at these Works, but the number of sizes and variety of patterns in this class has been very largely increased.

About the year 1872 the "Half Patent" styles (figs. 2 and 3) were taken up, and now a full line of these goods are manufactured, and are in great demand for the finer grade of carriages. The Iron Axles of this style are Case Hardened or Steel Converted when required. Parties ordering this style should always give the length of hub for which they are wanted.

Another style of axles made at these works is the "Iron Hub Axle," (fig 4,) which has been in use for many years on Trucks and Heavy Freight Wagons, Quarry Wagons, Mining Wagons, etc., but is gradually coming into use on Express and other Light Wagons, its great strength and durability being a recommendation for its use in all classes of work.

There are also made at these works, Axles for Steam Fire Engines, Hose Carriages, Extinguishers, Hook and Ladder Trucks, Stages, Hacks, &c., &c.; in short, Axles for almost every possible style of wheeled vehicle.

The Eggleston Patent Oiler, if so ordered can be applied to any axles made at the Concord Axle Works. The cuts of this device on this page need but little explanation. Fig. 1, represents the shape of the Oil Cup, Tube and Wick, detached from Axle. Fig. 2, shows the Axle, with the Eggleston Oiler complete. As an evidence of its utility it is stated that an axle with this attachment has been worked under a belt in the Works of the Auburn Prison a sufficient number of revolutions to have run it four thousand miles with one oiling and less than a teaspoonful of oil. It saves oil, time and labor, and is a valuable improvement for buggies, carriages, express wagons, stages, trucks, etc.

When the present management took charge of the Concord Axle Works it was decided to make a better article than was made at any other point. For about four years past, American iron of the best brands has been selected, and has proved to be admirably adapted for this use.

The high reputation gained by these goods, during the past ten years, has induced many manufacturers to put into the market an imitation Concord Axle, and in order to protect customers from deception, the patented Trade Mark of the works is now stamped on every piece of axle made at the Concord Axle Works. The trade may send orders to either of their selling agents.

View of D. Arthur Brown & Co.'s Axle Works, Concord, [Fisherville,] N. H.

Trade Mark.

FIG. 1.
FIG. 2.
Eggleston Patent Oiler.

Fig.1. The Original Concord Axle.

Fig. 2.
Concord Half Patent Axles.
Fig. 3.

Fig. 4. Concord Iron Hub Axles.

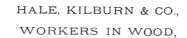

HALE, KILBURN & CO.,
WORKERS IN WOOD,
48 and 50 North Sixth Street,
Philadelphia, Pa.

—:o:—

Prominent among the many wood-working factories of Philadelphia, is the establishment of Hale, Kilburn & Co. Previous to 1868 the firm had been confined to very limited quarters, but in September of that year it extended its operations and took possession of its present location. The buildings now occupied by the firm were designed, erected and specially fitted to meet the requirements of their business. A brief description of the works, will enable the reader to form some idea of their capacity for turning out great quantities of the very best goods.

The building fronting on North Sixth Street, used as offices, salesrooms, packing and finishing rooms, together with the building in the rear, are each 45 x 100 feet, five stories in height and basement; on Filbert Street there are two buildings, each 30 x 90 feet and five stories high, the three last being used for manufacturing—the aggregate number of square feet of flooring being 86,000.

In fitting up this large establishment no expense has been spared, the machinery is of the most perfect character, and every device tending to lessen the cost of production has been adopted. In the selection of lumber the utmost care is exercised, and only perfect wood will be accepted; and every article produced by this firm is made of thoroughly seasoned lumber, kiln-dried in their own drying rooms, which are as nearly perfect as mere men can make them, and capable of drying at one time 300,000 feet. None but skilled workmen are employed and the whole business is so systematized that immense quantities of the best and finest goods can be turned out in the shortest possible time. The establishment gives employment to from 250 to 300 hands.

The grand aim of this house has been to produce the very best quality of work, and in this it has succeeded, no better goods being made anywhere than are produced by this firm. The excellence of

unfold as easily and as perfectly as the most expensive ones—the enhanced price representing merely the difference in the value of the woods used, and the cost of labor for the ornamental finish, and not any practical superiority in the working parts. Our cuts of the "Champion" as it appears when folded in its wardrobe shape, when partly unfolded, and when spread out a perfect bedstead, will give the reader an idea of its appearance, but to be thoroughly understood and appreciated it must be seen.

Hale's Flexible Top Spring Bed is another of the productions of this firm worthy of special mention. It is made of finely tempered steel wire springs, covered with a flexible top composed of wooden slats, so arranged as to form a flexible, thoroughly comfortable and cleanly spring bed. A comparison with others will clearly demonstrate its superiority.

Hales's Flexible Seat Chairs, Stools, Settees, etc., are not only pleasing to the eye, but their smooth, flexible seats make them easy resting places. They are durable, and it is claimed are, in every respect, superior to cane or other wooden seats. They have become very popular with the people, and their manufacture alone gives employment to many hands.

Hale's Tilting Chair (just patented) with the "flexible" seat, is a grand, good thing. It is readily adapted to the needs or whims of the sitter, so that almost any desired position may be attained at will without leaving the seat; its motions are easy, and taken all in all it may be ranked among the leading promoters of general comfort.

While Hale, Kilburn & Co., make specialties of the articles previously referred to, they by no means confine themselves to the manufacture of such goods. Every description of cabinet work is made at their establishment, and in their warerooms will be found everything necessary for the complete furnishing of either a small private residence or a large hotel. They are not only among the most extensive but the most comprehensive manufacturers in the country. One can purchase of this firm not only suites for parlor and dining room, but for the servants chambers, also; and small articles of house furnishing goods such as hat and clothes racks, towel stands and holders, umbrella stands, and all the thousand and one articles that are necessary for the complete furnishing of a house. In addition to the goods mentioned above, a complete assortment of easels, pedestals, music stands, etc., will always be found at their warerooms, and they are always prepared to manufacture such articles of new styles or designs at very short notice.

Recently the firm prepared themselves for manufacturing and fitting up every de-

their productions has created an immense business in supplying the constantly increasing demand. The cuts here presented convey but a faint idea of the style and beauty of their work, while we can but briefly mention in a general way a few of the principal goods made by them, viz:

Photograph and Picture Frames, comprising a large assortment of oval, square and rustic frames of every style; the solid oval (patented) especially being a very popular frame, in such demand as to tax to the utmost the facilities of the house for manufacturing them.

Walnut Mouldings in a great variety of styles, made from the choicest lumber, thoroughly dried, straight, smooth and perfect; and every lot guaranteed to match any previous one of the same pattern.

Mantel and Pier Mirror Frames, of the most beautiful and stylish designs; a varied stock of samples tastefully arranged in their magnificent warerooms, affords the visitor an opportunity of selecting the desired pattern, and in a very short time the order will be filled. Hale's Chameleon Mirror Frame is a specialty and the novelty of its design and rare beauty has attracted universal admiration. Window cornices are also furnished in the best and newest styles.

Among the patent specialties of which this firm are the sole proprietors and manufacturers and worthy of more than a passing notice, is the " Champion " Folding Bedstead and Crib, which is generally acknowledged by those who have examined it, to be one of the greatest inventions of the age, and the most perfect thing of its kind ever made. When folded (with bed and bed clothing all in their proper place) it presents the appearance of an ornamental wardrobe or closet, and does not seem out of place in or detract from the neat appearance of dining room, sitting room or parlor; when unfolded it is a symmetrical, perfect bedstead. The changes from closet to bed or from bed to closet are readily made, requiring neither great strength nor special skill. While the " Champion " is made in various designs, plain, handsome and very elaborate, to suit the tastes and fit the pockets of all classes, they are all equally perfect in their mechanism. The cheapest will fold and

scription of fancy cabinet and ornamental wood work, "Centennial" Show Cases, Druggists' Prescription Cases, and other work of a like character, which will be artistically and thoroughly done, in the quickest possible time.

The immense resources of this establishment in materials, skilled workmen, and ingenious labor saving machinery, enable it to produce the very highest class of work, and to do it rapidly and cheaply. It has been the constant aim of the firm from its first inception to make every article as nearly perfect as possible. They have never sacrificed thoroughness of workmanship to cheapness of production, and consequently the good name which came to them in their early years of business life has not been tarnished, but has grown brighter and better year by year.

Visitors to the city of Philadelphia, interested in this branch of industry, will do well to visit the large and completely equipped factories and magnificent warerooms of this firm, where they will receive a cordial welcome and kind attention.

Messrs. Hale, Kilburn & Co., have a handsome branch store at 613 Broadway, New York, where may be found a complete assortment of the different articles manufactured by them.

Hale, Kilburn & Co., may certainly be classed among the leading representative wood workers of America. All their special productions have become very popular; notably the " Champion " Folding Bedstead and Crib. Disinterested and competent furniture manufacturers and dealers have given it their unqualified approval, and from consumers it has received the warmest commendations. It is a most desirable article of furniture for use in offices, or by families occupying a suite of rooms, or by those who at times require additional bed-room, enabling them to have a handsomely furnished sitting room in day time, which at night is transformed into a perfect bed chamber. Indeed, all their special productions are vast improvements over the older styles which they are rapidly replacing.

Parties may obtain further information by calling at or addressing either of the firm's places of business.

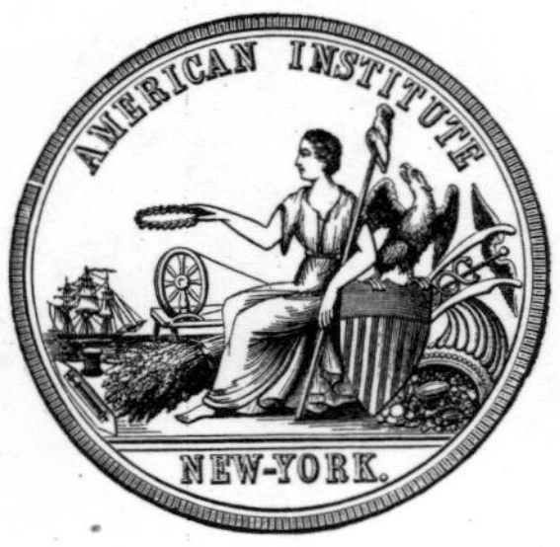

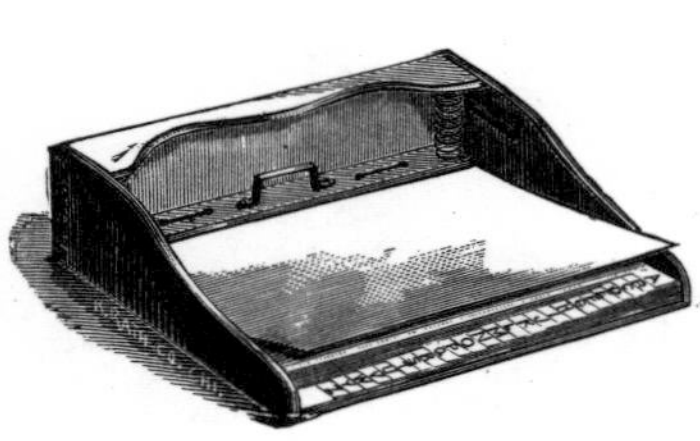

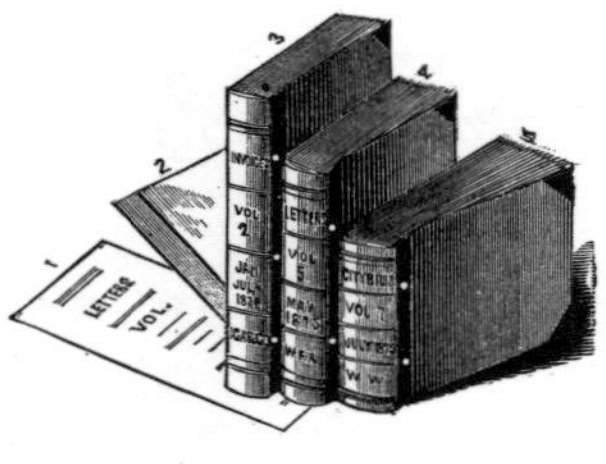

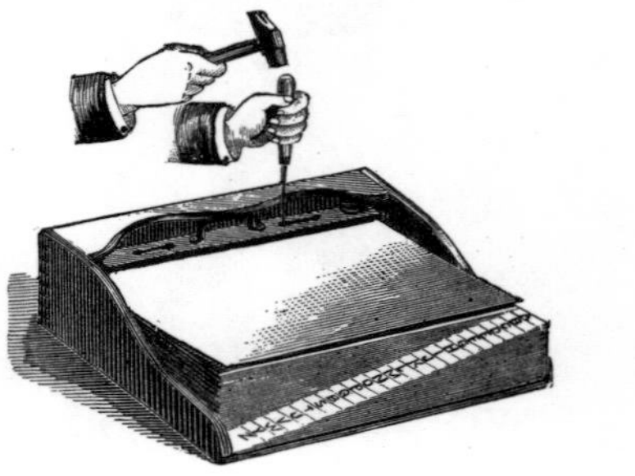

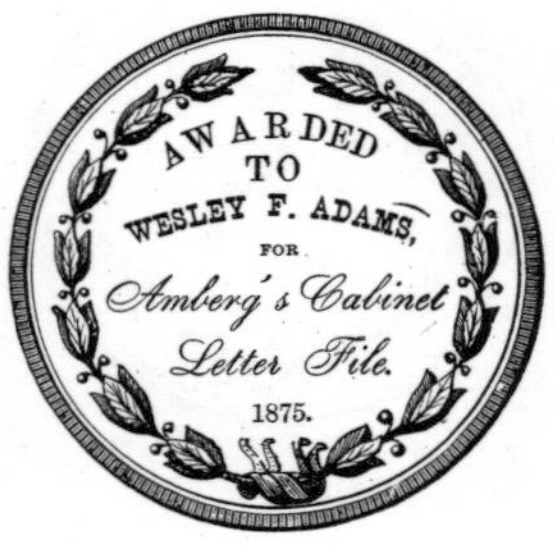

AMBERG'S PAT. "SELF-INDEXING" FILES & BINDERS,

Cabinet Letter Files, Etc.,

W. F. ADAMS, Gen'l Ag't, 59 MURRAY ST, NEW YORK.

——:o:——

Amberg's Self-Indexing Files and Binders when first introduced, like other new inventions, had to overcome the prejudices which long usage had created in favor of previously existing methods. They were not long in gaining a foothold, however, and within a short time they had largely displaced the imperfect methods of filing and binding that had preceded them. Then came a host of so-called "improvements" made by other parties; but the only improvements in these files that the public would have aught to do with were such as were made by the original inventors and manufacturers, or their agents. The files are made of black walnut, in the shape shown on the cut at the top of this article.

An "Indexicon" composed of a series of loose leaves, with pieces of "press board" on each side (which afterwards form the covers), is placed in the File under the pressing bar. A handle in the centre enables the bar to be raised for the purposes of filing underneath between the loose leaves in alphabetical order. The leaves of the "indexicon" being loose, will adjust themselves to the number of papers filed between them; letters may be withdrawn if necessary at any time prior to the binding of the accumulated papers. The File will hold about 600 sheets. The three sides of the box shape the volume squarely with smooth edges. The back of the volume, when bound, can be readily endorsed.

The Letter File and Binder, of which we give an engraving, is designed to meet the wants of both a small and reasonably large correspondence, and is the size usually purchased for filing letters. Its dimensions are 9 x 11 inches, allowing a letter sheet to be placed in sidewise, an open sheet of note, or two half sheets of note side by side, endwise.

Several sizes of these Files are made. There is a Bill Holder File and Binder, 7 by 9 inches, which is without a rival for filing ordinary bills, receipts, statements, etc., and is indispensible in large cities, where "city bills" or "memorandum bills" as they are termed, are numerous. Long invoices can also be filed by folding in centre, face outward. The alphabetical arrangement is such, that all the bills of each house can be kept together in the order of date, so that when statements are presented, they are in the proper order, and "checking off" requires scarcely any time, and is reduced to the simplest work imaginable. A Letter File and Binder, one inch larger each way than the one first described, is also made, and an Invoice File and Binder, 9 by 14 inches. It will hold without folding the longest invoices (half cap), one on a page; half length (or one-fourth cap) invoices, two on a page, and one-third length (or one-sixth cap) invoices,

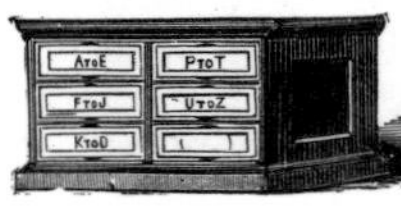

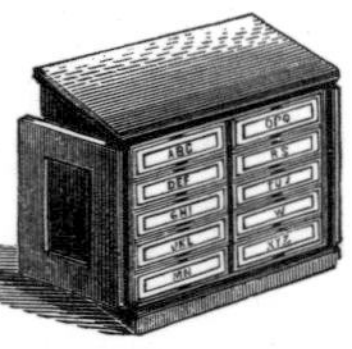

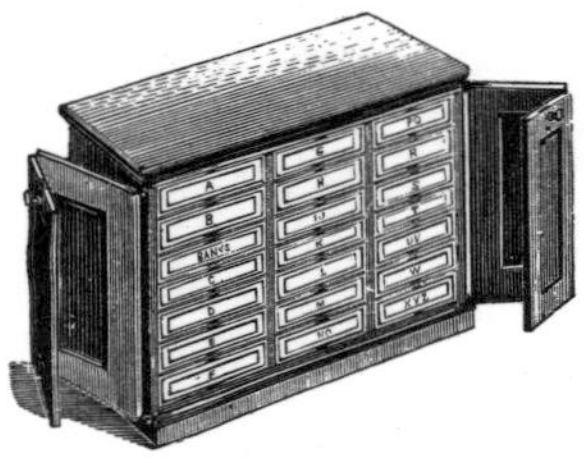

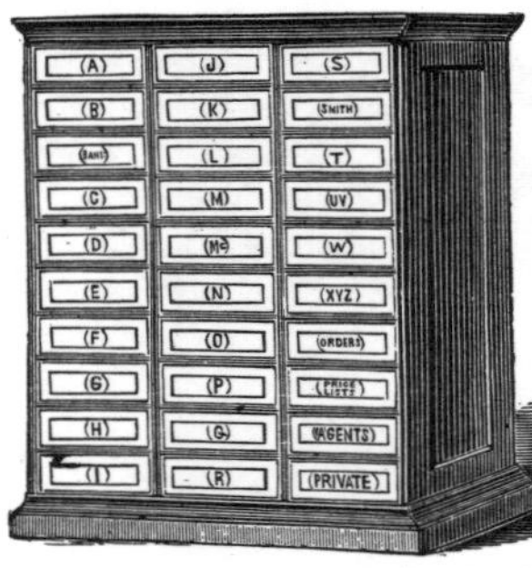

three on a page; legal or fools-cap paper when used by lawyers, as well as other papers.

Directions for Filing.—Turn to the proper letter of the alphabet and place the sheet to be filed about half way in, then raise the bar with your left hand, and with your right (finger tips being slightly moist) you can easily move it to its proper position. Always file papers against the back, and they will never slip out of themselves.

Position of Sheet in Filing.—Letter heads and sheets are always filed on the side. Note sheets with printed headings, file with printed heads outward, as they are more easily read than written names, otherwise use your own judgment. Invoices and bills, postal cards and the like, should always be filed with left margin inward.

Order of Filing.—There are two ways: 1st. In the order of date severally between the sheets of the indexicon, those of latest date being filed uppermost; and 2d, in the same order in which names are arranged in a directory; for example, those in the B space would be filed in the following order, the first named being uppermost, viz: Babbitt, Barry, Bassett, Benham, Berr, Bissell, Blair, A. B., Blair, & D., Bliss, Bowen, Browning, Busse, Byford.

Directions for Binding.—Place the File on a solid table or box, and be sure that the papers are properly filed against the back of the file, and evenly distributed; also, that so far as practicable they are placed against either the top or bottom edges. If your letters have been irregularly filed, or have been carelessly handled, take them out "in bulk," turn them upside down, take out bar and springs, and place the papers in properly one by one (or a few at a time), which will take but a few moments, then replace the bar and springs, and with the awl, which is furnished with the binder, punch in the centre of the holes in the bar, as shown in cut above, and insert the copper wires ∩ shape through each set of holes and twist on the bottom. Secure the end of the wire after twisting, by punching a small hole near the edge and turning in the points as shown.

For those who desire to have a nice, tasty binding, which is inexpensive and easily applied to the bound volumes, the manufacturers have perfected special binding covers, with printed back. Each cover consists of a back of cartridge paper, printed, similar to fig. 1 in the cut above, and two covers (figure 2) of stiff boards, each having a flexible join of canvas and binders' cloth; the sides are of marbled paper. These covers are easily applied by any one in a few minutes.

Amberg's Patent "Double Indexing" or Cabinet File, of which, also, we give illustrations, are designed for the use of Wholesale Houses, Banks, Railways, Insurance Offices, and others. Every one having a large correspondence has felt the necessity of some invention, which would facilitate the filing of letters rapidly and cheaply. To meet this long felt want Mr. Amberg has recently perfected a system, and submitted it to the utmost test, inviting criticism from the largest mercantile houses, business men, etc., all of whom pronounce the system perfect, simple and complete. Thirty-two different kinds are kept in stock, but they can be made in any desired shape or size. They are made of Black Walnut, and are a handsome piece of furniture.

BUILDERS' IRON FOUNDRY,

Z. Chafee, Ag't. N, T. Greene, Sup't.

Codding Street,

PROVIDENCE, R. I.

The term "Builders' Iron Foundry" applies not only to the establishment itself, it is also the style of the corporation that operates the works known by that name. The Company was organized in 1853, and, as the name implies, the originators designed to make architectural work their leading business. The idea of erecting iron buildings was then new and builders generally looked at the innovation with distrust. Many "reasons" were given why iron, and especially cast iron, could never become popular as a building material, but the lapse of a few years proved that iron fronts did not "crack" in frosty weather, and that in case of fire they did not "burst" and "fall to pieces"—consequently iron as a building material came into good repute. It would be needless at this late day to offer any arguments in favor of iron as a building material; a large proportion of the better class of buildings erected in the United States have been built in part, at least, of iron. We may, however, state a few of the leading reasons for its popularity: its economy of wall space; the facility with which it may be erected, and if occasion requires, taken down, removed, and re-erected; security against lightning; ease of thorough ventilation; imperviousness of material, saving contents from damp, decay, etc; durability; incombustibility; in none of these particulars is it excelled by any building material known, and no other combines them all to the same degree. Consequently

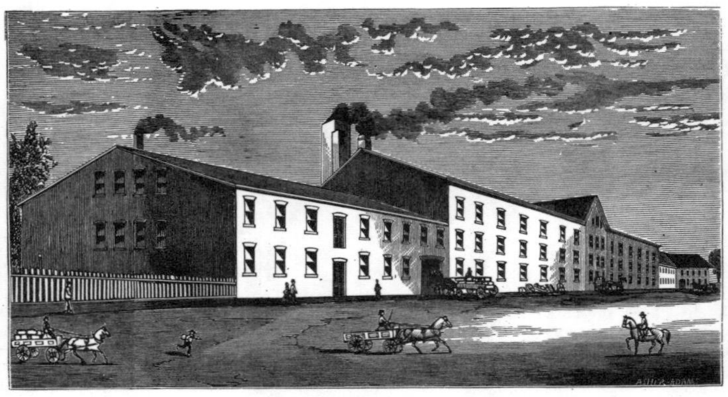

BUILDERS' IRON FOUNDRY, PROVIDENCE, RHODE ISLAND.

the demand for Architectural Iron Work is constantly increasing, and the Builders' Iron Foundry continues to make it a leading branch of their business.

The Foundry is equipped with two air furnaces of a capacity of twenty tons each, and these afford facilities for casting seventy tons per day. They have facilities for making all kinds of machine work and heavy castings. The casting of Bridge Piers has become an important branch of their business, and they have furnished large quantities within the past few years. Samples of this kind of work may be seen at the South Street Bridge, Philadelphia; Old Colony Railroad Bridge, Fall River; and Mobile Bridge, Tensaw River. The establishment is also fully prepared for casting Heavy Ordnance, of which they have produced large quantities, in sizes varying from a 32 pound to a 13 inch gun. In fact, they have facilities for making every description of casting from the smallest to the largest.

In addition to the Foundry proper, the Company have a Machine Shop completely equipped with first class tools and appliances of every description.

Within the space at our disposal we could not do the subject justice, we can only say that they are complete in every particular. The branches of business of which specialties are made, Architectural Iron Work, Bridge Piers, Heavy Machine Castings, and Ordnance, render it imperatively necessary that only the finest quality of iron should be used, from the very nature of most of their work—Architectural—they cannot use a poor metal, even if so disposed, as only the best qualities of iron will run into and completely fill the moulds where the architect has ornamented the design, nor can a smooth casting of flat surfaces be made with poor iron. This establishment has erected some of the finest iron fronts in the country, and they stand as lasting monuments of their skill.

CHASE TURBINE MANUFACTURING COMPANY,

Orange Mass,

——:o:——

Among the noted inventors and mechanics of New England, we must mention J.D. Chase and his sons Denison and Jefferson. Commencing business in their native town in Vermont, they soon gained an enviable reputation as builders of machinery—principally for wood workers—but the place was not favorably situated for an extensive business and they soon sought a wider field and a more convenient location. This they found at Orange, Massachusetts, to which point they removed some twelve years since and established themselves as machinists.

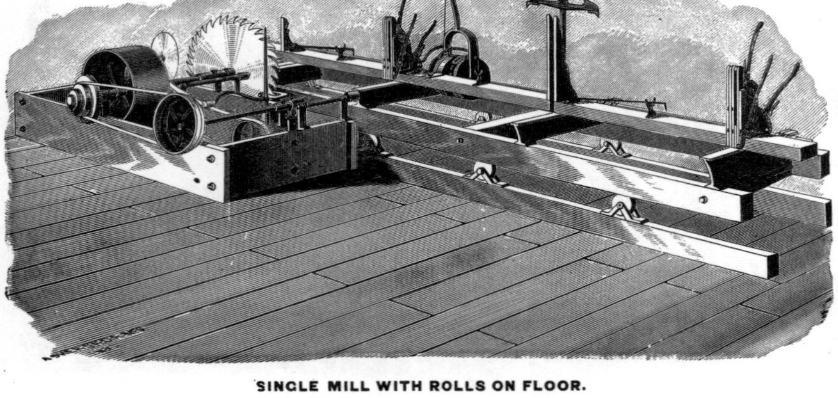

SINGLE MILL WITH ROLLS ON FLOOR.

The Chase Turbine Wheel is extensively used throughout New England; and in nearly every State in the Union and in the Canadas it is well represented. Many improvements have been made, and it has the reputation among manufacturers of being one of the most desirable Turbines in use.

The Messrs. Chase were pioneer builders of Circular Saw Mills in New England, and have ever been among the leaders in that line of production. They have made many valuable improvements, and a Chase Circular Saw Mill is claimed to be an indispensable requisite for lumber manufacturers. It is made in three sizes and each size is made both single and double; also, both with rolls in carriage, running on planed iron ways and the reverse. Among the numerous time and labor saving improvements in securing the log, is the Double Drop Dog, and Under Lift Dog, and Outset or Taper.

The Chase Automatic Stave Sawing Machine, though but a few years before the public, has a deserved preference wherever known. It is speedily adjusted to cut different lengths, and is admirably adapted to sawing small lumber for various purposes. They manufacture other machines for general purposes, but as our space is exhausted we must refer the reader for further information to the Chase Turbine Manufacturing Company, Orange, Mass., U. S. A.

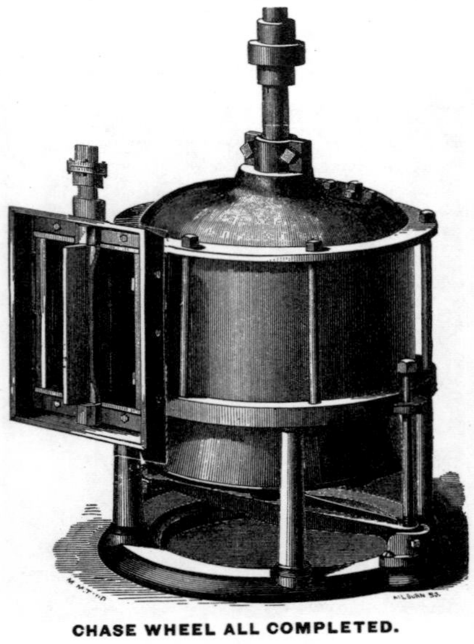

CHASE WHEEL ALL COMPLETED.

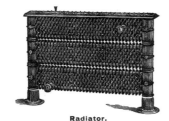

Radiator.

Gold's Hygeian Heater.

Dart's Combination Pipe Vise.

H. B. SMITH & CO.,

Manufacturers of

Steam & Water Heating Apparatus, and Gold's Hygeian Heater, etc.,

Westfield, Mass.

How to heat and ventilate our dwellings and public buildings in such a manner as to secure the desired temperature, equally distributed, and to avoid the introduction of super-heated and impure air, has been for many years the special study of some of our most noted physicians and scientists, and has called forth the best efforts of inventors.

The firm of H. B. Smith & Co., of Westfield, Massachusetts, was established in 1854, and has been since then engaged in the business of furnishing apparatus for heating purposes known as Gold's Patent Sectional Low Pressure Steam Heater, which has met with the most gratifying success. The great desideratum to be obtained in the heating of dwellings, hospitals—in fact all buildings occupied by man—is pure air, which is attained in this apparatus by the introduction of air from the outside, through the radiators as shown in the cut herewith.

The popularity of this Radiator, and its successful accomplishment of the purpose for which it was invented is fully proven by the fact that it has been selected by experts for introduction and use in some of the largest institutions in this country. Upwards of three thousand of them are in use in the Willard Asylum, at Ovid, New York; three thousand more in the Asylum at Morristown, New Jersey; they have also been adopted at the Northampton Asylum, Mass.; the Middletown, Conn.; the Utica Asylum, New York; and others in different parts of the country, while in the public schools of Brook-

lyn, New York, over fifteen thousand of them are in use. Many of the public buildings at Washington, and in other parts of the country are furnished with them. This new heating apparatus is the result of many years of careful study and experience by a practical man, Mr. S. F. Gold, who is well known throughout the country in connection with "Gold's Steam Heater" which is in extensive use, and was adopted in preference to all other methods of heating for many of the Government Buildings, including the Capitol.

The Hygeian Heater possesses qualities of sanitary nature, only heretofore found in "Steam Heaters" and "Hot Water Apparatus" without their expense and with an economical consumption of fuel. The radiating surfaces are so arranged that no portion of the metal comes in contact with the fire. The exterior surface, or that portion over which the air passes to be warmed, is nearly eight times greater in area than the interior surface; hence, no matter how hot the inner chamber may be, the outside or radiating surface will never become overheated. The small pins or projections on the outer surface, not only add to its area, but serve to draw the heat from the flanges and prevent the possibility of their warping; they also divide the air to be warmed into innumerable small bodies, thereby warming it more quickly and uniformly.

The radiators being in sections, facilitate the putting together, and, also, readily admits of a heater being enlarged or reduced in power by simply adding or removing one or more sections. A very important feature not found in other furnaces.

The "Hygeian" is a universal heater, as it may be used in any section of the country, being so arranged that with a slight alteration of the fire chamber it can be made to burn any kind of coal, coke or wood.

We know of no Hot Air Furnace that contains over one hundred and fifty feet of heating surface. Now a little calculation will show the merits at one point of the Hygeian Heater:—As the largest contains three hundred feet of radiating surface, it follows that if a certain room can be warmed by a furnace to a given temperature, a like room can be heated by the Hygeian as readily and have the temperature of the Heater not over half the intensity. In consequence of the low temperature at which the heat is given off the radiating surface, it necessitates the enlarging of the warm air registers.

Sectional View of Dwelling Warmed by the Hygeian Heater.

GEORGE WEST & SON,

Manufacturers of

MANILLA PAPER AND PAPER BAGS,

Ballston Spa, N. Y.

———:o:———

Many things with which we are familiar from every day contact are the least known to us, but which in their manufacture involve the investment of large capital, the use of ingenious machinery and the employment of many hands. Prominent among these is Manilla Paper and Paper Bags.

The Hon. George West, of Ballston, N. Y., senior partner of the firm whose title heads this article, was one of the first gentlemen to embark in the manufacture of Manilla Paper in this country, and has proved one of the most successful. The firm now own and operate no less than five paper mills and a paper bag factory.

The Stock, or raw material, is first cut or ground by machinery made for that purpose, and then placed in the large boiler previously mentioned where it remains several hours under a heavy pressure of steam, the boiler revolving continually that the various fibres composing the mass of stock may be seperated from their original positions, and each part receive an equal contact with the saturated steam and chemicals. When the steaming process is completed the stock is removed to the main building where three engines are in constant operation in washing and bleaching it, and reducing it to pulp. As soon as it is thoroughly washed and prepared it is passed into an adjoining room, where the Paper Machine is located. This machine receives the pulp upon a cylinder of peculiar construction, where it is formed into a thin sheet. A cloth belt receives this tender sheet from the cylinder and carries it to rollers through which it passes and is more compactly pressed together, and a large portion of the water taken from it. It is then passed through or between a number of steam-heated cylinders which dry it. It is now paper but is very rough, and to finish it, it is passed through a stack of calenders which impart a smooth surface. Thence it travels under revolving cutters which trim the sides, and cut it through the centre, dividing the strip into two parts which are wound on spindles connected with the machine and the paper is ready for use.

The Lower Mill is of about the same size as the Upper one, and contains also one boiler, three engines and one paper machine.

At Rock City Falls they have two more paper mills, known as the Empire and Excelsior, using about five tons of stock per day, running ten engines, and making three tons of paper daily. These mills

are built on a much larger scale than those at Middle Grove. At the Empire Mill we find the rotary steam boiler located in a room 64x45 feet, while the room containing the paper machine is 80x22.

The bag works are located adjoining the Empire mill, at this place, and employ between thirty and forty hands. There were seven machines running at the time of our visit. It would seem as if the product of one week's labor of the thirty five hands here employed in feeding and attending the rapidly working machinery would be sufficient to supply the entire demand for at least six months, but such is far from the fact; for with the 1,800,000 bags which these machines turn out per week, this firm have never yet been able to fill the orders which are constantly pouring in upon them. These machines

View of George West & Son's Manilla Paper Mills, Ballston Spa, N. Y.

take the paper from a roll, and require only two boys to superintend each. They are apparently very simple, yet very ingenious and complete in their operation. As the paper leaves the roll it passes up between rollers, and a grooved paste roll running on the edge, pastes it; a revolving cutter cuts off sufficient to form a bag, after which it runs along and thin irons turn up the sides so that a complete fold is formed, lapping the two edges near the center, to be pressed together by another roller, so that the paste holds them fast; then a cut is made for the bottom, which is pasted and lapped on as it passes, by a belt which runs over a large drum and delivers the bag to the boy standing ready to receive it. A bell rings, denoting when fifty bags are finished, the trouble of counting thus being avoided, and a great

deal of time and labor saved. The smallest machine, making bags of the sizes known as "quarter pounds" to "pounds," turn out 70,000 per day; but the machines making the larger sizes are not able to make so many. As before stated the production of all sizes is 1,800,000 bags per week. Some twenty different sizes are made, of two qualities of paper.

The other mill of the firm is situated below Rock City and is called the Pioneer Mill.

The aggregate production of all the mills is about five and a half tons per day, of which about half is consumed in the bag mill, and the remainder is shipped to Chicago and St. Louis. Messrs. George West & Son, are large importers of jute butts, which they find imparts great strength to their paper.

The firm have a number of fine teams constantly employed in moving the paper and bags manufactured, from the mills to the railroad depots.

Mr. West is an Englishman and a practical paper maker. He commenced operations in 1861 and has since then built up a large and flourishing business, which is a credit to himself and the town. In addition to the Mills he has an interest in the New York House where his paper and bags are sold, and where he also has machines for making satchel bottomed bags. He is also a part owner of the several patents for the manufacture of bags and the ingenious machinery for making them. He is a public spirited gentlemen and while he gives close attention to his large business, he finds time for the thorough enjoyment of a peculiarly pleasant home, and the recreation of travel abroad.

A few years ago Mr. West associated with him his son, George West, Jr., who assumes nearly the entire charge of the business at Rock City while his father attends to business matters in New York. That these gentlemen are not only thorough-going business men but men of high standing in the community may be inferred from the fact that Mr. West, Sr., for several consecutive terms, represented his district in the State Legislature, where he did good service for his constituents, while Mr. West, Jr., at the same time served his town as Supervisor. The former was placed in position and ably represented the Republican party, while the latter was a Democratic officer.

The firm of George West & Son have a reputation in business circles of which they may well be proud. They are straightforward in their dealings, and their word is considered as equal to their bond.

Those of our readers who spend their summer vacation at Saratoga or Ballston should not fail to make the acquaintance of these gentlemen. A visit to their mills and factory will amply repay those who make it, and we know of no place, within a short distance of these resorts, where more can be found to interest the visitors.

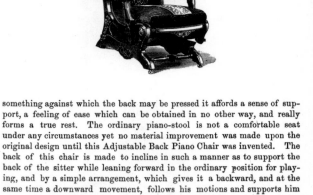

ALBERT BEST & CO.,

Manufacturers of

PARLOR FURNITURE,

SPECIALTIES:

PATENT ADJUSTABLE BACK PIANO CHAIRS, PATENT ROCKING CHAIR, and PATENT OFFICE CHAIR.

39 and 41 Perry Street, Buffalo, New York.

:o:

Among the most important of American industries we rank the manufacture of Cabinet Furniture and Chairs—important alike in the number of establishments, in the capital invested, and the number of hands employed. There are at present in operation in the United States over six thousand manufactories of Furniture and Chairs, many of them large establishments supplied with labor-saving machinery, which is operated by steam-engines and water-wheels aggregating about thirty-thousand horse-power. These factories afford employment to not less than fifty-five thousand hands, who receive wages amounting to nearly twenty-two million dollars a year. The capital invested in buildings, machinery, materials, stock, etc., is, in round numbers, forty-four million dollars. The value of the raw material consumed in the year 1875 was nearly twenty-five million dollars, and the goods produced were worth nearly seventy million dollars.

In the manufacture of furniture, as in other branches of business, there has been developed within a few years, a disposition on the part of proprietors to classify the general production, and devote each establishment to some special branch or class of work. Thus there are now factories devoted entirely to the manufacture of Parlor and Library Furniture, others to Chamber Furniture, still others that make Tables only, and a number that produce nothing but Chairs. Prominent among those engaged in the branch first named is the house whose name heads this article.

The firm of Albert Best & Co., of Buffalo, New York, was established in the year 1871, primarily for the purpose of manufacturing every description of Parlor and Library Furniture, for the trade, including in their list of productions one or two special articles. These are, however, incident to the business, and are most appropriately combined with the valuable list which they have to offer. They are the inventions and property of members of the firm, and are of such high utility that they deserve prominent notice. The first is a rocking chair on an entirely new but most admirable principle. It combines that ease of motion for which the old-style rocker was so famous, without the inconvenience of its long cumbersome rockers. It is a device so perfect and unique, as to merit investigation and its superior advantages cannot fail to be approved. We can best describe it by inserting the inventor's "claim:"

"My invention relates to that class of rocking-chairs which consists of a stationary base and an upper rocking portion resting upon the base, and connected thereto by flat or other suitable springs.

"Previous to my invention these springs have been rigidly secured to the base, which causes a short and hard rocking motion of the chair. In order to overcome this difficulty as much as possible, comparatively light springs have been hitherto employed, which is objectionable as such springs are more or less liable to be broken in moving the chair.

"The object of my improvement is to remedy these defects; and this invention consists in securing the connecting springs to a pivot or rocking support, whereby they are enabled to follow the movements of the rockers to a certain extent, being deflected only during the latter part of the rocking movement, thereby permitting the employment of heavier springs, without rendering the connection inconveniently stiff, and at the same time producing a long and easy rocking movement."

The second is a Piano Chair or Stool with an adjustable back which moves to suit the posture of the occupant and is a constant support. The practice of sitting at a piano or organ practising for hours together, without a support for the back is tiresome in the extreme, as every player well knows, and giving way to the tired feeling very many, especially young persons, attempt to rest or relieve themselves by assuming a position which is not only ungraceful, but unnatural and unhealthy, and are often permanently injured thereby. To rest the back, it is not always necessary to incline the body to the rear. The body may lean forward, but if there is a

something against which the back may be pressed it affords a sense of support, a feeling of ease which can be obtained in no other way, and really forms a true rest. The ordinary piano-stool is not a comfortable seat under any circumstances yet no material improvement was made upon the original design until this Adjustable Back Piano Chair was invented. The back of this chair is made to incline in such a manner as to support the back of the sitter while leaning forward in the ordinary position for playing, and by a simple arrangement, which gives it a backward, and at the same time a downward movement, follows his motions and supports him in any position, without the slightest interference with the freedom of his movements. Just how it does its work we cannot well explain without the use of diagrams; but it most assuredly does it, and that without the slightest effort on the part of the occupant.

Though this Chair has been before the public but a short time, it has already attracted marked attention, and has gained the highest approval of all who have tested it. We are confident that it will fully meet the needs of thousands who have long been hoping and anxiously looking for some such improvement, and that teachers, scholars, and finished amateur and professional players will alike welcome it.

It may be mentioned in this connection that the Chair is equally applicable to the Sewing Machine, and that the manufacturers are now manufacturing large quantities of Sewing Machine Chairs.

The Office Chair is made on essentially the same principle as the Piano Chair, and wherever it has been introduced is popular.

In addition to these specialties, the manufacture of which would alone be a large business, this firm are extensive manufacturers of parlor and library suits, centre tables, etc., in all the fashionable styles. They do not make any goods of low grades, but confine themselves to fine work, and the specialties previously mentioned. Their factory was erected with special reference to their business, and is completely equipped with the most approved wood-working machinery, and all the adjuncts that can aid a large force of skillful workmen in the rapid and cheap production of first-class goods. They have a very extensive trade with dealers South and West, and are constantly gaining new acquaintances and patrons. Their location insures the cheapest transportation, which enables them to secure material at the lowest figures, and to ship manufactured articles at the most favorable rates.

The firm is composed of George W. Tifft, Albert Best, and Leonard H. Best, gentlemen fully educated in the business, and alive to the wants of the trade.

The house has acquired a high reputation for the substantial character and elegance of design and finish of their productions, a reputation which they are determined to fully maintain.

ESTABLISHED 1806.

:o:

JOSEPH FOX & SON'S

MAMMOTH

Steam Cracker Manufactory.

J. FOX,

Inventor and Patentee of

FOX'S

Excelsior Cracker Machine.

600 & 602 State, & 8, 10, 12, 14 & 16 Elizabeth Sts.,

Lansingburgh, N. Y.

:o:

Seventy years of successful manufacture is conclusive evidence of the excellence of the merit of the thing produced, and is testimony such as few establishments in this country can offer. Among that few is the cracker manufactory of Joseph Fox, at Lansingburgh, New York, which was founded in 1806, and soon became noted for the superiority of its productions.

Mr. J. Fox, Sr., was the first to introduce the Sponge Butter Crackers, (then made entirely by hand) which were soon known over all the world as being the finest crackers made. Many improvements have been made in methods of manufacture since those days, and with each new process has come an improvement in the quality of the article produced, so that now Fox's Butter Crackers are really what their name indicates, "Excelsior."

The present proprietor, Mr. Joseph Fox, was brought up from infancy in this branch of business, and when he arrived at man's estate was thoroughly conversant with all that pertained to it. After seven long years, he produced the first working machine, making the crackers essentially the same as when made by hand, the machine automatically subjecting the materials to the same processes.

The first machine, patented February 1st, 1859, was a success, and readily produced results equivalent to the labor of thirty men, though it only required seven men to operate it, prepare the dough and attend to the baking. The Excelsior Cracker Machine completely revolutionized the business of biscuit and cracker making—not only adding

greatly to the quality of the goods, but reducing the cost of production.

The last "Improved" Machine, patented October 7th, 1873, is almost, if not quite, as great an advance upon the original machine as that was upon the old hand processes which it supplanted. The Improved Machine will do the work of sixty-eight men, and as it, like the old machine, only requires seven men to operate and attend it, it at once effects a saving in the cost of manufacture equal to the wages of forty-eight skilled workers.

In the Fox Cracker Manufactory three of these machines are kept running, doing the work of one hundred and eighty men, and though seven men are usually assigned to a single machine, only fifteen men are required to operate these three.

In connection with the bakery, Mr. Fox has a well appointed Machine Shop, where, under his immediate supervision, all of his Excelsior Cracker Machines are built. Each of these machines is composed of from twelve hundred to eighteen hundred separate pieces (the number varying with the size and capacity) and consequently are, in their first cost, somewhat expensive, but their original cost is of little consequence when compared with the value of the labor they save over the common cutting machine, which cuts from the sheet of dough. None of these last improved machines are in use outside of the Fox establishment, though many applications have been made for them, but Mr. Fox is still experimenting, believing that a still higher degree of perfection can be attained.

The Crackers manufactured at the Fox Bakery are known as the "Excelsior," that being a trade-mark registered in the United States Patent Office, April 17, 1873. The name of the machine is "Excelsior" and the quality of the goods produced from it certainly Excel. Parties desiring to purchase one of these machines and the right of manufacturing these crackers can do so by applying to the proprietor at Lansingburgh.

The extensive Cracker Bakery now occupied, of which a cut is presented on this page, was erected in 1861, and enlarged in 1868. One of the ovens in this establishment, is, we believe, the largest in the world.

Elastic Trusses and Abdominal Supporters,

Manufactured by the

ELASTIC TRUSS COMPANY,

683 Broadway, N. Y.

For many years we have been observant of various appliances known under the general technical name of "trusses," each successive device claiming to be superior to its predecessors; and often the claims were well founded; but all were crude efforts to the desired end, though not without merit. Their lamentable failures to effect radical cures in cases of Hernia, more or less serious, have of late years enlisted the labors of mechanical ingenuity, based on profound medical and surgical knowledge; and by dint of patient and costly experiment, guided by increased experience, a perfect mechanical appliance for the cure of Hernia has apparently been reached, in the invention now known as the Elastic Truss and Abdominal Supporter, manufactured by the Elastic Truss Company, incorporated under the laws of the State of New York.

We give illustrations of the Double Truss, with Supporter Brace; the Single Truss, with Brace Right Side; and the Umbilical or Naval Truss. The Elastic Truss is an Elastic Band united with a Flexible Body Brace and Adjustable Pads. It has no springs to press against the back, to pain and weaken it. Being of simple construction it is not liable to get out of order. It is claimed to be the cheapest perfect truss ever invented, and the most durable.

Eminent physicians and surgeons, men who rank as authorities in their profession, speak warm words for this truss, and express an opinion that it is destined to supersede all metallic or other contrivances for alleviating and permanently curing hernia, prolapsus uteri, and all weaknesses of the abdomen. It is perfectly adapted to the relief and cure of every description of rupture and abdominal feebleness; is in fact an infallible remedy for hernia. The truss firmly holds the rupture, in any possible position of the body; and it has achieved permanent cure where other means have proved useless. It has demonstrated the important fact that hernia can be cured as easily as a broken limb, if the pressure is continually and uniformly preserved day and night, till adhesion is perfected. This truss can be worn day and night, by children and adults, without inconvenience, and this constitutes one of its pre-eminent merits. The patient can easily adjust it as he likes, in the severest case of rupture, and yet be as comfortable as a well person, and take any reasonable amount of exercise; and when once adjusted, no accident or movement of the body can displace it.

The severe, hard, rigid pressure of metal trusses, often disturbs the electric current, sometimes inducing spinal disease and paralysis, and the metallic springs are to some the cause of almost continual pain and annoyance. They cannot be worn by night, as by day; and as this temporary removal of pressure allows the tissues to separate, their permanent healing is retarded, and frequently wholly prevented. Moreover, a metal truss if not properly conformed to the body, is liable to slip out of place, and thus, by wholly removing or unduly increasing pressure, it retards a cure, or hopelessly aggravates the rupture. From these faults the Elastic Truss is totally free, standing, sitting, or lying down, the wearer is reliably and comfortably braced and protected by this scientific invention. Under all circumstances it keeps its proper place and uniform pressure, and inevitably effects a cure, even in cases where another truss could not be worn at all. A "Single" Elastic Truss is perfectly adapted to cure rupture on one

Single Truss, with Brace Right Side.

Double Truss, with Supporter Brace.

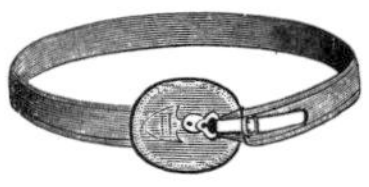

Umbilical or Navel Truss.

side; but in case of tendency to rupture upon the opposite side also, it is timely prevented or cured by wearing the "Double" Elastic Truss, which gives equal comfort and protection to both sides.

The Trusses and Supporters for adults are in three styles, varying in quality of materials, but are practically perfect, the prices varying from $5 to $8, $12 and $16. Infants' and Children's Trusses are from $4 to $6. They are always made with "Double" attachments; and a complete cure, even of the worst cases, is guaranteed, and without the slightest pain or discomfort to the child, even if only a week old.

The Elastic Abdominal Supporter, for the cure of prolapsus uteri, prolapsus ani, all descriptions of abdominal weakness, and female uterine complaints has already greatly diminished the prevalence of the above often fatal evils, and is fast superseding all other devices for their relief and cure. It so braces and guards the body as to double its natural power to endure fatigue and violent excrcise. It renders rupture impossible, and its value as a preventative in this respect is so well recognized that it is coming into general use in gymnasiums, and is worn by pedestrians, base-ball players, athletes, and others accustomed to excessive muscular efforts. For females it is an especially valuable relief and safe guard.

The following are a few brief excerpts from numerous testimonials, volunteered by some of the highest medical and surgical authorities:—J. M. Carnochan, M. D., says:—"The Elastic Truss possesses, in a high degree, all requisites claimed for other inventions for relief and cure of hernia." W. H. Burnham, M. D., writes:—"It is the only one entitled to the confidence of the public." George W. Brooks, M. D., declares it to be "One of the greatest remedial blessings conferred by genius upon the human race." L. T. Warner, M. D., says:—"Next to its efficiency, its comfort recommends it above all others." W. H. Scott, M. D., affirms that "It is designed to supplant all forms of Metallic Truss," and Thos. Stevens, writes, "It cured me of rupture and long continued gravel and kidney complaint. I am now seventy-four, and stronger than I was ten years ago." To the above might be added a host of convincing testimonials as to cures effected by the Elastic Truss and Abdominal Supporter, besides highly eulogistic reports from the Judges of the New York American Institute Fair and the Cincinnati Industrial Exposition, from both of which the Elastic Truss Company have received the highest premiums; together with numerous diplomas and medals awarded at all other Expositions where humanitarian inventions were exhibited.

Very inferior articles, under the name of "Elastic Truss," have been brought before the public; but only the genuine have the name of "The Elastic Truss Company," in gilt letters, in full upon them. The Company employ the best surgical talent and make no charge for examination or advice; or a trial at their offices; competent female assistants being always in attendance.

The General Superintendent of the Elastic Truss Company is G. V. House, M. D., at 683 Broadway, New York; the branch offices being at 129 Tremont Street, Boston; 1202 Chestnut Street, Philadelphia; 235 Pennsylvania Avenue, Washington; and 44 West Fourth Street, Cincinnati; with agencies in nearly every city in the Union.

Though before the public only six years, the immense demand, great improvements, increased facilities, and consequently moderate prices have been such that these important inventions are now known throughout the world, and are doing much to alleviate and cure some of the most prevalent "ills which flesh is heir to," sure, speedy, and painless, we wish them God-speed on their world-wide errands of mercy to both sexes and all ages, to all races and all classes of mankind.

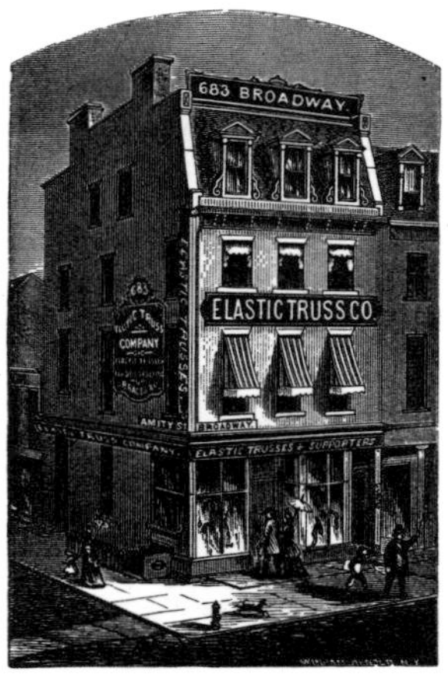

ELASTIC TRUSS COMPANY.

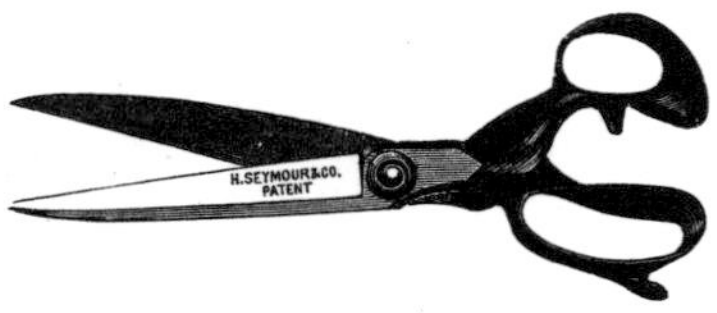

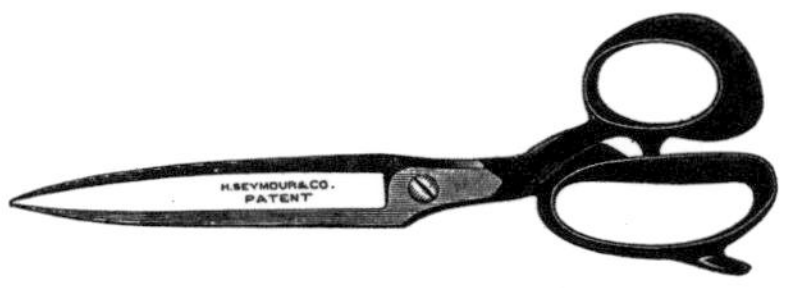

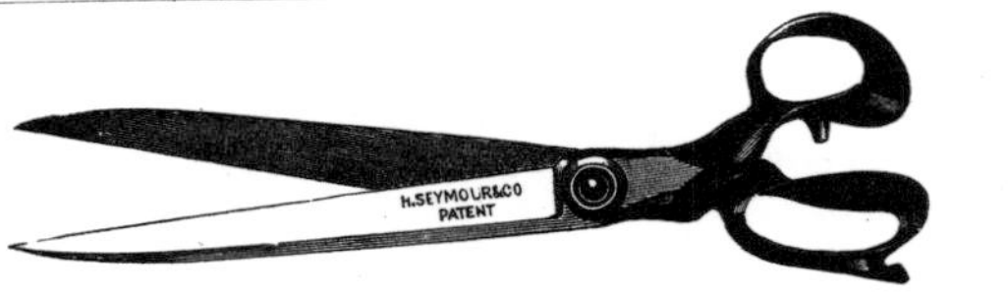

HENRY SEYMOUR & CO.,

Manufacturers of

SHEARS AND SCISSORS OF ALL KINDS,

29 & 31 Rose Street, New York.

If we may believe those veracious chroniclers, the historians, the art of making steel was known to some of the Oriental nations many centuries ago, and the famous blades of Damascus still flourish in the pages of romance, although the skill of her ancient artificers does not appear to be inherited by their descendants. In comparatively modern times the production of steel has been brought nearer to perfection by English manufacturers than by those of any other nation, and until within quite a recent period the supply of cutlery, shears, and edged tools generally, for the entire civilized world, has been principally derived from England. For several centuries the city of Sheffield has been especially famous for her manufactures of this description, that city still carries on an immense business in this line, although her former *prestige* has in a measure been lost, and it is now very generally conceded that American cutlery is fully equal to the English, and that in many articles manufactured from steel, shears and scissors, notably, our productions are vastly superior to those of England.

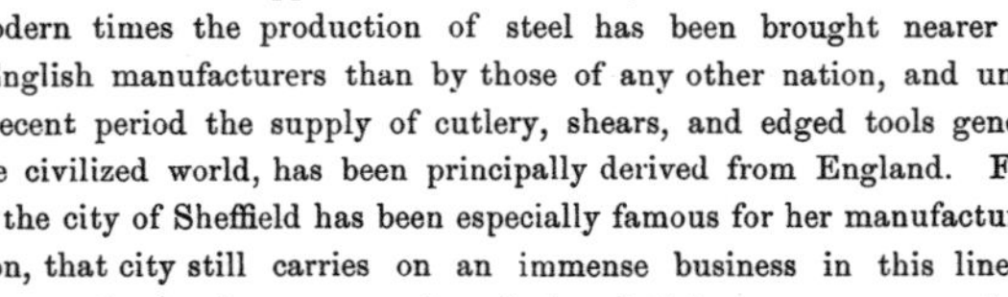

Within the last forty or fifty years the manufacture of shears and scissors has grown to a business of considerable magnitude in the United States, and is deserving of honorable mention in this record of the progress of American Industries.

Henry Seymour & Co, whose factory is located at Nos. 29 & 31 Rose Street, New York, have established for themselves the reputation of making goods of this character, equal, if not superior to any others in the market, whether of foreign or domestic production. They have originated and patented many improvements in the manufacture of shears and scissors, and make use of certain processes known only to themselves, particularly in the tempering and hardening of steel, whereby they give an extra quality and finish to their finest grades of goods.

Their factory comprises four spacious floors, and is fully equipped with steam driven machinery of the most improved description. They employ about 100 workmen, and are at present producing upwards of one hundred dozen pairs of shears and scissors per day. The steel used is the choicest quality of English, manufactured expressly for this firm. It comes in long, narrow bars, of various degrees of thickness, according to the different sizes of blades. The malleable iron castings are made to order at foundries which make a specialty of that kind of work.

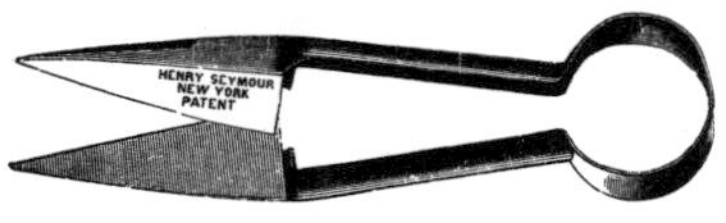

As will be seen by reference to the cuts here presented, Henry Seymour & Co. manufacture all descriptions of shears for tailors' and counting house use, straight and bent trimmers, ladies' scissors, button hole cutters, barbers' scissors, pocket scissors, tailors' points, tinners' and dental snips, lamp trimmers, pruning or sheep toe shears, etc., each of these in a number of sizes and qualities, so that the different varieties produced cannot be far from two hundred.

The larger sizes of shears and scissors receive most particular attention, and their tailors' shears especially have acquired a very high reputation. Large quantities of them are exported to England, and in Canada they have fairly run the English article out of the market. They also make a limited quantity of left handed shears, and finish some goods in nickel plate, especially for the South American market.

Another specialty of this firm, is the manufacture of sheep shears, which are pronounced by practical judges superior to anything of the kind, imported or domestic. They have been awarded numerous diplomas, first premiums and medals at the Fairs of the American Institute and at State Fairs in various parts of the Union, and have received the highest commendation from the best authorities among wool growers, not only in the United States but in foreign lands.

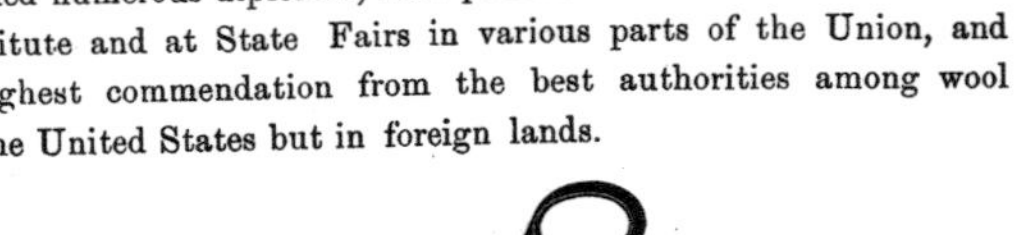

In addition to supplying the trade in all parts of the United States, this firm make large shipments of their general productions to Canada, Central and South America, Mexico, the leading countries of Europe, Australia, China, Japan, etc., and wherever their goods have been introduced they have met with that success which always accompanies merit.

The long experience of Messrs. Henry Seymour & Co.,—the business having been established in 1839,—acquaints them thoroughly with the requirements of the trade in different localities, and enables them to promptly fill orders, which smaller or younger houses would scarcely comprehend.

Their nearly forty years of business life have been successful years. Early in their career they gained a reputation for their goods which placed them in the front rank of their trade, and their constant aim since then, has been to fully maintain that superiority of material and workmanship, which first made their productions successful, and whenever possible, to improve the quality; at the same time introducing such improved processes in manufacture as will tend to a reduction of cost.

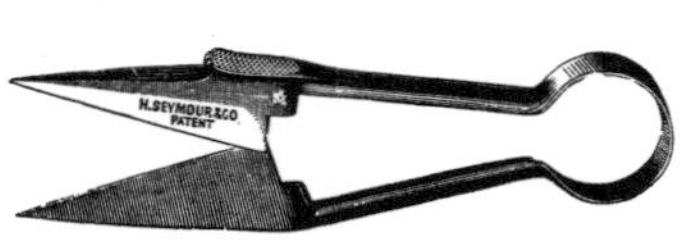

VIEW OF CONCORD GRANITE COMPANY'S QUARRIES, CONCORD, NEW HAMPSHIRE.

CONCORD GRANITE COMPANY,

Works, Concord, N. H.

E. C. Sargeant, Agent, Quincy, Mass.

At what remote period of antiquity the granite hills of New Hampshire assumed their present form, neither the ancient chronologer nor the modern scientist can assign a date; and for our purpose it is not essential to know. It is with the adaptation of granite for specific purposes, and the history of its being thus utilized, rather than the method or time of its creation that we now have to do.

Stone of different formations and qualities has been used for a great variety of purposes in all ages of the world. Relics of nations long since extinct, bear testimony to the fact that it was once used by men in savage and in civil life, for many purposes for which metallic substances have since been substituted.

The Pyramids of Egypt, so celebrated from remotest antiquity, are among the most illustrious works of art. The three principal ones are situated on a rock at the foot of some high mountains which bound the Nile. The building of them is supposed to have commenced about the time of the departure of the Children of Israel out of Egypt, nearly 1500 years before the Christian Era. The largest occupies about twelve acres of ground. It is constructed of stupendous blocks of stone; the length of its base is 746 feet; its perpendicular height 461 feet, with a platform on the top, 32 feet square.

In early times men dwelt in caves. The first buildings constructed were of wood and clay. Stone was used for buildings quite early among the Tyrians.

Stone buildings were introduced into England during the latter part of the seventh century, by Benedict, the monk. The first stone building in Ireland, was a Castle, built at Tuam, by the King of Connaught, in 1161. It was "so new and uncommon as to be called the *Wonderful Castle*."

Stone was also early used for many other purposes. A Stone Bridge built at Bow, near Stratford, by Queen Matilda, in the eleventh century, has been claimed to be the first structure of this kind, although a similar bridge exists at Crowland, which is believed to have been built about two hundred years earlier. Stone Chinaware was made by Wedgwood, in 1762. Artificial Stone for Statues was manufactured by a Neapolitan, and introduced into England during the year of the Declaration of the Independence of the American Colonies. Stone Paper was also made the same year.

Although all New England abounds in Granite, New Hampshire has been particularly designated and long and familiarly known to the civilized world as the "Granite State." More than two and one-half centuries have now past since the English emigrants sought their homes and constructed their rude dwellings beneath the shadows of her mountains and along the fertile banks of her rivers, yet, it is comparatively few years since their worthy descendants learned to look upon these granite hills as mines of wealth, rather than undesirable excrescences on the earth's surface, serving no higher purpose than to give variety to the landscape. It did not occur to the New Englanders of the last century that what was then looked upon as an index of poverty would be utilized by those who should come after them, for their pecuniary benefit. It would have required the exercise of a faith almost as strong as that which will remove mountains, to satisfy those early settlers that it was a feasible enterprise to convert mountains into cities.

It is true that stone was used to some extent in the construction of buildings in this country as early as the middle of the last century. King's Chapel, in Boston, erected in 1752, is probably the first building in New England, built from the native granite. When the proposition was made to construct this building of stone, a committee was sent to Quincy to ascertain if so large an amount of granite could be obtained in that vicinity. After a thorough investigation it was reported that sufficient granite could be found there to build two Churches as large as the one then contemplated.

Stones were not then split by wedges, as now; the process usually adopted being to build fires on or under them, the intensity of the heat causing the stone to split. In this way as will be readily seen, only an inferior quality of granite could be used. During the preceding century the Dutch settlers of New York, being accustomed to importing the yellow brick from their native land, also imported stone for building purposes rather than quarry it when the material was abundant in sight of their own homes. To encourage the introduction of stone from abroad it was placed on their free list. The present generation look upon such enterprises as the follies of their ancestors.

The preference of stone for purposes where strength and durability are desirable, has been acknowledged by all nations from the earliest historic ages. The proof of this is abundantly attested by the broken walls, demolished castles, towers and arches, now the only relics of nations and people long since extinct. But by what mechanical power the huge blocks of stone used in the construction of some of these works, were raised to their lofty resting places, is a marvel even to the inventive genius of the present age.

The necessity for importing material for building purposes no longer exists. Some manufactured marble, it is true, is still imported, but the amount of manufactured marble and other stone exported from the United States exceeds in value, the imports.

Brown freestone or sandstone has been very much used of late for building purposes in many of our larger cities. It is softer and of course more easily manipulated than granite; but is much more easily affected by the weather, and not unfrequently is caused to crumble and scale off from the effects of the frost.

The sandstone quarries on the Connecticut River, opposite Middletown, Conn., are among the oldest in the country, having been worked for more than a century; and stone is now taken from them at a depth of more than two hundred feet below the bed of the river. It is said that in 1802 there were found in these quarries, many feet below the surface, fossil footprints of gigantic birds; some of the prints measuring sixteen inches in length and ten in width, while the tracks were from three to six feet apart.

Many reasons may be assigned for the long delay in the introduction of granite for building purposes in this country. No one doubted its adaptation for such purposes; but while other material, although of far inferior quality could be made to serve as a substitute, with less expenditure of money and labor, it was not deemed expedient to hazard the expense of opening quarries, even under the most favorable circumstances.

The wooden buildings erected during the last century, had their foundations, as may still be seen in many places, prepared by the use of such surface stones as could be most easily procured from the fields and hillsides. No effort seems to have been made to prepare them for their positions by any artificial means. Split stone is almost never found in the foundations of buildings constructed prior to the present century.

In former years lumber for building material was usually found sufficiently abundant for that purpose, in the immediate vicinity of the best granite, consequently the necessity for using the latter in such localities did not seem to exist, and the facilities for transportation, at that time were not such as to justify the effort to remove it to any considerable distance.

The machinery, too, necessary for quarrying granite and removing such enormous blocks, often weighing many tons, as are used for pillars in many of our larger public buildings, was not then available. The first railroad built in the United States, less than fifty years ago, was for the special purpose of transporting granite from a quarry, to the navigable waters of the Neponset River, near Boston.

Since that time, and especially during the last twenty-five years, quarries of more or less importance for working the various kinds of stone found in this country have increased very rapidly; but, like efforts in most other branches of industry, comparatively few have become particularly conspicuous as to the quality or quantity of their productions. At the present time there are more than twenty-five hundred marble and stone works in the United States, the average annual products of which are about $10,000, being an aggregate of $25,000,000.

Limestone and white marbles abound in Vermont and most of Atlantic States, from Massachusetts to Georgia, also in Alabama. Maine produces a variety of gray and clouded limestone, which is quite extensively used for mantels. Beautiful variagated Marbles are quarried in the Carolinas, Virginia, Tennessee and California.

Granite abounds in all the New England States, in New York, on the Delaware Bay, in South Carolina, Georgia, California, and a few other States.

This branch of industry is fast becoming one of the most important in the country. New quarries are constantly being opened for the production of material for building and other purposes, in States where granite is unknown, or where it is found only of an inferior quality. Illinois produces a fair quality of Marble for building purposes, which is much used in Chicago and other cities. A handsome yellow stone found in Ohio is quite extensively used in Cincinnati and Cleveland.

The Concord Granite Company was organized under the laws of Massachusetts, in 1865. Its Quarry is favorably situated on Rattlesnake Hill, in Concord, near the capitol. It is easily accessible, affording the most favorable facilities, for shipment to all parts of the country. This quarry is the best in that vicinity, and being in excellent condition, the proprietors are enabled to furnish stock for the largest structures with unusual promptness.

The granite produced at this quarry is of a beautiful white, and has become so deservedly popular, that it is now extensively used in the construction of the finest buildings.

When run to their full capacity, these works afford employment to three hundred hands, and are capable of producing material to the value of $500,000 annually.

This Company furnished the granite for the Custom House in Portland, Maine, many of the beautiful and substantial stores of Boston, which are an ornament to the city and the admiration of visitors; also much of the material for the Public Buildings in Penn Square, Philadelphia.

They also furnished the granite for the Main Art Building for the Centennial Exposition at Philadelphia.

The works of this Company are so complete and perfect in all their appointments, and the facilities for shipping so excellent, that they are enabled to furnish granite for first-class buildings, cheaper, more promptly and consequently more satisfactorily than any other Company in the United States.

PERSECUTION OF NEW IDEAS.

Dr. C. L. Blood, Inventor of Oxygenized Air, for Diseases of the Throat and Lungs.

When Christ appeared, and inculcated precepts superior to those of the Jewish teachers, he was persecuted for blasphemy. What the Jews could not overthrow by the learning of their priests, they sought to subdue by physical power. The treacherous sword of injustice was unsheathed; Jesus was wrongfully accused, condemned and crucified His enemies believed their system of worship permanent and immutable, and treated him as a blasphemous impostor.

Abelard, for maintaining the rights of free inquiry, was condemned in solemn council. Farel, Lefevre, Hutton, Luther, Zwingle, Calvin, and a host of others, for lifting up the standard of independence, rejecting the infallibility of papacy, and condemning the unmeaning ceremony and legalized licentiousness of the church, were hunted down by mercenaries of the Pope, and menaced by the horrors of the Vatican. It was wrong for the human mind to assert its independence, and attempt to break loose from the restraints which had held the church and the world in darkness and degradation for centuries. Socrates taught the Athenians the existence of a supreme being, the source of all good, and the only true object of adoration. For this, he incurred the vengeance of those who should have rendered him gratitude, and was condemned to drink the juice of the hemlock.

When Descartes taught the doctrine of innate ideas he was declared an Atheist. The University of Paris became alarmed for the being of a God, and the purity of philosophy, and with all laudable zeal ordered the pestiferous works of the infidel author to be burned. It was but a short time, however, till this same infallible University adopted the very doctrine it had combated so lustily, and when Locke and Coudillac attacked it, the cry of materialism and fatalism was turned against them. The teachings of Aristotle were held for many years to be as permanent as the rock of truth. Francis I, passed a degree against Peter Raurno, interdicting him under pain of corporeal punishment, from uttering any more slanderous invectives against Aristotle, and other ancient authors, received and approved. About a century after, the Parliament of Paris passed a decree prohibiting any person, under pain of death, from holding or teaching any maxim at variance with the ancient and approved authors, especially the infallible Aristotle. More than a century after this, the medical faculty in Paris became alarmed for the safety of genuine medical science, and the Royal Academy of Medicine condemned inoculation as "murderous, criminal and magical." Jenner was threatened with disgrace if he did not cease annoying the quietude and self-complacency of his friends with the silly visionary subject of vaccination. Harvey for discovering the circulation of the blood, and announcing the heretical fact, was treated with scorn by medical brethren, deprived of his practice and driven into exile. It is a fact, containing an instructive moral, that not one of his contemporaries at the age of forty years, when Harvey made known his discovery, ever conceded its correctness. They were stable-minded men and despised being led astray like boys by the glare of novelties. When Columbus made application to the Sovereigns of Europe for assistance in his project of western discovery, he met with cold neglect, and repeated repulse. The earth was as flat as a board, and how could he get to the East Indies by sailing west, and as to finding land, that was only the day dreams of a visionary madman. All the philosophy of the past was not to be capsized to suit the fantasy of an adventurer. When the persevering Fulton proposed to make steam a mighty agent in the propulsion of vessels, his capacious minded countrymen laughed at him. Steam had never propelled vessels; therefore it never could. The conclusion was as natural as to look to the past for all wisdom, and Fulton was ridiculed and neglected, and at last died in poverty.

From the introduction of Oxygenized Air, until the present time, the Old School has been lavish and unscrupulous in bestowing upon its author and those engaged in its application, the vilest vituperations. Knaves, fools, quacks and every degrading epithet which jealousy, ignorance and blind fanatical superstition could invent, have been applied to them.

Notwithstanding this great opposition, those engaged in the Oxygenized Air practice have calmly pursued their labors, and thousands of victims to the old school practice, who were on the verge of the grave, have been saved. Thousands who were on the road to eternity from consumption and other supposed incurable diseases, are to-day sound in body, and are living monuments to the worth of Oxygenized Air.

Dr. Blood is one of the remarkable men of the age, of commanding presence, great intellectual attainments, a polished gentleman, and is one of the most successful physicians in the country, if not in the world.

It is more than an eighth of a century since Dr. Blood discovered a method for combining Oxygen and Nitrogen in such proportions as to make the Oxygen positively curative in its effects for diseases of the blood and lungs, and at the same time perfectly safe to inhale in any condition of health or disease.

When Dr. Blood began to advocate the merits of his invention for the cure of diseases of the respiratory organs, he was met at the threshold of his career by a storm of derision and bitterness which would have driven an ordinary man from his purpose. His offence was that he dared to doubt the plenary inspirations and traditions of dead and rotten medical authors, whose errors were to be held as sacred as the living truths of Deity. War was declared, and the decree of social ostracism and defamatory rebuke was to silence the audacious innovator.

There is scarce an exception to the rule that many who are so far in advance of the age in which they live, as to discover a new, or rather a before unknown principle, for nothing is absolutely new, are generally reviled.

Ambrose Pare introduced the ligature as a substitute for the painful mode of staunching the blood, after the amputation of a limb, viz: by applying boiling pitch to the surface of the stump. He was, in consequence, persecuted with remorseless rancor by the Faculty, who ridiculed the idea of putting the life of a person upon a thread, when boiling pitch had stood the test for centuries. The Jesuits of Peru introduced the Peruvian Bark (invaluable as a medicine), but being a remedy used by the Jesuits, the Protestants at once rejected the drug as an invention of the devil.

Dr. C. L. BLOOD,

Inventor of Oxygenized Air.

Dr. Gronevelt discovered the curative power of Cantharides in Dropsy. As soon as his cures began to be noised abroad he was commited to Newgate by warrant of the President of the College of Physicians.

Physicians of the Old School have always been at war with progress, equal rights, and human liberty. The doctors have but recently secured the passage of a law by the legislature of New York, making it an offence punishable by fine and imprisonment for a physician or citizen to prescribe a medicine without first securing a license from them to do so. Their next effort will probably be to secure a law to prohibit the people from taking a medicine without a written order from some member of the faculty.

Notwithstanding the opposition of the bigoted and ignorant portion of the medical profession against Dr. Blood in the introduction of his great discovery, its grand principle remained impregnable, behind which he felt himself secure and fortified against the assaults of a world of doctors, and he persevered on until now his Oxygenized Air is almost universally acknowledged the most important medical discovery of the age. Over two hundred regular physicians have adopted it as a practice, and nearly every city in America, and many in Europe, have an office and a physician devoted to its application.

Dr. Blood believes that if physicians of the old school would become less rigidly wedded to a dogmatic theory and system of treating diseases, suffering humanity would be greatly benefitted, He also believes that the rule of medical societies which does not allow its members to practice specialities, but compels them to treat all diseases, is productive of danger, suffering and death, as no physician is equally skillful in all diseases. He believes that this compulsory "general practice" destroys tens of thousands of lives every year. He also believes that the rule of medical societies which prohibits its members from advertising or making known to suffering humanity where they can be relieved or cured, is unjust and only calculated to gratify or benefit a few old fogy doctors who never should have been born. Dr. Blood also believes that there is no science or safety in the old school practice. How far his views are sustained by medical men of character and note the following testimony will show. Notwithstanding medical men are very severe on quacks, it is impossible to look into medical literature without finding it replete with virtual confessions that medical men are immensely indebted to what they call quacks.

Radcliff said that "when he died he would leave behind him the whole mystery of physics on half a sheet of paper." Sir Ashley Cooper is reported to have acknowledged that his "mistakes would fill a church yard." Prof. Jackson, of Philadelphia said that he "would rather see a patient die than call in another doctor when such a step might appear to imply any distrust of his own abilities."

One of the foremost English physicians and medical writers, Dr. James Johnson, says: "I declare my conscientious opinion, founded on long observation and reflection, that if there was not a single physician, surgeon, apothecary, chemist, druggist or drug, on the face of the earth there would be less sickness and less mortality than now obtains."

Prof. Magendic addressed his students at the medical college at Paris as follows; "Gentlemen, medicine is a great humbug. I know it is studied as a science. Doctors are mere imperics when they are not charlatans. We are as ignorant as men can be. Who knows anything in the world about medicine? There is no such thing as medical science. I grant you people are cured; but how? Nature does a great deal, imagination does a great deal, doctors do devilish little."

Dr. O. W. Holmes says, "Medicine is a grand colossal humbug." There was a certain pope who lost his physician, and to all who applied for the office, he put the question, "How many have you killed?" Each doctor in turn solemnly asseverated that he had "never killed anyone." An old doctor, with a big beard, came at last. "How many have you killed?" asked the pope. "Two thousand," said the old fellow, pulling his beard with both hands. The pope was pleased with the confession, and, believing he must be a man of experience at least took him as his physician.

Statistics claimed to be authentic show a mortality under homœopathy of about half—and in some diseases much less—than under allopathic treatment.

An allopathic physician in London sent to inspect the different cholera hospitals, concluded his report by avowing that, "if taken with the disease, he desired homœopathic treatment."

It is an alleged fact that Homœopathic Insurance Companies have about one-third the deaths on their homœopathic policies that they do among the policy holders treated by allopathy—the actual fact being that they charge on the former a considerable less premium for the risk. Researches into the respective results of homœopathic and allopathic private practice in New York City shows, for two years, thirty thousand three hundred and ninety-five deaths in the private practice of nine hundred and eighty-four allopathists and fifteen hundred and twenty in that of one hundred and fifty-six homœopathists, showing fifty-three per cent. in favor of homœopathy. Dr. Blood advocates the homœopathic treatment because if it does not always cure it does no harm.

Previous to Dr. Blood's discovery of Oxygenized Air, he was engaged in the regular practice of medicine, prescribing for his patients from formulas laid down in medical works, written by ignorant doctors who lived before it was discovered that the blood circulated through the system, and which he was educated to believe would cure the various ills to which humanity are subject. But in many cases, in place of seeing his patients recover as he anticipated and expected, he saw them grow worse under the treatment called scientific, but which he found a curse and a delusion. Being a man of strong integrity, he abandoned the practice, feeling if he could not labor to promote the physical welfare of suffering mankind, he would not assist in entailing misery on the already myriads of victims to pernicious drugs.

Since Dr. Blood commenced the Oxygenized Air practice he has treated personally over one hundred and twenty thousand patients, and in a majority of cases has obtained the finest results, restoring persons to health who had been drugged almost to death by other physicians and by them pronounced incurable. Unlike other physicians, Dr. Blood does not advise persons in the last stage of consumption to seek the air of the South or a trip across the briny deep, leaving home and kindred at the very time they most need their care, to risk their frail constitutions by perilous and exhausting journeys to far-off lands in pursuit of health; but, alas! where they too often meet with the sad fate of dying among strangers and in a strange land. If the disease in the lungs has not advanced too far, all the patient requires to regain his lost force and vitality is the soothing and purifying influence of Oxygenized Air, which, when taken into the lungs, sends the life blood gushing through the system and dyes their faded cheeks with the bloom of health.

What can be more natural, more simple and efficacious than the treatment of consumption by this method, by which the vital principle of life, Oxygen is conveyed directly into the lungs, and its life-giving properties brought to bear at once upon the seat of disease.

Dr. Blood, enabled by this great discovery to alleviate the sick and suffering, must have reflected on his own soul the benign smiles of those he has been the means of benefiting and a gratiful people will hand down to posterity the blessed name of the one who gave to humanity the great boon of Oxygenized Air.

OFFICE AND RESIDENCE OF Dr. C. L. BLOOD,

27 Bond St., near Broadway, New York City.

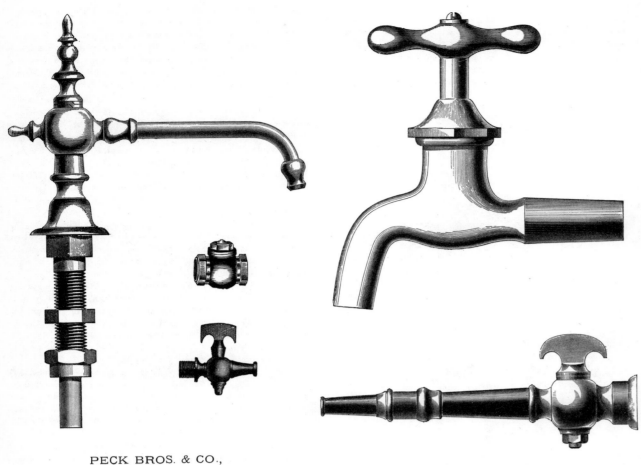

PECK BROS. & CO.,

Manufacturers of all kinds of Brass and Plated

Work for Water, Gas and Steam,

74 Franklin Street, New Haven, Conn.

New York Warehouse, 73 Beekman Street.

If the men who passed from earth a hundred years ago could revisit their old homes and note the changes which have taken place during their absence, we fancy they would be startled as well as pleased at the manifest progress the world has made. The steam engine was then in its infancy. Illuminating gas had scarcely been thought of, and the introduction of water into all the rooms of our dwellings would have been considered impracticable, if not impossible. During the last half century greater improvements have been made in our manner of living and working than was made in all previous time. One of the notable results of—and at the same time aid to—our advancement has been the constant tendency of men to

confine themselves to one special line of production. Our most successful manufacturers confine themselves to single classes of goods, though of many different patterns and adapted to many different uses.

The Peck Bros. & Co., since their organization in 1866, have followed this course. They have devoted themselves to the manufacture of Brass and Plated Work for Plumbers, Gas and Steam Fitters, Engine Builders, and Water and Gas Companies. Though there are older companies engaged in the same line of trade, and much rivalry among manufacturers of such goods, this company has, since first its wares were introduced, taken a prominent place among the leading firms of the country. Abundantly supplied with improved machinery and a full corps of skilled workmen, they are enabled to produce the very finest and best of work—work excelled by none.

In addition to the manufacture of Brass Goods they deal largely in all kinds of materials and supplies used by Plumbers, Gas and Steam Fitters, and kindred trades, such as Bath Tubs, Boilers, Water Closets, Iron and Earthen Ware, etc., in addition to which they constantly keep on hand a large stock of tools used in such callings. They have a branch warehouse in New York, at 73 Beekman Street, under the superintendence of Mr. A. T. Foster, where a full line of their goods can always be found.

Mr. H. F. Peck is the President, and Mr. John M. Peck the Secretary and Treasurer of the Company. With such men to guide the business we predict for this establishment a future fame as brilliant as its past record.

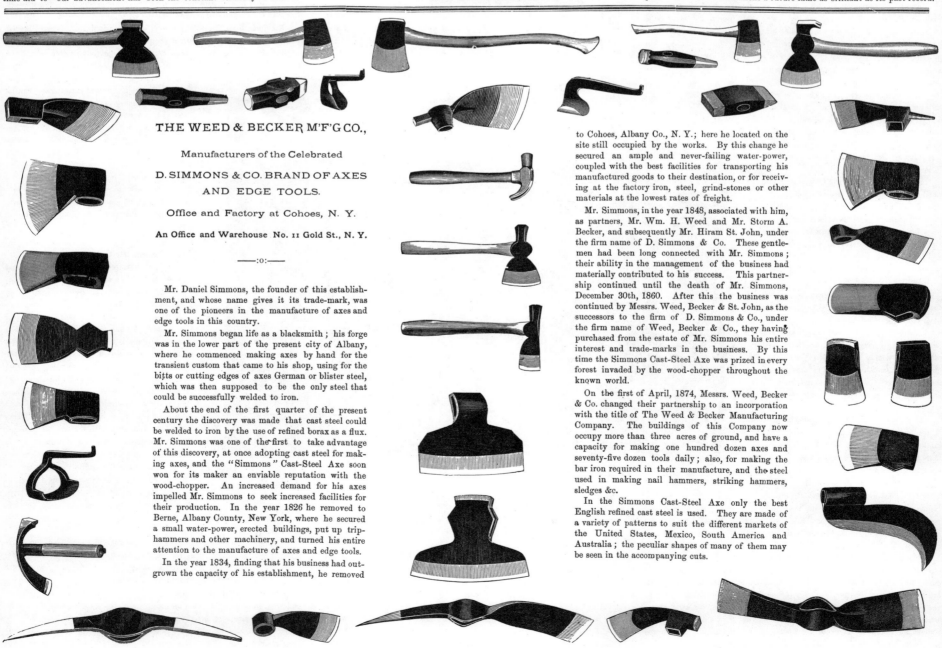

THE WEED & BECKER M'F'G CO.,

Manufacturers of the Celebrated

D. SIMMONS & CO. BRAND OF AXES

AND EDGE TOOLS.

Office and Factory at Cohoes, N. Y.

An Office and Warehouse No. 11 Gold St., N. Y.

Mr. Daniel Simmons, the founder of this establishment, and whose name gives it its trade-mark, was one of the pioneers in the manufacture of axes and edge tools in this country.

Mr. Simmons began life as a blacksmith; his forge was in the lower part of the present city of Albany, where he commenced making axes by hand for the transient custom that came to his shop, using for the bitts or cutting edges of axes German or blister steel, which was then supposed to be the only steel that could be successfully welded to iron.

About the end of the first quarter of the present century the discovery was made that cast steel could be welded to iron by the use of refined borax as a flux. Mr. Simmons was one of the first to take advantage of this discovery, at once adopting cast steel for making axes, and the "Simmons" Cast-Steel Axe soon won for its maker an enviable reputation with the wood-chopper. An increased demand for his axes impelled Mr. Simmons to seek increased facilities for their production. In the year 1826 he removed to Berne, Albany County, New York, where he secured a small water-power, erected buildings, put up trip-hammers and other machinery, and turned his entire attention to the manufacture of axes and edge tools.

In the year 1834, finding that his business had outgrown the capacity of his establishment, he removed

to Cohoes, Albany Co., N. Y.; here he located on the site still occupied by the works. By this change he secured an ample and never-failing water-power, coupled with the best facilities for transporting his manufactured goods to their destination, or for receiving at the factory iron, steel, grind-stones or other materials at the lowest rates of freight.

Mr. Simmons, in the year 1848, associated with him, as partners, Mr. Wm. H. Weed and Mr. Storm A. Becker, and subsequently Mr. Hiram St. John, under the firm name of D. Simmons & Co. These gentlemen had been long connected with Mr. Simmons; their ability in the management of the business had materially contributed to his success. This partnership continued until the death of Mr. Simmons, December 30th, 1860. After this the business was continued by Messrs. Weed, Becker & St. John, as the successors to the firm of D. Simmons & Co., under the firm name of Weed, Becker & Co., they having purchased from the estate of Mr. Simmons his entire interest and trade-marks in the business. By this time the Simmons Cast-Steel Axe was prized in every forest invaded by the wood-chopper throughout the known world.

On the first of April, 1874, Messrs. Weed, Becker & Co. changed their partnership to an incorporation with the title of The Weed & Becker Manufacturing Company. The buildings of this Company now occupy more than three acres of ground, and have a capacity for making one hundred dozen axes and seventy-five dozen tools daily; also, for making the bar iron required in their manufacture, and the steel used in making nail hammers, striking hammers, sledges &c.

In the Simmons Cast-Steel Axe only the best English refined cast steel is used. They are made of a variety of patterns to suit the different markets of the United States, Mexico, South America and Australia; the peculiar shapes of many of them may be seen in the accompanying cuts.

Carpenters' Mallet.

Hand Screw.

Iron Bound Mallet for Opening Cases.

Cabinet Maker's Clamp.

R. BLISS MANUFACTURING CO.,

Manufacturers of

HAND AND BENCH SCREWS, CLAMPS, CROQUET GAMES, BOYS' AND

YOUTH'S TOOL CHESTS, &c., &c.

Pawtucket, R. I.

—:o:—

Rufus Bliss, the founder of the business now conducted by the R. Bliss Manufacturing Company, was one of the pioneers in this country of the manufacture of wooden screws to be used as bench screws, or as hand screws or clamps for piano-forte and cabinet makers' use. In the establishment and subsequent prosecution of his business, Mr. Bliss enjoyed peculiar facilities for acquainting himself with the wants of the trades above named, by reason of his long acquaintance with Mr. Jonas Chickering, (the father of the Chickering pianos) and all the other piano-forte manufacturers in Boston. Through this acquaintance he had access to their workshops at all times, and becoming familiar with the wants of the workmen, he was enabled to devise and manufacture such appliances as would best aid them in the prosecution of their work. Mr. Bliss was a man of much energy and perseverance, with whom ultimate success was only a matter of time, and fortunately he has been succeeded by equally energetic and persevering men who have not only fully maintained but have added to the high reputation which the manufactures of Mr. Rufus Bliss attained years ago. Many of the simplest appliances used by the mechanics of to-day are of comparatively recent invention and among that number must be classed the modern hand screw and clamp used by fine wood workers, which are far superior in every respect to the devices previously in use. Even such implements as have not been greatly improved in principle, have been materially improved in methods of manufacture, and are afforded at less comparative cost.

In addition to their immense production of Hand and Bench Screws, and Clamps, for piano-forte and cabinet makers, Carpenters' Door Clamps, etc., the Company are large manufacturers of Apple Tree and Hickory Handles for chisels of various kinds, augurs, brad awls, files and other tools. Carpenters' Mallets, Tinners' Mallets, Carvers' Mallets, Jewelers' Mallets, Mallets of hickory, maple, box and lignumvitæ, Mallets handles to screw or to drive in, Mallets with malleable iron rings or without rings, round mallets or square mallets, in short, mallets of every description in immense quantities are turned out by the R. Bliss Manufacturing Company.

When Croquet Games were first introduced in this country, this Company was fortunate in possessing not only an abundance of material but peculiar facilities for manufacturing sets of the game; they at once added Croquet Games to their line of manufactures, and have since then been constantly producing a line of goods of that class, which are not excelled by any made. In the manufacture of their fine games they use the best Turkey Boxwood; and the best selections of Madagascar and Honduras Woods that the market affords. Weight and durability of material being of the first importance in the manufacture of Croquet Sets, American Rock Maple is doubtless as valuable a wood for the manufacture of Croquet Sets, as any known, except perhaps, Turkey boxwood, its solid, enduring qualities not being surpassed. The Company manufacture some twenty different grades of Croquet Sets, from the finest attainable down to the medium and cheaper grades. The fine sets are all made of the best material with first-class work in turning and polishing, and they are confidently recommended as the standard line of croquet games. The medium and cheaper grades are all durable, and are of varied designs. In addition to the Lawn Croquet Sets, the R. Bliss Manufacturing Company, produce a full line of Table Croquet Sets—some ten different styles—as carefully made as the field sets.

R. BLISS MANUFACTURING COMPANY'S WORKS, PAWTUCKET, R. I.

Another, and a very important branch of the Company's business is the manufacture of Tool Chests for Boys and Youth. The Boy's Tool Chest is made of fine hard wood with walnut trimmings, in nine different sizes—numbered from one to nine inclusive—the smallest size containing six tools, and the largest twenty tools. The Youths' Tool Chests comprise seven sizes—numbered from ten to sixteen inclusive—and contain from eighteen to forty-five tools. These Chests, like the ones previously mentioned, are substantially made of hard wood, trimmed with walnut, and the tools are not merely playthings, but are really useful implements such as are used by skilled mechanics. The Gents' Walnut Chests, number from twenty to twenty-five, and contain from twenty to sixty tools each, according to size and price, the larger sizes embracing everything likely to be of use to the amateur, or any but a working mechanic, while the sixty tool chest, is fully as complete as the kit of an ordinary workman.

For children the Company manufacture a variety of useful and instructive toys, such as Architectural Building Blocks, made of hard wood and smoothly finished, but not painted. These blocks while affording endless amusement for the little ones, are silent, but very effective educators. The baby boy or girl who amuses itself by arranging blocks in different positions—however crude the arrangement may be—is learning something. Unconsciously it is acquiring habits of thought, and developing perceptive faculties which otherwise would lie dormant perhaps for years. In its amusements it receives the first practical lessons of life, which others only understand after more or less rough experience. The man who so improves the games of childhood as to render them means of imparting information, or who devises an amusement which interests and instructs, is a teacher whose lessons will be remembered through life, and not a few of our most successful mechanics, inventors and business men can trace the development of their habits of thought and their quickness of perception back to the games of their childhood.

The R. Bliss Manufacturing Company have facilities for the production of goods in their line not surpassed by those of any house in this country, and whether it is Hand Screws or Clamps, Bench Screws, Handles for Tools, Mallets, Croquet Sets, Tool Chests or Toys, their manufactures, one and all, stand in the front rank in their class of goods, the same careful selection of material is made, and the same perfection of manufacture is arrived at, whether the article produced is large or small.

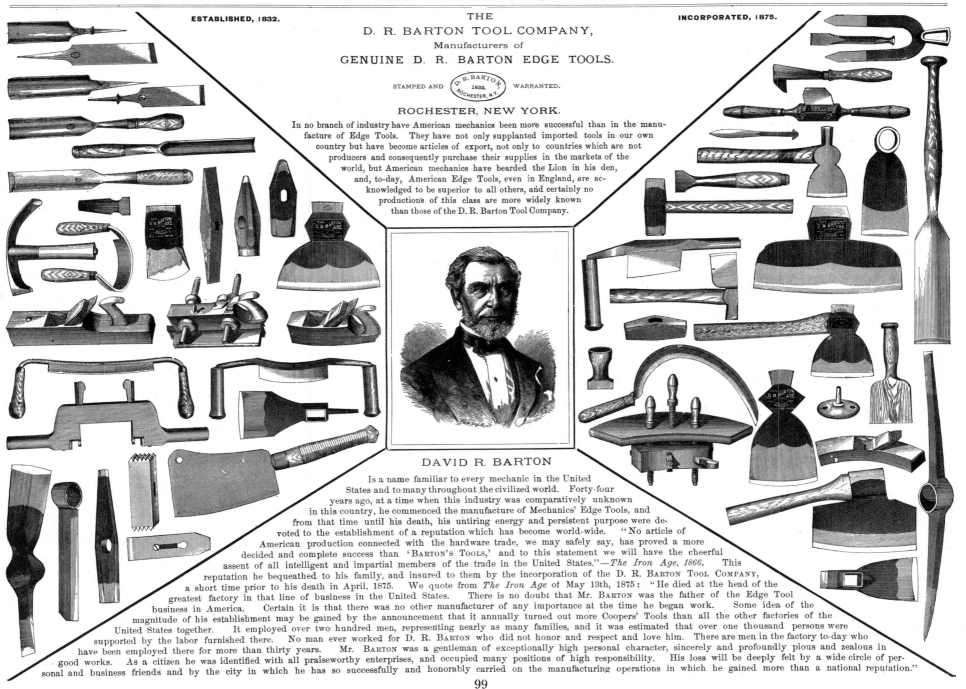

ESTABLISHED, 1832.   INCORPORATED, 1875.

THE
D. R. BARTON TOOL COMPANY,

Manufacturers of

GENUINE D. R. BARTON EDGE TOOLS.

STAMPED AND   *D. R. BARTON 1832 ROCHESTER, N.Y.*   WARRANTED.

ROCHESTER, NEW YORK.

In no branch of industry have American mechanics been more successful than in the manufacture of Edge Tools. They have not only supplanted imported tools in our own country but have become articles of export, not only to countries which are not producers and consequently purchase their supplies in the markets of the world, but American mechanics have bearded the Lion in his den, and, to-day, American Edge Tools, even in England, are acknowledged to be superior to all others, and certainly no productions of this class are more widely known than those of the D. R. Barton Tool Company.

DAVID R. BARTON

Is a name familiar to every mechanic in the United States and to many throughout the civilized world. Forty-four years ago, at a time when this industry was comparatively unknown in this country, he commenced the manufacture of Mechanics' Edge Tools, and from that time until his death, his untiring energy and persistent purpose were devoted to the establishment of a reputation which has become world-wide. "No article of American production connected with the hardware trade, we may safely say, has proved a more decided and complete success than 'BARTON'S TOOLS,' and to this statement we will have the cheerful assent of all intelligent and impartial members of the trade in the United States."—*The Iron Age*, 1866. This reputation he bequeathed to his family, and insured to them by the incorporation of the D. R. BARTON TOOL COMPANY, a short time prior to his death in April, 1875. We quote from *The Iron Age* of May 13th, 1875: "He died at the head of the greatest factory in that line of business in the United States. There is no doubt that Mr. BARTON was the father of the Edge Tool business in America. Certain it is that there was no other manufacturer of any importance at the time he began work. Some idea of the magnitude of his establishment may be gained by the announcement that it annually turned out more Coopers' Tools than all the other factories of the United States together. It employed over two hundred men, representing nearly as many families, and it was estimated that over one thousand persons were supported by the labor furnished there. No man ever worked for D. R. BARTON who did not honor and respect and love him. There are men in the factory to-day who have been employed there for more than thirty years. Mr. BARTON was a gentleman of exceptionally high personal character, sincerely and profoundly pious and zealous in good works. As a citizen he was identified with all praiseworthy enterprises, and occupied many positions of high responsibility. His loss will be deeply felt by a wide circle of personal and business friends and by the city in which he has so successfully and honorably carried on the manufacturing operations in which he gained more than a national reputation."

VIEW OF HAVEMEYERS & ELDERS SUGAR REFINERY, WILLIAMSBURGH, NEW YORK.

HAVEMEYERS & ELDERS,
SUGAR REFINERS.

Office, 98 Wall Street, New York.

Works, Williamsburgh, N. Y.

At what remote period of antiquity sugar was first known we have no positive information ; or from what substances and in what manner it was first obtained, history furnishes no reliable data. Strabo says it is supposed to have been known to the Ancient Jews. It was found in the East Indies by Nearchus, admiral of Alexander, 325 B. C.

Sugar was then, and for a long time subsequent, considered a neutral substance, without congeners ; but has of late years become the head of a numerous family, which is constantly increasing.

Lucan speaks of an Oriental nation in alliance with Pompey in the first century B. C. who used the juice of the cane as a common beverage. Pliny writes, about one century later that the best sugar in those days was made in India. It is held by some that the sugar produced in the first centuries of the Christian era, was purer and possessed more medical virtue than the unrefined sugars of the present day, from the fact that Galen, a distinguished physician of Rome, who died about A. D. 200 prescribed it as a medicine.

It is supposed to have been brought into Europe early in the seventh century from Asia. About the middle of the twelfth century, sugar-cane was transported from Tripoli and Syria, to Sicily, thence to Madeira, and finally to America. It is claimed that after repeated failures to cultivate it in Italy, the Portuguese and Spaniards brought it to America about 1510.

The process of refining sugar was known in England as early as the sixteenth century, although not utilized to any great extent until the following century.

This process is designed to remove those impurities, or adulterations found in raw sugar when imported and to produce clear white sugar of the various grades known as large crystal, " Coffee Sugar," crushed and pulverized sugar.

The establishment of sugar refineries in this country is of a more recent date than many of our great industries, yet very few people not particularly interested in this branch of business have any adequate conception as to its magnitude and utility.

We are unable to give statistics to show as definitely as we could wish the entire products of this branch of American industries, but will refer briefly to the business of a single refinery, that of Messrs. Havemeyers & Elder of Williamsburgh, N. Y.

This gigantic establishment is the largest of the kind, not only in this country but in the world. Its dimensions are such that no adequate conception of it can be formed, if we give the length and superfices in feet or even in yards, and the production in pounds. To give numbers which the mind can comprehend and retain we are compelled to give the data of measurement in rods and acres, and of the products in tons.

The entire premises may be divided into three portions.

1. The Sugar House proper in which the raw sugar is received, and after being treated and refined is turned out ready for the consumer. This portion of the works forms that imposing structure which is the most conspicuous object on the East River. It occupies the whole block between South Third and South Fourth Streets, and First Street and East River.

2. A series of buildings, serving for storage and other purposes, occupying the whole of another block between South Fourth and South Fifth Streets, and First Street and East River.

3. A third portion is the Bone black House and one of the boiler

houses. This portion covers about one half of the surface of the block between South Second and South Third Streets, and First Street and East River.

Besides the three portions already described this establishment includes an entire block, and portions of two other blocks equivalent to a whole one, between North Fourth and North Sixth Streets, and the East River, in which are the Cooper's Shops where barrels are manufactured by machinery, the stables for their truck horses of which there are sixty, and store rooms and other buildings.

The Sugar House and adjoining buildings cover a ground surface of two and one half acres. While the total surface of floors in the block occupied by the sugar house proper is five and one seventh acres. The surface of floors in the block between South Fourth and South Fifth Streets, amounts to two and one fifth acres, while the buildings on the lot where the Bone black house is situated have a floor surface of one and one seventh acres, making for the entire buildings an aggregate floor surface of about eight and one half acres.

Between North Fourth and North Sixth Streets, are grounds embracing two whole blocks, including a surface of four acres ; or a floor surface of seven acres, making a grand aggregate of floor surface belonging to this refinery of fifteen and one half acres.

The river front, which constantly presents a scene of bustle and activity from the great number of vessels of all sizes which are required to furnish this establishment with the raw materials, has a total length of twenty seven rods.

The buildings situated south of Grand Street are, as has been already stated, only a portion of those belonging to these premises.

The portion of this establishment north of Grand Street has also a river front of more than six rods, which added to that already referred to, gives a total river front of thirty three rods at the disposal of this firm.

The Refining of Sugar is, with very few exceptions the most important of our manufacturing enterprises.

The exceptions referred to are the industries relating to the mining of coal and iron, the manufactures of iron and the textile substances. The account we have given of the magnitude of the refinery of Messrs. Havemeyers & Elder, shows in some measure the importance of this branch of industry.

We will now give a few data which will afford a clearer comprehension of the extensive scale on which this business is conducted.

Three hundred tons of raw sugars are daily received at this establishment, and consequently about three hundred tons of refined sugars, on an average, leave the house daily. Allowing ten hours for a day's work, we see that thirty tons of stock go in and the same amount goes out of the house every working hour, or one ton every two minutes. Now if we bear in mind that it takes ten barrels of sugar such as are seen at the grocer's, to make a ton we shall see that five barrels full of raw sugar go into the refinery and five barrels of refined sugars come out every minute.

One of the principal agents in sugar refining is steam. This furnishes the necessary heat, the motive power for the engines, pumps, and other machinery. The quantity of steam used every twenty four hours if applied exclusively as a motive power, would be equivalent to twenty two hundred horse power. But about one fifth of this amount is used for propelling machinery, the balance being required to furnish the heat necessary for the various operations of refining.

The large amount of steam required for this establishment is produced in twenty four immense boilers, under which are burned not less than one hundred tons of coal per day, the smoke from which is discharged from two enormous chimneys, having a diameter of seven feet at the base, inside dimensions. One of these chimneys is one hundred and thirty feet high, and the other one hundred and forty feet.

The process of refining sugar involves many delicate questions of

chemistry and mechanics, and presents many difficult problems, which are daily being solved. It would be interesting to the reader, if it were possible to enter fully into the minutiæ concerning these operations. But the limit of this article will admit of only a brief description of this process of refining sugar.

The raw sugar comes in the shape of cane sugar from the West Indies and the East Indies, from Java, Manilla, from South America, and even from Egypt and China ; and the beet sugar from France and Germany. It is first taken from the hogsheads, boxes, bags or baskets in which it is originally contained and thrown into hot water to dissolve it.

It is next passed through appropriate filters made of cloth, from which the solution of raw sugar comes, still very dark, but clear or free from any suspended matter. This solution is now ready for going through what may be regarded as the most important operation of sugar refining, which is a filtration over bone black. This substance is made by burning bone until all the organic matter is destroyed, the residue being bone charcoal which is perfectly black.

This bone charcoal or bone black possesses the remarkable property of removing the coloring matter, a great many salts, and other impurities, not only from sugars but from many other liquids. To use the bone black, it is placed in very large iron vessels, or reservoirs. Over this the dark brown solution of raw sugar is allowed to run, when it becomes white, having not only lost its color, but also its bad taste, by which it is rendered sweeter and purer. To secure the refined sugar, it is now only necessary to remove the water, which is done by boiling it in very large vessels called vacuum pans. To these pans are attached powerful pumps which constantly remove the vapor from the boiling liquid ; thus removing almost entirely the action of the atmospheric pressure, enabling the liquid to boil at a low temperature, which allows the water to evaporate more rapidly and gives a better product to the refiner. A small quantity of water is left in the sugar after being boiled. This water dissolves a part of the sugar, forming a syrup which remains mixed with solid sugar and must be separated by draining out.

This draining is performed very rapidly by centrifugal machines, which spin around with the tremendous velocity of thirty revolutions per second. The result of this rapid spinning is that the sugar is retained in an appropriate vessel, and the syrup thrown out to be collected and boiled again, when fresh quantities of sugar are again separated.

The sugar of the various grades and the molasses are always put up in barrels to be sold. The barrels are all made at the Cooper's Shop already referred to, situated north of Grand Street. Two thousand barrels are required every day for the products of this institution.

We have now given but a brief review of the extent, and the productions of this vast enterprise. Yet we trust our readers will be able, in some measure to appreciate the blessings they enjoy for which they are indebted to the inventive genius of the originator of the process for refining sugar.

To no one house, probably are we more indebted for the improvements which have been devised and the fidelity with which they have been executed than to that, we have been considering. Enterprises like this requiring large investments of capital, and directly or indirectly the employment of such a vast amount of labor, are the motive power which has caused the rapid devolpment of the resources of our country for which it is now so justly celebrated.

We are not informed of the amount of capital required by this house but we may form some idea of the amount, when we consider the extent of their business which gives constant employment to two thousand men ; a number sufficiently large to fill an ordinary hall, or with their families to people a town as large as some of the county seats in this State. Besides the premises already described this house has an office, or place of business at 98 Wall Street, New York City.

Stationary Engine, with or without Variable Cut Off.

Portable Engine, Six to Thirty Horse Power

Agricultural Engine, Six to Twenty Horse Power.

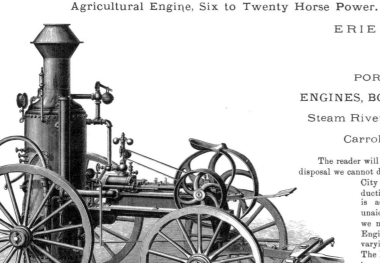

Light Agricultural Engine, Five to Ten Horse Power.

Detached Portable Engine,

This Engine is the same as are mounted on the Boiler for the Portable, showing the Steam Chest side of the Engine.

ERIE CITY IRON WORKS,

ERIE, PA.

Manufacturers of

PORTABLE AND STATIONARY

ENGINES, BOILERS & CIRCULAR SAW MILLS,

Steam Riveters, Torsion Spring Hammers and

Carroll's Patent Gang Saw Tables.

—:o:—

The reader will at once see that within the very limited space at our disposal we cannot describe the extensive establishment known as the Erie City Iron Works, nor catalogue their productions. The cuts with which this page is adorned must tell their own story unaided by any written descriptions; we may however say that the Stationary Engines are manufactured in 14 sizes, varying from 8-horse to 125-horse power; The Detached Portable Engines are built in six sizes, from 8-horse to 30-horse power.

The Works have the latest improvements in Circular Saw Mills, and can supply a full outfit for mills on short notice, they also are largely engaged in the manufacture of Shafting, Pulleys, Gearing, etc., but for further information we must refer the reader to the manufacturers themselves, who will, on application, send descriptive circulars and price lists. Address, Erie City Iron Works, Erie, Pa.

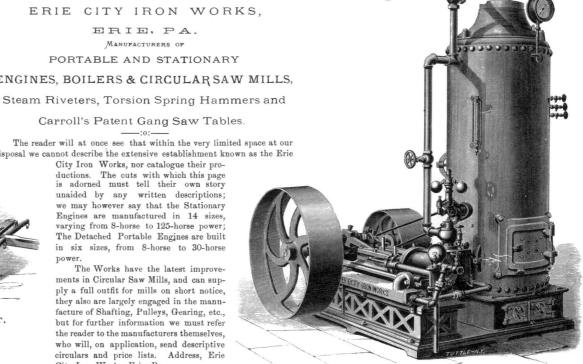

Semi-Portable Engine, Five to Ten Horse Power.

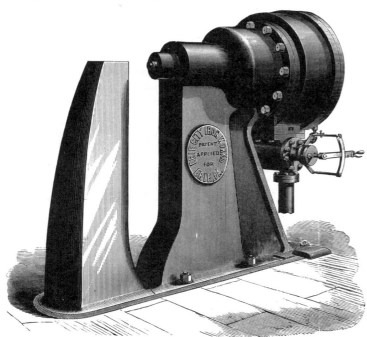

Direct Acting Steam Riveter.

Circular Saw Mill.

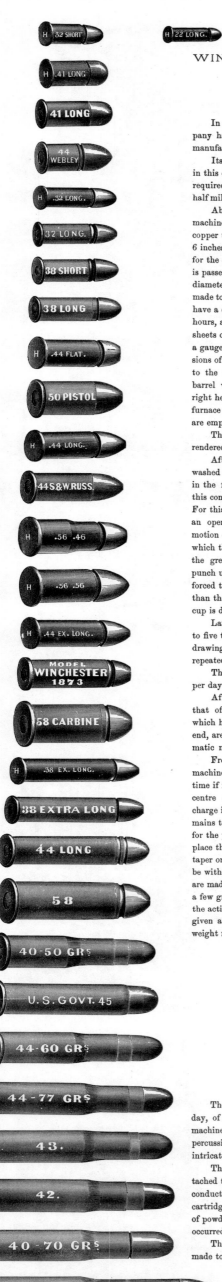

WINCHESTER REPEATING ARMS COMPANY.

New Haven, Conn., U. S. A.
Metallic Cartridges.

In addition to the production of Fire Arms, this Company have within a few years added to its business the manufacture of metallic cartridges.

Its present facilities, which are perhaps second to none in this country, if in the world, enable it to produce daily, if required, one million cartridges for military arms, and one half million for sporting rifles and pistols.

About one acre of floor room, and several hundred machines are devoted entirely to this work. The brass or copper used in the manufacture is received in strips, 5 to 6 inches wide and 5 or 6 feet long, of a thickness suitable for the cartridge for which it is intended. In this state, it is passed under a press, which cuts from it discs of a proper diameter, which are by the continued motion of the machine made to assume the form of a shallow cup. These machines have a capacity of from 30 to 50 thousand per day, of ten hours, and are operated by one man, who simply feeds the sheets of brass into the machine. He is provided also with a gauge, by which he can test from time to time the dimensions of the cups turned out. The cups are then removed to the annealing room, where they are heated in an iron barrel which is made to revolve over a fire. When the right heat is attained, by an ingenious arrangement of the furnace the barrel is rolled out of the furnace and the cups are emptied through a door in its side into a tank of water.

This is done to soften the brass, which has been rendered hard by the cupping operation.

After being removed from the tanks, the cups are washed to remove the oxidation which they have acquired in the furnace and are turned out shining like gold. In this condition they are submitted to the drawing process. For this purpose they are thrown upon a revolving table by an operative and placed with the open end upward. The motion of the table carries them against a curved guide by which they are presented one by one under a punch with the greatest regularity. By the rapid movement of the punch up and down the point are forced through a steel die having a diameter somewhat less than that of the cup and by this means the diameter of the cup is decreased and its length increased.

Large military cartridges are drawn in this way three to five times according to the length required; between each drawing operation the annealing and washing process is repeated.

These presses have a capacity of thirty to forty thousand per day and are operated by females.

After the necessary length, (somewhat greater than that of the finished shell) has been obtained, the cups which have now assumed the form of tubes closed at one end, are trimmed at the open end by swift running automatic machines.

From the trimmers they are passed to the "heading" machine by which the flange is formed, and at the same time if it be a central fire shell, the pocket is formed at the centre of the head, to contain the primer by which the charge is to be fired. After the heading operation it remains to pierce the shell at the bottom of the primer pocket for the passage of the flame from the primer to the powder, place the primer in the pocket and to taper the shell. The taper or conical form is given in order that the shell may be withdrawn easily from the gun after firing. The bullets are made by casting the lead into slugs which have a weight a few grains heavier than the ball. These are submitted to the action of a powerful press by which the exact form is given and the superfluous lead is pressed out leaving the weight required.

are charged with powder at once from a charger having a corresponding number of cells. The bullets are placed in a similar plate and superposed upon the plate containing the charged shells. The two plates are then placed under a press which at a single stroke forces each into the shell below.

Great care is taken in packing the finished cartridges to have neat and strong and attractive packages.

They are packed first in paper boxes, containing twenty to fifty, according to the size, symmetrically placed so that the box is filled.

The wooden cases are made by Dove-tailing the sides and ends together and screwing on the top and bottom, thus securing a more than ordinary strong case.

From one to ten thousand cartridges are contained in a wooden case.

The cartridge department of the business grew out of the necessity of having for use in the guns of their manufacture the most perfect and uniform cartridge that could be produced. Finding it impossible to procure from any manufacturer a cartridge possessing the desired qualities they undertook to make such an article in 1860.

For several years they made no cartridges except the sizes designed for their own make of guns.

The reputation that these cartridges obtained for their uniform qualities, created a demand for sizes adapted to other arms which should possess the same degree of excellence.

Yielding to this demand the production increased from a single variety till the present time, where at least seventy-five sizes and styles are made adapted to all the different known breech-loading guns.

The statistics of this branch of industry would be interesting but we omit any full statement and give but few figures. Of one size of pistol cartridge the annual production is about thirty millions.

For foreign governments they have and are executing contracts on orders of from fifty million to one hundred and fifty millions.

The end to be attained is to so make the cartridges that each of a given kind shall be as nearly a facsimile of every other as possible, and all absolutely perfect.

To attain this requires the use of none but the best material, a perfect and complete set of gauges, the machinery of the most accurate and approved make, the most constant care in inspection and constant testing.

All of these requirements are to be found in their fullest development in the works of this Company.

Much of their machinery is novel and the exclusive use of it secured to them by Letters Patent.

The cartridges are of two general classes, viz.: the Rim Fire and Central Fire.

The Rim fire all have the shell or case made of copper, and this is only designed to be used once, while the shell of the Central fire is made from brass, and is so constructed, that it can be reprimed and reloaded many times.

Both the weight and strength of metal in the latter allows this reloading to be repeated many times, in some cases the test has been carried as far as two hundred times, without showing any signs of deterioration in the shells.

The powder used is made expressly for this Company, and is of uniform strength and quality; the special size and quality varying as to the particular cartridges in which it is to be used. By automatic loading devices the quantity of powder placed in each cartridge cannot vary by more than a fraction of a grain.

The bullets are made from either pure soft lead, or lead hardened with tin, or antimony to conform to their special use and are brought to a perfect uniformity of size and weight by a recent and patented machine which is used exclusively by this company; So perfect is its work that taking one thousand bullets the standard weight of which is

These machines have a capacity of 55 thousand per day, of ten hours, one man tending from three to five machines. One large building is devoted to the making of percussion caps and primers and is filled with beautiful and intricate machinery, adapted for this purpose.

The loading of the cartridge is done in a building attached to one of the wings of the Armory, and is so carefully conducted that although fifty to three hundred thousand cartridges are loaded in each day, and several hundred tons of powder have been used there, no fatal accident has ever occurred.

The shells are placed in a plate pierced with holes made to fit the shells, and thus held, one or two hundred

four hundred and eighty grains each, the variations between the heaviest and lightest will not exceed one grain.

In order to make the reloading of the Central fire practicable, an instrument for the purpose has been devised and is manufactured by this company which is the most compact and complete of its kind yet produced it really combines three tools in one, that for removing the exploded primer, that for inserting the new primer and for fastening in the ball of the finished cartridge.

Further it can be used with any make of cartridge, no matter what the style of primer may be.

When put up for sale each Reloader is accompanied by a charge cup for measuring the powder, a wad cutter, bullet mould, or whatever may be needed to enable a person to make a perfect cartridge.

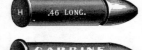

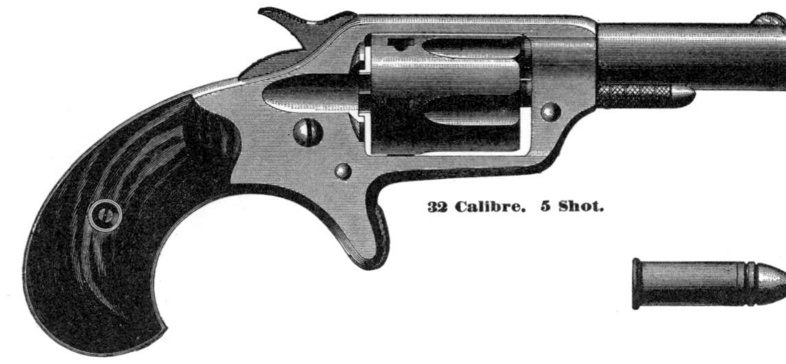

32 Calibre. 5 Shot.

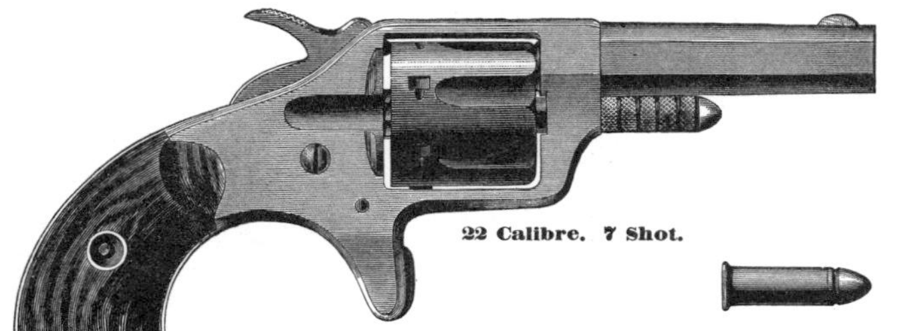

22 Calibre. 7 Shot.

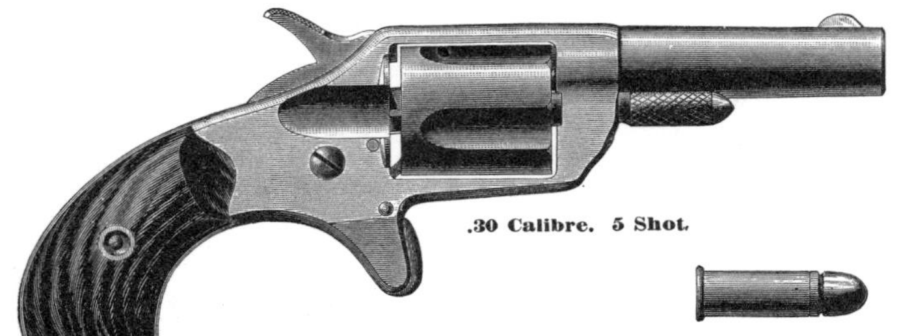

.30 Calibre. 5 Shot.

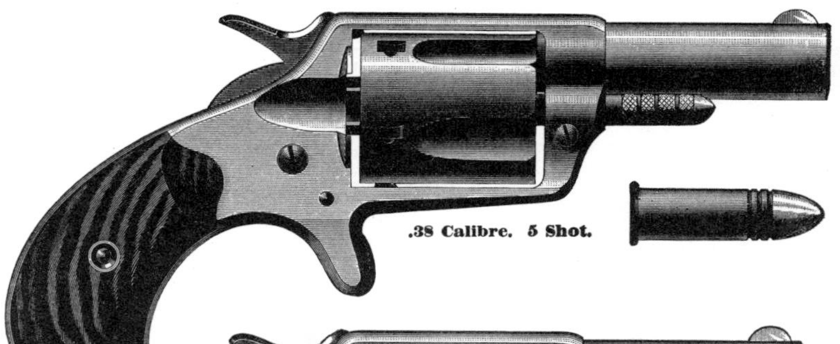

.38 Calibre. 5 Shot.

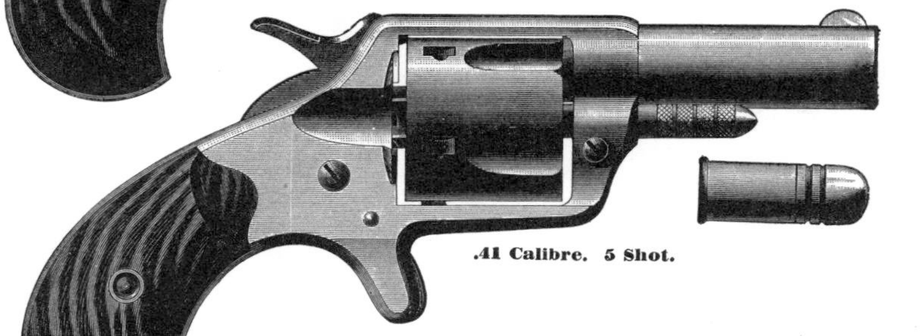

.41 Calibre. 5 Shot.

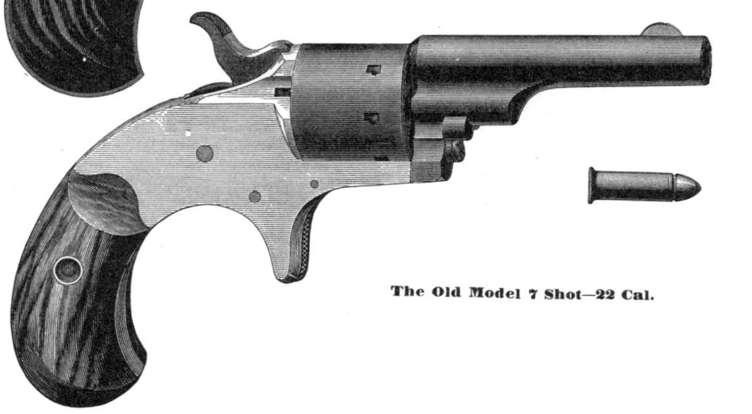

The Old Model 7 Shot—22 Cal.

SPIES, KISSAM & CO.,

279 Broadway, New York.

AGENTS FOR COLT'S FIRE ARMS CO.

The above named firm,who are the agents in New York for the Colt's Armory, have kindly furnished us with the cuts which adorn this page, of the latest style of pocket pistols manufactured and introduced by that famous Company. This new and beautiful arm is called Colt's New Line Solid Frame Revolver. The frames of these pistols are of wrought metal, and are case-hardened, a process which not only gives beauty of finish, but also subjects them to the closest inspection, so that if any imperfection exists it is at once discovered and the defective part condemned, thus rendering every pistol turned out absolutely perfect. All the pistols here represented, carry the long cartridges of appropriate size as well as the short range cartridges used by other revolvers. One of their marked qualities is the superior power of penetration which they possess.

The whole aim of manufacturers of pistols at the present time seems to be the concentration of as much positive value in strength, calibre, penetration and workmanship as possible in the least compass. The name of Colt, having been identified with the manufacture of revolvers since their first successful introduction, and his successors in the business having ever been imbued with the desire to excel, and having made many improvements from time to time on the original arm which rendered its inventor famous, their works need no word of special praise from us. Though many others have engaged in the manufacture of this class of weapons, yet the Colt Company still stands in the front rank.

In addition to those finished by the case-hardening process—which by epicures of mechanical work is considered the most tasteful—we were shown at the warerooms of Messrs. Spies, Kissam & Co., a rare collection of pistols in pearl and ivory stocks, inlaid with gold and silver, richly engraved and otherwise elaborately ornamented. Indeed some of them might very properly be called warlike jewelry.

If space permitted we would be pleased to give our readers a full account of the process of manufacture of these weapons as it could hardly fail to prove both interesting and instructive to the many who have not had an opportunity of visiting the armory of the Colt's Company, but must content ourselves with a very brief summary.

Each different part of the finished weapon is made by men who for years have done nothing but make that special piece. It is only by long, patient and studious practice that the workman can arrive at that perfection of skill which is necessary in the making of every different piece which forms a part of the finished whole. The slightest deviation from the pattern is readily discovered by skillful men whose whole duty is to detect and condemn imperfect work. Machinery as perfect as human skill can devise and construct, attended by men of trained experience, performs a very considerable portion of the work, and the whole is under the superintendance of thoroughly competent men. Case-hardening is one of the well kept secrets of the trade, and the workman who is an adapt in this art is justly proud of his skill.

At the warerooms of Messrs. Spies, Kissam & Co., will be found pistols of all sizes and degrees of finish. Gentlemanly attendants are ever ready to exhibit their treasures to the curious, and to supply customers with an article that will exactly suit them. Their large stock embraces every description of Colt's pistols, plain or as elaborately finished as the most fastidious could desire. We believe we can say that every article they sell will be found as represented, or absolutely perfect, without being accused of partizanship.

THE SHARPS RIFLE COMPANY,

E. G. Westcott, President,

ARMORY & OFFICE, HARTFORD, CONN.

The invention of breech-loading fire-arms dates back to a very remote period, but, to borrow an expression credited to Napoleon III, "Inventions that are before their age, remain useless until the stock of general knowledge comes up to their level."

There is reason to believe that gunpowder was employed in warfare, by the Chinese, more than two thousand years ago, but it does not seem to have become generally known until the latter part of the thirteenth or early in the fourteenth century. We have records of the use of Artillery in European warfare as early as 1327, and of small arms a few years later. The first attempts at improvement were confined to modes of firing, but the old match lock was retained until 1577, when it was superseded by the wheel or German lock. In this lock the rapid rotary motion of a wheel produced sparks which ignited the powder. About 1630 the flint lock was introduced. After this, and until 1840, when the percussion lock was adapted to military muskets, improvements were confined to lessening the weight of small arms and simplifying their mechanism.

Though the method of firing was, in the beginning, generally deemed of the greatest importance, there were those who endeavored to make other improvements, and breech-loading arms and revolvers were made at an early date, as is amply proved by the fact that among the relics of the past preserved in the *Musee dè Artillerie*, in Paris, is a breech-loading gun of the time of Henry II, prior to 1550, and a match-lock revolver of the same period. These inventions, however, were in advance of their times.

The honor of the successful introduction of breech-loading fire-arms, and of revolvers and repeating arms belongs to our own country, and we might say to our own times. In 1811 the United States Government issued its first patent for breech-loading fire-arms to one John H. Hall. In 1816 one hundred of these arms were made and issued to a company of riflemen (as indicated by official records) and were, after use for a short time, reported upon favorably. In 1825 two companies of United States troops, stationed at Fortress Monroe, were armed with Hall's rifles and had the same in use in 1827.

It was not until Sharps' Breech Loading Rifles were introduced that the old style of muzzle loaders was visibly affected by the new devices. This arm at once sprang into popular favor, and as early as 1850 it was generally conceded to be the best arm in use. In those days we had no railroads in our out-lying territories, and that vast chain that now links ocean to ocean was scarcely deemed possible by any but enthusiasts. Emigration was rapidly pushing westward, but as it advanced must fight for right of way. None of our American readers who have arrived at middle manhood can forget the stirring times when contending factions wrestled for supremacy on our then western border, nor will they forget that a Sharps Rifle was considered as of first importance in the outfit of the settlers in Kansas or Nebraska, while the man who would venture an overland journey to California, without such a companion, even though he formed one of a party of hardy frontiersmen, each of whom was well armed, would have been deemed insane or a fool.

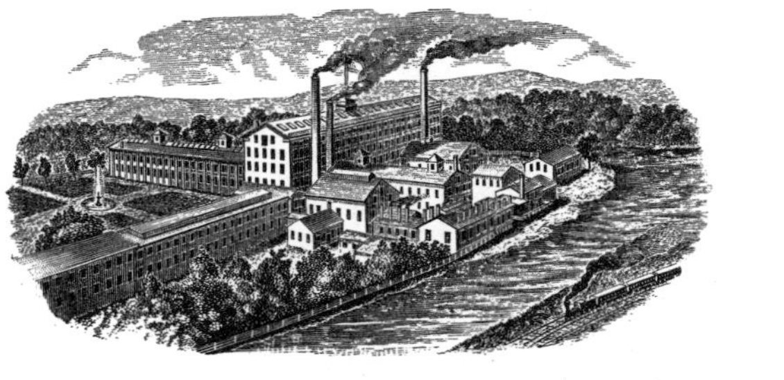

Armory of The Sharps Rifle Company.

Sharps' Rifle was introduced at a peculiarly favorable time; first, because the condition of affairs then demanded a perfect arm; and second, because filling the want, it was enabled to easily acquire the fame its merits warranted, and take a leading position among weapons of its class, a position which it still retains. Many different styles of breech-loaders have been made since the introduction of Sharps', but none have wrested from it one whit of the confidence which warriors, hunters and gentlemen sportsmen first reposed in it. Since the days of its first introduction it has been the aim of the owners of the patents under which it is made, to improve; in which they have been entirely successful, and though the original arm was deemed perfect, the present one is as far ahead of the original as it was then ahead of the old style of muzzle-loaders.

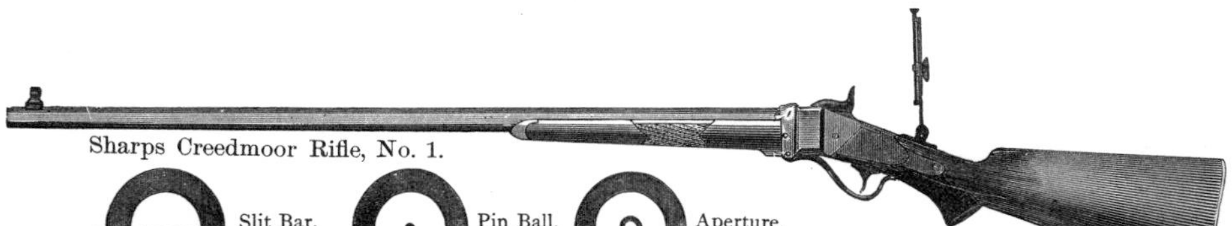

Sharps Creedmoor Rifle, No. 1.

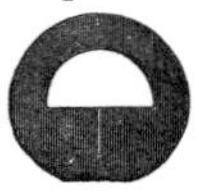

Slit Bar.

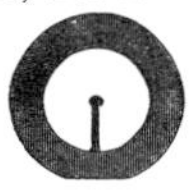

Pin Ball.

Aperture.

With the introduction of machinery the production of fire-arms has been much cheapened, as have all other manufactures to which this method has been applied. The Sharps Rifle Company in their extensive works at Hartford, Connecticut, have gathered together every machine and labor-saving contrivance that a liberal outlay of capital could purchase or construct, with the view of securing the utmost perfection in their productions, in regard to certainty and accuracy of action and lightness and gracefulness of form. The extent to which machinery is made to do the work which but a few years since could only be performed by human hands is one of the marvels of the age. Many articles which under the old system of manufacture were so expensive that only the wealthy could purchase, have, by this means, been so cheapened that those of very moderate means can now afford them. Not only has the introduction of machinery greatly cheapened the cost of production, but it has added immeasurably to the uniform accuracy of the articles produced. In no branch of industry has the effect of the introduction of machinery been more marked than in the manufacture of fire-arms, and probably no armory in the world is better supplied with ingenious labor-saving appliances than that of the Sharps Rifle Company. Skilled workmen who have matured in this Company's extensive establishment tend the unthinking machines and perform the manual labor necessary. After every process through which each separate part of the finished arm is passed it is critically examined by experts before it is accepted, and the whole establishment is supervised by men of many years experience.

When we take into consideratian the fact that the immense success which attended the first introduction of Sharps' Rifles, stimulated invention to such a degree, as to almost flood the land with new breech-loading arms, each of which, of course, claimed to be the best; and that the patent office at Washington has issued letters patent for over one thousand designs, either as original conceptions of or improvements in breech-loading systems, the fact that Sharps' Rifle still maintains its prestage—is, of itself proof of its superiority. Most of the new inventions utterly failed to stand the first really practical test, viz: continued use in the hands of the military, or of hunters and frontiersmen, and have long been forgotten. Others possessed some merit and are sometimes mentioned. But Sharps' Rifle after having been submitted to every test that experts in the trial of fire-arms could suggest, and better than that,an unblemished record of twenty-five years,still occupies the place it first assumed in the front rank of the breech-loading rifles of the world. If the same degree of inventive genius and mechanical skill which has marked the many improvements made in this arm under the auspices of the present manufacturers, is continued in the future, and that they will be none can doubt, we see no reason why the Sharps Rifle of the coming time should not fully maintain the leading position which it gained on its first introduction, and has since held against all competitors. Sharps' Rifles never shoot backward! For safety, accuracy simplicity and penetration, combined with excellence of workmanship they stand unsurpassed.

Those desirious of further information should send for an illustrated catalogue, which will more fully convey to the mind of the reader the many points of marked superiority which is possessed by this arm, than we can possibly do in the limited space at our disposal.

The Company have agents in all the principal cities of the Union, and their arms have been extensively introduced in foreign lands and may be purchased in all the European capitals.

ACTUAL SIZE OF CARTRIDGES.

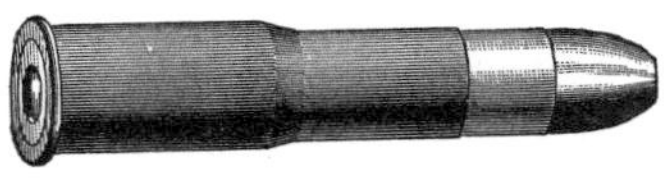

$\frac{40}{100}$ Calibre, 50 grains Powder.

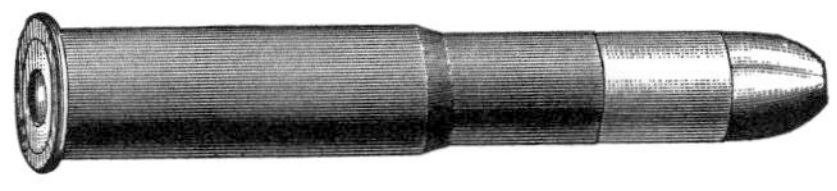

$\frac{44}{100}$ Calibre, 70 grains Powder.

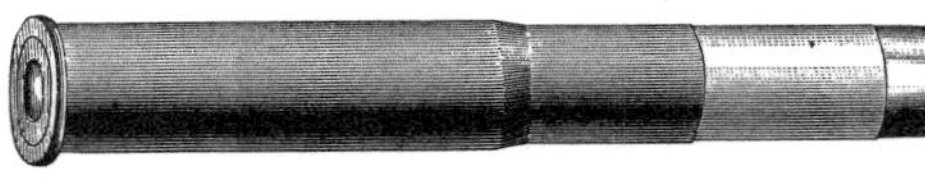

$\frac{44}{100}$ Calibre, 95 grains Powder.

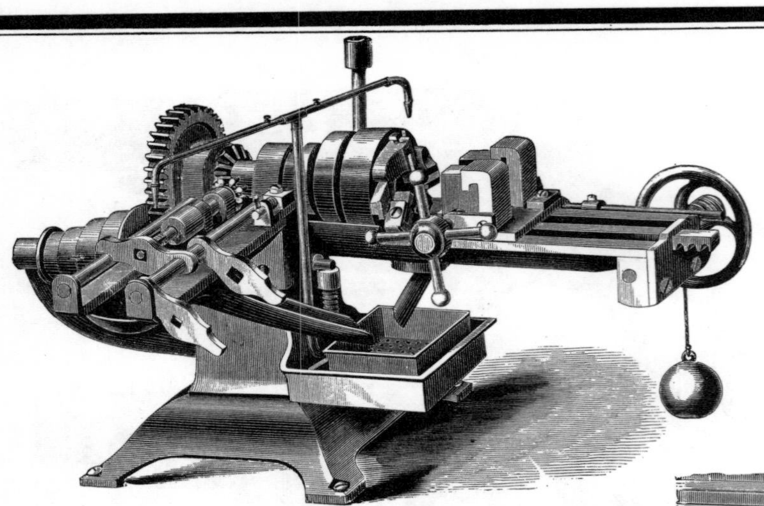

Schlenker's Revolving Die Automatic Bolt Cutter and Nut Tapping Machine.

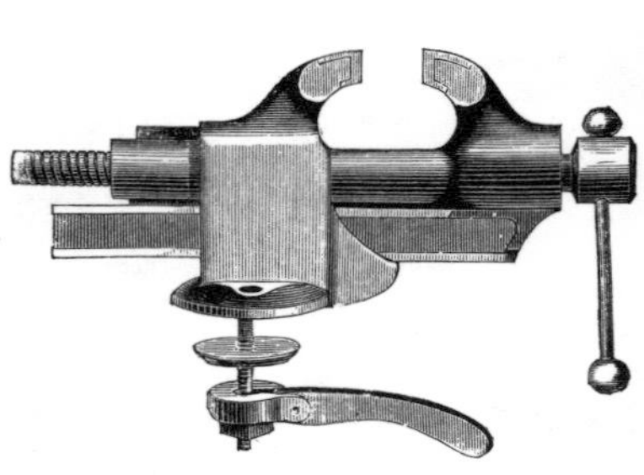

Howard Parallel Bench Vise.

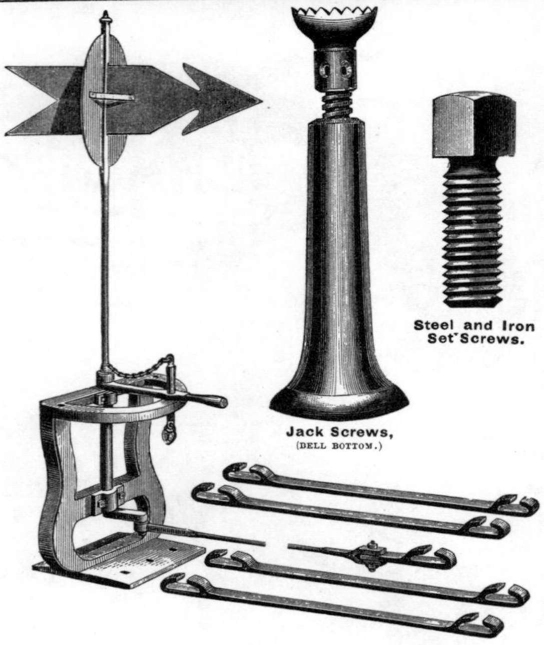

Steel and Iron Set Screws.

Jack Screws, (BELL BOTTOM.)

Railway Switch Stands.

HOWARD IRON WORKS, BUFFALO, N. Y.

R. L. Howard & Son., Proprietors.

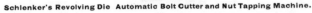

These works are owned and operated by General R. L. Howard & Son, who make a specialty of all kinds of iron work, engines, boilers, railroad frogs, switches and all railroad supplies, bark mills and tannery fixtures, jack and set screws, besides general job work, coach makers' vises, bolt cutters, elevators, &c. The works front on Chicago street, corner of Granger street on one side, and the Hamburg canal on the other. They are divided in the centre, which enables them to ship machinery, &c., with great facility. Prominent among their productions is the Bolt Cutting and Nut Tapping machine above represented, a recent invention of Mr. Erhard Schlenker, Sup't. of the Howard Iron Works. There are some 600 of his former Bolt Cutters in use in the best machine shops in the country, but we believe he has now made his *master piece* in the way of a Bolt Cutter. It is very simple and durable, and the work is performed with rapidity and excellence. The dies are opened and closed automatically, and can be changed quickly without removing a nut, bolt, or pin. The oil is pumped by an automatic pump, and is strained and used continuously without unnecessary waste. Nuts are tapped by this machine, which may be operated by any boy, tapping nuts and cutting bolts at the same time, with the same machine and the same power. It is claimed and acknowledged by the most skillful mechanics in the country, to be the best machine of its kind ever made, and must come into general use in all machine shops, where good work is required to be done with great rapidity. They also manufacture the Stationary Dies as usual.

This firm also manufacture their justly celebrated elevator, which has a safety lock on the counter poise, so that if the rope should break it is at once locked; the gearing is inside the drum, which revolves and over which the rope runs. Their elevators and hoisting machines have been placed in many buildings in all the important cities, and have given great satisfaction.

They are the owners of several very important improvements in apparatus of this kind, having spared no expense to possess themselves of every device which would aid them in attaining noiseless movement and perfect safety.

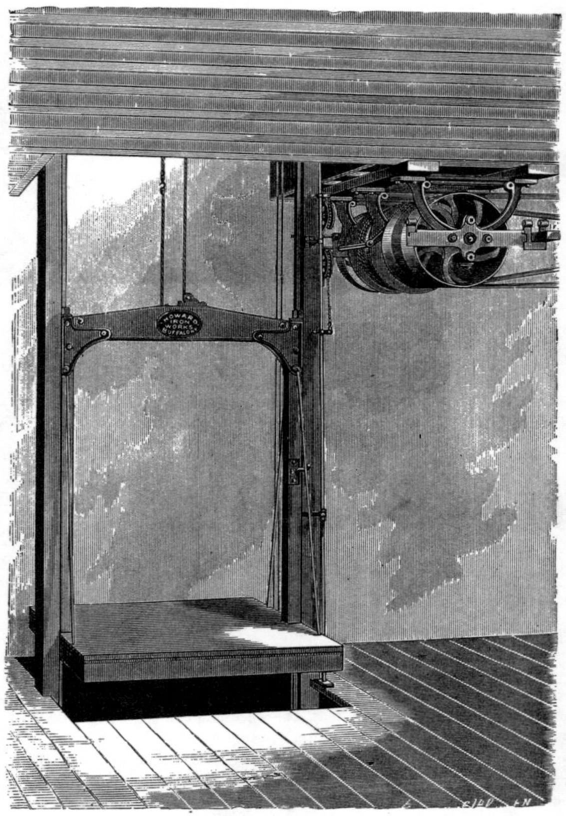

Howard Gear Hoisting Machine with Safety Attachment.

Hand Hoisters and Hoisters either for hand or power, and instantly changeable from one to the other, are manufactured by this firm.

Messrs. Howard & Son have had great experience in parallel bench vises, and seeing the need of some improvements, have succeeded in attaining them in their Vise illustrated in the above cut. They can now recommend it to the public, and it may be obtained either in iron or steel.

Our readers are referred to the catalogue of Messrs. R. L. Howard & Son, for a more full description of these and the other machinery which they manufacture extensively. It will be forwarded to any address.

General Howard, the senior partner, is an old resident of the City of Buffalo, and a very liberal and enterprising man. He was formerly engaged in the manufacture of mowing and reaping machines, but for the last ten years has made the present class of work his study, and consequently the firm make first-class work, which cannot be excelled anywhere.

The foundry is 165x40 feet, with two cupolas with capacity of 20 tons of iron per day. The blacksmith shop is 32x40 feet. There are cleaning and store rooms, also the room where the vises are made. Their engine is very fine, the invention of Mr. Schlenker, their Superintendent, a most ingenious and valuable mechanic; it is 24x40 inch cylinder; also two tubular boilers. The whole works cover an area of 525 feet by 100.

The firm transmit power to a tower which contains machinery constructed to drive a propeller wheel for pumping water into the canal; it is operated by a wire rope ½ an inch thick and 1,200 feet long; this runs at the rate of 36 miles an hour, and gives 65 horse-power.

All the machinery and castings turned out by this firm are of very superior quality.

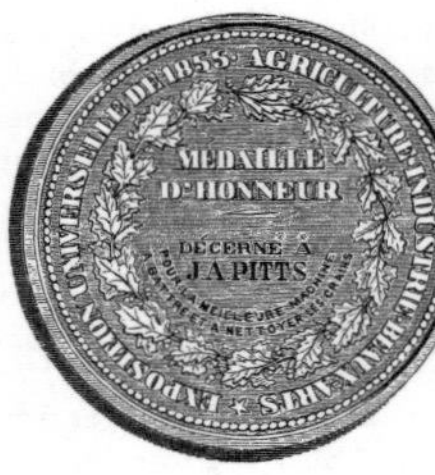

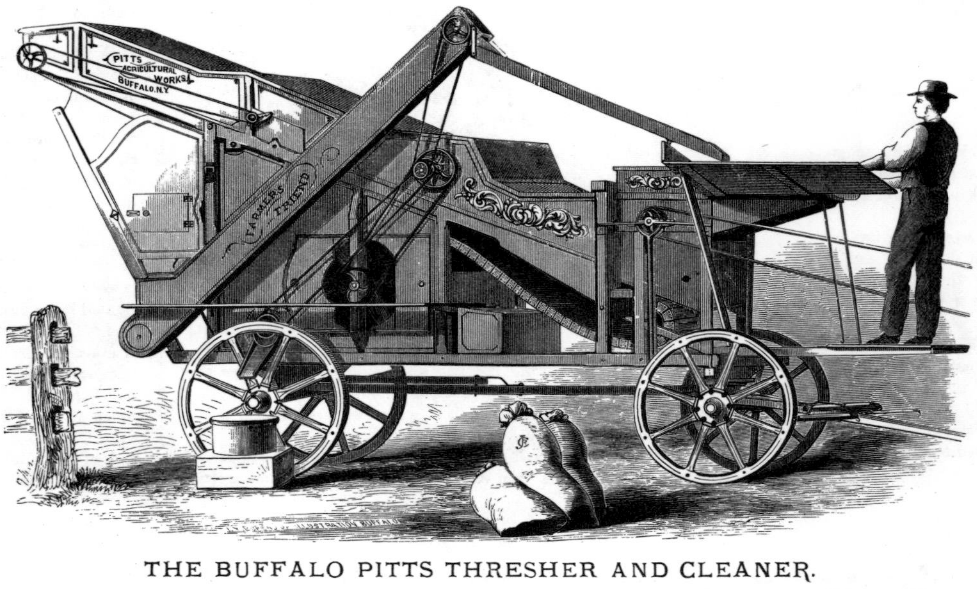

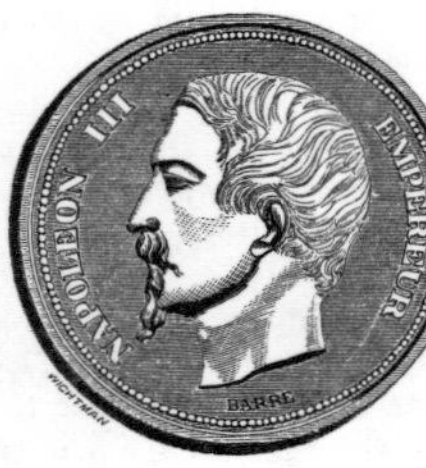

THE BUFFALO PITTS THRESHER AND CLEANER.

THE PITTS AGRICULTURAL WORKS,

JAMES BRAYLEY, Proprietor.

In a large portion of the world the primitive or simplest implements of husbandry are still retained. The plow now used generally in the Roman States, and indeed throughout Italy, is but a slight improvement on that used there two thousand years ago. In many countries the cereal crops are still harvested with a sickle, and the grain threshed, or rather tramped out, by horses and oxen.

The laborious method of threshing by flail was common until a comparatively recent period, and many of our readers will vividly remember the time, when, with the dawning of light on a winter morn, they repaired to the paternal barn to thresh. There was merry music in the well-timed strokes of the flail, and its use for a limited time was a healthful exercise, peculiarly adapted to the development of the muscles of the arm, but when one followed it day after day for weeks or months, it became excessively fatiguing, and the last flooring was always gladly welcomed.

Threshing finished, "cleaning up" commenced; a slow and laborious process. The time was, even in this country, when the mixed husks and grain were separated by throwing them up in the air, a shovelful at a time, trusting to the wind to blow the chaff away—and in some countries this primitive method is still followed—but winnowing machines or farming mills were soon invented and very generally adopted.

No mechanical inventions have so much aided in the development of the resources of our country as those relating to labor saving agricultural machinery, and in no department of manufacture has more rapid advancement been made. Prominent among the many labor saving machines for farmers' use is the Buffalo Pitts Thresher and Cleaner.

During the days of the old system of flail threshing, eight bushels of grain was considered a good days work for a man. Then followed the labor of cleaning up, which was not inconsiderable. If such processes were in use to-day, it would be simply impossible to market the present grain crops of the country, for the reason that the combined force of all the agricultural laborers in the United States, working steadily from the end of one harvest till the beginning of the next, could scarcely thresh and clean the production. In addition to the immense amount of manual labor saved by threshing machines, they effect a great saving of capital. The construction of all the barns and threshing floors on and in which to beat out the grain by hand, would involve an expenditure of many millions of dollars. In the grain producing regions of the West and Northwest, it is a small farm that has not eighty acres of cereals, while there are scores of farmers who count their acres sown to wheat by thousands, and thousands of others who have hundreds, not to mention the vast areas in barley, rye and oats.

The Buffalo Pitts Threshers and Cleaners may be driven by water, steam or horse power. They are made several different sizes, varying from twenty-four inch cylinder to forty inch cylinder, and will thresh and clean, fit for market, from three hundred to three thousand bushels of grain per day, the capacity of course varying with their size. Those of our readers who are agriculturists need not be told that this celebrated machine is a model of perfection, nor for them need we describe its operation, or note how well it does its work, for its reputation has extended over all this land, and the better class of farmers in foreign countries are not unfamiliar with its many points of merit. Still there are those for whose information we deem it well to state that among the many distinguishing excellencies of the Buffalo Pitts Thresher and Separator, are: It threshes clean; it extracts all the kernels from the head of every straw that passes through it; it does not mash or crack the berry but delivers it in a perfect state; it perfectly separates the grain from the chaff and delivers it in bags ready for market, saving entirely the labor incident to recleaning.

The machines are made of the very best materials, only the finest qualities of iron and steel are used, and the wood work is made of carefully selected woods, free from knots and checks and thoroughly seasoned. Only skilled labor is employed in the construction. Each different part of the machine is made by men who work continuously on that one part, by which the greatest possible degree of accuracy is obtained, and every part of each is an exact duplicate of the corresponding part in every other machine of the same size and class, thus rendering it easy in case of accident to replace the broken part.

Particular attention is paid to making changes necessary to adapt these machines to the grains of foreign countries.

The Pitts Double Pinion Horse Powers were specially invented for use with the threshing machine but are adapted for all purposes for which horse powers can be used. They are manufactured in large quantities at these works, and are in great demand. They are made with the same careful attention that is bestowed upon the thresher, varying in sizes from four to twelve horses. The various parts are all made in duplicate and extras can always be obtained.

Many thousands of the Buffalo Pitts Threshers and Cleaners, and Horse Powers, are in use in all parts of the country. Consequently there is a steady demand for extras or repairs. To meet this demand several parties in different sections of the States have embarked in their manufacture by means of patterns which are taken from genuine castings perhaps, but which are necessarily imperfect. In some cases too, owners of machines, parts of which are worn or broken, take the imperfect pieces to the nearest country foundry and have new castings made from the worn or broken ones. Such repairs, however, can never work true. There is but one way to obtain perfect duplicates, and that is to purchase them direct from the Pitts Agricultural Works or its duly accredited agents.

Mr. Brayley, with a view of assisting those who may need extras has published a neat pamphlet of about forty pages, in which are engravings of every separate part of all the threshing machines and powers manufactured by him; each engraving being numbered. The engravings are followed by lists of the names of the parts, with their numbers and the page upon which the engraving may be found also noted. By reference to this catalogue any one can, without chance of mistake, order the exact article desired, which will be shipped the day on which the order is received, and which, when put in place, will always exactly fit.

As will be seen from our engravings, the Pitts Thresher and Cleaner was awarded the medal of honor at the Paris Exposition, that being but one of the very many awards it has received from Industrial Exhibitions, Institutes and Fairs.

For descriptive circulars, price lists or any further information desired, address James Brayley, Proprietor Pitts Agricultural Works, Buffalo, N. Y.

Buckeye New Model Mower. Front View.

THE BUCKEYE MOWER AND REAPER,

Manufactured by

Adriance, Platt & Co., 165 Greenwich St., New York.

Manufactory, Poughkeepsie, N. Y.

Buckeye Harvester Mower, on Uneven Ground.

Buckeye Harvester Reaper. Rear View.

The vast extent of our territory, and the scarcity of laborers to develope its agricultural resources called into activity the inventive genius of Americans, which seems to have culminated in the machines represented on this page. It must be conceded that mowing and reaping machines are really of American origin.

The first American patent for a reaping machine was granted in 1833, fourteen years before the introduction of the first practical mowing machine. Like all other new inventions, these machines, while to a certain extent involving correct principles, were very imperfect in their application. Want of the power of adaptation to irregular surfaces, forbade their introduction where they were most needed.

The first machine that would work equally well on uneven and level ground was the Buckeye, introduced in 1857.

Two important original features, peculiar to the Buckeye machines, are two driving wheels, and a double jointed folding bar. The great value of these unique features will be fully appreciated by all who have used machines with a single driving wheel or a rigid cutting bar. When this bar is folded over on to the machine the weight is evenly balanced, and resting firmly and securely, is unaffected by any jarring in traveling over rough roads.

This machine was first brought prominently before the public at the Great National Field Trial at the United States Agricultural Society, held at Syracuse in 1857.

Only twenty-five Buckeye Mowers were built in 1857, but the success achieved at the Syracuse Trial gave them a notoriety, which induced the manufacturers to build fifteen hundred for the next harvest. Manufactories were soon established in different parts of the country, and machines turned out in greatly increased numbers; but the demand was constantly in advance of the supply and the sale has increased from twenty-five machines to thirty thousand in a single year. Their fame has spread all over the world, and the number in use can be counted by hundreds of thousands.

The Buckeye Self-Raking Reaper is too extensively and favorably known to need any special notice in this connection. The Dorsey principle of Sweep Rakes in which the same arms act as both reel and rake, has been almost universally adopted in all Self-raking Reapers, and this principle has been most perfectly and successfully applied in the Buckeye Machine.

The home demand for the Buckeye machines being so great as to require every available facility of the manufacturers to meet it, no effort was ever made on their part to create a foreign demand, yet the reputation of these machines became so favorable in Europe and other foreign countries that they were compelled to greatly enlarge their manufactories to supply the foreign market.

It has been awarded the highest premiums at the great National Field Trials in Germany, Holland, Norway, Sweden, Belgium, Prussia, Finland, Switzerland and in all parts of the United States.

Buckeye Mower on the Road.

Buckeye New Model Mower. Rear View.

Buckeye Harvester Reaper. Front View.

RUTH gleaning in the fields of Boaz, obtaining barely enough Grain for individual necessities.

THE CROOKED SICKLE. By systematic and hand labor small quantities of Grain were harvested by working from dawn to dark.

THE CRADLE. By which the farmer was enabled to raise small quantities of Grain for market.

A REAPING MACHINE, crude, rough, heavy and incomplete, but the dawning of a New Era in raising Grain.

The Johnston Harvester Company's Wrought Iron Mower.

THE JOHNSTON HARVESTER COMPANY'S

Contribution to the Progress of the Country.

Manufactory, Brockport, N. Y.

—:o:—

The earliest known reaping instrument of which we have record is the Sickle, which is still in common use in many parts of the Old World. When it was invented and introduced is not known, but that it was at a very early date is amply proven by the fact that it is mentioned in Hebrew legends and the Christian scriptures. That the sickle of the ancients was similar in shape to the sickle of modern times, and that it was used by hand only and not as part of a machine, is evident from the bas reliefs upon old Egyptian buildings and tombs where reapers are represented using sickles, some with smooth and others with serrated edges. In the "Gallery of Egyptian Antiquities," in the British Museum, London, England, two of

The Johnston Harvester Company's Wrought Iron Harvester.

these ancient Egyptian iron sickles, very much rusted, are on exhibition.

In the days when Ruth gleaned in the field of Boaz, and "Boaz commanded his young men, saying: Let her glean even among the sheaves, and reproach her not: And let fall also some of the handfuls of purpose for her and leave them, that she may glean them, and rebuke her not," the standing grain was cut by sickles. The most expert reaper with the sickle, would hardly fail, as he grasped the straw within his hand preparatory to cutting, to leave some ungathered, and yet, though Boaz commanded the reapers to "let fall also some of the handfuls of purpose for her," and though "she gleaned in the field until even, and beat out what she gleaned:" her gain was only "about an ephah of barley." An ephah is equal to three pecks, three and a quarter pints.

The first real improvement on the sickle was the cradle. Cradling is perhaps not less laborious, but it is a much more rapid process. The time was, and not very long ago, when as harvest time approached, expert cradlers were in great demand at wages from 50 to 100 per cent. higher than was paid for other farm labor, and the man who could cut three or four acres of average grain a day was considered a first-class man. In harvesting with the sickle, several cuttings of grain are laid upon each other until sufficient for a sheaf is obtained, when it is bound together generally by the cutter, though where many reapers are working in the same field the binding is sometimes done by others. When the cradle is used the grain is smoothly laid in a straight line and the cradler is followed by a raker and binder. By neither of these methods could one-tenth of the present grain crops of America be harvested.

Attempts were made as early as the first century to reap by machines, but from the descriptions of them handed down, they were so cumbersome, and from their imperfect method of operation so wasteful, that they were no improvement on the time-honored sickle. They would reap a field in less time, but the loss of grain more than counterbalanced the loss of time.

As early as 1799 a patent for a reaping machine was issued in England, and on May 17, 1803, a patent was granted to Richard French and J. T. Hawkins of New Jersey, but it was not until much later that a really effective reaper was produced.

In the great grain growing states of the Union, as the harvest time approaches the farmer begins to canvas the cities and villages for help, not to cut, but to bind and stack his crop. Lumbermen leave their mills and rafts, and mechanics their shops to supply the demand.

With a good team, a driver and a Johnston Self-Raking Harvester, the farmer of to-day can cut as much grain as half a dozen cradlers of a few years ago, and more than twice as much as was cut by the crude machines which marked the dawn of a new era in harvest labor.

The beautiful engravings on this page fairly illustrate perhaps the most important advancement that the world has made. Important not only in the manual labor saved to the agriculturist, but because it has directly benefitted every other class of people, in limiting the cost of the very staff of life—our daily bread. No men who ever lived are more entitled to honor for their good works than are the original inventors and improvers, and the manufacturers of modern harvesting machinery. Prominent among these is the Johnston Harvester Company, of Brockport, New York. Their machines have been long and favorably known to the farming public. Upon the first introduction of the Johnston Harvester, it received the unqualified endorsement of agriculturists generally, and soon became very popular; but the Company were not satisfied to rest upon their first successes. From year to year they have improved it, their desire being, if such a thing is possible, to make a machine absolutely perfect in all its parts. There is in the United States a large number of reaper manufacturers, and a score or more of large and wealthy firms, each of whom are constantly striving for supremacy; bearing this in mind, when we say that in 1874, at the most important public trial of reaping machinery held in the United States, the

The Johnston Harvester Company's Self Raking Single Reaper.

Johnston Reaper took the gold medal as shown above, the reader will be enabled to judge how near this Company have reached the goal of their ambition. In Europe, during the same year, (1874,) these machines were awarded nearly thirty first prizes, and in 1875 they were successful beyond all precedent.

The Johnston Harvester Company's Wrought Iron Harvester, and the one at the bottom of the page, (the Self Raking Single Reaper) have been pitted against every machine manufactured in the world and with the most astonishing success, carrying the palm from every field in Europe and wherever in America it could get a chance to compete. It lays a square and handsome gavel and will descend to the ground saving all the lodged and tangled grain. It is also very durable, runs without noise, and may be said to be the perfection of harvesting machinery.

The engraving between the medals represents the excellent and beautiful machine for cutting grass, built by this Company. It will secure and

The Johnston Harvester Company's Self Raking Reaper and Mower.

save the worst lodged and prostrate grass and clover. Runs easy and being made of wrought iron is very durable and strong.

The Self Raking Reaper and Mower combined, is a machine eminently adapted to the wants of the moderate farmer who requires one machine to do both haying and harvesting. It has been demonstrated on the fields of Europe and America to be as complete and successful a combined machine as any in the world. Made of wrought iron and steel of the best qualities, will work in either grass or grain as satisfactory as a separate machine. It has been awarded the highest premiums ever given and is exceedingly popular wherever it has been used.

In the manufacture of the various machines turned out by the Johnston Harvester Company, the utmost care is taken to secure perfect workmanship, and only the best of materials are used, and the farmer who purchases from them always obtains something durable.

One of the peculiar features of the Johnston machines, one which first gave prominence to the Johnston system of Raking is the facility with which they pick up and save lodged and tangled grain. They have even at trials successfully cut and saved grain that had been pressed down flat to the earth with a heavy roller. Their success in various parts of the world and especially in Europe, where they are greatly sought after, is a source of pride to the company that manufacture them, and their pride may well be shared in by their countrymen that the Centennial year of American Independence witnesses American Harvesting Machines the most successful and the most popular of any in the world—and we will add that in the front rank of all stand the various machines of The JOHNSTON HARVESTER COMPANY.

Steel Hoosier Plow.

Hillside Plow.

Improved Pelican Plow.

Globe Steel Cotton Blade.

Hillside Plow.

Colonel Double Shovel Plow.

Cast Road Scraper.

Buzzard Steel Cotton Sweep.

Patent Iron Centre Plow.

Iron Expanding Cultivators.

Dickson Steel Sweep.

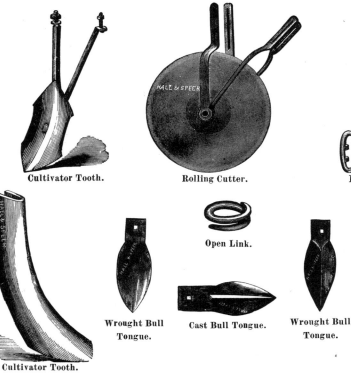

Cultivator Tooth.

Rolling Cutter.

Cast Skuter.

Plow Clevis, Wro't.

Open Link.

Cultivator Tooth.

Wrought Bull Tongue.

Cast Bull Tongue.

Wrought Bull Tongue.

Cultivator Tooth.

Iron Rail Road Colter Plow.

Soil and Sub-Soil Plow.

Centre Lever Plow.

Steel Sweep.

Hillside Plow.

Captain Double Shovel Plow.

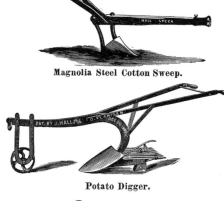

Wood Road Scraper.

Magnolia Steel Cotton Sweep.

Potato Digger.

Lone Star Steel Cotton Plow.

Steel Shovel.

Pittsburgh Globe Plow Works.

ALEXANDER SPEER & SONS,

Successors to HALL & SPEER,

PLOWS,

Plow Castings and Cultivators,

PITTSBURGH, PA.

On some of the ancient monuments of Egypt are graven representations of the plows in use at the period of their erection, and probably of the first devices for plowing ever used. The figures sometimes represent a plow formed of a crotched limb of a tree, and sometimes the body and root of a sapling; the part entering the ground is always represented as sharpened, a beam to draw by is generally, but not always, shown, and a handle to guide or hold it in place, the latter, in case there is a drawing beam, being generally a separate piece of wood bound to the other with thongs of leather or tough twigs.

Though wooden plows, made of three sticks—the beam, the handle, which is a crooked stick set into the beam, the lower end forming the share or digging point, and a brace connecting the two,—are still in use in Palestine, plows made of iron were evidently in use at a very early day. The earliest writers, sacred and profane, speak of plows as a well known instrument of husbandry, and frequently illustrate their meaning by reference to plows and plowing. *Job*, writing 1520 years before Christ, says: "They that plow iniquity and sow wickedness, reap the same," *Job* iv, 4. Solomon, 1000 years B. C., says: "The plowing of the wicked is sin." *Proverbs* xxi, 4. These quotations would have had equal force, of course, if there had been no plows but those made entirely of wood, but the prophet Joel, 800 years before Christ would hardly have used these words, even prophetically,

of plows very expensive. The farmer desired a plow that was light, strong, durable, and cheap, which was eventually furnished them in cast cast-steel.

In no country in the world is so large a number, or so great a variety of plows made as in the United States, for the simple reason that in no other land is there so great a variety of soil, or so much of it, to be plowed; and in no other country has the manufacture of plows attained such perfection as it has here, as is amply evidenced in the fact that American plows carry off the highest prizes in the International Exhibitions where they are practically tested. The Pittsburgh Globe Plow Works, engravings of a few of whose productions form the border surrounding this article, is one of the oldest, largest, most widely and favorably known of the plow manufacturing establishments of the United States, and is a fair representative of Pittsburgh's industrial growth.

The Globe Works were established nearly half a century ago, in the year 1828, by Mr. Samuel Hall. In 1845 he admitted to a cö-partnery interest in the business Mr. Alexander Speer, who had been for a number of years previously a practical worker at the trade, the style of the firm being Hall & Speer. Mr. Hall died in 1852, but the business was continued by Mr. Spear, without any change of proprietory title or interest until 1858, when John S. Hall, son of the founder of the concern, joined Mr. Speer in partnership. During these years the business of the house had grown to large proportions, and their wares were in common use through the South and West, while not a few had been shipped East and North, and some to foreign countries,—South America and Cuba. In 1873, Mr. Hall died, but previous to his decease he had disposed of his interest in the concern to Mr. Speer, who admitted his two sons, W. W. and J. T., into an interest in the business which has since been conducted under the firm name of Alexander Speer & Sons, these latter gentlemen, like their father, having been literally brought up to the trade.

Their present works were built and occupied by them

PITTSBURGH GLOBE PLOW WORKS, PITTSBURGH, PA.

if the people of his time would not understand their meaning, and they certainly could not have done so if metal plows had not then been in common use: "Beat your plow shares into swords and your pruning hooks into spears."*Joel* iii, 10. Isaiah, writing forty years later, tells of the coming time when the people "shall beat their swords into plow shares and their spears into pruning hooks," *Isaiah* ii, 4.

A complete history of the plow can never be written, for its use ante-dates all records, nor can we within the limited space at our disposal describe all the improvements in form or modes of manufacture that have been made within the past hundred years; suffice it to say that until quite recently all plows were very imperfect instruments, and that the greatest and the most valuable improvements have been made in this country. Thomas Jefferson, third President of the United States, was one of the early improvers of plows. In a communication to the French Institute he laid down practical and intelligible rules for shaping plows; in 1793 he practically tested his theory by causing several plows to be made after his patterns, which were used on his estates in Virginia.

In 1797 patents were granted to Charles Newbold, a farmer of New Jersey, who made the first cast iron plow; but he was in advance of the time, and after spending upwards of $30,000 in fruitless attempts to popularize it he gave up in despair. Others closely followed in his wake however. Improvements were made in form, but till within the memory of middle-aged men of to-day, wooden mould boards were in common use. Plows made entirely of cast iron succeeded these, then came the substitution of sheet steel, for those parts most liable to wear, the aim being to lessen the weight, but in gritty soils the thin sheet soon wore away, rendering that class

in 1870, and are to-day, in the completeness of their equipment for the prompt and perfect execution of all work belonging to the special line of trade which their proprietors seek to serve, unsurpassed, if indeed equaled, by any in Pittsburgh.

The principal lines of manufacture for which this firm are distinguished are Plows, Harrows, Cultivators Shovel-Plows, Road Scoops, Ice Plows, Railroad Grading Plows, etc., of which we give a number of illustrations, but to describe them would fill a good sized volume. From the cuts and the names beneath them we must leave the reader to draw his own conclusions as to the special purposes for which they are intended and their fitness for the work.

The quality and acceptability of the Plows made at this establishment is certified to by the fact that besides taking the Medal and Diploma at the World's Fair, at Hamburg, Germany, in 1863, and a Medal at the London, England, Exhibition of All Nations, in 1851, they have carried off Gold and Silver Medals and Diplomas at more than thirty State and County Fairs, in as many years, in the United States, as well as at the New York Exhibition of All Nations in 1855. But better than all these is that hearty endorsement of the Farmers of our country, evidenced by a constantly increasing demand for their goods, which proves that their general productions are of the highest quality, made of the best materials and in a workmanlike manner, else, in the face of strong competition their business would decay, instead of making steady growth. All the manufacturing operations are conducted under the personal supervision of the proprietors.

Strangers visiting Pittsburgh will find it very interesting to pay Messrs. Alexander Speer & Sons' Works a visit, as they take great pleasure in showing strangers through their immense establishment.

Dickson Steel Sweep.

Pea Vine Knife.

Black Land Plow.

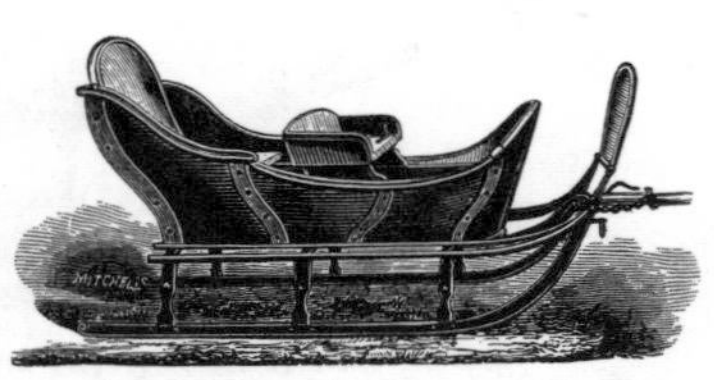

1816—THE SLEIGH OF THE PERIOD—1816.

ESTABLISHED 1813.

——:o:——

THE ALBANY COACH MANUFACTORY

——:o:——

JAMES GOOLD & CO.,

Manufacturers of

FINE CARRIAGES AND SLEIGHS,

Division, Union and Hamilton Sts., Albany, N Y.

——:o:——

Albany, which is at once the Capital of the State of New York and of Albany county, differs from most of the Capitals of the States in being a manufacturing centre of great importance. The last United States census returns show that there were in the county seven hundred and twenty-one manufacturing establishments of various kinds with a capital of $16,031,268, affording employment to 14,495 hands whose yearly pay roll amounts to about $6,000,000, the products being valued in round numbers at $25,000,000. There are eleven counties in the State which contain a greater number of manufacturing establishments, but in eight of these counties fewer hands are employed; New York, embracing the city of that name, Kings, which takes in Brooklyn, the second largest city in the State, and Rensselaer, which is only divided from Albany by the Hudson River, being the counties that employ a greater number. Four counties—Erie, which includes Buffalo, the third largest city in the State, Kings, New York and Renselaer, return products of greater value than Albany county, but only two of these, Kings and New York have as large a capital invested in manufactures, and they are the only ones that pay out a larger amount ot money in wages. Thus Albany judged by the amount of capital invested and the wages paid, is fairly entitled to rank as the third manufacturing county of the Empire State.

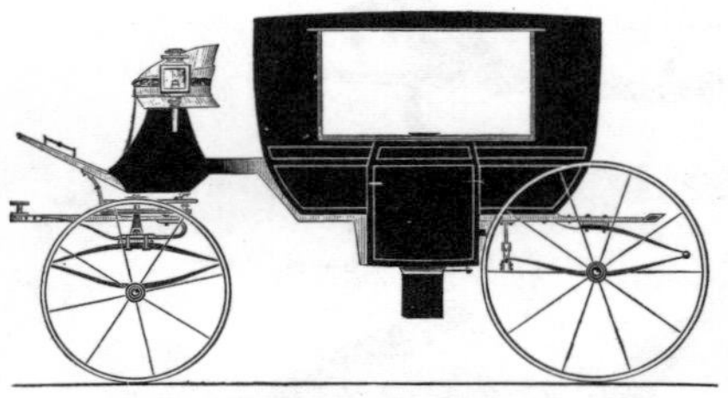

DRAWING ROOM COACH, [open].
Patented.

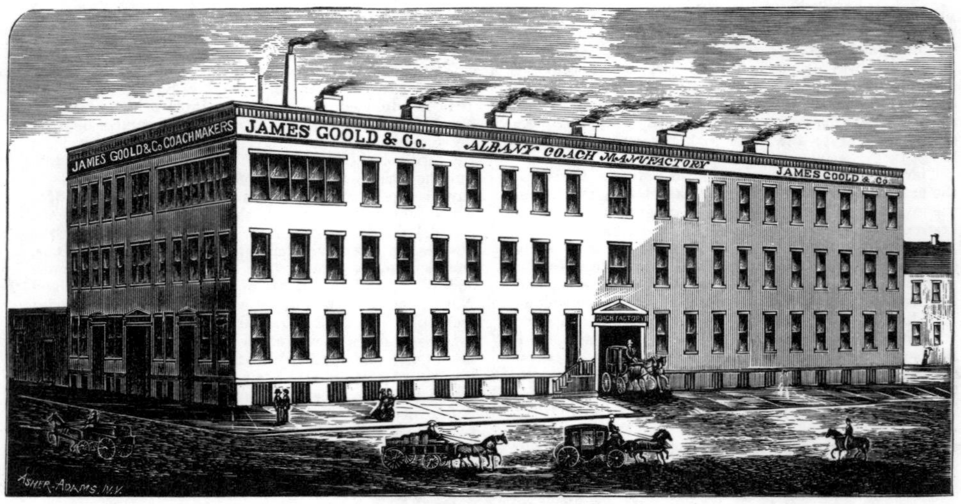

CARRIAGE MANUFACTORY OF JAMES GOOLD & CO.,
ALBANY, N. Y.

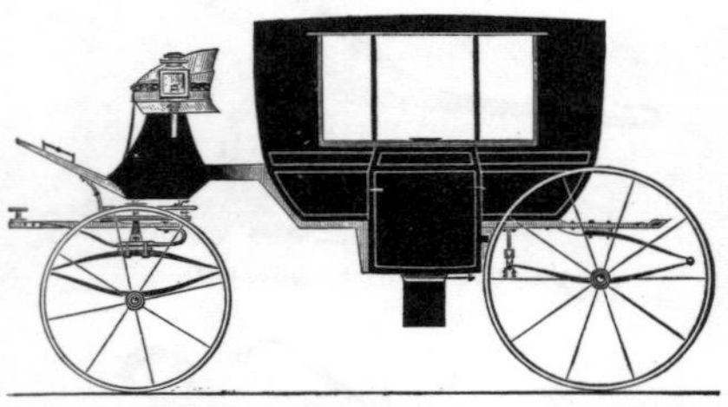

DRAWING ROOM COACH, [closed].
Patented.

It is not our intention in this article to sketch the progress of general manufactures in Albany (to do that we would be compelled to begin with its first settlement by the Dutch traders who, within a year after Hendrick Hudson first ascended the river, in 1609, had built themselves huts and began the business of buying skins from the Indians and established the industry of curing them, and preparing the furs for shipment to the old country, and trace it through the intervening two hundred and sixty-six years to the present time; the task is too great, we cannot undertake it,) but to briefly notice one of the largest and oldest established carriage manufactories, in the United States which is located here.

The Albany Carriage Manufactory was established in 1813 by James Goold, a native of New England, who had previously acquired a practical knowledge of carriage building in Pittsfield, Massachusetts, as an apprentice with the late Jason Clapp, and, after attaining his majority, as a fellow workman, for a season, in a shop in New Haven, Connecticut, with the late James Brewster, who in later years divided the honors with his contemporary, Jason Clapp, of Pittsfield, of being the most prominent carriage builders in the New England States.

For several years after its establishment the business of the Albany Coach Manufactory, as it was then commonly called, was conducted by Mr. Goold alone; afterwards, for a series of years in connection with his nephew, Mr. W. R. Bush, and son-in-law, Mr. J. N. Cutler, and later, with his son, Mr. John S. Goold. Mr. John S. Goold died in 1873; since then, with the aid of his grandson, Mr. John Chester Goold who is now a partner and the active manager of the business.

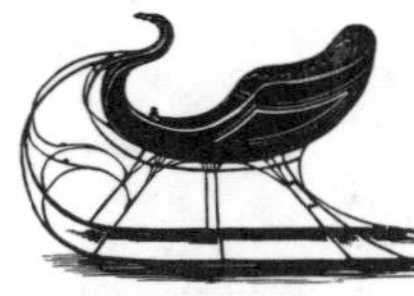

CUTTER. No. 1.

Mr. James Goold, in his younger days was a man in advance of the times; he was not content to merely keep pace with the demands of the public, and to build vehicles such as others built; his aim was to improve on the styles then in vogue, to preserve all the strength, but to design more graceful forms, and make them lighter but equally durable. The design and construction of Pleasure Sleighs, which previous to his improvements had presented a very unseemly appearance, as is amply testified to by the engraving of "The Sleigh of the Period—1816," at the top of this page, early engaged the attention of Mr. Goold, and has since been pursued as a special feature of his business. He has introduced many new designs, (more, perhaps than any other manufacturer) and each new form has been an improvement on the older ones, until the sleighs of the present time, as built at this establishment, are models of grace in form, beautiful in finish, and of world-wide reputation. Some of these designs are patented and are manufactured by no other maker; others are not thus protected, and are consequently used as models for others to build from. The production of this establishment embraces every description of pleasure sleigh from the diminutive Cutter to the largest sizes both open and closed.

From 1817 to 1831 the building of Stage Coaches for the mail service of the United States was prosecuted as an important branch of the business. Few of our readers whose recollections do not extend back to the time when all the mails were carried and most of the traveling done by Stage Coaches, have any idea of the immense number of such vehicles that were built every year. A number of large establishments were engaged in their construction affording employment to thousands of skilled mechanics, and necessitating the investment of large capital. It was, indeed, one of the leading industries of the country. But the grand onward march of improvement has changed all this, and though there is still a demand for stage coaches on the Western frontier, and in the older States even, a few are still used for transporting mails and passengers from railroad stations to interior villages, they are essentially a thing of the past. During the palmy days of Stage Coaching, Mr. Goold was one of the foremost builders, foremost alike in the quantity and qualtity of his productions. With the introduction of railroads, however, the demand for Stage Coaches declined, but a new, and as it has since proved a much larger branch of industry filled its place, the building of Railroad Cars.

Mr. Goold at once entered the new field of operations and in 1831 constructed the cars for the old Mohawk and Hudson River Railroad, running between Albany and Schenectady, by many claimed to have been the first Steam Railway in the United States, surely the second, and the first in the Northern States. The first cars were really coaches in shape and general appearance. The present style of long cars being of more recent date. Thus, the Albany Coach Manufactory instead of suffering a loss of patronage by the withdrawal of stage lines and the introduction of Steam Railroads, as did many of its old competitors, really increased its business, and for the ensuing forty years the building of Cars for Steam and Street Railroads formed an important branch of the business, but only a branch, for during all these years the construction of Carriages and Sleighs was carried

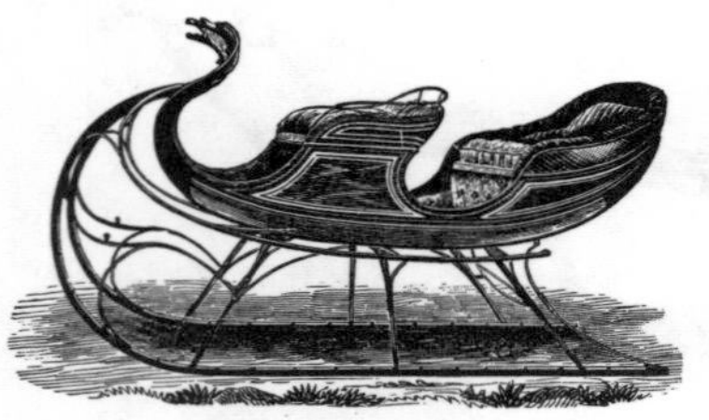

PONY SLEIGH, No. 3.

on with unabated vigor. During this time Cars were made for a number of Railroads in the United States, and Canada, and for several companies operating lines on the East and West coasts of South America.

The favorite line of production, however, was pleasure vehicles, and eventually all other manufactures were abandoned, and all the resources of the establishment were devoted to that branch of the business. Carriages and Sleighs of the best designs, are the only articles manufactured at the Albany Coach Manufactory at the present time, and we believe, that their productions in this chosen line, are not inferior in any respect to any made elsewhere.

To enumerate and describe all the styles of Carriages and Sleighs produced would occupy much more space than we have to spare, suffice it to say that they are numerous, and embrace everything that seems to us to be desirable. All of them are graceful in appearance, elegantly finished, and as light as is compatible with strength. Of the material used in their construction we need not speak, as the long continued success of the establishment is the best attainable proof of the perfection and durability of its work.

In the sixty-three years of its existence the Albany Coach Manufactory has passed through trials and changes by fire, and emerged in 1838 in the commodious and well arranged building represented in the engraving in the centre of this page. Mr. Goold, as we have previously said, when he laid the foundation of this business, early in life, was the possessor of ideas far in advance of the times, and if during all these years of active business life he has not kept ahead, he certainly has not fallen behind any of his competitors. It has been his good fortune to witness many great improvements in his line of business, new and better methods of construction, the introduction of machinery to do most of the heavy work, which in his younger days was done entirely by hand, scores—nay hundreds—of other improvements, and to his honor be it said that he has ever been among the very first to aid in the perfection of and to adopt in his own business all devices which could lighten the labor of his men, and produce as good results as were attained by the old methods. And equally careful has he been not to adopt any device, which in lessening the labor or cost of his productions, would in the slightest degree detract from their merit as perfect work. His constant aim has been (and it also has been the desire of those connected with him in business) to build the best possible vehicles, whether Stage Coaches, Railway Cars, Carriages or Sleighs, and to achieve that end no effort or expense has been or will be spared. The manufactory occupies nearly a square, bounded by Division, Union and Hamilton Streets, and is equipped with everything that can aid in, but contains nothing that can detract from, the excellence of its productions.

The active management of the business of the concern is now committed to the care of Mr. John Chester Goold, grand-son of its founder, who conducts it with the same careful attention that has distinguished his predecessors. It is not uncommon for young men who succeed to the control of an old established and highly esteemed business, to rely more upon the already acquired good name of the house for their success than upon their own effort. In this instance it is not so. It is the aim of Mr. John Chester Goold, not only to fully maintain the high reputation of the establishment and its productions, but, if possible to increase it.

Mr. James Goold, though far advanced in years, is statedly in his office, and continues a general supervision of the business, feeling a deep interest in the perpetuity of his name as connected with the Carriage Building of the United States.

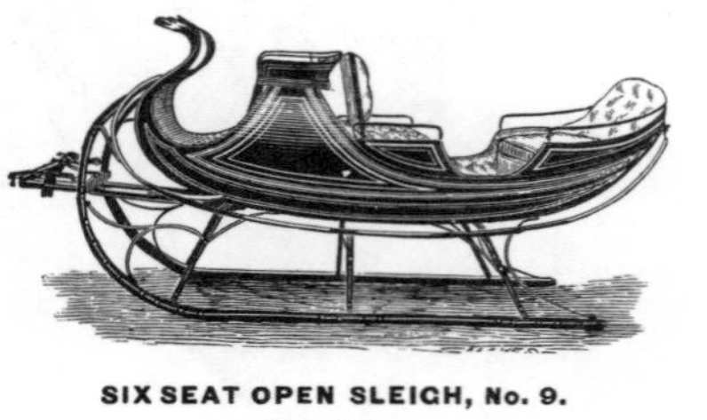

SIX SEAT OPEN SLEIGH, No. 9.
Patented.

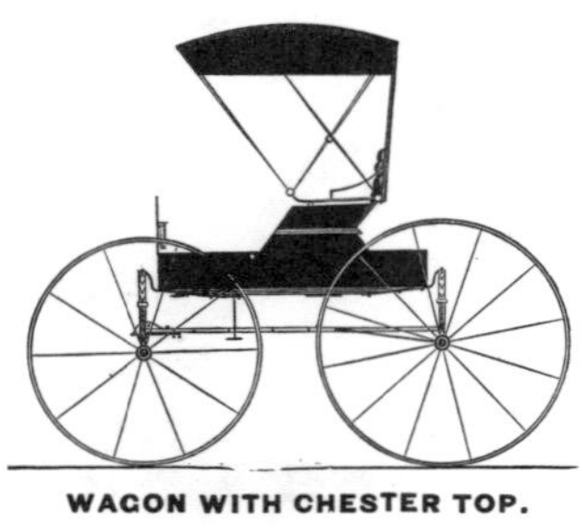

WAGON WITH CHESTER TOP.
Patented.

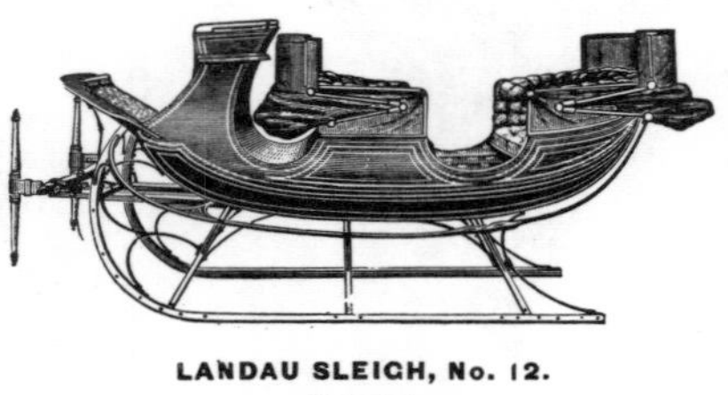

LANDAU SLEIGH, No. 12.
Patented.

Buffet Sideboard Safe, with top.

TRIPLE BANKERS' CHEST.

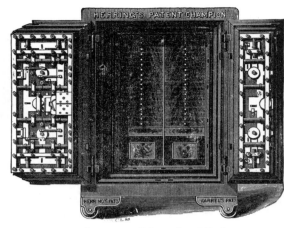

Improved Jewelers' Safe.

HERRING'S PATENT CHAMPION SAFES.

251 Broadway, New York.

It is an old and a true saying, that it is easier to get money than to keep it. The man who wastes his substance by prodigality, or embarks in illegitimate or hazardous enterprises is alone responsible for the losses he may sustain. But he, who through honest industry, frugality and constant application to business, accumulates a fortune, large or small, is bound by the laws of common prudence to secure the same from destruction by fire or from loss by theft.

History tells us that the Mint in the Tower of London, was anciently the depository of merchants' cash, until Charles I, laid his hands upon the money and destroyed the credit of the mint in 1640. The traders were then driven to find some other place of security for their gold, for if left at home, their apprentices or clerks frequently absconded with it to the army. They afterwards lodged it with the goldsmiths in Lombard Street, who were provided with strong chests or safes for their own valuable wares; this became the origin of banks and bank safes in England. But the introduction into this country of anything like a fire proof safe is of a comparatively recent date.

Paradoxical as it may seem, wood, a highly combustible material, afforded the first lining in this country for fire proof (?) safes. But the folly in this is not as great as might at first appear, as it is well known that wood, saturated with certain compounds, and protected from the atmosphere, to prevent igniting, is a very poor conductor of heat. Experience soon proved, however, that this was an unreliable protection against the ravages of fire.

The first substitute for wood for this purpose was plaster of paris or cement. It would be interesting here to narrate the manner in which the process for preparing this material was accidently discovered;

but our space will not admit of this, and we only refer to the discovery for the purpose of introducing the pioneer and most successful manufacturer of fire and burglar-proof safes and vaults in America—the senior member of the firm of Herrings & Farrel.

Although the safes manufactured by this firm have a world wide reputation and stand pre-eminently ahead of all competitors, comparatively few are aware of the rapid improvements made, and the high state of perfection attained in this important and now indispensable branch of industry.

It is but about thirty-five years, since the first safe filled with plaster of paris was manufactured, and that safe may now be seen in the store of Messrs. Herrings & Farrel in New York City.

The plaster of paris safe, or, as it is, perhaps better known, the "Wilder Patent" of 1843, acquired all the good reputation it ever had, through the influence of Mr. Silas C. Herring. It consisted simply of plaster of paris mixed with water; the former having the ability to absorb and retain a large amount of water.

The fiery ordeal to which so many safes were subjected in 1845, in New York and other places, proved the inability of most of them to accomplish the purpose for which they were designed. But the "Herring Salamander" achieved a success which won for it that enviable reputation which it still retains. At that time an increasing rivalry in the manufacture of safes commenced. But improvements were requisite to perfect what had been so well begun, and there was found a man to meet this, as well as all other emergencies. Mr. Herring led the van in these improvements, and has since secured several patents, until he has approximated very near, if he has not actually reached the point of perfection.

It was found that the water used with the plaster of paris, became of itself a destructive element by rusting, and destroying the efficiency of the metal with which it came in contact; hence, a dry safe became indispensable, to prevent rust and mould inside. This, Messrs. Herrings & Farrel have succeeded in securing, and until fire shall exceed its present heating

capacity ten fold it will prey in vain upon Herring's safes.

The demand for increased strength in safes seems to have been anticipated by the manufacturers of the Herring safe, and those now manufactured by this firm, are a marvel for strength as well as beauty of finish.

No cast iron is used on the corners or other parts of the safe exposed to the weight of falling iron, or stone walls as is the case with other safes, but solid, refined wrought iron.

But there is a foe more dangerous than fire to the safety of valuable treasures. The burglar, with a skill and determination worthy of a better purpose, and the constantly increasing facilities for accomplishing his designs, seems to bid defiance to all walls of stone or metal, and ordinary bank locks are to him no barriers.

The quality and reputation of the Herring burglar-proof safe are too well known to need any commendation from us. From the report of the great trial of United States against British safes, at the Paris exhibition in 1867 we learn that Herrings & Farrell's Fire-proof Safe, with Bankers' Chest inside, was the victor. It resisted for four hours and fourteen minutes, actual working time, all the skill and effort that could be brought to bear upon it by two English civil engineers and three picked experts, with the use of wedges, hammers, crow-bars, sledge hammers and other tools, one hundred and one in number, and weighing one hundred and seven and one-quarter pounds; the opportunity for using such tools is seldom enjoyed by burglars. The accompanying cuts clearly represent different views of some of the many varieties of safes manufactured by this firm; also their team of un-rivalled horses, which may be seen daily, pursuing their serpentine course along the crowded thoroughfares of the city, bearing to their destination those perfect safeguards against fire and robbers.

To those who would learn wisdom we will say hide not your treasures in the earth, like the foolish and unprofitable servant, but deposit them in a Herring Safe, where fire cannot consume, "where neither moth nor rust doth corrupt, and where thieves cannot break through and steal."

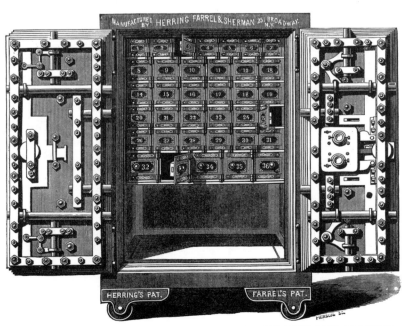

BANKERS' CHEST, CONTAINING SAFE DEPOSIT BOXES.

Patent Champion Safe, with Folding Doors and Double Bankers' Chest.

STEAM STONE CUTTER COMPANY,

Proprietors of Patents and Sole Manufacturers of

Wardwell's Stone Channeling and Quarrying

Machines,

Rutland, Vermont.

——:o:——

The largely increasing demand for stone for building and other purposes, calls for the introduction of labor saving devices, which, while increasing the supply, lowers the cost of production. To this class belong the machines herewith illustrated, which are extensively used for quarrying throughout the country. The following is a description of the Double Gang Machine, as represented mounted upon its track in the bed of the Quarry:—

The frame which supports the boiler, engine, and other machinery, consists of one piece of forged iron, weighing nearly a ton, thus furnishing great strength and durability. The engine is of six horse power; its shaft carrying a balance wheel A on each end, to which is attached an adjustable wrist pin plate. B and F are levers pivoted at their rear ends to the frame at C. The free end of the lever B passes through a sliding stirrup or swivel attached to the wrist pin, (not shown) giving an up and down motion to that end of the lever, as the balance wheel A revolves. The free end of the lower lever F passes through a mortice in back side of lower clamp G. Motion is communicated from the upper to the lower lever, by means of clasps, between which the rubber springs D and E are placed as shown in the engraving. The free end of the lever F actuates the gang of chisels, which consists of five bars of the best cast steel, sharpened at their lower ends, and clamped together by head and foot clamps; the whole sliding freely on the standard. Of the five chisels, two II have diagonal cutting edges, and three have their edges transverse. The middle chisel H extends the lowest, and altogether form a stepped arrangement each way from the centre; thus it will be seen that when the machine is moving forward the front three cutters, which includes the middle one H, operate; while moving in the opposite direction the other two with the middle one, H, perform the work.

The object of the diagonal cutting edges is to insure an even bottom to the channel. These bars of steel are from seven to fourteen feet in length, according to the depth of the channel to be cut. The upper end of these bars are serrated to match corresponding serrations in the head clamp, for the purpose of preventing any displacement of the cutters while in use. J, is a worm on the main shaft and actuates the toothed wheel K. The shaft of the latter extends diagonally downwards to the rear of the machine where it terminates in a bevel pinion; upon the rear axle are placed two beveled gears, one of which is shown in part at L. By means of the lever M, either of these beveled gears may be thrown into action with the pinion. When the machine is required to be stationary, these beveled gears are so placed as not to engage with the pinion. The short lever N, locks these beveled gears in either of the desired positions. The windlasses, OO, on each side of the machine, are for raising the gangs of cutters out of the channels.

The Double Gang Machine is 10 feet long. Three widths are made, respectively, to cut channels 4 feet 1 inch, 6 feet 3 inches, and 6 feet 7 inches apart, and cuts two channels at once. Its weight is four tons; shipping weight with all the fixtures, six tons. The Single Gang Machine is 7 feet long, width 6 feet, and it cuts either vertical or inclined channels down to 45 degrees, and the cutting apparatus with its operating machinery is made adjustable for operating upon either end of the machine, making it a right or left handed machine adapted to cut in all corners. Its weight is two and one-half tons, shipping weight, with fixtures, five tons. The Double Machine has a six horse horizontal boiler and engine, and the Single Machine a five horse vertical boiler and engine, and they are provided with patent lock-up safety valves set to carry eighty pounds of steam. They are supplied with 100 feet of track and a full set of tools and fixtures; the Double Machine with eight, and the Single with four gangs of cutters. They are locomotive and cut moving in either direction, they are reversed without stopping the cutters, and either or both sides of the Double Machine may be operated at pleasure. It requires two men to operate the Single and three men to operate the Double Machine, they use from three hundred to four hundred pounds of coal per day. The Single Machine strikes 150 and the double 300 blows, (150 on each side) per minute, and feed forward on the track ½ inch

at each stroke, or 6 feet per minute, and cut from ½ to 1 inch in depth (according to the stone) each time passing over. The Single Machine cuts from 30 to 50 square feet of channel in marble and limestone, and 80 to 100 in sandstone per day, equivalent to the labor of twenty-five men, and the Double Machine will accomplish about twice as much. It is estimated that channels 4 feet in depth can be cut by the Machines for one-quarter, and 6 feet deep for one-fifth the expense of hand labor. Channels can be cut by the machines within three inches of the parallel wall of a quarry, and they have been cut 13 feet deep. The channels cut are straight and true like a tooled face, and every foot of channel cut, makes two feet of cut surface upon the blocks, which is worth all it cost in cutting (incidental to quarrying) in the enhanced value of the stone, over that taken out by the old process. Each alternate tier of blocks can be cut to any desired width by placing the machine a greater or lesser distance from channels previously cut, or channels can be cut between, thus giving a great variety of sizes even with the Double Machine.

As to the capacity of these machines, we may mention that a Double Machine has cut in West Rutland (Vt.) Marble, 173 feet in one day of eleven hours; 859 feet in five days of eleven hours each, and has averaged 100 feet per day by the month.

As indicating the practical utility and value of these machines on different kinds of stone we make the following extracts: Mr. John N. Baxter, Superintendent of the Rutland Marble Company says: "I estimate that one of your Double Gang Machines will do the labor of forty men; and it is a fact well known in this community, that a marble quarry in this vicinity which was formerly worked by hand power and did not pay expenses, has been enabled by the use of your Machine alone to do a very successful and profitable business."

Mr. Edwin Walker, of Chicago and Lemont, Illinois, writes: "It has paid for itself in net earnings this season. I have lately bought another one, which is now at work in my Lake Superior Brown Sand Stone Quarry, and it is working perfectly."

We might add many other extracts fully as complimentary as the above, and publish a long list of the names of purchasers, in nearly every state in the Union, as references but deem it unnecessary. Parties desiring further information can readily obtain it from the headquarters of the Company.

THOMAS ROSS,

Manufacturer of

Merriman's Patent Gangs, Derricks, Traveling

Cranes, and Stone Working Machinery,

Rutland, Vermont.

The successful working of the Marble quarries of Vermont has largely added to the demand for stone working machinery of various kinds. Among the manufacturers of stone sawing and working machinery generally there are none whose productions are better known or more popular than those of Mr. Thomas Ross, of Rutland, Vermont.

For many years Mr. Ross has made a leading specialty of the manufacture of the Merriman Patent Gang, which is universally used in sawing marble throughout the entire marble producing district of Vermont, and is favorably known and extensively used in the largest and best marble sawing mills in all parts of the United States. Mr. Ross is the exclusive manufacturer of the Merriman Gang. He is also largely engaged in the construction of Derricks, Traveling Cranes, etc. Everything that is produced at the works of Mr. Ross is made of carefully selected materials and by skilled workmen. Perfection is the end sought after and the enviable reputation which the machinery here made has attained is positive proof that it has been very closely approached, as closely as human invention may ever hope to get.

Mr. Ross's location in the midst of extensive

quarrying interests, affords him superior advantages for studying the wants of quarrymen. In addition to his specialties of Stone Working Machinery, Mr. Ross does a general Foundry and Machine Business, making light and heavy castings of every description, Shafting, Pulleys, Gears, etc.

THE MERRIMAN PATENT GANG.

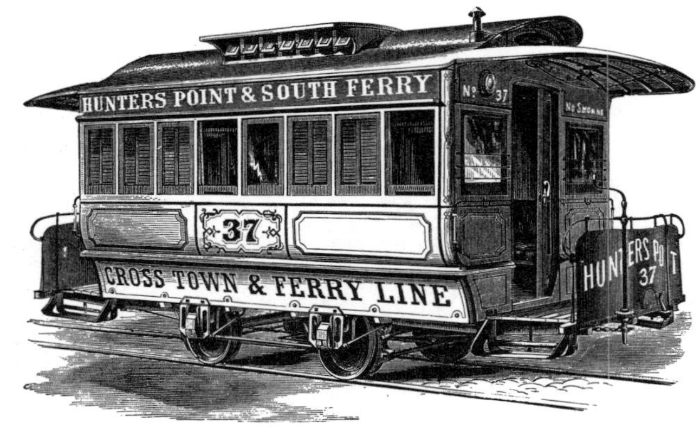

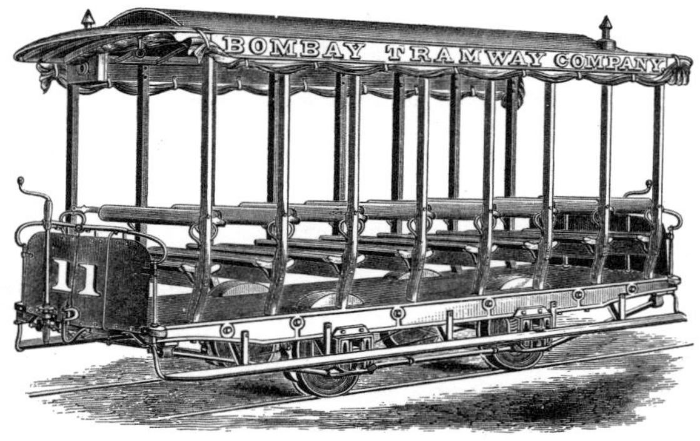

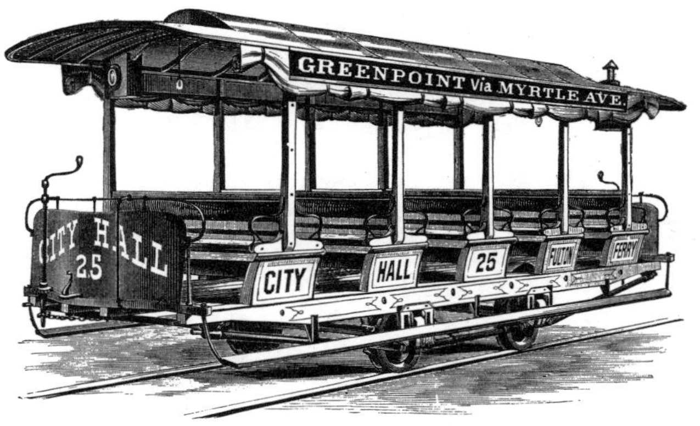

J. M. JONES & CO.,

Manufacturers of

STREET RAILWAY CARS,

West Troy, New York.

——:o:——

When those of us who have reached or passed the meridian of life let memory carry us back to the days and surroundings of our boyhood, our minds are filled with wonder at the progress the world has made within our time. But how few of us ever stop to consider any but the so-called "important" inventions or applications of principles. The history of the telegraph, for instance, is familiar to every reading person in the civilized world; but, contemporary with the telegraph came other improvements which have since been as universally adopted, and the good resulting from which has been as great, but of their history we have never thought it worth while to inquire. Many of these important improvements and inventions consist merely in a new method of applying a principle previously well known, or of grappling and controlling a force, a knowledge of whose existence and power was not new. The inventions connected with telegraphy extend no further than this: the power of electricity was known to men, and attempts had been made to utilize it long before the man who finally conquered and made it his servant had seen the light. These facts detract nothing from the fame of Morse, though others battled valiantly, the victory was his, and his is rightfully the crown.

Not less important than the improvements in the means of rapidly communicating information to points more or less distant, is the improvements in the methods of traveling. So far as these improvements relate to the ease and facility with which long journeys may be accomplished, they are generally appreciated and highly commended, but when it comes to the methods of going from home to business, or from business, home, we seldom pause to think how greatly we are in advance of our fathers.

Most of us will acknowledge it as true, that, too often, "familiarity breeds contempt." We are prone to lightly esteem that which is easily and cheaply attained, though its real value be ever so great, and do not stop to think of the advantages we have gained by its use; but, if deprived of it, how sorely it would be missed. Frequently the most common methods are the least appreciated, especially such as relate to small matters of every-day occurrence. And sometimes the introduction of the simplest improvements meet with the most, and the fiercest opposition.

These thoughts forced themselves upon us recently in a street railway car. It was uncomfortably full, yet every person in or on it, grumble though many did, was gaining an advantage by being there. We rank the introduction and popularization of street cars in our large cities, and horse railroads between the smaller villages, as among the most important improvements in methods that have been adopted within the last fifty years. Important, because they afford more rapid transit than is possible under the old system of stages or omnibuses; because they are more comfortable to ride in; because they require less power and it consequently costs less to run them, following which, the fare is proportionately lower, and the laborer, weary with the day's hard toil can afford to ride to his home in them.

Street Cars when first introduced were not popular. In the large cities those who were accustomed to ride in stages objected to the cars because they could not drive up to the curbstones and allow their passengers to step out on the sidewalk, and unimportant as that objection may now seem, it was so commonly made that many who should have been wiser, accepted it as a reason why street railways must prove unpopular, and one gentleman, who is now well-known to horse railway companies over all the world, rediculed the idea that street cars would ever be largely introduced in this or any other country, though he has since amassed a fortune in their manufacture.

The horse railway is pre-eminently an American institution. It was conceived and had its birth here, and not until it had become popular with us was it tried in other lands. Out of its success has sprung up a business of great importance, the manufacture of street cars, giving employment to hundreds of men and involving the investment of a large capital.

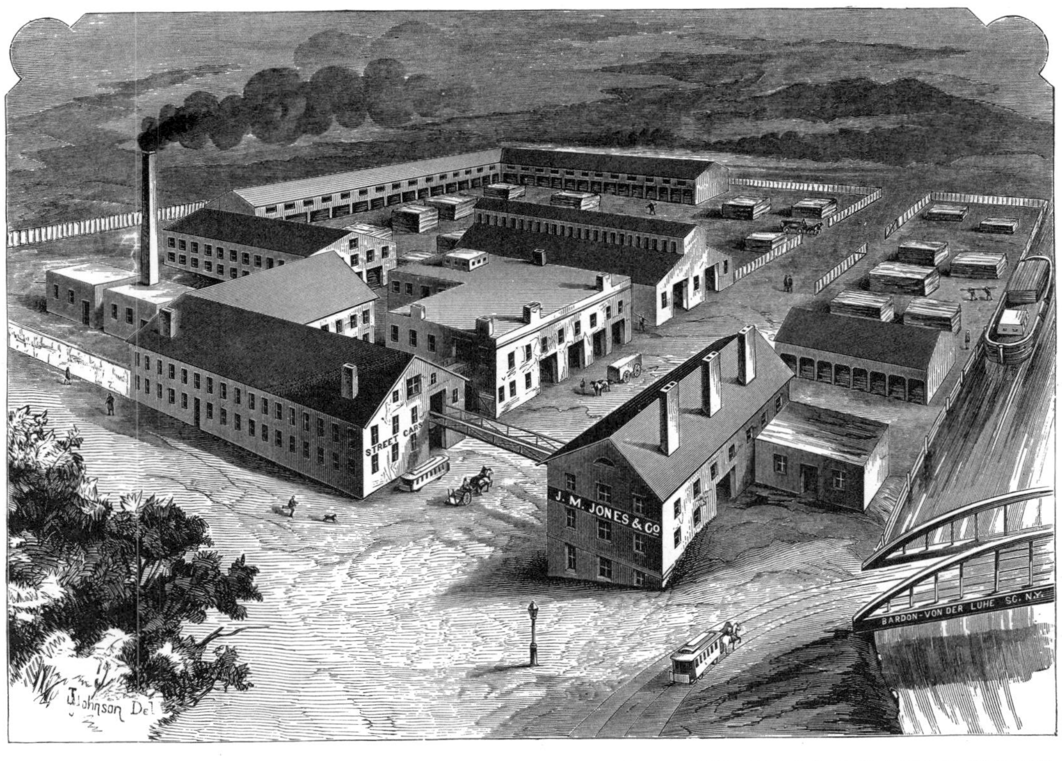

J. M. JONES & CO.'S STREET CAR MANUFACTORY, WEST TROY, NEW YORK.

The firm of J. M. Jones & Co., a fine engraving of whose establishment occupies the centre of this page, is, we believe, the only one in the country which devotes their entire attention to the building of horse cars. Their works are eligibly located on the McAdam Road, in the first ward of West Troy, New York, and are supplied with every appliance that can aid them in the pursuit of this their special branch of manufacture. The firm originated before horse cars were dreamed of, and originally consisted of Mr. Henry Whitbeck, and Mr. J. M. Jones, who in 1839, formed a co-partnership, and commenced the manufacture of carriages in an unpretending two-story building, measuring about forty feet square. The firm of Whitbeck & Jones was a success. Their productions became very popular, by reason of the elegance of their designs and the thoroughly workmanlike manner in which they were finished, and found ready sale, not only at home, but in distant sections of the country. The steady growth of their business made it necessary from time to time to add to their buildings and machinery, until the originally small shops developed into a thoroughly equipped establishment. The firm of Whitbeck & Jones continued until 1863, when Mr. Whitbeck, having acquired a competency retired, and Mr. George Lawrence, (since deceased) assumed an interest in the concern.

Upon the advent of Mr. Lawrence, the attention of the new firm was turned to the building of Street Cars, and the carriage business was abandoned. In the year 1864, Mr. Lawrence, on account of failing health, withdrew from the concern, Mr. J. M. Jones purchasing his interest, and associating his sons in the business with him.

Determined to turn out the best possible work and the best only, the firm secured the finest and best machinery that the skill of man has invented to aid them in their work, and so completely equipped their entire establishment, that in point of adaptation to the work performed, it is second to none in the country.

In conducting a business of the character and extent of that of this firm, many things, which to the superficial observer or the small manufacturer would seem of but secondary, become here of primary importance. For instance, the selection of materials. All are aware that to make a durable vehicle of any description it is necessary that the toughest and strongest wood and the finest quality of iron and steel should be used; but in the construction of street cars, weight is a very important consideration, and in the selection of material it is not only necessary to consider its strength, but its gravity, and the experienced builder rejects many a fine piece of wood whose only fault is its too great weight. In a large concern like this it is necessary to exercise the utmost care in the purchase of material, or there would soon be a large stock on hand, not fitted for the purpose for which it was bought. It is a mistaken notion that many men have, that wood, to be strong, must be heavy, or that the heavier it is the stronger. The difference of a hundred pounds weight in a car, is a matter of considerable importance to railroad companies. A car disproportionately heavy, faster wears out itself, the road on which it runs and the horses that draw it, and last though not least, makes far harder work for the driver who controls it, than one of proper weight. Few of those who daily travel on the street cars have ever thought of these facts, but a moment's reflection, however, will convince any intelligent man of their truth.

As Messrs. J. M. Jones & Co. do no business but that of manufacturing street cars, all their materials are selected with reference to that special work, and all their machinery is constructed with reference to its adaptability to making some particular part. Their workmen too, are so divided that the same men perform the same class of work day after day, year in and year out, their long practice resulting in the attainment of a skill which cannot be reached by men who work on a car to-day and a lumber wagon to-morrow. The result is that all the cars turned out by this firm are as near perfection as human hands can make them.

The marked superiority of their work has gained for this firm a success second to none. From the beginning of their new enterprise there has been a rapid and steady increase of business, and now their cars are doing satisfactory service throughout the United States and South America. The name of the establishment has penetrated even into the East Indies, which contribute largely to the patronage of the firm; and it is questionable whether any manufactory of any kind in the country can boast of a trade distributed over a greater extent of territory.

This wonderful growth of their business has, of course, necessitated a corresponding increase of their facilities for manufacturing, and the several buildings composing the concern cover an area of over four acres. A description of the shops and their contents, a glance at the ingenious machinery which "work and work but never tire," following a car through its various stages, would be interesting to the reader perhaps, but unfortunately would more than fill our space. Suffice it to say that it is the largest establishment, confining its business strictly to street cars, in the United States, and that there is but one firm engaged in the business, a New York establishment, which manufactures omnibuses as well as cars, that excels it in the amount of its productions.

The firm as it now stands, consists of J. M. Jones, the founder of the business and his sons, John H. Jones and Walter A. Jones. The proprietors are ably assisted by an experienced corps of foremen, who, like the proprietors, have been thoroughly educated to the business. As an evidence of the pleasant relations existing between the employers and employés, it will not be amiss to state that the superintendent of the painting department has been connected with the establishment for over thirty-five years, and that the superintendent of the trimming and blacksmithing shops can boast of thirty years devotion to the firm. In these facts we have evidence, first, of the skill and faithfulness of the men, and second of the honor of the employers, for had the men not been good men they would not have held their situations so long, and had the employers not been just they could not have retained such workmen. When there are honorable employers and skillful employés, good work is a natural consequence.

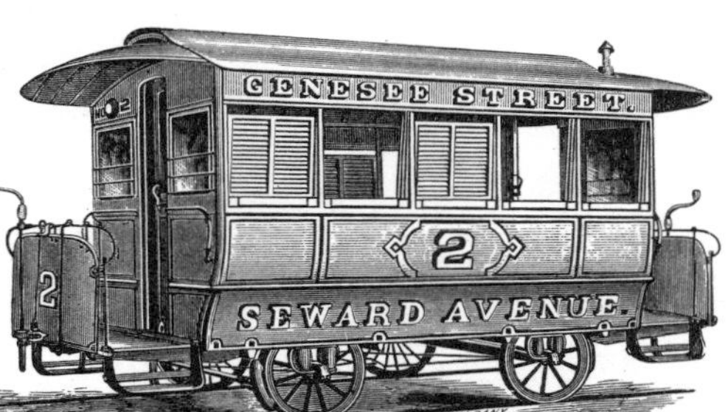

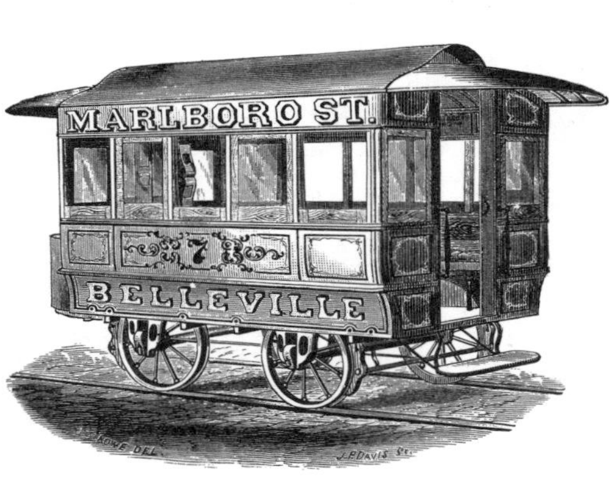

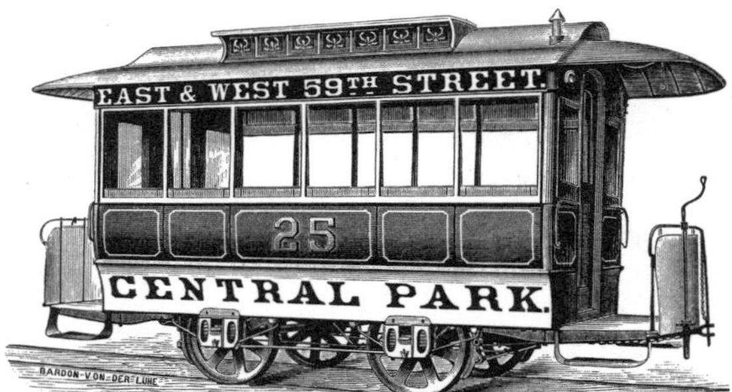

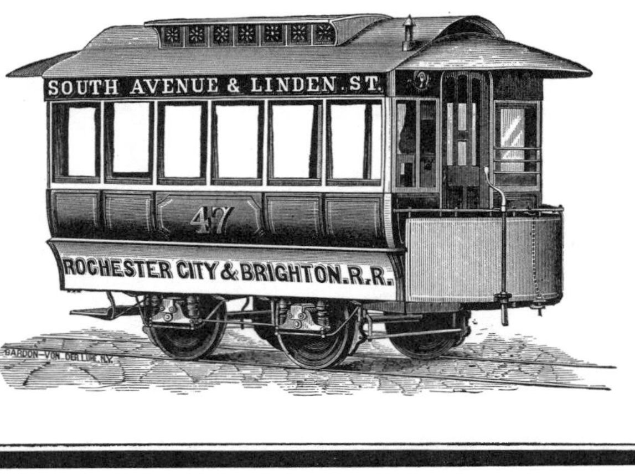

DECKER BROS., GRAND, SQUARE & UPRIGHT PIANOS,
33 Union Square, N. Y.

Prominent among the leading piano manufacturers of the world is the firm whose title heads this article. Conversant from their youth with every detail of the mechanism of a piano forte, and having filled the most responsible positions in the establishments of the best manufacturers of the time, the two brothers, David and John Jacob Decker, entered into business for themselves in 1862 with a ripened experience and a full appreciation of the æsthetic as well as the commercial possibilities of their work. They indulged in no rosy hope of sudden popularity and a quickly realized fortune. Their object was to produce the very best pianos in the world. They were fully aware that only the unerring test of time could prove the merits of their work, but were determined to ultimately reach the highest place. Practical artisans themselves, and familiar with the capabilities of every man employed in the business in New York, they secured the most skillful workmen for every department. Good mechanics prefer employment where their ability is not only well paid for but also appreciated and the Decker Brothers were so highly esteemed by the trade that leading journeymen in other establishments sought engagements with them. From these they selected the best. They were equally careful in the selection of material. Their motto from the beginning has been "the best cannot be too good."

Their first instruments astonished and delighted the musical profession, and in a few months they had an established reputation in art circles.

Their business has outstripped their most sanguine expectations, and the reputation is voluntarily accorded them by professionals and amateurs of making all their pianos of equal excellence and maintaining the highest standard of perfection in manufacture.

The Decker Brothers have made many important improvements in the manufacture of piano fortes which are secured to them by Letters Patent. Among these is an improved construction of the full metallic plate, whereby the strings are freed from contact with the iron frame and their connection with the tuning pins carried close to the wrest-plank. Decker Brothers' improved Agraffe is so constructed as to admit of its being fastened on the the wrest-plank instead of entering the iron plate, the only method before known; thus securing a sweeter, purer tone. Another patent is for an improvement in the motion of the hammer of an upright action; and for a new mode of adjusting the action in upright pianos whereby the whole action may be turned away from the strings to permit adjustment or repairs without removing it from the case. Still other patents have been granted to this firm for improvements in the application of the veneer to the cases. Under the old method nearly half an hour was required to do work which, by the new method, is better done in five minutes. Such results are not attainable except by the use of Decker Brothers' patents.

They manufacture the three styles of pianos, named the Grand, the Boudoir or Upright, and the Square. Their Concert Grands are unsurpassed in power and beauty of tone and are faultless in action. The Parlor Grands are especially designed for parlor use. They posses a fine body of tone, governed by an easy and durable action and in every respect are perfectly constructed. The Boudoir or Upright piano-forte has for years been admired for its compact construction and tasteful appearance but it lacked some of the qualities deemed

indispensable by artistic players. Decker Brothers, in their newly Patented Upright Pianos, have obviated the faults of the old style of boudoirs, and now offer an instrument possessing in a pre-eminent degree the matchless qualities of tone and action which characterize their Grands.

The Square Piano-fortes introduced by Decker Brothers in 1862, possess patented improvements to be found in no other pianos in the world. Their superior merits first brought the name of Decker into favor with the public and secured them the voluntary endorsement of the pro-

DECKER BROS.,
Warerooms, 33 Union Square, N. Y.

fession. Thousands of these instruments have been sold within the past few years, and in no cases have they failed to give the fullest satisfaction, or to realize the highest expectations of purchasers—a fact that can be substantiated by innumerable voluntary letters to the manufacturers. To meet the demand for a serviceable instrument for pupils, Messrs. Decker Brothers are manufacturing a Square piano-forte possessing all the advantages of their patented improvements, and differing from their parlor styles only in the expensive particular of exterior ornament. This School Piano-Forte has a beautifully finished black walnut case, while in point of tune, durability, excellence of material and thoroughness of workmanship, it is equal to their higher priced patterns.

The same superiority of workmanship and tone is uniformly maintained in all the several styles and varieties of the piano-forte made by this firm. The same rich singing quality of tone is found in their Square, Upright and Grand Pianos, varying only in fullness and power. This tone is peculiar to the Decker Brothers' instruments, and is easily distinguished by its brilliant purity, warmth, delicacy and expanding power. Its elastic nature renders it especially obedient to the requirements of the artist's fastidious taste, enabling him to graduate the power and volume of tone to the utmost limit of expression with absolute certainty and ease. This is particularly noticeable in their Upright, or Boudoir Pianos, and is most perfectly realized in their improved Concert Grands.

A requisite, second to none other, in a well made piano, is the Action. If this be inexact, in ever so slight a degree, the musical character of the instrument is lessened, and the task of the pianist increased. The unreliable character of even the best French Actions, imported for the use of American manufacturers, compelled the Messrs Decker to manufacture their own Actions. This they have done for a number of years, and to their scrupulous care in the mechanism of this prominent feature may be credited much of the success that has caused their instruments to be recognized in the highest musical circles, as the choicest known.

The Decker Brothers, 33 Union Square, New York, are the owners of the only patents issued by the United States Government to any one of the name of Decker, for improvements in piano-fortes. In all genuine Decker Brothers' Pianos, the following line appears cast upon the iron plate, on the inner left hand side of the instruments: "Decker Brothers' Patent, June 2d, 1863." As unscrupulous parties have offered inferior pianos to the public, naming their wares "Decker Pianos," purchasers should take care to see that the above line is plainly stamped upon the iron plate.

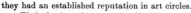

Clocks and Their Makers.

E. INGRAHAM & CO.,
Bristol, Conn.

As a result of the skill and enterprise of Connecticut artisans, good serviceable clocks are now made at so low a price that every family can afford to be the owner of a reliable time-piece.

Some seventy-five years ago the manufacture of hang-up wooden clocks was commenced in the town of Plymouth, Connecticut. It was a small beginning, made under many difficulties, but has grown to be a business of immense proportions.

At that time the entire mechanism of a clock was made by hand—the wheels and cogs were first marked out with compass and square, and then shaped with a fine saw—a slow, tedious, and expensive process. The movements of these clocks were sold for about twenty-five dollars. At a later date wooden clocks were made by machinery, and in a few years, competition among manufacturers became so great that the price of movements was reduced to five dollars each.

Yankee enterprise and ingenuity, not satisfied

MANUFACTORY OF E. INGRAHAM & CO., BRISTOL, CONN.

with what had been accomplished, adopted new materials for the works, invented new methods of manufacture, and revolutionized the trade by the introduction of one and eight day brass clocks, made by machinery, and the parts, (being facsimiles) interchangeable.

The history of clock making does as much credit to American intelligence and mechanical skill as that of any other manufacturing interest in America. The largest establishments in the world are located in Bristol, Plymouth, Waterbury, Ansonia and New Haven, Conn. Their production is colossal. Nearly all the clocks used in this country are manufactured in this state and large numbers are exported to foreign lands.

One of the oldest of these establishments is that of E. Ingraham & Co., located at Bristol. This firm manufacture reliable eight and one day spring time-pieces, their annual production exceeding one hundred thousand. All designs produced at their works are original with them and are covered by Letters Patent. The above cuts represent some of their styles. Had we attempted to illustrate all of them we might have filled a much larger space. Their designs are all neat and tasty, some of them elaborate, and the record of their clocks as timekeepers is unsurpassed.

In their works, an engraving of which is here presented, they give constant employment to a large number of hands. Their Clocks are widely known and highly commended by those who use them.

Tompkins' Brusher.

Tompkins' Spooler.

Tompkins' Knitter.

TOMPKINS' MACHINE SHOP.

Machinery for Manufacturers of Knit Goods,

Troy, New York.

—:o:—

The name of Clark Tompkins is intimately associated with the invention, improvement and perfecting of knitting machinery, and other machinery connected therewith.

Mr. Tompkins commenced business on the site of his present large establishment, on the bank of Poestenkill Creek, in the year 1846, in connection with Mr. Benjamin Marshall, the business being conducted under the name of the Empire Machine Company. The operations of the concern were mainly confined at first, to the production of mill gearing, to which they devoted special attention, and the pursuit of the general jobbing business. Soon the manufacture of looms for cotton and carpet mills was added, and also the production of wooden sign letters, in which business this was the pioneer establishment in this section.

In the year 1848, the original building, with its entire equipments, was destroyed by fire. With characteristic energy, the firm immediately commenced the reconstruction of the works, and they were soon completed, and furnished with new machinery and tools, and greatly increased general facilities. Shortly afterward the attention of Mr. Tompkins was directed to the wants of the hosiery manufacturers, who demanded a more efficient machine for knitting purposes than the old reciprocating "Jack and Sinker Frame," then in use. The hosiery manufacturers were beginning to prosper—the demand for knit goods was rapidly increasing—the public having outlived the prejudice, in this direction, generally evinced towards innovations, and Mr. Tompkins concluded that the wants of a class of manufacturers who were evidently destined to be among the most opulent in the country, were well worthy of consideration.

About the year 1853 the company imported specimens of what was known as the English horizontal knitting frame, with a view to construct the machine at their Troy works. A number of these were

manufactured and placed in the Cohoes knitting mills. The English machine was found deficient in many particulars, and Mr. Tompkins, in connection with John Johnson (the latter of carpet-loom celebrity), set to work to transform it into an upright machine. This they soon effected, and also added to the machine a device called a "take-up." This attachment consists of a series of rollers so arranged as to revolve in unison with the knitting cylinder, and to maintain a proper and uniform tension while taking up the cloth as it comes from the needles. To effect this required the exercise of great ingenuity, but the inventors named were equal to the task, and the "Upright Rotary Knitting Machine" came from their hands a perfect piece of mechanism, and was patented in the year 1855. Subsequently other important inventions relating to the manufacture of knit goods were made in the concern.

Sometime after having secured a patent on the Upright Rotary Knitting Machine, Messrs. Johnson & Tompkins became involved in a lawsuit

Tompkins' Winder.

with the makers of the "Gage" knitting frame, which was decided by the courts to be an infringement on their invention. Many machines now in operation throughout the country, known as the "Gage" frame, are simply imitations of the Tompkins machine. We understand that the Knitting Machine called the "Campbell & Clute Frame," is manufactured under license from C. Tompkins.

The "Tompkins Cone Winder" is an extremely simple machine. It operates without gears, and is so arranged as to allow each bobbin to act independently, so that an empty bobbin can be put on between two that are nearly full, and yet each one will be completely formed and filled requiring no skilled labor. The Cone Winder was invented to supply the deficiencies of the "Traverse and Cup Winders." Each Winder contains ten spindles, and one machine will rewind the yarn as rapidly as it can be made on a 250 spindle spinning-jack. This machine was patented by Messrs. Tompkins and Bradford in the year 1865. It was invented in response to the demands of manufacturers, who claimed that a perfect winder would save one-half the trouble and labor previously involved in the production of knit cloth.

Another ingenious machine manufactured at this establishment is the "Spooler" made for the purpose of winding skein thread on spools for the sewing machine. They are generally made for three spools, though they will be made to order for any number of spools. It is automatic, only requiring the attendant to keep the ends tied; the reels are light and adjustable to different sized skeins. The machine, according to the testimony of many users, is very desirable, cheap and capable of soon paying for itself.

The "Brusher" takes in any width cloth, from 24 inches down; brushes the cloth in a flattened web, works on both sides at once, cleans off the specks, burrs, seeds, &c.; raises a nap, restores the pliancy and softness of which the washing has deprived the goods, and leaves the web in a smooth roll, ready for the cutter.

The patronage of the establishment extends from Maine to California, and northward to Canada. No living manufacturer of machinery is better known to the producer of knit goods than Clark Tompkins, and to none are they more largely indebted for the beautiful and marvelously efficient mechanism which has enabled them to take a front place among the great "captains of industry."

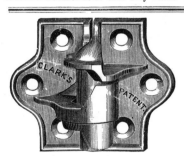

BUILDERS' HARDWARE,

Represented by

CLARK & COMPANY, BUFFALO, N. Y.

The nineteenth century has very properly been called the age of improvements. In every branch of industry rapid strides have been taken until at the present time we seem to have nearly reached perfection. In no branch of trade does this appear more clearly than in that of Builders Hardware a branch embracing articles too numerous to mention in detail but of the greatest importance in the make up of our modern luxurious dwellings and business blocks.

For many important improvements we are indebted to

Messrs. Clark & Co., who began the manufacture of hardware goods in Buffalo, about eight years since; being the first in that city to establish this branch of manufacture. Starting with very limited means, their business has gradually increased, until the demand for their goods has become very general and their sales now extend to every part of the Union.

Most of the articles manufactured by this firm have improvements over similar classes of goods in the market, and are protected by patents issued to and owned by members of the firm.

Constant additions are being made to their list of goods. The best quality of iron is used in the castings and great care is taken that none but perfect goods go into the market.

The works of the company are located on Niagara Street, one of the broad and business avenues of the city. The build-

Clark & Company, Builders' Hardware Manufactory, Buffalo, N. Y.

ings are of brick, and very commodious, well ventilated, and extend from street to street. The latest improved machinery is used in the special manufactures of the company.

The motive power is furnished by the Harris Corlis Engine of seventy-five horse power. Steam is supplied by the "Babcock & Wilcox Tubular Safety Steam Boiler," The "MacKenzie Patent Cupola Furnace and Blower" are used in melting the iron. From four to five tons are daily consumed in the manufacture of the castings.

This amount of iron would be moderate for floor moulded castings, but when it is considered that from ten to one hundred pieces are moulded in bench flasks about twelve inches square, some idea may be formed of the large quantities of goods daily produced.

Much experience, skill and inventive genius are possessed by the firm. They also employ a large number of skilled workmen in their manufactory. The material used, and the work of every description turned out, is of a superior quality.

Their goods are illustrated by Catalogue, which they issue annually; and supply on application for the benefit of their patrons and all others interested.

THE STURTEVANT BLOWER
and its Uses.

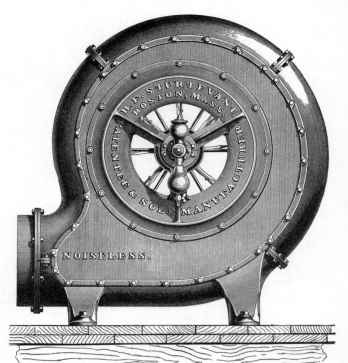

It is only within a few years that the air blast has been successfully applied to any but the simplest uses ; indeed, until quite recently its whole employment was confined to furnaces and forges for working metals, and its occasional use to increase the draught of the fires under steam boilers. Coarse fans generally constituted the mechanical device, or in cases where an especially strong blast was required, ordinary air pumps were substituted. Either method was crude and imperfect, and was generally so acknowledged, yet for many years no real improvement was made. The deficiency of the then existing apparatus for creating and conveying a blast of air to the point where it was needed was painfully manifest, and to overcome this deficiency Mr. B. F. Sturtevant, of Boston, devoted his attention, and after much careful study devised the ingenious mechanism now known as the Sturtevant Blower, and, in 1867, obtained his first patent thereon. Since that time Mr. Sturtevant has relaxed no effort to perfect his invention. He has made numerous improvements, and no less than thirty patents have been granted upon the original form.

Few inventions have so completely succeeded as has the Sturtevant Blower. It has at once received the earnest commendation of all who have become familiar with its operation and has entirely replaced the imperfect devices which were in use previous to its introduction. Other "fans," "injectors," "blowers," and "exhausters" have been invented and tested, but none has filled the place generally accorded to the Sturtevant. On this page we present engravings of several styles of these Pressure Blowers and Exhaust Fans, and have obtained from the inventor many facts, which added to the information we have gained by a personal inquiry among many prominent manufacturers and others who use them, enable us to present the following as prominent among the various uses to which the different styles of the Sturtevant Blower may be advantageously applied, believing that the information thus collected will prove a reliable reference for manufacturers and others, as we include in our lists only such uses as the machine has been successfully tested in.

B. F. STURTEVANT'S
PATENT
STEEL PRESSURE BLOWERS,
For Cupola Furnaces and Forges.

Pressure Blowers are used for supplying blast for forges, and for every description of furnace for smelting, melting, heating and converting all kinds of metals and ores, ranging from the jewelers blow-pipe through the long catalogue of silversmiths', coppersmiths', and blacksmiths' forges ; for forges and furnaces for manufacturing the steel and iron parts of agricultural implements, hardware and cutlery—from the plow to the pen-knife ; for blowing cupola furnaces in iron and brass foundries, and the forge and furnace fires, in steamship building and railroad repair shops, for Bessemer steel works, cast steel works, rolling mills ; for the manufacture of iron and steel rails, sheet-iron and boiler plates and merchant iron for making blast for steam-forges, for forging shafts for steamships, anchors, and other heavy work, and also for affording a blast for furnaces, for smelting and packing gold, silver, copper and lead ores, in fact for every purpose for which a blast can be used.

Exhaust Fans are employed for removing shavings from planing and moulding machines ; saw dust and dust from sand wheels, such as are used for polishing lasts, carriage spokes, shoe bottoms, felt hats, etc., and from emery wheels used for polishing cutlery, and all kinds of hardware ;—for exhausting smoke and the deleterious gases that are found in smith shops, manufacturing establishments and chemical works ;—steam and noxious vapors arising from paper machines, and found in all drying rooms, etc. Also for removing sweat from mill stones, offensive odors from try kettles, and dyeing establishments, for cleansing rag and cotton pickers, flax and rape machinery from dust, and for the thorough ventilation of coal and other mines and all underground apartments or cellars. As a means of exhausting impure air from public buildings or other places these Fans have no superior and many of them are in use for this purpose in various parts of the country. At the National Capitol, two of these Fans are in use in the Senate Chamber, and two in the House of Representatives, being driven by very powerful engines and capable of removing 1,800,000 cubic feet of foul air per hour.

B. F. STURTEVANT'S
IMPROVED FAN BLOWER,
For Boilers, Heating Furnaces and Ventilation.

An annoying defect of Fans, Blowers and Exhausters generally, is the howling noise they make while in operation. The Sturtevant Machines are noiseless. Necessarily, the strength of the blast depends upon the velocity of the fan, and the velocity in turn depends upon the amount of power expended in driving the machine ; but the Sturtevant Blowers and Exhaust Fans are so correctly constructed that they run with far less power than is required by others. They are in use in the largest establishments in every state and territory in the Union, and are gaining in popularity day by day as their merits become generally known, and though the first patent was only issued in 1867. Mr. Sturtevant has manufactured and sold over twelve thousand machines.

COUNTER-SHAFTS, HANGERS & PULLEYS,
As Furnished with the Sturtevant Pressure Blowers.

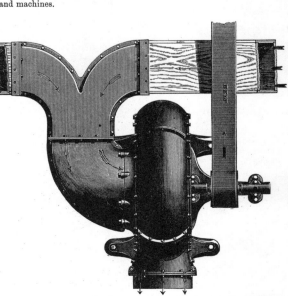

B. F. STURTEVANT'S PATENT EXHAUST FAN.—Nos. 70 & 72 SUDBURY STREET, BOSTON, MASSACHUSETTS.

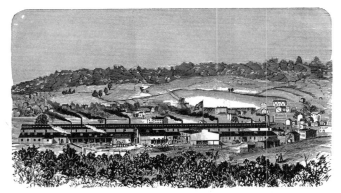

VIEW OF PATERSON IRON COMPANY'S WORKS.

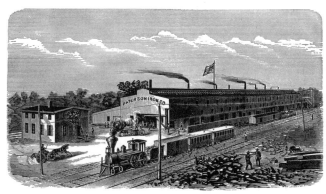

VIEW OF PATERSON IRON COMPANY'S WORKS.

PATERSON IRON COMPANY,

Manufacturers of

Railroad and Steamship Forgings, Heavy Machine Forgings, etc.,

Paterson, New Jersey. New York Office: 138 Chambers Street.

The Paterson Iron Company ranks prominently among the leading metal workers of the United States. They possess an equipment which in its completeness and extent is not surpassed. The attention of the Company is largely devoted to the manufacture of railroad and steamship forgings, such as locomotive frames, axles and tires; steamship shafts, anchors, etc.; together with every description of heavy forgings required in the erection of bridges and the construction of machinery for mining, excavating and dredging purposes. They have equipped their works with every mechanical appliance that can in any way expedite, or aid in attaining perfection.

The premises pertaining to the establishment comprise some twenty-five acres of land located at the eastern extremity of Paterson, and bordering upon the line of the Erie Railway, from which a branch track is extended through the grounds of the Company, affording them easy and ample facilities for the reception of crude materials and the shipment of finished productions.

The main building, containing the forging department and the machine shop is 530 feet long and 90 feet wide. A narrow railway extends the length of the forge shop, with switches leading to the shears, the steel shop and the blacksmithing department for the purpose of conveying materials and work from point to point.

The works contain twelve steam boilers, with an aggregate capacity of seven hundred horse power. For driving the shafting and blowers there are three engines, of twenty, thirty and sixty horse power, respectively. The forging is done by ten vertical steam hammers, which range in size from one thousand pounds to ten tons. Each hammer is operated by a separate engine, and near each stands a crane, by means of which the huge masses of iron are taken to and from the furnaces. The crane used in connection with the ten ton hammer is capable of sustaining a weight of one hundred tons. It is worked by two steam engines, one for moving the arm to and fro, the other for raising and lowering. With the attendance of one man, this immense machine easily performs the labor which would require twenty-five or thirty men with a crane worked by hand.

The stock used in these works is exclusively wrought scrap iron of the finest quality. The larger pieces of boiler iron, etc., are cut up by means of powerful shears, which will go through a four inch bar with the utmost ease. The scrap is piled up in masses weighing about one hundred and eighty pounds each, and ten or twelve of these piles are placed on a huge shovel, called a *peel,* and run into the furnace, where, in about an hour, the scrap becomes fused into slabs, which are removed with enormous tongs and swung under the hammers. Some of the forgings of the Company, such as shafts for ocean steamers, which sometimes weigh from twenty to twenty-five tons, are forty feet or more in length, requiring several days, sometimes even weeks, for their completion.

The Machine Shop is provided with the latest improved machinery, including a face lathe which swings fourteen feet; three slide lathes which admit, respectively, lengths of thirty-seven, forty and fifty feet; two lathes of smaller dimensions, four planers, the largest planing twenty-four feet in length; three slotting machines, capable of performing the heaviest work, boring, drilling and shaping machines, together with all the minor tools requisite for the complete finish of any piece of work.

An important item in the production of the Paterson Iron Company is crucible steel for the manufacture of shafts, axles, locomotive crank pins, connecting rods, etc. This steel which is of the very finest quality, and manufactured by them expressly for their own use, is first cast in ingots which are subsequently drawn into any required shape.

The Company are also the sole manufacturers of Marshall's Patent Anchor, which differs materially in its construction from any other in use, and is said to hold with much greater strength, while containing only about half the usual weight of metal. The flukes are so arranged that they can be folded into comparatively small compass, a consideration of importance on board ship, where deck room must be economized.

The character of the work turned out at this establishment is well known throughout the country, and in certain circles, their reputation extends all over the civilized world. The Company have furnished shafts, etc., for all the prominent steamship lines whose vessels land at ports in the U.S.

Within the very brief space at our disposal we cannot describe the works or business of this Company as fully as their size would warrant; the exterior and interior views presented will aid the reader at arriving at an approximate judgment of their extent and capacity.

INTERIOR VIEW OF PATERSON IRON COMPANY'S WORKS, PATERSON, NEW JERSEY, U. S. A.

L. GRAF & BRO.,

BOOT AND SHOE MANUFACTURERS,

44 to 54 Lincoln Street, Newark, N. J.

Salesroom, 16 Warren Street, New York.

——:o:——

To write a history of Boots and Shoes, tracing the progress that has been made in their manufacture, from the ancient days when sandals were worn down to the present time, would be the labor of years. Even to note the progress of the trade in this country, would require a good sized volume. Few persons not connected with the trade, or who have not put forth special effort to arrive at the truth, ever thought of the manufacture of Boots and Shoes as being a specially important branch of industry; yet the fact is that it affords employment to a greater number of operatives than any other single trade.

Reliable authorities estimate that there are now in the United States over twenty-six thousand establishments for the manufacture of Boots and Shoes, affording employment to one hundred and forty thousand hands, who each year work up materials valued at ninety-six million dollars, and receive wages amounting to not less than fifty-three million dollars. The capital invested in buildings, machinery, stock, etc., is estimated at fifty million dollars, and the manufactured products at one hundred and eighty-three million dollars.

These factories were scattered over all the States and Territories, including the District of Columbia, and in every State and Territory, excluding the District of Columbia, sewing or pegging machines, or both, were used in the manufacture; in all, 12,394 sewing machines and 901 pegging machines; 266 steam engines, and 24 water wheels, with a combined horse power of 3,055 furnishing the motor. The report divides the hands employed into three classes, viz:—males above sixteen years of age, 70,688; females above fifteen, 18,208; youth, 2,806; making a total of 91,702 hands. The capital invested in the business is set down at $37,519,019, and the wages paid during the year foots up $42,504,444. Materials valued at $80,502,718 were consumed in the manufacture, and 14,318,529 pairs of Boots, valued at $50,231,470, (about $3.50 per pair,) and 66,308,705 pair of Shoes, valued at $93,846,206 (about $1.41 per pair). In addition to these sums "other products" (chiefly repairing) to the value of $2,611,179, are reported, which swells the aggregate value of the productions of 3,151 establishments to $146,704,055, or an average of about $46,557 for each factory.

Prominent among these is the establishment of L. Graf & Brother, Newark, New Jersey. The business of this firm was established by Mr. Leopold Graf in the year 1857, and conducted by him until he was joined by his brother, Mr. Herman Graf, in 1860, when the present firm name was adopted. From the beginning the business of the firm has been a successful one, and has steadily increased until now it has assumed immense proportions.

The extensive brick buildings, a cut of which is here given, now occupied by them as a factory, forms one of the largest and most completely equipped Boot and Shoe Manufactories in the United States. These buildings were erected by the firm in the year 1871, they having entirely outgrown their old quarters, and more room and better facilities being necessary to enable them to keep pace with the steadily increasing demand.

In fitting up their manufactory no expense has been spared, and the machinery is of the latest and most approved character now in use in this line of trade, some of which is the invention of the senior member of the firm, Mr. Leopold Graf. The shoemakers' shop of fifty years ago and the shoe factory of to-day are two very different affairs. Then everything was done by hand, and he was considered a rapid workman who could make one pair of what where then called fine boots per day. Then the workman received the leather from the cutter's hands, and "fitted" and "bottomed" and "finished" and "treed" the work alone; now in the manufacture of a pair of boots they pass through a dozen or more hands, and half as many machines, and all the parts of the work are done by men specially skilled in that particular labor. Even such boots as are made entirely by hand, are not made, in large establishments at least, as they were made in olden time, by one man; the trade is divided, and it takes a "team," which may mean two, three or five men, according to the kind of work to be done to make a pair of boots or shoes.

A very considerable amount of the hardest labor is now done by machine. Sewing and pegging machines have been in use for several years, but within a short time several new machines have been introduced, and proved successful for performing other portions of the work.

They do their work, and do it well—better than it can be done by hand, more rapidly, and consequently at less expense. The establishment of L. Graf & Bro., is supplied with all these aids, and every device to lessen the cost of manufacture has been adopted by them, and they are thus enabled to produce goods so perfect in quality and so cheap, that it is difficult for others to successfully compete with them. The machinery is run by steam power.

This establishment affords employment to four hundred and fifty workmen selected for their special skill, and produces one thousand pair of Men's and Boys' Hand Sewed and Machine Sewed fine and medium grades of Boots and Shoes a day.

Messrs. L. Graf & Brother have salesmen constantly traveling.

VIEW OF L. GRAF & BRO.'S BOOT AND SHOE MANUFACTORY,
Newark, New Jersey.

EIGHT WHEEL LOCOMOTIVE.

THE MASON MACHINE WORKS,
Manufacturers of
Cotton Machinery, Locomotives, Car Wheels, &c.,
Taunton, Mass.

—:o:—

Taunton, situated on the Taunton River, at its junction with the Mill River, 35 miles south from Boston, is the seat of a number of very important manufactories. One of the most remarkable establishments in Taunton from whatever stand point we may view it, whether we regard its extent, the variety of its machinery, the number and excellence of its manufactures, or the celebrity of its founder, is the Mason Machine Works.

Richmond, machinists, he perfected the great invention of his life, the "Self-Acting Mule," a machine now so well known to all who are familiar with cotton machinery that a detailed description of it would be superfluous. Here, in 1842, when his employers had failed, he, through friendly assistance, became the principal owner and manager of the works. The prosperous times which succeeded the tariff of 1842, and the confidence of cotton and other manufacturers in the mechanical abilities of Mr. Mason at once secured for him a large and profitable business, which in a few years enabled him to erect after his own design the noble buildings known as the Mason Machine Works—the largest it has been said ever erected for the manufacture of machinery.

In 1852, Mr. Mason made an addition to the works previously erected, for the purpose of undertaking the business of building locomotives. There were already several large companies engaged in this branch of manufacture and it was a bold, and by some considered a rash move, to enter into competition with them, but Mr. Mason was convinced that there was room for great improvements in the model and construction of locomotives, and his great experience in other manufactures plainly proved that if such improvements were made, they would be appreciated and success would follow the undertaking. With him to devise was to execute, to project was to accomplish. In 1853 the first Mason Locomotive was brought out, and at once attracted attention. With characteristic fertility of genius he had stepped aside from the beaten track, and originated a new model, combining special beauty of external appearance with ex-

DOUBLE TRUCK LOCOMOTIVE.

gines, which carry their whole weight on the Drivers; the swivelling of the trucks enables it to pass the very sharpest curves with all the steadiness and smoothness of a passenger car; it will run either end first equally well, and on narrow gauge roads it is the only Locomotive whose method of construction admits of a wide and roomy firebox. These Locomotives have been used with great success for two or three years and their power for hauling heavy loads on severe grades and sharp curves is remarkable.

When the Locomotive branch of the business was firmly established, Mr. Mason made another step forward by equipping a foundry for the manufacture of Car Wheels. In this, as in everything else he attempts, his aim is improvement and the result success. His wheels are generally known as "Spoke," or "Tubular," in contradistinction to "Plate" wheels, a shape which it is said experiment

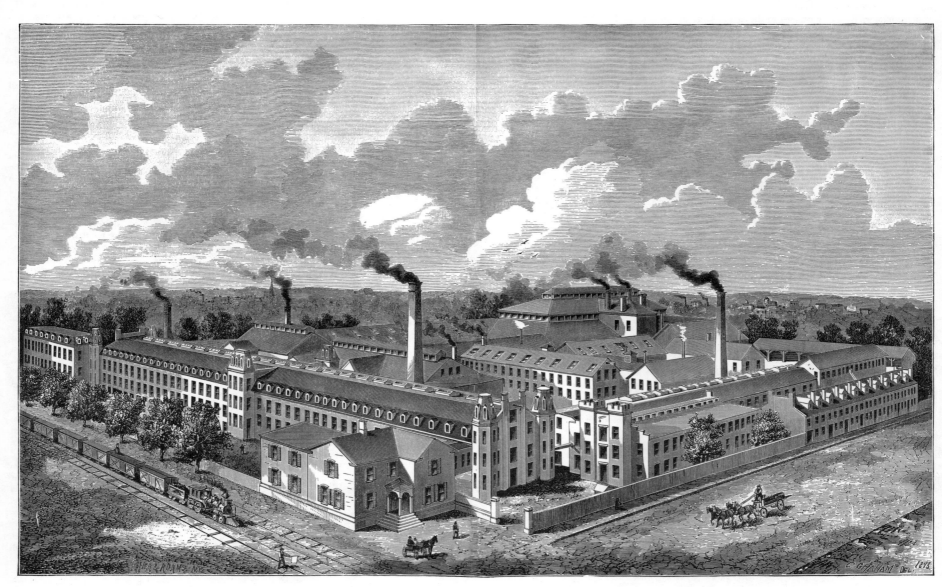

BIRDS-EYE VIEW OF THE MASON MACHINE WORKS, TAUNTON, MASSACHUSETTS.

William Mason, the founder of this splendid establishment, belongs to that class of intelligent and ingenious mechanics, who in spite of early disadvantages, and by the force of native genius leave their impression upon the age in which they live. The limited space at our disposal will not admit of our writing a biography of this eminent mechanic; therefore, suffice it to say, that after a boyhood spent successively in the blacksmith shop, the cotton mill and the machine shop, we find Mr. Mason in 1829, when about twenty-one years of age, in Canterbury, Conn., constructing and setting-up power looms for the manufacture of diaper-linen; and, at a later period, in Taunton, Mass., which, after many sad disappointments and crushing reverses caused by the failure of others, became the theatre of his future triumphs. It was here, while acting as foreman for Crocker &

cellence of workmanship. These points were apparent to the casual observer, but the trained mechanic and skilled engineer discovered other and more important improvements. The dome was placed exactly over the joint of the equalizing lever, between the drivers, the smoke-box cylinder and smoke stacks were placed in the same vertical line as the truck pintle, and the sand box was placed nearly midway between. The chimney, which although comparatively light, has necessarily the appearance of great weight, was thus brought directly over the truck, which supported its load with the symmetry of a pedestal in architecture. Mr. Mason entirely discarded all outward encumbrances, such as frames and their accompanying diagonal braces—resembling a ship's shrouds—thus leaving all the working parts in full view, and a clear range from end to end and under the boiler. The horizontal lines of his runningboard, hand-rail, feed-pipe, heighten the symmetry of the design, while the graceful forms and disposition of the details, give a finished expression to the whole, sufficient to raise it to the dignity of a work of genuine art.

It has been said of Mr. Mason, that "He has brought nearly all the credit upon New England engines that they are likely to retain, and he is probably the only New England builder who has left his mark on the American Locomotive."

Among the most recent of his valuable productions is the "Double Truck Locomotive," which has already attracted universal attention and has established itself on a successful career. The distinctive features of this locomotive are as follows: The Engine and Tender are framed together solid and carried on two trucks, one at either end; the Cylinders and running gear are framed into the forward or Driving Truck. The advantages gained are: The whole weight of the Engine is available for tractive power on the Drivers, while at the same time the length of the whole machine and the guiding of the rear truck prevent any of the oscillating motion common in all other en-

has proved to insure the greatest strength besides securing uniformity with the driving wheels.

At the outbreak of the Rebellion, when the Government was called upon to defend its existence, and it was found that there were but seventy thousand efficient muskets at the command of the authorities, Mr. Mason in common with many others set about providing the necessary facilities for the manufacture of fire-arms. He erected an armory and equipped it with the best machinery that could be obtained, some of which he further improved by original inventions, and while the war lasted and the demand continued, he manufactured Springfield Rifled Muskets at the rate of a hundred a day, but at the dawn of peace he joyfully relinquished this branch of his business, and the buildings are now occupied for other purposes.

COTTON CARD.

COTTON LOOM.

The Buck Range.

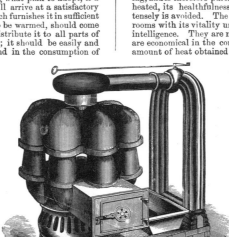

CULVER'S IMPROVED HOT AIR AND HOT WATER COMBINATION FURNACE.

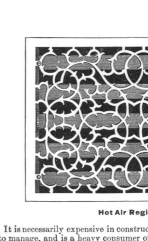

Hot Air Register.

The Simonds Manufacturing Company,
50 Cliff Street, New York.

How to heat our houses, with proper regard to economy and healthfulness, is a question of no small importance. So many systems, each claiming superiority over every other, have been devised of late, that persons seeking information on this subject are frequently bewildered by the arguments for this or that apparatus. In determining what plan to adopt, if a few requirements are kept in view, and a fair amount of judgment exercised, the purchaser will arrive at a satisfactory conclusion. A system should be adopted which does not destroy the vitality of the air, but which furnishes it in sufficient quantity at a moderate temperature, to promote healthfulness. To secure this end, the air to be warmed, should come from the outside of the building; it should secure a regular supply of heat, and uniformly distribute it to all parts of the building; the apparatus should be so simple in construction as to be easily managed; it should be easily and cheaply repaired; it should not be a producer of dirt; it should be economical in first cost, and in the consumption of fuel; it should be safe from accident, and, in any plan adopted, a proper regard should be had to ventilation. Any system of heating which combines these results, is a good one.

Grates furnish a "cheerful" fire and secure good ventilation, but they give very little heat in proportion to the coal consumed, "make dirt," do not uniformly warm the building, or even the room in which they are placed and require too much attention.

Stoves consume less coal than grates, but do not afford either their cheerfulness or ventilation; require about as much attention, and do not warm the whole building, unless one is placed in every room and passage.

There are many serious objections to the method of heating by steam, among which may be mentioned: the large original cost of fixtures; the great expense of keeping them in repair; their complicated character; the danger of explosions when in the hands of careless or inexperienced persons and the enormous consumption of fuel.

Any apparatus which depends entirely upon radiation from pipes filled with hot water for a supply of heat, is open to nearly all the objections urged against steam heat-

SIMOND'S PATENT.

Culver's New Pattern Sand-Joint Furnaces.

ing. It is necessarily expensive in construction and repairs; is difficult to manage, and is a heavy consumer of fuel.

Hot air furnaces, are, at least in cities, more generally used than any other method of heating, and, if properly constructed, they meet all the requirements laid down.

The following are among the advantages secured in using the furnaces made by the Simonds Manufacturing Company. The air to be heated is brought from the outside of the building, and is therefore pure. It is equally distributed to all parts of the hot-air chamber, so that, no part of it being overheated, its healthfulness is retained. The radiating surface being large, the necessity of heating the castings intensely is avoided. The castings are therefore durable, and, what is more important, the warm air is thrown into the rooms with its vitality unimpaired. They are simple in construction and easily managed by any person of ordinary intelligence. They are not liable to get out of order, and if out of order, can be easily and cheaply repaired. They are economical in the consumption of fuel, being so constructed that a perfect combustion is secured and the greatest amount of heat obtained from a given amount of coal. The dampers are so arranged as to make it possible to have a large or small fire, as the weather may require.

Our very limited space renders it impossible to mention many of the merits of the Culver and Simonds Furnaces manufactured by this company. They also manufacture registers and ventilators in great variety of size and design, cooking ranges, plain and enameled hoppers and urinals, flue and pipe dampers, cast iron pipe, etc., etc.

In 1845, when Canal Street was "up-town," Mr. David Culver came to New York and engaged in the manufacture of furnaces, ranges, registers, etc. His industry and integrity, together with the merit of the goods he manufactured, resulted, in a few years, in an established and prosperous business. He was succeeded by Mr. J. H. Simonds, and he, in turn, by the Simonds Manufacturing Company. This company is incorporated under the laws of New York, with a capital of $154,000.

Their works are in Jersey City, and though quite extensive, are generally occupied to their full capacity in supplying the demand for their goods. A full list of which can be procured on application, together with any other information pertaining to the business.

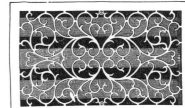

STEWART & CO.,
Proprietors of Manhattan Pottery, Drain Pipe and Terra Cotta Works.

Stewart & Co., are among the largest and most reliable manufacturers of clay goods in the world. Twenty-five years ago they established business in a small way and with many difficulties surrounding them, but their indomitable energy overcame all obstacles; the superiority of their productions created a great demand for them, and to-day, their immense works cover all the ground embraced in Nos. 540, 542, 544 and 546 West 19th Street, and 537, 539, 541 and 543 West 18th Street, with an office at 539 West 18th Street, and a down-town depot at 269 Pearl Street, New York. A business of such extent and importance can only be built up by long and persistent effort, aided by careful study of and intelligent ministration to the wants of the public.

Terra Cotta possesses many advantages over other materials used in the construction of artistic designs for the ornamentation of gardens, parks, etc. Among its points of excellence are: It is not affected by the most intense heat of summer, or the freezing cold

STEWART.

of winter; it is less expensive in the rough; being pliable, is easily moulded in any desirable form and, consequently, is cheaper.

From the cuts which adorn this page the reader will readily infer that Stewart & Co., are largely engaged in the manufacture of drain pipe. Their pipe is vitrified and double glazed, and is warranted to be perfectly indestructible, standing the action of the strongest acids and gases. Garden statuary of ancient and modern designs, in great variety; rustics, garden seats, hanging vases, etc., in perfect imitation of natural wood, and in numberless designs, have been introduced by them. Aquaria, with and without flower stands, for in and out door ornamentation; plain and ornamental chimney tops; greenhouse and oven tile; smoke and hot air flues; fire, range and stove brick, and, in fact, almost every thing manufactured of clay, useful or ornamental, are produced by them. Their work has stood the test of time and met the unqualified approval of a critical public. They need no higher praise. A visit to either of their places of business, or their catalogue and price list, (which they mail on application) will secure to our readers such further information in relation to Messrs. Stewart & Co., and their goods, as may be desired.

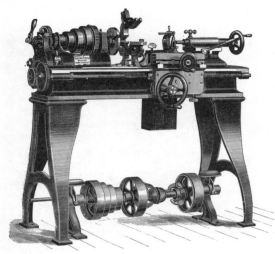

13 INCH WEIGHTED LATHE.

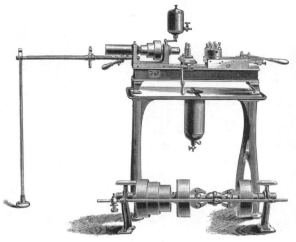

No. 1 SCREW MACHINE—WIRE FEED.

30 INCH PLANER.

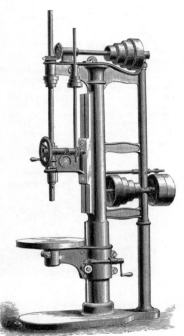

No. 2 UPRIGHT DRILL.

DROP HAMMER.

HYDRAULIC ADJUSTABLE PRESS.

No. 1 MILLING MACHINE.

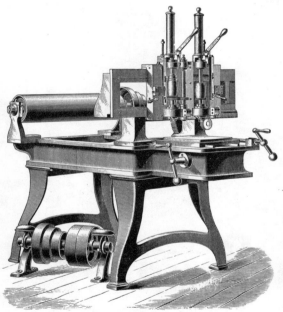

PROFILING MACHINE.

BLACKSMITH'S POWER SHEARS.

FOUR SPINDLE GANG DRILL.

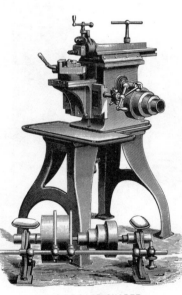

6 INCH PILLAR SHAPER.

THE PRATT & WHITNEY COMPANY,

HARTFORD, CONN.

—:o:—

In 1860 two Hartford mechanics began the manufacture of a patented attachment for looms, in connection with general machine jobbing. In 1861 they made gun machinery and were joined by a mechanic from New Britain, Conn. They soon began the manufacture of a patent rotary pump, and gradually extended their business, turning their attention mainly to the production of first-class tools adapted to the uses of the machinist and the gun maker. They aimed at producing intrinsically excellent tools of undeniable accuracy of working parts, perfection of fitting and adaptation of the completed machine to the work to be performed, in all of which they succeeded. There was no reason why they should not, for all of the firm were good workmen. Mr. F. A. Pratt was well known as a mechanic and inventor, before he became the head of the concern to which his name has been given. Mr. Amos Whitney is noted for his skill in contriving improved methods of doing work in the shop and his scrupulous care in the exactness of manipulation and finish. Mr. Monroe Stannard is known as well for his thoroughness as a practical mechanic as for his inventions of the rotary pump and motor bearing his name and his organ-blowing apparatus. These men began without capital, except an insignificant sum borrowed to start with, and now they manage the manufactures of an incorporated company holding a capital of $500,000, employing more than 300 men and turning out manufactures of a value of $500,000 yearly.

The Pratt & Whitney Company was incorporated in July, 1869. The three originators of the business, Messrs. Pratt, Whitney and Stannard, occupy respectively the positions of president and superintendents as well as directors.

The premises are on the north bank of Park River, on the line of the

New York and New Haven and Providence and Fishkill railroads, from which branch tracks run to the works. The locality is about an eighth of a mile from the Union Passenger Depot on Asylum Street. The main building is of brick, with Portland stone trimmings, four stories high, 225 by 45 feet, having an area in the aggregate of 40,500 square feet.

In addition is one of the finest foundries in New England, 120 by 60

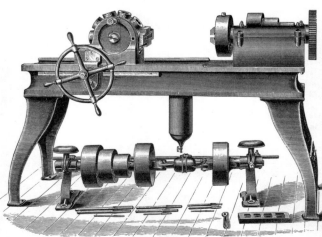

No. 3 (POWER) BOLT CUTTER.

feet, with cleaning and pickling rooms 48 by 40 feet, all built in the most substantial manner of brick, with walls twenty inches thick, and slate roof. A Woodruff & Beach engine of 60 horse power drives the machinery. A building supplementary to the foundry is used for core making. Immense ovens for baking cores capable of receiving the largest fabrications of this class, are connected with the foundry, which is furnished with a crane of fifteen tons lifting capacity. About four tons daily are turned out from this foundry, of first-class castings.

In the machinery department of the principal building are in constant use 200 lathes, 60 planers, 25 drills, and of milling, screw and other machines about 30. This does not comprehend vises and other hand tools not driven by power, or the machinery in the extensive pattern shop, which, by the way, is most complete in its arrangements and fittings for producing models and patterns for castings and forgings, as demanded by the exigencies and the exactions of the managers, who will not be satisfied with anything short of attainable perfection in the ultimate results of their work. In the forging shop, which is 175 x 42 feet, there are ten fires, a Marchand & Morgan steam hammer of 700 pounds, a Hotchkiss atmospheric hammer of 60 pounds for rapid work, 2 drop hammers, 1 tilt hammer and 1 shear.

For years the business of the firm has been largely the production of sewing machine tools and those for the general use of the machinist. To this category should be added tools for the manufacture of rifles and pistols, and special machinery for the production of appliances for the perfection of other manufactures or for particular uses. In the production of machinists' tools the company aims at simplicity, durability, convenience and adaptation to the work to be performed, rather than to show and surface finish. No ground or emery-surfaced bearing is permitted, but all the wearing surfaces are fitted by scraping. The perfection of the work and the easiness of the working of the lathes and planers made by the company, is so generally acknowledged that no particular description of their qualities need be introduced.

We cannot spare the space necessary to fully describe any, or even name all the different kinds of machinists' machinery and tools manufactured by The Pratt & Whitney Company. We give small cuts of a few of their machines, but for descriptions must refer the reader to the Company.

Head Dressing and Leveling Machine.

Barrel Power Windlass.

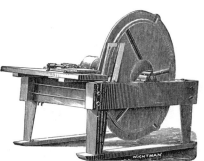

Machine for Dressing and Jointing Headings.

E. & B. HOLMES,

Manufacturers of

Barrel, Keg, Shook and Stave

Machinery.

BUFFALO, N. Y.

Our readers and especially those interested in the manufacture of barrels, or who use the article to any great extent in their various callings, are doubtless aware that there has been invented machinery by means of which the labor of skilled mechanics, may, in a great measure be dispensed with, and the work readily accomplished by ordinary laborers at a great reduction of cost.

We recently devoted a few hours to the inspection of a very extensive barrel factory, our object being to examine the operation and process of barrel making, as performed by the machinery illustrated on this page.

The staves are first perfectly finished on both sides at one and the same time, whether straight, crooked or winding, by the Machine for Dressing Rived and Sawed Staves.

They are next taken to another ma-

ends of the cask are formed to receive the barrel heads, finishing both ends at the same time at the rate of from 1,000 to 1,500 per day and chamfers, levels, howels and crozes a cask of imperfect periphery with the same exactness as if it were a perfect circle.

We now have the barrel completed excepting the heads and hoops.

Barrel heads are not made of a single piece but of two or more jointed and doweled together. To make the joints and prepare the pieces of heading for the dowel pins is the province of the Combined Fan and Heading Jointing and Dowel Boring Machine, which also blows all the dust and shavings made to the fuel room.

After the heading is doweled together in squares of proper size for making barrel heads the squares are passed through the Head Dressing and Leveling Machine which gives them a smooth and level surface, and finishes them at the rate of from 5,000 to 6,000 per day.

The next operation is turning the heads and beveling their edges ready for the cask, which is accomplished by the use of the machine for Turning Barrel Heads of all sizes. This machine after receiving the heads, finishes and discharges them at the rate of five tight or ten slack Barrel

Machine for Turning Barrel Heads of all sizes.

Machine for Sawing off Staves.

Chamfering, Howeling and Crozing Machine.

Combined Fan and Stave Jointing Machine.

Combined Fan, with Heading, Jointing and Dowel Boring Machine.

chine and jointed on their edges, and the correct bevel and bilge given, so that each piece is in proper form to take its place in making up the barrel, and all the debris is blown through conductors to the fuel room. This work is accomplished by the Combined Fan and Stave Jointer.

The staves are then set up in the lower head and quarter iron truss hoops, in the Barrel Setting up Form.

A rope is then passed around the flaring ends of the staves, and they are brought together ready to receive the upper head truss hoop by use of the Barrel Power Windlass.

It now assumes the form of a barrel and is next compressed endwise and made level so that the cask will assume a perpendicular position when upon its end. This is accomplished by the Machine for Leveling Barrels and casks.

For the next stage of the proceeding it is taken to the Chamfering, Howeling and Crozing Machine represented on this page in operation—an invention of extraordinary merit and ingenuity. By this machine the

Heads per minute. It will also make all sizes and is easily and speedily changed from one size to another by the turning of one hand wheel, and will make the heads oval or round as desired.

The combined Leveling and Trusshoop Driving Machine, herein illustrated, is for trussing Slack Barrels such as used for flour, sugar, salt, cement, &c. The machine receives the Barrel with all the trusshoops on it, but not driven, by operating the foot tredle and hand lever, the machine being in motion—the drivers being brought in contact with all the trusshoops and forcing them to their proper places—and at the same time levels the cask. This machine works at the rate of 2,000 barrels per day.

We have thus briefly described some of the leading features of a portion of the labor saving machinery for barrel making. Our space is too limited to permit us to enter into detail more largely but we refer the reader to the firm whose name heads this article, with the assurance that they will be pleased to furnish a catalogue fully describing the machinery manufactured by them.

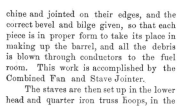

Truss Hoops. Barrel Setting-up Form.

Machine for Driving Truss Hoops.

Machine for Dressing, Rived and Sawed Staves.

Combined Barrel Leveling and Truss Hoop Driving Machine for Slack Work.

Machine for Dressing Sawed Staves.

DALTON AND PAPER.

—:o:—

Weston's Famous "Old Defiance Mills."

—:o:—

Paper derives its name from the Greek papyrus, an Egyptian plant which was so much used by the ancients in all kinds of writing. As our knowledge is derived from experience, it has been the effort of men of different ages to employ every possible expedient to preserve and give permanence to their ideas. Without the records of passing events, to be transmitted to future generations in a manner more permanent and reliable than by oral communication, history would be no more credible than Grecian or Roman mythology, or the uncertain narratives of tradition.

We learn that when the art of writing was once discovered, stones, brick, leather, stuccoed cloth, leaves and inner and outer bark of trees, plates of lead, wood, wax and ivory were all employed for its purpose. Among the relics of antiquity, especially in Egypt, are found pieces of pot-

kinds of paper; especially of the Egyptian papers, and the perfection to which the Chinese and Japanese have carried the art of paper-making, but it is more particularly of the manufacture of linen paper that we intend to speak in this article. More than one hundred different substances, many of them once considered worthless, have been utilized for the manufacture of paper of various grades and qualities. By far the largest portion of these belong to the vegetable kingdom; comparatively few to the animal kingdom, but still less to the mineral.

The invention of making paper from linen and cotton rags, as now manufactured throughout Europe, in the East Indies, and in America has been ascribed to different nations. Scaliger credits it to the Germans, but adduces no proof for his assertion. Moffei gives it to the Italians, and others to some Greek refugees at Bazil. Others claim that the honor belongs to the Chinese, who manufactured it in several provinces as we now do. But it is quite certain this invention was known in Europe before any communication was opened with China

It is claimed that a paper mill was in operation in Toledo, Spain, as early as 1085. The oldest specimen of paper made from linen, known to be in existence in Spain, is used to record a treaty of peace between the king of Aragon and Spain in 1178. The earliest English manuscripts on linen paper with a date that has been discovered is of the fourteenth year of Edward III. The introduction of this industry into France, Germany and Italy was as early as the fourteenth century.

Paper was made in England during the reign of Henry VII, but the first mill of importance was established during the reign of Elizabeth.

In 1693 the first paper mill in America was built at Roxborough, near Germantown, Penn. It is a singular fact, however, that printing had been introduced into the colonies fifty years before this time. A mill was constructed on Chester Creek, Delaware County, Penn, in 1714, from which the press of Benj. Franklin was supplied, and furnished the bank-note paper used for printing the continental currency. Of the sixty-three mills in operation in the colonies in 1787, forty-eight were in Penn., producing altogether, paper valued at about two hundred and fifty thousand dollars.

The rapid increase in paper-making during the present century, especially those qualities designed for newspapers and books, has been the result of an unprecedented increasing demand for these productions. In no

Of the particular line of goods made at this mill we have no hesitancy in saying there is none better. We have nowhere else seen any so remarkably and uniformly excellent in every respect, and that there is substantial foundation for this commendation, the many medals won in competitory exhibitions are ample proof. We give herewith *fac similes* of some of them. The business is that of making thoroughly good record and ledger paper, for State, county and government record books, banking and insurance ledgers, and for all those purposes where strength, solidity, durability and uniformity in quality and finish are so essential. To succeed in this is the aim of the proprietor, and with this end in view every stage in the processes which bring about the desired result, is under the most vigilant and skillful direction. Supervising all are Captain Weston's eye and hand, trained by many years of practical experience, and inspired by the praiseworthy determination to place his goods in the front rank and keep them there. He has met with grand success, and gained a name for his production with which he may feel more than gratified. In the market, to-day, the brand " Byron Weston's Linen Ledger Paper," is as certain a guaranty of value and reliable standard as is the " Victoria Rex " upon the coin sterling of Her Majesty's kingdom.

BYRON WESTON'S PAPER MILLS, DALTON, MASS.

tery, bearing inscriptions of soldiers' furloughs, orders of admission, memoranda accounts, etc. But these materials gave place in due time to paper of different kinds, successively from the Egyptian to that prepared from old rags.

For want of sufficient knowledge, as well as proper facilities for manufacturing paper for a long time after the invention of writing, the materials used for that purpose were such as required but little mechanical fashioning to fit them for the purpose designed.

It is not the design of this article to give the history of the invention and successive improvements in paper making, nor to enumerate the many kinds which have served their purpose and been more or less popular at different periods in the world's history. The following are perhaps most worthy of notice,—first, the Egyptian ; second, that made from cotton ; third, paper made from the inner bark of trees ; fourth, chinese paper ; fifth, Japanese paper ; and lastly, paper prepared from linen and cotton rags.

Would space allow, we might present our readers in this connection with an extended historical account of the origin and use of these various

country in the world are there as many papers published as in the United States. In fact more paper is manufactured in this country for that purpose than in England and France combined.

We wish in this connection to call the attention of our readers to a single manufactory of linen paper.

There are few business men in the country—certainly very few stationers—to whom the word Dalton will not at once suggest the article, Paper, and, uniting the two, Dalton-Paper, we have the pretty name of one of the best known Massachusetts towns. Dalton will not at once suggest the article, and with it the product that has made her famous, like Newcastle for coals, or Cheshire for cheese.

Dalton is, to be sure, only a rural bit of a village, modestly hiding among the Berkshire Hills, but the old Bay State does not contain a more healthful, prosperous or thrifty township. That part of its population dependent upon their labor for support finds constant and well remunerated employment in the factories and mills that make the sweet music of industry along her streams, while it is notable, too, how firm and safe have stood her manufacturers for generations, through the most threatening financial storms. Many are the commercial gales they have weathered without a shake or falter. There is always a demand for the best. In good times everybody wants the highest grade of goods, and in " dull times " the class of customers who understand that " the best is the cheapest " seek out the very best, and thus such productions as Dalton is renowned for have a market when there is none for the inferior products of rivals, and thus we may account for this unvarying thrift and unbroken prosperity. The wheels of her mills are kept running and the hum and rattle of busy machinery ceases not.

And so it has been for upwards of three-quarters of a century, for it was in 1800 that Zenas Crane, in the humblest way began the making of paper in Dalton. In 1809 David Carson built a mill, and from those early years there has been growth and extension as fast as the unexcelled excellence of the paper made here became more and more widely known. Since 1800 many mills have been erected, a fine example of which we give in the illustration adorning this page, the old " Defiance Mills " of Capt. Byron Weston.

Our illustration is a faithful picture of Mr. Weston's extensive and handsome establishment and its surroundings. A walk through the building reveals some of the secrets through which the manufactures of the mill have won their great repute. We notice scrupulous cleanliness everywhere; we see every employée diligent, attentive, in earnest in his work and doing it well; we find all the machinery in the best state of perfection, in superb order, and under the direction of veterans in the profession. In the stock room are bales upon bales of the first grades of new linen, which is the only material, excepting, of course, the necessary chemicals, used in making this paper. It is really what it purports to be, linen paper and nothing else, and in handling the beautiful sheets as they fall from the cutter of the new sixty-six inch Fourdrinier, we do not wonder that the maker can comply with perfect complacency with the law of Records which requires the name of the manufacturer and the year of its production to be " watermarked " in every sheet, for such paper honors a name, quite as much as any thing can honor it.

SKEIN SCREWS.

(Established 1863.)

Plumb, Burdict & Barnard,

Manufacturers of BOLTS & NUTS,

Buffalo, N. Y.

A celebrated writer recently designated the present as pre-eminently the "Silver Age," we think our time might better be denominated as the "Iron Age." Iron is the most widely diffused of all the metals, and forms a constituent part of almost everything we see about us in the material world. Intrinsically iron is the most valuable of metals, because adapted to a greater variety of use than any other. If gold and silver were as common and easily obtained as iron, their market price would scarcely reach the same relative proportion, reversed, as now: *i. e.*, a pound of iron would be worth as much more than a pound of gold or silver, as the gold and silver is now worth more than the iron, for the simple reason that gold and silver could not be put to the various uses to which iron is adapted.

CARRIAGE BOLTS.

Within the last fifty years great advances have been made in the manufacture of iron and iron goods. When the mature man of to-day was a boy there were few iron bridges and no iron vessels. Now the largest and best steamships that majestically ride upon the oceans are almost exclusively built of iron, and the great bridges that span mighty rivers, allowing lightning express trains to pass from shore to shore are constructed of the same material.

The almost numberless uses to which iron is put has been one of the best incentives to the inventive minds of the age, and ingenious machines have been constructed to fashion the metal into all conceivable shapes, without resorting to the slow and laborious forgings and other hand processes of the olden times. It is, comparatively but a few years since the expense attendant upon the erection of iron structures was so great as to deter many from its use, and no small part of this expense grew out of the method then in vogue of making the bolts and nuts, with which the various parts of the finished structure must be joined, by hand. In those days every bolt had its own special nut, and every nut its bolt, and no other bolt or nut would exactly fit this special pair.

But these things have been changed. By the aid of machinery any desired quantity of bolts of any given size or pattern may be made, and nuts furnished, cut with such accuracy that every nut will fit any bolt, so that in putting the parts of a bridge or other large structure together, no time is lost in the workman's hunt for bolts and nuts that will fit. Moreover, bolts and nuts manufactured by machinery are much cheaper than those made by hand, and between the saving in cost price and in cost of time in using, the introduction of machine made bolts and nuts has done much toward cheapening the construction of heavy iron work, and has so reduced the time necessary for their erection as to make it easier to build iron bridges, etc., than wooden ones. But the making of nuts and bolts is not confined to such as are needed in large structures, such as bridges, etc., carriage makers, machinists; indeed all who use nuts and bolts or screws in large numbers, almost universally purchase them from those who make their manufacture a specialty.

Perhaps no firm in this country has done more to bring about this state of affairs than have Plumb, Burdict & Barnard of Buffalo, N. Y. This firm was founded in 1863 by George C. Bell, who commenced business with two carriage bolt headers and two nut machines, with a capacity of making about 8,000 nuts and bolts per day. Mr. Ball's goods were favorably received and had soon acquired a reputation which occasioned a demand calling for increased facilities of manufacture, and in 1868 Mr. Ralph H. Plumb formed a co-partnership with him. In 1869 they purchased of Mr. Burdict his valuable patents for bolt and nut machines (Mr.

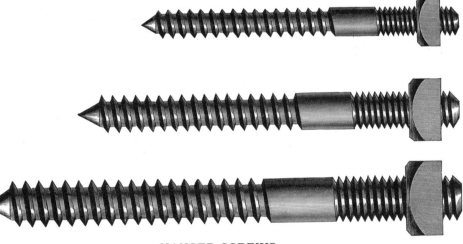

HANGER SCREWS.

B. becoming at that time a member of the firm) and commenced the manufacture of Machine Bolts, Coach and Skein Screws on a larger scale. This continued about two years, their business meantine constantly increasing, when Mr. Bell, the original founder of the business sold his interest in the American house, to his partners, Plumb & Burdict, and went to England, where he established a large manufactory, located at Saddleworth, Yorkshire, (Messrs. Plumb & Burdict retaining an interest in the English house. The English firm have been largely engaged in the manufacture of the celebrated Burdict's Patent Bolt Machines, which have been largely introduced in Europe, and indeed throughout the civilized world, their superiority being acknowledged wherever they are known.

Upon the retirement of Mr. Bell from the American house and the establishment of the English one, Messrs Plumb & Burdict admitted Mr. Barnard as a partner, the firm since that time having been known as Plumb, Burdict & Barnard. From its first inception this house has been a continued success. The high reputation earned by their first productions has been fully mantained, and to-day they occupy a proud position in the foremost ranks of American Manufacturers. From the small beginning of a modest shop with a capacity of 8,000 bolts and nuts per day they have steadily grown until now their works cover one half of the block bounded by Clinton, Eagle, Adams and Watson Streets, in the east part of Buffalo, and near the track of the New York Central Railroad Company, with a capacity of fully 100,000 bolts and screws, and four tons of nuts per day. Their goods have achieved a wide spread reputation, and their sales are not confined to the United States, but their productions are exported in immense quantities to Canada, Australia, South America and other foreign lands. In fact wherever American iron work is known, the goods of Plumb, Burdict & Barnard are rated as first in their class.

Success such as this can only be obtained by intelligent and persistent effort to produce the very best.

We present cuts of a few of the many bolts manufactured by this house. To describe or even enumerate the different kinds, or to suggest the various uses to which they may be applied, would more than fill the space at our disposal. Suffice it to say that their name is legion, and that the same care is bestowed upon every article they manufacture.

The firmly established reputation of this house is of itself a sufficient guarantee that those who patronize them will always find their works the best that highly improved machinery and skilled labor can produce.

As mechanics they have no superiors, and as business men they are too well and favorably known to need a word of commendation at our hands.

COACH SCREWS.

When we consider the highly important purpose served by bolts and screws, and the safety or destruction of life and property resulting from their efficiency or imperfection, we may in some measure approximate a proper appreciation of the necessity of perfect material and skilled labor in their production. An imperfect screw or a defective bolt may ruin an otherwise perfect structure, and cause the most disastrous results; hence the necessity of exercising the greatest care and judgment in the selection of material as well as the highest attainments in mechanism in its manipulation.

The honor of inventing the screw is usually ascribed to Archimedes, in the third century before the Christian Era, but we have reason to believe that its invention dates from a higher antiquity, and that to him belongs only the credit of classifying it as one of the mechanical powers, and of demonstrating a rule for calculating its efficiency.

Those of our readers who may desire further information in regard to the manufactures of this house, will receive polite attention by calling at their establishment or addressing them at Buffalo, N. Y.

MACHINE BOLTS.

MILWAUKEE IRON COMPANY,

Manufacturers of

IRON RAILS, FISH PLATES, CAR LINKS, MERCHANT BAR, HORSE SHOES AND PIG IRON.

Milwaukee, Wisconsin.

——:o:——

Iron is not only the most useful of all known metals, but is also one of the most generally diffused of all the products of Nature. In some form it is found in almost everything having a place in the organic or inorganic world. It is present not only in the tangible forms given to it by the aid of man, and in which all are familiar with it, but nature uses it as liberally and for as many different purposes. Scarcely a thing is visible around us into which iron does not enter. It is a component part of our life blood and forms no inconsiderable portion of our daily food. Not only is our sense of taste gratified, but the sense of sight, also, is gladdened by its presence, for many of the brilliant colors of the floral kingdom are attributable to it. Nor is it only in this world of ours that iron is found. Spectral analysis has traced its presence in nearly all the stars.

A history of the iron trade would be interesting but to trace the various improvements made in the methods of reducing ores and manufacturing iron, and note the haps and mishaps of their inventors, would much more than fill the space allotted to this article, consequently, we will confine ourselves to a very brief record of the business in this country.

From a tract entitled *A True Declaration of Virginia* published in 1610, we find that in that year, Thomas Gates testified before the Council in London, that in the country there were "divers minerals," especially "iron oare," some of which after being worked in England had been found to yield as good iron as any in the world. From a similar tract published in 1620, we find that among those recently sent to the colony there were "out of Sussex about forty, all famed to iron workes." Beverly, in his *History of Virginia*, speaks of an "iron works at Falling Creek, Jamestown River," which had attained "so near a perfection that they writ word to the Company in London that they did not doubt but to have plentiful provision of iron for them by the next Easter." This was in 1620. In 1621, three of the master workmen having died, the Company sent over Mr. John Berkeley, his son Maurice, and twenty other experienced workmen. On the 22d of May following, the whole settlement, comprising some four hundred persons, except a boy and a girl who managed to hide themselves, were massacred by the Indians, and the manufacture of iron was stopped and not renewed at this point until 1712. The early colonial governments were anxious to encourage the manufacture of iron, and the authorities of Virginia, avowedly to check too excessive attention to the raising of tobacco, and to encourage the consumption of iron and its manufacture into various articles needed for use, and which were then imported, in 1662 prohibited the exportation of iron under a penalty of a forfeiture of ten pounds of tobacco for every pound of iron exported. This tax was in force until 1682.

When the colonization of Massachusetts was actively begun, the manufacture of iron was counted upon as one of the prospective sources of profit, and experts were sent into the colony as early as 1628 to prospect and report to the Court of Assistants, in London. Whether these men discovered any mines does not appear, but no steps toward the manufacture of iron was taken for fifteen years.

In November, 1637, the General Court of Massachusetts granted to Abraham Shaw one-half of any "coles or yron stone wh[ch] shall bee found in any common ground whi[ch] is in the countrye's disposing."

In 1643, Mr. Bridges carried with him to England specimens of bog ore from the ponds, near Lynn, Massachusetts, and in connection with Winthrop, and others, formed a "Company of Undertakers for the Iron Works." One thousand pounds were subscribed, and with this capital and a corps of workmen, Winthrop returned to New England the same year. Subsequently others joined in the enterprise, and in 1663 the General Court granted them the exclusive privilege of making iron for twenty-one years, provided that within two years they made enough to supply the colony. They were allowed the use of any six locations not already granted, provided that within ten years they set up in each place a furnace and a forge, and "not a bloomery only." The stockholders were exempt from taxation on their stock, their agents from public charges, and they and their workmen from trainings.

In March 1637, Joseph Mallison, who was interested in a furnace at Duxbury, Mass., memorialized the legislature for a grant of unimproved lands, in consideration of his having introduced the use of sand moulds for casting hollow ware, such as pots and kettles, of which he claimed to be "the sole promoter, whereby the province saved annually at least twenty thousand pounds importations." This improvement he had made some years previously and in acknowledgement of his claim he was granted two hundred acres of unimproved land. The introduction of casting in sand instead of clay moulds has also been ascribed to Jeremy Florio, an Englishman.

In 1750, the British Parliment passed an act to encourage the importation from the colonies of pig and bar iron, and prohibiting the erection or working of in the colonies any slitting or rolling mills, plating forges or steel furnaces. At the time of the passage of this law there were found to be in existence in the colonies, two slitting mills at Middleboro, one at Hanover and one in Milton, as also a plating mill with a tilt hammer, and one steel furnace.

It will thus be seen that long before the United States, as such, had an existence the people were largely interested in the manufacture of iron, and that they were far advanced in their methods. With the growth of our country this industry has been removed from its old centres to larger and better paying fields. America is blessed with an abundance of iron ore diffused over all the land, and of a quality second to none in the world. It is found in every State and Territory in the Union, but for reasons which are apparent to all who give the subject a moment's thought, it is most profitably manufactured in the growing West, which teems with large deposits of the richest ores, and possesses the advantage of having, or being near to abundant supplies of suitable fuel for smelting purposes. Among the notable iron deposits of the West are those of Wisconsin. Previous to its admission as a State, the existence of valuable beds of iron ore within its limits was known, but it is only within a few years that their development has enlisted the active attention of many prominent business men, manufacturers and capatalists. True, some time since, at several points feeble efforts were made to utilize them, but no attempt on a large scale was made until the formation of the Milwaukee Iron Company. Near Ironton, Sauk County, beds of brown hematite occur, and from these, a little charcoal blast furnace has for some years smelted iron for

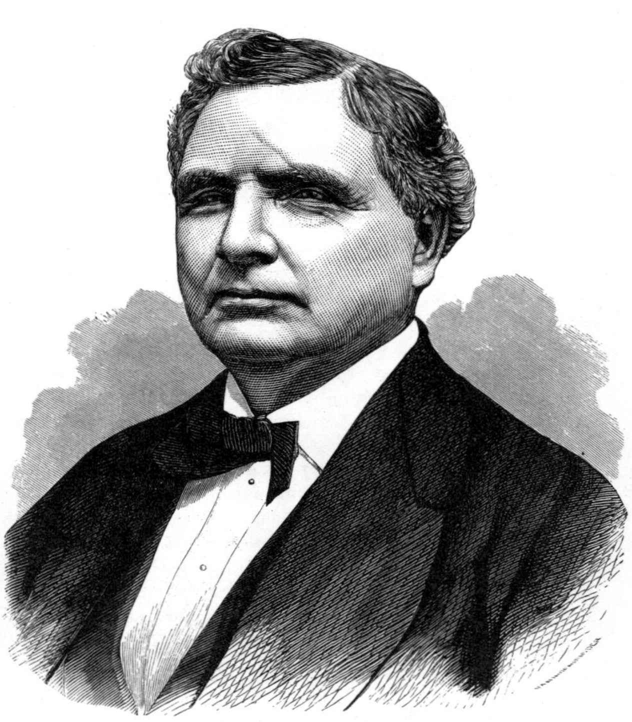

CAPT. E. B. WARD,
Founder of the Milwaukee Iron Company.

the supply of its small foundry and others in the vicinity. At Iron Ridge a vast deposit of oolitic hematite crops out at the surface and extends north and south, beneath the surface, many miles, a bed of clean ore of great width and depth. Two charcoal furnaces, at and near Iron Ridge, have for twenty years drawn their supplies from this bed. More recently effort was directed to the Black River Falls deposits, near the town of this name. The vast mounds at that point, almost wholly outcrops of purely silicious ore, yielding about 45 per cent., of pure metallic iron, induced the erection of a small charcoal furnace and a little city, Dannemora, to centre about it, but alas, Dannemora and its furnace have fallen in ruins and the other establishments maintain an existence only by reason of the light demands they make upon the accessible timbered regions. The larger furnaces at Iron Ridge and vicinity, with each succeeding year are more and more cut off by the rapidly diminishing forests from any hope for a much longer lease of profitable life.

It is easy, now to see that the Lake Shore of the State is the only region where the iron industry can be established in any magnitude to remain a permanent success. This was the shrewd observation of the late Capt. E. B. Ward, who, in canvassing the opportunities of the State for such enterprises readily chose Milwaukee as offering the greatest advantages:—embracing cheap transportation for fuel from Erie and Buffalo, as freight rates could in many cases be scarcely greater than cost of handling; otherwise the grain fleets must return from the Eastern ports of the lakes light or in ballast. Its comparative nearness to the Lake Superior Iron Ore Ports, Marquette and Escanaba, and the absence of all towage expenses from Escanaba would make the cost of ore transportation a minimum —below any competitive points. As a point for the manufacture of Railroad iron Milwaukee offered the greatest inducements. Two lines of railway, each having a length of thousands of miles, connect the city with the vast net-work of railways of the Western States. While its location so far West would enable it to rule out Eastern competitors by the high rates of freight over the intervening distance. With all this railway system for a market, the inducement was sufficient for the erection of a rail mill as the initial step in the enterprise.

The successful growth of the business is the best exemplification of the wisdom and foresight exercised by its founder. A site for the works was chosen just without the city limits. Of the large tract secured, fifty-two acres have been reserved for manufacturing purposes, so located that ample lake shore front would bound one side, which allows unlimited opportunity for a profitable disposition of all the refuse material, which so rapidly accumulates, often embarrassing or entailing great expense upon iron works. With this frontage on the lake and other water privileges, secured by a canal connecting with a tributary of the Milwaukee river and thus with the lake, opportunities are afforded far beyond probable requirements for all docks and the storage room needed for all raw materials as stock. The docks are all supplied with numerous economical appliances such as steam engines, cranes and trestle work, for unloading quite a fleet of vessels at the same time. From these docks a railway system connects all with the tracks encompassing the mills, as well as with the Chicago, Milwaukee and St. Paul and the Chicago and Northwestern Railroads, which intersect the site of the works. From the inception of the enterprise in 1866, when the Company received its charter from the State, there has been no check to its growth, no reverse, except the common tide of general depression which has overtaken all manufacturing interests. Beginning in 1866 with a capital of $250,000 it has gradually grown until it now possesses a capital of $1,500,000, representing actual value.

An immediate market offering for rails, this branch of the business first received attention and the erection of a suitable mill was commenced, at once, and completed in 1868. This mill is fully equipped with the most approved of modern rolling mill machinery and is one of the most perfect mills of its class in the country.

That the Company might provide its own pig iron needed for conversion into the puddled iron requisite for rail heads, an interest was secured in the iron ore bed, at Iron Ridge previously mentioned. An examination of the metal from the ore of this mine, which had hitherto been esteemed unfit for most purposes of manufacture, proved it eminently valuable for the purpose of head iron for rails. The crystalline texture of iron made by puddling or boiling it, its remarkable hardness and its readiness to weld, perfectly adapt it for head iron. For the smelting of this ore a blast furnace was built at the works in 1869. Contemporaneously a puddle mill was erected to work up the pig metal into iron for rail heads. From this date the growth of the establishment has been continuous. In 1871, a companion blast furnace was built, served by the same hoist as No. 1 furnace. At the same time an additional puddle mill was built to convert the product of this furnace. To enlarge the capacity of the rail mill making it adequate to the product of the two puddle mills, another mill was erected in 1872 to be devoted exclusively to the heating and rolling of metal for the heads and flanges of rails, called a top and bottom mill, thereby relieving the rail mill-roll train and engine of this work.

Subsequent additions have been made, extending the manufacture to finished merchant bar iron of all grades and sizes, to Fish Plates, Car Links, Horse Shoes, with the design of adding still other branches of manufacture in response to the demands of the market.

A concise statement of the number of the various furnaces, with the machinery appertaining, the annual consumption of material by them, and their capacity for finished product, will best show the magnitude to which the works have attained and is here appended: There are

2 Blast Furnaces.
1 Top and Bottom Mill.
2 Puddle Mills.
1 Rail Mill.
1 Merchant Mill.
1 Fish Plate Mill.
40 Puddle Furnaces.
23 Heating Furnaces.
57 Steam Engines.
61 Boilers.
18 Forge Fires.
16 Pumps.
2 Locomotives. These consume,
60,000 Tons Bituminous Coal.
7,300 " Anthracite Coal.
50,000 " Coke.
Iron Ridge and Similar Ore, 28,000 tons.
Lake Superior Ore, 18,500 "
Limestone 22,000 "
They yield a product of
33,000 Tons Pig Iron.
44,000 " Rails.
15,000 " Merchant Iron.
9,000 " Fish Plates.

The excess of metal is made up in part of old rails which are re-rolled and of scrap iron re-worked into merchant iron.

Very complete and extensive machine shops and blacksmith shops constitute a part of the establishment, ample for all manner of repairs and the building of any needed machinery. For the handling and storage of the raw material and finished product two locomotives are in constant service. The company have in use three or four miles of private railroad tracks and a full mile of elevated track upon high trestle work to facilitate and economize storage. A thousand workmen, many of them skilled laborers and mechanics, are employed immediately about the works, and of the five thousand or more dependent upon their labor some three thousand have homes in the thriving little village of Bay View, which has been an outgrowth of the enterprise. How wide reaching and how beneficient has been the impulse radiating throughout the state, and, indeed, the entire Northwest from this single enterprise would be no easy matter to estimate. In the collection of so much skilled labor, and making it a part and parcel of the population of the State it has enriched it by a wealth more active than that from any other source. By practical showing it has quickened the perception of the citizens of the State to a true estimate of the substantial value of a diversified industry.

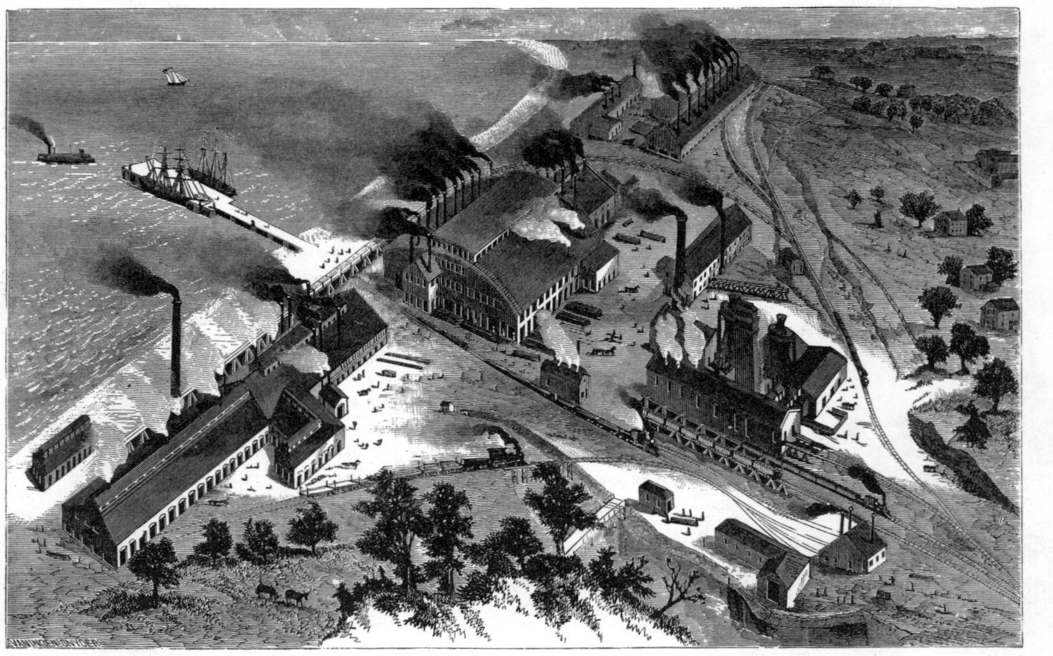

MILWAUKEE IRON CO.'S WORKS, MILWAUKEE, WIS.

SOUTH BOSTON IRON COMPANY,

Manufacturers of

Ordnance & Projectiles, Iron & Bronze Castings,

Boston, Mass

The South Boston Iron Company, also known as Cyrus Alger & Co.,

strength of ordinary castings, and is of the utmost importance in the manufacture of Ordnance.

The mortar gun "Columbiad," the largest iron gun that had then been cast in this country, was made under his supervision. It was of 12 inch caliber and had a range exceeding three miles. He also invented the method of making chilled rolls by which the face, or part subjected to great wear, is greatly hardened, without at all altering the natural density or strength of the other portions.

The first cannon ever Rifled in America, was made at these works in

We present on this page an exterior view of the works, from which the reader will be enabled to judge of their extent, while the interior views of the foundry and gun shop, with their mammoth cranes, and other appliances represented, will convey some idea of the magnitude of the operations. No establishment in the United States is more thoroughly equipped for the manufacture of Ordnance than this, and none has a better reputation at home and abroad.

From its capacity for furnishing ordnance and munitions, the importance of this establishment in a National point of view, in time of war,

VIEW OF WORKS OF THE SOUTH BOSTON IRON COMPANY, SOUTH BOSTON, MASSACHUSETTS,

was founded by Cyrus Alger, of Bridgewater, Massachusetts, in the year 1809, and soon attained a high reputation for the reliability and perfection of its work, such as Ordnance, Projectiles, Rolls, Hydraulic Presses, Heavy Geers, and castings for general machinery and ordinary trade purposes. Mr. Alger was one of the best practical Metallurgists of his day, and to him the world is indebted for the discovery of methods which have completely changed and vastly improved upon the old system of manufactures. He discovered a method of purifying cast-iron which gives it three times the

1834, and in 1836, Mr. Alger manufactured the first Malleable Iron Guns made in this country. He manufactured the first perfect Bronze Cannon for the United States Ordnance Department, and the world is indebted to him for numerous improvements in the construction of bomb shells and grenades, and in time fuses for the same. Our limited space forbids even a bare enumeration of his inventions.

Mr. Cyrus Alger died in the year 1856, and was succeeded by his Son, Mr. Francis Alger, who had attained eminence as a scientist, and was a thoroughly educated, practical mechanic,—the inventor of several improvements in the construction of shells for rifled guns and other projectiles, which were adopted by the United States Government. Mr. Francis Alger died in 1864.

The South Boston Iron Company have fully preserved and maintained the early reputation of the Alger Foundries, and the works have been extended and enlarged to a degree commensurate with the advancement and requirements of the times. They are located in South Boston and now cover some six acres of ground. They are completely equipped with all the appliances that can aid in the production of such manufactures as come within their line, and are capable of turning out annually one hundred 15 inch, or 25 ton guns, and an equal number of 9, 10, or 11 inch guns, made of iron; and 350 Bronze Guns for Field or Naval service, with their Carriages and Equipments, and a full compliment of Projectiles, in addition to 10,000 tons of general castings.

This Company has recently cast and finished a 12 inch Breech-Loading Steel-Lined Rifle, made after the Nathan Thompson system, which, when finished, weighed 42 tons. The rough block weighed 80 tons. Mr. Thompson, the patentee, was represented at the works by G. Leverick, Engineer, of New York, who, on the completion of the gun, under date of July 6th, 1875, wrote as follows:—

"I take pleasure in herewith certifying that the fabrication of the 12 inch Breech-Loading Rifle is complete, and in accordance with the specifications and drawings. In expressing my personal satisfaction therewith, I must also say that it is doubtful whether, there or abroad, the uniformity and strength of the materials, or the thoroughness and accuracy of the workmanship could have been equalled."

may be appreciated. Though specially fitted for the production of Guns and Projectiles of various descriptions, the manufactures of the Company are by no means limited to such articles. They are among the largest and most favorably known manufacturers of Chilled Rolls in the United States, the process of making which was introduced and patented by the founder of these works. Building Hydraulic Presses is another of their specialties; in fact, they do a very extensive foundry and machine business, affording employment to hundreds of skillful men.

Style B.

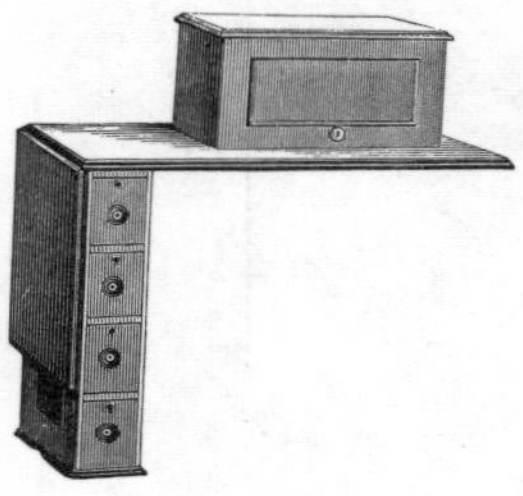

Plain Walnut, Table,
Drop-leaf and Paneled Cover, with Lock, Hinges, and Two, Three or Four side Drawers.

Style K.

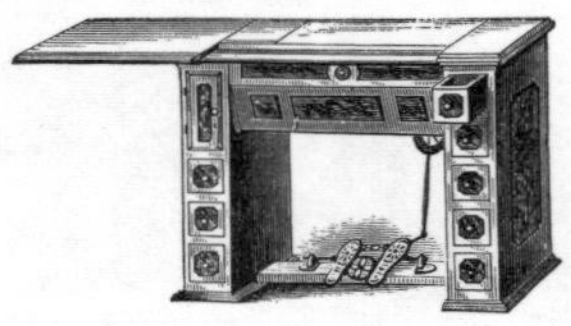

(OPEN.)
Cottage Cabinet,
Plain Walnut, Finished in Oil or Varnish.

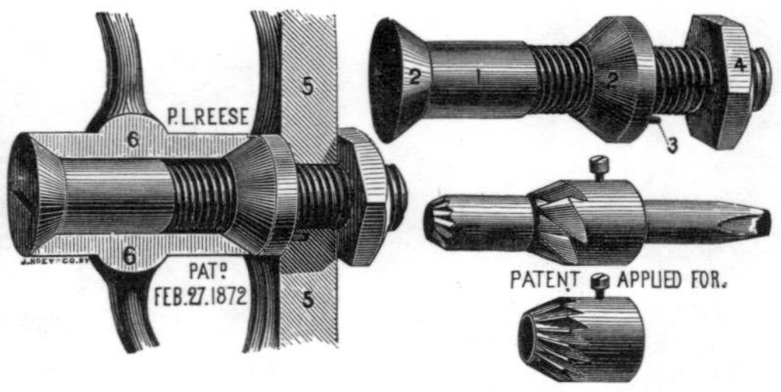

P. L. Reese's Patent Anti-Rattling Journal
Or Adjustable Axle, For taking up Lost Motion in the Band Wheel of Sewing Machines.

Style K.

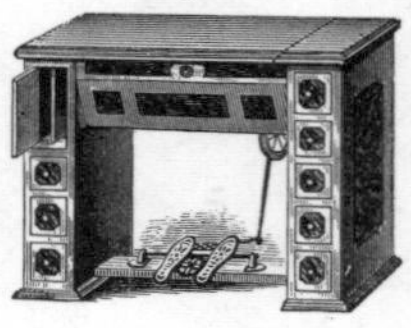

(CLOSED.)
Cottage Cabinet.
Fancy Walnut, Finished in Oil or Varnish. N. B.—Special Terms for Rosewood, Mahogany, or Inlaid Cabinets.

Style C.

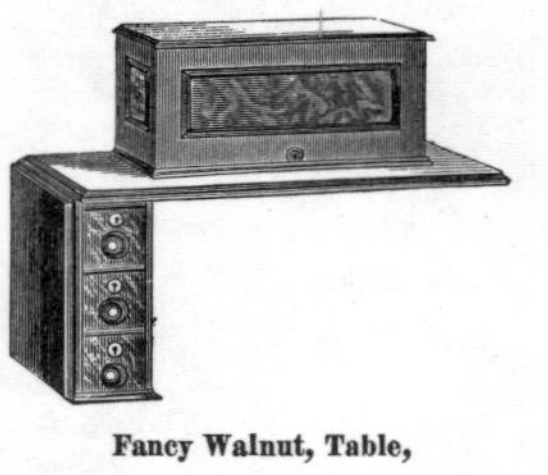

Fancy Walnut, Table,
Drop-leaf, and Cover, with Lock and Hinges, French Veneered Panels, and Two, Three or Four Drawers.

Style G.

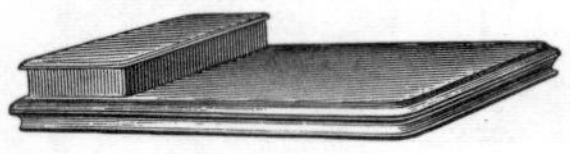

Plain Walnut, Table and Platform,
with or without cover.

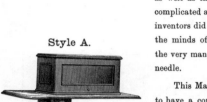

Style A.

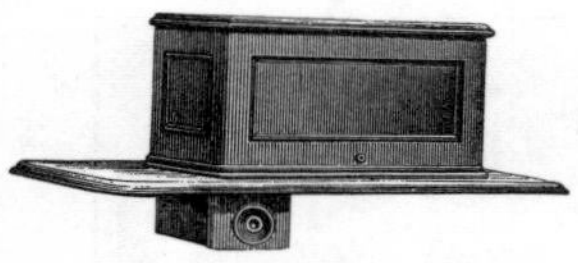

Plain Walnut, Table, Drawer, and Paneled Cover,
with Lock and Hinges, Finished in Oil or Varnish.

Style I.

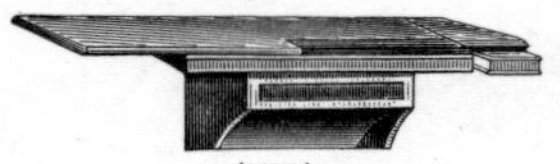

(OPEN.)
Cuthbert Cottage Table,
Plain Walnut, Finished in Oil or Varnish.

Style I.

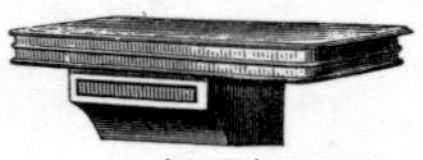

(CLOSED.)
Cuthbert Cottage Table,
Fancy Walnut, Finished in Oil or Varnish.

Style D.

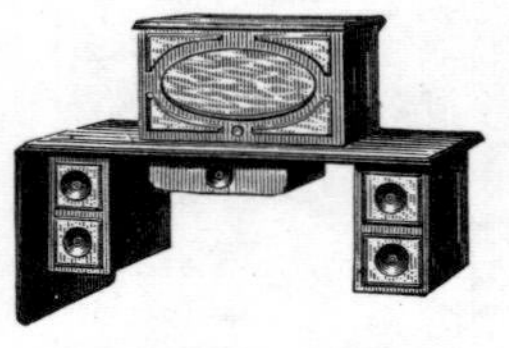

Fancy Walnut, Table,
Drop-Leaf and Cover, with Lock and Hinges, Front Ornamented with Fancy French Veneers, and Two Drawers on each side, finished in Oil or Varnish.

SEWING MACHINE CABINET WORK,

Manufactured by

VAN DYKE & DOWNS,

Nos. 473, 475 and 477 First Avenue, Cor. 28th St., N. Y.

The sewing machine is destined to immortality, not less because of its adaptation to human wants and necessities than of the improvements of which it is the occasion from year to year. Originally comparatively simple as well as imperfect in its construction, ends and aims, it has become a complicated and perfect machine, accomplishing purposes that its original inventors did not dream of. The idea of sewing by machinery had agitated the minds of inventors and others long before it came into practical use; the very many difficulties to be overcome being connected chiefly with the needle.

This Machine unlike many other useful and practical inventions seems to have a complete history. Its origin is remembered by those who are now enjoying its blessings, and its originator was personally known to many of them.

It is now about thirty-five years since two men,—a mechanic and a capitalist, in the City of Boston, attempted the production of a knitting machine, but proved incompetent for the task. Despairing of success by their own efforts, the result of their labors was brought to the attention of Ari Davis, an ingenious and eccentric man, who kept a shop in Cornhill, Boston, for the manufacture and repair of nautical instruments and philosophical apparatus. The shop's crew at once gathered about the knitting machine, to learn the principles of this attempted strange production.

Mr. Davis is reported to have broken in thus abruptly: "What are you bothering yourselves with a knitting machine for? Why don't you make a sewing machine?" "I wish I could," said the capitalist; "but it can't be done."

"O, yes it can," said Davis; I can make a sewing machine myself."

"Well," said the other, "you do it, Davis, and I'll insure you an independent fortune."

Although the conversation is said to have dropped there, and was never resumed, it was not without effect. Boastful as was Davis, he never attempted to construct a sewing machine; but among that group was a young man from the country, a new hand in the shop, who was much impressed by the emphatic assurance of the capitalist that a fortune was in store for the inventor of a sewing machine. The idea of sewing by the aid of a machine had never before occurred to him. This conversation, apparently accidental, and so trifling, no doubt was the origin of this indispensable household assistant. Whatever improvements may have been made since, it is now generally believed, and for all practical purposes admitted, that the late Elias Howe, Jr., was the original inventor of the sewing machine. His discovery, however, was mainly confined to the needle, and consisted wholly in the form of the needle and in the location of the eye. This difficulty overcome, the rest was comparatively easy, and from that day to this, improvement has followed improvement till now there is scarcely any sewing, embroidering, &c., that cannot be done by this ingenious machine and its attachments of various kinds.

We need not specify these in detail, as most people know what they are, and are more or less familiar with their operation. Suffice it to say they cover, nearly if not quite, the entire field of operations with the needle, accomplishing their work better, as a rule, than the latter can be done by hand. The triumphs in this direction are almost endless as well as complete, as every recurring fair, County, State or otherwise, fully demonstrates. The late fair of the American Institute was rich in demonstrations of this kind, much work of different kinds being exhibited, altogether superior to any that could have been done by hand.

The improvements referred to have extended to the cases of the sewing machine as well as its more material parts; many of the latter being highly ornamental as well as useful. The latest of those that have come under our notice are the Cottage Cabinet and Tables, manufactured by Messrs. Vandyke & Downs, and which were awarded the premium at the recent fair of the American Institute. The simple object of these improved cases is to increase the usefulness of the sewing machine as a whole, and to add to its ornamental character. We will give a brief description of both the cabinet and table, as the best means of conveying to our readers an idea of their usefulness and appearance.

The Cottage Cabinet when closed has somewhat the appearance of an ordinary secretary desk; and, except for the treadle underneath, would be readily mistaken for one.

On either end are rows of drawers or closed closets, according to fancy, which may be used for any purpose for which a secretary desk is used. The top is composed of one large leaf, which is movable, and one of smaller dimensions fixed and is so arranged that the large leaf can be swung around, forming an extra sized extension leaf for the support of the work while sewing. Beneath this cover is a deep box, into which the sewing machine when not in use is lowered. When required for use it is raised to its proper position, when it is ready for operation, the box in which it is enclosed is pushed back, telescoping in itself, and is out of the way of the operator. When the work is done the machine is again lowered into the box, the cover swung round to its proper position, when it becomes a table or desk for other purposes.

They are elegantly made in different kinds of wood, and are highly ornamental as well as useful. They can be used as checker and backgammon boards when the movable leaf is fitted for the purpose. It is the most perfect arrangement for a sewing machine ever introduced, and is adapted to any machine new or old. Any lady can have her machine, no matter of whose make, placed on a Cottage Cabinet by sending her order to the manufacturers or any sewing machine agent; the cabinets being sold by all sewing machine companies and agents.

The Cottage Table, so far as the top and box are concerned, is similar to the cabinet, and is managed in the same way; the standards being iron, as in the case of other sewing machines. When closed the machine is useful as a table for ordinary table work, writing, games, &c.; one end containing a drawer for thread and other articles used about the machine as in other cases.

This improvement, we understand, has proved a very great success; the demand for the table being so great as to compel the proprietors to establish a large factory for their manufacture. They occupy the premises on First Avenue indicated at the head of this article, the building being five stories in height, and replete with machinery adapted to the business. They give constant employment to a large number of hands, and the business may now be considered an established feature of our manufacturing system.

The firm employ none but first-class skilled workmen and use nothing but the very best of material, consequently every Cottage Cabinet, Table or other article turned out by them will be found to be very near perfection.

In conclusion we take pleasure in adding a word of praise clipped from the *Christian Intelligencer*:

The neatest thing in the way of a sewing machine case is that called "The Cottage Cabinet." It is made of black walnut and when closed looks like a cabinet desk; the machine is lowered into a drawer-like receptacle under the table. The large leaf is moved around over it, and forms an even and unincumbered surface, thus changing the sewing machine into a handsome piece of furniture. There are, besides, plenty of drawers and closets for spools, work, books, etc. Van Dyke & Downs, New York, are the manufacturers, and all sewing machine agencies can supply them.

Style H.

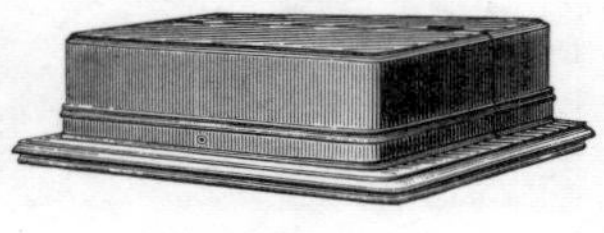

W. & W. Half Case,
Plain, Finished in Oil, or with Moulded Base Finished in Oil or Varnish.

Style F.

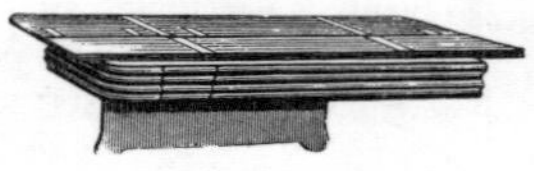

Fancy Walnut, Folding Cover,
with Silver Plated Lock and Hinges and French Walnut Veneered Panels, Finished in Oil or Varnish.

Style E.

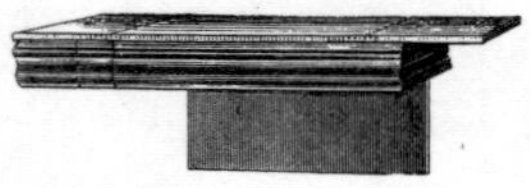

Plain Walnut, Folding Cover,
with Lock, Hinges, &c., Finished in Oil or Varnish.

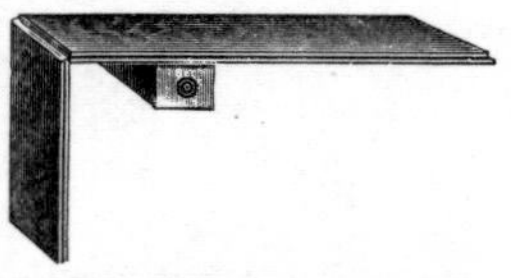

Plain and Built-up Black Walnut Tables,
with or without leaves, For all kinds of machines.

Style W.

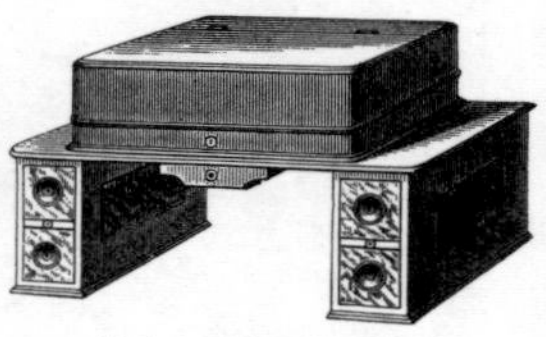

"W. & W." Half Cabinet,
Front and Back Ornamented with Fancy French Veneers and One or more Drawers on either or both sides, finished in Oil or Varnish.

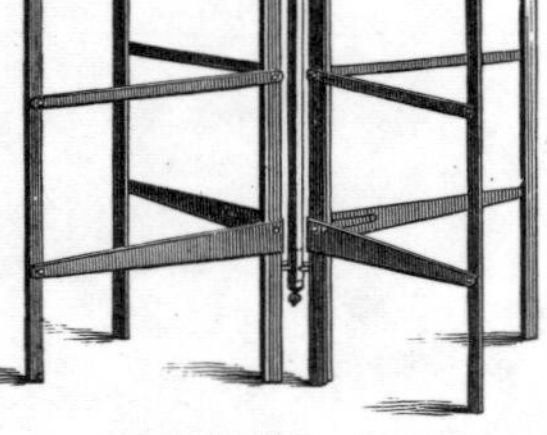

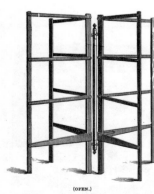

(OPEN.)
The "STAR" Clothes Horse.
As it appears when open and ready for use. It is very strong although so light that a child can handle it, does not get out of order, will not tip over and is ornamental as well as useful.

Style L.

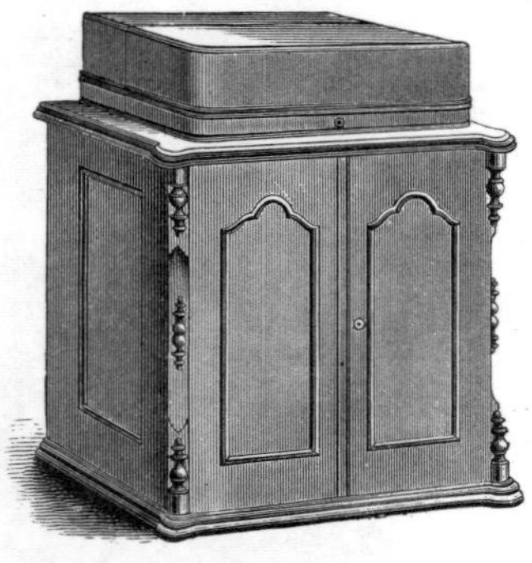

Plain Walnut Cabinet.
For "W. & W." Machines, Finished in Oil or Varnish.

Style M.

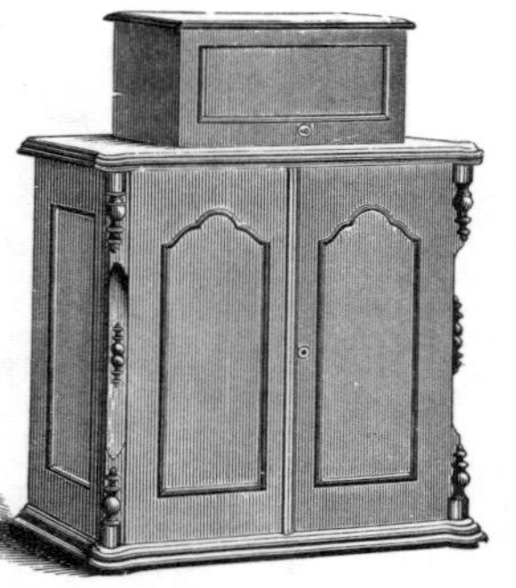

Plain Walnut Cabinet,
With either Box or Folding Top, Finished in Oil or Varnish.

Style O.

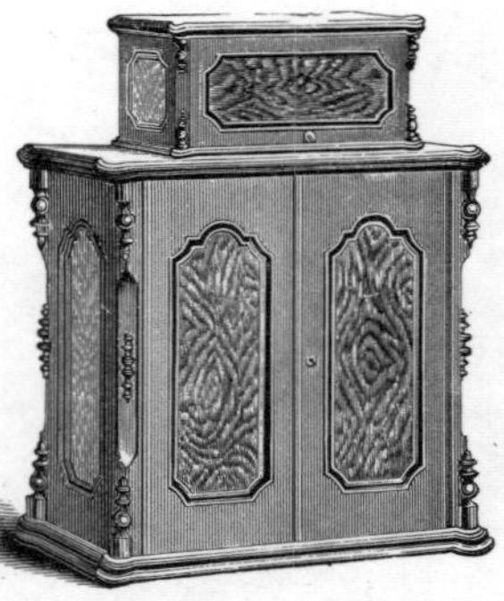

Fancy Walnut, Mahogany or Rosewood Cabinet,
Superbly Finished.

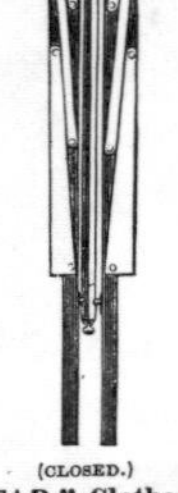

(CLOSED.)
The "STAR" Clothes Horse.
The above cut represents the "Star" Clothes Horse as it appears when closed, and gives a very correct idea of the smallness of the space it occupies when not in use.

Wm. H. JACKSON & CO.,

Manufacturers of
GRATES & FENDERS.

Union Square, near Broadway, N. Y.

[Established in Front Street, N. Y., in 1827.]

:0:

There is nothing, perhaps, which add so much to the brightness of home during the long winter evenings as a ruddy, blazing fire. A house may be sufficiently warmed by means of hot-air furnaces, steam heaters, or by stoves, but though the necessary heat is obtained from such appliances, they fail to diffuse with their warmth that look of cheerfulness and sense of comfort which one feels in the presence of an open fire; and, in properly planned and constructed houses, for this reason, if there were no others, grates will always be popular. We say "in properly planned and constructed houses" for the reason that within the past quarter of a century an antipathy to grates seems to have been developed among many architects and builders, and many houses have been erected in which grates cannot be successfully used, because the chimneys are narrow and crooked and lack the capacity to carry off the smoke and vapors generated by a grate fire. Straightway the fault is ascribed to the grate. It does not draw and must be imperfect in construction. Not so. No grate fire will ever smoke if there is a perfect draft to the chimney; and no grate can be so made that it will retain the vapors of combustion;

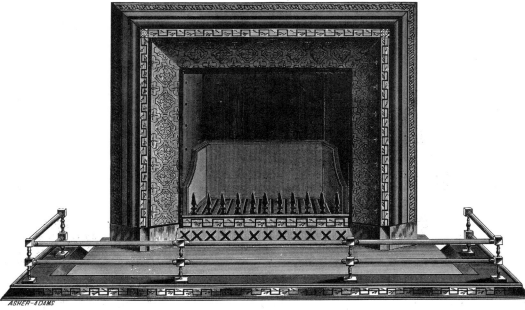

Drawing Room Grate.

of the largest and most widely known and popular manufacturers of Grates and Fenders in this country. Half a century of constant endeavor to understand the wants and completely fill the demands of the public; for

goods in their line has met with unqualified success, and they have grown to be leaders in their trade.

The engraving here presented of their elegant and spacious warerooms, will convey to the mind of the reader some idea of the magnitude of their business, but no attempt has been made to represent their work in detail which would be impossible in a cut of this size. The room in the foreground is occupied with samples of grates of various designs and styles of finish. Running through the centre, and on each side of the wareroom to the rear are large and expensive plate glass cases which are filled with samples of the most elegant pattern and finish, representing every style of architecture, and ranging in price from one hundred dollars to one thousand dollars each. We cannot, within the space at our disposal adequately describe the display; to be appreciated it must be seen, and we much doubt whether there are any who enter these warerooms for the first time who are not greatly surprised at the artistic beauty of many of the designs exhibited. The elaborate and expensive patterns kept under glass, will of course attracts the most attention, but in the front of the room where the less expensive kinds are shown, there are many beautiful designs. There is a large variety from which to choose, ranging in price from ten dollars for the complete grate suitable for an unpretentious home, to ten hundred dollars, for one intended for a palatial mansion.

In the immediate rear of the wareroom, and extending through to the next street, (18th Street,) is the manufactory, six stories in height.

VIEW OF WM. H. JACKSON & CO.'S SALESROOM, UNION SQUARE, NEAR BROADWAY, NEW YORK.

the smoke must either go up the chimney or out into the room.

We do not propose to discuss the relative merits and defects of the various methods of heating our houses, for present purposes it is only necessary to remark that none have ever questioned the healthfulness of warming by means of grate fires, and that among the advantages which are generally conceded as derived from their use, is perfect ventilation, soft and evenly diffused heat, and an air which is not deprived of its oxygen or humidity. Within the memory of those who have arrived at middle age the time was when all the better class of dwellings in cities were heated by grates or open fire places. Then came the era of stoves and hot-air furnaces, closely followed by steam heaters. As a people we are always ready to test the merits of every new invention, and so, the new methods of heating became popular, but the good old fashioned grate fire was never entirely discarded. In the early Autumn, before the weather is cold enough to warrant kindling the furnace fires, grates are indispensable; and within a few years many of our best families who had previously warmed their dwellings with furnace heat, have discarded it entirely and returned to the exclusive use of grates, as affording the most healthful, comfortable and cheerful fire attainable.

The firm of Wm. H. Jackson & Co., is one

Library or Dining Room Grate.

Here skilled mechanics, (many of whom have been in the employ of the firm upwards of twenty years) aided by the latest and most approved labor-saving machinery, produce the work. We cannot describe the different processes through which the numerous parts pass before the finished whole is produced, suffice it to say that after the various parts have been made, the work is fitted together in the rough from drawings if the design is new, or from sample if the same pattern has been made before. Having been assembled and fitted together, the pieces are taken apart, some to be simply filed and polished, others to be nickel plated, still others to be gold or silver plated, or bronzed or japanned, as the orders on hand may require. When each piece has safely passed through the various processes requisite to finish it, the parts are all collected together on the third floor, and then put together again, this time to form a completely finished and perfect grate. Experienced and skillful men only are employed, and when they pronounce the work finished it is examined by the foreman and if he finds it to be without flaw, it is approved, and sent to the store room on the second floor to await orders from the office for shipping.

This firm have facilities for manufacturing which are not surpassed by any in the business.

American Steam Gauge Co.,

OFFICE:

46 Chardon St., Boston, Mass.

J. C. Blaisdell, Pres't.   E. Burt Phillips, Treas.

H. K. Moore, Sup't.

—:o:—

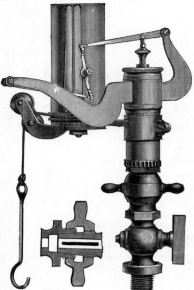

RICHARD'S INDICATOR.

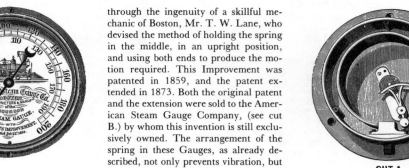

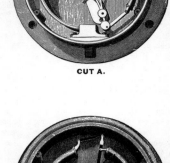

CUT A.

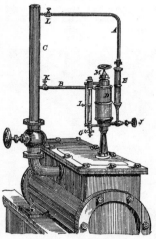

SEIBERT'S LUBRICATOR.

CUT B.

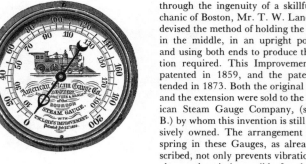

PRAY'S OILERS.

Probably no instrument connected with the use of steam as a motive power is of more importance than the Steam Gauge, and certainly no more reliable method of indicating pressure or vacuum has yet been discovered than that presented in the well known Bourbon Tube, either in the original or, far better, in that later form known as "Lane's Improvement."

Previous to 1849 there had been no practical instrument invented for the purpose of measuring and registering steam pressure, except the cumbrous mercurial column, and as this could only be used on stationary boilers, where economy of space was no object, the majority of engineers were never able to determine how much steam they had, and their only guard against explosion was the then very uncertain safety valve. In the year above mentioned, a gentleman named Eugene Bourdon, who was then engaged in the manufacture of stills, in Paris, France, discovered that a flattened tube, bent in a circular form and subjected to internal pressure, had a tendency to straighten itself, thereby producing the motion now utilized in the Bourdon and Lane Steam Gauges.

The discovery was purely accidental and would not have been made when it was, but for an error which occurred in M. Bourdon's establishment. Having completed a worm for a still which was to be shipped to the island of Cuba, he found its diameter to be greater than that of the cylinder which was to contain it, and to remedy this difficulty he flattened the worm on the outside until it was reduced to the proper dimensions. On placing the worm in the cylinder, and applying internal pressure, M. Bourdon was greatly surprised to discover that it exhibited a tendency to unwind. Being a man of marked ability, he at once perceived that here was a motion that could be turned to practical account, and he immediately set to work to devise a method of applying it for the purpose of indicating pressure. The result was the invention of the far famed Steam Gauge which bears his name.

The invention was patented in France by M. Bourdon, and was held in such high esteem by the Government of that country that the inventor was rewarded with the decoration of the Cross of the Legion of Honor. Engineers at once recognized it as one of the most valuable devices of the age, and M. Bourdon deservedly realized a handsome fortune from it.

In 1854, the American Steam Gauge Company purchased the patent right for the United States and began the manufacture of the instruments on a large scale. It was soon found, however, that the gauge as invented and constructed by Bourdon was not suitable for use on locomotives, because the spring, being fastened only at one end, was subject to too great a vibration, (see cut A.) This defect was soon obviated

through the ingenuity of a skillful mechanic of Boston, Mr. T. W. Lane, who devised the method of holding the spring in the middle, in an upright position, and using both ends to produce the motion required. This Improvement was patented in 1859, and the patent extended in 1873. Both the original patent and the extension were sold to the American Steam Gauge Company, (see cut B.) by whom this invention is still exclusively owned. The arrangement of the spring in these Gauges, as already described, not only prevents vibration, but also renders it impossible for the condensed steam to freeze in the tube when the gauge is not in use—very important advantages.

The manufacture of such delicate machinery as Steam Gauges requires the employment of the most experienced and skillful workmen, and the advantages possessed by the American Steam Gauge Company in this respect will be to some extent appreciated when we state that their principal employes have been in their service ever since the company was founded. The company have already manufactured nearly one hundred thousand gauges, and their sales are constantly increasing. It is a generally conceded fact that the greater the length of the spring the longer it will wear; and it is claimed that a spring of far greater length can be used in the same space by Mr. Lane's method than by any other known. The fact that this improvement is generally appreciated is amply attested by the large number of gauges of various other patterns which are sent to the works of the Company to be altered and fitted with the Lane Spring. The Gauges manufactured by this Company are all tested by a standard mercurial column, forty-six feet in height, and none that are not perfectly accurate are allowed to leave the works. As a proof of the merit of their productions the company refer with pride to the fact that the Hartford Steam Boiler Inspection and Insurance Company, have on file an accurate record of over twenty-three thousand gauges, and that they (the Hartford Steam Boiler Inspection Company) unhesitatingly affirm that the instruments manufactured by the American Steam Gauge Company are the best in use.

The American Steam Gauge Company also manufacture N. Seibert's Patent Steam Cylinder Lubricator, (for which R. F. Clark of Boston, Mass., office 48 Chardon Street, is General Agent,) and are also agents for the sale of the same. This is an invention which is acknowledged by the agents and engineers of a number of large corporations now using them, to far excel others which the same parties have tested, as to economy and utility. The proprietors warrant them to save fifty percent in oil over others which have been in use, and to lubricate perfectly at that. They are also the sole manufacturers of the Pray Oilers for lubricating shafting, etc., a valuable invention for the purpose for which it was designed.

In addition to the above this Company manufacture all kinds of instruments used in connection with Steamships, Locomotives, Engines, Water Works, etc., including the Combination Gauge.

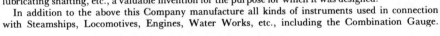

A. FIELD & SONS,

MANUFACTURERS OF TACKS AND NAILS,

Office and Factories, Taunton, Mass.,

Warehouse, 78 Chambers Street, New York.

—:o:—

The manufacture of Tacks has become an industry of far greater importance than is generally supposed. Tacks and small Nails enter into the manufacture of hundreds, nay, thousands of articles of every day use and consumption, and there is consequently increasing demand for them. Hundreds of men and boys are constantly employed in their manufacture, and when we stop to think that they are cut by Automatic Feeding Machines, each of which will cut 100,000, tacks per day, and that one boy will readily attend from three to five of these machines, we will begin to receive a faint idea of the millions of these little articles daily produced in this country.

We present on this page a cut of the extensive works of A. Field & Sons, who rank prominently among the best known manufacturers. A glance at the engraving will at once give the reader a fair idea of the size of the establishment and aid him in estimating the immense productions of this firm.

They manufacture tacks of every conceivable size, ranging from the almost infinitesimal, which will count nearly five thousand to the ounce, up to the largest sizes; they make them of every imaginable shape, and for every purpose for which tacks are used, and of

every material which is suitable for their manufacture. They are made of copper, iron and steel; some are tinned, others plated with copper, and still others, for the better kinds of work are finished with elaborate heads plated with the finer metals. We could scarcely give the names and weights of all the different styles made here, much less describe their uses, in the space to which this article must be limited. There are Swedes Iron Tacks for Upholsterers' use, Saddlers supply, Card Clothing, etc., American and Swedes Iron Shoe Nails, Zinc and Steel Shoe Nails, Carpet Tacks with or without leathers, Brush Tacks and Gimp Tacks, common and patent Brads, Finishing Nails, Annealed Trunk and Clout Nails, Hob and Hungarian Nails, Copper and Iron Boat Nails, patent Copper Plated Tacks and Nails, fine Two Penny and Three Penny Nails, Channel, Cigar Box and Chain Nails, Glaizer's Points, etc.; an assortment which is not excelled by any other manufacturer.

In this branch of industry the United States, confessedly stands at the head, and so far as other nations compete with us, it is by the use of American Machinery.

Previous to 1776 all nails had been forged, or pressed and finished by hand. Cut nails were unknown. In this year Jeremiah Wilkinson of Rhode Island invented a method of cutting tacks from sheet iron, and subsequently heading them. Later he applied the same method to the cutting of nails. The first machine for cutting nails, was invented about 1790, by Jacob Perkins of Connecticut, and was patented in 1795, this machine it was claimed could turn off 10,000, nails per day.

Since then many improvements have been made in machines for cutting tacks and nails, and scores of patents have been granted. As a result of this perfection of machinery, American tacks and nails have been manufactured at so slight a cost that an immense foreign demand has arisen for them and they are now shipped in large quantities, not only to the islands of the sea, and the States of South America, but to the manufacturing countries of Europe and to England.

Much of the machinery in the factories of Messrs. A. Field & Sons differs from that in use elsewhere, having been manufactured after their own patterns and under their own supervision. No effort has been spared to make their machinery

View of A. Field & Sons' Tack and Nail Manufactory, Taunton, Massachusetts.

perfect in every part. To the visitor, the cutting room is perhaps the most interesting department of the establishment; here are arranged scores of machines, each working with the precision of a clock, cutting and heading tacks or nails at the rate of from one thousand to fifteen hundred per hour or cutting shoe nails, which need no heading, at rates varying from fifteen hundred to three thousand per minute, according to the size of the nail and the material used.

This establishment was founded by Mr. Albert Field, who managed the business till his death, in 1866.

FOOS & JANE,

Representing

THE BOOKWALTER ENGINE.

The want of a small portable Engine and Boiler, so constructed as to be furnished at a price within the reach of every one, has long been felt. The Bookwalter Engine has been invented solely to fill this want, possessing, as it does, all the essential qualities of cheapness, simplicity, safety and economy in space. Messrs. Foos & Jayne, of 109 Liberty Street, New York, have displayed great sagacity and forethought by thus bringing into the market an engine so admirably adapted for light uses, where space and money are to be economized.

The Boiler is an *upright tubular*, of the form which experience has taught is *the most economical in the use of fuel*, and of greatest safety in operation.

The Engine, Bed-Plates, Pump, Governor, &c., are constructed and attached to the Boiler in the most simple and firm manner, so that the heat from the Boiler does not, by expansion, change the relation of the working parts to each other.

All the parts are made in exact duplicate, so that in case of breakage the owner can get a new part and replace it without having to go to a machine shop with the engine.

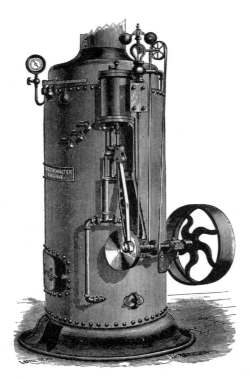

THE BOOKWALTER ENGINE.

Every Boiler and Engine is tested by hydraulic pressure, and also fired up and run, before leaving the works, to insure its perfect working in the hands of the purchaser.

We describe this Engine and Boiler thus minutely that our readers may understand their many advantages, as at this time the demand for small Engines of from three to five horse power is very great, and the enquiry comes up from all parts of the country, "where can small, cheap, economical, and safe steam power be had."

For further particulars the reader is referred to the catalogue and description issued by the firm above named and sent free on application.

STANLEY RULE & LEVEL COMPANY'S FACTORIES.

The Stanley Rule & Level Company, of New Britain, State of Connecticut, is one of the most prominent concerns in this country engaged in the manufacture of Improved Carpenters Tools. A view of their mammoth factories is given above. Some idea of the capacity of their works, as well as the demand for their excellent tools, may be had from the fact that in the year 1873, their sales included over 54,000 dozen Boxwood and Ivory Rules, 3,600 dozen Spirit Levels, 3,300 dozen Try Squares, 1,900 dozen T Bevels, 2,900 dozen Mallets, and corresponding quantities of all their regular goods. A specialty with the Company is the manufacture of "Bailey's Patent Adjustable Planes," several styles of which are illustrated on this page. The sale of these Planes has already exceeded 70,000. The primitive, and indeed the only method of adjusting planes, until these tools were invented, had been by the uncertain strokes given by a hammer. In the tools here represented, the plane-iron is secured in the stock by means of a cam,

while the thickness of shaving to be taken off any surface, can be readily controlled by the use of a thumb-screw, located just in front of the hand of the workman, and by which he can push down, or withdraw, the plane-iron as the nature of his work may require. A plane having a flexible face, for the use of stair builders, or indeed, all classes of builders having ornamental work coming under their hands, is shown near the top of this article. It can be used for planing all surfaces, whether concave or convex, and the plane-iron is adjusted by the same method as the other planes. While it is true that the greater part of the labor of preparing lumber, which was formerly done by hand labor, is now performed by machinery, leaving only the more delicate parts to be executed by the hand tools; this has only stimulated greater ingenuity in seeking for the better

adaptation of these tools to the needs of the men who use them. Full description of the peculiar features of the adjustable planes may be had from the illustrated circulars of the manufacturers. The Warerooms of the Company are at 35 Chambers Street, New York. Their tools may be found in the hands of all principal Hardware Dealers.

HARDICK'S PATENT DOUBLE-ACTING STEAM PUMP WORKS.

The Niagara Direct-Acting Steam Pump is an invention of the present progressive age, indicating, in its construction, an appreciation of the want of the times, viz: Machinery, so simple in its details of construction, that in new Mining and Oil Regions, &c., where Machine Shops are not yet opened, any man of ordinary intelligence may be able to put it together and take it apart as occasion may require; and in following, to a successful issue, the solution of this hitherto difficult problem in the manufacture of Steam Pumps, it will be observed while steadily keeping that in view in the manufacture of the Niagara Direct-Acting Pump, the matter of economy for the purchaser has also received due attention. If these considerations commend it in a new country—or field of enterprise—they are none the less applicable in older settled districts.

Among its advantages; so far as is consistent with durability, it is cast in separate parts, so that in case of accident or breakage, the immediate part affected need only be replaced, as its cylinders are separate from Bed-plate, Water Valve-chest, Discharge and Air-chamber; each being separate, is an important item of economy in severe climates, where by the action of frost, all metal vessels are liable to fracture.

Its arrangement of Patented Water-Valves is such that in case of obstructions entering the Valve Chamber through the suction pipe, (an annoyance to which all pumps are subject,) it becomes of the first importance to have, as in the case of this Pump, one whose valves may be taken out, cleaned and replaced in the shortest possible space of time, for which half a minute has been found on occasion sufficient; the accessibility of the valves is apparent by a glance at the bonnet of the Valve Chest. It will be seen, to extract water valves, it is only necessary to remove one nut, no further fastening being requisite, as the valves are four square pieces of metal, kept in place by bonnet shown in cut. Valves on each face present an accurately fitting surface to valve seat in chest, so that each of the four surfaces may be successfully used. When in the course of years these surfaces are exhausted, if emergency require, hard blocks of wood of like form and surface may be used with equal facility and reliability.

We might enumerate other advantages in favor of these truly valuable pumps, and this house has done much towards bringing to a high standard this important branch of industry. Mr. Charles B. Hardick's works are situated at No. 23, (old No. 9) Adams Street, Brooklyn, New York.

HARDICK'S NIAGARA DIRECT AND DOUBLE-ACTING PLUNGER PUMP.

Office, 23 Adams Street, Brooklyn, New York.

By the above cut it will readily be seen that all the advantages of the regular Direct-Acting Pump are combined in this Plunger Pump, with the only and important difference, that in the above there are no Piston Rings or Interior Packing, hence no necessity for removal of the Cylinder Heads, there being one Plunger operating both Cylinders, to pack which it is necessary to unscrew the Nuts shown at the center of Water Cylinder, slip the Caps of Stuffing Box back, insert the Packing in Stuffing Boxes, replace the Caps, and all is done. The superior advantages of this Pump will be readily appreciated by Miners, Steamboat and Saw Mill men, in whose operations the use of muddy and gritty water is unavoidable.

This establishment also manufacture the Niagara Direct-Acting Steam Pump, an invention of the present progressive age, indicating, in its construction, an appreciation of the wants of the times, viz: Machinery, so simple in its details of construction, that in new Mining and Oil Regions, &c., where Machine Shops are not yet opened, any man of ordinary intelligence can put it together and take it apart as occasion may require; and in following, to a successful issue, the solution of this hitherto difficult problem in the manufacture of Steam Pumps it will be observed that, in the manufacture of the Niagara Direct-Acting Pump, the matter of economy for the purchaser has also received due attention. These considerations commend it in a new country —or field of enterprise—and are none the less applicable in older settled districts.

Among its advantages: so far as consistent with durability, it is cast in separate parts, so that in case of accident or breakage, the immediate part affected need only be replaced, as its cylinders are separate from Bed-plate, Water Valve-chest, Discharge and Air-chamber; each being separate, is an important item of economy in severe climates, where, by the action of frost, all metallic vessels are liable to fracture.

It has a Patent Steam Valve, which insures its starting, whenever steam is let on—it matters not at what point of stroke the piston may be—hence impossible to set on the centre; and, moreover, can be run at any rate of speed, thus, when feeding the boiler, it can be made to run as fast or as slow as may be desired; in fact, it can be run so slow, without fear of stopping, that the motion is hardly perceptible; thus by a steady and certain supply of water to the boiler, economy and safety are both secured.

For Mines and Quarries, it has acquitted itself to the entire satisfaction of those who have used it, and proved peculiarly adapted; for should it become submerged in the mine, it will start upon turning on steam from the boiler at the top of the shaft, and work, notwithstanding the condensation of steam incident to carrying it to the pump.

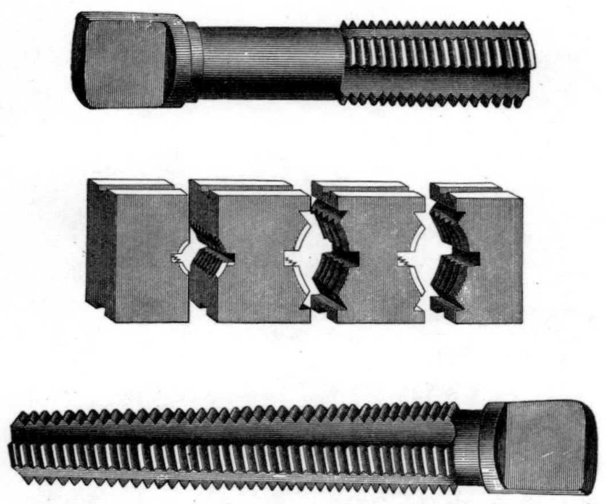

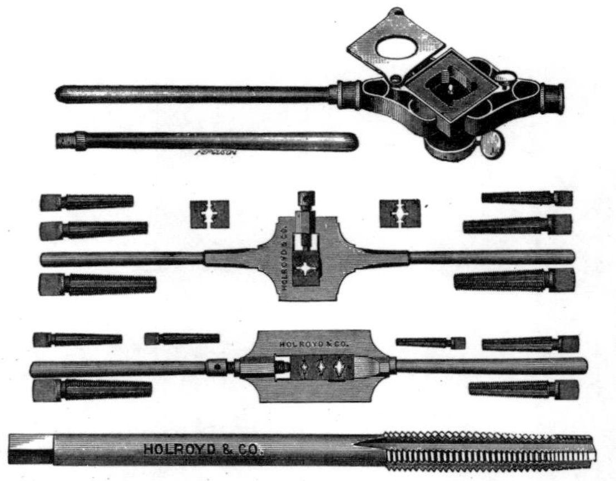

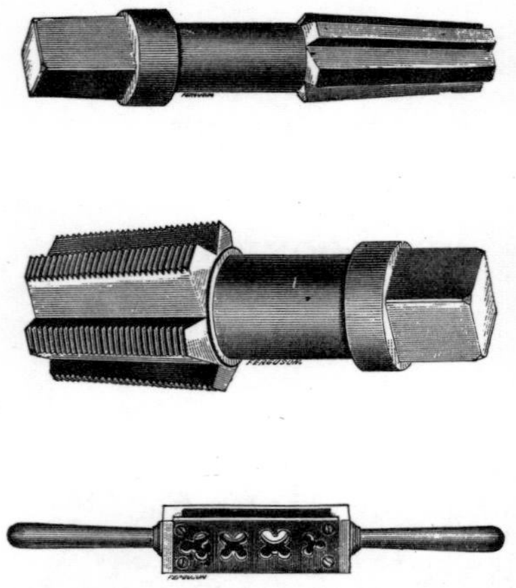

HOLROYD & CO., WATERFORD, N. Y.

Manufacturers of Stocks, Dies, etc.

We present our readers, in connection with this article, representations of a few of the many patterns of Stocks and Dies manufactured by the well known house of Holroyd & Co., Waterford, Saratoga County, N. Y. This firm was established in 1847, under the name of Platt & Holroyd. A few years later the present proprietors took the name of Holroyd & Co., by which they are still known. They commenced to manufacture with a determination to win a reputation for their products on their own merits. For that reason they very soon took a leading position in the manufacture of Stocks and Dies, which, by a faithful adherence to their original resolution, they still retain.

By allowing only first-class work to go into the market, their home trade increased rapidly, until it has become very large, while their goods find a ready sale and are well appreciated in Australia, South America, Canada, &c. Their extensive works are elaborately fitted up with the best and most approved machinery and tools known to the trade, many of which had their origin in their own establishment. Great care is exercised to select none but the best brands of steel, subjected to the severest tests.

By having a steady and increasing demand for their manufactures, they have been enabled to give constant employment to their employées, and have thus trained up a skilled and efficient corps of workmen, so essential to the proper manipulation of steel.

As a natural result of this care and steady adherence to their original intention their business in the manufacture and sale of taps alone has become immense, as has also that of plates and taps for cutting gas and steam pipes, of the latter of which they were among the first to introduce the manufacture into this country.

With the steadily increasing demand for their manufactures, Messrs. Holroyd & Co., have correspondingly increased their facilities for filling orders, and with constant care to keep a full and complete stock of all their wares in store, they are enabled to fill all orders with unusual promptness.

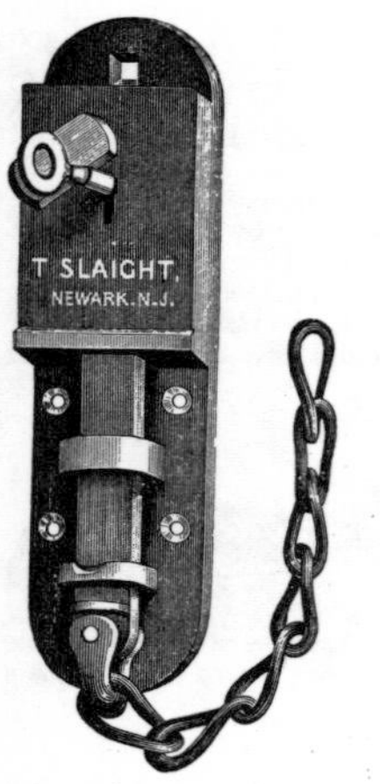

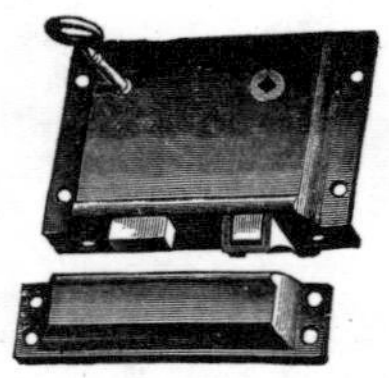

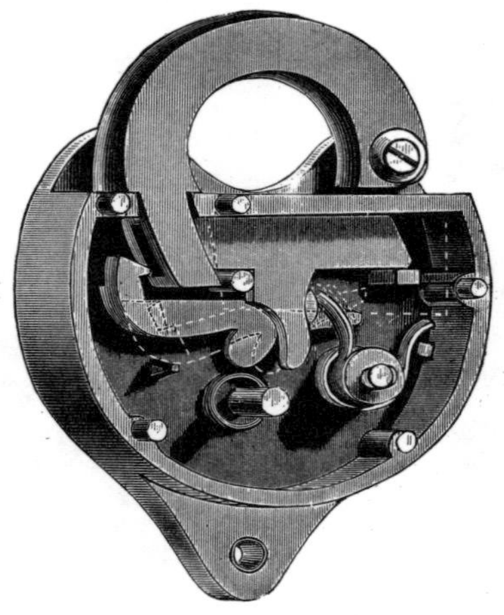

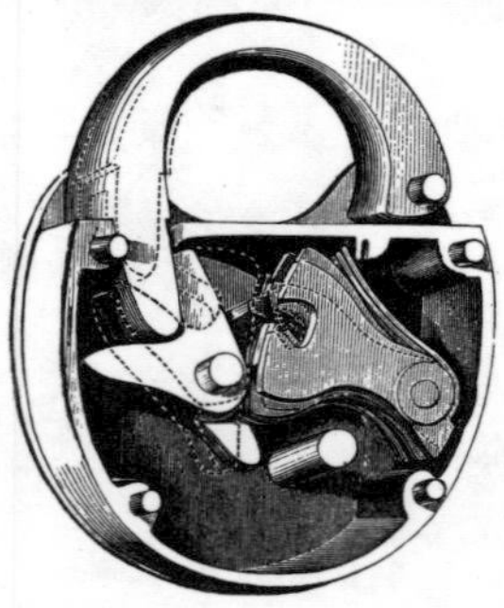

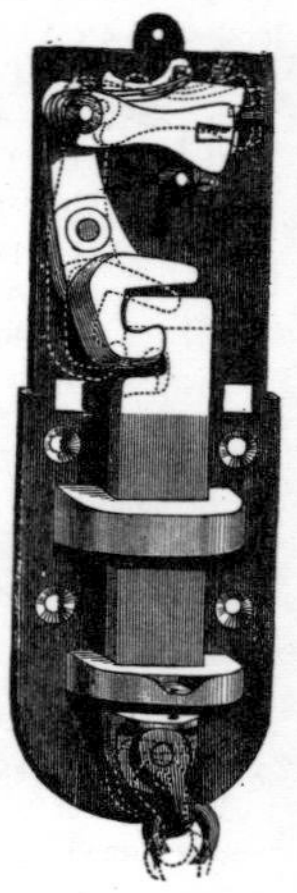

SELF-LOCKING SPRING PAD-LOCKS,

Manufactured by

THOS. SLAIGHT, NEWARK, N. J.

The rapid increase in thefts, robberies and kindred crimes, during the last few years, enhanced, no doubt, by the increased facilities for picking and forcing locks, has called into requisition all the inventive genius of lockmakers to secure greater safety for whatever needs the protection of lock and key.

Locks for railroad uses seem to have received special attention, until a high state of perfection has been reached. But in this as in other manufactures the reputation of the genuine often suffers by the attempts at imitation.

Many of the locks which are now manufactured are far less efficient than their outward appearance indicates. They often so far resemble the standard lock as to deceive experts, while the inside or invisible portion is very defective. To enable a mechanic to manufacture a lock that will defy the power of the burglar's "kit," it is indispensable that he have a practical experience as manufacturer, and a thorough knowledge of the ingenious devices to which the burglar resorts. We know of no one better qualified to meet those requisites than Mr. Thomas Slaight, of Newark, N. J. His practical experience commenced in 1835, and he established his manufactory in 1849. He has continued on until he has become proficient in all the details of this branch of mechanism; including, not only the manufacture of locks for Railroad uses, but for Banks, Steamboats, Prisons, Hotels, etc. These qualifications, not possessed by his competitors, should be appreciated by those in want of locks of any kind.

Mr. Slaight now holds twelve "Principal" patents on his own inventions, which he is manufacturing principally for railroad purposes. He was the first inventor of the Self-Locking Rack Tumbler Pad-Lock; also, the celebrated Antifriction Latch now in general use by railroad companies. His latest invention is a Rack Tumbler Master Key Lock. He can make almost any number of locks, every key different, and one Master Key, that will unlock them all without impairing the security of the locks in the least. He has also a patent Seal Holder, for sealing the key-hole of a padlock. This lock and seal are now used by the Internal Revenue Department of the U. S. and give better satisfaction than the glass or any other seal. The seal is made of paper and may be manufactured by the parties using it, and applied to any self-locking locks. Those in want of odd locks of any pattern should examine the samples of Mr. Slaight as he makes a specialty of manufacturing that class of work.

CRACKER MACHINERY,

Manufactured by

J. W. RUGER & CO.,

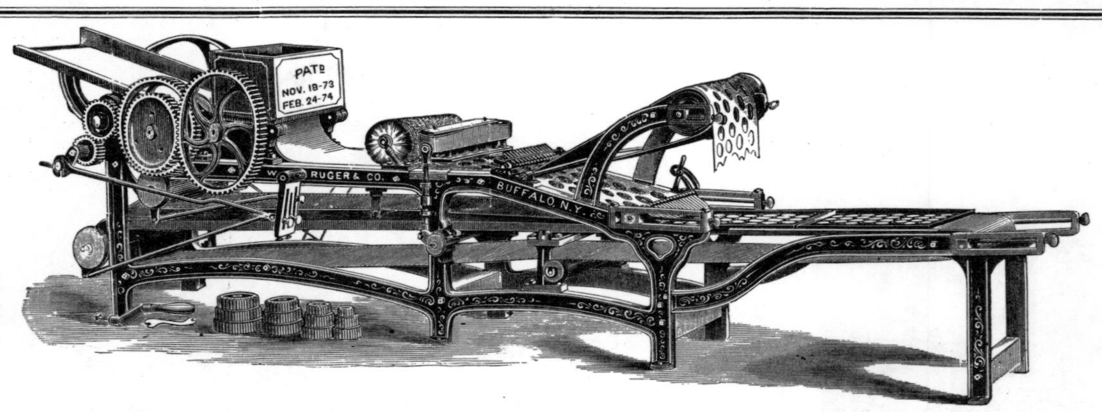

Eureka Cracker Machine with Fuller's Patent Soft Dough Sheeter Attachment.

At what time in the history of man the art of making bread was first developed, or by what process the conversion of grain into bread was first accomplished, history does not inform us. Contemporaneous with the record of the introduction of the human race into the world, we find the irrevocable decree, "In the sweat of thy face shalt thou eat bread, till thou return unto the ground."

But as the word bread is often used to denote food of all kinds, animal and vegetable, we will not claim a literal rendering of the above quotation.

The first person named in history, so far as we have any knowledge, who taught men the art of husbandry and the art of making bread from wheat, was Ching-Hong the successor of Fohi; the latter, supposed by many to be the Noah of the bible, and founder and first monarch of China. The same man is also reported to have taught the Chinese the art of making wine from rice. As Noah died 1998 years before the Christian era, the art of bread-making may claim a very great antiquity.

The art of baking bread was also known in patriarchal times among the Hebrews before they left Egypt 1491, B. C. It became a profession at Rome before the conquest of Macedon, 148 B. C., and soon after that event, large numbers of Greek bakers came to Rome, obtained special privileges, and soon secured the monopoly of the baking trade.

During the siege of Paris by Henry IV, at the commencement of the fifteenth century owing to the famine that then raged, bread, which had been sold while any remained, for a crown a pound was made from the bones of the charnel of the Holy Innocents.

In Iceland, codfish beaten to powder, is made into bread, and in Ireland, potato-bread is not uncommon. Prior to 1302 the London bakers were not allowed to sell bread in their own shops.

The English bakers are known to have made bread with yeast as early as 1634.

In 1856 or 1857 Dr. Dauglish patented a mode of making "aerated bread," in which carbonic acid gas is combined with water and mixed with the flour, which is said to possess the advantages of cleanliness, rapidity and uniformity.

Of the origin of bread-making machinery, and its gradual development and improvement, history furnishes but little information; but that its introduction is of comparatively modern date must be admitted by all, and that its development in this country has been rapid, and has reached a high state of perfection is equally true.

As one of the most prominent and favorably known houses in the manufacture of Cracker Machines, we present our readers with a brief sketch of the firm of J. W. Ruger & Co. of Buffalo, N. Y.

As early as 1856 Messrs. J. S. and J. W. Ruger were employed as journeymen by Messrs. Gage Brothers, of Rochester, N. Y., in a small shop, manufacturing Cracker Machines. About this time commenced what is known as the great panic of 1857, when Gage Brothers concluded to discharge their employées and close their shop.

The Messrs. Ruger having a practical and thorough knowledge of the business, and six hundred dollars in cash, opened a small shop and commenced manufacturing what is known as the number one Cracker Machine, the largest machine for that purpose then made. Until that time crackers were mostly made by hand power. But the demand for them increased rapidly, and a heavier machine, adapted for steam power, became a necessity; to meet which they improved their number one and manufactured their number two machine, and soon after enlarged the latter to what is now known as number three. In 1860, very favorable inducements having been offered them, they removed their works to Buffalo, N. Y. Soon after this, on the breaking out of the war the demand for hard bread increased so rapidly, that to manufacture it, machines of greater strength and capacity became indispensable. To meet this demand Messrs. Ruger produced their number four machine with many improvements This machine was received with such favor that the manufacturers were compelled to double their facilities for manufacturing, to meet the demand.

In August, 1866 J. S. Ruger retired from the firm, and A. Ruger a junior brother was admitted, and the firm name changed to J. W. Ruger & Co. In 1873 they perfected their celebrated number five, self-scraping and panning, plain and fancy cracker machine, and secured the exclusive right to manufacture and sell the McKenzie Reel Oven. Owing to the rapid increase in the demand for these machines, the manufacturers were compelled to rebuild their works on a much larger scale, and to run them to their full capacity to fill their orders.

During the present year they have secured the exclusive control of Fuller's Patent Sheeter and Mitchell's Patent Steaming Machine for soft cakes. They are now prepared to offer bakers the most complete assortment of machines and tools adapted to their business anywhere to be found.

With their unrivaled facilities for manufacturing, their long experience and personal attention to this class of goods as a specialty, we think the most incredulous may be convinced of their ability to furnish the very best class of bakers' machinery to be found in this country. We might enter more into details in our description of the manufactory of this firm; but the limits of the space allotted will not permit. It is much safer to rely upon those who have had long experience as manufacturers than upon those less favorably known. Parties interested should send for an illustrated Catalogue.

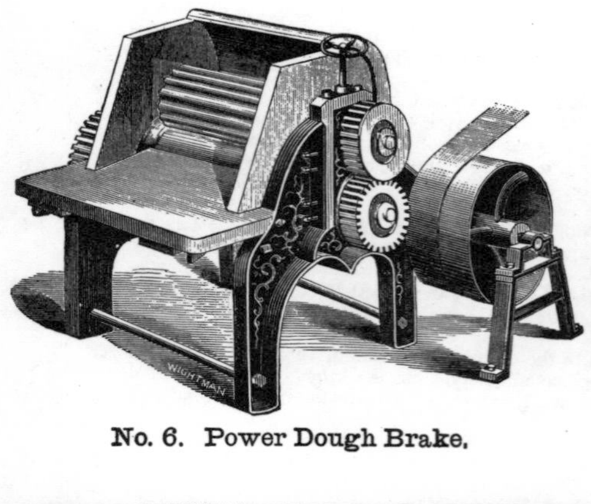

No. 6. Power Dough Brake.

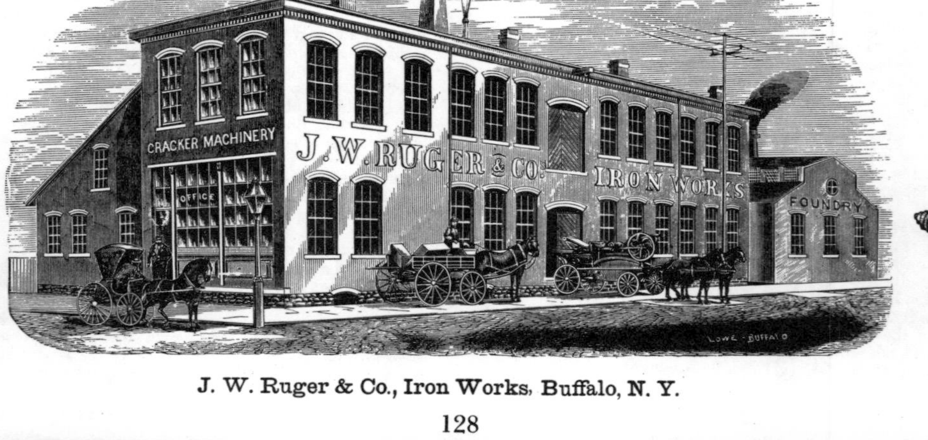

J. W. Ruger & Co., Iron Works, Buffalo, N. Y.

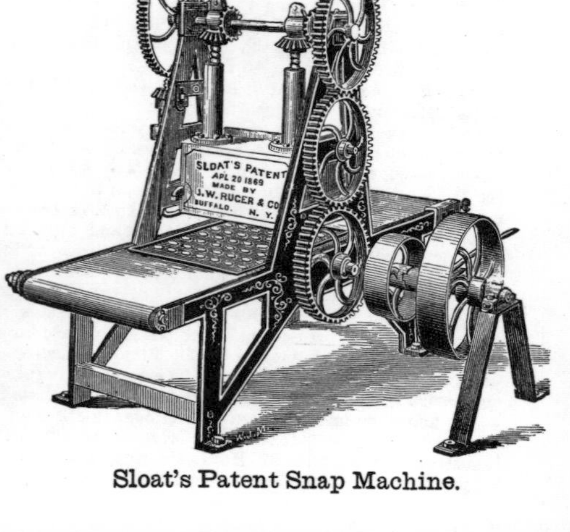

Sloat's Patent Snap Machine.

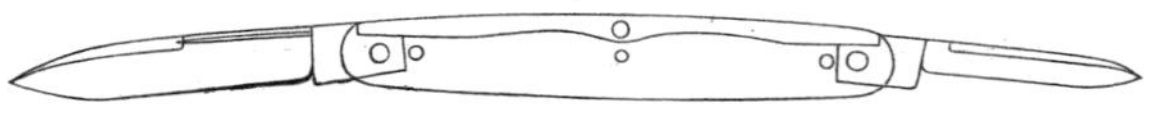

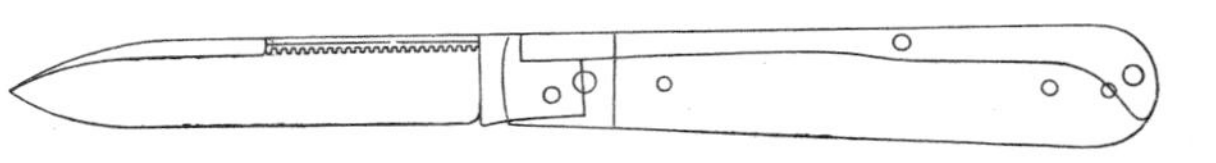

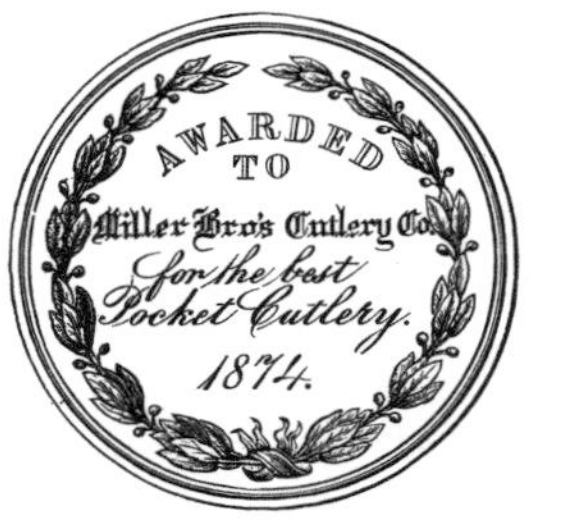

Miller Brothers Cutlery Co.,

Manufacturers of

Patent Fine Pocket Cutlery.

West Meriden Conn.

——:o:——

The Miller Brothers Cutlery Co. was organized in January, 1870, for the purpose of manufacturing Pocket Cutlery, under patents granted to Wm. H. & G. W. Miller, who had previously been engaged in the manufacture on the American or Interchangeable plan.

The Company made a modest commencement at Yalesville, in the town of Wallingford. After perfecting their machinery and tools and successfully demonstrating the feasibility of the plan of manufacture, they increased their capital stock, purchased the shops at West Meriden, formerly occupied by Pratt, Reed & Co. in the manufacture of Ivory Goods, and commenced moving their works in July, 1872, since which time the business of the Company has steadily increased—from the manufacture of forty dozen knives per day in 1873, to one hundred dozen knives per day in 1875, reaching during the month of November, 1875, an average production of one hundred and twenty-five dozen per day.

A peculiarity of their mode of manufacture is that all the parts are made to gauge and are uniformly alike and complete before they are given out to the Cutler, who assembles the knife together. The covering of the handle is attached to the scales or sides of the knife with screws after the other parts have been riveted together enabling them to make as strong and durable a knife as can be made.

The knives of this Company are not only accurate in their working parts but the quality of the blades is equal to the best in the market. S. & C. Wardlow's Blade Steel is used, and the method of hardening and tempering adopted is not surpassed by any process

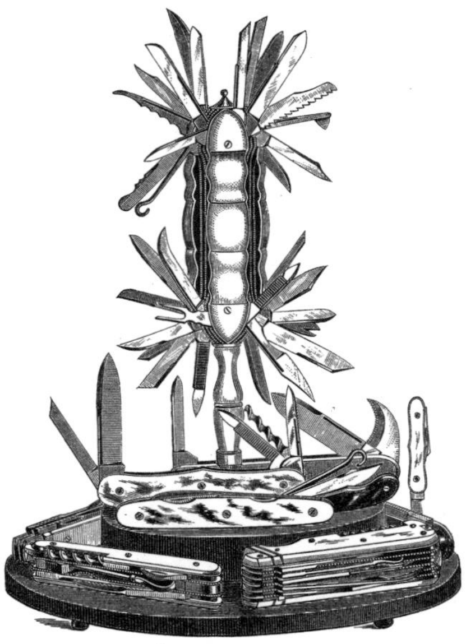

yet introduced. The blades are heated in an oven and the temperature so regulated that it is impossible to overheat the steel in hardening; the temper is drawn by color and pyrometer test, which method gives as uniform results as any yet discovered.

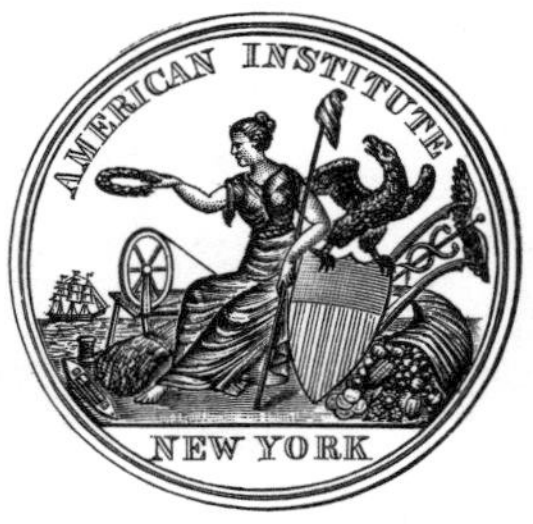

We copy the following compliment from the report of the judges at the 43d Exhibition of the American Institute, held in the city of New York, October, 1874.

"The Miller Brothers Cutlery Co., West Meriden, Conn., appears as the representative of what is known as the American feature in Cutlery, the interchangeableness of parts. Presuming that the materials and workmanship are, in other respects, equal to the best, we regard this interchangeable feature as deserving of special attention.

"We recommend the interchangeable feature in the Pocket Cutlery as an advance in the art of which it is a representative.

"We consider this interchangeable Cutlery a product of superior merit; the best of its kind on exhibition, or in common use. A Silver Medal awarded."

The adaptation of machinery to the manufacture of Cutlery marks a new era in the business and was inaugurated by this firm. It must necessarily confer benefits of the utmost general importance. By its introduction a much higher finish is attained and the greatest possible precision is secured. The various parts of the knife are made absolutely interchangeable, so that if any portion should be broken, a corresponding part can be instantly adjusted. A remarkable feature is that in some of the finer qualities of knives the back and sides are formed from a single piece of metal imparting a strength not attainable by any other means.

The works of the Miller Brothers Cutlery Co., denote in every department a thoroughness and excellence which is not excelled, anywhere, and the high and wide reputation which their goods have already attained is another proof, that merit always insures success.

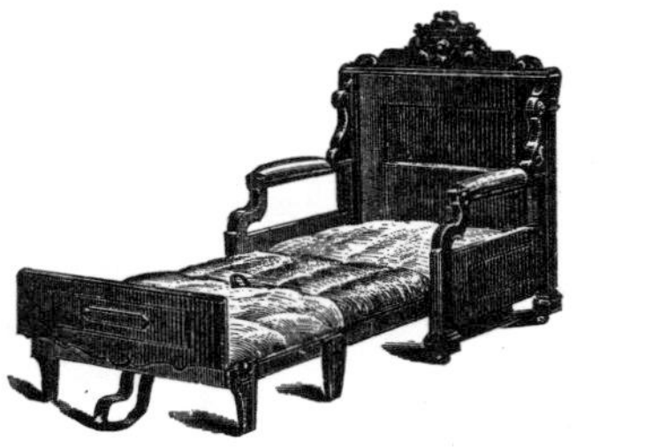

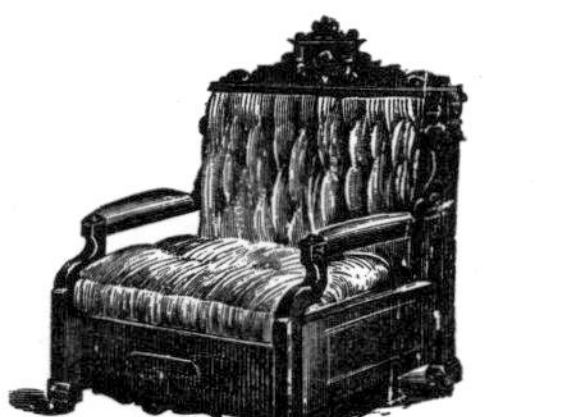

SMITH'S PARLOR BED,

Depot: 816 Broadway.

Near Twelfth Street, New York.

For several years Mr. G. W. Smith has made the construction of parlor beds a special study. During that time he has designed and patented several different styles of parlor beds, the most popular of which is the Smith Sofa Bed above illustrated. As will be seen by reference to the cuts, it is by day an elegant, as well as a useful article of furniture for the parlor or sitting room, which at night is transformed into a luxurious bed. These beds are made in three sizes, viz: 2 feet 6 inches, 4 feet, and 4 feet 6 inches wide, by 6 feet 2 inches long, with clothes box under the seat. A comparison of the difference in the cost of the separate articles which are combined in this bed itself would result about as follows: A sofa, $40; a bedstead, $18; a fair mattress, say $25; giving a total of $83; while the expense of a Smith Sofa Bed, of full size, which within itself combines all these articles, is only $65, a saving of $18 in the cost, and a gain which cannot easily be computed, in enabling the housekeeper to convert a perfectly furnished parlor into as perfectly furnished a bedroom without moving any article into or out of the apartment. In addition to the Sofa Bed there are several other styles, which when not in use as beds and closed, simulate, book cases and bureaus of different patterns, at prices ranging from $30 to $150 varying with size and the degree of elaborateness with which finished.

Mr. Smith received premiums at the Fairs of the American Institute in 1873 and 1874, but the best proof of the merits of his goods is his ever increasing sales. Those interested may obtain a catalogue and price list by mail, by sending their address to Mr. G W. Smith, 816 Broadway, near 12th Street, N. Y.

The "Broadway"

Folding and Adjustable Table,

816 Broadway, New York.

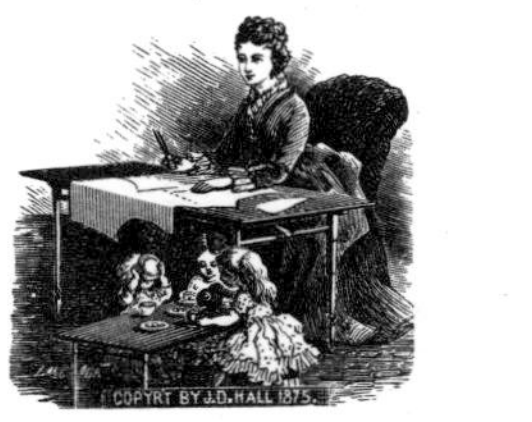

In dress-making, prior to the invention of the low, portable table, various devices or makeshifts were from time to time resorted to. Every lady is familiar with the uncomfortable and often ludicrous operations of cutting and basting garments on a floor and over a bed or piano; and many of them have vivid remembrances of how one tires the limbs, another the back, a third the arms. From these ills, the common lap board has afforded but partial relief. It is too small for cutting any but small patterns, and the constrained position which it enforces upon its holder renders its use always irksome. But in favor of the little table it is difficult to say too much. It is so completely adapted to so great a variety of uses, that we hardly know where to begin in enumerating them. Every member of a family has a frequent demand for it. It can be folded so as to occupy but little space, and is so light as to be easily moved from room to room, up stairs or down stairs, by ladies or children. As each table is furnished with casters it can, when unfolded, be moved back and forward, or to either side at the will of the operator without changing the position of the individual.

There have been a number of attempts made to introduce other tables intended for the purposes which this table so completely fills, a few of which are still offered. That this may be readily distinguished from all other similar productions, the proprietor has adopted for it the distinctive name of the "Broadway." Those who desire a perfect portable sewing and game table, if they buy one that combines these three peculiarities, viz.:—casters, a yard measure in either black or gold figures, on the top surface, and the word "Broadway" painted in plain letters upon the face of each draw, will be sure to get a Broadway Table, and not an inferior one.

Another useful implement is the Galloping Bias Maker, a perfect machine for marking off folds, flounces, plaits and tucks, both "on the bias" and on the square. It is convenient, rapid and perfect in its operation. Bias strips cut by this machine are perfectly true, hence there is no waste of goods. It will often save its cost in preparing the trimmings for a single garment. It is indispensable not only to all dressmakers, but also to every family in which dress and cloak-making is done. For further particulars in regard to either of these articles call upon, or address John D. Hall, 816 Broadway, New York.

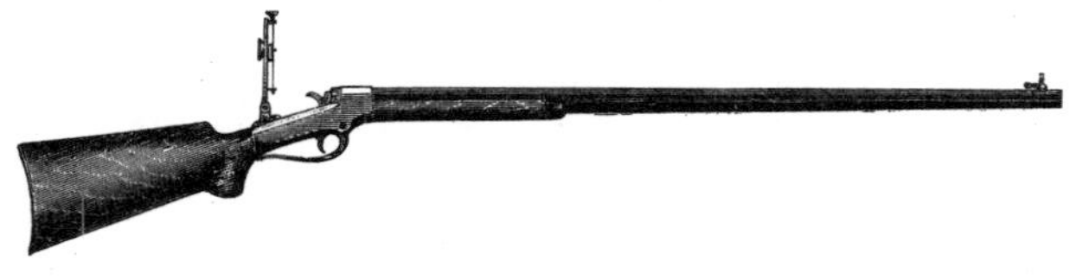

J. M. MARLIN,

Manufacturer of

BALLARD RIFLES, "STANDARD," "O K,"

and other Revolvers,

Best Steel Gun Barrels Made to Order,

NEW HAVEN, CONNECTICUT.

——:o:——

The number of Breech-Loading Fire Arms, which, within a comparatively few years, have been introduced to and tested by a discriminating public is far greater than most of our readers would suppose. Scores of inventors have taken out letters patent for original designs, or improvements, so called, on already existing arms, of which, by far the largest number have proved valueless; and of all the styles of Breech-Loading Guns that have been offered, less than a dozen have attained success. Prominent among this fortunate few is the Ballard Rifle, which, when it was first put upon the market, attracted the attention of sportsmen and hunters, and was by them pronounced second to none manufactured. Since that time many improvements have been made in the lock mechanism of this gun, and the manufacturer has endeavored to make it as nearly perfect as possible. With this end in view he has supplied his armory with all the latest and most approved devices for manufacturing the various, parts, and has secured the most skillfull workmen that money could hire. The materials used are of the very best quality—the barrels of steel—frames of wrought iron, and in every process of manufacture the utmost care is exercised. The Ballard Rifle as a long range gun has few equals and no superior.

In addition to the number of Ballard Rifles produced, Mr. Marlin, at his works, manufactures Revolvers of several kinds. The "Standard" and "O. K." being, perhaps, the styles most widely known. The "Little Joker" Revolver, is a neat and handy weapon, and does good service.

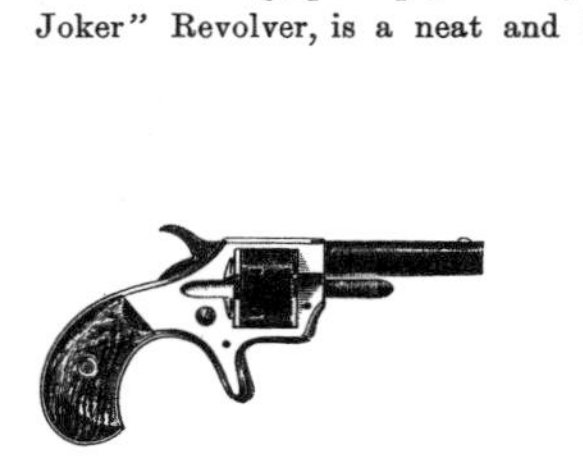

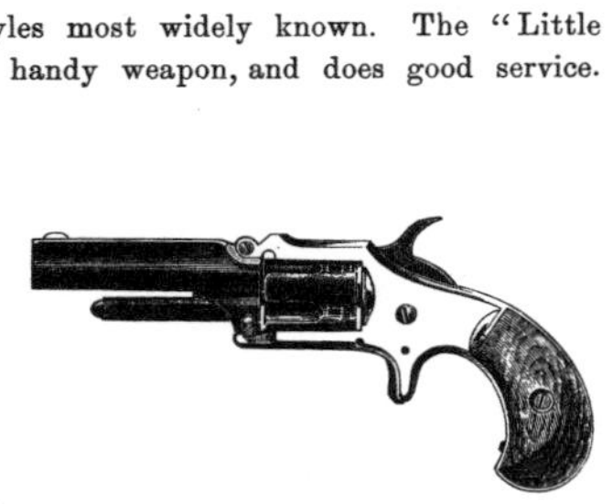

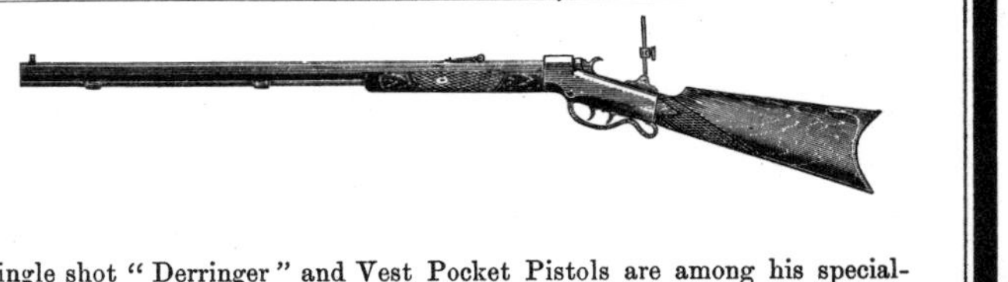

Single shot "Derringer" and Vest Pocket Pistols are among his specialties, and all the articles produced at this establishment hold the same high place in the estimation of the public. The Standard Revolvers are made in three sizes, viz: Twenty-two, Thirty, and Thirty-two, One-hundredths, caliber, all using the long cartridge, and all manufactured of the very best materials and with the same care that is bestowed upon the Ballard Rifle.

These arms are known and used not only in every part of the United States and Territories, but over all our civilized world. They do not belong to that class of productions which are gotten up for show purposes; they are made for use, and the hardy hunters of the Great West find in Ballard's Rifles, and the Standard Revolvers, arms not liable to foul or get out of order, reliable pieces that wear for years, outlasting many higher priced styles. It is from our frontiersmen that we gain the most valuable information as to the relative merits of the various styles of arms. The practical use which a gun or pistol receives at their hands is a far more thorough test of its value than the experimental trials of ordnance boards or judges at fairs, and when we find it to be the verdict of the Scouts of the Plains and the Hunters of the Western Mountains that these arms are perfectly reliable, we must receive their verdict as final.

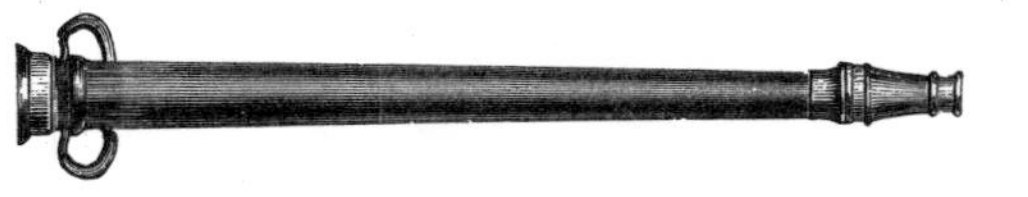

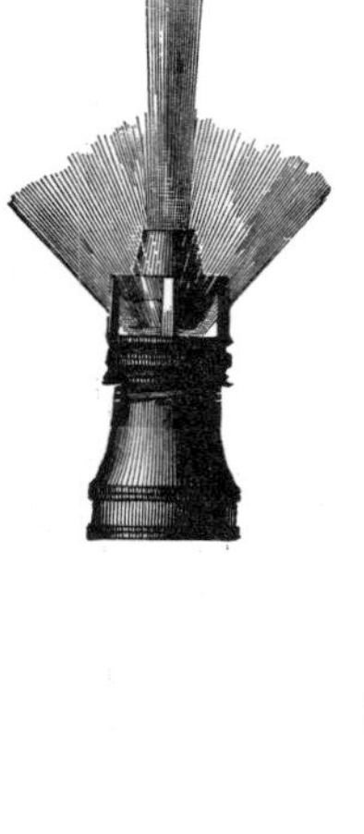

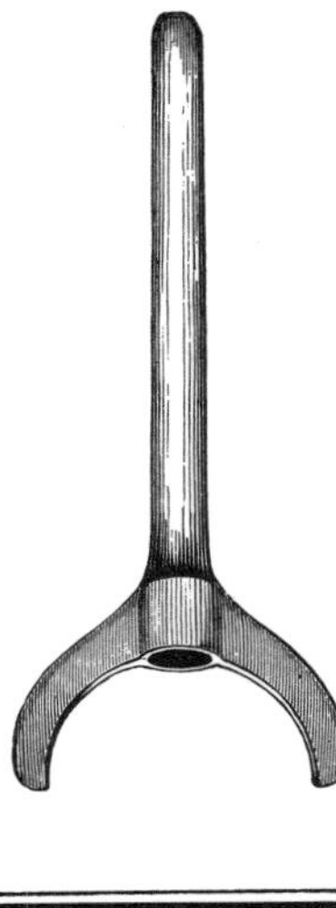

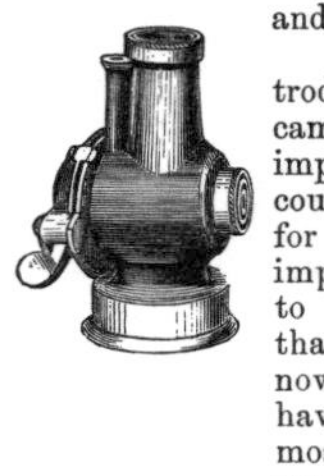

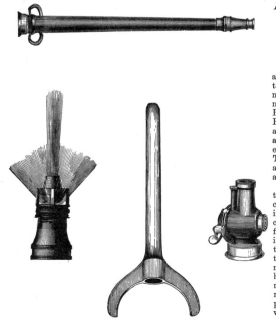

ALLEN FIRE DEPARTMENT SUPPLY CO.,

Cor. Eddy & Friendship Sts.,

Providence, R. I.

Within the limited space to which this article must be confined we can but briefly refer to the principal articles manufactnred and furnished by the above named company. They manufacture and deal in Steam Fire Engines, Hose Carriages, Steam Pumps, Relief Valves Hydrants, Piping, Fire Extinguishers, Hose of all kinds, Hose Couplings, Discharge Pipes, and a general line of articles used by fire departments, embracing many specialties of great value. The goods manufactured by this Company are covered by more than twenty-five patents, and improvements are constantly being made.

The Allen Patent Coupling when first introduced, some eight years ago, immediately became popular, but since then has been greatly improved. Starting with the assumption that a coupling with screw connection was best adapted for general use, every effort has been made to improve the method of attaching the coupling to the hose. The Company have tried more than fifty different styles of couplings, and those now manufactured embody all the points that have proved valuable. The Spray Nozzle is a most admirable contrivance by which the pipeman is protected from heat, so that he can approach close to the fire and direct the stream where it will prove most effective. The Automatic Relief Valve, places the control of the supply of water under the direction of the pipeman, enabling him in a moment's time to shut off the stream without interrupting the working of the engine.

This Company supply a large number of other establishments dealing in fire department supplies with, Piping, Hydrants, Balconies, Fire Escapes and everything needed for fighting fire. They deal largely in Fire Hose of all standard makes, including Rubber Hose, 2, 3, 4, and 5 ply, and ranging from ½ to 3 inches in diameter; Patent Carbolized Hose, (which is chemically prepared to prevent mildew, dry and wet rot, and also the deterioration of the rubber) 2, 3 and 4 ply; Linen Hose, Rubber Lined Linen Hose, and Oak Tanned Leather Hose. They make Suction Hose to order on spirally wound galvanized iron, from ¾ to 6 inches, the smaller sizes on spiral brass wire if preferred; they also make a Patent Smooth Bore Suction Hose, which is stronger and more flexible than ordinary suction hose, and through which the water passes with less friction.

The Company operates a large and completely fitted Machine Shop on general machine work, and an extensive Brass Foundry and Finishing Shop, where a large business in the manufacture of Plumbers' Fittings, etc., forms an important part of their establishment.

The Company was incorporated in 1872, with an authorized capital of $200,000. Mr. A. Work is General Manager, and Samuel G. Colwell is the Treasurer.

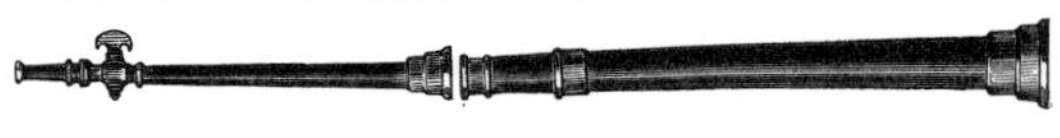

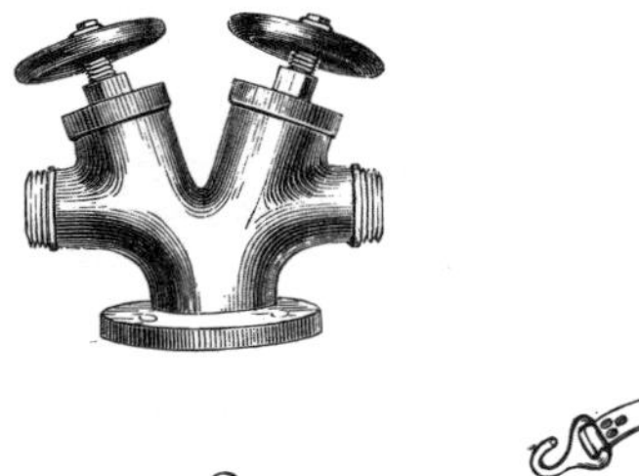

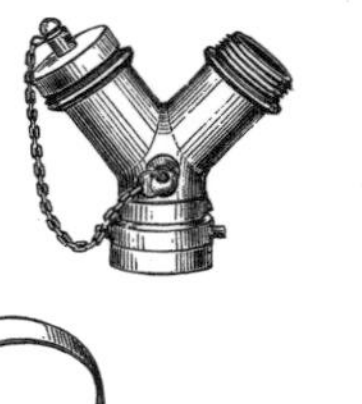

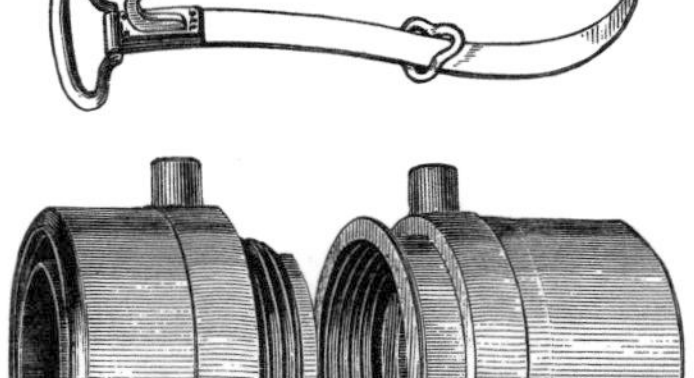

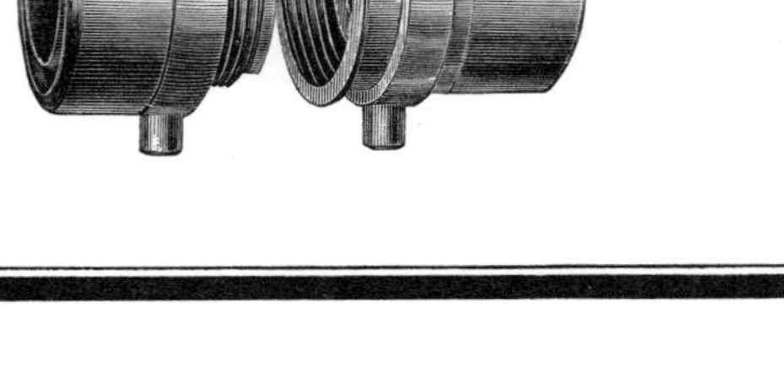

THE LAMB KNITTING MACHINE MANU-FACTURING COMPANY,

Chicopee Falls, Massachusetts.

Lamb's Family Knitting Machine, which has completely revolutionized the art of knitting, is constructed upon the novel and simple principle of employing two straight, parallel rows of needles, sufficiently near to each other to connect the two rows of knitting at either end, but far enough apart to allow the fabric to pass down between them as it is knitted. The needle is automatic. The two rows of needles are placed opposite each other, in grooves in an iron needle-bed, the two sides of which slope from each other like the roof of a house, and are separated at the ridge or center, where the needles form the stitches. Back and forth over the needle-bed a carriage is propelled by a crank. This carriage contains, under each side an automatic Cam—one for each row of needles—for operating the needles up and down in their grooves.

As the carriage is driven over the needle-bed, the needles are moved up, fed by yarn, and drawn down almost simultaneously,—all the needles forming stitches by one revolution of the crank.

The Cam is so constructed that by adjusting a Camstop, which can be done without stopping the machine, the Cam is opened or closed, (but engages the needles only when open) so as continuously to operate the front row of needles toward the left, then the back row toward the right, forming a perfect Tubular or Circular Web; or to operate both rows together in one direction, then one row in the other, making the Double Flat Web or Afghan stitch; or to operate both rows together in both directions, making the Ribbed or Seamed Flat Web; or to operate forward and back, first one row and then the other, so as to connect the two rows of knitting at one end, and leave them open at the other,

forming the Wide Flat Web—thus producing "four different webs." In knitting these webs, if every second, third, or fourth needle, or combinations of them, in one or both rows, be not used, an almost unlimited variety of rare and beautiful stitches are produced, such as the Shell Stitch, Unique Stitch, Raised Plaid Stitch, Nubia Stitch, Tidy Stitch, etc. Only those needles that are moved up within range of the cam are used. As any number of needles, in one or both rows, can thus be employed at the start, and the number be increased or diminished at any time, so any size of work, tubular or flat, can be set up, and widened or narrowed to any extent.

The machine sets up its own work. The stitches being made the same as in hand-knitting with no tension on the yarn, the fabric is equally durable. The length of the stitches is regulated by turning a thumb screw, so as to knit all sizes and kinds of yarn, woolen, cotton, or linen, home spun or machine spun, making the fabrics as tight or loose as desired; and as it knits a web either tubular or flat, single or double, ribbed, plain or fancy, in any desired shape, by narrowing and widening, it produces with equal facility, Hosiery, Gloves, Mittens, Shawls, Hoods and Muffs, Nubias Cardigan Jackets, Afghans, Counterpanes,—in fact every variety of staple and fancy knit goods. It also knits elegant trimmings for all its own articles, such as the plain ruffle, double ruffle, borders, fringes, etc.

The machine knits a stocking in two ways. By one method the toe is formed first, the foot and gore next; then the heels is knit, the calf is widened and the stocking completed, except to bind off the top and close the heel. By the other method the leg is knit first, the top being bound off or finished in setting it up, the heel is turned and closed with the Heeling Attachment, (making the regular, square, capped heel, the same as in the famous "Shaker Sock,") and the toe completely narrowed off—thus finishing the stocking in the machine ready for wearing.

The machine is constructed in the most solid and substantial manner, and, with ordinary usage, will last a life-time. It has no complicated parts, and as now improved, is so simple and so easy to manage, that it may be operated by a child ten years old without liability of getting out of order. With each machine is furnished a Book of Instructions, which contains a Table of Sizes for hosiery, mittens, and gloves, giving the exact number of needles to be set up. The rules for shirts, drawers, shawls, etc., are equally simple and explicit. The needles are registered, so that the operator can see at a glance how many are in use, while a Counter, records on a dial, the number of rounds that are knitted. By this perfect arrangement, an inexperienced operator can proportion any garment, and knit two or more precisely alike. The ordinary speed of the machine, is from eight to nine thousand loops a minute—producing over two yards of plain work in ten minutes, or a pair of men's socks in twenty minutes.

The Lamb Knitting Machine is certainly a pronounced success, and ranks highly among the most meritorious labor-saving devices of the age. It is one of the few machines which lighten the labor of our farmers' wives and daughters. Within the past ten years, this machine has been exhibited and placed in competition with others at all the leading fairs and exhibitions in the world, and has been awarded during that time 19 gold metals, (including one from the Vienna Exposition and one from the Great German Fair, at Berlin, Prussia.

WORKS OF THE LAMB KNITTING MACHINE MANUFACTURING COMPANY, CHICOPEE FALLS, MASS.

NEW HAVEN WHEEL COMPANY,

New Haven, Conn.

—:o:—

The wheel business was started on a part of the premises now occupied by the above Company in 1845, by Mr. Zelotes Day, who began at once to make wheels by machinery, but found it very up-hill work to sell them, owing to the deep-seated old-time prejudice in favor of hand made wheels. Machine made wheels were fought against by the public as an innovation that must be put down; it therefore is not strange that between 1845 and 1853 the business changed hands a number of times. By the latter year, however, machine made wheels had so demonstrated their superiority, both in appearance and durability that quite a trade had been built up, and a number of spirited men were venturesome enough to go ahead and form a Joint Stock Company under the title of "New Haven Wheel Company."

The new Company cast about for a competent and thorough business manager. They found such an one in the person of Hon. Henry G. Lewis, a lawyer by profession and then clerk of the Courts; now President of the Company and Mayor of New Haven. Mr. Lewis was elected Secretary and Treasurer of the Company and at once gave his whole attention to the duties of these positions, and by his vigorous exertions the business was largely increased. The panic of 1857 however retarded matters considerably and it had hardly recovered from the evil effects of that before the civil war came on, causing enormous losses to the company, especially through its

Southern customers, and almost destroying its entire trade; it was consequently in a very languishing state untill the peace of 1865 again gave it a prospering trade. During this year important changes were made in the company's ownership and management. Mayor Lewis was elected President and Edward E. Bradley, who had been with the company for some five years previous Secretary and Treasurer. The concern now entered on a new lease of life, and from a

business of say 25 sets of wheels per week, which had been increased to perhaps 50 sets at the time of the change, it grew rapidly up to 200 sets per week, besides quantities of parts. This large business continued down to September, 1874, when about two-thirds of their works were destroyed by fire, some \$200,000 worth of property being devoured by the fiery element in the space of five hours. Among the buildings destroyed was the original factory in which the business was started in 1845.

The wonderful energy and recuperative force of the Company had

now ample opportunity for action and was fully displayed. In eighty days from the date of the fire over one-half million of bricks were laid and the present buildings were the result. The Company by buying out a smaller wheel concern, the week following the fire were able to keep their customers fairly supplied until their new works were started, so that it can be reasonably said that no break of consequence, or serious inconvenience resulted.

Very early in 1875, the Company started in their new works with increased facilities and a full line of orders. The capacity now of this mammoth concern is four hundred sets of wheels per week, besides quantities of parts sold to carriage makers, small wheel makers, &c. The Company now send their goods not only throughout the United States, from Maine to California, but to foreign parts, Australia, Europe, South America, Mexico, &c.

Being one of the oldest wheel concerns in the country, and their work being so favorably and thoroughly known over so great a territory, their trade is not so liable to the great fluctuations that occur to most manufacturers. They, perhaps, occupy the most favorable position of any concern in their line in this country, as regards facilities, experience, ability, &c. The machinery used in the manufacture of wheels is a marvel of perfection and is driven by a Harris Corliss Engine of 200 Horse Power.

Each part passes through many processes before appearing in the finished wheel, some fifteen operations being required on a spoke alone. We here present a view of the works. The Company intend placing sample sets of wheels in the Centennial Exhibition, where our readers may see them.

Manufactory of the New Haven Wheel Company, New Haven, Conn.

A Scientific System of Physical Training.

CUMULATIVE EXERCISE,

Popularly known as

"THE HEALTH-LIFT," or "LIFTING-CURE,"

Developed in the

REACTIONARY LIFTER,

Manufactured and Sold by

THE HEALTH-LIFT COMPANY,

No. 46 East Fourteenth Street, New York.

:o:

The Origin of the Health-Lift.

In 1855, Dr. George B. Windship, of Boston, commenced lifting as a means of muscular development. Most are familiar with his story. "A puny, sickly, diminutive youth, subject to intense nervousness, headache, indigestion, dyspepsia, and a weak circulation, as well as to the taunts of his classmates for being the smallest man in his class at Harvard College, was driven to the cultivation of his 'muscle' by the petty tyranny of one of his college-mates; making, on one occasion, after unusual abuse, the following promise to a sympathizing chum: 'Wait two years, and I promise you I will either make my tormentor apologize, or give him such a thrashing as he will remember for the rest of his life.'"

Tardy revenge: but young Windship was as sure as he was slow, and at the end of two years, with broadened shoulders and developed muscles, the young athlete sought his old enemy and received his apology.

In his "Autobiographical Sketches of a Strength-Seeker," he says:

"I have only to add that we parted without a collision, and that, in my heart, I could not help thanking him for the service he had rendered in inciting me to the regimen which had resulted so beneficially to my health.

"The impetus given to my gymnastic education by the little incident I have just related, was continued without abatement through my whole college life. Gradually I acquired the reputation of being the strongest man in my class. I discovered that with every day's development of my strength, there was an increase of my ability to resist and overcome all fleshly ailments, pains and infirmities,—a discovery which subsequent experience has so amply confirmed, that, if I were called upon to condense the proposition which sums it up into a formula, it would be in these words: 'Strength is Health.'"

The Health-Lift has grown out of Dr. Windship's gymnastic training; he developed a very useful lifting apparatus, and were it not for its great cost it would be more generally used. Dr. Windship confined his practice to the cure of patients by the use of his "Graduated Yoke Lifting," as he calls it. Latterly, however, he has adopted the Reactionary, giving high testimony in its favor, and preference over all other machines. He makes use of it in his gymnasium.

The impetus given by Dr. Windship to this new and unique form of exercise created much interest and enthusiasm, and it was predicted by many that the Health-Lift would eventually take the place of all other forms of gymnastics. Even at this early day, the prophecy seems to have been warranted.

From time to time various machines for lifting have been devised, but few had merit enough to warrant other than an ephemeral existence; they were expensive, complicated, bungling, ugly. The most objectionable of all was the dead-weight, centre-lift, necessitating the cockscrew twist of the spine.

Since the appearance of the Side-Lift or Reactionary, nearly all the others have been withdrawn. It is cheaper, more compact and beautiful than others, and with its late improvements is complete and perfect in every particular. It is believed that it can not be superseded.

The Rationale of Lifting.

Cumulative Exercise, while improving the health, will Double the Actual Strength in three months;—occupies only Ten Minutes once a day;—furnishes a safe and valuable mode of Physical Training;—is adapted to both Ladies and Gentlemen, requiring no change of dress;—does not fatigue nor exhaust, but by equalizing and improving the circulation of the blood, refreshes and invigorates;—and finally, is daily recommended by leading physicians to those suffering from want of tone and vigor, or from Dyspepsia and other forms of Indigestion, or from various deseases of the Nervous System, or from the class of ailments caused by torpor or Congestion of the Liver—in short, it is warmly approved by the Medical Profession as a most efficient, safe, and simple means of preventing diseases arising from sedentary habits.

Lifting is a system of harmonious and simultaneous exercise of the whole body. Every muscle is brought into use at once, and each in proportion to its relative strength. And so connected are the vital organs with the muscular tissue of the body, that when all the muscles simultaneously and harmoniously act, the organs themselves receive their appropriate amount of exercise. So distributed is this effort that there is no danger of injurious strains or rupture. It strengthens the weak organs, and expels disease by a gradual, co-operative exercise of the whole body. The strength of the whole body is augmented and equalized, the weak parts are built up, disease is expelled, and the individual becomes uniformly strong, and consequently healthy. It develops power chiefly at the vital centres. All the voluntary and respiratory muscles are brought into harmonious play, expanding the chest, augmenting the breathing capacity, aerating the blood, equalizing the circulation, warming the extremities, and thus vitalizing every part; and by determining action and circulation to the whole surface, increases the relative amount of blood in the extreme capillary vessels, thereby removing internal congestions wherever located, and accelerating the nutrition of every organ.

READY TO LIFT.

It is a true exercise, a correct developing agency, a safe method of cure. It is an equalizer and invigorator—a reconstructor of the tissues of the body and brain. It invokes all hygienic agencies, especially pure air, pure water, healthful food, sun, air and water baths, abundant sleep, rest, and recreation. It increases the healthy action of the brain correspondingly with that of the body. All the elements of a perfect manhood are increased, including not only intellectual vigor, but moral power and social purity. For as certainly as disease favors an abnormal condition of the mind as well as the body, so surely does an increase of health and strength become a promoter of virtue. In a word, it is putting a man in possession of himself.

The Health-Lift is one of the greatest inventions of the age, and it is second to none in importance, as it is a direct appliance for the culture and improvement of the human race. It is good for everybody, and should be used by all. The following are among

The Results that Follow Lifting.

1. It causes an equal circulation of the blood to all parts of the system. 2. It expands the lungs and increases the respiration. 3. It infuses more oxygen into the muscles, and thus purifies the tissues of the body. 4. It tones and builds up the whole system when purified. 5. It will double the strength in a few months. 6. It steadies and regulates the heart's action. 7. It does all these by a practice of only ten minutes once a day. 8. It will, by the above principles, cure many of the ills to which flesh is heir, especially when chronic, and resulting from derangement of the circulation.

The Health-Lift competes, and most successfully, with every proposed method of purifying the blood and giving vitality to the system, both general and local. It will in many cases do all that is claimed for medicine, electricity, movement cure, baths, and other forms of treatment. It produces power, energy, and vitality; it promotes physiological action, and thereby raises the standard of health; it impels the blood in its course, changes interstitial fluids, produces chemical action, and performs other duties serviceable to vitality; it is the greatest aid to the circulation, removing all local impediments.

It removes local congestion and chronic inflamation. It increases the oxidizing function. It causes the absorption and disappearance of solid and fluid accumulation. It diminishes chronic nervous irritability. It supplies a most efficacious remedy for paralysis, if taken in time. It cures deformities, liberates adhering and contracted fibres, renders mechanical and instrumental supports unnecessary. It increases muscle, hardens the flesh, perfects digestion and nutrition. In short, it promotes the healthy action of every function of the body.

THE REACTIONARY LIFTER.

What it is.

The Reactionary Lifter is the response which science and inventive talent have made to the demand for an instrument which would make this exercise popular and convenient. It is a portable, compact, and graceful apparatus for taking exercise in the safest and best possible manner. It has a combination of levers and a movable fulcrum, adjusted instantly, by which exercise varied in amount from twenty to twelve hundred pounds may be taken, being thereby suited to the weakest woman or the strongest man; and yet the instrument weighs only a little more than one hundred pounds.

Its exact dimensions are thirty-six inches long, eighteen inches wide, fourteen inches high. Its handles can be let down, so that it may be easily rolled under a table or bed if desirable. It can be readily transported from place to place, or trundled about the house on its castors. It is japanned to save it from rusting, and is beautifully finished in black and gold. It is highly ornamental and graceful in appearance, and may be placed without inconvenience in a hall, study, office, or bed-room. The "cuts" on this page illustrate its appearance and mode of use.

Its adjustment is so simple that a child can readily understand and manage it. It possesses the elasticity of rubber without its objections.

It has side-handles, therefore enabling all to use it with the body in the only natural and proper position for lifting, avoiding the unnatural and painful twist of the spine.

Only ten minutes once a day is required for all needed exercise on this apparatus. It affords to all who use it the best means of physical development and healthful exercise.

In the household, in the study or office it is a source of relief to overtaxed brains, and tired bodies. Every school and college should have one and make its use a daily duty, for we should teach and develope the physical as well as the mental powers of our youth.

Accompanying each machine is an illustrated "Manual," giving plain and full directions for its use. The "Manual" will be sent free to anyone wishing to investigate further before purchasing.

There are over two thousand Reactionary Lifters in constant and permanent use, giving entire satisfaction. Their sale has now reached one hundred per month, and the demand for them is constantly increasing. Important changes and improvements have lately been made in this machine, lessening its weight, greatly improving its finish and appearance, introducing a new self-locking fulcrum or slide, so that it cannot get out of order. Its adjustment is much more easy, the handles have been very materially improved, and it is now pronounced a perfect machine.

The Reactionary Lifter was patented by the inventor, Rev. C. H. Mann. The sole right to manufacture and sell these machines has been purchased by the Health-Lift Co., of New York, a joint stock corporation, having a capital of $200,000, and possessing every facility for introducing this valuable invention to the world at large. It has already organized nearly one hundred agencies in as many of the principal cities of the United States. and is constantly adding to their number. The demand for an article of this kind is unprecedented. The many who have and are using this machine, with marvelous results, will bear witness to all that is claimed for it. Its cost is only one hundred dollars.

If, in addition to its merits as a system of exercise, means so simple as those of the Health-Lift shall be found to produce tangible and uniform results, to check and even eradicate the most formidable disease, to secure immunity from sickness, and, finally, to bestow a freshness, vigor and endurance which make physical labor light and mental exertion pleasant, it must, in the language of a recent editorial in one of our leading dailies, be conceded "that such a system is not alone an individual blessing, but a wide spread benefit to the community. Its claims demand rigorous scrutiny from press and public. If baseless, their existence can but be ephemeral; if well founded, no reward is too great for him who shall have urged them, and so fulfilled the demand for a practical form of physical exercise, which is every day emphasized by some new case of a merchant breaking down at his desk, lawyer in his office, or minister in his pulpit, under the pressure, nowhere higher, nowhere more dangerous, than in our own city."

What is said of it.

Many eminent physicians, clergymen and lawyers have testified to the merits of the Health-Lift, some in letters to the Company, others in communications to magazines and newspapers. From a mass of such testimonials we select the following from Rev. J. F. W. Ware, D. D., Pastor of the Arlington Street Church, Boston, Mass. Dr. Ware has been a regular, paying subscriber at the Boston Agency of the Health-Lift Co., for three years, and is, therefore, qualified to speak, and has done so solely with the view of interesting others in what he found of great benefit. He was under no obligation to write and did so unsolicited. His article appeared in the *Atlantic Monthly*, February 1875, without the knowledge of anyone interested. These significant facts should give great weight to every word it contains.

"In common with many others, I had heard vaguely of this thing, with the same sort of vague indifference or skepticism with which one almost always hears of new things. The chance word of a friend at the right moment—the word in season—followed by the prompt "come with me now," led to the mysteries and blessings of the lift.

"Never shall I forget the sensations of my first lift and my introduction to parts of myself unknown or forgotten.

"It sent a glow all over the body that was as luscious and cheery as any that have been told of by the Turkish bath enthusiasts, and then—I am afraid it may betray me—an exhilaration purer and more subtle and enduring than that of best champagne. My experience has been a record of many joys, joys that come of soothing and strengthing to a fagged brain, and a weary body, and a pestered soul. I take my lift before my late dinner, when the day's work is done. I carry to it whatever weariness the day has made —of body, of brain, of heart—and I go away another than the man I came. Headache, limbache, heartache are gone, or toned down to easy bearing, and a new counteractant vigor set to work in all the pulses. It seems to get behind the heart, and bolster that first seat of power and action. It is the best of rest.

"The Health-Lift is the gradual, easy, complete waking up of every torpid molecule in brain, liver, and blood, the sending through and possessing the entire man with a new sense, a recreating him then and there, so that he turns from his few minutes at his Lift a new creation.

"It rouses the universal lethargy of the body; it sends the stagnant blood to the places nature intended it for; routs it from its hiding, its loafing places, and sends it to its duties; it removes surplus fat or distributes it; it decreases the girth of men growing portly and increases the girth of the lungs of men growing hollow; it helps digestion, increases the power and endurance of the voice, and sets one up generally. These are things whereunto I individually bear witness. Others have there other say. As I walk from my lift into the air I feel as if I could carry Atlas—his load—without stooping; I feel life down to the uttermost filament of my lungs, the glory and the joy of mere being. I feel so perpendicular as if I must be nadir and zenith to the universe. Amid all summer luxury and enjoyment I have felt the need of and have missed my daily lift.

"If we were only doing about these bodies somewhat near what we ought to do, every community would have a lift-club and careful attendant. It should be a public institution as much as a school is. It would be to many a man an addition, if not to the length of his days, to the value of his life; would furnish him with sensations, the like of which he has not had since he parted with the supplenets and the enterprise of boyhood. It will renew lost vigor better than voyage or nostrum; but the better work of it may be in keeping one from losing the vigor which at best is slowly regained, in pursuit of which so many lose the patience, perseverance, and faith which are vital to recovery. The Lift works slowly, as all real beneficences do, and its demand of you is patient perseverance

"It would be a great thing to have these Lifts attached to banks and buildings where many men are employed, who are burning life out at both ends; it would be a great step in political shrewdness to plant them next door to where young men do congregate, rather than she too eager and tempting saloons. Fathers would do well to send their growing boys and girls. Parishes would be wise if they made it a part of their duty to see that their minister took his Lift, and paid his bill for it to boot, if he be not able fairly to do it himself. And as things go, it would not be a bad idea to attach a Health-Lift to the church appointments, kitchens and parlors to set up the social thing that a man is even in his religion; why not set the man up in the physical things that he is, and that his religion needs him to be? A good lift of a Sunday morning before going to church would have a wonderfully clearing influence. There would be less sleeping, less indifference, less fault-finding, better chance for good all around. We should have men, women, ministers roused, wide awake, alert, good-humored and making the best of themselves and of everybody else. There isn't a great deal of use in talking about worshiping in spirit, when the body is tormenting you with its apathy, and the only real incense you lay upon the altar is an indigestion. I believe in worship and all that, but my creed is not complete until I have written it—I believe in the Health-Lift."

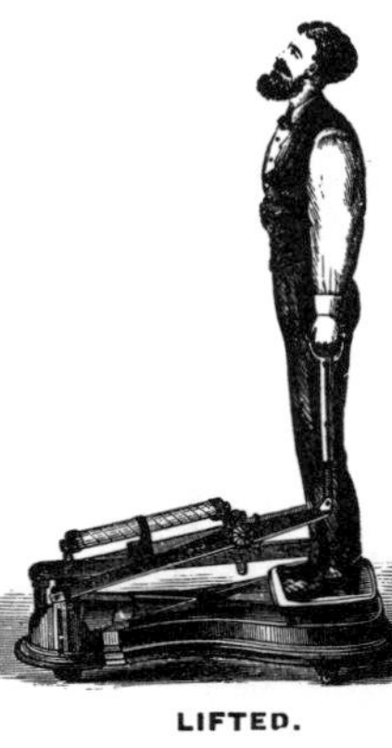

LIFTED.

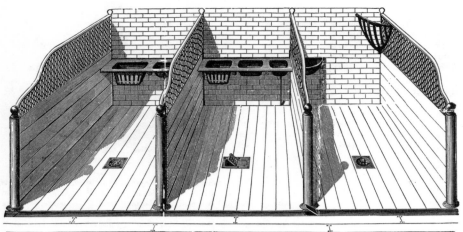

A Range of Open Stalls.   A Range of Loose Box Stalls.

SAMUEL S. BENT, GLOBE IRON FOUNDRY, NEW YORK. MANUFACTURER OF IMPROVED STABLE FIXTURES ETC.

Stable fixtures like other branches of industry have only gained in point of adaptation, elegance and cheapness, since they have become a specialty. The honor belongs to Samuel S. Bent, who has for twenty-eight years been devoted to fine castings and to have organized the manufacture of Stable Fittings in a separate line of industry, embracing an infinite variety of articles useful as well as ornamental, conducive to the health of the horse as well as to its comfort. Mr. Bent has furnished the conveniences of many of the largest livery stables in the United States, as well as some of the most elegant private stables of our prominent citizens. These fixtures

form one of the many attractions of the beautiful grounds of Mr. Frank Leslie, on the Saratoga Lake which the proprietor takes pleasure in explaining to the visitor. Mr. Bent is a practical man, making an especial study of every individual case of stable or buildings by adapting his fixtures, so as to conform to the plans which any locality may require, the sense and the taste and wishes of the gentleman applying to him for his work and attention. This model foundry was established in 1843, and is located at Nos. 408 to 422 East 26th Street, New York.

Complete Bed.   National Bed.   Folding National Bed

THE WOVEN WIRE MATTRESS CO., HARTFORD, CONN., AND CHICAGO, ILL.

This Company was organized March 23rd, 1869. From the beginning, the Woven Wire Mattress has met with popular favor, as an article of household use and it is said to be unsurpassed for beauty, cleanliness, durability and luxury. After six years experience the company feel justified in claiming for the Woven Wire Mattress that it is the best sleeping arrangement in the world. From time to time valuable improvements have been added making it more desirable. No labor or expense has been spared to bring it up to the present high degree of perfection. A heavy reduction in the prices has been made each year, so that the present cost of a Woven Wire Mattress is but a trifle more than the cheapest article in the market, taking into consideration that a hair mattress weighing only fifteen or twenty pounds at farthest, is sufficient to make it one of the most comfortable beds in existence. In the Woven Wire Mattress an invention is perfected which secures all the requisites of a bed combining elasticity and softness with a perfect regard for hygienic laws, together with durability and simplicity of construction. In the short time it has been before the public it has been fully recognized by those who un-

derstand and appreciate the comfort and luxury of a perfect bed. The fabric is so made that it can be rolled up like a piece of cloth and shipped in small bulk to any part of the country; its attachment to the frame when necessary and its disengagement being a simple matter of a few moments. The hygienic properties of the Woven Wire Mattress are perfect. Their metallic nature offers no texture of animal or vegetable fibres to absorb and retain the emanations from the body while the accuracy with which the frame fits affords no cracks or crevices for the gathering of dust or the harboring of vermin. The entire bed is open to the free circulation of air, and can at any moment be thoroughly examined. All sizes of these beds are made at short notice, for convenience of handling—in houses with narrow stairways—and moving. Iron beds complete for hospital uses, strong and durable. The improved or National Mattress, the standard bed of the United States. Address The Woven Wire Mattress Co., 175 Pearl St., Hartford, Conn., and 286 State Street, Chicago, Ill.

 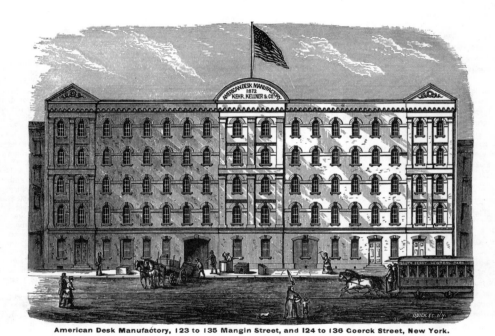

American Desk Manufactory, 123 to 135 Mangin Street, and 124 to 136 Coerck Street, New York.

KEHR, KELLNER & CO.,

Representing the Desk and Office Furniture Business of New York.

This extensive establishment is composed of Peter Kehr, John A. Kellner and Louis Ott. They are all practical mechanics and thoroughly conversant with every branch of their business. The firm was organized in 1865 with limited capital, therefore the business was at first started upon a small scale, but with a sure foundation, backed up by skill, energy and perseverance. They make a specialty of manufacturing office and library furniture of a very superior quality and finish, their desks being unsurpassed by any in America, in fact their work is at the present time in use in every part of this country.

By assiduous personal attention and by satisfying the wants of the trade, they secured a heavy patronage from the furniture dealers throughout the United States, and succeeded thus in making rapid progress from year to year.

With the increase of capital, luxurious business houses have sprang up all over the country, and the devotees of commerce spending most of their time in their office, look to convenience and even comfort in articles of office furniture. With the spread of culture a private library became part of every gentleman's house. This firm, by making a specialty of this kind of furniture made vast improvements upon the old styles and invented many new patterns of office and library furniture, suited for different uses and different styles of architecture and tastes, which

secured them an immense trade extending to every part of the Union.

They had to enlarge their facilities, which they accomplished by the purchase of 14 lots of ground in the city of New York, upon which they erected their present large warehouses and factories.

On the first day of January, 1874, the facilities of this firm for manufacturing consisted in the following dimensions in square feet: one five story factory, 130 x 25; one four story factory, 130 x 40 ; one five story ware-house, 156 x 40; one engine house, 35 x 50; 10,000 feet of lumber sheds, 8,500 feet of yard room: equivalent when in full operation to 35,700 square feet for manufacturing purposes, 4,500 square feet for machinery, 19,000 square feet for warerooms, 5,000 square feet for packing and shipping rooms, 10,000 square feet for lumber sheds, 1,000 square feet for office room, 2,000 square feet for veneer legs and moulding room, 35,000 cubic feet for drying room.

This house employs 300 men, and turns out every week on an average 175 to 200 desks, of which they have frequently over 100 different styles on exhibition in their ware-rooms.

Machinery is used exclusively for cutting out the work in the rough, the real work being performed by hand. There is not a hole bored nor a single shaving made in this factory by machinery, the object being to make the work more durable and give it a more graceful appearance than if performed by machinery, the stiff or ever repeated lines of which offend the artistic eye of the lover of the truly beautiful in form.

For further information concerning the manufacture of office and library furniture, we refer to the published catalogue of this house, which may be obtained gratuitously by applying for the same to the American Desk Manufactory of Kehr, Kellner & Co., 123 to 135 Mangin Street, and 124 to 136 Goerck Street.

Chandeliers, Gas Fixtures and Bronze Ornaments and Fine Clocks.

Manufactured by

MITCHELL, VANCE & CO.,

No. 597 Broadway, New York.

—:o:—

" The prayer of Ajax was for light,
Through all that dark and desperate fight,
The blackness of that noon-day night,
He asked but the return of sight,
To see his foeman's face."

Light is the friend of man. Darkness is his foe. Artificial illumination engages the best scientific and mechanical skill of our time. It is not too much to say that it is an essential part of our civilization.

Rude and simple as were the lights used by the ancients, they displayed great skill in the design and manufacture of metal lamps and vessels for holding oil.

The public use of gas for illumination has hardly seen its semi-centennial. It was introduced in London in 1814; Paris, 1820; Boston, 1822; New York, 1827; Philadelphia, 1835.

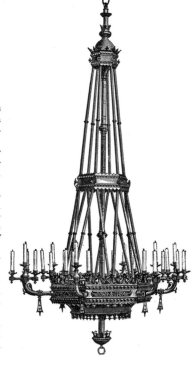

talents of their artists and workmen they are without superiors in this or any other country. They unquestionably stand in the front ranks of those who have labored successfully to elevate the standard of their business.

In full appreciation of the growing refinement and delicacy of taste everywhere exhibited, they have sought to merit their share of the encouragement and patronage which wealth and culture are extending to all branches of artistic industry.

They first organized in the year 1854, under the corporate laws of Connecticut, as Mitchell, Bailey & Co., the late John S. Mitchell being at the head of the organization. In the year 1860, Sam'l B. H. Vance having been connected with the business from the beginning, the new copartnership firm of Mitchell, Vance & Co. was formed. In 1873 this copartnership was dissolved, and a corporation under the laws of New York was organized.

Upon the death of John S. Mitchell, (Feb. 1st, 1875,) Charles Benedict was made President; Sam'l B. H. Vance, Vice-President; Edgar M. Smith, Secretary and Treasurer. Trustees: Charles Benedict, Edward A. Mitchell, Sam'l B. H. Vance, Dennis C. Wilcox and Edgar M. Smith. The reputation of these gentlemen for business ability and integrity is a guarantee that the interests entrusted to their charge will

View of Mitchell, Vance & Co.'s Factory and Foundry, New York.

Its use, however, seems to have gone forward hand in hand with those scientific discoveries and mechanical inventions which have marked the general progress of the last half century. Its great advantages over other means of illumination seems to have given both stimulus and reward to mechanical and artistic skill. Few branches of industry have accomplished more to make their specialties complete in arrangement and perfect in principle and utility. It may be added, few, if any, more decidedly affect the comforts, conveniences and pleasures of society.

The great importance of public and domestic illumination properly demands Gas Fixtures and appliances, useful and complete in character and ornamental in effect. Occupying as they do, the most conspicuous and prominent position in public buildings the highest artistic talent finds suitable opportunity for the display of its best skill in their production.

Mechanical ingenuity of the highest order is also demanded for the construction of fixtures required to keep under safe control so subtle, and, possibly so mischievous an agent as illuminating gas.

In order fully to meet those requirements, both artistic and mechanical, Mitchell, Vance & Co. have for years, in the most painstaking and conscientious manner, devoted their best skill and ability.

In the extent and completeness of their works; in the numbers and varied

not suffer from inattention to its details or from want of sagacity in management.

Beside Gas Fixtures, Clocks and Bronzes, Mitchell, Vance & Co., manufacture in the best spirit and style of workmanship, all objects of Decorative Art, in metal, necessary for the furniture or embellishment of Churches, Public and Private Buildings.

Artists, native and foreign, are constantly employed in designing and moulding subjects to be produced in both Real and Imitation Bronze.

At two successive exhibitions of the American Institute this firm was awarded the highest medals for Crystals and Metal Gas Fixtures, and the same award was made for Fine Bronzes and Fine Metal and Marble Clocks.

The Warerooms of Mitchell, Vance & Co., are situated at No. 597 Broadway, extending to 140 Mercer Street, comprising seven stories, each 25 x 200 feet, and are used solely for the display and sale of the articles of their own manufacture, where everything pertaining to the various branches of their business may be seen in endless variety of design and excellence of finish.

The above engraving represents their extensive Factories and Foundry situated on Twenty-fourth and Twenty-fifth Streets and Tenth Avenue, New York City.

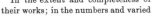

BAXTER
STEAM ENGINE.

Horizontal View of Tubular Boiler.

We have examined this engine with care and believe it to contain all the advantages that an engine of this character can possibly have. It is too much to say that no improvement is possible, but we confess ourselves unable to see where or how any substantial improvement can be made. The principal points aimed at by inventors has been to generate the largest amount of steam in the smallest possible space, and by the consumption of the least amount of fuel. The Baxter Engine does that, by methods so entirely unique, as to take it altogether out of the category of ordinary engines.

Before proceeding to the detailed description of this beautiful piece of mechanism, it is proper to say while it is the happy invention of Mr. Baxter, to whom great credit is due, its comparative perfection, and its present wide popularity, is due to the sagacity and intelligence of others. It is one thing to invent a machine, but quite another, to render it practical. Mr. Baxter has been eminently fortunate in the direction he has succeeded in giving to the introduction and manufacture of his engine.

It is difficult to convince an incredulous public of the value of an invention until it has been practically demonstrated. This requires business talent, capital, patience, and perseverance, which supported by an intelligent appreciation of the thing invented, serve as a stimulus to press on against all obstacles, until, in spite of unfair criticisms, success crowns the effort.

BAXTER ENGINE.

The first cut represents the completed engine; it is of a portable character, and occupies very little space indeed. The engine proper is immediately over the fire box and boiler, as will more fully appear in the second cut. It has the necessary valves, guages, band and fly wheels, governor, cranks, piston, cylinder, &c., all within the size of the upright boiler below, arranged as never before in the history of steam engineering. It occupies less space than other engines of like capacity and power. Access to the fire box is had through the iron door near the bottom of the boiler.

The second cut shows the internal mechanism and arrangement of the various parts, not shown in the first cut. The fire box occupies the center of the boiler, the coal grate and ash box being below. The boiler being of the tubular pattern, the flames and heated gases rise to the top of the fire chamber and are deflected downward through the tubes, as indicated by the arrows in the cut, passing thence through proper connections into the outer space surrounding the boiler, into the smoke pipe. The water surrounds the fire box entirely, the tubes, and also to the heating surface of the outer chamber of the boiler. The cold water, supplied at the bottom, is also heated before it enters into the main body of the boiler, effecting an economy.

Interior View of Boiler Furnace, Cylinder Valves, &c.

COLT'S PATENT FIRE-ARMS MANU-
FACTURING COMPANY.
Hartford, Conn.

The beautiful engraving of the works of the above named corporation, here presented, will convey a faint idea of the magnitude of its operations.

Col. Samuel Colt, while a young man, paid much attention to the study of fire arms. In a paper read before the Institution of Civil Engineers, in London, in 1851, he presented the best history of the early attempts to produce breech loading small arms, that has ever been written. In this paper Col. Colt says, "after much reflection and repeated trials, I effected an arrangement of the construction of revolving fire arms without having seen or been aware, at that period (1829), of any arm more effective than a double-barreled having ever been constructed.

Col. Colt, when his inventions were first made, was without the pecuniary means to practically test their efficacy. To obtain money he assiduously pursued his calling as a scientific lecturer and from its rewards procured the funds necessary to manufacture specimen arms. In 1836 he received his first patent from the United States.

After procuring his first patent, Col. Colt's lack of means placed him in the situation of most successful inventors, and his only course was to engage the attention of capitalists to form a company to make and introduce his arms to the public.

Indomitable energy and perserverance soon accomplished this, and the Patent Arms Com-

pany was established in 1836 at Paterson, New Jersey.

In 1837 the Seminole Indians, retreating into the "Everglades," defied the power of the United States. The Government applied to Col. Colt, who went to the seat of war with his repeating arms. It was glorious success for the government but disastrous to Col. Colt; the closing of the war destroyed the market for the arms.

From the failure of the Paterson Company until 1847 none of these arms were made. In the meantime, the demand from Texas, where they had been adopted in both Army and Navy, had drained the market. In the above year, when the Mexican Campaign commenced, Gen. Taylor dispatched Capt. Walker of the Texan Rangers to procure a supply of revolvers from Col. Colt. Not one could be found; but the Colonel soon prepared for the emergency, and this case presents a striking instance of the extraordinary energy and determination of purpose so prominent in his character. He was looked upon as a ruined man; but he thought otherwise, knowing that his eventual triumph depended upon himself and that here was the opportunity to retrieve the embarrassments he had been drawn into by the acts of the corporation. He temporarily hired an armory at Whitneyville, Connecticut, and shortly afterwards established the nucleus of the present works at Hartford, Connecticut.

Colt produces from 250 to 350 Gatling Guns, 300 Baxter Steam Engines, 350 Gally's Universal Printing Presses, 5,000 Conductors' Punches, 200,000 to 300,000 one inch metallic cartridges for Gatling Guns and small metallic cartridges for Pistols, besides forgings for rings for Cotton Machines, Carriage Fittings, &c. Iron and Brass Foundries, are attached to the works.

COLT'S PATENT ARMS COMPANY'S MANUFACTORY, HARTFORD, CONN.

THE HILLS
"ARCHIMEDEAN" LAWN MOWER.

A celebrated florist says, "The space in front of the house, and generally the sides exposed to view from the street should be in grass. No arrangement of beds, or borders of box, or anything else, will look so neat and tasteful as a well kept plot of grass." The last five words of the quotation are important ones. Until the introduction of the Hills Archimedean Lawn Mower it was no easy task to have a "well kept piece of grass."

This little machine is now so well known throughout the United States, that it requires but little description on our part. Its invention gave to the American people a practical hand Lawn Mower, and it was at once adopted here, and also in Europe.

It is now celebrated all over Europe, being used on nearly all the public parks in Great Britain, on the boulevards in Paris, and for the beautiful gardens in Constantinople. It is acknowledged to be a perfect Lawn Mower. Its chief features are simplicity of construction, perfectness of manufacture, ease of operating, easy way of sharpening the knives when dull, and particularly its adapting itself to slopes, undulating lawns, ridges and valleys.

This machine was the first balanced Lawn Mower invented, operated by an adjustable handle, which can be raised or lowered at the will of the operator, allowing the machine to adapt itself to the surface of the ground, preserving a beautiful level cut. The height of cut is regulated by shoes in front, which glide along the surface of the lawn, causing it to run steadier than with a wheel, preventing the knife from cutting the turf.

The Croquet Mower, a beautiful little machine, was first placed in the market in 1873, and during the first season became very popular. It cuts a swath ten inches wide and in every respect is equal to the larger sizes, only being reduced in weight to correspond with width of cut. It is light running and durable and can easily be operated by a lad or miss of ten. A patent guard on the front of the machine to protect shrubbery from being injured by coming in contact with the knives is of great value, and has only to be seen to be appreciated. This guard may be obtained from the company or any of its agents, and is applicable to the larger sized machines. The wonderful success which has attended the introduction of this machine, has induced others to attempt the manufacture of similar ones.

"Archimedean" Horse Power Lawn Mower.

The method of sharpening a Lawn Mower when it becomes dull, is of the greatest importance to every one owning a machine. A valuable feature in the Hills "Archimedean" Lawn Mower, is that the knives can be sharpened without removing them. This is easily and quickly accomplished by placing oil and emery on the cutters, and reversing the motion, thereby giving the knives a smooth and keen cutting edge, and keeping them perfectly true, without which no Lawn Mower will cut the grass clean and do good work; thus experiencing none of the trouble and vexation caused by taking out the knives and grinding them on a grindstone.

Their new machine is durable and beautiful in its proportions, and is claimed to be the lightest draft machine in the world of its capacity. Columbus Ryan Esq., superintendent of public parks in the city of New York, whose knowledge of lawn culture and lawn mowers is unquestioned, and whose great experience and good judgment is a sufficient guarantee, after testing it, says it is superior to any they ever used before.

All the improvements that experience could suggest, have been added to these machines. They are supplied with patent noiseless ratchet, fine steel knives, covered gears, and a simple method for putting the machine in and out of gear. A tool-box is attached, on the back part of the machine to keep the tools, oil can, &c., necessary in its use, always with the machine. Two sizes are manufactured, one cutting a swath twenty-eight inches wide, and one thirty-two inches, either of which is easily operated by a pony or small horse, and with but little labor. The machines are warranted perfect in all their parts; directions for using and keeping in order are sent with every machine. They are manufactured by the Colt's Patent Fire Arms Manufacturing Company, a guarantee of perfection.

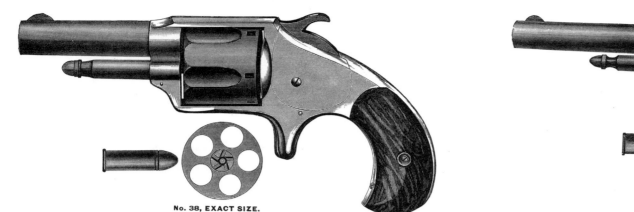

NO. 38, EXACT SIZE.   No. 32, EXACT SIZE.

SAVAGE & SMITH,
Manufacturers of
Breech-Loading Cartridge Revolvers, Sporting Gun
Locks, Washer Cutters, etc.,
ROCK FALLS, Near Middletown, CONN.
——:o:——

The village of Rock Fall is situated on the line of the Boston and New York Air Line Railroad, three and one half miles west of Middletown, and is a fair representative of the many wide-awake and thriving villages with which Connecticut is studded. The large establishment of the firm whose name heads this article was erected here in 1840, and since then has been used for the manufacture of Pistols for the United States Government, and private parties.

The firm, consisting of E. B. Savage and Otis A. Smith, are now manufacturing many first-class articles, but make a specialty of their superior Revolver, and in this department both gentlemen are perfectly at home, Mr. Savage having been brought up in the business by his father, Edward Savage, the well known manufacturer of fire-arms for the United States Government, who succeeded his father, one of the oldest, if not the oldest manufacturer of fire arms in America. Mr. Smith is perfectly familiar with all classes of fire-arms, and the inventor of several important improvements in pistols, to which he has given his special attention. After years of careful study, he perfected the model patented by him, April 15, 1873, and which

has since become immensely popular because of its convenient size, its graceful form, its strength, beauty of finish and durability.

Smith's Patent Revolvers are now produced in four sizes, of 22, 32, 38 and 41 calibre, here represented by cuts of exact proportions. These Pistols are of superior

workmanship throughout, the manufacturers not having fallen into a too prevailing idea of the day, that it is necessary to make a poor weapon in order to make it cheap. They use only the best of materials in its construction; all the parts are fitted to gauge, and none are used that have not passed the critical examination of competent inspectors. Consequently the finished product is a perfected arm, a pocket pistol adapted to meet the wants of every gentleman or lady who desires a reliable and ever present protector.

During the past few years, so largely has their business increased, Messrs. Savage & Smith have been obliged to make several important additions to their building, and to add largely to their machinery and tools. Their establishment is now amply provided with gun and pistol machinery of the latest and most improved patterns, and with complete sets of special tools for making every separate part of these Revolvers.

Soon after this arm was introduced, the firm received orders for thirty thousand at one time, and they now have facilities for promptly filling orders of almost any size.

The manufacture of the Sporting Gun Lock was commenced in 1866, until then almost an untried experiment in this country, it being necessary to compete with English and German hand made locks. The enterprise proved successful, however, and Messrs. Savage & Smith now make over thirty different varieties from Bar, Side and Back Action patterns, Rough and Filed, Polished and Engraved, either Right or Left hand,—for Sporting Rifles and Shot Guns, both single and double barrels, which find a ready sale throughout the United States.

Another useful article needs mention, the King & Smith Patent Washer Cutter, used in cutting leather washers for Carriages, Pump Packing, Valves etc., this is meeting with a ready sale and promises to be an important branch of their business.

No. 41, EXACT SIZE.

No. 22 EXACT SIZE.

 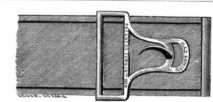

THE RUSSELL MANUFACTURING CO.,
Middletown, Conn.

The Russell Manufacturing Company, the principal factories of which are in Middletown, Connecticut, owes its position as a successful, and, in its specialties, leading manufacturing company in the United States, to Hon. Henry G. Hubbard, its President and largest stockholder. Such, indeed, has been his relation to its development, that one well acquainted with the facts, said: "He is the Russell Company."

The first factory building of the Company, erected in 1834, was of brick 80 feet long, 30 feet wide and 3 stories high, located at the South Farms in Middletown, on a mill-privilege, then belonging to Hon. Samuel Russell. These gentlemen obtained a charter and organized the Company, owning themselves nine-tenths of the stock. The capital was $40,000, representing the privilege, building, and the real estate connected therewith; also, certain machinery, material and stock, into possession of which they had come as creditors of the insolvent firm of Spaulding & Collis, manufacturers of non-elastic web and suspenders. Having removed this machinery to their factory, the Company commenced to manufacture the same line of goods, employing Mr. Spaulding as superintendent. At the end of two years the liabilities of the Company exceeded its assets by more than $20,000, and it was doubtful whether the whole property—real estate, machinery, stock, everything—could be sold for an amount sufficient to pay the indebtedness.

At this juncture, in April, 1836, Henry G. Hubbard, a nephew of Hon. S. D. Hubbard, then twenty-one years of age, was invited to take charge of the business. Accepting the position, he addressed himself with all his energies to acquiring a thorough knowledge of the machinery and the mechanical methods involved in the manufacture, his previous experience having been wholly mercantile. In 1841, he commenced the manufacture of elastic web, which had not been previously attempted in this country except to a very limited extent, and on hand looms, a single strip at a time. Securing the services of a Scotch weaver, and obtaining from

him information as to the process of cutting and otherwise preparing rubber threads for weaving then in use in England, he very soon devised machinery which enabled him to weave the web in power looms, and his factory became the pioneer in this country, and, it is believed, in the world, in manufacturing elastic web by power.

In 1853 he purchased the Hon. S. D. Hubbard's interest in the Company, and in 1857 that of Hon. Samuel Russell. He has not at any time called for additional capital, but, solely out of the profits, has liquidated the debt, purchased the water privileges, purchased and erected additional factory buildings, and increased the capital to $300,000, besides making, from year to year, liberal dividends to the stockholders. The number of looms has been increased from twelve to two hundred and sixty, with a corresponding increase of subsidary machinery, and the number of employes has been increased from thirty to five hundred. All the operations necessary to finishing the goods, from the raw material, except the spinning of worsted and linen yarns, are performed in the mills of the Company.

In addition to the mill first built which has been enlarged, other buildings have been erected at the original privilege. These are devoted to weaving elastic and non-elastic web for various purposes, to the making up of suspenders, to dyeing of yarns, and to the repairing of old and the construction of new machinery. At this point, also, are the central office of the Company and the storehouses for raw material and for manufactured goods. At the privilege above the original one, is a factory devoted to weaving web, elastic and non-elastic, and at the next privilege below, one devoted to spinning, etc. The latter work is also done at a factory at Higganum, six miles below Middletown, and at another factory erected by the Company on the site of the old Falls factory in Middlefield. At Staddle's Hill, a large factory was built in 1865, in the most thorough and substantial manner, for

the manufacture of skirt tape, the whole expense of the building and machinery having been realized from the profits of the manufacture for two years. This mill is now devoted to the manufacture of non-elastic web.

About two-thirds of the whole production consists of suspender-web and suspenders. They are of staple quality, it being Mr. Hubbard's policy to make and sell large quantities of these, rather than to cater to the comparatively limited demand for those of fancy style and high price. Within this chosen range the goods have always taken the highest rank, being of attractive patterns and of bright showy colors.

The non-elastic webs for boot and gaiter straps have deservedly taken a leading position in the trade. Lighter webs for binding, stay-webs, etc., are made in large quantities, and at prices which render difficult, if they do not defy competition. In the line of non-elastic webs, may be mentioned, also, a variety of wide webs, designed for slippers, and affording a material both durable and of pleasing patterns. The rein and girth webs are in great variety, and are recognized as of the highest quality. In connection with the girth-webs, an elastic-web is made for inserting in girths used to confine blankets on horses when in their stalls, permitting the girths to yield thereby promoting the comfort of the animal. A considerable business has also been developed in the manufacture of a heavy cotton web, to take the place of leather in the harness for horses and mules, and is used largely in the Southern States. An especially noteworthy style of web is made from 5 to 20 inches wide and from two to five-ply, the latter being a half inch thick, and is used by manufacturers of Steam Fire Engine Hose. It readily bears a pressure of 700 lbs. to the square inch and is woven so closely as to be quite impervious to water, but security in this respect is increased by coating the inside with India-rubber and vulcanizing it. An advantage of this hose is that it requires no great labor in cleaning it after use, or the application of grease or other material for its preservation, as in the case of leather hose. This hose was original with Mr. Hubbard.

The Company has as its agents, Messrs. Sawyer & Judson, 76 Worth St., New York. Sales are also made directly to jobbers and manufacturers in different parts of the country, from its office in Middletown, Connecticut.

VIEW OF THE RUSSELL MANUFACTURING COMPANY'S WORKS, MIDDLETOWN, CONNECTICUT, U. S. A.

Remington Breech Loading Double Barrelled Gun. Open to receive Cartridge.

Remington Breech-Loading Double Barrelled Shot Gun.

Cartridge Case for Above Gun.

Remington Breech Loading Double Barrelled Gun. Sectional View.

Cartridge Cases for Above Gun.

Cartridge for Long Range Rifle.

E. REMINGTON & SONS.

Breech Loading Fire-Arms, Agricultural Machinery and Sewing Machines, Ilion, N. Y.

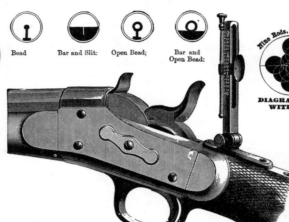

Bead   Bar and Slit.   Open Bead;   Bar and Open Bead:

Remington Creedmoor Rifle.

DIAGRAMS OF TARGETS MADE WITH A REMINGTON RIFLE.

The principle of breech-loading, applied to small arms, did not meet with approval until this century. The first recorded patent in the United States was dated May 21st, 1911, and John H. Hall, of North Yarmouth, was the inventor and patentee of the first breech-loading fire-arm which received attention from the U.S. Government.

The Remington Breech-Loading Rifle, furnished in greater numbers to troops than any other arm, with the exception of the needle-gun, is one of the most recent inventions of its class. Its first public appearance was in 1865. Its record shows its adoption by Denmark, Spain, Sweden, Greece, France, Rome, Egypt, Japan, South American Republics, the United States (both for army and navy use) and by several of the States for use of the militia.

At the Imperial Paris Exposition of 1867, the Remington competed with other systems from England, Austria, Belgium, and the United States. The report of the commission, which was composed of representatives of France, England, Austria, Belgium, Spain, Italy, Holland, Prussia, Russia and Sweden, was in favor of the Remington, which received the highest trophy awarded military and sporting arms.

The Remington sporting rifles and shot guns are as well known as the military arm. Since their introduction they have always been popular. The first point to which an observer's attention is directed in a breech-loading gun is the breech action, or the device for opening and closing the rear end of the barrel. It is important that this should be strong, simple, and easily operated. All these requirements are filled in a marked degree by the improved Remington.

All the Remington Rifles, except the Creedmoor Rifle, are furnished, unless otherwise ordered, with a plain bead fore sight and open rear sight. When so ordered the fore sight can be replaced by the Beach Combination Sight, which fits in the cut made in the barrel for our regular bead sight, and a peep rear sight can be attached.

For the Creedmoor Rifles, new long range front and rear sights have been made. The front sight has a wind-gauge adjustment, and when so ordered, is provided with spirit-level and extra discs of the several forms in use. The rear sight is hinged to a base piece and is provided with a screw adjustment and vernier for reading elevations to minutes.

In the construction of the front sight care has been taken to get it as low down on the barrel as possible. The bead with which these sights are usually made is well protected by a long projecting hood, the importance of which will readily be understood by any one who will contrast the clear black outline given by a well covered sight with the gray surface shown by a sight such as those used in many of the imported rifles.

To adjust the rear sight, the eye-piece is first loosened, then, when the sight is properly set by means of the screw, the eye-piece is tightened and holds the slide firmly, irrespective of the screw, which is intended only for convenience in adjusting the eye-piece.

The rear sight is graduated into degrees and minutes by means of a vernier scale. Each minute of elevation corresponds to about two inches for each one hundred yards of range. From the nature of the case it is impossible to construct a table of elevations which shall be exactly correct for more than one single gun; nor will any two men shoot exactly alike with the same gun.

The beautiful double-barreled shot guns manufactured by this firm are special favorites, and in points of excellence are surpassed by none.

In the production of these arms no expense or trouble is spared. An elaborate and complete set of machinery and gauges has been made, by means of which all the parts are produced exactly alike, and interchangeable, thus insuring great accuracy and uniformity in the character of work produced, affording great facility to the sportsman. The workmen are skilled men who have spent many years in this branch of industry, and the utmost care is exercised in every department to secure excellence. Many thousands of these arms are sold yearly.

Another branch of manufacture which has naturally grown in connection with the manufacture of breech-loading fire arms, is Metallic Cartridges.

In the early history of breech-loaders, one of the chief difficulties was that of obtaining a reliable cartridge. This was so impressed upon the attention of the Messrs. Remington, they are prepared to furnish ammunition used with their arms. The "special" cartridges used at Creedmoor with the Remington "Creedmoor" Rifle, are all made by the Messrs. Remington.

The Messrs. Remington are rapidly acquiring a new fame. For years gentlemen have praised their arms, but now the former praise is eclipsed by the ladies who are warm in commendation of a sewing machine known as the "Remington," a cut of which is shown on this page.

The Remington Sewing Machines are rapidly gaining favor in every household where they are introduced. They are silent and smooth while in motion, positive proof that they will continue to run well for years without expense.

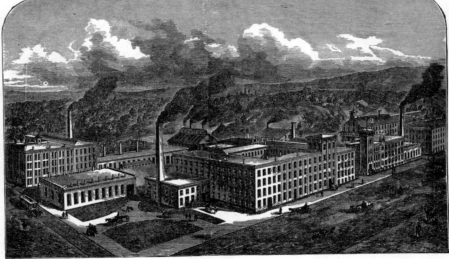

Remington Armory, Ilion, New York.

The Remington Sewing Machines were invented by Mr. J. T. Jones, who is well known in the trade throughout the world as one of the pioneer inventors.

This machine is capable of a range and variety of work such as was once thought impossible to perform by machinery. It is remarkable not only for this, but also for the variety and different kinds of texture which it will sew with equal facility and perfection, using silk twist, linen or cotton thread, fine or coarse, making the interlocked-elastic stitch, aline on both sides of the fabric sewn. Thus beaver cloth or leather may be sewn with great strength and uniformity of stitch; and in a moment this willing and never-wearying instrument may be adjusted for fine work on gauze or gossamer tissue, or the tucking of tarletan, or ruffling, or almost any other work which delicate fingers have been known to perform. It has a straight needle, perpendicular action, automatic drop feed.

It is every way completely and tastefully ornamented in various styles, and at an expense that is put upon very few machines in the market.

But the Messrs. Remington do not stop even here. They are among the largest and best known manufacturers of agricultural machinery in the country, and the same high degree of excellence which they have acquired in their other branches of industry is fully maintained here. Among the many agricultural implements manufactured by them are the celebrated Mohawk Valley Patent Clippers and the Ilion Iron Beam Patent Clipper Plows. A full and complete description of them is unnecessary, as they are known and used all over the United States. No less than sixteen different sizes of these plows are manufactured, and there is no conceivable quality of soil to which some of them are not adapted. They also manufacture Sayre's Patent Horse Hoe for weeding, hoeing and hilling corn, cotton, tobacco and potatoes, which for surface culture in light soils has no superior; Solid Steel Teeth Cultivators, for one and two horses; sho-

Mohawk Valley Clipper Plow.

Needle Cotton Gin, with Condenser.

vel and double shovel plows and cultivators of various names and kinds, steel shovel plows, wheel cultivator and horse hoe blades, steel shares, harrow teeth and harrows, solid steel cultivator teeth, cast standards with reversible point, oval and diamond; wrought standards with reversible point, cast steel hand hoes with solid shanks or sockets; Scattergood's American Needle Cotton Gin, a machine whose many points of excellence have been fully recognized; Daniel Judd's Improved Patent Excavator, which has been thoroughly tested and in every case gave perfect satisfaction. Nor does the list stop here. Bridge building is an important branch of their work. Whipple's patent iron bridges have been in use about thirty years and have been thoroughly tested. They are in use on all canals of New York State and have given complete satisfaction. Mr. John M. Whipple has made iron bridges a special study for twenty-five years.

These mammoth works are turning out, among other goods, a yearly product of about 2,500 mowers and reapers, 5,000 plows, 800 cultivators, 30,000 to 40,000 cultivator teeth, 500 cotton gins, 10,000 dozen hoes and rakes, a large quantity of bridge work, besides immense quantities of extras of all sorts made and sold separately. Special attention is given manufacture of cotton gins, steel plows, mowers and cultivators. Their products are sent east, west, north and south, and wherever used have given perfect satisfaction. The Remingtons make only superior articles.

The Remington Sewing Machine.

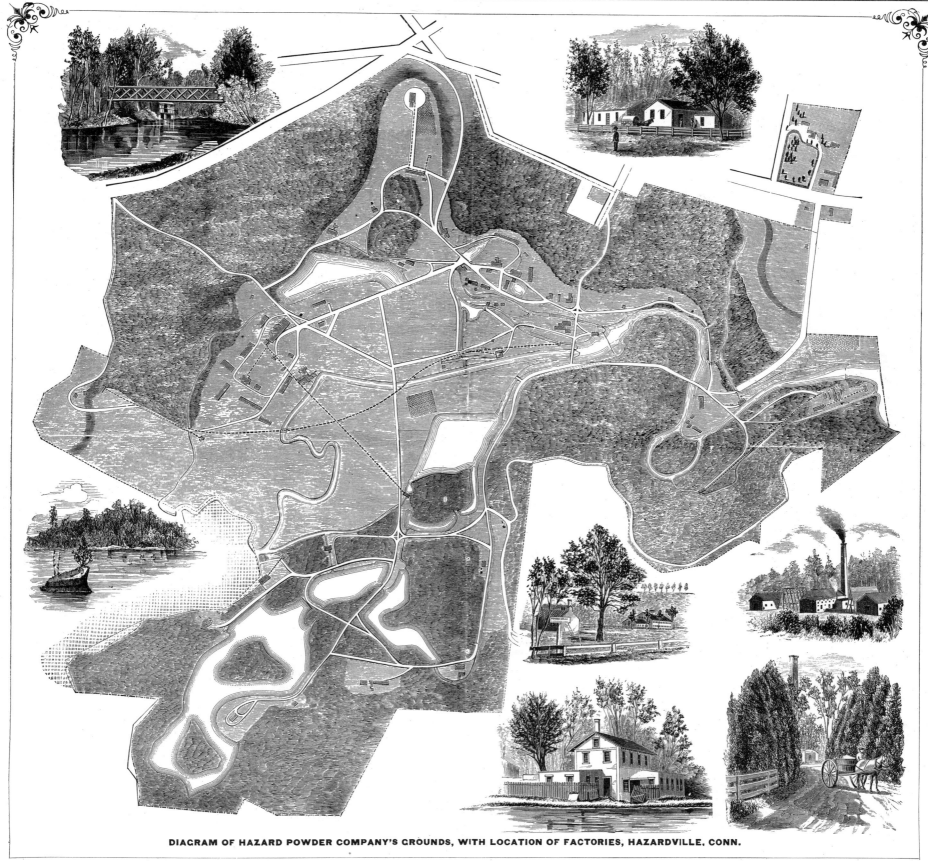

DIAGRAM OF HAZARD POWDER COMPANY'S GROUNDS, WITH LOCATION OF FACTORIES, HAZARDVILLE. CONN.

THE HAZARD POWDER COMPANY,

OFFICE, 88 WALL STREET, NEW YORK.

Among the appliances indispensable to the sporting, mining and railroad interests of the United States, and for purposes of offensive and defensive warfare, the article of Gunpowder suitable for heavy ordinance and small arms as also for blasting takes a conspicious rank. Its manufacture is prosecuted by numerous companies and firms of greater or less experience or means.

In localities where large amounts of Blasting Powder are continually required for mining purposes, establishments of lesser magnitude spring up in secluded valleys furnishing available water power, and in a crude and common fashion the ingredients of Nitrate of Soda, Charcoal and Sulphur, are mixed in sheds and shanties with the simplest possible machinery, involving perhaps, a larger personal risk, but operated at inconsiderable outlay of capital. For immediate use, generally within a few days of its fabrication, this primitive mode of manufacture will answer fairly for a neighborhood where the better and more expensively manufactured article could not conveniently be furnished, but the powder so made possesses but limited explosive force and is destitute of durability or of power to resist moisture or endure transportation, and commands no trade beyond the immediate vicinity of its manufacture. While these establishments are comparatively numerous, the standard manufactories involving extensive outlay of capital in machinery and buildings, and furnishing powder, for all the varied demands of peace or war, whether at home or abroad, which is capable of enduring exposure to climatic influences, and brought by the ability of the experts employed, up to the highest possible standard—such manufactories are few—and in the United States cannot be said to exceed eight in number. Among these there is a very considerable disparity in the extent of works and business and of capital employed, the latter ranging from several thousand dollars to several millions.

It is not our design to explain the process of the manufacture of Gunpowder, that is the province of Text-Books and Encyclopedias. The ingredients are well known and for centuries have been invariable. They are "Nitrate of Potash," (or "Saltpetre,") "Charcoal" and "Sulphur." For ordinary blasting purposes only, Nitrate of Soda is substituted for Nitrate of Potash, its sole recommendation

being its reduced cost. On the other hand its tendency to absorb moisture is very great and often in exposed places baffles the best care of the manufacturer or consumer. For durability it is far inferior to the first named ingredient, "Saltpetre." While for Blasting and Gun-powder the proportions of ingredients used by different manufacturers are almost identical, the quality of the manufactured article is largely influenced by the amount of intelligence and experience displayed in its more intricate manipulation.

In the details of its fabrication new discoveries are constantly being applied, and the uninitiated would be surprised at the amount of judgment demanded of the experts upon whom the more delicate details of the manufacture devolve. The processes through which each of the ingredients is compelled to pass to attain the highest stage of purity, the mode of admixture, the time they remain under the rolls, the pressure to which subjected, the graining and sifting, glazing and drying, each one of these influenced by the weight, humidity or dryness of the atmosphere at the time, are all subjects for special intelligence and the brain is ransacked to develope formula for these and numberless other details of the manufacture, all of which to a greater or less degree modify the manufactured articles and gain for the manufacturers the special reputation they value. This knowledge and experience is the work of a life time spent in the business, as well by the manufacturers as by their employees and constitutes a reasonable assurance to the purchaser that old established companies as a rule produce the most reliable and satisfactory Gunpowders. While an observance of these minutiae is indispensable in the manufacture of Military and Sporting Powders, it is not specially demanded for the commoner styles of Blasting Powder, which nevertheless, in the case of the more extensive companies, receives the benefit of the knowledge possessed by the experts of the establishment, and issues from its precincts endowed with some fruits of the peculiar intelligence and skill expended ordinarily upon more aristocratic brands.

But we must leave our comment upon the manufacture of Gun-powder to call attention specially to the views presented upon this page which illustrate better than we can describe the vast extent and ramifications of a well organized Gunpowder manufactory. Among those which have acquired prominence in the United States, the establishments of the Hazard Powder Company, at Hazardville, Scitico and Burnside in Connecticut take a very conspicuous stand.

Starting with a small local mill in the town of Enfield, Connecticut, in 1833, the energy and ability of its well-known proprietor, A. G. Hazard, and the company he organized some ten years later, extended the sales of their product to every part of the world, and established a reputation for their manufacture second to none.

The Hazard Powder Company's main works are situated upon the Scantic River at "Hazardville" in the town of Enfield, Connecticut. They also have mills at "Scitico" about three miles, and at "Burnside" about fourteen miles distant in the same State. Together, these cover an area of about two and one quarter miles long by about one-half mile wide.

The motive power at Hazardville is furnished by three dams, six canals and three large artificial reservoir ponds or lakes. There are five steam engines two of which are of one hundred horse power, the others somewhat smaller, made by the Novelty Works, N. Y., and Woodruff Iron Works Hartford, Conn.; also twenty-three turbine wheels and seven tub wheels.

These Mills consist in part of twenty-two pairs of rolling mills with iron wheels six to seven feet in diameter, and weighing about fifteen tons per pair; five different granulating houses; six hydraulic presses of four hundred to five hundred tons working power each; three screw presses; some forty pulverizing, mixing, dusting, drying, glazing, sorting and packing houses; five refineries and leach houses; seven cooper shops and keg houses; iron and wood machine shops; fourteen sheds for powder wood, fire wood, hard coal, lumber and framing; twenty-four storehouses for charcoal, brimstone, saltpetre, nitrate soda, &c.; four charcoal burning houses; besides "proof houses" "watch houses" magazines, charge houses, foundry, blacksmith shop, stables, barns, nineteen dwelling houses and other minor buildings,—in all over two hundred buildings.

Alongside of these works and as the result of their establishment, has grown up the village of "Hazardville" now numbering a population of about eight hundred souls, having several handsome churches, an institute for literary purposes, a large district school, and the usual quota of stores and factories. It is accessible by the New York, New Haven and Hartford Railroad, and by the Connecticut River, both of which pass close to the West of it, while the Connecticut Central Railroad connecting with Hartford and Springfield, runs through the village, thus bringing it into full and direct communication with the main railways and water lines.

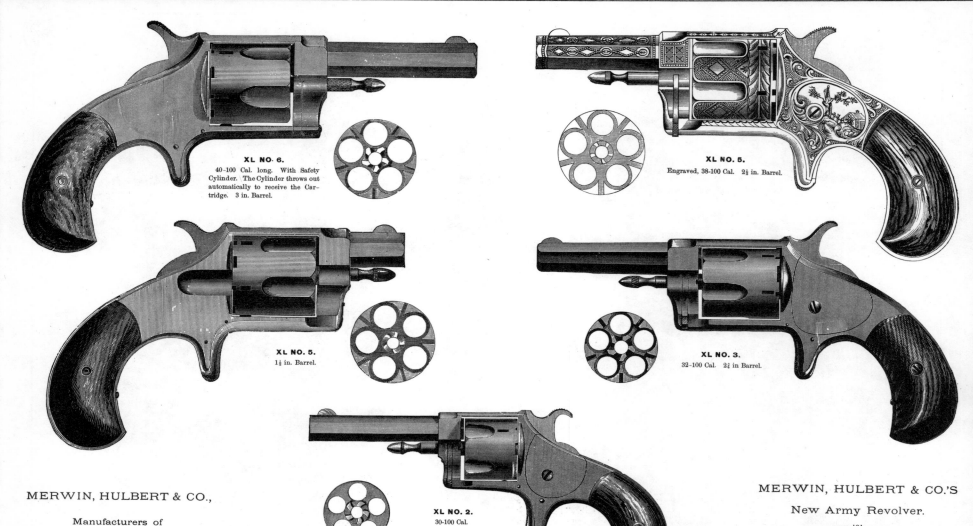

XL NO. 6.
40-100 Cal. long. With Safety Cylinder. The Cylinder throws out automatically to receive the Cartridge. 3 in. Barrel.

XL NO. 5.
Engraved, 38-100 Cal. 2¼ in. Barrel.

XL NO. 5.
1½ in. Barrel.

XL NO. 3.
32-100 Cal. 2¾ in Barrel.

XL NO. 2.
30-100 Cal.

MERWIN, HULBERT & CO.,

Manufacturers of

XL, and Blue Jacket Revolvers.

——:o:——

The firm above named manufacture XL Nos. 1, 2, 3, 4, 5, 6 and 7, XL Navy and Police Revolvers, XL Derringers, XL Vest Pocket Pistol, Expert, Single Shot Pistol, Pointer Single Shot Pistol, Bonnie Blue Single Shot, and other Pistols; Phœnix Breech Loading Rifles, Phœnix Single Breech Loading Shot Guns. The Revolvers are all made at one factory and under the same inspection. They are made in calibres, 22, 30, 32, 38 and 41, and in 1½, 2, 2¼, 3 and 4 inch barrels, and are of superior quality and low in price. All the XL Revolvers have a safety rest for the hammer in the solid part of the cylinder.

Attached to XL 2, 3 and 5 Revolver is a Patent Safety Lock, that the owner can lock or unlock in a second of time, but so secretive is its action that one not knowing it would find great difficulty in releasing the hammer from the safety notch. These Revolvers, when locked, can be laid away with confidence that no injury can arise from any handling or carelessness, and when placed in the pocket no premature explosion can take place.

The XL Navy Revolver, 6 Shot, 6 inch Barrel, (a cut of which is presented below) shoots the 38-calibre rifle ball, long or short cartridges. Is adapted for the Holster, and especially desirable for Police, Mounted Men and Prison Guards.

It is provided with a Safety Rest for the hammer, making it entirely safe to carry when loaded, has a perfect shell extractor, and is loaded without removing the cylinder.

MERWIN, HULBERT & CO.'S

New Army Revolver.

——:o:——

This weapon ejects the shell simultaneously. It is very simple but strong in construction, having Wrought Iron Frame and Barrel and best Steel Working Parts, and will commend itself for the following peculiarities.

When closed no part of the Cartridges are exposed.

After firing, when drawn forward for the purpose of withdrawing the shells the movement cleans the centre stem and cylinder. At an actual test by firing 200 rounds, the last shells were ejected as easily, and the parts worked as smoothly, as on the first round.

It can be taken apart, without screw driver, by simply pressing the barrel spring and withdrawing the centre-stem, from the Barrel, leaving the arm in three parts, viz: Frame, Barrel, Cylinder.

It has no Spiral Springs, the ejector is of solid iron, worked out of the recoil shield, and is absolute in its work.

The Barrel has a nose cap fitted to go on the cylinder, shutting off all escape of gas into the lower part of the Barrel.

The Centre Stem will bear a strain of 5,000 pounds.

The cylinder is adapted to use a cartridge having five grains more powder than any now in use for an Army Revolver.

MERWIN, HULBERT & CO.'S
NEW ARMY REVOLVER,
6 Shots, 44-100 Cal, Centre Fire. Half Size, Drawn at an Angle of 60 Degrees, Showing the turning aside for the purpose of drawing the shells. (Ready for delivery Jan. 1877.)

THE EVANS MAGAZINE RIFLE. CARRYING THIRTY-FOUR ROUNDS. CENTRE FIRE CARTRIDGES. 44-100 Cal.
MERWIN, HULBERT & CO., SOLE AGENTS.

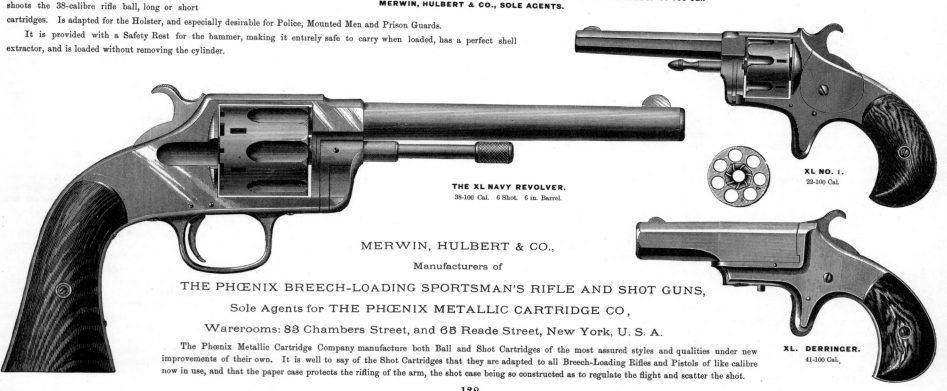

THE XL NAVY REVOLVER.
38-100 Cal. 6 Shot. 6 in. Barrel.

XL NO. 1.
22-100 Cal.

XL. DERRINGER.
41-100 Cal.

MERWIN, HULBERT & CO.,

Manufacturers of

THE PHŒNIX BREECH-LOADING SPORTSMAN'S RIFLE AND SHOT GUNS,

Sole Agents for THE PHŒNIX METALLIC CARTRIDGE CO,

Warerooms: 83 Chambers Street, and 65 Reade Street, New York, U. S. A.

The Phœnix Metallic Cartridge Company manufacture both Ball and Shot Cartridges of the most assured styles and qualities under new improvements of their own. It is well to say of the Shot Cartridges that they are adapted to all Breech-Loading Rifles and Pistols of like calibre now in use, and that the paper case protects the rifling of the arm, the shot case being so constructed as to regulate the flight and scatter the shot.

WM. E. CLARKE,

REGISTERED PHARMACIST,

And Proprietor of

"HUNT'S REMEDY,"

Laboratory, 319 South Main Street,

PROVIDENCE, R. I.

——:o:——

To be perfectly healthy, every part of the human body must possess two essential conditions: free circulation and perfect absorption. If the former be imperfect, congestion of the parts will, and death may, ensue; if the latter, the blood becomes charged with a poisonous material intended for discharge by one or the other of the excretory organs. The principal excretory organs are the lungs, skin, liver, and the kidneys, the last named being as important as either of the others and subject to as many diseases, though these facts are not generally known outside the medical profession. The masses of our people are ever guarding against a possible diseased condition of the other organs named; they carefully avoid drafts, wet feet, and whatever else may, or they fancy may, result in "catching cold," lest diseased lungs should follow. They are at infinite pains to bathe and rub the skin, that through its numberless pores Nature may expel the effete matters for which they are the proper passages. If there is any derangement of the bowels, or headache, or any unusual feeling for which they can ascribe no cause, straightway the liver is supposed to be out of order, and medicine is taken to correct the evil. But if there comes a pain or a dragging sensation in the back just over the hips, it is attributed to some heavy lift or sudden wrench that occurred days, weeks, months, or even years previously; or, if there is an unnatural retention, or a frequent desire to void urine, it is seldom even noticed until it has become painful, and then is ascribed to drinking too much or too little water and not to a diseased condition of any special portion of the system. Diseases of the kidneys are as susceptible of cure as any other functional disorders, if treated in good time; yet Bright's Disease, Diabetes, and Dropsy are generally looked upon as exceedingly dangerous, if not absolutely incurable diseases, for the simple reason that before they assert themselves with sufficient force to awaken attention they have generally been quietly running their course for a long time—frequently for months, sometimes for years—and have become so firmly seated as not to be easily dislodged.

It is not our intention at this time to write a treatise on medicine, but being aware of the immense number of persons suffering from fully developed diseases of the Kidneys, Bladder, and Urinary Organs, and being fully convinced that a still greater multitude have contracted (without being aware of the fact) such diseases in their first stages, we deem it a duty to warn them of their danger, that they may see the necessity of taking immediate measures to arrest the disease and be restored to a state of perfect health, and at the same time to bring to their notice a medical preparation of inestimable value to them, known as "Hunt's Remedy."

This remedy was originally prescribed by an eminent physician for a case of Dropsy in Mrs. Hunt's family. John Hunt, aged about forty-five, of a stout and plethoric habit, was seized with a sudden attack of general dropsy, which in a few days threatened his life; the ordinary remedies had all proved inefficacious, and under their use the patient was fast falling into an alarming state. The dropsy was general and extensive, legs swelled to an enormous size, almost total suppression of the urine, loss of breath, and the water increasing rapidly. He was entirely unable to lie down in bed, and was forced to remain night and day in a sitting posture. This state of things continued until, by the advice of the physician alluded to, the present remedy was tried. In consequence of its peculiar nature it was necessary to prepare it with great care, and in order to insure this it was intrusted to the family of Mr. Hunt to procure and compound it.

The remedy was administered, and almost from the moment of its reception a decided improvement became manifest. The kidneys were immediately affected and roused to action; in place of almost complete retention of water, urine was passing by quarts, the swelling of the legs rapidly subsided, the lungs were freed and resumed their healthy and agreeable action; the flesh of the limbs resumed its elasticity, no "caking" remaining, and he was rapidly convalescing, when, unfortunately, he gave up the remedy for a short time.

It was unfortunate, for the curative process was arrested, the kidneys flagged in their action, again becoming torpid, the water increased with frightful rapidity, and he soon again found himself in a very alarming state. The Remedy was again had recourse to, and by its persevering use, disease was a second time subdued. But this was a most aggravated and severe case, and it took all the virtues of the Remedy, combined with care and time, to eradicate the effects of the disease. But through a persevering use of it a permanent cure was effected, and he resumed his active out-of-door occupation within a short time—a well man.

THIS TEAM HAS BEEN ON THE ROAD ADVERTISING.

This is the manner in which the Remedy was brought into notice, and since then, for a period of twenty-five years, the medicine has been prepared after the same approved formula by Mrs. Hunt, and used by our first physicians in their private practice for Dropsy and other affections of the kidneys. It has been widely and favorably known and extensively used since that time, by all classes, both with and without the advice of physicians, and has been the means of saving from a lingering and frightful disease and untimely death, many of our most estimable and well-known citizens.

Mr. Wm. E. Clarke, Pharmacist, the proprietor of the celebrated remedy for all diseases of the kidneys and kindred complaints, known as "Hunt's Remedy," has been compelled by the large and constantly increasing demand for that valuable and standard medicine to establish a new and enlarged laboratory for its manufacture. For that purpose he has taken a portion of "Carrington Block," No. 319 South Main Street, Providence, Rhode Island, which he has just completely fitted up with every facility for his increasing business.

The new laboratory comprises the whole building of five stories. The fifth, or upper floor, where all the supplies and ingredients are kept, and the Remedy compounded, is the laboratory proper. Around three sides of this room are ranged thirty-four casks, in which it is stored as it is compounded, and from which it is drawn, alternately, through a filter, into a large tank on the floor below. From this tank the perfected medicine flows through hose to a "Patent Automatic Bottle-Filler" standing on one end of a long table, which fills six bottles at once, each with exactly the same quantity and without any possible waste. From this machine the bottles, as filled, are passed down the table to be corked, one man filling as fast as three can cork them up. They are then passed along to the lower end of the table, where they are taken by girls, a six cent revenue stamp placed on each bottle, and each labelled and wrapped in two wrappers. Next the filled and labelled bottles are sent by a railway to another room, on the same floor, where they are packed in neatly labelled paper boxes, six in each, and each box strongly and securely tied up.

From this room these filled paper boxes are sent by an elevator to the floor below, where they are packed in sawdust, in wooden cases holding one, two, or three dozen each, and thence sent to the lower floor to be taken away from the rear entrance of the laboratory for shipment.

A large supply of empty bottles with the name "Wm. E. Clarke," proprietor, blown in the glass in each one, are stored on the lower floor, where they are thoroughly washed in Pawtuxet water (which is introduced in every story), before using, with a patent and effective washing machine, and are then sent to the laboratory by the elevator, as they may be required.

The office of the new establishment is the front room on the first floor from the street, and is tastefully and conveniently fitted up for the business and accommodation of patrons and visitors. The room in rear of the office is used as a store-room of the Remedy when ready for the market.

The whole of Mr. Clarke's new laboratory is very conveniently arranged for the manufacture and sale of the Remedy, systematically and economically, under the personal direction and supervision of the proprietor, as the business is now so large as to require his whole time and attention.

Hunt's Remedy has gained for itself a reputation second to that of no popular compound that we know of. It is not a "cure-all;" it is not recommended as a never failing specific for "all the ills that flesh is heir to." It is simply a scientifically prepared compound for the cure of diseases of certain portions of the human system, to wit: the kidneys, the bladder, and the other urinary organs. Its wide fame rests solely on its merits as a medicine. By many who should be competent judges it is considered the only known Remedy for Bright's Disease. It has cured every case of Dropsy in which it has been given; Irritation of the Neck of the Bladder and Inflammation of the Kidneys, Ulceration of the Kidneys and Bladder, Diabetes, Difficulty of holding the Urine, in Stricture, in Seminal Weakness, Retention of Urine, Diseases of the Prostate Gland, Stone in the Bladder, Gravel, Brick Dust Deposit and Mucous or Milky Discharges, and for Enfeebled and Delicate Constitutions of both sexes, attended with the following symptoms: Loss of Power, Loss of Memory, Difficulty of Breathing, Weak Nerves, Wakefulness, Painful and Dragging Sensation in the Back or Lions, Flushing of the Body, Eruptions on the Face, Pallid Countenance, Lassitude of the System, etc. Those afflicted should lose no time in testing its efficiency.

The cut in the centre of this article represents a team and wagon which has been on the road advertising Hunt's Remedy since June, 1875, and which up to December 31st, had traveled over 5,000 miles, and distributed over 100,000 thirty-six page pamphlets describing the Remedy.

The original cost of the team and equipment complete was $2,500. The body of the wagon is painted lake color, gold letters, shaded black. The dome is silver plated, running gear black, striped with red. The horses are dark bay.

ARCHITECTURAL IRON WORKS.

This well known Corporation has been in existence about twenty years, and is the successor of the firm of Daniel D. Badger & Co., who had been for a period of years engaged in the Iron business, and had made a specialty of Iron Work for buildings. Mr. Badger, the President of this Company, is regarded as the pioneer of Iron Architecture in America. This Company may therefore claim to be the oldest establishment of its kind in our country, and to have had the largest experience.

The works of the Company are situated in the City of New York on 14th Street near the East River, occupying about fifty lots of 100 by 25 feet each covered with their buildings. The area of these lots and the floors of the buildings exceed four acres. The shops are fitted with all kinds of machinery required for the work to be done, and have every improvement and facility for making Iron Work for all kinds of buildings, as well as for many other purposes.

The various departments are conducted by skilled and experienced workmen, and the Company is thus enabled to perform the several branches of work for all iron structures from the inception, designing, drafting, patterning, casting, fitting and setting, to the final completion for occupancy.

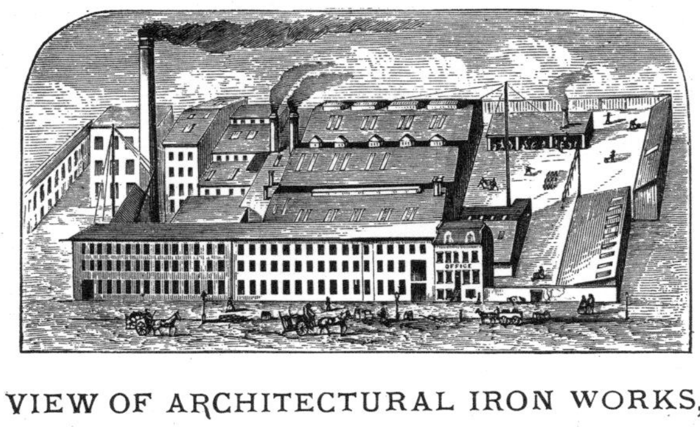

VIEW OF ARCHITECTURAL IRON WORKS,
New York.

It has the capacity to employ more than a thousand men, and to produce thousands of tons of iron work annually. It will be seen that, for the successful conduct of a business of this magnitude, a large capital, extended facilities and a large experience are needed, and that therefore this establishment possesses many advantages which commend it to the notice of all owners, capitalists and corporations, designing to erect iron buildings of any description.

Iron architecture encountered at the time of its introduction the bitterest opposition from builders, insurance companies, fire departments and the public generally; but it has been persisted in by its originators and tested by use, until at length all objections to it have been removed, and it is now conceded that iron is entitled to be regarded as one of the most useful and enduring of known building materials.

A brief enumeration of the advantages of the use of iron will confirm this assertion.

It possesses the greatest possible strength in proportion to its weight and bulk. Hence, it allows of grace and lightness of construction, the greatest possible amount of beautiful ornamentation; it will be obvious that the cost of elaborate designs in stone or any other durable material executed by the chisel, will exceed that of castings of iron, and hence that iron is cheaper for work of an ornamental character. It may be added that iron admits of more delicate tracery and sharper outlines than any other material.

Iron is of course incombustible, and, though it may be affected by intense heat, it is far more nearly fire proof than stone, granite, marble and other building materials.

One of the great advantages arising from the use of iron is that it admits of unusual rapidity of construction and erection.

The sanitary advantages of the use of iron deserve also to be considered. Occupying but small space in piers and columns, it freely admits the air and light which are both essential to health.

As a final argument in favor of its use, it may be stated that iron always has a value, and the old material finds an immediate sale. When iron work becomes defaced, it can be easily restored to its pristine appearance by a fresh coat of paint.

Iron has of late years been used to advantage and with general approval for many purposes, among which may be enumerated the following: store fronts, hotels, depots, grain warehouses, public buildings, roofs, domes, verandas, balustrades, stairways, columns, capitols, arches, window lintels and sills, sashes, doors, brackets, guards, lamp posts, railings, crestings, bank counters, rolling shutters, venetian blinds, patent lights, sidewalks, bridges, light houses, churches, ferry houses, arsenals, etc., etc.

This company has during the last twenty years erected a great number of iron buildings in all the principal cities and towns throughout our country, of a great variety of styles, designed by the best architects.

Among these may be mentioned the Grand Central Depot, an illustration of which will be seen on this page, Manhattan Market, 800 feet long, 200 feet wide, 100 feet high; Hudson River Railroad Depot, St. John's Park; Kemp Building, Singer's Sewing Machine Company Building, Gilsey House, Seamen's Bank for Savings, Atlantic Savings Bank, etc., in the City of New York, Post Office and Sub-Treasury, Boston Post Building, Stores for Hunnewell estate, Messrs. Fitch, Snow, White, Rich, Gray, Hawley, Folsom & Martin and others in Boston. Congressional Library, Conservatory, etc., in Washington. Buildings in Chicago, Philadelphia, Troy, Rochester, Springfield, New Haven, New Orleans, and indeed in almost every section of our country, and even in distant lands.

Their facilities for furnishing the iron work for building purposes, of a superior quality and finish, are unsurpassed in this country, as their long experience in architect work has been used to the very best advantage, in bringing forward improvements of great importance and architectural beauty. For particulars address the company as above.

GRAND CENTRAL DEPOT, NEW YORK.
IRON WORK CONSTRUCTED BY ARCHITECTURAL IRON WORKS.

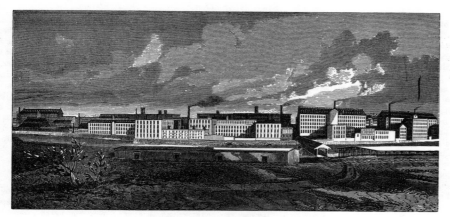

AMOSKEAG MANUF'C CO.'S MILLS.
View from West Side of the River.

AMOSKEAC MANUF'C CO.
Counting House and Buildings on Upper Canal.

AMOSKEAG MANUFACTURING CO.,

Manchester, N. H.

MANUFACTURERS OF

Tickings, Denims, Drillings, Sheetings, Flannels, Ginghams, Fancy Shirtings, Bags, etc.

ALSO, MANUFACTURERS OF

Steam Fire Engines, Hose Carriages, Machinery, Tools, Turbine Wheels, Mill Work, and Castings of Every Description.

——:o:——

WM. AMORY, TREASURER,   E. A. STRAW, AGENT,
60 State Street, Boston, Mass.   Manchester, N. H.

GARDNER, BREWER & CO., SELLING AGENTS,

Federal Street, Boston.   62 Leonard Street, New York.

——:o:——

The Amoskeag Manufacturing Company, Manchester, N. H., is one of the earliest, most extensive, and best known establishments for the manufacture of Cotton Goods in the United States. The first Cotton Mills at Amoskeag Falls, on the Merrimac River, near the site of the present city of Manchester, were built in 1809, and were purchased in 1825, by a private company, two members of which were members of the firm from which has descended the present firm of Gardner, Brewer & Co., now the selling agents of the Amoskeag Company.

In 1831, the Amoskeag Manufacturing Company was incorporated by the legislature of New Hampshire, with a capital of one million dollars, which has at various times been increased, its present capital being three millions. one of the first operations of this Company was the purchase of all the Water Power of the Merrimac River from Manchester to Concord; a power which at Manchester alone is estimated at over 10,000 horse power.

On the organization of the Company in 1831, it had in operation three small wooden Mills, containing about 12,000 spindles, and situated at the foot of Amoskeag Falls, about a mile to the North of the present site of its works, and on the opposite side of the river; these Mills were long since destroyed by fire. During the intervening period of nearly half a century, the Company have built and put in operation seven new Mills, containing an aggregate of 135,000 Spindles and 4,000 Looms; and have built two Machine shops and a Foundry, making, as required, nearly all the Machinery in use in the Mills, and manufacturing also Locomotives, Heavy Tools, etc., which have since 1859 been superseded in great part by the building of Steam Fire Engines.

During this long and busy period, and through all the extensions and changes of the works, the standard goods manufactured by the Company have remained almost without change, except such as might be due to improved processes and machinery; and they offer to-day Tickings and other goods exactly as made in 1831; goods which have stood the test of nearly fifty years competition and experience, and stand to-day confessedly at the head of the market, and not excelled by any other goods of the same class wherever made. Within the last six years the Mills of the Company have been thoroughly renovated, and in many cases entirely re-built; and all old or worn machinery has been replaced by machines of new and improved patterns. In this work and in the erection of the Gingham Mills about two millions of dollars have been expended and everything connected with the manufacture of cloth is now practically new. The annual production of the Company's Mills is now about twelve millions of pounds or thirty-six millions of yards, and their yearly consumption of Cotton is thirty thousand bales.

Among the earliest operations of the Company, after its incorporation in 1831, was the purchase of nearly two thousand five hundred acres of land on both sides of the river, on which they laid out a town with public squares, and sites for churches, schools, etc. The first sales of lots were made in 1838, and by these and subsequent sales nearly all the land comprising the site of the present city of Manchester—a city of thirty thousand inhabitants—was brought into the market all the public squares, and nearly all the sites of churches, schools, etc., having been donated by the Company to the City, or to religious societies.

Meanwhile, during the years from 1836 to 1840, a stone dam was built across the Merrimack; the two canals, having an aggregate length of nearly two and one-half miles, were finished, and the Company commenced the building of Mills and Boarding Houses on the sites thus made available. All or nearly all the Mills, Mill-Boarding House Blocks, and other such buildings in the city have been built by them, either for themselves, or under contracts with other corporations.

The first Mills built on the east side of the river were sold to the Stark Mills Company in 1838 and 1839. The Company then finished, in 1841, two mills just below these for their own use. Afterwards, in 1845, were built by contract, the Manchester Mill and Printery, and in this way

FIRST AND SECOND-CLASS DOUBLE PLUNGER ENGINE, CRANE-NECK FRAME.

the Company have, from time to time, erected nearly all the Mills (running about 350,000 Spindles), with their Boarding and Store Houses, and a large portion of the Machine Shops, Work Shops, etc., which are now in Manchester.

One of the late operations of the Company in this direction was the building of a stone dam across the river, by which they obtain a fall of fifty-five feet, and are also enabled, by means of the pond formed above the dam, so to economize the water as to make the minimum flow of the river equal to two thousand cubic feet per second of working time.

The Machine Shops of the Amoskeag Company are two in number, and were built, one in 1842, and the second in 1848, to accomodate an increasing business. The Foundry adjoining was built in 1842 and re-built in 1848. The original design of these shops was to furnish the machinery required for the Mills then in course of construction by the Company, but the business was gradually enlarged and there were also made Locomotive and Stationary Engines, Boilers, Heavy Tools, Turbine Wheels, etc. During the late war the shops made some forty thousand stand of arms for the United States and also some turret work for the Monitors.

These Shops now employ about four hundred and fifty men who have

been in great part occupied during the past few years in building and repairing Machinery for the Mills; a large force however have been constantly employed in the manufacture of the Amoskeag Steam Fire Engines and Hose Carriages. Of the former, over five hundred have been built up to the present time, and sent to all parts of the United State as well as abroad.

Of the principal cities using these Engines, New York City has forty-nine, Boston twenty, Brooklyn nineteen, New Orleans eighteen, Pittsburgh fourteen, San Francisco thirteen, and Philadelphia twelve.

The Company have recently perfected a self-propelling Steam Fire Engine, several of which are in use in Boston, New York and Detroit, and which have thus far given perfect satisfaction.

The Company guarantee every machine from their works to be as nearly perfect as can be secured by the utmost care in the selection of materials and in the workmanship. Circulars giving full particulars will be sent on application to the Agent at the works in Manchester.

The Amoskeag Company is most extensively engaged in the manufacture of Cotton Goods of almost every description, and of these they have steadily increased the quantity, variety and quality of their products since the formation of the Company in 1831.

The first Mills of the Company on the east side of the Merrimack River on the present site of their works were built in 1841, and the original Mills on the west side of the stream, at the foot of the Falls, were destroyed by fire a few years later. The present mill yards of the Company cover an aggregate of about thirty acres, and contain seven large Mills with the necessary store houses and other smaller buildings used in connection with them.

These Mills are now running one hundred and thirty-five thousand Spindles and four thousand Looms and produce about seven hundred thousand yards of Goods per week, including all varieties of Tickings, Denims, Drilling, Cotton Flannels, Fancy Shirting, Stripes, Sheeting and Ginghams. Constant employment is furnished to thirty-four hundred operatives.

The Tickings of the Amoskeag Company (A C A) have long had a very high reputation: The manufacture of these Tickings exactly as now made, was commenced by the Company in 1832, and has been continued in constantly increasing quantities up to the present date; they are very generally considered to be the best Tickings in the market, and notwithstanding the numerous imitations of other manufacturers, and the most bare-faced infringements of the trade-mark, the demand for them has more than kept pace with the Company's ability to supply them.

The Amoskeag Company commenced the manufacture of Ginghams in 1868 with 20 looms, and from their first introduction the demand for these goods has so steadily and rapidly increased that the Company have now 1700 Gingham looms in operation : 800 looms of this number, with all the necessary adjuncts and preparatory machinery, have been added to the works during the year 1875, and the Company are now prepared to supply all possible orders promptly, their production of these goods being not less than 12,000,000 yards per annum. As with the other goods so with the Ginghams: The standard of quality has been and will be strictly maintained.

The Company has also recently given particular attention to the manufacture of Fancy Shirting Stripes, and Cotton Flannels; of these latter they now make no less than eleven varieties. The Amoskeag Denims and Drillings have for years been standard goods in all the markets of the United States; of the former the Company now makes about four and one half millions of yards yearly, of the latter about two millions of yards.

In conclusion, the Amoskeag Company, with a reputation of nearly fifty years standing, and having recently added to their works the latest and most improved machinery, and greatly increased their facilities for manufacturing in all the departments of their mills, assure all consumers that they may confidently rely on all goods bearing the mark "Amoskeag" as being, as nearly as possible, perfect of their kind.

AMOSKEAG MANUF'C CO.'S MILLS.
Upper Yard.

AMOSKEAC MANUF'C CO.'
Machine Shops and Lower Mill Yard.

BUTTON ENGINE WORKS,

L. Button & Son, Proprietors, Waterford, N. Y.

Established 1834.

Really effective Fire Engines are of comparatively recent introduction. True the Romans, during the later days of the Empire, paid some attention to the devising of means to raise water to a considerable height, with the view of extinguishing fires, but their appliances reached no greater perfection than a kind of hose, made from the entrails of an ox, one end of which was attached to a bag filled with water. By pressing upon the bag, the water could be forced through the tube to a height of twenty feet, but it was not deemed safe to attempt to raise it a greater distance lest the hose should burst.

The first machines intended to put out fires, of which we have any reliable notice were in use in Augsburg, Germany, in 1518. They were called "instruments for fires" and "water syringes useful at fires." Casper Schott describes one of these which he saw in Nüremberg, in 1657, and says that forty years previous he had seen one in Konigshofen. He describes the one in Nüremberg as having a water-box eight feet long, four feet high and two feet wide. The pump was worked by twenty-eight men and threw a stream of water, one inch in diameter, a distance of eighty feet.

Comparing this rude machine with the powerful Steam Fire Engines of the present day, one must marvel at the dullness of inventive genius of the olden time, as well as be astonished at the rapid advancement made in this class of machinery within a few years.

To Mr. L. Button, the senior partner of the firm of L. Button & Son, we are largely indebted for the marked improvements recently made in Fire Apparatus. He commenced the manufacture of Hand Fire Engines in 1834, as partner in the firm of Wm. Platt & Co. In 1841, Mr. Platt relinquished his interest in the business and from

that time Mr. Button's name has stood at the head of the firm. In 1846 Mr. Button drew the plans for a pump for Hand Engines. Water has been fairly thrown by them 220 feet high and 240 feet horizontally.

There have been made and sold at the Button Engine Works over 2,000 Hand and Steam Fire Engines, Hose Carriages and Hook and Ladder Trucks. The long experience and superior facilities of this firm enable them to supply the wants of Fire Departments with thoroughly efficient apparatus on the best of terms. The merit of their engines is amply proven by the fact that during the past twenty-five years more than three-fourths of all the prizes awarded at Firemen's Tournaments have been taken by engines of their manufacture.

Since 1863 Messrs. L. Button & Son have paid special attention to the manufacture of Steam Fire Engines, and with marked success. They are made with large wheels, and an arched frame, with the weight of the boiler on the rear and the entire works on the forward axle, so that the forward wheels can turn quite around, thereby enabling the operator to turn the engine around in its length. The boiler is an upright tubular, with submerged combustion chamber.

The flues are of copper, which has these advantages over iron: It will not corrode, is a better conductor of heat, and, when allowed to expand freely, will bear a higher degree of heat without injury. The pumps are made of the best bronze metal, mixed and cast in their own establishment and under the direct supervision of the firm. Piston pumps are used and they are models of perfect construction. The Button Engines will draw and force water through 200 feet of hose with five pounds of steam, and do good fire service with thirty pounds, while the boiler presents sufficient fire surface to generate as much steam as can be used at any pressure.

Those to whom the selection and purchase of Steam Fire Engines is intrusted often find it impossible to determine from the evidence furnished by different manufacturers, which kind it is best to buy, and competitive trials are frequently resorted to as a test of the merits of each. Messrs. L. Button are always willing to furnish opportunities for comparison with other engines, but do not advocate such trials.

The legitimate use of a Steam Fire Engine is to put out fires, and the engine best adapted to that purpose is the best engine, and the true way of arriving at the merits of such an engine is to thoroughly test it in the manner in which it will be used at fires. Such a test can be more thoroughly made by examining each Engine separately, than by placing them side by side, and merely noting the size of the stream and the distance attained by each competitor.

There are many things to be taken into consideration in determining the relative merits of Steam Fire Engines. For instance, the pressure of steam required to produce a given result, strength, compactness of form, the facility with which they can be moved, the liability to wear, the kind and qualities of material used in their construction, etc.

Messrs. L. Button & Son, manufacture Steam Fire Engines of different weights and powers, but do not name them as first, second and third class machines as other makers do. All their Steam Fire Engines are first-class, but the largest and heaviest are of course most powerful.

Improved Cloth Washer.

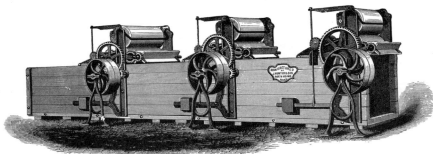

Wool Scouring and Washing Machine.

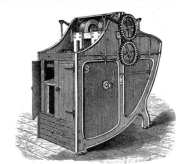

Improved Rotary Fulling Mill.

JAMES HUNTER & SON,

Manufacturers of Wool Scouring and Washing Machines, Fulling Mills & Cloth Washers.

North Adams, Mass.

Few manufacturers of woolen goods, who have not given the subject special attention, are aware how much wool is lost in the old method of washing. Observations at the rinse-box will readily convince the prudent that a less wasteful method should be adopted. Messrs. James Hunter & Son are now manufacturing a Wool Scour-

ing and Washing Machine which does its work in a superior manner and not one particle of the wool is lost. Manufacturers who have tested it thoroughly, estimate that by its use they save from one to two per cent. of wool.

In this machine the wool is compressed between iron rollers, and is completely freed from lumps of manure and other filth, thereby saving the wool which under the old method must be cut off and thrown away.

Another important advantage is that it throws the wool off straight, free and open, and in a well prepared state for working or dyeing. The entire satisfaction expressed by all who have used this machine, and the rapidity with which it is being adopted, warrants

us in asserting that it is to the interest of every woolen manufacturer to examine its merits.

Hunter's New Improved Cloth Washer is vastly superior to the old washer. The frame is of iron; the casings hard pine. The rollers are iron covered with wood so that the end of the wood is presented to the cloth. The bottom rollers have iron or bronze flanges, as desired. The top rollers are weighted down by eliptic springs and geared together.

Hunter's Patent Improved French Rotary Fulling Mill manufactured by the same enterprising firm, is very popular with manufacturers of woolen goods. The frame is of iron, the casings of hard pine. The rollers are cast iron, clothed in oak.

The C. W. ROBERTS

PIPE CUTTING AND THREADING MACHINE AND VICE.

Manufactured and For Sale by

N. W. FROST & CO., COHOES, NEW YORK.

This ingenious little machine is pre-eminently adapted for use by steam and gas fitters and gas companies; in machine shops or in mills, or other large establishments doing their own fitting, wherever introduced, it is considered indispensable. To practical men it commends itself on account of its simplicity, portability, ease of management, adaptability to all kinds of work and its cheapness.

The construction of this machine is very simple and easily understood, and any man or boy of ordinary capacity can successfully operate it. It can be slipped apart in three pieces and carried with ease by a boy from floor to floor of a building where work is to be done, or carried from job to job in different parts of the city or town. One piece of the machine forms an excellent vise for screwing fittings off or off, or for doing any work for which a pipe fitter uses a vise. Its attendance require so small an outlay of physical strength that by its use one man can now do with ease the work that under the old

system required two, effecting thereby a great saving of time and consequently a like saving of money.

The simplicity of this machine is one of the many things that recommend it to the trade. It is simply a modification of the stocks and vise, with a movable gear attached, to give the power required to cut large pipes with ease.

In a word, this machine gives the stocks, with the cutting apparatus added, the only difference between this and the old stocks being that the stocks have handles, and this is made in the form of a gear, and instead of turning with the handles, you mesh the pinion with a cutting gear and turn the crank, which enables (as we have previously mentioned) one man to do as much work as two could turn off with the stocks. The tool used for cutting off is a square nosed lathe tool and it makes a clean, square cut, leaving no burr.

This machine has been submitted to the most severe tests, both as to its strength and its utility, and has always proven itself equal to the emergency.

Our limited space prevents us from giving a more detailed description of it, but as a matter of interest we feel called upon to note the extremely low price at which it is sold, viz: No. 1, Pipe Threading Machine and Vise, $55; Dies cutting from ¾ to 2 inches, $15. No. 2, Pipe Cutting and Threading Machine and Vise, $95; with full set of Nipple Collars; Dies cutting from ¾ to 2 inches, $15. No. 3, Pipe Cutting and Threading Machine and Vise, $225; with full set of Nipple Collars.

DROP CENTRE LANDAU.

LANDAULET.

LADIES' PHAETON.

BROUGHAM.

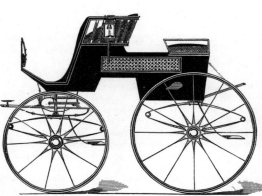

STANHOPE DOG CART.

WM. H. BRADLEY & CO.,
Manufacturers of
CARRIAGES AND ROAD WAGONS,
61 to 66 Chapel Street, New Haven, Ct.

One of the oldest establishments of the city of New Haven, Conn., and, perhaps, the oldest Carriage Factory in this country, is that of Wm. H. Bradley & Co., the business having been originally established by Mr. James Brewster, in 1810, and carried on by him alone for nearly twenty years. During this time large numbers of carriages were shipped to Boston, Charleston and New Orleans and a trade was begun with Cuba, Mexico, and the States of South America, which soon became a prominent part of the business. In the year 1827 Mr. Brewster opened a Repository in New York City, and employed Mr. John R. Lawrence as salesman, until the year 1829, when a partnership was formed under the firm name of Brewster & Lawrence. In 1830, Mr. Solomon Collis, who had been Mr. Brewster's bookkeeper, since the year 1821, was made a partner also, and, until the year 1839, the firm was Brewster & Collis, at New Haven, and Brewster & Lawrence, in New York. It was under these names that the great reputation for the beauty and quality of the work was first attained. On the first of February, 1837, Mr. Brewster retired from the firm.

The business was then conducted under the name of Lawrence & Collis in New York, and Collis & Lawrence in New Haven, until the year 1850, when, owing to ill-health, Mr. Collis sold his interest in New Haven to Mr. Wm. H. Bradley, and in New York to Mr. Lawrence. The latter, soon after connected with himself Mr. S. A. Durbrow, and his son, Mr. John Lawrence, under the firm of John R. Lawrence & Co., while at New Haven the firm was Lawrence & Bradley, until January, 1857, when Mr. William B. Pardee became a partner, under the name of Lawrence, Bradley & Pardee.

T CART.

At this time the business had so largely grown that more room was demanded and the factory was enlarged to its present size and beautiful proportions—220 feet on Chapel Street, by 280 feet on Hamilton Street, more than doubling its former manufacturing facilities.

After December 31, 1870, the business came under the control and sole ownership of Mr. Wm. H. Bradley, and so continued until July, 1872, when Mr Wilder H. Pray became associated in the business, forming the firm of Wm. H. Bradley & Co. During all these years the business has been continually increasing and they have manufactured and continue to manufacture four, six and eight Spring Landaus, Coaches, Clarences, Barouches, Victorias, four and six seat Park Phaetons, Square, Round and Octagon Front Coupes and Landaulets, Coupelets, Drags, Perithrons, Dog Carts and T Carts, four and six seat Rockaways, Chariotees, Broughams and all styles of light Carriages for Ladies', Gentlemen's and Children's Driving.

Messrs. Wm. H. Bradley & Co., have facilities for manufacturing which are seldom surpassed, in this or any other country. Their factory is fully equipped with such appliances as can aid in the rapid production of thoroughly good work, but they do not trust to lifeless machinery and thoughtless boys, the labor which only skilled workmen can properly perform. The utmost care is exercised in every department of manufacture, under the immediate supervision of members of the firm.

Particular attention is given to the execution of orders for foreign markets, and their export trade has become a prominent feature of their business. They have designed and are constantly manufacturing vehicles specially adapted to the climates and roads of other lands, and their goods are favorably known in all parts of the civilized world.

In addition to carriages and other vehicles, Messrs. Wm. H. Bradley & Co., keep constantly on hand a full assortment of Harness, Whips, Mats, Canopies, Umbrellas, and a general assortment of Carriage Furniture of the finest quality.

GLASS FRONT DROP CENTRE LANDAU.

ROAD WAGON.

OCTAGON FRONT COUPE.

GRAND VICTORIA.

ROAD WAGON, WITH TOP.

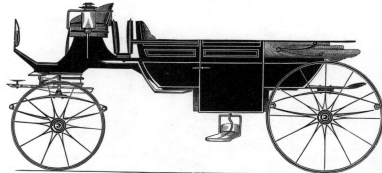

GLASS FRONT LANDAU, OPEN.

FIVE CLASS LANDAU, No. 57.

HEARSE, No. 47.

CLOSE QUARTER LANDAU, No. 3.

JAMES CUNNINGHAM & SON,

Manufacturers of

FINE CARRIAGES AND HEARSES,

No. 3 Canal Street, Rochester, New York

—:o:—

The senior partner of the present firm of James Cunningham & Son has been for many years actively engaged in the business of manufacturing Carriages, having been a member of the old firm of Kerr, Cunningham & Co. which was fully organized and commenced operations, May 1st, 1838.

This firm continued to manufacture some four years, when it was dissolved, Mr. Cunningham continuing the business which he successfully conducted alone until May 1st, 1865, when he admitted his son as a partner, since which time the house has been continuously known as James Cunningham & Son.

From a comparatively small beginning the business has grown to immense proportions, and the little shop of less then forty years ago has expanded year by year, until now the magnificent buildings shown in our illustration are none too large. If the buildings comprising their present works were stretched in a straight line their united length would measure about 1,000 feet; one-half the length being six stories in height, and 45 feet wide; the remaining half three stories in height and 66 feet wide; affording a floor area of nearly seven acres, and furnishing ample room for the constant employment of 700 men. All these structures are built in the most substantial manner. The walls are of brick and stone laid in cement and mortar, and are of unusual thickness, and in their erection neither pains nor expense were spared to render them strong enough to bear the immense weight resting upon them, durable enough to withstand the wear of Time and successfully battle against the destructive elements, including fire.

In these days of progress, labor saving machinery has become so important an element of production that when we say this or that establishment employs a given number of men we really convey but little information as to its capacity. Work that but a few years since was done entirely by hand labor, is now almost as entirely done by machinery. Men, of course, are required to watch and direct the machines, sometimes two or more to a single one—while sometimes a single man can oversee three or four of these silent workers—but the number of men employed, in

of the present century proves that labor saving machines, absolutely increases the demand for and the value of skilled labor. The machinery of this establishment, if run to its full capacity, would supply work for 1,000 men, and at that rate, the production of the establishment would be equal to the labor of 7,000 men if the work was all done by hand. We cannot name, much less describe all these machines within the space assigned to this article, suffice it to say that the equipment of the factory is complete.

With such facilities for manufacture, backed up by thirty-eight years of practical experience in the business, and a capital of nearly half a million dollars invested in buildings, machinery and stock, this firm are enabled to produce the best possible goods at the lowest prices, and to do this has been their constant aim.

The reputation of Messrs. James Cunningham & Son does not rest on the excellence of any single production, but on the general perfection of all their work, which embraces every style of carriage in use at the present time, and, if ordered, such as were used forty years ago or at any time since. We present on this page sketches of a few of their present productions but only a few, as the reader will readily infer from the number attached to each name. They have constantly in stock a large assortment of Family Carriages, Light Buggies and Phætons. Five Glass Landaus, of various styles and forms, Landaulets, in many designs, Landaus, close and open quarters, Barouches of different styles, Coupes and Coupe-Rockaways, four and six passenger, also all varieties of Light Buggies, in fact almost every description of Vehicle for family or pleasure riding may be found in their spacious warerooms.

Messrs. James Cunningham & Son are not only manufactures, but Designers, and they are thus enabled to give shape to the peculiar ideas of customers, and build any kind of Carriage their patrons may suggest. The most eccentric and the most fastidious can through them procure exactly the style desired.

The manufacture of Carriages for the pleasure and convenience of the living is the leading branch of their business, but not all of it. We can hardly say they minister to the comfort of the dead, or afford them aught of pleasure in providing chaste and fitting conveyances for the last dread ride to the grave, but it does seem to us that the least the living can do, is to provide a funeral car in keeping with the station the deceased held in life.

Few manufacturers have given any attention to Hearses but this firm have made their construction a special feature of their business, and their productions in that line are very models of fitness.

VIEW OF CARRIAGE REPOSITORY AND MANUFACTORY OF JAMES CUNNINGHAM & SON, ROCHESTER, NEW YORK.

proportion to the amount of work done, is infinitely less then it was; and for this reason in estimating the possible production of an establishment engaged in any manufacturing business it is essential that the machinery employed should enter into the calculation. Men really do little else than to supply and watch the machines that do the bulk of the work, and to assemble their products together into a finished whole.

The works of Messers. James Cunningham & Son are exceptionally well provided with labor saving machinery—much of it of their own invention devised to meet their own special wants, patented but not sold to other parties, being used exclusively in their own factory. Some of these machines will do the work of one hundred men. The immense saving in the cost of production where such devices are largely employed must be apparent to every thinking man nor does it work a harm to the skillful mechanics. From the decreased cost, springs an increased demand, and the experience

3-4 SIZE LANDAULET. No. 1.

GLASS FRONT LANDAU, No. 70.

BERLIN COACH, No 73.

COURELETTE, No. 75.

DROP FRONT BERLIN, No. 74.

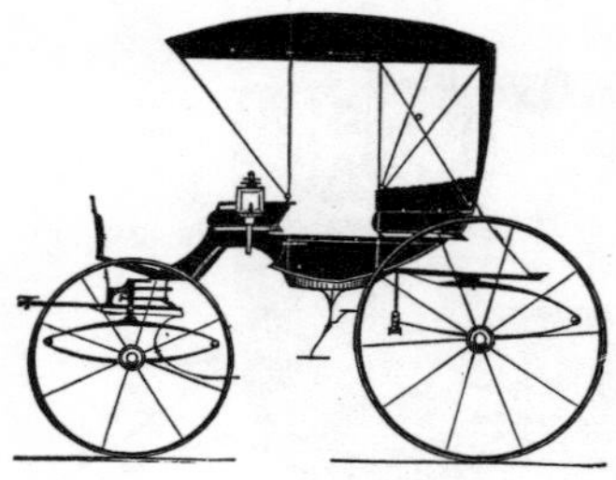

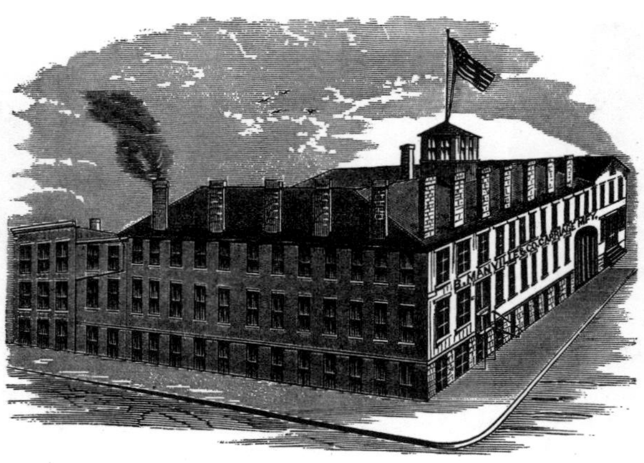

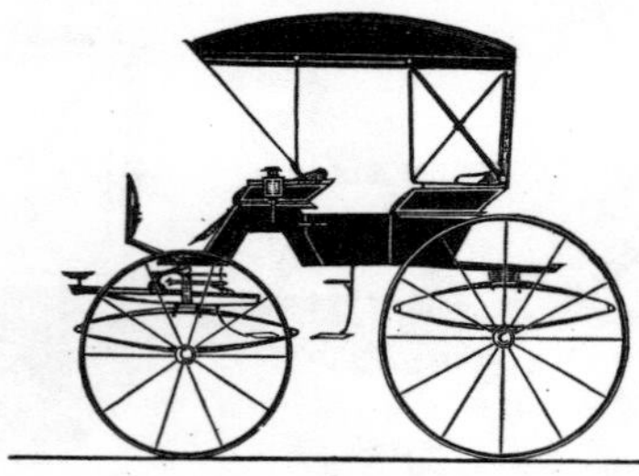

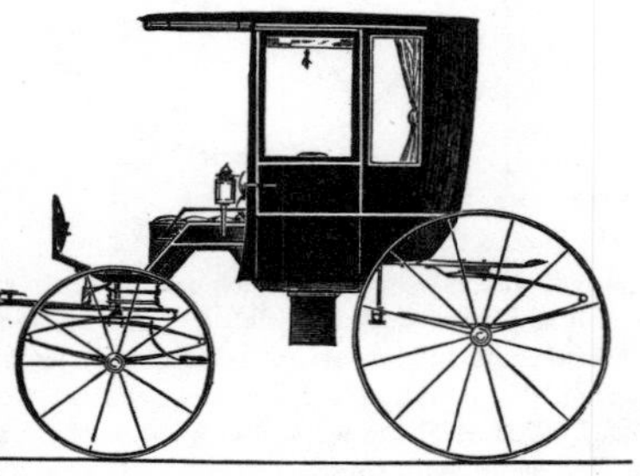

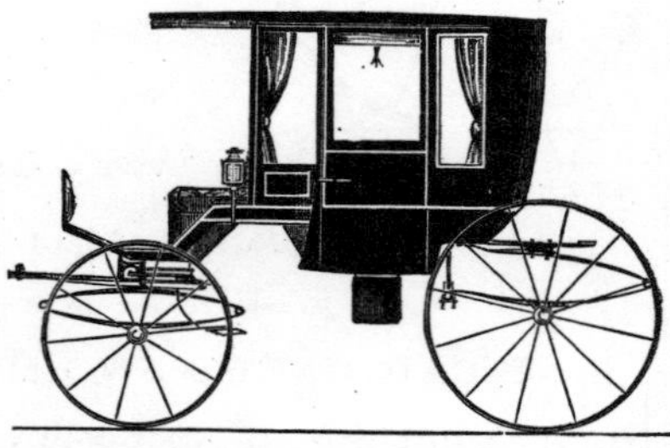

B. MANVILLE & CO.,

Manufacturers of

FINE FAMILY CARRIAGES,

20 to 28 Wooster St., New Haven, Conn.

——:o:——

In 1855, the above named well known firm began the manufacture of Four and Six Seat Carriages, specially adapted for family use, and of such style that the owner could drive and at the same time be with the family. Since then this class of vehicles has received their sole attention, Rockaways being their chief specialty, though they make numerous other styles. Their trade extends all over the United States, and as they have carefully studied the requirements of every section of the country, they are enabled to produce carriages which in adaptability to section, lightness, strength, beauty of design and comfortableness are not excelled. Their manufacturing facilities are complete, and they execute orders with promptness. Catalogues furnished to applicants.

COBB & DREW'S

TACK AND RIVET WORKS,

Manufacturers of

NORWAY IRON RIVETS,

Copper, Brass and Tinned Rivets,

Tacks, Brads, Nails, &c.

PLYMOUTH, MASS.

——:o:——

The firm of Cobb & Drew was established in the year 1848 for the purpose of manufacturing stoves and castings, and were not engaged in the making of rivets until 1860. The rivet business was from the commencement a success, and in a short time they added the manufacture of tacks and nails. These branches of the business grew so rapidly that they disposed of the stove and foundry business in the year 1866, and have since confined their attention entirely to Rivets, Tacks and Nails.

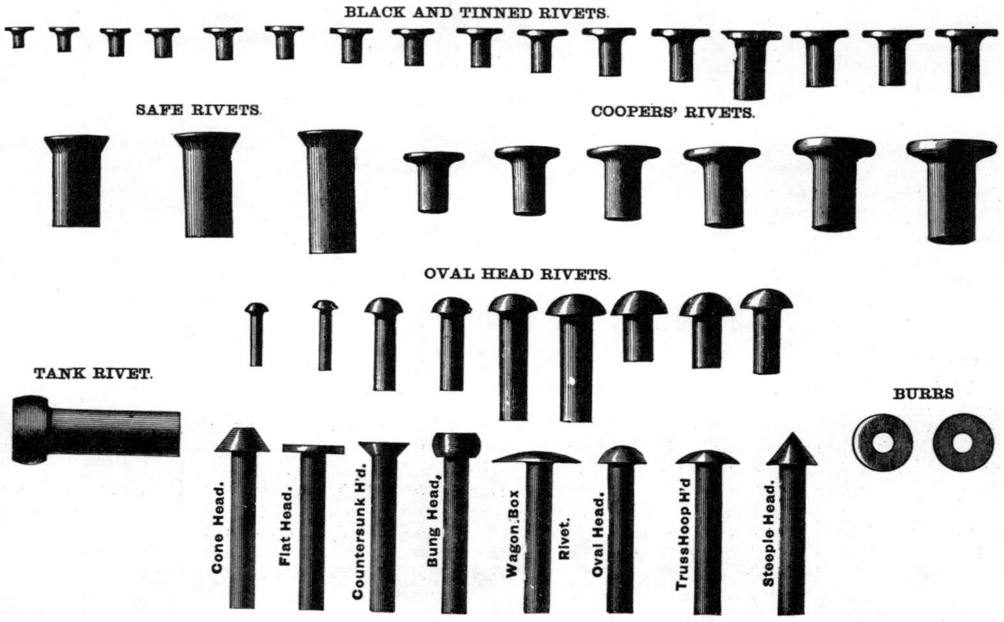

BLACK AND TINNED RIVETS.
SAFE RIVETS.
COOPERS' RIVETS.
OVAL HEAD RIVETS.
TANK RIVET.
BURRS
Cone Head.
Flat Head.
Countersunk H'd.
Bung Head.
Wagon Box
Rivet.
Oval Head.
TrussHoop H'd
Steeple Head.

From the styles presented on this page the reader will form but a very imperfect idea of the varieties and styles of their productions. They manufacture a full assortment of Rivets, from the smallest, suitable for manufacturers of Dolls up to the three-eight inch Boiler Rivet, and of any desired length and style of head; also, Tacks, Brads and Nails of every variety.

In the manufacture of their goods the establishment uses large quantities of Norway Iron for the greater part, and for the balance the best of American Iron, and consumes five hundred tons or more per annum.

The works are completely supplied with the best of machinery for the rapid production of perfect goods, and comprise a building 90x40 feet, with an L of 60x25 feet, two stories in height for the factory; also a building 50x50 feet, used for Annealing, Tinning Rooms and Blacksmith Shop, etc., also commodious Packing Shop and Store Houses.

Both steam and water power is used, and it requires from seventy-five to one hundred horse power to run their machinery. Usually about thirty-five hands are employed.

The reputation of their goods is such that they sell them in every State and Territory of the Union, and largely export them to the South American States, to Australia and other foreign countries.

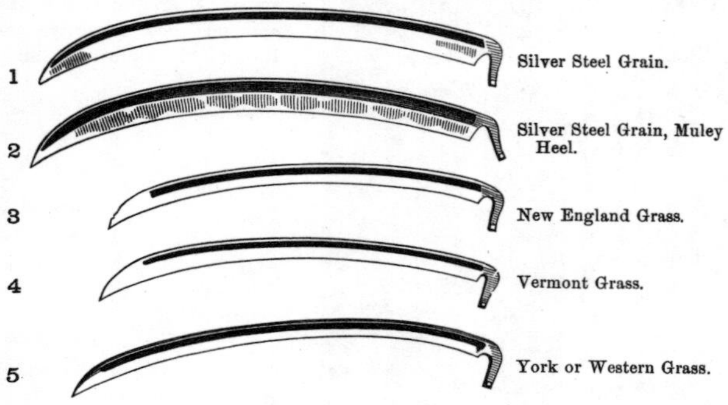

1 Silver Steel Grain.
2 Silver Steel Grain, Muley Heel.
3 New England Grass.
4 Vermont Grass.
5 York or Western Grass.

BEARDSLEY SCYTHE COMPANY,

Manufacturers of

GRAIN, LAWN, BUSH AND WEED SCYTHES,

Hay Knives, etc., etc,

WEST WINSTED, CONN.

——:o:——

Until the closing year of the last century, the scythe was strictly a hand made tool, wrought out in smith shops with sledge and hammers and ground on a stone turned by a hand crank, or hung on the shaft of a flutter wheel, without gearing or other appliances. The first establishment in this country for drawing and plating the scythe under trip hammers, and grinding it on a geared stone—water power being used as a motor—was erected by Robert Orr, of Bridgewater, Mass., during, or soon after the close of the Revolution. The second like establishment was built by Col. Robert Boyd, on or near the west bank of the Hudson, previous to 1790; and the third was built in Winsted, Conn., by Jenkins & Boyd, precise date not known. In 1802 or 1803 Merritt Bull, an early apprentice of Jenkins & Boyd, erected a scythe shop in what is now known as West Winsted, Conn., which he conducted until his death, in 1824, when the works were acquired by S. & M. Rockwell, and formed the starting point of the large and prosperous establishment, built up and managed by the successive firms of Rockwell & Hinsdale, Hinsdale & Beardsley, Elliot Beardsley, and the Beardsley Scythe Company.

The methods of manufacturing Scythes have been greatly improved since these works were first established, by the invention of special machinery. The first of these improvements, in date and perhaps in importance, was a spring die with attachments to the trip-hammer for holding the back, and setting down and smoothing the web of the scythe—a very slow and laborous process when performed with a hand hammer. The next important improvement consisted in shaping and finishing the point by a series of light tilt hammers. Then came a machine for turning and finishing the heel, which was soon followed by another for turning up the back of the scythe. Following this came an ingenious machine to spin the straw rope with which the scythes are bound up in packages of a dozen, and as a supplement to that came another for binding the scythes up in bundles, doing the work more rapidly and making a much firmer package than hand labor. The latest and certainly one of the most important improvements is that of drawing the welded scythe rods through rolls, producing a uniform and tapered rod, much faster and better than those made by the old and slow process of drawing with a hammer. The greater part of these improvements originated in Winsted. In the process of manufacture a scythe passes through some eighteen different operations.

The Beardsley Scythe Company, have a capacity to manufacture about 10,000 dozen scythes per annum. The works are supplied with both steam and water power, and all their facilities are such that, when under a pressure of orders they can turn out immense quantities of goods.

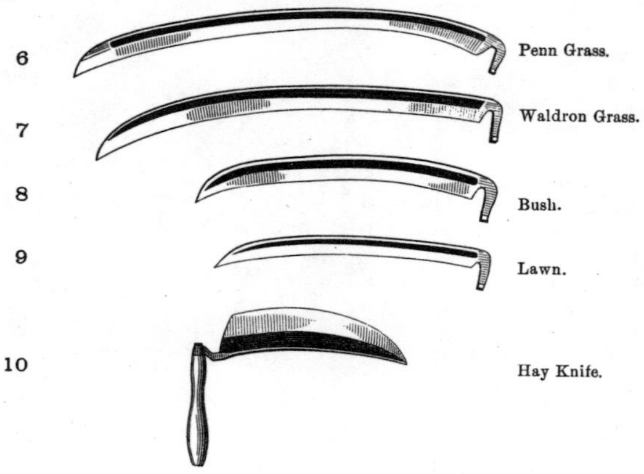

6 Penn Grass.
7 Waldron Grass.
8 Bush.
9 Lawn.
10 Hay Knife.

In their manufactures the Company use the best Swedish iron and English cast steel, imported expressly for their use. They manufacture a full assortment of Grain, Grass, Lawn, Bush, and Weed Scythes, Hay Knives, Corn Knives, Bush Hooks and Grass Hooks.

The well and favorably known brands of "Clipper," "Emperor," "Silver Steel," "Beardsley's Golden Trimmer," "Harvest Victor," "Eclipse," and others, which in quality are excelled by none, are manufactured by this Company.

HENRY ROBERTS,

WIRE MANUFACTURER,

39 OLIVER STREET, NEWARK, N. J.

——:o:——

The process for drawing wire is said to have been invented early in the fifteenth century, by Rodolph, of Nuremberg. The original method of manufacturing wire was to beat gold into thin plates and cut it into wires.

Gold was first made into wire in Italy about 1350. This has been considered the purest of all metals, for which reason it has been from the earliest ages recognized, by nearly all nations as the most valuable.

Fourcroy, says, an ounce of gold is sufficient to gild a silver wire thirteen hundred miles in length ; and such is its tenacity, that a wire the one eighteenth part of an inch will bear the weight of five hundred pounds, without breaking.

It was not until about the sixteenth century that machinery was used to any considerable extent in the manufacture of wire ; Germany being the first to introduce it. The first wire mill in England was not erected until near the middle of the seventeenth century.

The purposes for which wire has been found adapted, and to which it has consequently been applied, having increased so rapidly during the last century, correspondingly increased facilities for its manufacture became a necessity. Few, if any branches of metal manufacture have become more universal. It is made of all sizes and capacities from the hair-like wire for scientific purposes to the powerful cable for suspending Bridges. Platinum is the heaviest of all metals, except Osmium, which is the heaviest metal known, and was discovered in platinum ore, in 1804. Platinum is now claimed to be the most ductile, and from this metal the finest wire is made. The ductility of other metals takes precedence in the following order,—Gold, Silver, Copper, Steel, Iron, Brass and Zinc.

The machinery required for manufacturing wire is not as intricate as is required in many other departments of manufacture, as the process of wire-drawing is quite simple. The iron rods, varying in thickness from one-fourth to one-half inch, are first annealed, and then, drawn by powerful machinery through dies, consisting of holes in steel plates. These dies gradually decrease in size in proportion to the required fineness of the wire.

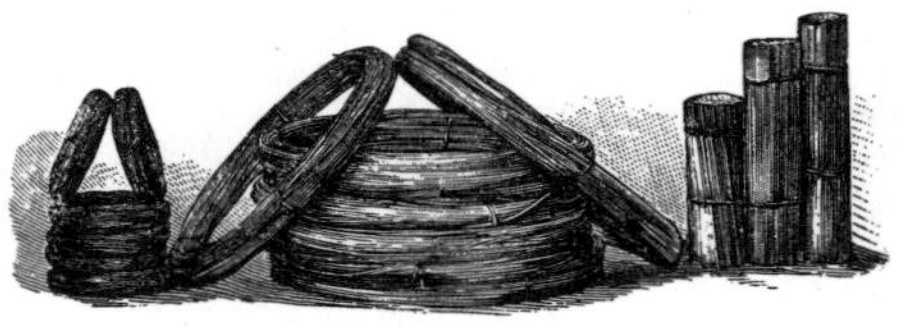

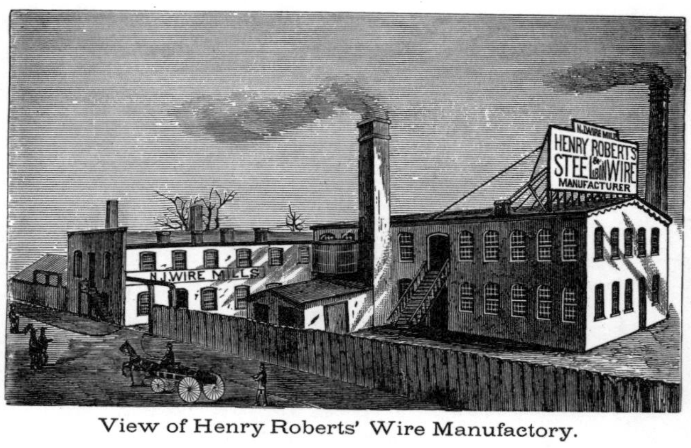

HENRY ROBERTS
STEEL WIRE
MANUFACTURER
N.J. WIRE MILLS

View of Henry Roberts' Wire Manufactory.

Prominent among the manufacturers of wire from Iron and Steel, is Mr. Henry Roberts, Proprietor of the New Jersey Wire Mill, of Newark, New Jersey. This house was established in 1858, by the firm of Laffey, Hughes & Roberts, who were afterwards succeeded by Hughes & Roberts, and in 1864 Mr. Roberts became sole Proprietor.

Although the productions of this Mill consist entirely of Cast Steel, Bessemer Steel and Iron of all grades, from the Best Norway to Common Scrap Iron. The purposes to which it is applied are very numerous. The wire is made of the best material, and in all sizes, from 0000 to No. 40, enabling Mr. Roberts to supply Steel and Iron Wire for nearly all purposes to which it is applied. Finer wires, however, are made to order. Among the kinds of wire which Mr. Roberts makes a specialty, are the Copper Covered Wire for Pail Bails, Wire for Carpet-Bag Frames, for Mosquito Netting, Bolting Cloths ; also an extra quality of Tinned Wire for Lanterns. Fine Wire for Bonnet Wire, also Wire for Paint Brush Ferules.

In the manufacture of Cast Steel and Bessemer Steel, Mr. Roberts makes a large quantity for Umbrella Ribs and Stretchers, for Sewing Machine Needles, Fish Hooks, etc. The Bessemer Steel is made extensively for Bed and Sofa Springs, this having taken the place of iron wire entirely.

In covering wire with other metals, and in finishing processes, Mr. Roberts excels. The annealing furnaces of the mill have a capacity of 12 tons of iron and $1\frac{3}{4}$ tons of steel per day. The mill has facilities for making 150 tons of wire per month or 1,800 tons per year. The market for these goods extends over the whole country, and to show the standard quality of the wire, it is only necessary to state that Mr. Roberts employs no traveling salesmen, orders being received direct at the factory. The working force numbers 50 hands, and the weekly pay roll is $900. The aggregate value of yearly productions reaches $200,000. Mr. Roberts has the only iron and steel wire manufactory in Newark, and his production will doubtless increase as the wants of the country require.

FAIRBANKS' STANDARD SCALES,

Manufactory, St. Johnsbury, Vt.

Warehouses in all the principal cities in the United States.

Also in London, England, and Montreal, Canada.

There was doubtless a time in the history of man when there existed no necessity for ascertaining the quantity or value of the products of agriculture or manufacture by weight or measure. When this period terminated we have no means of knowing; but that there arose a necessity for weighing and measuring articles of merchandise, early in the history of the race, we have abundant proof. Various theories have been advanced regarding the primitive method of meeting this necessity, but it is quite certain that not until a comparatively recent date, was any method devised by which anything more than an approximate accuracy could be secured.

The principle in mechanics upon which the modern balance scales are based is that of the lever, the invention of which is credited to Archimedes in the early part of the third century, B. C. He laid the foundation of nearly all those inventions the further prosecution of which was the boast of the seventeenth century. It is quite probable that the earliest method of ascertaining the weight of articles was by balancing them in each hand, by which a general idea of the comparative weight could be obtained, but nothing like strict accuracy could be obtained. In this manner the basis would naturally be laid for the discovery of the steel yard, which, in its various modified forms, is at present the most generally used contrivance for weighing.

The instrument used by the ancients which is translated *balance* in the Pentateuch, was doubtless the steelyard, which is but a suspended lever. This instrument is known to have been in use among the Egyptians long before the time of Archimedes, although the law of the lever was not fully demonstrated until his time.

From the time of Archimedes until the seventeenth century many of the laws of mechanics were understood and practically applied, but it was not until the latter date that anything like a scientific character was given to the study of mechanics.

It is to the philosopher Galileo and his successors, that we are indebted for our present positive methods for investigating the laws of force and motion.

In no way can we contrast more vividly the standard of modern society with that of the ancients, and thus appreciate the wonderful progress that has been made, even during the last two centuries, since the days of Galileo, than in the general habits of accuracy introduced into modern life, by the ability to measure and weigh correctly. This constant approximation to strict accuracy in commercial transactions, and the duties of domestic life, has led to a higher appreciation of the merits of weight rather than measure, in securing this end. To such a high state of perfection have the instruments for ascertaining the value of any commodity by its weight, been brought, that many articles which but a few years since, had their value known in trade only by measure, now have their legal standard quantities determined by weight.

There is no mechanical achievement of more importance in commercial transactions, and none that has required a higher quality of more than three hundred, from the delicate standard required by the druggist and the banker, to those of enormous proportions required for the use of railroads, canals and other transportation companies, sometimes requiring a capacity for weighing three hundred tons at a time.

The demand for the Fairbanks Scales has constantly increased as their reputation became more extended, until the present production of more than fifty thousand scales annually with an aggregate value of $2,000,000 is not sufficient to supply the market. Their reputation and appreciation are not confined to this country, nor even to America; they find a demand in China, India, Persia, Australia, Turkey and Arabia—where for want of better facilities for transportation, they are carried on mules' and camels backs far beyond the reach of railroads or water communication. They have already found a market in the Barbary States, Cape Colony, Sandwich Islands, Isle of France, all the South American States, and all the great commercial nations of the earth. They are adapted to the standard of all nations and marked with the signs of each. The metric system which has now been adopted by about 350,000,000 of the worlds population requires that the scales for use in many countries, especially in Europe, India and South America, should be based on that system, which has accordingly been done. Many of their scales are fitted with double beams, giving both the common and the metric system, thus facilitating the comparison and use of each.

One of the leading instrumentalities in the establishment of the enviable reputation these scales have acquired is the severity of the test to which they are subjected before they are allowed to leave the factory. Not the most unimportant part of the

material or mechanism, is allowed to be approved until it has been tested in every possible manner which human ingenuity can devise and found to be perfect. Another commendable feature peculiar to this establishment, and which is sure to strengthen the confidence of purchasers in the perfection of these scales, is the mutual interest everywhere apparent among proprietors and mechanics for the success of the business.

None but a higher class of workmen are employed, men who are willing to have their merits measured by their success; men of that order of intelligence who can appreciate the fact, overlooked by too many of the ordinary mechanics of the present time, that "nothing is so successful as success," and that this cannot be achieved by employer or employé without the co-operation of both; and this mutual effort is a striking characteristic observed in every department of this manufactory.

It should also be said, to the credit of the founders and later proprietors of this establishment, that the policy adopted toward the men in their employ has been such as to incite a spirit of enterprise and habits of economy, the result of which is now apparent in their fine cottage homes which their own industry has secured. It cannot be denied that the thrift and enterprise, the advanced state of moral and intellectual culture, for which the village of St. Johnsbury is so distinguished are but the legitimate results of the well-directed business capacity and extensive munificence of this company. These facts are the principal solution of an enigma which has long puzzled the larger portion of manufacturers. It has been a marvel how this Company could conduct their business economically and successfully so far from navigation or any great commercial centre.

Other manufacturers of heavy articles, often requiring the transportation of far less tonnage, have been compelled to seek more eligible localities, near tidewater or in the immediate vicinity of the place where the material for their manufactures is produced.

FAIRBANKS' SCALE MANUFACTORY, ST. JOHNSBURY, VERMONT.

genius for its conception, or of mechanical ingenuity for its development, than the Fairbanks Scales, now so universally known and practically applied. It is nearly fifty years since the manufactory of the Fairbanks Scales was established in the quiet village of St. Johnsbury, in the north-east part of the state of Vermont. Here from small beginnings has arisen the largest manufactory of scales in the world. The establishment covers an area of more than ten acres, and gives employment to about six hundred men, to which if we add the number of four hundred or more employed in branch departments elsewhere we have the total of about one thousand men who receive employment directly or indirectly from this house. The scales are of all sizes, constituting a variety of more than

The rapid extension of railroads for the past twenty-five years has called into requisition a great variety of platform scales of larger capacity than was hitherto required. This demand has been promptly and successfully met by this manufactory, and the number of the Fairbanks Patent Iron Frame Track Scales, now in use by leading railway and manufacturing companies is nearly two thousand. These vary in length of platform from twelve to one hundred and twenty-three feet, the larger portion of which vary from twenty-four to forty-two feet.

PROVIDENCE STEAM AND GAS PIPE CO.,

Providence, R. I.

—:o:—

The Providence Steam and Gas Pipe Company operate one of the largest manufacturing establishments of its kind in the United States, and since its first organization has been and still is constantly adding to its facilities for production in order to meet the requirements of the rapidly increasing business. The Company is favorably known in almost every manufacturing community in New England, for their successful application of the most approved methods in the equipment of manufacturing establishments with Steam Heating, Lighting and Sprinkling (for protection against fire) Apparatus. They are large builders of Coal Gas Works for cities and towns, having been for many years past engaged in the erection of such works in various parts of the country. Steam Heating Apparatus for public buildings is another important feature of their business. A specialty, however, is made of furnishing manufactories with Fire Protection, Heat and Light.

A glance at the accompanying engravings will enable the reader to form a very correct idea of the manner in which Sprinkling Piping and Steam Heating Apparatus is arranged by the Company. In the matter of Sprinkling Piping, for protection against fire, water is brought to a Receiver located in a tower, hall or other easily accessible point, and distributed from thence, by means of independent Wrought Iron Supply Mains, to the different systems of Perforated Wrought Iron Pipes which run lengthwise or crosswise of the room or rooms to be protected, and are so arranged that only that portion of the room where the fire actually exists need be subjected to the drenching by water. These perforated pipes are run at a proper distance from the ceiling of the rooms, and their top surfaces, looking up to the ceiling, are perforated at proper intervals by conically shaped orifices, the diameter of the holes at the apex of the cone being one-fourteenth of an inch. The ceilings, beams and side walls of the room are completely covered by the spreading of the water over their surfaces, the angles of the perforations in the pipes being such as to procure a thorough protection. The end sought to be accomplished by this arrangement of perforated pipes is that in all cases there shall be such a distribution of water upon the exposed surfaces overhead, that it (the water) shall strike them with such force and at such angles as to entirely cover and thoroughly wet the surfaces, and drop and run down the sides and upon the floor of the room. To facilitate the easy and rapid passage of the water with as little loss of head in its distribution as possible: long Radii Water Fittings, such as Elbows, Crosses, Tees, etc., have been designed and adapted to this work.

This system of perforated pipes so arranged that a copious supply of water can be in a moment's time directed to the point where it is needed, without flooding an entire building, or indeed wetting any portion of the room in which the fire is, other than that in immediate danger, possesses many marked advantages over the ordinary methods of fighting fire. It not only affords a perfect protection against loss by fire, but renders entirely unnecessary that flooding of an entire establishment which generally follows the attempt to extinguish a fire originating in one of the upper stories, where steam pumps or fire engines are used, and a few large streams are depended upon. Wherever this system has been adopted a large reduction of insurance rates has been effected in both mutual and stock companies.

Steam heating by utilization of the waste or exhaust steam from the engine has been extensively and successfully introduced by this Company in the largest and best manufactories in New England and elsewhere. By their peculiar system of piping they are enabled to utilize the exhaust steam with little or no back pressure on the piston of the engine. By their system the pressure is reduced to less than one pound per square inch, and a great saving in the consumption of fuel is the natural result. The Company are now using one inch and one and one-quarter inch pipes for radiation where much larger sizes were formerly put up, and the small pipes afford the best results.

The Petroleum Oil Gas Works manufactured by this Company have been in successful operation nearly a score of years. Illuminating gas, made of coal, is composed of carburetted hydrogen, carbonic oxide and olefiant gas, the last being the principal agent in producing light. Gas made from petroleum contains all these elements, but has a larger percentage of olefiant gas, and therefore gives a more brilliant and much whiter light. Light is in this manner obtained at less than one-fourth the average cost of coal gas. The illuminating power of this gas is much superior to that of coal gas, while the steadiness and whiteness of the light, renders it soft, and far less trying to the eye. Many of the largest manufactories in New England have put in these works, and others are rapidly following their example with highly satisfactory results. Even in the largest cities, these works are being largely introduced in hotels, manufacturing establishments, etc., as they afford a purer and a much cheaper gas than is supplied by gas companies. The gas is particularly adapted for brazing, soldering and singeing for mechanical purposes.

The Company's business career has been an eminently successful one, and their operations from a comparatively small beginning have grown to large proportions. Their success, however, has not been beyond their just deserts.

Providence Steam and Gas Pipe Co., Providence, Rhode Island.

W. H. HILL,

Successor to HILL, DEVOE & CO.,

ENVELOPE MANUFACTURER,

Worcester, Mass.

—:o:—

To write a history of the envelope manufactory of Mr. W. H. Hill, a cut of whose establishment is here presented, would be to write a complete history of the envelope business of the United States, and such an article would much more than fill the limited space at our disposal. Suffice it then to say, that its record dates back to the very beginning of the trade, and that it was one of the first, if not the very first house established in this country, for the manufacture of machine made envelopes and envelope making machinery.

The business was begun in the year 1846, by Dr. Hawes, (who was the inventor of the first envelope-folding machine, which he used,) and has been successfully continued since that time. Messrs. Trumbull & Hartshorn were the proprietors for a time, and became very popular in the trade, but, in August, 1865, they sold the business to Messrs. Hill, Devoe & Co., who proved worthy successors, and were forced to largely add to the manufacturing facilities of the concern in order to meet the constantly increasing demand for their productions. They continued the business until January 1, 1875, when the present proprietor, Mr. W. H. Hill, purchased the entire establishment, since which time many improvements have been made in the machinery, and in all the processes of manufacture, and the business has grown to immense proportions.

The envelope machinery used in this establishment is quite different from that used in other manufacturing establishments. Mr. Hill builds his own machines, having a completely appointed machine shop on the premises for that especial purpose; they cannot be made elsewhere, nor does he offer them for sale, but builds them solely for his own exclusive use, consequently, in his special line of production he need fear no rivalry.

The goods manufactured by this house are not forced upon buyers by traveling agents, nor placed in the hands of commission merchants. Mr. Hill finds enough to do to fill orders constantly sent to him by the leading paper and stationery firms of the country, and is not forced to resort to any of the devices which some others employ to "make" trade. The present production of the establishment is over 750,000 envelopes per day, which, if need be, can be increased to 830,000, indeed, at times, 5,000,000 envelopes have been made here in a single week. It is not possible, however, to always run an establishment of this kind at its greatest capacity, the disabling of a single folding machine for instance, would decrease the day's work about 80,000 envelopes, and as such accidents sometimes happen, the factory is now running at about its average capacity. The business, however, is increasing so rapidly that a larger manufactory will soon be erected and equipped with the facilities for turning out from one and a half to two million envelopes per day.

Over fifteen hundred different styles of envelopes are manufactured by Mr. Hill, and from so vast an assortment of sizes and shapes, colors, materials and qualities of the various materials, it seems as though all might readily be suited, there are envelopes for druggists, perfumers, glove makers, and dealers in fancy goods, note, letter and official envelopes of many sizes, wedding envelopes, mourning envelopes—there are parchment

View of the Envelope Manufactory of W. H. Hill, Worcester, Mass.

envelopes, cloth-lined envelopes, envelopes seemingly for every conceivable use, and yet new styles are constantly being added.

The last United States census reports twenty-two envelope manufacturing establishments, fifteen of which employ steam or water power. The total production is stated at $2,277,541, but we believe these figures to be considerably below the real value of the goods in first hands.

The total production, of course, is added to with each succeeding year; a few new factories have recently sprung up and old ones have enlarged their facilities, but the business of Mr. Hill is steadily increasing at a much more rapid rate than the mere increase of consumption would warrant, if that increase was equally divided among leading manufacturers, consequently we must infer that his great success is due to the superior quality of the goods produced at his establishment. Long continued success is always positive proof of merit, and real merit always succeeds.

With the most improved machinery; with skillful workers, and all the aids that long experience in the business can give, Mr. Hill has facilities for the rapid and cheap production of first-class goods, not excelled by those of any other manufacturer. He purchases the finest qualities of raw material in large quantities at the lowest prices, manufactures at the minimum cost, and consequently can and does furnish strictly first-class goods at rates as low as any.

For further information parties should apply either personally or by mail to W. H. Hill, Worcester, Mass.

"TELESCOPING" ON AMERICAN RAILROADS.

Its Cause and Cure.

The present inhabitants of the earth and those who are to follow them through the decades of time, are now and will be more indebted to the middle half of the present century for valuable inventions than to any full century preceding it. So rapid has been the change wrought by inventive genius, that mankind has been, as it were, transformed; the management of the great business interests of trade, commerce and the industries of civilized nations have undergone a change such as only the silent, working forces of genius could command; and to-day we look back to fifty years ago, and exclaim, that without the telegraph and the aid of steam this earth would be a chaos.

Railroading began with the use of horse power to be supplanted by locomotives, and the first cars used were the bodies of old cast off stage coaches placed upon a frame work, which in turn rode upon axles and wheels. These cheaply constructed vehicles had necessarily to be coupled together, which was easily done with hook and chain, and it so happened that the point of contact or coupling of the frames, was two feet and nine inches above the track; which has ever remained the standard height of car couplers. On English roads the introduction was the same but as there has been no change in the form of running gear, there has been no trouble arising therefrom, and the only change made has been in the method of coupling the cars together; the chain and hook giving place to the double acting screw, with compression buffers on each corner, which being forced together by the screw in the center, holds the cars firmly together thereby preventing lateral jerking and oscillation. The result of this was that English trains became noted for speed and safety. On the other hand the spirit of improvement in America would not rest and an entire new style of cars was adopted. The bodies were made long and high and airy; with doors in each end opening upon a platform from which steps communicated with the ground. These bodies were placed on two independent trucks of four wheels each, made so as to sway on a center bearing, in order to turn curves easily without straining the truck or axle bearings. This was necessary owing to the great length of the car bodies and the curves of American roadways. This important change had the effect to raise the underside of the car bodies several inches above the coupling point of the older cars, and a compromise was effected by placing the platform below the line of the car sills and below them the draw-head, placing the point of contact between the cars about sixteen inches below the plane of the car sills. These sills therefore constituted the resisting line of strength and any deflection from this line produced weakness, increasing in ratio with the deflection. Thus it is shown how a great error of construction crept into being, and by it came all the horrible results of telescoping of cars.

In the foregoing the one great error in American car construction has been briefly noticed; an error that led to serious results and demanded a remedy, which, thanks to the genius of Col. Ezra Miller, is now being placed upon every railroad in the United States. This remedy is simple: only a change of platforms and couplers, with the addition of compression buffers, forming what is widely known as the "Miller Platform." It consists of four sills, twelve inches in depth by four inches in thickness, butting six inches against the end sill of the car, the two center sills being connected by truss and suspender beams. From the truss beam strong iron trusses extend over or through the end sill and fasten to the transom of the car. The buffer which forms the point of contact, is placed on a line with the car sills, resting against a spring beam, thus keeping up a continuous line of resistance, while the coupling-hooks are placed five inches below the buffer-beams, and two feet and nine inches above the track. The hooks and buffers are so arranged that when the hooks are coupled together, a compression of several thousand pounds is caused from the action of the springs, connected to the hooks and buffers, and which holds the car steadily in place, preventing oscillation and lateral jerking, as experienced in all slack couplings. All danger in coupling cars is avoided as simply pushing one against the other does the work most effectually, and the hooks interlocking beneath the buffer-beams admit of no lapping of platforms while the direct line of contact through the train prevents telescoping in case of accident.

The Miller Platform is now in use upon nearly every American railroad and its value cannot be computed in dollars and cents. It is the greatest blessing yet conferred upon the travelling public, for not only is it a preventive of accident, but it renders travelling much less fatigueing, in doing away with osciliation and lateral jerking.

There are hundreds of well known instances wherein the Miller Platform has been the means of preventing the most horrible accidents. On all the great lines of travel it is a common thing to meet with employés who claim that they owe the preservation of their lives to it, it having become so widely known for its great value as a life-saving car attachment.

Ezra Miller was born in Bergen County, New Jersey, on the shore of the Hudson river, opposite the upper part of the city of New York, on the 12th day of May, 1812.

He gained a wide knowledge of men, a classical education; mastered the sciences, and, though educated for a physician and surgeon, he very naturally inclined to mathematics, and became a civil engineer second to none in the profession.

In the month of April, 1848, he removed to Rock County, Wisconsin, establishing himself with his family at the new town of Magnolia. While a member of the Legislature, Col. Miller espoused the cause of internal improvement and became the champion of every project for establishing the railroad system of the State on a firm and substantial basis, which would open up its great wealth of soil and timber to the markets of the East and secure to the inhabitants the just and equitable order of things that has been a credit to its growing commonwealth. It was during the celebration of the opening of one of the important railroad lines that he became impressed with the great error of car construction, in an accident where cars were telescoped and over sixty persons were killed and wounded, and barely escaping with his life, he determined to effect a remedy. After a thorough investigation, followed by numerous experiments, he presented to the world his present system of car coupling.

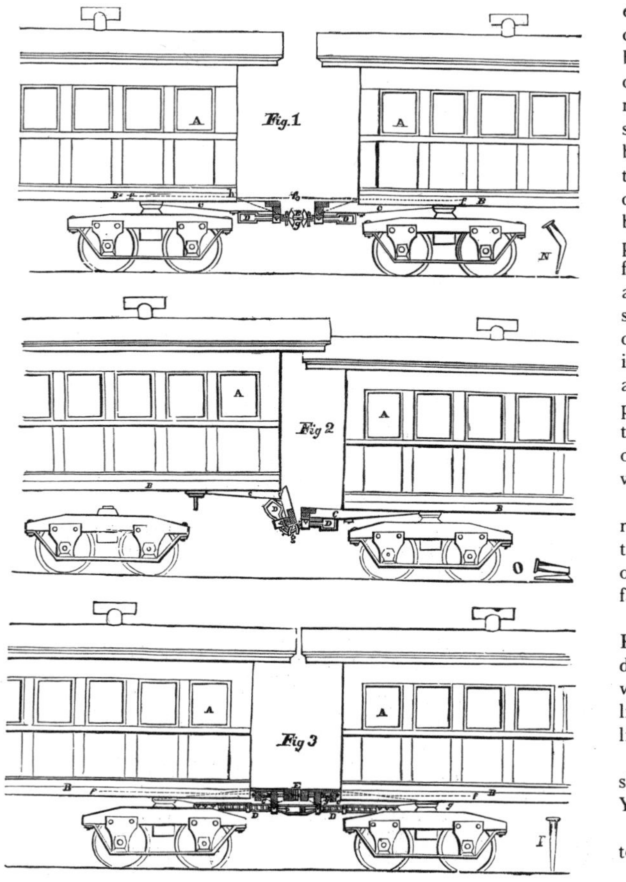

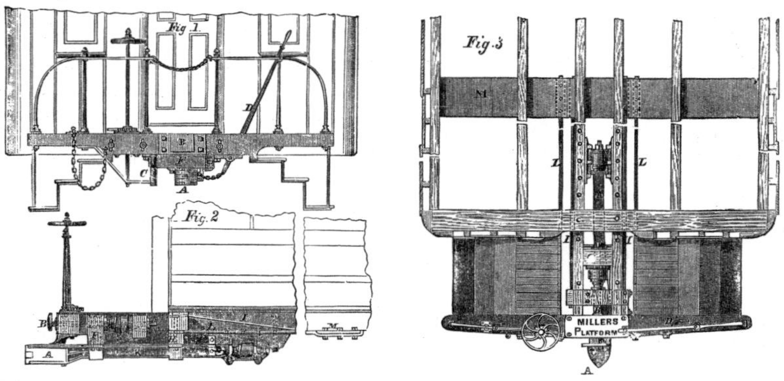

Illustrations showing Col. Miller's Construction for the Prevention of Telescoping Railroad Cars.

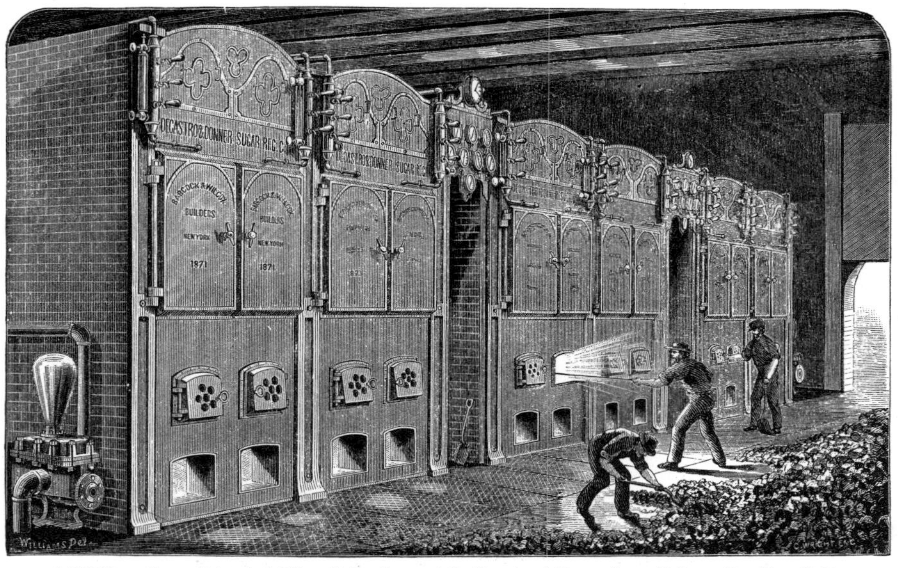

A 900 Horse Power Babcock & Wilcox Boiler, in use at the Decastro & Donner Sugar Refinery, Brooklyn, N. Y.

BABCOCK & WILCOX,

Patent Tubulous Steam Boiler

30 CORTLANDT ST., N. Y.

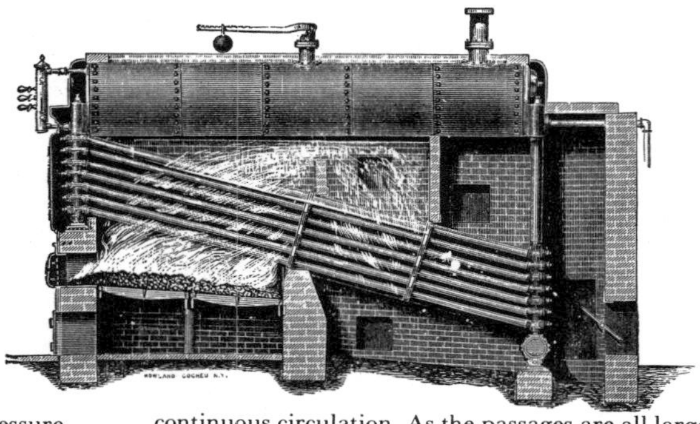

This boiler is composed of lap welded wrought iron boiler tubes, placed in an inclined position and connected with each other, and with a horizontal steam and water drum, by vertical steel castings at each end, while a mud-drum connects the tubes at the lower end. The tubes are "staggered" (or so placed that one row comes over the spaces of the previous row), and are fitted with hand holes at each end for cleaning. They are tested and made tight under a hydrostatic pressure of 500 pounds per square inch, iron to iron, and without rubber packing, putty or other perishable substances.

The fire is made under the front and higher end of the tubes, and the products of combustion pass up between the tubes into a combustion chamber under the steam and water drum.

The water being inside the tubes, as it is heated tends to rise toward the higher end, and as it is converted into steam rises through the vertical passages into the drum above the tubes where the steam separates from the water and the latter flows back to the rear and down again through the tubes, in a continuous circulation. As the passages are all large and free this circulation is very rapid, and secures three very important advantages: 1st. It sweeps away every particle of steam as fast as formed, and supplies its place with a particle of water, thereby absorbing the heat of the fire to the best advantage. 2d. It causes a thorough commingling of the water throughout the boiler and a consequent equal temperature, thus preventing those very serious strains from unequal expansion, which are a frequent cause of explosions. 3d. The rapid circulation prevents, to a great degree, the formation of deposits or incrustations upon the heating surfaces. Over 15,000 horse power of these boilers in operation.

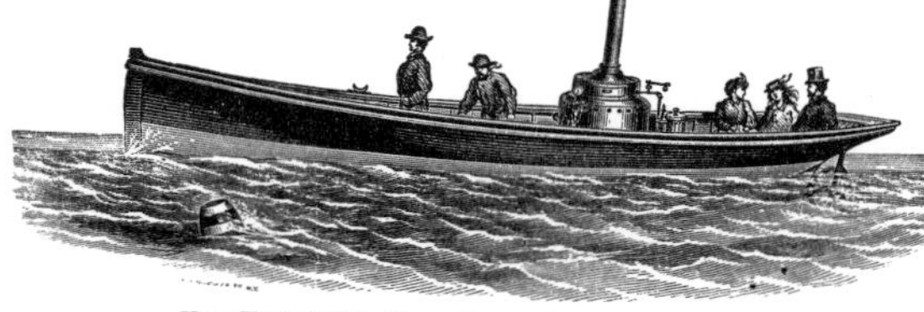

New York Safety Steam Power Co's. Steam Launches.

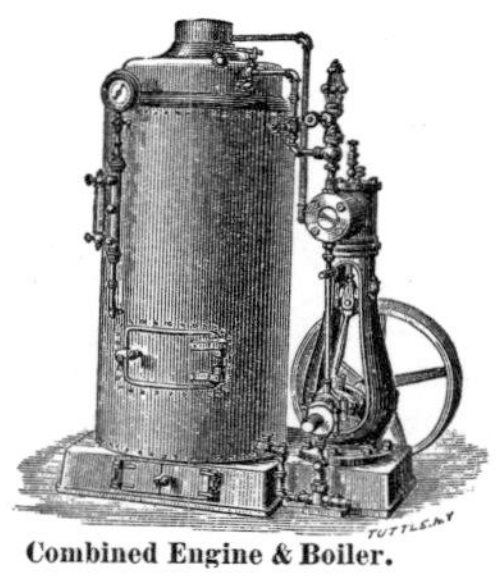

Combined Engine & Boiler.

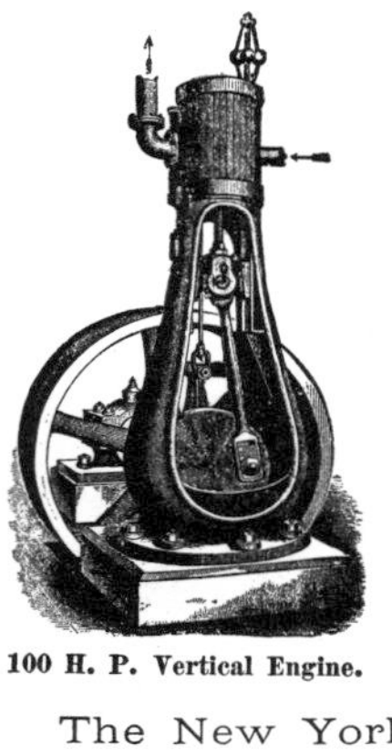

100 H. P. Vertical Engine.

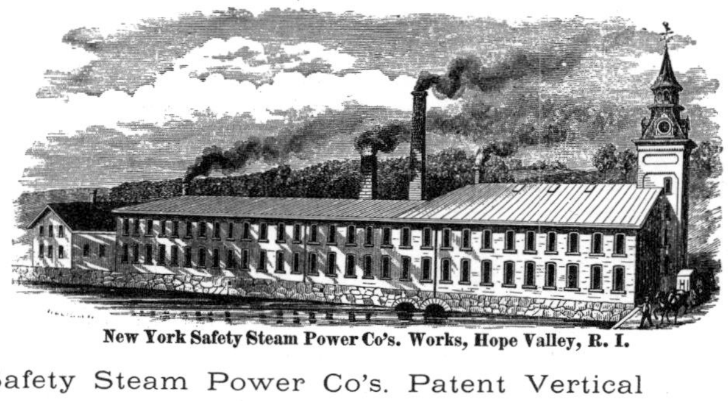

New York Safety Steam Power Co's. Works, Hope Valley, R. I.

The New York Safety Steam Power Co's. Patent Vertical Steam Engine, 30 Cortlandt St., N. Y.

The Vertical Engine possesses advantages peculiarly fitting it for many locations. It has already won its way to universal favor on board of the finest screw steamers, where its continuous and rapid working, during long and stormy passages, proves it to be peculiarly fitted to sustain severe labor for long periods. There is no style of engine which occupies so little room; in which the strains are so well resisted by the framing; or in which the friction is so small and the endurance of all the parts so well secured.

These engines are built in quantities and the parts duplicated by special machinery, which secures great accuracy and uniformity of workmanship, and allows of any part being quickly and cheaply replaced, when worn or broken by accident.

All the bearing surfaces are made extra large and are accurately fitted; and the best quality of Babbitt Metal only used for the journal bearings.

Being attached to one base, the combined Engine and boiler is easily transported, occupies little space, and may very readily be mounted upon wheels, rendering it peculiarly adapted for agricultural purposes.

This Company give special attention to machinery for Pleasure Yachts, Tugs, and small Steamers, and are prepared to furnish any desired size at short notice. For these purposes their larger engines are fitted with self-adjusting bearings, giving them a degree of flexibility in every direction peculiarly adapting them to marine use.

They are now able to furnish light and graceful boats of remarkable swiftness, and with such improved and simplified machinery as to run on a very small consumption of fuel and be easily managed by any one with a little instruction. These boats are fitted with light and strong boilers, able to make a large amount of dry steam with little fuel, and a light engine, capable of running at a high speed without shake or jar, and using steam very economically.

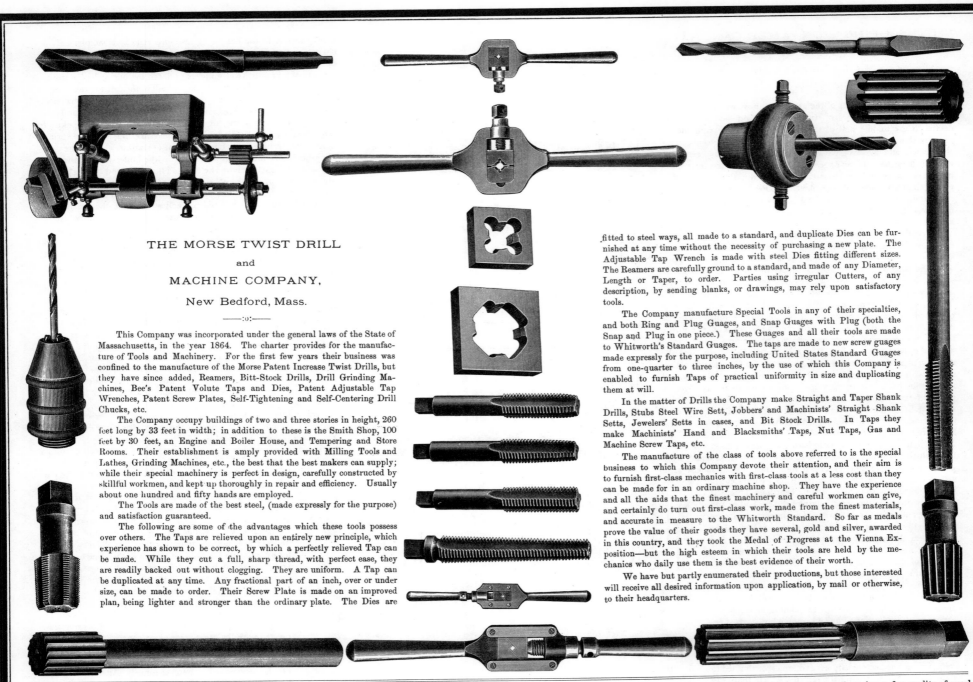

THE MORSE TWIST DRILL

and

MACHINE COMPANY,

New Bedford, Mass.

—:o:—

This Company was incorporated under the general laws of the State of Massachusetts, in the year 1864. The charter provides for the manufacture of Tools and Machinery. For the first few years their business was confined to the manufacture of the Morse Patent Increase Twist Drills, but they have since added, Reamers, Bitt-Stock Drills, Drill Grinding Machines, Bee's Patent Volute Taps and Dies, Patent Adjustable Tap Wrenches, Patent Screw Plates, Self-Tightening and Self-Centering Drill Chucks, etc.

The Company occupy buildings of two and three stories in height, 260 feet long by 33 feet in width; in addition to these is the Smith Shop, 100 feet by 30 feet, an Engine and Boiler House, and Tempering and Store Rooms. Their establishment is amply provided with Milling Tools and Lathes, Grinding Machines, etc., the best that the best makers can supply; while their special machinery is perfect in design, carefully constructed by skillful workmen, and kept up thoroughly in repair and efficiency. Usually about one hundred and fifty hands are employed.

The Tools are made of the best steel, (made expressly for the purpose) and satisfaction guaranteed.

The following are some of the advantages which these tools possess over others. The Taps are relieved upon an entirely new principle, which experience has shown to be correct, by which a perfectly relieved Tap can be made. While they cut a full, sharp thread, with perfect ease, they are readily backed out without clogging. They are uniform. A Tap can be duplicated at any time. Any fractional part of an inch, over or under size, can be made to order. Their Screw Plate is made on an improved plan, being lighter and stronger than the ordinary plate. The Dies are fitted to steel ways, all made to a standard, and duplicate Dies can be furnished at any time without the necessity of purchasing a new plate. The Adjustable Tap Wrench is made with steel Dies fitting different sizes. The Reamers are carefully ground to a standard, and made of any Diameter, Length or Taper, to order. Parties using irregular Cutters, of any description, by sending blanks, or drawings, may rely upon satisfactory tools.

The Company manufacture Special Tools in any of their specialties, and both Ring and Plug Guages, and Snap and Plug Guages with Plug (both the Snap and Plug in one piece.) These Guages and all their tools are made to Whitworth's Standard Guages. The taps are made to new screw guages made expressly for the purpose, including United States Standard Guages from one-quarter to three inches, by the use of which this Company is enabled to furnish Taps of practical uniformity in size and duplicating them at will.

In the matter of Drills the Company make Straight and Taper Shank Drills, Stubs Steel Wire Sett, Jobbers' and Machinists' Straight Shank Setts, Jewelers' Setts in cases, and Bit Stock Drills. In Taps they make Machinists' Hand and Blacksmiths' Taps, Nut Taps, Gas and Machine Screw Taps, etc.

The manufacture of the class of tools above referred to is the special business to which this Company devote their attention, and their aim is to furnish first-class mechanics with first-class tools at a less cost than they can be made for in an ordinary machine shop. They have the experience and all the aids that the finest machinery and careful workmen can give, and certainly do turn out first-class work, made from the finest materials, and accurate in measure to the Whitworth Standard. So far as medals prove the value of their goods they have several, gold and silver, awarded in this country, and they took the Medal of Progress at the Vienna Exposition—but the high esteem in which their tools are held by the mechanics who daily use them is the best evidence of their worth.

We have but partly enumerated their productions, but those interested will receive all desired information upon application, by mail or otherwise, to their headquarters.

THOMAS DAVIS,

Manufacturer of

PEARL BUTTONS AND STUDS,

Newark, N. J.

—:o:—

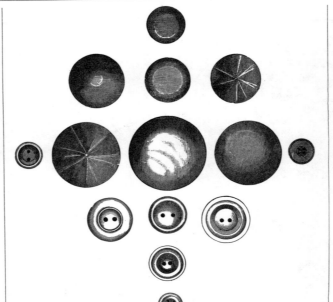

In speaking of buttons a recent writer says:—"It might not be too much too say that the Romans retained the use of the toga chiefly because they had not yet discovered any inexpensive way of making buttons. Had they been able to fasten their garments by some simpler method than that of brooches or strings, the dress coat and the waistcoat would not have remained undiscovered until modern times." Comparing ancient and modern costumes, or the present style of dress in the East with the prevailing mode in Europe or the United States, the most marked difference is in the degree of looseness. Among the ancients, as in the East at the present time, the dress is flowing and is worn as drapery, while among civilized nations, the dress is made to closely fit the person, and the writer above quoted, ascribes this difference in style to buttons. How far buttons are entitled to credit for this change of style we will not undertake to determine, but we do know that, though of comparatively recent origin, they play a very important part in the world of fashion, and that in their manufacture many hundreds of thousands of dollars are invested and some of the best skill of the world is employed.

Nearly a century ago, Mr. James Davis, Sr., became identified with the manufacture of buttons in Birmingham, England. His son James Jr., Davis, successfully pursued the same industry, and his grandson, Thomas Davis, following in the footsteps of his ancestors, is the well known manufacturer whose name heads this article.

Mr. Thomas Davis settled in the United States in the year 1852, and immediately began the business of manufacturing a fine quality of pearl buttons and studs, which soon attracted the attention of buyers and became very popular. Since then his business has grown immensely, and now ranks among the largest of this special class. Mr. Davis manufactures from three to four hundred different styles and sizes of buttons and studs, and in addition a general line of pearl work.

In the manufacture of the finest goods, the choicest Manilla Pearl Shells are used exclusively, and so extensive has the business become, that there is annually consumed in the establishment of Mr. Davis from forty to fifty thousand pounds of these shells, which cost in the rough from seventy to seventy-five cents per pound, or in round numbers twenty-three thousand dollars. For a cheaper class of goods Bombay shells are used to the extent of fifteen thousand pounds per annum, and in addition large quantities of Japanese and Ballonia Shells, etc.

The manufacture of this class of goods is partly done by machinery. It requires some thirty hands to attend the machinery employed by Mr. Davis, and the aggregate product of finished goods is so large that if stated here many of our readers would question the correctness of the figures.

We present on this page cuts of a few of the styles of buttons produced by Mr. Davis, but a mere engraving, while it may clearly show the size and shape, cannot show the beauty and brilliancy of a stud or button made of fine pearl. Mr. Davis' productions are remarkable for the beauty of the material of which they are made, for their really artistic design, and for the perfection of their finish. These desirable qualities are duly appreciated by the public, and consequently there is always a demand for his goods. They are known to dealers and consumers almost everywhere, and are to be found in nearly every city and town in every state and territory of the Union, and are largely exported to foreign countries.

MUNSON BROTHERS,

MILL FURNISHING ESTABLISHMENT,

Cor. Broadway and Erie Canal, Utica, New York.

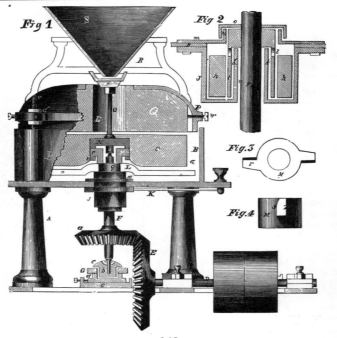

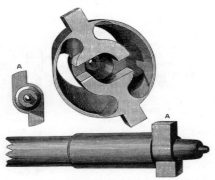

The founder of the celebrated firm of Munson Brothers, Mr. Alfred Munson, in the year 1825, established himself in Utica, N. Y., as a manufacturer of Burr Mill Stones, and was undoubtedly one of the first makers of that peculiar article known as French Burr, most of the mill stones formerly produced in this country having been made from our common American rock-stone. From its beginning the business was a success, and within a few years the demand for French Burrs had become so great that Mr. Munson was induced to associate with him, in their manufacture, Mr. Martin Hart, under the firm name of Hart & Munson. Subsequently Edmund C. Munson, a nephew, and Alexander Hart, a son of the former partners, took possession, continuing the old firm name, but later, other changes were made and the present style adopted.

Under the new management the business increased very rapidly, largely owing to the genius and inventive skill of Mr. Edmund Munson. His first great improvement consisted of a machine for Balancing and Finishing Burr Mill Stones; the Stones were placed on a Circular Face Plate, and while being balanced and finished they were made with both running and standing balance, and this together with the superior skill and judgment displayed in selecting and matching the stock for the building of the stones, secured for them a reputation second to that of no other maker. Then came the Patent Eye and Spindle, the greatest improvement in hanging Mill Stones ever invented. They prevent any filling or clogging in the eye or cramping of the driving parts. They do not require resetting as the stone wears away as the old style does, but will remain in place until a stone is worn out. They grind cooler and easier, with less power, and this together with the rapidity of grinding, makes the Eye and Spindle one of the most valuable improvements for the milling public. In addition to this Mr. Munson invented and patented what he calls his Hollow Necked Spindle and Oil Tight Bush. The Spindle is made of wrought iron and is provided with a collar or bearing which is forged solid on the Spindle, and is fitted within the Bush. The Bush is of square form, inside of which Babbitt metal boxes are placed and adjusted snugly against the collar by keys or screws; the collar is hollow and open at the lower end, leaving a space all around between it and the Spindle. The Bush is provided with a central vertical tube around which the collar works, the tube passing up between the collar and the bottom of the Spindle. The Collar within the Bush forms the bearing surface of the Spindle. The Bush is covered with a cap having a circular opening in its center through which the Spindle passes. This Spindle and Bush has been conceded by those having them in use to be the best thing out. Munson Brothers also present a Portable Wheat Flouring and Corn Grinding Mill, an invention which is certainly worthy of attention. Its peculiar advantage over others now in use, are summed up in the following merits which it is claimed are peculiar to it, and which Mr. Munson designated in his patent, viz: self-adjusting, perfect in balance, self-lubricating, simple in construction, durable in material, rapid in grinding, and does not choke. It has received the highest premiums and awards wherever exhibited, and they safely place it in competition with any mill ever produced.

BROOKLYN LIFE INSURANCE COMPANY.

Office, 320 & 322 Broadway, New York.

We are indebted to the Brooklyn Life Insurance Company for this fine representation of the Brooklyn Bridge, which will ere long afford a new means of communication between New York and her sister city. The view is from the Brooklyn side of the river, and affords an excellent idea of this grand work. The towers are to be 278 feet in height. The length of the great span which crosses the river is 1,600 feet and its approach on the New York side is to start from near the City Hall, and ascend in the intervening distance. The elevation of the centre of the bridge above the water will be 130 feet, and the roadway 80 feet wide. The view from this bridge will be one of the finest in the world. The structure when completed will be a grand monument to the architecture and skill of the nineteenth century, and only equalled by another enterprise founded upon as solid a foundation and destined to achieve as great results. We refer to the Brooklyn Life Insurance Co., which was incorporated in 1864 with a paid up capital of $125,000. Ten years have now elapsed and we find it to be the peoples favorite, firmly rooted with an accumulated capital of $2,500,000, proving it to be the most popular plan of life insurance known, combining to the policy-holders the advantages of a paid up cash capital, and an equitable share of such surplus as may be earned: the benefits of both the stock and the mutual systems are thus obtained, while their disadvantages are avoided.

The directors of the Brooklyn Life are men of wealth and experience—gentlemen of acknowledged repute and highly honored in our community. In their capacity as directors, their self interest as stock-holders and policy-holders compels them to a close supervision over the affairs of the company. The history of the life insurance business has fully proven that no companies are so judiciously managed, as those in which the control is vested in stock-holding directors who are personally responsible for any impairment of the necessary reserve.

This company initiated the well known and universally approved feature entitled the endorsed and guaranteed surrender-value plan. Any one of its policies has a value as definite and imperishable as gold. If the insured dies it is good to his heirs for the amount on its face, with all its dividends and additions. If the policy-holder is driven at any time by pecuniary distress to sell his policy, its value is not a problem which the actuary of the company alone can solve for him, he can find it in a moment on the policy itself, where it was written by the officers of the company when issued.

Parties owning these Policies can save them from forfeiture in the day of extreme need, by borrowing on them as collateral, or they may be used as stocks and bonds are used, as security for temporary loans

—the guarantee of the Company plainly endorsed affording evidence of their cash value. It is good at all times and anywhere for an expressed and definite value, increasing constantly during the life of the holder and at his death proving a fortune to his widow and children who might otherwise be the victims of want, debasement and misery.

Of the many plans and features devised in recent times to better the practice and popularize the extension of life insurance, this is the only one which has met with no disapproval.

Universal commendation has been accorded it by the Press, the Insurance Department, and the very best Actuaries. So striking is its justice and its desirability that for several years persistent efforts have been made in the interests of Policy-holders, to render the plan obligatory by legislative enactment upon all the life companies of New York State.

The present rates of the Brooklyn Life are deduced from American experience in life insurance, and are based upon the standard Table of Mortality adopted by the New York State Insurance Department.

The premiums for insurance in the Brooklyn Life are payable in cash exclusively. Premiums may be paid annually, or semi-annually or quarterly.

None but Eligible candidates are admitted; but when once accepted the policy-holder is treated with a fairness, friendliness and liberality which have made its members earnest, grateful and effective life insurance advocates. The policies are absolutely non-forfeitable after having attained a surrender value, and the company is always ready to pay such value in cash, or in lieu thereof, a paid-up Policy for such proportionate amount of the original Policy, as the number of annual payments really made bears to the whole number which would be required by the terms of the original Policy.

The surplus is divided yearly, on the first day of March, and is paid on all Policies at the settlement of the third annual premium, and annually thereafter if earned. Return-premiums (dividends) are paid, and due only, when the succeeding premiums are settled. If the premiums be paid quarterly, the return-premium, if taken in cash, will be paid in the same manner; if the premiums be paid semi-annually, the return-premium will be thus settled: so that the settlement of the return-premiums—when used to diminish future premiums—transpires on the date of, and in the manner of, the payment of the premiums coming due in the year of the distribution. Return premiums may be applied to diminishing succeeding premiums, or to increase the amount of insurance.

The Brooklyn Life issues policies of the following kinds: Ordinary Life; Life in one, five, ten, fifteen or twenty payments; Ordinary Joint Life and Ten-Payment Joint Life; Ordinary Endowment; Ten-Payment Endowment; and Term. We have not room to describe these different kinds of policies; full information can be obtained at the Company's office, 320 & 322 Broadway, N. Y., or of its local agents.

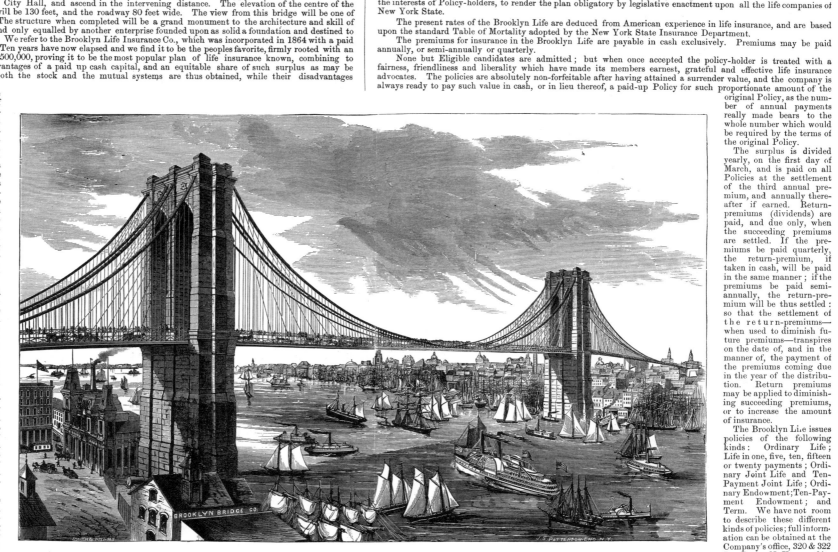

View of the BROOKLYN BRIDGE, New York.

JAMES CLAYTON'S PUMP WORKS,

BROOKLYN, N. Y.

———

The use of machine drills for boring blast holes, is now so common that we are not surprised to see a new compressor enter the field. One of these was made for Messrs. Dillon Clyde & Co., the contractors for sinking the Harlem Railroad tracks in Fourth Avenue, New York, and its manufacturer is Mr. J. Clayton, of Brooklyn. The machine comprises two horizontal steam cylinders of 18 in. diameter and 14 in. stroke, and two air cylinders of 16 in. diameter, the cranks running at right angles to each other. The designer has introduced his patent yoke motion and also his patent sliding journal box. The latter consists of a taper wedge lying along the side of a taper journal box, the latter being held in position by a standing bolt, and the former by a flange on the top of the wedge. The yoke underneath has a broad face and runs on a guide which steadies it perfectly, preventing all rocking motion. This guide is furnished with adjustable screws, so that the weight of the piston rods and yoke is carried squarely on the guide. The piston and rods are made precisely alike, and of equal weights. They are so well supported on their guides, that there is no fear of their wearing down the lower side of the cylinders.

In the heads of the compressor-cylinder are valves, which

CLAYTON'S AIR COMPRESSOR.

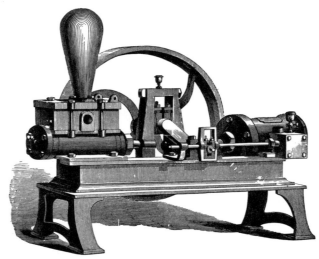

CLAYTON'S STEAM PUMP.

are a new device, admirably adapted to the purpose. The object sought in their design has been to provide a valve which should be delicate enough to open with the least pressure, so as to insure the complete filling of the compressor cylinder with the greatest pressure of free air, and they can be examined when the machine is running by taking off the outside covers. The compressor piston is packed with hemp prepared with a particular composition which Mr. Clayton will supply. It is quite effective as a lubricant, is semi-elastic, and will work without water and not cut the cylinder. This is the best and simplest packing ever invented.

Water enters the compressing cylinder at each stroke, serving to cool the air, secure lubrication and finally to fill up the free space behind the piston, thus causing the expulsion of all the air. It will be seen, therefore, that this, the latest of the compressors, adopts, like all the others, the principle of cooling the air. Though the machine takes little room, it has proved itself quite effective. One compressor can be disconnected from the other in a few minutes, so that if one should need repairs, it could be done without altogether stopping the works; in fact by running faster with one compressor in most cases there would be no delay at all.

Circulars and any other information in regard to the compressor may be obtained of J. Clayton, 14 and 16 Water St., Brooklyn, N. Y.

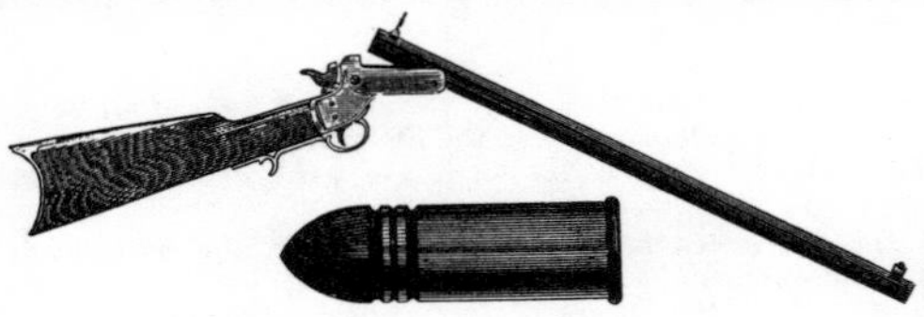

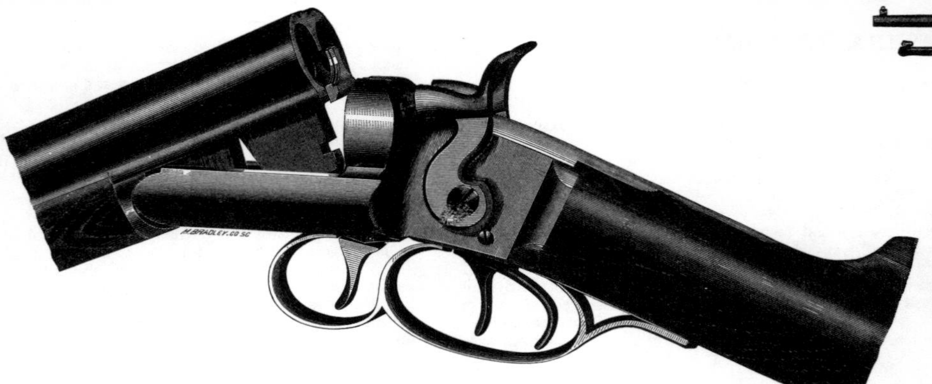

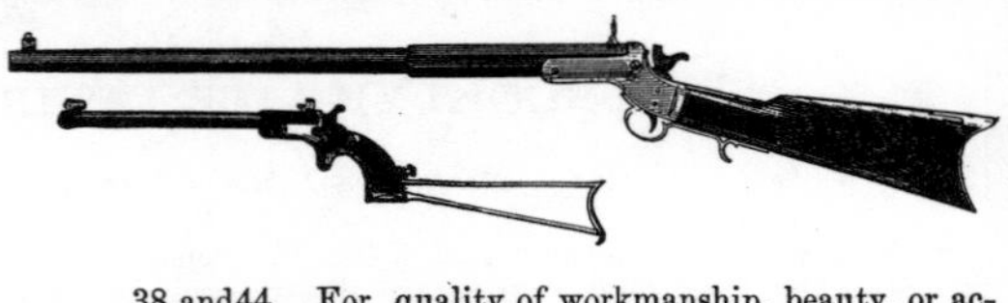

J. STEVENS & CO.,

Manufacturers of

Patent Breech-Loading Fire Arms,

Chicopee Falls, Mass., U. S. A.

——:o:——

Mr. J. Stevens, the inventor of the celebrated Stevens' Breech-Loading Fire Arms began the manufacture of Pocket Pistols at Chicopee Falls, Mass, in 1864, employing at that time but four men, associating with himself, Mr. Wm. B. Fay, both being practical workmen on fire arms of many years experience. In 1865, Mr. James E. Taylor became a partner in the concern, acting as business manager. From this time the business has rapidly increased. The Arms made by them are all breech-loading, and all (except pocket pistols) designed for sporting purposes.

In 1867, the celebrated Pocket Rifle was brought out by Mr. Stevens and soon became very popular. Orange Judd, Esq., of the *American Agriculturist* offered it as a premium to subscribers, and from 6,000 to 7,000 were sold far and near, also 40,000 pocket pistols. The Pocket Rifle (old model) is a remarkable little arm. The largest size—barrel 10 inches long, caliber 22—weighs but 11 ounces. The new model is larger and heavier than the old, and is made in sizes varying from a 10 inch barrel (the entire arm weighing 2 pounds) up to 18 inches, caliber 22 and 32.

Later they brought out the noted "Hunter's Pet" a rifle with skeleton breech, but a full size rifle barrel and the stock and breech rest made strong in proportion to the barrel; with lock, firing pin and barrel same as Sporting Rifle, suitable for large game at long range.

In 1872, they introduced a new and elegant Sporting Rifle with barrels from 24 to 32 inches long; nickel plated gun metal frame and trimmings; to work as delicately as a hair trigger; fixed ammunition, calibre 22, 32, 38 and 44. For quality of workmanship, beauty, or accurate shooting it is not surpassed.

The Sporting Rifle is also made with Centre Fire Reloading Shell, and interchangeable Shot Barrel. The owner of this combined arm has a gun adapted to all possible wants, and at reasonable cost.

They also make a Single Barrel Breech-Loading Shot Gun, operating on the same plan as the Sporting Rifle. They are made of the best materials, and for strength and beauty are not excelled. A rifle barrel is furnished to go with this gun when desired.

During the year 1876, they intend to put into the market a Double Barrel Breech-Loading Shot Gun, also a heavy rifle to shoot 1,000 yards and fully meet the requirements of the National Rifle Association.

In addition to the production of arms, etc., they are the only manufacturers of "Spring Calipers and Dividers" in this country, and make large quantities of small tools for machinists' use.

Messrs. J. Stevens & Co., in their various manufactures from the smallest to the most pretentious have established so high a standard of excellence and adhered to it so persistently, that with no other effort, their productions have obtained a wide and enviable notoriety.

Mr. Charles Folsom, of 53 Chambers Street, New York, acts as their General Agent for the United States and Europe.

RHODE ISLAND BRAIDING MACHINE CO.,

No. 89 Aborn Street, Providence, R. I.

The manufacture of Braiding Machines, for the production of worsted dress braids began in the United States in the year 1861. Previous to that time smaller Braiders for the covering of whips and hoop skirt wire, and the production of shoe and corset lacings and other small wares had been somewhat extensively made and used in New England, but the broader braids were all imported; the construction of machinery for their manufacture not being understood in this country.

In 1861, after much labor and experiment, Mr. G. K. Winchester, of Providence, R. I., one of the members of the Company above named, succeeded in developing and advancing the Braider substantially to its present effective condition. This achievement was largely the result of a happy combination of previous partial successes introduced by other parties, which, combined with important improvements of his own, supplemented by some knowledge of the English machine, a cumbrous and expensive affair not in use in this country—enabled him to construct a Braider far superior to any of foreign make, and rendering easy the establishment of another industry of considerable importance.

It is now fifteen years since Mr. H. N. Daggett, who may be called the pioneer in this branch of industry, commenced, in Attleboro', Massachusetts, operating the first machines of American make designed for the manufacture of worsted dress braids. Since the initiatory enterprise of Mr. Daggett, factories or mills for the prosecution of this line of industry have been established in various parts of the United States and Canada, though, with one or two exceptions, the business seems to prove uncongenial in localities outside of New England. The principal braid factories of the country at this time are to be found in Attleboro', Massachusetts; Providence, Pawtucket and Woonsocket, in Rhode Island; Lawrence and Lowell in Massachusetts; Hartford, Connecticut and Philadelphia, Pa. From the mills in these cities come the great bulk of all the dress and fancy braids consumed in the country; though some of the richer varieties are still imported, but even these, through the increasing skill and constant improvement in machinery will soon, doubtless, be manufactured in this country.

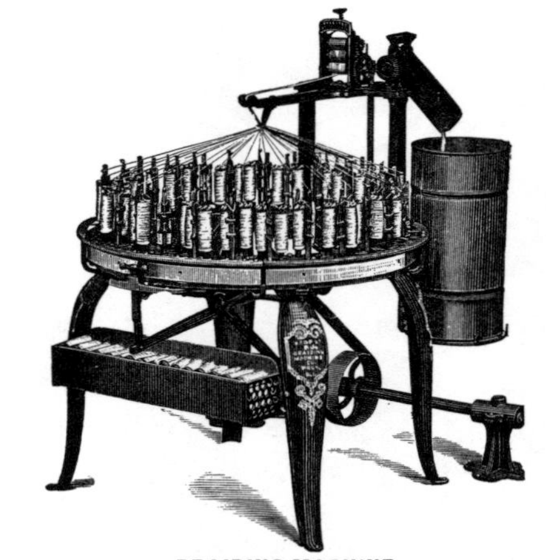

BRAIDING MACHINE.

Though the establishment and growth of the manufacture of braids in the United States may be attributable to the protection from foreign markets afforded by a high tariff, the home competition is now so sharp, and the business has attained to such proportions, that the child of fifteen years ago has well nigh attained to a state independent of parental or governmental protection necessary to the stage of infancy.

The Braiding Machine such as is shown in the accompanying engraving—a 53 strand Braider—(the great majority of all the machines in use being of this class) consumes from one and a quarter to one and a half pounds of yarn a day, (10 hours), equivalent to from two hundred to two hundred and fifty yards of braid in that time. The machines when running are usually attended by girls, sixteen, twenty, and sometimes a greater number of machines being committed to the care of a single hand, her labors being supplemented by those of the bobbin boy, the singeing machine, the dyer and the packer. Only combing wools, or those of long fibre are used in the manufacture of braids, there being certain breeds of sheep whose wool is specially suited to this purpose. Some fine varieties of braid are made from the fleece of the alpaca or Peruvian sheep, also from the hair of the Mo, or Turkish Goat—hence the names alpaca and mohair braids.

This Company, besides manufacturing every variety of machine used in the production of regular and fancy braids, are constantly constructing machines designed for use in various other departments of industry, among these are the following:

The Cocoa or Coir Braider, a machine weighing some six hundred lbs., with which the coarse Cocoa and Coir yarns are laid up into braid for mats and matting. These machines have been successfully introduced in the Coir Factories in Philadelphia, New York, Cincinnati and those in the vicinity of Boston. The Winder, a machine auxilliary to the above, which fills the bobbins evenly and compactly with the coir yarn preparatory to use upon the braider.

The Steam Packing Braider, a machine whose purpose is seen in its name is made of various sizes, capable of producing tubing from the smallest diameter to that of four inches.

The Coverer and Twister is a machine which, combining these two operations, produces a handsome silk or worsted faced picture or dress cord.

The "Hercules" Braider is a machine which produces a line or cord specially suited to clothes line or sash cord purposes, from the fact that they are free from the liability to untwist and kink incident to the use of most other lines. The product of this machine is known as the "Hercules Line."

At their spacious and convenient works in Providence, the proprietors would take pleasure in exhibiting to all interested, samples of many of these machines in operation, and are prepared to fill orders for the same with dispatch.

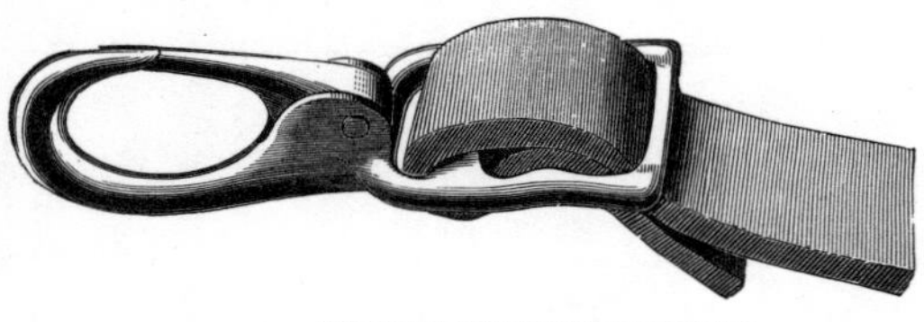

BUCKLE SNAP WITH STRAP.

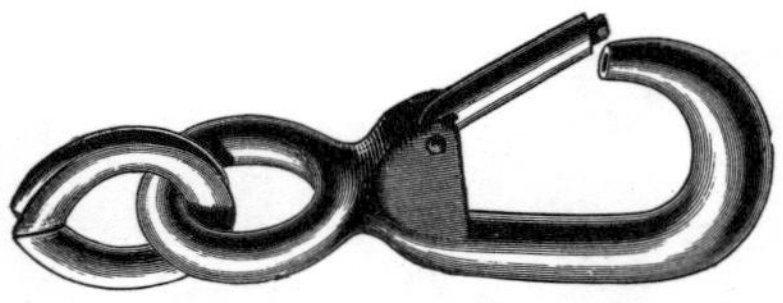

SELF MOUSING SLIP HOOK.

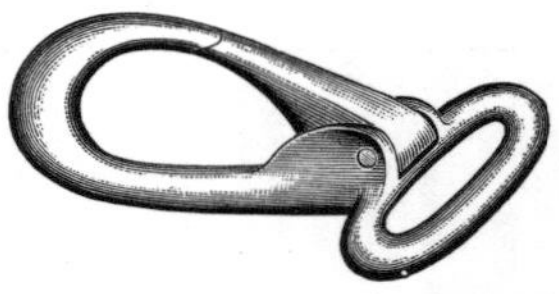

HENSHAW'S PATENT HARNESS SNAP.

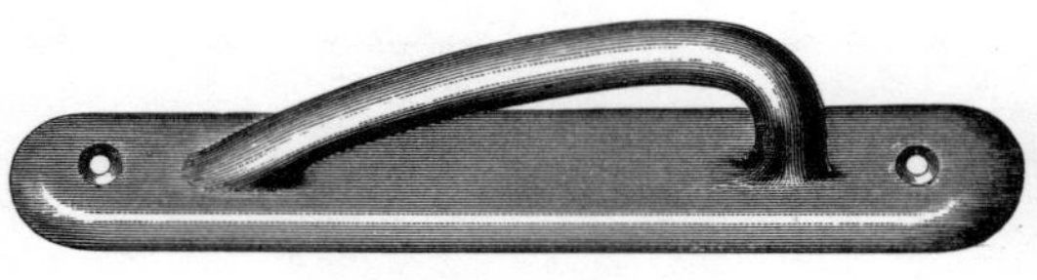

HOLDBACK IRON.

MIDDLETOWN TOOL COMPANY,

Manufacturers of

SUPERIOR PLANE IRONS,

Henshaw's Patent Harness Snaps, Patent Buckle Snaps, German Harness Snaps, Centennial Baby Snaps, Henshaw's Gaff-Topsail Self-Mousing Ship Hooks, Washer Cutters, etc.

Middletown, Conn., U. S. A.

The business now conducted by the Middletown Tool Company was founded by Mr. Austin Baldwin. The Baldwin Tool Company was formed in 1854, and established works, the ownership of which was transferred to the present corporation in 1864, who have largely increased the business and established the highest reputation for their productions. The works, tenements, etc., of the Company occupy about four acres of land in the town of Middletown. The main factory is 225 feet long and 30 feet in width, with two wings, one 25x45 feet, the other 16x20 feet. A portion of the building is but one story high, other parts are two and three stories. The manufactures of the Company embrace a wide range of goods, but lack of space prevents us from more than merely mentioning a few of their specialties:

Foremost among these are Plane Irons, their list embracing every variety and size. They use the best stock the market affords, paying the highest price, and employing first-class workmen; and claim to make the largest variety of Irons that is offered. They make special Irons on receipt of patterns or models. The constant increase in their sales in all kinds of Plane Irons furnish most gratifying proof that their efforts to make them superior to all others, both foreign and domestic, are being recognized, both at home and abroad, the Company having a considerable export trade.

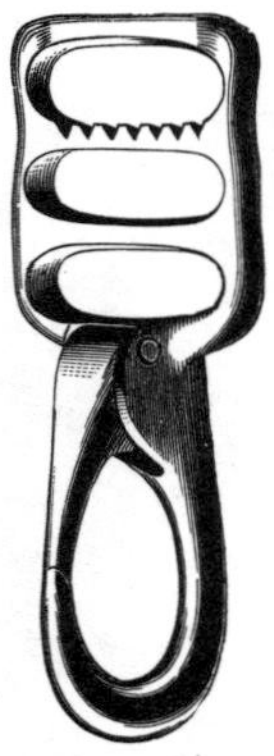

BUCKLE SNAP. Without Strap.

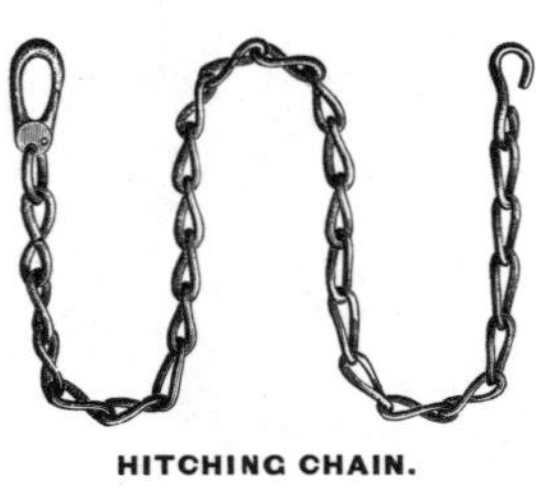

HITCHING CHAIN.

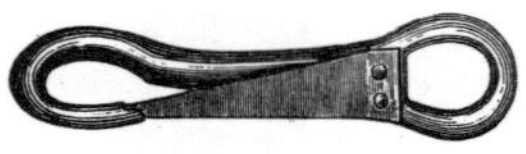

CENTENNIAL BABY SNAP.

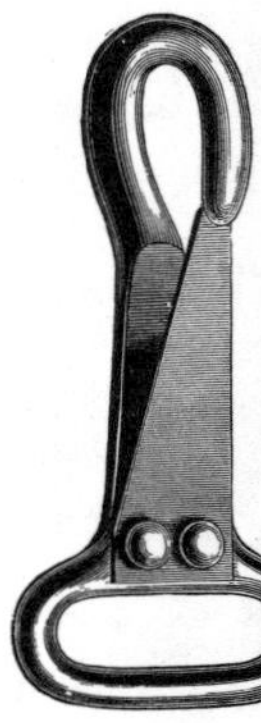

GERMAN HARNESS SNAP.

Harness Snaps.—Of these most useful little articles, they make a long line, under the names of Henshaw's Patent Harness Snaps, German Harness Snaps, etc. They have made several important changes in these Snaps, and greatly improved their patterns and methods of manufacture, so that in point of utilty, general appearance, fineness of finish and durability they cannot be excelled,

The Company have just introduced a Patent Buckle Snap for Reins, Tie Reins, Check Straps and wherever it is necessary to attach a snap to anything by buckles, rivets, or sewing. From cuts here shown it will easily be seen how readily the attachment is made, and once made it is perfectly strong and safe, and is less expensive and more convenient than the usual mode of attachment.

The "Centennial" Baby Snaps, are for dog chains, hanging bird cages, and other purposes requiring a small light snap.

Other specialties worthy of notice are their Holdback Irons, made of Malleable Iron; they are stronger and cheaper than leather, absolutely safe, and never wear out. Hitching Chains, snap and chain both tinned, and especially suitable for posts exposed to the weather. They also manufacture several kinds of Washer Cutters, and a variety of other small but useful articles which we have not room to enumerate.

J. A. BROWN & CO.,

(Established in 1858.)

Sole Manufacturers of the

Ladd Patent Stiffened Gold Watch Cases,

Adapted to the various American made Movements.

——:o:——

OFFICE: *11 Maiden Lane, New York.* FACTORY; *104 Eddy St., Providence, R. I.*

J. H. BIGELOW, Agent at New York.

——:o:——

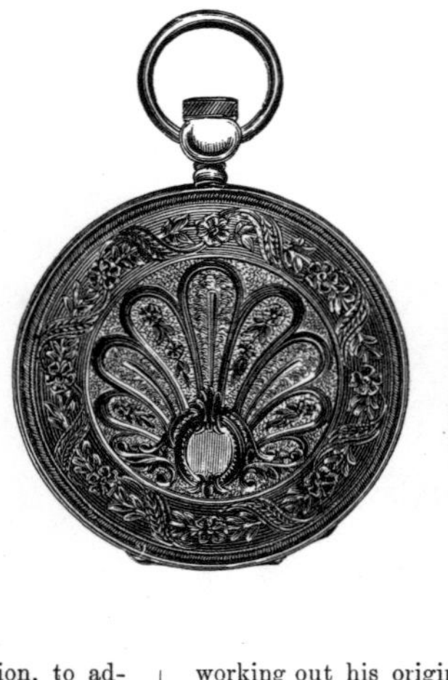

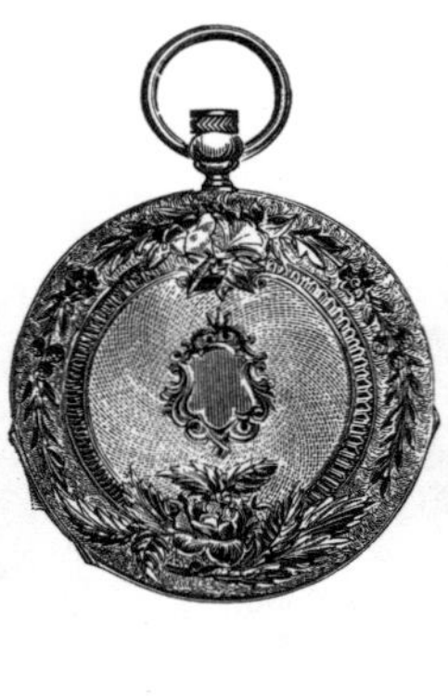

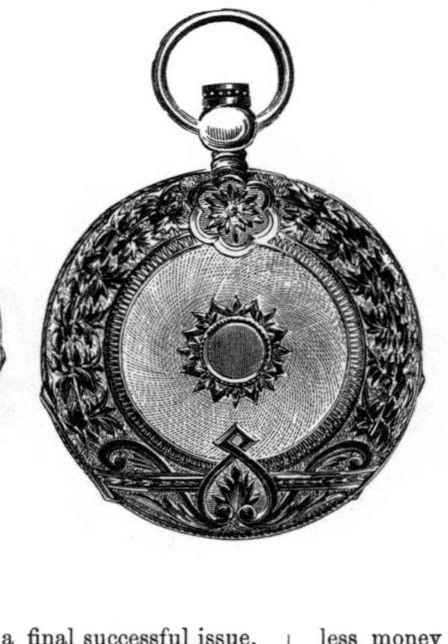

In the year 1853, Mr. George W. Ladd, a practical watchmaker of Providence, R. I., conceived the idea of, and commenced the experimental work for making a serviceable Stiffened Gold Watch Case, substantially as the Ladd Patent Case is now made, the gold on which should be of sufficient thickness to wear for a lifetime, yet the cost of which would be reduced enough, by stiffening with composition, to admit of purchase by any person of moderate means or desires—at about one-third to one-half the cost of a solid gold case.

His business demanding all his time and attention, and being without the requisite means to conduct the costly experiments necessary before success could be assured, the idea remained in abeyance (though taken up at intervals in slack business seasons) until the winter of 1864-65, when, in connection with Mr. J. A. Brown, of the same city, he began anew working out his original conception, bringing it to a final successful issue, over many and various obstacles and discouragements, early in the spring of 1867. A patent covering the method of construction was then applied for, which was granted June 11th, of that year, and a re-issue was afterwards obtained, dated May 4th, 1869, covering the article itself.

These Cases are made from thick plates of gold and nickel composition, "sweated" or soldered together, forming a solid bar of metal which is rolled to the required thickness for use. The nickel composition (forming the centre material) is like gold in the qualities of toughness and springiness, and makes the case equally as stiff and as strong as would the gold it displaces. The greatest thickness of gold is on the outside, where the wear upon a watch case is mainly felt. They are fitted with Mr. Ladd's improved spring, forged from a single piece of steel, secured without screws. They are as strongly and thoroughly built, and finished in a manner as workmanlike, as if of solid gold, and are adapted to the movements of the different American watch companies, being more than commonly uniform and accurate as to fitting. They can be procured of the watch and jewelry dealers throughout the United States and British Provinces. Full descriptive circulars will be sent on application.

Messrs. J. A. Brown & Co., were originally engaged in the manufacture of Lockets, which they made a specialty, and possessing processes peculiar to and invented by themselves, (by which a better article for less money is produced, than by other methods) they were enabled by these superior advantages to establish in the winter of 1860-61 an office in London, England, for the sale of their goods, to which they soon after added Pencil Cases. The firm are believed to be entitled to the credit of being the first exporters to England and the Continent of Europe, of American manufactures in the Jewelry line—a branch of business which has since increased to respectable dimensions.

No. 0, REGULATOR.

THE ITHACA CALENDAR CLOCK CO.,

MANUFACTORY AT

Ithaca, Tompkins County, N. Y.

—:o:—

The first calendar carried by clock machinery in America, was invented by Mr. J. H. Hawes, of Ithaca, New York, and patented in the year 1853. This calendar was imperfect, as it would not make the change of the 29th of February, in leap year. In 1854, Mr. W. H. Akins, invented an improvement on this calendar, automatic in its operations, re-adjusting itself

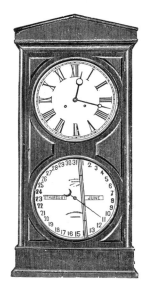

No. 3, REGULATOR.

Company was first established, and though from the first they were obliged to compete with old established and wealthy companies whose productions were favorably known, yet they have succeeded not only in introducing, but in creating a large and growing demand for their clocks in all parts of the United States, in South America and in Europe. That excellence in quality makes reputation, and that success always follows merit, are among the clearest business propositions. For accuracy of time, for reliability of calendar, for beauty of design, for cheapness and durability, the Ithaca Calendar Clock Company challenge competition.

In offering their manufactures to the public, the Ithaca Calendar Clock Company take pride in referring to the fact that where their clocks are best known they are most admired, and that they are gaining rapidly in public favor as is evidenced by the constantly increasing business of the Company, and by the very many voluntary testimonials received from jewelers and others.

No. I, REGULATOR.

costing $200 to $500 in very many jewelry establishments where economy is an object, while even in appearance, the No. 1 will compare favorably with many more expensive ones.

In response to the call of the times for progress and improvement, this Company have recently introduced a novel and beautiful style of Parlor Clock which is commanding a large sale and to the description of which they ask attention. The case is 20 inches high, of Black Walnut, with Ebony Trimmings and elaborate carvings; 5 inch Time Dial with Nickel Plated Sash, and 8 inch Glass Calendar Dial; Nickel Plated Bell, Calendar and Pendulum Rod, with Glass Ball. A small cut of this style of Parlor Clock will be found near the bottom of the centre column of this page.

The Company have also adopted at considerable expense, yet without

OFFICE OR SALESROOM CLOCK.

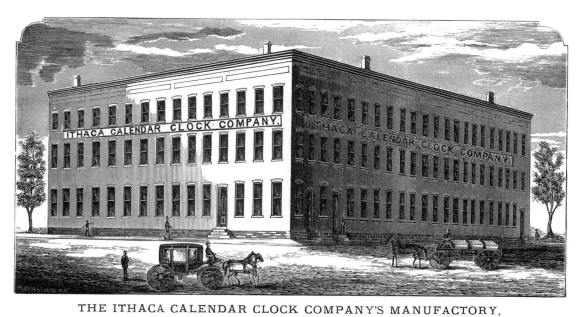

THE ITHACA CALENDAR CLOCK COMPANY'S MANUFACTORY,
Ithaca, New York, U. S. A.

HANGING LIBRARY CLOCK.

to show all the changes, including the 29th of February. This calendar was purchased by Messrs. Huntington & Platts, and was by them placed in the hands of Messrs. Mix Brothers, of Ithaca, for manufacture. Still further improvements were made by the Mix Brothers, for which patents were granted in 1860 and 1862. Messrs. Huntington & Platts continued the manufacture of large Bank Calendar Clocks for a year or two, and then disposed of their patents to the Seth Thomas Clock Company, of Connecticut.

During the years 1864 and 1865, Mr. Horton, of Ithaca, invented a new and almost perfect Perpetual Calendar, and in April, 1865, obtained his first patent, in eight distinct claims. In August, 1868, he associated a few gentlemen with himself, and organized a firm under the name of the "Ithaca Calendar Clock Company."

The Company immediately began the manufacture of Calendar Clocks under the patent of Mr. Horton. The beginning was rather modest, their factory consisting of a single room, and their capital reaching the enormous sum of $800. In a short time, however, as soon as the merits of their clocks became known, more room was needed and a larger capital required to enable them to keep pace with the demand for their productions. These wants were readily filled, and the business has since grown from year to year, until it has now become one of the largest and most favorably known in its line of productions in the United States.

Though it is but little over ten years since the Ithaca Calendar Clock

It is now admitted by all conversant with the matter, that the Calendar Clock is an article of great utility and convenience, and it is not difficult to foresee that at no very distant day it will take the place of the ordinary clock in every case where a valuable piece of furniture as well as a good time-piece is wanted. And among the very few really good Perpetual Calendars now in the market, this company claim for theirs decided superiority in essential points, among which are the following:

First. The parts, by means of which the changes are made, are held securely fast at all times—the changes being made instantaneously, leaving no appreciable time during which the parts can be displaced by jar or touch.

Second. The time movement is never in any sensible degree taxed or

PARLOR CLOCK.

drawn upon by the calendar, the force required to make the changes being so slight that the power of an ordinary watch would be sufficient for the purpose. This essential point has been gained by distributing the labor through a period of eighteen hours, and by the use of simple mechanical devices for diminishing the amount of labor to be performed.

This Company use none but fine thirty day and eight day time movements which they guarantee to perform with more than ordinary exactitude and to fill every reasonable requirement. They invite particular attention to the very fine eight day Regulator Movement used in Nos. 1, 2 and 3, which is sufficiently close as a time-keeper to answer in place of a Regulator

advance in price, the use of Nickel Plated Sash in place of the ordinary brass, on all their clocks on which brass sash have been used hitherto. This improvement combines beauty with utility in a high degree, it being well known that nickel plate will not tarnish like the ordinary brass finish, and it is readily cleaned when spotted by exposure to flies, etc.

The Ithaca Calendar Clock Company, believe themselves authorized to claim priority in the use of Nickel Plated Sash and Matting in the regular manufacture of clocks, and they feel satisfied that the trade and the public will appreciate the value of this novelty.

The assortment of cases consists of eleven different styles, which are adapted for use in dwellings, offices, stores, banks, insurance offices—in short, wherever a record of time is desirable.

To insure the perfection of the Calendar, they have devised and patented a machine by which they test every Calendar before offering it for sale, by running it by steam power equivalent to a period of eight years, the daily change being made once in five seconds.

The manufactures of this Company are protected by the re-issue of the original Akins & Burritt patent, dated Nov. 2d, 1860, for twenty-one years from Sept. 19th, 1854, and by the two patents of H. B. Horton, dated April 18th, 1865, and August 28th, 1866, comprising in all twenty patent claims on the calendar machine alone; and also by the patent of H. B. Horton and M. L. Wood, for testing and proving Calendar Clocks by power, dated 11th June, 1867, and by the patent of H. B. Horton, for Swinging Pendulum Rod in front of dial, dated Jan. 4, 1870.

OFFICE CLOCK.

OCTAGON.

CONTINENTAL LIFE INSURANCE COMPANY OF NEW YORK.

The offices of this Company are in the Continental Building, at Nos. 22, 24, and 26 Nassau Street, New York. See cut above.

They have issued in all 61,800 policies. In 1873, they issued 7,220 policies, insuring to the amount of $13,864,762. The officers are:—L. W. Frost, President. M. B. Wynkoop, Vice-President. J. P. Rogers, Secretary, S. C. Chandler, Jr., Actuary. E. Herrick, M. D., Medical Examiner. Whitney & Betts, Counsel.

MARCHALL & SMITH'S PIANO FORTES.

These Pianos combine every improvement in tone, touch, power and beauty, and have everywhere won for themselves a reputation for unrivalled excellence and durability. They are all large size, 7 1-3 octaves, with overstrung bass, full iron frames, French grand action, fret desk, carved pedal, solid rosewood mouldings, ivory key fronts, capped hammers, agraffe treble, and have every modern improvement.

The Marchall and Smith Pianoforte Company, have a world-wide reputation for making a first class piano, equal in tone and finish to any manufactured in the country.

BELVEDERE HOUSE,
Cor. Irving Place and Fifteenth Street, N. Y.

This popular hotel is situated on the corner of Fifteenth Street and Irving Place, where Mr. Jos. Wehrle, the proprietor, has made extensive improvements for accommodation of his guests.

It is a deservedly popular house, especially among artists in the musical profession. Parties desiring a home in the metropolis will find this hotel convenient to places of amusement, and near some half dozen lines of street cars and omnibuses.

SCIENCE AND ART.

Marion and its Temple of Labor.

While the world-traveled stranger is being whirled out of Jersey City, just beyond the western verge of that expanding hive of industry, the first object of beauty that strikes his eye is a vast but airy structure, chiefly of glass and iron, lifting its chaste proportions from a garden lawn of several acres.

It seems as it built for a colossal conservatory, or a summer palace for a prince of fairy tale; which it were our traveler could not guess. But what would be his astonishment if told that this structure of such wondrous beauty, held six hundred artisans of both sexes, moving intelligently among nearly as many curious and tireless machines, doing the work of one hundred thousand human hands, and that there were sent from this scene of enchanted labor a quarter of a thousand perfect watches in silver, and gold, and precious stones, every twenty-four hours. The first thought of our traveler would be about horology in former ages, and American watches made by perfected machinery in 1874.

The difficulties which attended the final establishment of a fixed standard of time are inconceivable in our day, just as the importance of accurate time-keeping is incalculable. Without a reliable measure of time there could be no union of action among men. The vast net-work of railways, steam lines and telegraphs, which are now making a brotherhood of men in business and feeling, would beget nothing but inconceivable disaster. Nor could the triumphs of modern science over the stubborn forces of nature on earth, or in the stellar universe, have been won. And yet man began his observations and experiments in this unknown field without a single ascertained landmark, wholly unconscious even of the period when he commenced his own existence—with no idea of time, or natural or mechanical means

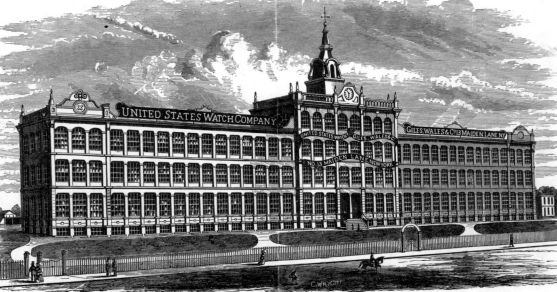

MANUFACTORY OF THE UNITED STATES WATCH COMPANY.

near approach to perfection. Scores of these watches will follow their wearers around the sun—a circuit of over four hundred million miles—and not make a variation of five seconds; while on the same long journey the magnet may vary a million of times. Never did a devout Heathen or an illuminated Christian, worship so unwaveringly his idol or his God.

The extraordinary record of these Watches as the time-keepers in the pockets of the American public, including many of the leading men of our country, R. R. Engineers, Cunductors, Expressmen, and others whose occupation renders it absolutely necessary they should have the most accurate time, speaks volumes.

It has remained for this Company to supply two serious wants, long felt by both dealer and consumer, but which have heretofore been unattained. One of these is a Patent Reversible Barrel, to prevent damage to the train in case of breaking the mainspring. This (which they now put in all of their watches) is quite an ingenious contrivance, extremely simple, and so arranged that it is always free and ready to act, even though the watch may have run for years, unlike other appliances for similar purposes, which, after the watch has been wound a few times, become set and entirely useless, so far as accomplishing the purpose intended. The other is a Patent Double Index Regulator, beautiful in design and finish, while in novelty of construction and the results obtained, it is a little Wonder, and we are sure will be hailed with delight, not only by watch wearers, who appreciate fine time, but by the seller, who with the old style of regulator, is often exceedingly annoyed (even with watches that are otherwise fine), and, in fact, is often unable, after repeated trials and consuming much time, to touch the regulator fine enough for a small variation, getting it first too far one way, and then to far the other, backwards and forwards, sometimes for months.

for fixing its beginning, or measuring its flight. He had to make an alphabet from the sun, moon and stars, and create a language, harmonious and universal, by which to read, arrest and fix the hurrying movements of the whole physical creation.

Shepherds watching the stars, five thousand years ago, on the plains of Chaldea, traced imaginary forms in the sky, and named them after the animals in their various herds, and, by the aid of the hand and the stars, fixed the first rude measure of time. Then came the noon-mark, and the dial and the flowing tide of sand or water; and finally, at the close of the tenth century, the discovery of the balance clock with weights, and eight hundred years later the improved pendulum clock, and the balance spring clock, or watch for the pocket. The mechanical principle of time-keeping consists of the uniform division of a constant force in a given time, so that a vibratory or reciprocating movement is continually changed into rotary motion. The agent for doing this is called an escapement, and when this delicate point was reached the great invention was made.

There could be only one thing lacking, and that, like so many things, was to be achieved by American genius—viz: making watches by machinery. England, France and Switzerland chiefly supplied the world with watches until the American discovery. Since 1812 we imported up to last year probably over $300,000,000 worth, nine-tenths worthless as time-keepers and costing more than the original outlay in trying to make them go in some sort of correspondence with the motions of the solar system.

The American Watch is an absolute triumph of science and art. A thousand from the same model could be distinguished from each other only by the number. Being made with the precision of unvarying machinery, perfect uniformity is secured, and if the first is made right, all the rest must be.

This grand result—this new miracle—is performed nearly a hundred thousand fresh times every year in that fairy Palace of Labor in Marion. Hitherto the magnetic needle has been considered the only perfect type of unchangeable fidelity. But we must give up the comparison, for the variations of the magnet are endless. Its main fidelity is towards the North Star. But it yields to so many other attractions that, if followed implicity, it would sweep all navigation from ocean. But the Creator's latest and grandest work is the genius of man, which atones for the otherwise imperfect reliability of the magnet. The Marion pocket watch seems to us a

This house makes a specialty of Stem Winders, for which they own patents, and the mechanism of which, for simplicity, durability, strength and smoothness of action, excels anything yet produced, either at home or abroad, and is becoming quite a feature in the trade—so much so that prominent dealers predict that in less than five years there will be none but stem-winding watches sold. This Company, we observe, has taken the front rank among American manufacturers. At the first Fairs held in different parts of the country, where there has been great competition in this line, the Marion (Giles, Wales & Co.) United States Watches have been regarded as greatly superior in every particular to any on exhibition, and have been awarded the first premiums, over all competitors, at a Fair of Cincinnati Industrial Exposition, Ohio; Ohio Mechanics' Institute, Cincinnati, Ohio; at "Louisiana State Fair," New Orleans, La.; at "Texas State Fair," Houston, Texas, 1871; at New Jersey State Fair, 1872, and Iowa State Fair, 1872.

In conclusion we will introduce the individual members of this model Establishment, that our readers may appreciate the skill, perseverance and manly qualities possessed in so large a degree by each individual Member as a Citizen.

Mr. Giles, being left an orphan at the age of eight years, and being the oldest male member of a family of seven children, it became incumbent on him, with his eldest sister, to provide for and superintend the education of the rest. Feeling his responsibilities as a son and a brother, he determined on learning the manufacturing of watch-work, with the idea, at some future day, of controlling the destinies of a watch manufactory. The manufactory, now completed, stands to-day a monument to the skill and determination of its worthy head.

W. A. Wales, Esq., is a gentleman who, once met, is not easily forgotten. Having experienced all the disadvantages possible in his early efforts to rise, he is always ready to cheer and encourage the young man, striving to win himself position.

In G. C. F. Wright, Esq., the junior member of the firm, we find all the elements of the true business man. Bold and determined in the prosecution of trade, genial, generous and decided in character, he has won for himself a host of friends, both in active and private life.

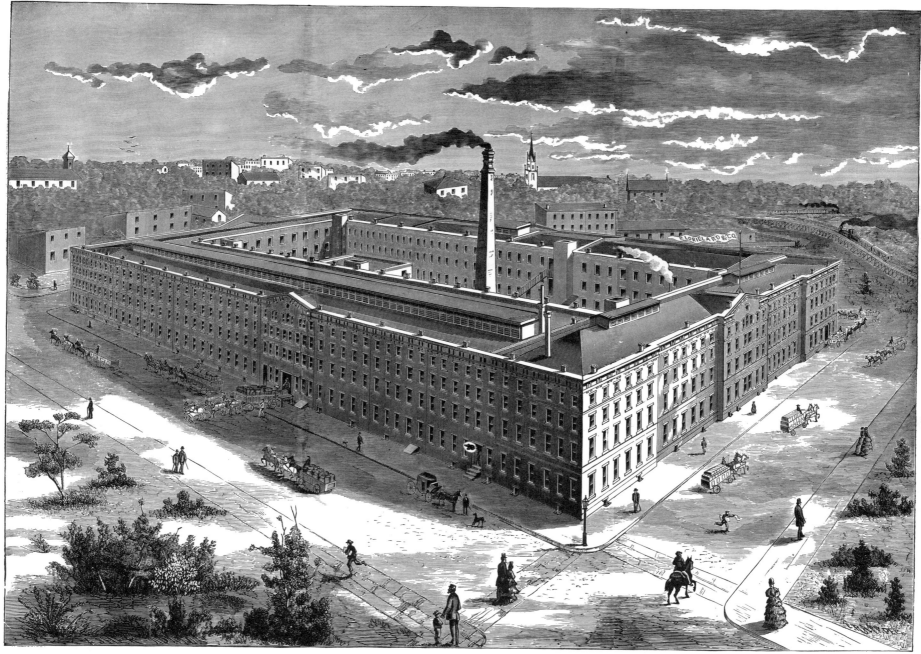

BIRDS-EYE VIEW OF P. LORILLARD & CO.'S TOBACCO MANUFACTORY, JERSEY CITY, N. J.

P. LORILLARD & CO.,

Manufacturers of

SMOKING AND CHEWING TOBACCOS, AND

SNUFF,

16, 18 and 20 Chambers Street, New York.

——:o:——

Factory, Jersey City, N. J.

——:o:——

It is not within the province of this work to give a detailed history of the discovery and introduction of tobacco, nor yet to enter into argument as to its harmlessness but a brief sketch of its introduction and a reference to the manner of its reception when first introduced to the civilized nations of Europe will not be out of place.

All users of the "weed" are aware that it is an "original" American production, and that long before the existence of the United States was thought of it was introduced into Europe by the discoverers and explorers of the New World. The term "Tobacco" did not originally apply to the plant, but to the pipe in which it was smoked; for want of a better name the Spaniards adopted it for the weed itself. Some derive the word from *Tobaco*, a province of Yucatan, where it is said to have been first found by the Spaniards; others from the Island of Tobago, one of the Caribbees. But these derivations are very doubtful. The botanical name, *Nicotina*, was given to it in honor of Jean Nicot, of Nismes, in Lanquedoc, who as an agent of the King of France, in Portugal, procured seeds of the plant from a Dutchman who had obtained them in Florida, and transmitted them to his sovereign in the year 1560.

The discoverers of America introduced the habit of smoking into Spain and Portugal, from whence it spread to other parts of the Continent, and though a very expensive one, soon became a very common habit. Columbus found the natives of Hispaniola smoking a plant "the perfume of which was fragrant and grateful," which from the earliest ages had been offered as incense to their gods, and the first English colonists to America found that pipes and tobacco held an important place in all transactions with the Indians.

The colony which Sir Walter Raleigh sent to Virginia, returned to the mother country in 1586, and introduced the habit into England. Hariot, the historian of that expedition carefully observed the culture of tobacco, and its effects upon those who used it, and after personal experiment, became a firm believer in its medicinal and healing virtues. Raleigh described it as "Rest to the weary, to the hungry, food."

Before the successful establishment of the Virginia Colony in the year 1606, the tobacco imported into England was procured through Spaniards, from the West India Islands. Its use by the masses of the people in England encountered great opposition. King James called it a "precious stink," and in the year 1604, without the consent of

Parliament, he raised the duty from two pence to six shillings and ten pence a pound. In the communication on this occasion addressed to the Lord Treasurer, he said, that: "Tobacco being a drug of late years found out, and brought from foreign parts in small quantities, was taken and used by the better sort, both then and now only as physic to preserve health; but that persons of mean condition now consumed their wages and time in smoking tobacco, to their great injury and the general corruption." Its cultivation was forbidden in England, and plants then growing were ordered to be torn up. Burton speaks of tobacco in mingled praise and condemnation, calling it "divine, rare, super-excellent tobacco, which goes far beyond all their panaceas, potable gold, philosophers stones—a sovereign remedy to all diseases," if "opportunely taken," but in the same paragraph he says that when abused by men who "take it as tinkers do ale, 'tis a plague, a mischief, * * * the ruin and overthrow of body and soul."

But kingly censure, and the writings of learned men who pointed out the harm that might arise from its too common use, seemed only to bring tobacco into higher favor and more general use.

The large amount of capital employed in the cultivation and manufacture of tobacco, and the untold millions of pounds consumed in all parts of the world, clearly indicates that it is profitable to the producer and a source of pleasure to the consumer. And though it has been condemned as unhealthy and immoral, the force of the arguments against it always ends in *smoke*. A greater number of learned men have spoken in its favor than have condemned it, and the great masses of the people in all parts of the world are habitual users of it, which is by far the most practical endorsement.

Lord Bacon may or may not have written Shakespeare, but he certainly did write "Tobacco comforteth the spirits and dischargeth weariness, which it worketh partly by opening but chiefly by the opiate virtue which condenseth the spirits." In reference to the universality of its use. Byron speaks of the "short frail pipe," which "puffed where'er winds rise or waters roll," and "wafted smoke from Portsmouth to the pole."—And apostrophises "sublime Tobacco," as "divine in hookas, glorious in a pipe."

Few persons not engaged in the tobacco business have a just conception of its importance in a commercial or industrial point of view. While tobacco is raised to some extent in almost every country, the United States is by far the largest producer, a large proportion of what is consumed in Europe being grown in this country. The colonists of Virginia, in the year 1815, seem to have become "Tobacco mad," and Bancroft tells us that—"The fields, the gardens, the public squares and even the streets of Jamestown were planted with tobacco," and "it eventually became not only the staple but the currency of the colony. From the earliest settlement of Virginia, therefore, tobacco has been a very important article in the agricultural and commercial interests of the country. In the early days the culture of tobacco was confined almost entirely to Virginia, but was soon diffused over other portions of the South, where it exclusively remained until quite recently. Now, however, it is largely grown for the general market in many of the Northern States, notably Con-

necticut and Massachusetts, and is raised to some extent in every State in the Union. The average tobacco crop of the United States for several years has been, in round numbers, 275,000,000 pounds, valued at $33,000,000. In the year 1871, there was exported from this country 185,748,881 pounds of leaf tobacco, 365,000 cigars, 20,181 pounds of snuff, and other manufactured tobacco, to the total value of $22,705,225. In 1870, there was exported from the United States to England and the British possessions 54,433,695 pounds of tobacco, 84,000 cigars and 12,670 pounds of snuff. The City of Bremen was supplied with 41,977,412 pounds of tobacco; Italy with 27,629,871 pounds, and France 24,387,339 pounds.

These figures will enable the reader to form an idea of the gigantic proportions which the culture and manufacture of tobacco has assumed,—millions of acres are devoted to its culture, and millions of hands are employed in its manufacture. The commercial intercourse created by the demand for it, employs a large shipping interest, and the home trade of the countries to which we export it gives employment to myriads of men, women and children.

There is no name connected with the tobacco business, more widely or more favorably known than that of Lorillard; and widely known because identified with the trade longer, we believe, than any other in this country, and favorably, because from the beginning it has always been attached to goods of the finest quality and has never been identified with inferior articles.

In 1760 Pierre Lorillard a French Huguenot, commenced business in a modest way on what was then known as the High Road to Boston,—Chatham street, near Tryon row. The venture was a successful one, and the founder of the house which has since become so famous, did a thriving trade and grew in riches. After the death of Pierre Lorillard the business was continued by his widow, who eventually bequeathed it to her sons Peter and George, who conducted it until 1832 when George died, and Peter continued it alone until he gave it up to his son, another Peter, who carried it on for about thirty years when he relinquished it to his eldest sons Peter Jr., and George L. Lorillard. During all these years the business had steadily grown and the fame of the house had spread all over the civilized world. Each succeeding generation felt a pride in the good name earned by its predecessors, and was anxious not only to maintain the ancient prestige, but to add to it.

In 1868 George L. Lorillard retired from the firm; Charles Siedler was admitted as a partner under the name of P. Lorillard, and in 1870 the first name was changed to P. Lorillard & Co.

Of Plug Tobacco alone this firm produced about 5,000,000 pounds in 1874, while of Fine Cut Tobacco, Smoking Tobacco and Snuff, they sold nearly 5,000,000 pounds more.

Their trade is constantly growing in volume, and as their goods are not the lowest in price, is it not ample proof that quality will tell, and that every manufacturer should adopt their motto, "to excel and not to undersell."

The Internal Revenue Taxes paid the United States Government by P. Lorillard & Co., amounts to about $2,000,000 per annum, and is the best proof of the popularity of their goods.

STEINWAY & SONS,
Piano Manufacturers.
New York.

We have the evidence of modern refinement on every hand. The luxuries of a wealthy age are the unmistakeable signs by which the rapid march of civilization is marked. From the days in the history of our country when the Pilgrim fathers first landed in New England, or the early Dutch settlers on Manhattan Island, down to the present period there has been one continuous onward and progressive movement which has impelled the people of this great country towards those ever ripening harvest fields which commerce, labor, art, science, capital and culture have prepared for the present and future generations. In the workshops, in the places of amusement and even in the sacred edifices, the growth of refinement is everywhere visible in our midst.

The cultivation of the most refined taste naturally creates a desire for a supply of those enjoyments upon which such tastes depend and on which they are fed. The keen intelligence displayed by many of

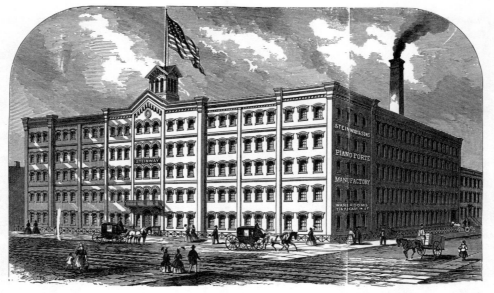

STEINWAY & SONS, PIANO FORTE MANUFACTORY.

STEINWAY GRAND PIANO.

STEINWAY UPRIGHT PIANO.

STEINWAY SQUARE PIANO.

those who have been led to make this their adopted country, has led them to cater for and satisfactorily supply these yearnings of refinement; and foremost among these, in the race of energy, enterprise and inventive skill are the Messrs. Steinway & Sons, of New York.

Since they began business—about twenty-one years ago, they have manufactured and sold thirty thousand pianos, which are distributed all over the world: some are delighting Imperial ears in Russia, some are heard in the palaces of Queen Victoria, in the saloons of Ex-Queen Isabella of Spain, and of those of the high aristocracy of Paris, Berlin and Vienna, they are found in the far inland depths of Asiatic Russia and British India; they are seen at the exhibition of models for study and example at Stuttgart; they are used as the best instrument by the greatest scientist of the age, Professor Helmholz at the Berlin University. The parlors of the best American families number them as their choicest ornaments; they are heard in the studios of the most renowned artists at home and abroad; they are used in public, whenever accessible by Franz Liszt, Rubinstein, Kullak, Henselt, Jaell, Marmontel, Mesdames Krebs, Mehlig, and Essipoff—but best of all they are to be found in twenty-five thousand homes of the people of America.

The Messrs. Steinway have earned and achieved their brilliantly unexampled success by first aiming at perfection in their Art and then by untiring energy, patient study and persevering skill in accomplishing it. From the outset they marked out a path for themselves and have steadily adhered to it; they aimed at an enduring reputation by the perfection of their instruments and their lasting quality which has stood the test and trial of any and every climate. Other manufacturers have made a profession of cheapness, the main inducement to purchasers and have paid little regard to the excellence of their workmanship or to the proper and enduring qualities of the materials used, whilst Messrs. Steinway & Sons, guided by finer perceptions and truer principles, have preferred to make their pianos lasting monuments of perfect artistic merit, rather then valueless articles which in a short time disgrace their makers and disappoint their owners. Mark the result of this foresight, they now make and sell more pianos, than almost all the other New York manufacturers combined and their factory is not only the largest, but the most complete in the world.

In the limited space at our disposal we cannot at length describe their elegant building in Fourteenth Street, widely known as Steinway Hall or their mammoth factory which is immense in its proportions; but must confine ourselves to such other facts in the history of the firm which we deem of interest to our readers.

Steinway & Sons made their first pianos in America in 1853, but being entirely unknown in the trade, they gained but little reputation as manufacturers, until 1855 when they placed one of their best instruments in the New York Crystal Palace exhibition. The result of this, their first effort to popularize their pianos may be learned from the following extract from the report on musical instruments. A member of the musical jury says, "They were pursuing their rounds, and performing their duties with an ease and facility that promised a speedy termination to their labors, when suddenly they came upon an instrument that, from its external appearance,—solidly rich, yet free from the frippery that was then rather in fashion,—attracted their attention. One of the company opened the case, and carelessly struck a few chords. The others were doing the same with its neighbors, but somehow they ceased to chatter when the other instrument began to speak. One by one the jurors gathered round the strange polyphonist, and, without a word being spoken, every one knew that it was the best pianoforte in the exhibition. The jurors were true to their duties. It is possible that some of them had predilections in favor of other makers; it is certain that one of them had—the writer of the present notice. But when the time for the award came, there was no argument, no discussion, no bare presentment of minor claims; nothing in fact, but a hearty indorsement of the singular merits of the strange instrument."

The reputation of the Steinway piano being thus fully established, the progress of the business of the firm from that time has been very rapid.

From the year 1855 to 1862 the Messrs. Steinway received no less than thirty-five first premiums (Gold and Silver Medals,) at the principal Fairs in this country and in addition thereto were awarded a First Prize Medal at the International Exhibition at London in 1862 in competition with two hundred and sixty-nine pianos from all parts of the civilized world, and as stated in the report of the Jury for powerful, clear, brilliant and sympathetic tone with excellence of workmanship as shown in Grand and Square Pianos. Their crowning triumph was however achieved at the Universal Exposition at Paris in 1867 where—by the unanimous verdict of the International Jury, Steinway & Sons were awarded the First of the Grand Gold Medals of Honor for the greatest excellence in all three styles exhibited namely: Grand, Square and Upright Pianos. The official report of the International Jury on Musical instruments at the Paris Exposition, says, as follows:

"The Pianos of Messrs. Steinway & Sons are equally endowed with the splendid sonority of the instruments of their competitor; they also possess that seizing large-

ness and volume of tone, hitherto unknown, which fills the greatest space. Brilliant in the treble, singing in the middle, and formidable in the bass, this sonority acts with irresistible power on the organs of hearing. In regard to expression, delicate shading, variety of accentuation, the instruments of Messrs. Steinway have over those of their American competitors an advantage which cannot be contested. The blow of the hammer is heard much less, and the pianist feels under his hands an action subtle and easy, which permits him at will to be powerful or light, vehement or graceful."

"These Pianos are at the same time the instrument of the virtuoso who wishes to astonish by the eclat of his execution, and of the artist who applies his talent to the music of thought and sentiment, bequeathed to us by the illustrious masters—in one word, they are at the same time the Pianos for the concert-room and the parlor, possessing an unexceptional sonority."

Though Messrs. Steinway did not exhibit at the Vienna Exposition in 1873 owing to the unsatisfactory state of the Austrian patent laws, the Jury unanimously adopted and signed the following

STEINWAY GRAND PIANO.

STEINWAY UPRIGHT PIANO.

STEINWAY SQUARE PIANO.

flattering resolution:

"It is much to be deplored that the celebrated inaugurators of the new system in Piano-making, Messrs Steinway & Sons, of New York, to whom the entire art of Piano-making is so greatly indebted, have not exhibited."

In conclusion we have the pleasure to submit to our readers an unsolicited communication received from one of the greatest pianists of the age regarding the Steinway Pianos.

New York, May 24, 1873. Messrs. Steinway & Sons. Gentlemen,—On the eve of returning to Europe, I deem it my pleasant duty to express to you my most heartfelt thanks for all the kindness and courtesy you have shown me during my stay in the United States; but, also, and above all, for your unrivalled Piano-fortes, which once more have done full justice to their world-wide reputation, both for excellence and capacity of enduring the severest trials, for during all my long and difficult journeys all over America, in a very inclement season, I used and have been enabled to use your pianos exclusively in my 215 concerts, and also in private, with the most eminent satisfaction and effect. Yours very truly,
ANTON RUBINSTEIN.

STEINWAY & SONS, PIANO WAREROOMS,
Steinway Hall, New York.

Dixon's Patent Crucible Turning Machine, Making 400 Crucibles per day, with two unskilled hands.

Dixon's Stove Polish Labeling Room, 150 Feet in Length.

Dixon's Pencil Machine, Finishing 132 Per Minute.

PENCILS, CRUCIBLES, STOVE POLISH,

Represented by

The JOSEPH DIXON CRUCIBLE COMPANY,

ORESTES CLEVELAND, President,

JERSEY CITY, N. J.

Previous to 1827 the Graphite Crucibles used in the United States were made at Obernzell, Bavaria, and imported through Rotterdam; hence they were called Dutch pots. In that year the late Mr. Joseph Dixon, then a machinist and worker in metals in Salem, Mass., becoming dissatisfied with the want of reliability in the Bavarian Crucibles, which would run with great care but four or five meltings, undertook to produce crucibles that could be used with more safety. He experimented with the Graphite found in the State of New Hampshire, and in October produced Crucibles much superior to the imported, being less liable to crack and able to stand many many more meltings. About 1830 he procured the first shipment of Graphite or Plumbago, as it was called in commerce, ever sent from the Island of Ceylon to the United States. His success in using it gave character to the Ceylon Graphite, and during the succeeding forty-five years the world was supplied with foliated graphite from that source. Mr. Dixon removed to Jersey City and established himself in the manufacture of crucibles of a quality that soon drove the foreign article entirely out of the American market. Twenty years afterwards their fame spread abroad and an agency for the sale of them was undertaken by Morgan & Reese in London. The success was such that in 1854 Morgan proposed to start the manufacture there in order to save the freight. Mr. Dixon sent out a workman to give instructions, and the present Battersea works, were thus started. In the meantime the works at Jersey City were steadily gaining, the manufacture of the now celebrated "Dixon's Stove Polish" having been added as a regular branch. In 1858 the Hon. Orestes Cleveland purchased the interest of Mr. Dixon's partner and undertook the management of the business, under the firm name of Joseph Dixon & Co. From that moment the business started up and the firm soon became prominent in trade as the largest dealers in, and consumers of, Graphite in the world, which position the house has maintained to the present time.

The "Dixon" Crucibles have a world-wide reputation. They are made the capacity of one pound to that of six hundred pounds of melted metal. Special shapes for melting, and retorts and chemical ware, are made to order. In the Stove Polish department the sale is enormous, amounting to about *six millions of packages per annum.* A specialty is made of the fine grades of Graphite for electrotyping, lubricating, paint, and for a thousand other uses, and the Graphite is prepared for the Trade for all purposes, making the Company really the head-quarters for Graphite in this country. To accomplish this result the Dixon Company purchased the extensive mining property, mills and water power at Ticonderoga in the State of New York, of the American Graphite Company, producing the finest Graphite in the world, not excepting the celebrated Alibert Mine in Siberia. It was the extraordinary quality of the Ticonderoga Graphite that led the Hon. Orestes Cleveland, President of the Dixon Company, to take up the manufacture of fine pencils, in which, after many years of patience, perseverance and outlay, he has been successful. He has produced the very finest grades of pencils, manufactured entirely by machinery, more perfect in style and finish, with leads more uniform and lasting, and of a greater strength and smoothness than attained by any other pencil maker.

The Company has prize medals from all the great exhibitions in different parts of the world, more than fifty in number. The one at Vienna in 1873, granted a Medal for the Dixon Crucibles, one for Electrotyping Graphite, and the Grand "Medal for Progress" to Dixon's American Graphite Pencils, over all the European makers. These pencils have been in the market less than two years, and have already taken their position at the head of the trade. This is perhaps partly due to the fact that the Dixon Company are the only pencil makers in the world who have Graphite mines of their own, and partly to the fact that Mr. Cleveland has made Graphite a study, and is perhaps the only real expert in the whole trade, in the examination and selection of the different grades and varieties of natural Graphite. He is preparing a complete and exhaustive work on Graphite and its uses, to be published at an early day, from the manuscript of which the articles "Graphite" and "Pencil," in Knight's Mechanical Dictionary were taken. The Dixon Company may be said to be the founders of the trade in this country, and now stand at the Head of the Graphite industry of the World.

The Company has a capital of $750,000, and the works are very extensive, fronting on Railroad Avenue, Putnam and Wayne Streets, Jersey City, driven by two large engines; also a mill at Ticonderoga, 90 feet square and six stories high, driven by a water wheel of 100 horse power. At the Ticonderoga Mill the very fine grades are produced, by wet grinding, some grades bringing a very high price, that for photographers selling at $7.50 to $10.00 per pound, and it has been retailed at one dollar per ounce, the price of pure silver.

These fine grades are produced by great labor, and exhaustive manipulations in purifying. The Graphite is reduced in water to an impalpable powder, and brought to a white heat several times in the course of its subsequent treatment, until at last it makes a point that shows less than one-thirtieth of one per cent of impurity, and leaves the least perceptible ash.

In the pencil department, Mr. Cleveland has substituted most ingenious automatic machines for hand labor, and it is worth a visit to the works to see beautifully finished pencils leave a machine at the rate of 132 per minute.

We have been "through" Dixon's plumbago mill, and a great black, noisy, bewildering place it is. You go from one building to another, up stairs here and down yonder, coming out first on Railroad Avenue, then on Putnam Street, and then again on Wayne Street, till a stranger would be utterly unable to find his way back to the office without a pilot. The works have been in operation nearly half a century, and the business transactions reach nearly all parts of the civilized world.

From the offices of the Company on Railroad Avenue, we enter the crucible turning shop, 140 feet long, on Putnam Street; one side is devoted to the operation of "turning," while the other is filled, from floor to ceiling with frames for drying the crucibles, retorts and other apparatus for melting and refining. From here we enter the large interior building that holds the heavy mixers and other machinery. The mixers consist of two huge cast-iron curbs, holding two and three tons each, which contain the clay and plumbago for the making of crucibles. The mixing is performed by great iron arms, so arranged in these curbs as to work the composition over and over, as a woman kneads dough. In the basement is the eighty horse power engine, with a fly-wheel fourteen feet in diameter, and a driving pulley eight feet, carrying a great leather belt, twenty-four inches wide, that leads off into darkness and drives all the vast detail of machinery. Next, we enter the boiler room, containing three boilers, each thirty-six feet long. In another department is storage for a thousand barrels of plumbago. A steam elevator takes us to the second floor, where we find, to our unaccustomed eyes, Pandemonium let loose. The noise is so tremendous that you cannot hear your own voice. Here are three cast iron mills revolving rapidly, in each of which are four thirty-two pound cannon balls. There is a Bogardus mill, and further on a powerful crushing machine called a "breaker." Into this machine lumps of plumbago are put, which come out broken to the size of kernels of corn; it then goes into the mills, where it is ground to a fine powder ready for the different articles to be manufactured— crucibles, stove polish, pencils, lubricating plumbago, etc. On the next floor above is the stove polish department. The plumbago comes up from the mills bolow through an elevator, is dumped into the hopper above, a complicated mass of cog-wheels, arms, pulleys, plungers, feeders, rolls and lifters, all in rapid motion, and is brought out on a table in front of the machine in small solid cubes, at the rate of four thousand per hour, each cube weighing exactly a quarter of a pound. From here we enter the labeling department where about thirty girls work at wrapping the cubes in their blue papers, and pasting the little yellow labels on the ends, when they are ready for the market. In another large room adjoining is the box shop—the company make their own boxes for packing, and use over three hundred per day. By a private door we enter another room: here is where the plans for making pencils by machinery have been worked out under Mr. Cleveland's own eye. In this room are three turning lathes, a planer, a portable forge, vises and tools without end. We cross the yard from these buildings and enter a new brick building put up expressly for the pencil department. The basement is devoted to staining the wood and artificial drying. Every piece of the cedar undergoes a careful examination before going to the machines. On the main floor the wood passes through a machine which planes and grooves the pieces ready for the leads. They are landed in another room where the leads are laid in, and the parts are glued together. Passing into another room they go through a "shaping" machine, and fall into baskets that carry them up on the next floor; here the unfinished pencils are piled into a hopper, and hardly stop a moment until they are varnished, dried, polished, the ends cut smooth and even, and the gold stamp put on, and then they are finished, no hand labor being used until they are put up in packages of a dozen each, these packages put into boxes of six dozen each; and these boxes wrapped, labeled, and packed for shipping.

In 1830, the late Mr. Dixon undertook to make pencils by machinery, but the trade wanted a foreign label put on them, under the idea that an American pencil would not sell, which so disgusted the expert mechanic that he quit all further attempt at pencil making. His plan was to put his own name on every article that left his hands finished, and he was never ashamed of his productions or of his name as a scientific mechanic. The present process of converting iron into steel in the crucible, was his own invention, although patented by a mason working on his furnaces.

The Dixon Company has one of the most complete establishments in the country, with every modern appliance for handling materials, and the offices are not excelled for convenience and elegance by any we ever visited. Strangers, and especially ladies, are shown through these most interesting works with a politeness that takes us back to the olden time, when politeness was the rule and not the exception in trade.

The mines of the company form what is known on the map of Essex County, in the State of New York, as the Black Lead Mountain, back of the village of Ticonderoga, and the immense mill for water grinding is on the outlet of Lake George into Lake Champlain, the Company owning one side of that outlet, perhaps one of the finest and most reliable water-powers in the country, holding steady at six thousand horse power, winter and summer. The mining property covers fourteen hundred acres and comprises veins of both the foliated Graphite like the Ceylon, and the granulated like the Alibert deposit in Siberia, but of a quality much finer than that from either of these celebrated sources.

The trade of the Dixon Company extends to nearly every civilized country, and covers every known branch in which Graphite is used.

THE JOSEPH DIXON CRUCIBLE COMPANY'S WORKS, JERSEY CITY, N. J.

VOLNEY W. MASON & CO.,

Manufacturers of Patent

FRICTION PULLEYS, FRICTION CLUTCHES

For Connecting Shafting and Gearing,

HOISTING MACHINERY & ELEVATORS,

Shafting, Hangers and Gearing,

Lafayette Street, Providence, R. I., U. S. A.

——:o:——

Fairbairn, in *Machinery of Transmission* in speaking of "Disengaging and Re-engaging Gearing" says: "This is an important branch of Mill Work, requiring careful consideration and the utmost exactitude of construction when ponderous machinery, has to be started without endangering the shafts and wheels. This is most strikingly exemplified in the case of Powder Mills, where trains of edge stones are employed for grinding the gun powder, and in Rolling and Calendering Machinery, which requires well fitted Friction Clutches to communicate the motion by a slow and progressive acceleration from a state of rest to the required velocity." The manufacture of a really effective and reliable Friction Clutch was commenced in the year 1860, by the firm whose name heads this article, as a special branch of their business, and now "Mason's Patent Friction Clutches" are used in nearly every place in the United States where manufacturing is carried on, and also in Canada, the Republics of South America, and in Europe, furnishing as they do a very perfect method for starting and stopping all kinds of machinery without sudden shock or jar.

Since they were first introduced, many important improvements have been made in their construction, as well as in the machinery, especially Hoisting Machinery for elevators and other purposes, to which they are applied. The firm make it a study in all cases to provide clutches that are fully equal to and specially adapted for the services they have to perform, and their fifteen years of practical experience in this line of business enables them to readily determine as to the proper construction and sizes necessary for every different use. Over one hundred different styles or patterns are made adapted to every description of service for which Friction Clutches are required.

The simplicity and effectiveness of the mechanism embraced in their construction commend them to all practical mechanics. The Friction Clutches may be started as quickly or as gradually as may be desired, by varying the movement of the shipper, working it quickly to start light running machines, and slowly to get up speed gradually in heavy machinery.

These Friction Clutches are made with four segments, also, extra heavy patterns designed for connecting lines of shafting without stopping engine or motive power, or slacking speed when started, for connecting Steam Engines and Water Wheels so as to use them connected or independent of each other as required; also for starting Force Pumps, Picker Rooms in Mills and Heavy Machinery of every kind, such as is used in Print Works, Bleacheries, Paper Mills, Rolling Mills, Powder Mills, Circular Saw Mills, &c. Also for Hoisting Purposes in Mines, Quarries, Packing Houses, Elevators, and for all places where power is available for hoisting.

The engraving represents a new, improved Patent Hoisting Machine for Elevators, manufactured by this firm, with which is furnished an improved Platform of new pattern with extra strong safety connections. This Hoisting Machine has an independent Stop Motion to insure the stopping of the machine, and platform at the top and bottom of the hatchway, should the hoisting wire rope become disarranged or inoperative. This Stop Motion acts independent of the shipper rope stops, and prevents the machine from running or unwinding the hoisting rope after the platform has arrived at the top or bottom of the hatchway. All the bearings of the machine being contained in the single iron frame, strongly bolted together, they are not liable to get out of line, and the entire machine is easily put up or taken down. These machines are very solid and compact and take up but little room. The best quality of iron, steel, and composition metal is used in their construction, and every piece is finished to gauge, so that it can readily be replaced when worn.

The firm also manufacture Gearing and Drums of different sizes, and will furnish Counter Shafts, Shafting, Gearing, Hangers and Pulleys to order. They will furnish estimates on application, and promptly attend to all orders and correspondence.

JOHN AUSTIN & CO.,

Gold and Silver Refiners, Assayers and Smelters,

74 CLIFFORD STREET, PROVIDENCE, R. I.

——:o:——

Since this firm was established in 1861, they have made many improvements in methods, so that operations which then took several days to perform, are now done in a few minutes, and have been forced to add to their facilities to keep pace with their steadily increasing business, which now amounts to $1,000,000 per year. A specialty with them is the refining of jewelers' waste, such as sweeps, sink, clippings, etc. These having been got into proper shape, the metals are melted together, and afterwards separated, one by one. The baser metals having been eliminated, the gold and silver are left fine.

ORGANIZED IN 1851.

——:o:——

PHŒNIX MUTUAL LIFE INSURANCE CO,

Hartford, Connecticut.

Assets, - - - - -	$11,000,000.
No. of Policy-Holders, - -	33,000.

A. C. Goodman, Pres't. J. B. Bunce, Vice-Pres't. J. M. Holcombe, Sec'y.

——:o:——

An examination of the annual reports of this Company show that it has steadily and surely progressed since its organization nearly a quarter of a century ago, and that, while it guarantees ample security to Policy-holders, it affords insurance at the lowest possible rates.

The Company has issued over ninety thousand policies, has paid to its policy-holders in dividends and death losses, more than ten million dollars, and stands to-day on a surer foundation than ever.

J. E. ROBINSON,

Patent Sand and Air Chambers and Artesian Wells,

Office, 1120 Washington St, Boston, Mass.

——:o:——

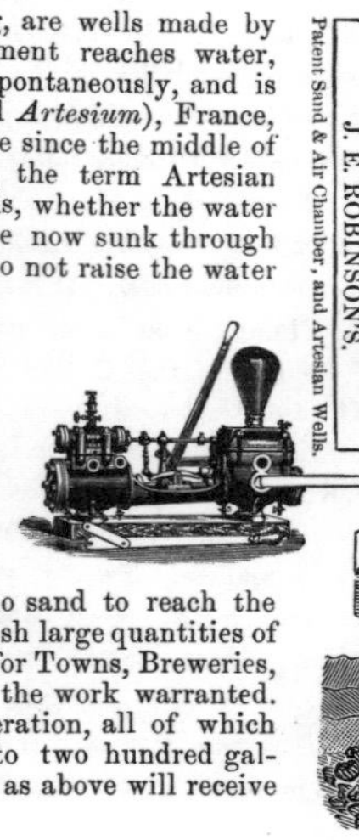

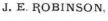

Artesian wells, properly speaking, are wells made by boring into the earth till the instrument reaches water, which from internal pressure flows spontaneously, and is derived from *Artois* (anciently called *Artesium*), France, where many such wells have been made since the middle of the last century. Recently, however, the term Artesian has been applied to all deep bored wells, whether the water overflows or not, and as such wells are now sunk through clay, sand or rock, and many of them do not raise the water to the surface, the term is also applied to the tubing with which the well is cased and to the appliances connected therewith necessary to draw the water.

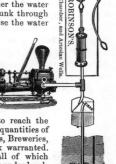

Mr. J. E. Robinson warrants his Patent Sand and Air Chamber and Artesian Wells to give from two to twenty times as much water as common strainer wells. They never give out or run down, nor injure the best steam or force pump, as they allow no sand to reach the pump. He is ready to contract to furnish large quantities of pure water, drawn from mother earth, for Towns, Breweries, Factories, etc., at the lowest price and the work warranted. He has over six hundred wells in operation, all of which give satisfaction, pumping from five to two hundred gallons per minute. All orders addressed as above will receive immediate personal attention.

CURTIS & ARNOLD,

GOLD AND SILVER REFINERS,

ASSAYERS AND SWEEP SMELTERS,

And Dealers in Bullion.

No. 236 Eddy Street, Providence, Rhode Island.

——:o:——

Providence, Rhode Island, is, in proportion to its population, one of the wealthiest and most enterprising of American cities, the greater part of its capital and enterprise being invested in manufactures. Competent authorities have estimated that if all the wealth of the city could be equally divided among its inhabitants, each man, woman and child would be entitled to nearly seventeen hundred dollars, or, computing families at five persons, each head of a family would be worth nearly eight thousand five hundred dollars—an average fully equal, we believe, to that of any city in the world.

Providence is specially noted for its extensive production of Jewelry and Silverware, leading all other cities in the United States. Over one hundred manufacturing jewelers have factories and shops in Providence, while at Attleboro' but a few miles distant, there are some sixty more. This large aggregation of consumers rendered necessary the establish-

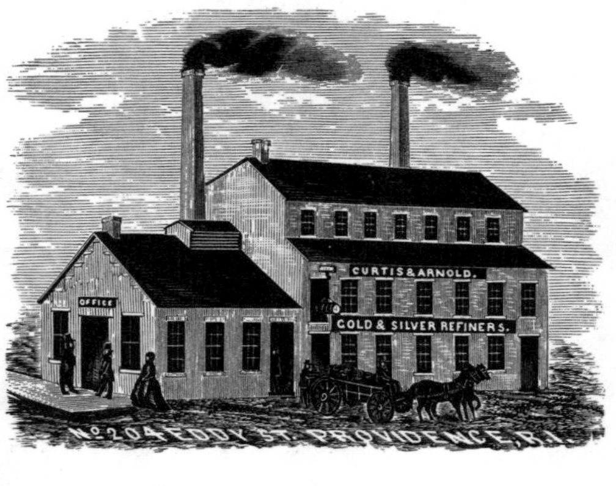

ment of works for assaying ores, smelting and refining—and especially for extracting from the sweepings and other waste of the manufacturing establishments—the precious metals. The art or science of refining and smelting jewelers' sweeps, polishings and metal refuse is, however, comparatively new in Providence, the first attempt not having been made until about the year 1845. The apparatus used was of the crudest description and the science imperfectly understood, the only aim being to save the gold and silver from the most valuable portion of the Jewelers' and Silversmiths' waste. Thus a large percentage of the real value of the materials operated upon was entirely lost. Since the above date, educated and thoughtful men have made the process of eliminating gold and silver from ores, Jewelers' and Photographers' waste, and all other materials containing them, a subject of careful study and costly experiment, with such happy practical results, that now the science seems to be thoroughly understood.

Prominent among these successful investigators is the firm of Curtis & Arnold, who established themselves in Providence, as Assayers and Smelters, a number of years ago, with an intelligent comprehension of the needs of the trade, and a determination to overcome all obstacles that might present themselves. Constant application to business and their sterling integrity have won for them deserved success. They have adopted the most perfect processes and in addition to saving the precious metals, they extract or convert into valuable products, all the base metals that may be contained in the material upon which they operate. For instance, the iron eliminated is converted into Sulphate of Iron, or, as it is more commonly called, Copperas; the Copper becomes Sulphate of Copper, or Blue Vitriol; of Tin they make Tin Crystals, and so on to the end of the list. Nothing of any value is lost.

The large number of manufacturing jewelers and silversmiths in Providence and Attleboro', of which we have previously spoken, all of whom have considerable quantities of "waste" to be refined, would, alone, ensure for Messrs. Curtis & Arnold a large business, but in addition to their local trade, they are constantly in receipt of consignments from all parts of the United States and the Canadas. Providence, New York, and Newark, N. J., are, we believe, the only cities in this country where this business is carried on, while every city and village has jewelers who repair, if they do not manufacture, and who, consequently, have waste to smelt and refine, making an aggregate of immense value, of which Providence probably secures the largest amount.

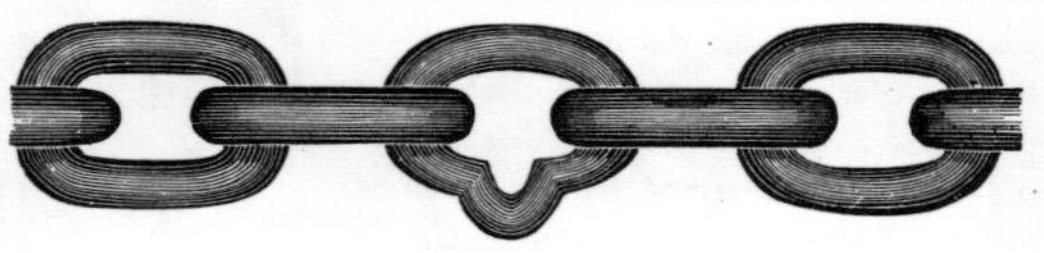

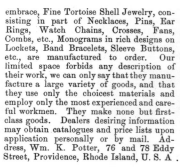

PROVIDENCE SHELL WORK
S.F.K.
TRADE MARK

Providence Shell Works,

William K. Potter, Prop'r.

——:o:——

This business was established in 1827 by Claflen & Bowen, since which time it has passed through many changes—changes of fashion and changes of ownership. Mr. Wm. K. Potter is the surviving partner of the old and well known firm of Samuel F. Knight & Co., and continues the business with the determination to fully maintain the reputation which was gained by his predecessors.

The manufactures of the establishment embrace, Fine Tortoise Shell Jewelry, consisting in part of Necklaces, Pins, Ear Rings, Watch Chains, Crosses, Fans, Combs, etc., Monograms in rich designs on Lockets, Band Bracelets, Sleeve Buttons, etc., are manufactured to order. Our limited space forbids any description of their work, we can only say that they manufacture a large variety of goods, and that they use only the choicest materials and employ only the most experienced and careful workmen. They make none but first-class goods. Dealers desiring information may obtain catalogues and price lists upon application personally or by mail. Address, Wm. K. Potter, 76 and 78 Eddy Street, Providence, Rhode Island, U. S. A.

LEATHER BELTS
AS A MEANS OF
Transmitting Power.

The inherent force or power of steam was known and written of by Hero, or Heron, a philosopher of Alexandria, who lived in the third century before Christ. He describes several applications of the mechanical effects of steam but no attempt to store up, control and apply this force to any useful purpose seems to have been made until the second century of the Christian era. We are too apt to lose sight of the wide difference between discoveries and the applications of principles which utilize the thing discovered and renders it subservient to the will of man.

Not less important than the means of gathering, and storing up power, is the method of transmitting it. When the power of steam was first practically applied to useful purposes it was by means of direct gearing—wheels meshed into other wheels, and the use of belts was unthought of. The loss of power by friction of the interlocking parts was known, but it was not deemed possible to overcome this waste except so far as the liberal use of lubricants would accomplish it. The compensating power of the adhesion from which friction is, in part, evolved was unthought of, and the man who would have suggested that such a force could be saved and so applied as to render much of the gearing unnecessary, would have been deemed mad. Cogs were considered so indispensable to the practical transmission or application of power, and so entirely misunderstood was adhesive force, that when steam railroads were first thought of, the idea of constructing an engine which would be able to move itself, much more draw a load after it, was ridiculed without measure.

The forces of gravitation and adhesion, which cause the locomotive to so closely cling to the rails as to give it drawing power, are practically the same as those employed in the transmission of power by belts, and subject to the same conditions.

While the advantages of belts over close gearing as a means of transmitting power is now generally conceded in this country, there are few who are aware how great a saving is effected by their use, nor in how many different ways this saving is effected. We can hardly hope to enumerate and explain within the limits of this article all the benefits accruing from their use, but will endeavor to present a few of them: Among the most generally recognized advantages of the belt system is the facility with which, without stopping the revolutions of a shaft, by the shifting of a belt from one section of a cone pulley to another the speed of any single machine in a well appointed factory can be altered at the will of the operator.

The breakage, loosening, or slipping of a belt is readily remedied without at all interfering with the operation of any machine other than that to which it supplies power, while in geared shafting the snapping of a cog causes the stoppage of all the machines obtaining power from that shaft until the broken gear is replaced.

In the event of the breakage of the main belt which transmits the power from the engine to all the other machines which it supplies, it takes much less time and labor to splice or lace the belt than it would to remove a broken gear and replace it with a new one.

Again, belts are less expensive in their first cost than gearing. In transmitting power from shaft to shaft by means of cog gearing it is generally necessary to use a third shaft and two sets of cog wheels to form the connection.

Belts do not wear faster than cog gearing, and are not as liable to accident. For instance, the dropping of a wrench between cogs would inevitably stop the machinery at once, or break the cogs and thus render it necessary to shut down for repairs, while if the same body was dropped between a belt and pulley the belt would give sufficiently to carry it through without injury. But supposing belts to

PAW PAW TANNERY, PAW PAW, VIRGINIA.

MANUFACTORY, 206 to 216 ELDRIDGE ST., N. Y.

cost the same as cog gearing, to wear more rapidly and to be equally liable to accidents, the difference in time consumed in replacing and repairing is largely in favor of belting.

Experts figure the resistence of the two systems as about equal. Cog gearing, according to their figures having a slight advantage where large powers and low speeds are combined but belts being preferable in rapid velocities.

A Leather belt will safely and continuously resist a strain of three hundred and fifty pounds per square inch of section, and a section of .2 of an inch will transmit the equivalent of a horse power at a velocity of one thousand feet per minute over a wooden drum, and of .4 of a square inch over a turned cast iron pully.

These facts sufficiently demonstrate the capacity of belts to safely convey to any distance any desired amount of power, the only limit being their size.

The length of life of a well made and properly cared for leather belt has not yet been determined, but we know that there are leather belts still doing daily duty that have been in constant use for thirty years.

HOW LEATHER BELTS ARE MADE.

When belts were first used as a means of transmitting power, leather was selected as the most suitable material. In those days mill men and others using belts purchased ordinary sole leather, from which they made their own belts, and very poor belts they were.

Some forty years ago, Mr. William Kumble, late of the City of New York,—having noticed the growing popularity of belting, notwithstanding the very imperfect method of manufacture, and being fully convinced that, if properly made, it would soon supersede the then existing means of transmitting power—determined to make the manufacture of leather belting a specialty.

Mr. Kumble's idea was to select his leather with special reference to the making of belts, (to so treat it as to render it softer and more pliable than ordinary sole leather,) and to use only the best parts of the hide. He also paid attention to so stretching the strips that when placed upon the pulleys they would draw evenly.

But since these early days the methods of manufacture of belting have greatly improved. The prime requisites of a leather belt are strength, flexibility and elasticity, and to secure these the best quality of hides should be used.

Careful manufacturers use scarcely one-third of the area of a hide for belting, all that portion from the horns to the shoulders, and all the skirts are waste. From the remaining portion strips are cut lengthwise the hide. These are stretched by powerful machinery and retained at the utmost tension they will stand without injuring the fibre. These pieces are jointed and secured so as to present an even surface to the pulley and the belt runs as though it was one piece.

The most perfect belt, especially where great power is to be conveyed, is two-ply. The parts are so lapped that the joints on one side are equi-distant from the joints on the other side. The result is a band of immense strength, perfect in its drawing lines.

The well-known house of J. B. Hoyt & Co., commenced the business of manufacturing leather belting in 1848, and in 1850 began to tan leather for band purposes. Their business has been a constantly increasing one, so that they now tan over 100,000 hides per year.

The firm occupy as a warehouse, the large building known as 28 and 30 Spruce Street, New York. They also own choice oak lands in the regions of Southern Pennsylvania, Western Maryland and West Virginia, and have no difficulty in procuring ample supplies, of the very best bark. Every branch of the manufacture is under the personal supervision of the members of the firm, from the selection of the green hides to the completed belt, and their twenty-seven years of business, place them among the most reliable belt makers in this country.

WILLS CREEK TANNERY, CUMBERLAND, MARYLAND.

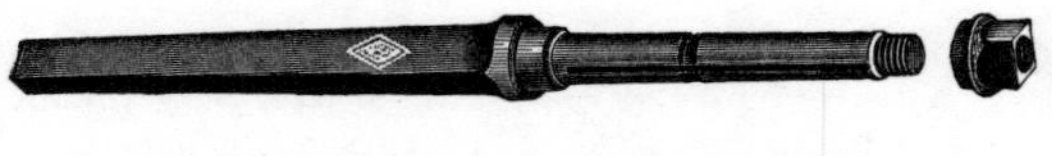

AXLE WITH BOX AND NUT REMOVED.

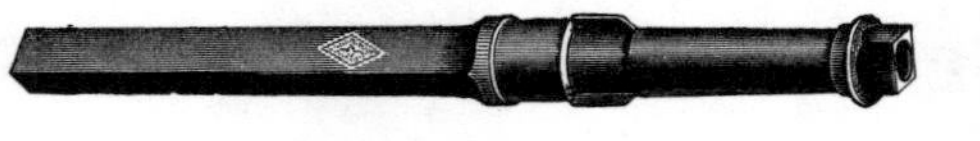

SWELLED TAPER AXLES.

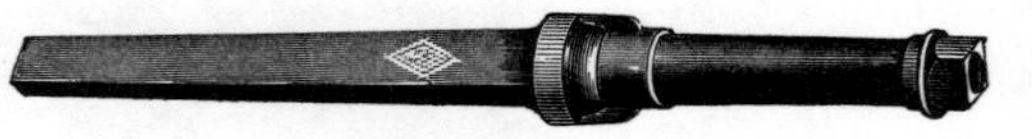

HALF PATENT AXLE.

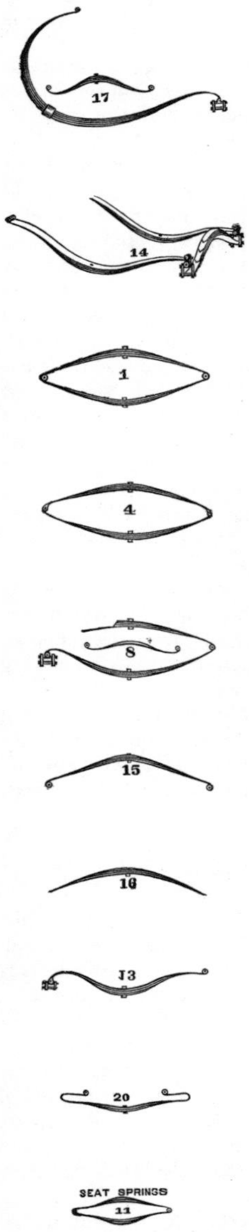

FORT PLAIN SPRING AND AXLE WORKS.

CLARK, SMITH & CO.,

Manufacturers of

CARRIAGE & WAGON SPRINGS & AXLES,

Fort Plain, New York.

—:o:—

So many different mechanical operations contribute toward the construction of carriages, wagons and other vehicles, that it would be next to impossible for all branches of the work to be carried on in any one establishment, and moreover, experience has conculsively shown that greater proficiency is attained by restricting attention to some special department of production. Among the most important items in this connection is the manufacture of springs and axles, for upon their strength and durability the serviceableness of all kinds of vehicles mainly depends.

One of the most extensive manufactories in the country, devoted to this speciality, is the Fort Plain Spring and Axle Works, Fort Plain, New York. The business was established about eight years ago, and for the last five years has been carried on by the present proprietors, Messrs. Clark, Smith & Co. The excellent character of the goods manufactured by this firm is evident from the fact that during all this period their works have been run to their full capacity, and there has been no falling off in the demand, even during the seasons of the greatest business depression.

The village of Fort Plain, situated upon the line of the New York Central Railroad, about sixty miles west of Albany, is advantageously located for manufacturing purposes, having ample transportation facilities, not only by rail, but by water, being intersected by the Erie Canal, which affords every convenience for the reception of heavy freight, such as coal, iron, etc.

The factory premises owned by Messrs. Clark, Smith & Co. embraces about three acres of land, lying a short distance from the railroad, fronting on Willett Street and bounded on the rear by the Canal. The accompanying illustration, though small, affords a very correct view of the factory buildings. The main structure is three hundred and eighty feet in length by fifty feet in width, and one story in height, with the exception of the central portion which, for the length of seventy-five feet, is two stories high. Extending toward the rear are two wings, each fifty by seventy-five feet in area.

The eastern end of the main building is the Spring Shop, which is completely equipped with the most improved machinery and mechanical appliances for the manufacture of all styles and sizes of carriage, wagon, sulky, cart, truck and omnibus springs; elliptic, Concord sides, platform, French scroll, etc., made from the best brands of English and Swedish steel, oil tempered, and warranted to be fully equal in quality and finish to any goods in the market.

The advantage of oil over water, in the tempering of steel, is shown by the comparative tensile strength resulting from the two processes. Hardening in water reduces the strength of steel, while it is greatly increased by being hardened in oil. Reliable scientific authorities state that the reduction of strength by hardening in water is twenty per cent, while the use of oil gives an increased strength of seventy-nine per cent.

But to return to our description of the works: the ground floor of the central part of the factory—aside from spacious business offices—is devoted to the turning, grinding and finishing of Iron and Steel Axles, of all sizes, from those of the smallest dimensions, adapted to light wagons and sulkies, to the heaviest required for carts, trucks and coaches. The machinery in this department includes twenty turning lathes, twelve grinding lathes, two patent machines for finishing nuts, each doing the work of at least four men; a new machine for turning small axles, holding them firmly and ensuring true work; together with many other mechanical devices of original construction. Nearly all the machines and tools used in the works are made and repaired on the premises. The upper floor of this building is occupied for the manufacture and storage of patterns.

The western end of the main factory is the Forging and Blacksmithing Department. It is equipped with six fires, one vertical and three horizontal trip hammers, heavy shears, capable of cutting three inch iron; and all the other requisites for the heavier portion of the axle work. The iron used is of the best quality manufactured for their special use by the Corning and Burden Works, Troy, New York.

The west wing contains the engine and boiler room and the Foundry. The boilers are of sufficient capacity to operate an engine of eighty horse power and furnish steam for the establishment. Water for the boilers is supplied from an exhaustless well on the premises. For protection against fire there is a powerful steam pump, capable of throwing five streams of one and one-half inches each, drawing the water from the Canal. Three hundred and fifty feet of hose are constantly in readiness for use. The Foundry is completely equipped for the casting of Axle Boxes of all sizes and descriptions; a feature seldom found in axle works, as the majority of manufacturers have their Boxes cast by outside parties.

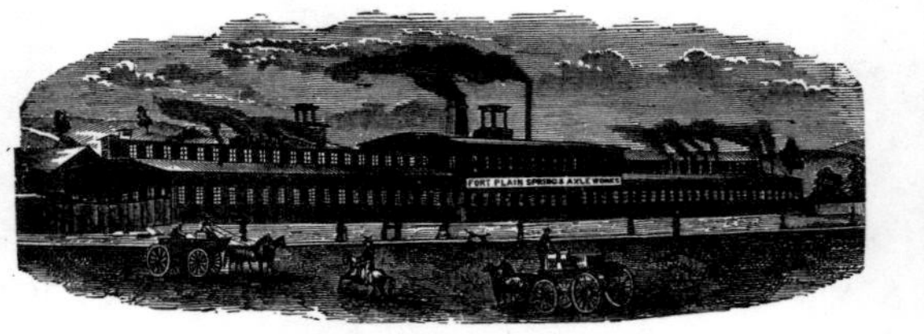

FORT PLAIN SPRING AND AXLE WORKS.

The eastern wing is for the storage of finished goods and their packing and shipment.

The arrangement of the entire works is most systematic throughout, each successive step in the manufacturing processes leading gradually from the raw material to the finished goods, without unnecessary handling or any loss of time or labor.

The extent of the production may be inferred from the following partial statistics of the materials used. There are annually worked up one thousand tons of bar iron, five hundred tons of steel, one hundred and fifty tons of pig-iron; fifty grindstones, weighing three tons each, are annually required, and the yearly consumption of coal is about fifteen hundred tons.

The number of operatives employed is upward of one hundred, and the weekly pay roll averages $1,200. Great care is taken in the selection of the most experienced workmen, and it would be difficult to find an equal number of good mechanics in any similar establishment in the country.

The Spring Shop contains some of the finest machinery ever built for this branch of manufacture. All the Springs are subjected to the most thorough tests, being placed under a much heavier pressure than they will ever be called upon to sustain in actual use, and none are suffered to pass inspection that are not perfect in every particular.

Heavy Platform Springs constitute a somewhat prominent specialty, and of this style alone the production for the present season will not be less than ten thousand sets. All shipments are made from the factory direct, and the widely extended reputation of the goods manufactured by this firm is indicated by the fact that they regularly fill orders for nearly all the States and Territories in the Union, ship largely to Canada and the British Provinces, besides making frequent consignments to the Sandwich Islands, Australia and other foreign countries.

In concluding this sketch of Messrs. Clark, Smith & Co.'s works, we need only add that the trade will find them always prepared to fill orders for Springs and Axles of any of the standard styles, upon the most reasonable terms, and with the utmost promptness, and of a quality unsurpassed.

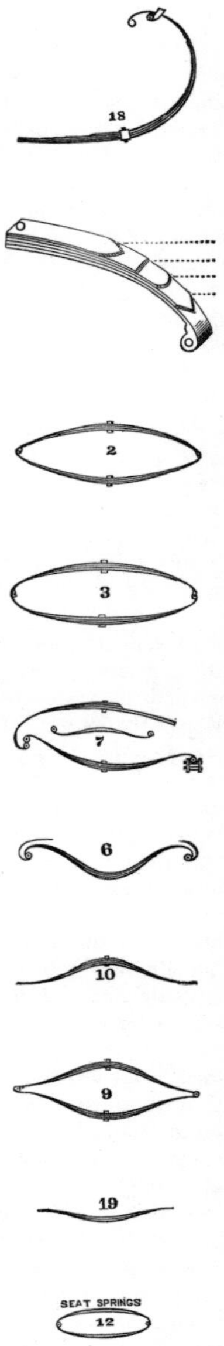

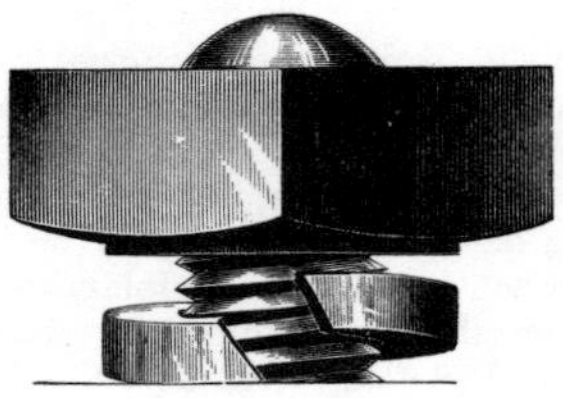

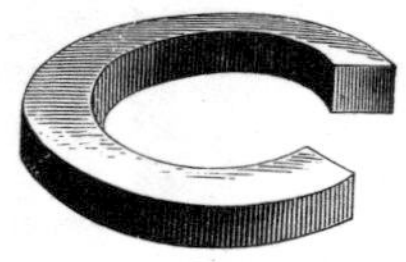

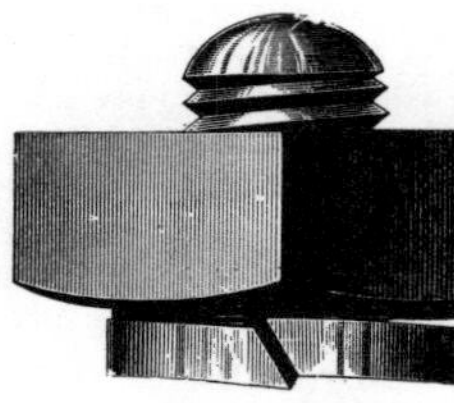

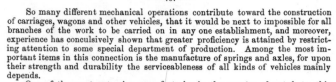

VERONA TOOL WORKS.

METCALF, PAUL & COMPANY,

WORKS: Verona, Penn'a. OFFICE: 331 Penn Ave., Pittsburgh, Pa.

Manufacturers of

RAILROAD TRACK TOOLS,

The Standard Solid Eye, Solid Cast Steel Tamping and Clay Picks, Improved Claw Bars, The Pat. Verona Nut Lock, Mining and Blacksmith's Tools.

The success achieved by our steel manufacturers within the last twelve or thirteen years—and especially within the last four or five—in not only producing as good steel as the very best of foreign make, but in actually surpassing it in some respects, has entirely revolutionized the old condition of things, the imported material is growing "beautifully less" in our markets every year, while our exports of the article are steadily increasing. Previous to this change we were largely dependent upon foreign manufacturers not only for our supply of steel, but also for the tools made of it, especially for those required for hard work, such as sledges, hammers, axes, heavy chisels, picks, etc. In railway and mining tools of this class we were sadly behind the European manufacturers in point of quality. It is no wonder then that one of the fruits of this industrial independence should be seen in the tool trade, and it is still less a wonder that the city of Pittsburgh, wherein the best American steel is made, should reveal the latter fact in the most prominent degree.

As a distinct branch of trade, tool making is one of Pittsburgh's most recent accomplishments, but already it is represented by some four or five large and responsible manufacturing establishments, each distinguished for certain special lines of production. The foremost of these, in point of achievement above competition, seems to be the Verona Tool Works, of Messrs. Metcalf, Paul & Co., situated at Verona, on the line of the Allegheny Valley Railroad, ten miles north of Pittsburgh, the principal business office being at the corner of Penn Avenue and 10th Street, Pittsburgh.

For a long time the necessity for a great improvement in this class of work was seriously felt by all the railroad companies, the tools which they required to use for track work being made mainly of iron and therefore weak. The introduction of steel rails enhanced the difficulty, and it was found that only tools made of the very best quality of steel and with extraordinary care would meet the want. To supply this need was the purpose of Messrs. Metcalf & Paul in starting their works, and understanding well the nature of the difficulty involved in their undertaking, they were resolved to spare no pains or expense in seeking to accomplish their object; in other words, they fully realized the necessity for the production of a class of tools not hitherto made in this country.

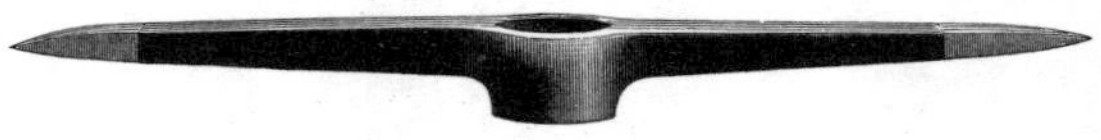

MINERS' PICK.
Straight.

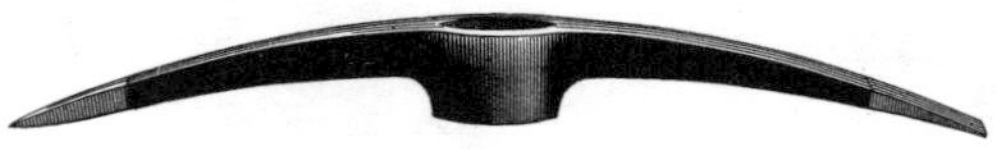

RAILROAD CLAY PICK.
Solid Eye. Solid Cast Steel.

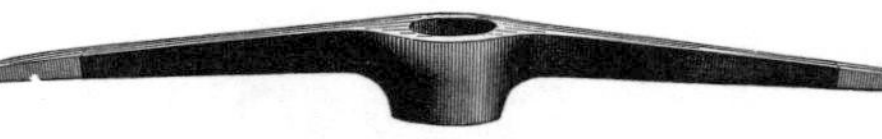

MINERS' PICK.
Curved.

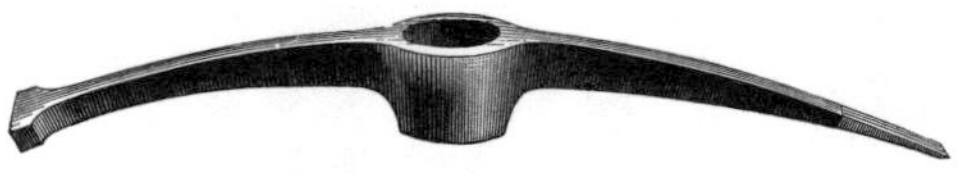

THE VERONA TAMPING PICK.
Solid Steel. Solid Eye.

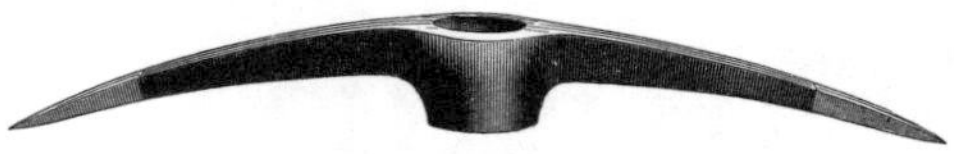

MINERS' PICK.
Surface.

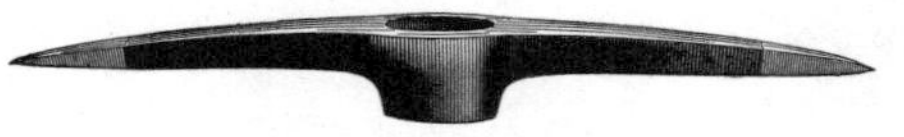

MINERS' PICK.
Drifting.

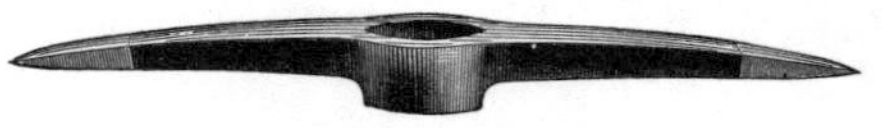

COAL PICK.

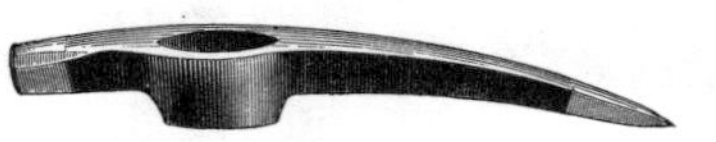

ORE HAMMER PICK.

Providing themselves, therefore, with every requisite appliance in the way of machinery, using only the very best of cast steel, and employing the most skilled labor to be procured, and subjecting every piece of work to the severest test in order to prove equal to the requirements of the service for which it was designed, they soon found a ready market for their productions, and secured a trade which has elevated them to the prominence that we have above indicated.

Messrs. Metcalf, Paul & Co. make a specialty in Railroad Track Tools, embracing every description of tools used by track layers; they also largely manufacture Blacksmith, Stone mason and Mining tools. It would be impossible to describe all their productions within the brief space at our disposal, but deem it a duty to call attention to their various styles of Picks. These Picks are made of solid Cast Steel, and, though their first cost may be greater, they are really cheaper than any iron pick can be. One of them will do the work of six iron picks. They cannot be broken by any legitimate use to which they may be put, and they will stand harder usage than other picks. To miners and contractors who have their work at a distance from a forge, these picks will be particularly valuable, and far more than save their extra cost by their durability and not being required to send them to the smith for repairs, as is caused in the iron pick, by broken points, etc. In these goods, as well as the sledge, hammers, etc., for miners, smiths, and masons, this establishment uses none but the best selected cast-steel, and fully guarantees every article of its manufacture, when stamped with its trade mark.

The *British Mail*, (London, England,) of Jan. 31, '76, in describing these tools, says: "These are made by compression in a series of dies, the invention of Messrs. Metcalf, Paul & Co., of cast steel, solid eye, and guaranteed impossible to break, especially in the eye, by any usage to which a pick can be put. Messrs. Metcalf, Paul & Co. are the first, and, we believe, the only concern that has succeeded in putting in the market a perfect, solid eye, solid steel pick. They have spent much time and money in perfecting this article, and now have a pick, at a not large advance on a first class iron pick, that will last (one of them) as long as six iron picks. The reports from those who have used these picks are unanimous, that they are perfect, the standard far better and cheaper than iron. Workmen must have a good pick, one that will not break in the eye, the first desideratum being a perfectly reliable article, which it has been impossible to get hitherto. Specimens of these picks may be seen in our offices; we have had them thoroughly tested, and can speak authoritatively about their excellence."

When an English mechanic's journal pays such a tribute to American tools, they must be of far more than ordinary excellence.

Of their Patent Verona Nut Lock, the Track Chisels, Napping Hammers, Spike Mauls, Claw Bars, Sledges, etc., we can only say that they are perfect.

The works at Verona, as we have already intimated, are as complete in their arrangements for the perfect and prompt execution of all the class of work for which they are designed as modern ingenuity and skill can make them and have a capacity for any demand that may be made on them.

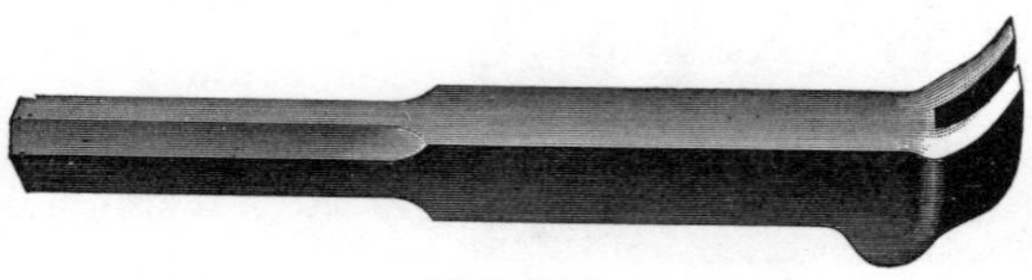

CLAW BAR.
Solid Cast Steel.

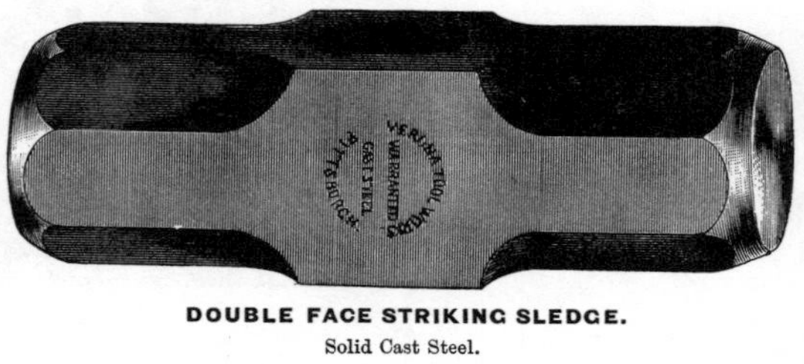

DOUBLE FACE STRIKING SLEDGE.
Solid Cast Steel.

THE YALE LOCK MANUF'G CO.,

Stamford, Conn.

HENRY R. TOWNE, Pres't.

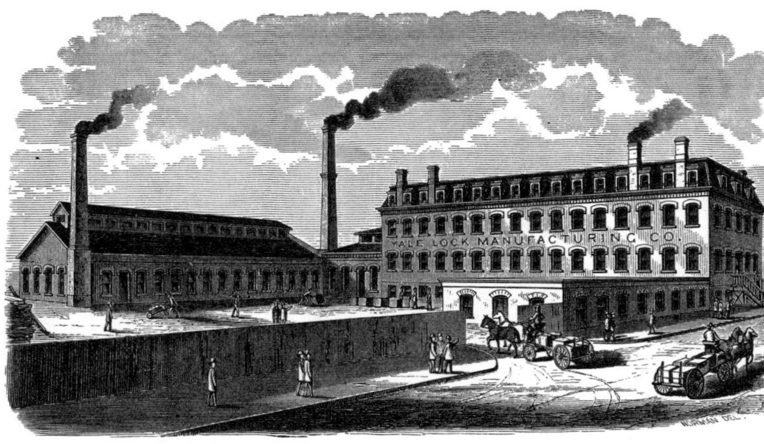

View of the Yale Lock Manufacturing Company's Works.

The need of locks and keys dates back to early days, and it would add an interesting chapter to the history of the mechanic arts could we trace the growth of human invention in this field.

Researches among the antiquities of the Oriental Nations, disclose the fact that the manufacture and use of locks were not unknown, even in pre-historic times. The ancient Egyptians with whom originated many of the "Lost Arts," are credited with the invention of a lock, which, in a crude form, is strikingly similar to the famous Yale Lock, and which probably presented as serious an obstacle to the felonious attempts of the Theban or Alexendrian burglar as the later devices of Bramah, Yale or Hobbs do to those of the modern house breaker.

No material improvement in the manufacture of locks was effected until 1784, in which year was invented the famous Bramah lock, so called from its inventor, the security of which was such as to prompt the offering of a reward of two hundred pounds to any one who should succeed in picking it. This was accomplished, however, by Mr. Hobbs, the American lockmaker, in 1851, and in the London Exhibition of 1856 at the Crystal Palace, Mr. Hobbs exhibited locks which fairly established the supremacy of American lockmakers.

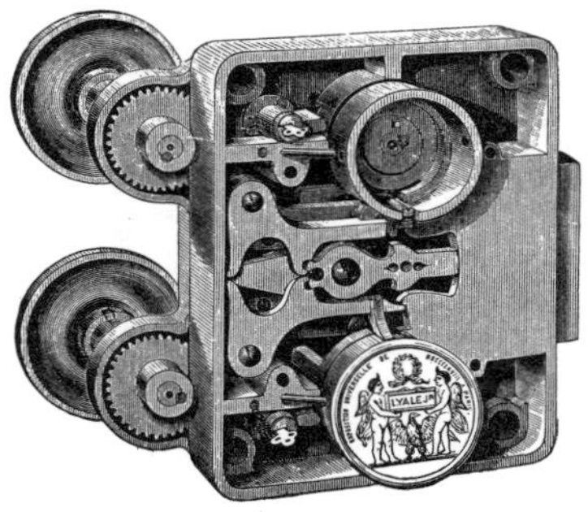

Yale Bank Lock.

In this branch of manufactures, as in most others, competitors for the highest distinction are numerous; but for ingenuity of design, excellence of material, absolute security, and above all finished workmanship, none sustain a higher and more deserved reputation than the celebrated Yale Lock Manufacturing Company.

The business conducted by this Company was founded upwards of thirty years ago but the present Company was not organized until 1868, in which year the erection of the works, at Stamford, Conn., was commenced. In 1869, the Company commenced business with a force of thirty men; but the superior quality of their products caused a steady and constant demand for them, which required a corresponding increase of labor until they now employ from one hundred and twenty-five to one hundred and fifty hands, and the area covered by their shops has more than doubled.

The buildings of the Company are all substantial brick structures, and being situated but a short distance from the Railroad Depot, form an important feature of the place.

The Yale Locks, as first made by the inventor, the late Linus Yale, Senior, nearly thirty years ago, were a great improvement over their predecessors, but their range of application was limited, and their costliness, prevented their general adoption. Subsequently, Linus Yale, Jr. a son of the above, engaged in the lock manufacture and soon became celebrated for the ingenious and complicated Bank Locks which he invented and which in their day were the best in the market. Passing from locks of this class which were necessarily very expensive (a single lock costing from $100 to $400) and the market for which was therefore limited, Mr. Yale invented in 1860 the lock with which his name has since become so widely identified and which is now made in such variety of forms as to adapt it to almost every use, from a ladies jewelry case or a tradesman's cash drawer to the heaviest house and store-doors.

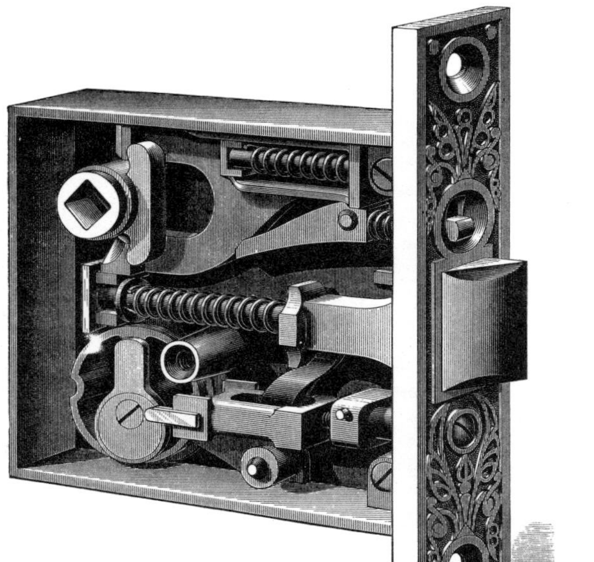

This lock, which is known as a "Pin Lock," was similar in some respects to that made by Linus Yale, Sr., but possessed the distinctive and desirable feature of a key of thin flat steel, less than an inch and a half long, and weighing but a fraction of an ounce as shown in the accompanying cut.

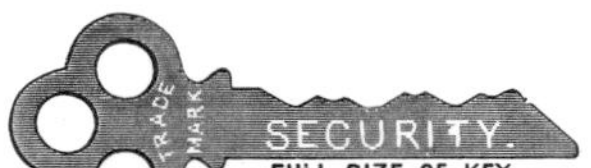

FULL SIZE OF KEY.

All other locks at that time and nearly all others now manufactured, have required heavy keys and the thicker the door, the longer must be the key to reach the lock, while in the Yale Lock the Escutcheon or Tumbler-Case, which contains the mechanism to be acted on by the key, is placed close to the outer face of the door, so that the length of the key remains the same whether the door be one inch or one foot in thickness.

In general terms we may designate the distinctive peculiarities of the Yale lock as being the arrangement of the parts acted upon by the key, and the shape and size of the key itself. The form of the lock and many details of construction of course vary with the intended use, and may not differ essentially from those of other locks except in superiority of design and more thoroughly finished workmanship.

These prominent features may be illustrated by the description of a Yale mortise night latch, an escutcheon of this kind being applicable to almost any style of mortise or rim lock; flush locks—for drawers, desks, etc. —differing only in having the body of the lock contain the mechanism which is here enclosed in a separate escutcheon.

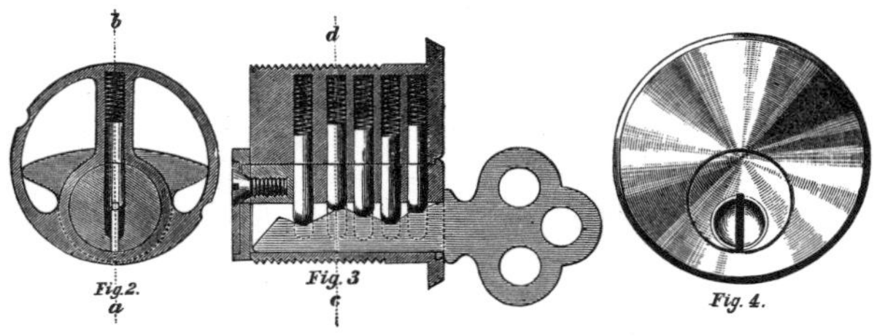

Sectional view of the escutcheon of a Yale Night Latch, showing the principle of construction embodied in all the Yale Locks.

The escutcheon consists, as will be seen from an examination of the above cuts, of an exterior shell of cylindrical form, containing in its lower part a smaller cylinder, from which rises a rib of metal containing the "pin chambers," and within which is the "plug," attached to the inner end of which is the cam that imparts motion to the bolt, as shown in interior view of mortise night latch, shown in left hand corner below, where the back end of escutcheon is seen projecting into lock case.

The escutcheon contains five holes, or "pin chambers," each formed partly in the shell and partly in the plug, therefore a pin which filled one of these holes would prevent the rotation of the plug, but if the pin were cut in two, the joint corresponding with that between the plug and its hole, the plug could revolve freely, carrying with it one-half of the pin, and leaving the other half in that part of the pin-chamber contained in the shell. Such is precisely the construction of the lock and its great element of security.

Each pin is in two parts—the upper termed the "driver," the lower the "pin"—and above each driver is a light spring, tending to press drivers and pins downward. In this position the drivers intersect the joint between the shell and the plug, completely preventing the rotation of the latter. If, by the insertion of a knife blade, or other instrument in the key hole, the pins are all raised as high as they will go, it will be found that they bar the motion of the plug as effectually as the drivers did, or if four of the pins are elevated to their proper position, the fifth will still prevent the revolution of the plug.

To open the lock, therefore all the pins must be raised simultaneously to just the proper height, which can be done only by the right key, since a variation of one-fiftieth of an inch in the elevation of either of the pins will prevent the opening of the lock. This explains the immense variety of keys and wide range of permutations of which the Yale lock is susceptible, surpassing the capabilities of any other lock now made.

The Yale Locks are made in some three hundred different styles and varieties, thus adapting them to almost every conceivable use; but the form of key and construction of the parts acted upon by it are essentially the same throughout the whole series, included in which are many specialties, such as locks for Safe Deposit Vaults, Prisons, Insane Asylums, Reform Schools, Hotels and a special line of Freight Car Locks of an entirely new design.

The manufacture of Burglar Proof Bank and Safe Locks is carried to great perfection by this Company. The most important of these is what is known as the Yale Double Dial Lock, represented in the accompanying cut. The distinctive feature of this lock, is the double principle whereby one common bolt is controlled by two entirely independent locks, which may be set on different combinations, thus affording access to two different persons, and avoiding danger of being "locked out," the great trouble hitherto arising from combination locks. Each dial operates a distinct four tumbler lock, capable of 100,000,000 changes, every combination of which is available. These are pronounced the most perfect locks in the world.

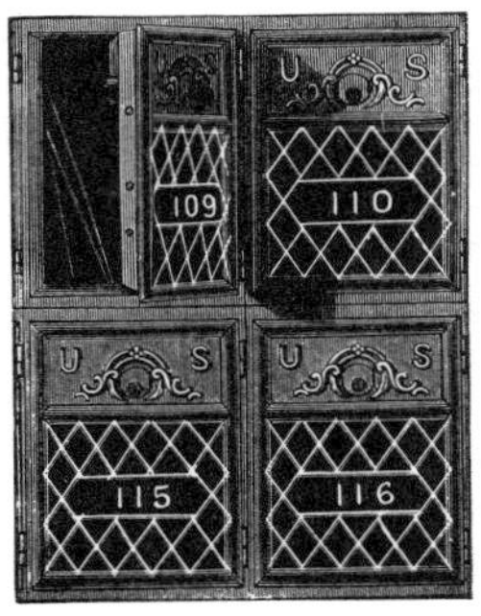

Yale Post Office Boxes.

Another leading feature, or specialty, is the manufacture of Post Office Lock Boxes, Drawers, Call Boxes, furniture and equipments complete. The demand for this class of work has necessitated large additions to the company's facilities for manufacturing. Over 50,000 of their lock boxes, as represented in the accompanying cut are now in use by the Post Office Departments of the United States and Canada, and they supply Post Masters with every thing for the entire furnishing of offices.

Their Prison Locks are so constructed, that instead of being attached to the door, as usual, they are built into the masonry of the cell wall, the bolt projecting into the door jam, thus rendering any attempt to tamper with the mechanism of the lock entirely futile. These locks are each furnished with six pins or tumblers capable of more than one million changes, and they are absolutely impervious to any attack from within or without. Want of space prevents our giving further details of their extensive Lock manufacturing business; but we wish to call the attention of our readers to another department of manufacture, which this Company has recently combined with its other business, viz: Real Bronze Ornamental Hardware.

This class of goods has during the past few years come into almost exclusive use for the finest class of residences and public buildings, and is a notable instance of the application of art to the purposes of utility. The character of the work is indicated by the illustration below which represents a Real Bronze Door Knob, and the goods as made by this Company are all of genuine bronze, of a rich golden color, and in elegance of design, richness of color and perfection of finish they are entirely unsurpassed.

The particular specialty of the Yale Lock Manufacturing Company, and its constant aim, is the doing of thoroughly good work, and it is intended that in the future, even more than in the past, its name shall be a synonym for excellence.

Mr. Henry R. Towne has been President of the Company since the death of Mr. Linus Yale Jr. in 1869, and now controls the business.

Parties interested in this department of manufactures should order one of the Company's beautifully illustrated catalogues, containing much specific information to which we are unable even to refer.

Their principal office is at the works in Stamford, Conn.; the New York salesroom is at No. 298 Broadway.

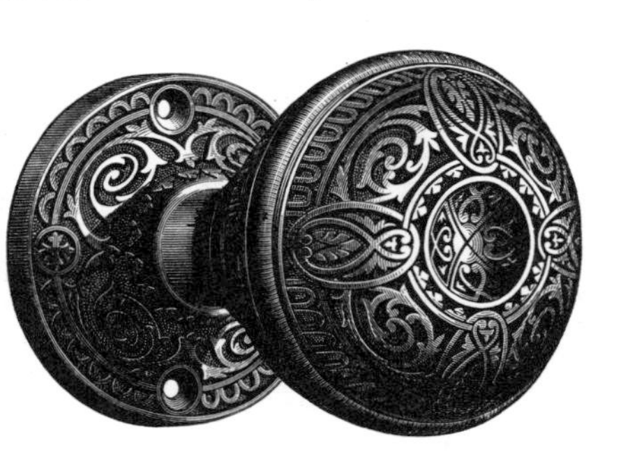

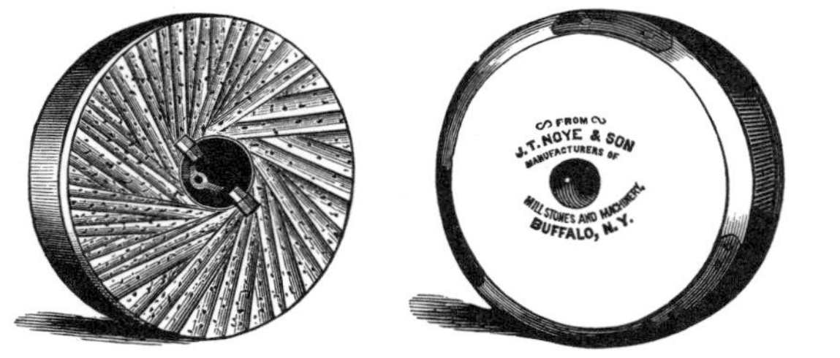

French Burr Mill Stones. Showing Furrowed Face and the Back with Running Balance Boxes.

FLOURING & GRIST MILL MACHINERY,

Represented by

Messrs. J. T. Noye & Son, Buffalo, N. Y.

The manufacture of machinery for Flouring and Grist Mills, has never in this country received attention as an independent branch of industry until the establishment of that business by Mr. J. T. Noye, of Buffalo, N. Y.

The manufacture of Burr Millstones had been, and is still carried on in a small way in different parts of the country; but Mr. Noye was the first to combine the manufacture of all the machinery required in a mill, and we believe the present firm is the only one thus engaged up to this time.

To the casual observer it would seem that no great variety of labor would be called into requisition to furnish the outfit for a flouring mill, but to one who has visited the manufactory of Messrs. Noye & Son it is evident that few branches, claiming to be specialties, cover such a variety of machinery and call into use so many kinds of mechanical labor.

END VIEW.

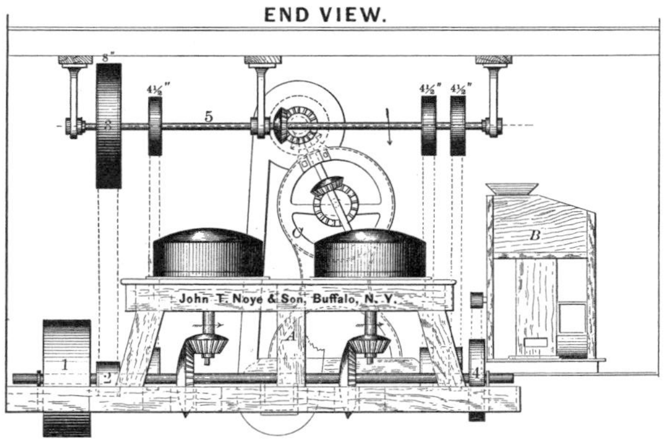

Complete Custom Mill of Two Pairs of Burrs: All the machinery located on one floor.

The part of the business which is of most interest to the general public is the Stone Department. All the stone is quarried in France, within a radius of one hundred miles of Paris. No stone suitable for the purpose has yet been discovered anywhere else in the world. This stone is of a silicious nature and remarkable for its cellular formation, which gives to the surface, a sharp, roughened surface, however much it may be worn. It is mostly quarried in blocks of a size which require from thirty to forty to make a single pair of millstones.

Other portions of their establishment comprise the foundry, machine shop, millwright shop, pattern shop, tin and blacksmith shops; employing in all about one hundred and twenty-five men.

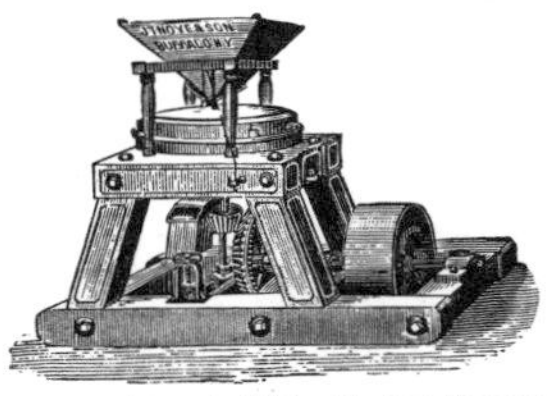

Portable Oil Bush Mill. Under Runner.

In the drafting room are planned and matured the orders which set the whole establishment in motion. Here all the details of a mill are laid out on paper. The dimensions of every piece of machinery to be used, and its relation to the whole, are accurately indicated before any portion of the work is commenced; thus ensuring accuracy in execution of an order, and enabling a purchaser to put the machinery in its proper position in his building.

Messrs. Noye & Son have furnished the millstones and machinery for most of the large flouring mills in this country. Among the most important and best known are: The Brooklyn City Mills, Atlantic Dock Mills, Brooklyn; Washburn Mills, and Aukuy & Bros., of Minneapolis, Indianna; Haxall Mills, of forty-eight pair of burrs, Richmond, Va.; and Thornton & Chester's Mills, of Buffalo, N. Y.

For newly settled country, and for grinding feed they make portable mills of six varities and of eleven different sizes. Our illustrations show one of these mills.

They also make mills for grinding paint, spices and drugs which are very successful.

The line of gearing and pulley patterns (all live patterns) represented in the catalogue of Messrs. Noye & Son is said to be the best in the United States for variety and adaptation to its use.

The firm issue a handsome illustrated catalogue which can be obtained on application at their office, or by letter, addressing Jno. T. Noye & Son, Buffalo, N. Y.

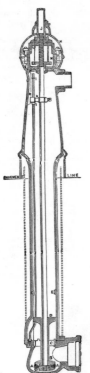

Fire Hydrant.

Brass Valve.

Brass Valve.

Iron Valve with Indicator, Showing position of Gate.

Half Gate and Wedges.

VIEW OF THE LUDLOW VALVE MANF'G CO'S WORKS, TROY, N. Y.

Fire Hydrant.

Single Gate Valve.

Half Gate and Wedges.

Double Gate Valve.

Rear of Single Valve Case.

WATER, GAS & STEAM VALVES, AND FIRE HYDRANTS,

Represented by

LUDLOW VALVE M'F'G. COMPANY,

938 to 954 River St., and 67 to 83 Vail Ave.,

TROY, N. Y.

The introduction of water and gas into nearly all the cities and towns of any note throughout the Union, and the greatly increased use of steam, have given rise to several distinct and important branches of industry in the production of machinery and apparatus for these purposes. One of these, and probably the most extensive establishment in the United States—if not in the world—devoted to the making of Brass and Iron Valves, Fire Hydrants, and Railroad water Columns as a specialty, is the Ludlow Valve Manufacturing Company of Troy N. Y.—whose President was the pioneer in the manufacture of slide valves with a gate made in more than one piece. The business originated some fifteen years since in Waterford, near Troy, and promised so well that a Company was soon after formed to develop the business.

A few years ago the manufacture of valves was commenced at Troy by the firm of Brown & Co., who purchased spacious buildings and made preparations for the prosecution of the business upon an extensive plan, but about two years since, having been unsuccessful in their contest with the Ludlow Valve Co., they sold their entire establishment, including grounds, buildings, tools, machinery, patterns and patents to said Co., who immediately proceeded to enlarge the works, and introduce the latest improved machinery ; the entire equipment being of the best possible description, and supposed to be unequaled by anything in a similar line in the United States.

Thus far, by the combination of hard work and skill in making improvements, the Company have achieved a remarkable success which has enabled them to keep well in advance of all competitors in this important branch of industry, their sales steadily increasing each year, being materially larger for the year 1874 than in any previous twelve months, notwithstanding the wide spread commercial stagnation.

The factory premises occupy an area of about 270x325 feet, fronting on two streets just above the line dividing Troy and Lansingburgh, and comprise a large machine shop, fully equipped with valuable machinery, much of it made and adapted specially for their own manufacture, also an Iron Foundry, Brass Foundry, Pattern House, Storage Facilities, &c. The Company have also an ample cash capital.

In the line of Brass Valves are included all sizes from one half inch to three inch, while larger ones are made to order. They are of good steam metal, usually with double gates. The Iron Valves range from one and a half to forty-eight inches inside diameter.

These valves give a straight unobstructed opening of the full size of pipe, and are made full bronze mounted, (not with yellow brass) partially bronze mounted, or all iron; double or single gate, with screwed sockets, flange, hub or spigot, with screwed stem opening to right or left, with sliding stem or sliding stem and lever, also with hand wheel or nut for wrench.

When this Company commenced the making of valves, there were no straight way valves in the market, excepting those having a solid gate in one piece, and their introduction of the double valves, for which they have three patents, was an important improvement. The double iron gates, from three inch inclusive, and the single ones from ten inch inclusive, upward, move between closely fitting parallel faces, rendering them self cleaning from any foreign matter that may adhere to them. Gas and Water Companies will find this a feature of importance. The double water valves possess a marked advantage from the peculiarity of their construction, the gates being kept in line by the parallel seats, while in valves with wedging seats, the water has a tendency to crowd the gates to one side, thereby wearing out the stems more rapidly. All the wedges in the double water valves are of solid brass.

These valves also have an advantage in the independent play of the wedges, relieving the gates of much of the friction in closing and opening. Every valve is carefully tested before leaving the works.

The Company make for attachment to their valves, when desired, indicators to show the position of the gate; also, valves with plain sliding stem, operated by a lever with a simple arrangement for holding the gate firmly wherever desired They also make to order brass or iron valves of special size or finish, also valves and hydrants of the Brown patents, owned by them.

The Company's new style of fire hydrant embraces many distinctive features of value and is considered the most effective and durable Hydrant in the market.

They are made in eight styles, three with four and a half inch, the others with five and a half inch stand pipe. The standard length is five feet from the pavement to bottom of hydrant. The opening through the seat in the smaller sizes, is three and seven-eighths, through the larger four and one eighth inches. From the latter both valves and the seat can be removed without digging ; from the former both valves, but not the seat.

The Company's goods are largely used by gas and water companies, steam fitters and manufacturing concerns in all parts of the country, and abundant testimonials can be given to their excellence.

Possessing long practical experience, ample manufacturing facilities, with energy and enterprise, the Ludlow Valve Manufacturing Company cannot fail to retain the leading position they have so worthily won.

The officers of the Company are H. G. Ludlow, President; D. J. Johnston, V. President; M. D. Schoonmaker, Treasurer.

Double Gate Valve.

Hydraulic Main Dip Regulator.

Lever Valve.

Standard, with Patent Indicator.

Single Gate Valve.

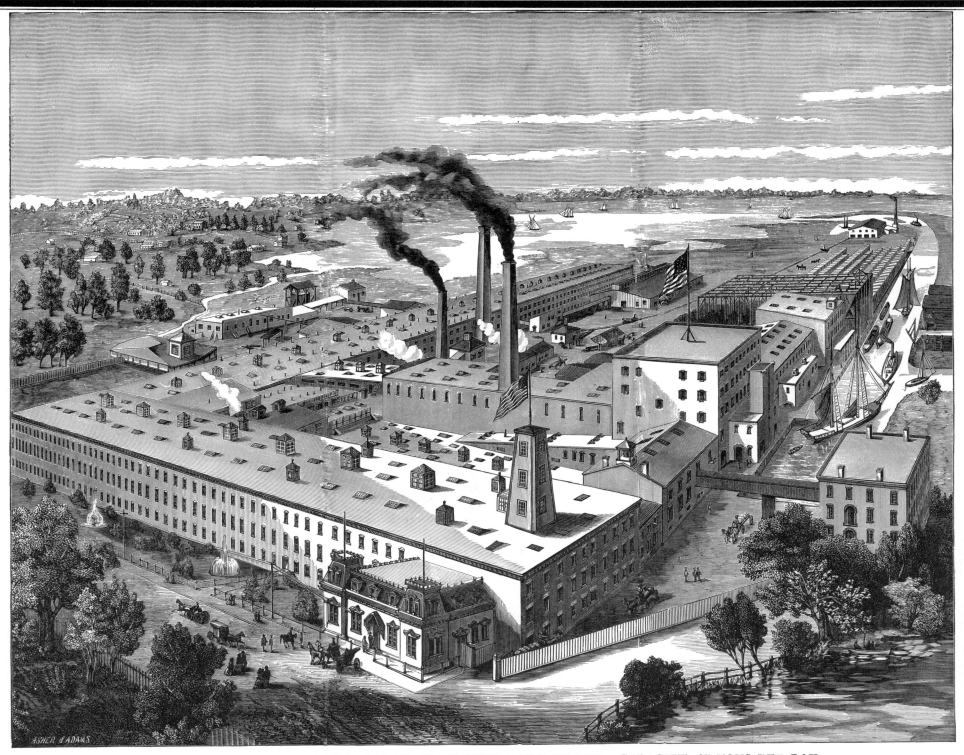

DURYEAS' GLEN COVE STARCH WORKS, GLEN COVE, LONG ISLAND. CAPACITY, 45 TONS PER DAY.

GLEN COVE MANUFACTURING COMPANY,

Manufacturers of

Duryeas' Satin Gloss and Superior Starch for the Laundry, and Duryeas' Improved Corn Starch and Maizena for Food.

Wm. Duryea. Gen'l Agent, 29, 31 & 33 Park Place, New York.

The very extensive and complete works of the Glen Cove Manufacturing Company, represented in the above engraving were erected in 1855 for the practice of a process mechanically and chemically new, having for its object the production of a quality of starch superior to any previously produced. It is unnecessary for us to comment on the success of the under-taking, as the quality of the goods emanating from the works, viz: Duryeas' Satin Gloss Starch, and Superior Starch, for the Laundry, and Duryeas' Improved Corn Starch and Maizena for food, have gained a world wide celebrity. These manufactures have been placed in competition with like goods of other makers at all the leading expositions of the world, with decisions in their favor as evidenced by medals, cuts of which appear below; the prize medal having been awarded to these productions in every instance of competition. At Paris in 1867 they received the unqualified approbation of "Perfection of Preparation."

Few persons who have not given the subject special attention have an approximately correct idea of the vast amount of Starch daily consumed in the United States.—Competent authorities have estimated it at two hundred tons, of which the Glen Cove Works has a capacity to manufacture forty-five tons. There are some three or four large manufacturers in this country and hosts of smaller ones, but there are none great or small, whose productions are more widely and favorably known than are those of the Glen Cove Manufacturing Company. A glance at our engraving will convey an idea of the size of the works, which are completely fitted with every appliance that can aid in the production of absolutely perfect goods.

The demand for Duryeas' Starch is so wide spread and so extensive that the Company have established home offices as follows:—

General Depot, 29, 31 & 33 Park Place, New York.
132 South Water Street, Chicago, Illinois.
503 North Second Street, St. Louis, Missouri.
Corner of Water and Chestnut Streets, Philadelphia, Pennsylvania.
144 State Street, Boston, Massachusetts.
109 California Street, San Francisco.
78 Gravier Street, New Orleans.
And Foreign Offices at :
33 East Cheap, London, E. C.
36 St. Mary-at Hill, London, England.
17 Greenside Place, Edinburgh, Scotland.
39 Admirality Street, Hamburgh, Germany.
Andre & Co., Antwerp.

FAC-SIMILE OF PRIZE MEDALS

Awarded to the

MESSRS. DURYEA

OVER ALL COMPETITORS FOR THE "PERFECTION OF QUALITY" OF THEIR GOODS.

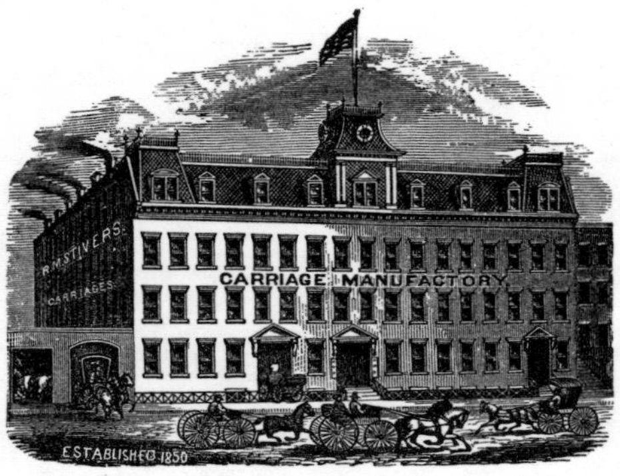

R. M. STIVERS,

CARRIAGE MANUFACTURER,

144, 146, 148, 150 and 152 East 31st Street, N. Y.

—:o:—

ESTABLISHED IN NEW YORK TWENTY-SIX YEARS.

—:o:—

The above engraving represents the extensive carriage manufactory of R. M. Stivers, who is one of the most popular builders in this country, he having achieved within a comparatively few years a world wide reputation for fine work and upright dealing. Mr. Stivers came to New York in 1850 with a (borrowed) capital of one hundred dollars, and embarked in business.

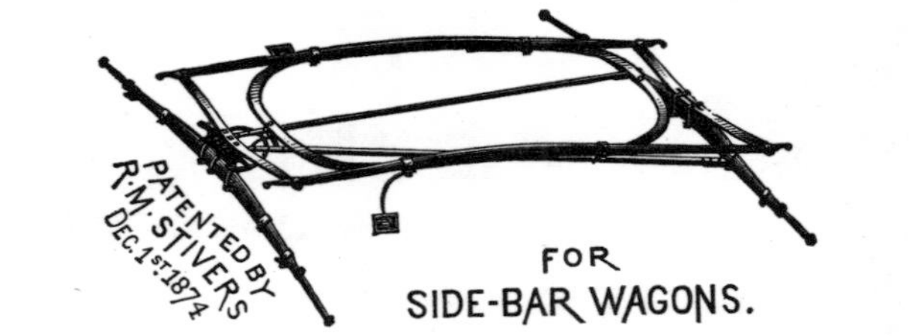

His indefatigable energy, pluck and indomitable courage overcame all difficulties. With "Excelsior" as his motto, he slowly but surely climbed from the lowest round of the ladder, to a position second to that of none in his line of specialties, viz: the production of the finest carriages for road and park driving. In the warerooms connected with his factory, which covers an area equal to four hundred feet long by twenty-five feet in width, will always be found an assortment of elegant work in the newest and latest designs. It will repay all visitors to New York City to visit this factory; the business is a feature of the city, and the building one of its many ornamental structures. Mr. Stivers is of a genial nature and has a hearty welcome for all who call at his works, whether they come as buyers or merely as visitors.

He is the inventor and patentee of several improvements in pleasure work; one a shifting rail for buggy tops; another, for the prevention of all rattle in the fifth wheels; a third, for the concealing of all bolt heads, nuts, etc., so that the outlines of the woodwork remain unbroken; his last and most important invention, being a circular combination spring for improving the riding of side-bar wagons, which he patented December 1st, 1874. The old-style side-bar wagon was complained of as riding hard, stiff and shaky. To obviate these objections, Mr. Stivers invented his spring improvement, and now produces a side-bar wagon (which, by the way, is the fashionable wagon) that rides easy, soft and pleasant, and still retains all of

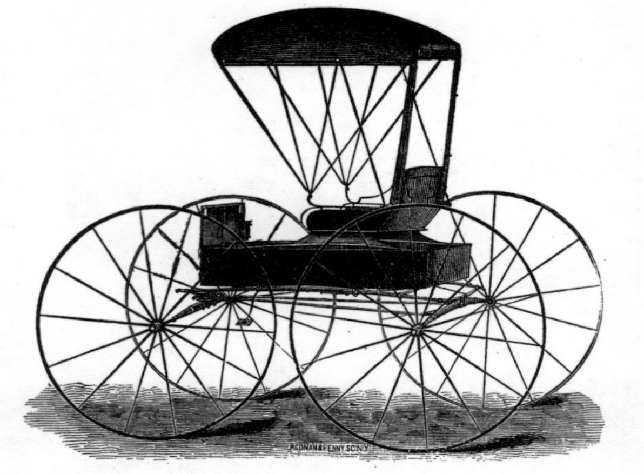

those qualities so necessary to make a perfect speed wagon. This invention is well worthy of investigation by all who desire to see a really perfect wagon.

No branch of industry, perhaps, has made more rapid strides during the last fifty years than carriage building, and it is very generally admitted that no country excels our own in the production of vehicles combining graceful proportions with extreme lightness, great strength, and beauty of finish. American carriages and pleasure wagons are used everywhere, and the productions of Mr. Stivers rank with the best productions of the oldest American manufacturers.

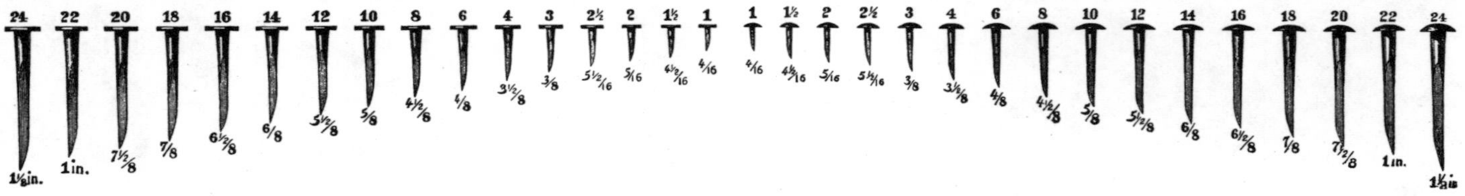

AMERICAN TACK COMPANY,

Factory, Fairhaven, Mass.

SALESROOM, 117 CHAMBERS ST., N. Y.

—:o:—

The United States are far in advance of the balance of the world in the manufacture of nails and tacks, in consequence of the superiority of their mechanical appliances. Recently the American Automatic Feeding Nail and Tack Machines have been introduced in England, but the operatives there are opposed to them and prefer their own machines, which requires a "feeder" to "turn plate" to every machine, while one boy can tend four tack or two nail machines of the American self-feeding patterns. By the use of these Automatic Feeding Machines, capable of turning out 100,000 tacks per day, manufacturers are enabled to make more and better work, with less physical exertion than can be produced by the hand fed machines of Europe.

Prominent among the manufacturers of America is the American Tack Company, engravings of a few of whose productions are presented above. This Company commenced operations in 1865, with fifty machines for tacks and fifteen for small nails, but as their productions became known, the demand for them so increased that they were forced to add to their manufacturing facilities, and they now run seventy-five tack and twenty-five nail machines.

The officers of the Company are: Chas. E. Brigham, of Boston, President; J. A. Beauvais, of New Bedford, Treasurer; and C. D. Hunt, Agent and Manager, gentlemen well and favorably known in business circles. The factory is 250 feet long, 40 feet wide and three stories high, making the entire floor length 750 feet. In addition to the main building are the engine house, pickling house, annealing house, store houses, blacksmith shop and other necessary buildings.

The above cut represents the principal sizes of the regular tacks, flat heads, and oval heads manufactured by this Company. They make, however, much smaller tacks than the one ounce, (which count one thousand to the ounce,) their smallest size counting 4,800 to the ounce, and the largest are much larger than the twenty-four ounce. They manufacture every variety and style of tack, including those known as Upholsterer's, Gimp, Lace, Trimmer's, Card, Pail, Cheese Box and Looking-glass Tacks, Finishing, Trunk and Clout Nails; Hungarian, Channel, Cigar Box and Chair Nails; Iron, Zinc, Steel and Copper Shoe Nails; Polished and blued 2d and 3d Nails; Boat Nails of copper and iron, and any size or style of tack or nail will be made to sample.

In the manufacture of these different classes of goods, the American Tack Company annually consumes over 1000 tons of iron, one-half of which is imported from Sweden, while the other half is selected from the best brands of American manufacture. Large quanties of copper, zinc, steel and tin are also used. The iron is imported in bars, and rolled to the proper thickness before going to the factory, where it is stripped to suitable width and cut into tacks or nails.

The Company own some fifteen acres of ground fronting the water, and have a fine wharf on their own premises from which they ship goods direct to New York, Philadelphia and other points. Their goods are used in every State and Territory in the Union, and are largely exported to South America, and indeed all foreign countries using tacks, including England, Germany, France, Switzerland and other European states.

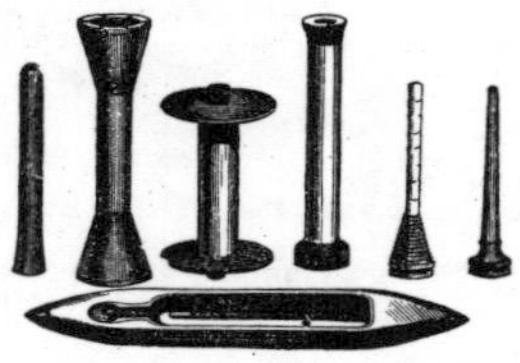

JAMES BALDWIN & CO.,

Manufacturers of Every Description of Bobbins, Spools, and Shuttles, with all the Latest Improvements, for Silk, Linen, Cotton and Woolen Mills.

Manchester, N. H.

Mr. James Baldwin, the senior partner of the above named firm, has been practically engaged in the manufacture of Bobbins and Shuttles over forty years, and is one of the oldest and most successful men in this business in the United States—the celebrated Baldwin Patent Shuttle, of which he is the patentee, having added largely to his fame. The present firm commenced business in 1859, and in 1870 entered largely into the manufacture of Jack Spools with Baldwin's Patent Nut, which is claimed to be the best device yet known for holding on and strengthening the heads. A great advantage gained in their method of manufacture is that the spools can be shipped in parts, reducing the bulk of packages, rendering them less liable to breakage, and also saving a large percentage of the freight, especially when shipped to distant points. The parts are readily adjusted at the mills where used, and, when heads are worn out or broken in use, they can easily be repaired, as the manufacturers are always ready to furnish extra heads to fit the barrels. Messrs. James Baldwin & Co., also manufacture Bass' Patent Filling Bobbins, and are at all times prepared to supply mills with their goods at short notice and at lowest prices.

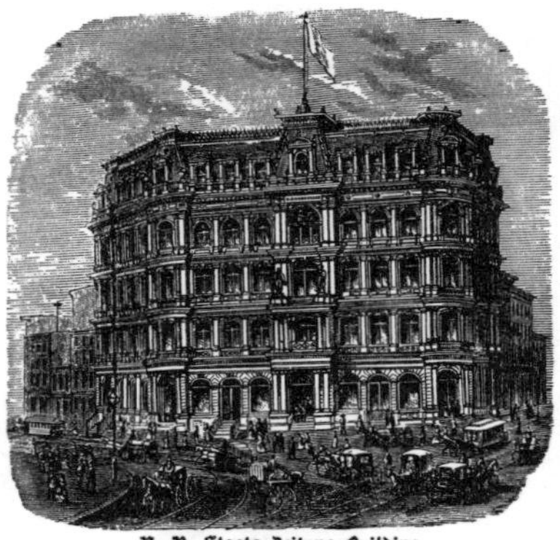

N. Y. Staats-Zeitung Building.

N. Y. STAATS ZEITUNG,

The New York *Staats Zeitung* building on Tyron Row at the junction of Chatham and Centre Streets, opposite City Hall, is one of the most tasteful and splendid buildings in New York. The style of architecture is Renaissance and not only the whole of the building, but every particular shows a cultivated taste and a successful effort to unite beauty with utility. It is fire-proof in every particular and the interior arrangements are in strict harmony with the outside appearance. The building was especially erected for the publication of the *New Yorker Staats Zeitung*, one of the oldest and the most widely circulated German papers published in the United States, and the press rooms, the publication office, the editorial and compositors departments are the best adapted of any newspaper establishment.

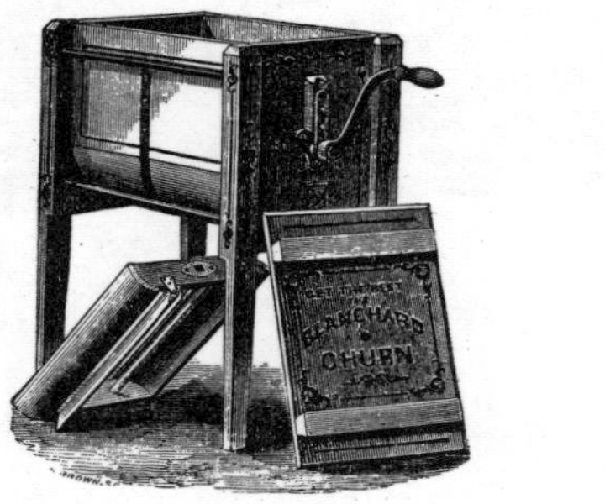

THE BLANCHARD CHURN,

Porter Blanchard's Sons, Sole Manufacturers,

Concord, N. H.

Among the many labor-saving contrivances invented by Yankee ingenuity, none have been more universally adopted in our country homes than the Blanchard Churn. Porter Blanchard commenced making churns in 1818, which soon became famous. The Blanchard Churn has kept pace with the times, and it is still confidently claimed to be the best in use. The present firm make its manufacture their sole business, occupying an extensive steam factory and employing a large number of hands. Their long experience, the conscientious care taken in the selection of material and in its manufacture, and the acknowledged superiority of the principles upon which this churn is constructed, render its continued popularity as sure as its past success. It is made in seven sizes, and is really an automatic butter maker. Those interested should send for the "New Butter Manual" and descriptive circulars.

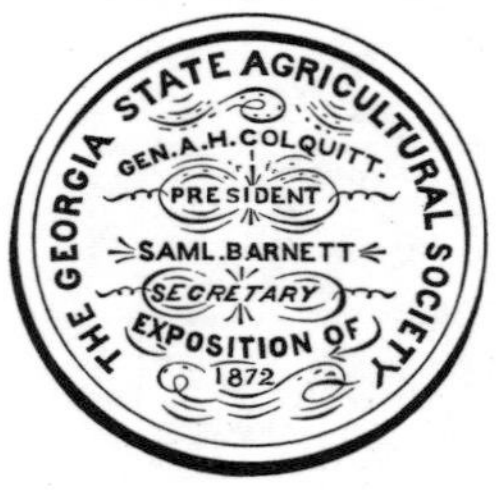

The Improved

"FAIRHAVEN" PRINTING PRESS,

Manufactured by the

BOSTON AND FAIRHAVEN IRON WORKS,

Fairhaven, Mass.

—:o:—

The town of Fairhaven is situated in Southern Massachusetts, near the mouth of the Acushnet River, emptying into Buzzard's Bay. It is excellently situated for manufacturing purposes, and having a splendid harbor, possesses superior facilities for shipping its productions either by rail or boat to New York or Boston. Fairhaven was a place of some importance in colonial times, and was attacked by the British forces during the Revolution.

Prominent among the manufacturing establishments which have developed since those early days is the Boston and Fairhaven Iron Works, having foundry and machine shop facilities not excelled in Southern Massachusetts. The Company makes a specialty of the "Fairhaven" Printing Press, represented in the above cut.

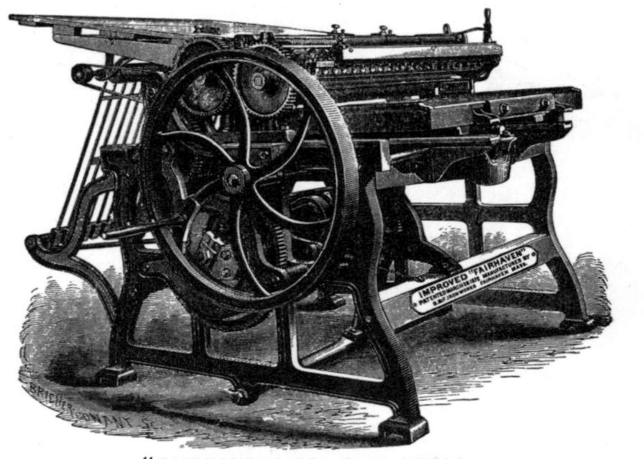

"FAIRHAVEN" PRINTING PRESS.

With the development of our country there has grown up a demand for printed matter in enormous quantities and of a superior quality, which demand could only be met by such improvements in the printing press as would enable more rapid work than could be obtained by hand presses. New styles of presses of different patterns were built, but it was not till within a few years that a thoroughly reliable press could be bought at a price within the means of publishers outside the large cities. The thousands of printers and publishers in smaller cities and villages who were obliged to use the hand press found it difficult to "work off" the increasing editions of their papers on time, and utterly impossible to supply the de-

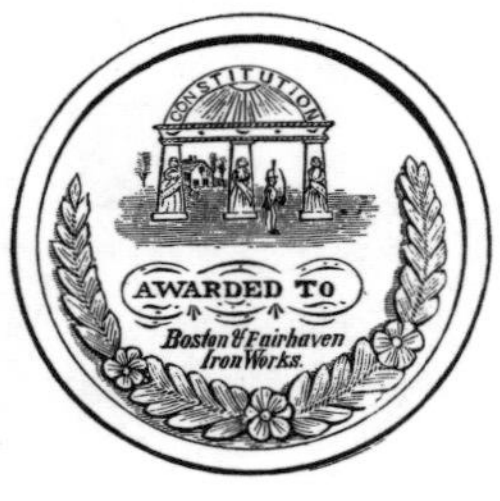

mands for job printing at prices approximating to those ruling in larger places, until inventive genius was stimulated to produce something which readily filled their want. This the "Fairhaven" Press does to perfection. It is compact in form, simple in construction, easily understood, and we do not think it possible to make a press of its size and weight requiring less power to run it. It may be driven by steam or by hand, and is capable of a speed of 1000 per hour by the former and 800 by the latter. It has a perfect roller and cylinder distribution; the fountain could not be improved, and the whole inking apparatus is under control of the feeder, who, without leaving his place, can instantly cut off the color. The impression, too, can be thrown off at will, and every misfed sheet be saved, and all the advantages of a high-priced "trip" press, in the additional rollings of forms for fine work, is gained. The sheets are delivered as accurately as though piled by hand. It is about seven years since these presses were first introduced—now they are in use from Maine to California and have given universal satisfaction. The tokens of their appreciation embrace not only the testimonials of many printers but medals and diplomas, among which are those of the Georgia State Fair, held at Atlanta. Job printers and proprietors of country newspapers will find this press especially adapted to their wants.

PERKINS CHEESE FACTORY

W. C. & W. L. PERKINS, Proprietors.

Cazenovia, Madison Co., N. Y.

——:o:——

Cazenovia is one of the prettiest little villages in Central New York, nestling among the hills of Madison County, on the banks of Chittenango Creek and at the southern extremity of a beautiful lake (Cazenovia Lake) five miles in length and one in breadth; on the line of the Syracuse and Chenango and the Cazenovia, Canastota, and De Ruyter Railroads, it has connection with trunk lines leading in all directions, and is thus afforded the choice of markets for its productions. The streets of the village are well laid out and kept scrupulously clean—cozy houses with neatly kept flower gardens and miniature parks in front, the crystal lake at the foot of its principal street with its fleet of little yachts belonging to private parties and boating clubs, the many trim row boats for practice or fisher's use, the tiny steamers, as complete in their appointments as the larger ones that ply the waters of the great lakes, its many beautiful drives in every direction—all tend to make it a favorite place of resort during the summer season for pleasure seekers from the larger cities.

Several factories, mills and manufacturing shops, are located here, and they are rapidly increasing in size and number; the magnificent water power, which is rapidly being developed making a peculiarly favorable point for the establishment of large industries, and it is predicted that Cazenovia will soon rank not only as the most beautiful but as one of the most important manufacturing towns in the State.

The surrounding country is agriculturally very rich, and is divided mainly into small but productive farms. There is little or no "scientific" farming done, no new-fangled methods are adopted until their superiority over the old ones have been uncontestably proven;—the owner of each homestead is a "practical" not a "theoretical" farmer, and the result is a population generally well-to-do, a large proportion even wealthy. Madison County is essentially a Dairy County, and though the raising of grains and root crops are not neglected, the wealth of the people is largely drawn from their Dairy products, the most important of which is Cheese, and to Cheese we propose to devote the balance of this article.

Messrs. W. C. & W. L. Perkins, proprietors of the celebrated Perkins Cheese Factory, Cazenovia, New York, have occupied their present premises (about one mile south of the village) more than fifty years, and during all that time have been engaged in the manufacture of Butter and Cheese. For more than forty years these products of their place were made in the old-fashioned (home-made) way, but thinking that perhaps as good if not a better article could be made at a less cost, by newer processes, and by working larger quantities of milk, they, as an experiment, commenced drawing milk to a Cheese Factory. From long previous experience and observation they had learned just what results could be obtained from a given quantity of milk under the old manipulation, and were pleased to find that the factory process gave far better results, in quantity and quality of product, and that these better results were attained with much less labor. They continued to draw their milk to the factory about three years, but as it was situated at a considerable distance from their place, and as their neighbors urged them to institute a factory more conveniently located, they for these and other minor considerations, determined to do so, and, in the Spring of 1869, they opened a factory which formed the nucleus of their present completely appointed establishment.

While perfectly familiar with home-made processes of manufacture, factory methods were comparatively new to them, and as their hopes of success could only be based on the superior quality of their production, and they were determined to succeed, they engaged experienced cheese makers to superintend the work. From the beginning the enterprise was a success, and Perkins Cheese soon held a high place in the market; but the proprietors were not satisfied with merely maintaining the quality of the products at the standard first accorded them, they thought it could be improved, and reasoned that the employes who made good cheese in 1869 should be able to make much better in 1872. The workman however, like the great mass of employes, argued that if they made as good as others, it was good enough, and therefore did not give the work that care and attention necessary to produce better results. Messrs. Perkins desire was, not to make

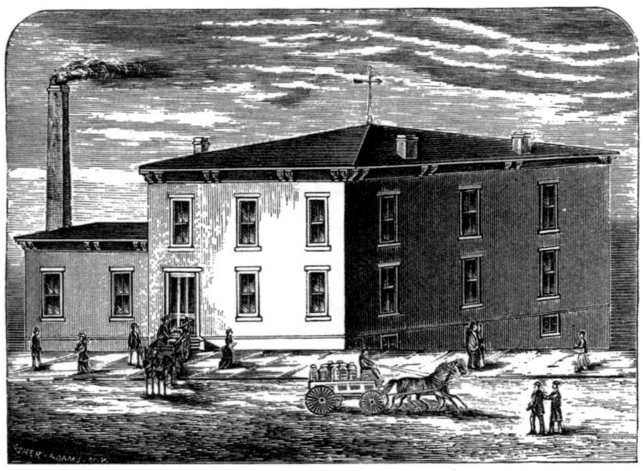

THE PERKINS CHEESE FACTORY, CAZENOVIA, MADISON CO. N. Y.

good cheese, merely, but the best, and that they might more easily accomplish this, in 1873, the junior member of the firm assumed the sole supervision of the factory work.

The great majority of Cheese Factories are owned by associations of farmers who employ professional cheese makers, paying them stated salaries, or so much per hundred pounds. If either of these modes of payment is adopted, the superintendent's interest is to fit the cheese for market as rapidly as possible, and to get rid of it as soon as there is a shipment ready —with regard only to the current price, and sometimes without regard even to that—so as to be freed from the care of it, for here his interest ends. In the Perkins Factory the proprietors own by far the largest proportion of the milk consumed, and the patrons know that their cheese will be well cared for, and held in store until what seems to be the most favorable time to sell, without regard to the extra work such retention may entail upon the firm. The interest of the proprietors of the factory and of the Dairymen who contribute milk are identical and cannot be divided until the product is sold, consequently the proprietors cannot be careless of their patrons interest without at the same time sacrificing their own. For essentially the same reasons, milk producers who contribute to, and cheese buyers who purchase the product of this factory, can always rely upon obtaining the best returns for the capital invested, whether it be milk, as material for, or money as the purchase price of the product, because it is to the interest of the proprietors and managers of the factory to produce and sell the very best; the best brings the highest price to the manufacturer, and pays the highest profit to the buyer, and therefore always finds a ready sale.

The first building used by Messrs. Perkins for a curing house had originally been a dwelling, and was remodeled for cheese purposes. It soon however became inadequate, and being flattered by the annual cheese buyers, as to the superior quality of their product and urged to erect a larger, more attractive and commodious building, believing too that it was to their own interest and that of their patrons,(many of whom derive the major portion of their yearly income from the products of the factory) to have a building specially adapted to and equipped for the business, they, in 1875, erected a two story brick building with a commodious cellar underneath, the whole perfectly ventilated, and furnished with the most approved appliances. In their new house they have met with even greater success than in the old one. The cheese cures perfectly. It is not very warm during the hottest day, nor very cool at night. The mold that often attacks cheese in wooden buildings during warm weather, did not occur on those cured in this building during the past season, (1875). Some July cheese cured in a wooden dryhouse which had became "off flavor" and quite "sharp," were stored in the basement, and became quite "mild."

Cheese that had been cured and boxed were stored here for months, and the shrinkage was much less than is usally allowed. Here the cream can be raised upon the milk and stored until it is properly changed ready for churning without danger of the temperature raising above churning point even in the hottests weather. It is believed that for the manufacture of butter and cheese this factory has advantages unsurpassed, indeed, those who should know, and who have no interest other than as buyers, say it is the best built and most perfectly equipped factory known.

By leaving orders parties can have such styles of Cheese and Butter made as best suits their trade. The cows from which the milk is taken are thorough-bred Jerseys, Devons, New York and Kentucky Durhams with grades of each.

Some estimate of the magnitude of the Cheese trade of the State of New York will be gathered from the following carefully compiled figures. There were in the State April 1, 1876, 1,022 Cheese Factories, which consumed the milk of 459,900 cows, and produced during the preceeding year 160,965,000 pounds of Cheese, which, estimated at an average value of 12 cents per pound, was worth $19,315,800. Cheese was manufactured in private dairies to the extent of $3,219,300, making the total Cheese interest of the State, $22,535,100. The number of Milch Cows in the State is in round numbers, 2,000,000. The Butter produced was valued at $37,084,-048. The value of the milk sold and consumed we have no reliable data for, but estimating it at one cent per day for each inhabitant, which certainly is not too high, it amounts to $16,000,000. Commissioner Wells in his report upon the Industry, Trade and Commerce of the United States for 1869, puts the value of the dairy products of the Country at $400,000,000.

PEARL HOMINY,

Manufactured by the

BALTIMORE PEARL HOMINY COMPANY.

——:o:——

The United States Census Report states the principal cereal productions of the country as follows: Wheat, 287,745,626, bushels; Oats, 282,107,-157 bushels; Barley, 29,761,305 bushels; Rye, 16,918,759, bushels; Buckwheat, 9,821,721 bushels, making a total of 626,354,568 bushels. The production of Corn was 760,944,549 bushels, an excess of 134,589,981 bushels over the combined yield of the five grains first named; if the production of Rye had been four times as great, (67,675,036 bushels), Buckwheat three times as great, (29,465,163 bushels), and Barley three times as great (89,283.915 bushels), Corn would have still been, 4,667,625 bushels ahead. Much of this immense yearly yield, is of course, used in manufactures, not eatable; as much more is fed to cattle and swine, but many millions of bushels are manufactured into food for man, ground into meal or flour, converted into starch, or cracked into hominy. Of all the cereals used for food, Corn is the most nutritious and the most healthful; it contains 34 per cent. of nitrogen to feed muscular growth, 40 per cent. of carbon for flesh, and 4 per cent. of phosphorus for the brain, a ratio of food elements, better by far than that of any other grain.

Hominy is at once the simplest and the best preparation of Corn for food, and is also the cheapest. In the bill of fare of the farmer, the mechanic, or laboring man it finds a prominent place, because it is nutritious—because it supplies food for overworked muscles and it has a place on the table of the wealthy, because it is delicious; in fact it is the food for the million—equally adapted for the home of elegance or the abode of indigence.

Many of our readers of middle age can doubtless well remember how Hominy was made in their young days. It was usually pounded in a mortar with a pestal, and came forth bruised, partly broken or in whole grains, with the hull but partially peeled from the Corn. This is now cnanged, however, and the preparation of Hominy has become a business of great importance The largest manufacturing Hominy Mill in the world, we believe, is that of the Baltimore Pearl Hominy Company, and for perfection of grade and quantity of yield it certainly has no superior.

The Mill is situated at the extreme north bounds of the city, the furthest point north of North Street. Strangers will find it by following North Street to its place of location on Jones Falls, which stream, when full, gives motive power to the Mills, but when the water is low the Company have recourse to steam power, and the machinery of their extensive Mill (or mills) is driven by two steam engines, one of 150 horse power, another 100 horse power. The magnitude of the interests involved in this enterprise called for that combination and organized system so common to the extensive interests which underlie the movements of those industries which necessitate large investments and wholesale operations. Accordingly a Company was formed which is ably presided over by Mr. V. Winters with Mr. Robert McGregor, as Treasurer and Manager.

The grounds are 1,400 by 200 feet; the main building 125 by 80 feet, 3½ stories high, with basement or cellar; attached to which is a one-story brick wareroom, 70 by 45 feet; the engine and boiler house, 35 by 45 feet, which attaches to the building on the north. These buildings are of modern style, massive in construction, and entirely fire-proof. Two water wheels, ninety and seventy-five horse power respectively, together with two engines with a combined force of 250 horse power, by which to give accelerated speed or power to the grinding of Grits, Pearl Hominy, Pearl Meal, Corn Flour, etc. Thus we have a dim outline of a ponderous establishment which runs twelve Buckeye Hominy Mills; grinds 2,500 bushels of Corn per day, whilst five burr mill stones have a capacity of 300 barrels of Corn Meal at the same time. Likewise, the Company have in their basement a kiln for drying Corn, in which 400 barrels can be dried daily.

In addition to Pearl Hominy, the Company makes Pearl Meal. Of this last named article of food some fifty barrels per day are ground. Also Corn Flour which is decidedly whiter than wheat flour, and is used for admixture with flour, by which combination, bread is obtained which retains moisture and freshness even longer than when made wholly of wheat flour.

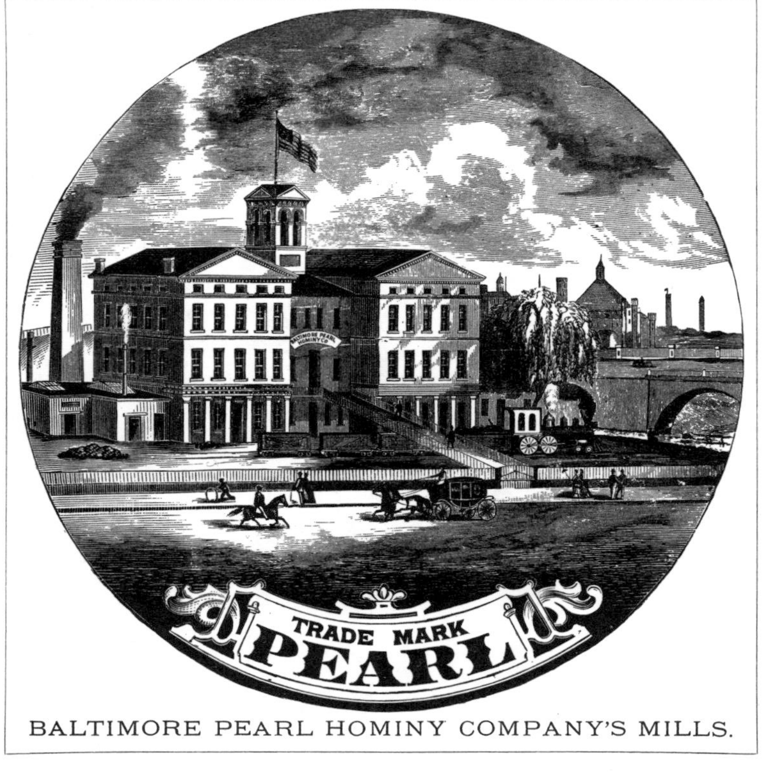

BALTIMORE PEARL HOMINY COMPANY'S MILLS.

The Company make a food for stock, composed of the heart and hull of Corn, which is relished by the cattle, and which forms for them a rich and cheap article of subsistance.

Preparatory to making Hominy the Corn is run through Cleaners before it reaches the Mills, and is carried to the different stories of the building by elevators. The process of grinding by the Buckeye Mills, separates the solid portion of the cereal from the husk and heart, thus leaving nothing but the solid grain to go into their marketable Hominy, which gives the Grits or Pearl Hominy, or Corn Flour, such exquisite beauty, adds to its nutritive qualities, or, rather, eliminates all the indigestable portions and renders it capable of withstanding all changes of weather or climate without deterioration. The Company have evidence in their posession of Hominy having kept seventeen months, during which time the ship which freighted it had passed the tropics, and doubled Cape Horn; and still the writer says, "notwithstanding its passage through the tropics and the fact that it is seventeen months old, it is as white and sweet as ever."

Messrs. Warden, Merritt & Co., the well known Commission Merchants of Baltimore, write:—"It affords us great pleasure to contribute our testimony to the superiority of your products. Being, as we are aware, manufactured of the very choicest materials to be had in the country, and by the most approved method, there is nothing better to be had. From your extreme care in the selection of your raw materials, located as you are, where the best of Corn is to be had, we should say that you are in a position to defy competition."

Messrs. James E. Morris & Co., of 194 Chambers Street, New York, write:—"Our business, that of supplying vessels sailing to all parts of the world, has subjected it (Pearl Hominy) to various changes of climate and temperature, and the result has without exception been entirely satisfactory."

We might add many other complimentary letters, but deem it unnecessary. The following well known firms highly recommend it, and to name them is enough to satisfy any who might doubt that the Pearl Hominy is an article of superior excellence. J. M. Parr & Son, Baltimore; McDowell, Lockwood & Co., New York; Charles S. Brown & Co., Baltimore; Dusenbury Brothers, New York; Harvey & Sisler, Wilmington, Del.; Richard & Co., Jacksonville, Florida; Henry C. Kellogg & Co., Philadelphia, Pa.; Alfred Smith & Co., Paris, France.

Within the past few months the Company have received applications from London, Hamburg, and Paris for agencies for the sale of their Pearl Hominy and other productions, which are well and favorably known in all the leading cities of the Old World. The Company have on file at their office letters similar to those above quoted, from leading firms in Great Britian and on the Continent of Europe, and, without any attempt to "push" it, a large foreign demand has been created, which is constantly increasing. The Company own the right to sell the Buckeye Hominy Mill over the United States. Its superior qualities entitle it to all praise. Interested parties should not fail to call at the Company's extensive works when they visit Baltimore.

THE MANUFACTORY, WAREHOUSES AND TRADE OF B. T. BABBITT.

Of this justly noted successful and enterprising merchant, we give an extended notice for the benefit of the young men of our day who are starting in mercantile pursuits.

All things considered, one of the most remarkable instances of well directed business energy, sagacity and enterprise ever witnessed in America, is that of Mr. B. T. Babbitt, whose name heads this article. The age, we are aware, is fruitful of great names. We have still among us a Stewart, a Claflin, a Vanderbilt and others, but these men built upon foundations already established, and their remarkable talents have been exhibited in simply enlarging their business to magnificent proportions. They are princes in their way, but they have simply builded upon foundations thoroughly laid by others. Mr. Babbitt, on the other hand, has largely established his own business. We can do the young men of this age no greater service, than to set before them, briefly, and in a general way, the business and career of this remarkable man.

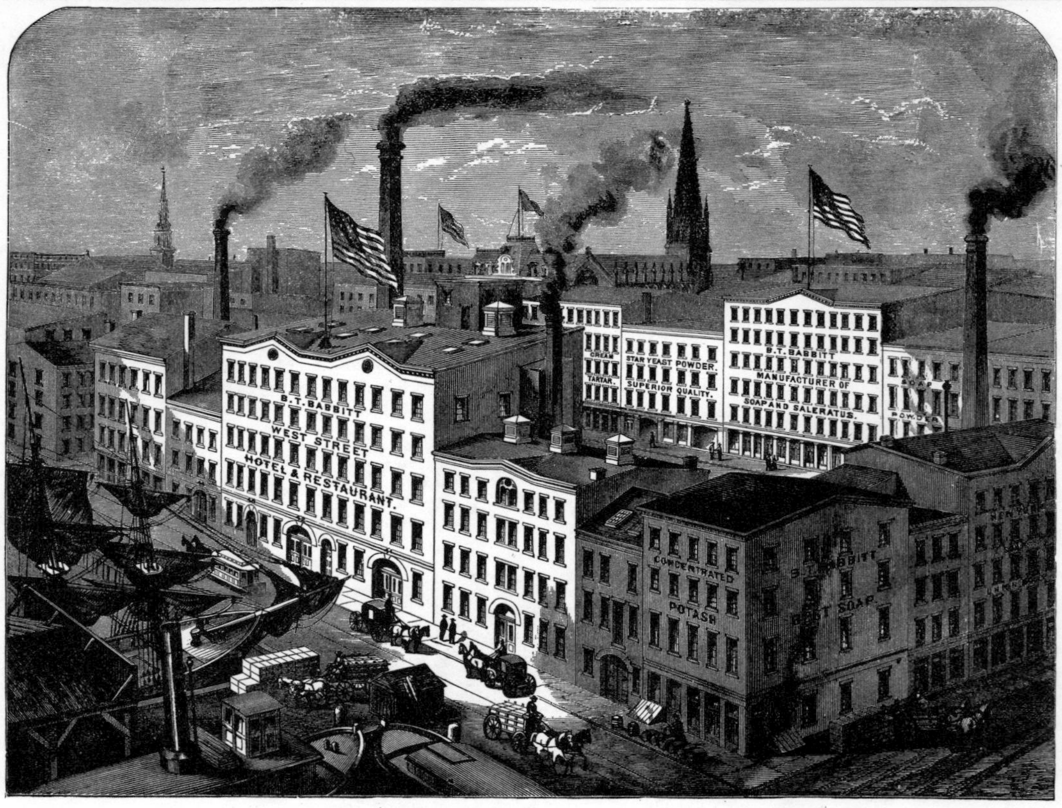

B. T. BABBITT'S BUILDINGS, New York City.

Mr. Babbitt was born at Westmoreland, N.Y., in 1811, and is, therefore now sixty-three years of age. He is yet hale and in the full vigor of manhood and possession of all his powers. As will be inferred, his habits are simple and correct. As a rule, no great results in any of the pursuits of life, are otherwise obtained. He commenced his career as a farmer; graduated from that to a blacksmith shop in Utica; turned his attention subsequently to machinery; and later still to the manufacture of threshing machines; the latter pursuit being carried on at Little Falls, Herkimer County. It was inevitable that a man of this character should find his way to this city as the only proper field for his energy and enterprise.

Mr. Babbitt left his business at Little Falls (which had been reasonably successful) in the hands of one whom he regarded as a friend, came to New York in 1843, and immediately established himself at 68 Washington Street, as a manufacturer of Saleratus. He supposed himself at this time worth at least $10,000; but the friend whom he had entrusted with his business at Little Falls proved recreant to his trust, collected and spent his money, and failed. Mr. Babbitt had, therefore, so far as capital was concerned, to commence his business career anew. He had literally nothing, thus in fact starting with less than nothing but an indomitable will, energy and ambition. In such a man's case these are all that are necessary. Failure, in this way, was but a stepping stone to success. He commenced in a small way, in a two-story building, 25x100 feet. His business rapidly increased and in a short time he added the manufacture of his since famous Soap Powder to the first article. Little by little his business crept up in the face of strong competition, by the then large manufacturers who prophesied the early sinking of the little boat which he thus launched upon the stormy waters.

While strong competing houses were working and planning to accomplish this, their young rival was laboring with his mechanical brain, working out new problems of manufactures, improvements, machinery, etc., and kept constantly adding to his business facilities, space and machinery, purchasing and leasing additional buildings (these lots being then worth $250 each), economizing his expenditures at every point, sleeping at his office, and, as he has ever since done, kept his business under his own immediate supervision.

While progressing satisfactorily under these conditions, to the surprise of everyone—especially his competitors in trade—he invented and perfected the plan of making pure Salaratus from soda ash instead of pearl ash, from which it had been made. Pearl ash brought at that time 9 1/2 cents per pound, while soda ash sold for 2 1/2 cents, a difference of 7 cents per pound. Through this discovery Mr. B. at once controlled the chief part of the trade in this line throughout the country.

Babbitt's Soap became a household word. Building after building was added to the already large establishment. Every improvement in machinery and otherwise was made, and no money spared to make this already vast establishment the first in its line in the nation.

Mr. Babbitt now manufactures in addition to the three articles named, viz: Saleratus, Soap Powder and Soap; concentrated potash, concentrated soft soap, star yeast-powder, lion coffee, hotel and family toilet soaps, super carbonate of soda, cream of tartar, sal-soda, etc. His gigantic establishment now occupies nineteen full city lots.

We have already enumerated the different articles manufactured by Mr. Babbitt. We will now speak a little more in detail. The manufacture of soap is the largest and most important specialty of the business, and is conducted on a scale that approaches the sublime. The works for this purpose are by far the largest in the world. For this purpose alone five enormous kettles, made of heavy boiler iron, are employed, each of which is thirty feet in depth and twenty feet in diameter, having each a capacity of 500,000 pounds; and the whole having an aggregate capacity of 2,500,000 pounds.

The stock out of which all their soap is made, is pure while tallow, purchased and received in barrels or casks. To transfer the tallow to the soap kettles, several barrels or casks are arranged upon a platform, with the bung holes downward; steam pipes are then inserted, connecting with the boilers, and the rapidly melted tallow flows in streams into large iron reservoirs and thence into the kettles. The lye is made from potash and lime, in iron tanks on the upper floor and conveyed in pipes to the kettles. The former is known as caustic soda, and comes in large iron drums. The vast cauldron having been filled, the steam is turned on, and 500,000 pounds of soapy materials boil at once. While one is being filled or prepared another is perhaps boiling and another giving up its finished contents, and thus the work constantly proceeds upon a scale of wholly unparalleled magnitude.

5,000,000 pounds of soap can be manufactured per month, and the cost of the raw materials to fill each kettle for a single boiling, is not less than $36,000. The material in filling the largest kettle costs the enormous sum of $50,000. Such an establishment and facilities are worthy an age of ocean telegraphs and continental railways. The aid of steam and machinery is required to empty kettles, as it would be impossible to ladle material out in the ordinary way.

The soap frames are large shallow iron boxes each made in five pieces, so as to be taken apart when the soap is hard; each holds 1,500 pounds. In these the soap cools and hardens. It is then cut by wire into bars, and wrapped and packed for market. A series of rooms of this immense concern is devoted to the manufacture of toilet soaps; an article for which Mr. Babbitt is held in deserved repute throughout the entire country. These soaps are made from vegetable oil, from which all impurities have been removed, by heat, in the process of manufacture. The agreeable fragrance, the soft, healing detergent qualities of this soap are too well known to be specially referred to. Its most astonishing quality considering the expensive materials used in its manufacture, is its cheapness. Among the interesting appliances in this department are the curious soap engines, into which the bars of equal weight are placed, and receive by powerful compression, without loss of weight, their peculiar oblong form with rounded corners, and the imprint of excellence "Babbitt's Best Soap." These beautiful cakes are placed in racks in immense quantities, wrapped in colored paper, and packed 100 three-quarter pound cakes, in each box. The production of this article is immense, nearly 1,000 boxes, per day. All the other articles manufactured by Mr. Babbitt, are manufactured upon a scale of relative magnificence. Nothing is done piecemeal or by halves. Every modern convenience and appliance is used, while all are the result of the inventive skill and ingenuity of Mr. Babbitt himself.

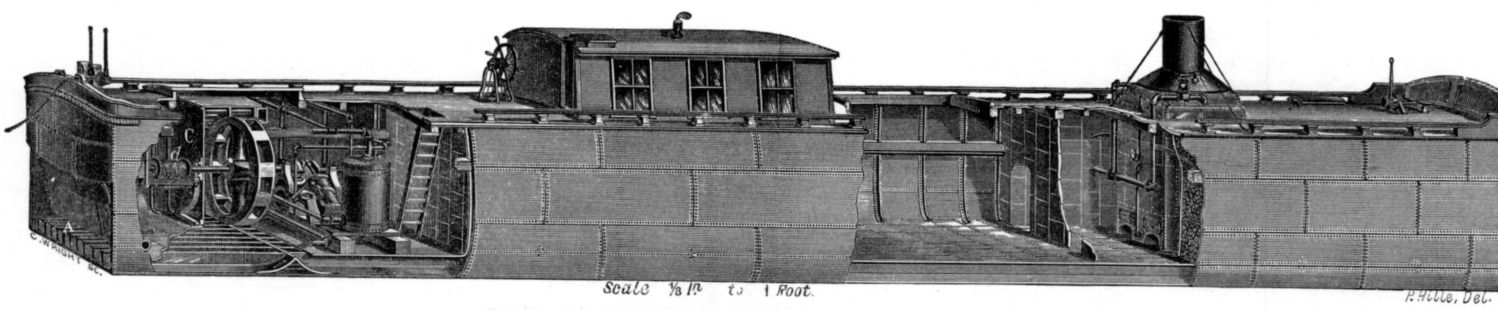

B. T. BABBITT'S STEAM CANAL BOAT

On this page will also be found a cut of a steam canal boat, which, in addition to his many other enterprising achievements, Mr. Babbitt proposes to confer upon the commerce of the country.

It will be remembered that the State Government offers a reward of $100,000 for the best practical plan for utilizing steam power on our canals, and Mr. Babbitt feels confident that his invention fills the requirements called for, and that he will reap the reward. The insuperable objection to all steam canal boats, yet tried, has been the washing away of the canal banks by the disturbing action of the propellor on the water. Mr. Babbitt's boat is so constructed, that unlike all other vessels, its bow does not break water at all, but glides along making scarcely a ripple on the surface. This extraordinary and seemingly impracticable effect is produced by a scientific plan at once novel and ingenious. The boat is square at the bow. Underneath the bottom is what may be designated a chamber, or false bottom, twelve inches high and seventeen feet three inches wide. In this and near the bow of the boat is placed a powerful rotary pump, five feet in diameter and four feet wide, of 400 horse power, having a *suction* capacity of 90,000 cubic feet per minute. By the action of these pumps a vacuum is created and at the same time the water in front of the boat is sucked into the chamber, and thus leaves no resistance to the bow of the boat, which is thus easily and rapidly propelled. The water being pressed out of the stern and filling the vacuum, will also by its reaction add powerfully to the speed of the vessel.

Mr. Babbitt claims that this new principle can also be applied to ocean steamships and will revolutionize this mode of transit by nearly doubling its present rate of speed. He has perfect confidence that by this plan the Atlantic can easily be crossed in five or six days. We earnestly hope that his most sanguine anticipations may be fully realized in this most important matter.

B. T. BABBITT'S COMBINED STEAM GENERATOR, CONDENSER, AND STEAM HEATER FOR BUILDINGS.

After many years of experience as a practical engineer, and a thorough study and comprehension of the scientific principles which govern the circulation of heated air through flues and passages, it has been rendered possible to invent the steam-generating, condensing and heating apparatus, illustrated in the fine engraving in this circular. It is, in itself, a study which will be found most profitable for all who are endeavoring to gain correct ideas upon the subjects of heating and ventilation.

Whatever opinion may be held in regard to the merits of the steam-generator herein illustrated, we think there can be no doubt whatever as to the value of the same construction when used as a surface condenser—cold air being the condensing agent.

We also think it would be difficult to conceive of any way in which a greater amount of cooling surface could be obtained in proportion to the weight of metal used. We hope to be able to explain the action of this apparatus without letters of reference, so that all may comprehend its principles by reading the following description.

To the extreme left of the engraving is situated the steam boiler and furnace, which is constructed with a bottom manifold or heat drum, occupying a position horizontally below the grates, from which rises a series of upright manifolds or pipes, with horizontal pipes extending internally therefrom. From the top of each upright manifold extends a small pipe, connecting with the steam drum, which is placed in the top of the arch. All these parts are constructed in such a manner that the pipes are secured at one end only, and are arranged in such a way that it is claimed a perfect circulation is secured through all parts of the boiler. The upright manifolds are made in a zig-zag form, so that the heat is compelled to come in contact with all the horizontal pipes. The feed-water enters the bottom manifold, and passes thence through the upright manifolds, supplying the side pipes, which are subjected to the action of the fire. The steam generated in these pipes passes from the top of the upright manifold through the several small pipes into the steam drum, the small pipes having sufficient length to allow the upright manifold to expand or contract without straining any other part of the boiler. The objects sought in the construction are safety, perfectly independent expansion, and economy in the use of fuel.

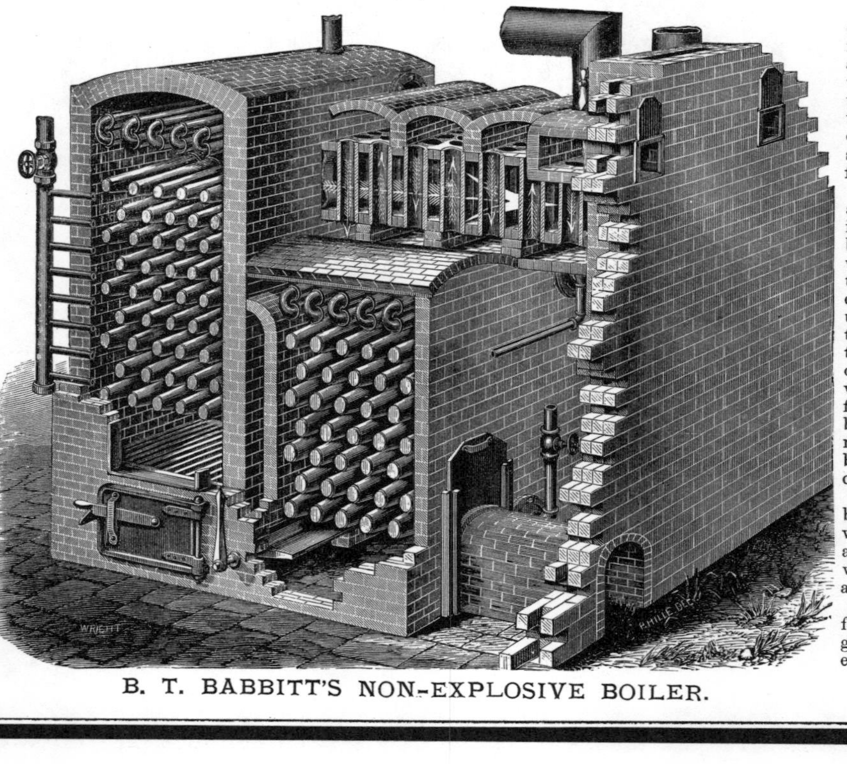

B. T. BABBITT'S NON-EXPLOSIVE BOILER.

It is claimed that the boiler will, without danger of explosion, allow a greater variation of the height of the water contained therein than any other boiler hitherto made, the variation admissible being from four to six feet. It is, moreover, evident that when the water is high, more of the horizontal pipes are filled, and that hence there will be a greater generation of steam under these circumstances than when the water is low, this being the reverse of what is usually met with in boilers. The circulation in the boiler is so thorough that it will deposit all the sediment in the mud drum at the bottom of the boiler below the fire, and in a line with the blow-off cock, so that the sediment may be removed at any time. The verticle manifolds are attached to the lower manifolds by suitable flanges and bolts. These are the only packed joints, and they are below the fire—copper packing invariably used. It is practically a non-explosive boiler, as no rupture can take place unless the parts be heated red-hot, and then cold water forced in. Even under such circumstances, there could not follow any serious damage.

The boiler is tested to a pressure of 60 0lbs. to the square inch before leaving the works at Whitesboro, N. Y. The rapidity with which steam can be generated is something quite remarkable, as is also the amount of true evaporation claimed per pound of fuel, which is nearer the theoretical maximum than has been attained by any boiler yet produced.

Thus we are enabled on this page to give some of the leading features of Mr. B. T. Babbitt's business career and inventive genius. A straightforward, upright business life, crowned with eminent success, and worthy of imitation.

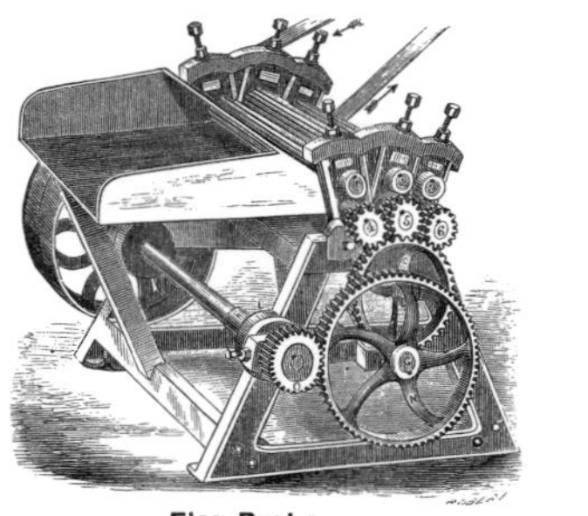

Flax Brake.

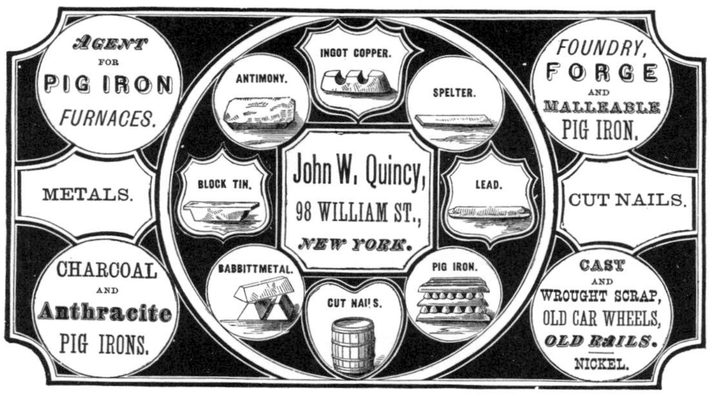

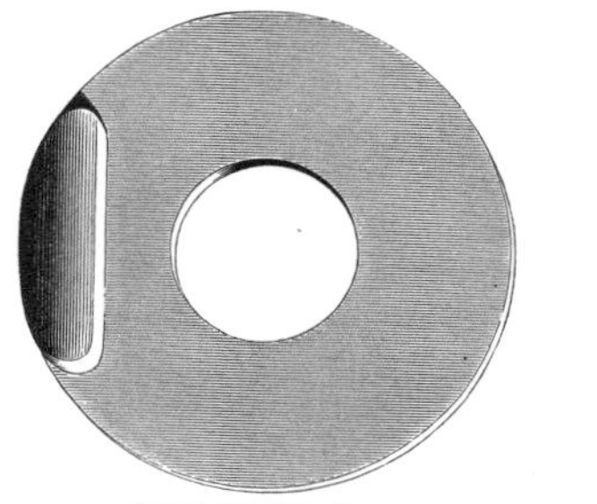

Lock Nut Washer.

JOHN W. QUINCY, METALS AND HARDWARE.

98 William and 41 Platt Sts., New York.

This well-known house, one of the oldest in the American hardware trade, was founded in 1837. The original firm name was Davenport & Quincy, later Davenport, Quincy & Co., afterwards Quincy & Delapierre, then John W. Quincy & Co., and is now John W. Quincy.

It is interesting and instructive to learn the various phrases through which trade has passed from those whose experience embrace half a century, and it is only by comparing the present with the past that we are enabled to fully appreciate the rapid advance of American industry.

Mr. Quincy's business experience extends back to the time when there were no railroads, no canals, no telegraphs. In those days in the wholesale hardware trade a business of $100,000 a year was considered large, and twice that amount enormous. Then profits were about one hundred per cent., and it was safe to sell to everybody, the margin being so great as to admit of considerable loss and yet enable every attentive business man to amass a competence.

Goods were then transported from the warehouses and stores of the larger cities to the interior country in carts or wagons drawn by horses and oxen over rough roads, one, two, perhaps three hundred miles or more, and woe to the packer of hardware who had not learned to pack so close that a mouse could not find its way through the box, or the constant jar from so long a trip would strip the goods of their papers, and a fearful conglomeration of cut tacks, screws, brads, butts, locks, etc., would be the result.

But time advanced; the Erie Canal became the great forwarder of goods in 1832; steamboats gradually improved in point of comfort and speed; stage coaches came to be driven at the rate of nearly eight miles per hour; and when express speed was required, relays of horses were provided and riders made the distance between New York and New Orleans several days quicker than the mails. Then came railroads, bringing a celerity of communication before undreamt of and which it was thought could not be exceeded, till unexpectedly the telegraph was introduced. "What had God wrought?"—the first words flashed over the wires by the immortal Morse, still vividly remains fixed upon the minds of those who remember our then slow method of communication.

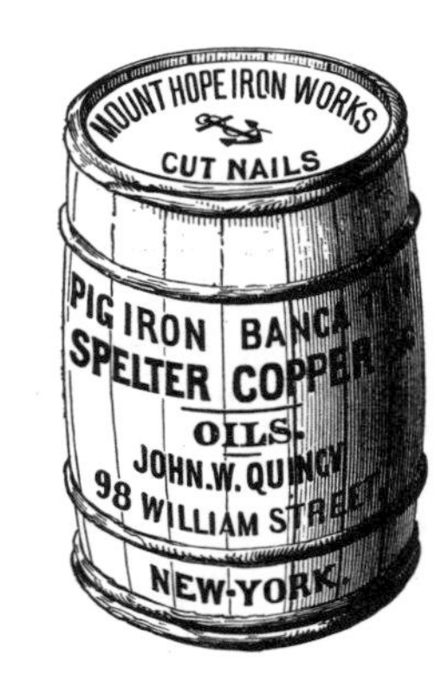

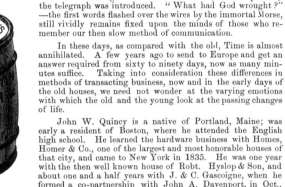

In these days, as compared with the old, Time is almost annihilated. A few years ago to send to Europe and get an answer required from sixty to ninety days, now as many minutes suffice. Taking into consideration these differences in methods of transacting business, now and in the early days of the old houses, we need not wonder at the varying emotions with which the old and the young look at the passing changes of life.

John W. Quincy is a native of Portland, Maine; was early a resident of Boston, where he attended the English high school. He learned the hardware business with Homes, Homer & Co., one of the largest and most honorable houses of that city, and came to New York in 1835. He was one year with the then well known house of Robt. Hyslop & Son, and about one and a half years with J. & C. Gascoigne, when he formed a co-partnership with John A. Davenport, in Oct., 1837.

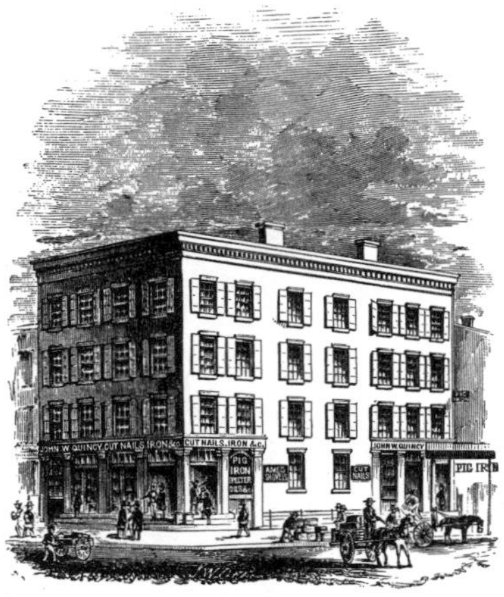

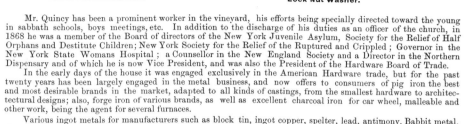

Store of John W. Quincy, 98 William St. N. Y.

Mr. Quincy has been a prominent worker in the vineyard, his efforts being specially directed toward the young in sabbath schools, boys meetings, etc. In addition to the discharge of his duties as an officer of the church, in 1868 he was a member of the Board of directors of the New York Juvenile Asylum, Society for the Relief of Half Orphans and Destitute Children; New York Society for the Relief of the Ruptured and Crippled; Governor in the New York State Womans Hospital; a Counsellor in the New England Society and a Director in the Northern Dispensary and of which he is now Vice President, and was also the President of the Hardware Board of Trade.

In the early days of the house it was engaged exclusively in the American Hardware trade, but for the past twenty years has been largely engaged in the metal business, and now offers to consumers of pig iron the best and most desirable brands in the market, adapted to all kinds of castings, from the smallest hardware to architectectural designs; also, forge iron of various brands, as well as excellent charcoal iron for car wheel, malleable and other work, being the agent for several furnaces.

Various ingot metals for manufacturers such as block tin, ingot copper, spelter, lead, antimony, Babbit metal, etc., are also constantly on hand. A large assortment of superior cut nails forms a part of their stock.

The house of John W. Quincy is the only agent for Mallory & Sandford's Patent Brakers for flax, hemp, rannie, mallow, etc., also Fibre Machines for tropical plants. These machines are patented and largely used in Europe as well as in this country, and are said to be the best in use.

Prominent among their specialties is Gibbs Patent Lock Nut and Washer for rails. A lip in the washer holds the nut from turning, and the washer is bent into a groove rolled in the fish plate. This is cheap, durable and effective, invented by a railroad engineer, and is generally approved, being found good practically. The American Institute reported this in 1871, as the most perfect lock-nut on exhibition. It has not been exhibited since that time. The above cut represents the full size of washer, can be made for any size nut. The cut below represents the washer as applied to the rail. They are now in general use and have always given entire satisfaction.

This house, has always paid one hundred cents on the dollar. It has gone through the various panics and times of commercial disaster since its foundation, unharmed. It has witnessed the downfall of strong houses, the pride of the trade, some through financial distress, others by the withdrawal of the strong arms which had guarded them in the days of prosperity by death or retirement from business, and still others through that entire revolution in trade which has rendered old paths impracticable, but it still stands a proud monument to the energy, business capacity and high moral character of its original founder, John W. Quincy.

We might largely extend this article but space forbids, therefore, those interested should go to 98 William Street, New York, the store of John W. Quincy one of the pioneers in this important industry, and see for themselves the immense strides made in the improvement of American Hardware, and they would find themselves amply repaid for their trouble, as they will there find, in great variety, an immense stock of almost everything in the metal line to select from and at prices to suit the times.

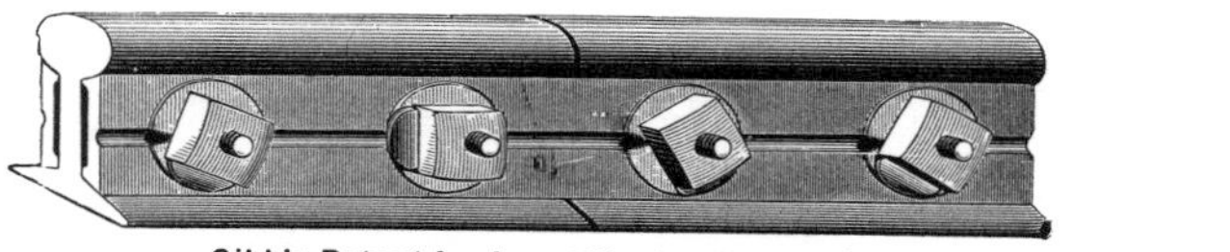

Gibb's Patent Lock and Washer for Rails.

Manhattan Fire Brick and Clay Retort Works.

Maurer & Weber, Proprietors.

Important among the many manufactures of the United States, is that of Fire Brick, Tiles, Retorts, etc. Until within a comparatively few years our people were largely dependent upon foreign makers for their supply of such articles, but recent discoveries of very superior clay and improvements in the manipulation of the raw material, have so enhanced the value of our home productions that now American goods are sought in preference to imported.

Among the most prominent firms engaged in this branch of manufacture are Maurer & Weber, (a very fine engraving of whose works is here presented,) who began operations in the year 1863. The superiority of their productions was so apparent that from the first they found a ready market for their wares; and soon established a business second to none of its kind in the country. The establishment comprises five large buildings, having a frontage on East Fifteenth Street of two hundred feet, on Avenue C, fifty feet, extending through the block; on Sixteenth Street, twenty-five feet. The huge chimney, which is seen for miles around, rises to the height of one hundred and fifty-four feet and was built after a model by Mr. Weber, one of the firm. About sixty men are constantly employed, and a large steam engine furnishes the power necessary to operate the machinery.

The extent of the business can be more correctly judged of when we say that the establishment is capable of turning out eight thousand ordinary sized fire brick per day in the manufacture of which from thirty to thirty-five tons of clay are consumed, a ton making from two hundred and seventy-five to three hundred and fifty common sized bricks. The clays are brought from Amboy, New Jersey where the firm have a large clay bank (thirty-five acres) of the best qualities. A number of suitable vessels are constantly employed in the transportation of the clay to New York.

In order to meet the requirements of the trade, Messrs. Maurer & Weber usually carry a stock of about fifty thousand brick, of all sizes, varying in

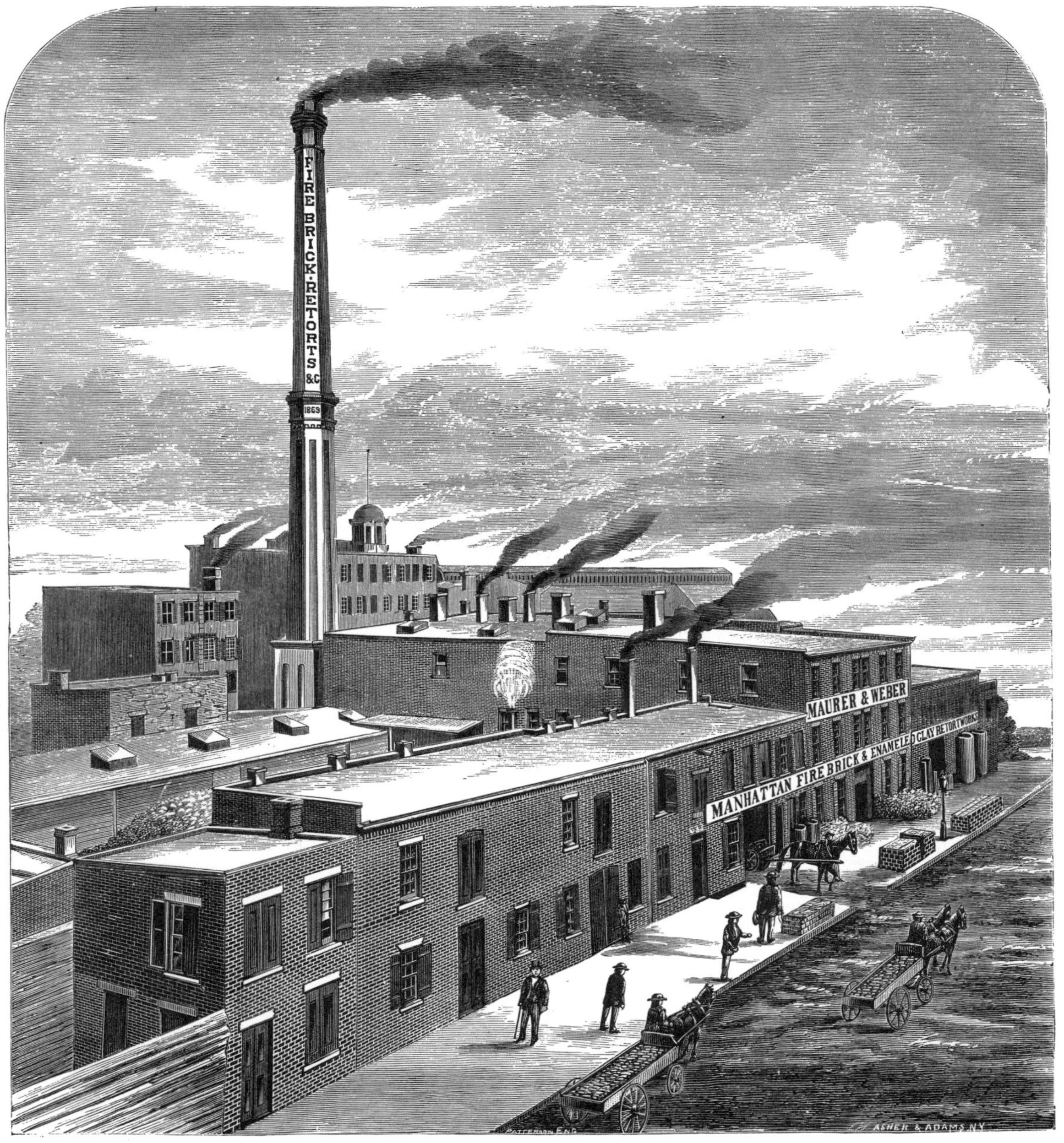

Manhattan Fire Brick and Enameled Clay Retort Works, Maurer & Weber, Proprietors.

weight from seven to several hundred pounds. They have three large kilns each holding about thirty thousand bricks, under each of which six fires are kept constantly burning.

They also make Retorts and Tiles for gas works and all kinds of furnaces where an intense and continuous heat is required. Many of the largest gas houses in the country obtain their Retorts from these works, preferring their manufacture to all others. Mr. P. B. Brunner, formerly Engineer of the City Gas Company at San Francisco, California, and now Superintendent of the Pacific Rolling Mill, in a letter to Messrs Maurer & Weber, says: "We have forty-eight benches of your retorts at work, and thus far have not had a single one cracked, in short, I never have, even with the celebrated Belgian Retorts, had such luck." Certainly a high commendation from a competent authority.

Messrs. Maurer & Weber have in operation a machine of their own invention, with which they can press about eight thousand brick per day, whereas by the old hand method twenty-five hundred was a good days work for two men. This is a most important invention and improvement. Everything about the establishment evinces the determination of these gentlemen to produce the best possible grade of goods. They manufacture Fire Bricks of all sizes, Arch Bricks, Bull Heads, Pier or Jamb Bricks, Key Bricks, Soap Bricks, Split Bricks, besides Cupola, etc. Tiles groved, or in any desired shape or size are made to order.

The amount of stock, daily manufactured, large as it is, is scarcely sufficient to supply their numerous customers and they employ labor-saving machines as far as possible, to facilitate the rapid and perfect construction of the various articles which they manufacture. The productions of the Messrs. Maurer & Weber being bona fide home productions and not excelled by any of foreign make, the American people may well feel proud of their enterprise. It reflects credit alike upon themselves and the nation.

Further particulars may be obtained by addressing Messrs. Maurer & Weber, Manhattan Fire Brick and Clay Retort Works, 633 East Fifteenth Street, New York.

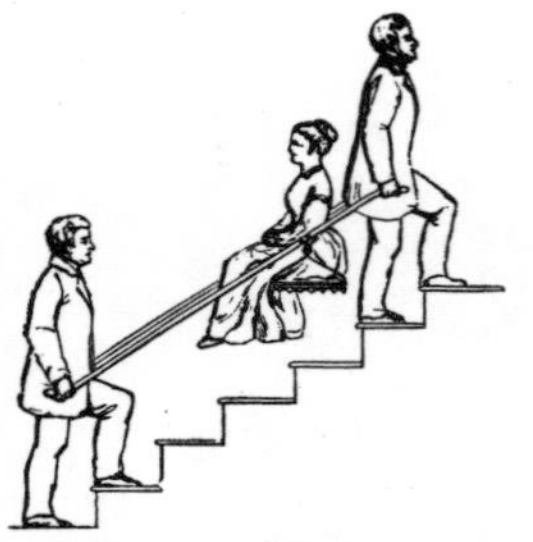

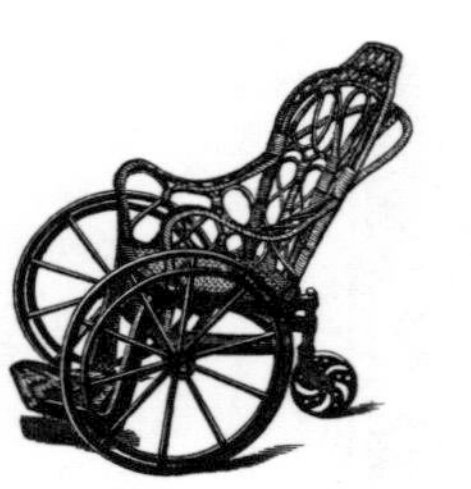

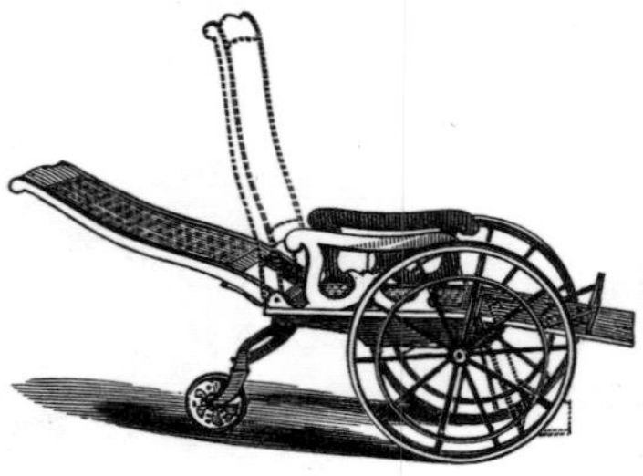

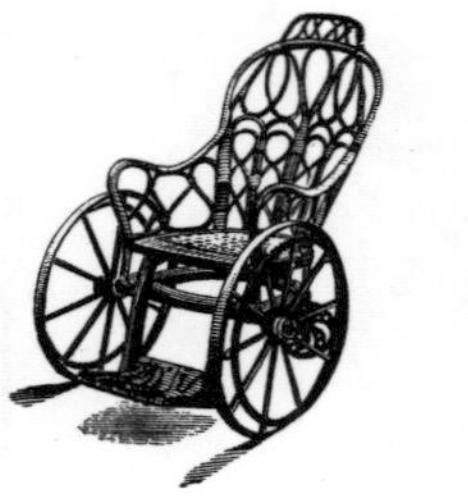

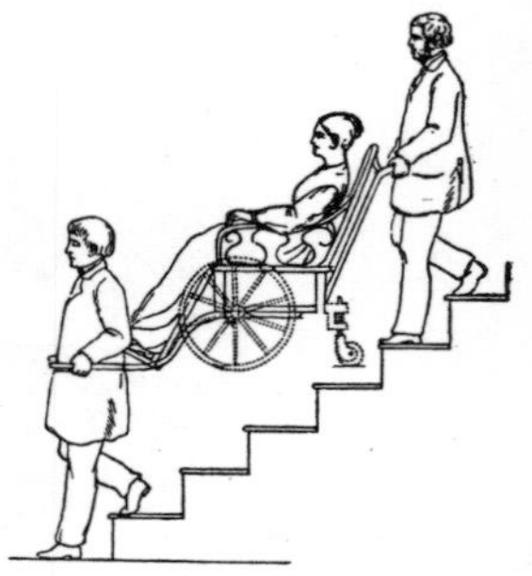

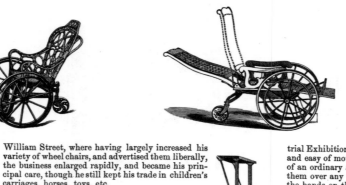

SELF PROPELLING CHAIRS,

For Invalids and Cripples.

S. A. SMITH, Manufacturer,

No. 32 Platt St., N. Y.

This business is now an independent one, and produces, nothing but, "Wheel Chairs," and their auxillaries, except a Bed-chair to support the invalid at any angle in bed, and the Sedan Chair, as shown above.

The business originated about the year 1864, by Stephen Wm. Smith, Esq., introducing an Invalid's Wheel Chair, just patented, in connection with his business of Patent Cantering Horses at No. 498 Broadway, perhaps he sold no more than six of these chairs when, in 1865, he moved to No. 90 William Street, where having largely increased his variety of wheel chairs, and advertised them liberally, the business enlarged rapidly, and became his principal care, though he still kept his trade in children's carriages, horses, toys, etc.

In July 1871, Stephen Wm. Smith died, leaving in consequence of his perservering and extensive advertising, and by sustaining his well known reputation for honorable dealings and substantial workmanship, a well established business, which has since, under the firm name of S. A. Smith, assumed still greater proportions. The move to the present location No. 32 Platt Street, was made in 1874, when, of all that branch relating to children's amusement, the Patent Self-Operating Swing (see cut) only, was retained. This swing is under the entire control of the occupant, whether child or adult.

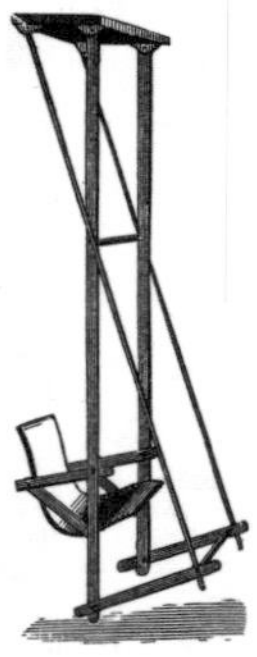

Mr. Smith's chairs have received diplomas at the American Institute Fair, and Brooklyn Industrial Exhibition, as being durable, light, comfortable, and easy of motion; any person having the strength of an ordinary 5 year old child can propel and guide them over any smooth ground, simply by the use of the hands on the side wheels.

The back wheel swivels in every direction, following the motion of the side wheels, so that by turning one wheel forward and the other backward, the chair may be turned around in its own space. Only the best of materials are used in the construction of these chairs; the axles are of wrought iron, with right and left turned nuts, and wrought iron boxes turned on steel mandrils; the side wheels have cornered felloes, shaved spokes, square mortise in hubs, welded iron tires, etc.

In addition to the many kinds of Self-Propelling Chairs, various styles of the celebrated English Bath Chair, designed to be pushed, are also manufactured here.

Of the recent improvements may be mentioned the Iron Portable Handles, to be attached to the chairs, for carrying purposes; as shown above; the new Canopy Sun Shade and the very essential and highly important Rubber Tires, made of vulcanized rubber, cured for this special purpose, and secured to the wheels, by a method, which was only arrived at after, at least 3 years of costly experimenting. All kinds of special and curious Wheel Chairs, Mr. Smith is constantly making to order, and chairs of his make are in use in all quarters of the globe; the flow of letters, pouring gratitude and blessings for the benefits his chairs have conferred, is never ending.

Mr. Smith's illustrated catalogue and price-list, with full description of the various styles, may be had on application.

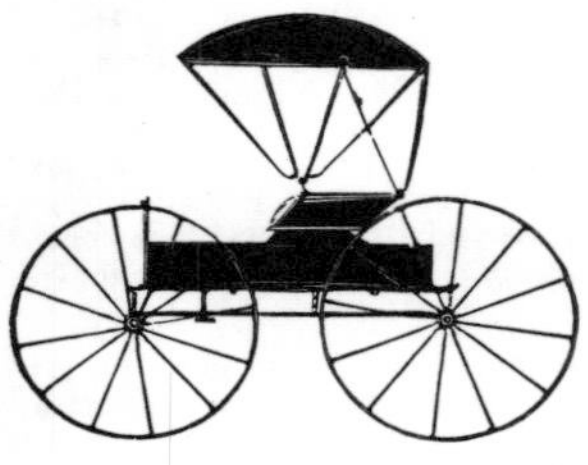

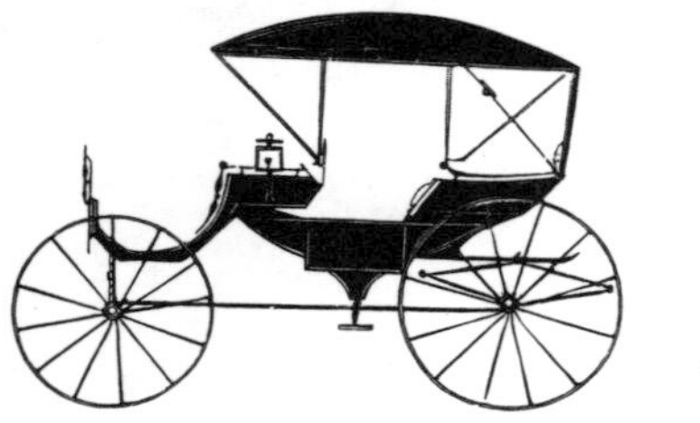

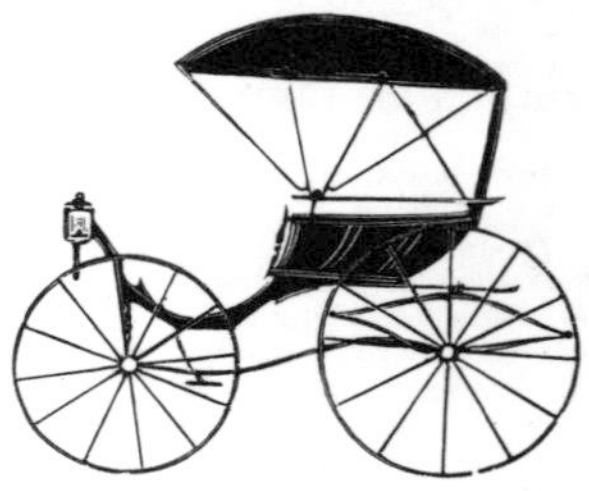

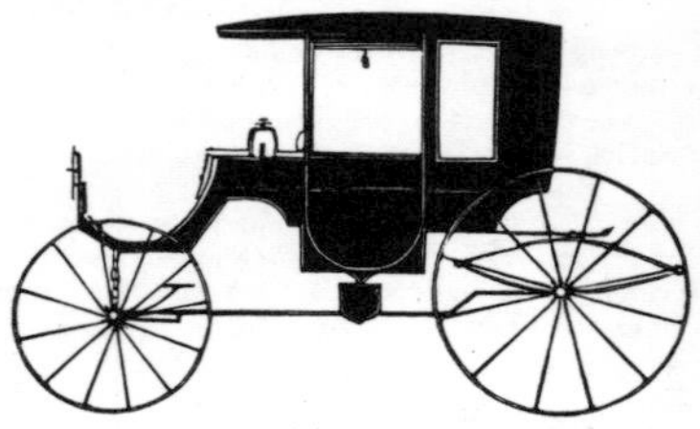

GREGG & BOWE COACH WORKS,

Cor. Eighth and Orange St., Wilmington, Del.

One of the finest warerooms in this country for the display and sale of carriages, is that of Gregg & Bowe, of Wilmington, Del., and those of our readers who visit Wilmington should not fail to call at the establishment, which is located at the southwest corner of Eighth and Orange Streets. The building fronts 165 feet 6 inches on Eighth Street and 154 feet on Orange; it is three stories high within the brick walls, the Mansard roof forming another story, and with the exception of a part of the first floor is occupied exclusively by the firm. The office is on Orange Street, where the visitor will be likely to find either member of the firm, pleasant, corteous and always ready to exhibit the large assortment of beautifully designed and finely finished carriages of a great variety of styles, with which their warerooms are filled, of whose many merits they have but little to say, leaving their productions to speak for themselves.

In April, 1855, Alexander Jamison, the gentleman with whom Messrs. Gregg & Bowe served their apprenticeship together, having deceased, they bought out the business, which was not at that time very extensive. The

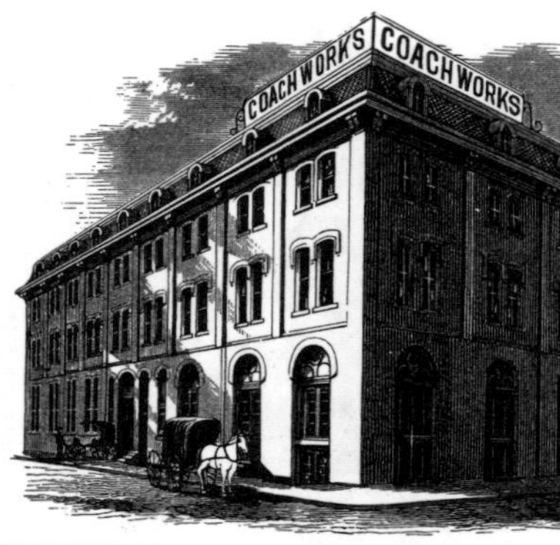

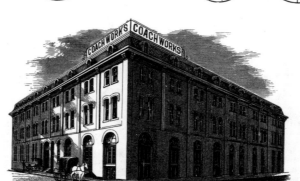

young firm determined to improve and extend their facilities and by manufacturing the best possible carriages, to build up a larger and consequently more profitable business. They have succeeded beyond their most sanguine expectation, and their carriages may now be found in nearly every State and Territory in the Union, in China, and in the South American States.

A large portion of their trade is done by correspondence. Having photographs of every style of carriage which they manufacture, purchasers by selecting the kind of vehicle they wish, and designating how many and about the average weight they wish it to carry; how painted, whether plain or showy, color of trimming, width of track, style of mounting, etc., may order by mail, and Messrs. Gregg & Bowe guarantee to fill it satisfactorily.

A portion of the first floor of the large building previously spoken of—165x52 feet—is occupied as a market, and divided into 123 stalls, the income from which is sufficient to pay all the expenses on the entire building, thus leaving the firm rent free. The wareroom is directly over and of the same dimensions as the market. All the balance of the building is used in the manufacture of their work, and for the storage of material. A large stock of select lumber is constantly kept and their facilities are such that they always have plenty of thoroughly seasoned wood on hand, and none but perfect materials ever enter into any of their work.

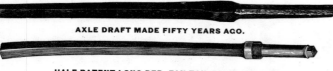

AXLE DRAFT MADE FIFTY YEARS AGO.

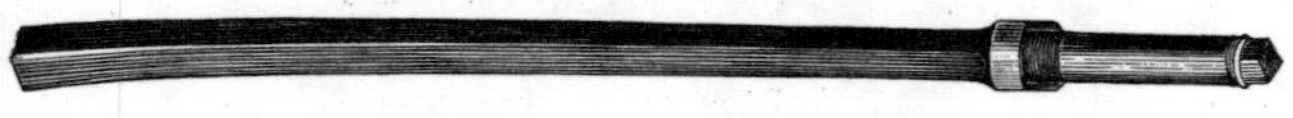

HALF PATENT LONG BED, FAN TAIL SOLID END NUT.

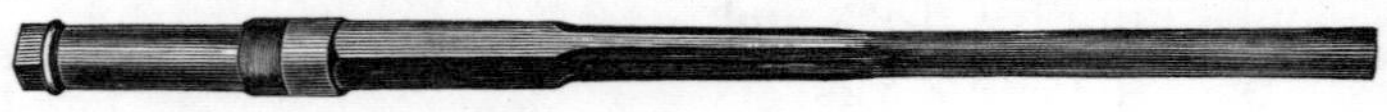

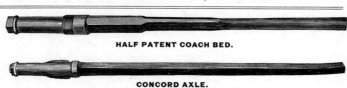

HALF PATENT COACH BED.

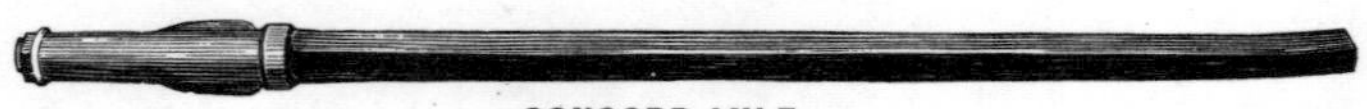

CONCORD AXLE.

R. COOK & SONS,

Manufacturers of

SOLID COLLAR IRON AXLES,

Winsted, Conn.

The firm of R. Cook & Sons was established in 1839 for the purpose of making carriage and wagon axles, and their works are probably the oldest in the business in the United States, conducted continuously under the same name.

The head of the firm, Reuben Cook, in company with Bunce & Seymour, of Hartford, Conn., in 1811 began the manufacture of iron, on the site now occupied by the Axle Factory, from Red Salisbury, or Hematite ore, which was hauled some thirty miles across the country.

After reducing the ore to refined metal, the iron was sent to Springfield, Mass., where it was used mainly in the manufacture of guns. About one-third of the entire production not being quite fine enough for gun-barrels, was used for tires, crowbars, sleigh-shoes, plow-molds and mill-cranks.

About 1825 Mr. Cook began making axle drafts, similar to those shown in the cut of axle made fifty years ago. The arms were forged eight-sided by a hammer with a straight die, and were subsequently rounded as well as possible by the blacksmiths who purchased them. In 1832 he built a shop in addition to the forge, and began making mill irons and cranks, etc. In the same year he swaged the arms of axles round, under the hammer, in dies made for that purpose and was, as we are informed the first to adopt that improved method. In 1839 the present firm was organized, and the business of making entirely finished axles was begun.

R. Cook & Sons were among the first to appreciate the advantages of a solid collar for Half Patent Axles over the welded collar universally used before, and soon as they were devised, began their manufacture and have continued to make a specialty of Solid Collar Axles ever since.

Axles can be made in this manner only from iron that is tough and free from flaws. Poor iron cannot be used, for the simple reason that if an inferior bar should accidentally be placed in the workmen's hands it would at once develope its weakness. To make an inch axle a bar of iron one inch and a half square is swaged down to the proper size, a process which only the very toughest and strongest iron could undergo. There can be no question of the superiority of this method of making axles. Upsetting to produce an imitation of the solid collar, or a welded collar, however closely it may be fitted, does not effect the same result that is attained in the Solid Collar Axle.

Charles Cook, of this firm, was the inventor of the case hardened wrought iron pipe box, the first ever made, the patent for which he sold to other parties who are now using it for extra fine carriage axles, with great success.

The founder of this firm, Reuben Cook, died in March, 1872, the business descending to his sons and partners, Charles and John R. Cook, who worthily succeed their honored father in its management, retaining the firm name, which during the past thirty-six years has become so widely and favorably known for the perfectness of its manufactures and its honorable dealings, fully determined to maintain the excellence, and consequently the popularity, of their goods.

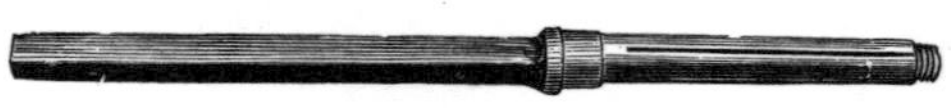

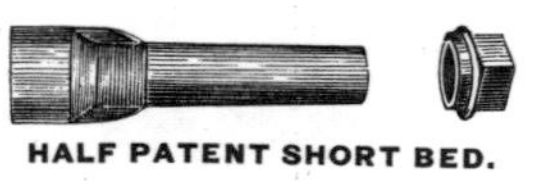

HALF PATENT SHORT BED.

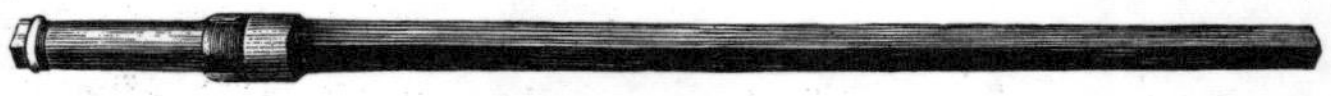

HALF PATENT LONG BED.

MAYNARD RIFLE TARGETS.

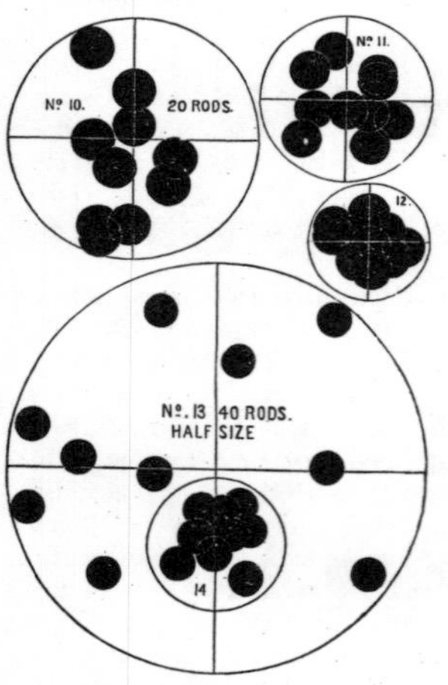

Ten Consecutive Shots each.

No. 13 - - - - - - - - -	40 Rods.
Nos. 10 and 11 - - - - - -	20 Rods.
Nos. 12 and 14 - - - - -	10 Rods

Maynard's Patent Breech-Loading Rifles and Shot Guns,

Manufactured by the

MASSACHUSETTS ARMS CO.

Chicopee Falls, Mass.

The Maynard Sporting Rifle was invented by Dr. Edward Maynard, of Washington, D. C., in 1851. As originally constructed it contained a primer magazine, which is now superseded by the use of central fire capped cartridges. H. W. S. Cleveland in his *Hints to Riflemen*, published in New York and London, in 1864, says: "It is certainly one of the most ingeniously contrived instruments of the kind which have yet been produced. Indeed, it combines so many ingenious arrangements, which together result in the production of a weapon whose efficiency and strength are quite as remarkable as its perfect simplicity, that it is only by a careful examination and study of its various parts and their workings, that one can properly estimate the amount of brain work involved in its construction."

As now manufactured, many valuable improvements, recently perfected by the inventor and secured by letters patent, have been introduced, which place this arm at the present time, among the most popular in use.

It is a breech-loader, operated by throwing down the trigger guard, which acts as a lever to lock the barrel to the frame. The movement of the lever is also connected with an arrangement by which the hammer and firing pin are held in position, so as to secure the arm from premature or accidental discharge.

By the removal of a single pin, the barrel may in a few seconds be disconnected from the stock, and another of different length or calibre

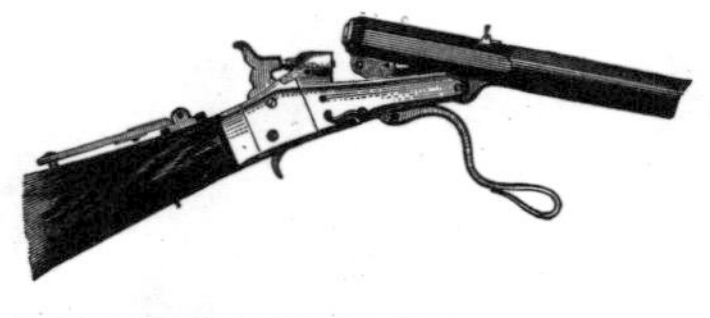

MAYNARD'S PATENT BREECH-LOADING RIFLES AND SHOT GUNS.

substituted, either for the use of shot or ball as may be desired.

The arm is in reality a Combination Gun, readily adapted for hunting large or small game, or for target practice, at any required distance; its peculiar construction making it applicable for the widest possible range of service. Results corresponding with the annexed diagram of targets may readily be secured with an arm weighing but seven and one-half pounds.

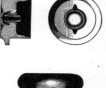

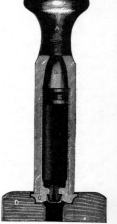

The cartridge constitutes a very important feature of Dr. Maynard's invention, being so constructed that by means of a simple instrument the ball is placed mathematically exact in its position, and so held that it cannot be moved after being placed in the chamber in any direction, except with a perfect true delivery through the calibre of the barrel.

The shell is a brass cylinder with a solid end, to which a thick brass head is lapped on and firmly soldered. A steel cone is driven into the centre of the head, rivited fast and so placed in position that the primer does not rest upon it, but impinges upon the sides of the cavity surrounding it, thus rendering it water proof and gas tight.

The simple device of a slot milled into the head of the cartridge,—the invention of W. F. Parker, of West Meriden, Connecticut, affords means of removing the cap after explosion, which will be readily appreciated by the practical sportsman.

The ease with which the cartridges are loaded may be seen by reference to the accompanying cut: The cap or primer is forced to its place, the charge of powder is then poured into the shell "C," and after it is put upon the block "D" with a hole in the center so that nothing can come in contact with the primer,—the bullet "B" is dropped into the loader "A" to give an accurate position, and with a blow of the hand compressed into its proper position in the shell. Each cartridge case is serviceable for many hundred discharges.

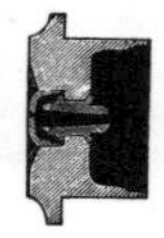

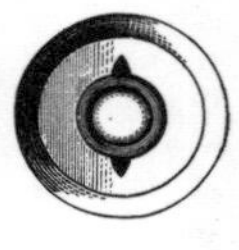

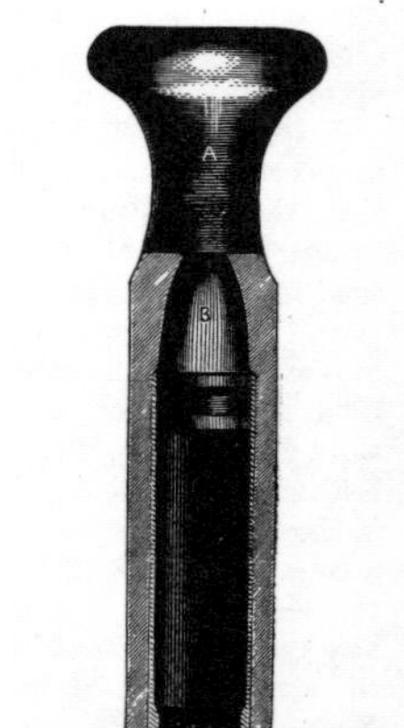

20 Inch Planer.

THE PRATT & WHITNEY COMPANY,
Hartford Conn.

AMATEUR FOOT LATHE.

Engine Lathe.

Pillar Shaper.

In 1860 two Hartford mechanics began the manufacture of a patented attachment for looms, in connection with general machine jobbing. In 1861 they made gun machinery and were joined by a mechanic from New Britain, Conn. They soon began the manufacture of a patent rotary pump, and gradually extended their business, turning their attention mainly to the production of first-class tools adapted to the uses of the machinist and the gun maker. They aimed at producing intrinsically excellent tools of undeniable accuracy of working parts, perfection of fitting and adaptation of the completed machine to the work to be performed, in all of which they succeeded. There was no reason why they should not, for all of the firm were good workmen. Mr. F. A. Pratt was well known as a mechanic and inventor, before he became the head of the concern to which his name has been given. Mr. Amos Whitney is noted for his skill in contriving improved methods of doing work in the shop and his scrupulous care in the exactness of manipulation and finish. Mr. Monroe Stannard is known as well for his thoroughness as a practical mechanic as for his inventions of the rotary pump and motor bearing his name and his organ-blowing apparatus. These men began without capital, except an insignificant sum borrowed to start with, and now they manage the manufactures of an incorporated company holding a capital of $400,000, employing at least 300 men and turning out manufactures of a value of $500,000 yearly.

The Pratt & Whitney Company was incorporated in July, 1869. The three originators of the business, Messrs. Pratt, Whitney and Stannard, occupy respectively the positions of president and superintendents as well as directors. Mr. E. G. Parkhurst is also superintendent of one department of the machine shop. Messrs. S. W. Bishop and C. H. Porter manage the foundry. Mr. R. F. Blodgett is secretary and treasurer.

The premises are on the north bank of Park River, on the line of the New York and New Haven and Providence and Fishkill railroads, from which branch tracks run to the works. The locality is about an eighth of a mile from the Union Passenger Depot on Asylum Street. The main building is of brick, with Portland stone trimmings, four stories high, 225 by 45 feet, having an area in the aggregate of 40,500 square feet.

In addition is one of the finest foundries in New England, 120 by 60 feet, with cleaning and pickling rooms 48 by 40 feet, all built in the most substantial manner of brick, with walls twenty inches thick, and slate roof. A Woodruff & Beach engine of 60 horse power drives the machinery. A building supplementary to the foundry is used for core making. Immense ovens for baking cores capable of receiving the largest fabrications of this class, are connected with the foundry, which is furnished with a crane of fifteen tons lifting capacity. About four tons daily are turned out from this foundry, of first-class castings.

UPRIGHT DRILL.

In the machinery department of the principal building are in constant use 200 lathes, 60 planers, 25 drills, and of milling, screw and other machines about 30. This does not comprehend vises and other hand tools not driven by power, or the machinery in the extensive pattern shop, which, by the way, is most complete in its arrangements and fittings for producing models and patterns for castings and forgings, as demanded by the exigencies and the exactions of the managers, who will not be satisfied with anything short of attainable perfection in the ultimate results of their work. In the forging shop, which is 175 x 42 feet, there are ten fires, a Marchand & Morgan steam hammer of 700 pounds, a Hotchkiss atmospheric hammer of 60 pounds for rapid work, and two drop hammers.

For years the business of the firm has been largely the production of sewing machine tools and those for the general use of the machinist. To this category should be added tools for the manufacture of rifles and pistols, and special machinery for the production of appliances for the perfection of other manufactures or for particular uses. In the production of machinists' tools the company aims at simplicity, durability, convenience and adaptation to the work to be performed, rather than to show and surface finish. No ground or emery-surfaced bearing is permitted, but all the wearing surfaces are fitted by scraping. The perfection of the work and the easiness of the working of the lathes and planers made by the company, is so generally acknowledged that no particular description of their qualities need be introduced.

The lathes manufactured by this company comprise all the gradations of the spinning, chucking, traverse, hand, and turning lathe, up to the engine lathe of 13,250 pounds weight. A new style of lathe for turning pulleys has just been completed, which is also adapted to chucking and facing, that weighs five tons, having an automatic cross feed, the tool carriage being fixed and the feed traversing by a slide rest longitudinally or transversely, while the head stocks are movable on the ways.

We cannot spare the space necessary to fully describe any, or even name all the different kinds of machinists' machinery and tools manufactured by The Pratt & Whitney Company. We give small cuts of a few of their machines, but for descriptions must refer the reader to the Company. Among the many labor saving and powerful mechanisms produced by them, is a style of blacksmiths' power shears worthy of special mention; possessing, as it does, compactness, capacity, strength, durability and efficiency. Two cutters on either end of the rocking bar or blade, one for rounds, the other for squares and flats, are always in place, and can be used separately, or by two persons at the same time.

They are also largely engaged in the manufacture of a drop hammer, which possesses great power. It is readily set in operation and its motion is controlled by the foot of the attendant. We would be pleased to describe it fully, but only have room to advise those in want of such a machine to consult with The Pratt & Whitney Company, before purchasing elsewhere.

GROCERS' TRIP SCALE.

PATENT BALANCE OR SCALE BEAM.

UNION SCALE.

BALANCES & SCALES.
John Chatillon & Sons, Manufacturers, 91 and 93 Cliff St., N. Y.

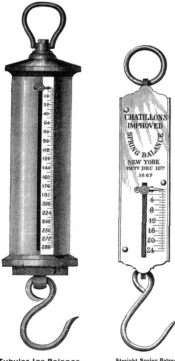

Tubular Ice Balance.   **Straight Spring Balance.**

SASH BALANCE.

Among the important manufactures of our country may be mentioned that of the above named goods. We find that the use of scales dates far back into antiquity, their importance being shown by the fact that the ancient astronomers used the term *libra* (the balance) to designate one of the signs of the zodiac.

Space will not permit us to go into a detailed description of the various changes and improvements that have been made in instruments for weighing. John Chatillon & Sons, New York, are successors to the late Mr. John Chatillon, the founder of this house, who began making scale beams about the year 1835, and in a few years added the manufacture of spring balances.

In the introduction into this market of American made spring balances, manufacturers had many difficulties to contend with. They were deemed unreliable. It was very difficult to convince the people that a balance could be made in which the spring would preserve its original elasticity for any length of time, though they could but acknowledge that the new balance was correct. The idea was new and the public had to be educated up to the point where they would recognize the great improvement. Sellers were afraid that a constant breakage of springs would be a source of expense to them. There were those who were willing to concede that such scales might be made absolutely correct in their recorded results, and that they might also be so constructed as not easily to break or get out of order; but the majority of this class had little faith in American skill. Again, the importation of foreign scales was at that time a large business, and dealers in the foreign articles were loud in their condemnation of the American, and eloquent in their praise of foreign goods.

Notwithstanding the prejudice of consumers in favor of imported scales and the competition of the importers, the manufacture of these goods has constantly increased and the superiority of American goods has become so apparent, that foreign scales have been driven out of the market altogether. Instead of importing we now export, and the reputation of American scales is everywhere very high.

Messrs. John Chatillon & Sons are among the oldest and largest manufacturers, dealers in and exporters of spring balances and scales in the country. The accompanying cuts show some of their leading styles of goods, such as are generally in use. They manufacture every variety of spring balances, combining elegance with utility; lightness with strength and durability; and are constantly improving and adding to their already large line of goods, being determined to maintain the standard of excellence they have achieved.

They also manufacture extensively patent balances, and union and counter scales. On their union and counter scales they use a seamless scoop (patented); a great improvement on the old style, presenting a much better appearance as well as being stronger and more easily kept clean. Their latest improvement is an enameled scale pan which they use in connection with their sash balance. This pan is made of heavy sheet iron covered with white porcelain enamel, the bows being nickel plated on brass. They also manufacture large quantities of tempered steel spiral springs for other parties, who compliment them as making the best spiral springs in the country.

The fame of this firm extends throughout the world, their goods are known and used everywhere, and none speak of them but to praise. A visit to their warerooms, 91 and 93 Cliff Street, New York, would be interesting and instructive even to the casual caller, and profitable to those who desire goods in their line. The first will receive courteous treatment and the latter will find articles that are thoroughly reliable.

Spiral Springs.

MOUNT HOPE HOUSE,

Hooper & Son, Prop's.,

Fall River, Mass.

—:o:—

This popular hotel is centrally located in the business part of the city and affords ample accommodations for permanent and transient boarders. It is one of the most cozy, home-like houses in New England; one of those rare hotels in which the traveler instinctively feels that "all his wants will here be cared for—his every need supplied."

MANSION HOUSE,

A. G. Baily, Proprietor,

Williamstown, Berkshire Co., Mass.

—:o:—

The delightful climate and the grand mountain scenery of Northern Berkshire, annually draws to that section a host of summer visitors, who find in the Mansion House a pleasant home. The beauty of Williamstown in natural scenery is unrivaled. The house is within five minutes walk of four churches, post office, telegraph office, and the College buildings and grounds, and within six miles of the famous Hoosac Tunnel. Greylock, the highest mountain in Massachusetts, is about the same distance, and surrounding it in all directions is a picture unsurpassed for grandeur and beauty. The house remains open all the year, and is first-class in every respect.

EAGLE HOTEL.

John A White, Prop.,

Concord, New Hampshire.

—:o:—

Concord, the Capital of New Hampshire, has several institutions of which it is justly proud, prominent among which is the far famed Eagle Hotel, an engraving of which we present above. This hotel is situated directly opposite the Capitol, and is as fine a house as can be found in New England, outside of Boston. Mr. John A. White, the gentlemanly proprietor, considering the comfort of his guests of paramount importance, has fitted his house with every convenience, and leaves nothing undone to render the Eagle a first-class hotel.

MERRIMAC HOUSE,

Emery & Nute, Proprietors,

Monument Square, opp. Merrimac St. Depot, Lowell, Mass.

—:o:—

The present proprietors of the above named well known hotel have remodeled and refurnished it throughout, rendering it one of the neatest and best hotels in the State. Located as it is in the very heart of the business centre of the city, fitted with every modern improvement that can add to the comfort or convenience of its guests, with tables abundantly supplied with the choicest viands the market affords, and polite and attentive servants, all under the immediate supervision of the popular proprietors, the business man or tourist will here find a pleasant and convenient stopping place.

PHENIX HOTEL,

J R. Crocker, Proprietor,

Concord, New Hampshire.

—:o:—

This Hotel is one of the best known points in the Capital of the Old Granite State. For more than half a century it has been in active operation. It was kept by the Hutchison family for thirty years. In 1858 it was rebuilt, heated by steam, and modern improvements introduced. Connected with the hotel is a brick fire-proof stable, said to be the best in the State.

CITY HOTEL,

A. L. Bliss, Proprietor,

Taunton, Mass.

—:o:—

This commodious house is the only first-class hotel in the city, is pleasantly located, fronting the park, and in the centre of business. It contains all the modern improvements and conveniences, including a Telegraph Office, Billiard Hall, Barber Shop, Bathing Rooms, etc., and ranks as a first-class hotel in every respect. It affords every comfort and convenience of a private home for permanent boarders—and transient guests can find no better resting place.

MASSASOIT HOUSE,

M. & E. S. Chapin, Proprietors,

Springfield, Mass.

—:o:—

Springfield is one of the finest cities in New England, and the tourist will here find many points of interest that will well repay a visit. The Government Armory and Arsenal will readily suggest itself to the stranger, and there are many other places in the city and its immediate vicinity equally worthy of attention. But the most important point for the dusty traveler is a good hotel. Such an institution is the Massasoit House, and Springfield has as much reason to be proud of it as of any of its other notable places. This truly first-class hotel is directly opposite the Union Railroad Depot, and is in the business center of the city. Its spacious, airy and handsomely furnished apartments, its tables liberally supplied with the choicest edibles, skillfully cooked and neatly served, and during the thirty-one years Messrs. M. & E. S. Chapin have owned and managed it, it has achieved a reputation second to no hotel in the state, a reputation it will surely maintain.

ARNOLD HOUSE,

Streeter & Swift, Proprietors,

North Adams, Mass.

—:o:—

North Adams, nestled among the mountains of Berkshire, in northwestern Massachusetts, is a prominent station on the Hoosac Tunnel route from Boston to the West. The Tunnel just completed by the State at a cost of $14,000,000 is less than two miles distant from the village. The Arnold House, one of the largest hotels in Western Massachusetts, is first-class in all respects. Its advantageous location, ample accommodations, and their own experience, enable the proprietors to provide everything necessary for the comfort and convenience of its guests.

CITY HOTEL,

F. A. McLaughlin, Proprietor,

Manchester, N. H.

—:o:—

A thriving, busy town is Manchester, New Hampshire, a place well worthy of an extended notice, but as we have determined to devote this page to a brief mention of a few important hotels, we must, for the time, neglect the manufacturing interests of the place to speak of the City Hotel. This old and well known house has recently been newly fitted up, and in the completeness of its appointments now ranks with the first hotels of the land. The City Hotel has been favorably known for more than thirty years, and many of the old time visitors to Manchester consider it a kind of second home. It is a good place to stop at.

GREYLOCK HALL,

Streeter & Swift, Proprietors,

Williamstown, Mass.

—:o:—

A summer resort in the most beautiful part of Northern Berkshire. The Warm Springs which determined the location of this house and which have proved beneficial for rheumatism and cutaneous affections, have been made available by extensive bathing houses. A mountain stream runs through the grounds and a fine grove of tall pines affords a cool retreat for summer days. The location commands a view of the whole Williamstown Valley, and of Graylock and the Taghanic Mountains beyond. This house has all the appliances to make it attractive and comfortable.

WAUREGAN HOUSE,

C. W. Johnson, Proprietor,

Norwich, Conn.

—:o:—

We heartily commend the Wauregan House as being first-class in every respect. Business men and tourists will here find ample accomodations and every attention. During the summer season it has become a kind of headquarters for pleasure seekers on their way to Watch Hill, R. I., which, as a desirable resting place during the heated term, is too well known to need extended notice. It combines a superb ocean beach, magnificent sea views, and every facility for surf-bathing, sailing and fishing. One great advantage to be noticed, is the entire freedom from the usual pest of the seaside, mosquitoes. The Atlantic House at Watch Hill, C. W. Johnson & Co. Proprietors, is a model hotel, and consequently a popular sea-side resort.

TREMONT HOUSE,

Gilman Scripture, Prop., Nashua, New Hampshire.

Located corner Main and Pearl Streets, in the business centre of the city, fitted with all modern improvements, the Tremont richly deserves the patronage of travelers.

BATES HOUSE,
Rutland, Vermont.
W. F. Page, Proprietor.
—:o:—

This splendid Hotel is located in the business centre of the town, nearly opposite the Railroad Depot, and is one of the best kept hotels in the State. It contains one hundred and fifty neatly furnished rooms, light and airy in summer, and heated by steam (without any extra charge to guests) in winter. In a few words: the Bates House is a model of neatness, convenience and comfort. The culinary department is conducted in the most approved style, and the tables are supplied with all the luxuries and substantials of the season. Commercial travelers will find the Bates House conveniently situated for their business and provided with good sample rooms.

Mr. Page has had many years' experience as a hotel keeper, and we assure travelers that at his hands they will receive every attention.

CLARENDON HOTEL,
Saratoga Springs, New York.
Chas. E. Leland, Prop.
—:o:—

The Clarendon is beautifully situated on Broadway, opposite Congress Grove. Its apartments are spacious and handsomely furnished, and there is about the place an air of quiet elegance, which renders it specially popular among the oldest and most wealthy families who yearly visit the Springs. The famous Washington or Champagne Spring is on its grounds. The name of Charles E. Leland, its proprietor, is a sufficient guarantee that it is perfect in all the requisites of a hotel.

PARKER HOUSE,
Purchase St., cor. Middle and Elm Sts., New Bedford, Mass.
H. M. Brownell, Prop.
—:o:—

The above named well known house has recently been extensively altered, improved, and newly furnished, and ranks in every particular as first-class. Visitors to New Bedford will find here every comfort of a home.

The Sea View House, Oak Bluffs, Martha's Vineyard, an engraving of which is given above, is owned and managed by the proprietor of the Parker House.

The Sea View House is a truly first-class Hotel where the visitor may find a quiet and healthful resting place.

SCOVILL HOUSE,
Waterbury, Conn.
D Dolittle, Proprietor.
—:o:—

The Scovill House is frequently spoken of as the Hotel of Waterbury. It is situated near the business centre of the city, facing as handsome a green as eye ever looked upon. Mr. Dolittle, the proprietor, is a genial host, and looks well to the comfort of his numerous guests.

The Montvert Hotel is conducted by the same gentleman. This elegant Hotel is situated 3,800 feet above the sea, in the most picturesque part of Rutland County. The building is four stories in height, and is finished and furnished on the latest and most approved plan, having every modern convenience. Contains 225 rooms; baths in the house and is lighted by gas.

The village of Middleton is nestled among the hills, in a romantically beautiful location. The scenery from the hotel is attractive beyond description, and it is worth the tourist's while to visit this spot if only to witness the beautiful sunsets, which are as charming as in the mountains of the Old World. Valuable Mineral Springs add to the attractiveness of the place. In connection with the Springs is a bath house, where hot mineral waters may be had.

CITY HOTEL,
Providence, Rhode Island.
L. H. Humphreys, Proprietor.
—:o:—

Mr. Humphreys is also proprietor of the Rock Point Hotel, on Narragansett Bay, between Providence and Newport—a popular summer resort. Both of these hotels are first-class in every respect.

TAYLOR'S HOTEL,
Jersey City, New Jersey.
Lyman Fish, Prop.
—:o:—

This popular Hotel is conducted on the European plan—a system which has become very popular with business men and travelers and which is rapidly gaining favor with families who decline house-keeping. It is conveniently located, being opposite the Pennsylvania and Lehigh Valley Depots, and near the New Jersey Central, Morris & Essex, New York & Erie and Northern Railroad Depots; it is but a short distance to the piers of the Cunard Steamers, and within twelve minutes of Wall Street, Canal Street, and the City Hall, New York, and is therefore specially well located for merchants and others visiting New York and having business in the lower part of the city. It is open at all hours, and affords its guests all the accomodations and conveniences to be found in a first-class hotel.

MARSDEN'S HOTEL,
Ballston, N. Y.
James E. Marsden, Proprietor
—:o:—

Marsden's Hotel is situated on Bath Street, directly opposite the Depot, and in the business centre of the village. Mr. Marsden, the genial proprietor, has ministered to the wants of the traveling public for many years, and thoroughly learned the art of keeping a hotel. The perfect manner in which this house is fitted up and furnished, combined with the happy faculty which Mr. Marsden possesses of making his guests feel perfectly at home, and its excellent location for both business and pleasure travelers, makes it a most convenient and comfortable resort. The rooms are lofty and well ventilated, the tables are bountifully supplied with the best the markets afford, the waiters are polite and attentive—well, in a word, it is a good place to stop at. Attached to the hotel is a fine livery stable, where the most stylish turnouts can be obtained at all times. There are many pleasant drives in the immediate vicinity of Ballston, and with Marsden's Hotel as a head-quarters, the pleasure seeker may spend pleasant days in this vicinity, without suffering the inconvenience of the larger hotels.

PROSPECT PARK HOTEL,
Catskill, New York. John Breasted, Proprietor.
—:o:—

The views from this Hotel are unsurpassed in extent and beauty. The annually increasing tide of visitors to this region—drawn hither in pursuit of health and pleasure—has amply vindicated its right to the title of the Switzerland of America.

The location is a judicious selection from the Prospect Hill property, in the village of Catskill, and the site, with its surroundings occupies twenty acres. It has a commanding view of the River in front and for miles north and south, and the grand old Mountains in the back ground. It is easily accessible by train and by boat.

MANCHESTER HOUSE,
Manchester, N. H.
Wm. Shepherd. Proprietor.
—:o:—

This House, situated at the corner of Elm and Merrimack Streets, is not only conveniently located, but is a peculiarly well kept Hotel. Established in 1839, it is well known to the traveling public, and no Hotel in New Hampshire has a better reputation than the Manchester House.

ALDRICH HOUSE,
Providence, R. I.
L. M. Thayer, Prop.
—:o:—

This is the largest Hotel in Rhode Island. It is located at 31 and 33 Washington Street, within three minutes of the depot and convenient to business. Recently enlarged, renovated and refurnished, it offers unsurpassed accommodations for travelers. Mr. Thayer is also the proprietor of the well known Long Meadow House, Warwick, R. I., on the West Shore of Narragansett Bay, ten miles from Providence, and one mile from Rocky Point.

EXCHANGE HOTEL,
Binghamton, N. Y.
J. G. Devoe, Proprietor.
—:o:—

Binghamton is one of the handsomest and most enterprising places in the interior of the State of New York, and in the summer season is resorted to by thousands who seek the rest and comfort which can only be found in semi-rural cities.

The Exchange Hotel is located in the business centre of the city—a short ride from the depot—and is one of the best and most popular Hotels in the State.

Major Field, a veteran in the business, is Caterer, and the thousands of his friends need no other assurance of a most excellent table—general comfort and satisfaction.

MANSION FARM HOUSE,
Locust Valley, L I.
Fitzhugh Smith, Prop.
—:o:—

The Mansion Farm House, or, as it is frequently called, Fitzhugh Smith's Hotel, is situated in a section of country which abounds with picturesque scenery, magnificent views, delightful drives and is within a short distance of Long Island Sound, where may be enjoyed the luxury of sea bathing. It is accessible by boat or cars, and is especially convenient for those wishing a quiet country home so near the city that they may daily journey back and forth.

BUTTERFIELD HOUSE,
Utica, N. Y.
C. A. Linsley & Co., Prop.
—:o:—

A thriving place is the city of Utica, and wide-awake are the people who live there. Few cities of its size can compete with it in a business point of view, and we think none excel it. There is a solidity about Utica that is not to be found in many cities of greater population. Its business men are solid—its buildings are solid, and it has in the Butterfield House an eminently solid Hotel, a place where one can take solid comfort.

Under the management of C. A. Linsley & Co., the Butterfield House ranks high among the Hotels of the State. They are thoughtful and careful landlords, and leave nothing undone that could minister to the wants and comfort of their guests, and consequently the House is popular among travelers. It is conveniently located and complete in all its appointments.

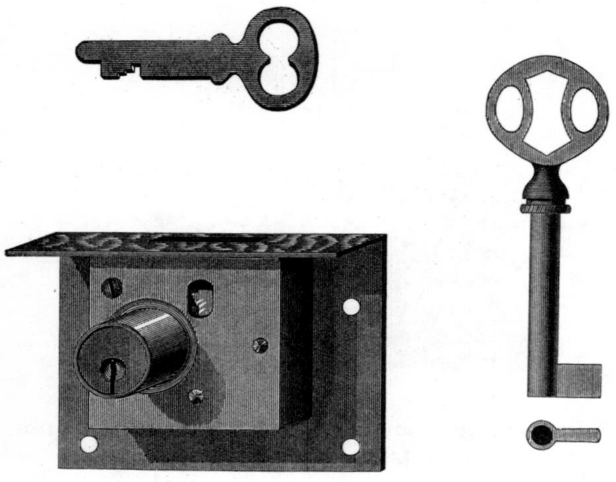

DRAWER LOCK.

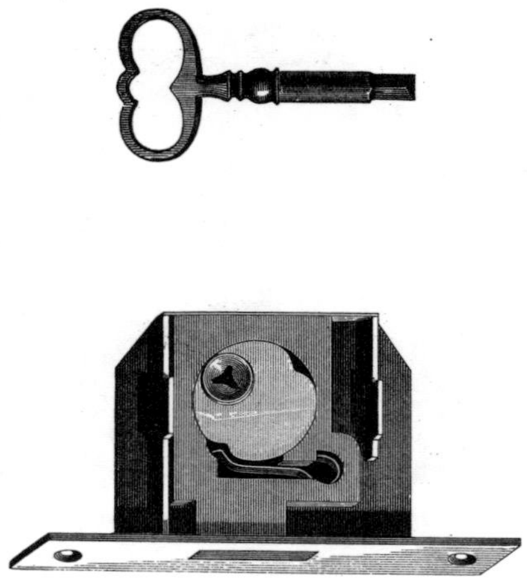

SEWING MACHINE LOCK.

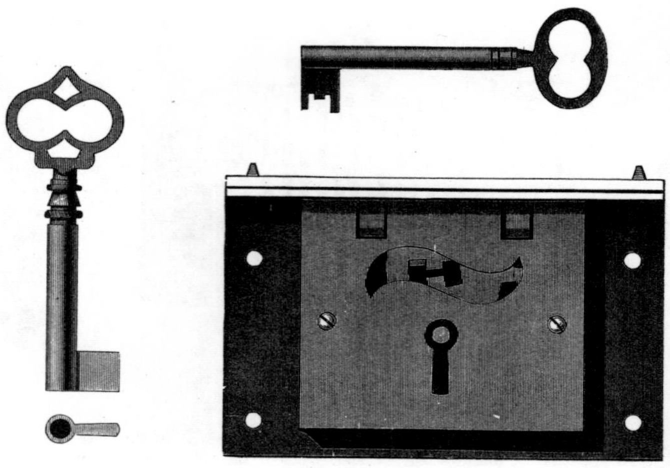

CHEST LOCK.

THE EAGLE LOCK COMPANY,

Terryville, Conn.

When locks were first invented, or by whom, is not known, but that they were in use at a very early date is abundantly proven.

Wilkinson, in his *Manners and Customs of the Ancient Egyptians* describes a key made of iron which he found in the ruins of Thebes, and which had a shank five inches long. The handle consisted of a loop at one end of the shank, which at the other end was turned at a right angle, and furnished with three teeth or points to fit into corresponding cavities in the lock. Other keys have also been found and described, from which it is evident that the Egyptians, at a very early date, were acquainted with some of the principles which have been generally supposed to be distinctive of modern improvements in locks, for instance: that of tumblers, which hold the bolt in place until they are first moved by the key. In fact, rudely constructed locks upon this principle were in use by several of the nations of Europe during the middle ages. In some unaccountable manner, however, all knowledge of the plan was lost, and, though rude tumbler locks were made centuries ago, as made to-day, they are essentially a modern invention.

In the Bible, Judges iii, 23, Ehud is represented as locking the doors; further on in the same chapter we are told that Ehud's servants "took a key and opened them," (the doors) and in many other places in the Old Testament keys are spoken of in such connections as to prove that locks were commonly used.

Homer in the *Odyssey*, speaks of Penelope as opening a wardrobe with a brazen key, made crooked and provided with a handle of ivory.

Locks have been discovered in the ruins of Herculaneum and Pompeii, showing that the ancient Romans were familiar with their use; and in Great Britian keys have been found which dated back to the Roman occupation of that country.

Among the Chinese, lock-making has been well known for centuries, and locks constructed upon the principle of the famous Bramah lock, which was invented in England in 1784, have been made in the "flowery kingdom," of wood, from very early times.

Though locks have been made and used for almost countless years, it is only within a short time that they have been other than clumsily constructed affairs, and it was not until after the establishment of the business of lock-making in this country, that any really perfect locks were ever made.

The Eagle Lock Company, a cut of whose factory at Terryville, Conn., is presented on this page, is the outgrowth of perhaps the first attempt made to establish the business of lock making in the United States.

In the year 1832, an English lock-smith came to this country, and connecting himself with a man of limited means, commenced the manufacture of cabinet locks, at Watertown, Conn. He commenced with one hundred different patterns, improving slightly upon the old English method of hand work. At the end of one year, as nothing had been sold, they found themselves short of funds, and sold out to Eli Terry, 2d, who soon after transferred the business to Lewis, McKee & Co., of Terryville, a company organized for this purpose, and composed of men who had previously been engaged in the clock business. They removed the business to Terryville, taking the Englishman with them.

This company was, of course, entirely without experience, and had everything to learn. They found themselves ignorant of the nature of their materials, and the best manner of working them; and the thousand and one little matters of practice, that seem simple enough now, were the fruits of long, laborious, and often unsuccessful trial.

Their workmen were, with one exception, wholly unacquainted with the business, and he only in the old English ways, and the tools they made and used were bungling and ill adapted to the purposes for which they were intended. Their machinery was rude in form, and inconvenient in practice. For years after they commenced they had no engine-lathe, and such a thing was scarcely known in all the manufactories of the State. For a long time they used only hand presses, cutting out the heavy parts with immense labor, though they were the first to introduce the power press, now universally used in manufacturing every variety of hardware. They imported some of their lock-plates already bent up—for the significant reason, that they could import them cheaper than they could the raw stock. The work produced, of course, partook somewhat of the nature of their machinery and lacked finish. Knowing nothing of the demands of the trade, they made many goods not at all adapted to the wants of the country.

Thus equipped, they made their appearance in a market stuffed with English goods. Here they met with a decided rebuff. It is difficult, at this day, to conceive of the inveterate prejudice that existed, against American manufactures at that time. Hardware men would scarcely look at an American lock, and the man who offered them felt called upon to make a hasty retreat, fearing "extra inducements." The idea that Americans could compete successfully with the English in the manufacture of locks was generally scouted by dealers. A few commission houses were willing to take them, and work them off one by one, but the sales were very slow. The consequence of this, as the reader will readily foresee, was that the Company's resources were locked up in piles of unsaleable goods, and bankruptcy stared them in the face. Such was the position of affairs in 1841, when Eli Terry, 2d, the President of the Company, died. In the settlement of his estate, the concern was bought by Lewis & Gaylord, for six cents on the dollar of the capital stock.

The new Company progressed slowly, adding new and improved machinery, introducing styles of locks better suited to the trade, and putting their price where it would meet the English competition. In 1849, Mr. Lewis died, and the Lewis Lock Company was formed, the stock being taken principally by his heirs and the surviving partner.

In the meantime, Bucknell, McKee & Co. had started the first manufactory of trunk locks in this country. They availed themselves of the experience gained in making cabinet locks, but failed to make the business pay. About 1840, they sold out to Warren Goodwin, who removed to Wolcotville, where he was soon after burned out, and afterwards returned to Terryville. Meanwhile Williams, McKee & Co., had commenced the business anew at Terryville, where they continued till 1846, and then sold out to James Terry & Co.

Each of these companies met with the same difficulties in the shop and in the market, that were encountered by Lewis, McKee & Co., and they were barely able to pay their debts and make no dividend. Jas. Terry & Co., added to their business the manufacture of Carpet Bag Frames, which they conducted principally at Newark, and they also made a few Cabinet Locks.

In 1854, the two companies united under their present name. In all of these changes the original owners and workmen were retained. Some of them still remain with the company; others have passed away.

During these more than forty years there has been a constant improvement, not only in the systems and methods of manufacture, but in the style and quality of the goods produced. Locks of American manufacture are no longer viewed with distrust by dealers and consumers; on the contrary, they have entirely displaced foreign goods, and an English or French trunk or cabinet lock, offered for sale in this country, would now be deemed a curiosity; not only this, they have become an article of export, and the Eagle Lock Company are constantly shipping their goods to the Canadas, Mexico, the States of South America, to England and to nearly all the nations of Europe. Indeed, over all the world, American Locks, like American Sewing Machines and American Clocks, have become immensely popular and are recognized standards of excellence by which other like productions must be judged; and the locks manufactured by this Company have been referred to as a standard by the United States Government.

The business has grown from the small beginning made in 1832, when a single man turned out more work, than the market could absorb, to very large proportions, giving employment to hundreds of hands, each of whom aided by the appliances now in use, can produce ten times as many locks, as could be made by the old method.

When the present Company succeeded to the business, a small stream furnished them abundant water power, interrupted at long intervals by severe drouth, but they long since outgrew the stream and now use the water only as an auxillary to a sixty-five horse power steam engine.

The works comprise two large Factories, a Brass Foundry, Japanning and Tempering Shops, a store house for iron and brass in the rough, and other necessary buildings. In addition to these are the office and store-rooms for manufactured goods.

The manufactories are fully equipped with the finest machinery, devised and constructed to meet the peculiar wants of the business. The workmen employed are skillful and experienced, and everything that can aid in the production of perfect work, is supplied by the Company. The business is completely systematized. Every man has a special kind of labor to perform, and each machine is intended for some particular branch of the work. There is no time wasted; the work moves swiftly on from department to department until finished.

The Company now manufacture nearly eight hundred (800) different varieties of locks and keys. These are all of the smaller kinds, designed for trunks, cupboards, chests, wardrobes, drawers and general furniture. They embrace a wide range of designs, from the plainest and least expensive to the most elegant and costly, but all are perfect of their kind. One not acquainted with the business would hardly imagine that there was any need for so great a number of designs for small locks. Our impression when we first saw the statement was that the number must embrace door locks and pad locks of all descriptions; but investigation proved that we were mistaken and that only small locks are manufactured by the Company. Each lock has its name and number, for instance, "Trunk Lock 73," "Piano Lock 102," "Drawer Lock 300," Camp Desk 296," Chest, Cupboard, Till, Tin Box, and so on, each followed by a number. From such an immense variety surely everybody can be suited we thought, and yet we find that the Company are continually making improvements; adding new sizes and styles, and extending their facilities for manufacturing, being determined not only to maintain the high reputation which they have achieved in the past, but to add to it day by day.

To commend the productions of this Company to dealers in locks would be superfluous, for every hardware man knows that the goods supplied by this Company are not surpassed by any made in the world.

The high esteem in which they are held is the result of persistent and long continued efforts on the part of the Company to meet and fill the wants of the public. Such a result surely follows every honest, manly effort to succeed. We commend them as a fitting example for the young business men of the country to follow.

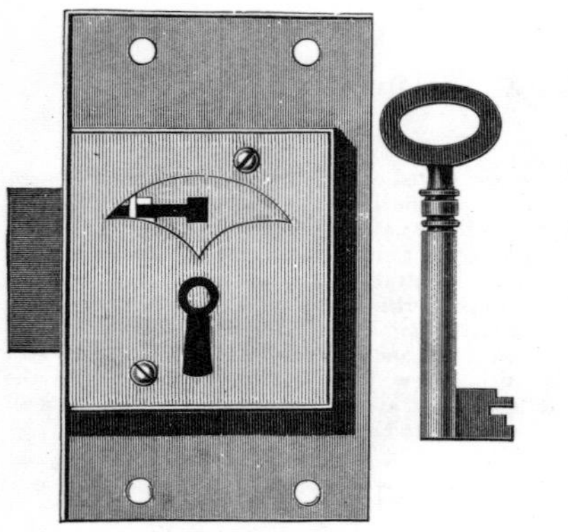

CUPBOARD LOCK.

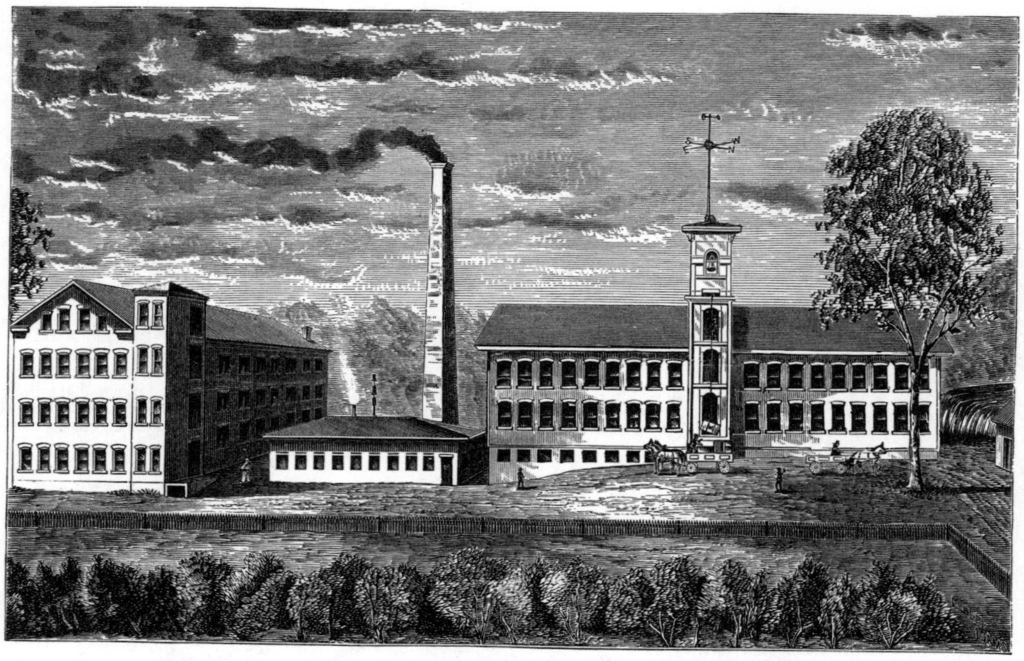

View of Eagle Lock Company's Works, Terryville, Conn.

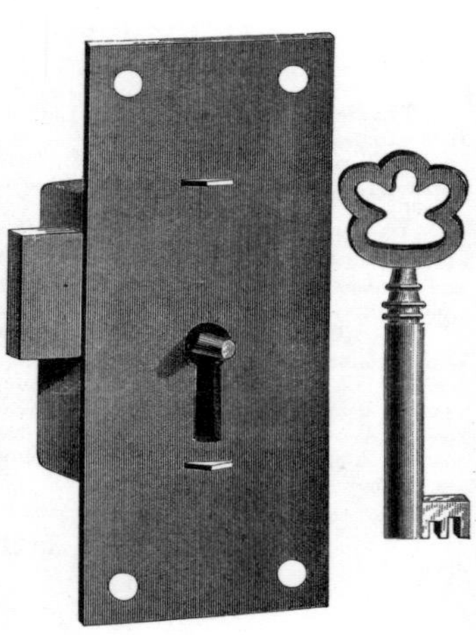

WARDROBE LOCK.

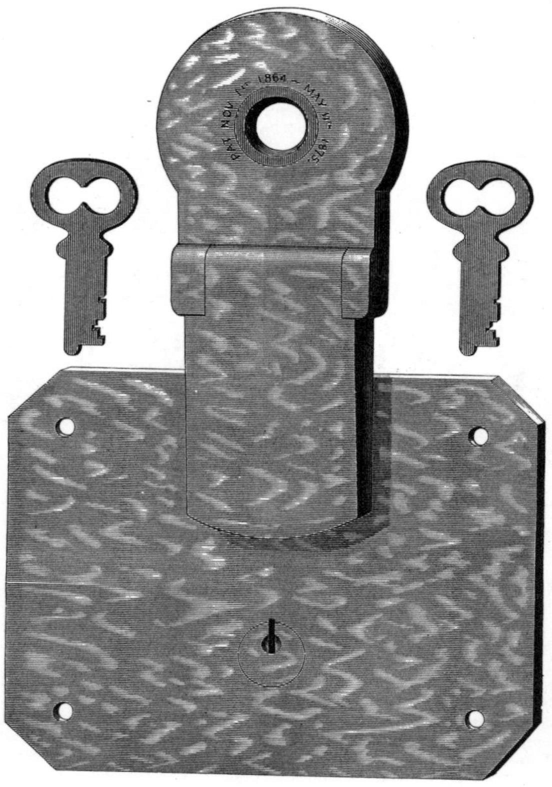

TRUNK LOCK.

A. W. FABER'S LEAD PENCILS.

New York Branch House, Eberhard Faber,

133 William Street.

Like most articles that depend for their existence upon mechanical skill, the pencil is entirely a product of modern times; the ancients knew not either the Lead Pencil in its present form, or the use of lead in any shape for the purposes of art or writing. It was not until the middle ages that we hear of lead being used for either of these purposes, nor was it then the article now made into pencils, but the *metallic* lead, which differs from the former in almost everything except appearance. To this outward similarity, however, with the metallic lead, the pencil lead or black lead owes its common name—the scientific name being *graphite*. Its composition is a mixture of carbon with a small quantity of iron.

Metallic lead was used by the ancients, cast into sharp-edged disks, for ruling the parchment of manuscripts; but the first knowledge of drawings in lead is contemporaneous with the earliest development of modern art. Mention is made of works by masters of the fourteenth and fifteenth centuries which appear to have been produced by some pencil-like instrument on paper surfaced with chalk.

The Italians used at that time what was called a *stile* composed of metallic lead and tin, which had the advantage that its marks could be partially erased with soft bread-crumbs. Vasari, in speaking of an artist of the sixteenth century, commends the versatility which enabled him to excel at the same time in the use of the *stile*, the quill, and both black and red chalk.

But all these different materials were almost immediately discarded on the discovery of the celebrated black lead mines of Borrowdale, in the County of Cumberland, England, in the year 1564, which was followed the very next year by the manufacture of the first lead pencils, substantially such as we use at the present day. The manufacture remained for nearly two centuries exclusively an English one, or until the mine (although allowed by Government to remain open not more than six weeks during the year) became exhausted.

Long before the final exhaustion of the Borrowdale mine, processes were invented for cleaning and refining the impure refuse. The purified powder was pressed into a substantial cake which could be cut like the native ore, but the material produced by this process was found to be deficient in strength. A variety of ingredients were then tried in the hope that by combining them with the finely powdered lead, the necessary consistency might be obtained; but the mark always remained faint.

In France the happy suggestion was first made to mix the purified lead with clay, and the process proved a complete success. It not only gave necessary consistency to the lead without materially diminishing its writing qualities, but was soon found to furnish also the means of making a lead of every degree of hardness or softness—a most desirable result.

This process of mixing and preparing the lead remains in principle essentially unaltered at the present day and is briefly as follows:

The lead, which comes from the different mines in every imaginable quality, is carefully assorted, crushed, and by a well-known process of washing or sluicing, freed from all impurities, and separated into different degrees of fineness. The clay is submitted to a somewhat similar treatment. These two essential raw materials are then spread out in shallow pans and dried at a low temperature. They are next mixed, wetted, and ground in heavy mills for many hours at a time. When the requisite degree of fineness and eveness is obtained, the mass is kneaded like dough into a cake. This cake is placed in a cast-iron cylinder, and by a severe but slow pressure is squeezed through a small hole at the bottom, from which it issues in the shape of a continuous thread. It is now straightened out and cut into the requisite lengths. It is then dried in a moderate temperature, and, when perfectly dry, packed in crucibles, hermetically sealed, and submitted to a high heat in ovens of a peculiar construction.

The lead is now finished, with the exception of the trying, which is the most responsible operation, and requires the greatest skill.

After trying, the finished lead is ready for the wood. This is cedar-wood, none other having been found that possesses in the same degree the two essential qualities of extreme fineness of grain and perfect softness under the knife. The large blocks of cedar, the best of which comes from Florida, are cut up into small slabs of the length of a pencil and about the width of six. After being seasoned, the slab is grooved for the reception of the lead, a preparation of glue is then dexterously poured through the grooves, the leads carefully laid into them and covered with another slab, which is securely glued to the first.

It now passes under peculiarly shaped knives which form half the diameter of six pencils, and being reversed passes again under the shaping knives, and the lead pencil is to all intents and purposes finished.

It still, however, has to undergo all that large variety of processes which change it into the smooth, polished, stamped, gilt, headed, and in fact, completed article, which every one handles with pleasure and satisfaction, without pausing to consider how many industrious pairs of hands have contributed to its production.

To any one familiar with the leading characteristics of the principal modern nations, even this slight and imperfect description will amply explain why the Pencil manufacture, beginning in England, and improved in France, should have made its final home in Germany. It is a manufacture in which success depends preëminently upon constant watchfulness and the most conscientious care,—and these are the qualities which distinguish the German race above all others.

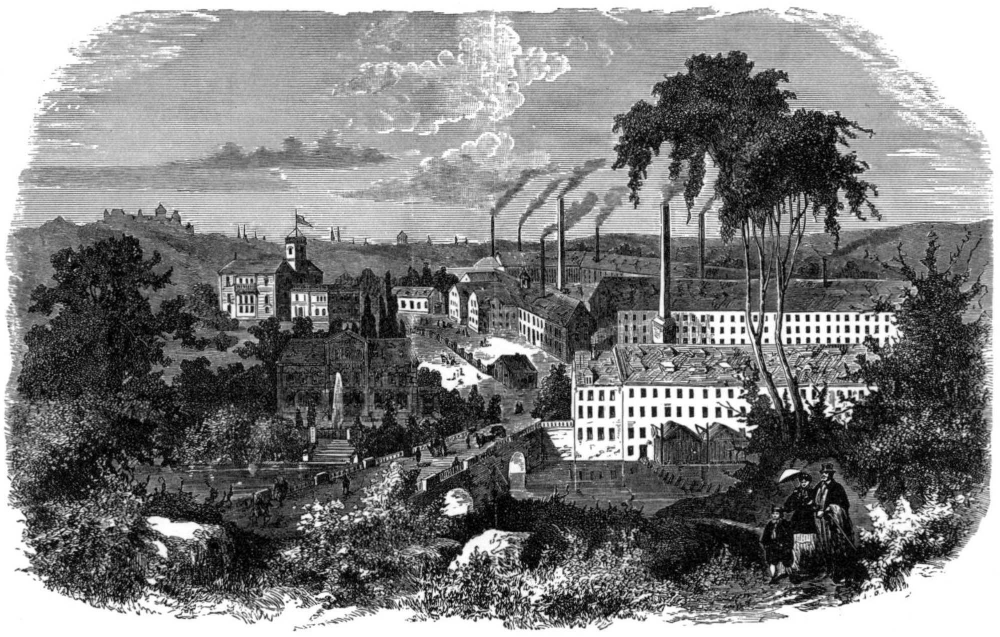

A. W. Faber's Lead Pencil Factory at Stein, near Nürnberg, Bavaria, Germany.
ESTABLISHED 1761.

In the manufacture of lead pencils, the house of A. W. Faber, has for many years enjoyed a monopoly with which none are dissatisfied, a phenomenon well deserving the thoughtful inquiry of every merchant and manufacturer; for if such marked success can be achieved by one business firm, why may not others attain as proud positions in their respective branches of industry by pursuing the same honorable course. The name "Faber" has become almost synonymous with "pencils"; and is familiar as a "household word," wherever civilization has carried the art of writing.

The unparalleled reputation of this firm is a natural consequence of the uniform superiority of the goods they manufacture; their unwavering adherence to the principle that quality is the great desideratum, and that finish or show should be only in proportion to quality, and not assume its place; the unvarying straightforwardness and fairness which characterize all their dealings, and make their name as perfect a guaranty of superiority as any article can bear; and finally, their system of branch houses and branch agencies which enables them to carry out the same principles in every country with which they deal to any extent.

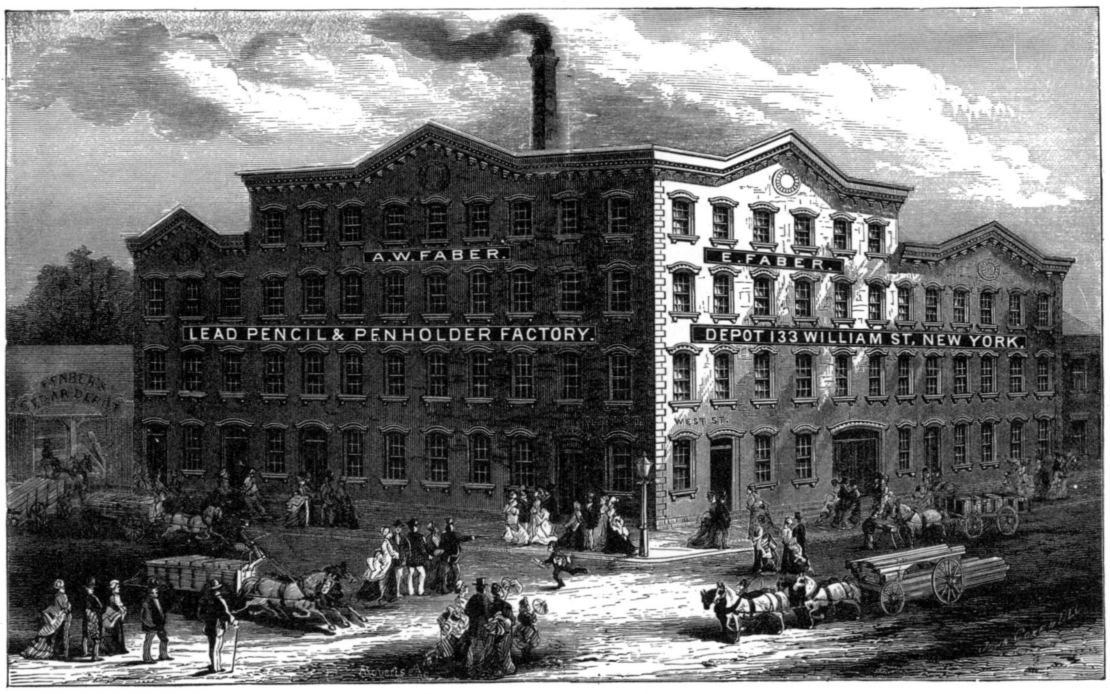

A. W. Faber's Branch Lead Pencil and Penholder Manufactory, Brooklyn, N. Y.
ESTABLISHED 1861.

The history of the house has been almost identical with that of the lead pencil for more than a century. In the year 1761 Caspar Faber settled in the little village of Stein, near Nürnberg, Bavaria, and commenced the manufacture of Faber's pencils. Four generations of the Faber family have since succeeded to the business and have labored continuously to improve the quality of their products; the result being the general acknowledgement of their unvaried excellence, compelling the implicit confidence of both dealer and consumer.

Architects, draftsmen, engineers, and others whose business necessitates the use of large numbers of pencils, and of greatly varying degrees of softness, proclaim them to be the very best. The academies of Paris, Berlin, Dresden, Rome and Munich recommend them particularly. Artists of world wide renown—Horace Vernet, Ingres, Meissonier, Cornelius, Von Kaulbach, Bendemann, Lessing, Von Kreling, Von Seitz, Overbeck, Wilson, and many others, have long since pronounced them superior to all others, and the juries of the Industrial exhibitions in Germany, France, England, Austria and America have awarded these pencils the first prizes.

No faultless article can be made unless every component part is of the highest order ot merit. The manufacturers of the A. W. Faber pencils being well aware of this fact, have spared neither pains nor money to secure the best possible materials.

The lead used for their finest pencils is brought at great expense from the celebrated Alibert mines in Asiatic Siberia, the discoverer, Mr. John Peter Alibert, having, in 1856, bound himself by a contract, endorsed and sanctioned by the Russian Government, the terms of which are such that the Siberian lead, so far as it is suitable for the manufacture of pencils is furnished now, and for all future time, exclusively for the A. W. Faber Lead Pencils.

Good wood, equally with good lead, is essential to a perfect pencil. Ever alive to secure to his factories only the best of a material of such vital importance, Mr. Eberhard Faber, who established the present branch house at 133 William Street, New York in 1851, has since his arrival in this country in 1849, given his special attention to furnishing the Florida red, or pencil cedar as it is called. Cargoes are exported by him to Bremen, and other German ports, Havre, Liverpool, etc., for the supply, not only of the European factory, but for the pencil and other trades generally, in the different countries. He also recently established at Cedar Keys, on the west coast of Florida, a cedar yard and saw mill for the purpose of freeing the large logs, near the place of their growth, of all their useless parts, knowing from long experience the great expense and loss attending the transportation of the wood intact. In his saw mill he also reduces the wood to the small suitable slabs above mentioned, preparatory to the other manipulations by which they are finally transformed into pencils.

The American demand for Fabers Lead Pencils had become so great and was so rapidly increasing, that in 1861, Mr. Eberhard Faber deemed it necessary to establish a branch factory in this country. To insure its successful operation many difficulties had to be encountered and overcome. The cost of labor is so much higher in this country than in Europe, that machinery had to be devised and constructed to automatically perform the work, which is done so cheaply by hand labor in the old country. In fact, the whole process of manufacture as it was known until then, had to be changed from its foundation. The necessary machinery was invented, the new factory put in successful operation, and Mr. Faber had the satisfaction of knowing that he could not only make pencils in this country cheaper, but also of a much better and more uniform finish than any before produced. He thus became the pioneer in a branch of industry then comparatively unknown to our shores, and by uniting American ingenuity with European experience has supplied the public for many years with American Lead Pencils, made in European style.

The house of A. W. Faber have their principal manufactory at Stein, near Nürnberg, Bavaria, which was established in 1761, and has since been in constant operation. We hardly think that Caspar Faber, the founder, ever even hoped that the little works he opened would grow to such immense proportions, or that the local fame which he soon gained would continue to extend until his name should be known throughout the civilized world—more generally known perhaps than that of any other manufacturer who ever lived.

This firm also have a large slate factory at Geroldsgrün, Bavaria, which produces school and other slates in great variety and of the finest description. Colored Chalk, Crayon and Slate Pencils are also made in their European factories, while the celebrated A. W. Faber Rubber Bands and Artist's Rubber, and the E. Faber Penholders are supplied by their respective works here.

An idea of the immense business done by the house will be better conveyed to the mind of the reader by mentioning the style and location of their largest establishments, which, in addition to the above, are: House in Paris, A. W. Faber, 55 Boulevard de Strasbourg; house in London, A. W. Faber, Queen Victoria St., and Bennet's Hill, E. C.; agency in Vienna, Stadt Schellinggasse 12; house in New York, Eberhard Faber, 133 William St.

The Bartlett Galvanic Battery.

Case of Electrodes.

Manufactory and Office.

Galvano-Caustic Battery.

Cabinet Regulator and Batteries.

Galvano-Faradic Manufacturing Company.

167 East 34th Street, New York.

The Galvano-Faradic Manufacturing Company, of New York City, established in 1870, for the construction of Electro Medical Instruments, are the most extensive manufacturers of the kind in the world, and construct the greatest variety of apparatus. Of these the principal machines are the Galvanic, Electro-Magnetic, Galvano-Caustic, Cabinet Combination and Permanent Batteries; to which are added a great variety of accessory instruments for the more scientific and exact application of the electric current to the human body.

Electro-Therapeutics, although comparatively a modern science, has spread over all the enlightened countries of the world until it has become a regular and essential part of medical study, and is certain ever to continue so.

The first mention we have of electricity as a remedial agent, it is true, carries us back to a remote period, when shocks were given to patients from the Torpedo or Electric Ray, found in the Mediterranean, and the Malapterurus, or Electric Shad, found in the Nile—creatures provided with a natural apparatus bearing a strange analogy to those constructed by human hands.

No. 2 Electro-Magnetic Machine.

New Combination Regulator.

No. 3 Electro-Magnetic Machine.

Galvanic Cell.

No. 4 Electro-Magnetic Machine.

Needles and Holder.

But it was not until after the memorable discoveries of Franklin, Galvani and Volta that the scientific world became interested in the matter; then, calling to their aid the Electrifying Machine and Voltaic Pile, physicians began to carefully study the effects of electrical currents upon disease. Some discouragement, as is usual in the introduction of new methods, attended the first attempts to effect cures through the agency of electricity, and in a short time it fell so far into discredit as to discourage experimental inquiry. It was not until some forty years later—about forty years ago—that Duchenne, an eminent French scientist, discovered the method of limiting the application to the diseased organ, by which the remedial effect was

greatly increased. Duchenne's discovery gave a new impetus to the science. He continued his experiments and was assisted in his efforts to arrive at a perfect knowledge of the power and uses of the currents by some of the first makers of electrical instruments in Paris. But, other scientists taking up the inquiry—notably such men as Du Bois, Raymond, Stöhrer, Neef and others in Germany, and Faraday in England—great advances were made, and many new varieties of machines constructed, with still improving parts, down to our own day, and our own country.

The Galvano-Faradic Company takes its title from the two most eminent of the discoverers, Galvani and Faraday; and, in emulation of these great men and of the others herein alluded to, have labored to improve the various apparatus, in which they have been so peculiarly successful that their machines have attained a world-wide celebrity, and are now in general use.

Considered simply in a mechanical point of view, they are beautiful inventions, singularly precise in their movements, and variable to an almost infinite degree in their effect; so that while America may claim the honor of having been among the first nations that endeavored to cure disease by electricity, she is also among the foremost in constructing thoroughly efficacious appliances for so important a purpose.

The engravings presented on this page represent but a few of the many varieties of electrical machines and appliances manufactured by the Galvano-Faradic Manufacturing Company. They occupy the large building situated at the corner of Third Avenue and Thirty-fourth Street, New York City, and keep in constant employ a large force of skillful and scientific workmen, who are taxed to their utmost capacity to keep pace with the constantly increasing demand for their instruments.

The Company will, on application, furnish any of our readers who may desire to know more of electricity as a remedial agent, and the best methods of applying it, with all required information.

A Broken Belt--All Hands Idle--Moral: Buy the Best Belt.

Hose Making.

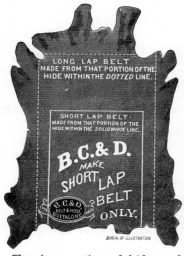

Showing portion of hide used for making Short Lap Belt.

BICKFORD, CURTISS & DEMING,

Manufacturers of

LEATHER BELTING & HOSE,

Nos. 53 and 55 Exchange Street, Buffalo, New York.

Few employers realize the loss of time and money occasioned by the use of a defective belt. One not properly stretched needs a piece cut out to take up the slack, many times oftener than a well stretched one. A dozen men idle about a machine waiting for a broken or slack belt to be repaired, will waste in fifteen minutes the time of one man three hours; this added to the value of the time of the idle machine and the mischief idle hands get into would more than pay the difference between a poor and a good belt.

There are few things that show the progress made in the use of machinery in this country more than the use of belting.

One hundred years ago power was communicated almost entirely by cog wheels. The smooth running and noiseless belt of this day was unknown.

Fifty years ago there was no such thing as a belt factory, and none used except home made ones—strips of leather roughly fastened together, and not stretched till after being put into service, and becoming so crooked as to be as likely to run off from as on the pully—

Even thirty-five years ago a large part of the belts used in the Mills of New England were made and repaired in New York City, and not till about that time was leather stretched by machinery before being made into belting. Now there are many millions of dollars invested in this business, and the hides from near two thousand cattle made into belt every day.

There is cheating in all trades, even belt making. A hide may be

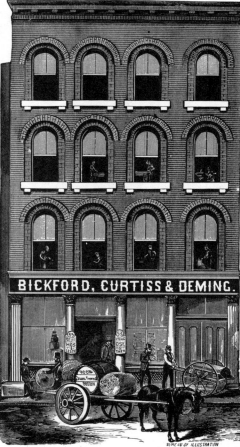

Belting and Hose Warerooms, Buffalo, N. Y.

tanned in three or four weeks by the use of chemicals, and can be made to resemble the pure oak leather tanned in the good old fashioned process by use of bark, which requires many months.

The old way is the only one to make durable leather. Then the hides tanned in the very best manner can be so cut that belts made from them will not be worth half as much as others made from the same hides with the inferior parts left out, as will be seen by a study of the above diagram.

The leather in the neck and shoulder is not firm and solid, as it is in the central part of the hide, or that inside the solid lines. If both parts are used the belt is like a chain, having four sound links and a fifth one unsound, evidently the whole is no better than the weakest part.

The "B. C. & D." belt, or the Best, Cheapest and most Durable belt made by Bickford, Curtiss & Deming, is made only from that part of the hides inside of the solid lines in the above diagram. Then each lap or joint is made from leather equally firm and hard and all are of uniform length and termed "short lap."

The most of belting is made having every alternate lap made from the neck or shoulder or that part of the hide between the solid and dotted lines, and therefore made several times longer, and doubled on account of the thinness and sponginess of the leather and termed "long lap."

B. C. & D. have been established in the Belt and Hose business in Buffalo, New York, since 1867, Mr. Bickford having had eighteen years previous experience in the business in the largest manufacturing town in New England. They believed there were but two courses to pursue, either to make the very best article and find those customers who cared most for quality, or else, to make the poorest and look for customers among those that cared most for price. They chose the former course.

B. C. & D. also believe their motto, "Best is Cheapest because most Durable," is as applicable to leather hose as to belting. There is as small a proportion of a hide—not forty per cent.—put in their hose as in the belts manufactured by them. For particulars, price list, &c., address as per heading of this article.

Established 1855. Incorporated 1875.

TIVOLI HOSIERY MILLS.

ROOT MANUFACTURING COMPANY.

JOSIAH G. ROOT, President, ANDREW J. ROOT, Treas. and Gen'l Manager.
SAMUEL G. ROOT, Superintendent. GEO. WATERMAN, Jr., Secretary.

Manufacturers of

Ladies', Gent's, Youth's and Children's Fine

WOOL AND MERINO KNIT UNDERWEAR.

——:o:——

In the early colonial days, the "Cahoos" or Falls of the *Maquaskil* (Mohawk River) and the adjacent country were noted for their wild but wonderously beautiful scenery. Moore, the Irish poet, during his visit to America, drew the inspiration for one of his finest poems from a view of this cataract, and in a note appended to it, says:—"There is a dreamy and savage character in the country immediately above these Falls which is more in harmony with the wildness of such a scene, than the cultivated lands in the neighborhood of Niagara." It is not our intention, however, to enter very largely into a description of the natural beauties of this section when in its prestine glory, but to briefly glance at the history of its development, and perhaps no better evidence of the rapid but substantial growth of the manufacturing interests of our country can be given than is to be found in the advancement of the city of Cohoes and its industries.

Previous to 1811 the present site of the city was simply a wilderness, skirted by a vast unappropriated water power, and only known in the world at large through such descriptions of its wonders and beauties, as had been given by tourists and travelers who had been compelled by circumstances or prompted by curiosity to visit the vicinity. The first extensive attempt at manufacturing was made in 1811 by the "Cohoes Manufacturing Company," which was incorporated "for the purpose of manufacturing cotton, woolen and linen goods, bar iron, nail rods, hoop iron and iron-mongry." A factory and several dwellings were built; and a wing dam extending into the river was erected, and operations commenced. These manufactures were too diversified in character however, to be successfully carried on by one management, and in 1827, after the destruction of their factory by fire, the company failed, and the property was sold to the Cohoes Company, who further developed the water power, and for a time manufactured extensively, in addition to supplying power to others; but as the industrial interests of the place commenced to develop the association gradually relinquished manufacturing and finally confined itself entirely to furnishing power.

INTERIOR VIEW OF KNITTING ROOM, TIVOLI HOSIERY MILLS.

The early growth of the town was not very rapid. In 1830, in what now constitutes the principal manufacturing portion of Cohoes, there were not fifty inhabitants, and in the entire present corporate limits there was not to exceed one hundred and fifty. In 1831, there was neither post office, church, tavern or store in the locality where now the principal business of the city is transacted. When in 1832, Mr. Egbert Egberts, the father of the knitting business in America, made his appearance in Cohoes and set up his knitting frames, the introduction of the new industry gave an impetus to the growth of the town, and Cohoes from the establishment of this, the first knitting mill in the country, has enjoyed a continuous prosperity which has scarcely been rippled by the panics that have so sorely crippled other manufacturing towns, and has increased in population from a mere handful of people to a city of about 25,000 inhabitants.

Cohoes not only inaugurated the knitting business of this country, but has since maintained the lead, and now produces fully one-third of all the hosiery manufactured in the United States. At the present time there are no less than eighteen knitting establishments in the city, prominent among which are the Tivoli Hosiery Mills, owned and operated by the Root Manufacturing Company.

These mills were originally established by Josiah G. Root, of Albany, N. Y., in the year 1855, and to-day, stand among the knitting mills of Cohoes, third in order of establishment, and in capacity, appointments and appurtenances, and quality of goods produced, rank with the best in the United States. In the year 1860, Mr. Root admitted his sons, Messrs. A. J. and S. G. Root, into partnership and the firm name became J. G. Root & Sons, under which title the business was continued until the year 1869, when Mr. Josiah G. Root retired, and the style was changed to J. G. Root's Sons, and so continued until the formation of the present Company.

On the 2d day of April, 1874, the mills were entirely destroyed by fire. But Josiah G. Root's Sons are not men who are paralyzed by such calamities. The sudden destruction of their works with all the costly machinery with which they were amply supplied, and the loss of the stock of manufactured goods on hand was a severe blow but did not demoralize them. Active and vigorous, full of enterprise, and with a business standing which ranked high, they had the will and the means to make good their serious losses, and immediately began the erection of the present magnificent establishment known as the Tivoli Hosiery Mills upon the site occupied by the old ones. The new mills are built upon the most approved plans, not only for convenience and adaptability to the business, but with special reference to security against fire. Upon their completion the Root Manufacturing Company was organized and immediately stocked the structure with the latest and most approved machinery for the manufacture of the special lines of goods to which they have since devoted their attention. Neither pains nor expense have been spared to procure the very best of everything that could in any way tend to the absolute perfection of their productions. Skilled labor of the highest class is employed, and the utmost care is exercised in the selection of the material and its subsequent conversion into marketable goods. The high rank which their manufactures have obtained is *prima facia* evidence of their superiority.

The capacity of the Tivoli Hosiery Mills is fifteen sets of machinery, to operate which they employ three hundred hands, whose wages aggregate one hundred thousand dollars per annum. Their annual production is forty-five thousand dozen of fine wool and merino knit underwear, valued at half a million dollars, for which they not only find a ready market, but frequently are unable to supply the demand.

TIVOLI HOSIERY MILLS, COHOES, NEW YORK.

DONAGAN & DAVIS,

GRANITE QUARRY,

Concord, N. H.

——:o:——

As the Nation advances in years and the wealth of our people increases, there is a growing desire manifested on all sides to erect a better and more substantial class of buildings than were common at an earlier date. True, the sturdy men who first settled the country, coming from a fatherland where massive structures of stone and brick were common, built many of their first dwellings in imitation of those in the old home; but those who were not wealthy could hardly afford to pay for the labor necessary to build a stone house and contented themselves with the less substantial but more easily erected and inexpensive wooden structure. The first stone houses were built of broken boulders, or of the common rock formation in their immediate vicinity, and though they were substantial and comfortable, they did not present a handsome appearance. There seems to have been but little effort made to discover whether the better classes of stone could be found in the country or not; the man who built a stone house took the first material that presented itself, or, if rich and proud, imported it from the old country. The authorities favored the erection of stone or brick buildings and, to cheapen their cost, the Dutch of New York from the earliest date of their settlement imported yellow brick from Holland, and, in 1648 put stone to the free list to encourage its introduction from abroad. Subsequent to this a number of buildings were erected on Manhattan Island of imported stone, though close by, in New Jersey, literal "free-stone" might have been had for the quarrying.

In all the colonies, however, timber was plenty, and as it required far less labor and time to erect a log cabin, or, in later times, a shingled or clapboarded house, than a stone or brick one, wood became the common building material. But as the population of the cities and towns increased, it became necessary to build more compactly, and the greater danger from fire among wooden structures awakened a desire to use less inflammable materials. Brick yards were established, quarries of granite, marble, freestone and slate were opened, and, as it was soon proven that an abundant supply of durable building material could be taken from the ground, in the larger places wood was almost entirely discarded by common consent. But as there are always a few who, regardless of the rights of others, and blind to their own interests, are willing to put up flimsy wooden structures, the local authorities of all the cities and villages of importance throughout the United States have enacted ordinances prohibiting the erection of such buildings.

The destructive conflagrations which have within the last fifty years made sad havoc in some of our principal cities and almost entirely destroyed several smaller towns, have resulted in an increased disposition to erect only fire-proof buildings, and in all the cities, and in most of the villages of importance, there are structures so substantially built, and of such indestructable materials as to defy the fire-fiend and withstand the wear of Time for ages. Nearly all the really first-class buildings erected within the past few years are, at least partly constructed of granite. Many fine structures which to the passer-by seem to be entirely of brick, or iron, rest on foundations of huge slabs of granite, without which their great weight would cause them to settle in the yielding earth. The general verdict of architects and builders that no other material combines the many good points of granite, and the growing desire to use the best, has developed an industry of gigantic proportions in the quarrying of this stone. One of the most popular firms in the granite business is Donagan & Davis, of Concord, N. H. Operating one of the largest quarries of the choicest granite in the Granite State, and having supplied themselves with all the improved appliances which can aid them in taking it from its native bed and fashioning it for the builders' use, the promptness with which they fill orders and the strict honesty of their dealings, have made them prominently and favorably known.

Messrs. Donagan & Davis have furnished the whole or a portion of the granite for many of the largest and best public and private buildings in the country, and to these they refer as tangible proofs of their skill and the excellence of their material. The U. S. Custom House, Portland, Maine, the Public Ledger Building in Philadelphia, the Equitable Building and the German Savings Bank, New York, received granite from these quarries. Such buildings furnish endorsements which, though mute, are stronger than written or spoken words.

The ease with which granite can be transported from the quarries to all parts of the country, as a consequence of the rapid extension of railroads, has greatly promoted its general use. The stone is now loaded on the cars at the quarries and, without being disturbed, may be delivered almost anywhere within the Union or the Canadas. It is not many years since the blocks had to be drawn many miles by teams before a car could be reached, and if the shipment was to a distant point, the expense of frequent handling made the cost of transportation so great that many who ackowledged the worth of granite as a building material were deterred from using it. This drawback having been swept away, there is no longer any valid reason why inferior stones should be used and, consequently, within a few years, the demand for granite has more than doubled and is still increasing.

With the greater demand came a necessity for labor-saving appliances, and, following that necessity, many devices were invented which have aided in developing the quarries and cheapening their products. Messrs. Donagan & Davis have taken advantage of all these aids, and are always prepared to furnish builders at short notice, and at prices as low as is compatible with excellence of material and workmanship.

VIEW OF DONAGAN & DAVIS' GRANITE QUARRY, CONCORD, N. H.

SWAMSCOT MACHINE COMPANY,

Manufacturers of

Steam Engines, Steam Boilers, Steam and Water Pipe, Gas Works and Gas Holders, Steam Heating Apparatus and General Machine Work.

SOUTH NEWMARKET, NEW HAMPSHIRE.

——:o:——

South Newmarket is one of the most active and wide-awake towns of the Old Granite State; one of her many gems of which she is justly proud. It is situate in Rockingham County, upon the Swamscot River, a branch of the Piscatuqua, which furnishes a water communication with Portsmouth and the ocean, it is navigable for vessels drawing eleven feet of water, and is also on the line of the Boston and Maine Railroad, which affords easy and direct communication with both Boston, Mass., and Portland, Maine. South Newmarket was originally embraced in the township of Newmarket, but, in 1850, was incorporated as a separate town, since which time it has grown apace, increasing rapidly in population and in material wealth, a result largely due to the establishment and successful operation of the extensive works of the Swamscot Machine Company, and the impetus it has naturally imparted to other branches of industry.

As early as 1830 Iron Works were established in South Newmarket for the manufacture of Stoves, and to make castings for Cotton and Woolen Mills, and for heavy machinery. Considerable quantities of such work were turned out, but the production did not fully meet the demand for a variety of machine work of which the town and adjacent county had need.

To more fully supply this want the Swamscot Machine Company was organized, and, in 1849, incorporated by the State Legislature. The first efforts of the Company were confined to the production of Tools and Mill Machinery, to which has since been added a long line of Special Machines, and a great variety of Iron and Brass Work, the business having grown to proportions, doubtless, far exceeding the original anticipations of its founders

Intelligent, persistent, honest effort, is, however, always successful, and as, from the beginning, it has been the determination of the managers of the Company to produce the best possible work, and the best only, to accomplish which neither capital nor labor has been spared, the growth of their business is scarcely a marvel. It is simply the recognition which is a natural sequence of merit—the reward that ever follows worth. This extension of the business of the Company, both in the variety and the value of its productions, has steadily increased, year by year, until it has

now reached a point which places it in a prominent position among the leading mechanical industries of the country, and, as such, worthy of more than passing notice.

In 1865 the Swamscot Machine Company purchased the Iron Foundry Works, previously mentioned, and united it to their extensive Machine Shops, the two combined forming a specially complete establishment, enabling them to perform, upon their own premises, all the labor (from the drawing of plans, making the necessary patterns, moulding and casting, or forging the various parts down to and including the last finishing and ornamental touches) incident to the construction of almost every description of machinery.

The works of the Company, an engraving of which graces the centre of this page, cover an area of about six acres of ground, and are located on both sides of the Boston and Maine Railroad. To say that they are supplied with all the appliances that can lighten the labor of the employés, or aid them in any way in the rapid production of perfect work is an assertion so general in its character, as to scarcely do justice to the completeness of their equipment, while to describe the various devices and aids employed would much more than fill the space allotted to this article. Suffice it to say, that there are huge steam shears to cut heavy plates of boiler-iron to the required shapes and sizes, rolls to give them the required curve, drilling machines and steam punches to make the necessary holes for rivets;—there are great planers and lathes, steam hammers, traveling cranes to lift and move heavy forgings, as necessity requires, and all the latest and most approved devices that can be successfully used in general machine-work, and, in addition to these, a number of peculiar machines and tools adapted to their special classes of production.

The Company annually turn out a large number of Steam Engines, of various sizes and of perfect pattern; they are also largely engaged in the construction of Steam Boilers of any required capacity, and, as fitting adjuncts to this class of their business, they are extensive manufacturers

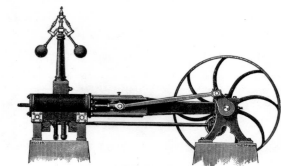

complete equipment of the establishment with improved appliances of every description, by the aid of which they not only secure more perfect work, but lighten the labor of their employés, and greatly enhance their capacity for production. Still another is in the pains that are taken to secure and retain the services of the most skillful mechanics, and the prompt dismissal of all who prove incompetent, careless, or in any way unreliable.

The smaller towns and villages of this and every other country possess marked advantages over the principal cities in the character of their laboring classes. To use an expressive, if not an elegant phrase, " they average better." Many of the mechanics employed by the Swamscot Machine Company served their apprenticeship and have since continuously labored in their shops, and not a few of them own the neat and comfortable homes in which they live. Such men have an interest in the town and all that pertains to it, but especially in the reputation of the works that affords them steady and profitable employment, which the traveling mechanic, who floats from one large city to another, never feels. The village mechanic looks upon himself as a part and parcel of the establishment, and feels that he has a personal interest in its success entirely outside and independent of the wages earned. Its good reputation reflects credit upon him, or its bad name is his disgrace. The unsteady class of workmen who congregate in cities view the thing in a different light. A situation to them is only an opportunity to secure so much money for so many hours of time. The extent of their interest in the work performed is bounded only by the wages paid. The quality of their work, if it will only pass, is with them a matter of little consideration. We do not claim that the larger cities have no workmen as skillful as those of the villages, but we do claim that among the mechanics of small towns there is a

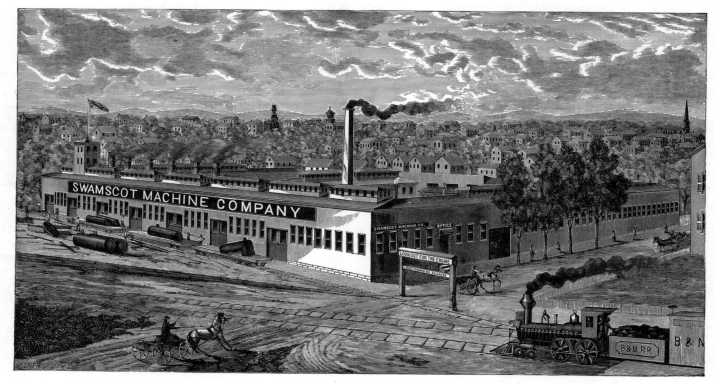

View of Swamscot Machine Company's Works, South Newmarket, New Hampshire, U. S. A.

of Lap-Welded Wrought Iron Water and Steam Pipes, and every description of Brass and Iron Steam Fittings. A very important line of their business is the building of Gas Works and Gas Holders, a branch of iron work in which but few establishments in this country are engaged, requiring, as it does, special machinery and facilities not commonly possessed. Steam Heating Apparatus for public buildings, factories, and dwellings is another of the special branches to which attention is paid at these works, and in which they have been peculiarly successful. Then they make Machinists' Machinery, such as Boiler Plate Planers, etc., and are large manufacturers of Mill Machinery and Appliances, such as Bleaching Kiers, Dye Becks, Hot Room Furnaces, Steam and Ageing Boxes for Print Works, etc., and a variety of general machine work which we cannot specifically mention.

The wide range of the products of the Swamscot Machine Company is somewhat remarkable, but still more noticeable is the fact that in every branch of their business they are acknowledged as leaders. Many establishments are noted for the superiority of some one production, or class of productions; for their steam-engines or their boilers, or the two combined; for their mill machinery or for some special machine, but there are few that have the reputation of excelling in so great a variety of work. This high and well-earned reputation is the result of good management on the part of the Company. To begin with, the location of their works was wisely selected. They have all the facilities for communication with the outside world, by land or sea, that could be desired, and, consequently, have no difficulty in readily and cheaply securing supplies of crude material, or shipping their finished products, while the capital invested in grounds and buildings is infinitely less than would be necessary to secure as eligible quarters in any of the large cities. Another evidence of good management is found in the liberal outlay that has been made from time to time in the

larger percentage of good ones than is found in the cities.

South Newmarket is peculiarly fortunate in possessing the Works of the Swamscot Machine Company, and numbering among its inhabitants the hundreds of steady, honest men, who comprise its working force. The town is amply provided with schools and churches, the spires of three of the latter being discernable in the background of our engraving, and is, in every respect, a perfect model of a thriving New England village To say more would be superfluous.

EDWARD MILLER & CO.,

Brass and Bronze Works and Rolling Mill,

MERIDEN, CONN.

—:o:—

Among the mills and factories of Meriden, Conn., there are none better deserving notice than the Brass and Bronze Works, and Rolling Mills of Edward Miller & Co. These works, though now among the largest of their class in this country had a very humble origin, and the success which has attended them is attributable to the indefatigable energy, the mechanical skill and the sterling business talents of the gentlemen whose name heads the style of the Company.

The business was begun in a very small way, in the year 1844, by Mr. Horatio N. Howard, who opened a small shop and began the manufacture of Lamp Screws, Oil Screws and Candle Stick Springs, little dreaming that he was laying the corner stone of an establishment whose good name would be well known throughout the United States and extend to foreign lands.

In 1845 Mr. Edward Miller succeeded Mr. Howard, and for a short time labored under the same difficulties that had beset his predecessor—lack of facilities for turning out large quantities of goods. Finishing brass with a hand lathe, and other appliances as primitive, is hard work and slow, and Mr. Miller in the beginning was forced to use such for lack of means to get a better power. But fatiguing as was the labor of the first few months of his business venture, and small as was the quantity of goods produced, he was not discouraged. There was a ready market for his wares at paying prices—the demand largely exceeded the supply, and he was soon enabled to (and the business required that he should) increase his facilities. The first addition was a "horse power." With this aid his products were greatly increased but the demand increased still more—his old quarters were not large enough, and he erected a small shop and introduced steam power.

In the new quarters Mr. Miller manufactured a greater variety of goods, screws becoming a specialty. When camphene and burning fluid were introduced as illuminating agents he turned his attention to the production of burners adapted to them.

The burning fluid gave such a superior light without smoke or ordor, and was so much cleaner and better to handle than whale oil, it became a gr t favorite for household use, almost entirely superseding tallow dip candles and whale oil as illuminating agents for home use. This greatly increased the demand for burners suitable to burn the various fluids that were used, and Mr. Miller gave this class of burners his special attention; the demand for them soon become so great as to seriously tax the resources of the factory.

While in the full tide of success, disaster came. In the early spring of 1857 the new shop was destroyed by fire. To witness the destruction of one's accumulations after years of unceasing labor has, to say the least, a tendency to discourage most men, but in this case it seemed to act as a stimulant, inciting to stronger effort and infusing greater energy. New quarters were promptly obtained, and the business pushed ahead with, if possible, more vigor than before.

When Kerosene oil, distilled from bituminous coal, was first introduced as an illuminating agent, (some years before the Petroleum fields of Pennsylvania were worked,) Mr. Miller added the manufacture of Kerosene Burners to his already extensive business. And here we deem it only just to that gentleman to remark, that he was the first man in America to enter into the manufacture of such burners, and that he undoubtedly made the first Kerosene Burner ever made in this country. His friends make this claim for him, and we have never heard it disputed. Kerosene distilled from coal was more expensive than fluid, and the latter was most generally used by the masses of the people,consequently for some years after the production of the Kerosene Burner, the fluid burners were made in immense quantities. With the development of the oil fields, and the improved methods of refining which closely followed, Petroleum was cheapened and soon became the common illuminating agent. Then came a demand for Kerosene Burners which taxed Mr. Miller's establishment to its utmost

capacity. Other workers in brass began the manufacture of burners, and were sucessful; no one concern could supply the demand—but the reputation of the goods turned out here, after years of comparison and competition with those of other make, is not excelled by those of any other house.

In 1866 the business had assumed such large proportions that Mr.

Edward Miller & Co.'s Brass and Bronze Works and Rolling Mills.

Miller deemed it best to divide the cares and responsibilities with others. Consequently a Joint Stock Company was organized, under the name of Edward Miller & Co.; the previous style having been Edward Miller, and the Stockholders deeming it best to preserve the name so widely and favorably known in the business. The Company immediately increased the capacity of the works, and the same success which had attended the earlier years of the business has continued since. In 1868—'69 a large Brass Rolling Mill

was erected and the manufacture of Sheet Brass, etc., was begun on an extensive scale.

The productions of the Company embrace a great variety of articles which we cannot well enumerate in detail. Prominent among there manufactures are the articles previously mentioned, Lamp Trimmings of every description, and a line of highly ornamental Bronze Lamps. Tinners' Hardware, also forms an important feature of their business, and the number of Spun Brass Kettles they produce is simply enormous.

The reader will notice that this page is beautified with engravings of ornamental designs. These cuts represent a few selected from a very large assortment of artistic works in bronze manufactured by this Company. It has been, and still is a fault with our people that they are disposed to bestow most of their praise and patronage upon foreign works, to the exclusion of American. We import yearly many millions of dollars worth of goods which could be, and in many instances are as well made and as finely finished here as in foreign lands, but at a much higher price the "imported" article is selected. There are some manufacturers who pander to this bad taste by labelling their productions with foreign marks, thus fostering the evil of which they complain, while others place their goods beside the imported articles and confidently await a final verdict in their favor. In the world of art, especially, is this patronization of foreign productions noticable, and to such an extent is it carried that there are those who are always ready to believe that any price of art work attributed to or claimed by an American was really designed and executed by some needy but talented Italian or Frenchman who, for a price, sold the fame that was justly his.

Edward Miller & Co., are large manufacturers of Bronze Ornaments, Statuettes, etc. Some of these are reproductions of the works of famous artists, embracing not only their best original ideal conceptions, but busts and full length representations of the renowned statesmen, poets and warriors of the world. They also produce an infinite variety of mantel and desk ornaments of every description, Vases, Urns, Pitchers, antique, and of modern designs—the conceptions of their own corps of artists—Birds and Animals, single and in groups. No works of like character whether produced in foreign lands or our own, excel those of this Company. In their fidelity to nature, their clearness of outline, their gracefulness of design and the truly artistic finish in every particular which marks them, they cannot be surpased. Jewelers and dealers in works of art and ornament, throughout the country, keep a full line of these goods on hand.

The birds-eye view of the works of the Company presented on this page is drawn on a small scale but is still large enough to convey to the mind of the reader some idea of the size of the establishment. The various departments are completely equipped with all the devices that can aid in the rapid and inexpensive production of thoroughly first-class work. It is a rule in the production of their goods, that excellence is the grand aim to be attained, and the high esteem in which their goods of every description are universally held by dealers and consumers warrant us in asserting that they fully realize the end sought. These works afford employment for from three hundred and fifty to four hundred skilled artizans. Their goods are in demand in every State and Territory of the Union, and are largely exported to foreign lands, and immense as the business has already become it is still constantly increasing. The Company does not call to its aid any of those outside influences which some manufacturers make use of,—they do not represent their work as being of foreign origin, nor appropriate the styles of others, but rely solely upon the merit of their productions for success. Following this course Mr. Miller, when sole proprietor of the works, (from the time he personally ran the single foot lathe that the establishment owned down to the time when the business had outgrown the capacity of any one man to conduct it alone,) achieved a reputation for himself and his productions, which the corporation could not afford to sacrifice. There is the same careful attention paid to the most minute details of the business, from the mixing of the native metals which form the alloy, to the final finishing of the smallest article they produce. There is the same earnest endeavor to attain perfection—and we believe this Company has as nearly reached it as it is possible for mere men to do.

GEO. MATHER'S SONS, MANUFACTURERS OF FINE PRINTING AND LITHOGRAPHIC INKS,

Factory, Sixth and Provost Streets, Jersey City.

Office and Salesrooms, 60 John Street, New York.

PRINTING INK.

The history of the art of printing has been so frequently and so exhaustively written up that we do not deem it necessary to here investigate the proofs offered in support—nor express an opinion as to the relative merits—of the claims of priority of discovery entered for Koster, of Harlaem; Mentelin, of Strasbourg; and Guttenberg, of Mentz; nor yet to give any account of their early struggles. The invention of movable metal types, the dates at which different styles of letter have been introduced, and by whom, are matters of history—facts within the reach of all who desire the information. So, too, of the printing press. No class of machinery has been more thoroughly explained, and if the masses of the people are not as well informed in relation to its mechanism as they are in relation to that of the steam engine, it is because they have not been at the same pains to learn the facts.

All are aware and ready to acknowledge that through the facilities afforded by the art of printing for the rapid and cheap diffusion of information, mankind has been more rapidly advanced than would have been possible by any other means, and so confessedly great is the power wielded through books and papers, that the Press has come to be generally recognized as "The lever that moves the world."

Guttenberg, Koster, Mentelin, Faust, Schœffer, Nicholas Jenson,

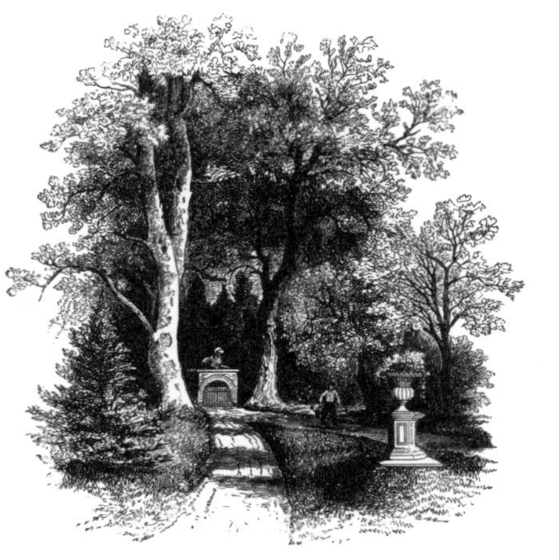

Aldus Manutius and William Caxton, will always be revered as Fathers or early disciples of the art; and, among the first inventors of printing machinery, the names of the Earl of Stanhope and William Nicholson, of England; Frederick König, of Saxony; George Clymer, of Philadelphia, Pennsylvania; and Isaac Adams, of Boston, Massachusetts, U. S. A., stand out prominently. These names are all well known; the histories of the men and their inventions have been written and re-written, and the general public are generally acquainted therewith, while the names of the more recent inventors are "familiar as household words" to-day, and will be handed down to future generations for all time to come.

The history of paper is equally well known, the materials of which the various kinds are made, and the processes through which they pass have been described frequently and with the utmost minuteness, and the important relation it holds to printing is thoroughly appreciated. But the type, the presses and the paper are not the only materials required to transform thoughts into words that can be read. There is one other article as essential as either of the above named—and yet, to those unacquainted with the business, of such seemingly slight importance that it is rarely thought of—Ink.

Ink, to the average mind is simply so much "'some kind of coloring matter, and some kind of oil,' used to daub on the types and thence be transferred to the paper in waiting for it." Few, except those interested in its manufacture, and the more philosophical of those who win livlihoods in its use, have ever attempted to trace the steps by which it has become one of the most perfect and expensive compounds in existence, and fewer still have even the most remote idea of the prominent position held by Printers' Ink among the materials consumed in the world of art.

In the olden time each master printer prepared his own inks, and right good care did he take that no other became possessed of his formulas and processes. As to the ingredients and their proportions, the secrets have been well kept, and though a number of recipes were published in England and France, from 1683 down to 1832, not one of them names a combination of materials or describes a process of manufacture which would result in the production of an ink that could be worked with the printing machinery of to-day. Nor does it seem possible that either of them could have been worked in the manner then employed with results as fine as were achieved by some of the early masters, for we must acknowledge that the first printers did very neat press work, and used inks the color of which have not been materially impaired by time. We do know, however, that until a comparatively recent date the ingredients of which the ink was composed were ground together by hand on flat stones, as the fine colors of painters are ground, but further than this, and that nut or linseed oil, (boiled or burned) and lamp black were used, we knew absolutely nothing of either the materials or methods of manufacture.

But the Ink of the Fathers, though it doubtlessly fully met the requirements of their times, would not answer now, and for several reasons: The character of the work to be performed is different, and all the methods of operation have changed. Within the memory of living printers the trade has been completely revolutionized; power presses of various kinds have superseded the hand press of a few years ago, and the finest classes of work are now done on cylinders. With this last change came a pressing necessity for an ink very different from any previously known—finer in quality, easier to work, and more intense in color.

Taking this page as an example, we will endeavor to explain the difference in the method of printing on a hand press and a cylinder press, at least so far as the application of color and the means of taking the impression are concerned, and if we do this so that the reader understands it we shall have explained why the new presses require a better quality of ink than the old ones did. Premising that the bed of each press is flat, and contains a form or electrotype plate of this page, we will proceed to take an imaginary impression from each, beginning with the old hand press.

There are men working at the trade to-day who can well remember when the face of the type or engraving was covered with ink by gently tapping it with leather balls which had previously taken their "color" from a stone on which the ink was spread. The process was slow, but, if, for instance, a "form" was being "worked" which contained both heavy lines and light ones, it enabled the operator to spread the "color" as liberally on the large lines and as sparingly on the small ones as was necessary to produce the proper degree of light and shade; or, where the black spots were too small to be touched by the ball without endangering the filling up of fine lines close by, as for instance in the cut of the "Willow Spring," on the upper left hand corner of this page, the finger was frequently used. Even after the days of leather balls had passed away and composition rollers had come into use as a means of inking the face of the type, parts of a form could receive such additional rolling as was necessary to produce the desired effects. Then the entire page was subjected to pressure at once, and the pressman could "dwell" upon the impression for such length of time as was necessary to enable the paper to absorb the extra "color."

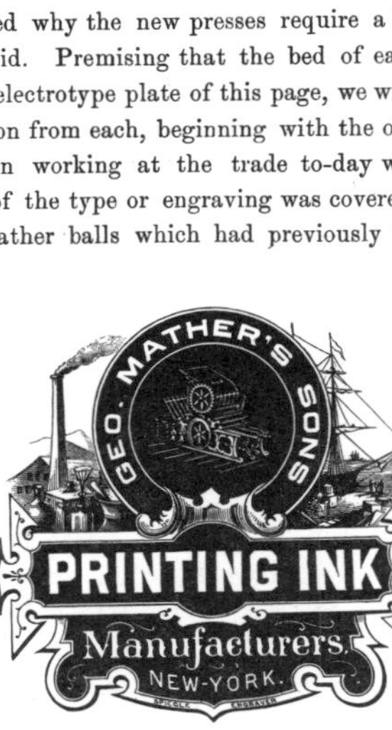

With a cylinder press the form is rolled a given number of times, and every part of it is rolled alike; it cannot be rolled in spots: it may be rolled twice, or four times, or six times, but one corner cannot be rolled and the other part left untouched, while on the hand press any portion may receive extra rolling and consequently extra "color." On this page the rollers first touch the form on the outside of the right hand column, roll across the page and back again, making at least two rollings, but the number may be repeated as often as the pressman deems advisable. The impression in this case is taken by running the bed containing the form under a revolving cylinder which holds the sheet, consequently the impression is taken a little at a time, and if "color" was spread as thickly on the plate as might safely be done with a hand press, the tendency of the cylindrical impression would be to force the ink sufficiently over the edge of the line containing it to cause a blur.

Engraving on wood is done in relief, that is, every black line is a raised line in the block or plate and every spot or line of white shows

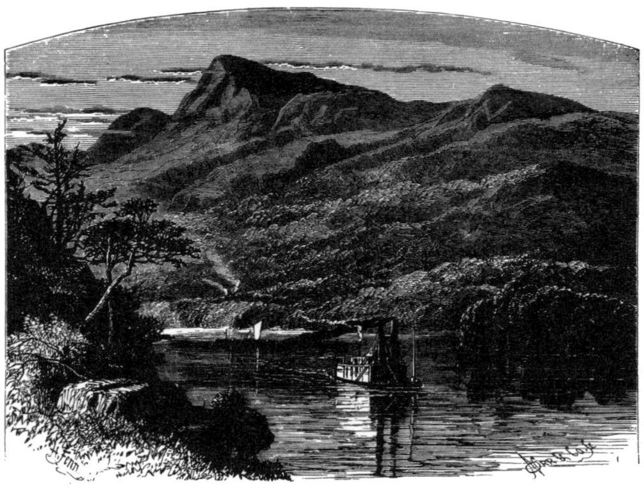

where the wood has been cut away. If the reader will now examine the engravings presented on this page it will be seen that in each one of them there is some place entirely black, and that crossing or against the darkest parts, are very fine light lines running close together. It will also be noticed that every line stands out clear and distinct, that there is no blur, no cloudiness, no indefinable something—one hardly knows what—that mars too many fine engravings. This sharpness of line could not be secured but for the superior quality of the ink used.

For many years there existed a rivalry among the printers and ink manufacturers of Germany, France, Holland and England in the production of fine inks, and within our memory, considerable quantities of ink intended for the very finest printing were imported from France and

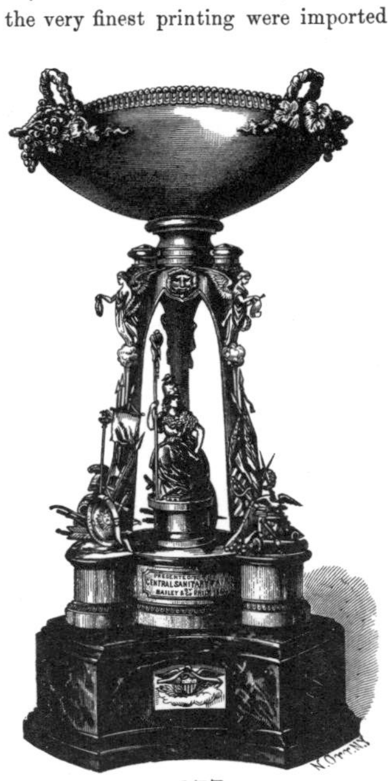

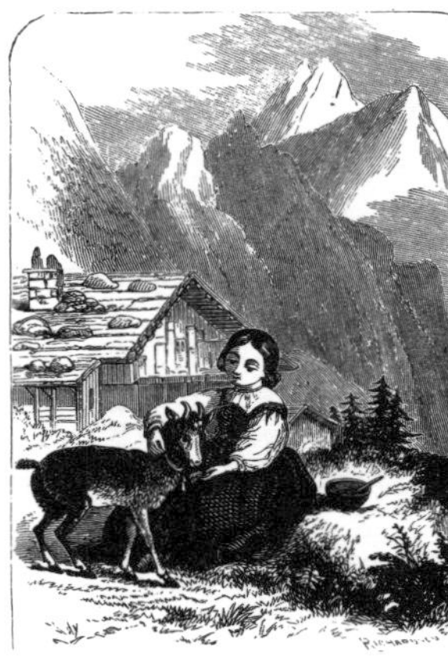

England. But to-day, keeping pace with the rapid progress which America has made in every branch of the typographical art, and with the necessity for such progress involved in the fact that we have demanded far more work than any other nation, and have been willing to pay better prices to secure supreme excellence—to-day we stand at the head of the manufacture of printing inks in the world.

In nearly all the large cities of the country there are manufactories of printing ink more or less extensive, but what could be called the "great houses" of the trade, need fewer than the fingers on a man's hand to count. Both Philadelphia and Boston have had their "masters" in the art; but from its metropolitan position, New York soon became the leader of the manufacture in this country, and has since held the place of prominence.

The first factory, still in existence, for the manufacture of printers' ink in New York, was established April 1, 1816, by George Mather; it was located on Green Street, near Prince, and was continued there until about the year 1840 or '41 when the business was moved to Front and South Streets, where it remained some ten years, and continued to grow until another change of base was necessary. In 1852, or thereabouts, the works were removed from New York to Jersey City, where they have since been continuously located, on ground now forming the corner of Sixth and Provost Streets.

In January, 1857, Mr. George Mather, the founder of the house, retired from active business and was succeeded by his sons, S. Talmage Mather and D. W. C. Mather, and his son-in-law, R. N. Perlee, under the firm name of George Mather's Sons. Coming into posession of a business firmly established on that sure foundation which sterling integrity always lays, the new firm determed to fully mantain the high reputation which Mather's Inks had already acheived, and, if possible, to improve their quality. About this time ornamental printing in colors became popular—and the demand for colored inks increased to such an extent that it soon became necessary to enlarge their building and increase their facilities for manufacturing Colored Printing Inks.

A little later, Steam Lithographic Presses were successfully introduced, following which came a demand for Lithographic Inks, to supply which they were obliged to make still further additions to their works.

George Mather's Sons manufacture various grades of Lithographic and Printing Inks, but make a specialty of the finer qaulities. Their colored inks have been too long and favorably known to need any special mention, while their Black Wood Cut Ink speaks for itself. Those of our readers who are familiar with Appleton's Picturesque America, Picturesque Europe, the Aldine, the Art Journal, and other works of that class which we might name, must have noticed the marked clearness with which the wood cuts are printed, and if the trouble is taken to compare them with other wood engravings equally well cut, but worked in other lands or with other inks, none can fail to remark the superiority of the American work. The publications above named are printed with Geo. Mather's Sons $5.00 Extra Fine Wood Cut Ink. Cheaper qualities of wood cut inks are made with which very fine work is done; so fine, in some instances, that only experts could detect the difference. Harper's Weekly, Frank Leslie's Illustrated Newspaper, the Christian Weekly, and many of the choicest School Books of the day are printed with other grades of their Wood Cut Ink.

Many inks of other manufacture in a short time become dull and yellow. A marked peculiarity of George Mather's Sons Inks is that they retain their lustre and density of color.

Few of our readers who are not in some way connected with the typographic art, we venture to say, have ever thought that printers' ink was so expensive. Five dollars seems a great price to pay for one pound of ink, but there are printing inks of yet higher price, $10, $20, $30,—and still we have not mentioned the top figure,—but these prices are for colored inks; on the other hand, plain black ink, such as is used in printing the huge editions of the leading daily papers, can be bought at from ten to twenty cents a pound.

The cuts on this page are, to all intents and purposes, trade-marks of the firm of Geo. Mather's Sons, appearing in their specimen book, for which they were selected for the reason that they are peculiary difficult subjects to print, being specially liable to "fill up," because of the fineness of the white lines that break into or adjoin the darkest portions of the pictures. The New York office of the firm is 60 John Street.

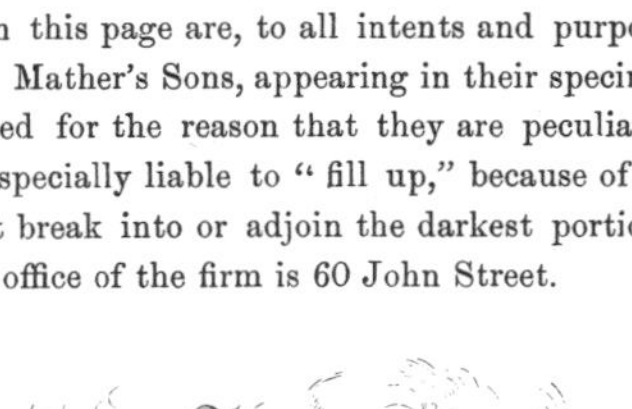

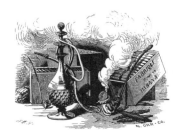

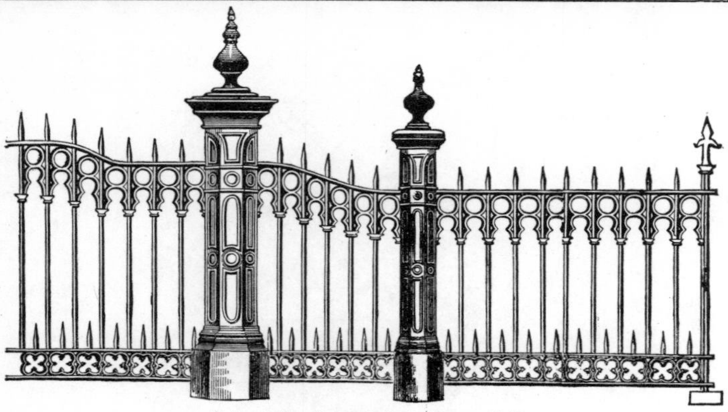

Gate at the Cathedral at Albany, N. Y.

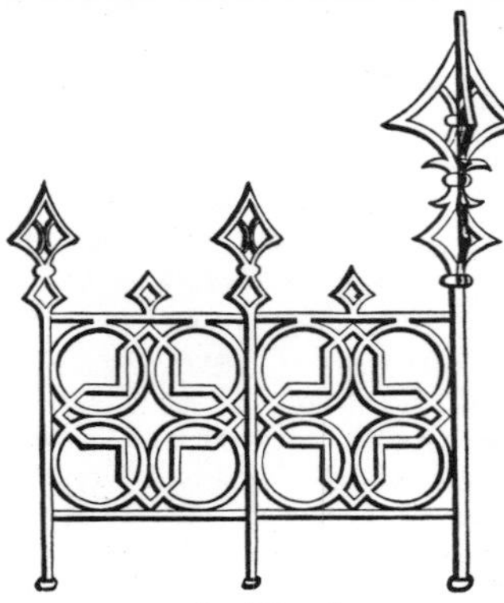

Roof Cresting.

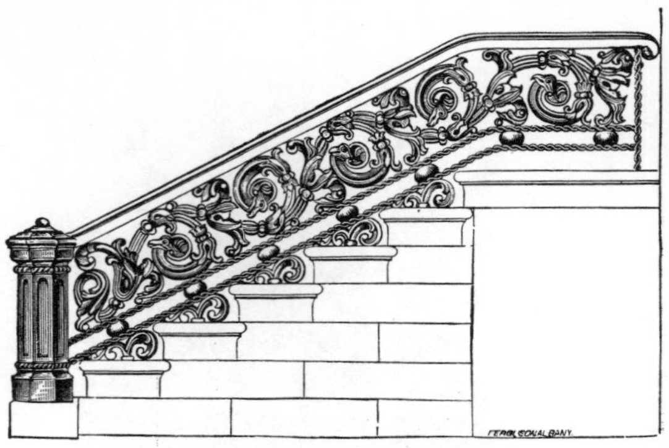

New York State Capitol Stoop Railing.

ALBANY IRON AND MACHINE WORKS AND FOUNDRY,

Albany, New York.

The Albany Iron and Machine Works were established in 1847, by Starks & Pruyn, who were succeeded by the well known firm of Pruyn & Lansing, under whose management they were conducted until 1865, when the present energetic proprietor, Henry C. Haskell, came into possession of them.

These extensive works are located at 50, 52, 54 and 56 Liberty, and Nos. 4, 6 & 8 Pruyn Streets, near the steamboat landing, and consist of machine, boiler, blacksmith, railing, pattern and bolt shops, and foundry, which combine every improved mechanical contrivance likely to facilitate expedition and perfect workmanship. In the various departments about two hundred men are usually employed in the manufacture of marine, stationary, and portable engines, boilers and general machinery, forging of all kinds, ornamental and plain railing, balconies, etc., patterns and models of all kinds, bridge and truss bolts, in fact iron and brass work of every description.

At the Albany Iron and Machine Works may be found an extensive assortment of the most approved patterns for high and low pressure engines from one-half to two hundred and fifty horse power and upwards, and additions are constantly made combining all the latest and most important improvements for the minimum economical productions of power.

Mr. Haskell constructed the splendid engine now in the government printing office at Washington, which is a low pressure beam engine of one hundred and fifty horse power; twenty-six inches bore and three and a half feet stroke; it is fitted with the celebrated Stevens' cut off, and all the latest improvements, and the excellence of its working capacity has fully sustained the high reputation which had previously been accorded to Mr. Haskell, as one of the first steam engine builders in the country.

He also manufactures the celebrated Babcock & Wilcox patent stationary steam engine, which is noted for its perfection of workmanship, and boilers for marine, stationary, and portable engines of every style and kind; also tanks and all articles made of plate iron. A general assortment of steam boilers, consisting of upright and horizontal tubular, flue and locomotive varieties, may always be found at these works.

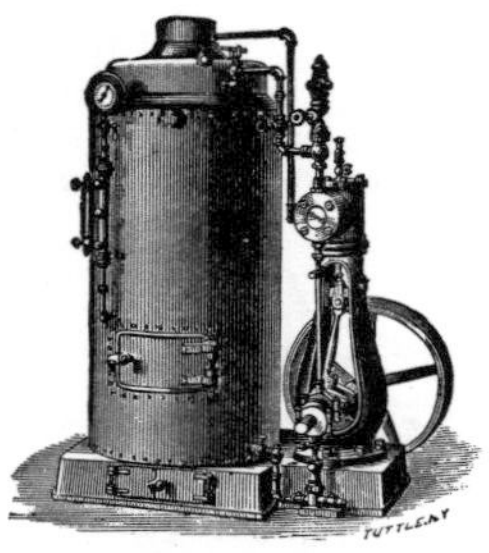

Upright Engine.

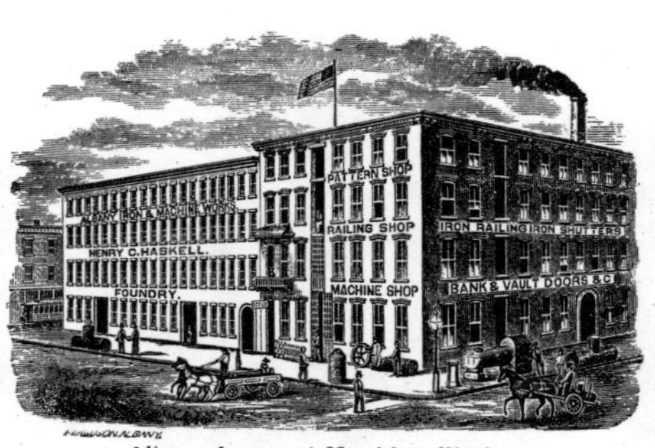

Albany Iron and Machine Works.

In the manufacture of iron bridges, Mr. Haskell controls an immense business. Many of the bridges for the canals of the State of New York, and for the New York Central, Hudson River, Erie, and Rensselaer and Saratoga Railroads; also numerous highway bridges in different localities, were manufactured at his establishment.

Special attention is paid to the manufacture of Iron Roofing, in which branch of the business Mr. Haskell has been very successful. Among the many specimens of his handiwork in this line, may be mentioned the roof of the engine house of the Brooklyn Navy Yard. Bridge and roof bolts of every description are manufactured at the Albany Iron and Machine Works in immense quantities, many of the principal railroad companies, and leading bridge and roof builders of the country receiving their supplies directly from them.

Other productions of these Works are Fire and Burglar Proof Bank Vaults and Vault Doors, Iron Doors and Shutters, in which department Mr. Haskell has been eminently successful. The vaults of many of the largest banks in the country have been constructed by him. Under special license from the owners of the patent, he is enabled to manufacture Burglar Proof Vaults filled with chilled Iron, the most efficient barrier to the depredations of the burglar ever introduced.

In the department devoted to Railing work, there is a very large selection of choice patterns, the accumulation of many years, to which are constantly being added other most beautiful designs for church, park, area, stoop, cemetery and counter railings, balconies and verandahs, roof crestings, etc. Mr. Haskell furnished the iron fences of the Albany Cathedral, and the railings for most of the bridges which span the various canals of New York, also the Railing for the new Iron Bridge over the Hudson River at Albany.

The iron beams in the New State Capitol at Albany, were erected by Mr. Haskell. Our limited space renders it impossible to enumerate all the articles manufactured here. Their name is legion.

The vast resources of this establishment, with the enterprise of the proprietor and the evidences which he has given of his ability as a manufacturer, open a range of progression too wide to admit of theoretical boundary, for he not only offers invaluable facilities to his patrons, but all his work tends to the ennobling of the arts and sciences generally, and the consequent greatness and grandeur of the country.

THE ALBANY STEAM TRAP.

James H. Blessing, Inventor.

Townsend & Blessing, Manufacturers, Albany, New York.

In the various uses to which steam has been applied as a heating agent, the removal of the water from the pipes as rapidly as it forms from condensation, and retaining as far as possible the boiler pressure, has always been the grand difficulty. To accomplish this purpose, "Traps" of various kinds, and of much ingenuity, have been devised; but most of which have failed to successfully accomplish the end sought to be achieved, namely, the automatic and simultaneous removal of the water as it condenses from the steam in the Heating Coils, the boiler pressure remaining about the same.

A Trap is now presented, which, without opening to the atmosphere in any manner, not only does this, but also returns the very same water of condensation to the boiler from which it before issued in the shape of steam, without any loss whatever, and at a temperature a few degrees less than that of the steam itself; without the intervention of any other mechanical agent, the Trap silently and automatically doing it all, and returning to the boiler even the steam used as the actuating agent. It performs this work equally well whether the heating coils are above or below the water level of the boiler. In cases where the coils are all above the water level of the boiler, and where the water from condensation is sought to be returned to the boiler by "direct circulation," as it is termed, this Trap is of the first importance.

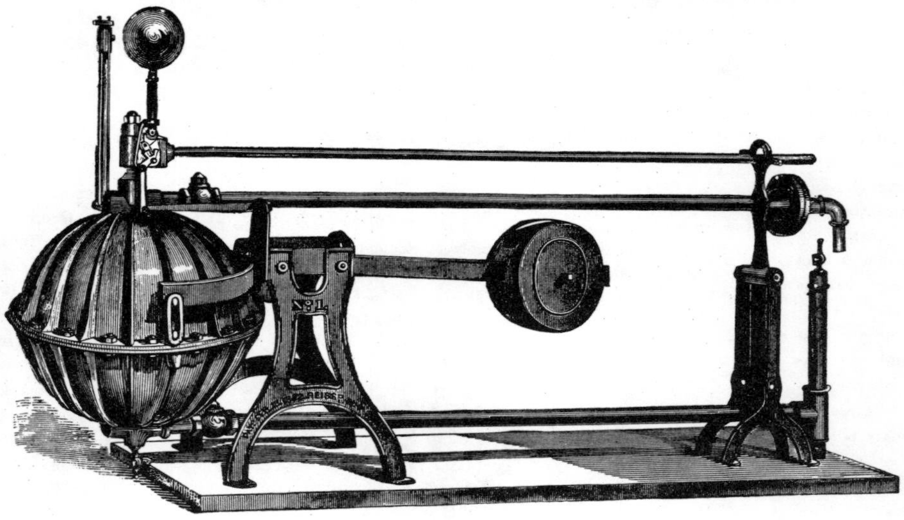

FIGURE 1.

THE ALBANY STEAM TRAP.

By its use the greater or less supply of heat to a building is perfectly within control, through the partial opening or closing of the valve which admits the steam to the coils, without the possibility of the water of condensation "backing up" in the coils, or of the water in the boiler leaving it and entering the coils. It will be remarked here how important is this feature of the Trap, especially in cases where it is necessary to carry a high boiler pressure in order to run an engine in addition to the supply of steam for heating purposes.

This Trap is represented in the accompanying engravings, and its construction will no doubt be readily understood from the same and the following explanation: premising that the three connecting pipes which are broken apart in the engraving, Figure 1, are, in reality, extended sufficiently far horizontally to give them elasticity enough to allow the apparatus to operate easily.

It consists essentially of a hollow globe, supported by one end of a lever and counterbalanced by a weight at the other. The topmost pipe is connected with the steam space of the boiler, and is opened and closed to the globe by the automatic weighted valve seen on the top of the same. The larger pipe beneath supplies the globe or trap with the condense water from the heating apparatus. It is provided with a check valve opening inward. The pipe at the bottom connects the globe with the water space of the boiler, and is furnished with a check valve opening outward. The operation is as follows: When the globe becomes filled with a certain weight of the condense water, it overbalances the weight at the other end of the lever, and descends. In descending, it moves the mechanism of the steam valve sufficiently to shift the center of gravity of the attached weight beyond its supporting point, which causes the ball to fall and open the steam valve. The steam pressure closes the check valve in the supply pipe, and allows the water in the trap to flow into the boiler through the bottom pipe, the check valve of which opens to let it pass. When the globe has lost sufficient weight through the escape of the water, it is raised again by the weighted lever, and the steam valve is shut by the operation of its attendant mechanism. The water of condensation is again admitted by the opening of the check valve in the supply pipe, and the operation is repeated continuously.

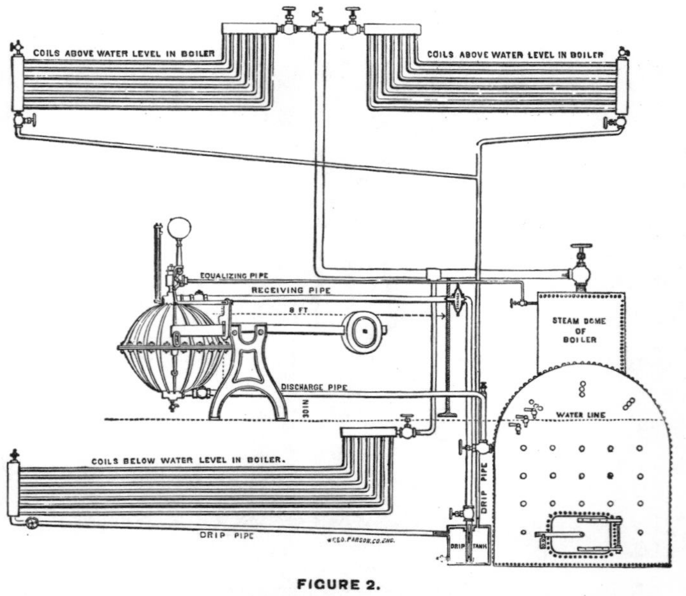

FIGURE 2.

Showing the attachment of Trap to Boiler and System of Coils.

The steam valve apparatus is so nicely adjusted, that the machine cannot, by any possibility, rest on a center. The valve must always be fully opened or closely shut. An air valve is also attached to the globe, by which the air is expelled.

The inventor estimates that the use of this trap secures a saving of certainly not less than from fifteen to twenty-five per cent. over any other method of returning water of condensation to the boiler, where the coils are below the water level. Where the coils are all above the water line, and the return is made by "direct circulation," a large saving is still effected by using the trap, as its action is such as to force a continual circulation without intermission, and thereby to keep the coils nearly up to boiler heat all the time. He claims, as a consequence, that a given space may be heated to a given temperature with one-fourth less pipe by this method, than by any other. The invention, which was patented by Mr. James H Blessing, Feb. 13, 1872, has been satisfactorily in practical operation in a variety of manufacturing and other establishments for the past two years.

Among the many uses to which this particular Trap may be most advantageously and economically applied, are the following, viz: To return to the boiler the water of condensation from the "paper dryers," in mills for the manufacture of paper, and in augmenting their drying capacity and in performing the same service in connection with "drying rooms," in cotton, woolen and other mills; In connection with "steam tables" in hotels, with "brewer's kettles," etc. It has proved to be especially advantageous in draining coils in connection with vacuum pans, etc., in sugar houses and refineries, and, in a word, in all cases where steam is used for heating purposes, by any mechanical device whatever.

This ingenious machine is manufactured at the well-known Townsend furnace, Albany, New York. Messrs. Townsend & Jackson, the proprietors of these famous works, are thoroughly practical men. Every article of their manufacture is constructed of the best material obtainable. They employ only skillful workmen, who are furnished with every mechanical aid in the execution of their labor, and the entire establishment is conducted under their personal supervision.

Our limited space will not permit us to enumerate the different kinds of machines made, and other work performed, at the Townsend Furnace, much less describe them or mention their many merits. Suffice it to say that each is perfect in its class Messrs. Townsend & Blessing make a specialty of the Albany Steam Trap, which is manufactured for them by Messrs. Townsend & Jackson at the Townsend Furnace, the success of which has been beyond their most sanguine expectations. The perfect manner in which it performs its work, made it popular upon its first introduction, and the test of time has since stamped it as one of the most practical inventions of the age. All who have used it, warmly commend its merits, and the proprietors have very many highly flattering testimonials.

Further information may be obtained by application to Townsend Townsend & Blessing, Furnace, Albany, N. Y.

VIEW OF T. KINGSFORD & SON'S OSWEGO STARCH FACTORY, OSWEGO, N. Y.

OSWEGO STARCH FACTORY,

Oswego, New York.

T. KINGSFORD & SON PROPRIETORS.

Warerooms, 146 Duane Street, New York.

E. C. Chapin, Agent.

——:o:——

Among the many almost indispensable articles for the household, but few are recognized of greater necessity, or serve a more important purpose than starch. It has long been a prominent article of trade, and occupied an important place among our domestic manufactures. There is scarcely a household in the land where it does not find a market; but aside from its ordinary use in the family or laundry, its demand for cotton manufactures is almost unlimited.

It is not our purpose, in this article, to attempt to give a history of the origin and progress of the manufacture of starch, but shall dwell more at length upon the origin and wonderful success of the establishment.

Kingsford's Oswego Starch has become a household word, not only in this country but in other lands. The success which has attended this manufactory since its origin until the present time, shows in a striking manner what genius and energy accompanied by a liberal spirit of enterprise can accomplish, when honestly and judiciously applied. Mr. Thomas Kingsford, the founder of this establishment, was an English chemist, who came to the United States more than thirty years ago. He soon applied himself to experimenting in starch-making, and made the discovery that Indian corn contained the purest and strongest substance for the production of starch, provided it could be obtained in its original purity, which was found to be a process very difficult of execution. But by persevering effort, he finally succeeded in his purpose and commenced the manufacture of Corn Starch on a small scale. The article thus produced was said to be the most perfect starch ever manufactured, either for the use of manufacturers or for the laundry. To Mr. Kingsford, is justly accredited the honor of being the sole inventor of the manufacture of this delicate and highly appreciated article of Corn Starch. It is now about a third of a century since this important discovery was made; since which time it has been the constant aim and purpose of the inventor and his successors, to exhaust all the resources of skill and science, if necessary, to bring this article to the highest attainable degree of perfection. How far they have succeeded in accomplishing this purpose, is shown by a strict analysis of one thousand ounces of starch, in which but two ounces of foreign material were found, showing a much higher degree of purity than has ever before been attained.

Mr. Kingsford being now satisfied with the success of his experiments, and fully convinced that Corn Starch must take the preference to all others, determined to increase his facilities for manufacturing, and perfect what had been so well begun. A site affording an abundance of pure air and water was indispensable, and with the flattering prospect that the great popularity of the article produced would eventually necessitate extensive facilities for manufacturing, it

was decided after careful investigation that the place most fully possessing these pre-requisites, was on the banks of the Oswego River, near the shores of Lake Ontario. Experience has since proved the wisdom of this selection. Here was commenced, on a limited scale, but in a permanent manner, and with a view to future extension, what has now become one of the most extensive starch manufactories in the world.

This like many other articles for domestic purposes, has become so common from the fact of its necessity, that comparatively few people ever give a thought to the method of its production, and scarcely a thought to the source from whence it is derived. It is an easy process, requiring no unusual skill to produce what is often used as a substitute for pure starch, and this is produced from a variety of vegetable substances; but to manufacture an article that is what its name implies, pure starch, is an art which few people possess.

The present factory buildings are 615 feet in front, and extend back 200 feet to the Oswego River. Some of the buildings are seven stories high, containing an aggregate of 521,000 square feet of flooring, equal to more than twelve acres. They contain 600 cisterns or vats, having an aggregate capacity of 2,500,000 gallons, for the purpose of cleansing the starch from all impurities; a very essential feature in the production of a pure article, and one which has had much to do in establishing the enviable reputation of the Kingsfords' Oswego Starch.

The establishment contains force pumps capable of raising 523,000 gallons per hour. The gutters for distributing the starch have an aggregate length of over three miles. The length of the water pipes is equal to about three and one-fourth miles, and varies in diameter, from two to sixteen inches. Twenty pairs of Burr Stone and six pairs of heavy iron rollers are required to grind the corn. The entire length of shafting is more than three miles, connected by 1,960 gear wheels. To warm the buildings and dry the starch, requires more than twenty miles of steam pipe. For propelling the machinery, twelve turbine water wheels, of fifty horse power each, and steam engines of 800 horse power are required.

This establishment has the capacity for using 950,000 bushels of Indian Corn annually, which will produce some 10,300 tons of starch, equivalent to nearly thirty-four tons for each working day, which is said to be about one half of the entire amount of Corn Starch manufactured in the United States. To dry this vast amount of starch requires 5,000 tons of coal annually. More than 600 operatives are employed about these works. To pack this amount of starch requires 300,000 pounds of wrapping paper, and 4,000,000 feet of lumber for boxes. The demand has become so great that it cannot be fully met even with these facilities.

The buildings are of stone and brick, substantially built, and the internal arrangements such as to render them nearly fire-proof. The store-house, with a capacity for storing 450,000 boxes of starch, is entirely proof against fire. It has no windows and only sufficient door room to receive and deliver the boxes. Notwithstanding this comparative safety against destruction or damage by fire, the proprietors of this establishment have organized a Fire Engine Company of one hundred men, with Mr. Kingsford at the head, who are fully equipped, thoroughly drilled, their rooms nicely fitted up and

supplied with every convenience, and facility for extinguishing fire, rendering them as efficient and in every way as well organized and equipped as any Metropolitan Company. The Company is now incorporated into the City Fire Department, and is designated as the Kingsford Fire Company, Number Five. The flag from their engine house is distinctly seen in the accompanying engraving.

Kingsford's Silver Gloss Starch has been placed on exhibition in nearly all parts of the civilized world, in competition with that of other manufacturers, and always with entire success, as the many first and highest prize medals bear testimony. At the World's Fair in Europe, it was brought in competition with similar products of the world, and received the medal of superiority.

Notwithstanding the superior excellence of Kingsford's Silver Gloss Starch, and the beautiful finish it gives to linen, it is afforded at a price, but little, if any, in advance of the ordinary grades, and when we consider that on account of its superior strength it requires a less quantity, it is very apparent that in point of economy it is better to use this than inferior grades, and that in this instance the best is literally the cheapest.

It is a notable fact that while the American people import European manufactures to a very large amount, they are to a great extent the luxuries rather than the necessities of life; those articles in the production of which cheap labor is brought in competition with the higher prices in our own country, rather than where the inventive genius of Europe and America strives for the mastery. Products requiring a high order of inventive genius and skilled mechanism, in machinery, and articles of necessity in domestic economy, are produced in this country in such perfection and at such cost, as not only to supply all home demands, but to find a ready and extensive market against all competition in other countries.

For manufacturing purposes, such as color printing, stiffening and dressing linen, finishing cotton, woolen and silk goods, and for the numberless uses for which it is required, no starch has been produced superior to Kingsford's, as it is entirely free from acids and all foreign substances that injure the material. The high standing and reputation of Kingsford's Oswego Starch is fully proven by the fact, that the largest manufacturers in Europe and America who have used it for many years and carefully tested its qualities in their various goods, speaks in the highest terms of its merits and superiority. It has also been found to be a good preservative from mildew in the finest and most delicate linens and muslins which are so liable to be thus injured during transportation on long voyages.

Kingsford's Oswego Corn Starch for Puddings, Blanc Mange, Ice Cream, &c., is the original, having been manufactured since 1848. It is perfectly pure and clear, and will keep sweet in any climate for years. The Pulverized Corn Starch for Puddings, Custards, &c., is considered a great delicacy, and is pronounced by the most eminent physicians equal to arrow root for invalids and for infants' food.

A portion of these extensive Oswego Works is set apart for making the Kingsford Oswego Prepared Corn, which is the first of this article ever used for food. Although Mr. Kingsford has since had many imitators, both in this country and in Europe, his productions still preserve their well earned reputation of being the original and the best, not one having as yet been found that could stand the analytical test to which Kingsford's is subjected with entire success.

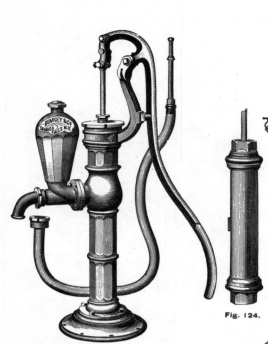

Fig. 124.

Fig. 118. RUMSEY' PAT. ENGINE WELL PUMP.
Standard and Cylinder, for Deep Wells.

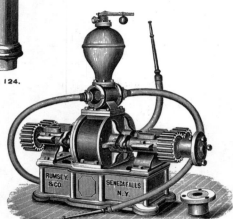

Fig. 199. ROTARY FIRE PUMPS.

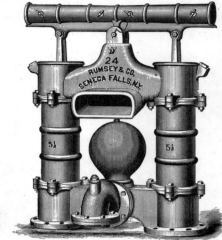

Fig. 262. EAGLE TWO CYLINDER SHIP'S MAIN PUMP.

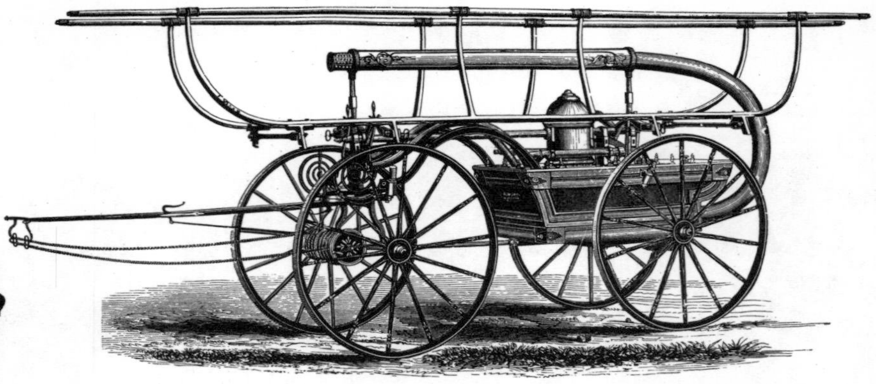

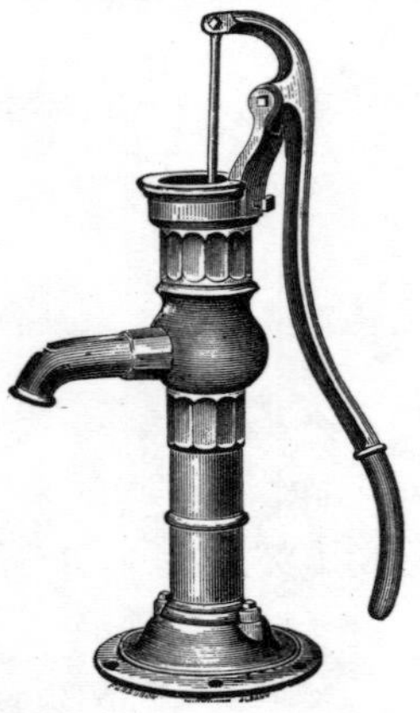

Fig. 248. CRANE NECK STYLE FIRE ENGINE. WITH FOLDING BRAKES.

Fig. 171. PACIFIC RAIL ROAD FORCE PUMP.
Double-Acting—On Base—For Hand and Power.

Fig. 209. HYDRAULIC RAM.

Fig. 101. CISTERN PUMP.

Pump and Fire Engine Works of Rumsey & Co., Seneca Falls, N. Y., U. S. A.

Fig. 165.
STEAM BOILER FORCE PUMP.

Fig. 104. FOUNTAIN CISTERN PUMPS,

RUMSEY & COMPANY, [Limited,]
SENECA FALLS PUMP & FIRE ENGINE WORKS,
Seneca Falls, New York, U. S. A.

The Seneca Falls Pump and Fire Engine Works is claimed to be the most extensive establishment of its kind in the known world. Their range of production embraces almost every conceivable variety of hydraulic machinery and metal pumps for lifting or forcing fluids of every description from any depth or to any height. Their illustrated catalogues contain cuts, descriptions and prices of nearly eight hundred different styles of pumps adapted to every use, and ranging in price from three dollars to six hundred dollars each. Many of our readers will doubtless be surprised at the number and styles of patterns turned out at this establishment, but it is still more wonderful, that in this single branch of their business, Rumsey & Company manufacture from 1,000 to 1,500 pumps per week, or in round numbers, about 70,000 each year. At first glance these figures seem almost fabulous, but it must be remembered that the demand for these goods is not confined to our own country—it extends over all the civilized world, the business of the firm having assumed such proportions in foreign lands that they have established branch houses in Liverpool, England; Madrid, Spain; and Hamburg, Germany, where full lines of their goods are constantly kept in stock, and from which other points in the Old World are supplied.

In addition to this immense production of pumps, Messrs. Rumsey & Co., are among the largest manufacturers of Fire Engines, Hose Carts, Hook and Ladder

Fig. 99. PITCHER SPOUT PUMP.

Trucks and Hose Carriages in the United States, and are always prepared to fully or partly equip the Fire Departments of cities and towns, large or small, with all needed supplies. The fire laddies of America have so long held the Rumsey apparatus in high esteem that words of commendation from us would be superfluous.

The firm also manufacture Steel Amalgam Bells, suitable for churches, academies, factories, etc., which in power and purity of tone are not surpassed.

We regret that the space at our disposal is so limited as to prevent the insertion of a description of the extensive works where the above mentioned goods are manufactured. We can only say that it is one of the model establishments of the United States. It is provided with all the latest and best labor-saving appliances, employs a large force of skilled workmen, and it is so systematically arranged that the work progresses from stage to stage very rapidly, but without any appearance of hurry and bustle. No article is ever shipped from the works until it has been inspected by competent judges and pronounced perfect, and the rigid adherance to this rule has contributed largely to the past success, and will in the future fully maintain the high reputation of their productions.

Messrs. Rumsey & Company, in addition to their works at Seneca Falls, and their foreign depots previously mentioned, have branch houses in the United States at 93 Liberty Street, New York City; at Chicago, Illinois; St. Louis, Missouri, and San Francisco, California.

Fig. 133. FORCE PUMP WITH COCK.

STEEL AMALGAM BELLS,
For Churches, Academies, Factories, Shops, &c.

EXCELSIOR HORIZONTAL DOUBLE ACTING FORCE PUMP.

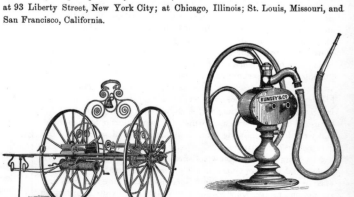

Fig. 250. BALANCED HOSE CART.

Fig. 196.
ROTARY HAND FORCE PUMP.
For Cisterns and Shallow Wells.

SILSBY MANUFACTURING COMPANY,

Island Works, Seneca Falls, New York, U. S. A.

Builders of the Celebrated

SILSBY ROTARY STEAM FIRE ENGINE.

H. C. SILSBY. HORACE SILSBY. CHARLES T. SILSBY.

——:o:——

Fire, when under the complete control of man, is certainly one of his most valuable servants; so valuable that we can scarcely wonder at the veneration in which it was held by the ancients, who generally ascribed its discovery to the agency of the gods. While some of the nations of the East accepted it as a symbol of the divine power which created and sustained the universe, others going a step further, saw in the leaping flames Divinity itself. Fire worship is not a myth, and in nearly, if not quite, all the barbarous or semi-civilized nations of the earth to-day, fire is looked upon with mingled veneration and awe. We certainly can conceive of no more perfect symbol of infinite power than fire affords. Confined to the limits within which it is beneficial to man, who can estimate its value? who can number the advantages daily and hourly derived from its use? or, when it bursts those bounds, and becomes man's master instead of his slave, who can measure its destructive force, or express its terrors?

In the early days when the great mass of mankind lead a wandering life, living in tents, and but few were gathered together in communities, fire seemed to possess but few attributes of evil, but as population increased, and towns and cities were built; as wealth was gathered, and immense values were stored within limits more confined, as industries increased and labor became specialized; as the ever onward march of improvement advanced, and fire was applied to other uses than the mere preparation of food or the warming of chilled bodies—in a few words, as men attained a higher civilization, the terrors of fire asserted themselves, and it became a symbol of destruction rather than of service, and the more cultivated nations, though deriving from its use far greater blessings than their fathers had done, viewed it rather as demoniac than godly.

There is scarcely a city on the face of the globe, old enough to have a history, that has not suffered from a great fire, the date of which forms so marked an era in its history, that the time of other occurances are computed from it.

The great fire of London, in 1666, which reduced about five-sixths of the city to ruins, is as much a part of English history as the accession of a new monarch to the throne, and we venture the assertion that the average foreign visitor to London is quite as thoroughly posted while there in relation to its boundaries, the loss sustained in life and money, the suffering it caused, and the ultimate advantages which grew out of it, in the better building of new London, as he is in relation to any event in English history.

In how many cities and villages in our own country, too, are epochs fixed by great fires? It is not uncommon, for instance, in New York city to hear a man say, this occurred before the first great fire, (1835), or that happened after the second great fire, (1848). In Portland, Maine, in Chicago, Ills., and in Boston, Mass., as well as in New York, conflagrations have occurred, which are frequently referred to in all parts of the country, as the "great fire" in this or that place, and which have been viewed not merely as local disasters, but as national calamities. While in places where no sweeping devastation has entitled them to such extended fame, there have been hundreds of fires as disastrous to the smaller communities, as were these famous ones to the larger towns.

How to fight fire most effectively has, since an early date, been the subject of much study. Water, of course, suggested itself but in the early days some of the most important properties of water were unknown—for instance, that enclosed in pipes or other ducts of sufficient strength, it would rise to the level of its source—consequently, the conveyance of water in large quantities any considerable distance, could only be accomplished at a great outlay. Nor was any method known, even when an abundance of the fluid was near at hand, of throwing or forcing it to any height or distance.

The use of the siphon was known at a very early date, and it doubtless was the first appliance used for raising water. Then came the suggestion of filling a bag with water, and attaching to it a hose made from the intestines of an ox, through which water was forced by applying pressure to the bag. Neither the siphon or the device last mentioned were originally intended for use at fires, the former, before its introduction into the houses of Rome having been employed as a means of transferring water from one recepticle to another, and the latter was first suggested as a means of supplying water to beseiged places—they were, doubtless, both used for that purpose, however, and certainly were the most effective means then known.

The first fire engines of which we have an authentic account were used in Germany, in 1518, and were simply huge syringes—nothing more. Engines which threw a continuous stream of water were used in Paris in 1684, and in 1699 the King of France appointed an officer whose special duty it was to construct and keep in repair, and operate at fires the "portable pumps" which were then in the royal service.

It was a long time before the improved methods of extinguishing fires known on the continent were introduced into England, and up to the close of the sixteenth century we have no accounts of the use of any apparatus in London except a kind of syringe which held but a few quarts of water. Three men were required to work them; two, one on each side, to hold the "engine" in their hands, while the third applied the requisite power to the piston, and forced out the water in a stream. Even at this time it does not seem to have been known that water would rise in a vacuum, for when the instrument had discharged its contents, instead of placing its nozzle in a vessel of water, and by pulling the piston back, allowing the fluid to enter and fill the pipe, the piston was entirely withdrawn, and the water dipped up or poured into the tube. Some of these primitive fire extinguishers are still preserved. Subsequently these syringes were improved, being fitted with a portable cistern, and the pistons arranged so as to be worked by levers. No further advance seems to have been made in the principles or methods of constructing fire apparatus until about the end of the seventeenth century when one Newshan invented and patented a new engine, which was a decided improvement on all preceding it. Briefly, it was a cistern on wheels, holding several barrels of water. It had pumps and an air chamber, and threw a much steadier stream than had been before attained. It was also provided with a suction hose, with which to draw water from cisterns if they chanced to be located within a convenient distance of the fire, or, if not, the water-box was filled with water brought in buckets. Up until the beginning of the nineteenth century, no radical change was made in fire engines, several improvements were made in the manner of working them, to be sure, but the principle of all were substantially the same as that of the one just described.

In the early part of the present century, an improvement was made, which consisted in the arrangement of a number of force pumps around a central air chamber. Each of these pumps could be worked independently of the others, and as but one man was required to work each pump, the engine could be operated, and a considerable stream of water thrown without waiting for the arrival of the force required to work the entire machine. The hand fire engines in general use until within a comparatively few years, even in the largest cities, and still doing good service in many of the smaller towns, may be generally described as a water box containing two vertical double-acting pumps, with an air chamber. The pumps are worked by brakes, consisting of a long handle running parallel with the engine, and operated by men standing on the ground, or, in the largest and most powerful ones, the brakes run across the ends of the machine, having double arms, with a platform on the water box, so that while half the men stand on the ground the other half occupy places on the engine itself, and double the power can be applied.

These machines are, many of them, very powerful, but in all the larger places, in this country at least, they have given place to the much more powerful and reliable Steam Fire Engines.

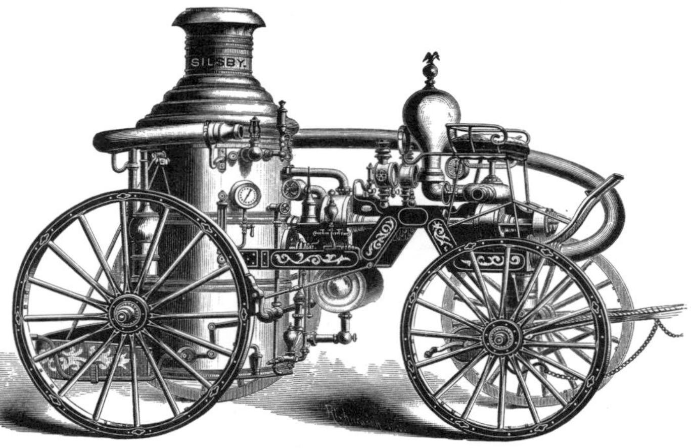

SILSBY ROTARY STEAM FIRE ENGINE,

Manufactured by the Silsby Manufacturing Company.

The first attempt to build a Steam Fire Engine was made by Mr. Braithwaite, of London, England, in 1830. The first engine weighed about five thousand pounds; the boiler was upright, but it took twenty minutes to generate sufficient steam to work the engine, and the utmost power was less than six horse. It threw water at the rate of about one hundred and fifty gallons per minute, to a height of from eighty to ninety feet. Cumbersome as it was to move, slow in making steam, and small as were the results after it was put in operation, compared with the Steam Fire Engines of to-day, it was still a vast improvement then, and others were constructed upon the same general principles, one in 1832, for the King of Prussia.

The great fire in New York, in 1835, first fully aroused our people to the necessity of providing more ample means for arresting it. Powerful engines, whose motive power would not tire. Premiums were offered as inducements to inventors to furnish plans for steam fire engines, and in 1841, a number of Insurance Companies associated themselves together, and contracted with Mr. Hodges for the construction of such an engine. In due time it was completed, and on several occasions it did excellent service, but it was too heavy to be rapidly moved to the point where needed, and was soon abandoned as being practically worthless for a service where speed of movement is so important an element of success.

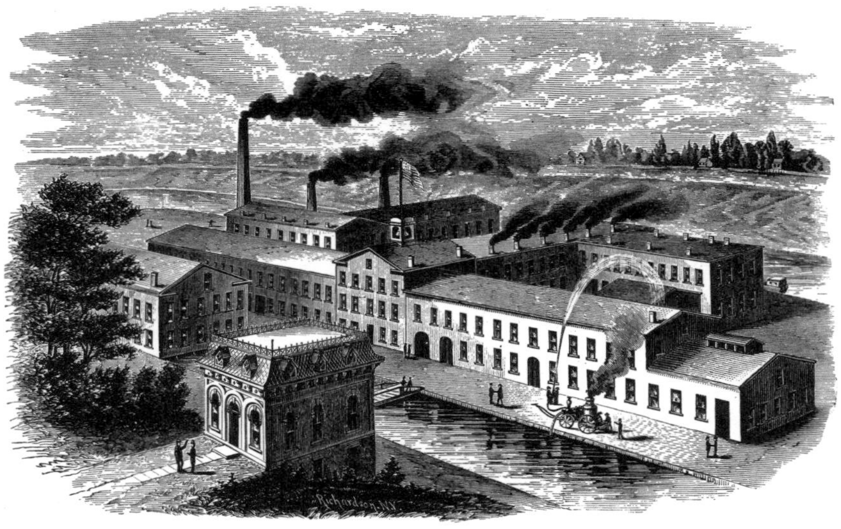

VIEW OF THE SILSBY MANUFACTURING CO.'S WORKS,

Seneca Falls, New York, U. S. A.

To Cincinnati, Ohio, belongs the credit of having organized the first Steam Fire Department in the United States, in 1853. The first engines used there were very heavy, weighing about twelve tons, and though their own steam was applied as a propelling force, still four powerful horses were required to move them. What was required was an engine light in weight, strong in its parts, and powerful in action, rapid in the generation and economical in the consumption of steam, and from the time when the possibility of using steam fire engines was first canvassed, there had been a number of busy brains actively at work devising plans by which these requisites to complete success could be best arrived at.

Among the first to engage in this branch of manufacture was the Silsby Manufacturing Company, proprietors of the famous "Island Works," Seneca Falls, N. Y., their determination being then, as now, to build the best possible machines, and none but the best. As previously stated the pumps of hand fire engines had been, generally, single or double-acting force-pumps, provided with an air-chamber to secure a continuous flow of water, and most builders of Steam Fire Engines determined to follow in the old track, at least as far as the means of forcing a stream was concerned. Pumps of this character are objectionable from the complication of their parts and the use of many valves which are liable to get out of order. The Silsby Manufacturing Company, therefore, would have none of them, but invented for their apparatus a rotary pump, which, without doubt, secures the effective production of the largest amount of work with an expenditure of the least amount of force. This effect was precisely what was desired in a Steam Fire Engine, and the leading feature or characteristic which has given these engines their superior efficiency and popularity, is the rotary principle involved in the construction.

Under the auspices of the Silsby Manufacturing Company, Rotary Steam Fire Engines have been brought to so high a degree of perfection that they have achieved a complete and lasting victory over those known as reciprocating engines. Not only are the difficulties growing out of the expansion and contraction of parts entirely obviated, but there is no packing to be looked after, no ill-working valves to be put in order, and besides there is an immense power utilized by the rotary which is entirely lost by the reciprocating principle of constructing pumps. This saving of power is so great that competent judges, who are familiar with the practical workings of both systems, confidently assert that the Silsby Rotary Engines require from 50 to 75 per cent. less pressure of steam to do a given amount of work than is required to accomplish the same result with pumps of other style; that they will do fire duty through longer lines of leading hose than others, and that they will throw a much larger quantity of water to a far greater distance, while all concede that without any possible injury to their mechanism, they will pump dirty or sandy water, that would soon cut a piston pump all to pieces.

These manifest advantages of the Silsby Rotary Steam Fire Engine have not, could not have been overlooked, by the firemen of our country even had they desired to ignore them. They are points of excellence which force themselves upon all discerning men, and merits which must be acknowledged; but in all other respects, as well as the more correct principle upon which their pumps are constructed, these engines are built in the best possible manner, no effort being spared to render them equally perfect in every part, and to make them in design, material and workmanship very models of modern scientific and mechanical skill.

We do not deem it necessary here to state what special metals are used for this or that part of these Engines, nor to particularly describe the boiler or fire box. The shape and general appearance of the Engine will be more fully conveyed to the mind of the reader by the engraving presented on this page, than we could hope to do without its aid, while to attempt to give a minute description of its mechanism without the aid of drawings of the various parts (and these we do not possess) would be futile.

Upwards of five hundred Silsby Rotary Steam Fire Engines are now in active and successful service in the United States and Canada. They have been thoroughly tested during the last eighteen years, and have during that time given universal satisfaction. When their manufacture was first begun, the Company fully determined to place them, if possible, beyond all successful competition, a purpose which seems to have been accomplished. They have been tried under all conceivable circumstances, and, both in practical use and for experiment have been subjected to all kinds of hard treatment, but they have not failed, and are confidently claimed to be the most durable, reliable and efficient Steam Fire Engines built.

In the rapid growth of villages and towns in this country, especially through the West, it not unfrequently happens that the organization of a fire department and the purchase of proper apparatus for the suppression of fire is entirely lost sight of until, in the midst of a fancied security from danger, the torch is accidentally applied, and in a few minutes, or at most hours, the garnered wealth of years of toil is crumbled into ashes and scattered by the winds. Then the impoverished people bestir themselves, and in hot haste appliances are ordered with which to protect themselves when next the danger approaches. In many instances such as this, the purchase of the needed apparatus is entrusted to parties who have no practical knowledge of what is really required, and who in their desire to promptly secure the needed protection, purchase inferior or worn out apparatus from other corporations, much to their subsequent sorrow. As a rule, we believe it better to purchase entirely new engines from reputable makers and suggest that in all cases a test of the absolute merits of the machines should be made before purchase. It is of the utmost importance that every village should have some means of fighting fire, and it is equally important that the weapons should be reliable ones. It is cheaper to purchase a good machine which will surely be ready for service when needed than to accept a poor one, which may fail at the most critical moment. There are scores of towns of considerable importance in our most populous sections of country, which though they have an engine, or an apology for one, and an ample supply of water close at hand, are practically without any protection against fire, simply because their machine lacks power to throw water a sufficient distance to meet emergencies that may at any time arise. In many towns, too, the organization of a fire department and the purchase of a Silsby Rotary Steam Engine, the merits of which are well known to the Underwriters of America, would decrease the rates of insurance sufficiently to reimburse them within a single year.

Thus an efficient department, well supplied with the best known appliances for suppressing fire, is not only a protection against loss when danger approaches, but is a paying investment under ordinary circumstances, as it lessens the expense of that, at best only partial, assurance against loss, which the best insurance companies will give. It is always the cheapest in the end to buy the best in the beginning. And in purchasing fire department supplies, it is always better to purchase, so far as possible, at first hands, or to obtain the entire equipment through the manufacturers of the leading articles.

The Island Works are devoted exclusively to the manufacture of Rotary Steam Fire Engines, Rotary Pumps, Hose Carts, Hose, and Fire Department Supplies, of which a full line are constantly on hand, or will be promptly furnished to order. It is manifestly to the interest of the proprietors that all the other productions of the establishment should maintain the same high standard of excellence that has been so generally accorded to their Rotary Steam Fire Engines, consequently no effort is spared to render all their goods equally perfect.

The factories, of which we herewith furnish an engraving, are among the most methodically arranged and completely furnished manufacturing establishments in the country. All the mechanical devices that can lighten the physical labor of the workman or aid in the rapid production of perfect work, find a place there, but no mere money-saving machine, which only speeds production without making it perfectly accurate, is tolerated. The force of mechanics comprise many of the most skillful workers in the country, many of them having been in the employ of the Company since the days of their apprenticeship, while others who entered the establishment in middle life, have grown gray in the service. Such workmen have an interest in the good name of the Company which ordinary mechanics do not possess.

Those desiring further information in regard to their manufactures, by addressing the Silsby Manufacturing Company, Seneca Falls, N. Y., U. S. A., will by return of mail receive their illustrated catalogue and circular, and such further information by letter as their inquiries may call for.

HOLYOKE MACHINE COMPANY,
Holyoke, Massachusetts,
Manufacturers of
Paper Machinery, Hydraulic Presses,
Turbine Water Wheels and
Mill Work,
also
Ball's Patent Steam Stamping Machines
For Crushing Ores and Minerals.

C. H. Heywood, Pres.   Stephen Holman, Treas.
S. F. Stebbins, Agent.   N. H. Whitten, Eng'r.

——:o:——

Until the year 1831, the immense water power of the Connecticut River, at Holyoke, Massachusetts, estimated at fully twenty thousand horse power, was allowed to run entirely to waste, over what was known as the Great Rapids, or Falls of South Hadley. These rapids extended a distance of a mile and a half with a total fall of sixty feet. In 1831, a company was organized for the purpose of utilizing a portion of the power by the construction of wing dams and the diversion of a portion of the water into canals and its subsequent use as a motor for a small paper mill and a cotton mill. In 1846, a company was chartered with a capital of four millions of dollars for the purpose of damming the entire stream, and by a system of canals utilizing all the power.

The first dam was completed on the 19th day of November, 1848. During the month of October a great freshet had occured and it was known that the dam had sustained some injuries; though they were not believed to be serious. When the gates were closed however, and the water had gathered until it had risen nearly at the top of the dam, the structure gave way and the rushing waters in a few moments destroyed the labor of a year.

Disheartening as was this disaster, the company was not discouraged. Work was immediately begun on a new dam, which was completed in less than a year, and which has since withstood the immense pressure of the entire volume of the Connecticut River without sustaining any material injury, though from time to time it has been repaired and strengthened.

The general plan of the company for the improvement of the water power, and its complete utilization, comprehended not only the building of the dam, but the construction of ample canals, and the erection of mills and factories. In fact everything requisite for the building up of an important manufacturing town was planned on a scale commensurate with the immense power to be used. A large Machine Shop and Foundry were soon built, designed to furnish all the machinery required in the equipment of the mills which it was proposed to erect and operate, to keep the same in repair, and to do general machine work. Operations were continued until, during the great financial reverses of 1857, the principal promotors of the enterprise became involved in difficulties which resulted in the transfer of the land and water power with all the improvements, including the Machine Shop and Foundry with their appurtenances to a new company known as the Holyoke Water Power Company.

The new Water Power Company, in 1868, caused the dam, which had then stood twenty years, to be carefully examined and it was found that it required repairing. Some of the front timbers had been loosened and worn away by the concussions of the heavy blocks of ice which successive spring floods had hurled against them, and the rock foundation of the dam was being undermined by the force of the falling water. As first built, the dam presented a perpendicular front on the side down stream. The bed of the river at this point is of rock, but is full of seams, and the tremendous force of the falling water had been sufficient to displace large masses of stone, some of them several tons in weight, and to sink a great hole along the entire front of the dam. To remedy this a new front was built with a gradual slope, presenting an inclined plane for the overflow. This

Boyden's Turbine Water Wheel.

The Gould Patent Pulping Engine.

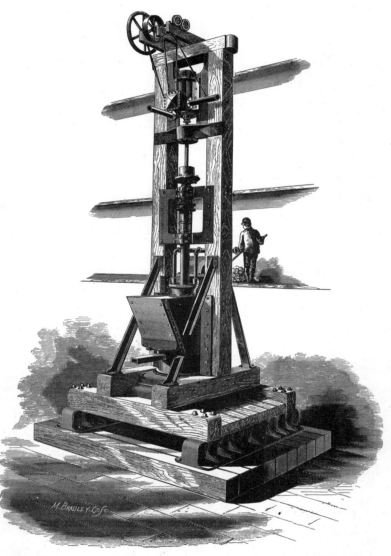

Prospective View of Ball's Steam Stamping Machine,
For Crushing Ores and Minerals.

strengthening of the dam was effected at a cost of about $400,000, but the money was well spent, for it renders it one of the strongest works of the kind in the world. The power is distributed by means of three canals at different levels and furnishes in the aggregate about eight miles of available sites for mills.

The Machine Shop property was purchased by Mr. John C. Whitin, who, in 1863, sold the real estate to a company, the building to be fitted up for the manufacture of cotton thread and yarn, he removing the machinery belonging to the shop. The closing of the machine shop was regarded by all the mill men and manufacturers of the vicinity as not only depriving them of a great convenience as individuals, but as a serious blow at the ultimate prosperity of the town, and the establishment of a new one soon began to be discussed.

Nearly all the capital invested in the different manufacturing establishments in Holyoke at that time had been derived from other places, and the successful, permanent centering of a very large manufacturing interest at this point was deemed as a doubtful experiment; still the large number of the mills at that time already in operation, and the prospective improvement of the numerous mill sites and abundant water power seemed to present a promising field for mechanical industries and to render the establishment of machine shops an absolute necessity.

The Holyoke Machine Company was organized in 1863 with a cash capital of $30,000; suitable buildings were at once erected, and business was commenced October 1st, before the old shop was closed. In 1864, the capital was increased to $40,000. At first the business was limited to the making of castings, shafting and mill work and to general jobbing, but the rapid growth of the paper interest, the multiplication of mills along the banks of the Housatonic and Connecticut Rivers, and the development of Holyoke as one of the largest and most important paper producing towns in the country, led the Company to engage in the manufacture of Paper Mill Machinery and Turbine Water Wheels. In a few years these branches of their business had increased to such an extent that additional facilities were required, and, in 1871, the capital was increased to $80,000, and the shops were enlarged. But this increase of capital and enlargement of facilities were not commensurate with the steady growth of the business, and in 1872, the capital was again increased, this time to

$150,000, and further additions were made to the shops, so that now the buildings are more than three times their original size. The establishment is one of the most complete of its kind in the country, being fitted up with the most approved modern appliances that can aid in the rapid execution of perfect work.

The Company has also built a fine brick block on Main Street, opposite their works, occupied as stores on the first floor and as tenements in the upper stories.

The rapid growth of the manufacturing interests of the city has developed for the Company a large business in supplying the water wheels, gearing and shafting necessary to make available and transmit the immense power which Nature has here furnished. Much of the machinery in use in the mills located at Holyoke and vicinity was manufactured by this Company, and their trade is rapidly extending. During the past year, in addition to their very extensive local business, they have shipped machinery to the Southern States, to the West—as far as California—to Canada, Nova Scotia, and to Europe.

The business that was commenced in a small way, merely to supply a local demand, has increased year by year, until it has grown to large proportions, and is extensively known. This rapid but permanent growth is the direct result of the determination by the management of the Company to excel. They have been careful to introduce no new device which they did not know to be meritorious, and their productions are noted for their thorough workmanship. Success always follows such persistent, honest effort.

Among the important specialties of the Holyoke Machine Company is the celebrated Turbine Water Wheel, generally known as Boyden's Improved Fourneyron's Turbine, of which they have built a large number within the last five years for manufacturing companies in New England and in some other States. These wheels are highly commended by those who constantly use them, for their admirable construction and remarkable economy in the use of water.

The Company also build two other Turbine Wheels, under license from the patentees, which, though offered at a less price than the Boyden Wheels, hold a prominent place in the front rank of modern turbines for simplicity of construction and economy. These are known as Risdon's Improved Turbine, and the Dayton American Turbine.

In the line of paper making machinery there are several important improvements recently patented, the right to manufacture which is exclusively vested in this Company. The Improved Calenders made by the Company have gained such a reputation for thorough excellence and convenience, that notwithstanding the depressed state of the paper trade, the demand for them has steadily increased. The manufacture of paper rolls for calender machinery has become so large a business with them that they now keep two hydraulic presses of great strength in operation pressing the rolls.

Gould's Patent Pulp Engine, made by this Company is attracting considerable attention among paper mill owners; it has been introduced in a number of establishments, and wherever it has been tested, has proved highly satisfactory. This is not an auxiliary engine, but takes the washed stock direct from the drains and reduces it to a pulp of any required degree of fineness; and it requires but a small portion of the room necessary for working the same amount of stock with the old style engine.

This Company also manufactures the well known Littlefield Pumps, which are too well known to need a word of praise from us; Hydraulic Presses, and the famous Holyoke Elevators.

Recently the Company completed arrangements with the proprietor by which they have secured the exclusive right to manufacture Ball's Improved Steam Stamping Machines for crushing ores and minerals. This machine has stood the test of twenty years use in copper and gold mines, and stands to-day unsurpassed in thoroughness of work, in economy, durability and convenience. It works on the principle of the direct steam hammer, is adapted to wet or dry crushing, and no material has yet been found too refractory to be successfully worked by it. Five sizes are made, ranging in capacity from fifteen to one hundred and twenty tons of the hardest rock in twenty-four hours.

In addition to the special machines above mentioned the Company have ample facilities for building first-class machinery of every description. Their foundry and machine shops are complete in all their appointments, and they constantly employ a large force of thoroughly competent workmen, men who take a pride in doing good work. It ever has been, and is the aim of the Company, to have everything that leaves their establishment bear its own recommendation. They desire to be judged by their works and only by their works.

Patent Improved Web Super Calender.

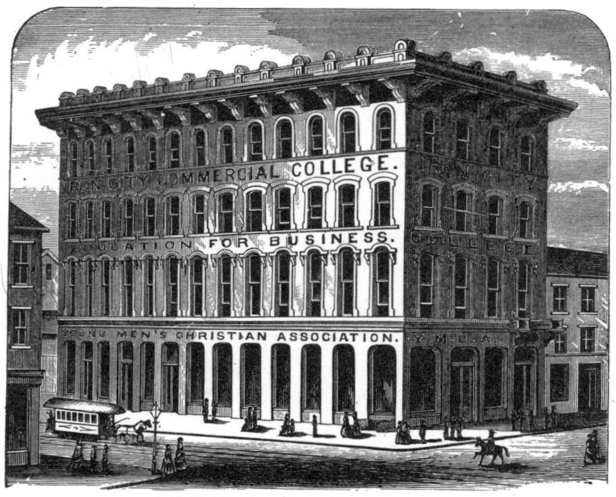

IRON CITY COLLEGE,

Cor. Penn Avenue and Sixth Street, Pittsburgh, Penn.

This popular and successful Business College was founded in 1855. There is scarcely a city or large town in the United States, that does not count among its most successful business men, graduates of this institution. Its course of study and system of business training is thorough and eminently practical, and hundreds of bankers, merchants, and other business men owe much of their success to an adherence to the teachings received here. Those desirious of obtaining further information should address the Principal, Prof J. C. Smith, A. M., Pittsburgh, Pa.

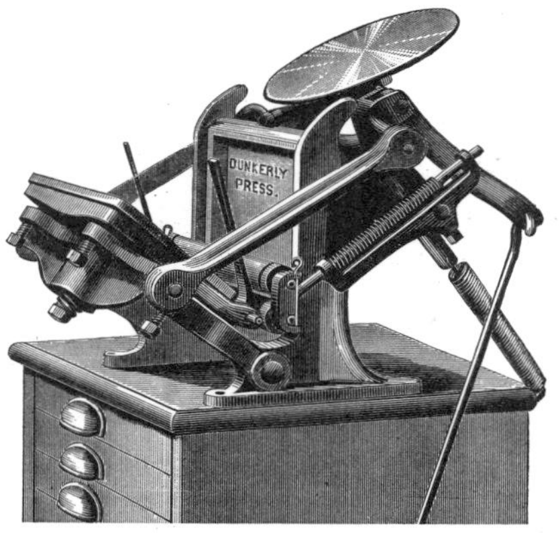

THE DUNKERLY SELF-INKING PRESS,

207 Dyer Street, Providence, R. I.

Mr. W. H. Dunkerly, was, we believe, the first to introduce an Amatuer Self-Inking Printing Press, there being no self-inking press in the market, when his was first offered, six years ago, for a less price than $250. Mr. Dunkerly's Presses are very strong—and print full size of chase without springing the bed, and are sold at the following prices: Size inside of chase, 4½ by 6½ inches; cabinet, 12 cases; iron treadle, $16. Size 7 by 10 inches; cabinet, 12 cases; iron treadle, $38. Rotary Power, $75. Steam Power, $85. He also makes the "Boss" Press, price $1, and is now successfully experimenting on a press to print two colors at one impression.

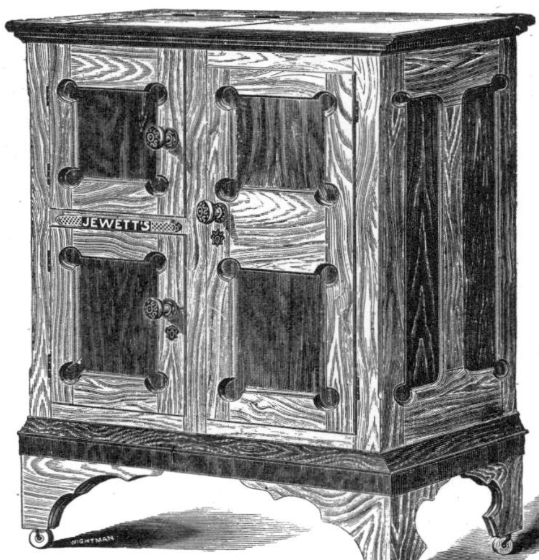

JOHN C. JEWETT & SONS,

323 to 331 Washington and 86 to 90 Ellicott Sts., Buffalo, N. Y.

Jewett's Patent Refrigerators, Filters and Coolers have no superiors. In addition to these the firm are large manufacturers of Toilet Ware, Bird Cages, etc. Illustrated catalogues sent to dealers on application.

SOLE LEATHER CHAMPION WASHER TRADE MARK

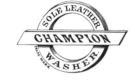

J. R. READ,

MANUFACTURER OF

CHAMPION AXLE WASHERS,

Also, Leather Washers for all Purposes,

135 South Main St., Providence, Rhode Island.

Few persons have the most remote idea of the number of Washers annually used in the United States, but if the reader will reflect for a few moments—think of the many purposes for which they are used—they will be convinced that hundreds of thousands are used daily and hundreds of millions every year. Every maker or owner of a vehicle uses them, pump makers, machinists, and other mechanics almost without number use them; indeed, they are used everywhere, and to a greater or less extent by almost everybody. Mr. J. R. Read, has been for a long time engaged in the business of manufacturing them, and constant consumers have learned that they can buy the best Sole Leather Washers accurately made to size, cheaper than they can make poor and ill-shaped ones themselves. Mr. Read's Washers are made of the best sole leather, to supply a demand long felt for a Washer that will fit nicely and give the best results. He makes over 400 regular sizes, and frequently makes special sizes varying from the regular only the sixteenth part of an inch, to meet the requirements of fine axles. Sole Leather Washers are his specialty—and the Champion has the reputation of being the best Washer made.

AMERICAN WORSTED COMPANY,

Woonsocket, R. I.

——:o:——

It must be manifest to the reader that within the very limited space at our disposal we cannot describe the manufactures, much less the numerous processes through which the wool must pass before it emerges in the beautiful finished Braids and Yarns of this Company. Unable to do the subject justice, we deem it best not to attempt any description of methods, nor is it necessary that we should speak a word in praise of their goods. Every merchant who deals in such articles is well aware of their extended popularity, and that the Company are possessed of unexcelled manufacturing facilities, and commercially ranks among the leading houses in their line in the United States, and nearly every lady in our broad land is thoroughly convinced that goods bearing the trade mark of the American Worsted Company are of superior excellence.

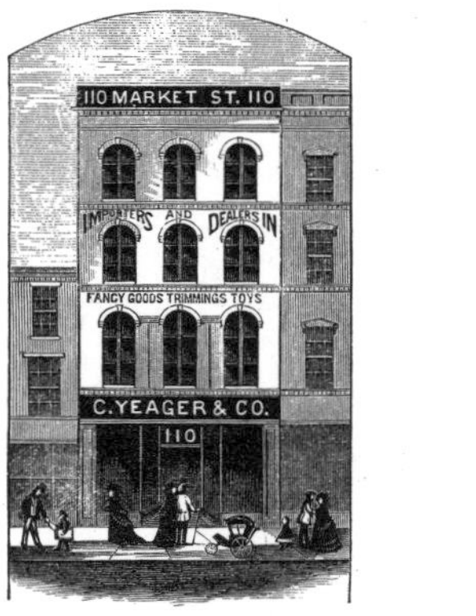

C. YEAGER & CO.,

IMPORTERS AND DEALERS IN

Dry Goods, Fancy Goods, Trimmings and Hosiery,

No. 110 MARKET STREET,

Bet. Fifth Ave. & Liberty St., PITTSBURGH, PA.

The above named house is so widely and so favorably known that we deem it unnecessary to write any history or speak any word of praise.

TOTTEN & CO.,

FULTON FOUNDRY,

Pittsburgh, Pa.

Pittsburgh, from the extent of its iron manufactories, is frequently spoken of as the Birmingham of America, and fittingly so, for in the extent

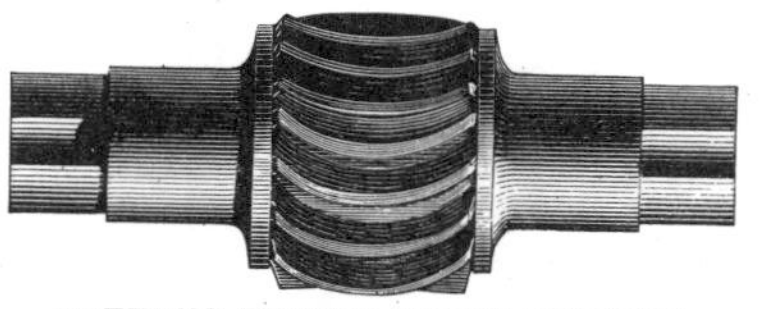

LETZKUS CURVED TOOTH GEARING.

and variety of its iron productions, it doubtless excels all other American as Birmingham does all other English cities. Foremost in rank among the many important iron manufacturing establishments of Pittsburgh, judged by the value and extent of its special productions, is the Fulton Foundry. The

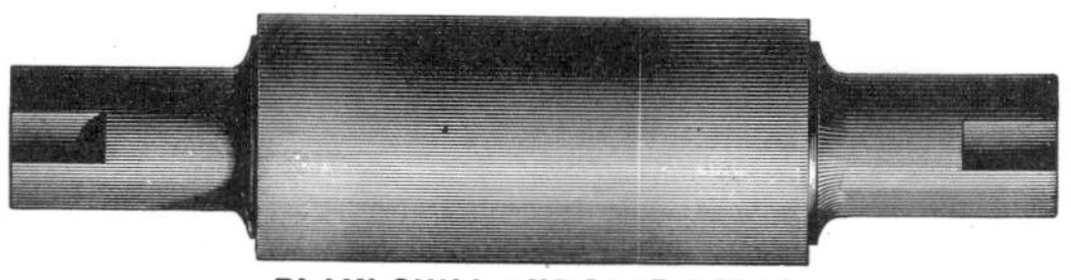

PLAIN CHILL AND SAND ROLLS.

present organization of this establishment was effected in 1866, but the practical experience of the proprietors far ante-dates that time, the managing member of the firm having been in early life connected with the Fort Pitt Cannon Foundry, of which his father was one of the originators. The works cover nearly three acres of ground and are eligibly located with reference to leading railroads which afford connections with all parts of the country.

Rolling Mill and Blast Furnace Machinery are the leading productions of the Fulton Foundry, in the manufacture of which they have attained a success not surpassed by any. During the past ten years they have erected and completely equipped thirty first-class rolling mills, being more than one-half of all the increased rolling mill capacity of the whole United States during that time, and have successfully introduced many important improvements in forms and methods of construction.

Among the modern devices for Rolling Mill Pinions none is more deserving than the Curved Tooth Pinion, and none has met with more marked success. Being a perfect arch the tooth is of great strength. It is mechanically as well as theoretically correct. It makes all "Back Lash" impossible, and prevents the pinions from marking the iron.

Another important discovery to Rolling Mill owners was that grooves might be cast in Chilled Rolls, instead of casting the Roll plain and then turning them out. Mr. Totten was the first to successfully accomplish this. Rolls made in this way soon pay for themselves in the cost of dressing alone, and, as must be apparent to all, the greater hardness of the wearing surfaces of grooves chilled in casting, that evenness of density of face which cannot be obtained in turned grooves, renders them far more durable, enabling them to do, it is estimated, twelve times the work that can be got out of an ordinary Roll made in the old style.

The proprietors of the Fulton Foundry also claim the honor of asserting the feasibility, and proving the practicability of making Chilled Rolls of any required diameter—after it had been tried and abandoned by one of the oldest makers. They were the the first to make a Chill Roll 31⅝ inches in diameter, and this, so far as we can learn, has never yet been equalled by any other maker. Great as have been the advances in Rolling Machinery during the past ten years, the mills previously erected still use Straight-Cog Pinions as per sketch, these are made by Totten & Co., in every variety.

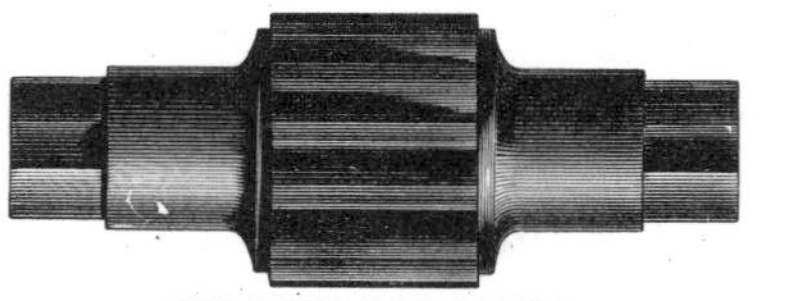

STRAIGHT COG PINION.

They are supplied with every facility, including the latest and most approved patterns, for the rapid and successful production of all articles within their chosen line of industry—the manufacture of first-class Rolling Mill and Blast Furnace Machinery.

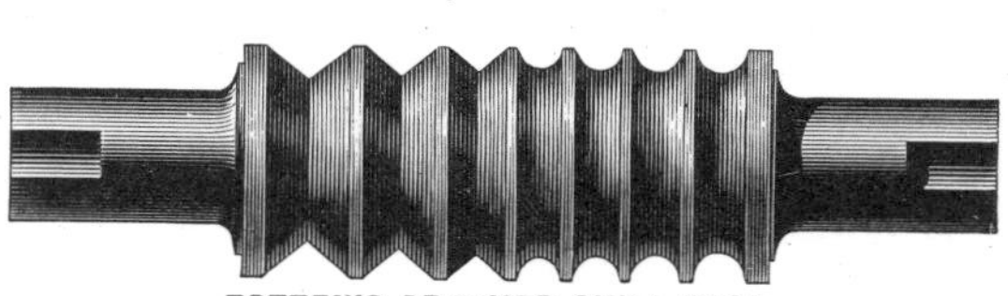

TOTTEN'S GROOVED CHILL ROLL.

THE KIDD IRON WORKS,

WILLIAM GLEASON, Proprietor.

Brown's Race, Rochester, N. Y.

——:o:——

The Kidd Iron Works, now owned by Mr. William Gleason, were formerly operated by a stock company engaged in the manufacture of car wheels and machinist's tools, with Mr. Gleason, who was a stockholder, as superintendent of the establishment. It is not our intention to give a complete history of the Company, suffice it to say that after a time they abandoned the manufacture of car wheels and that Mr. Gleason, who had previously been engaged in the tool trade, succeeded to that portion of the Company's business which he has since successfully carried on. An ingenious inventor and a thorough practical mechanic he has made many new and useful improvements in old and some entirely new machines of special merit, and all the productions of his establishment are noted for the accuracy with which they are made and for their great strength and durability.

The Elevating Tool Post for Lathes, patented in 1867, is one of the best devices of the kind in use. Mr. Gleason also has a patented Screw Cutting Lathe which greatly shortens labor. The slide block that holds the tool is connected with the handle that opens and shuts the shear nut; the same operation that opens the nut also releases the tool from the work, and replaces it when closed. This Lathe took the highest premium at the Fair of the American Institute, in New York, in 1874. Mr. Gleason has also a patented, Traverse Drill, and other inventions which we cannot describe for lack of room.

His latest invention is the Gear Dressing Machine, of which the cut presented herewith is a fair representation. This being an entirely new machine, we subjoin a brief description of its construction and make mention of some of the kinds of work it will do. It will dress either iron or wood—spur or bevel—and gives the perfect reducing cut to the latter,

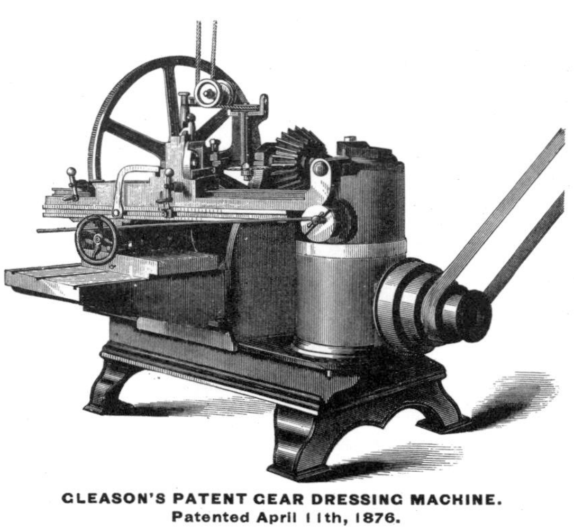

GLEASON'S PATENT GEAR DRESSING MACHINE.
Patented April 11th, 1876.

making the small end of the cog of the same proportionate shape as the large end. The motion is transmitted to the slide that holds the tool block by a central shaft, so that the bar can be swung to any desired angle or bevel; it is also hinged so as to permit of vertical movement. The form is placed at or near the bar and can be moved to or from the centre, consequently wheels of different pitches can be planed with the same form. To dress a spur gear the head is moved crossways on the frame and the bar is swung parallel to the spindle and remains stationary. The tool block is fitted so as to move over a form. For dressing wood or core bevels a bracket which takes a small circular saw is held in the tool post, receiving a quick rotary motion from the counter shaft over head, which is also made to swing to any desired angle. The reciprocating motion is kept and it is fed the same as if dressing iron, only much quicker. A shape tool can be used for dressing wood spur gears. Patterns can be made and other works of that description readily done on this machine. The work is done very rapidly and the changes are easily and quickly made. Messrs. John T. Noye & Son, of Buffalo, N. Y., purchased the first of these machines made, and the Straub Mill Company, of Cincinnati, Ohio, and Messrs. Philo Ferriss & Son, of Ypsilanti, Michigan, are also using them to their entire satisfaction.

Mr. Gleason makes it a special point to have all the tools manufactured at his establishment accurate in every part; all the small feed gears and racks are made either of steel or wrought iron, as is most desirable, and they are all cut to exact measurement. The planers run noiseless and shift easily.

This new machine has already attracted the attention of some of the best mechanics in the country and received their endorsement, and as it becomes better known we predict for it a popularity second to that of no machine of its class. Those interested should address the proprietor, William Gleason, Brown's Race, Rochester, New York.

URBANA WINE CO., HAMMONDSPORT, N. Y.

URBANA WINE COMPANY,

Hammondsport, Steuben County, New York.

Though some of the early colonists of Virginia made "wine of faire qualitie," as the records state, from the native wild grape of the forest, and subsequently a much better article from "tame (cultivated) grapes," and though at an early date the peculiar adaptability

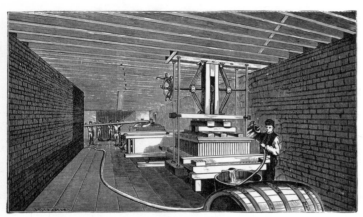

PRESS ROOM.

of many sections of our country to the culture of the grape was well known, yet few attempts were made to introduce the new industry until within a comparatively few years. In the spring of 1804, a party of emigrants from Switzerland settled on land in Indiana, under grants made by Congress for the purpose of encouraging the cultivation of the vine and the making of wine. The settlement was first known as New Switzerland, but the town was subsequently named Vevay. The grape culture was carried on first with the Maderia and other foreign varieties, but afterwards with the native Cape or Schuylkill grape, the superiority of which was strictly main-

BOTTLING CHAMPAGNE.

tained by the founder of the colony. In 1810, the colony had eight acres of vineyard from which they made 2,400 gallons of wine. In 1818, nearly 5,000 gallons were made, but the wine was of inferior quality and the settlers became discouraged; about 1820 they abandoned the wine business.

In 1820, Mr. John Adlum, of the District of Columbia, called the attention of Congress to the fact that he had succeeded in making "wine of superior quality" from native grapes. Mr. Adlum was one of the early promoters of wine manufacture in this country. About 1823, Nicholas Longworth, of Cincinnati, made his first essay in wine making, using the Schuylkill, Muscadel, or Vevay grape.

The first wines manufactured in this country were "very poor stuff," (the poorest of them were never worse than many imported and "doctored" wines sold in the United States at the present time), but within the past ten years, as fine wines have been made in the United States as have been produced in the most favored vine growing districts of Europe. Many Americans will be slow to accept this assertion, but the fact is that a large portion of our people are in many things blindly prejudiced against their own country. Before any attempts were made in this country to manufacture wines for the market, certain French and German wines had become popular with our people, and deservingly so; when the first American wines were introduced it soon became a general conviction that fine wines could not be made in the United States, and American wines became a scorn. The great difficulty with the early wine makers of this country was that they lacked the knowledge that can only be gained by experience; within the past few years that knowledge has been gained, and American wines are now rising in public favor, to such an extent that at a conference of

wine makers in Europe, it was gravely announced that the day was not far distant when they would lose almost entirely their great American trade. The fact is that the connoisseurs of the Old World having tested the quality of American wines, and found them in nowise inferior to their own productions, they naturally expect that our people will appreciate their excellence.

A Champagne or sparkling wine is necessarily a manufactured wine to a certain extent. Those best acquainted with foreign champagnes know that they are made from wines without flavor or bouquet; consequently, all that must be made by flavoring extracts or essences, making, instead of a pure and healthful wine, a compound that is frequently deleterious.

American wines need no such doctoring, especially those grown in Urbana and vicinity. We have only to skillfully combine the Delaware, Iona, Catawba, Walter and Isabella to produce a bouquet unequalled, without additions, for a most perfect wine. To show that these wines are kept in a state of purity, we give the Company's process of handling in full, which is precisely like the most approved French method, with this exception: The French finishing syrup is flavored or compounded, while theirs is perfectly pure.

The grapes, after being cut, are carefully sorted; perfect ones are run through a small mill which breaks the skins so the juice can be more readily pressed out. From the press the must is conducted through rubber hose into the large casks for fermentation, which brings out its wine qualities. By very much the larger part of the juice of the fully ripened grape is Nature's own arch solvent, pure water; but mingled with this water are other elements, the chief of which is sugar, a relatively small percentage of tartaric acid, and numerous other substances which aid in giving color, flavor and fragrance to the fruit. In the early stage of the formation of the grape the acid preponderates, but as it matures the sugar accumulates rapidly and the acid is overborne or masked, if not actually converted into sugar. After the rich juice of the perfectly ripened grape has remained in the vat or cask, in a moderately warm temperature for a time, fermentation begins, the sugar is further decarbonized and alcohol is formed. In order that grape-juice may be converted into wine of good quality by the natural process of fermentation, it is found that it must not have more than five parts in each one thousand of tartaric acid, or twenty per cent. of sugar. When the must of the grape contains the appropriate twenty per cent. of sugar the result of the fermentation is a wine which has eleven per cent. of absolute alcohol, or nineteen per cent. by volume, of proof spirit. This is as high a proportion of alcohol as can be produced by natural fermentation, and it becomes the standard of the highest strength of natural wines. All alcohol contained in wines beyond this proportion must have been added to the wine. The reason for this is that in the presence of this quantity of spirits, all further conversion of sugar into alcohol is arrested. If a rich juice containing more than twenty per cent. of sugar is fermented there always remains a considerable amount of unconverted sugar in the wine, and this remainder is prevented from further change by the presence of the spirit. The natural wines which have a strength of eleven or twelve per cent. of absolute alcohol, rarely contain more than one half of one per cent. of unconverted sugar.

When the expressed juice has safely passed through its first fermentation and is ripe for bottling, each cask of wine is carefully analyzed, the proportion of acid and sugar each contains is noted, the quantity of spirit, the differences in flavor, are all studied, and then with consummate skill they are so combined as to bring out the most perfect bouquet for a fine Champagne, and to produce the proper amount of effervesence for a good sparkling, and this last is a matter of much moment; too much would burst all the bottles, too little produce a lifeless wine. It is in this skillful combination at the time of bottling that the secret of how to make a fine Champagne is hidden. A fine sparkling wine can only be produced by combining pure natural wines of the highest quality. When filled, bottles are piled where the temperature is warm, causing a second fermentation of the wine in the bottle, which produces carbonic acid gas.

When the fermentation is perfected, the bottles are lowered into cool vaults to mature from one to two years. In the meantime the

VINEYARD AND LAKE VIEW.

sediment, which is a product of all fermentation, has settled on the side of the bottles. When wanted for use the bottles are marked and placed on sediment racks neck downwards and shaken twice each day from three to four weeks, working the sediment on the corks. When the wine is required for shipment, it is taken to the finishing room, where each bottle is seized by an expert, who eases the cork, which flies with a loud report. A small quantity of champagne follows, removing the sediment with it. It is then passed to the doser's hands, who inserts the syrup. The bottle then passes into the hands of the corker, who closes it with a large cork of finest quality. The

STILL WINE VAULT.

tying and wiring comes next. Now all is secure, but the bottle does not rest; it is well shaken, mixing the syrup thoroughly with the wine. Then the finale, which is labeling, putting on the foil, wrapping, and packing in cases for shipment.

We have been thus particular in describing the process of manufacture adopted by the Urbana Wine Company—the "Old Style," as it is sometimes called, because most American manufacturers have adopted the New Style, or quick process, which requires but a few words to describe. The wine is bottled and a gas made by combining oil of vitrol and marble dust is injected into the bottle. Spar-

FINISHING CHAMPAGNE.

kling can be made in this way in a few hours.

In addition to the brands of Champagne made by the Company, are Still Wines, of which we can make but brief mention.

Their Sweet Catawba has become a national wine. It is heavy, fine flavored, and will keep in every style of package, in any climate. It is fast taking the place of the sherry most frequently met with in this market, and is much cheaper and better.

Their Port, always good, has been greatly improved in the last two years by adding wine from new black grapes now being grown in their locality. It is made from a combination of several varieties fermented on the skins, which gives a heavy dark color. No coloring material whatever being used, it will draw down perfectly clear. It is used largely for medicinal and sacramental purposes.

The Company also make a Dry Catawba which ranks with many of the better grades of Rhine wines, and is often preferred on account of its superior fine, fruity flavor.

Their Brandy is a pure distillation from the last pressing of the grapes. Its purity in all respects makes it a valuable medical agent, and it is mostly sold for that purpose.

American wines are rapidly growing in public favor and we confidently predict that the time is not far distant when native wines, such as are manufactured by the Urbana Wine Company will displace the "doctored" products of Europe.

Frequently American Wines have been bottled under foreign names, some manufacturers finding that the easiest way of profitably disposing of their stock. The Urbana Wine Company will not pursue such a course, well knowing that when fairly tested beside foreign wines the verdict of experts will be in favor of their product.

CHAMPAGNE VAULT.

HAMMONDSPORT WINE CELLAR

G. H. WHEELER, Prop'r,

G. H. Wheeler, Jr., Sup't and Gen'l Manager,

HAMMONDSPORT, STEUBEN CO., N. Y.

——:o:——

To write a history of wine would really be to write a history of the world; the oldest records known to man, both sacred and profane, frequently speak of wine in such a manner as to irresistably convey the impression that even then wine had long been known to and commonly used by man. Wine is mentioned in the Bible more than one hundred times, and all ancient writers make frequent mention of it. Of the exact signification of the word as used in various places in the Scriptures, much has been written, but the generally received opinion is that the term wine refers to the juice of the grape, sometimes unfermented, but generally fermented. Other fruits have been used for wine making, strawberries, raspberries, blackberries, gooseberries, currants, etc., but such wines are always known by the name of the fruit from which they are made, while the simple term wine, when used without a prefix, is understood to mean a wine made of grapes.

The geographical range of the grape is very great. At a very early day after the first settlement of the American colonies wine was made from the native grapes that were everywhere found in abundance. Then slips of better kinds of "tame" grapes, as the cultivated varieties were then and still are commonly called in some sections, were imported from the mother countries and a much better class of wine was made from their products. As the settlements advanced further into the interior, and the population was added to by emigrants from the wine producing districts of Europe, more attention was paid to grape culture, and the manufacture of wine as a business, began to be talked of. It was not until comparatively recently, however, that any really effective steps were taken to develop the wine making resources of the United States.

It is our intention merely to call attention to one of the finest grape growing and wine producing districts in this country, situate in the township of Urbana, Steuben County, State of New York—a section frequently and fittingly spoken of as "The Vineyard of the Empire State."

The township of Urbana, was formed from Bath, April 17, 1822. Urbana lies at the head of Crooked Lake. The surface of the town is divided by Pleasant Valley into two series of highlands whose summits rise from eight hundred to one thousand feet above the level of the lake. Cold Spring Lake takes its rise in this valley, emptying into Crooked Lake. The soil in the valleys is alluvial, and on the hill-tops a heavy gravelly loam. From their sheltered situation the slopes of the hills descending to the south and east, are especially adapted to the culture of the grape, the climate and soil being all that could be desired for that purpose. When the country was first settled this section soon became noted for its superior grapes, and since then its fame has yearly increased. No attempt to raise grapes on a large scale, either for market as grapes or to be converted into wine, seems to have been made until about 1855. In 1858, some thirty acres of these hillsides had been converted into vineyards. The yield was so great and the quality of the grapes so eminently superior, that the land owners of that district began to think that grape culture would probably pay. In 1858, the number of acres devoted to grape culture was double that of the preceding year; and with each succeeding year the average has been extended, until now all that section of country which is eligibly located, amounting to several thousand acres has become a vineyard, and wine making has become a business of great importance.

Hammondsport was incorporated as a village, June 16, 1856. Situated in the very midst of the vintage grounds, and having superior facilities for transporting the products of the surrounding country to a waiting market, the Wine business naturally settled here. The village is a most attractive one, neatly laid out, the streets broad, well

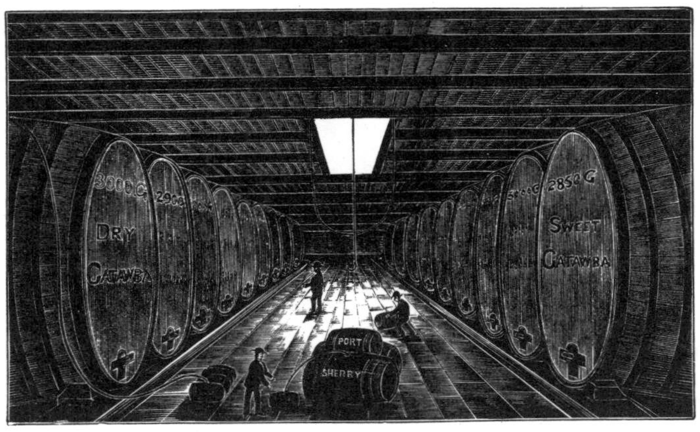

VIEW OF HAMMONDSPORT WINE CELLAR.

shaded and kept scrupulously clean, and the cozy looking houses embowered in trees, with flower gardens or neatly trimmed lawns in front, plainly reveal to the stranger that he is among people of thrift and culture. There are schools, churches and workshops, all speaking volumes in their way. A daily line of steamboats plies between Hammondsport and Pen Yan, an important station on the line of the Elmira, Jefferson, and Canandaigua Railroad, affording connection with the New York Central Railroad and its connections. The Bath and Hammondsport Railroad, from Hammondsport to Bath, connects, at the latter place, with the Rochester Division of the Erie Railway.

As we have previously said, a leading business of Hammondsport is the manufacture of Pure Wines and Brandies from the luscious grapes grown in the immediate vicinity. Prominent among these establishments, and to which we desire to call the reader's attention, is the one known as the Hammondsport Wine Cellar. Not a few connoisseurs have pronounced the various wines hailing from this Cellar unsurpassed by any produced either in the New World or the Old.

The quality of a wine does not depend alone upon the quality of the grape from which it is pressed. Of course the finest grapes, that is those possessing the correct relative proportions of water, sugar, acid and the various other substances that Nature has cunningly mixed together, to give color, flavor and fragrance to the fruit and its juices, will make the best wine, and yet as fine grapes as ever grew, have at times produced as poor wine as ever was made, simply because it was not matured and perfected under intelligent and skillful management. The pure juice of the grape, after it is expressed from the fruit, needs constant care and attention or it will rapidly deteriorate, and that which properly managed would have made an excellent wine, will surely become absolutely worthless.

American Wines within the last few years have risen rapidly in popular favor, and bid fair at no very distant day to almost entirely supplant foreign production. In the front rank of the most celebrated American Wines are those of the Hammondsport Wine Cellar, and in recommending them we are but echoing the endorsement they have received wherever they are known. The wines of this establishment for the present season, will be found even more complete in flavor, body and in general appearance than any vintage heretofore offered by them.

With the accumulated experience of many years in this business, and without change in management during the entire period, the proprietor of the Hammondsport Wine Cellar is now enabled to make the productions of his establishment, unexceptionally first-class in every particular.

Having in the past given such general satisfaction in the leading brand of the Cellar, *Sweet Catawba,* the proprietor feels confident that he has touched the key note, and that he now offers an article well nigh perfect, and difficult to improve upon.

Centennial Red is a sweet wine, similar in flavor to Sweet Catawba, and is especially designed for this season's trade, being a shade lower in price than the first named wine, but fully equal to it in purity and quality.

Nonpariel, also a sweet red wine is a fine summer drink of good body and flavor, and an astringency peculiar only to this brand.

The *American Port and Sherry* of this establishment are manufactured by a process peculiar to it. These wines are thoroughly pure and are steadily growing in public favor: we especially recommend them to the Drug Trade, for medicinal purposes.

The choice stock of *Brandy,* the proprietor claims is superior to any Grape Brandy offered to the public. It is manufactured in limited quantities only, and expressly for medicinal use.

The capacity of the Hammondsport Wine Cellar (100,000 gallons), its adaptation to the maturing of wines, are unsurpassed in its locality.

In ordering, the reader will please bear in mind that this is an individual establishment, not a firm nor a company, and that the proprietor and managers are men of long experience.

NATIONAL YEAST COMPANY.

Seneca Falls, N. Y.

MANUFACTURERS OF DRY HOP YEAST.

——:o:——

Good bread is indeed "the staff of life." Poor bread is a "broken reed." It is notorious that hardiest soldiers are those who have the best commissary department. The ancients called the stomach the seat of the intellect, and, speaking figuratively, they were not far from correct. To ignore the wants of the stomach, or in any way ill treat it, is to derange the brain. The connection between these organs is close and sensitive, and a very large percentage of all brain diseases are directly traceable to a disordered stomach, arising from the use of unwholesome articles of food; indeed the whole man, in his physical, mental and moral nature, is controlled in a large degree by the food he eats. Among civilized nations bread, in its various forms, is the most important food element, and it is therefore not surprising that great improvements should be made in the methods of its preparation. The men who made such discoveries and improvements may not become as famous as a Franklin, a Fulton or a Morse; but are no less deserving.

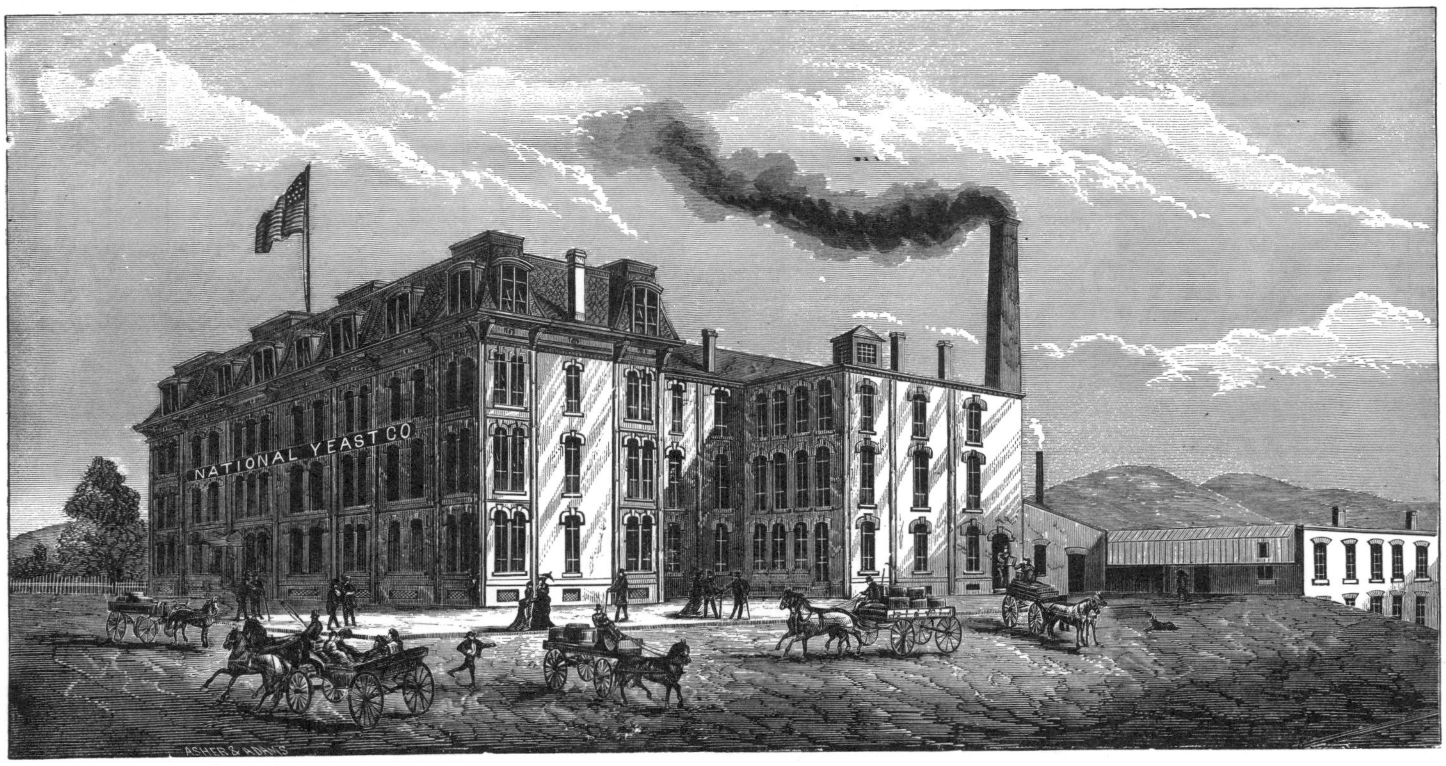

NATIONAL YEAST COMPANY'S MANUFACTORY, SENECA FALLS, NEW YORK.

The term "National," as applied to this Company, is not a mis-nomer. Its field of operation is the United States; its products are found all over the Union. Yeast made by this Company is used very extensively; for, once finding its way to the kitchen and its merits practically tested, the delicious bread and pastry it produces so strongly recommend it, thereafter it is deemed indispensable.

Great discoveries are sometimes the result of accident, but are generally the legitimate result of skillful and laborious research. Of the latter class is the National Dry Hop Yeast. It was only after a long series of practical experiments, and a thorough investigation of the general nature and the peculiarities of all the different kinds of leaven, and their healthful and harmful effects, that this celebrated article was produced. Confident of its superiority, and that a practical test of its value in the homes of the people would soon render it popular, the Company began the distribution of "trail packages," consisting of two cakes of Yeast with printed directions for their use, which were gratuitously distributed. Since then several millions of such packages have been distributed each year, and the investment has proved a paying one. Anxious that the public should be informed of their excellence, they have given away thousands of dollars worth of these small packages, which were tested, and being found superior to other preparations, the recipients have become regular consumers and the thousands of dollars sown as seed have yielded an abundant harvest.

This Company began manufacturing at Seneca Falls, N. Y., in 1870 in a small building. The first year their business necessitated the erection of a large brick building, five stories high. Now a group of elegant establishments handsomely finished, with Mansard roofs, are occupied. They are all of brick, with modern improvements for heating, ventilating, cleansing and purifying the whole, and are all fully equipped with the most approved appliances that can in any way aid in the manufacture, packing and shipping of their products. The Company have good reason to be proud of their efficient workmen to whose promptness, regularity and thoroughness is largely due to the high standard of excellence which the National Dry Hop Yeast maintains. Agents are constantly on the road taking orders; many buyers send their orders direct to the Company's Office at Seneca Falls. Car loads of these Yeast Cakes are shipped daily, and millions of packages are sent every year to all parts of the United States.

The Boston Board of Health, during the fifteen months ending April 25, 1874, had their attention repeatedly called to the unusual mortality among the infants and children of that city and vicinity. Determined, if possible, to discover the cause, all kinds of food liable to adulteration were submitted to eminent chemists for analysis. Samples were purchased in open market, and no seller had the least intimation of the severe test his goods were to be subjected to. This Yeast came forth with no taint or suspicion attached to it.

During the past five years these Yeast Cakes have been exhibited at a large number of State Fairs, and bread raised with them has been made and baked on the grounds in the presence of multitudes, always with success, and in every instance they have been flatteringly recognized by the committee.

The only place where the National Dry Hop Yeast is manufactured is at Seneca Falls, New York. But why not locate factories in the West where grain is cheaper, saving transportation and reducing the cost? Suffice it to say, that the Company will not take the risk of damaged products and reputation by having a number of factories, when they can manufacture all that may be required in a locality that affords them the best water and a climate most favorable to their operations.

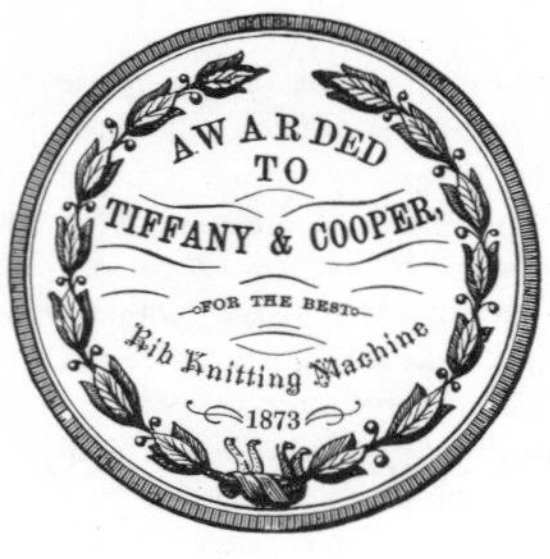
AWARDED
TO
TIFFANY & COOPER
FOR THE BEST
Rib Knitting Machine
1873

TIFFANY & COOPER,

Builders of

FLAT RIB KNITTING MACHINERY,

For Manufacturing all varieties of Plain and Fancy Ribbed Goods.

BENNINGTON, VERMONT

——:o:——

The development of machinery by means of which the process of knitting could be accomplished automatically has, during a period of three hundred years, or more, engaged the attention of some of the best mechanics, most ingenious inventors, and most noted patrons of industry. Since the days of William Lee, of Nottinghamshire, England, who constructed, about 1589, a square knitting frame, operated by the hands and feet, which produced a straight flat web, the progress toward the ingenious Flat Rib Knitting Machine of the present day has been slow and tedious.

About 1717, Strutt and Woolatt added a second set of needles to the Lee machine by which combination they were enabled to make ribbed goods. For this improvement they received British patents in 1758 and 1759. This machine was generally adopted in Derbyshire, England, and was known as the "Derby Rib."

In 1831, Timothy Baily, of Albany, N. Y., succeeded in applying power to the old stocking frame of Lee, thus making the first power machine ever constructed. In 1847, Benjamin Baily, obtained a patent in Great Britain for constructing the "Derby Rib" machine so that it could be driven by power instead of by the hands and feet of the operator as theretofore, and in 1851, John Pepper received a United States patent.

In 1835, Joseph Powell received a United States patent for a power rib knitting machine having two sets of parallel vertically moving and rocking spring barbed needles. In the same year Benjamin Baily obtained an English patent for a power rib knitting machine in which two sets of spring barbed needles had endwise and rocking movements across each other in connection with fixed pressers.

In 1851, Eli Tiffany came to this country from Yorkshire, England, and commenced the business of learning to knit by machinery at Waterbury, Connecticut, working on flat power knitting machines which produced a very plain article of goods for shirts and drawers. After about six years service in the capacity of a practical knitter, the crudeness, imperfections and defective operation of all the then existing machines stimulated him to bend his energies toward perfecting a new machine for making ribbed work, which should preserve the best elements of the old rib machines without their defects, and at the same time be operated automatically. Having in the years of his early experience accumulated a small capital, he, in the year 1857, addressed himself exclusively to the task of developing his idea of an automatic power rib knitting machine, and after about twelve months of unremitting labor and experiment he succeeded in producing a successfully operating rib knitting machine, which was brought out at Glastenbury, Connecticut, in the year 1858.

The characteristic features of this machine which rendered it preeminent over its predecessors were the knitting of ribs with "welts" and "slack courses" and the manipulation of two sets of stationary spring barbed needles crossing each other at right angles, by a single presser bar having two separate movements in a direction diagonal to the two sets of needles. This machine, which was subsequently enlarged and improved, as above illustrated, was patented May 1, 1860. On the 30th of April, 1874, an extension of this patent for the term of seven years was granted.

Many valuable improvements have been made in these machines since the issuing of the patent.

The working parts are so constructed that they can be taken out

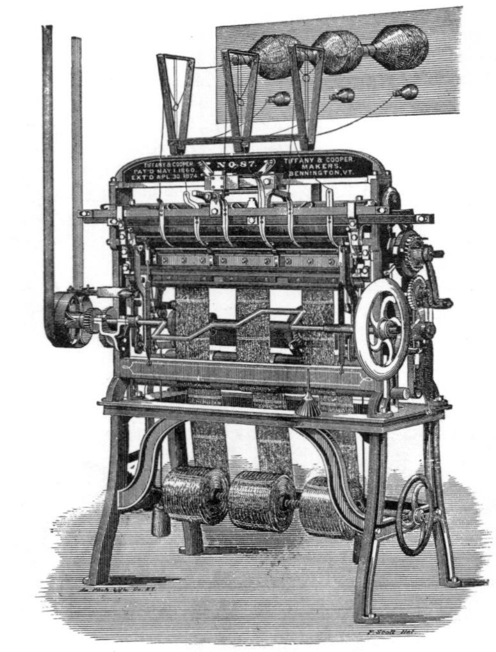

TIFFANY'S IMPROVED MACHINE

For Knitting Ribbed Shirt Cuffs, Drawers' Bottoms, Wristlets, Gaiters, &c.

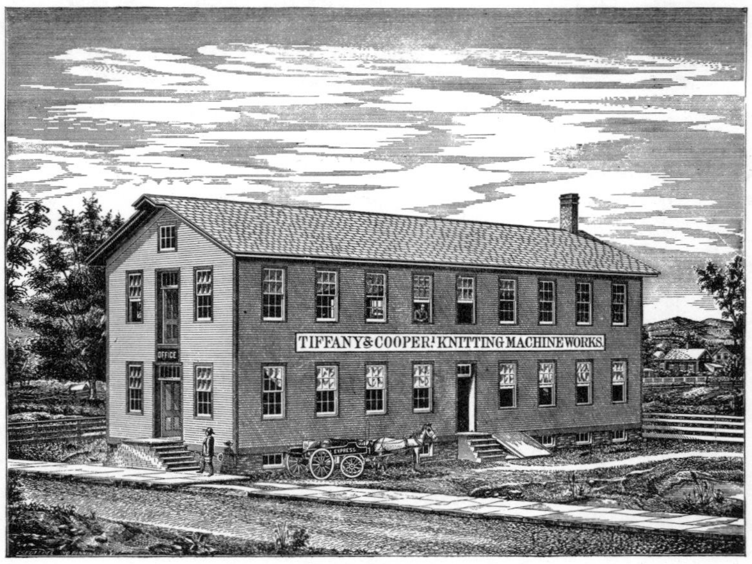
TIFFANY & COOPER'S KNITTING MACHINE WORKS
OFFICE

TIFFANY & COOPER'S WORKS, BENNINGTON, VT.

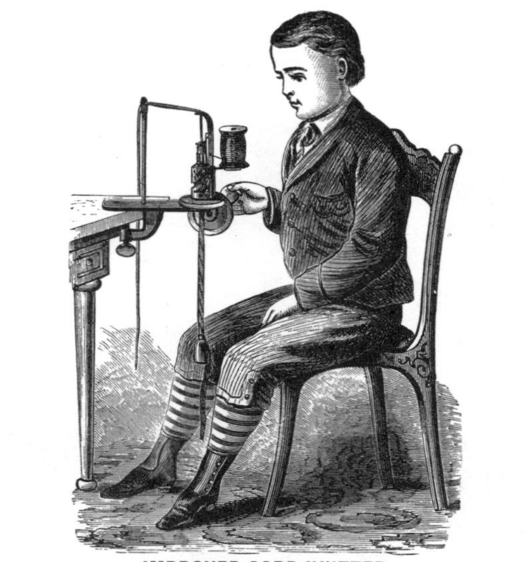

IMPROVED CORD KNITTER.

For making Picture and Curtain Cords, Watch Guards, Fancy Trimming, &c.

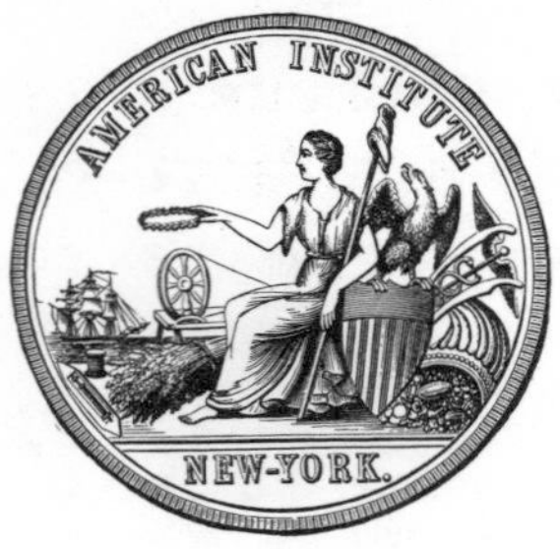
AMERICAN INSTITUTE
NEW-YORK

and replaced or repaired without disturbing the adjacent parts. The springing or bending of the needles, which in other machines necessitates immediate repair or change, involving a stoppage, is in this machine provided for, by operating the needles in ways or slots, so that at each movement, the needle, if bent or sprung, is brought back to its proper working position. Each needle is separately placed in a slot cut in a brass plate and secured by a cap and screw (not cast in lead as in other machines), and can be instantly withdrawn and replaced.

Each machine is provided with an adjustable device for regulating the tension of the stitch, which consists of a spring and set screw attached to the back needle bar, and arranged to regulate elevation and depression of the falling bar, so that a tight or loose fabric can be made. Every machine is provided with an automatic take-up.

Another important feature is the device for disconnecting the slur bar from various appendages which it actuates, so that when the yarn breaks or runs out, the slur bar can be drawn back and sinkers elevated so that the end of the yarn may be recovered and spliced.

The slur cocks are made of the best steel, highly finished, and are so hardened that years of wear makes but little or no impression on them, and are so fitted that they can be easily taken out and replaced.

The accompanying engraving gives a very clear idea of the general features of this machine, although many attachments are added, by the use of which a variety of work in colors and styles can be made. The attachments for making fancy colored goods are few and simple, and consist of an additional thread guide bar, rack wheels, pins and a series of blocks in chain form, working in connection therewith and forming a constituent part of what the manufacturers term the "end tackle."

The machine occupies about two and one-half by five feet of floor space, knits three breadths of shirt cuffs or drawer bottoms at once, and does nearly three-fourths as much work as the ten-section frame formerly built by the same firm; the original cost is only about one-third, and the running expenses are much less for the same quantity of work. It is estimated that nearly two hundred thousand dollars are annually saved in the United States by the use of the machines which have been built under this patent.

A four-section machine for making shirt cuffs for fine goods is also built. It is a convenient and valuable machine for manufacturers whose business require a frame especially adapted to knitting fine shirt cuffs, as there is no time lost in changing from one style of work to another.

The three-section machine can be built to make fancy ribbed cuffs, wristlets, gaiters and stockings, in three colors of any desired pattern; the work will be of a more even grade than that made on hand machines, while the quantity will be more than three times as great. A change from one pattern to another is readily made by the operator, and by a simple mechanical contrivance, the different colors are taken up and used without stopping the machine.

They also build to order a frame for making flat ribbed shirts and borders for the bottom of plain knit shirts. These borders, being elastic, keep the shirt in its place (a great comfort to the wearer), and add to its finish and durability.

A very ingenious and useful device recently introduced by this enterprising firm is styled Tiffany's Patent Knitting Machine, an illustration of which is presented. This machine is used by manufacturers for making Fancy Trimmings, Corset Laces &c., by Dressmakers for making Dress and Cloak Trimmings, by Jewelers for making Watch Guards, and by Furniture Dealers for Picture and Curtain Cord. It can be run by hand or power; when run by power it will make five hundred Watch Guards in one day, or six hundred yards of Picture Cord in the same time. It will also knit over and around wire or rubber goods, and will make cord suitable for making Tidies, Lamp Mats, &c. The price of the Knitting Machine is $3.00.

CHARLES COOPER,

Manufacturer of all varieties of Spring Needles for Knitting Machinery.

BENNINGTON, VERMONT.

——:o:——

The importance of using perfect needles is fully appreciated by every hosiery manufacturer. In manufacturing all varieties of goods the outlay for needles, together with the damage resulting from the use of inferior ones, forms no inconsiderable item in the cost of production. During the late war, the excess of the demand for knit goods over the supply called into operation all the knitting machinery of the country, and consequently created a market for needles which had never before existed, and which the establishments then engaged in manufacturing a first class quality of needles were unable to supply. This condition of affairs called into the field a host of needle manufacturers who supplied the demand with very inferior articles at exorbitant prices but after the close of the war and the abatement of this extraordinary demand, the price of machine needles fell accordingly. The strife among needle makers then was to see who could produce the cheapest article and in this struggle the character and quality of the needle, as might have been expected was sacrificed.

Mr. Cooper, a descendant from a long line of English needle makers, and himself from boyhood, a practical machine needle maker, then operating in the State of Connecticut, declined to become a party to this unworthy competition, and continued to keep up the quality and reputation which his needles had then attained by carefully selecting the finest qualities of

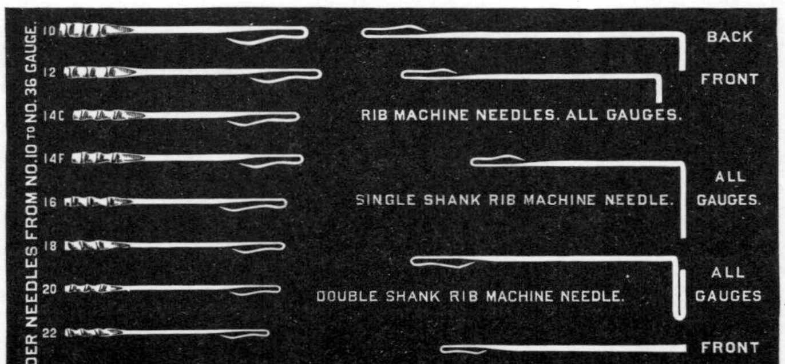
CYLINDER NEEDLES FROM NO.10 TO NO.36 GAUGE.
10
12
14C
14F
16
18
20
22
30
35
BACK
FRONT
RIB MACHINE NEEDLES. ALL GAUGES.
ALL GAUGES.
SINGLE SHANK RIB MACHINE NEEDLE.
ALL GAUGES
DOUBLE SHANK RIB MACHINE NEEDLE.
FRONT
BACK
HAND-FRAME NEEDLES.

steel, by employing none but the most expert workmen; by giving his personal and undivided attention to the supervision of his business, and tolerating no introduction of labor saving machinery or other innovations in the process of manufacture except such as by the test of long experience had demonstrated their superiority over hand labor. Of course he could not in this way make an article of goods which could be sold in competition with the inferior needles of other manufacturers, but the hosiery makers in a majority of instances have demonstrated to their own satisfaction the fact that Mr. Cooper's needles even at the enhanced prices, are greatly to be preferred to those of other manufacturers, and in the end prove to be the cheapest.

Mr. Cooper removed his business from Thompsonville, Connecticut, to Bennington, Vermont, in the year 1868, since which time it has been steadily increasing and has from time to time made successive enlargements of his factory necessary to accommodate his increasing patronage. He manufactures exclusively on orders, and keeps no needles in stock. All his work is guaranteed and he has one uniform price to all customers.

A circumstance which speaks well for his establishment is the fact that a large proportion of the men now working in his factory have been in his employ for the last fifteen years. This is a perfect assurance to purchasers that the high quality of his productions, which has gained for Mr. Cooper so good a reputation among hosiery makers all over the country, has been fully maintained and that they will not deteriorate. Having secured the services of competent workmen he retains them by rendering their situations pleasant and remunerative. His mechanics are as much interested in the superiority of their productions as he is; which is a perfect guard against careless workmanship.

AMES MANUFACTURING COMPANY,
Chicopee, Massachusetts.

Manufacturers of

Machinery, Machinists' Tools, Gun Stocking Machinery, Boyden Turbine Water
Wheels, Power Pumps, Bronze Cannon, Bronze Statuary, Iron and Brass
Castings, Regulation, Presentation and Society Swords

of all descriptions

—:o:—

Of the many establishments in Massachusetts, not one has been longer or more favorably known than the Ames Manufacturing Company of Chicopee. Its origin dates back as far as 1791, when N. P. Ames, Sr., opened a shop for the manufacture of edge tools, and for doing blacksmith and general mill work, in Chelmsford, (now Lowell), Mass. In 1829, he and his sons, N. P. Ames, Jr., and James T. Ames, removed their works to Chicopee Falls, and continued the same general business until 1831, when they began the manufacture of swords for the Government. In this latter department of their business they were eminently successful, and the high reputation they then acquired as makers of swords of the best quality—finely tempered, elegant in pattern and finish—has ever since been fully maintained, and since that time a very large proportion of all the swords used in the United States by the army and navy, by the militia of the various states, and by societies,—have been manufactured at these works.

In 1834 the firm removed to their present site in Chicopee, (the location then being known as Cabotville,) and were together with James K. Mills and Edmund Dwight, incorporated under the name of the Ames Manufacturing Company, with a capital of $30,000. The management of the company devolved upon N. P. Ames, son of the original founder of the business, assisted by his brother, James T. Ames.

In 1836 the Company added to the list of its productions, Bronze Cannon, for the manufacture of which they soon became justly celebrated, During the late civil war the Government crowded the company with orders for Cannon and Projectiles, and, at the request of the officers of the ordnance department, Mr. N. P. Ames visited Europe, and spent a year in examining works of a similar nature in the old world, with a view of adopting any improved methods of manufacture he might there find.

During the year 1842, the capital of the Company was increased to $75,000, and a number of new manufactures were added to its list of productions. The rapid expansion of the business of the Company soon made a still larger capital necessary, and in 1846 it was again increased, this time to $200,000. The same year the declining health of Mr. N. P. Ames compelled him to retire from the management of the business of the corporation, and Mr. James T. Ames was chosen as his successor, which position he has held nearly all the time since. In 1849 the capital was further increased to $250,000. The Company had at this time very largely increased its facilities for the manufacture of machinery and all articles usually produced at first class machine shops. The list of machines made was, and still is, very extensive, including Lathes, Planing Machines, etc., for other workers in metals, Machinists' Tools, Mill Machinery and special machines made only to order. It was about this time (1849) that they began the manufacture of the "Boyden Turbine Water Wheel," also of Cotton Machinery.

The Boyden Wheel, as manufactured by this Company, was soon generally adopted by the large Cotton Mills in the vicinity of the Company's works, and was, and still is unsurpassed if not unequalled for efficiency and economy in the use of water as well as for durability. These wheels, of from one hundred to five hundred horse power, have been in use in the large Cotton Mills of Cohoes, New York, Holyoke and Chicopee, Massachusetts, and in various other manufacturing towns from ten to twenty years without any necessity for repair,—not having deteriorated through wear, notwithstanding their long and constant use, nor through the breakage of any essential parts—and are as efficient today as ever they were.

The United States Government, had, for some time previously, employed the

Equestrian Statue of Washington, in Public Garden, Boston, Mass.

When the Ames Manufacturing Company essayed the casting of large Bronze works, they not only invited criticism, but they challenged it, and placing their works in competition with the best productions of European founders, even the most unfriendly were forced to acknowledge that the comparison reflected no discredit on the plucky men who dared attempt it. Since then the Company has achieved a world-wide fame, of which they may well be proud, for the perfection of the most minute details of their casts. Among its many celebrated productions may be mentioned the Collossal Statue of De Witt Clinton, in Greenwood Cemetery, Brooklyn, N. Y., after the model of H. K. Bowne, artist; the Equestrian Statue of Washington, in Fourteenth Street, (Union Square), New York, designed by the same artist; the Franklin Statue, and the Equestrian Statue of Washington, at Boston, Mass., from the design of T. Ball, artist; the doors of the Capitol at Washington, from the model of Crawford; the elaborate monument to President Lincoln, at Springfield, Illinois, and Soldiers' Monuments erected in various parts of the country. These works are, each and every one of them, perfect so far as the founder's skill can render them so, and such faults as either of them may possess, are attributable to the artist who designed the model, and not to the founder who cast it.

In 1858 the United States Government sent Mr. James T. Ames to England to procure machinery for rolling gun barrels. Mr. Ames was peculiarly fortunate in securing models of the most approved machinery for that purpose then in existence, and the company furnished the machinery required for the armories at Springfield, Mass., and Harpers' Ferry, Va., in such season as to render them far more effective in the production of muskets during the late war than they otherwise would have been, to the great advantage of the Government. During the continuance of the war, the Company constantly employed a large force of skilled men, in the manufacture of Swords, Bronze Cannon, Projectiles, and machinery for the manufacture of small arms, and was thus of the utmost use and importance to the country. The Company are now pursuing the business of manufacturing the various articles previously mentioned in the sketch, but, with the changes in the times, have altered to some extent the character of their goods. That is, as the demands of the Government have lessened for Army Swords, the Company has bestowed greater attention upon the manufacture of Society, Militia and Ornamental Swords, though their production in these lines has always been large and their styles greatly admired for their elegance of design and beauty of finish. In the manufacture of presentation swords, this Company has been very fortunate. As early as 1840, they were commissioned by the State of Virginia to furnish six swords at a cost of one thousand dollars each, for presentation to as many of her historical heroes, and in 1848 Congress gave a like commission to the Company. Its books show orders from many of the States of the Union, and from foreign countries for articles of the finest workmanship.

This Company is entitled to the credit of having introduced or of being among the first to test the merits of many new machines, methods and processes of manufacture which have since been generally adopted, so that the entire people have been indirectly benefited through their enterprise. Much of the work turned out by them is ornamental, plated or gilded, and to their efforts to discover a method of applying a coating of precious to bases of coarser metal—to their enterprise in thoroughly testing every new plan offered, may be traced the introduction of the present generally used process of electro-plating, as they were the first to introduce it in this country, in the year 1839.

Mr. N. P. Ames possessed a peculiar genius for the establishment and subsequent management of a great work like this; the remarkable success and world-wide fame of the undertaking are largely due to his masterly power, skill, knowledge and taste, which has been ably seconded and followed by his successor.

The Company is now employing large forces of skilled workmen in the production of Swords, Machinery, Machinists' Tools, Wheels, Bronze Works, etc., and its present productions are models of fine workmanship.

Company in the construction of special machinery for use in the National Armories, as also had private companies and firms engaged in the manufacture of small arms, when, in 1853, the English Government, through its commissioners sent to this country for the purpose of investigating American methods of gun-making by machinery, selected this Company as the fittest parties to furnish Gun Stocking and other machinery for a small-arms factory at Enfield, near Woolwich, England. This enterprise of the British Government was surprisingly successful and popular in England, and was the beginning of a large foreign demand for machinery of like character. The interchangable or American system has been adopted all over the world, and naturally the machinery necessary, or at least the first sets used in each country, has been purchased of the American manufacturer.

REGULATION ARMY SWORD.

During the same year, (1853), the Company prepared its foundry for the production of Statuary and other works of art in bronze and iron. This undertaking though not involving a greater outlay of capital, perhaps, than several others of their added industries, was attended with a peculiar risk not easily estimated. The Company had an established fame for the superiority of all its productions which was exceedingly valuable, but a failure in the new line would dim the lustre of that good name, and doubtless diminish the demand for their other products. The Company had no fear of failure, but their friends had, and there were not a few who predicted that their efforts to gain a footing in art circles, and take a place among the few really successful bronze founders of the world, would result in dire disaster.

GUN STOCKING MACHINE.

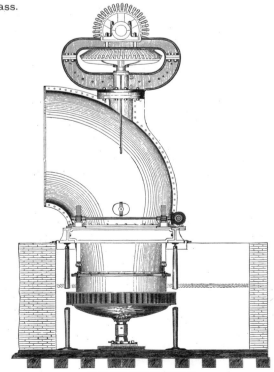

BOYDEN TURBINE WHEEL.

THE DECORATION OF THE LEGION OF HONOR,
Conferred by the Emperor of France upon WALTER A. WOOD, in Connection with the PARIS EXPOSITION, 1867.

CHAIN RAKE SELF DELIVERY REAPER.

THE DECORATION OF THE IMPERIAL ORDER OF FRANCIS JOSEPH,
Conferred by the Emperor of Austria, upon ¡WALTER A. WOOD, in Connection with the VIENNA EXHIBITION, 1873.

WALTER A. WOOD'S
HARVESTING MACHINES,
COMPRISING
Iron Mowers, Self-Rake Reapers, Self-Rake Reapers and Mowers Combined, Harvesters and Self-Binders Combined.
Manufactured Exclusively By
WALTER A. WOOD
Mowing and Reaping Machine Co.,
General Office and Manufactory,
Hoosick Falls, New York, U. S. A.

IRON FRAME MOWER WITH MANUAL DELIVERY REAPING ATTACHMENT.

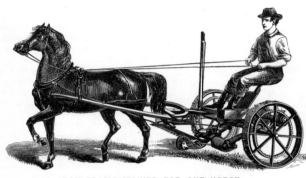

IRON FRAME MOWER FOR ONE HORSE.

IRON FRAME MOWER FOR TWO HORSES.

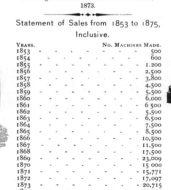

MOWING ATTACHMENT FOR CHAIN RAKE REAPER.

SWEEP RAKE SELF DELIVERY REAPER ON THE ROAD.

WALTER A. WOOD'S
HARVESTING MACHINES.

The evidence of the success of these Machines, and of their unrivaled superiority in merit and public favor, does not rest upon any bare assertion, but upon facts. It is apparent that the best possible test of merit in Harvesting Machines is their success in practical use, demonstrated by a steady and increasing demand for them.

No better evidence of success in that regard could be put before the public than the preceeding statement of the number of Walter A. Wood's Harvesting Machines manufactured and sold from 1853, year by year, to 1875—inclusive—showing, as it does, the marvelous growth of the

GRAND DIPLOMA OF HONOR,
The Highest Award at Vienna Exhibition, 1873.

Statement of Sales from 1853 to 1875, Inclusive.

Years.		No. Machines Made.
1853	- - - - - -	500
1854	- - - - - -	600
1855	- - - - - -	1,200
1856	- - - - - -	2,500
1857	- - - - - -	3,800
1858	- - - - - -	4,500
1859	- - - - - -	5,500
1860	- - - - - -	6,000
1861	- - - - - -	6,500
1862	- - - - - -	5,500
1863	- - - - - -	6,500
1864	- - - - - -	7,500
1865	- - - - - -	8,500
1866	- - - - - -	10,500
1867	- - - - - -	11,500
1868	- - - - - -	17,500
1869	- - - - - -	23,000
1870	- - - - - -	15,000
1871	- - - - - -	15,771
1872	- - - - - -	17,097
1873	- - - - - -	20,715
1874	- - - - - -	20,430
1875	- - - - - -	23,507
		234,120

HARVESTER AND SELF BINDER COMBINED.

business, resulting from the constantly increasing demand for these Machines.

Walter A. Wood's Mowing and Reaping Machines have been awarded the highest prizes ever offered in America, Great Britain, France, Germany, Russia, Switzerland, Belgium, Holland, Sweden and Denmark. Prior to 1874, these machines had received more than 750 first-class County, District and State Prizes, thereby attesting their great superiority over all other machines.

Continued success at important Field Trials in Europe. These machines were awarded in

1873, 54 First Prizes;
1874, 71 First Prizes;
1875, 61 First Prizes;

Total, 186 First Prizes in three years.

GOLD MEDAL

HIGHEST AWARD PARIS EXPOSITION, 1867.

GOLD MEDAL

HIGHEST AWARD PARIS EXPOSITION, 1867.

HEADER.

Index